TWELFTH EDITION

Food for Fifty

Mary Molt, Ph.D., R.D.

Assistant Director, Housing and Dining Services

Assistant Professor of Hotel,
Restaurant and Institution Management,
and Dietetics

Kansas State University

PEARSON

Prentice
Hall

Upper Saddle River, New Jersey 07458

Library of Congress Cataloging-in-Publication Data

Molt, Mary.
  Food for fifty/Mary Molt.—12th ed.
    p. cm.
  Includes index.
  ISBN 0-13-113871-5
  1. Quantity cookery. 2. Menus.   I. Title.

TX820.M57 2005
641.5'7–dc22   2004058733

Executive Editor: Vernon R. Anthony
Associate Editor: Linda Cupp
Editorial Assistant: Beth Dyke
Production Editor: Janet Kiefer, Carlisle Publishers Services
Production Liaison: Janice Stangel
Director of Production & Manufacturing: Bruce Johnson
Managing Editor: Mary Carnis
Manufacturing Manager: Ilene Sanford
Manufacturing Buyer: Cathleen Petersen
Creative Design Director: Cheryl Asherman
Cover Design Coordinator: Miguel Ortiz
Cover Designer: Joseph DePinho
Cover Photo: Courtesy of Getty Images; photographer Sandra Ivany
Senior Marketing Manager: Ryan DeGrote
Senior Marketing Coordinator: Elizabeth Farrell
Marketing Assistant: Les Roberts
Composition: Carlisle Publishers Services
Printer/Binder: Courier

This book was set in 10/12 New Baskerville by Carlisle Communications, LTD and was printed and bound by Courier. The cover was printed by Coral Graphics.

Pearson Education Ltd.
Pearson Education Singapore, Pte. Ltd.
Pearson Education Canada, Ltd.
Pearson Education—Japan

Pearson Education Australia PTY, Limited
Pearson Education North Asia Ltd.
Pearson Educacíon de Mexico, S.A. de C.V.
Pearson Education Malaysia, Pte. Ltd.

0-13-113871-5

To the many talented Kansas State University Housing and Dining Services dietitians and food service professionals that I have had the privilege to learn from.

Contents

Tables   *xi*

Figures   *xiv*

Color Photographs   *xv*

Preface   *xvii*

About the Author   *xxi*

PART I

Planning Meals   1

CHAPTER ONE

Planning Menus and Planning Special Meals and Receptions   3

Menu Planning   3

Types of Menus   3
Factors Affecting Menu Planning   5

    Clientele   5
    Type of Foodservice   6
    Financial Limitations   6
    Food Availability   7
    Production Capabilities   7

       Available Equipment   7
       Number and Experience of Employees   7
       Distribution of Work   9

Menu Planning Procedures   9

    Plan for Variety and Good Nutrition   9
    Plan for Eye Appeal   9
    Plan for Contrast in Texture and Flavor   9
    Plan for Consumer Acceptance   9
    Plan for Financial, Production, and Service
       Limitations   10
    Plan for Minimizing Leftovers   10

    Steps in Menu Planning   10

       Determine a Time Period   10
       Proceed Systematically   10
       Evaluate the Completed Menu   10

Menu Planning for Different Types of Foodservice   11
    Elementary and Secondary Schools   11

       National School Lunch Program   11
       School Breakfast Program   11

    Child and Adult Care Food Programs   11
    Colleges and Universities   14
    Commercial Foodservices   15
    Hospitals   18
    Foodservices Serving Older Adults and the
       Disabled   20

Planning Special Meals and Receptions   22

Planning Responsibilities   22
Receptions and Teas   23
Coffees and Brunches   23
Buffet Dinners and Luncheons   25

    Menu Planning   27
    Table and Space Arrangement   27
    Food Presentation and Service   28

Banquet Service   30

    Preparation of the Dining Room   30
    Setting the Tables   30
    Seating Arrangement   31
    Service Counter Setup for Served Meals   31
    Table Service   32
       Plate Presentation   35

Styles of Service   35
Wine and Bar Service   36

    Wine and Food Pairings   36
    Bar Service   36

PART II

Food Production Information   39

CHAPTER TWO

Food Production Information   41

    General Information   41
    Specific Food Information   43
    Quality Food Evaluation Information   43

The Recipe: Development, Construction, and Adjustment   **43**

Recipe Development and Construction   43
Recipe Adjustment   44
   Converting from U.S. Measurement to Metric   44
   Converting from Weight to Measure   45
   Increasing and Decreasing Recipe Yields   45
      Factor Method   45
      Percentage Method   46
   Enlarging Home-Size Recipes   47
   Reducing Fat, Sodium, and Sugar   48
   Direct-Reading Measurement Tables   50
      Directions for Using Tables 2.1 and 2.2   50
      Directions for Using Table 2.3   59

Amounts of Food to Serve, Yield and Food Equivalent Information   **64**

Weights, Measures, and Guides for Cooking/Baking Temperatures   **88**

Food Safety   **100**

CHAPTER THREE

Food Product Information   **109**

Dairy—Eggs, Cheese, Milk, and Milk Products   **109**

Eggs   109
   Egg Purchasing and Storage   110
      Fresh Eggs   110
      Processed Eggs   110
Cheese   111
   Natural Cheese   111
   Processed Cheese   111
      Purchasing   111
      Storage   117
Milk   117
   Purchasing and Storage   117
Cream   118
   Purchasing and Storage   118
Butter   119
   Purchasing and Storage   119

Grains, Pasta, Flours and Other Starches   **119**

Grains   119
   Purchasing and Storage   120
Pasta   122
   Purchasing and Storage   122
Flours, Meals, and Other Starches   127

Meat—Beef, Lamb, Pork, Veal   **127**

Meat—Beef, Lamb, Pork, Veal   127
   Purchasing   128
   Storage   129

Poultry   **133**

Poultry   133
   Purchasing   133
   Storage   133

Fish and Shellfish   **135**

Fish and Shellfish   135
   Purchasing   136
   Storing   140

Fresh Produce; Canned, Frozen Fruits and Vegetables; Dried Lentils, Beans, and Peas   **141**

Fresh Produce   141
Fresh Fruit—Pre-preparation Guidelines and General Information   146
Fresh Vegetables—Pre-preparation Guidelines and General Information   153
Fresh Herbs and Flowers   166
Canned and Frozen Fruits and Vegetables   172
Tofu and Dried Beans, Lentils, and Peas   173

Food Production and Service Staples   **174**

Coffee and Tea   174
Condiments and Vinegars   175
Dried Herbs, Spices, and Seasonings   175
   Herbs and Spices   175
   Salt and Pepper   182
Nuts and Seeds   184
Extracts, Alcohol, and Sweeteners   187
Fats   187

CHAPTER FOUR

Production Fundamentals   **189**

Production and Kitchen Readiness   189
   Assemble Tools and Equipment   189
   Gather Ingredients   190
   Complete Pre-preparation Steps and Prepare Sub-Recipes; Prepare Par Levels of Seasonings and Food Staples   190
   Weigh and Measure Ingredients   190
   Clean the Workplace and Keep It Orderly   190
Production Scheduling   190
Cooking Methods and Terms   191
   Dry Heat Cooking Methods   193
   Broiling, Griddle Broiling/Pan Broiling, Grilling, and Barbequing   193
      Roasting and Broiling   194
      Frying   195
   Moist Heat Cooking Methods   197
      Blanching and Parboiling   197
      Braising   198
      Boiling   198
      Poaching   199
      Simmering   199

Steaming, en Papillote, and
Pan Steaming   199
Stewing   200
Evaluating Food for Quality   200
Bread   201
Desserts   201
Entrees   201
Soups   201
Vegetables/Starches   201

CHAPTER FIVE

Knives and Other Equipment   205

Knife Identification, Knife Care
and Safety, and Knife Skills   205
Knife Identification   205
Knife Care and Safety   206
Knife Skills—Gripping, Guiding, Cutting   209
Hand Tools and Small Equipment   215
Basic Hand Tools (non-mechanical)   215
Pans   218

PART III

Recipes   223

Recipe Information   224
Yield   224
Ingredients   224
Weights and Measures   225
Cooking Time and Temperature   225
Critical Control Points   225
Abbreviations Used in Recipes   225
Basic Recipes   225

CHAPTER SIX

Appetizers, Hors d'oeuvres, and Special Event Foods   227

Appetizer Recipes   232

CHAPTER SEVEN

Beverages   245

Coffee   245
Tea   246
Punch   246
Wine   246
Beverage Recipes   247

CHAPTER EIGHT

Breads   263

Quick Breads   263
Methods of Mixing   263
Muffin Method   263
Biscuit Method   264
Conventional Cake Method   264
Yeast Breads   264
Ingredients   264
Flour   264
Yeast   264
Liquid   264
Other Ingredients   265
Bread Bases   265
Mixing the Dough   265
Fermentation of Dough   266
Shaping, Proofing, and Baking   266
Freezing Yeast Doughs and Breads   266
Quick Bread Recipes   268
Yeast Bread Recipes   299
Fillings or Toppings for Coffee
Cake and Sweet Rolls   317

CHAPTER NINE

Desserts   319

Cakes and Icings   319
Methods of Mixing Batter
or Shortened Cakes   319
Conventional Method   319
Dough-Batter Method   319
Dry Blending and Wetting Method   319
Muffin Method   320
Methods of Mixing Foam
or Sponge Cakes   320
Angel Food Cakes   320
Sponge Cakes   320
Cake Mixes   320
Scaling Batter   320
Pan Preparation   320
Scaling   320
Baking   322
Cooling and Removing from Pans   322
Icing and Fillings   322
Cookies   325
Proportion of Ingredients   325
Methods of Mixing   325
Shaping   325
Baking   325
Storing   325

Pies   327
    Ingredients   327
    Mixing   327
Other Desserts   328
Cake Recipes   328
Icing Recipes   352
Filling Recipes   359
Drop Cookie Recipes   364
Bar Cookie Recipes   377
Pressed, Molded, and Rolled
    Cookie Recipes   383
Pie Recipes   389
Other Dessert Recipes   416

CHAPTER TEN

Eggs and Cheese   **437**

Egg, Cheese, Milk Cookery   437
    Egg Cookery   437
    Cheese Cookery   437
    Milk Cookery   438
Egg and Cheese Recipes   439

CHAPTER ELEVEN

Fish and Shellfish   **457**

Cooking Methods   457
    Baking   457
        Fish Fillets   457
        Whole Fish for Buffet Display   458
    Broiling   458
    En Papillote   458
    Frying   458
        Pan Frying and Sautéing   458
        Deep-Fat Frying   458
        Oven Frying   458
    Microwave   459
        Primary Cooking Guidelines   459
    Oven Steaming   459
    Poaching   459
        Acidulated Water   460
        Court Bouillon   460
        Bouquet garni   460
Fish and Shellfish Recipes   460

CHAPTER TWELVE

Meat   **479**

Time and Temperature Timetables
    and Guidelines   479

Degree of Doneness   479
Beef Recipes   488
Veal Recipes   512
Pork Recipes   514

CHAPTER THIRTEEN

Poultry   **527**

Handling Poultry Safely   527
Cooking Methods   527
    Broiling or Grilling   527
    Deep-Fat Frying   528
    Pan Frying   528
    Oven Frying   531
    Braising   531
        Braising Whole Poultry   531
        Braising Cut-up Poultry   531
    Stewing or Simmering and Poaching   531
        Stewing or Simmering   531
        Poaching   531
    Roasting   532
Poultry Recipes   535

CHAPTER FOURTEEN

*Pasta, Rice, Cereals, and Foods
with Grains, Beans, and Tofu*   **559**

Pasta   559
Rice   559
Cereals   559
Beans   560
Pasta Recipes   561
Rice Recipes   594
Cereal and Grain Recipes   611
Bean and Tofu Recipes   627

CHAPTER FIFTEEN

Salad and Salad Dressings   **639**

Salads   639
Arranged Salads   639
Salad Bars   640
Salad Ingredients   641
Salad Dressings   641
Vegetable and Pasta Salad Recipes   642
Gelatin Salad Recipes   667
Fruit Salad Recipes   670
Entree Salad Recipes   677
Relish Recipes   693
Salad Dressing Recipes   699

CHAPTER SIXTEEN

Sandwiches   **713**

Preparation of Ingredients   713

    Breads   713
    Spreads   713
    Fillings   713
    Vegetable Accompaniments   714

Preparation of Sandwiches   714

    Closed Sandwiches   714
    Grilled and Toasted Sandwiches   714
    Open-Faced Hot Sandwiches   714
    Canapés   714
    Ribbon Sandwiches   714
    Checkerboard Sandwiches   714
    Rolled Sandwiches   715

Freezing Sandwiches   715
Sandwich Recipes   716

CHAPTER SEVENTEEN

*Sauces, Marinades, Rubs,
and Seasonings*   **747**

Entree and Vegetable Sauces   747
Dessert Sauces   748
Marinade, Rubs, and Seasonings   748
Entree and Vegetable Sauce Recipes   748
Dessert Sauce Recipes   773
Marinade, Rub, and Seasoning Recipes   779

CHAPTER EIGHTEEN

Soups   **789**

Types of Soups   789
Commercial Soup Bases   790

Serving and Holding Soups   790
Stock Soup Recipes   790
Cream Soup Recipes   810
Chowder Recipes   815
Chilled Soup Recipes   821

CHAPTER NINETEEN

Vegetables   **823**

Fresh and Frozen Vegetables   823

    Directions for Boiling   824
    Directions for Steaming   824
    Directions for Stir-Frying   824

Canned Vegetables   824

    Directions for Heating   824

        Stockpot or Steam-Jacketed Kettle   824
        Steamer or Oven   826

Dried Vegetables   826

    Directions for Cooking   826

Vegetable Recipes   827

APPENDIX A

*Suggested Menu Items
and Garnishes*   **885**

APPENDIX B

*Glossary of Menu
and Cooking Terms*   **893**

Index   **903**

Tables

Menu Planning Information

Table 1.1	Types of menu patterns	4
Table 1.2	Servings required for the food groups in the Food Guide Pyramid	6
Table 1.3	Serving sizes for foods in the Food Guide Pyramid	7
Table 1.4	Food practices of different religions	8
Table 1.5	Comparison of school foodservice menu planning systems	12
Table 1.6	Age group nutrient standards for NuMenus and Assisted NuMenus (1)	14
Table 1.7	Grade group nutrient standards for NuMenus, Assisted NuMenus, and food-based menu planning (1)	15
Table 1.8	Food-based menu meal plans	16
Table 1.9	Child care meal pattern	18
Table 1.10	Adult care meal pattern	20

Wine and Bar Information

Table 1.11	Wine and food pairing guide	24
Table 1.12	Wine purchasing guide	26
Table 1.13	Guidelines for stocking a bar	37

General Information

Table 2.1	Direct-reading table for adjusting weight ingredients of recipes divisible by 25	52
Table 2.2	Direct-reading table for adjusting recipes with ingredient amounts given in volume measurement and divisible by 25	54
Table 2.3	Direct-reading table for increasing home-size recipes with ingredient amounts given in volume measurement and divisible by 8	60
Table 2.4	Amounts of food to serve 50	64
Table 2.5	Food weights and approximate equivalents in measure	75
Table 2.6	Ingredient substitutions (approximate)	85
Table 2.7	Ingredient proportions	87
Table 2.8	Ounces, decimal equivalents of a pound and grams (rounded)	88
Table 2.9	Basic equivalents in measures and weights	89
Table 2.10	Guide for rounding off weights and measures	89
Table 2.11	Weights (1–16 oz) and approximate measure equivalents for commonly used foods	90
Table 2.12	Common can sizes	94
Table 2.13	Metric equivalents for weights, measure, and temperature	95
Table 2.14	Temperatures used for food preparation	96
Table 2.15	Convection oven baking times and temperatures	97
Table 2.16	Deep-fat frying temperatures	98
Table 2.17	Coatings for deep-fat fried foods	99
Table 2.18	Guidelines for reducing the risk of food-borne illness	100
Table 2.19	Instructions for calibrating a probe (stem) food thermometer	101
Table 2.20	Cold food storage temperatures	102
Table 2.21	Refrigerator defrosting times for meats, seafood, and poultry	102
Table 2.22	Temperatures and bacteria growth	102
Table 2.23	Safe internal temperatures for cooked foods	103
Table 2.24	Food serving temperatures and holding times	104
Table 2.25	Food cooling and storage procedures	105

Table 2.26   Time and temperature standards
              for reducing food safety hazards of
              potentially hazardous foods (PHF)   106
Table 2.27   Water activity (A$_W$) of selected
              foods   106
Table 2.28   pH values of selected foods   107
Table 2.29   Potentially hazardous foods   107

Specific Food Information

Table 3.1   Quality characteristics for
              chicken egg grades   110
Table 3.2   Guide for selecting natural and
              processed cheeses   112
Table 3.3   Types of milk products   118
Table 3.4   Types of cream products   119
Table 3.5   Flours, meals, and other starches   127
Table 3.6   Quality and yield grades for meat   128
Table 3.7   Categories and classes of poultry   134
Table 3.8   Fish buying guide   137
Table 3.9   Marketing sizes for oysters   139
Table 3.10   Count and descriptive names
              for raw shrimp (not peeled)   140
Table 3.11   Shellfish buying guide   140
Table 3.12   Yield, availability, and storage
              of fresh fruits and vegetables   142
Table 3.13   Descriptions of greens for
              cooking, salad greens,
              and lettuces   155
Table 3.14   Common types of mushroom   161
Table 3.15   Chile pepper varieties   163
Table 3.16   Fresh herb descriptions, flavor,
              and usage   167
Table 3.17   Edible flowers   172
Table 3.18   Common varieties of dried beans,
              lentils, and peas   173
Table 3.19   Teaspoons per ounce for dry
              herbs and spices   176
Table 3.20   Herb and spice usage for different
              categories of food   178
Table 3.21   Regional flavorings   182
Table 3.22   Salt and pepper seasonings   183
Table 3.23   Nuts and seeds   184
Table 3.24   Sugars and syrups   187
Table 3.25   Approximate smoke points
              of selected fats   188

Quality Food Evaluation Information

Table 4.1   Primary heat transfer for
              basic cooking methods   191
Table 4.2   Names and suggested cooking
              methods for beef cuts   192
Table 4.3   Evaluating food using sensory
              attributes   202
Table 4.4   Evaluating food products during
              preparation and service   203
Table 4.5   Quality food evaluation form   204

Equipment Information

Table 5.1   Pan capacities for baked products   219
Table 5.2   Counter pan capacities   220
Table 5.3   Dipper equivalents   220
Table 5.4   Ladle equivalents   221
Table 5.5   Recommended mixer bowl and
              steam-jacketed kettle sizes for
              selected products   221
Table 5.6   Large equipment requirements
              for basic cooking techniques   222

Recipe Specific Information

Table 6.1   Suggestions for appetizers   228
Table 6.2   Number of hors d'oeuvres and
              appetizers to prepare per person   229
Table 6.3   Meat, cheese, and vegetable trays   230
Table 6.4   Name suggestions for hors
              d'oeuvres and appetizers   231
Table 9.1   Approximate scaling weights
              and yields for cakes   322
Table 9.2   Approximate scaling weights
              for icings and fillings   323
Table 9.3   Guide for using frozen fruit in
              pies and cobblers (seven 9-inch pies) 398
Table 11.1   Fin fish cooking guide   457
Table 11.2   Methods of cooking fin fish
              and shellfish   458
Table 11.3   Timetable for steaming fish
              and shellfish   459
Table 12.1   Timetable for roasting beef   480
Table 12.2   Timetable for roasting lamb
              and veal   481
Table 12.3   Timetable for roasting pork in
              conventional oven   482

Table 12.4   Timetable for roasting pork in
convection oven   482

Table 12.5   Timetable for broiling meat   483

Table 12.6   Timetable for griddle-broiling
meat (surface 400°–450°F)   485

Table 12.7   Timetable for direct grilling steak   486

Table 12.8   Timetable for braising meat   487

Table 12.9   Timetable for cooking meat in
liquid (large cuts and stews)   487

Table 12.10   Portioning guidelines for pizza   506

Table 12.11   Approximate temperatures
and times for cooking pizza   508

Table 13.1   Cooking methods for poultry   528

Table 13.2   Roasting guide for poultry
(defrosted)   532

Table 14.1   Basic proportions and yields for
converted rice   560

Table 15.1   Basic salad bar components   640

Table 19.1   Timetable for boiling or steaming
fresh and frozen vegetables   825

Table 19.2   Timetable for roasting vegetables   883

Figures

Figure 1.1   Food pyramid   5

Figure 1.2   Table arrangement for a reception or tea   26

Figure 1.3   Table arrangement for buffet service, single line   27

Figure 1.4   Table arrangement for buffet service, single serving line using two 8 foot × 30 inch tables   28

Figure 1.5   Table arrangement for buffet service, double line   29

Figure 1.6   Table arrangement for buffet service, double serving line using one side of two 8 foot × 30 inch tables and a small 30-inch-radius half-round table   29

Figure 1.7   Table arrangement for buffet service, double straight-line for serving large numbers   30

Figure 1.8   Cover for a served meal   31

Figure 1.9   Basic napkin folds   32

Figure 1.10   Placement of food and cover for a served meal   34

Figure 3.1   Chicken egg size designations and weight per dozen eggs   110

Figure 3.2   Shapes and descriptions of selected pasta   123

Figure 3.3   Quality grade and yield stamps for meat   128

Figure 3.4   Primal and retail cuts of beef   129

Figure 3.5   Primal and retail cuts of lamb   130

Figure 3.6   Primal and retail cuts of pork   131

Figure 3.7   Primal and retail cuts of veal   132

Figure 3.8   USDA inspection stamp for poultry   133

Figure 3.9   USDA grade shield for poultry   133

Figure 3.10   Processed Under Federal Inspection (PUFI) mark for fish and shellfish   135

Figure 3.11   Product inspection stamp for fish and shellfish   135

Figure 3.12   Grade A stamp for fish and shellfish   135

Figure 3.13   Peeling and sectioning grapefruit   148

Figure 3.14   Preparing fresh pineapple   153

Figure 3.15   Preparing leaf lettuce   159

Figure 3.16   Coring head lettuce   160

Figure 5.1   Sharpening a knife using a stone   207

Figure 5.2   Honing a knife using a steel   208

Figure 5.3   Identification of the parts of a chef's knife   209

Figure 8.1   Shaping bread loaves   300

Figure 8.2   Shaping bowknot rolls   310

Figure 8.3   Braiding yeast dough   310

Figure 8.4   Shaping and panning cloverleaf rolls   310

Figure 8.5   Shaping crescent rolls   310

Figure 8.6   Shaping Parker House rolls   311

Figure 8.7   Preparing cinnamon rolls   316

Figure 9.1   Layering and icing a sheet cake   321

Figure 9.2   Suggested cutting configurations for cakes   323

Figure 9.3   Rolling and filling a jelly roll   350

Figure 9.4   Preparing pastry for a baked pie shell   390

Figure 9.5   Preparing pastry for a two-crust pie   392

Figure 12.1   Shaping meat loaf   498

Figure 13.1   Cutting up a whole chicken   529

Figure 13.2   Breading techniques for poultry   530

Figure 13.3   Carving a turkey   533

Figure 13.4   Skinning and boning a turkey breast   534

Figure 15.1   Suggested salad bar arrangement   640

Color Photographs

Cheeses, Fruits, Vegetables, and Herbs
(following p. 138)

Breads *(following p. 266)*

Exhibit I   Bread Loaves

Exhibit II   Bread Shapes

Exhibit III   Bread Shapes

Exhibit IV   Yeast Bread Variations

Exhibit V   Quick Breads

Meats *(following p. 522)*

Exhibit VI   Beef Steak Color Guide

Exhibit VII   Plate Garnishes

Exhibit VIII   Sandwich Presentations

Exhibit IX   Sandwich Presentations

Garnishes and Plate Presentations
(following p. 682)

Exhibit X   Entree Salads

Exhibit XI   Entree Salads

Exhibit XII   Entree Salads

Exhibit XIII   Fruit and Vegetable Garnishes

Preface

For nearly 70 years, *Food for Fifty* has been used as a resource for students in quantity food production and food production management courses, and for persons employed in foodservice management positions. The book is designed to provide food professionals with quantity recipes that they can prepare, confident of quality outcomes, and with information that will make their jobs easier. Since the book's origin, revisions have been made to keep abreast of the changing foodservice industry. In this twelfth edition, new recipes have been added that reflect current food preferences and modern eating styles, including meatless and vegan recipes. In addition, a longtime goal of *Food for Fifty* is to provide basic standardized recipes that can be adapted to produce foods similar to those shown in popular magazines, home-size cookbooks, and trade publications. The basic recipes and straightforward production guides will assist production staff in making an endless variety of food products. New and expanded food production information includes food safety guidelines, food evaluation forms, discussion about the basic foods used in food preparation, and food production fundamentals. Knife use and care, and information about equipment is included. Color visuals in the basic foods section add to *Food for Fifty's* usefulness as a teaching text and foodservice resource.

ORGANIZATION OF THE BOOK

Food for Fifty is divided into three major sections. Part One, "Planning the Menu and Planning Special Meals and Receptions," offers guidelines and procedures for planning meals, with special consideration given to different types of foodservices. Planning and serving special foodservice events such as receptions, buffets, and banquets are discussed, and guidelines for planning are provided.

Part Two, "Food Production Information," is a guide to planning and preparing food in quantity. This part has four sections. In Section A, the guidelines and tables are useful for developing, constructing, and adjusting recipes. Directions for increasing recipe yields are helpful when adapting recipes given in this book to different yields and for increasing home-sized recipes for quantity production. Suggestions for reducing fat, sodium, and sugar are useful for providing food choices that help clientele meet the dietary guidelines for Americans. Section B provides a comprehensive table of amounts of food needed to serve 50 people and information for making food substitutions and weight and measure conversions. Section C includes tables for weights and measures, and cooking and baking temperature guides. Section D has many food safety guidelines that are useful for developing Hazard Analysis Critical Control Point (HACCP) plans. This section also includes a discussion of basic food products and production fundamentals such as kitchen readiness, production scheduling, cooking methods, and food evaluation. Knife care and descriptions for basic knife cuts will be helpful for teaching inexperienced food production staff or students. A visual description of small equipment used in food production is in this section.

Part Three, "Recipes," includes a wide variety of tested recipes given in yields of approximately 50 portions and many suggestions for variations of the basic recipes. Recipes are organized according to menu categories. Most recipe chapters begin with general timetables and cooking guidelines for preparing the recipes in that chapter.

At the back of the book is a list of menu planning suggestions and garnishes (Appendix A) and a glossary of menu and cooking terms (Appendix B).

DISTINCTIVE FEATURES OF THE BOOK

Food for Fifty has been recognized for many years as a dependable resource for students and food production managers. Part Two is considered by many to be an indispensable reference for food production information. The various tables are helpful for menu planning and purchasing, and when making food production assignments.

Dietitians, foodservice managers, and faculty members have, for many years, depended on the standardized recipes in *Food for Fifty*. Recipes are written in an easy-to-read format with standardized procedures that allow quality products to be prepared consistently. Suggested variations for many of the recipes increase the value of the recipe section. In this revised book, recipes now include new foods on the market and foods appropriate for helping clientele meet their dietary standards. This new edition serves to increase *Food for Fifty's* value as a resource for a broad variety of recipes. The nutrition information will be helpful in planning and preparing foods for clientele with different needs. Food production, service, and storage procedures will be useful for developing Hazard Analysis Critical Control Point (HACCP) plans.

Menu planning information is given in concise terms in Part One. The discussion of planning procedures and the menu suggestion list in Appendix A are helpful to students and to foodservice managers whose responsibilities include menu planning. Many foodservices are called upon today to provide food for special events such as holiday meals, buffets, and coffees, receptions, and teas. Part One offers suggestions for menus, organization, and service of these functions.

Many four color pictures present the reader with attractive photo inserts of breads, meats, produce, and salads. The pictures are provided to generate ideas and offer creative food production and service suggestions. Other color photos used in the book will help describe food products.

USING THE BOOK

Food for Fifty is written for many users. Students in quantity food production and foodservice management use the text as a resource for learning the standards, skills, and techniques inherent in quality food production. Instructors find beneficial the basic menu planning and food production features that equip them with the tools necessary for designing teaching modules and supervising laboratories. The reliability of the recipes, tables, and charts in the book allows instructors to make assignments with confidence of a quality outcome. Additionally, the text provides a resource for instructing students on how to plan and serve special foodservice functions. Foodservice administrators, managers, and supervisors are also users of the text. *Food for Fifty* is a comprehensive resource for quantity recipes and technical food production information. The book serves as a foundation for the food production system.

The uses for *Food for Fifty* as both an instructional text and food production resource are unlimited. We believe the following examples of how the text can be used address many of the book's strengths.

- Amounts of food to purchase may be easily determined. Accurate calculations are achieved by using the purchasing and yield information in Part Two and the standardized recipes in Part Three.

- While the recipes yield approximately 50 servings, they can be adjusted easily for other yields by using the recipe extension procedures in Part Two.

- Menu planning is simplified by the lists of food item names, by menu categories, in both Appendix A and the Index. *Food for Fifty* also provides a comprehensive file of standardized recipes that can support the menu plan. General information on writing menus for various kinds of foodservices is included in the text.

- General descriptive and purchasing information about the basic foods used to produce recipes, descriptions for cooking methods, and knife care and use will be helpful resources for a variety of users.

- Mise en place discussion and production scheduling techniques will help students understand and apply kitchen readiness principles.

- Recipes and ideas from trade and popular food magazines and cookbooks can be produced in quantity by adapting the basic standardized recipes in *Food for Fifty*.

- Variations are included for most recipes. Users are given suggestions for producing food products consistent with contemporary eating trends.

- Quality standards for food products may be established by using standardized recipes that produce a consistent quality product. Specific standards are available for some product categories. Evaluation forms are available for students to use as guidelines for evaluating food quality.

- Food costs are easily established for recipes. Each recipe includes specific portion size information and instructions for ensuring accurate yields.

- Efficient labor procedures were considered for all recipes. Students and foodservice operators may use the recipes as a model for making products using the minimum amount of labor.

- Standardized recipes assure that accurate nutrition values can be assigned to serving portions. Users of the book can review the recipe's nutrient values and make adjustments, if required, for a specific population.

- *Food for Fifty* can be used for planning teas, receptions, and special functions. Part One brings together general information and guidelines useful for organizing events. Parts Two and Three support the planning function with food production information.

- Using *Food for Fifty* as a resource to direct accurate food production techniques is intended in the design of the recipes. Each recipe can be used for communicating the techniques necessary for producing a quality product. In addition, the material prefacing each recipe category and Chapter Three provides general text information that supports the standardized techniques specified in the recipes.

ACKNOWLEDGMENTS

Kansas State University's residence hall dining program "make-it-from-scratch" culture and high quality standards have for nearly 70 years helped shape *Food for Fifty*. It is with sincere appreciation for the support and encouragement from John Pence, associate director of Housing and Dining Services, for continuing to value this endeavor. Special acknowledgment is given to John and his management staff for their support, advice, and creative ideas. Without their help, this twelfth edition of *Food for Fifty* would not have been possible. Appreciation is extended also to the many colleagues, family, and friends who have, through the course of association with the author, made this revision of *Food for Fifty* possible.

We would also like to thank the reviewers for *Food for Fifty, 12/e* including

Geralyn H. Farley, Purdue University, Calumet

Nancy Brenowitz, University of Maryland

Nelda Downer, Oklahoma State University, Okmulgee

Janet B. Andersen, Utah State University

Laura McKnight, Idaho State University

H. G. Parsa, The Ohio State University

Jeanne Florini, St. Louis Community College at Florissant Valley

About the Author

Mary Molt, Ph.D., R.D., L.D., is assistant director of Housing and Dining Services and assistant professor of Hotel, Restaurant, Institution Management, and Dietetics (HRIMD), Kansas State University. She holds a bachelor's degree from the University of Nebraska—Kearney, a master's degree from Oklahoma State University, and a Ph.D. from Kansas State University. Dr. Molt has 31 years of professional experience at Kansas State University, with a joint appointment in academe and food service administration. Current responsibilities include team teaching Food Production Management, assisting with supervised practice experiences for senior students in Dietetics, and directing management activities for three residence hall dining centers serving more than 8,000 meals per day. Dr. Molt is active in the American Dietetic Association, Kansas Dietetic Association, and the National Association of College and University Food Services (NACUFS). Twice she was recognized with the NACUFS Richard Lichtenfelt Award for outstanding service to the association. In 1995, Dr. Molt received the Theodore W. Minah Award, the highest honor given by NACUFS, for exceptional contribution to the food service industry. The Award For Excellence in the Practice of Management was given to Dr. Molt in 1997 by the American Dietetic Association. She serves on several University committees, advises students in *Kappa Omicron Nu,* and holds membership in several honor societies including *Kappa Omicron Nu, Delta Kappa Gamma, Phi Upsilon Omicron,* and *Phi Kappa Phi.*

PART I

Planning Meals

Chapter   1   *Planning the Menus and Planning Special Meals and Receptions*   3

Planning Menus and Planning Special Meals and Receptions

G. Huntington / Pearson Education Corporate Digital Archive

Menu planning and serving special events are functions by which foodservice organizations are judged. The information in this chapter provides guidelines for planning menus, special meals, and receptions.

This chapter includes the following topics:

- Menu Planning: Types of Menus; Factors Affecting Planning; Planning Procedures; Planning for Different Types of Foodservices
- Planning Special Meals and Receptions: Planning Responsibilities; Receptions and Teas; Coffees and Brunches; Buffet Meals; Banquet Service; Styles of Service; Wine and Bar Service

Menu Planning

Food eaten outside the home has become an integral part of the American lifestyle. Patrons expect to have food choices that are creative, exciting, and nutritious. Menu writers are challenged to plan innovative menus that support the goals of the organization and that cater to customers' preferences.

A well-planned menu is the cornerstone of a successful foodservice and the focal point from which many activities originate. An understanding of menu types, factors affecting menu planning, and planning procedures is important before menu writing can begin.

TYPES OF MENUS

The menu is an outline of food items to be included in each meal or, in the broader sense, a list of all food items offered by a foodservice. Types of menus used in foodservices may be classified as static or set, cycle, or single use. Menus may be further categorized according to the degree of choice as selective or nonselective and by the method of pricing.

Static or *set menus* include the same menu items every day, but with a variety of choices, the exact number depending on the type of foodservice. Most commercial foodservices use this type of menu, and an increasing number of hospitals have adopted this static or restaurant-style menu pattern. Some restaurants change a few foods within a set menu to provide additional variety or to take advantage of special purchases and seasonal foods.

A *cycle menu* is a carefully planned series of menus that offer different items from day to day for one week, two weeks, or some other time period, after which the menus are repeated. The length of the cycle depends on the type of foodservice. A short cycle is appropriate for foodservices having a frequent clientele turnover, such as hospitals. If a short cycle is used for patient meals, a longer cycle is necessary for the employees' and visitors' foodservice. In extended care facilities, the cycle usually is four to six weeks. Using a cycle with numbers of days not divisible by seven ensures that the same menu is not served on the same day of the week.

Restaurants may prefer to use monthly or seasonal cycles or may use the same menu throughout the year. Many foodservices recognize seasonal changes by having spring, summer, autumn, and winter cycles.

Cycle menus save time for the planner and are effective tools for food and labor cost control, forecasting, and purchasing. Repetition of the same or nearly the same menu helps standardize preparation procedures and gives the employees an opportunity to become more efficient through repeated use of familiar recipes. Menus can become monotonous and repetitious, however, if not carefully planned. Regardless of the cycle length, menus should be constantly reviewed and updated. Each day's menu should be analyzed shortly after service, and any production problems or negative clientele feedback should be noted and corrections made before the next cycle. The menu planner must allow flexibility for changes due to holidays, special occasions, leftover food, and inability to obtain specific food items for production.

Selective menus offer two or more items within each category. Foods from which the individual patron may choose a well-balanced meal should be included. Most commercial and noncommercial foodservices use this type of menu extensively. Table 1.1 gives a suggested pattern for a selective menu, using the same format for lunch and dinner.

Nonselective menus have a single item in each menu category. To ensure nutritional adequacy, foods from each of the basic food groups should be included. Table 1.1 gives a general pattern for a nonselective menu. A nonselective menu may be modified to include a limited selection; for example, two entrees may be offered or a choice of two vegetables may be given. A soup and salad may be offered as an alternative to an entree and vegetable for those who wish a lighter meal.

Menus may also be classified by method of pricing. *Á la carte menus* price food items separately; the customer chooses menu items individually. *Table d'hôte menus* include the complete meal at a fixed price. It is common for foodservices that use a table d'hôte menu to offer more than one choice of complete menu. Banquet menus are examples of this strategy. *Pre fixe menus* are similar to table d'hôte menus in that the price for the meal is fixed. A pre fixe menu may offer choice within a menu category. *Du jour menus* are planned, written, and priced daily.

TABLE 1.1   Types of menu patterns

Nonselective menu pattern		
Breakfast	**Lunch**	**Dinner**
Fruit	Soup (optional)	Soup (optional)
Cereal	Entree	Entree
Protein item	Salad and/or vegetable	Two vegetables (one may be potato or starch food)
Bread, butter or margarine	Bread, butter or margarine	Salad
Beverage	Fruit or other light dessert	Bread, butter or margarine
	Beverage	Dessert
		Beverage

Selective menu pattern[a]	
Breakfast	**Lunch and dinner**
Fruits: 2 or more juices, fresh fruit in season	Soups: 1 cream, 1 broth
Cereals: cooked, choice of cold cereals	Entrees: at least 2 meats, 1 meatless, 1 meat extender, poultry or fish, and a cold plate
Entrees: eggs, bacon, ham, or sausage, potatoes, breakfast casserole	Sandwiches: 1 hot, 1 or more cold
Breads: toast, white and whole grain; one or more hot breads	Rice or pasta: in addition to or as alternative to potatoes
Beverages: coffee, decaffeinated coffee, tea, milk (whole and lowfat)	Vegetables: 3 or 4, including potatoes in some form
	Salads: 4 to 10, including entree, tossed green, vegetable, gelatin, fruit, cottage cheese, relishes
	Breads: 2 to 3, including white and whole grain, 1 hot bread
	Desserts: 4 to 8, including 2-crust pie, soft pie, cake and/or cookies, pudding, yogurt, ice cream or sherbet, fruit
	Beverages: coffee, decaffeinated coffee, tea, milk (whole and low fat), fruit juice or fruit flavored drinks

[a]Menu variety may be increased or decreased to fit the demands of the foodservice.

FACTORS AFFECTING MENU PLANNING

The production and service of food begins with the menu, which determines the foods to be purchased, the personnel needed and their work schedules, and the equipment necessary for production and service of the food. The menu is closely tied to financial management and marketing and, in a new foodservice, influences the design of the kitchen and selection of equipment. The menu, however, must be one that meets clientele expectations and that can be produced within facility constraints and demands. A number of factors must be considered when planning a menu.

Clientele

The menu planner must consider the makeup of the group to be served—age, gender, nutritional needs, food habits and customs, and individual preferences. This is especially important if the foodservice offers limited food choices, as in some extended care facilities, child care centers, and retirement complexes. Menus for this type of foodservice are planned to meet the needs of the majority of patrons, with enough flexibility to satisfy everyone. Planning menus for foodser-vices with a static population requires strict attention to the complete nutritional needs of the group. Such menus also must offer enough variety to minimize monotony and keep satisfaction high.

The Dietary Guidelines for Americans established by the U.S. Department of Agriculture and U.S. Department of Health and Human Services has helped to set in motion a national emphasis on good nutrition and healthful eating. Clientele's awareness of the relationship between food and health challenges food and nutrition professionals to use the guidelines when planning menus. The Dietary Guidelines for Americans (2000):

Aim for fitness

- Aim for a healthy weight.
- Be physically active each day.

Build a healthy base

- Let the Food Guide Pyramid guide your food choices. (Figure 1.1)
- Choose a variety of grains daily, especially whole grains.
- Choose a variety of fruits and vegetables daily.
- Keep food safe to eat.

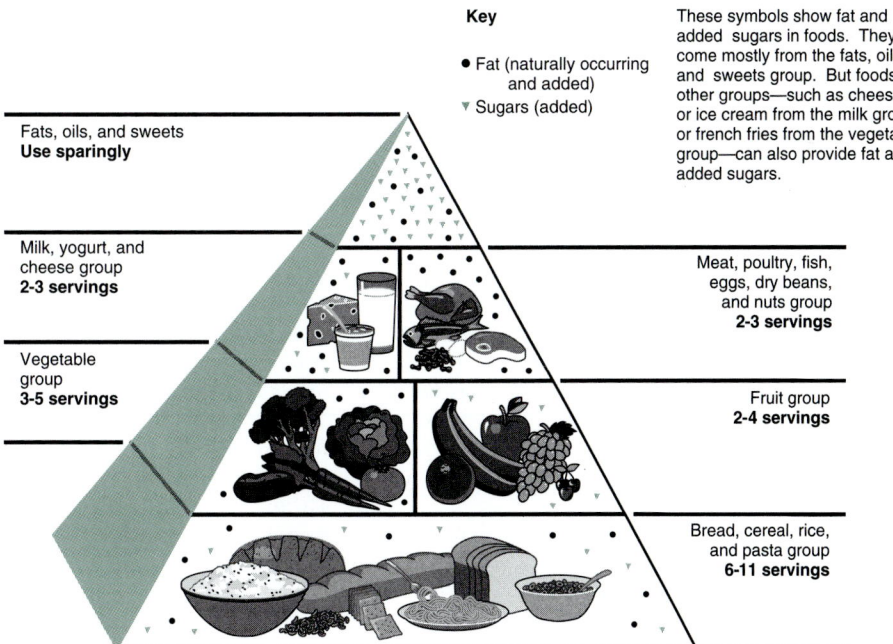

Key

- Fat (naturally occurring and added)
- ▼ Sugars (added)

These symbols show fat and added sugars in foods. They come mostly from the fats, oils, and sweets group. But foods in other groups—such as cheese or ice cream from the milk group or french fries from the vegetable group—can also provide fat and added sugars.

Fats, oils, and sweets
Use sparingly

Milk, yogurt, and cheese group
2-3 servings

Vegetable group
3-5 servings

Meat, poultry, fish, eggs, dry beans, and nuts group
2-3 servings

Fruit group
2-4 servings

Bread, cereal, rice, and pasta group
6-11 servings

Looking at the Pieces of the Pyramid

The Food Guide Pyramid emphasizes foods from the five major food groups shown in the three lower sections of the Pyramid. Each of these food groups provides some, but not all, of the nutrients you need. Foods in one group cannot replace those in another. No one of these major food groups is more important than another—for good health, you need them all.

FIGURE 1.1   Food pyramid. U.S. Department of Agriculture and U.S. Department of Health and Human Services.

Choose sensibly

- Choose a diet that is low in saturated fat and cholesterol and moderate in total fat.
- Choose beverages and foods to moderate your intake of sugars.
- Choose and prepare foods with less salt.
- If you drink alcoholic beverages, do so in moderation.

The Food Guide Pyramid (Figure 1.1) has been widely distributed and is often used by clientele for directing their food choices. The pyramid and serving guidelines (Tables 1.2 and 1.3) will be useful when planning healthful menus that support clientele eating according to the Dietary Guidelines for Americans.

Clients are increasingly more knowledgeable about new and different foods and desire greater variety and an opportunity to select foods representing new culinary styles. Ethnic, meatless, and regional foods are popular, and menus should incorporate choices from these categories. See p. 182 for flavor profiles of foods from different countries.

Vegetarian preferences are varied and savvy menu planners consider the preferences of their vegetarian clientele. *Vegans* eat plant products only, *lacto-vegetarians* eat plant and dairy products, *lacto-ovo-vegetarians* eat plant, dairy, and eggs. *Pesco-vegetarians* eat fish and plant products and may or may not eat dairy and egg. Religious customs are important in menu planning also. Table 1.4 identifies food practices of different religions.

Planning acceptable menus requires the menu planner to be aware of food preferences and to periodically evaluate clientele acceptance of foods and food combinations. Plate waste analysis, customer preference surveys, food usage data, meal census informa-tion, and informational interactions with clients are a few ways to assess menu acceptability.

Popular magazines, recently published cookbooks, and themes for new dining establishments reflect contemporary food interests of consumers and can be used as menu planning tools. Menu choices should include current dining trends; often slight adjustments or name modifications to existing recipes will satisfy clientele requirements for contemporary menu items.

Type of Foodservice

Menu plans cannot be generalized to a specific type of foodservice because of the wide variety of clientele most operations serve. Most college foodservices offer menu choices similar to commercial restaurants. Hospital menus for general diet patients may be no different from those in any other segment of the foodservice industry. School foodservice menus reflect offerings similar to foods available in the commercial market. Philosophy and specific limitations of individual foodservices provide more direction for the menu writer than does the type of foodservice.

Financial Limitations

The budget plays a critical role in planning menus. The costs of food, labor, and supplies for menu items must be considered in relation to projected income and expenses. In some foodservices, a raw food cost allowance per meal or per day may be determined. Although the daily food cost may fluctuate, the cumulative average for a week or a month must stay within the daily allowance. Offering a high-priced item along with a popular low-cost item will help balance costs. This is especially true with buffets, or when food amounts are not restricted.

TABLE 1.2   Servings required for the food groups in the Food Guide Pyramid

Food group	Children ages 2 to 6 years, women, some older adults (about 1,600 calories)	Older children, teen girls, active women, most men (about 2,200 calories)	Teen boys, active men (about 2,800 calories)
Bread, Cereal, Rice, and Pasta (Grains Group)—especially whole grain	6	9	11
Vegetable Group	3	4	5
Fruit Group	2	3	4
Milk, Yogurt, and Cheese (Milk Group)— preferably fat-free or low-fat	2 or 3*	2 or 3*	2 or 3*
Meat, Poultry, Fish, Dry Beans, Eggs, and Nuts (Meat and Beans Group)— preferably lean or low-fat	2, for a total of 5 ounces	2, for a total of 6 ounces	3, for a total of 7 ounces

Adapted from U.S. Department of Agriculture, Center for Nutrition Policy and Promotion. The Food Guide Pyramid, Home and Garden Bulletin Number 252, 1996.

* The number of servings depends on your age. Older children and teenagers (ages 9–18 years) and adults over the age of 50 need 3 servings daily. Others need 2 servings daily. During pregnancy and lactation, the recommended number of milk group servings is the same as for nonpregnant women.

TABLE 1.3   **Serving sizes for foods in the Food Guide Pyramid**

BREAD, CEREAL, RICE, PASTA GROUP

- 1 slice of bread
- About 1 cup of ready-to-eat cereal
- ½ cup of cooked cereal, rice, or pasta

VEGETABLE GROUP

- ½ cup of raw leafy vegetables
- ½ cup of chopped, cooked, or canned fruit
- ¾ cup of fruit juice

FRUIT GROUP

- 1 medium apple, banana, orange, pear
- ½ cup of chopped, cooked, or canned fruit
- ¾ cup of fruit juice

MILK, YOGURT, AND CHEESE GROUP*

- 1 cup of milk** or yogurt**
- 1½ ounces of natural cheese** (such as Cheddar)
- 2 ounces of processed cheese** (such as American)

MEAT, POULTRY, FISH, DRY BEANS, EGGS, AND NUT GROUP

- 2–3 ounces of cooked lean meat, poultry, or fish
- ½ cup of cooked dry beans*** or ½ cup of tofu counts as 1 ounce of lean meat
- 2½ ounce soyburger or 1 egg counts as 1 ounce of lean meat
- 2 tablespoons of peanut butter or ⅓ cup of nuts counts as 1 ounce of meat

From the Dietary Guidelines for America, Fifth Edition 2000, Home and Garden Bulletin No. 232. United States Department of Agriculture and United States Department of Health and Human Services.
* This includes lactose-free and lactose-reduced milk products. One cup of soy-based beverage with added calcium is an option for those who prefer a non-dairy source of calcium.
** Choose fat-free or reduced-fat dairy products most often.
*** Dry beans, peas, and lentils can be counted as a serving in either the meat and beans group or the vegetable group. As a vegetable, ½ cup of cooked, dry beans counts as 1 serving. As a meat substitute, 1 cup of cooked, dry beans counts as 1 serving (2 ounces of meat).

In commercial foodservices, the amount of money that can be spent on food is based on projected income from the sale of food. Food and labor costs are used in establishing the selling price, which often must be within a predetermined range, thus making the choice of menu items important. Forecasted need and menu mix, in relation to cost, must be considered.

Food Availability

While most foods are available year-round, there may be differences in quality and price. Peak seasons for fresh fruits and produce should be known when planning menus. Seasonal price differences occur also for non-produce food products, such as fresh fish and poultry. Locally grown food products, often available at farmers markets, should be considered; they are usually very fresh, good quality, and reasonably priced.

Production Capabilities

Available Equipment

The type, size, and amount of food preparation, holding, and transporting equipment available is an important factor in planning menus that can be produced. Special attention should be given to oven capacity, number of grills or fryers, refrigerator and freezer facilities, number and size of steam-jacketed kettles and steamers, and availability and capacity of mixers. Certain combinations of menu items often must be avoided because of lack of production equipment or serving pans and dishes.

Number and Experience of Employees

The person-hours of labor available and the efficiency and skill of employees are important factors to consider when deciding on the variety and complexity of the menu. Understanding the relationship between

TABLE 1.4 Food practices of different religions

BUDDHISM

Much variability exists between areas of the country and the sect. Generally Buddhists do not eat meat, especially beef as the cow is considered sacred. Dairy products, eggs, and some fish are usually eaten.

CHURCH OF JESUS CHRIST OF THE LATTER DAY SAINTS (MORMON)

Prohibit the use of coffee, tea, and alcoholic beverages. Many Mormons refrain from drinking any beverage with caffeine.

EASTERN ORTHODOX

On fast days and periods of fast, meat, fish, and animal products are not eaten. Shellfish is allowed. Fast days include most Wednesdays and Fridays (except during the fast-free week following Christmas and Easter), Eve of Theophany, Beheading of John the Baptist, and the Elevation of the Holy Cross. Fast periods include Advent, Great Lent, Fast of the Apostles, and Fast of the Dormition of the Holy Theotokos.

HINDU

Most Hindus follow a vegetarian diet. If meat is eaten, beef and pork is forbidden. The cow is considered sacred.

JUDAISM

Orthodox and some conservative Jews follow Jewish dietary laws that define the use of animal products. Permitted are mammals that have cloven hooves and chew a cud (e.g., cattle, goats, sheep), poultry with a crop and gizzard (e.g., chickens, ducks, geese, turkeys) and their eggs. Fish must have fins and scales. Meat and dairy products are not eaten together, and separate kitchen equipment is required for preparing meat and dairy products.

Jewish religious holidays with food element include:

Rosh Hashanah—Challah (braided egg bread) and apples dipped in honey are common menu items.
Yom Kippur—A day of fasting. A light meal is served after sundown.
Hanukkah—Latkes (potato pancakes) are often served.
Passover—Seder meal may be served. The foods for a Seder meal are specified.

MUSLIM

Prohibited foods include pigs and any animal that catches food with its mouth or talons (birds of prey). Some Muslims will eat only meat slaughtered according to a prescribed method. Very devout Muslims do not drink alcoholic beverages, coffee, or tea. During the month-long fasting period of Ramadan, Muslims over the age of 15 may eat only during the time before sunrise and after sunset.

PROTESTANT

Dietary customs vary among denominations.

ROMAN CATHOLIC

Few dietary restrictions are stipulated. Catholics between the ages of 14 and 60 are required to abstain from eating meat on Ash Wednesday, Good Friday, and during the Fridays of Lent. Some Catholics may abstain from eating meat every Friday throughout the year.

SEVENTH-DAY ADVENTISTS

Coffee, tea, alcoholic beverages, pork, and shellfish are not eaten. Milk and eggs are permitted. Many Seventh-Day Adventists do not eat meat or animal products. See Judaism for animal products that are permitted.

menu and personnel will help the planner develop menus that can be prepared by the available staff.

Distribution of Work

Menus should be planned to distribute the work evenly among the different areas of preparation. In determining a day's work load, the menu planner should consider not only one day's menu but also any preparation necessary for meals for the following day. Care should be exercised so menus are not planned that create an excessive work load for employees one day and underutilize them the next. To introduce variety in the menu, a limited number of foods requiring time-consuming processes may be included if combined with other food items that require minimum preparation. Some foods require last-minute cooking to ensure high quality. To avoid confusion and delayed meal service, the menu should be planned to balance items that may be prepared early and those that must be cooked just prior to serving.

MENU PLANNING PROCEDURES

Menu planning follows no absolute rules as long as clientele needs are satisfied and organization goals are met. It is suggested that menu planning be done without interruptions and that the following materials be available to the menu writer.

1. Menu forms as prescribed by type and needs of the foodservice.
2. Standardized recipe file.
3. Current trade periodicals and other foodservice publications.
4. Menu suggestions (Appendix A).
5. Previous menus.
6. Menu evaluation data to include customer and staff feedback.
7. Dietary Guidelines for Americans (full document available at www.usda.gov).

The following general guidelines should be considered when planning a menu.

Plan for Variety and Good Nutrition

1. Include a wide variety of foods from day to day to ensure adequate nutrients. Unless you provide a choice, avoid the same form of food on consecutive days; for example, meat loaf on one day and spaghetti and meatballs the next.
2. Include foods that will allow clientele to meet the Dietary Guidelines for Americans as established by the U.S. Department of Agriculture and the U.S. Department of Health and Human Services (see p. 5 for guidelines).
3. Avoid repeating the same food on the same day of the week. For this reason, a short cycle where the days are divisible by seven is undesirable.
4. Vary the method of preparation. For example, serve vegetables raw or cooked, seasoned, stir-fried, marinated, or with a sauce.
5. Introduce new foods regularly and, on a selective menu, pair a new food with a familiar well-liked food.

Plan for Eye Appeal

1. Try to visualize the appearance of the food on the plate.
2. Use at least one or two colorful foods on each menu.
3. Use colorful foods in combination with foods having little color.
4. When serving more than one vegetable, serve one green and one nongreen vegetable. Avoid serving vegetables that are the same color as the entree.
5. Vary the shapes of food.

Plan for Contrast in Texture and Flavor

1. Offer crisp foods with soft foods.
2. Use strong- and mild-flavored foods together.
3. Balance light and heavy foods; for example, in a nonselective menu pair light desserts with hearty entrees.
4. Avoid repeating foods with similar cooking methods.
5. Avoid using the same herbs and spices in foods served together on the same plate.
6. Avoid serving very strong foods with delicate entrees.

Plan for Consumer Acceptance

1. Include food combinations most acceptable to the clientele.
2. The completed menu should, if possible, have a predominance of familiar and well-accepted menu items, with the introduction of new or less well-liked foods spaced throughout the menu period.
3. In nonselective menus, it is important that the less popular foods be accompanied by some that are well liked by the majority of the clientele.
4. Periodically assess the food preferences of the consumers.

Plan for Financial, Production, and Service Limitations

1. Include food combinations that can be prepared with available personnel and equipment.
2. Select menu items that will keep food costs within the budget allowance.

Plan for Minimizing Leftovers

1. Plan menu items so as much edible trim as possible can be incorporated into another menu item; for example, meat scraps in soup or other dishes, raw meat trim in stew.
2. Plan menu item combinations so leftovers can be avoided; for example, batch production considerations, lead items complemented by secondary items.
3. Plan the menu to use leftover menu items in a different form; for example, roast turkey followed by turkey salad sandwich rather than the reverse order.
4. Carefully plan menu to use perishable ingredients that have a minimum order quantity greater than the amount needed for a specific recipe.

Steps in Menu Planning

Determine a Time Period

Plan menus for at least a week at a time, preferably longer. If a cycle menu is being planned, decide on the length of the cycle. Decide on the meal pattern before beginning.

Proceed Systematically

Select menu items systematically. Entrees are selected first because they are the central focus of a meal and form the framework of the menu plan. Other foods are then chosen that complement the entree.

Entrees.   Select meat and other entrees for the entire cycle or length of time for which menus are being planned. If planning a week's menus only, choose entrees for a month or longer, then complete the menus as needed. In this way, an entree cycle can be developed that would simplify planning each week's menus. Since entrees usually are the most expensive food on the menu, cost can be controlled to a great extent through careful planning at this point. A balance between high- and low-priced items will average out the cost over the week or period covered by the cycle.

On a selective menu, offer at least one meat and one meatless entree, along with poultry and fish to complete the number of entrees required.

Be specific about method of preparation when recording the menu; for example, show pork chops as baked, stuffed, barbecued, breaded, or prepared using another method.

Soups and Sandwiches.   Plan soups and sandwiches at the same time as entrees if they are to be offered as a main dish in lieu of meat or other entree. On a selective menu, offer a cream soup and a stock soup. In a cafeteria, a variety of sandwiches may be offered that may not change from day to day.

Vegetables.   Select vegetables that are compatible with the entrees. Potatoes, rice, or pasta may be included as one choice. On a selective menu, pair a popular vegetable with one that is less well liked.

Salads.   If only one salad is to be offered, select one that complements or is a contrast in texture to the other menu items. On a selective menu, include a green salad and fruit, vegetable, and gelatin salads to complete the desired number. Certain salad items may be offered daily such as tossed salad, cottage cheese, or cabbage slaw; or a salad bar may be a standard menu feature. See p. 640 for salad bar suggestions.

Breads.   Vary the kinds of breads offered or provide a choice of white or whole grain bread and a hot bread.

Desserts.   If no choice is offered, plan a light dessert with a hearty meal and a rich dessert when the rest of the meal is not too heavy. On a selective menu, include a two-crust pie, a soft pie, cake, pudding, and a gelatin dessert. Ice cream, yogurt, baked custard, and fruit may be offered daily.

Breakfast Items.   Certain breakfast foods such as cooked and cold cereal, toast, and fruit juices may be standard. Variety may be introduced through a choice of entrees, hot breads, and fresh fruits.

Beverages.   A choice of beverages usually is provided. Coffee, decaffeinated coffee, tea, and milk, including lowfat, usually are offered. Lemonade, soft drinks, fruit punch, and a variety of juices may be included also.

Evaluate the Completed Menu

After the menu has been planned, check carefully to see if it has met the established criteria. Evaluate the menu again after the meals have been served. Make notations of satisfactory menus and difficulties encountered in production and service of the meals. If the cycle is to be repeated, desired alterations should be noted.

The responsibility of the menu planner does not end with the writing of the menu. The task is completed only when the food has been prepared and served and the reaction of the consumer noted.

MENU PLANNING FOR DIFFERENT TYPES OF FOODSERVICE

Elementary and Secondary Schools

National School Lunch Program

The National School Lunch Program (NSLP) is designed to provide nutritious, reasonably priced lunches to children in schools and residential child care centers, to contribute to a better understanding of good nutrition, and to foster good food habits. School foodservice is an integral part of the child's education.

The nutrition goals of the NSLP are designed to provide adequate calories and nutrients for specific age groups of children while reducing fat and saturated fat to recommended levels. The goals are based on the Recommended Dietary Allowances (RDA) (⅓ RDA for lunch, ¼ RDA for breakfast), children's calorie (energy) requirements, and the Dietary Guidelines for Americans (p. 5). USDA nutrient standards for the NSLP set target goals for calories, calcium, iron, protein, and vitamins A and C. Standards also specify that no more than 30 percent of calories come from fat and less than 10 percent of the fat calories come from saturated fat. States are required to establish their own nutrient standards for carbohydrates, cholesterol, fiber, and sodium.

Three menu planning systems that meet federal guidelines are compared in Table 1.5. Enhanced Food-Based Menu Planning requires specific food group components in specific amounts for different established age/grade groups. Nutrient Standard Menu Planning (NSMP) uses computerized nutrient analysis of menus. This planning system uses a simplified menu pattern which requires that lunches include an entree and milk. Other food items may be added to the menu. When averaged over a week, the menus must meet the nutrient standards and calorie requirements for specific age/grade groups. NSMP and Assisted Nutrient Standard Menu Planning (Assisted NSMP) are exactly alike except an outside consultant or other agency performs all functions of menu planning and nutrient analysis.

Not represented in Table 1.5 is the Traditional Food-Based Menu Planning system, used since the National School Lunch Program was established in 1946. Although the Traditional Food-Based Menu Planning system is still an option, it is used infrequently because of the difficulty in complying with the Dietary Guidelines. This system was designed to provide, over time, the RDA for key nutrients but without consideration for calorie needs or dietary fat.

To qualify for reimbursement, a school is required to use the framework specified in this table and to meet the minimum nutrition standard requirements, Tables 1.6 and 1.7. Other foods may be added to improve acceptability and to satisfy students' appetites.

An "offer versus serve" provision allows students to choose fewer than all the food items offered. However, they must select a specified minimum amount of food in order for the lunch to be reimbursed. Schools are required to implement the "offer versus serve" provision for senior high school students. The implementation of this provision in middle, junior high, and elementary schools is left to the discretion of the local school food authorities.

The cycle menu is used to some extent in school foodservices, and many schools are using selective menus in which students may choose from two items of comparable nutritional value for part of the menu; for example, a student may have a choice of two vegetables and two fruits. Some schools offer multiple menus in which more than one complete menu that meets federal requirements is offered, such as a chef's salad or soup and sandwich meal. À la carte items are also provided in many schools. The more menu choices provided to students, the better their participation in the school foodservice programs.

Many foods on the Suggested Menu Items listed in Appendix A are suitable for school lunches. Keep in mind the nutrition requirements, cost, labor and equipment restraints, and food preferences of the age group served. Adding options such as salad bars, special day celebrations, or ethnic and international food promotions allows the school foodservice operation to compete with the commercial food industry.

School Breakfast Program

The importance of students eating a nutritious breakfast cannot be overemphasized. Breakfast furnishes fuel for the morning, when students do most of their learning. In 1975, Congress passed an amendment that made the School Breakfast Program (SBP) a permanent part of the Child Nutrition Act. All public and nonprofit private schools may participate in the SBP.

The School Breakfast Pattern for the various age groups is found in Table 1.8 on p. 16. To qualify for reimbursement, a school is required to use this framework and to meet the minimum requirements, but other foods may be added to help improve acceptability and to satisfy students' appetites. Offer versus serve is also available to any school in the SBP, whereby students can refuse some items comprising a school breakfast. School breakfast requires little additional labor from the school foodservice operation.

Child and Adult Care Food Program

The Child and Adult Care Food Program (CACFP) was founded in 1968 to provide federal funds for meals

TABLE 1.5   Comparison of school foodservice menu planning systems

	Enhanced food-based menu planning	*Assisted nutrient standard menu planning ("Assisted NuMenus")*	*Nutrient standard menu planning ("NuMenus")*
Meals are planned based on . . .	Enhanced Meal Pattern (must meet nutritional standards)	Required nutrient levels averaged over a school week	Required nutrient levels averaged over a school week
Reimbursable lunch requirements under "offer vs. serve"	Offer a minimum of 5 food items: • 1 meat/meat alt. • 2 vegetables/fruits • 1 grain/bread • 1 milk Senior high students must accept 3 food items. Students below senior high must accept 3 or 4 food items at the discretion of the School Food Authority.	• Schools must offer students at least 3 menu items: an entree, fluid milk, and another menu item. • Students must select at least 2 of the 3 menu items; 1 of the 2 must be an entree. • If more than 3 menu items are offered as a meal unit, students may decline no more than 2 menu items of the meal unit (entree must be selected).	• Schools must offer students at least 3 menu items: an entree, fluid milk, and another menu item. • Students must select at least 2 of the 3 menu items; 1 of the 2 must be an entree. • If more than 3 menu items are offered as a meal unit, students may decline no more than 2 menu items of the meal unit (entree must be selected).

Reimbursable breakfast requirements under "offer vs. serve"	Offer a minimum of 4 food items:
	• 1 milk
	• 1 vegetable/fruit
	• 1 of the 3 following combinations:
	    1 meat/meat alt. AND
	    1 bread/bread alt.
	    OR
	    2 meat/meat alt.
	    OR
	    2 bread/bread alt.
	
	Students must accept 3 food items.
		• Schools must offer fluid milk as a beverage or on cereal or both. Must offer at least 2 side dishes.
		• Students may decline a maximum of 1 menu item out of the 3 or more required menu items offered.
			• Schools must offer fluid milk as a beverage or on cereal or both. Must offer at least 2 side dishes.
			• Students may decline a maximum of 1 menu item out of the 3 or more required menu items offered.

Menu items credited toward nutrient standard requirements	Only USDA-approved foods count toward meeting meal pattern.	All menu items count.	All menu items count.
Computer needs	Not required	Not required because nutrient analysis may be done by another school, a consultant, or a school food co-op.	Required—District must have computer hardware and USDA approved nutrient analysis software.
Recordkeeping	• Production records document quantities planned and served. • CN label or product analysis required for pre-prepared items. • Recipes and nutritional analysis of pre-prepared items.	• Production records document quantities planned and served. • Nutrient analysis required at school level.	• Production records document quantities planned and served. • Nutrient analysis required at school level.

TABLE 1.5   *continued*

	Enhanced food-based menu planning	Assisted nutrient standard menu planning ("Assisted NuMenus")	Nutrient standard menu planning ("NuMenus")
Age/grade groupings (lunch)	Three grade groups are required: • Preschool • K–6 • 7–12 Four grade groups are optional: • Preschool • K–3 • 4–6 • 7–12 *Breakfast Required* • Preschool • K–12 • 7–12 (optional)	Opt. 1—Grade Groups: • Preschool • K–6 (optional: K–3 and 4–6) • 7–12 Opt. 2—Age Groups: • 3–6 • 7–10 • 11–13 • 14 and older Opt. 3—Create custom groups *Breakfast Required* • K–12 • 7–12 (optional)	Opt. 1—Grade Groups: • Preschool • K–6 (optional: K–3 and 4–6) • 7–12 Opt. 2—Age Groups: • 3–6 • 7–10 • 11–13 • 14 and older Opt. 3—Create custom groups *Breakfast Required* • K–12 • 7–12 (optional)
Meeting Dietary Guidelines	• Schools must meet Dietary Guidelines. Nutrient analysis is optional. • State educaton agency will conduct nutrient analysis to determine if Dietary Guidelines are met.	• Schools must meet Dietary Guidelines and are required to provide nutrient analysis at school level. Schools must document that they have served the recipes and menus used in the nutrient analysis. • State educaton agency will review nutrient analysis to determine if Dietary Guidelines are met.	• Schools must meet Dietary Guidelines and are required to do nutrient analysis at school level. • State educaton agency will review nutrient analysis to determine if Dietary Guidelines are met.
Advantages	Requires minimal training and change for local personnel.	Requires minimal training and change for local personnel. Menus will comply with the DGA.	Local district retains flexibility and control. Menus will comply with the DGA.
Disadvantages	School will not know if it is meeting the DGA until it is reviewed by state education agency. Length of education agency review will increase substantially to allow time to perform nutrient analysis. Due to length of time between reviews, problems could go uncorrected for long periods.	Costs may be incurred to have an outside party perform nutrient analysis. If a food vendor performs nutrient analysis, there may be financial implications. For example, schools might be required to use specified products. Schools will lose some control and flexibility.	Costs will be incurred for hardware and software. Personnel will need to spend time learning the software and setting up the system (i.e., entering local recipe and product data).

Source: Kansas State Department of Education (KSDE) and USDA

Notes: • DGA—Dietary Guidelines for Americans.
   • NSMP—Nutrient Standard Menu Planning, which means planning menus that provide adequate nutrients to meet the Dietary Guidelines for Americans.
   • NuMenus—USDA's term for NSMP.
   • Assisted NuMenus and Assisted NSMP—refers to nutrient analysis of school menus performed by another school, a consultant, or a school food co-op.
   • Other menu planning systems may meet federal guidelines.

TABLE 1.6   Age group nutrient standards for NuMenus and Assisted NuMenus (1)

Nutrients and energy allowances	Ages 3–6	Ages 7–10	Ages 11–13	Ages 14 and above
SCHOOL BREAKFAST				
Energy allowances/calories	419	500	588	625
Total fat (as a percent of actual total food energy)	(2)	(2)	(2)	(2)
Saturated fat (as a percent of actual total food energy)	(3)	(3)	(3)	(3)
Protein (g)	5.50	7.00	11.25	12.50
Calcium (mg)	200	200	300	300
Iron (mg)	2.5	2.5	3.4	3.4
Vitamin A (RE)	119	175	225	225
Vitamin C (mg)	11.00	11.25	12.50	14.40
SCHOOL LUNCH				
Energy allowance/calories	558	667	783	846
Total fat (as a percent of actual total food energy)	(2)	(2)	(2)	(2)
Saturated fat (as a percent of actual total food energy)	(3)	(3)	(3)	(3)
Protein (g)	7.3	9.3	15.0	16.7
Calcium (mg)	267	267	400	400
Iron (mg)	2.5	2.5	3.4	3.4
Vitamin A (RE)	158	233	300	300
Vitamin C (mg)	14.6	15.0	16.7	19.2

Source: U.S. Department of Agriculture

(1) School week averages for age groups.

(2) Not to exceed 30 percent over a school week.

(3) Less than 10 percent over a school week. Grams of fat will vary depending on calories offered.

and snacks to licensed public and nonprofit child care centers, and to family and group child care homes for preschool children. Funds are also provided for meals and snacks served at after-school programs for school-age children, and at adult day care centers serving chronically impaired adults or people over age 60.

To meet the nutritional needs of children and adults, specified meal patterns are followed. The required portion sizes for young children differ slightly between CACFP and school nutrition programs. CACFP Meal Pattern requirements are shown in Tables 1.9 and 1.10.

In planning food for children, their total daily food requirements should be considered. The combination of meals and snacks will vary according to the age group, their time of arrival at the center, and their length of stay. It is important that the planner consider the nutritional needs of the children, their food preferences, regional food habits, equipment, personnel, and other management functions.

Young children need nutritious foods at frequent intervals, but it is important to schedule the service of food to allow sufficient time between meals and supplements. Young children enjoy food they can handle easily. Finger food, snacks, and bite-size pieces are most popular. Banana slices, berries, dried peaches or pears, fresh fruit wedges, carrot and celery sticks, cheese cubes, and crackers are examples of finger foods.

Those responsible for foodservice in child care centers should provide the opportunity for children to learn about the foods they eat so they can begin to make wise, nutritious choices.

Colleges and Universities

College and university foodservice menus are representative of the marked change in the college foodservice industry over the last decade. The college customer on most campuses has several menu options: board plan cafeterias, snack bars, specialty shops, food courts, convenience stores, vending operations, cash cafeterias, and fine dining restaurants. Commonplace, too, are catering operations that support social, athletic, and university events both on and off campus.

More than one menu type may be appropriate for these varied functions because the menu must support many objectives. For example, a serving area may provide traditional board, cash meals, and carry-out food options from a single location. The success of these

TABLE 1.7   Grade group nutrient standards for NuMenus, Assisted NuMenus, and food-based menu planning (1)

Nutrients and energy allowances	Preschool	Grades K–6	Grades 7–12	Option for Grades K–3
SCHOOL BREAKFAST				
Energy allowances/calories	388	554	618	
Total fat (as a percent of actual total food energy)	(2)	(2)	(2)	
Saturated fat (as a percent of actual total food energy)	(3)	(3)	(3)	
Protein (g)	5	10	12	
Calcium (mg)	200	257	300	
Iron (mg)	2.5	3.0	3.4	
Vitamin A (RE)	113	197	225	
Vitamin C (mg)	11	13	14	
SCHOOL LUNCH				
Energy allowance/calories	517	664	825	633
Total fat (as a percent of actual total food energy)	(2)	(2)	(2)	(2)
Saturated fat (as a percent of actual total food energy)	(3)	(3)	(3)	(3)
Protein (g)	7	10	16	9
Calcium (mg)	267	286	400	267
Iron (mg)	3.3	3.5	4.5	3.3
Vitamin A (RE)	150	224	300	200
Vitamin C (mg)	14	15	18	15

Source: U.S. Department of Agriculture
(1) School week averages for grade groups.
(2) Not to exceed 30 percent over a school week.
(3) Less than 10 percent over a school week. Grams of fat will vary depending on calories offered.

complex operations is closely linked to the menu design and the ability of the menu writer to satisfy both facility and customer objectives.

The selective menu pattern in Table 1.1 may be used for designing a traditional cycle menu. With today's campus diner, however, the most successful menus offer extensive variety daily. Menus must be exciting and creative and reflect choices that parallel student preferences. Basing menu decisions on accurate food trend data is necessary.

Consideration for good nutrition is important for all menu writers but offers a special challenge when the customer is generally from a healthy population and often between 18 and 28 years old. Customers of this age are more apt to make choices based on impulse preference than are clientele from a population having health and dietary concerns. The menu, to be successful, must allow for customer satisfaction and at the same time reflect the principles of sound nutrition and quality nutritious food. Customer input is necessary for designing menus that allow this to happen. See p. 5 for the Dietary Guidelines for Americans.

The following section, "Commercial Foodservices," includes additional information appropriate to the college and university market.

Commercial Foodservices

Menu planning for commercial foodservices varies according to the type and size of operation, its goals, and the expected check average. Menus range from the fast-food concept of a limited menu for high volume and quick service to the table d'hôte menu of a formal seated-service restaurant.

The basic rules of menu planning apply to commercial foodservices. Type of foodservice must be determined, financial goals decided, production and service capabilities analyzed, and labor needs addressed. Assessing clientele wants is especially important and should be assessed accurately, using proven research procedures.

Commercial customers make choices daily about what and where to eat and the amount of money they will spend. It is often not enough for the menu planner to follow all the rules that make production and

TABLE 1.8 Food-based menu meal plans

	Minimum quantities for enhanced food-based menus			
	Required			Option
	Ages 1–2	Preschool	Grades K–12	Grades 7–12
BREAKFAST				
Milk (Fluid) (As a beverage, on cereal or both)	½ cup	¾ cup	8 fl oz	8 fl oz
Juice/Fruit/Vegetable Fruit and/or vegetable; or full-strength fruit juice or vegetable juice	¼ cup	½ cup	½ cup	½ cup
Select *one* serving from each of the following components or *two* from one component:				
Grains/Breads[a] One of the following or an equivalent combination:				
Whole grain or enriched bread, whole grain or enriched biscuit/ roll, muffin, etc.	½ serving	½ serving	1 serving	1 serving
Whole grain, enriched or fortified cereal	¼ cup or ⅓ oz	⅓ cup or ½ oz	¾ cup or 1 oz	¾ cup or 1 oz
				Plus an additional serving of one of the grains/breads above
Meat or Meat Alternates				
Meat/poultry or fish	½ oz	½ oz	1 oz	1 oz
Cheese	½ oz	½ oz	1 oz	1 oz
Egg (large)	½	½	½	½
Peanut butter or other nut or seed butters	1 Tbsp	1 Tbsp	2 Tbsp	2 Tbsp
Cooked dry beans and peas	2 Tbsp	2 Tbsp	4 Tbsp	4 Tbsp
Nut and/or seeds (as listed in program guidance) [b]	½ oz	½ oz	1 oz	1 oz
Yogurt (plain or flavored, sweetened or unsweetened)[c]	2 oz or ¼ cup	2 oz or ¼ cup	4 oz or ½ cup	4 oz or ½ cup

[a] Grain/bread requirements are based on the weight of the enriched flour or whole grain in the product.
[b] No more than 1 oz of nuts and/or seeds may be served in any one meal.
[c] Frozen yogurt may not be counted.

TABLE 1.8   *continued*

	Minimum quantities for enhanced food-based menus				
	Required				Option
	Ages 1–2	*Preschool*	*Grades K–6*	*Grades 7–12*	*Grades K–3*
LUNCH					
Milk (as a beverage)	6 fl oz	6 fl oz	8 fl oz	8 fl oz	8 fl oz
Meat or Meat Alternate (quantity of the edible portion as served)					
Lean meat, poultry, or fish	1 oz	1½ oz	2 oz	2 oz	1½ oz
Cheese	1 oz	1½ oz	2 oz	2 oz	1½ oz
Large egg	½	¾	1	1	¾
Cooked dry beans or peas	¼ cup	⅜ cup	½ cup	½ cup	⅜ cup
Peanut butter or other nut or seed butters	2 Tbsp	3 Tbsp	4 Tbsp	4 Tbsp	3 Tbsp
Yogurt (plain or flavored, unsweetened or sweetened)	4 oz or ½ cup	6 oz or ¾ cup	8 oz or 1 cup	8 oz or 1 cup	6 oz or ¾ cup
The following may be used to meet no more than 50% of the requirement and must be used in combination with any of the above:					
Peanuts, soynuts, tree nuts, or seeds, as listed in program guidance, or an equivalent quantity of any combination of the above meat/meat alternate (1 ounce of nuts/ seeds = 1 ounce of cooked lean meat, poultry, or fish).	½ oz = 50%	¾ oz = 50%	1 oz = 50%	1 oz = 50%	¾ oz = 50%
Vegetables/Fruits (2 or more servings of vegetables or fruits or both)	½ cup	½ cup	¾ cup plus extra ½ cup over a week[d]	1 cup	¾ cup
Grains/Breads Must be enriched or whole grain. A serving is a slice of bread or an equivalent serving of biscuits, rolls, etc., or ½ cup of cooked rice, macaroni, noodles, other pasta products or cereal grains.[a]	5 servings per week[d] Minimum of ½ per day[e]	8 servings per week[d] Minimum of 1 per day[e]	12 servings per week[d] Minimum of 1 per day[e]	15 servings per week[d] Minimum of 1 per day[e]	10 servings per week[d] Minimum of 1 per day[e]

Source: U.S. Department of Agriculture
[d] For the purposes of this chart, a week equals five days.
[e] Up to one grains/breads serving per day may be a dessert.

TABLE 1.9   Child care meal pattern

Breakfast for children			
Select all three components for a reimbursable meal			
Food components	*Ages 1–2*	*Ages 3–5*	*Ages 6–12*[1]
1 milk			
Fluid milk	½ cup	¾ cup	1 cup
1 fruit/vegetable			
Juice,[2] fruit and/or vegetable	¼ cup	½ cup	½ cup
1 grains/bread[3]			
bread or	½ slice	½ slice	1 slice
cornbread or biscuit or roll or muffin or	½ serving	½ serving	1 serving
cold dry cereal or	¼ cup	⅓ cup	¾ cup
hot cooked cereal or	¼ cup	¼ cup	½ cup
pasta or noodles or grains	¼ cup	¼ cup	½ cup

Snack for children			
Select two of the four components for a reimbursable snack			
Food components	*Ages 1–2*	*Ages 3–5*	*Ages 6–12*[1]
1 milk			
Fluid milk	½ cup	½ cup	1 cup
1 fruit/vegetable			
Juice,[2] fruit and/or vegetable	½ cup	½ cup	¾ cup
1 grains/bread[3]			
Bread or	½ slice	½ slice	1 slice
cornbread or biscuit or roll or muffin or	½ serving	½ serving	1 serving
cold dry cereal or	¼ cup	⅓ cup	¾ cup
hot cooked cereal or	¼ cup	¼ cup	½ cup
pasta or noodles or grains	¼ cup	¼ cup	½ cup
1 meat/meal alternate			
Meat or poultry or fish[4] or	½ oz	½ oz	1 oz
alternate protein product or	½ oz	½ oz	1 oz
cheese or	½ oz	½ oz	1 oz
egg[5] or	½	½	½
cooked dry beans or peas or	⅛ cup	⅛ cup	¼ cup
peanut or other nut or seed butters or	1 Tbsp	1 Tbsp	2 Tbsp
nuts and/or seeds or	½ oz	½ oz	1 oz
yogurt[6]	2 oz	2 oz	4 oz

service possible without special consideration for the role the menu plays in making the commercial food-service operation successful. A few guidelines that should be followed in designing the commercial menu are:

- Decide what to serve and what to charge. Market research is necessary to assess accurately what customers will purchase.

- Design the presentation of the menu suitable to the operation. The layout and overall design should be readable and attractive, and should support marketing goals.

- Determine the sequence of food items on the menu. A generally accepted sequence is appetizers or foods eaten first, then soups, entrees, and desserts. Within this order, salads, side orders, and beverages must be placed. Foods listed first within each category are selected most often so consideration should be given to this placement.

- Write the menu names to describe the foods offered accurately and to merchandise the food item and the operation. The importance of the menu to create atmosphere and serve as a marketing and advertising tool cannot be overemphasized.

Hospitals

Although hospital menus may be more complex, the principles of meal planning for health care facilities are the same as those for other types of foodservices. Foods must be provided for many kinds of diets, ranging from

TABLE 1.9   *continued*

Food components	Lunch or supper for children Select all four components for a reimbursable meal		
	Ages 1–2	*Ages 3–5*	*Ages 6–12[1]*
1 milk			
Fluid milk	½ cup	¾ cup	1 cup
1 fruit/vegetable			
Juice,[2] fruit and/or vegetable	¼ cup	½ cup	¾ cup
1 grains/bread[3]			
Bread or	½ slice	½ slice	1 slice
cornbread or biscuit or roll or muffin or	½ serving	½ serving	1 serving
cold dry cereal or	¼ cup	⅓ cup	¾ cup
hot cooked cereal or	¼ cup	¼ cup	½ cup
pasta or noodles or grains	¼ cup	¼ cup	½ cup
1 meat/meal alternate			
Meat or poultry or fish[4] or	1 oz	1½ oz	2 oz
alternate protein product or	2 oz	1½ oz	2 oz
cheese or	1 oz	1½ oz	2 oz
egg[5] or	½	¾	1
cooked dry beans or peas or	¼ cup	⅜ cup	½ cup
peanut or other nut or seed butters or	2 Tbsp	3 Tbsp	4 Tbsp
nuts and/or seeds or	½ oz	¾ oz	1 oz
yogurt[6]	4 oz	6 oz	8 oz

From USDA Child and Adult Care Food Programs

[1] Children age 12 and older may be served larger portions based on their greater food needs. They may not be served less than the minimum quantities listed in this column.

[2] Fruit or vegetable juice must be full-strength. Juice cannot be served when milk is the only other snack component.

[3] Breads and grains must be made from whole-grain or enriched meal or flour. Cereal must be whole-grain or enriched or fortified.

[4] A serving consists of the edible portion of cooked lean meat or poultry or fish.

[5] One-half egg meets the required minimum amount (one ounce or less) of meat alternate.

[6] Yogurt may be plain or flavored, unsweetened or sweetened.

liquid, ground, soft, or regular, to bland, low sodium, low carbohydrate, or fat restricted, with a wide range in caloric requirements. In addition, a cafeteria generally is available for hospital personnel and visitors.

Like college and university foodservices, hospitals are adopting more characteristics of the commercial foodservice. More emphasis is being placed on developing innovative menus and on offering new and creative food items. Many hospitals use catering and other services as revenue centers.

Cycle menus are widely used in health care facilities. The length of patient stay is an important factor in determining the length of the cycle. In an acute care hospital, where the average length of stay may be three to five days, a short cycle could be used. In an extended care facility a longer cycle would be more satisfactory. If a short cycle is used for patient meals, a longer cycle would be required for the employee cafeteria.

When developing a hospital meal pattern, the first step is to plan a regular or normal diet that will supply all food essentials necessary for good nutrition. This pattern then becomes the foundation for most diets required for therapeutic purposes and is the core of all meal planning in a hospital of any type or size. Patients requiring other than a normal diet will receive various modifications of the regular diet to fit their particular needs.

In planning a normal or regular diet, meals should be planned for each day as a unit. Each day's menu then can be checked to be sure that all essential foods have been included. A suggested three-meal-a-day menu pattern for a normal diet is given in Table 1.1.

The selective menu adds much to the satisfaction of patients and also helps to prevent waste. Choices that appeal to various patients usually can be made available with little extra work, if careful planning is used in pairing items on the menu. The main items on the selective

TABLE 1.10   Adult care meal pattern

Breakfast for adults		
Select all three components for a reimbursable meal		
1 milk	1 cup	fluid milk
1 fruit/vegetable	½ cup	juice,[1] fruit and/or vegetable
1 grains/bread [2]	2 slices	bread or
	2 servings	cornbread or biscuit or roll or muffin or
	1½ cups	cold dry cereal or
	1 cup	hot cooked cereal or
	1 cup	pasta or noodles or grains

Lunch for adults		
Select all four components for a reimbursable meal		
1 milk	1 cup	fluid milk
2 fruit/vegetable	1 cup	juice,[1] fruit and/or vegetable
1 grains/bread[2]	2 slices	bread or
	2 servings	cornbread or biscuit or roll or muffin or
	1½ cups	cold dry cereal or
	1 cup	hot cooked cereal or
	1 cup	pasta or noodles or grains
1 meat/meat alternate	2 oz	lean meat or poultry or fish[3] or
	2 oz	alternate protein product or
	2 oz	cheese or
	1	egg or
	½ cup	cooked dry beans or peas or
	4 Tbsp	peanut or other nut or seed butter or
	1 oz	nuts and/or seeds[4] or
	8 oz	yogurt[5]

Supper for adults		
Select all three components for a reimbursable meal		
2 fruit/vegetable	1 cup	juice,[1] fruit and/or vegetable
1 grains/bread[2]	2 slices	bread or
	2 servings	cornbread or biscuit or roll or muffin or
	1½ cups	cold dry cereal or
	1 cup	hot cooked cereal or
	1 cup	pasta or noodles or grains
1 meat/meat alternate	2 oz	lean meat or poultry or fish[3] or
	2 oz	alternate protein product or
	2 oz	cheese or
	1	egg or
	½ cup	cooked dry beans or peas or
	4 Tbsp	peanut or other nut or seed butter or
	1 oz	nuts and/or seeds[4] or
	8 oz	yogurt[5]

menu are the same as those on the general menu. Some items, such as the choice of meat and vegetables, may be the same as foods prepared for one of the modified diets or for the cafeteria. Other choices may be soup or fruit juice, or fruit or ice cream in place of a prepared dessert. On the dinner menu, choices of light or more hearty foods may do much to promote patient acceptance. Some hospitals have adopted a selective menu similar to the table d'hôte menu of the commercial sector. The same menu is offered daily but with a wide enough variety of choices that the patient can select a different meal each day. Patients may order any food item on the menu unless it is restricted on their diets.

Foodservices Serving Older Adults and the Disabled

Good menu planning is an important factor in meeting the nutritional needs as well as many social and psychological needs of older adults eating meals in ex-

TABLE 1.10 *continued*

		Snacks for adults
		Select two of the four components for a reimbursable snack

1 milk	1 cup	fluid milk
1 fruit/vegetable	½ cup	juice,[1] fruit and/or vegetable
1 grains/bread[2]	1 slice	bread or
	1 serving	cornbread or biscuit or roll or muffin or
	¾ cup	cold dry cereal or
	½ cup	hot cooked cereal or
	½ cup	pasta or noodles or grains
1 meat/meat alternate	1 oz	lean meat or poultry or fish[3] or
	1 oz	alternate protein product or
	1 oz	cheese or
	½	egg or
	¼ cup	cooked dry beans or peas or
	2 Tbsp	peanut or other nut or seed butter or
	1 oz	nuts and/or seeds[4] or
	4 oz	yogurt[5]

From USDA Child and Adult Care Food Program

[1] Fruit or vegetable juice must be full-strength.

[2] Breads and grains must be made from whole-grain or enriched meal or flour. Cereal must be whole-grain or enriched or fortified.

[3] A serving consists of the edible portion of cooked lean meat or poultry or fish.

[4] Nuts and seeds may meet only one-half of the total meat/meat alternate serving and must be combined with another meat/meat alternate to fulfill the supper requirement.

[5] Yogurt may be plain or flavored, unsweetened or sweetened.

tended care facilities, retirement communities, or congregate dining sites, or in their homes via home-delivery programs. The menu planning guidelines discussed earlier in this chapter will also be helpful when writing menus for the older and sometimes disabled adult clientele. When planning menus for older adults, it is especially important to get their input during the menu-writing process and their evaluation after the meals are served. Input mechanisms may include advisory councils, focus groups, suggestion boxes, or formal and informal surveys. Feedback may also be provided by production staff, service or support staff, and drivers that deliver meals in home-delivery programs.

Menu planners for older adults should be aware of the challenges unique to this age group. The habits and food preferences that have developed through the years may influence but should not determine entirely the meals planned for them. Healthy adults, regardless of age, need nutritious meals and, in planning the day's food, the basic pattern for the normal diet should be followed. Individual needs of the group members, such as difficulty in chewing, special dietary requirements, and limited mobility and activity, must also be considered.

In extended care facilities and retirement communities, at least three well-planned meals should be served daily, with hot food at each meal. The menu pattern can follow a pattern similar to that of the regular hospital diet (p. 4), with adjustments in portions and some modification for residents with individual eating problems. If a non-selective menu is used, some system for choice will add to the residents' acceptance of the food. Choice may be provided by offering popular menu items daily in addition to a set menu, or through a choice of two items in each menu category for one meal a day. To improve satisfaction, long term care facilities that offer a non-selective menu should consider using a four- to five-week cycle or longer and changing it seasonally. Holidays and special events are opportunities for adding menu variety to non-selective menus and should be planned within each cycle.

Foodservice programs producing food for the older adult population should plan menus that follow the Dietary Guidelines for Americans. (See Figure 1.1; Tables 1.2 and 1.3) The regulatory requirement for following the guidelines may vary among states.

USDA's Child and Adult Care Food Program (CACFP) is directed toward child and adult care food programs and was discussed on p. 11. Table 1.10 provides guidelines for adult care menu planning.

The Older Americans Act (OAA) provides for nutritional services for older or disabled adults in either congregate settings or as home-delivered meals. The Act requires that nutrition programs meet the Dietary Guidelines for Americans and the Recommended Dietary Allowances (RDAs) established by the Food and Nutrition Board, Institute of Medicine, National Academy of Sciences. The Dietary Reference Intakes (DRI's) were published as an update to the older RDAs and because they reflect new dietary information they should be used in place of the RDAs. Each meal must provide a minimum of one-third of the daily recommended dietary allowances, totaling 100 percent when three meals are served. In addition to meeting these guidelines, the menus for OAA programs should follow the menu-writing guidelines discussed earlier in this chapter.

Planning Special Meals and Receptions

Planning special meals and receptions is a function of nearly every foodservice. The types of functions may include coffees, teas, receptions, brunches, buffets, banquets, and catered events. Regardless of the type of service provided, considerable planning is required to ensure a successful foodservice event.

PLANNING RESPONSIBILITIES

Careful planning is important to the success of any special event. The major responsibilities of the foodservice staff in charge of a special meal or other function are as follows:

- Confer with representatives of the group to be served to determine the type of function or theme; date, time and place; number to be served; service desired; event's agenda; any special dietary needs of guests; budget range; and financial arrangements. Understanding the client expectations is important. For events off-premise, a site visit is recommended to clarify details such as electrical and water sources, guest access and traffic flow, catering access and staff parking, kitchen availability or staging area, and storage for supplies.

- Plan the menu with the client or client's representative. Provide creative ideas that harmonize with those of the client. Plan menus that can be produced with the resources available. If the event is off-premise, food that can be prepared ahead of time and transported easily should be planned. Duplicate copies of the menu plans should be signed and kept by the client and the foodservice director. This procedure confirms the agreement and may prevent a misunderstanding of details and last-minute changes.

- Determine food quantities and estimated cost of food to be served. Criteria to consider when planning food quantities for events include the age of the guests, gender, any pre- and post-event functions, length of the event, and type of service (buffet, sit-down, etc.). A general guideline is to prepare 20 percent more food for events with 20 guests, 15 percent more for 50 guests, 10 percent more for 100 guests. Events with more than 100 guests generally require preparing 5–10 percent more food than the guaranteed number.

- Place food orders. It is important that orders for foods not normally used be made early enough to ensure delivery.

- Prepare the dish and equipment list and make arrangements for obtaining any additional items needed. A list including the amount and kind of linen, dishes, silverware, glassware, serving utensils, and tables and chairs required should be compiled by the manager and arrangements made for assembling these at least one day before they are to be used. Success of a special event is often evaluated by the creative use of different sizes and shapes of dishes and the methods used to present the food to guests.

- Prepare work schedules. A detailed work schedule includes preparation, cooking, serving, room setup, and cleanup assignments. If workers are inexperienced, the schedule should indicate a time for each task, detailed procedures, and other special instructions. For a seated service luncheon or dinner, assign personnel to the serving counter from which plates will be filled. Assign and instruct servers for dining room service. See pp. 30–35 for directions for table setting and service.

- Supervise the setup of the room and the preparation and service of food. Complete the setup approximately one hour before guests arrive. Give last-minute attention to plate garnishes and food presentation. See Exhibits VII, VIII, IX, X, XI, XII and XIII in the color insert for examples of nicely garnished and attractively presented food.

- Supervise the dishwashing and cleanup of preparation and service areas.

- Prepare and keep on file a detailed report, including menu, number of guaranteed guests and actual attendance, quantity of food prepared and leftover amounts, income and expenses, and recommended changes and useful comments for service of similar events in the future. Record any unusual factors that may have affected consumption or attendance; for example, weather, gender of guests, or any unusual circumstances regarding the event.

- Follow up with the client after the event to evaluate the success from the customer's point of view. Record information that can be used for future events.

RECEPTIONS AND TEAS

Receptions and teas may vary in degree of formality and may accommodate a few or many guests. The menu may be simple or elaborate and should be planned according to the type of event; the time of day; the number, age, and gender of guests to be served; and the money and labor available.

One or two beverages usually are offered—coffee and tea or coffee and punch. The menu may be limited to an attractive dessert, with nuts and mints, or it may include several kinds of sandwiches, cookies, or cakes. The following are suggested choices for a reception or tea:

Beverages:
Coffee, tea, hot spiced tea or cider, punch, wine.
See Tables 1.11 and 1.12 on pp. 24 and 26 for wine purchasing and selection guides. See p. 261 for nonalcoholic cocktail suggestions.

Breads:
Open-face sandwiches spread with a variety of fillings and decorated attractively.
Rolled, ribbon, checkerboard, or pinwheel sandwiches.
Nut bread or fruit bread sandwiches with cream cheese or marmalade filling, cut in squares, triangles, round, or oblong shapes.
Cheese wafers or cheese straws.
Miniature cream puffs filled with chicken or fish salad.
Petite biscuits with sliced meat or salad filling.

Dips:
Dips with cheese, cream cheese, yogurt, or sour cream base served with crisp raw vegetables, fruits, and/or crackers and chips.

Cakes, cookies, and tarts:
Petits fours or small decorated cupcakes.
Meringue shells with whipped cream and fruit fillings.
Small pecan or fruit tarts.
Small tea cookies that offer a variety of shapes, flavors, and colors.

Nuts and candies:
Salted, toasted, or spiced nuts.
Candied orange or grapefruit peel.
Mints in pastel colors.

Figure 1.2 suggests a table arrangement for a reception or tea, using two lines of service and set up so that a guest may start by placing a beverage cup on a plate, then selecting food items. The silverware and napkin usually are last. Placing the cup on the plate first ensures adequate space for both food and beverage. If only one or two food selections are offered, beverages may be served last. Use Figure 1.2 as a guide, but start with plates and end with the beverage or beverages.

The table covering, centerpiece, tea service, silverware, and serving dishes should be attractive, and the food should be colorful and interestingly arranged. To prevent a crowded appearance, there should be a limited amount of silverware, china, napkins, and food on the table when the serving begins. A small serving table with extra china and silverware near the tea table is a convenience. Replacements of small dishes and appointments are brought on trays from the kitchen. If two beverages are served, they are placed at either end of the table. Cookies, sandwiches, and other foods should be arranged so they do not appear crowded. It is best to use small serving plates and replace them frequently so there is an assortment of food at all times. Arrangements should be made for people to pour the beverages, and employees or hostesses should be assigned to replenish the tea table and to take empty plates from guests.

COFFEES AND BRUNCHES

Coffees and brunches are easy and popular ways to entertain a few or many guests. An ample supply of hot, fresh coffee is necessary, and an alternate choice of tea and/or decaffeinated coffee may be offered. Flavored coffees and teas are popular beverage choices. One or more hot breads are served, and the menu may be expanded to include fresh fruit or juice. A fruit tray, with bite-size pieces of fresh fruit arranged on a silver or other appropriate tray, is an attractive centerpiece and an interesting addition to a coffee hour or brunch.

Brunch, a meal combining breakfast and lunch, usually includes a wider variety of food than does a coffee. The menu may consist of foods normally served at breakfast or may resemble a luncheon menu, depending partly on the hour of service. It may be quite simple, consisting of fruits, hot breads, and coffee; or it may be a more substantial meal that will replace lunch. The food usually is placed on a buffet table for self-service, but may be served to guests seated at tables. Brunch often starts with fruit juice or sparkling wines served to guests before they go to the buffet table. The main entree may be one or several that are typical of breakfast, such as eggs in some form, bacon, ham, sausage, or a breakfast casserole; or a luncheon-type entree of chicken, turkey, or fish. An assortment of breads usually is offered. A dessert may be served if the

TABLE 1.11   Wine and food pairing guide

		Appetizers (light)	Cheese (mild)	Cheese (strong)	Pasta (light)
WHITE WINES (DRY)	Chablis (light bodied)	X	X		X
	Sauvignon Blanc (medium bodied)	X	X		X
	Fume Blanc (medium bodied)		X		X
	Pinot Blanc (medium bodied)		X		
	Pinot Gris (medium bodied)				X
	Chardonnay (full bodied)		X	X	
	Viognier (full bodied)		X		
WHITE WINES (SLIGHTLY SWEET)	Johannisberg Riesling (light bodied)	X			
	Gewürztraminer (light bodied)	X	X		
	Chenin Blanc (medium bodied)	X	X		X
	Ice Wines (medium bodied)			X	
WHITE WINES (SWEET)	Sauternes (medium bodied)			X	
RED WINES	Gamay-Beaujolais (light bodied)	X	X		X
	Pinot Noir (medium bodied)		X		
	Merlot (medium bodied)		X	X	
	Zinfandel (medium bodied)			X	
	Syrah/Shiraz (medium bodied)	X	X		
	Cabernet Sauvignon (full bodied)			X	
	Sangiovese/Chianti (light)	X	X		X
ROSE WINES	White Zinfandel and other "blush" wines (light bodied)	X	X		X
SPARKLING WINES AND CHAMPAGNE	Brut	X			
	Asti Spumante				
FORTIFIED DESSERT WINES	Port			X	
	Sherry	X (before dinner)			

meal is scheduled late in the morning, but it should be light. Suggested foods for coffee hours and brunches are as follows:

Fruits and juices:

Orange, pineapple, or tomato juice.
Fresh fruit cup or fresh berries.
Melon wedges, fruit kebobs.
Orange juice, champagne punch.

Fruit trays:

Fresh pineapple chunks, banana wedges, orange sections, fresh strawberries, kiwi fruit, mangos, carambola (star fruit).

Apple slices, honeydew melon wedges, kiwi fruit, and frosted grapes.
Plums or bing cherries, pear slices, cantaloupe wedges, green grapes, and cheese cubes.

Entrees:

Canadian bacon, grilled ham, sausage patties on apple rings.
Small biscuits with ham slice.
Scrambled eggs, egg and sausage casserole, omelets.
Cheese and broccoli strata, quiche, cheese soufflé, crepes, broiled or grilled chicken breast on rice or pasta.

TABLE 1.11 *continued*

Pasta (robust)	Beef	Lamb	Pork/ veal	Ham	Poultry	Seafood (heavy sauce)	Seafood (light or no sauce)	Tuna/ salmon	Fruits/ desserts
			X		X		X	X	
			X	X	X		X	X	
			X		X		X	X	
X			X	X	X	X	X	X	
			X	X	X	X			
X		X	X		X	X			
X		X	X		X	X		X	
	X		X	X	X		X	X	X
					X			X	
			X	X	X		X		
									X (after dinner)
									X
	X		X	X	X		X	X	X
X	X	X	X	X	X	X		X	
	X								
X	X	X	X		X				
X	X	X	X	X	X			X	
	X								
X	X	X		X	X	X		X	
			X	X	X	X	X		X
					X	X	X	X	
									X (fruits)
									X
									X (after dinner)

Note: • Serving temperatures: dry whites and roses, 44°–54°F; light-bodied reds, 50°–55°F; medium-bodied to full-bodied reds, 55°–65°F; sweet wines, 41°–47°F; sweet fortified wines (port), room temperature; sparkling wines, 41°–47°F.

Breads:
> Small pecan or orange rolls, scones, kolaches, toasted English muffins or bagels with marmalade and/or cream cheese.
> Coffee cake, Danish pastry.
> Small doughnuts or doughnut holes, cinnamon puffs.
> Small nut or fruit bread sandwiches.

Desserts:
> Fresh pineapple and berries, ambrosia, sherbet.
> Strawberry-sour cream crepes, fruit and cheese platters.
> Cookies or small cakes.

BUFFET DINNERS AND LUNCHEONS

Buffet dinners and luncheons provide a means of serving relatively large groups of people with a minimum of service personnel. The ability to offer a variety of foods makes buffets popular.

The steps to planning a buffet include theme development and menu planning, tables and space arrangement, food presentation, and service. The steps are not

TABLE 1.12   Wine purchasing guide

Size	Volume (ounces)	Servings per container[a]	
		Dinner	Cocktail
187.5 milliliters (split)	6.35	1½	2
375 milliliters (half)	12.7	3	4
750 milliliters (standard)	25.4	6	8
1 liter	33.8	8	11
1.5 liters (magnum)	50.7	12	17
3 liters	101.4	25	34
4 liters	135.2	34	45

[a]Number of servings per container is based on dinner portion size 4 oz, cocktail portion size 3 oz. If larger or smaller glasses are used, adjustment in the servings per container will need to be made.

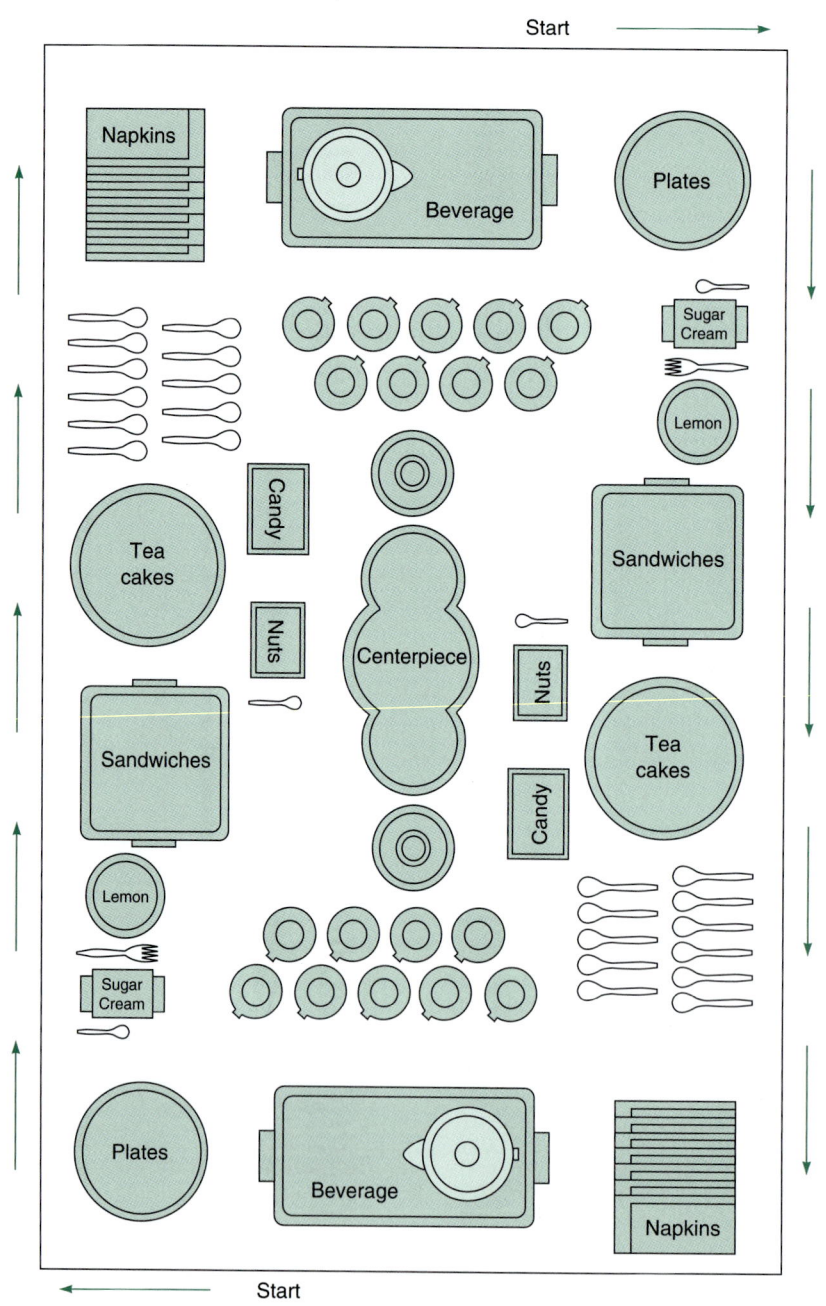

FIGURE 1.2   Table arrangement for a reception or tea.

independent of each other and so must be considered together.

Menu Planning

The number of selections offered may depend on preparation time, space on the buffet table, and the equipment available for preparation and service. Client or guest expectations also must be considered. At a minimum, food selections on a buffet should be two or three entrees (beef, poultry, and if a third, fish, shellfish, or pork), one nonmeat entree, one or two starches (potato, pasta, rice), one or two vegetables (green and nongreen), two or three salads, relishes, hot bread, dessert, and beverage.

Plan a menu that is easy for guests to serve themselves. For example, avoid foods that are soft and runny on the plate. Foods that require extra silverware, such as bread and butter spreaders and cocktail forks, usually are not served.

Plan hot foods that hold well and serve easily. Rare meat, delicate pasta such as capellini, and French fries do not hold well on a buffet line. Select instead foods that will hold their quality when held hot such as braised meat, large roasts, rigatoni pasta, and baked potatoes.

Choose foods that have different cooking methods, colors, and textures. Avoid serving a creamed vegetable with sauced meat items, strong-flavored vegetables with delicate entrees, or deep-fried potatoes with fried vegetables.

Balancing expensive items with popular less-expensive items will help achieve financial goals. Foods appropriate for buffets may be selected from the Suggested Menu Items in Appendix A. Consider religious customs when planning the menu. See p. 8.

Table and Space Arrangement

Buffet tables and food items may be arranged in several ways. Figures 1.3 and 1.4 illustrate a buffet arrangement with one service line. A double line, as shown in Figures 1.5 and 1.6, will speed service but requires more space and duplicate serving dishes. Figure 1.7 illustrates a straight-line simple buffet arrangement, used when large groups serve themselves from both sides of the table. For a large group requiring a more elaborate buffet, it is advisable to set up several serving stations, each serving different food items. A typical four-station buffet for serving 200 people includes:

Salad station (round 72-inch table):

Salad plates, several salads, fresh fruit, bread and butters/spreads, salad dressings, and crackers and cheeses.

First entree station (two serpentine tables arranged in an S shape):

Plates, display cooking station (stir-fry perhaps), chafing pans for entree accompaniments (pasta, rice, sauces), antipasto, breads, and butter/spreads.

Second entree station (see Figure 1.4 for table requirement):

Plates, carving station, chafing pans for entree accompaniments (vegetables, potatoes/starches), sauces, breads, and butter/spreads.

Dessert station (see Figure 1.6 for table requirement):

Plates, desserts and dessert sauces, cups and saucers, coffee/tea, and beverage condiments (sugar cubes, sweeteners, cream, whipped cream, citrus peel, cinnamon sticks, cinnamon, nutmeg, chocolate shavings).

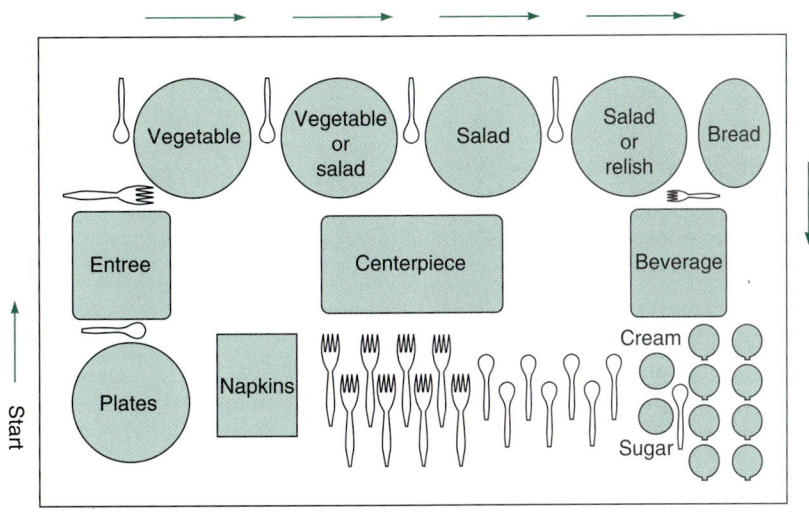

FIGURE 1.3 Table arrangement for buffet service, single line. Beverages may be served at tables. Desserts may be served from a dessert table or to guests at the individual tables. Suitable for serving very small numbers.

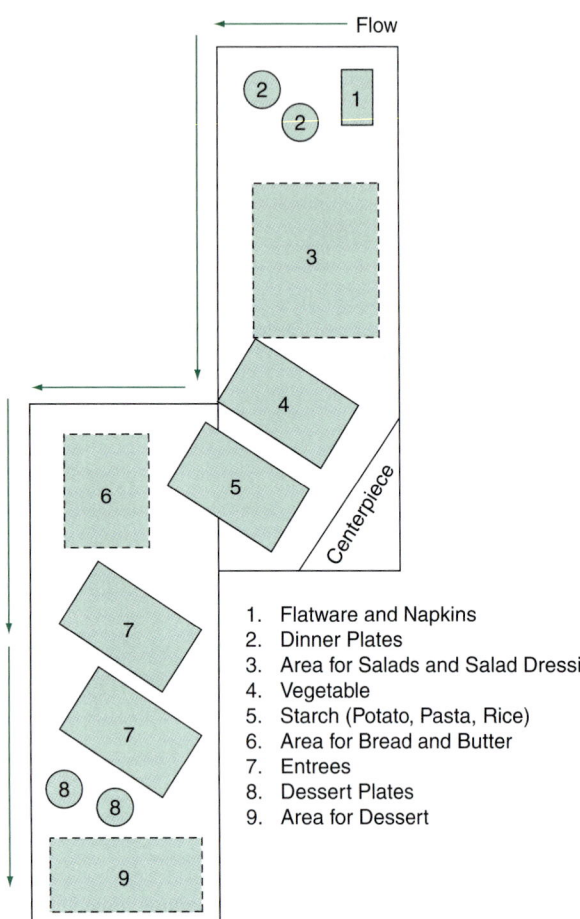

1. Flatware and Napkins
2. Dinner Plates
3. Area for Salads and Salad Dressing
4. Vegetable
5. Starch (Potato, Pasta, Rice)
6. Area for Bread and Butter
7. Entrees
8. Dessert Plates
9. Area for Dessert

FIGURE 1.4   Table arrangement for buffet service, single serving line using two 8 foot × 30 inch tables. Shorter tables may be used if desserts are served to guests or served from a separate table. This straight-line agrrangement is suitable for serving 50 or fewer people.

All tables should include at least one centerpiece. Beverages other than coffee and tea should be served by the wait staff or at another table.

Food Presentation and Service

The success of a buffet meal depends not only on the quality of the food, but also on the attractiveness of the buffet table. Visual appeal may be increased by placing trays and chafing dishes at an angle to the table, raising trays on one or two corners so they slant toward guests, and displaying food trays and pans at different levels. Interesting colors may be introduced in the table covering, the serving dishes, the food, and the decorations.

The attractiveness of cold food plates and platters can be enhanced by carefully selecting the foods to include. Consider choosing *items* that are seasonal, practical, properly sized, and both traditional and non-traditional. The number of items on the platter should provide a full but not over-crowded display. Some open

spaces heighten the display's attractiveness. *Flavor* enhances a platter when the foods selected are fresh and compatible. *Color* combinations that exhibit natural tones and vibrant colors provide attractive displays. *Texture* is achieved by varying the cooking methods and choosing foods with different textures. *Height* adds interest and visual appeal to food on a platter. Consider choosing foods with natural height differences. The *shape* of the food should be natural and not contrived. This can be accomplished by using a combination of cut, molded, loose, and whole food items.

Designing attractive cold platters requires applying some general principles. Buffet platters have three elements—a centerpiece or focal point, the main item, and a garnish.

The centerpiece may be an uncut piece of the main item (e.g., whole cheese, small roast), an item related to the main item, a sauce or condiment for the main item, or a decorative-only item such as fresh flowers in a vegetable vase. Not all platters require a centerpiece but all should have a focal point. The centerpiece should compliment the main item and not dominate the platter.

The main item should be arranged artistically, keeping in mind that food should be easy for guests to handle and self-serve. Another goal is to have the platters look nice throughout the serving period. Arranging foods in curves or with angled lines gives a sense of motion and adds to the design's artistry.

The garnish serves the same function as for plated meals (p. 35) and should enhance and not overpower the platter. Platters with adequate color and texture may not need a garnish. See Exhibit VII in the color insert for table and garnish ideas.

When arranging foods and other items on the buffet table consider *flow* of people through the line. The order of food should be logical. A generally accepted procedure is to arrange the food in the same order as if it were a served meal. Placing condiments and side dishes near the food they will accompany is suggested. Panning foods together that are intended to be served together is a presentation style that enhances food appeal and helps guests select food items more quickly. For example, chicken breasts, rice pilaf, and grilled vegetables could be placed together in the same chafing pan.

Using an 11-inch plate is satisfactory for most buffets. If using a smaller plate, then consider placing salad plates alongside the salads. If dessert is served on the buffet table, then plates should be placed on the buffet table near the desserts. Desserts may be placed on a separate table from which guests will later serve themselves. An attractive dessert table will make a lasting impression on guests.

Make room between serving pans for ease of serving and for changing pans of food. Adequate *spacing* will be achieved when approximately one linear foot of space is allowed for each item on the buffet.

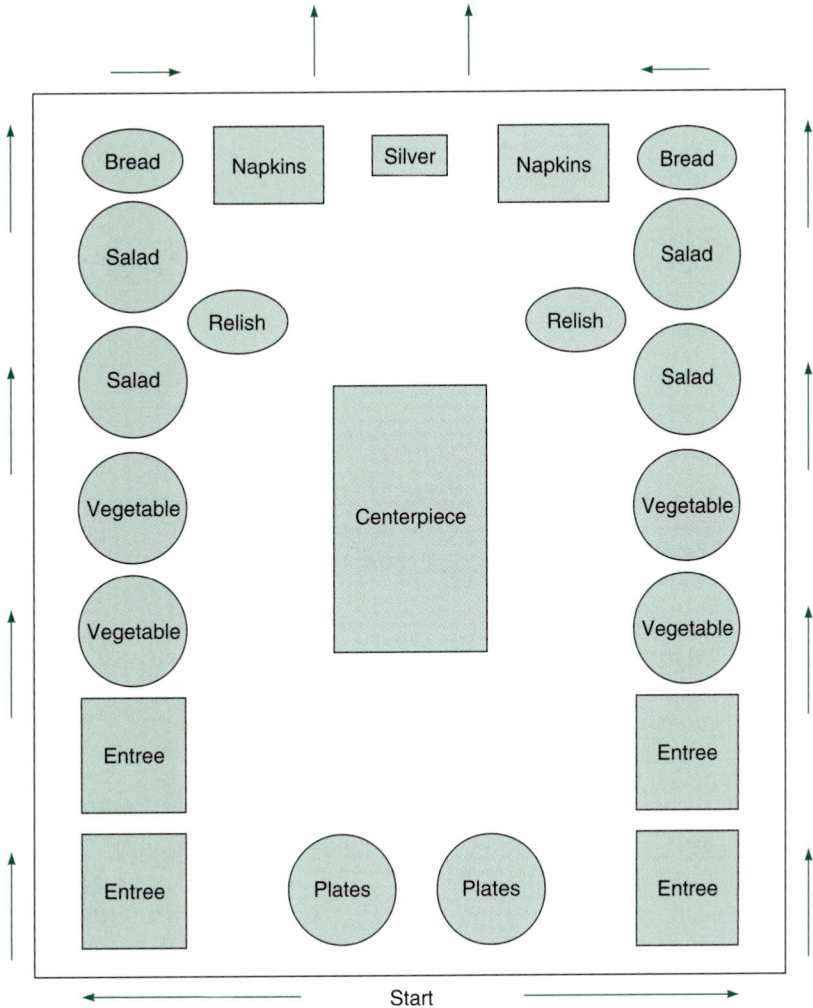

FIGURE 1.5   Table arrangement for buffet service, double line. Beverages may be served at tables. Desserts may be served from a dessert table or to guests at the individual tables. Suitable for serving small numbers.

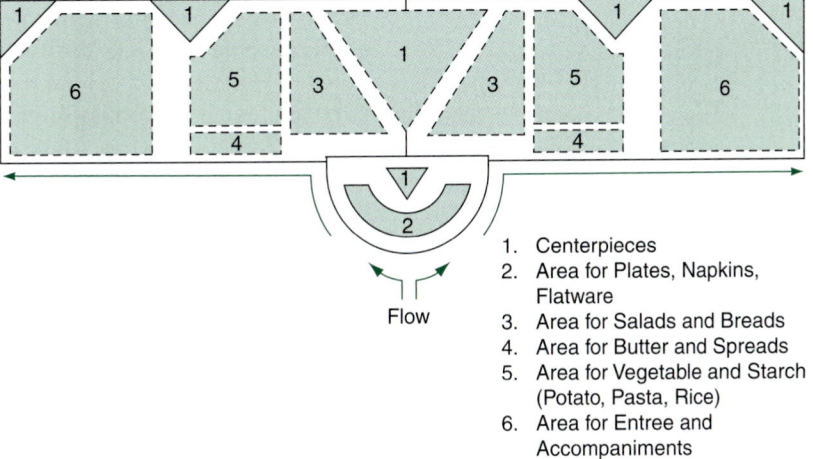

1. Centerpieces
2. Area for Plates, Napkins, Flatware
3. Area for Salads and Breads
4. Area for Butter and Spreads
5. Area for Vegetable and Starch (Potato, Pasta, Rice)
6. Area for Entree and Accompaniments

FIGURE 1.6   Table arrangement for buffet service, double serving line using one side of two 8 foot × 30 inch tables and a small 30-inch-radius half-round table. Small tables may be added to each end if dessert is served. Arrangement is suitable for serving 150 people.

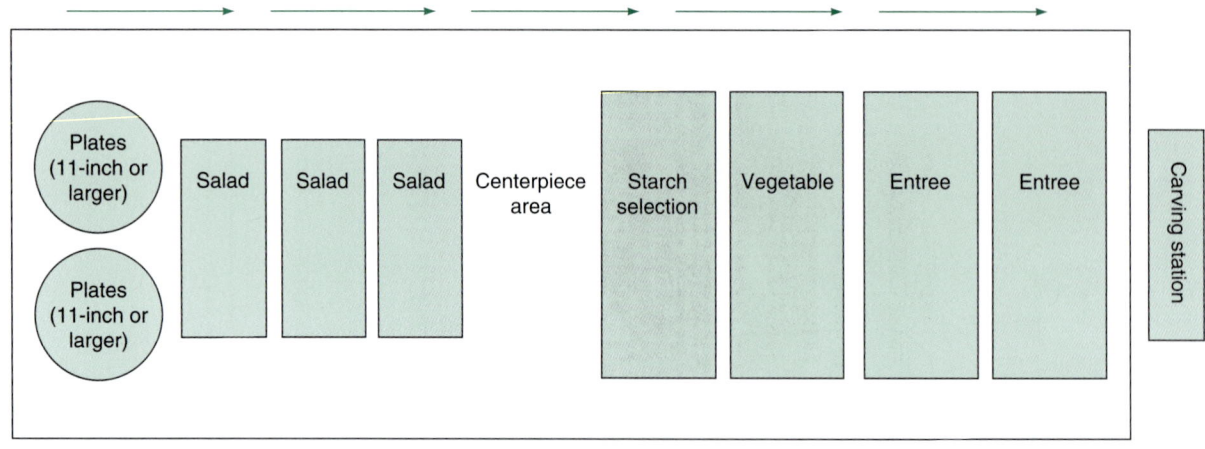

FIGURE 1.7   Table arrangement for buffet service, double straight-line for serving large numbers. Guests serve themselves from either side of a single line of food items. Napkins, silverware, bread and butter, and beverages are usually placed at each table. Desserts may be served at a separate table or individually to each guest.

Buffets can become messy if foods are placed out of guests' *reach*. If possible, avoid placing food so guests must reach over other food items; however, when placing food behind other food is unavoidable, use care to put messy serving items to the front of the table. Elevating the food to the back of the table will help reduce drips and spills and also adds to the attractiveness of the food display. Elevation can be achieved by draping tablecloths or napkins over different-size cans or boxes.

Centerpieces and *decorations* add to the visual appeal of a buffet table and can be used to carry out a menu theme. Both should be sized appropriately for the space and not interfere with the service of the food.

Labeling food items that are unusual or not easily recognized is recommended. Because some people are allergic to nuts, it is advisable to identify products that contain nuts.

BANQUET SERVICE

Although table service for banquets in hotels and many other commercial foodservices may be elaborate, a simplified service may be the most practical for foodservices in which only an occasional banquet is served. The discussion of table setting and plate service that follows is intended primarily for this type of facility.

Preparation of the Dining Room

Tables and chairs should be arranged to allow adequate space for serving after the guests are seated. Chairs should be placed so that the front edge of each touches or is just below the tablecloth. If there is to be a head table, it should be placed so that it is easily seen by the guests, with a podium and microphone available for the program. Audiovisual equipment, if needed, should be

properly placed and adjusted. Serving stands, conveniently placed, facilitate service. Such provisions are especially important when the distance to the kitchen or staging area is great.

Setting the Tables

Tablecloth.   Tablecloths generally are used for banquets, although place mats make an attractive table setting when the finish of the table top permits and the meal is informal. Place the cloth on the table so that the center lengthwise fold falls exactly in the middle of the table and the four corners are an equal distance from the floor. The cloth should extend 6 to 12 inches over the table top and should not touch the chair seat.

The Cover.   The plate, silverware, glasses, and napkin to be used by each person are known as the cover (see Figure 1.8). Consider 20 inches of table space as the smallest permissible allowance for each cover; 25 to 30 inches is better. Place all silverware and dishes required for one cover as close together as possible without crowding.

Silverware.   Place knives, forks, and spoons about 1 inch from the edge of the table and in the order of their use (see Figure 1.8). Some prefer to place the salad or dessert fork next to the plate as the menu dictates. If the menu requires no knife, omit it from the cover. When cocktail forks are used, they are placed at the extreme right of the cover. If a butter spreader is used, lay it across the upper right side of the bread and butter plate with the cutting edge toward the center of the plate. It may be placed straight across the top of the plate or with the handle at a convenient angle. Dessert silverware often is not placed on the table when the cover is laid, except when the amount of silver required for the entire meal is small or when it is necessary to simplify the service. If a dessert

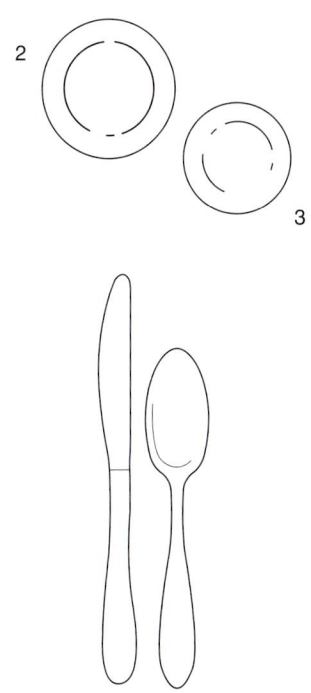

FIGURE 1.8   Cover for a served meal: (1) bread and butter plate, with butter knife; (2) water glass; (3) wine glass; (4) napkin; (5) salad fork; (6) dinner fork; (7) knife; (8) teaspoon.

fork is used, it is sometimes placed in the area above the dinner plate so the guest will use it for the final course.

Napkin.   Place the napkin at the left of the fork with the loose corner at the lower right and the open edges next to the edge of the table and the plate. It may be placed between the knife and fork if space is limited, and it may be folded into an accordion shape and placed upright. See Figure 1.9 for basic napkin folds.

Glasses.   Place the water glass at the tip of the knife or slightly to the right. Goblets and footed tumblers often are preferred for luncheon or dinner and should be used for a formal dinner. Wine glasses are placed to the right of and slightly below the water glass.

Bread and Butter Plate.   Place the bread and butter plate at the tip of the fork or slightly to the left.

Salt and Pepper.   Salt and pepper shakers should be provided for every six covers. They should be placed parallel to the edge of the table and in line with sugar bowls and creamers.

Decorations.   Some attractive decorations should be provided for the center of the table. A centerpiece should be low so the view across the table will not be obstructed. Candles should not be used in the dayime unless the lighting is inadequate or the day is dark.

When used, they should be the sole source of light. Do not mix candlelight and daylight or candlelight and electric light. Tall candles in low holders should be high enough so that the flame is not on a level with the eyes of the guests. If place cards are used, they are set on the napkin or above the cover.

Seating Arrangement

The guest of honor, if a woman, usually is seated to the right of the host; if a man, to the right of the hostess. At banquets and public dinners, a man is seated to the left of his partner. Customs for seating guests may be different in countries other than the United States.

Service Counter Setup for Served Meals

Food should be served from hot counters or hot holding equipment. Some provision also must be made for keeping plates and cups hot. For serving 50 plates or less, the plan should provide one person to serve each food item. Such an arrangement for serving is termed a setup. For 60 to 100 persons, two setups should be provided to hasten service. For more than 100 persons, it is well to provide additional setups.

Food is placed on the hot counter in the following order: meat, potato or substitute, vegetables, sauces, and garnish. The supervisor should

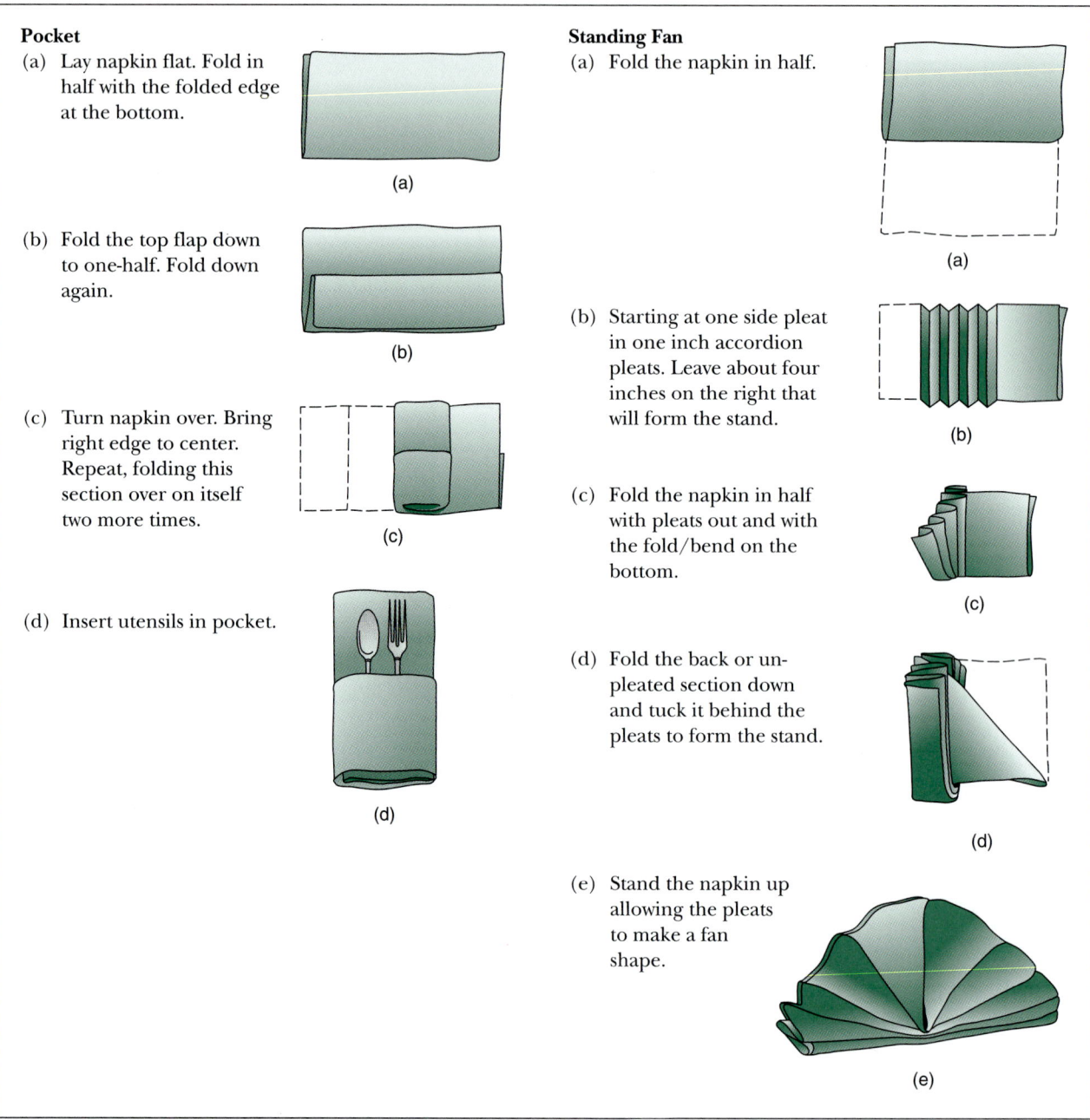

Pocket

(a) Lay napkin flat. Fold in half with the folded edge at the bottom.

(a)

(b) Fold the top flap down to one-half. Fold down again.

(b)

(c) Turn napkin over. Bring right edge to center. Repeat, folding this section over on itself two more times.

(c)

(d) Insert utensils in pocket.

(d)

Standing Fan

(a) Fold the napkin in half.

(a)

(b) Starting at one side pleat in one inch accordion pleats. Leave about four inches on the right that will form the stand.

(b)

(c) Fold the napkin in half with pleats out and with the fold/bend on the bottom.

(c)

(d) Fold the back or un-pleated section down and tuck it behind the pleats to form the stand.

(d)

(e) Stand the napkin up allowing the pleats to make a fan shape.

(e)

FIGURE 1.9   Basic napkin folds.

demonstrate the size of portions to be given and their arrangement on the plate. There should be a checker at the end of the line to remove with a damp cloth any food spots from the plate and to check the plate for completeness, arrangement, and uniformity of servings. The importance of standardized servings and food arrangement can hardly be overemphasized; these factors can determine the enjoyment of the guests and the financial success or failure of a meal.

Table Service

1. Service personnel should report to the supervisor to receive final instructions at least 15 minutes before the time set for serving the banquet.

2. If the salad is to be on the table when the guests arrive, it should be placed there by the service personnel not more than 15 minutes before serving time. It should be placed to the left of the fork (Figure 1.10). If space does not permit this arrange-

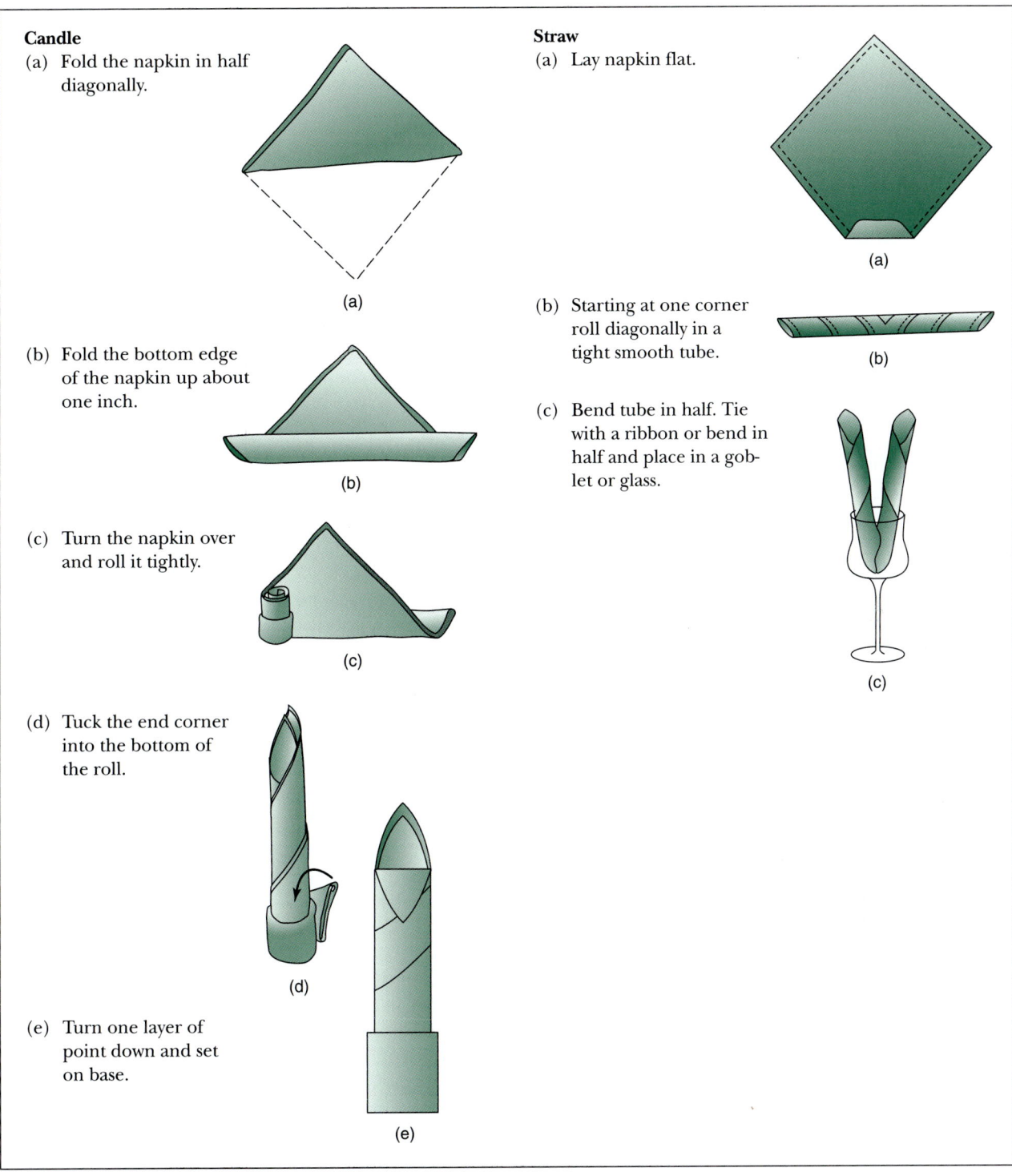

Candle

(a) Fold the napkin in half diagonally.

(b) Fold the bottom edge of the napkin up about one inch.

(c) Turn the napkin over and roll it tightly.

(d) Tuck the end corner into the bottom of the roll.

(e) Turn one layer of point down and set on base.

Straw

(a) Lay napkin flat.

(b) Starting at one corner roll diagonally in a tight smooth tube.

(c) Bend tube in half. Tie with a ribbon or bend in half and place in a goblet or glass.

FIGURE 1.9 Basic napkin folds.

ment, place the salad plate at the tip of the fork and the bread and butter plate, if used, directly above the dinner plate between the water glass and the salad plate. If the salad is to be served as a separate course, it is placed between the knife and the fork, then removed before the main course is served.

3. Place creamer beside the sugar bowl.

4. Place relishes on the table, if desired.

5. For small dinners, the first course may be placed on the table before dinner is announced. For large banquets, however, it is best to wait until the guests

FIGURE 1.10   Placement of food and cover for a served meal: (1) bread and butter plate; (2) water glass; (3) wine glass; (4) salad plate; (5) dinner plate; (6) cup and saucer. The salad is placed at the left of the fork when salad and beverage are both served with the main course. If space does not permit, place salad plate at tip of fork and bread and butter plate, if used, above the dinner plate.

are seated. Hot soups or plated appetizers are served after the guests are seated. A first course of beverages and appetizers may be offered as the guests arrive in the reception area.

6. Place butter on the right side of the bread and butter plate. If no bread and butter plate is used and the salad is to be on the table when guests arrive, the butter may be placed on the side of the salad plate. This procedure is often necessary where dishes and table space are limited. Butter may also be arranged on a serving plate and passed.

7. Place glasses filled with ice water on the table just before guests are seated.

8. When the guests are seated, service personnel line up in the kitchen for trays containing the first course. A general rule is to schedule one waiter for each one to two tables and one busperson for every two tables. It is helpful if two persons work together, one carrying the tray and the other placing the food. Place the cocktail glasses, soup dishes, or canapé plates on the service plates, which are already on the table.

9. Serve food from the guest's left with the left hand. Serve beverages from the guest's right with the right hand. Proceed counterclockwise.

10. Serve the head table first, progressing in order to the other tables. To minimize the disruption of

guests, it is preferable to have the head table the one farthest from the kitchen entrance.

11. When the guests have finished the first course, service personnel remove the dishes from the right.

12. For the main course, plates may be brought to the dining room on plate carriers or on trays holding several plates and set on tray stands. Each worker serves the plates to a specified group of guests.

   An alternate method often is used in serving large groups. A tray of filled plates is brought from the kitchen by bus personnel to a particular station in the dining room, from which the plates are served. The dining room service personnel remain at their stations during the serving period.

13. Place the plate 1 inch from the edge of the table with the meat nearest the guest.

14. As soon as a table has been served with dinner plates and salad, specially appointed workers should follow immediately with rolls. Coffee may be served at this time or with dessert.

15. Place the coffee cups at the right of the spoons with the handles toward the right at about the 5 o'clock position. If the coffee is served with the main course, the cup and saucer may be placed on the table with the rest of the cover. If it is served with the dessert only, the cups are not placed on the table until the dessert is served.

16. Serve rolls at least twice. Offer them from the left at a convenient height and distance. Plates or baskets of rolls may be placed on the table to be passed by the guests.

17. Refill water glasses as necessary. If the tables are crowded, it may be necessary to remove the glasses from the table to fill them. Handle the glass near the base.

18. Refill coffee cups as necessary. Do not remove cups from table when filling.

19. At the end of the course, remove all dishes and food belonging to that course. Remove dishes from the guest's right.

20. If the silverware for the dessert was not placed on the table when the table was set, take it in on a tray and place it at the right of the cover.

21. Serve desserts two at a time and in the same order that the plates were served. Place the dessert in front of the guest in the most attractive manner. For example, place cheesecake wedges so the tip is pointing toward the guest.

22. If possible, clear the table except for decorations before the program begins. The handling of dishes should cease before the program starts.

Plate Presentation

Balancing food items on a plate is a fundamental element in making food look appealing. The general principles are similar to those of menu planning: balancing colors, shapes, textures, and flavors. See menu planning procedures on p. 9.

Portion size plays a role in a plate's attractiveness. Food should fit on the plate's eating surface without making it look overcrowded or too small. The entree should be the focal point and should be larger than the accompaniments.

Food can be arranged on a plate following a variety of plating styles. Regardless of the style, however, the guest should be able to eat the meal comfortably and conveniently. The type of food being served must also be considered when plating. Following are some common plating styles:

- The plate is divided into thirds with the entree, vegetable, and starch item placed on each third. When served, the entree is placed nearest the guest with the garnish towards the rear of the plate. This classic plating style has widespread use.

- The entree is served in the center of the plate with only a sauce or simple garnish.

- The entree is served in the center of the plate with vegetables placed around it. The vegetables may be placed randomly or in an arranged pattern. Food

that is randomly placed should be neat and orderly and not appear sloppy or haphazard.

- The entree is leaned against a generous amount of vegetables or starch that has been placed in the center of the plate. Additional vegetables, sauce, and a garnish surround the entree.

- The entree is stacked on top of the starch or vegetable accompaniment. A sauce and garnish is added around the entree.

- The vegetable or starch is in the center of the plate with the entree placed neatly around it. A sauce under the vegetable or starch is common.

- Slices of the entree are shingled on top of vegetables or a starch, and the garnish is placed to one side.

Regardless of the plating style, a few general guidelines will assure the food's attractiveness.

1. Place the food on the plate's eating surface and not on the rim. The rim may be used for a simple garnish such as chopped fresh herbs.

2. Food should look balanced on the plate without the appearance of a heavy or a light side.

3. The food should be convenient to eat. Guests should not need to rearrange the food, dismantle an arranged or stacked display, or reorient the plate on the table before they begin eating.

4. Each food should maintain its own identity. This is accomplished by keeping space between items or by neatly placing foods close together. Sauces should not hide food's color, flavor, or shape.

5. The entree should serve as the focal point while working in harmony with the accompaniments so the plate has unity and cohesiveness. The accompaniments may serve as the garnish.

6. The garnish should contribute flavor, texture, and visual appeal to food. Garnishes should be appropriate for the food being served, and their placement should be carefully planned. Non-functional garnishes that add color but serve no other purpose and nonedible garnishes are not recommended. A garnish is not required or recommended if the plate is attractive without a garnish. Attractiveness can be achieved by using a plating style that complements the foods being served and by planning the accompaniments carefully.

STYLES OF SERVICE

The style of service will have an impact on the menu items and on the equipment and labor required to serve the meal. Following are some common styles of service.

American or Plate Service. Food items are placed on plates and delivered to guests. An attractive placement of food and garnish is important. Basic service rules for American service include:

- Serve food from the guest's left with the left hand (remember to leave on left). Serve women first and proceed counterclockwise. If the host or hostess is known, begin to his or her right.
- Serve beverage from the guest's right with the right hand.
- Clear dishes from the guest's right (remember to remove on right). Do not stack dishes or scrape plates in sight of guests.

Buffet. Food is prepared in the kitchen and arranged in serving pans for guests to serve themselves or to be served by service personnel. Appetizers, soups, and salads may be served at guests' tables prior to going through the buffet.

English. Platters of food are placed in front of the host or hostess who places the food on individual plates. Whole pieces of food may be cut by the host or hostess. A waiter generally receives the filled plates and delivers them to the guests.

Family Service. Food is placed in bowls and platters on each table. Guests serve themselves.

French. Food is partially prepared in the kitchen and finished in the dining room in view of the guests. A variation of the French style is to carve or serve fully cooked food from a cart at table side.

Russian. Individual portions of food are transferred by a waiter from a platter to the guest's plate.

WINE AND BAR SERVICE

Alcoholic beverages are often a part of special-event menus. Following are some basic guidelines for pairing wine with food and for setting up a bar.

Wine and Food Pairings

No hard and fast rules exist for selecting wines to serve with various foods. Generally accepted practice and the personal taste and experience of the client should be considered when selecting wines. Table 1.11 provides guidelines for pairing food with some commonly requested wines. Table 1.12 gives the amount of wine in different-size bottles.

Bar Service

Bars should be stationed so guests see them upon arrival. The location should be away from the dining area and buffet.

The number of bars and bartenders should be based on the number of guests. A general guideline is one bar per every 100 people with no more than two bartenders per bar. For 50 people, one bartender is usually adequate. The volume expected and type of beverages served should be considered when deciding when to add additional bars or bartenders.

The kind of liquor and amount of bar stock depends on the type and length of function and the guests being served. Table 1.13 provides general guidelines for stocking a bar. Glassware should be appropriate for the beverages being served.

State and local laws regarding alcohol service must be followed. Know the laws and educate employees about the laws before serving alcohol.

TABLE 1.13   **Guidelines for stocking a bar**

Item	Approximate stocking quantities for 50 people[a]	Item	Approximate stocking quantities for 50 people[a]
LIQUOR		**MIXERS**	
Beer, regular	18 cans	Cola	12 cans
Beer, light	36 cans	Diet cola	12 cans
Beer, nonalcoholic	3 cans	Non-cola, clear	6 cans
Bourbon	$\frac{1}{2}$ bottle	Diet non-cola, clear	3 cans
Gin	1 bottle	Club soda	3 liters
Rum	$\frac{1}{2}$ bottle	Gingerale	3 liters
Scotch	$\frac{1}{2}$ bottle	Tonic	6 liters
Vermouth, dry	1 partial bottle	Blood mary mix[b]	2 quarts
Vermouth, sweet	1 partial bottle	Orange juice	1 gallon
Vodka[b]	$\frac{1}{2}$ bottle	Cranberry juice	1 quart
Whiskey	$\frac{1}{2}$ bottle	Grapefruit juice	1 quart
Wine, white (chardonnay)	3 bottles	**GARNISHES**	
Wine, blush (white zinfandel)	1–2 bottles	Celery sticks	
Wine, red (cabernet sauvignon) (or merlot)	1–2 bottles	Cherries with stems	8 ounces
		Lemons	5
		Limes	3
		Oranges	3
		Stuffed green olives	6 ounces

[a] Quantities are generous. For bars located close to replenishment stock, the recommended quantity can be reduced.

[b] For morning events increase the vodka and bloody mary mix and the orange juice.

Champagne, sparkling wine, or fruit schnapps may be added for events such as receptions and weddings.

Note: For each guest estimate one mixed drink, one beer, or two glasses of wine per hour. For guests not drinking alcoholic beverages, have available three or four cans of soda or sparkling water. Plan 10 oz mixer, two to three glasses, and 1 lb ice per person.

PART II

Food Production Information

Chapter 2	Food Production Information	41
Chapter 3	Food Product Information	109
Chapter 4	Production Fundamentals	189
Chapter 5	Knives and Other Equipment	205

Food Production Information

Chapter **2**

Food Production Information

Ian O'Leary © Dorling Kindersley

The information in this chapter is presented as a guide for ordering food, for adjusting recipes, and for planning, preparing, and serving food. The chapter includes the following topics:

- The Recipe: Development, Construction, and Adjustment (p. 43)
- Amounts of Food to Serve, Yield and Food Equivalent Information (p. 64)
- Weights, Measures, and Guides for Cooking/Baking Temperatures (p. 88)
- Food Safety (p. 100)

Quantities of food to prepare are based on 50 average-size portions, as are most of the recipes, but adjustments may need to be made to fit individual situations. Rarely is 50 the exact number to be served, and the portion size will vary according to the type of foodservice and the needs of the individuals in the group. Tables are included in this chapter that will assist with these recipe adjustments.

Most ingredients in the recipes are given in weights, but if volume measurements (teaspoons, tablespoons, cups, quarts, or gallons) are to be used, tables in this section will assist in converting from weights to measures. Metric measures are not used in the recipes, but charts for converting to metric are included.

Basic information on cooking temperatures, food equivalents and substitutions, and equipment capacity

is also given. A guide for using herbs and spices and a glossary of cooking and menu terms are found at the end of the book.

General Information

Tables 2.1–2.3—Direct-Reading Tables for Adjusting Recipes. These tables include amounts of ingredients needed for varying portions, from 25 to 500. Table 2.1 (p. 52) is used when ingredient amounts are given in *weights* and portion yields are divisible by 25. In Table 2.2 (p. 54) ingredients are stated in *volume* measurement (teaspoons, tablespoons, cups, quarts, and gallons) and portions are divisible by 25. Table 2.3 (p. 60) is especially useful when enlarging home-sized recipes. Ingredients are in *volume* measurement for yields from 8 to 96 portions.

Table 2.4—Amounts of Food to Serve 50. This table (p. 64) suggests amounts of food to purchase and prepare for 50 persons, based on the portion size listed in the table. If larger or smaller servings are needed or if the number of portions required is other than 50, an adjustment in the amount to prepare or purchase must be made. Because preparation losses must be considered in determining the amount to purchase for 50 portions, the ready-to-serve raw yield or the yield of cooked product is given for some products, with the amount as purchased (AP) to buy. The yields, which are given in decimal parts of a pound, can be converted to ounces by using Table 2.8. (p. 88).

Table 2.5—Food Weights and Approximate Equivalents in Measure. Information in this table (pp. 75) is useful when converting recipe ingredients from weight to measure or vice versa and is helpful in adjusting or enlarging recipes.

Table 2.6—Ingredient Substitutions. This table (pp. 85) is useful when it is necessary to substitute one ingredient for another in a recipe.

Table 2.7—Ingredient Proportions. This table (p. 87) gives the relative proportion of ingredients in preparing certain types of foods. It is useful when evaluating recipes for the proper amount of leavening agents, seasonings, and thickening agents.

Table 2.8—Ounces and Decimal Equivalents of a Pound. This table (p. 88) is useful when increasing or decreasing recipes. The multiplication or division of pounds and ounces is simplified if the ounces are converted first to decimal parts of a pound.

Table 2.9—Basic Equivalents in Measures and Weights. Table 2.9 (p. 89) is useful when converting measures (gallons, quarts, or cups) to smaller units such as cups, tablespoons, or teaspoons. Metric equivalents are given for commonly used weights and measures.

Table 2.10—Guide for Rounding Off Weights and Measures. When enlarging home-sized recipes, the resulting quantities may be difficult to measure. Table 2.10 (p. 89) aids in rounding fractions and complex measurements into amounts that are as simple as possible to weight or measure while maintaining the accuracy needed for quality control.

Table 2.11—Weight and Approximate Measure Equivalents for Commonly Used Foods. In Table 2.11 (p. 90), the equivalent measures (teaspoons, tablespoons, and cups) are given for selected ingredients, such as flour, salt, and sugar, that appear repeatedly in recipes. This information is the same as that given in Table 2.5 except that the equivalents are given for weights from 1 to 16 ounces.

Table 2.12—Common Can Sizes. Can sizes, with approximate weight or measure and number of portions, are included in this table (p. 94) as a purchasing guide.

Table 2.13—Metric Equivalents for Weight, Measure, and Temperature. Table 2.13 (p. 95) provides information that will be helpful in converting weights,

measures, and temperatures as given in recipes to metric equivalents.

Table 2.14—Temperatures Used for Food Preparation. Information in this table (p. 96) identifies temperature guidelines for cooking food.

Table 2.15—Convection Oven Baking Times and Temperatures. Information in this table (p. 97) is useful when using convection ovens. Times and temperatures in recipes included in *Food for Fifty* have been tested using conventional ovens.

Table 2.16—Deep-Fat Frying Temperatures. Table 2.16 (p. 98) provides guidelines for the deep-fat frying of different types of menu items.

Table 2.17—Coatings for Deep-Fat Fried Foods. Proportions of ingredients are given (p. 99) for typical coatings for deep-fat fried foods.

Table 2.18—General Guidelines for Handling Food Safely. This table (p. 100) describes practices that are essential for handling food safely.

Table 2.19—Instructions for Calibrating a Probe (stem) Thermometer. Step-by-step procedures for calibrating a probe thermometer are given (p. 101).

Table 2.20—Cold Food Storage Temperatures. Recommended refrigerator and freezer storage time and temperatures are given (p. 102) for safe storage of foods.

Table 2.21—Refrigerator Defrosting Times for Meats, Seafood, and Poultry. Approximate defrosting times are given (p. 102) for roasts, chops, steaks, and poultry.

Table 2.22—Temperatures and Bacteria Growth. The relationships between temperature and bacteria growth are given (p. 102).

Table 2.23—Safe Internal Temperatures for Cooked Foods. Table 2.23 (p. 103) provides safe end-point cooking temperatures for meats, fish, and poultry.

Table 2.24—Food Serving Temperatures and Holding Times. Serving temperatures in this table (p. 104) are those recommended for optimum food quality and safety.

Table 2.25—Food Cooling and Storage Procedures. Recommended procedures for safely cooling foods are provided (p. 105).

Table 2.26—Time and Temperature Standards for Reducing Food Safety Hazards of Potentially Hazardous Foods (PHF). Table 2.26 (p. 106) provides information that will be helpful in developing a Hazard Analysis Critical Control Point (HACCP) plan.

Table 2.27—Water Activity (A_W) of Selected Foods. This table (p. 106) provides the water activity of selected foods.

Table 2.28—pH Values of Selected Foods. This table (p. 107) provides the pH value of selected foods.

Table 2.29—Potentially Hazardous Foods. This table (p. 107) identifies potentially hazardous foods.

Specific Food Information

Tables 3.1 to 3.25. The tables in Chapter 3 provide information helpful for ordering and specifying and for using and storing food products.

- Quality characteristics of egg grades (p. 110).
- Selecting cheeses (p. 112).
- Types of milk products (p. 118).
- Types of cream products (p. 119).
- Flours, meals, and other starches (p. 127).
- Quality and yield grades for meat (p. 128).
- Categories and classes of poultry (p. 134).
- Fish buying guide (p. 137).
- Marketing sizes for oysters (p. 139).
- Count and names for shrimp (p. 140).
- Shellfish buying guide (p. 140).
- Yield, availability, and storage of fresh fruits and vegetables (p. 142).
- Descriptions of greens for cooking, salad greens, and lettuces (p. 155).
- Chile pepper varieties (p. 163).
- Common types of mushrooms (p. 161).
- Herb descriptions, flavor, and usage (p. 167).
- Edible flowers (p. 172).
- Dried beans, lentils, and peas (p. 173).
- Tsp. per oz. for dry herbs and spices (p. 176).
- Herb and spice usage (p. 178).
- Regional flavorings (p. 182).
- Salt and pepper seasonings (p. 183).
- Nuts and seeds (p. 184).
- Sugars and syrups (p. 187).
- Smoke points of selected fats (p. 188).

Table 4.1—Primary Heat Transfer for Basic Cooking Methods. The method for heat transfer using basic cooking methods is given in this table (p. 191).

Table 4.2—Names and Suggested Cooking Methods for Beef Cuts. Suggested cooking methods for beef is given in this table (p. 192).

Quality Food Evaluation Information

Tables 4.3 to 4.5. The tables provide guidelines for evaluating food for quality.

- Evaluating food using sensory attributes (p. 202).
- Evaluating food products during preparation and service (p. 203).
- Quality food evaluation form (p. 204).

Table 5.1—Pan Capacities for Baked Products. This table (p. 219) gives the maximum capacity of different-sized pans for baking breads, cakes, or pies and is useful when enlarging or adjusting recipes.

Table 5.2—Counter Pan Capacities. Capacities, suggested uses, and number of portions for different sizes of counter pans are given in this table (p. 220).

Table 5.3—Dipper Equivalents. Approximate measure and weight for different-sized dippers (scoops) are given (p. 220). Suggested uses for different food products are also included.

Table 5.4—Ladle Equivalents. Table 5.4 (p. 221) gives measures and approximate weights for different-sized ladles and the size to use for different menu items.

Table 5.5—Recommended Mixer Bowl and Steam-Jacketed Kettle Sizes for Selected Products. This table (p. 221) is helpful in determining the size of mixer bowl and steam-jacketed kettle needed for selected food items in portions ranging from 50 to 500. If the equipment on hand is not large enough for the amount required, the recipe may need to be made in two or three batches.

Table 5.6—Large-equipment Requirements for Basic Cooking Techniques. The equipment requirements for cooking using basic cooking techniques are identified in this table (p. 222).

The Recipe: Development, Construction, and Adjustment

RECIPE DEVELOPMENT AND CONSTRUCTION

Recipe files are a valuable resource for food production staff when general principles of recipe development and construction are used. Following are suggestions for writing quantity recipes.

A standard recipe format includes a *recipe title* that is simple and factual, and that describes the food and indicates the main ingredients and general method of preparation. Products with names that are generally understood, such as chili, do not need additional descriptors. Recipe titles should provide the information necessary to locate a particular recipe in the file. *Indexing* recipes so they can be quickly retrieved is useful.

Names of *ingredients* should be consistent and listed in the order in which they are used in preparation. List first the ingredients that require pre-preparation for a later step so they will be ready when needed. Using a descriptive word before the ingredient tells what kind and form of food is purchased, or the cooking required before the food is used in the recipe; for example, diced tomatoes, cooked chicken. The descriptive words used after the ingredient indicate what preparation is necessary to make the food different from the form as purchased or pre-prepared; for example, cooked chicken, diced, or diced tomatoes, drained. For additional clarification, ingredients showing a weight gain or loss during preparation are often marked AP (as purchased) or EP (edible portion). For example, if a chili recipe specifies ground beef, 10 lb (AP), it will improve clarity to also specify the EP weight, 6 lb 8 oz (EP). The AP to EP conversion is variable because of product differences such as the amount of fat in the ground beef. Variance may also be caused by the different procedures followed when preparing products, such as the amount of waste in paring vegetables and fruits or the length of time a product is cooked (roast beef).

List *weights* when possible. *Measures* should be given in terms of standard measuring utensils such as cups, quarts, and gallons.

Portion size is the amount served to each customer and *yield* is the total batch weight or number of servings the recipe will make. The portion size may be described in counts, measure, or weight. Identifying *serving utensils* that are correctly sized for the portion size will aid in making yield predictions accurate. Over or under yielding can often be explained by comparing the size of portion served with the portion size specified in the recipe.

Procedures are written in sequential order. Directions should be simple and easy to understand, and placed with the ingredients involved in the production step. The side-by-side format for ingredients and procedures as used in this book is easy for production staff to follow. Some recipe software packages are designed so the procedures follow the recipe ingredients at the bottom of the recipe. When possible, each production step should begin with an action verb such as *blend, add, mix,* or *stir*. Keep directions short. Descriptive terms should be used in the procedure steps only when needed for clarity. It is helpful if basic procedures and terminology are uniform for all recipes using similar products or similar production steps. For example, the procedures for making sweet roll and loaf bread dough are similar, so the procedures should be written in a similar way.

Timing information for such procedures as mixing, cooking, and marinating is important. Including *scaling or panning instructions* as a procedure step will improve recipe yield accuracy.

Food safety information (HACCP standards) such as end-point cooking temperatures, cold and hot holding temperatures, and safe handling procedures are important to include on each recipe. Highlighting recipe procedures that are Critical Control Points (CCPs) reinforces food safety practices.

Writing *quality standards* on the recipe gives production staff a basis for evaluating the finished product. Quality standards are especially helpful to less experienced production staff and when recipes are either new or made infrequently. See p. 201 for examples of quality standards for selected products. For several recipes in this book, quality standards follow the recipe.

Equipment should be grouped in a way that simplifies gathering for production use. Identify oven temperatures for baked products.

RECIPE ADJUSTMENT

Recipes often need to be adjusted to meet the requirements of an individual foodservice. For example, the number of portions may need to be increased from 50 to the exact number to be served, or an adjustment in portion size might better reflect the policy of the dining facility or the requirements of the clientele. Portions for recipes in this book are average sized.

Enlarging home-size recipes may require converting household measurements to weights and adjusting certain ingredient proportions as the recipes are expanded. These procedures, as well as directions for converting to metric weights and measures, are explained in the pages that follow.

Converting from U.S. Measurement to Metric

Two approaches are possible for converting recipes from U.S. to metric measures: soft conversion and hard conversion. *Soft conversion* translates weights and measures into their exact metric equivalents. An ounce would become 28.3 grams; a quart would be 0.95 liter. This method produces numbers that may be awkward to work with, and equipment may not be available to measure ingredients to the degree of accuracy required.

Hard conversion changes weights and measures to round metric sizes. For example, a 1-ounce portion would convert to either 25 or 30 grams, but not to 28.3 gams; 1 quart would be changed to 1 liter. This method may be satisfactory for recipes that are not sensitive to formula adjustments, such as soups and beverages, but may not be suitable for cakes, breads, and other products in which accurate ingredient ratios are critical. Testing recipes to evaluate acceptability is recommended when using the hard conversion method. (Table 2.13 shows metric conversions.)

Converting from Weight to Measure

Quantities of most dry ingredients in recipes in this book are given by weight in ounces and pounds. If accurate scales are not available, however, or if scales do not have graduations for weighing small amounts, then the weights of ingredients may need to be converted to measures. A number of tables will be helpful:

- *Table 2.5*—Food Weights and Approximate Equivalents in Measure (p. 75)
- *Table 2.8*—Ounces, Decimal Equivalents of a Pound, and Grams (Rounded) (p. 88)
- *Table 2.9*—Basic Equivalents in Measures and Weights (p. 89)
- *Table 2.10*—Guide for Rounding Off Weights and Measures (p. 89)
- *Table 2.11*—Weight (1–16 oz) and Measure Equivalents for Commonly Used Foods (p. 90)

The following example illustrates the procedure for converting ingredients in Baking Powder Biscuits (p. 268) from weight to measure.

- Change 5 pounds flour to measure by multiplying by 4 cups. Turn to Table 2.5 (p. 75).
- The resulting 20 cups would be equivalent to 5 quarts. See Table 2.9 (p. 89). For ingredients other than flour, a gallon measure should be used.
- By referring to Table 2.11 (p. 90) the 5 ounces of baking powder and 1 pound 4 ounces of shortening may be converted quickly by finding the amount in the appropriate column or adding the columns together. The same information is included in the longer table (Table 2.5, p. 75), but for conversion of small amounts of commonly used foods, Table 2.11 (p. 90) is useful.

Increasing and Decreasing Recipe Yields

It may be necessary to change recipe yields in this book to meet the needs of individual situations. Recipes may need to be adjusted to produce batch sizes compatible with preparation equipment, such as mixers, ovens, and steam-jacketed kettles, or consistent with pan sizes available. See Tables 5.1, 5.2, 5.5 (pp. 219, 220, 221) for recommended equipment sizes and pan size capacities. Recipes may also need adjustment as portion sizes are increased or decreased or as purchase units for ingredients change. Three methods commonly used to adjust recipe yields are the *factor method,* the *percentage method,* and *direct-reading tables*.

Factor Method

In the factor method, a conversion factor is determined and multiplied by each ingredient in the recipe. This process is explained in the following steps and in the Factor Method Table example.

Step 1a When portion size remains the same.

Divide the desired yield by the known yield of the recipe being adjusted to determine the conversion factor. For example, to increase a 50-portion recipe to 125 portions, divide 125 by 50 for a factor of 2.5.

desired yield (125) ÷ known yield (50) = conversion factor (2.5)

Step 1b When portion size changes.

Recipe portion sizes may need to be changed for plate coverage reasons, because of the clientele being served or to comply with the foodservice facility's objectives. To determine a conversion factor for a recipe that requires a different portion size from the original recipe, one must determine the yield of the original and the new recipe. Determine the yield of the existing recipe by multiplying the number of portions by the portion size. Determine the yield desired in the new recipe by multiplying the number of portions desired by the new portion size. To increase a 50-portion recipe with 3-oz portions to 125 portions each with 4 oz:

original recipe yield
(50 × 3-oz portion) = 150 oz
new recipe desired yield
(125 × 4-oz portions) = 500 oz

Determine the conversion factor by dividing the desired yield by the known yield of the recipe being adjusted.

desired yield (500 oz) ÷ known yield (150 oz) = conversion factor (3.3)

Step 2 Whenever possible, convert ingredients to weight. Making this conversion will provide a number (weight) that is generally easier to use than volume measurement amounts that are not measurable using conventional volume measurement equipment (for example: $2\frac{1}{5}$ cups, $2\frac{1}{3}$ teaspoons). Any unit can be used, however, as long as the same unit is used in both the new and the old recipes. Some ingredients may be too small to convert to weight and should be left in measure.

Step 3   Multiply the amount of each ingredient in the original recipe by the factor. To work with decimal parts of a pound instead of ounces for this multiplication, Table 2.8 (p. 88) will be helpful.

Step 4   Add together the weights of all ingredients in the original recipe and multiply by the factor. Multiply the pounds and ounces separately.

Step 5   Add together the new weights of all ingredients for the adjusted recipe. If the answers in Steps 4 and 5 are not the same, an error exists and the calculations should be checked. (A slight difference may exist because of rounding the figures.)

Step 6   Change weights of any ingredients that can be more easily measured than weighed.

Step 7   Check all amounts and use Table 2.10 (p. 89) for rounding off unnecessary fractions to simplify weights or measures as far as accuracy permits.

The table below illustrates the procedure for adjusting Baking Powder Biscuits from 100 biscuits to 500, using the factor method of adjustment.

Percentage Method

The percentage method of recipe adjustment often is desirable, especially for large-volume production where batch sizes may vary greatly. For most large-volume foodservices, a computer software package with a recipe adjustment module has eliminated the need to hand calculate recipe yields. Some computer systems use the percentage system for their method of adjustment.

The percentage method of adjustment requires that ingredient percentages be established only once; they remain the same for all future adjustments. Recipe increases and decreases are made by multiplying the percentage of each ingredient by

the total weight desired. Checking ingredients for proper recipe balance is possible, because the percentage of each ingredient is available. The percentage method of adjustment is explained in the following steps:

Step 1   Convert all ingredients from measure or pounds and ounces to pounds and tenths of a pound (see Tables 2.5 and 2.8). Make desired equivalent ingredient substitutions such as frozen whole eggs for fresh eggs, nonfat dry milk and water for liquid milk. Use edible portion (EP) weights when a difference exists between EP and as purchased (AP) weights (see Table 2.4). Individual meat items and other meats in entree recipes that do not require the meat to be cooked prior to combining with other ingredients are calculated on AP weight. Examples are pork chops, meat loaf, and Salisbury steak.

Step 2   Total the weight of ingredients in the recipe, using EP weight where applicable.

Step 3   Calculate the percentage of each ingredient in relation to the total weight, using the following formula:

$$\frac{\text{individual ingredient weight}}{\text{total weight}} = \text{percentage of each ingredient}$$

The sum of the percentages must equal 100.

Step 4   Check the ratio of ingredients. Standards have been established for ingredient proportions of many items. The ingredients should be in proper balance before going further.

Step 5   Establish the weight needed to give the desired number of servings. The weight will be determined by portion size multiplied by the desired number of servings to be prepared. This weight may need to be adjusted because

Factor Method Table

Step 1: Derive the factor	Ingredients	Original recipe	Step 2: Convert to weight	Step 3: Multiply by factor	Steps 6 and 7: Change to measure and simplify
$\frac{500 \text{ (new)}}{100 \text{ (original)}} = 5$ (factor)	Flour, all-purpose	5 lb	5 lb	25 lb	25 lb
	Baking powder	5 oz	5 oz	25 oz	1 lb 9 oz
	Salt	2 Tbsp	1⅓ oz	6½ oz	6½ oz
	Shortening, hydrogenated	1 lb 4 oz	1 lb 4 oz	6 lb 4 oz	6 lb 4 oz
	Milk	1¾ qt	<u>3 lb 8 oz</u>	<u>17 lb 8 oz</u>	2 gal + ¾ qt
Steps 4 and 5: Total weight			10 lb 2 oz	50 lb 11 oz	

of pan sizes or equipment capacity (see Tables 5.1, 5.2, and 5.5).

Step 6 Handling loss must be added to the weight needed. It may vary from 1 to 10 percent, depending on the product. Similar items produce predictable losses, and with some experimentation these losses can be assigned accurately. The formula for incorporating handling loss is as follows:

$$\text{total weight needed} = \frac{\text{desired yield}}{100 \text{ percent} - \text{assigned}\atop\text{handling loss percent}}$$

For example, cake has a handling loss of approximately 2 percent, and 72 lb of batter is needed to make nine $18 \times 26 \times 2$-inch pans. To determine the total amount of batter to be made, divide 72 lb by 98 percent (100 percent less 2 percent handling loss). Using this formula, as demonstrated in the Percentage Method Table, a recipe calculated for 73.47 lb of batter is needed.

Step 7 Multiply each ingredient percentage by the total weight to give the exact amount of each ingredient needed. The total weight of ingredients should equal the weight needed as calculated in Step 6. Once the percentages of a recipe have been established, any number of servings can be calculated, and the ratio of ingredients to the total will remain the same.

Step 8 Unless scales are calibrated to read in pounds and tenths of a pound, convert to pounds and ounces (Table 2.8, p. 88) or to measure (Table 2.5, p. 75). Use Table 2.10, p. 89 for rounding off unnecessary fractions. If volume measurements are required, Table 2.5, p. 75 is helpful.

The example in the Percentage Method Table illustrates the procedure for adjusting Baking Powder Biscuits from 100 biscuits to 500, using the percentage method of adjustment.

Enlarging Home-Size Recipes

Before enlarging a small recipe, be sure the recipe is appropriate for large-quantity production and that the same quality can be achieved in the larger amount. Appropriate equipment and pans also must be available. Quantity production procedures used in the particular foodservice may need to replace small-scale techniques.

Percentage Method Table

Ingredients	Original recipe	Step 1: Convert to decimal weights	Step 3: Calculate percentage	Step 7: Calculate weights	Step 8: Convert to pounds and ounces
Flour, all-purpose	5 lb	5.0 lb	49.276	25.52 lb	25 lb 8 oz
Baking powder	5 oz	0.313 lb	3.085	1.60 lb	1 lb 10 oz
Salt	2 Tbsp	0.0839 lb	0.827	0.43 lb	6¾ oz
Shortening, hydrogenated	1 lb 4 oz	1.25 lb	12.319	6.38 lb	6 lb 6 oz
Milk	1¾ qt	<u>3.5 lb</u>	<u>34.493</u>	<u>17.86 lb</u>	2¼ gal

Step 2:
Total weight   10.1469 lb   100.00   51.79 lb

Step 4:
Check ratio of ingredients to see if they are within acceptable guidelines.

Step 5:
Establish needed weight: $\dfrac{10.1469 \ (\text{total weight of 100 biscuits})}{100} = 0.1015 \text{ lb (weight per biscuit)}$

500 (desired yield) $\times$ 0.1015 lb = 50.75 lb of dough needed before handling loss

Step 6:
Calculate handling loss. Estimated handling loss 2 percent:

$\dfrac{50.75 \text{ lb (desired yield)}}{98 \text{ percent} \atop (100 \text{ percent} - 2 \text{ percent})} = 51.79 \text{ lb total dough needed}$

Enlarging a small-quantity recipe in steps is more likely to be successful than increasing size too quickly. Following are suggestions for expanding home-size recipes:

Step 1   Prepare the product in the amount of the original recipe, following the quantities and procedures exactly and noting any procedures that are unclear or any problems that occur during preparation.

Step 2   Evaluate the product and decide if it is acceptable for the foodservice. If adjustments are necessary, revise the recipe and make the product again. Prepare the small-size amount until the product is satisfactory.

Step 3   Double the recipe or expand to an appropriate amount for the pan size that will be used, and prepare the product, making notations on the recipe of any changes you make. For example, additional cooking time may be needed for the larger amount. Use Table 2.3 on p. 60 for increasing recipe size. Evaluate the product and record the yield, portion size, and acceptability.

Step 4   Double the recipe again, or if the product is to be baked, calculate the quantities needed to prepare one baking pan of the size that will be used in the foodservice. Use Table 2.3 on p. 60 for increasing recipe size. If ingredients are to be weighed, home-size measures should be converted to pounds and ounces or to pounds and tenths of a pound before proceeding further. Prepare and evaluate the product as before.

Step 5   If the product is satisfactory, continue to enlarge by increments of 25 portions or by pans until approximately 100 portions are prepared. Recipes with larger yields should be evaluated for acceptability and adjustment made each time the yield is increased significantly.

When increasing or decreasing recipe yields, it is important to evaluate if changes are also needed in equipment or in the procedures that specify a time, such as mixing, baking, boiling, and so forth. Quality problems arise if the equipment used is too large or too small. It may become necessary to use equipment to mix an amount of product that could be hand mixed in a smaller amount. Pie crust or muffins are examples of products that would likely require an equipment change when increasing a yield from a small amount to a volume amount.

Production time does not increase proportionately as yields increase. The cooking time and timing for various steps may, however, change as yields increase or decrease and as production equipment and pan sizes change.

Reducing Fat, Sodium, and Sugar

It is often necessary to reduce the fat, sodium, and sugar content of recipes to meet the nutritional goals of an individual foodservice. Some changes in appearance, taste, or quality can be expected, and recipe experimentation is advised.

Flavorful commercial bases may be used to compensate for a decreased amount of fat in savory products. Minor's Flavor Concentrates manufactured by Nestlé are examples of products that add depth of flavor; for example, Chipotle, Herb de Provence, Ranchero, Roasted Red Pepper, Sun Dried Tomato Pesto. Several good quality commercial vegetarian bases also add flavor when fat and sodium are reduced. The amount of sodium varies among brands and varieties of bases, and should be evaluated when reduced sodium is a goal.

Adjusting the amount of spices or using flavorings such as lemon extract may enhance a food without adding additional fat, sodium, or sugar. The depth of flavor added by dried or fresh herbs and spices may compensate for reduced fat, sodium, or sugar. See p. 175 for uses of dried herbs and spices. The spice blends on pp. 177 and 782 are appropriate for adding flavors to foods.

Fresh fruits and vegetables may be used to add flavor. Some common vegetables that add a distinct flavor are garlic, fresh ginger, onions, mushrooms, and tomatoes. Lemons, limes, and oranges, or wines, liqueurs, and vinegars add flavor to desserts, main dishes, and sauces, and in some products may compensate for reduced fat, sodium, or sugar.

Following are specific suggestions to decrease the fat, sodium, or sugar content of recipes.

Decreasing fat in meat, fish, and poultry dishes

- Use lean cuts of meat with the visible fat trimmed.
- Use a lower grade of meat (usually less fat) for products where moist heat cooking methods are used.
- Remove skin and excess fat from poultry. To retain moisture, poultry may be roasted with the skin on and removed prior to serving.
- Substitute poaching, grilling, baking, roasting, or broiling for frying.
- Substitute ground poultry for part or all of the ground beef in casseroles.
- Use extra-lean ground beef in casseroles. Rinsing cooked ground beef will remove fat but is not generally recommended because of the flavor loss and also because the fat is added to the waste water.

- Moisten meats with wine, stock, or citrus juice instead of high-fat drippings, and season with herbs.
- Pour fat from baking and roasting pans before deglazing or using the drippings for sauces and gravies.
- Add raw meat to stews and sauces without browning first with added fat.
- When appropriate, substitute vegetables for some of the meat in a recipe.

Decreasing fat in egg products

- Replace some of the egg yolks with egg whites or egg substitutes. This may not be appropriate for all baked products. One should begin by replacing a small amount of egg yolk and increasing the amount replaced each time to determine a suitable limit.

Decreasing fat in sauces and soups

- Reduce the amount of fat used to sauté vegetables. To prevent burning, cook over medium heat and stir often. Covering the pan may also prevent burning but the moisture that accumulates may reduce caramelization and flavor development.
- Substitute low-fat or nonfat milk or evaporated skim milk for whole milk or cream. Low-fat milk products will curdle easier than whole milk and cream. They should be added at the last possible minute, heated slowly and gently, and held as short a time as possible.
- Substitute low-fat cheese for whole milk cheeses.
- Substitute part or all plain low-fat or nonfat yogurt for sour cream. In cooked sauces, add 1 tablespoon of cornstarch to each cup of yogurt before heating. Heat slowly and gently, do not boil, and add at the last possible minute.
- When feasible, refrigerate soups, stews, and stocks until fat congeals on top and skim it off. When it is not possible to refrigerate product, use a ladle to skim as much fat as possible from the top.
- Thicken sauces with cornstarch, arrowroot, or flour paste instead of a roux. For additional flavor, add wines, herbs, and concentrated bases. Puréed vegetables and starchy products such as potatoes, cooked legumes, barley, and rice may be used in place of roux to thicken some soups and sauces.
- Replace a traditional marinade or vinaigrette with a marinade or vinaigrette that has had up to half of the oil replaced with a starch-thickened liquid such as wine or fruit juice.
- Substitute fresh fruit or vegetable salsa or chutney for sauces made with fat.

Decreasing fat in salad dressings

- Substitute half of the oil with vinegar, lemon juice, vegetable juice, fruit juice, or plain low-fat yogurt.
- Use low-fat or nonfat mayonnaise and cream cheese.

Decreasing fat in baking

- Use a silicone baking mat, silicone parchment paper, or a food-release cooking spray instead of greasing a pan.
- Use fruit purées such as applesauce, mashed bananas, and commercially sold prune purée to replace fat in some quick bread, bar cookie, and cake recipes. The amount of fat that can be replaced varies among recipes. Begin by replacing a small amount of fat and increasing the amount replaced each time to determine a suitable limit.

Decreasing sodium

- Build a depth of flavor with herbs and spices and reduce salt. See pp. 177–181 for suggestions.
- Make stocks or use a reduced-salt commercial base.
- Purchase low- or reduced-sodium products. Make products from scratch rather than using convenience foods that often are higher in sodium.
- Rinse highly salted products.
- In some cases, salted products can be added to enhance flavor and provide some salt without adding more salt. Examples of products that may be appropriate to use are anchovies, capers in brine (rinsed), mustard, olives, pickles, soy and fish sauce, and some cheeses such as Parmesan and Romano.

Decreasing sugar

- Reduce the amount of sugar in recipes. The amount of sugar that can be replaced varies among recipes. Begin by decreasing a small amount of sugar and decreasing more each time to determine a suitable limit. Because sugar is important to the quality of baked products it may not be possible to reduce a large amount of sugar.
- Caramelize natural sugars in vegetables and fruits and reduce the added sugar for products that already have added sugar.
- Add spices that enhance sweet foods, and reduce the sugar. Spices that enhance sweetness in foods include allspice, cardamom, cinnamon, ginger, nutmeg, mace, and vanilla.
- Substituting honey, maple syrup, or molasses for part of the sugar in some products may provide enough flavor for the sugar and the resulting sweetness to be reduced.

- When appropriate, reduce the amount of sugar in a sweet product and serve it at room or warm temperature (foods taste sweeter at warm temperatures).
- Whenever possible, substitute fruit and fruit juices for sugar.

Direct-Reading Measurement Tables

Recipe adjustment may be made by using tables that have been developed for different numbers of portions. Using these charts requires minimal calculation. Table 2.1 can be used when the desired yields are divisible by 25 and the ingredients are given in *weights*. Table 2.2 is used when recipe ingredients are given in *volume measurements* and the yields can be divided by 25. Table 2.3 has yields that can be divided by 8 and is useful in enlarging home-size recipes. Following are instructions for using direct-reading measurement tables.

Directions for Using Tables 2.1 and 2.2

The choice of Tables 2.1 or 2.2 depends on whether the recipe ingredients are given in weights (ounces and pounds) or in volume measurements (teaspoons, tablespoons, cups, quarts, or gallons). Table 2.1 is used for converting weighed ingredients using recipe yields that are divisible by 25. Table 2.2 is used for converting volume measures of ingredients using recipe yields that are divisible by 25. To adjust recipes, follow these steps:

1. Locate the column that corresponds to the original yield of the recipe to be adjusted. For example, assume the original recipe yields 100 portions. Locate the "100" column across the top of the chart on Table 2.1.

2. Go down this column to the amount of the ingredient required (or to the closest number to that figure) in the recipe to be adjusted. If the recipe for 100 portions requires 21 lb of ground beef, for example, go down the column headed 100 to the figure "21."

3. Then go across the page, in line with that amount, to the column that is headed to correspond with the yield desired. For example, if only 75 portions are desired, begin with the 21 lb figure in the "100" column and slide across to the column headed "75" and read that figure. It indicates that 15 lb 12 oz of ground beef would be required to make 75 portions with this recipe.

4. Record this figure as the amount of the ingredient required for the new yield of the recipe. Repeat steps 1, 2, and 3 for each ingredient in the original recipe to obtain the adjusted ingredient weight needed for the new yield. Follow the same procedure using Table 2.2 in adjusting ingredient amounts indicated in volume measures. Yields can be either increased or decreased in this manner.

5. If two columns need to be combined to obtain the desired yield, follow steps 1 through 4 and add together the amounts given in the two columns to obtain the amount required for the adjusted yield. For example, to find the amount of ground beef for 225 portions of our hypothetical recipe, locate the figures in columns headed "200" and "25" and add them together. In this example it would be 42 lb + 5 lb 4 oz, so the required total for ground beef would be 47 lb 4 oz.

6. The figures given in these tables are given in exact weights including fractional ounces. After making yield adjustments for every ingredient, refer to Table 2.10 for rounding off fractional amounts that are not of sufficient proportion to change product quality.

Abbreviations used in the charts include the following:

- oz = ounce
- lb = pound
- tsp = teaspoon
- Tbsp = tablespoon
- qt = quart
- gal = gallon
- (r) = slightly rounded
- (s) = scant

Equivalents helpful in using the charts include:

- 3 tsp = 1 Tbsp
- 4 Tbsp = ¼ cup
- 5 Tbsp + 1 tsp = ⅓ cup
- 8 Tbsp = ½ cup
- 10 Tbsp + 2 tsp = ⅔ cup
- 12 Tbsp = ¾ cup
- 16 Tbsp = 1 cup
- 4 cups = 1 qt
- 4 qt = 1 gal

TABLE 2.1   Direct-reading table for adjusting weight ingredients of recipes divisible by 25[a]

25	50	75	100	200	300	400	500
*[b]	*	*	¼ oz	½ oz	¾ oz	1 oz	1¼ oz
*	*	*	½ oz	1 oz	1½ oz	2 oz	2½ oz
*	*	*	¾ oz	1½ oz	2¼ oz	3 oz	3¾ oz
¼ oz	½ oz	¾ oz	1 oz	2 oz	3 oz	4 oz	5 oz
*	*	*	1¼ oz	2½ oz	3¾ oz	5 oz	6¼ oz
*	¾ oz	*	1½ oz	3 oz	4½ oz	6 oz	7½ oz
*	*	*	1¾ oz	3½ oz	5¼ oz	7 oz	8¾ oz
½ oz	1 oz	1½ oz	2 oz	4 oz	6 oz	8 oz	10 oz
*	*	1¾ oz	2¼ oz	4½ oz	6¾ oz	9 oz	11¼ oz
*	1¼ oz	2 oz	2½ oz	5 oz	7½ oz	10 oz	12½ oz
*	*	2 oz	2¾ oz	5½ oz	8¼ oz	11 oz	13¾ oz
¾ oz	1½ oz	2¼ oz	3 oz	6 oz	9 oz	12 oz	15 oz
*	*	2½ oz	3¼ oz	6½ oz	9¾ oz	13 oz	1 lb ¼ oz
*	1¾ oz	2¾ oz	3½ oz	7 oz	10½ oz	14 oz	1 lb 1½ oz
1 oz	2 oz	2¾ oz	3¾ oz	7½ oz	11¼ oz	15 oz	1 lb 2¾ oz
1 oz	2 oz	3 oz	4 oz	8 oz	12 oz	1 lb	1 lb 4 oz
1 oz	2¼ oz	3¼ oz	4¼ oz	8½ oz	12¾ oz	1 lb 1 oz	1 lb 5¼ oz
*	2½ oz	3½ oz	4½ oz	9 oz	13½ oz	1 lb 2 oz	1 lb 6½ oz
*	2½ oz	3½ oz	4¾ oz	9½ oz	14¼ oz	1 lb 3 oz	1 lb 7¾ oz
1¼ oz	2½ oz	3¾ oz	5 oz	10 oz	15 oz	1 lb 4 oz	1 lb 9 oz
*	2¾ oz	4¼ oz	5½ oz	11 oz	1 lb ½ oz	1 lb 6 oz	1 lb 11½ oz
1½ oz	3 oz	4½ oz	6 oz	12 oz	1 lb 2 oz	1 lb 8 oz	1 lb 14 oz
*	3¼ oz	4¾ oz	6½ oz	13 oz	1 lb 3½ oz	1 lb 10 oz	2 lb ½ oz
1¾ oz	3¾ oz	5¼ oz	7 oz	14 oz	1 lb 5 oz	1 lb 12 oz	2 lb 3 oz
2 oz	3¾ oz	5¾ oz	7½ oz	15 oz	1 lb 6½ oz	1 lb 14 oz	2 lb 5½ oz
2 oz	4 oz	6 oz	8 oz	1 lb	1 lb 8 oz	2 lb	2 lb 8 oz
2¼ oz	4¼ oz	6½ oz	8½ oz	1 lb 1 oz	1 lb 9½ oz	2 lb 2 oz	2 lb 10½ oz
2¼ oz	4½ oz	6¾ oz	9 oz	1 lb 2 oz	1 lb 11 oz	2 lb 4 oz	2 lb 13 oz
2½ oz	4¾ oz	7¼ oz	9½ oz	1 lb 3 oz	1 lb 12½ oz	2 lb 6 oz	2 lb 15½ oz
2½ oz	5 oz	7½ oz	10 oz	1 lb 4 oz	1 lb 14 oz	2 lb 8 oz	3 lb 2 oz
2¾ oz	5½ oz	8¼ oz	11 oz	1 lb 6 oz	2 lb 1 oz	2 lb 12 oz	3 lb 7 oz
3 oz	6 oz	9 oz	12 oz	1 lb 8 oz	2 lb 4 oz	3 lb	3 lb 12 oz
3¼ oz	6½ oz	9¾ oz	13 oz	1 lb 10 oz	2 lb 7 oz	3 lb 4 oz	4 lb 1 oz
3½ oz	7 oz	10½ oz	14 oz	1 lb 12 oz	2 lb 10 oz	3 lb 8 oz	4 lb 6 oz
3¾ oz	7½ oz	11¼ oz	15 oz	1 lb 14 oz	2 lb 13 oz	3 lb 12 oz	4 lb 11 oz
4 oz	8 oz	12 oz	1 lb	2 lb	3 lb	4 lb	5 lb
4½ oz	9 oz	13½ oz	1 lb 2 oz	2 lb 4 oz	3 lb 6 oz	4 lb 8 oz	5 lb 10 oz
5 oz	10 oz	15 oz	1 lb 4 oz	2 lb 8 oz	3 lb 12 oz	5 lb	6 lb 4 oz
5½ oz	11 oz	1 lb ½ oz	1 lb 6 oz	2 lb 12 oz	4 lb 2 oz	5 lb 8 oz	6 lb 14 oz
6 oz	12 oz	1 lb 2 oz	1 lb 8 oz	3 lb	4 lb 8 oz	6 lb	7 lb 8 oz
6½ oz	13 oz	1 lb 3½ oz	1 lb 10 oz	3 lb 4 oz	4 lb 14 oz	6 lb 8 oz	8 lb 2 oz
7 oz	14 oz	1 lb 5 oz	1 lb 12 oz	3 lb 8 oz	5 lb 4 oz	7 lb	8 lb 12 oz
7½ oz	15 oz	1 lb 6½ oz	1 lb 14 oz	3 lb 12 oz	5 lb 10 oz	7 lb 8 oz	9 lb 6 oz
8 oz	1 lb	1 lb 8 oz	2 lb	4 lb	6 lb	8 lb	10 lb
8½ oz	1 lb 1 oz	1 lb 9½ oz	2 lb 2 oz	4 lb 4 oz	6 lb 6 oz	8 lb 8 oz	10 lb 10 oz
9 oz	1 lb 2 oz	1 lb 11 oz	2 lb 4 oz	4 lb 8 oz	6 lb 12 oz	9 lb	11 lb 4 oz
9½ oz	1 lb 3 oz	1 lb 12½ oz	2 lb 6 oz	4 lb 12 oz	7 lb 2 oz	9 lb 8 oz	11 lb 14 oz
10 oz	1 lb 4 oz	1 lb 14 oz	2 lb 8 oz	5 lb	7 lb 8 oz	10 lb	12 lb 8 oz
11 oz	1 lb 6 oz	2 lb 1 oz	2 lb 12 oz	5 lb 8 oz	8 lb 4 oz	11 lb	13 lb 12 oz

[a]To be used with Table 2.2, which is similarly constructed for volume measures.
[b]An asterisk(*) means these amounts cannot be weighed accurately without introducing errors.

TABLE 2.1   *continued*

25	50	75	100	200	300	400	500
12 oz	1 lb 8 oz	2 lb 4 oz	3 lb	6 lb	9 lb	12 lb	15 lb
13 oz	1 lb 10 oz	2 lb 7 oz	3 lb 4 oz	6 lb 8 oz	9 lb 12 oz	13 lb	16 lb 4 oz
14 oz	1 lb 12 oz	2 lb 10 oz	3 lb 8 oz	7 lb	10 lb 8 oz	14 lb	17 lb 8 oz
15 oz	1 lb 14 oz	2 lb 13 oz	3 lb 12 oz	7 lb 8 oz	11 lb 4 oz	15 lb	18 lb 12 oz
1 lb	2 lb	3 lb	4 lb	8 lb	12 lb	16 lb	20 lb
1 lb 1 oz	2 lb 2 oz	3 lb 3 oz	4 lb 4 oz	8 lb 8 oz	12 lb 12 oz	17 lb	21 lb 4 oz
1 lb 2 oz	2 lb 4 oz	3 lb 6 oz	4 lb 8 oz	9 lb	13 lb 8 oz	18 lb	22 lb 8 oz
1 lb 3 oz	2 lb 6 oz	3 lb 9 oz	4 lb 12 oz	9 lb 8 oz	14 lb 4 oz	19 lb	23 lb 12 oz
1 lb 4 oz	2 lb 8 oz	3 lb 12 oz	5 lb	10 lb	15 lb	20 lb	25 lb
1 lb 5 oz	2 lb 10 oz	3 lb 15 oz	5 lb 4 oz	10 lb 8 oz	15 lb 12 oz	21 lb	26 lb 4 oz
1 lb 6 oz	2 lb 12 oz	4 lb 2 oz	5 lb 8 oz	11 lb	16 lb 8 oz	22 lb	27 lb 8 oz
1 lb 7 oz	2 lb 14 oz	4 lb 5 oz	5 lb 12 oz	11 lb 8 oz	17 lb 4 oz	23 lb	28 lb 12 oz
1 lb 8 oz	3 lb	4 lb 8 oz	6 lb	12 lb	18 lb	24 lb	30 lb
1 lb 10 oz	3 lb 4 oz	4 lb 14 oz	6 lb 8 oz	13 lb	19 lb 8 oz	26 lb	32 lb 8 oz
1 lb 12 oz	3 lb 8 oz	5 lb 4 oz	7 lb	14 lb	21 lb	28 lb	35 lb
1 lb 14 oz	3 lb 12 oz	5 lb 10 oz	7 lb 8 oz	15 lb	22 lb 8 oz	30 lb	37 lb 8 oz
2 lb	4 lb	6 lb	8 lb	16 lb	24 lb	32 lb	40 lb
2 lb 2 oz	4 lb 4 oz	6 lb 6 oz	8 lb 8 oz	17 lb	25 lb 8 oz	34 lb	42 lb 8 oz
2 lb 4 oz	4 lb 8 oz	6 lb 12 oz	9 lb	18 lb	27 lb	36 lb	45 lb
2 lb 6 oz	4 lb 12 oz	7 lb 2 oz	9 lb 8 oz	19 lb	28 lb 8 oz	38 lb	47 lb 8 oz
2 lb 8 oz	5 lb	7 lb 8 oz	10 lb	20 lb	30 lb	40 lb	50 lb
2 lb 12 oz	5 lb 8 oz	8 lb 4 oz	11 lb	22 lb	33 lb	44 lb	55 lb
3 lb	6 lb	9 lb	12 lb	24 lb	36 lb	48 lb	60 lb
3 lb 4 oz	6 lb 8 oz	9 lb 12 oz	13 lb	26 lb	39 lb	52 lb	65 lb
3 lb 8 oz	7 lb	10 lb 8 oz	14 lb	28 lb	42 lb	56 lb	70 lb
3 lb 12 oz	7 lb 8 oz	11 lb 4 oz	15 lb	30 lb	45 lb	60 lb	75 lb
4 lb	8 lb	12 lb	16 lb	32 lb	48 lb	64 lb	80 lb
4 lb 4 oz	8 lb 8 oz	12 lb 12 oz	17 lb	34 lb	51 lb	68 lb	85 lb
4 lb 8 oz	9 lb	13 lb 8 oz	18 lb	36 lb	54 lb	72 lb	90 lb
4 lb 12 oz	9 lb 8 oz	14 lb 2 oz	19 lb	38 lb	57 lb	76 lb	95 lb
5 lb	10 lb	15 lb	20 lb	40 lb	60 lb	80 lb	100 lb
5 lb 4 oz	10 lb 8 oz	15 lb 12 oz	21 lb	42 lb	63 lb	84 lb	105 lb
5 lb 8 oz	11 lb	16 lb 8 oz	22 lb	44 lb	66 lb	88 lb	110 lb
5 lb 12 oz	11 lb 8 oz	17 lb 4 oz	23 lb	46 lb	69 lb	92 lb	115 lb
6 lb	12 lb	18 lb	24 lb	48 lb	72 lb	96 lb	120 lb
6 lb 4 oz	12 lb 8 oz	18 lb 12 oz	25 lb	50 lb	75 lb	100 lb	125 lb
7 lb 8 oz	15 lb	22 lb 8 oz	30 lb	60 lb	90 lb	120 lb	150 lb
8 lb 12 oz	17 lb 8 oz	26 lb 4 oz	35 lb	70 lb	105 lb	140 lb	175 lb
10 lb	20 lb	30 lb	40 lb	80 lb	120 lb	160 lb	200 lb
11 lb 4 oz	22 lb 8 oz	33 lb 12 oz	45 lb	90 lb	135 lb	180 lb	225 lb
12 lb 8 oz	25 lb	37 lb 8 oz	50 lb	100 lb	150 lb	200 lb	250 lb

TABLE 2.2   **Direct-reading table for adjusting recipes with ingredient amounts given in volume measurement and divisible by 25[a]**

25	50	75	100
¼ tsp	½ tsp	¾ tsp	1 tsp
¼ tsp (r)	½ tsp (r)	1 tsp (s)	1¼ tsp
¼ tsp + ⅛ tsp	¾ tsp	1 tsp + ⅛ tsp	1½ tsp
½ tsp (s)	¾ tsp (r)	1¼ tsp (r)	1¾ tsp
½ tsp	1 tsp	1½ tsp	2 tsp
½ tsp (r)	1 tsp + ⅛ tsp	1¾ tsp (s)	2¼ tsp
½ tsp + ⅛ tsp	1¼ tsp	2 tsp (s)	2½ tsp
¾ tsp (s)	1¼ tsp + ⅛ tsp	2 tsp (r)	2¾ tsp
¾ tsp	1½ tsp	2¼ tsp	1 Tbsp
1 tsp + ⅛ tsp	2¼ tsp	1 Tbsp + ¼ tsp + ⅛ tsp	1½ Tbsp
1½ tsp	1 Tbsp	1½ Tbsp	2 Tbsp
1¾ tsp + ⅛ tsp	1 Tbsp + ¾ tsp	1 Tbsp + 2½ tsp + ⅛ tsp	2½ Tbsp
2¼ tsp	1½ Tbsp	2 Tbsp + ¾ tsp	3 Tbsp
2¼ tsp + ⅛ tsp	1 Tbsp + 2¼ tsp	2 Tbsp + 1⅛ tsp	3½ Tbsp
1 Tbsp	2 Tbsp	3 Tbsp	½ cup
1 Tbsp + 1 tsp	2 Tbsp + 2 tsp	¼ cup	⅓ cup
2 Tbsp	¼ cup	¼ cup + 2 Tbsp	½ cup
2 Tbsp + 2 tsp	⅓ cup	½ cup	⅔ cup
3 Tbsp	6 Tbsp	½ cup + 1 Tbsp	¾ cup
¼ cup	½ cup	¾ cup	1 cup
¼ cup + 1 Tbsp	½ cup + 2 Tbsp	¾ cup + 3 Tbsp	1¼ cups
⅓ cup	⅔ cup	1 cup	1⅓ cups
⅓ cup + 2 tsp	¾ cup	1 cup + 2 Tbsp	1½ cups
6 Tbsp + 2 tsp	¾ cup + 4 tsp	1¼ cups	1⅔ cups
¼ cup + 3 Tbsp	¾ cup + 2 Tbsp	1¼ cups + 1 Tbsp	1¾ cups
½ cup	1 cup	1½ cups	2 cups
½ cup + 1 Tbsp	1 cup + 2 Tbsp	1½ cups + 3 Tbsp	2¼ cups
½ cup + 4 tsp	1 cup + 2 Tbsp + 2 tsp	1¾ cups	2⅓ cups
½ cup + 2 Tbsp	1¼ cups	1¾ cups + 2 Tbsp	2½ cups
⅔ cup	1⅓ cups	2 cups	2⅔ cups
½ cup + 3 Tbsp	1¼ cups + 2 Tbsp	2 cups + 1 Tbsp	2¾ cups
¾ cup	1½ cups	2¼ cups	3 cups
¾ cup + 1 Tbsp	1½ cups + 2 Tbsp	2¼ cups + 3 Tbsp	3¼ cups
¾ cup + 4 tsp	1⅔ cups	2½ cups	3⅓ cups
¾ cup + 2 Tbsp	1¾ cups	2½ cups + 2 Tbsp	3½ cups

[a]To be used with Table 2.1, which is similarly constructed for weight measures.

TABLE 2.2 *continued*

200	300	400	500
2 tsp	1 Tbsp	1 Tbsp + 1 tsp	1 Tbsp + 2 tsp
2½ tsp	1 Tbsp + ¾ tsp	1 Tbsp + 2 tsp	2 Tbsp + ¼ tsp
1 Tbsp	1½ Tbsp	2 Tbsp	2½ Tbsp
1 Tbsp + ½ tsp	1 Tbsp + 2¼ tsp	2 Tbsp + 1 tsp	2 Tbsp + 2¾ tsp
1 Tbsp + 1 tsp	2 Tbsp	2 Tbsp + 2 tsp	3 Tbsp + 1 tsp
1½ Tbsp	2 Tbsp + ¾ tsp	3 Tbsp	3 Tbsp + 2¼ tsp
1 Tbsp + 2 tsp	2½ Tbsp	3 Tbsp + 1 tsp	4 Tbsp + ½ tsp
1 Tbsp + 2½ tsp	2 Tbsp + 2¼ tsp	3 Tbsp + 2 tsp	4 Tbsp + 1¾ tsp
2 Tbsp	3 Tbsp	¼ cup	5 Tbsp
3 Tbsp	¼ cup + 1½ tsp	⅓ cup + 2 tsp	¼ cup + 3½ Tbsp
¼ cup	¼ cup + 2 Tbsp	½ cup	½ cup + 2 Tbsp
¼ cup + 1 Tbsp	¼ cup + 3½ Tbsp	½ cup + 2 Tbsp	¾ cup + ½ Tbsp
⅓ cup + 2 tsp	½ cup + 1 Tbsp	¾ cup	¾ cup + 3 Tbsp
¼ cup + 3 Tbsp	½ cup + 2½ Tbsp	¾ cup + 2 Tbsp	1 cup + 1½ Tbsp
½ cup	¾ cup	1 cup	1¼ cups
⅔ cup	1 cup	1⅓ cups	1⅔ cups
1 cup	1½ cups	2 cups	2½ cups
1⅓ cups	2 cups	2⅔ cups	3⅓ cups
1½ cups	2¼ cups	3 cups	3¾ cups
2 cups	3 cups	1 qt	1¼ qt
2½ cups	3¾ cups	1¼ qt	1½ qt + ¼ cup
2⅔ cups	1 qt	1¼ qt + ⅓ cup	1½ qt + ⅔ cup
3 cups	1 qt + ½ cup	1½ qt	1¾ qt + ½ cup
3⅓ cups	1¼ qt	1½ qt + ⅔ cup	2 qt + ⅓ cup
3½ cups	1¼ qt + ¼ cup	1¾ qt	2 qt + ¾ cup
1 qt	1½ qt	2 qt	2½ qt
1 qt + ½ cup	1½ qt + ¾ cup	2¼ qt	2¼ qt + ¼ cup
1 qt + ⅔ cup	1¾ qt	2¼ qt + ⅓ cup	2¾ qt + ⅔ cup
1¼ qt	1¾ qt + ½ cup	2½ qt	3 qt + ½ cups
1¼ qt + ⅓ cup	2 qt	2½ qt+ ⅔ cup	3qt + 1⅓ cups
1¼ qt + ½ cup	2 qt + ¼ cup	2¾ qt	3¼ qt + ¾ cup
1½ qt	2¼ qt	3 qt	3¾ qt
1½ qt + ½ cup	2¼ qt + ¾ cup	3¼ qt	1 gal + ¼ cup
1½ qt + ⅔ cup	2½ qt	3¼ qt + ⅓ cup	1 gal + ⅔ cup
1¾ qt	2½ qt + ½ cup	3½ qt	1 gal + 1½ cups

continues

TABLE 2.2   *continued*

25	50	75	100
¾ cup + 2 Tbsp + 2½ tsp	1¾ cups + 4 tsp	2¾ cups + ½ tsp	3⅔ cups
¾ cup + 3 Tbsp	1¾ cups + 2 Tbsp	2¾ cups + 1 Tbsp	3¾ cups
1 cup	2 cups	3 cups	1 qt
1¼ cups	2½ cups	3¾ cups	1¼ qt
1½ cups	3 cups	1 qt + ½ cup	1½ qt
1¾ cups	3½ cups	1¼ qt + ¼ cup	1¾ qt
2 cups	1 qt	1½ qt	2 qt
2¼ cups	1 qt + ½ cup	1½ qt + ¾ cup	2¼ qt
2½ cups	1¼ qt	1¾ qt + ½ cup	2½ qt
2¾ cups	1¼ qt + ½ cup	2 qt + ¼ cup	2¾ qt
3 cups	1½ qt	2¼ qt	3 qt
3¼ cups	1½ qt + ½ cup	2¼ qt + ¾ cup	3¼ qt
3½ cups	1¾ qt	2½ qt + ½ cup	3½ qt
3¾ cups	1¾ qt + ½ cup	2¾ qt + ¼ cup	3¾ qt
1 qt	2 qt	3 qt	1 gal
1¼ qt	2½ qt	3¾ qt	1¼ gal
1½ qt	3 qt	1 gal + 2 cups	1½ gal
1¾ qt	3½ qt	1¼ gal + 1 cup	1¾ gal
2 qt	1 gal	1½ gal	2 gal
2¼ qt	1 gal + 2 cups	1½ gal + 3 cups	2¼ gal
2½ qt	1¼ gal	1¾ gal + 2 cups	2½ gal
2¾ qt	1¼ gal + 2 cups	2 gal + 1 cup	2¾ gal
3 qt	1½ gal	2¼ gal	3 gal
3 qt + 1 cup	1½ gal + 2 cups	2¼ gal + 3 cups	3¼ gal
3½ qt	1¾ gal	2½ gal + 2 cups	3½ gal
3½ qt + 1 cup	1¾ gal + 2 cups	2¾ gal + 1 cup	3¾ gal
1 gal	2 gal	3 gal	4 gal
1 gal + 1 cup	2 gal + 2 cups	3 gal + 3 cups	4¼ gal
1 gal + 2 cups	2¼ gal	3¼ gal + 2 cups	4½ gal
1 gal + 3 cups	2¼ gal + 2 cups	3½ gal + 1 cup	4¾ gal
1¼ gal	2½ gal	3¾ gal	5 gal
1¼ gal + 1 cup	2½ gal + 2 cups	3¾ gal + 3 cups	5¼ gal

TABLE 2.2   *continued*

200	300	400	500
1¾ qt + ⅓ cup	2¾ qt	3½ qt + ⅔ cup	1 gal + 1⅔ cups
1¾ qt + ½ cup	2 qt + 3¼ cup	3 qt + 3 cups	1 gal + 2¾ cups
2 qt	3 qt	1 gal	1¼ gal
2½ qt	3¾ qt	1¼ gal	1½ gal + 1 cup
3 qt	1 gal + 2 cups	1½ gal	1¾ gal + 2 cups
3½ qt	1¼ gal + 1 cup	1¾ gal	2 gal + 3 cups
1 gal	1½ gal	2 gal	2½ gal
1 gal + 2 cups	1½ gal + 3 cups	2¼ gal	2¾ gal + 1 cup
1¼ gal	1¾ gal + 2 cups	2½ gal	3 gal + 2 cups
1¼ gal + 2 cups	2 gal + 1 cup	2¾ gal	3¼ gal + 3 cups
1½ gal	2¼ gal	3 gal	3¾ gal
1½ gal + 2 cups	2¼ gal + 3 cups	3¼ gal	4 gal + 1 cup
1¾ gal	2½ gal + 2 cups	3½ gal	4¼ gal + 2 cups
1¾ gal + 2 cups	2¾ gal + 1 cup	3¾ gal	4½ gal + 3 cups
2 gal	3 gal	4 gal	5 gal
2½ gal	3¾ gal	5 gal	6¼ gal
3 gal	4½ gal	6 gal	7½ gal
3½ gal	5¼ gal	7 gal	8¾ gal
4 gal	6 gal	8 gal	10 gal
4½ gal	6¾ gal	9 gal	11¼ gal
5 gal	7½ gal	10 gal	12½ gal
5½ gal	8¼ gal	11 gal	13¾ gal
6 gal	9 gal	12 gal	15 gal
6½ gal	9¾ gal	13 gal	16¼ gal
7 gal	10½ gal	14 gal	17½ gal
7½ gal	11¼ gal	15 gal	18¾ gal
8 gal	12 gal	16 gal	20 gal
8½ gal	12¾ gal	17 gal	21¼ gal
9 gal	13½ gal	18 gal	22½ gal
9½ gal	14¼ gal	19 gal	23¾ gal
10 gal	15 gal	20 gal	25 gal
10½ gal	15¾ gal	21 gal	26¼ gal

continues

TABLE 2.2   *continued*

25	50	75	100
1¼ gal + 2 cups	2¾ gal	4 gal + 2 cups	5½ gal
1¼ gal + 3 cups	2¾ gal + 2 cups	4¼ gal + 1 cup	5¾ gal
1½ gal	3 gal	4½ gal	6 gal
1½ gal + 1 cup	3 gal + 2 cups	4½ gal + 3 cups	6¼ gal
1½ gal + 2 cups	3¼ gal	4¾ gal + 2 cups	6½ gal
1½ gal + 3 cups	3¼ gal + 2 cups	5 gal + 1 cup	6¾ gal
1¾ gal	3½ gal	5¼ gal	7 gal

TABLE 2.2   *continued*

200	300	400	500
11 gal	16½ gal	22 gal	27½ gal
11½ gal	17¼ gal	23 gal	28¾ gal
12 gal	18 gal	24 gal	30 gal
12½ gal	18¾ gal	25 gal	31¼ gal
13 gal	19½ gal	26 gal	32½ gal
13½ gal	20¼ gal	27 gal	33¾ gal
14 gal	21 gal	28 gal	35 gal

Used with permission from *Quantity Food Preparation: Standardizing Recipes and Controlling Ingredients.* Copyright 1983 by the American Dietetic Association, Chicago.

Directions for Using Table 2.3

Many quantity recipes can be expanded from home-size recipes. Table 2.3 is useful when enlarging small-quantity recipes. Instructions for using this table follow:

1. Locate column that corresponds to the yield of the recipe to be increased. For example, if the recipe yields 8 portions, use the figures in the first column under the heading 8.

2. Locate the ingredient amount for each ingredient to be adjusted. Example: The original recipe of 8 portions calls for 1 Tbsp sugar; find 1 Tbsp in the column marked 8.

3. Locate the amount on the same line under the heading for the desired yield. Example: To increase the original recipe for 8 servings to 24, locate under the 24 column heading the number on the same line with the 1 Tbsp in the 8 column. In the case of 1 Tbsp sugar for 8 portions the enlarged amount is 3 Tbsp.

4. Repeat this procedure for each ingredient in the recipe. Refer to Table 2.10 for rounding off awkward fractions and complicated measurements.

Abbreviations in this table include:

- tsp = teaspoon
- Tbsp = tablespoon
- qt = quart
- gal = gallon
- (b) = too small for accurate measure; use caution
- (r) = slightly rounded
- (s) = scant

Measuring spoon sizes are:

- 1 Tbsp
- 1 tsp
- ½ tsp
- ¼ tsp
- for ¾ tsp combine ½ tsp + ¼ tsp
- for ⅛ tsp use half of the ¼ tsp

Equivalents include:

- 3 tsp = 1 Tbsp
- 4 Tbsp = ¼ cup
- 5 Tbsp + 1 tsp = ⅓ cup
- 8 Tbsp = ½ cup
- 10 Tbsp + 2 tsp = ⅔ cup
- 12 Tbsp = ¾ cup
- 16 Tbsp = 1 cup
- 4 cups = 1 qt
- 4 qt = 1 gal

TABLE 2.3   Direct-reading table for increasing home-size recipes with ingredient amounts given in volume measurement and divisible by 8

8	16	24	32
(b)	(b)	⅛ tsp	⅛ tsp (r)
(b)	⅛ tsp (r)	¼ tsp	¼ tsp(r)
¼ tsp (s)	¼ tsp (r)	½ tsp	¾ tsp (s)
¼ tsp	½ tsp	¾ tsp	1 tsp
¼ tsp (r)	¾ tsp(r)	1 tsp	1¼ tsp(r)
½ tsp (s)	¾ tsp (r)	1¼ tsp	1¾ tsp (s)
½ tsp	1 tsp	1½ tsp	2 tsp
½ tsp (r)	1¼ tsp (s)	1¾ tsp	2¼ tsp (r)
¾ tsp (s)	1¼ tsp (r)	2 tsp	2¾ tsp (r)
¾ tsp	1½ tsp	2¼ tsp	1 Tbsp
¾ tsp (r)	1¾ tsp (s)	2½ tsp	1 Tbsp + ¼ tsp (r)
1 tsp (s)	1¾ tsp (r)	2¾ tsp	1 Tbsp + ¾ tsp (s)
1 tsp	2 tsp	1 Tbsp	1 Tbsp + 1 tsp
1½ tsp	1 Tbsp	1½ Tbsp	2 Tbsp
2 tsp	1 Tbsp + 1 tsp	2 Tbsp	2 Tbsp + 2 tsp
2½ tsp	1 Tbsp + 2 tsp	2½ Tbsp	3 Tbsp + 1 tsp
1 Tbsp	2 Tbsp	3 Tbsp	¼ cup
1 Tbsp + ½ tsp	2 Tbsp + 1 tsp	3½ Tbsp	¼ cup + 2 tsp
1 Tbsp + 1 tsp	2 Tbsp + 2 tsp	¼ cup	⅓ cup
1 Tbsp + 2¼ tsp	3 Tbsp + 2¾ tsp	⅓ cup	¼ cup + 3 Tbsp
2 Tbsp + 2 tsp	⅓ cup	½ cup	⅔ cup
3 Tbsp + 1¾ tsp	⅓ cup + 5 tsp	⅔ cup	¾ cup + 2 Tbsp
¼ cup	½ cup	¾ cup	1 cup
⅓ cup	⅔ cup	1 cup	1⅓ cups
⅓ cup + 4 tsp	¾ cup + 4 tsp	1¼ cups	1⅔ cups
⅓ cup + 5¼ tsp	⅔ cup + 3½ Tbsp	1⅓ cups	1¾ cups + 1¼ tsp
½ cup	1 cup	1½ cups	2 cups
½ cup + 2¼ tsp	1 cup + 5¼ tsp	1⅔ cups	2 cups + 3½ Tbsp
½ cup + 4 tsp	1 cup + 3 Tbsp	1¾ cups	2⅓ cups
⅔ cup	1⅓ cups	2 cups	2⅔ cups

TABLE 2.3   *continued*

48	64	96
¼ tsp	¼ tsp (r)	½ tsp
½ tsp	¾ tsp (s)	1 tsp
1 tsp	1¼ tsp (r)	2 tsp
1½ tsp	2 tsp	1 Tbsp
2 tsp	2¾ tsp (s)	1 Tbsp + 1 tsp
2½ tsp	1 Tbsp + ¼ tsp	1 Tbsp + 2 tsp
1 Tbsp	1 Tbsp + 1 tsp	2 Tbsp
1 Tbsp + ½ tsp	1 Tbsp + 1¾ tsp	2 Tbsp + 1 tsp
1 Tbsp + 1 tsp	1 Tbsp + 2¼ tsp	2 Tbsp + 2 tsp
1 Tbsp + 1½ tsp	2 Tbsp	3 Tbsp
1 Tbsp + 2 tsp	2 Tbsp + ¾ tsp	3 Tbsp + 1 tsp
1 Tbsp + 2½ tsp	2 Tbsp + 1¼ tsp	3 Tbsp + 2 tsp
2 Tbsp	2 Tbsp + 2 tsp	¼ cup
3 Tbsp	¼ cup	⅓ cup + 2 tsp
¼ cup	⅓ cup	½ cup
¼ cup + 1 Tbsp	⅓ cup + 4 tsp	½ cup + 2 Tbsp
⅓ cup + 2 tsp	½ cup	¾ cup
¼ cup + 3 Tbsp	½ cup + 4 tsp	¾ cup + 2 Tbsp
½ cup	⅔ cup	1 cup
⅔ cup	¾ cup + 2 Tbsp	1⅓ cups
1 cup	1⅓ cups	2 cups
1⅓ cups	1¾ cups	2⅔ cups
1½ cups	2 cups	3 cups
2 cups	2⅔ cups	1 qt
2½ cups	3⅓ cups	1¼ qt
2⅔ cups	3½ cups + 2½ tsp	1¼ qt + ⅓ cup
3 cups	1 qt	1½ qt
3⅓ cups	4¼ cups + 3 Tbsp	1½ qt + ⅔ cup
3½ cups	1 qt + ⅔ cups	1¾ qt
1 qt	1¼ qt + ⅓ cup	2 qt

continues

TABLE 2.3 *continued*

8	16	24	32
¾ cup	1½ cups	2¼ cups	3 cups
¾ cup + 1¼ tsp	1½ cups + 2¾ tsp	2⅓ cups	3 cups + 2 Tbsp
¾ cup + 4 tsp	1⅔ cups	2½ cups	3⅓ cups
⅔ cup + 3½ Tbsp	1¾ cups + 1¼ tsp	2⅔ cups	3½ cups + 1 Tbsp
⅔ cup + ¼ cup	1¾ cups + 4 tsp	2¾ cups	3⅔ cups
1 cup	2 cups	3 cups	1 qt
1 cup + 4 tsp	2 cups + 2½ Tbsp	3¼ cups	1 qt + ⅓ cup
1 cup + 5¼ tsp	2 cups + 3½ Tbsp	3⅓ cups	4¼ cups + 3 Tbsp
1 cup + 2 Tbsp + 2 tsp	2¼ cups + 4 tsp	3½ cups	1 qt + ⅔ cup
1 cup + 3½ Tbsp	2¼ cups + 3 Tbsp	3⅔ cups	4¾ cups + 2 Tbsp
1¼ cups	2½ cups	3¾ cups	1¼ qt
1⅓ cups	2⅔ cups	1 qt	1¼ qt + ⅓ cup
1⅔ cups	3⅓ cups	1¼ qt	1½ qt + ⅔ cup
2 cups	1 qt	1½ qt	2 qt
2⅓ cups	1 qt + ⅔ cup	1¾ qt	2¼ qt + ⅓ cup
2⅔ cups	1¼ qt + ⅓ cup	2 qt	2½ qt + ⅔ cup
3 cups	1½ qt	2¼ qt	3 qt
3⅓ cups	1½ qt + ⅔ cup	2½ qt	3¼ qt + ⅓ cup
3⅔ cups	1¾ qt + ⅓ cup	2¾ qt	3½ qt + ⅔ cup
1 qt	2 qt	3 qt	1 gal
1 qt + ⅓ cup	2 qt + ⅔ cup	3¼ qt	1 gal + 1⅓ cups
1 qt + ⅔ cup	2¼ qt + ⅓ cup	3½ qt	1 gal + 2⅔ cup
1¼ qt	2½ qt	3¾ qt	1¼ gal
1¼ qt + ⅓ cup	2½ qt + ⅔ cup	1 gal	1¼ gal + 1⅓ cups
1½ qt + ⅔ cup	3¼ qt + ⅓ cup	1¼ gal	1½ gal + 2⅔ cups
2 qt	1 gal	1½ gal	2 gal

TABLE 2.3   *continued*

48	64	96
1 qt + ½ cup	1½ qt	2¼ qt
1 qt + ⅔ cup	1½ qt + ¼ cup	2¼ qt + ⅓ cup
1¼ qt	1½ qt + ⅔ cup	2½ qt
1¼ qt + ⅓ cup	1¾ qt + 2 Tbsp	2½ qt + ⅔ cup
1¼ qt + ½ cup	1¾ qt + ⅓ cup	2¾ qt
1½ qt	2 qt	3 qt
1½ qt + ½ cup	2 qt + ⅔ cup	3¼ qt
1½ qt + ⅔ cup	2 qt + ¾ cup + 2 Tbsp	3¼ qt + ⅓ cup
1¾ qt	2¼ qt + ⅓ cup	3½ qt
1¾ qt + ⅓ cup	2¼ qt + ¾ cup	3 qt + 2⅔ cups
1¾ qt + ½ cup	2½ qt	3 qt + 3 cups
2 qt	2¾ qt + ⅓ cup	1 gal
2½ qt	3¼ qt + ⅓ cup	1¼ gal
3 qt	1 gal	1½ gal
3½ qt	1 gal + 2⅔ cups	1¾ gal
1 gal	1¼ gal + 1⅓ cups	2 gal
1 gal + 2 cups	1½ gal	2¼ gal
1¼ gal	1½ gal + 2⅔ cups	2½ gal
1¼ gal + 2 cups	1¾ gal + 1⅓ cups	2¾ gal
1½ gal	2 gal	3 gal
1½ gal + 2 cups	2 gal + 2⅔ cups	3¼ gal
1¾ gal	2¼ gal + 1⅓ cups	3½ gal
1¾ gal + 2 cups	2½ gal	3¾ gal
2 gal	2½ gal + 2⅔ cups	4 gal
2½ gal	3¼ gal + 1⅓ cups	5 gal
3 gal	4 gal	6 gal

Amounts of Food to Serve, Yield and Food Equivalent Information

TABLE 2.4 Amounts of food to serve 50[a]

Food	Serving portion	Amount for 50 portions	Miscellaneous information
BEVERAGES			
Cider	4 oz (½ cup)	2 gal	64 4-oz portions
Cocoa	6 oz (¾ cup)	2½ gal	50 6-oz portions
Unsweetened powder		8 oz	
Instant mix		2½ lb	
Coffee	6 oz (¾ cup)	2½ gal	
Regular or urn grind		1–1½ lb	
Freeze-dried		2–3 oz	
Instant		3 oz	
Lemonade	8 oz (1 cup)	3 gal	48 8-oz portions
Frozen concentrate		3 32-oz cans	dilute 1:4 parts water
Orange juice, see Juices			
Punch	4 oz (½ cup)	2–2½ gal	1 gal yields 32 4-oz portions
Tea			2½ gal yields 50 4-oz portions plus 30 refills
Hot	6 oz (¾ cup)	2½ gal	
Bulk		2 oz	Amount may vary with quality of tea
Iced	8 oz (1 cup)	3 gal	48 8-oz portions
1-oz bag		6 bags	6 1-oz bags make 3 gal
Instant		1–1½ oz	
Wine	See Tables 1.11 and 1.12		
BREAD AND CRACKERS			
Biscuits, baking powder	1 biscuit	4½ doz	
Dough ready for baking		5 lb	
Mix		2½ lb	
Bread			
1½-lb loaf	1 slice	2½ loaves	24 slices per loaf
2-lb pullman	1 slice	1½ loaves	36 slices per loaf
Breads, quick 5 × 9 × 2¾-inch loaves	1 slice	4 loaves	16 slices per loaf
Coffee cake, 12 × 18 × 2 inches	3 × 2¼ inches	2 pans	Cut 4 × 8
Batter, ready to bake		5–6 lb per pan	
Crackers			
Graham	2 crackers	1¾–2 lb	60–65 per lb
Saltines	4 crackers	1½ lb	150–160 per lb
Soda	2 crackers	1½–2 lb	65 per lb
Muffins	1 muffin	4½ doz	
Batter, ready to bake		5 lb	
Mix		3½ lb	
Pancakes	3½ oz	7 qt batter	2 4-inch cakes
Mix		6 lb	
Rolls			
Breakfast, 3 oz	1 roll	4½ doz	
Dinner, 1½ oz	1 roll	4½ doz	
Frozen dough		10 lb	
Mix		5 lb	
Toast			
French	2 slices	7 lb bread	
Buttered or cinnamon	2 slices	7 lb bread	
Waffles	3 oz	6 qt batter	1 waffle

[a]Abbreviations used: AP, as purchased; EP, edible portion.

TABLE 2.4 *continued*

Food	Serving portion	Amount for 50 portions	Miscellaneous information
CEREALS			
Cooked cereal	⅔ cup	2 lb	2 gal cooked
Hominy grits	⅔ cup	2 lb	2 gal cooked
Cold cereal, flakes, crisp	1 oz (½–¾ cup)	3 lb	
Rice	½ cup	3–4 lb	6–8 qt cooked
See also Pasta			
DAIRY PRODUCTS			
Butter or margarine			
For sandwiches		1 lb	To butter 100 slices
For table	1–2 pats	1–1½ lb	
For vegetables	½–1 tsp	4–8 oz	
Cheese, cheddar, Monterey Jack, Swiss, provolone	1–1½ oz	3–5 lb	For sandwich or with cold cuts
Sandwich slices	1 oz	3¼ lb	
Cottage	2 oz (No. 20 dipper)	6½ lb	For salad or side dish
Cream	½ oz	2 lb	For salad or garnish
Dessert (cream, blue, Camembert)	1 oz	3 lb	
Cream			
Coffee		1–1½ qt	
Whipping	2 Tbsp	1½ pt	1½ qt whipped
Ice cream or sherbet, bulk	No. 12 dipper	2½ gal	Dish or sundae
	No. 16 dipper	1½ gal	With cake or cookie
	No. 20 dipper	1¼ gal	For à la mode
Milk			
Fluid	8 oz (1 cup)	3 gal	
Nonfat dry	8 oz (1 cup)	3 lb	3.5 oz (1⅓ cups) dry milk per qt of water. Volume may vary with brand.
Nondairy creamer	1 tsp	3 oz	
Sherbet			See Ice cream
Sour cream	1 oz (2 Tbsp)	3 lb	For baked potato
	1 tsp	8 oz	For garnish
Whipped topping mix			
Dry	2 Tbsp	5 oz	
Frozen	2 Tbsp	18 oz (1½ qt)	
Liquid	2 Tbsp	1½ pt	1½ qt whipped
Yogurt	8 oz (1 cup)	25 lb	
DESSERTS			
Cakes			
Angel food	1 oz	3–4 10-inch cakes	12–14 cuts per cake
Pound or loaf, 5 × 9 inches	3 oz	4 loaves	
Sheet, 12 × 18 × 2 inches	3 × 2¼ inches	2 pans	Cut 4 × 8
Batter, ready to bake		4–5 lb each	
Sheet, 18 × 26 × 2 inches	3 × 2½ inches	1 pan	Cut 6 × 10
Batter, ready to bake		8–10 lb	
Cake mixes			
Angel food		4 lb	
Chocolate, white, yellow		5 lb	

continues

TABLE 2.4 *continued*

Food	Serving portion	Amount for 50 portions	Miscellaneous information
Pies, 8 inch	⅙ pie	9 pies	Cut 6 pieces per pie
Filling			
Chiffon	3 cups per pie	6 qt	
Cream or custard	3 cups per pie	6 qt	
Fruit	3 cups (1 lb 8 oz) per pie	6 qt (10–12 lb)	
Meringue	4 oz per pie	2 lb	
Pastry			
1 crust	5 oz per pie	2 lb 8 oz	
2 crust	9 oz per pie	4 lb 8 oz	
Pies, 9 inch	⅛ pie	7 pies	Cut 8 pieces per pie
Filling			
Chiffon	3¾ cups per pie	6–7 qt	
Cream or custard	3¾ cups per pie	6–7 qt	
Fruit	3¾–4 cups (1 lb 14 oz)	6–7 qt (10–12 lb)	
Meringue	5–6 oz per pie	2–2¼ lb	
Pastry			
1 crust	9 oz per pie	4 lb	
2 crust	16 oz per pie	7 lb	
Puddings	½ cup (4 oz)	6¼ qt	No. 10 dipper
Toppings, sauce	2–3 Tbsp	2–3 qt	

EGGS

Food	Serving portion	Amount for 50 portions	Miscellaneous information
Eggs			
In shell	1 egg	4½ doz	
Fresh or frozen, whole	1 egg	5 lb (2½ qt)	

FISH AND SHELLFISH

Food	Serving portion	Amount for 50 portions	Miscellaneous information
Fish			
Fillets and steaks, 4 per lb	3 oz	14–16 lb	1 lb AP = 0.70 lb cooked fish
Whole, dressed	3 oz	40 lb	1 lb AP = 0.27 lb cooked fish
Lobster, meat only	4 oz	50 whole lobsters	1 lb lobster = approx. 4 oz meat
Oysters, shucked	3–4 oz	1½–2 gal	1 lb AP = 0.38 lb cooked oysters
Scallops, frozen, to fry	3 oz	10–12 lb	
Shrimp			
Raw, in shell	2 oz	12½ lb	1 lb AP = 0.54 lb
	3 oz	18–20 lb	cooked shrimp
Raw, peeled and cleaned	3 oz	16 lb	1 lb peeled = 0.62 lb cooked shrimp
Cooked, peeled and cleaned	3 oz	10 lb	1 lb AP = 1.00 lb cooked shrimp

FRUITS

Food	Serving portion	Amount for 50 portions	Miscellaneous information
Canned			
For pies, see Desserts			
For salad or dessert	3–4 oz (½ cup)	2–2½ No. 10 cans	For fruits such as peach or pear halves and sliced pineapple, depends on count per can

TABLE 2.4 *continued*

Food	Serving portion	Amount for 50 portions	Miscellaneous information
Fresh			
Apples	1 apple	½ box	Size 113
9 8-inch pies	⅙ pie	14–16 lb AP	1 lb AP = 0.91 lb ready to cook or
7 9-inch pies	⅛ pie	16 lb AP	serve raw with peels; 0.78 lb pared, cooked
Salad or dessert	3–3½ oz	15 lb AP	
Apricots	2	9 lb AP	Medium size 12 per lb
Avocado	½	25 avocados	Medium size 2 per lb
Salad	3 slices	12 avocados	1 lb AP = 0.67 lb ready to serve raw
Bananas	1	16 lb AP	Small, 5–6 inch 1 lb AP = 0.65 lb ready to serve raw
Salad	3 oz	10 lb AP	Medium 7–8 inch, 3 per lb
Blueberries	4 oz	12–14 lb AP	1 lb AP = 0.96 lb ready to serve raw
Cherries, sweet	3 oz	10 lb AP	1 lb AP = 0.98 lb ready to serve with pits; 0.84 lb pitted
Cranberries, for sauce	¼ cup	4 lb AP	1 lb AP = 0.95 lb ready to cook
Fruit cup (mixed fruits)	3 oz (⅓ cup)	9 lb (6 qt)	
Grapefruit	½	25 fruit	64 to 80 size
Salad	5 sections	21 fruit	12 sections per fruit 1 lb AP = 0.52 lb ready to serve raw
Grapes, seedless	4 oz	12–15 lb AP	1 lb AP = 0.97 lb ready to serve raw
With seeds			1 lb AP = 0.89 lb raw seeded
Kiwi	1 slice, as garnish	6–8 fruit	7–8 slices per fruit
Lemons			
For tea or fish	⅙ lemon	8–10 lemons	Medium, size 165
For lemonade	8-oz glass	3 doz	Medium, size 165
Limes			
Garnish	1 wedge	13 limes	4 wedges per lime
Limeade	8-oz glass	4½ doz	
Mangoes, cubed or sliced	½ cup	12½ lb AP	1 lb AP = 0.69 lb ready to serve raw
Melon			
Cantaloupe	½ melon	25 melons	
Fruit cup		5 melons	1 lb AP = 0.52 lb ready to serve raw
Salad slices		6 melons	
Casaba, honeydew, or persian	½ melon	7 melons	1 lb AP = 0.46 lb ready to serve raw
Watermelon	12–16 oz	38–50 lb AP	1 lb AP = 0.57 lb fruit without rind
Nectarines	1 nectarine (5 oz)	15–16 lb AP	1 lb AP = 0.91 lb ready to serve raw
Oranges	1 orange	½ box	Size 113
Juice	4 oz (½ cup)	6¼ qt	16–18 doz size 113
Sections	5 sections	18 oranges	Size 150; 1 lb AP = 0.40 lb ready to serve, without membrane

continues

TABLE 2.4 *continued*

Food	Serving portion	Amount for 50 portions	Miscellaneous information
Peaches	1 peach (4–5 oz)	12–15 lb AP	
Diced or sliced	½ cup	20 lb AP	1 lb AP = 0.76 lb ready to cook or serve raw
Pears	1 pear (5–6 oz)	17–19 lb AP	1 lb AP = 0.92 lb ready to cook or serve raw, unpared; 0.78 lb pared
Salad	3 slices	15–17 lb AP	8–10 slices per pear
Pineapple, cubed	½ cup	24 lb AP (6 pineapples)	1 lb AP = 0.54 lb ready to serve raw
Plums, Italian or purple	2 plums	12½ lb AP	Medium size, 8 per lb 1 lb AP = 0.94 lb ready to cook or serve raw
Rhubarb, 9 8-inch pies	⅙ pie	10–12 lb AP	1 lb AP = 0.86 lb ready to cook
7 9-inch pies	⅛ pie	12 lb AP	
Sauce	½ cup	14 lb AP	
Strawberries	4 oz	14 lb AP	1 lb AP = 0.88 lb ready to serve raw
Garnish	1 berry	1 qt AP	1 qt AP = about 1.32 lb ready to serve raw
Shortcake	¾ cup	8–9 qt AP	
Sundaes	½–¾ cup	6–8 qt AP	
Strawberries, frozen			
For pies, see Desserts			
For salad or dessert	4 oz (½ cup)	13–15 lb	
For topping	1½ oz	5 lb	

JUICES

Food	Serving portion	Amount for 50 portions	Miscellaneous information
Fruit or vegetable	4 oz (½ cup)	6¼ qt	
	6 oz (¾ cup)	9½ qt	
Canned	4 oz	4 46-oz cans	
	6 oz	7 46-oz cans	
Frozen	4 oz	4–5 12-oz cans	Dilute 1:3 parts water
		2 32-oz cans	Dilute 1:3 parts water
	6 oz	7 12-oz cans	Dilute 1:3 parts water
		3 32-oz cans	Dilute 1:3 parts water

MEAT

Beef

Food	Serving portion	Amount for 50 portions	Miscellaneous information
Brisket, corned, boneless	3 oz EP	25–30 lb AP	1 lb AP = 0.42 lb cooked lean meat
Brisket, fresh, boneless	3 oz EP	25–30 lb AP	1 lb AP = 0.46 lb cooked lean meat
Cubed, 1 inch, for stew	3 oz EP	12–15 lb AP	1 lb AP = 0.56 lb cooked lean meat
Ground (73% lean)	3 oz EP	13–15 lb AP	1 lb AP = 0.68 lb cooked meat
Lean (80% lean)	3 oz EP	11–13 lb AP	1 lb AP = 0.77 lb cooked meat
Extra lean (85% lean)	3 oz EP	11–12 lb AP	1 lb AP = 0.80 lb cooked meat
Liver	3½ oz EP	16 lb AP	1 lb AP = 0.70 lb cooked liver
Roast			
Chuck, pot roast, boneless	3 oz EP	18 lb AP	1 lb AP = 0.70 lb lean cooked meat
With bone	3 oz EP	20–22 lb AP	1 lb AP = 0.45 lb cooked lean meat
Rib, standing	6 oz EP	45–50 lb AP	Bone in, oven prepared
Ribeye	3 oz EP	13–15 lb AP	1 lb AP = 0.73 lb lean cooked meat

TABLE 2.4 *continued*

Food	Serving portion	Amount for 50 portions	Miscellaneous information
Roasts, continued			
Round, bottom boneless	3 oz EP	15–18 lb AP	1 lb AP = 0.70 lb cooked lean meat
Inside, boneless	3 oz EP	15–18 lb AP	1 lb AP = 0.70 lb cooked meat
Rump, boneless	3 oz EP	16–18 lb AP	1 lb AP = 0.62 lb cooked lean meat
Sirloin, boneless, trimmed	3 oz EP	16–18 lb AP	1 lb AP = 0.61 lb cooked lean meat
Short ribs, trimmed	3 oz EP	38–40 lb AP	1 lb AP = 0.25 lb cooked meat
Steaks			
Cubed, 4 per lb	3 oz EP	17 lb AP	
Flank, 4 per lb	3 oz EP	17 lb AP	1 lb AP = 0.67 lb cooked lean meat
Loin strip	8 oz AP	25 lb AP	Short cut, bone in
Round, boneless, 3 per lb	3½ oz EP	18–20 lb AP	1 lb AP = 0.59 lb cooked lean meat
Sirloin, boneless	3½ oz EP	14–16 lb AP	1 lb AP = 0.75 lb cooked lean meat
Tenderloin, trimmed	4 oz EP	14 lb AP	1 lb AP = 0.90 lb cooked lean meat
T-bone	8 oz AP	25 lb AP	
	12 oz AP	36–38 AP	
Lamb			
Chops, rib, 4 per lb	2 each	25 lb AP	1 lb AP = 0.46 lb cooked lean meat
Roast, leg, boneless	3 oz EP	15 lb AP	1 lb AP = 0.61 lb cooked lean meat
With bone	3 oz EP	22 lb AP	1 lb AP = 0.45 lb cooked lean meat
Pork, Fresh			
Chops, loin, with bone, 3 per lb	1 chop	17 lb AP	1 lb AP = 0.41 lb cooked lean meat
Cutlets, 3 or 4 per lb	3–3½ oz EP	12–15 lb AP	1 lb AP = 0.75 lb cooked meat
Ham, whole boneless	3 oz EP	18–20 lb AP	1 lb AP = 0.53 lb cooked lean meat
With bone	3 oz EP	20–22 lb AP	1 lb AP = 0.46 lb cooked lean meat
Shoulder, Boston butt, boneless	3 oz EP	18–20 lb AP	1 lb AP = 0.54 lb cooked lean meat
With bone	3 oz EP	19–21 lb AP	1 lb AP = 0.50 lb cooked lean meat
Shoulder, picnic, boneless	3 oz EP	20–22 lb AP	1 lb AP = 0.46 lb cooked lean meat
With bone	3 oz EP	25 lb AP	1 lb AP = 0.38 lb cooked lean meat

continues

TABLE 2.4 *continued*

Food	Serving portion	Amount for 50 portions	Miscellaneous information
Roast, loin, boneless	3 oz EP	18–20 lb AP	1 lb AP = 0.54 lb cooked lean meat
With bone	3 oz EP	22–24 lb AP	1 lb AP = 0.41 lb cooked lean meat
Sausage, bulk	2-oz patty	12½–15 lb AP	1 lb AP = 0.47 lb cooked lean meat
Links, 12–16 per lb	2 links	7–8 lb AP	1 lb AP = 0.47 lb cooked lean meat
Spareribs	8–12 oz AP	25–40 lb AP	1 lb AP = 0.39 lb cooked meat
Pork, Cured			
Bacon, sliced			
Hotel pack	2 slices	4–5 lb	24 slices per lb
Sliced	2 slices	5–6 lb	17–20 slices per lb
Canadian	2 slices (2 oz)	10 lb	16 slices per lb
Ham, boneless	3 oz EP	15 lb AP	1 lb AP = 0.63 lb cooked lean meat
With bone	3 oz EP	18–20 lb AP	1 lb AP = 0.53 lb cooked lean meat
Fully cooked, ready to eat	3 oz EP	15 lb AP	
Pullman, canned	3 oz EP	12–15 lb AP	1 lb AP = 0.64 lb cooked lean meat
Shoulder, Boston butt, boneless	3 oz EP	16 lb AP	1 lb AP = 0.60 lb cooked lean meat
Shoulder, picnic, boneless	3 oz EP	18 lb AP	1 lb AP = 0.53 lb cooked lean meat
Variety and Luncheon Meats			
Braunschweiger	2 oz	7 lb	
Frankfurters			
8 per lb	2 franks	12½ lb	
10 per lb	2 franks	10 lb	
Knockwurst	3 oz	10 lb	
Sliced luncheon meat	1 oz	3¼ lb	16 slices per lb
Veal			
Cubed, 1-inch, for stew	2 oz EP	12–15 lb AP	1 lb AP = 0.65 lb cooked lean meat
Cutlets, 3 or 4 per lb	3–3½ oz EP	12½–15 lb AP	1 lb AP = 0.80 lb cooked lean meat
Ground	3–4 oz EP	15–18 lb AP	1 lb AP = 0.73 lb cooked lean meat
Roast, leg, boneless	3 oz EP	15–18 lb AP	1 lb AP = 0.61 lb cooked lean meat
Shoulder, boneless	3 oz EP	18 lb AP	1 lb AP = 0.59 lb cooked lean meat

TABLE 2.4   *continued*

Food	Serving portion	Amount for 50 portions	Miscellaneous information
PASTA			
Macaroni, noodles, and spaghetti	4 oz	4½–5 lb dry	12 lb cooked
In casseroles	2 oz	2–3 lb dry	6–7 lb cooked
POULTRY			
Chicken			
Fryer parts			
½ breast (without back)	5 oz AP	15–16 lb AP	1 lb AP = 0.66 lb cooked chicken
1 drumstick and thigh	6 oz AP	19–20 lb AP	
1 drumstick	3 oz AP	10 lb AP	1 lb AP = 0.49 lb cooked chicken
1 thigh	3 oz AP	10–11 lb AP	1 lb AP = 0.50 lb cooked chicken
2 wings	5 oz AP	15 lb AP	1 lb AP = 0.34 lb cooked chicken
Whole	¼ fryer	13 fryers	3½ lb each
	½ fryer	25 fryers	2–3 lb each
Whole, for stewing	3 oz cooked chicken without bone	26–28 lb AP	1 lb AP = 0.36 lb cooked chicken, not using neck and giblets; 0.41 lb using neck meat and giblets
Cooked, diced	2 oz	6 lb 4 oz	
Turkey, dressed, whole for roasting	3 oz EP (slices)	50 lb AP	1 lb AP = 0.53 lb cooked turkey with skin, without neck and giblets; without skin 0.47 lb
Boneless roll, raw	3–4 oz EP	16–18 lb AP	1 lb AP = 0.66 lb cooked turkey meat
Boneless roll, cooked	3–4 oz EP	12–15 lb AP	1 lb AP = 0.92 lb cooked turkey meat
Breasts, whole, raw	3 oz EP	19 lb AP	1 lb AP = 0.64 lb turkey meat with skin; 0.57 lb without skin
Leg quarters	3 oz EP	19 lb AP	1 lb AP = 0.53 lb cooked turkey; without skin 0.48 lb
Ground	3 oz EP	11–12 lb	1 lb AP = 0.85 lb cooked meat
Tenderloin (steaks)	4 oz	14–15 lb	1 lb AP = 0.90 lb cooked meat
Wings	3–4 oz EP	30 lb	1 lb AP = 0.32 lb cooked meat (without skin)
Turkey ham, cooked	1½ oz	5 lb	
Turkey, cooked, cubed	1½–2 oz	5–6 lb EP (18–20 lb AP)	3¾–4½ qt
Canned, see Chicken			
RELISHES			
Catsup	1 oz	½ No. 10 can	1 No. 10 can = about 12 cups
	1 oz	4 14-oz bottles	
Mustard, prepared	½ tsp	½ cup	
Olives, green, whole	3	2 qt	88–90 per qt
Ripe, whole or pitted	3	1½ qt	120–150 per qt
Pickles, dill, whole	1 pickle	2½ qt	
Dill or sweet, sliced	1 oz	2¼ qt	
Pickle relish	1 oz	2 qt	1 gal = about 58 oz drained

continues

TABLE 2.4 *continued*

Food	Serving portion	Amount for 50 portions	Miscellaneous information
SALADS AND SALAD DRESSINGS			
Salads			
Bulky vegetable	1 cup	3 gal	
Fish or meat	½ cup	6–7 qt	
Fruit	⅓ cup	4¼ qt	
Gelatin	½ cup	1 12 × 20 × 2-inch pan	24-oz pkg flavored gelatin, 1 gal liquid
Potato	½ cup	6–7 qt	
Dressings			
Mixed in salad			
French, thin	1 Tbsp	3–4 cups	
Mayonnaise	1–2 Tbsp	1 qt	
Self-service			
Thousand Island, Roquefort, or Ranch	1–2 Tbsp	1½–2 qt	
French	1 Tbsp	1–1½ qt	
SAUCES			
Gravy	3–4 Tbsp	3–4 qt	
Meat accompaniment	2 Tbsp	2 qt	
Pudding	2–3 Tbsp	2–3 qt	
Salsa	2–3 Tbsp	2–3 qt	Condiment for Mexican entrees
Vegetable	2–3 Tbsp	2–3 qt	
SOUPS			
Soup			
First course	½–1 cup (4–8 oz)	2–3¼ gal	
Main course	1 cup (8 oz)	3¼ gal	
Soup			
Concentrated	1 cup (8 oz)	5 46-oz cans	
Soup base, paste		10 oz	For 2½ gal soup
SUGARS, JELLIES, SWEETS, NUTS			
Candies, small	2 each	1 lb	
Honey	2 Tbsp	5 lb (2 qt)	
Jam or jelly	1 Tbsp	2–3 lb	
Marshmallows	3	1–1½ lb	
Nuts, mixed	1½ Tbsp	1–1½ lb	
Sugar, cubes	1–2 cubes	1½ lb	
Granulated	1½ tsp	12 oz	
Syrup	¼ cup	3 qt	
Toppings for dessert	2 Tbsp	1½–2 qt	
VEGETABLES			
Canned	2½ oz	2 No. 10 cans	Most vegetables yield 60–70 oz drained weight
Dried			
Dehydrated potatoes			
Diced or sliced	3–4 oz	2–2½ lb AP	
Instant for mashing	4 oz	2–2¼ lb AP	
Dried beans	4 oz	5–6 lb AP	
Split peas or lentils	4 oz	4 lb AP	
Fresh			
Alfalfa sprouts	2 Tbsp	1 lb	

TABLE 2.4 *continued*

Food	Serving portion	Amount for 50 portions	Miscellaneous information
Vegetables, fresh, continued			
Asparagus	3 oz	18–20 lb AP	1 lb AP = 0.53 lb ready to cook; 0.50 lb cooked
Beans, green or wax	3 oz	10–12 lb AP	1 lb AP = 0.88 lb ready to cook
Bean sprouts	2 Tbsp	12 oz	
Beets, topped	3 oz	12–14 lb AP	1 lb AP = 0.77 lb peeled; 0.73 lb cooked slices
Broccoli	3 oz	16–20 lb AP	1 lb AP = 0.81 lb ready to cook
Brussels sprouts	3 oz	12–14 lb AP	1 lb AP = 0.76 lb ready to cook
Cabbage			
Green	1 wedge or 3 oz shredded	12–14 lb AP	1 lb AP = 0.89 lb ready to cook or serve raw
Red, chopped or shredded	2 oz	10 lb AP	1 lb AP = 0.64 lb ready to cook or serve raw
Carrots, without tops	3 oz	14–16 lb AP	1 lb AP = 0.70 lb ready to cook or serve raw; 0.60 lb cooked
Strips for relish	3 strips, 4 × ½ inch	4–5 lb	
Cauliflower	3 oz	16–18 lb AP	1 lb AP = 0.62 lb ready to cook or serve raw; 0.61 lb cooked
Salad pieces	¼ cup	8 lb AP	1 medium head = about 6 cups (50–75 florets)
Celery, sliced	3 oz	12 lb AP	1 lb AP = 0.83 lb ready to cook or serve raw; 0.74 lb cooked
Sticks for relishes	4 sticks, 4 × ½ inch	4–5 lb AP	
Celery cabbage	2 oz	9 lb AP	1 lb AP = 0.93 lb ready to serve raw
Corn, on cob	1 ear	5 doz (25 lb with husks)	1 lb AP = 0.33 lb EP cooked
Cucumbers	1½ oz	5–6 lb AP	1 lb AP = 0.84 lb pared ready to serve raw
Eggplant	3 oz	12–15 lb AP	1 lb AP = 0.81 lb ready to cook
Endive, escarole	½ cup	8–10 lb AP	1 lb AP = 0.78 lb ready to serve
Lettuce			
Iceberg, wedges	⅙ head	8–10 heads	24 heads per crate
Broken, for salad	1 cup (2½ oz)	9½ lb AP	1 lb AP = 0.76 lb ready to serve
Garnish	1 leaf	4–5 lb AP	
Leaf, for garnish	1 leaf	3–4 lb AP	1 lb AP = 0.66 lb ready to serve
Bibb	2½ oz	9 lb	
Romaine, for salad	2½ oz	9 lb AP	1 lb AP = 0.64 lb ready to serve
Mushrooms, sliced	3 oz	12 lb AP	1 lb AP = 0.90 lb ready to serve raw or cook; 0.22 lb cooked
For sauce	1 oz	3–4 lb AP	
Onions			
Green, chopped for salad	¼ cup (with tops)	3½–4 lb AP	1 lb AP = 0.83 lb ready to serve raw with tops; 0.37 lb without tops
Mature	2 oz	7–8 lb AP	1 lb AP = 0.88 lb ready to serve raw or cook; 0.78 lb cooked
Whole, to bake	1 medium	12–15 lb AP	
Parsley, for garnish or seasoning		2 lb AP	1 lb AP = 0.92 lb ready to serve raw
Parsnips	3 oz	12–15 lb AP	1 lb AP = 0.83 lb ready to cook
Peppers, green, red, and yellow strips	3 strips	4–5 lb AP	1 lb AP = 0.80 lb ready to cook or serve raw; 0.73 lb cooked
Chopped for salads	½ oz	1–2 AP	

continues

TABLE 2.4   *continued*

Food	Serving portion	Amount for 50 portions	Miscellaneous information
Vegetables, fresh, continued			
Potatoes, sweet, or yams to bake	1 potato (4½–5 oz)	18–20 lb AP	1 lb AP = 0.61 lb baked, without skins
Candied	4 oz	20–25 lb AP	1 lb AP = 0.80 lb peeled, ready to cook
Mashed	4 oz	18 lb AP	
Potatoes, white, baked	1 potato	17–25 lb AP	1 lb AP = 0.74 lb baked potato without skins
Mashed	4 oz (½ cup)	15 lb AP	1 lb AP = 0.81 lb ready to cook pared
Steamed	4 oz (1 potato)	16–17 lb AP	
French fried	4–5 oz	16–20 lb AP	1 lb AP = 0.81 lb ready to cook
Radishes, without tops, for relishes	2 oz	6 lb AP	1 lb AP = 0.94 lb ready to serve raw
Salad greens	3 oz	10 lb	
Spinach	3 oz	12 lb AP	1 lb AP = 0.88 lb ready to cook or serve raw
For salad	1 oz	4–5 lb AP	
Squash, summer, yellow	3 oz	10 lb AP	1 lb AP = 0.95 lb ready to cook; 0.83 lb cooked
Zucchini	3 oz	10 lb AP	1 lb AP = 0.94 lb ready to cook; 0.86 lb cooked
Squash, winter, acorn	½ squash	20–25 lb AP	1 lb AP = 0.87 lb ready to cook in skin
Butternut	3 oz	12 lb AP	1 lb AP = 0.84 lb ready to cook pared
Hubbard, baked	2½-inch square	20–25 lb	
Mashed	3 oz	15 lb AP	1 lb AP = 0.64 lb ready to cook pared
Tomatoes	1 small	20 lb AP	
Sliced, salad	3 slices	15 lb AP	1 lb AP = 0.90 lb ready to cook or serve raw
Diced	½ cup	12–15 lb AP	1 lb AP = 0.75 lb peeled and seeded
Cherry, salad	1 oz	4 lb AP	1 lb AP = 0.97 lb stemmed
Turnips	3 oz	12–15 lb AP	1 lb AP = 0.79 lb ready to cook or serve raw; 0.78 lb cooked
Watercress	1½ oz	4–5 lb AP	1 lb AP = 0.92 lb ready to serve raw
Yams, see Potatoes, sweet			
Frozen			
Asparagus spears	3 oz	10 lb	
Beans, cut green or lima	3 oz	10 lb	
Broccoli	3 oz	10 lb	
Brussels sprouts	3 oz	10 lb	
Cauliflower	3 oz	10 lb	
Corn, whole kernel	3 oz	10 lb	
Peas	3 oz	10 lb	
Potatoes			
French fried	4 oz	12–13 lb	
Hashed brown	4 oz	12–13 lb	
Spinach	3 oz	10 lb	
MISCELLANEOUS			
Ice			
For water glasses	3–4 oz	10–12 lb	
For punch bowl		10 lb	
Potato chips	1 oz	3 lb	

TABLE 2.5 Food weights and approximate equivalents in measure

Food	Weight	Approximate measure
Alfalfa sprouts	1 lb	6 cups
Allspice, ground	1 oz	4½ Tbsp
Almonds, blanched, slivered, chopped	1 lb	3½ cups
Apples, canned, pie pack	1 lb	2 cups
Apples, fresh, AP[a]	1 lb	3 medium (113)
Apples, fresh, pared and sliced	1 lb	2¾ cups
Apples, pared and diced, 1½-inch cubes	1 lb	3 cups
Applesauce	1 lb	2 cups
Apricots, canned halves, without juice	1 lb	2 cups or 12–20 halves
Apricots, canned, pie pack	1 lb	2 cups
Apricots, dried, AP	1 lb	3 cups
Apricots, dried, cooked, without juice	1 lb	4½–5 cups
Apricots, fresh	1 lb	5–8 apricots (large) 8–10 (medium)
Apricots, sliced	1 lb	3 cups
Asparagus, canned, cuts	1 lb	2½ cups
Asparagus, canned tips, drained	1 lb	16–20 stalks
Asparagus, fresh	1 lb	16–20 stalks
Avocado	1 lb	2 medium
Bacon bits	1 lb	3⅓ cups
Bacon, cooked	1 lb	85–95 slices
Bacon, uncooked	1 lb	14–25 slices
Bacon, uncooked, diced	1 lb	2¼ cups
Baking powder	1 oz	2⅓ Tbsp
Baking powder	1 lb	2⅓ cups
Baking soda	1 oz	2⅓ Tbsp
Baking soda	1 lb	2⅓ cups
Bananas, AP	1 lb	3 medium
Bananas, diced	1 lb	2½–3 cups
Bananas, mashed	1 lb	2 cups
Barbecue sauce	1 lb	2 cups
Barley, pearl	1 lb	2¼ cups
Basil, sweet, dried	1 oz	1⅓ cups
Basil leaves, fresh (loosely packed)	1 oz	¾ cup, 40 medium leaves
Bay leaves	1 oz	2 cups
Beans, baked	1 lb	2 cups
Beans, garbanzo, canned	1 lb	2½ cups
Beans, Great Northern, dried, AP	1 lb	2½ cups
Beans, green, cut, cooked	1 lb	3 cups
Beans, green, cut, frozen	1 lb	3 cups
Beans, kidney, dried, AP	1 lb	2½ cups
Beans, kidney, dried, 1 lb AP, after cooking	2 lb 6 oz	6–7 cups
Beans, lima, dried, AP	1 lb	2½ cups
Beans, lima, dried, 1 lb AP, after cooking	2 lb 9 oz	6 cups

[a]AP denotes "as purchased," which refers to the status of the product before it is peeled, hulled, cored, or otherwise prepared for cooking.

continues

TABLE 2.5 *continued*

Food	Weight	Approximate measure
Beans, lima, fresh, canned, or frozen	1 lb	3 cups
Beans, navy or black turtle, dried, AP	1 lb	2¼ cups
Beans, navy, dried, 1 lb AP, after cooking	2 lb 3 oz	5½–6 cups
Beans, pinto, dried, AP	1 lb	2½ cups
Bean sprouts, canned, drained	1 lb	1 qt
Bean sprouts, fresh	1 lb	2 qt
Beef, cooked, diced	1 lb	3 cups
Beef, dried, solid pack	1 lb	3¾ cups
Beef, ground, raw	1 lb	2 cups
Beef base (paste)	1 lb	2½ cups
Beets, cooked, diced, or sliced	1 lb	2½–3 cups
Beets, fresh, medium	1 lb	3–4 beets
Blackberries, fresh, frozen, IQF[b]	1 lb	3½ cups
Blackberries or boysenberries, pie pack	1 lb	2½ cups
Blackeyed peas, dried	1 lb	2¾ cups
Blueberries, canned	1 lb	2 cups
Blueberries, fresh, frozen, IQF	1 lb	2½ cups
Bran, all bran	1 lb	2 qt
Bran flakes	1 lb	3 qt
Bread, dry, broken	1 lb	8–9 cups
Bread, fresh	1 lb	8 oz dry crumbs
Bread, loaf	1 lb	16–18 slices, ½ inch each
Bread, sandwich	2 lb	36–40 slices, thin
Bread, soft, broken	1 lb	2½ qt
Bread crumbs, dry, ground	1 lb	4 cups (1 qt)
Bread crumbs, soft	1 lb	2 qt
Broccoli, florets	1 lb	4 cups
Broccoli, head	1 lb	1 medium
Brussels sprouts, AP	1 lb	1 qt
Butter	1 lb	2 cups 4 4 oz sticks
Buttermilk, dry	1 oz	¼ cup
Buttermilk, dry	1 lb	4 cups
Butterscotch chips	1 lb	2⅔ cups
Cabbage, raw, shredded	1 lb	1 qt lightly packed
Cabbage, AP, shredded, cooked	1 lb	1½ cups
Cake crumbs, soft	1 lb	6 cups
Cake mix	1 lb	4 cups
Cantaloupe	3 lb	1 melon, 6-inch diameter
Caraway seeds	1 oz	4 Tbsp
Cardamom, ground	1 oz	4½ Tbsp
Carrots, diced, cooked	1 lb	3 cups
Carrots, diced, raw	1 lb	3–3¼ cups
Carrots, fresh	1 lb	4–5 medium
Carrots, ground, raw, EP[c]	1 lb	3 cups

[b]IQF denotes "individually quick frozen."
[c]EP denotes "edible portion," or the status of the product after it has been prepared for cooking or for serving raw.

TABLE 2.5 *continued*

Food	Weight	Approximate measure
Carrots, shredded	1 lb	4 cups
Carrots, sliced, frozen	1 lb	3½ cups
Catsup	1 lb	2 cups
Cauliflower, florets	1 lb	4 cups
Cauliflower, head	1 lb	1 medium
Cayenne pepper	1 oz	4½ Tbsp
Celery, chopped	1 lb	3 cups
Celery, diced	1 lb (1–2 bunches)	1 qt
Celery cabbage, shredded	1 lb	6 cups
Celery flakes, dried	1 oz	1⅓ cups
Celery salt	1 oz	2 Tbsp
Celery seed	1 oz	4 Tbsp
Cheese, cheddar or Swiss, shredded	1 lb	4 cups
Cheese, cottage	1 lb	2 cups
Cheese, cream	1 lb	2 cups
Cheese, loaf, slices	1 lb	16–20 slices
Cheese, mozzarella, shredded	1 lb	3½ cups
Cheese, parmesan or Romano, commercially grated	1 lb	3½ cups
Cheese, parmesan or Romano, freshly grated	1 lb	7–8 cups
Cherries, glacé, candied	1 lb	96 cherries or 2½ cups
Cherries, maraschino, drained	1 lb	50–60 cherries
Cherries, red, frozen	1 lb	2 cups
Cherries, red, pie pack, drained	1 lb	2½ cups
Cherries, Royal Anne, drained	1 lb	2½ cups
Cherries, sweet fresh	1 lb	45 cherries
Chervil	1 oz	2 cups
Chicken, cooked, cubed	1 lb	3 cups
Chicken, ready to cook	4–4½ lb	1 qt cooked, diced
Chicken base (paste)	1 lb	1¾ cups
Chili powder	1 oz	4 Tbsp
Chili sauce	1 lb	1⅓ cups
Chilis, green, diced	1 lb	2 cups
Chives, freeze-dried	1 oz	3½ cups
Chives, frozen	1 oz	⅓ cup
Chocolate, baking	1 lb	16 squares
Chocolate, grated	1 lb	3½ cups
Chocolate, melted	1 lb	2 cups (scant)
Chocolate chips	1 lb	2⅔ cups
Chocolate wafers	1 lb	4 cups crumbs
Cilantro, fresh	1 oz	¾ cup
Cilantro, dried	1 oz	1⅓ cups
Cinnamon, ground	1 oz	4 Tbsp
Cinnamon, ground	1 lb	4 cups
Cinnamon sticks	1 oz	10 pieces
Citron, dried, chopped	1 lb	2½ cups
Cloves, ground	1 oz	4 Tbsp
Cloves, whole	1 oz	5 Tbsp or 500 cloves

continues

TABLE 2.5 *continued*

Food	Weight	Approximate measure
Cocoa	1 lb	$4\frac{1}{2}$ cups
Coconut, flaked or shredded	1 lb	$4\frac{3}{4}$ cups
Coffee, ground coarse	1 lb	$5–5\frac{1}{2}$ cups
Coffee, instant	1 oz	$\frac{1}{2}$ cup
Coffee, whole beans	1 lb	$6–6\frac{1}{2}$ cups
Coriander seed, whole	1 oz	6 Tbsp
ground	1 oz	5 Tbsp
Corn, cream style, canned	1 lb	2 cups
Corn, whole kernel, canned, drained	1 lb	3 cups
Corn, whole kernel, frozen	1 lb	3 cups
Cornflake crumbs	1 lb	$4\frac{1}{2}$ cups
Cornflakes	1 lb	4 qt
Cornmeal, coarse	1 lb	3 cups
Cornmeal, 1 lb AP, dry, after cooking	6 lb	3 qt
Cornstarch	1 oz	$3\frac{1}{2}$ Tbsp
Cornstarch	1 lb	$3\frac{1}{2}$ cups
Corn syrup	1 lb	$1\frac{1}{2}$ cups
Couscous	1 lb	$2\frac{1}{4}$ cups
Crab in shell	1 lb	$\frac{1}{2}$ cup cooked meat
Crabmeat, flaked	1 lb	$3\frac{1}{2}$ cups
Cracked wheat	1 lb	$3\frac{1}{2}$ cups
Cracker crumbs, medium fine	1 lb	5–6 cups
Crackers, $2\frac{5}{8} \times 2\frac{5}{8}$ inch	1 lb	65 crackers
Crackers, graham	1 lb	60–65 crackers
Crackers, graham, crumbs	1 lb	4 cups
Crackers, saltines, 2×2 inch	1 lb	150–160 crackers
Cranberries, cooked	1 lb	$1\frac{3}{4}$ cups
Cranberries, raw	1 lb	4 cups
Cranberry relish	1 lb	$1\frac{3}{4}$ cups
Cranberry sauce, jellied	1 lb	2 cups
Cream of tartar	1 oz	3 Tbsp
Cream of Wheat or farina, quick, AP	1 lb	$2\frac{2}{3}$ cups
Cream of Wheat or farina, 1 lb AP, after cooking	8 lb	1 gal
Cream, sour	1 lb	2 cups
Cream, whipping	1 pt	1 qt whipped
Croutons	1 lb	$2\frac{1}{4}$ qt
Cucumbers	1 lb	2–3 large
Cucumbers, diced, EP	1 lb	3 cups
Cucumbers, sliced	1 lb	50–60 slices
Cumin, ground	1 oz	4 Tbsp
Currants, dried	1 lb	3 cups
Curry powder	1 oz	$4\frac{1}{2}$ Tbsp
Dates, pitted	1 lb	$2\frac{1}{2}$ cups
Dill seed	1 oz	$4\frac{1}{2}$ Tbsp
Dill weed	1 oz	$\frac{3}{4}$ cup
Eggplant	1 lb	8 slices, $4 \times \frac{1}{2}$ inch
Eggplant	1 lb	1 qt diced
Eggs, dried, whites	1 lb	5 cups
Eggs, dried, whole	1 lb	$5\frac{1}{3}$ cups

TABLE 2.5 *continued*

Food	Weight	Approximate measure
Eggs, dried, yolks	1 lb	5⅔ cups
Eggs, hard-cooked, chopped	1 lb	2⅔ cups
Eggs, hard-cooked, chopped	1 doz	3½ cups
Eggs, shelled, fresh or frozen, whole	1 lb (approximately 1¾ oz per egg)	2 cups (8–10 eggs)
Eggs, shelled, fresh or frozen, whites	1 lb (approximately 1–1¼ oz per white)	2 cups (16–18 eggs)
Eggs, shelled, fresh or frozen, yolks	1 lb (approximately ½–¾ oz per yolk)	2 cups (22–26 eggs)
Eggs, whole, in shell[d]	1 lb	8–10 large eggs
Fennel seed	1 oz	4 Tbsp
Figs, dry, cut fine	1 lb	2½ cups
Flour, all-purpose or bread	1 lb	4 cups
Flour, cake or pastry, unsifted	1 lb	3¾ cups
Flour, rye	1 lb	4 cups
Flour, whole wheat	1 lb	3¾–4 cups
Garlic, fresh	1 oz	6 large cloves
Garlic, fresh, minced	1 oz	3 Tbsp
Garlic powder	1 oz	3 Tbsp
Garlic salt	1 oz	2 Tbsp
Gelatin, granulated, flavored	1 lb	2¼ cups
Gelatin, granulated, unflavored	1 oz	3 Tbsp
Gelatin, granulated, unflavored	1 lb	3 cups
Ginger, candied, chopped	1 oz	2 Tbsp
Ginger, fresh, sliced	1 lb	3 cups
Ginger, ground	1 oz	4 Tbsp
Ginger, ground	1 lb	4 cups
Graham cracker crumbs	1 lb	4 cups
Grapefruit, medium	1 lb	1 grapefruit, 10-12 sections, ⅔ cup juice
Grapefruit sections	1 lb	2 cups
Grapes, cut, seeded, EP	1 lb	2¾ cups
Grapes, on stem	1 lb	1 qt
Grapes, seedless, fresh	1 lb	3 cups
Grits, hominy	1 lb	3 cups
Grits, hominy, 1 lb AP, after cooking	6½ lb	3¼ qt
Ham, cooked, diced	1 lb	3 cups
Ham, cooked, ground	1 lb	2½ cups
Hazelnuts (shelled)	1 lb	3½ cups
Hominy, canned	1 lb	3 cups
Hominy grits, see Grits		
Honey	1 lb	1⅓ cups
Horseradish, prepared	1 oz	2 Tbsp

[d]One case (30 doz) eggs weighs approximately 41–43 lb and yields approximately 35 lb liquid whole eggs.

continues

TABLE 2.5   *continued*

Food	Weight	Approximate measure
Ice cream	4½–6 lb	1 gal
Jam, jelly	1 lb	1⅓–1½ cups
Kiwi	1 lb	5 kiwi
Lemon juice	1 lb	2 cups (8–10 lemons)
Lemon peel, dried	1 oz	4 Tbsp
Lemon peel, fresh	1 oz	4 Tbsp
Lemon peel, fresh	1 lemon	2 Tbsp
Lemons, size 165	1 lb	4–5 lemons yield ¾ cup juice
Lettuce, average head	2 lb	1 head
Lettuce, chopped or shredded	1 lb	6–8 cups
Lettuce, leaf	1 lb	25–30 salad garnishes
Limes, fresh	1 lb	5 limes, 15–20 thin slices yield, ⅞ cup juice
Macaroni, 1-inch pieces, dry	1 lb	4 cups
Macaroni, 1 lb AP, after cooking	3 lb	2–2¼ qt
Macaroni, cooked	1 lb	3 cups
Mace	1 oz	4½ Tbsp
Mango	1 lb	1 large, 2 small
Margarine	1 lb	2 cups
Margarine, whipped	1 lb	2⅔ cups
Marjoram leaves, dried	1 oz	1 cup
Marshmallows (1¼ inch)	1 lb	80–90
Marshmallows, miniature (10 miniature = 1 regular)	1 lb	8 cups
	1 oz	52
Mayonnaise	1 lb	2 cups (scant)
Meat, cooked, chopped	1 lb	2 cups
Milk, evaporated	1 lb	1¾ cups
Milk, fluid, whole	1 lb	2 cups
Milk, nonfat, dry	1 lb	6 cups
Milk, nonfat, dry	1 oz	6 Tbsp
Milk, sweetened, condensed	1 lb	1½ cups
Mincemeat	1 lb	2 cups
Molasses	1 lb	1⅓ cups
Monosodium glutamate	1 oz	2 Tbsp
Mushrooms, (whole fresh)	1 lb	Small 75 each Medium 40 each Large 20 each
Mushrooms, canned	1 lb	2 cups
Mushrooms, fresh, sliced	1 lb	5 cups raw (1¾ cups cooked)
Mustard, ground, dry	1 oz	5 Tbsp
Mustard, ground, dry	1 lb	5 cups
Mustard, prepared	1 oz	2 Tbsp
Mustard seed	1 oz	2½ Tbsp
Noodles, cooked	1 lb	2¾ cups
Noodles, 1 lb AP, after cooking	3 lb	2 qt
Nutmeats	1 lb	4 cups
Nutmeg, ground	1 oz	3½ Tbsp
Oats, rolled, quick, AP	1 lb	5⅓ cups
Oats, rolled, 1 lb AP, after cooking	2½ lb	4 qt

TABLE 2.5 *continued*

Food	Weight	Approximate measure
Oil, vegetable	1 lb	2–2⅛ cups
Olives, AP	1 lb	⅔ cup chopped
Olives, green, small size, drained	1 lb	160 olives
Olives, green, stuffed	1 lb	2½ cups
Olives, ripe, sliced	1 lb	3⅓ cups
Olives, ripe, small size, drained	1 lb	140 small, 110 medium, 90 large olives
Onions, dehydrated	1 lb	8 lb raw (equivalent)
Onions, dehydrated, chopped	1 oz	5 Tbsp
Onions, dehydrated, chopped	1 lb	5–6 cups
Onions, fresh, chopped	1 lb	2½–3 cups
Onions, green, sliced	1 lb	2½–3 cups
Onions, mature, AP	1 lb	4–5 medium
Onion powder	1 oz	3 Tbsp
Onion salt	1 oz	2½ Tbsp
Onion soup mix	1 oz	2½ Tbsp
Onion soup mix	1 lb	2⅔ cups
Orange juice, frozen	6 oz	3 cups reconstituted
Orange juice, frozen	32 oz	4 qt reconstituted
Orange peel, dried	1 oz	4 Tbsp
Orange peel, fresh	1 medium orange	3 Tbsp grated peel
Oranges, medium (size 113)	1 lb	3–4 oranges, unpeeled; 5 oranges, peeled; 10–11 sections each; yield, 1 cup juice
Oranges	1 lb	2 cups bite-size pieces
Oregano, ground	1 oz	5 Tbsp
Oregano, leaf	1 oz	¾ cup
Orzo	1 lb	2¼ cups
Oysters, shucked	1 lb	2 cups
Paprika, ground	1 oz	4 Tbsp
Parsley, coarsely chopped	1 oz	¾ cup
Parsley flakes, dry	1 oz	1⅓ cups
Parsnips, AP	1 lb	4 medium
Pasta	1 lb	see p. 561
Peaches, canned, sliced, drained	1 lb	2 cups
Peaches, fresh, AP	1 lb	3 medium
Peaches, sliced, frozen	1 lb	2 cups
Peanut butter	1 lb	2 cups
Peanuts, chopped, no skins	1 lb	3 cups
Peanuts, shelled	1 lb	3¼ cups
Pears, canned, drained, diced	1 lb	2½ cups
Pears, canned, large halves, drained	1 lb 14 oz	1 qt (9 halves)
Pears, fresh AP	1 lb	3 medium
Peas, cooked, drained	1 lb	2¼ cups
Peas, dried, 1 lb after cooking	2½ lb	5½ cups
Peas, split, dried, AP	1 lb	2⅓ cups
Pecans, chopped	1 lb	4 cups
Pecans, shelled, pieces	1 lb	4 cups
Pepper, cayenne	1 oz	5 Tbsp
Pepper, crushed, red	1 oz	6 Tbsp

continues

TABLE 2.5   *continued*

Food	Weight	Approximate measure
Pepper, ground, black or white	1 oz	4 Tbsp
Pepper, ground, black or white	1 lb	4 cups
Peppercorns	1 oz	6 Tbsp
Peppers, green	1 lb	2–3 medium
Peppers, green, chopped	1 lb	3 cups
Peppers, green, dried flakes	1 oz	¾ cup
Peppers, jalapeño	1 lb	16 medium
Pickle relish	1 lb	2 cups
Pickles, chopped	1 lb	3 cups
Pickles, halves, 3 inch	1 lb	3 cups or 36 halves
Pimento, chopped	1 lb	2 cups
Pineapple, canned, crushed	1 lb	2 cups
Pineapple, canned, slices, drained	1 lb	8–12 slices
Pineapple, canned, tidbits	1 lb	2 cups
Pineapple, fresh	2–4 lb	1 pineapple, 2–4 cups, cubed
Pineapple, frozen, chunks	1 lb	2 cups
Plums	1 lb	6 medium
Poppy seed	1 oz	3 Tbsp
Potato chips	1 lb	4–5 qt
Potato chips, crushed	1 lb	2 qt
Potatoes, dehydrated, diced	1 lb	5⅛ cups
Potatoes, dehydrated, flakes	1 lb	5 cups
Potatoes, dehydrated, granules	1 lb	2¼ cups
Potatoes, dehydrated, slices	1 lb	9⅔ cups
Potatoes, fresh, white, AP	1 lb	3 medium
Potatoes, fresh, white, cooked	1 lb	2½ cups
Potatoes, raw, white, cubed	1 lb	2⅔ cups
Potatoes, sweet	1 lb	3 medium
Potatoes, sweet, cooked	1 lb	2 cups
Poultry seasoning, ground	1 oz	6 Tbsp
Prunes, dried, size 30/40, AP	1 lb	2½ cups
Prunes, dried, 1 lb AP, after cooking	2 lb	3–4 cups
Prunes, pitted, cooked	1 lb	3¼ cups
Pudding mix, dry, instant	1 lb	2½ cups
Pudding mix, dry, regular	1 lb	2¼ cups
Pumpkin, cooked	1 lb	2 cups
Quinoa, AP	1 lb	2¼ cups
Radishes, AP	1 lb	45–50
Raisins, AP	1 lb	3 cups
Raisins, 1 lb AP, after cooking	1 lb 12 oz	1 qt
Raisins, chopped	1 lb	2⅔ cups
Raspberries, fresh AP, or frozen IQF	1 lb	3 cups
Raspberries, with syrup	1 lb	2 cups
Red-hots	1 lb	2¼ cups
Rhubarb, raw, 1-inch pieces	1 lb	4 cups
Rhubarb, 1 lb EP, after cooking		2½ cups
Rice, Aborio	1 lb	2¼ cups
Rice, brown, AP	1 lb	2½ cups
Rice, converted, AP	1 lb	2½ cups

TABLE 2.5 *continued*

Food	Weight	Approximate measure
Rice, cooked	1 lb	2¼ cups
Rice, 1 lb AP, after cooking	3½ lb	2 qt
Rice, precooked, AP	1 lb	4½ cups
Rice, regular, AP	1 lb	2⅓ cups
Rice, wild	1 lb	2⅔ cups
Rice, wild, 1 lb AP, after cooking	1 lb	5 cups
Rice cereal, crisp	1 lb	4 qt
Rosemary leaves	1 oz	9 Tbsp
Rutabagas, raw, cubed, EP	1 lb	3⅓ cups
Sage, finely ground	1 oz	8 Tbsp (½ cup)
Sage, rubbed	1 oz	⅔ cup
Salad dressing, cooked	1 lb	2 cups
Salmon, canned	1 lb	2 cups
Salt (table)	1 oz	1½ Tbsp
Salt (table)	1 lb	1½ cups
Sale (Kosher, Diamond Crystal)	1 lb	3 cups
Sauerkraut	1 lb	3 cups packed
Sausage, bulk, AP	1 lb	2 cups
Sausages, link, small	1 lb	16–17 links
Sesame seed	1 oz	3 Tbsp
Sherbet	6 lb	1 gal
Shortening, hydrogenated fat	1 lb	2¼ cups
Shrimp, cleaned, cooked, peeled	1 lb	3¼ cups
Soda, baking	1 oz	2⅓ Tbsp
Spaghetti, cooked	1 lb	2⅔ cups
Spaghetti, 1 lb AP, after cooking	3 lb	2 qt
Spinach, canned or frozen	1 lb	2 cups
Spinach, raw	1 lb	5 qt lightly packed
Spinach, raw, chopped	1 lb	3¼ qt
Spinach, 1 lb AP, after cooking	13 oz	2¾ cups
Squash, Hubbard, cooked	1 lb	2 cups
Squash, summer, fresh	1 lb	4 cups
Starch, waxy maize	1 oz	3 Tbsp
Strawberries, fresh or frozen, IQF	1 lb	3 cups
Strawberries, sliced, frozen, with syrup	1 lb	2 cups
Suet, ground	1 lb	3¾ cups
Sugar, brown, lightly packed	1 lb	3 cups
Sugar, brown, solid pack	1 lb	2 cups
Sugar, cubes	1 lb	96 cubes
Sugar, granulated	1 lb	2¼ cups
Sugar, granulated	1 oz	2¼ Tbsp
Sugar, powdered, unsifted	1 lb	3¼ cups
Sugar, powdered, XXXX sifted	1 lb	3¾ cups
Syrup, corn or maple	1 lb	1½ cups
Tapioca, quick cooking	1 lb	3 cups
Tapioca, 1 lb AP, after cooking		7½ cups
Tarragon, leaf	1 oz	1 cup

continues

TABLE 2.5 *continued*

Food	Weight	Approximate measure
Tea, bulk	1 lb	6 cups
Tea, instant	1 oz	½ cup
Thyme, ground	1 oz	6 Tbsp
Thyme, leaves	1 oz	¾ cup
Tomatoes, canned	1 lb	2 cups
Tomatoes, fresh	1 lb	2–3 medium, 12 slices
Tomatoes, fresh, diced	1 lb	2¼ cups
Tomatoes, fresh plum	1 lb	6 medium
Tomato paste	1 lb	2 cups
Tortillas, corn, 8 inch	1 lb	16
Tortillas, flour, 8 inch	1 lb	12
Tortillas, flour, 10 inch	1 lb	9
Tuna, canned	1 lb	2 cups
Turkey, AP, dressed weight	14 lb	11–12 cups diced, cooked meat
Turmeric, ground	1 oz	4 Tbsp
Turnips, AP	1 lb	2–3
Vanilla and other extracts	1 oz	2 Tbsp
Vinegar	1 lb	2 cups
Walnuts, English, shelled	1 lb	4 cups
Water	1 lb	2 cups
Watercress, EP	1 oz	½ cup
Watermelon	1 lb	1-inch slice, 6-inch diameter
Wheat germ	1 lb	5⅓ cups
Whipped topping, liquid	1 lb	2 cups
Yeast, compressed	1 oz	1 pkg
Yeast, dry	¼ oz	1 envelope
Yeast, dry, regular or instant	1 oz	3 Tbsp + 1 tsp
Yeast, dry, regular or instant	1 lb	3⅓ cups
Yogurt	1 lb	2 cups
Zucchini, fresh, shredded	1 lb	3¼ cups

TABLE 2.6 Ingredient substitutions (approximate)

Recipe item	Amount	Substitute ingredient
Baking powder	1 tsp	¼ tsp baking soda + ½ tsp cream of tartar ¼ tsp baking soda + ½ cup buttermilk or sour milk (to replace ½ cup of the liquid)
Butter or margarine	1 lb	14 oz hydrogenated shortening + 1 tsp salt 14 oz (1⅜ cups) oil + 1 tsp salt
Buttermilk	1 cup	1 Tbsp lemon juice or vinegar + enough whole milk to make 1 cup (let stand 5 min before using) or 1 cup unflavored yogurt
Celery, fresh	8 oz	4 oz celery flakes, dry
Chocolate, unsweetened	1 oz (1 square)	3 Tbsp cocoa + 1 Tbsp (½ oz) fat
Cocoa	3 Tbsp	1 oz chocolate; reduce fat in recipe by 1 Tbsp
Cornstarch (thickening)	1 Tbsp 1 oz 1 Tbsp 1 oz	2 Tbsp flour, all-purpose 2 oz flour, all purpose 2 tsp waxy maize starch ¾ oz waxy maize starch

Cream
  Half and half
  Whipping
	
	1 cup
	1 cup
		
		¾ cup milk + 2–3 Tbsp fat
		¾ cup milk + ⅓ cup fat

Flour, all-purpose	1 cup (4 oz)	1½ cups bread flour 1 cup + 2 Tbsp cake flour 1 cup rye or whole wheat flour 1 cup less 2 Tbsp cornmeal 1 cup rolled oats 1½ cups bread crumbs
Flour, all-purpose (thickening)	1 oz	1⅓ oz quick-cooking tapioca ½ cup cornmeal ⅔ oz cornstarch ½ oz waxy maize starch, arrowroot ¾ oz bread crumbs
Flour, cake	1 cup (4 oz)	1 cup less 2 Tbsp all-purpose flour
Garlic	1 medium clove	⅛ tsp garlic powder ½ tsp garlic, minced, dry ½ tsp garlic salt
Green peppers, fresh, chopped	8 oz EP	1 oz green pepper flakes, dry
Herbs, fresh	1 Tbsp	1 tsp whole dried ¼ tsp ground
Honey	1 cup	1¼ cups granulated sugar + ¼ cup liquid
Milk, fluid, whole	1 cup 1 qt	1 oz (⅓ cup) nonfat dry milk + water to make 1 cup + 1 Tbsp fat (optional) ½ cup evaporated milk + ½ cup water 4 oz nonfat dry milk + water to make 1 qt + 1¼ oz fat (optional)

continues

TABLE 2.6   *continued*

Recipe item	Amount	Substitute ingredient
Milk, sour[a]	1 cup	1 Tbsp vinegar or lemon juice + sweet milk to make 1 cup
Mushrooms, fresh	1 lb (6 cups)	3 cups processed mushrooms
Onions, fresh, chopped	8 oz EP	1 oz dehydrated onions, chopped or minced[b]
Parsley, fresh, chopped	8 oz EP	3 oz parsley flakes, dry
Sour cream	1 cup	1 cup yogurt
Stock, chicken or beef	1 gal	3 oz concentrated soup base + 1 gal water (commercial products may vary in strength; follow manufacturer's directions)
Sugar, brown	1 cup	1 cup granulated sugar + 2 Tbsp molasses
Sugar, granulated	1 cup (8 oz)	1⅓ cups brown sugar 1½ cups powdered sugar 1¼–1½ cups corn syrup less ¼–½ cup liquid in recipe 1 cup honey less ¼–⅓ cup liquid in recipe 1⅓ cups molasses less ⅓ cup liquid in recipe
Tapioca, quick-cooking	1 Tbsp	1 Tbsp all-purpose flour (for thickening)
Yeast, active dry	¼ oz (1 pkg) 1 oz	1 cake compressed 2 oz compressed
Yeast, instant		See manufacturer's directions for conversion from active dry or compressed

[a]To substitute buttermilk or sour milk for sweet milk, add ½ tsp baking soda and decrease baking powder by 2 tsp per cup of milk.

[b]Rehydrate onions unless they are to be used in a recipe in which there is a large volume of liquid. To rehydrate, cover onions with water, using the ratio of 1 oz dehydrated onions (½ cup) to ¾ cup of water.
Let stand 20–30 minutes.

TABLE 2.7   Ingredient proportions

Function	Ingredient	Relative proportion
Leavening agents	Baking powder	1½–2 Tbsp to 1 lb flour
	Baking soda	2 tsp to 1 qt sour milk or molasses
	Yeast	½–1 envelope dry (⅛–¼ oz) to 1 lb flour (varies with ingredients and time allowed)
Seasonings	Salt	1–2 tsp to 1 lb flour 1¼ tsp to 1 lb meat 2 tsp to 1 qt water (for cereal) 2½ tsp to 1 pt liquid (for rolls)
Thickening agents	Eggs	4–6 whole eggs to 1 qt milk 8–12 egg yolks to 1 qt milk 8–12 egg whites to 1 qt milk
	Flour	½ oz to 1 qt liquid—very thin sauce (cream soups, starchy vegetables) 1 oz to 1 qt liquid—thin sauce (cream soups, nonstarchy vegetables) 2 oz to 1 qt liquid—medium sauce (creamed foods, gravy) 3–4 oz to 1 qt liquid—thick sauce (soufflés) 4–5 oz to 1 qt liquid—very thick sauce (croquettes) 1 lb to 1 qt liquid—pour batter (popovers) 2 lb to 1 qt liquid—drop batter (cake muffins) 3 lb to 1 qt liquid—soft dough (biscuits, rolls) 4 lb to 1 qt liquid—stiff dough (pastry, cookies, noodles)
	Gelatin, granulated, unflavored	2 Tbsp to 1 qt liquid—plain gelatins (gelatin and fruit juices) 2 Tbsp to 1 qt liquid—whips (gelatin and fruit juices whipped) 3 Tbsp to 1 qt liquid—fruit gelatins (gelatin, fruit juices, and chopped fruit) 3 Tbsp to 1 qt liquid—vegetable gelatins (gelatin, liquid, and chopped vegetables) 3 Tbsp to 1 qt liquid—sponges (gelatin, fruit juice, and beaten egg whites) 4 Tbsp to 1 qt liquid—Bavarian cream (gelatin, fruit juice, fruit pulp, and whipped cream)

Note: • See Table 2.6 for ingredient substitutions.

Weights, Measures, and Guides for Cooking/Baking Temperatures

TABLE 2.8   Ounces, decimal equivalents of a pound and grams (rounded)

Ounces	Decimal part of a pound	Grams (rounded)	Ounces	Decimal part of a pound	Grams (rounded)	Ounces	Decimal part of a pound	Grams (rounded)
¼	0.016		5¾	0.359		11¼	0.703	
½	0.031		6	0.375	170	11½	0.719	
¾	0.047		6¼	0.391		11¾	0.734	
1	0.063	28	6½	0.406		12	0.750	340
1¼	0.078		6¾	0.422		12¼	0.766	
1½	0.094		7	0.438	198	12½	0.781	
1¾	0.109		7¼	0.453		12¾	0.797	
2	0.125	57	7½	0.469		13	0.813	367
2¼	0.141		7¾	0.484		13¼	0.828	
2½	0.156		8	0.500	227	13½	0.844	
2¾	0.172		8¼	0.516		13¾	0.859	
3	0.188	85	8½	0.531		14	0.875	397
3¼	0.203		8¾	0.547		14¼	0.891	
3½	0.219		9	0.563	255	14½	0.906	
3¾	0.234		9¼	0.578		14¾	0.922	
4	0.250	113	9½	0.594		15	0.938	425
4¼	0.266		9¾	0.609		15¼	0.953	
4½	0.281		10	0.625	284	15½	0.969	
4¾	0.297		10¼	0.641		15¾	0.984	
5	0.313	142	10½	0.656		16	1.000	454
5¼	0.328		10¾	0.672				
5½	0.344		11	0.688	312			

Note: • This table is useful when increasing or decreasing recipes. The multiplication or division of pounds and ounces is simplified if the ounces are converted to decimal parts of a pound. For example, when multiplying 1 lb 9 oz by 3, first change the 9 oz to 0.563 lb, using the table. Thus, the 1 lb 9 oz becomes 1.563 lb, which multiplied by 3 is 4.683 lb or 4 lb 11 oz.

TABLE 2.9   Basic equivalents in measures and weights

Equivalents	Abbreviations used in this book[a]	
1 Tbsp = 3 tsp, in liquids ½ fl oz	bu	bushel
⅛ cup = 2 Tbsp, in liquids 1 fl oz	fl oz	fluid ounce
¼ cup = 4 Tbsp, in liquids 2 fl oz	gal	gallon
⅓ cup = 5 Tbsp + 1 tsp	g	gram
½ cup = 8 Tbsp, in liquids 4 fl oz	kg	kilogram
⅔ cup = 10 Tbsp + 2 tsp	L	liter
¾ cup = 12 Tbsp, in liquids 6 fl oz	lb	pound
1 cup = 16 Tbsp, in liquids 8 fl oz	mL	milliliter
1 pt = 2 cups, in liquids 16 fl oz	oz	ounce
1 qt = 2 pt = 4 cups	pk	peck
1 gal = 4 qt	pt	pint
1 lb = 16 oz	qt	quart
1 pk = 8 qt, approximately 12½ lb	Tbsp	tablespoon
1 bu = 4 pk, approximately 50 lb	tsp	teaspoon

METRIC

1 g = 0.035 oz	1 tsp = 5 mL
1 kg = 2.2 lb (35 oz)	1 Tbsp = 15 mL
1 oz = 28 g	1 cup = 240 mL
1 lb = 454 g	1 qt = 0.95 L
1 mL = ⅕ tsp	1 gal = 3.8 L
1 L = 1.06 qt (34 fluid oz)	

[a]Periods are not necessary in abbreviations for quantity recipes.

TABLE 2.10   Guide for rounding off weights and measures

If the total amount of an ingredient is	Round it to
WEIGHTS	
Less than 2 oz	Measure unless weight is ¼-, ½-, or ¾-oz amounts
2–10 oz	Closest ¼ oz or convert to measure
More than 10 oz but less than 2 lb 8 oz	Closest ½ oz
2 lb 8 oz–5 lb	Closest full ounce
More than 5 lb	Closest ¼ lb
MEASURES	
Less than 1 Tbsp	Closest ⅛ tsp
More than 1 Tbsp but less than 3 Tbsp	Closest ¼ tsp
3 Tbsp–½ cup	Closest ½ tsp or convert to weight
More than ½ cup but less than ¾ cup	Closest full tsp or convert to weight
More than ¾ cup but less than 2 cups	Closest full Tbsp or convert to weight
2 cups–2 qt	Nearest ¼ cup
More than 2 qt but less than 4 qt	Nearest ½ cup
1–2 gal	Nearest full cup or ¼ qt
More than 2 gal but less than 10 gal[a]	Nearest full quart
More than 10 gal but less than 20 gal[a]	Closest ½ gal
More than 20 gal[a]	Closest full gallon

[a]For baked goods or products in which accurate ratios are critical, always round to the nearest full cup or ¼ qt.

Note: • This table is intended to aid in rounding fractions and complex measurements into amounts that are as simple as possible to weigh or measure while maintaining the accuracy needed for quality control.

TABLE 2.11   Weight (1–16 oz) and approximate measure equivalents for commonly used foods

Food item	1 oz	2 oz	3 oz	4 oz
Baking powder	2⅓ Tbsp	¼ cup + 1 tsp	⅓ cup + 2 Tbsp	½ cup + 1 Tbsp
Baking soda	2⅓ Tbsp	¼ cup + 1 tsp	⅓ cup + 2 Tbsp	½ cup + 1 Tbsp
Bread crumbs, dry	¼ cup	½ cup	¾ cup	1 cup
Butter or margarine	2 Tbsp	¼ cup	⅓ cup + 2 tsp	½ cup
Celery, chopped	¼ cup	½ cup	¾ cup	1 cup
Cornstarch	3½ Tbsp	⅓ cup + 2 Tbsp	⅔ cup	¾ cup + 2 Tbsp
Eggs, whole, whites or yolks, fresh or frozen	2 Tbsp	¼ cup	⅓ cup + 2 tsp	½ cup
Flour, all-purpose, unsifted	¼ cup	½ cup	¾ cup	1 cup
Flour, cake, unsifted	¼ cup	½ cup	½ cup + 3 Tbsp	¾ cup + 3 Tbsp
Milk, nonfat dry	⅓ cup	¾ cup	1 cup + 2 Tbsp	1½ cups
Nutmeats	¼ cup	½ cup	¾ cup	1 cup
Onion, chopped	3 Tbsp	⅓ cup + 2 tsp	½ cup + 1 Tbsp	¾ cup
Salt	1½ Tbsp	3 Tbsp	¼ cup + 1½ tsp	⅓ cup + 2 tsp
Shortening, hydro-genated fat	2 Tbsp + 1 tsp	¼ cup + 2 tsp	⅓ cup + 2 Tbsp	½ cup + 1 Tbsp
Sugar, brown, light pack	3 Tbsp	⅓ cup + 2 tsp	½ cup + 1 Tbsp	¾ cup
Sugar, granulated	2¼ Tbsp	¼ cup	¼ cup + 3 Tbsp	½ cup + 1 Tbsp
Sugar, powdered	3 Tbsp	⅓ cup + 2 tsp	½ cup + 1 tsp	¾ cup
Yeast, dry	3 Tbsp + 1 tsp	⅓ cup + 1 Tbsp	½ cup + 2 Tbsp	⅔ cup + 1 Tbsp

TABLE 2.11   *continued*

5 oz	6 oz	7 oz	8 oz
¾ cup	¾ cup + 2 Tbsp	1 cup + 1 tsp	1 cup + 3 Tbsp
¾ cup	¾ cup + 2 Tbsp	1 cup + 1 tsp	1 cup + 3 Tbsp
1¼ cups	1½ cups	1¾ cups	2 cups
½ cup + 2 Tbsp	¾ cup	¾ cup + 2 Tbsp	1 cup
1¼ cups	1½ cups	1¾ cups	2 cups
1 cup + 2 Tbsp	1¼ cups + 1 Tbsp	1½ cups + 1 Tbsp	1¾ cups
½ cup + 2 Tbsp	¾ cup	¾ cup + 2 Tbsp	1 cup
1¼ cups	1½ cups	1¾ cups	2 cups
1 cup + 3 Tbsp	1¼ cups + 3 Tbsp	1½ cups + 2 Tbsp	1¾ cups + 2 Tbsp
1¾ cups + 2 Tbsp	2¼ cups	2½ cups + 2 Tbsp	3 cups
1¼ cups	1½ cups	1¾ cups	2 cups
¾ cup + 3 Tbsp	1 cup + 2 Tbsp	1¼ cups + 1 Tbsp	1½ cups
⅓ cup + 2 Tbsp	½ cup + 1 Tbsp	⅔ cup	¾ cup
⅔ cup + 1 Tbsp	¾ cup + 2 Tbsp	1 cup	1 cup + 2 Tbsp
¾ cup + 3 Tbsp	1 cup + 2 Tbsp	1¼ cups + 1 Tbsp	1½ cups
½ cup + 3 Tbsp	¾ cup + 2 Tbsp	1 cup	1 cup + 2 Tbsp
¾ cup + 3 Tbsp	1 cup + 2 Tbsp	1¼ cups + 1 Tbsp	1½ cups
1 cup + 2 tsp	1¼ cups	1½ cups	1⅔ cups

continues

TABLE 2.11 *continued*

Food item	9 oz	10 oz	11 oz	12 oz
Baking powder	1¼ cups + 1 Tbsp	1½ cups	1½ cups + 2 Tbsp	1¾ cups
Baking soda	1¼ cups + 1 Tbsp	1½ cups	1½ cups + 2 Tbsp	1¾ cups
Bread crumbs, dry	2¼ cups	2½ cups	2¾ cups	3 cups
Butter or margarine	1 cup + 2 Tbsp	1¼ cups	1⅓ cups + 1 Tbsp	1½ cups
Celery, chopped	2¼ cups	2½ cups	2¾ cups	3 cups
Cornstarch	2 cups	2 cups + 3 Tbsp	2⅓ cups + 2 Tbsp	2½ cups + 2 Tbsp
Eggs, whole, whites or yolks, fresh or frozen	1 cup + 2 Tbsp	1¼ cups	1⅓ cups + 1 Tbsp	1½ cups
Flour, all-purpose, unsifted	2¼ cups	2½ cups	2¾ cups	3 cups
Flour, cake, unsifted	2 cups + 2 Tbsp	2¼ cups + 2 Tbsp	2½ cups + 1 Tbsp	2¾ cups
Milk, nonfat dry	3¼ cups + 2 Tbsp	3¾ cups	4 cups + 2 Tbsp	4½ cups
Nutmeats	2¼ cups	2½ cups	2¾ cups	3 cups
Onion, chopped	1⅔ cups	1¾ cups + 2 Tbsp	2 cups + 1 Tbsp	2¼ cups
Salt	¾ cup + 2 Tbsp	¾ cup + 3 Tbsp	1 cup + 1 Tbsp	1 cup + 2 Tbsp
Shortening, hydrogenated fat	1¼ cups	1⅓ cups + 1 Tbsp	1½ cups + 1 Tbsp	1⅔ cups
Sugar, brown, light pack	1⅔ cups	1¾ cups + 2 Tbsp	2 cups + 1 Tbsp	2¼ cups
Sugar, granulated	1¼ cups	1¼ cups + 3 Tbsp	1½ cups + 1 Tbsp	1½ cups + 3 Tbsp
Sugar, powdered	1⅔ cups	1¾ cups + 2 Tbsp	2 cups + 1 Tbsp	2¼ cups
Yeast, dry	1¾ cups + 2 Tbsp	2 cups + 1 Tbsp	2¼ cups + 1 Tbsp	2½ cups

TABLE 2.11 *continued*

13 oz	14 oz	15 oz	16 oz
1¾ cups + 2 Tbsp	2 cups + 1 Tbsp	2 cups + 3 Tbsp	2⅓ cups
1¾ cups + 2 Tbsp	2 cups + 1 Tbsp	2 cups + 3 Tbsp	2⅓ cups
3¼ cups	3½ cups	3¾ cups	4 cups
1½ cups + 2 Tbsp	1¾ cups	1¾ cups + 2 Tbsp	2 cups
3¼ cups	3½ cups	3¾ cups	4 cups
2¾ cups + 2 Tbsp	3 cups + 1 Tbsp	3¼ cups + 1½ tsp	3½ cups
1½ cups + 2 Tbsp	1¾ cups	1¾ cups + 2 Tbsp	2 cups
3¼ cups	3½ cups	3¾ cups	4 cups
3 cups + 1 Tbsp	3¼ cups + 1 Tbsp	3½ cups	3¾ cups
4¾ cups + 2 Tbsp	5¼ cups	5½ cups + 2 Tbsp	6 cups
3¼ cups	3½ cups	3¾ cups	4 cups
2⅓ cups + 2 Tbsp	2½ cups + 2 Tbsp	2¾ cups + 1 Tbsp	3 cups
1¼ cups	1¼ cups + 1 Tbsp	1⅓ cups + 1 Tbsp	1½ cups
1¾ cups + 1 Tbsp	2 cups	2 cups + 2 Tbsp	2¼ cups
2⅓ cups + 2 Tbsp	2½ cups + 2 Tbsp	2¾ cups + 1 Tbsp	3 cups
1¾ cups + 1 Tbsp	2 cups	2 cups + 2 Tbsp	2¼ cups
2⅓ cups + 2 Tbsp	2½ cups + 2 Tbsp	2¾ cups + 1 Tbsp	3 cups
2⅔ cups + 1 Tbsp	2¾ cups + 3 Tbsp	3 cups + 2 Tbsp	3⅓ cups

TABLE 2.12   Common can sizes

Can size (industry term)	Approximate net weight or fluid measure	Approximate cups per can	Approximate number of 4-oz portions	Cans per case	Principal products
No. 10	6 lb/7 lb 5 oz	12–13	25	6	Institutional size for fruits, vegetables
No. 5 Squat	4–4¼ lb	8	16–20		Institutional size for canned fish, sweet potatoes
No. 3 Cyl	46 fl oz or 51 oz	5¾	10–12	12	Fruit and vegetable juices, condensed soups
No. 2½	26–30 oz	3½	5–7	24	Fruits, some vegetables
No. 2	18 fl oz or 20 oz	2½	5	24	Juices, fruits, ready-to-serve soups
No. 303	1 lb	2	4	24 or 36	Fruits, vegetables, ready-to-serve soups
No. 300	14–16 oz	1¾	3–4	24	Some fruits and meat products
No. 1 (Picnic)	10½–12 oz	1¼	2–3	48	Condensed soups
8 oz	8 oz	1	2	48 or 72	Ready-to-serve soups, fruits, vegetables

Note: • When substituting one can for another size, one No. 10 can is approximately equivalent to:
   7 No. 303 (1 lb) cans
   5 No. 2 (1 lb 4 oz) cans
   4 No. 2½ (1 lb 13 oz) cans
   2 No. 3 (46 to 50 oz) cans

TABLE 2.13   Metric equivalents for weight, measure, and temperature

Weight		Measure		Temperature	
U.S.	Metric[a]	U.S.	Metric[b]	°F[c]	°C[d]
1 oz	28 g	1 tsp	5 mL	32	0
1½ oz	43 g	1 Tbsp	15 mL	100	38
2 oz	57 g	¼ cup (4 Tbsp)	60 mL	150	65
2½ oz	70 g	⅓ cup (5⅓ Tbsp)	80 mL	200	95
3 oz	85 g	½ cup (8 Tbsp)	120 mL	250	121
3½ oz	100 g	⅔ cup (10⅔ Tbsp)	160 mL	275	135
4 oz (¼ lb)	114 g	¾ cup (12 Tbsp)	180 mL	300	150
5 oz	142 g	1 cup (16 Tbsp)	240 mL	325	165
6 oz	170 g	2 cups (1 pint)	480 mL	350	175
7 oz	198 g	4 cups (1 qt)	0.95 L	375	190
8 oz (½ lb)	227 g	2 qt (½ gal)	1.89 L	400	205
9 oz	255 g	4 qt (1 gal)	3.79 L	425	220
10 oz	284 g			450	230
11 oz	312 g			475	245
12 oz (¾ lb)	340 g			500	260
13 oz	369 g				
14 oz	397 g				
15 oz	425 g				
1 lb (16 oz)	454 g				
2 lb	908 g				
2 lb 4 oz	1.02 kg				

[a]Basic formula used to calculate metric weights: 1 oz = 28.35 g. Resulting figures were rounded to nearest gram and to two decimal places for kilograms. Abbreviations used: oz = ounce; lb = pound; g = gram; kg = kilogram. To change grams to kilograms, move decimal three places to left: e.g., 28 g = 0.028 kg.

[b]Basic formulas used to calculate metric volume: 1 Tbsp = 14.8 mL, rounded to 15 mL; 1 cup = 237 mL, rounded to 240 mL; 1 qt = 0.95 L (4 × 237 ÷ 1000). Abbreviations used: tsp = teaspoon; Tbsp = tablespoon; pt = pint; qt = quart; gal = gallon; mL = milliliter; L = liter.

[c]To convert from °C to °F, the following formula is used: (°C × $\frac{9}{5}$) + 32 = °F.

[d]To convert from °F to °C, the following formula is used: (°F − 32) × $\frac{5}{9}$ = °C.

TABLE 2.14 Temperatures used for food preparation

	°F	Notes
OVEN		
Extremely Hot	500–525	Pocket Flat Breads (Pita)
Very Hot	450–475	Pizza
Hot	400–425	Biscuits, Pie Pastry
Moderate	350–375	Cakes
Slow	300–325	Large Roasts, Poultry
DEEP-FAT FRYING		
Hot	395	French-fried Potatoes
Moderate	375	Battered Foods (Vegetables)
Low	350	Chicken, Fish
SUGAR COOKERY		
Caramelization	338	
Hard Crack	310	Candy Brittles
Soft Crack	290	Taffy
Hard Ball	266	Divinity
Firm Ball	248	Caramels
Soft Ball	239	Fudge
Very Soft Ball	234	Fondant
WATER TEMPERATURES		
Boiling	212	0 lbs pressure at sea level (see note)
Simmering	185–210	
Scalding	149	
Lukewarm	104	

Note: Boiling temperature varies slightly at higher altitudes.

TABLE 2.15   Convection oven baking times and temperatures

| Product | Oven temperature | | Approximate baking time |
	°F	°C	
MEATS			
Steamship round (50 lb, medium)	250–275	120–135	8–9 hr
Rolled beef roast (12–15 lb)	275	135	2½ hr
Standing rib, choice (20 lb, trimmed, rare)	250–300	120–150	2¾ hr
Lasagna	250–275	130	90 min
Hot dogs, 10 per lb (18 × 26-inch pan)	325	165	10–15 min
Baked stuffed pork chops	375	190	20–30 min
Bacon (on racks in 18 × 26-inch pans)	400	205	5–7 min
POULTRY			
Chicken breast and thigh	350	175	40 min
Chicken (2½ lb quartered)	350	175	30 min
Turkey, rolled (18-lb rolls)	310	155	3¾ hr
Turkey, whole (16–20 lb)	275–300	135–150	4–5 hr
FISH AND SHELLFISH			
Halibut steaks, codfish (frozen 5 oz)	350	175	20 min
Lobster tails (frozen)	425	220	9 min
POTATOES			
Baked potatoes (120 count)	400	205	50 min
Oven-roasted potatoes (sliced or diced)	325	165	10 min
BAKED GOODS			
Frozen pies (22 oz)	400	205	30–35 min
Frozen pies (46 oz)	350	175	45–50 min
Fresh apple pie (20 oz)	350–375	175–190	25–30 min
Pumpkin pies	300	150	30–35 min
Fruit cobbler	300	150	30 min
Apple turnovers	350	175	15 min
Corn bread	335	170	20–25 min
Bread (24 1-lb loaves)	350	175	30 min
French bread	375	190	18–20 min
Yeast rolls	350	175	25 min
Croissant	325	165	15–18 min
Danish	335	170	12 min
Sheet cakes (5 lb batter per pan)	325	165	20–25 min
Chocolate cake	335	170	20 min
Fruit cakes	275	135	70 min
Brownies	325	165	20 min
Cookies	325–350	165–175	10–15 min
Cream puffs	350	175	20–25 min

Notes: • Actual times and temperatures may vary from those shown. They are affected by weight of load, temperature of the product, recipe, and type of pan.
  • For menu items not listed, use recommended time and temperature for conventional oven but reduce the temperature setting by 25°–50°F and reduce the total bake/roast time by approximately 10–15 percent.
  • The recipes in Food for Fifty were standardized using a conventional oven.

TABLE 2.16 Deep-fat frying temperatures

Type of product	Preparation[a]	Temperature[b] °F	Temperature[b] °C	Frying time[c] (minutes)
BREADS				
Doughnuts	See p. 294	375	190	3–5
French toast	See p. 296	360	180	3–4
Fritters	See p. 297	375	190	2–5
Sandwiches	Batter	350–375	175–190	3–4
FISH				
Fillets or pieces	Egg and crumb or batter	360–375	180–190	4–6
Oysters	Egg and crumb	375	190	2–4
Scallops	Egg and crumb	360–375	180–190	3–4
Shrimp	Batter or egg and crumb	360–375	180–190	3–5
FRUIT				
Bananas	Batter	375	190	1–3
POULTRY				
Chicken, pieces	Light coating or egg and crumb			
Fryers (1½–2 lb)		350	175	10–12
Fryers (2–2½ lb)		350	175	12–15
Chicken, half	Light coating or egg and crumb			
Fryers (1½–2 lb)		350	175	12–15
Turkey or chicken cutlets	Egg and crumb	325–350	165–175	5–8
VEGETABLES				
Cauliflower, precooked	See p. 851	370	185	3–5
Eggplant	See p. 851	370	185	5–7
Mushrooms	See p. 851	370	185	4–6
Onion Rings	Batter	350	175	3–4
Potatoes, ½-inch strips	See p. 857			
Complete fry		365	182	6–8
Blanching		360	180	3–5
Browning		375	190	2–3
Frozen, fat blanched		375	190	2–3
Zucchini	See p. 851	370	185	4–6

[a]See Table 2.17 for light coating, egg and crumb, and batter.

[b]If food is frozen, use lower temperature than listed and allow additional cooking time. At high altitudes, the lower boiling point of water in foods requires lowering of temperatures for deep-fat frying.

[c]The exact frying time will vary with the equipment used, size and temperature of the food pieces, and the amount of food placed in fryer at one time. If fryer is overloaded, foods may become grease-soaked.

Note: • Use frying fat with a high smoking temperature (see p. 188). Filter fat regularly, at least daily or more often if fryer is in constant use. The breakdown of fat may be caused by using the fat for too long a period, cooking food at too high a temperature, failing to filter the fat regularly, or inadvertently getting salt into the fryer when salting food.

TABLE 2.17   Coatings for deep-fat fried foods

Ingredient	Light coating[d]	Egg and crumb[e]	Batter[f]
Egg[a]		3	6
Milk[b]	1 cup	1 cup	2 cups
Flour, all-purpose or whole wheat	1 lb	8 oz (optional)	12 oz
Salt[c]	2 tsp	1 tsp	2 tsp
Bread crumbs, fine		12 oz	
Baking powder			2 tsp
Shortening, melted, or vegetable oil			3 Tbsp
Seasonings		As desired	

[a]Cholesterol can be lowered by substituting egg whites for all or part of the eggs.
[b]Water may be substituted for milk, except in batter.
[c]Seasoned salt (p. 781) may be substituted.
[d]Dip prepared food in milk. Dredge with seasoned flour.
[e]Dip prepared food in flour (may omit), then in mixture of beaten egg and milk. Drain. Roll in crumbs to cover (see Figure 13.2).
[f]Combine flour, salt, and baking powder. Add milk, beaten eggs, and shortening. Dip prepared foods in batter.

Food Safety

Preventing food-borne illness requires that correct procedures be established and followed for purchas-ing, storing, preparing, and serving food safely. Table 2.18 identifies general guidelines that will help reduce the risk of food-borne illness.

It is important to understand food safety terms when interpreting and applying food safety principles in a food

TABLE 2.18   Guidelines for reducing the risk of food-borne illness

PURCHASING/RECEIVING FOOD

- Purchase food products from reputable processors and distributors who apply HACCP principles.
- Upon delivery, visually inspect perishable food products for packaging defects (holes or tears) or for any sign of temperature abuse (for frozen products: ice crystals from product thawing and re-freezing, re-frozen liquid inside box or stained box from a defrosted product, partially defrosted or defrosted contents). Refrigerated foods should be received at 41°F or below, frozen foods at 0°F or below.
- Upon delivery, assess perishable food quality by odor, sight, and touch.
- Require distributors to include a "sell by" or "use by" date on perishable food items and a code for tracking the product.
- Record delivery date for perishable food products. Save shellfish tags for 90 days.

STORING FOOD

- Store perishable food immediately upon delivery in the freezer (0°F or below) or refrigerator (41°F or below).
- Prevent cross-contamination by storing cooked food above raw food and by storing raw meats on the lowest refrigerator shelf.
- Label and date foods that are removed from their original package.
- Store perishable food so oldest will be used first.

PREPARING FOOD

Food Preparation Procedures

- Wash hands before handling food, after handling raw food, and after touching anything that might contaminate hands.
- Process food in small batches, taking only small amounts of food out of the refrigerator at one time.
- Wash fruits and vegetables in cool running water before cutting, mixing with other foods, or serving whole.
- Keep juices from raw meat, poultry, and fish from contacting other foods.
- Keep everything that touches food clean—utensils, pans, bowls, countertops, hands, gloves.
- Use tongs, disposable gloves on hands, or other methods to keep bare hands from touching ready-to-eat foods.
- Use separate cutting boards and utensils for cooked and uncooked meat, poultry, and fish and for raw and ready-to-eat foods.
- Avoid preparing raw and cooked foods in the same work area and store raw and cooked foods in separate areas.
- Sanitize all utensils, pans, bowls, and food contact surfaces after being used for preparing potentially hazardous foods and before coming in contact with raw or ready-to-eat foods.

Cooking Procedures

- Batch cook whenever possible and prepare food as close to service as feasible.
- Cook all meat to the required internal temperature to kill harmful organisms (see Table 2.23 on p. 103. Measure internal temperature in several places.
- Use an accurate thermometer or thermocouple to measure internal temperature of potentially hazardous foods. Do not rely on color to determine whether meat, chicken, or fish has reached the correct end-point temperature. See p. 101 for how to calibrate a stem or probe thermometer.
- Wash and sanitize thermometers after each use.

SERVING FOOD

- Keep potentially hazardous food either at or below 41°F or above 140°F. Take food temperatures every 30 to 45 minutes when being served from a hot serving counter or steam table or from a cold serving area such as a salad bar.
- When replenishing food on a buffet, do not mix fresh food with food that has been out for service. Do not mix raw food with cooked food.
- Use pans that are as small as feasible and replace pans of food often.
- Cover food whenever possible and protect with sneeze guards.
- Use tongs, disposable gloves on hands, or other method to keep bare hands from touching ready-to-eat foods.

LEFTOVER FOOD

- Freeze or refrigerate leftovers immediately. Follow established guidelines for cooling food quickly, p. 105. Reheat foods one time only to 165°F (within 2 hours).

production setting. Knowing basic food safety terms also gives food production employees a common language to use when communicating food safety concepts.

Critical Control Point (CCP)—A step or procedure in the food handling process where food safety hazards can be eliminated, prevented, or reduced to acceptable levels. CCPs are steps or procedures that, if not performed, might result in a hazard that would not be prevented in a later step. Food handling procedures at a CCP should kill bacteria (cooking) or prevent or slow the growth of bacteria (cold storage or hot holding).

Critical Limits—A maximum or minimum value to which a hazard must be controlled at a CCP to minimize the risk of food-borne illness. Critical limits commonly established to eliminate hazards include standards related to time, temperature, pH, and water activity. All standards for CCPs must be as specific as possible and easily measured or monitored.

Cross-Contamination—The transfer of harmful substances (usually biological) from one food to another by means as hands, equipment, utensils.

Control Points (CP)—A step or procedure in the food handling process where food safety hazards can be controlled. Loss of control at a Control Point does not lead to an unacceptable health risk because a step or procedure to eliminate, reduce, or limit food safety hazards will follow.

Clean—Absence of visible soil, usually in reference to equipment, dishes, and flatware.

Danger Zone—The temperature at which potentially hazardous foods support rapid growth of harmful microorganisms, between 41°F and 140°F. Potentially Hazardous Foods (PHF) should be heated or cooled so they pass through the temperature danger zone as quickly as possible.

HACCP—Hazard Analysis Critical Control Points is an evaluation system to identify, monitor, and control food contamination risks in food service establishments. The seven steps to an HACCP system include (1) assessing hazards, (2) identifying CCPs, (3) establishing critical limits, (4) developing procedures to monitor CCPs, (5) taking corrective action (when deviations from the standard are identified), (6) setting up a record keeping system, and (7) developing an HACCP verification plan.

Hazards (in Food)—Food contamination can be caused by biological, chemical, and physical hazards. Biological hazards include harmful bacteria, viruses, parasites, fungi, molds, or yeasts. Chemical hazards include toxins, pesticides, food additives, cleaning compounds, and heavy metals such as mercury. Physical hazards include foreign objects in food such as broken glass, metal shavings, staples, toothpicks/wood, and stones.

pH—A measure of a food product's acidity or alkalinity expressed on a scale of 0 to 14. A pH of 7 is considered neutral. Microorganism growth is slowed when a product moves below or above the pH that is ideal for growth. At or below 4.6 pH (acidic medium), disease-causing organisms grow very slowly.

Potentially Hazardous Foods (PHF)—Any food or food ingredient capable of supporting the growth of microorganisms. Potentially hazardous foods include foods of animal origin (raw or cooked) and foods of plant origin that have been heat treated. Included also are raw seed sprouts, cut melon, and garlic and oil mixtures. See p. 107 for a more complete list of potentially hazardous foods.

Sanitary—Disease causing microorganisms are reduced to safe levels.

Water Activity—Bacteria require water activity (A_W) greater than .85 to grow. (Water has an A_W of 1.0.) Water activity explains why some dried foods such as beans or rice are not potentially hazardous but become so when re-hydrated.

Probe or stem thermometers can get out of calibration easily and must be handled with care. For accurate temperatures, calibrate probe thermometers each day, or more often if dropped or handled roughly. Table 2.19 gives instructions for calibrating probe thermometers.

TABLE 2.19   Instructions for calibrating a probe (stem) food thermometer

1. Fill a medium-sized glass with ice and add water to fill glass.
2. Place thermometer in glass of ice water.
3. Wait 3 minutes. Stir water occasionally.
4. After 3 minutes, thermometer should read 32°F.

If thermometer is out of calibration (does not read 32°F after 3 minutes):

1. Place thermometer back in ice water (add more ice if necessary for a high ratio of ice to water). Wait 2 to 3 minutes.
2. Using an adjustable wrench or pliers, turn the adjustable nut on the back side of the thermometer until the needle reads 32°F. (Always purchase adjustable stem thermometers.)
3. Add more ice to the glass if necessary and wait 3 minutes, stir occasionally.
4. If the thermometer needle does not read 32°F, repeat process.

TABLE 2.20 Cold food storage temperatures

Food	Refrigerator		Freezer	
	°F	Days	°F	Months
DAIRY/EGGS				
Ice cream			−10	3
Milk	32	7		
Eggs in shell	40	21		
Raw yolks/whites	40	2–4		
Liquid pasteurized (opened)	40	3		
FRESH MEATS				
Beef roast/steaks	32	3–5	0 to −20	6–12
Pork roast	32	3–5	0 to −20	3–6
Pork chops	32	3–5	0 to −20	3–4
Hamburger/ground pork/ ground lamb	32	1–2	0 to −20	3–4
Beef cubes	32	1–2	0 to −20	3–4
Lamb roasts/chops	32	2–3	0 to −20	6–9
Vacuum-packaged cuts	28–32	16–21	0 to −20	6–12
COOKED MEATS				
Browned meats	35	3–4	0 to −20	2–3
Bacon	35	7	0 to −20	1
Frankfurters				
Unopened package	32	14	0 to −20	1–2
Opened package	32	7	0 to −20	1–2
Lamb	32	3–4	0 to −20	2–3
Luncheon meats	32	3–5	0 to −20	1–2
FRESH POULTRY AND FISH				
Chicken/turkey				
Whole	32	1–2	0 to −20	12
Pieces	32	1–2	0 to −20	9
Fish	32	1	0 to −20	3
COOKED POULTRY				
With broth or gravy	35	1–2	0 to −20	6
Pieces, no gravy	35	3–4	0 to −20	4
Cooked dishes	35	3–4	0 to −20	4–6
Fried chicken	35	3–4	0 to −20	4

TABLE 2.21 Refrigerator defrosting times for meats, seafood, and poultry

Food	Approximate defrosting time (in refrigerator)
Large roast	4–7 hours per pound
Small roast	3–5 hours per pound
Chop or steak, 1-inch thick	12–14 total hours
Chicken, whole	1 day
pieces	8–12 total hours
Turkey, whole	
8–12 lb	1–2 days
12–16 lb	2–3 days
16–20 lb	3–4 days
20–24 lb	4–5 days
Seafood, whole, steaks	12–24 total hours
blocks, large whole	1–2 days

TABLE 2.22 Temperatures and bacteria growth

Temperature °F	Bacteria activity
212	Most bacteria destroyed
140 and above	Low survival rate, prevent bacteria growth
120–140	Survival and growth
60–120	Reproduce rapidly (99°F ideal for growth)
40–140	Survival and growth
32–40	Slow growth rate

TABLE 2.23   Safe internal temperatures for cooked foods

Food	Internal temperature
POULTRY	
Boneless, ground, stuffed	165°F for 15 sec
Bone-in pieces	170°F
Whole birds	180°F
GROUND/CHOPPED/TENDERIZED MEAT	
Beef, pork, sausage, lamb, fish	155°F for 15 sec (see Notes)
PORK	
Pork, ham	145°F for 15 sec
BEEF/VEAL/LAMB	
Steaks, chops, roasts (see Notes)	145°F for 15 sec
FISH	
Solid	145°F for 15 sec
Stuffed	165°F
OTHER	
Reheated foods	165°F for 15 sec (within 2 hr)
Stuffed pasta, stuffed meat	165°F for 15 sec
Eggs	155°F for 15 sec
Dairy, pasta, grains, rice	145°F for 15 sec

Note: • Whole beef and pork roasts are considered safe if cooked in a preheated oven and held for a specified length of time, as shown below:

Oven Type	Oven Temperature Based on Roast Weight	
	Less than 4.5 kg (10 lbs)	4.5 kg (10 lbs) or more
Still Dry	177°C (350°F) or more	121°C (250°F) or more
Convection	163°C (325°F) or more	121°C (250°F) or more
High Humidity[1]	121°C (250°F) or less	121°C (250°F) or less

[1]Relative humidity greater than 90% for at least 1 hour as measured in the cooking chamber or exit of the oven; or in a moisture-impermeable bag that provides 100% humidity.

Note: See Table 2.19, p. 101, for instruction for calibrating a probe (stem) thermometer.

Temperature °C (°F)	Time[1] in Minutes	Temperature °C (°F)	Time[1] in Minutes	Temperature °C (°F)	Time[1] in Minutes
54 (130)	121	58 (136)	32	61 (142)	8
56 (132)	77	59 (138)	19	62 (144)	5
57 (134)	47	60 (140)	12	63 (145)	3

[1]Holding time may include postoven heat rise.

• To obtain an even temperature throughout the product, foods cooked in a microwave oven must be stirred once or twice during the cooking process and held covered for 2 minutes after cooking. When using a microwave oven, end-point temperature should reach 165°F in all parts of the food.
• Current USDA regulations recommend cooking ground meat to 160°F, therefore removing the 15-second time requirement.

TABLE 2.24   Food serving temperatures and holding times

Food	Serving temp °F[a]	Approximate holding time
BEVERAGES		
Cold drinks—juices	40	30 min, if poured
Hot drinks	185	30–45 min
Coffee[b]	185	Hot plate, 20 min
		Insulated pot, 2 hr
DAIRY		
Ice cream	10	6–8 hr, dipped
Milk	34–38	
DESSERTS		
Pudding and refrigerator desserts	41 or less	
Pastries and cakes[c]	60–70	
ENTREES, SOUP		
Beef, roast[d]	150	10–15 min
Casseroles, stews	170–180	30–45 min
Chicken, baked	160	20–30 min
Eggs, scrambled	160	10–15 min
Ham, pork roast	160	10–15 min
Sandwiches, hot	160	10–15 min
Soup	170–180	45–60 min[e]
SALADS		
All cold	41 or less	
SAUCES, VEGETABLES		
Hot sauces	145	30–60 min
Cold sauces	below 41	
Gravy	180	30–60 min
Vegetables in cream sauce	145–160	15–30 min
Vegetables unseasoned	160–170	15–20 min
Whipped potatoes	160–170	15–20 min

[a]See Table 2.19, p. 101, for instructions for calibrating a probe (stem) thermometer.
[b]Coffee brewing temperature is 195°–200°F.
[c]Some pastries may be served warm, 100°–125°F, but food products that are potential food safety risks should not be held at temperatures between 41° and 140°F. Examples are custard or pumpkin pie.
[d]Temperature will depend on the doneness of meat. Rare roast beef may be served at a temperature lower than 150°F but does pose some food safety risk.
[e]Cream soups will curdle if held at a too-high a temperature or held too long. Broth soups can be held for a longer time and at a highter temperature than cream soups.

TABLE 2.25   Food cooling and storage procedures

Standard: Cooked potentially hazardous foods (PHF) must be cooled from 140°F to 70°F within 2 hours, and then from 70°F to 41°F within an additional 4 hours (or from 140°F to 41°F within 4 hours total). PHF prepared from ingredients normally stored at room temperature, such as canned tuna, must be cooled from 70°F to 41°F within 4 hours. **(Cooling food following the two-stage cooling method, cooling first to 70°F within 2 hours, and then from 70°F to 41°F within an additional 4 hours offers the greatest protection against microbial growth.)**

METHODS FOR COOLING HOT FOODS

A. Procedure: Cut large food items into smaller pieces.
   Application: large roasts, whole poultry or fish

B. Procedure: Pour hot, thick foods into clean, chilled, shallow, stainless steel pans, to no
         more than 2 inches deep.
   Application: stews, chili, pasta casseroles, pudding

C. Procedure: Pour hot, thin foods into clean pans or pots, to no more than 3 inches deep.
   Application: broth soups, thin sauces

D. Procedure: Set pan of food in an ice water bath (set pan with hot food inside another
         pan filled with ice). Stir both the hot food and the ice. Replace ice as it
         melts.
   Application: pourable thin or thick foods

E. Procedure: Delete part of the water in the recipe and add as ice in the cooling step. The
         weight of the ice should be equal to the water deleted from the recipe.
   Application: thick, pourable foods such as chili and pasta sauces that may be prepared,
         cooled, and heated for service at a later time

METHODS FOR CHILLING COLD FOODS

A. Chill ingredients thoroughly before combining (i.e., salad dressings, tuna, hard-cooked
   eggs, canned kidney beans).

B. Put dense products into clean, chilled, shallow, stainless steel pans to no more than
   2 inches deep.

Notes: • Hot foods will cool faster if loosely covered or uncovered. Protect uncovered food from
      contamination. Cover food tightly after chilling.
    • Small amounts of food will cool more rapidly than large amounts. Whenever possible divide
      food into small amounts.
    • Allow air to circulate around pans. Do not stack pans.
    • Chilling time can be shortened by stirring foods with a clean utensil once or twice during
      cooling.

TABLE 2.26   **Time and temperature standards for reducing food safety hazards of potentially hazardous foods (PHF)**

Step	*Standard*
Receiving	Frozen foods at 0°F or below
	Refrigerated foods at 41°F or below
Storage	Frozen foods at 0°F or below
	Refrigerated foods at 41°F or below for 7 calendar days or 45°F for 4 calendar days (The calendar day counting period begins as day 1 on the day the food is refrigerated.)
Thawing	In refrigerator at 41°F or below
	Under potable, running cold water (70°F or less) for not more than 2 hours
Food Production	
Pre-preparation	Keep all PHF at 41°F or below or at 140°F or above throughout pre-preparation time. Cool cooked products rapidly to 70°F within 2 hours and from 70°F to 41°F or below in 4 additional hours or less.
Preparation	*Cold foods:* Rapid cooling to 41°F or below
	Hot foods: Cook to internal temperatures specified in the recipe (reheated foods to 165°F). Maintain hot holding temperature at or above 140°F (see Notes).
Postproduction	Cool leftover food rapidly to 70°F within 2 hours and from 70°F to 41°F or less in 4 additional hours or less.
	Store cooked food in clean shallow pans or containers that are no more than 4 inches deep with a product depth of no more than 2 inches. If product is thick, stir frequently until cooled.
Serving	Maintain internal temperature at 140°F or more or 41°F or less (see Notes). Do not mix old product with freshly cooked product.
Cooling	Cool rapidly to 70°F within 2 hours and from 70°F to 41°F or less in 4 additional hours or less (see Postproduction).

Notes:
- In some locations, regulatory agencies will permit time to be used as control rather than holding temperatures. For time to be used as a control, the following conditions must be met: (1) The product must be marked with the time it is removed from temperature control; and (2) the product will be cooked and served or discarded within 4 hours.
- Measure all temperatures with a cleaned and sanitized stem thermometer or thermocouple thermometer.

TABLE 2.27   **Water activity (A_w) of selected foods**

Foods	*Water activity*
Crackers	.10
Fresh Fruits	.91–1.00
Meats	
Cured	.87–.95
Fresh	.95–1.00
Sweets	
Jam	.75–80
Honey	.54–.75

Note:
- Salt and sugar solutions as well as drying reduce the water that is available for bacteria to grow. Most bacteria will not grow with a water activity below 0.85 A_w, yeast below 0.88 A_w, and molds below 0.82 A_w.

TABLE 2.28   pH values of selected foods

PROTEIN

Chicken	6.2–6.7
Fish	6.6–6.8
Ground Beef	5.1–6.3
Ham	5.9–6.1

DAIRY

Buttermilk	4.5
Cheese	4.9–5.9
Milk	6.6–7.0
Yogurt	3.8–4.2

FRUITS AND VEGETABLES

Vegetables	4.2–6.5
Tomatoes, fresh	4.2–4.9
Fruits	2.0–6.7
Orange Juice	4.0
Grapefruit	3.6

OTHER

Mayonnaise	3.0–4.1
Salad Dressing	3.2–4.0

Note: • Food's pH value has an effect on microbial growth. Most bacteria grow when food pH values are between 5.5 and 8.0. Disease-causing organisms grow very slowly in foods with a pH value below 4.6. Spoilage yeasts grow best when food pH are between 4.0 and 6.5 and spoilage molds between 4.5 and 6.8.

TABLE 2.29   Potentially hazardous foods

FOODS FROM RAW OR HEAT-TREATED ANIMAL SOURCES

Cheese (soft, unripened, and ripened hard cheeses that have been cut or opened)
Eggs
Fish, shellfish, crustacea
Meat
Milk
Poultry

FOODS FROM HEAT-TREATED PLANT SOURCES

Cooked beans
Cooked pasta
Cooked potatoes
Cooked rice
Soy products (i.e., Tofu)

RAW PLANT SOURCE PRODUCTS

Melon (cut)
Seed sprouts

OTHER

Fresh garlic in oil
Rehydrated cooked and dried vegetables (onions)

Notes: • A potentially hazardous food (PHF) is any food that can support rapid bacterial growth and cause food-borne illness. Foods that do not support bacterial growth are those with a pH 4.6 or below (acid foods) and those with a water activity (A_w) of 0.85 or less (dried, salted, sugared foods).
• Any PHF in a food renders it potentially hazardous (for example, bread dressing, casserole, creamed and broth soups, gravies, and cream filling).
• Bacteria live well in PHF because they often are protein rich, moist, and neutral or low acid. PHFs are especially able to support bacteria growth when held in the temperature danger zone (41°F–140°F) for more than 4 hours (cumulative during the **entire** food handling process).
• This table provides examples of PHFs and is not intended to be an all-inclusive list of specific foods and food products.

CHAPTER 3

Food Product Information

Gerald Lopez © Dorling Kindersley

This chapter provides descriptive information and general purchasing and storage guidelines about the basic foods used as ingredients in *Food For Fifty* recipes. Cooking timetables precede the recipes in the chapters that follow. General food production techniques that are applicable to products in the basic food categories are presented in Chapter 4 p. 189.

The chapter includes the following topics:

- Dairy—Eggs, Cheese, Milk, and Milk Products (p. 109)
- Grains, Pasta, Flours, and Other Starches (p. 119)
- Meat (Beef, Lamb, Pork, Veal), Poultry, Fish, Shellfish, and Crustaceans (p. 127)
- Fresh Produce; Canned, Frozen Fruits and Vegetables; Tofu and Dried Beans, Lentils, and Peas (p. 141)
- Vinegars, Condiments, Dried Seasonings, Nuts, and Food Staples (p. 175)

Dairy—Eggs, Cheese, Milk, and Milk Products

- General Information
- Purchasing and Storage
- Cooking and Recipes (see Chapter, 10, p. 437)

EGGS

Eggs are considered a staple in quantity food production kitchens because of their versatility and the number of functions they serve in the preparation of recipes. Eggs are used to make *emulsions* by aiding in the dispersion of one liquid within another with which it is usually not mixable. *Foams* for making food products such as angel food cakes, meringues, and souffles are formed by incorporating air into egg whites.

Egg protein *coagulates* on heating to provide a structure for food products such as omelets and custards, and for meat and vegetable breading. The temperature at which egg protein coagulates and the time required for coagulation depends in part on the amount of egg in the mixture. Diluting egg protein with milk or adding sugar increases the temperature at which coagulation occurs. Undiluted egg white begins to coagulate and turn from a clear liquid to white at about 140°F. At about 149°F, the whites become opaque and firm. Egg yolk protein denatures and thickens at a slightly higher temperature than whites. Coagulation of egg yolk begins at about 149°F and loses its fluidity at 158°F. Egg protein heated at a high temperature becomes very firm and tough, as compared with the soft, tender texture obtained when heated at a lower temperature.

Soup stock can be *clarified* by adding egg whites and straining them out after they coagulate from being heated. The *flavor* of eggs alone, the flavor and *color* they add to other products and their *nutritional* value also add to eggs' appeal for use in food products.

Chicken eggs are graded following standards established by the U.S. Department of Agriculture. Quality characteristics for the different grades are identified in Table 3.1. Grade AA and A eggs are suitable for any use and especially when appearance is important. Because Grade B eggs are generally used for processed egg products they are not usually available as shell eggs. All grades of eggs have the same nutritional values.

Weight per dozen determines the size designation assigned to shell eggs. Size descriptions change at 3 ounce per dozen intervals. See Figure 3.1. The size of an egg is not related to the egg's quality grade.

Egg Purchasing and Storage

Fresh Eggs

Fresh eggs deteriorate rapidly at room temperatures. They should be shipped in refrigerated trucks and kept at 33°–38°F or below. If kept under proper refrigeration, they will retain their quality for 3–4 weeks. Eggs should be kept in their cartons or cases to prevent loss of moisture and, because the shell is porous, should be stored away from foods with strong odors. Eggs should not be washed prior to storage.

Processed Eggs

Although fresh shell eggs are used extensively for table service, processed eggs are convenient to use in many food products. They eliminate the time-consuming task and the food safety risk of breaking and storing eggs. Whole eggs, whites, and yolks are available in liquid, frozen, and dried forms. All eggs must be processed in sanitary facilities under USDA supervision and must bear the USDA inspection mark. They must be pasteurized and are routinely analyzed for bacterial contamination.

Frozen Eggs and Liquid Eggs.   Because food safety regulations prohibit pooling eggs in quantity (breaking raw eggs into a container and storing them until needed), food service operations often choose to use frozen eggs or unfrozen liquid eggs in place of fresh eggs for many recipes. Eggs may be purchased as frozen or liquid whole eggs (combined yolks and whites), in the form of whites or yolks, and as blended egg products such as scrambled egg mix. High-quality eggs are used for liquid and frozen eggs making them suitable for use in omelets, scrambled eggs, and baking. Because frozen egg yolks become viscous and gelatinous when thawed, they usually have added sugar, syrup, or salt and are generally used for baked products. Frozen liquid eggs are available in several container sizes. Because they are highly perishable, only sizes that can be used within 2 to 3 days after thawing should be purchased. The shelf life of liquid pasteurized eggs varies among processors, and their guidelines should be followed.

Frozen eggs should be kept frozen (shelf life 1 year) at 0°F or below and defrosted in the refrigera-

---

TABLE 3.1   Quality characteristics for chicken egg grades

Quality characteristics	Grade AA	Grade A	Grade B
Spread	Compact	Spreads slightly	Considerable spread
Egg White	Thick; firm	Clear; reasonably firm	Clear; thin
Egg Yolk	Firm; centered; round, stands very high; free from defects	Firm; stands high; free from defects	Flattened; enlarged
Shell	Clean; standard egg shape; unbroken	Clean; standard egg shape; unbroken	May be slightly stained; irregular shape permissible; unbroken

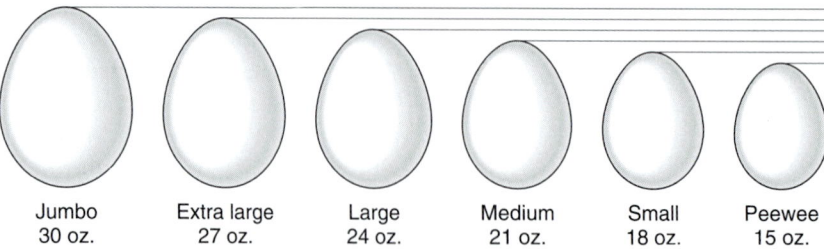

| Jumbo 30 oz. | Extra large 27 oz. | Large 24 oz. | Medium 21 oz. | Small 18 oz. | Peewee 15 oz. |

FIGURE 3.1   Chicken egg size designations and weight per dozen eggs

Notes: • Table provides additional information on weights for whole eggs, whites, and yolks.
   • Because sizes of eggs may differ, recipes specifying the amount of egg by weight are more accurate than those specifying the number of eggs.

tor. Large 30 lb containers of egg products may take 2–3 days to defrost. Quart or half gallon boxes will defrost in 24 hours or less. The maximum shelf life for liquid pasteurized eggs can be realized when stored in their original containers at 34–36°F.

Frozen hard-cooked eggs (diced, sliced, whole) and pre-cooked products such as crepes, omelets, quiche, and egg breakfast sandwiches are available. Quality differences among manufacturers should be evaluated carefully before purchases are made.

Dried Eggs.   Dried powdered eggs are used less frequently than frozen and fresh eggs—primarily for baking. Because dried eggs are very stable if kept tightly sealed, dry, and cool (preferably below 50°F), they are convenient when there is a lack of freezer and refrigerator space, such as on a ship, or when food is being prepared in a remote or isolated location. Dried eggs should be reconstituted only in the quantity that will be used immediately. In baking, dried eggs can be combined with the other dry ingredients in the recipe and the amount of water needed to reconstitute can be added with the other liquid ingredients.

CHEESE

Cheese is an excellent source of calcium and protein. It is a versatile food when used alone or as an ingredient in meal parts from appetizers to desserts. Understanding the characteristics of different cheeses is important for menu planning and for preparing quality food products that use cheese as an ingredient.

Natural Cheese

The type of milk used and the aging process will determine the flavor and texture of cheese. All *natural cheeses* are made in a similar way. The steps include:

- promoting curd formation in milk by adding a lactic-acid producing bacteria or a coagulating enzyme (generally rennet, a natural enzyme extracted from cow stomachs)
- draining the whey (liquid) from the curd
- heating the curd to force additional whey from the curd
- draining, salting, and pressing and shaping the curd
- aging (ripening) the curds (Some cheeses are not ripened and some are inoculated with a specially selected mold prior to ripening.)

Natural cheese can be classified according to the type of milk used (cow, goat, sheep), its texture (soft, semi-soft, hard, grating), or the ripening process.

Fresh cheeses are unripened and without a rind. They range in consistency from creamy and smooth to curd mixtures. Fresh cheeses have a shorter shelf life than harder cheeses, making it important to use them by the use-by date on the package. A high moisture content (40–80 percent) makes them highly perishable.

Soft cheeses have been ripened briefly and are characterized by their thin skin, creamy texture, and relatively high moisture content (50–75 percent). Soft cheeses ripen very quickly and are at their peak for only a short time. When cut, some fully ripe soft cheese such as Brie and Camembert will ooze slightly but will not run. Ripe soft cheese will be springy or feel spongy to the touch and have a nutty, aromatic smell.

Semi-soft cheeses are ripened, have a lower moisture content (40–50 percent) than soft cheese and therefore hold their shape when sliced or cut. Mild and smooth characterizes semi-soft cheeses.

Firm cheeses are low in moisture (30–40 percent) and often high in fat. They are aged for a longer time than softer cheeses and range in texture from crumbly to flexible and able to be sliced.

Hard grating cheeses are aged for a long period of time until they have a dry, granular texture. They have a low moisture content (30 percent) and will keep for extended periods of time when kept tightly wrapped in a refrigerator.

Blue-veined cheeses range in texture from smooth and creamy to dry and crumbly. A special mold is injected prior to ripening to give the cheeses a characteristic blue vein. The moisture content (40–50 percent) is similar to other semi-soft cheeses.

Processed Cheese

Pasteurized *processed cheese* is made differently than natural cheeses. Processed cheese is made by mixing different cheeses using a heat process and adding emulsifiers, flavoring, and coloring. The cheese is poured in a mold and allowed to harden. Because the product is pasteurized, it will not ripen. Flavor depends on the cheeses that were combined to make the product. Processed cheese is often salty and may have a moisture content of up to 40 percent.

Pasteurized *processed cheese foods* and *cheese spreads* contain less cheese than processed cheese but are produced in the same way. Cream, milk (whole, skim, or nonfat solids), whey, and other foods, such as chopped olives, may be added. Cheese food is milder and melts more quickly than processed cheese because of a higher moisture content. Cheese spreads have the highest moisture content, are usually spreadable, and melt very easily.

Purchasing

Choosing cheeses for cooking or for eating requires a knowledge of different cheeses and their unique characteristics. Table 3.2 provides a guide for selecting natural and processed cheeses.

TABLE 3.2   Guide for selecting natural and processed cheeses

FRESH CHEESE

Cheese type/milk used	Fat (approx.)	Characteristics	Purchasing notes	Mode of serving
Chèvre (general goat cheese)	6 grams/oz	Mild, soft (very fresh) to tangy, crumbly (when older)	Variety of shapes (cones, discs, logs). Short shelf life.	General cooking.
Cottage (whole or skim cow's)	5 grams/oz (creamed)	Mild, slightly acid flavor; soft, texture with tender curds of varying size; white to creamy white	In carton of varying sizes. Short shelf life.	As side, mixed with fruit or vegetables, in dips.
Cream (cow's plus cream)	10 grams/oz	Delicate, slightly acid flavor; smooth texture; white	Block, in loaf.	As such, in salads, on sandwiches in dips, on crackers, on sweet breads, in desserts.
Feta (sheep's, goat's, cow's)	6 grams/oz	Salty; soft, flaky, similar to very dry high-acid cottage cheese; becomes sharper with age; tangy; white	Block. Stored in brine water for a 5–6 week shelf life.	In salads, on pizza. Melts easily for fillings and sauces.
Mascarpone (cow's)	70–75% fat	Very mild, sweet, slightly tangy; soft, extremely smooth and creamy; pale yellow or ivory	Bulk or tubs. Highly perishable.	As such, with fruit, spread on bread, in desserts (tiramisù).
Mozzarella (cow's or buffalo's)	5 grams/oz (part skim) 40–45% fat	Delicate; mild, bland flavor; tender plastic-like texture, becomes elastic-like when heated; creamy white	Fresh in irregular balls or braided. Best eaten soon after making. Purchased shredded or sliced.	Fresh in salads, sliced with olive oil, sliced on sandwiches, shredded on pizza, in/on casseroles.
Neufchâtel (cow's)	7 grams/oz	Mild, slightly acidic; soft and creamy, similar to cream cheese but lower in milk-fat	Block, in loaf.	As such, in salads, in dips, on sandwiches, in desserts.
Ricotta (cow's)	10 grams/oz (part skim)	Bland, slightly sweet; soft curds; moist to slightly dry, grainy; similar to cottage cheese but dry; white or ivory	In carton of varying sizes. Short shelf life.	As such; in salads, in cooked foods (ravioli, lasagna).

SOFT CHEESE

Cheese type/milk used	Fat (approx.)	Characteristics	Purchasing notes	Mode of serving
Bel Paese (cow's)	50% fat	Mild to moderately robust; soft to medium firm, smooth waxy body; creamy yellow interior	Small wheels, wedges.	On crackers, with fruit, in sandwiches, as dessert.
Brie (cow's)	8 grams/oz 60% fat	Mild to pungent; soft, smooth; creamy yellow interior, edible thin white crust	Round flat disk (2–4 lbs each).	Appetizer, sauces, with fruit, dessert.
Boursin (cow's)	75% fat	Mild; smooth; creamy; often flavored with herbs, garlic, peppers	Small foil wrapped cylinders.	Breakfast, with fruit, as filling for baked chicken breasts.

TABLE 3.2   *continued*

SOFT CHEESE—CONTINUED

Cheese type/milk used	Fat (approx.)	Characteristics	Purchasing notes	Mode of serving
Camembert (cow's)	45% fat	Mild to tangy flavor; smooth texture; creamy yellow interior; edible thin white crust	Small, round oval disks. Overripens easily.	As such (dessert), with fruit.
Limburger (cow's)	8 grams/oz	Very strong flavor and pungent aroma; soft, smooth, and waxy; light yellow interior, brown exterior	Small cube, block.	Appetizers, with crackers, dark breads, dessert.

SEMI-SOFT CHEESE INCLUDING BLUE/BLEU-VEINED CHEESE

Cheese type/milk used	Fat (approx.)	Characteristics	Purchasing notes	Mode of serving
Blue (spelled Bleu when imported) (cow's or goat's)	8 grams/oz	Tangy, piquant, sharp; possibly crumbly; creamy white with blue veins and marbling	Cylindrical shape, wedges.	Appetizers, salads, dips, salad dressings, sandwiches, with fruit, dessert.
Brick (cow's)	8 grams/oz	Mild to moderately sharp (depending on age); light yellow; semi-soft to firm, elastic; creamy yellow	Loaf, brick, slices.	Appetizers, sandwiches, snacks, dessert.
Danish Blue (cow's)	8 grams/oz	Strong, sharp, salty; white with blue veins and marbling	Cylindrical shape, wedges, blocks.	Appetizers, salads, dips, salad dressings, sandwiches, dessert.
Fontina (cow's)	45% fat	Nutty, rich; medium yellow to pale gold; dense interior with a few small holes	Wheel.	Added to soups and sauces, sandwiches, dessert.
Gorgonzola (cow's)	48% fat	Tangy, piquant; creamier than other blues with more pungent flavor; creamy white interior streaked with blue-green veins	Cylindrical shape, wedges, oblong.	Appetizers, salads, dips, salad dressings, sandwiches, dessert.
Maytag Blue (cow's)	5 grams/oz	Strong, salty; harder than other blue cheeses; creamy white or light yellow with blue veins and marbling	Cylindrical shape, wedges	Appetizers, dips, salads, salad dressing, with fruits (pears, apples), dessert.
Havarti (cow's)	45–60% fat	Mild flavor; buttery, creamy texture, often with added dill, caraway seeds, peppers; pale yellow with small irregular holes	Rounds, wheels, rectangular blocks, loaves.	Appetizers, sandwiches.

continues

TABLE 3.2 *continued*

Cheese type/milk used	Fat (approx.)	Characteristics	Purchasing notes	Mode of serving
Monterey Jack (cow's)	9 grams/oz 50% fat	Semi-soft to very hard (depending on age); mild to pungent; smooth texture, small openings throughout, creamy white to light yellow	Wheel, block.	Sandwiches, in Mexican dishes.
Muenster (cow's)	5 grams/oz	Mild and mellow to pungent (depending on age); smooth, waxy, small holes; creamy white to light yellow	Wheel, block.	Appetizers, sandwiches, with fruit, dessert.
Port du Salut (cow's)	50%	Smooth, buttery, rich; small openings; mellow to robust; creamy white or pale yellow interior, edible orange rind	Wheel or cylinder.	Appetizers, with fruit, dessert.
Roquefort (sheep's)	45% fat	Sharp, peppery, piquant flavor; semi-soft, pasty, sometimes crumbly texture; white interior streaked with blue-green veins of mold (See Blue)	Cylindrical shape, wedges. Imported only from France.	Appetizers, salads, dips, salad dressings, sandwiches, dessert.
Stilton (cow's)	45% fat	Pungent, tangy, rich; milder than Roquefort and Gorgonzola; crumbly, harder than Roquefort; medium yellow with blue-green marbling (See Blue)	Cylindrical shape, wedges. Imported only from England.	Appetizers, salads, dessert.

TABLE 3.2   *continued*

Cheese type/milk used	Fat (approx.)	Characteristics	Purchasing notes	Mode of serving
Cheddar (cow's)	45–50% fat 9 grams/oz	Mild to very sharp depending on age; hard to soft depending on age; firm, smooth; can be crumbly; creamy white (not dyed) to medium yellow-orange	Wheel.	Appetizers, sandwiches, sauces, grating, dessert.
Colby (cow's)	9 grams/oz	Mild to mellow flavor, similar to cheddar; softer body and more open texture than cheddar; light cream to orange	Block.	As such, in sandwiches, cooked foods.
Edam (cow's)	7 grams/oz	Mellow, nutlike, sometimes salty flavor; rather firm, rubbery texture, creamy yellow or medium yellow-orange interior; surface coated with red wax	Loaf or sphere. May be coated with wax. Usually shaped like a flattened ball.	Appetizers, on crackers, with fresh fruit, dessert.
Emmenthaler/ Swiss (cow's)	45% fat 8 grams/oz	Sweet, nutlike; shiny, smooth, hard; large round gas holes or eyes; pale yellow	Wheel.	Appetizers, in salads, sandwiches, fondue, with fruit and nuts.
Gouda (cow's)	7 grams/oz	Mellow, nutlike; smooth, hard; may have tiny holes; creamy yellow or medium yellow-orange interior	Wheel. Red wax coating, usually shaped like a flattened ball.	Appetizers, with fresh fruit, in cooked dishes.
Gruyére (cow's)	45–50% fat	Sweet, nutlike; moist; highly flavored; small well-spaced holes; pale yellow	Wheel.	Appetizers, in sauces, dessert.
Jarlsberg (cow's)	45–50% fat	Mild, delicate sweet flavor; large holes, hard; light yellow; resembles Emmenthaler	Wheel. Coated with yellow wax.	Sandwiches, cooked dishes.

continues

TABLE 3.2 *continued*

FIRM CHEESE—CONTINUED

Cheese type/milk used	Fat (approx.)	Characteristics	Purchasing notes	Mode of serving
Provolone (cow's)	45% fat	Mild to sharp depending on age; hard, elastic; light yellow to golden brown	Various shapes (pear, sausage, round).	Sandwiches, cooked dishes, pasta dishes, pizza.

HARD GRATING CHEESE

Cheese type/milk used	Fat (approx.)	Characteristics	Purchasing notes	Mode of serving
Asiago (cow's)	30% fat	Rich, nutty flavor; mild (young) sharp (aged); hard for grating after 2 years aging, cheddar-like and crumbly after 1 year aging; melts easily; light yellow	Cylinder or flat block.	Sliced with fruits (young), grated in soups and pastas (aged), sauces.
Parmesan/Parmesan Reggiano (cow's)	32–35% fat 7 grams/oz	Sharp, complex, distinctive flavor; very hard, granular texture; light yellow	Cylinder, wheel. Parmesan Reggiano imported only (France).	Grated in soups, with pasta, on salads and vegetables, on pizza, in lasagna, in cooking.
Romano/Pecorino (cow's, sheep's, goat's)	35% fat	Very sharp, piquant flavor, tangy; very hard, brittle, granular texture; yellowish white	Cylinder.	Grated on salads, soups, pasta, pizza.

PROCESSED CHEESE

Cheese type/milk used	Fat (approx.)	Characteristics	Purchasing notes	Mode of serving
American (cow's)	9 grams/oz	Mild flavor; semi-soft to soft; smooth, plastic body; processed; creamy white or yellow-orange	Blocks, sliced or unsliced.	In sandwiches, on crackers, for cooking (melts quickly and smoothly).

Storage

Cheese should be stored in a refrigerator and wrapped tightly to keep out moisture and any refrigerator odors that may be present. Soft and unripened cheeses with a high moisture content are perishable and should be used within 7 to 10 days. Aged cheeses with a lower moisture content can be kept for several weeks or longer.

Some cheeses are made using special molds (Blue, Brie, Camembert, Gorgonzola, Roquefort, Stilton) and will have mold on the interior and exterior. The mold on these cheeses is safe to eat. Molds that are not part of the manufacturing process (wild molds) are undesirable when growing on the surface of cheese. Mold on hard cheeses such as cheddar can be cut off and the cheese safely used. If cheese is soft or unripened, or if mold permeates deeply into the cheese, it should be discarded because the mold cannot be removed completely.

Freezing cheese may cause the texture to become crumbly and mealy. Hard and cheddar-like cheeses are the most successfully frozen and should be thawed very slowly in the refrigerator to reduce the detrimental effects of freezing.

Cheese flavors are more pronounced if served at cool room but not cold temperatures. Taking cheese from the refrigerator approximately 30 minutes prior to serving is recommended. Cottage and cream cheese is an exception and should be served cold.

MILK

Milk is an ingredient in many dishes. Because it is highly perishable, strict food safety and sanitation standards must be followed in processing plants and throughout the distribution and foodservice systems.

Whole milk is graded according to standards recommended by the U.S. Public Health Service and voluntarily adopted by most local and state governments. Grades are assigned based on bacteria count. Grade A milk has the lowest bacteria count and is the fluid milk sold in the retail and commercial markets. Quality standards for dry milk are set by the USDA, and manufacturers who use the USDA grade or quality shield on a product label must follow USDA processing guidelines.

All Grade A fluid milk and milk products purchased commercially for drinking and cooking are *pasteurized* or heated to a specified temperature for a designated period of time. Pasteurization destroys pathogenic bacteria, most nonpathogenic bacteria, and enzymes that cause spoilage. The term *ultra-pasteurization* refers to a process in which milk is heated and held at a higher temperature for a shorter length of time than in regular pasteurization. Virtually all bacteria is destroyed during this process. Ultra-pasteurization is often used for whipping cream, half and half cream, and individual coffee creamers. *Ultra-high-temperature processing* is achieved by heating and holding milk at a high-enough temperature to kill all bacteria. Milk that has been ultra-high-temperature processed and packaged in sterilized containers is shelf stable and can be held without refrigeration for at least 3 months. Once opened, however, it must be refrigerated and used within a few days. Flavor changes can be noticed when milk is heated; ultra-high-temperature processed milk has a slightly sweet taste.

Most milk available commercially has been *homogenized* by a process that divides and disperses milk fat globules so the fat and the liquid portions of the milk do not separate. The homogenization process causes milk to have a whiter color, a more uniform consistency, and a richer flavor.

Milk-fat can be removed from milk to make a variety of fat-reduced products available. Table 3.3 identifies fluid milk products with varying amounts of milk-fat. Filled and imitation milk products resemble milk. In filled milk, milk-fat is replaced by another fat, often coconut oil, or a specially developed soybean, corn, or cottonseed oil. Imitation milk resembles milk but contains no milk products. Milk derivatives, however, are sometimes used as the protein source, and some imitation milks may contain whey products.

A curdled appearance is the undesirable result of milk protein coagulation caused by heat, acid, salts, and phenolic compounds in fruits and vegetables. Curdling is usually caused by a combination of these factors and can be reduced by heating milk products at a low or moderate temperature for the shortest time possible.

Purchasing and Storage

Many types of milk are available for serving as a beverage or for cooking purposes. Table 3.3 describes a variety of milk products.

Fluid milk is a potentially hazardous food and proper purchasing and storage procedures are important. When kept between 35 and 40°F, fluid milk will keep for a week, and buttermilk for 2 to 3 weeks. Shelf-stable milk (evaporated, condensed, and dry) will keep for 3–6 months unopened in cool 60–70°F temperature storage and 3 to 5 days when reconstituted and held at 35–40°F. Most milk products are date stamped to facilitate rotation of stock. All milk products will absorb flavor from strong foods and refrigerator odors if not tightly covered. Freezing milk, which causes fat globules to coalesce, is not recommended. Frozen milk can, however, be used in baking and in other products where some fat separation will not be noticed.

TABLE 3.3   Types of milk products

Fluid milk	% Milk-fat	Description
Milk	3.25	The term *milk* refers to *whole milk*. Contains 8.0 grams of total fat and 150 kilocalories per 1 cup (240 mL). States may establish a minimum for milk-fat in whole milk. Federal standards specify a minimum of 3.25%.
Reduced-fat	2	Synonymous terms are *low-fat 2%*, and *less-fat milk*. Contains 4.7 grams total fat and 122 kilocalories per 1 cup (240 mL).
Low-fat	1	Synonymous term is *low-fat 1% milk*. Contains 2.6 grams total fat and 102 kilocalories per 1 cup (240 mL).
Skim	0.5	Synonymous terms are *fat-free, zero-fat, no-fat*, and *nonfat milk*. Less than 0.5 grams total fat and 80 kilocalories per 1 cup (240 mL).

Concentrated fluid milk	% Milk-fat	Description
Evaporated	7.5 (whole)	Approximately 60% of the water removed.
Sweetened condensed	8 (whole)	15% sugar is added to whole or skim milk, which is concentrated to one-third of its volume.

Dry milk	Description
Nonfat	Made from nonfat skim in a process that removes water. Disperses rapidly in cold water. 1 1/3 cups of nonfat dry milk will make 1 quart of fluid milk.
Whole or low-fat	Dried whole or low-fat milk has a shorter shelf life because of the fat content, and it disperses slowly in warm water.
Buttermilk	Processed the same as other dried milk and made from the liquid remaining after butter is produced from cream. Proportions may vary but generally 1 cup of dried buttermilk powder will make 1 quart of fluid buttermilk. Dried buttermilk is usually mixed with the recipe's dry ingredients and water added with the liquid ingredients.

Cultured milk	Description
Acidophilus milk	Cultured by adding lactobacillus acidophilus bacteria to pasteurized skim or low-fat milk. Health benefit claims exist for drinking acidophilus milk and introducing lactobacillus acidophilus bacteria into the intestine.
Buttermilk	Cultured by adding streptococcus lactis bacteria to pasteurized skim or low-fat milk. Cultured buttermilk is thick and tart.
Yogurt	Cultured from whole, low-fat, or skim milk. A mixed culture is usually added. The resulting product is thick and tangy.

CREAM

Cream is produced by separating milk-fat from whole milk. The resulting products are used extensively in foodservice operations to give flavor, richness, and body to sauces, soups, and desserts. Table 3.4 identifies cream products with varying amounts of milk-fat.

Cream with a high milk-fat percentage is thicker than cream with low milk-fat. Temperature also affects cream thickness because the fat globules firm up and become more viscous when cold. Both high milk-fat content (at least 30%) and firm fat globules (35–40°F) are required to successfully trap air into cream for whipped cream.

Purchasing and Storage

Cream is marketed in several forms as identified in Table 3.4. When more milk-fat is present, the price is generally higher. Cream will absorb flavors from strong foods or from the refrigerator if not tightly covered. It can be stored at 35–40°F for 3 weeks. Ultra-pasteurized cream will keep for 4 weeks. Most cream products are date stamped for keeping stock rotated. Cream may separate when frozen; freezing is not recommended.

TABLE 3.4   Types of cream products

Cream	% Milk-fat	Description
Half-and-half	10.5–18	A mixture of milk and cream. Used in place of light cream or coffee cream.
Light, coffee, or table cream	18–30	A lower milk-fat cream; not for whipping
Cream	18 minimum	General name used when milk-fat is more than 18%.
Light whipping cream or whipping cream	30–36	The minimum milk-fat required for whipping.
Heavy whipping cream or heavy cream	36 minimum	Whips easily and holds its whipped shape longer than cream with less milk-fat.
Crème fraîche	36 minimum	A high milk-fat cultured cream product, thinner than sour cream with a similar but less tart flavor and velvety texture. Because of its high fat content, it will not curdle easily when used in cooked products. When not available commercially, crème fraîche can be made. See note at bottom of table.
Sour cream	18–22	Sweet cream cultured by adding streptococcus lactis bacteria to light cream. Tangy, tart flavor.

Note: To make crème fraîche, use the following proportions and procedure. *Proportions:* 16 fluid ounces (2 cups) of heavy cream (preferably not ultra-pasteurized) to 1 fluid oz (2 tablespoons) buttermilk (with active culture present). *Procedure:* Warm cream to 100°F (43°C), remove from heat, and stir in buttermilk. Cover loosely and let mixture stand at room temperature until it thickens slightly (6–24 hours). Refrigerate after thickening. Use within 3 to 5 days.

BUTTER

Butter is produced by agitating cream until the liquid separates from the milk-fat or butterfat. Butter contains 80 percent milk-fat, not more than 16 percent water and 2 to 4 percent milk solids. Butter is hard when chilled and soft at room temperature, and it melts at approximately 93°F. The smoke point of butter is lower than most other fats (see p. 188, smoke points of selected fats).

Grading is not mandatory but most manufacturers choose to have their product graded according to federal standards so they can use the USDA label. USDA Grades A and AA butters are made with sweet cream and are used most often. Grade AA butter is of superior quality, with a fresh sweet flavor and aroma, smooth creamy texture, and the best color. Grade A butter is good quality and has a pleasing flavor and a smooth texture. Grade B butter is made from sour cream and is used most often by commercial food manufacturers.

Purchasing and Storage

Butter for foodservice use is generally marketed in quarter pound cubes, four per box, and either salted or unsalted. If salt has been added, it should be only slightly detectable and not salty. Salt will increase the shelf-life slightly and may mask subtle unpleasant flavors. Butter color will vary among manufacturers and will depend on the time of year, the breed of cow, and the food the cow eats. Unsalted butter is sometimes referred to as sweet butter; however the designation indicates only that the butter was made from sweet cream and not sour cream. When unsalted butter is required, it is important to specify unsalted.

European-style butter has a higher milk-fat content—usually between 82 and 86 percent—without added salt. It may be churned from cultured cream, which gives it a more pronounced flavor. Whipped butter has air incorporated into it for easier spreading. Clarified butter is made by heating whole butter gently and separating the fat (clarified butter) from the water and milk solids (yield approximately 75 percent).

Butter will easily absorb flavors from strong foods or refrigerator and freezer odors. When tightly covered and held between 32 and 35°F butter will keep for 4 weeks. At 0°F or below, it will keep for 6 months.

Grains, Pasta, Flours, and Other Starches

- General Information
- Purchasing and Storage
- Cooking and Recipes (see Chapter 14, p. 559)

GRAINS

Grains are the edible seeds of a variety of grasses that are used extensively on menus because of their nutritional attributes and versatility. Grains are available whole or milled into various shapes and sizes. The milling process determines the characteristics of the end product and the uses for which it is suitable. Basic milling processes include cracking, grinding, hulling, and pearling. Cracking breaks open the grains, grinding reduces the grain to small particles of differing degrees of fineness, hulling removes the protective husk or covering, and pearling removes most or all of the hull, bran, and germ.

All grains have a similar structure. An outer layer of papery skin called *bran* covers the grain. Bran has very little flavor and is a good source of fiber. *Endosperm* is the starchy, central portion of the grain that contains most of the grain's starch and protein but very little fat or minerals. White flour is primarily from the endosperm. The *germ* is the embryo of the plant and is rich in protein, fats, and minerals. The germ remains in whole-meal flour but is removed partially or entirely from white flour. Because of the high fat content, grain products that contain the germ portion will become rancid if exposed to air or stored for a long period of time.

Grain products are often enriched by adding back in the nutrients that were removed by the milling process. Enrichment standards for wheat flour include adding thiamin, riboflavin, niacin, iron, and folic acid to white flour. Some grain products are fortified with vitamins and minerals beyond the enrichment standards.

Grains are often used as thickening agents because the starch granules absorb water and swell when heated with liquid. Common grain thickening agents are cornstarch and wheat flour.

Purchasing and Storage

The most common cereal grains are barley, corn, oats, rice, rye, and wheat. Other grains that are gaining in popularity include amaranth, buckwheat/kasha (which is considered with grains but is not a type of wheat or even a grain), millet, and quinoa.

Amaranth is an old grain (very tiny seeds) regaining popularity because of health claims. It is not readily available in all markets.

Barley is a grain with a sweet earthy flavor and a chewy-to-soft texture. A softer texture will result from cooking barley in a large amount of liquid, as in a soup. Pearled barley is the usual form used in cooking. In processing pearled barley, the outer hull

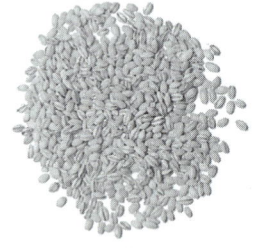
Barley

is removed, leaving a small, round, white pearl of grain. Barley is used in soups and is also used like rice in pilafs. It requires a longer cooking time than rice.

Buckwheat/Kasha is not a grain, but rather fruit from a plant. It has a distinctive nutty, earthy flavor. Whole buckwheat kernels are called groats. Kasha is the whole roasted buckwheat groat with a dark reddish brown color

Buckwheat/Kasha

that is most often used as a side dish or in a salad. Whole kasha remains in separate grains after cooking. Raw buckwheat groats are ground into flour and used for griddle cakes and blinis, and in pasta. Because of its sandy texture and the absence of the gluten necessary for structure, buckwheat flour should be used with wheat flour in recipes.

Corn is a grain food that is eaten both as a vegetable (sweet corn) and as a dried grain product (from field corn). In its dried form, corn is marketed in several ways. *Cornmeal* is made by drying and grinding field corn into coarse or fine grinds. White and yellow cornmeal are most common,

Cornmeal

but blue cornmeal is available in some markets, especially in the Southwest area of the United States. Cornmeal has a sweet starchy flavor and a gritty texture. It can be used in quick breads and flat breads but, because it does not contain gluten, it must be combined with wheat flour for yeast breads. It is the main ingredient in grits, polenta, and mush.

Hominy is the endosperm of the corn kernel that is removed from the bran and germ by a drying and soaking process using lime or lye. Dried hominy can be ground into grits (hominy grits) or into a flour (masa harina), which is used for making many Mexican and Southwestern dishes. Hominy has a soft, chewy, starchy texture when cooked. Cooked hominy is generally purchased canned. Hominy is also known as pozole.

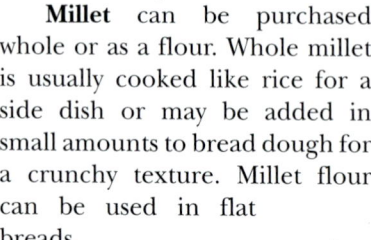
Hominy

Millet can be purchased whole or as a flour. Whole millet is usually cooked like rice for a side dish or may be added in small amounts to bread dough for a crunchy texture. Millet flour can be used in flat breads.

Grits

Oats are a whole-grain product used for hot cereal and in many baked goods. *Rolled* or *old-fashioned oats* are made from whole oat

Millet

Oats

kernels, with only the husks removed (oat groats), that have been steamed, then rolled into flat flakes. *Quick-cooking oats* (quick oats) are rolled oats cut into smaller pieces to reduce the cooking time. *Instant oats* have been partially cooked and dried before rolling. They need only to be rehydrated in boiling water. Rolled and quick-cooking oats are interchangeable with a slightly different texture resulting. Instant oats should not be substituted for rolled or quick-cooking oats.

Quinoa (keen-wa) is the seed of a South American plant similar to spinach and is not botanically a grain. The small flattened spheri-cal seeds are used similar to rice. Because they have a naturally bitter outer cover-ing, they should be rinsed several times before cook-ing. Quinoa seeds range in color from dark brown to almost white (considered superior). They become translucent when cooked and will absorb water at twice their volume (1 cup dry equals 2 cups cooked).

Quinoa

Rice is the seed of an semi-aquatic plant grown in several areas of the United States and in many coun-tries. Although rice fits into the foods of most cultures, it is always associated with Asian and Spanish cuisines. Rice's versatility makes it an important food staple throughout the world.

Three major types of rice are available. *Long-grain rice* cooks up firm and fluffy with grains that are in-clined to separate. Overcooking or excessive stirring while cooking will cause long-grain rice to become sticky. Long-grain rice is excellent for serving as a side dish, in salads, and in casseroles. It retains its texture when held on a steam table or buffet line. *Medium-grain rice* cooks up tender and moist, with the grains tending to cling together. Medium-grain rice becomes sticky when cool, so it is best served hot. It requires less water to prepare than long-grain rice. Medium-grain rice has a higher starch content than long-grain rice. The small, nearly round kernels of *short-grain rice* become very tender and sticky when cooked. Risotto, sushi, and rice pudding are made with short-grain rice. Short-grain rice has a high starch content.

Processing procedures differ to produce rice with different characteristics. *Brown rice* is the whole unpol-ished grain with only the outer husks and a small amount of bran removed. It has a nut-like flavor and a slightly chewy texture. Brown rice is available in short, medium, or long grain. Shelf life of brown rice is shorter than that of white rice because of the oil content.

Brown Rice

Regular or *white rice* has been milled or polished to remove the outer husk and layers of bran. Regular or white rice is sometimes called *polished rice*. Both brown and white rice can be processed into con-verted and instant or quick-cooking rice.

Converted (parboiled) rice undergoes a steam pressure process and is dried before milling. Af-ter cooking, the grains of converted rice remain separate and plump. Con-verted rice has good hold-ing quality after cooking. It is neither pre-cooked nor instant and requires a longer cooking time than regular or milled white rice. Converted rice is most often used in foodservice.

Converted Rice

Precooked (instant) rice has been milled, cooked, and dehydrated. It needs only to be rehydrated to be ready to use. Precooked rice does not hold well after cook-ing; the grains quickly loose their shape and become soft and mushy.

During the milling process, white rice and con-verted rice are often enriched to replace the vitamins and minerals lost in the milling process when the bran and germ portion of the grain are removed. Vitamins and minerals are usually added to the outside of the kernel in the form of a white powdery substance. To re-tain the vitamins and minerals, white rice and con-verted rice should not be rinsed before or after cooking.

Many varieties of rice are imported to the United States or grown domestically. Following are the vari-eties often used in foodservice.

Aromatic or fragrant rices have subtle floral, nutty, or earthy nuances. *Basmati* cooks to a dry, fluffy texture with separate grains similar to regular long-grain rice. Basmati rice is extra long-grained. *Thai jasmine* or *jasmine* long-grain rice cooks up soft and tender. It is very fragrant with a more sub-tle flavor than basmati.

Basmati Rice

Italian short-grain rice has polished white kernels that are a little longer than they are wide. Aborio rice, used for risotto, is a common short-grain rice. It is very sticky with a white color.

Aborio Rice

Spanish rice is similar to Italian short-grain rice but, when cooked, it is a little lighter in texture. Spanish rice absorbs liquid evenly and retains an al dente mouthfeel. Grana and Valencia are two rice varieties often used for making Spanish paella.

Sticky or *glutinous rice*, also called *sweet rice*, becomes extremely sticky when cooked. Sticky rice is used almost exclusively for Asian cooking and often for dessert dishes. The grains become bouncy and full when cooked. Sticky or glutinous rice has a high starch content and pearly white color.

Wild rice is not a rice but a seed of an aquatic reed-like grass. It has long, unpolished kernels; an intense nutty flavor; a dark brown to black color; and a firm, chewy texture. Wild rice is usually combined with other rices and ingredients for stuffing, salads, and side dishes. The

Wild Rice

longer grains are considered the best quality. Wild rice should be rinsed before using.

Rye is a grain used primarily as a flour for making bread. It is available in three grades—light, medium, and dark—and either flaked or as a pearled grain.

Wheat is a widely cultivated plant used for food products throughout the world. In addition to a wide range of flours, other wheat products are available for use in recipes.

Bulgur is the whole wheat kernel or wheat berry that has the bran removed. It is steam cooked and dried before being ground to various degrees of coarseness. It has a nut-like texture and flavor. Because bulgur is precooked, it cooks faster than whole

Bulgur

wheat. Whole wheat and bulgur are not interchangeable in recipes. Bulgur is often used in recipes originating in Turkey, Greece, the Middle East, and North Africa. Tabbouleh is a well-known ethnic salad using bulgur.

Couscous is the endosperm of a durum wheat berry that is steamed and pressed to form granular pellets of various sizes and then dried. Most couscous is pre-cooked (instant couscous) and needs only to be moistened with hot or boiling liquid and held for 5

Couscous

minutes. The process for cooking couscous that has not been pre-cooked requires fairly long periods of soaking and steaming.

Cracked wheat and whole wheat is the whole kernel of wheat (wheat berry) without the bran removed. The wheat berry is either left whole or broken into varying degrees of coarseness without first cooking. To soften the kernels, wheat berries should be soaked for 24 hours before being cooked in double their volume of water.

Wheat germ contains the fat from the wheat kernel and is a good source of protein, fiber, B and E vitamins, and iron. It can be substituted for approximately 20 to 30 percent of the flour in bread. It can be purchased defatted for longer storage—up to 6 months.

All grain products should be stored in a cool, dry, well-ventilated location. Because they have a higher oil content than highly processed grains, the shelf live of whole grain products will be extended if refrigerated.

PASTA

Pasta is a generic name for a basic dough mixture of durum semolina or other high-protein hard wheat flour and water. With the exception of noodles, which usually contain eggs, the various pasta products are made from the same basic dough. Flavor variations are many and include carrot, cracked black pepper, herb, garlic, lemon-pepper, tomato, and spinach.

Asian-style pastas are different from Italian pastas in that they may be made with rice, bean, and buckwheat flour as well as wheat flour. *Asian wheat noodles* or *Asian egg noodles* are known as *somen noodles* when thin and *udon noodles* when thick. Thin *rice noodles* are often fried in hot fat and cook very quickly to a white, puffy, crunchy product. *Bean starch noodles,* also known as *bean threads, cellophane noodles,* and *glass noodles,* are thin transparent noodles made from mung beans and can be fried in the same way as rice noodles. Buckwheat flour noodles are known as *soba noodles.*

Purchasing and Storage

Pasta shapes can be categorized into five basic groups: string (e.g., spaghetti), ribbon (e.g., noodles), tubes (e.g., penne), shapes (e.g., radiatore), and mini pastas (e.g., acini). There are hundreds of pasta shapes. The shapes used most often in foodservices appear in Figure 3.2. Pasta may be purchased fresh, frozen, or dry. Pre-cooked pasta is available in some markets.

Dry pasta will keep for several months when stored in a cool, dry, well-ventilated storage area. Fresh pasta should be wrapped tightly and stored in a refrigerator. Because fresh pasta is perishable, it should be used within 2 or 3 days.

Name	*Shape*	*Description*
Alphabets		Miniature pasta in letter shapes. Used in soups.
Bow ties, farfalle		Bow-shaped noodles. Used with entree sauces and also soups or salads.
Capellini, angel hair	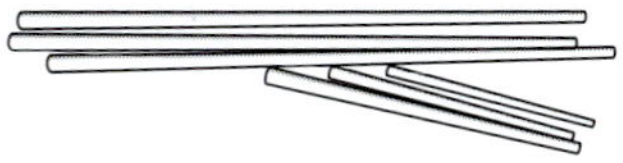	Delicate long thin threads. Used with light sauces.
Cavatappi	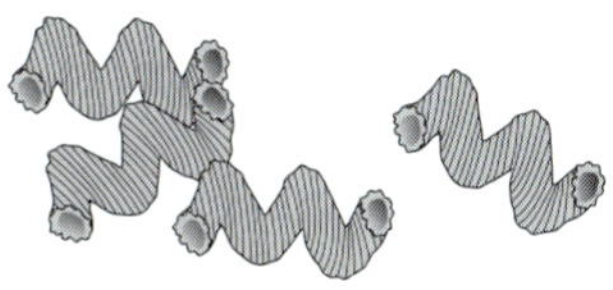	Spiral, ridged tubes (corkscrews). Used in casseroles and with sauces.
Conchiglie, shells	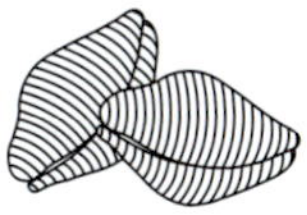	Shell shaped. Used with sauces; larger shells stuffed, smaller shells used in salads. Jumbo shells stuffed with cheese, meat, vegetables.
Dumplings	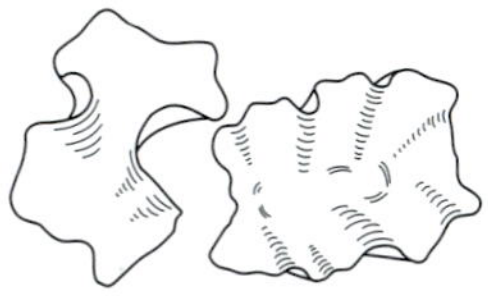	Flat, with rippled edges. Used in soups and baked casseroles.
Fettuccine	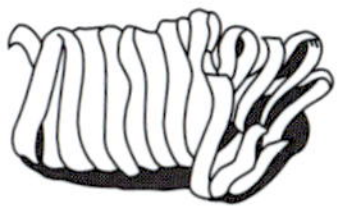	Pasta shaped like ribbons, slightly thick. Used with heavy creams or meat sauces.
Fusilli		Long strands of spiraled spaghetti, corkscrew shaped. Used with thick cream sauces or casseroles. Break into soups.

FIGURE 3.2   Shapes and descriptions of selected pasta.

continues

Name	Shape	Description
Kluski		Long narrow egg noodles, with homemade appearance. Used for soups, baked casseroles, and with cream sauces.
Lasagna	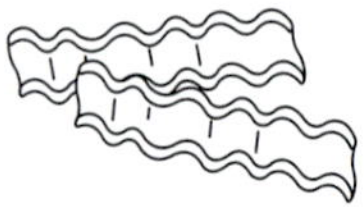	Wide, long, flat noodles with wavy edges. Baked layered with cheeses and sauces.
Linguine	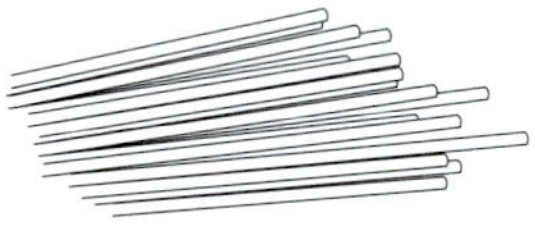	Thin narrow rods, slightly flattened. Used with all sauces, especially cream sauces.
Elbow macaroni		Short tubes that are slightly curved. Used in salads and casseroles.
Macaroni	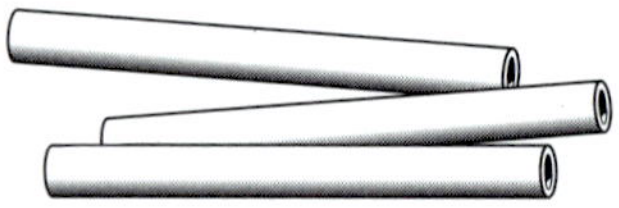	Long hollow round tubes, straight cut ends. Baked in casseroles or with sauces.
Manicotti		Giant pasta tubes. Stuffed with cheese or meat fillings.
Mostaccioli	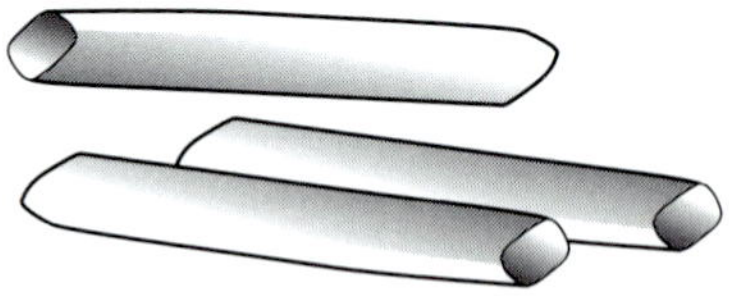	Medium-sized hollow tubes, ends cut diagonally. Used in baked casseroles or with sauces.

FIGURE 3.2   *Continued*

Name	Shape	Description
Noodles	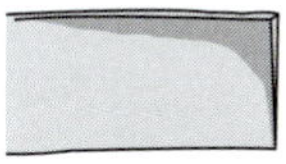 X-Wide Noodles  Wide Noodles  Medium Noodles	Narrow flat pasta; typically contains egg. Used in a variety of casseroles, with sauces, and as a side dish.
Orecchiette	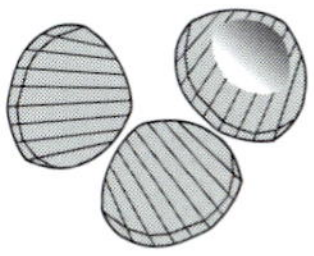	Ear shaped. Used in casseroles, with sauces.
Pastina (tiny dough) Ditalini	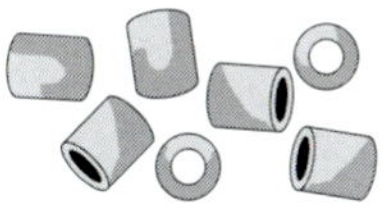	Used in soups and salads. Very short hollow tube.
Orzo		Shaped like rice. Used in soups, salads, and as a side dish.
Stelline		Star shaped.
Acini	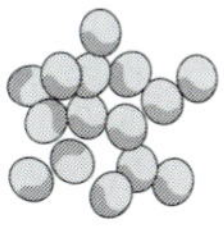	Small round shape.
Penne rigate	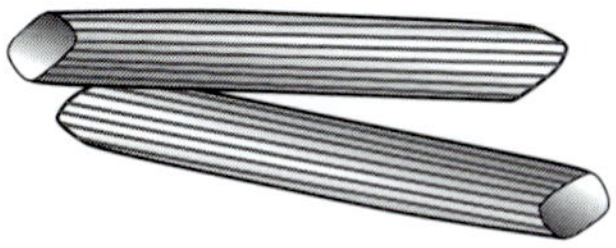	Grooved medium-size hollow tubes, ends cut diagonally. Used in baked casseroles or with sauces.
Radiatore	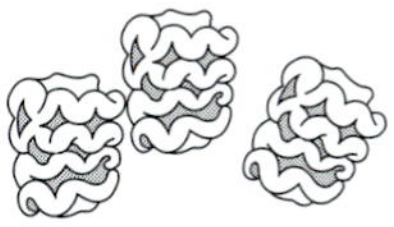	Frilly shaped pasta, short, thick, and compact. Used for salads, casseroles, with sauces, and in soups.
Rigatoni	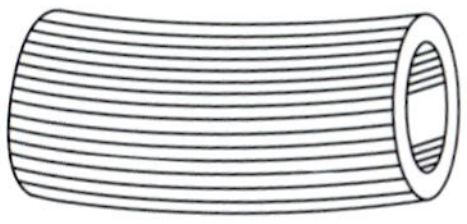	Large ribbed hollow tubes. Used in baked casseroles or with sauces.

FIGURE 3.2

continues

Name	Shape	Description
Rotini		Spiraled pasta. Used in baked casseroles or with salads.
Spaghetti	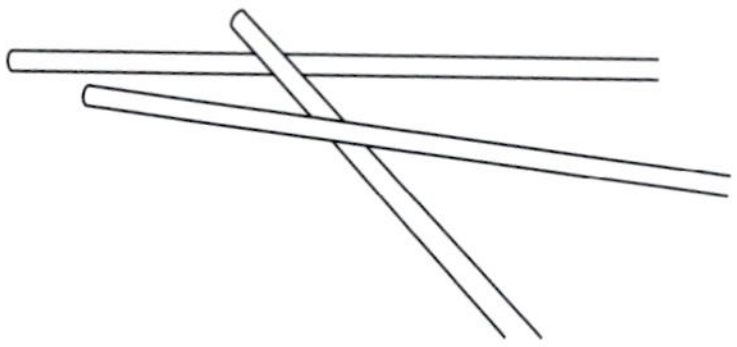	Long round rods. Used with all sauces, especially tomato. Used in casseroles.
Spaghettini	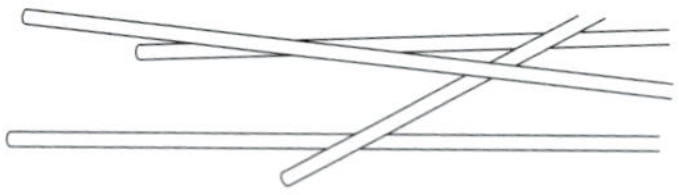	Thin round rods. Used like spaghetti, typically with light sauces.
Vermicelli	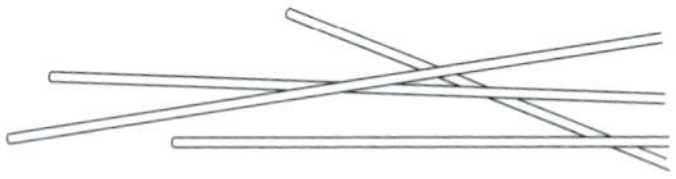	Extra thin spaghetti-like rods. Used with light delicate sauces.
Wagon wheels		Die-cut shape resembling wheels. Used with sauces, in salads and soups.
Ziti	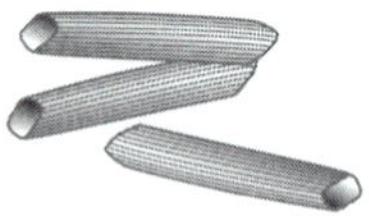	Short, hollow, round, medium-size tubes with straight cut ends; resembles large macaroni. Used in baked casseroles or with sauces.

FIGURE 3.2   *Continued*

FLOURS, MEALS, AND OTHER STARCHES

Flours, meals, and starches are staples in food production kitchens. They are used for breads and baked sweet goods, and for thickening fillings, soups, and sauces. Table 3.5 identifies flours, meals, and starches.

Meat—Beef, Lamb, Pork, Veal

- General Information
- Purchasing
- Storage
- Cooking Methods (see Chapter 4, p. 189)
- Recipes (see Chapter 12, p. 479)

MEAT—BEEF, LAMB, PORK, VEAL

The quality of cooked meat depends on the quality purchased, the storage and handling of the meat after delivery, and cooking methods. All meats marketed in interstate commerce in the United States must meet federal inspection standards for wholesomeness. This

TABLE 3.5   Flours, meals, and other starches

FLOURS/MEALS/STARCHES

Wheat flours

All-purpose	Several flours blended to yield a flour with lower protein content than bread flour. For general foodservice use including breads, pastries, and basic cakes.
Bread	A high-protein white flour made from hard wheat. Used for bread products in which gluten development is desirable. Produces a bread with high volume.
Cake	A very low-protein white flour made from soft wheat. Used for delicate and fine-textured cakes where gluten development is undesirable.
Enriched	Enriched flour has iron and B vitamins added. Flour sold in interstate commerce must be enriched with iron, thiamin, riboflavin, niacin, and folic acid. Vitamin D and calcium are optional additions.
Instant	All-purpose flour that has been processed by moistening and re-drying to produce a product that flows freely without packing. Because it blends easily with liquids it is used for thickening sauces and gravies. Instant flour is not interchangeable with other flours for baking.
Gluten	Wheat flour mixed with dried extracted gluten to increase the protein content. Used to adjust the protein levels of various doughs.
Pasta	Flour made from hard durum wheat. Makes a sturdy dough desirable for pasta.
Pastry	A low-protein white flour usually made with soft wheat. Used for pastries and cookies where gluten development is undesirable.
Self-rising	A white flour that has leavening agents and salt added.
Whole wheat	Also called graham flour. Flour made by grinding the entire wheat kernel to different degrees of fineness. Higher in fiber than white flour because whole wheat flour contains the bran.

Other flours

Amaranth flour	Made by grinding amaranth seed. High content of the amino acid lysine. Added to wheat bread and other baked products for its nutritional contribution.
Buckwheat flour	Contains no gluten. Used primarily in pancakes and waffles.
Corn flour	Corn flour is a fine grind of cornmeal made from either white or yellow corn. Contains no gluten so it must be added to wheat flour when used in yeast breads. Used primarily for quick breads.
Masa harina flour	Masa harina is a flour made from finely ground hominy. Used for making tortillas, tamales, and other Southwestern dishes.
Potato flour	Primarily potato starch.
Rice flour	Primarily rice starch.
Rye flour	Results from sifting rye meal. Contains small amount of gluten but is usually combined with wheat flour in baking.
Soy flour	A flour made from soybeans. High in protein but contains no gluten and must be used with wheat flour in breads.
Triticale flour	Made from a grain that is a cross between wheat and rye. Some varieties contain enough gluten to make a satisfactory yeast bread.

Other starches

Arrowroot	A fine starchy powder made from the root of a tropical plant. Used as a thickener.
Filé	Fine powder made from sassafras leaves. Used as a thickener, especially in gumbo.

requirement covers all processed meat products and fresh and frozen meats. Meat slaughtered, processed, and sold within a given state must be inspected using criteria at least equal to federal inspection standards. Government inspection of all meat is mandatory.

Quality grading helps predict the palatability of meat. Beef grades are based on two factors: the amount of marbling present and the age of the animal. Marbling is judged by the amount of inter- and intramuscular fat in the meat. Each grade denotes a specific level of quality as determined by the USDA.

Yield grading is a system used for some meats that estimates the percentage of boneless and closely trimmed foodservice cuts that can be obtained from a carcass. These grades identify carcasses for differences in cutability or yield and are applied by the USDA grading service. Meat grading is voluntary. Table 3.6 identifies quality and yield grades used for meat. Grade and yield stamps are shown in Figure 3.3.

Special types of meat are available, such as "certified angus beef," "organic," and "natural." Meats marked with these or other special designations are often more expensive. To help recoup the cost, the special distinctions should be obvious to customers. Before using the special distinctions, know what standards are implied. Standards for organic and natural are not well established and may vary among producers or distributors.

Wet aging or *dry aging* may be used to improve the tenderness and flavor of beef. Pork, veal, and lamb are usually not aged because they are slaughtered at a relatively young age when the meat is most tender. Wet aging occurs in the vacuum package in which the meat is sealed. Dry aging is the process of holding meat, uncovered in a sanitary environment, under controlled temperature and humidity for 3 to 4 weeks. Meat is tenderized and undergoes a flavor change because natural enzymes and microorganisms begin to break down the meat tissue. Because of the more intense flavor and tenderness of dry-aged meat, it can be effectively merchandised on a menu and priced higher than wet-aged products. Weight loss during the dry aging process reduces the yield and makes dry-aged meat more expensive than wet-aged meat.

Purchasing

Meat for foodservice use is available in primal (wholesale) cuts, subprimals, and portioned or retail cuts. The chuck, loin, rib, and round are the major wholesale cuts of beef, making up 76% of the carcass. The primal cuts for beef, lamb, pork, and veal are shown in Figures 3.4, 3.5, 3.6, and 3.7.

Subprimals are produced by breaking down the primals into smaller cuts. Portioned or retail cuts are processed from subprimals into individual steaks, chops, and other products. For example, a strip loin (subprimal cut) is processed from the loin (primal cut) and may be further fabricated into a Kansas City Strip Steak (portioned or retail cut). Decisions about whether to purchase large or small cuts must be based on the skills of employees to break down larger cuts, the ability to use the trim and bones, the amount of available refrigeration storage, the volume of meat used, and the cost difference that considers both product and labor costs. Portion cuts generally have the advantage of being more uniform, making costs more easily controlled. Their packaging often allows for safer, more efficient storage.

The National Association of Meat Purveyors (NAMP) publishes a *Meat Buyers Guide* that identifies meat products and cuts. Because the guide is based on USDA's Institutional Meat Purchasing Specifications (IMPS) and is used universally in the foodservice industry, it is a useful communication tool for purchasing personnel and vendors. Recipes and pro-

TABLE 3.6   Quality and yield grades for meat

Beef*	Veal	Pork	Lamb
		Quality grades	
Prime	Prime	U.S. No. 1	Prime
Choice	Choice	U.S. No. 2	Choice
Select	Good	U.S. No. 3	Good
Standard	Standard	U.S. No. 4	Utility
		Yield grades **	
1	na	na	1
2	na	na	2
3	na	na	3
4	na	na	4
5	na	na	5

* Commercial, Utility, Cutter, and Canner (for beef) and Utility (for veal) are lower grades and not purchased for general foodservice use.

** Number 1 represents the greatest yield (most lean), number 5 the smallest yield (least lean).

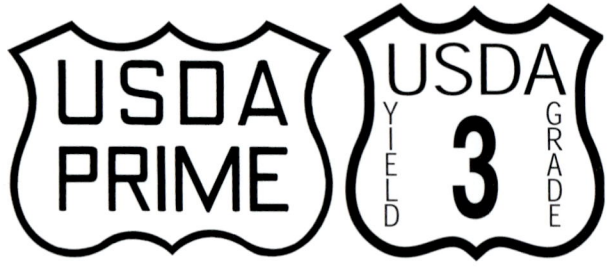

FIGURE 3.3   Quality grade and yield stamps for meat.

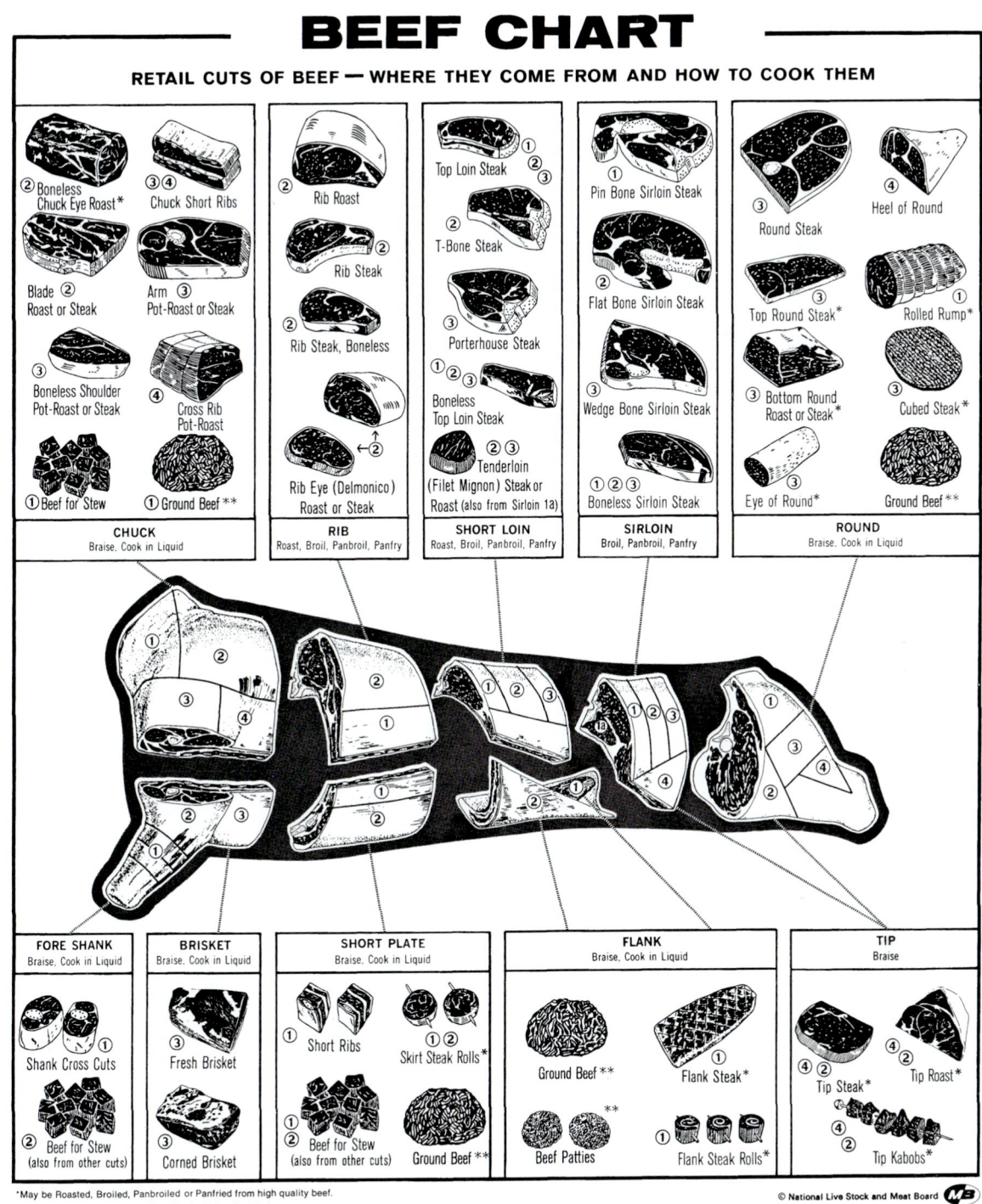

FIGURE 3.4 Primal and retail cuts of beef (Courtesy Cattlemen's Beef Board).

cedures may be standardized using specific IMPS/NAMP numbers. For example, a rib roast may be prepared from either an IMPS/NAMP number 109 or 112. Number 109 is a 16–22 lb oven-ready rib roast and number 112 a 6–8 lb rib eye roll. Yield and production procedures will differ between the two rib roasts. All purchasing offices should have a copy of the *Meat Buyers Guide*.

Storage

Storing meat in a refrigerator at a cold temperature is necessary to retard bacterial growth and slow the action of muscle enzymes. Store fresh meat loosely covered with waxed paper at a temperature of 28–32°F with a relative humidity of 85–90 percent. Vacuum-packaged meat should remain in its sealed package until used.

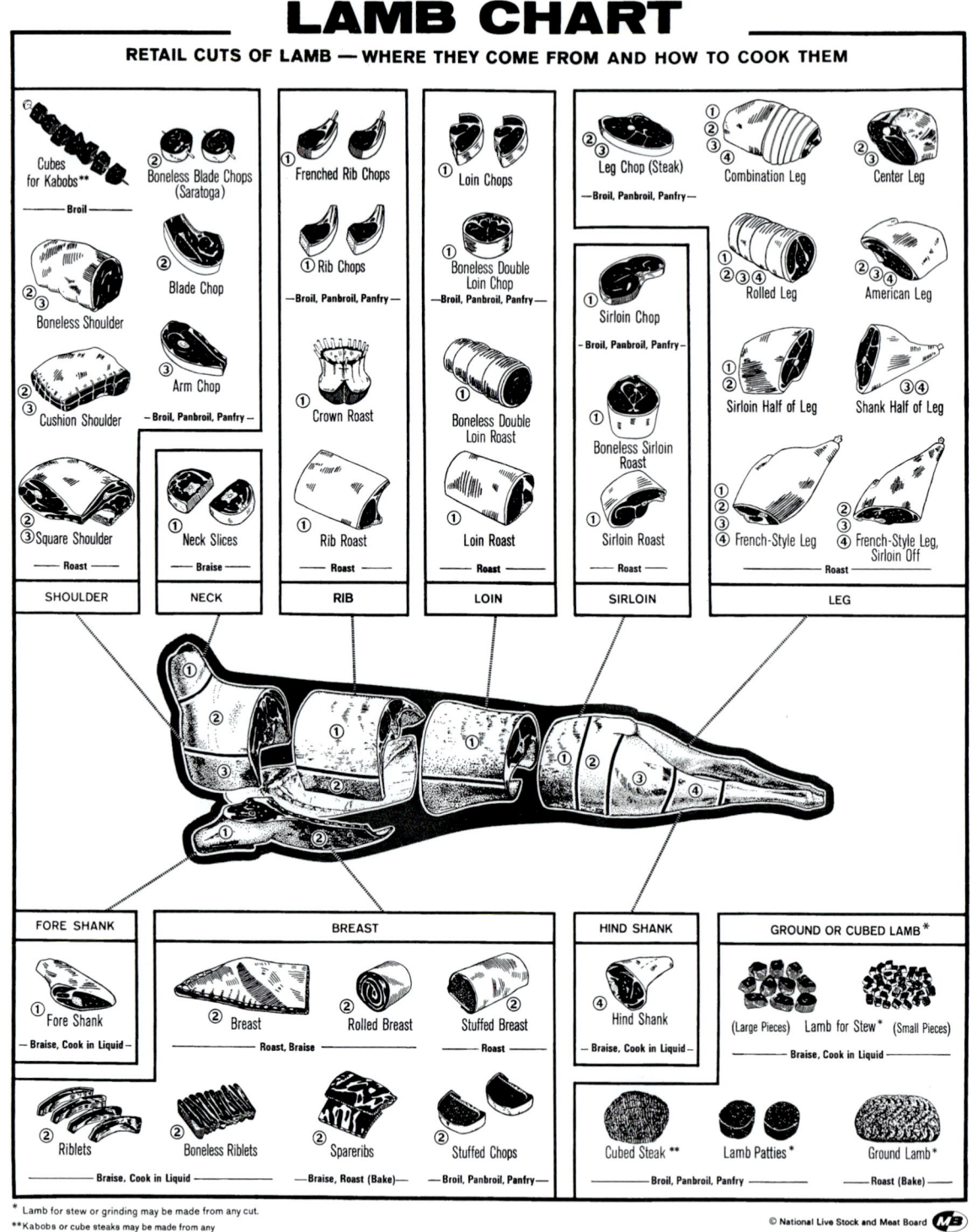

FIGURE 3.5   Primal and retail cuts of lamb (American Lamb Board).

Fresh meat should be used as soon after purchase as possible, not more than 3–4 days later. Fresh meat stored in a vacuum package (seal unbroken) will keep up to 21 days in the refrigerator. Once the vacuum seal is broken the meat should be used within 3–4 days.

Frozen meat requires a uniform holding temperature of 0°F or below. It should be well wrapped to exclude air and keep in moisture. When stored improperly, frozen meat may develop freezer burn causing the surface to discolor and look dehydrated.

PORK CHART

RETAIL CUTS OF PORK — WHERE THEY COME FROM AND HOW TO COOK THEM

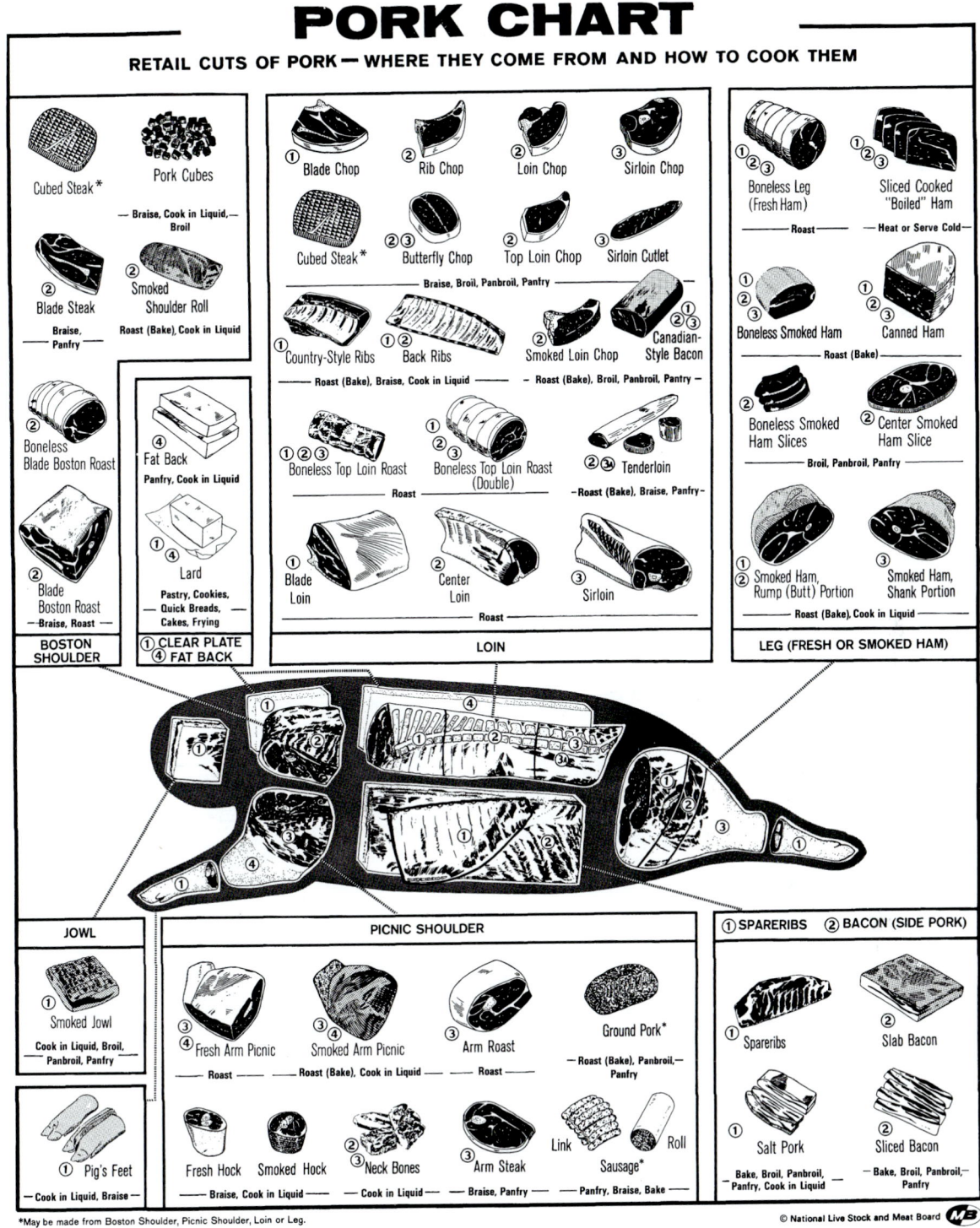

FIGURE 3.6   Primal and retail cuts of pork (Courtesy National Pork Board).

Fresh meat kept frozen at 0°F may be successfully stored for 6 months, and fresh beef kept frozen at −10°F for a year. Frozen meat should be kept wrapped while defrosting in a refrigerator at 30–35°F and should be cooked soon after defrosting. Once thawed, it should not be refrozen. Refreezing will result in some moisture loss and could pose a health risk if the total thawed time exceeds acceptable standards. Cooked meat may be frozen, provided it is frozen soon after cooking and cooling.

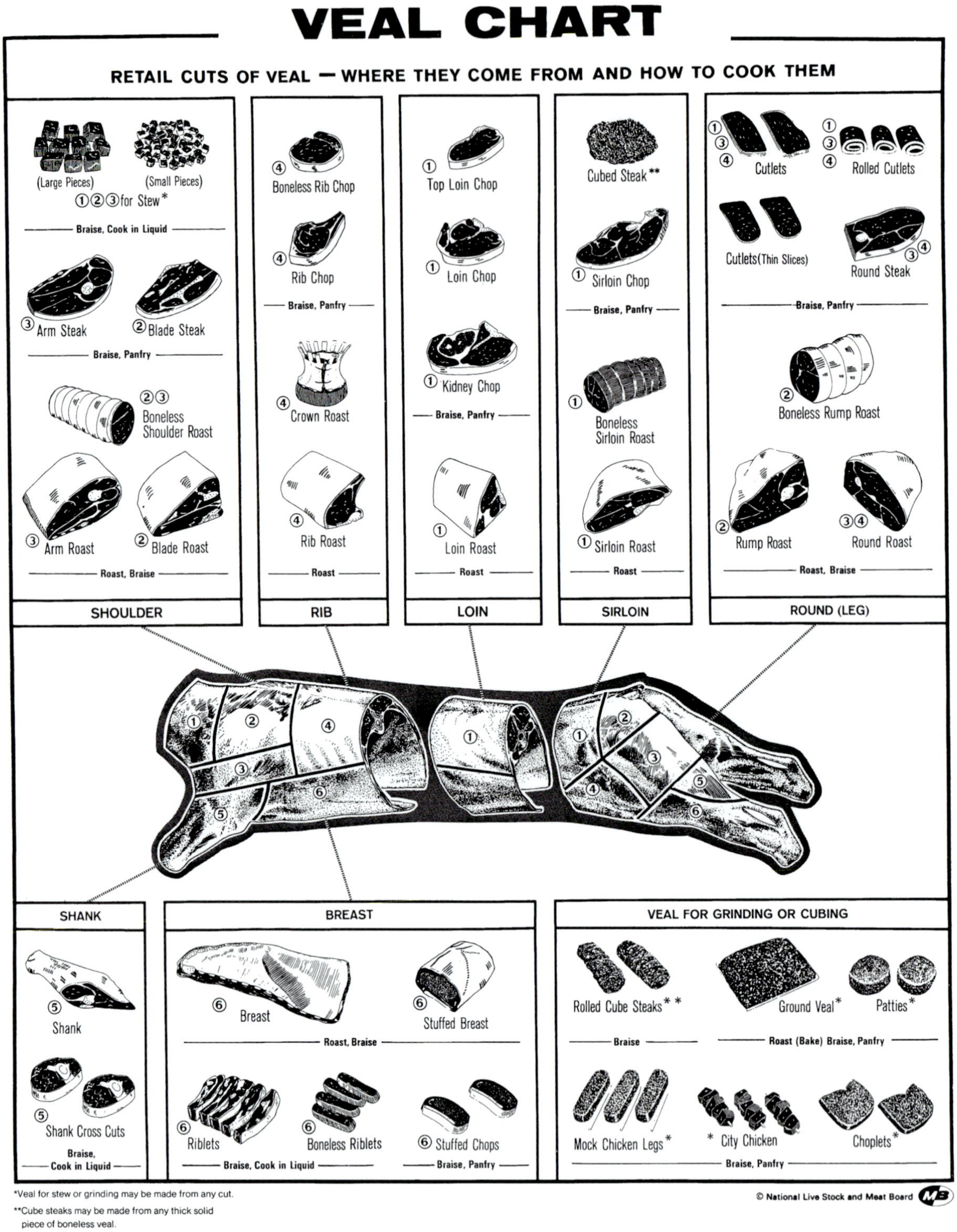

VEAL CHART

RETAIL CUTS OF VEAL — WHERE THEY COME FROM AND HOW TO COOK THEM

FIGURE 3.7   Primal and retail cuts of veal (Courtesy Cattlemen's Beef Board).

Meat that is frozen using equipment that freezes it quickly is superior to meat frozen in conventional freezers. For best quality, meat should be frozen quickly and thawed slowly. Quick freezing reduces the size of ice crystals, thereby lessening the number of ruptured muscle tissue cells and the amount of liquid lost during defrosting.

Cured meats and cured and smoked meats such as ham and bacon, sausages, and dried beef require refrigerator storage. Although ham, bacon, and other cured meats can be frozen, freezing should only be for short periods, since undesirable flavor changes occur because of their salt, spice, and fat content.

Poultry

- General Information
- Purchasing
- Storage and Safe Handling
- Cooking Methods (see Chapter 4, p. 189)
- Recipes (see Chapter 13, p. 527)

POULTRY

Poultry includes many different species of birds that are bred for eating. The popularity of poultry on menus results from its year-around availability, variety, relatively low cost, versatility, and customers' perceptions of a lower fat entree choice.

Federal law requires that all poultry sold for public consumption must be inspected by the USDA. Inspections ensure wholesomeness and that the products were processed according to USDA sanitary guidelines. Inspection involves only properties related to wholesomeness, not quality. Figure 3.8 illustrates a USDA inspection stamp for poultry that can be found on a hang tag attached to the bird or on the packaging label.

Grading poultry for quality is a voluntary but standard practice for most processors. USDA grades (A, B, or C) are identified by a shield-shaped hang tag attached to the bird or printed on the package label. See Figure 3.9. Grade A poultry is sold almost exclusively in wholesale and retail outlets. Lower grades are processed into poultry products, soups, etc. Quality grades are not meant to grade tenderness but rather to grade overall quality related to bird confirmation, thickness of flesh, fat covering, exposed flesh from skin tears, discolorations, feathers, and broken or disjointed bones.

FIGURE 3.8   USDA inspection stamp for poultry.

Grade Mark

FIGURE 3.9   USDA grade shield for poultry.

Purchasing

Poultry is available in many forms—fresh or frozen, whole or cut-up, bone-in or boneless, cooked or raw. The variety of cooked and processed poultry products continues to increase, opening up opportunities for new and labor-saving menu options. Decisions about whether to purchase whole or cut-up birds or raw or cooked products must be based on the menu, the skills of employees to cut whole birds into pieces, the ability to use the boney pieces for stock, the amount of refrigeration storage space, the volume of poultry used, and the difference in both product and labor costs. Portion cuts generally have the advantage of being more uniform, making costs easier to control, and their packaging often allows for safer storage. Figure 13.1, p. 529 illustrates procedures for cutting chickens into pieces.

Poultry is divided into six categories. Chicken, duck, goose, and turkey are the most commonly used, and guinea and pigeon are less common. The categories are subdivided into classes and are based primarily on age. Table 3.7 identifies the various categories and classes of poultry.

Storage

All poultry is highly perishable. Caution regarding cleanliness and temperature control should be exercised in storing as well as throughout the pre-preparation and cooking processes. Fresh chilled poultry should be stored at a temperature of 28–32°F and used within one to two days. Fresh turkeys can be kept for up to 4 days at these temperatures. Frozen poultry can be kept hard frozen at 0°F or less for up to 6 months. Once thawed, poultry may be kept safely for 24 hours at 32°F before cooking. Poultry should never be refrozen.

Poultry should be defrosted in a refrigerator. Place covered or wrapped poultry on trays to catch any drippings and arrange on refrigerator shelves so that air can circulate. Never thaw or store raw poultry so that the drippings will come in contact with cooked foods

TABLE 3.7   Categories and classes of poultry

	Weight	*Description*
CHICKEN CLASSES		
Cornish Game Hen	2 lbs or less	(Or Rock Cornish game hen) Young or immature Cornish chicken or Cornish and White Rock chicken (5–6 weeks). Very tender and flavorful. Suitable for all cooking techniques. Often roasted and served whole.
Broiler or Fryer	3½ lbs or less	Young (under 13 weeks), soft, pliable, smooth-textured skin and flexible breastbone cartilage. Tender and flavorful. Most versatile, suitable for all cooking techniques.
Roaster	3½–5 lbs	(Or roasting chicken) Young (3–5 months), soft, pliable, smooth-textured skin and somewhat less flexible breastbone cartilage than broiler or fryer. Tender and flavorful. Suitable for all cooking techniques.
Capon	6–10 lbs	Surgically unsexed male bird, under 8 months old. Soft, pliable, smooth-textured skin. Tender and flavorful. Usually roasted.
Stewing Hen	3½–8 lbs	Mature female (more than 10 months). Flavorful and less tender than roaster with non-flexible breastbone tip. Generally stewed or braised.
DUCK CLASSES		
Broiler or Fryer	2–4 lbs	Young (8 weeks or less), very tender. Usually roasted at high temperature but suitable for all cooking techniques.
Roaster	4–6 lbs	Young (16 weeks or less), tender, rich flavor, usually roasted.
Mature	4–6 lbs	Older bird (6 months or older). Toughened flesh, usually braised.
GOOSE CLASSES		
Young Goose	6–12 lbs	Tender, usually roasted.
Mature Goose	10–16 lbs	Toughened flesh. Usually braised or stewed.
TURKEY CLASSES		
Fryer-roaster	4–9 lbs	Immature bird (16 weeks or less), soft, pliable, smooth textured skin and flexible breastbone cartilage. Tender and flavorful. Meat can be cut into scallops and sautéd or pan-fried.
Young	8–22 lbs	Fully mature (8 months or less), soft, pliable smooth-textured skin, and somewhat flexible breastbone. Tender. Usually roasted. Sex designation is optional.
Yearling	10–30 lbs	Fully mature (15 months or less). Reasonably smooth-textured skin. Reasonably tender. Roasted or stewed. Sex designation is optional.
Mature	10–30 lbs	Older bird (over 15 months). Tough and usually ground or used as processed products.

Notes: • Pigeon (mature bird), squab (immature pigeon that has not begun to fly), and guinea fowl (domestic descendant of a game bird and related to a pheasant) are less common poultry choices. The meat of squab (4 weeks old or less) and young guinea fowl (3 months) is tender but toughens and darkens with age. Pigeon and squab are often considered a game bird along with partridge, pheasant, and quail.
  • Ratites are not considered a poultry class. They are flightless birds that include emu (native to Australia), ostrich (native to Africa), and rhea (native to South America). The meat is dark. Tenderness varies depending on where the meat is cut from the bird.

or foods ready to eat. Allow thawing time of 1 to 2 days for whole chickens and turkey roasts, and one day or less for cut-up chickens or small poultry pieces. Whole turkeys require approximately 5 hours thawing time for every pound of bird. Poultry should be completely thawed before cooking to ensure all parts will reach safe end-point temperatures. See Table 2.21, p. 102 for approximate defrosting times for poultry.

Handling poultry safely must always be a consideration because poultry is a potentially hazardous food and a potential carrier of illness-causing microorganisms, particularly salmonella bacteria. Good handling practices include the following:

• Keep fresh poultry refrigerated in the coldest part of the refrigerator (28–32°F). Limit the amount of time during production that poultry is held outside of refrigeration to 1 hour.

• Thaw poultry under refrigerated temperatures. (See Table 2.21 for approximate thawing times for poultry.)

- Keep raw poultry and raw poultry juices away from other foods, particularly cooked foods and foods ready to eat.
- Wash hands frequently and wash and sanitize countertops, cloths, cutting boards, knives, and other utensils used in preparing raw poultry before they come in contact with other raw or cooked foods.

Fish and Shellfish

- General Information
- Purchasing
- Storage
- Cooking Methods (see Chapter 4, p. 193)
- Recipes (see Chapter 11, p. 457)

FISH AND SHELLFISH

Fish and shellfish have increased in popularity on menus and, because of a reduced supply, have become increasingly expensive. On-ship and other processing technology and efficient transportation methods have, however, made a good quality and wide variety of fish and shellfish available to foodservice operators. In most markets, fish and shellfish are available as never frozen and sold as fresh or chilled, quickly frozen within hours of being caught and sold as flash frozen and fresh frozen, denoting they were frozen when fresh but not as quickly as flash frozen.

Fish and shellfish inspection by the U.S. Department of Commerce (USDC) is voluntary. Products inspected and certified under the USDC Seafood Inspection Program that meet all requirements and criteria specified can display the official marks or statements associated with the program.

Figures 3.10 and 3.11 illustrates a "Processed Under Federal Inspection" (PUFI) mark that can be used on labels of fish and shellfish processed under the USDC inspection program. This inspection covers processing plant, product, and processing methods from the time raw fish arrives at the plant to the final product. The inspection mark signifies that the product is certified to be safe, wholesome, and correctly labeled; conforms to quality and other criteria in the approved specification; and has been officially inspected in a USDC sanitarily approved facility under Federal inspection.

Fish sampled from a specific lot of finished product and meeting the standards and criteria can display a "Lot Inspection Mark." This inspection evaluates whether the product complies with purchase agreement specifications (such as condition of the product, weight, labeling), packaging standards, or other criteria determined by the customer paying for the inspection service.

Only fish and shellfish processed under the USDC Seafood Inspection Program in a sanitarily approved facility are eligible for grading (Figure 3.11). The grades assigned to fish are A, B, or C. Grade A products are sold primarily on the wholesale and retail market. Grade B and C products are generally processed or canned. An A Grade stamp is illustrated in Figure 3.12.

Fish and shellfish used in foodservice operations can be divided into four categories: fish, mollusks, crustaceans, and cephalopods. Fish may be either round or flat. *Round fish* have eyes on both sides of their head and swim vertically. *Flatfish* spend most of their life laying on their side on the ocean floor. They have asymmetrical bodies with both eyes on the same

FIGURE 3.11 Product inspection stamp for fish and shellfish.

FIGURE 3.10 Processed Under Federal Inspection (PUFI) mark for fish and shellfish.

FIGURE 3.12 Grade A stamp for fish and shellfish.

side of their head. The underside of flatfish is white and the top side is dark colored.

Mollusks are soft-bodied shellfish covered by a shell. Univalves such as abalone, snails, and conch are single-shelled. Bivalves are characterized by two shells joined by a hinge such as clams, mussels, oysters, and scallops.

Abalone   Blue Mussels

Crustaceans have a hard, jointed outer shell. Crabs, crayfish, lobster, and shrimp are examples of crustaceans.

Crayfish

Cephalopods have tentacles attached directly to the head. They have no hard outer shell but a single internal shell called a cuttlebone. Octopus and squid are cephalopods.

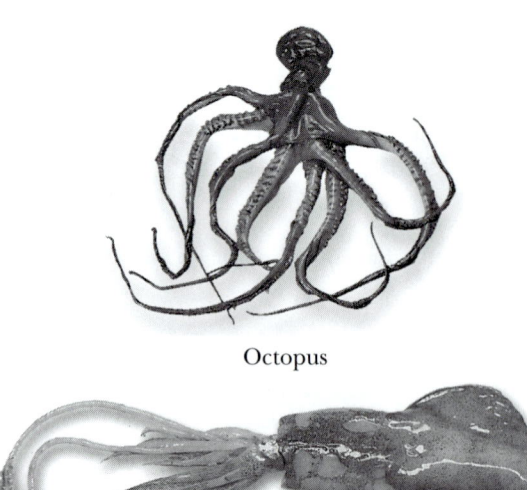

Octopus

Squid

Purchasing

Because fresh fish and shellfish are highly perishable, it is important to know how to identify freshness. The following criteria can be used to determine freshness:

1. *Smell.* Fish should not have a strong fishy smell or ammonia-like odor. A fresh, clean sea smell is acceptable. Regardless of the other indicators, a fish with very strong odors should be rejected or discarded.

2. *Eyes.* The eyes should be clear and bulge a little. Sunken and cloudy eyes indicate the fish is beginning to lose moisture and deteriorate. Only a few fish, such as walleye, have naturally cloudy eyes.

3. *Gills.* Bright red to maroon colored gills that are moist and fresh looking are a sign of freshness. Slimy and brown or grey gills are a sign of age.

4. *Flesh and Texture.* The flesh should be shiny with no brownish or yellowish discoloration. Firm, elastic flesh denotes freshness. A finger indentation should spring back after the flesh is depressed.

5. *Fins, Scales, Skin.* Fins and tails should be moist and flexible. They should not be ragged. Scales on fish with scales should be moist looking and firmly attached. The skin on fish without scales should be slick and moist.

6. *Movement.* Shellfish should be purchased live. Lobster and crab should be active and move about. Clams, mussels, and oysters should be tightly closed or snap shut when tapped with a finger.

Market Forms—Following are the most common market forms of fin fish.

Aberdeen Cuts—Rhombus-shaped cuts from a block of frozen fish are known as Aberdeen cuts; sides may be squared off or cut with a tapered edge. These usually are breaded or battered. Also called diamond cuts, French cuts.

Bits or Nuggets—Small pieces of fish breaded or coated with batter; usually weighing one ounce or less each. Shapes may be round, square, or irregular. Some are cut from regular blocks of fish; others are cut from frozen blocks of minced fish.

Boneless Fillet——The pinbones are removed from the fillet. Boneless fillets need not be completely boneless; U.S. Federal Grade Standards allow for an occasional small bone in Grade A fillets.

Drawn Fish—Drawn fish have the entrails, gills, and scales removed.

Fillet—A slice of fish flesh of irregular size and shape that is removed from the carcass by a cut made parallel to the backbone. Varies in size from 2–12 ounces.

Fingers—Fingers are irregular-shaped pieces of fish, similar to a long, thin fillet, that are breaded or battered. Weight per piece varies; usually available in portions of 1–3 ounces.

Fish Sticks—Sticks are rectangles of fish cut from a frozen block, usually 2 × 3 inches, weighing 1–2 ounces each, and breaded or battered.

Headed and Gutted—Head, tails, fins, and viscera have been removed before sale.

Portion—Usually a square or rectangle, cut from a block of frozen fish. Weights vary. Unbreaded or breaded.

Steaks—Slices of dressed fish, ready for cooking. Salmon, halibut, swordfish, and other large fish are commonly processed and sold as steaks.

Whole or Round Fish—Fish are sold just as they come from the water. Must be dressed before cooking.

The cost per edible portion in terms of both convenience and waste should be considered when deciding which form of fish to buy. Whole or round fish yield about 50 percent edible flesh after they have been eviscerated and scaled, and the head and fins have been removed; headed and gutted fish yield 70 percent; steaks 90 percent; and fillets and portions 100 percent. The standard on breaded portions is 25 percent breading and 75 percent fish when raw; 35 percent breading and 65 percent fish when oven finished. Battered portions are typically 50 percent batter and 50 percent fish. If portions are cut from whole fish, the heads, tails, and other trim should be used to make fish stock.

Table 3.8 identifies the usual market forms and characteristics of fish.

TABLE 3.8   Fish buying guide

Species	Fat or lean	Usual market forms	Characteristics
Bass, Sea	Fat	Fillets, steaks, whole, pan-dressed	Flaky, white; rich flavor
Bluefish	Fat	Fillets	Dark, turning light when cooked; mild
Catfish	Lean	Whole, dressed, fillets	Firm flesh; abundant flavor (fresh water fish)
Cod	Lean	Fillets, steaks, breaded portions	Mild flavor; soft white meat, flakes easily
Dolphin (mahimahi)	Lean	Fillets	Firm, white meat, flaky; delicate flavor
Flounder	Lean	Whole, pan-dressed, fillets, breaded	Delicate flavor; white flesh
Grouper	Lean	Whole, steaks, fillets	Firm white flesh; mild
Haddock	Lean	Whole, steaks, fillets, breaded portions	Firm white flesh; mild
Halibut	Lean	Steaks, fillets	Fine texture, snow white; mild delicate flavor
Monkfish	Lean	Fillets, tail only	Very firm, white flesh; mild flavor
Orange roughy	Lean	Fillets	Snow white flesh; delicate almost bland flavor
Perch, lake	Lean	Dressed, fillets	Firm flesh; sweet flavor (fresh water fish)
Perch, ocean	Lean	Whole, fillets, breaded fillets and portions	Firm, white, flaky; mild flavor
Pike, walleye	Lean	Whole, fillets, round	Snowy white meat; sweet flavor (fresh water fish)
Pollack	Lean	Fillets, breaded, portions	Firm, white; mild flavor
Pompano	Fat	Whole, fillets	Firm, white; full flavor
Redfish	Lean	Whole, fillets	Light firm flesh; sweet flavor
Red Snapper	Lean	Dressed, fillets, portions	Firm white flesh, flaky; mild, sweet flavor
Salmon, Atlantic	Fat	Dressed, steaks	Firm flesh, rich pink color; distinctive rich flavor
Salmon, Coho (or Silver)	Fat	Drawn, dressed, steaks, fillets	Firm flesh, pinkish flesh; distinctive salmon flavor
Salmon, King (or Chinook)	Fat	Drawn, dressed, steaks, fillets	Firm flesh, red-orange, flaky, distinctive rich flavor
Scrod (small Cod or Haddock)	Lean	Fillets, steaks, breaded portions	Firm, white flesh; mild
Shark	Fat	Steaks	Firm texture, white flesh; mild
Sole	Lean	Whole, fillets	Firm white flesh; delicate flavor
Swordfish	Fat	Steaks	Very firm texture, white when cooked; sweet
Tilapia	Lean	Whole, fillets	Firm texture, white; sweet flavor (farm raised only)
Trout, lake	Fat	Whole, drawn, fillets	Firm texture; rich flavor (fresh water fish)
Trout, rainbow	Lean	Whole, dressed, boned, fillets	Light delicate flesh; mild flavor (fresh water fish)
Tuna (ahi)	Fat	Steaks	Very firm, light grey when cooked; mild flavor
Turbot	Lean	Fillets	Firm, white; mild flavor
Whitefish	Fat	Whole, drawn, dressed, fillets	Tender white flesh; rich flavor (fresh water fish)
Whiting	Lean	Drawn, fillets, breaded portions	Firm texture, abundant flavor

Market Forms—Following are the most common market forms of shellfish.

Clams—Clams are available alive in the shell; shucked, fresh or frozen; and canned, whole or chopped.

Littlenecks

Cherrystones

Soft -Shell Clams

Crabs—Crabs may be purchased alive, but most are marketed cooked and frozen in the shell, as crab legs or claws, or as frozen or canned crab meat.

Blue Crab

Soft Shell Crabs

Dungeness Crab

King Crab Legs

Snow Crab Legs

Lobsters—Northern lobsters are marketed alive in the shell or as cooked meat, fresh or frozen. Rock or spiny lobsters are marketed only as lobster tails, usually individually quick frozen (IQF).

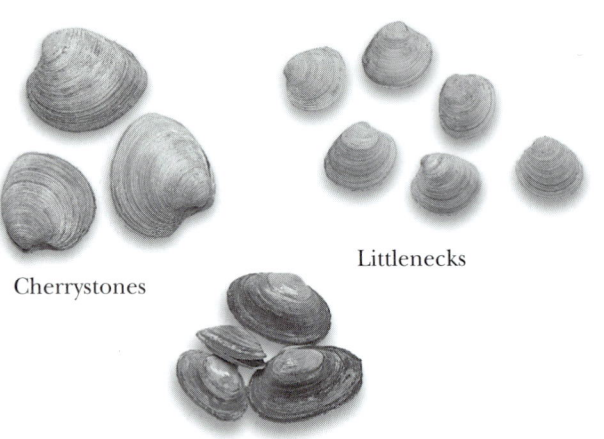

Maine Lobster

Oysters—Oysters are marketed alive in the shell; shucked, fresh, or frozen; and canned. Eastern oysters are larger and more readily available than Pacific oysters. Sizes of Eastern and Gulf oysters are given in Table 3.9.

Gulf Oysters

Bluepoint Oysters

Stone Crab Claws

CHEESES

Brie

Boursin

Gorgonzola

Havarti

Monterey Jack

Roquefort

Stilton

Cheddar

Emmenthaler (Swiss)

Gruyére

Asiago

Provolone

Parmigiano–Reggiano (Parmesan)

Shallots

Spinach

Acorn Squash

Banana Squash

Butternut Squash

Spaghetti Squash

Yellow Crookneck Squash

Tomatillos

Zucchini

Tomatoes

Turnips

Watercress

MUSHROOMS

White Mushrooms

Enokidake Mushroom

Oyster Mushroom

Morel Mushrooms

Portabella Mushroom

Shiitake Mushrooms

TABLE 3.9   Marketing sizes for oysters

Eastern and Gulf oysters		
Size	*Count per gallon*	*Pacific oysters sizes**
Counts or extra large	160 or less	Extra large
Extra selects or large	160–210	Large
Selects or medium (preferred for frying)	210–300	Medium
Standards or small	300–500	Small
Very small	over 500	Extra small

Based on information from the National Fisheries Institute, Washington, D.C.
*Pacific oysters generally do not require count per gallon sizing.

Scallops—Scallops are always sold shucked and are available fresh, by the gallon or pound; and frozen, as individually quick frozen (IQF), in 3- to 5-pound units, or frozen in block form in 5–pound units. Frozen breaded scallops for deep-fat frying are typically sold in 2½- to 3-pound units. They may be breaded whole or cut from a frozen block in uniform pieces for breading. Large sea scallops are graded in sizes from 10–70 count per pound; bay scallops are smaller and graded in sizes from 70–120 per pound.

Sea Scallops

Shrimp—Shrimp are available raw or cooked, fresh or frozen, shelled or in the shell. Raw shrimp in the shell are called green shrimp. Peeled and deveined (P&D) shrimp have had both the shell and sand vein removed. Peeled, deveined, and cooked (P&DC) shrimp have been cooked. Other terms used to specify the method of processing are butterfly (also called split or fantail), in which the shrimp have been cut along the vein; butterfly breaded, which are split part way through on the vein side, and spread open, then breaded; whole breaded, which are headless, usually deveined, and available tail on or off. Shrimp are sold by size or count per pound. The larger shrimp cost more than the smaller ones. The name prawn is usually given to large shrimp designated as jumbo or larger. Count and descriptive names for raw shrimp are given in Table 3.10.

Shellfish—Table 3.11 identifies market forms and characteristics of shellfish.

Tiger Shrimp

Green Headless Shrimp

Shrimp

Prawn

TABLE 3.10   Count and descriptive names for raw shrimp (not peeled)

Name	Count per pound
Extra colossal	Less than 10
Colossal	10–15
Extra jumbo	16–20
Jumbo	21–25
Extra large	26–30
Large	31–35
Medium large	36–50
Small	51–60
Extra small	More than 60

Note: Count per pound is more descriptive and a more accurate way to specify size.

Storing

Seafood must be stored at temperatures between 30 and 34°F to keep it safe and of a high quality. Fresh fish should be used within 2 to 3 days after receipt. The following procedures for storing fresh fish will help maintain freshness.

1. Upon receipt, check the fish for freshness. See p. 136 for criteria used to evaluate freshness. Fish may be rinsed but should be handled quickly to keep it cold, between 30 and 34°F.

2. Fresh fish should be shipped on a bed of shaved or chipped ice. Place the fish in a perforated pan and repack it with shaved or chipped ice. Be careful to pack ice completely around the fish and into the open belly of the fish. Position the fish so melting ice will drain from around the fish through the holes in the perforated pan. Fresh fish purchased as fillets or steaks and shellfish purchased out of the shell should be placed in waterproof packages before being packed in ice.

3. Set the perforated pan inside a solid pan with some distance between the bottom of the perforated pan and the solid pan. Water should drain away from the fish to prevent texture and flavor loss.

4. Drain and add shaved or chipped ice as necessary to keep the fish surrounded in ice and away from water.

Clams, mussels, and oysters should not be iced. They should be kept in the same bags or boxes in which they were delivered and stored with high humidity at a temperature between 35 and 40°F. Clams, mussels, and oysters will stay alive for 5 to 7 days under ideal storage conditions.

Crabs, lobsters, and other live shellfish should be delivered wrapped in moist seaweed or damp paper. If a saltwater tank is not available, they can be stored in their shipping container at 39 to 45°F for 3 to 5 days. Saltwater crustaceans will not live if stored in fresh water.

Discard shellfish if they are not alive or if their shells are cracked or broken. When alive, the shells of shellfish will close when tapped. Live crabs and lobsters should move about.

Frozen fish and shellfish stored at −20 to 0°F and covered adequately to protect it from freezer burn can

TABLE 3.11   Shellfish buying guide

Common name	Usual market forms	Characteristics
Abalone	Meat in shell	Tough flesh; delicate sweet flavor
Clams, quahog	Bushel, shucked	Large size, hard shell, chewy; not as sweet as other clams.
Clams, littleneck	Bushel	Small; sweet
Clams, cherrystone	Bushel	Slightly larger than littleneck; sweet
Clams, softshell	Bushel, shucked	Tender; sweet
Conch	Bushel	Very firm, chewy texture; sweet flavor
Crabs, blue, hardshell	Bushel, frozen meat	Tender; sweet
Crabs, blue, soft shell	Dozen	Tender; sweet
Crabs, rock	Bushel	Firm texture; sweet claw meat
Crabs, Dungeness	Whole	Firm texture; very sweet white meat
Crabs, king	Legs only	Firm texture; sweet white meat
Lobsters	Whole	Firm texture; very sweet flavor
Lobsters, spiny	Tails only	Firm texture, stringy; sweet
Mussels	Bushel	Slightly tough texture; sweet
Oysters	Bushel/sack/gallon	Range from firm to tender; slightly salty
Scallops, bay	Gallon	Very tender; very sweet (smaller than sea scallops)
Scallops, ocean	Gallon	Tender; sweet (larger than bay scallops)
Shrimp	By count (see Table 3.10)	Firm texture; white sweet meat

be stored for up to six months. Once thawed, fish should be treated as fresh.

Fresh Produce; Canned, Frozen Fruits and Vegetables; Dried Lentils, Beans, and Peas

- Fresh Produce—Grades, Yields, Availability, Storage
- Fresh Fruits, Vegetables, Herbs, and Edible Flowers—Pre-preparation Guidelines and General Information
- Canned and Frozen Fruits and Vegetables
- Tofu and Dried Beans, Lentils, and Peas
- Cooking and Recipes (see Chapters 14, 19; pp. 559, 823)

FRESH PRODUCE

Fresh produce is used in every menu category and is a staple in all foodservice kitchens. Because of its various menu applications, seasonal nature, and perishable characteristics, it is important for food production staff to have sufficient information for purchasing, storing, preparing, and handling produce correctly. This chapter provides the general information necessary for using fresh fruits and vegetables while meeting the quality standards required in today's competitive market place.

Fresh fruits and vegetables may be graded under the USDA voluntary grading program. Size, color, uniformity of shape, general appearance, maturity, and absence of defects are evaluated to assign grades to fresh produce. The USDA grades for all fresh fruits and vegetables are U.S. Fancy, U.S. No. 1, U.S. No. 2, and U.S. No. 3. U.S. No. 1 is the grade most often found on fresh fruits and vegetables. Not all grades are used for every fruit and vegetable classification and not all fruits and vegetables are graded.

Several factors should be considered before specifying a grade when purchasing fruits and vegetables.

- Purchasing top quality grades at the peak of harvest may not add the same value as it will during non-peak times. Time of year has a direct impact on the availability, price, quality, and appearance of fresh produce.
- Suppliers rarely sell all grades of produce. Communicating standards and product expectations to suppliers may achieve quality and value objectives.
- Suppliers may sell their products under a name or grade that is different from the USDA grade. Using common nomenclature is important.
- How fruits and vegetables will be used should be considered. For products in which exterior appearance is important (i.e., for individual fruit sales) the top-quality grade, and usually highest cost, may be appropriate. If appearance is not important, a lower-quality grade with a lower cost should be specified.

Fresh-cut or pre-cleaned produce is used in many foodservice operations and is one of the fastest growing segments of the produce industry. Because of the large demand and the production capabilities of large produce processors, the cost of some fresh-cut produce may be less than its uncut counterparts. When evaluating suppliers, it is important to ask questions about the reputation of the processors and to ask for documentation that they follow an approved HACCP plan. Assurance should be provided that safe raw produce is processed correctly in a clean, cold processing facility and distributed in a way that quality and product safety standards are met.

Table 3.12 provides yield, availability, and storage information for fresh fruits and vegetables.

This table provides information to calculate the amount of AP (as purchased) fruits and vegetables needed to yield the EP (edible portion) weight specified in a recipe. The information may also be used to calculate the approximate EP yield from AP fruits and vegetables. Because fruits and vegetables vary in size and quality and because processing procedures and techniques differ, the EP yields in this table are approximate.

- To calculate the amount of AP product needed to yield a specified amount of EP product, divide the desired EP weight by the figure given in the table. For example, the recipe for Mashed Potatoes on p. 856 specifies 12 lbs EP potatoes. To calculate the amount of potatoes to purchase (AP), divide 12 lbs by the number associated with white potatoes in the table (12 ÷ 0.81 = 14.8 lbs). In this example 15 lbs of potatoes would be purchased in order to yield the 12 lbs of peeled potatoes specified in the recipe.
- To calculate the amount of EP product that AP product will yield, multiply the AP weight by the figure given in the table. For example, to calculate the amount of peeled potatoes that a 15-lb bag of AP potatoes will yield, multiple the number associated with white potatoes by 15 lbs (15 × 0.81 = 12.15 lbs). In this example, 15 lbs of potatoes will yield 12 pounds of peeled potatoes.

TABLE 3.12   Yield, availability, and storage of fresh fruits and vegetables

Fruit/vegetable	Yield*	Availability	Storage (Raw, before paring, cutting, or processing.)	Ethylene
Apples	0.78	Some variety available year around. Peak: fall	35–40°F	Produces: Yes Sensitive: Yes
Apricots	0.76	Available May–Aug. Peak: Jun–Jul	32–36°F Ripen at room temperature	Produces: Yes Sensitive: Yes
Artichoke	0.35	Year around Peak: Mar–May	32–36°F	Produces: No Sensitive: No
Asparagus	0.60	Year around Peak: Mar–Jun	35–40°F	Produces: No Sensitive: Yes
Avocado	0.60	Hass variety available year around Peak: Dec–Apr	45–50°F unripe 34–38°F ripe	Produces: Yes Sensitive: Yes
Bananas (also see plantains)	0.65	Year around	60–65°F Do not refrigerate or store below 58°F	Produces: Yes Sensitive: No (after ripening)
Beans, green or wax	0.88	Year around Peak: May–Oct	45–50°F	Produces: No Sensitive: Yes
Beets, without tops	0.77	Year around	32–36°F	Produces: No
Beets, with tops	0.45	Peak: May–Oct		Sensitive: No
Belgian endive	0.95	Year around	32–36°F	Produces: No Sensitive: Yes
Blackberries	0.95	Jun–Oct	32–36°F	Produces: Low Sensitive: No
Blueberries	0.95	Jun–Oct Peak: late summer	32–36°F	Produces: Low Sensitive: No
Bok choy	0.75	Year around	32–36°F	Produces: No Sensitive: Yes
Broccoli	0.70	Year around	32–36°F	Produces: No Sensitive: Yes
Brussels sprouts	0.76	Year around Peak: Oct–Feb	32–36°F	Produces: No Sensitive: Yes
Cabbage, green (head)	0.80	Year around	32–36°F	Produces: No Sensitive: Yes
Cabbage, red (head)	0.64	Year around	32–36°F	Produces: No Sensitive: Yes
Cabbage, Savoy	0.75	Year around Peak: Aug–Apr	32–36°F	Produces: No Sensitive: Yes
Cantaloupe, peeled	0.52	Peak: Jun–Nov	32–36°F	Produces: Yes Sensitive: No
Carambola (star fruit)	0.92	Jul–Feb	45–50°F	Produces: Low Sensitive: No
Carrots	0.70	Year around	32–36°F	Produces: No Sensitive: Yes
Cauliflower	0.60	Year around Peak: Oct–Feb	32–36°F	Produces: No Sensitive: Yes
Celeriac (celery root)	0.75	Oct–Apr	32–36°F	Produces: No Sensitive: Yes
Celery	0.75	Year around	32–36°F	Produces: No Sensitive: Yes
Chard, Swiss	0.92	Year around Peak: Jul–Dec	32–36°F	Produces: No Sensitive: Yes
Cherries (sweet), pitted	0.80	May–Aug	32–36°F	Produces: Low Sensitive: No
Chicory	0.78	Year around	32–36°F	Produces: No Sensitive: Yes
Coconut		Year around	32–36°F	Produces: No Sensitive: No

TABLE 3.12   *continued*

Fruit/Vegetable	Yield[*]	Availability	Storage (Raw, before paring, cutting, or processing.)	Ethylene
Collards, leaves	0.57	Year around	32–36°F	Produces: No
Collards, leaves & stems	0.74	Peak: Dec–Apr		Sensitive: Yes
Corn, sweet	0.48	Year around	32–36°F	Produces: No
		Peak: Jun–Sep		Sensitive: No
Cranberries	0.95	Sep–Jan	45–50°F	Produces: No
		Peak: Nov–Dec		Sensitive: No
Cucumbers, peeled	0.84	Year around	45–50°F	Produces: Low
Cucumbers, peeled & seeded	0.68	Peak: Apr–Oct		Sensitive: Yes
Eggplant, unpeeled	0.85	Year around	45–50°F	Produces: No
Eggplant, peeled	0.70	Peak: Jul–Sep	Do not store below 45°F	Sensitive: Yes
Endive (curly) and Escarole	0.78	Year around	32–36°F	Produces: No
				Sensitive: Yes
Endive, Belgian	0.90	Year around	32–36°F	Produces: No
				Sensitive: Yes
Fennel (bulb)	0.45	Peak: Sep–May	32–36°F	
Figs	0.80	Jun–Oct	32–36°F	Produces: Yes
				Sensitive: No
Garlic cloves	0.85	Year around	32–36°F	Produces: No
				Sensitive: No
Ginger root	0.77	Year around	60–65°F	Produces: No
			Do not store below 55°F	Sensitive: No
Grapefruit (sections)	0.52	Year around	45–50°F	Produces: Low
		Peak: Jan–Apr		Sensitive: Yes
Grapes			32–36°F	Produces: Low
Champagne	0.92	Late summer		Sensitive: Yes
Seedless, red and green	0.94	Year around		
		Peak: Jun–Dec		
Herbs		Year around	Basil: 45–50°F	Produces: No
Basil (leaves)	0.68		Others: 32–36°F	Sensitive: Yes
Chives (minced)	0.89			
Cilantro (leaves)	0.65			
Dill (leaves)	0.44			
Mint (leaves)	0.83			
Oregano (leaves)	0.45			
Parsley (leaves)	0.68			
Rosemary (leaves)	0.45			
Thyme (leaves)	0.67			
Honeydew melon, peeled	0.66	Peak: May–Jan	60–65°F	Produces: Yes
				Sensitive: Yes
Jicama	0.80	Year around	60–65°F	Produces: No
		Peak: Jan–May		Sensitive: No
Kale	0.67	Year around	32–36°F	Produces: No
		Peak: Dec–Mar		Sensitive: No
Kiwi, peeled	0.80	Year around	32–36°F	Produces: Yes
		Peak: Oct–May	Ripen at room temperature	Sensitive: Yes
Kohlrabi	0.55	Year around	32–36°F	Produces: No
		Peak: Jun–Aug		Sensitive: No
Kumquat	0.98	Oct–Jun	45–50°F	Produces: No
		Peak: Jan–Mar	Do not store below 41°F	Sensitive: No
Leeks	0.50	Oct–Jun	32–36°F	Produces: No
		Peak: Oct–Dec		Sensitive: Yes

continues

TABLE 3.12   *continued*

Fruit/vegetable	Yield*	Availability	Storage (Raw, before paring, cutting, or processing.)	Ethylene
Lettuce, head	0.76	Year around	32–36°F	Produces: No Sensitive: Yes
Lettuce, leaf	0.66	Year around	32–36°F	Produces: No Sensitive: Yes
Lettuce, romaine	0.64	Year around	32–36°F	Produces: No Sensitive: Yes
Lemons/limes, sliced	0.78	Year around	45–55°F	Produces: Yes
Lemons/limes, wedges	0.90	Peak: Apr–Jul		Sensitive: Yes
Mangos	0.62	Year around Peak: May–Sep	60–65°F	Produces: Yes Sensitive: Yes
Melon (Casaba, Crenshaw, Juan Canary, Persian, Santa Claus)	0.55	Peak: Jun–Oct	60–65°F	Produces: Yes Sensitive: Yes
Mushrooms, trimmed	0.90	Year around	32–36°F	Produces: No Sensitive: No
Napa cabbage	0.75	Year around	32–36°F	Produces: No Sensitive: Yes
Nectarines	0.90	May–Sep Peak: Jul–Aug	65–72°F to ripen Chill damage between 36–46°F. Store unripe fruit 32–36°F	Produces: Yes Sensitive: Yes
Okra	0.85	Year around Peak: Jul–Oct	45–50°F	Produces: Low Sensitive: Yes
Onions, green (scallions)	0.70	Year around Peak: Summer	32–36°F	Produces: No Sensitive: Yes
Onions, mature	0.88	Year around Sweet peak: Apr–Aug	60–65°F	Produces: No Sensitive: No
Orange sections	0.40	Year around Peak navels: Nov–May	45–50°F	Produces: Low Sensitive: Yes
Papaya	0.70	Year around Peak: Feb–Apr	60–65°F	Produces: Yes Sensitive: Yes
Parsnips	0.75	Oct–Mar	32–36°F	Produces: No Sensitive: Yes
Peaches	0.76	May–Sep Peak: Jul–Sep	65–70°F to ripen Chill damage between 36–46°F. Store unripe fruit 32–36°F	Produces: Yes Sensitive: Yes
Pears	0.80	Some varieties available year around. Peak: Anjou, Oct–May; Bartlett, Aug–Dec; Bosc, Sep–May; Comice, Oct–Feb	60–70°F to ripen Store unripe fruit 32°F	Produces: Yes Sensitive: Yes
Peas, Green	0.38	Year around Peak: Mar–Apr	32–36°F	Produces: No Sensitive: Yes
Peppers, chile	0.85	Year around Peak: Jul–Sep	45–50°F	Produces: No Sensitive: Yes
Peppers, sweet bell	0.80	Year around Peak: Jul–Nov	45–50°F	Produces: No Sensitive: No
Persimmon	0.75	Sep–Dec	60–65°F to ripen Store unripe fruit 32–36°F	Produces: Yes Sensitive: Yes
Pineapple	0.50	Year around Peak: Mar–Jun	45–50°F Do not store below 45°F	Produces: Low Sensitive: No
Plantains	0.65	Year around	60–65°F Do not store below 56°F	Produces: Yes Sensitive: Yes

TABLE 3.12   *continued*

Fruit/vegetable	Yield*	Availability	Storage (Raw, before paring, cutting, or processing.)	Ethylene

Plums	0.85	May–Oct
		Peak: Aug–Sep
			65–70°F to ripen
			Chill damage between
			   36–46°F. Store unripe
			   fruit 32–36°F
				Produces: Yes
				Sensitive: Yes

Pomegranates	0.58	Aug–Dec Peak: Oct–Dec	45°F Do not store below 41°F	Produces: No Sensitive: No
Potatoes, sweet	0.80	Year around	60–65°F Do not store below 54°F	Produces: No Sensitive: Yes
Potatoes, white	0.81	Year around	60–65°F Do not store below 42°F	Produces: No Sensitive: Yes
Radishes	0.94	Year around	32–36°F	Produces: No Sensitive: Yes
Raspberries	0.95	Peak: Jun–Sep	32–36°F	Produces: Low Sensitive: No
Rhubarb	0.86	Year around Peak: late spring, early summer	32–36°F	Produces: No Sensitive: No
Rutabagas	0.79	Year around Peak: Jan–Mar	32–36°F	Produces: No Sensitive: Yes
Salsify (Black or White)	0.65	Sep–May	32–36°F	Produces: No Sensitive: No
Spinach	0.80	Year around	32–36°F	Produces: No Sensitive: Yes
Sprouts	0.95	Year around	32–36°F	Produces: No Sensitive: Yes
Squash, acorn	0.80	Year around Peak: Oct–Mar	60–65°F Do not store below 50°F	Produces: No Sensitive: Yes
Squash, butternut	0.84	Year around Peak: Oct–Mar	60–65°F Do not store below 50°F	Produces: No Sensitive: Yes
Squash, Hubbard	0.64	Year around Peak: Oct–Mar	60–65°F Do not store below 50°F	Produces: No Sensitive: Yes
Squash, summer	0.95	Year around Peak: Apr–Sep	45–50°F	Produces: No Sensitive: Yes
Squash, zucchini	0.94	Year around Peak: Apr–Sep	45–50°F	Produces: No Sensitive: Yes
Strawberries	0.88	Year around Peak: May–Jun	32–36°F	Produces: Low Sensitive: No
Tangerines/Tangelos	0.40	Peak: Oct–May	45–50°F Do not store below 38°F	Produces: Low Sensitive: Yes
Tomatillo	0.75	Year around Peak: Jul–Oct	45–50°F Do not store below 45°F	Produces: No Sensitive: No
Tomatoes	0.80	Year around	60–65°F Do not store below 50°F	Produces: Yes Sensitive: Yes (when green)
Turnips	0.79	Year around Peak: Apr–May; Sep–Oct	32–36°F	Produces: No Sensitive: Yes
Watermelon	0.57	Year around Peak: Jun–Oct	45–50°F Do not store below 41°F	Produces: No Sensitive: No

*For percent yield, multiply the number by 100. For example: Apple yield = 78% (.78 × 100). Table represents the weight of ready to cook or ready to serve raw from 1 lb as purchased.

FRESH FRUIT— PRE-PREPARATION GUIDELINES AND GENERAL INFORMATION

A variety of fresh fruits are available year around to be used as ingredients in food products or as stand-alone menu items. Regardless of how fresh fruit is used, it must be handled and prepared in a way that retains its quality characteristics. The following information will help food service operators serve the highest quality fruit.

Apples—Wash, pare, core, and remove bruises and spots. If the skins are tender and color appropriate, do not pare. To dice, cut into rings and dice with sectional cutter. Drop diced pieces into salad dressing, lemon, pineapple, or other acid fruit juice to prevent discoloration. If diced apple is placed in fruit juice, drain before using in a salad. To section, cut into uniform pieces, with widest part of the section not more than 1/2 inch thick. Remove core from each section. Varieties that are commonly available include:

Braeburn—Red to red with greenish gold areas on the skin. For eating out of hand and salads.

Fuji—Red to yellow-green with red highlights. Sweet-spicy flavor. For eating out of hand and cooking.

Gala—Heart-shaped. Yellow-orange color with red strips. Crisp with sweet flavor. For eating out of hand and salads.

Gala

Golden delicious—Yellow-green skin with freckling. Sweet, firm flesh. All-purpose apple for eating out of hand or cooking.

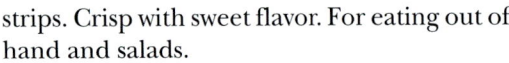

Rome

Red Delicious

Granny Smith

Golden Delicious

Granny Smith—Bright green skin with pink blush. Very crisp texture; tart. For eating out of hand, salads, and cooking.

Jonathan—Bright red skin with firm, juicy, tart to acidic flesh. For cooking and eating out of hand.

McIntosh—Red and green colored flesh. Slightly tart to acidic. For eating out of hand and salads.

McIntosh

Northern spy—Firm, juicy, tart. For pies.

Red delicious—Deep red skin, speckled with yellow. Mild, sweet, juicy. For eating out of hand and salads.

Rome beauty—Bright red skin. Tart-sweet, firm flesh. For baking and cooking.

Winesap—Bright red skin. Tart-sweet, firm flesh. All-purpose apple for baking and cooking.

Apricots—Wash before cutting by carefully and very quickly rinsing in cool water. Cut into halves or sections and remove seed. Thin velvety skin and not usually peeled. Most flavorful when served at room temperature.

Apricots

Avocados—Wash before cutting. Peel as close to serving as possible. To prevent browning, dip into dressing or lemon juice. To remove seed, cut avocado in half and while grasping both halves carefully rotate halves in opposite directions (pit will remain in one half). Remove the pit from the avocado half by striking the seed sharply with the cutting edge of a chef knife and rotating the knife and seed to loosen the seed. Peel leathery skin from the pulp. Serve avocados by the half or cut into cubes, slices, or other shape. If not served soon after cutting, dip avocado in lemon juice to keep it from turning brown. Botanically avocados are fruits but they are usually served as vegetables.

Avocados

Bananas—Wash before cutting or serving as whole fruit. As close to serving as possible, remove skins and bruised or discolored parts. Cut into strips, sections, or slices. Dip each piece in pineapple juice, or other acid fruit juice to prevent discoloration. (Also see plantains.)

Bananas

Berries—Wash berries (except cranberries) by carefully and very quickly dipping into cool water and draining completely in a single layer. Wash just before using as they soften quickly after washing. Do not let them soak in water. Cranberries are not fragile and should be thoroughly rinsed before using. Berries that are commonly available when in season include the following:

Blackberries—Deep purple to black color. Larger than raspberries. Loganberries, marionberries, and boysenberries are blackberry hybrids. Range from sweet to tart depending on variety.

Blackberries

Blueberries—Dark blue or purple with dusty silver-blue bloom. Firm and range from pea to thumbnail size.

Blueberries

Cranberries—Shiny, round, firm berry, red to maroon in color. White flesh with a distinct sour-tart flavor.

Currants—Tiny fruit that grows in grape-like clusters. May be black, red, or white in color. Dried currants are made from a variety of grape and not from currants.

Cranberries

White Currants

Red Currants

Raspberries—Red is the most common color with golden and black available in some markets. Dime to small quarter size fruit with very fine hairs on the surface. Cloudberries and dewberries are types of raspberries.

Raspberries

Strawberries—Shiny red, heart-shaped berry. Ranges in size from quarter to nearly egg size.

Strawberries

Cherries—Wash by submerging and swishing once or twice in cool water. After washing, drain completely, cut in half, and remove seed or use a cherry pitter.

Rainier Cherries

Bing Cherries

Citrus—All citrus fruits should be washed before cutting or serving as whole fruit. Citrus fruits are characterized by juicy pulp and a rind, with only the **zest** (thin outer portion) having the fruit's characteristic color and oils that add flavor and aroma to foods. The rind's **pith** (thick inner portion) is bitter and not often used in recipes.

Citrus Zest (fine)

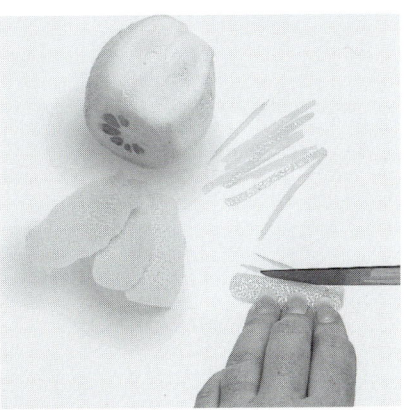

Citrus Zest (Strips)

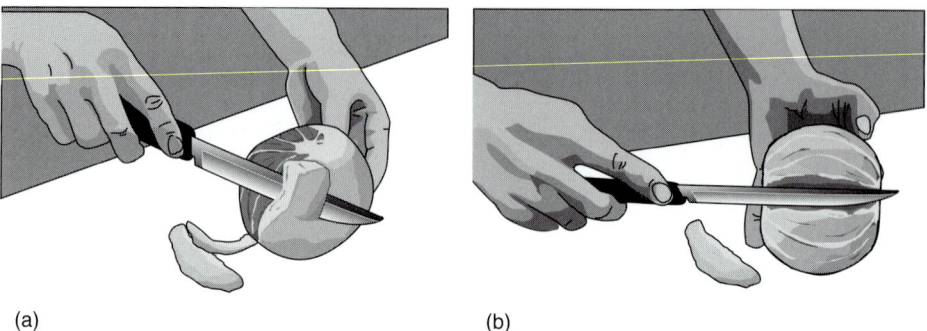

(a)   (b)

FIGURE 3.13   Peeling and sectioning grapefruit: (a) Cut layer of peel from top and bottom of grapefruit. Using a sharp knife, remove peel. Cut with a downward stroke deeply enough to remove all the white membrane. (b) Section grapefruit by cutting along membrane of one section to the center of the fruit. Turn the knife and force the blade along the membrane of the next section.

To section grapefruit, cut off a thick layer of skin from the top and bottom. Place grapefruit on cutting board, start at the top, and cut toward the board (Figure 3.13). Always cut with a downward stroke and deeply enough to remove the pith. Turn grapefruit while cutting. When paring is completed and pulp is exposed, remove sections by cutting along the membrane of one section to the center of the fruit. Other citrus fruit may be sectioned, but generally the membrane between sections is not removed. Common citrus fruits include

Grapefruits—White grapefruit has a light yellow flesh. Pink/red grapefruit's flesh varies from a light rosy pink to ruby red. Grapefruit is softball sized and should be heavy for its size. All grapefruit is tart, but pink grapefruit is usually sweeter than white.

White Grapefruit

Red Grapefruit

Kumquats—Small, oblong-shaped, bright golden-orange colored fruit. The fruit's sweet thin skin and tart flesh are both edible. Fresh whole or sliced kumquats are appropriate garnishes for meats and fruit platters. Preserves and marmalades may be made using kumquats.

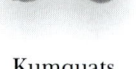

Kumquats

Lemons—Oval-shaped fruit with a bright yellow to yellow-green skin. Used to flavor and garnish foods but because of their tart flavor are not generally eaten raw. Meyers lemons are sweeter than regular lemons and considered superior for delicate desserts.

Lemons

Limes—Similar shape as a lemon but smaller. Skin ranges in color from dark to light green. Key limes are thin-skinned with a light yellow-green color and sweet tart flavor. Persian limes are a dark green with a thin, smooth, shiny skin and sweet-tart flavor.

Limes

Oranges—Round fruit with an orange skin or peel and orange flesh. Colors will vary by variety and growing factors. Naval oranges are juicy and sweet with few seeds and have the thickest skin of all oranges, making them easy to peel. Valencia oranges are juicy and sweet with some seeds and thin skin. Blood oranges have a thin orange-red skin and dark maroon-red flesh that may look streaked. Blood oranges are smaller than other oranges.

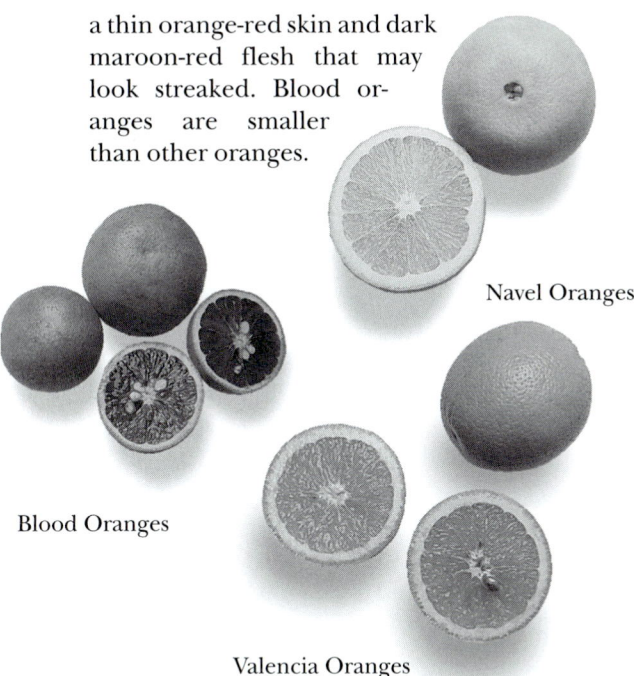

Navel Oranges

Blood Oranges

Valencia Oranges

Tangerines/Tangelos/Mandarins—All have red-orange skin and resemble an orange. Tangerine skin is loosely attached to the fruit and easy to peel from the pulp. It is characterized by a sweet, mellow flavor and has seeds. Tangelos (a grapefruit-tangerine hybrid) are characterized by a knob-like formation at the stem end of the fruit and have a tart-sweet flavor and few seeds. Mandarins are rounder and larger than tangerines, peel easily, are tart or tart-sweet in flavor, and may have some seeds.

Tangerines

Grapes—Grapes should be washed thoroughly by submerging and swishing in cool water once or twice and draining completely. Small clusters can be cut from the larger clusters by using a kitchen sheers or sharp knife. Grapes may be seedless or with seeds. When fresh, grapes are firmly attached to the stem and have no browning where attached to the stem. Common table grapes used in foodservices include:

Champagne—Very small, red to light purple seedless grape, always in tight clusters, and most often used on fruit and cheese platters or as a garnish. The small stems attaching the tiny grapes to the larger stem are very tender and can easily be stripped from the grapes.

Green/White Table (seedless)—Thompson seedless is a leading variety of green grapes that are eaten fresh and dried to make raisins. Most have a crisp texture and sweet flavor.

Thompson Seedless Grapes

Red Table (seedless)—Red flame is a leading variety. Large, round, and slightly tart flavor. Variegated color.

Red Flame Grapes

Purple/Black (seed-in)—Important varieties include Concord, Red Emperor, and Ribier. Most are in season during the fall months.

Concord Grapes

Kiwi—Wash before cutting by rinsing quickly in cool water. Remove fuzzy skin with a very sharp paring knife. Slice, chop, dice, or cut into wedges. May cut in half cross-wise without peeling and serve with a spoon to dip out the pulp.

Kiwi

Mango—Wash before cutting by rinsing quickly in cool water. Cut in half by carefully sliding a sharp knife along both sides of the flat side of the seed. Scoop the flesh out of the shell. To cut into chunks, peel back the skin from each mango half and cut as desired.

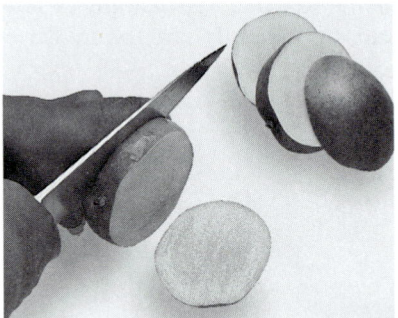

Mango

a. Cut along flat sides of pit.

b. Score flesh.

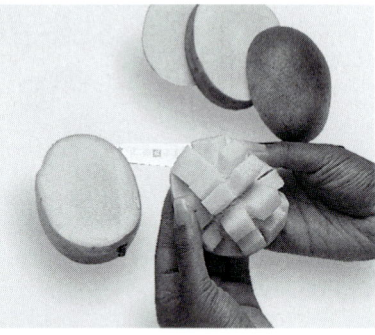

c. Remove cubes.

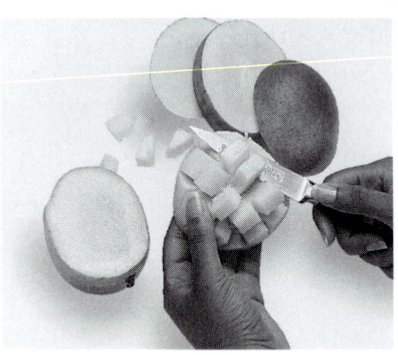

Melons—Because melon grows directly on the ground and the rind can harbor disease-causing bacteria, it is important to thoroughly wash melons before cutting. Melon with a hollow cavity filled with seeds should be cut in half and the seeds scooped out. Cut in wedges (skin on or off), dice, cube, or make into balls using a melon ball cutter or spoon. Melon with the rind on should not be stacked in a way that the rind comes in contact with the flesh that will be eaten. A discussion of common melon follows.

Cantaloupe—Round in shape. Creamy colored rind with good netting or webbing. Peach-colored flesh. When ripe, the stem end should be smooth and slightly depressed.

Cantaloupes

Casaba—Large round in shape. Yellow, slightly ridged rind. Creamy-white flesh.

Casaba

Crenshaw—Large and rounded with a slightly pointed stem end. Smooth golden-green rind with a golden-pink to creamy white flesh.

Crenshaw

Honeydew—Large round shape. Smooth creamy yellow-green rind. Light green flesh. Orange-fleshed honeydew has a flavor similar to a cantaloupe.

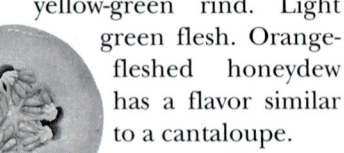

Green Honeydew

Gold Honeydew

Juan Canary—Oblong in shape. Yellow rind and creamy white flesh.

Persian—Globe shaped with a dark to light-green rind (turns lighter as it ripens) and light brown netting. Pink-orange flesh.

Santa Claus—Oblong in shape. Mottled green and yellow rind. Light green flesh.

Santa Claus

Watermelon—Large round or oblong shape. Rind color ranges from light to dark green. Most common has red flesh with black mature seeds. Some watermelon has yellow to bright orange flesh.

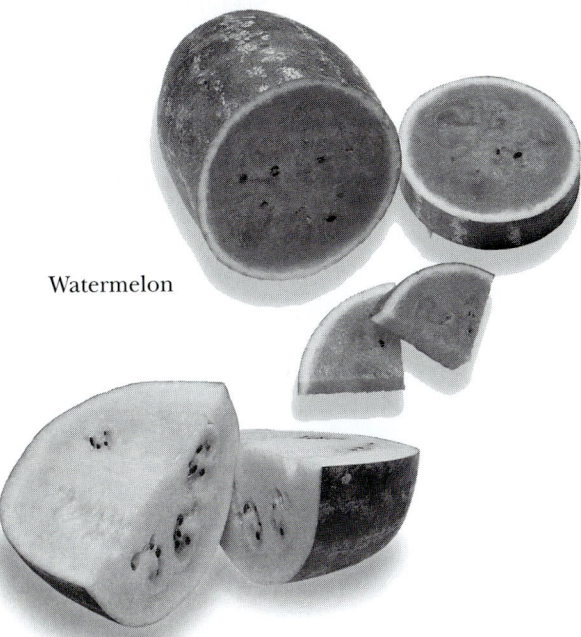

Watermelon

Gold Watermelon

Nectarines—Wash before cutting or serving as whole fruit by rinsing in cool water, being careful not to bruise. Cut into wedges or slices. Drop into acid fruit juice to prevent discoloration. Similar to peaches in shape, color, and flavor. Smooth skinned and usually not peeled.

Nectarines

Papaya—Wash before cutting. Cut papaya in half lengthwise, scoop out the seeds if desired, or leave in as they are edible. For rings carefully scoop out the seeds after cutting the papaya into circles.

Papayas

Peaches—Wash before cutting or serving as whole fruit by rinsing in cool water, being careful not to bruise. Remove the seed and smooth fuzzy skin just before serving. Dip pared fruit into acid fruit juice to prevent discoloration. Flesh ranges in color from white, to creamy yellow, to yellow-orange. When ripe, the fruit is soft, fragrant, and sweet to slightly tart depending on variety.

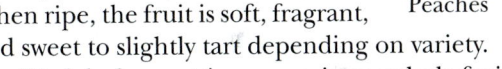

Peaches

Pears—Wash before cutting or serving as whole fruit by rinsing in cool water, being careful not to bruise. Peel and remove core and seeds a short time before serving. Cut into halves, wedges, or slices. Dip cut surface of fruit into an acid fruit juice to prevent discoloration. Common pear varieties include:

Anjou—Egg shaped with thin, light green skin. Skin color does not change as fruit ripens.

Anjou

Red Anjou

Asian—Also called Chinese pear. Apple shape and texture with a pear flavor. Yellow skin.

Asian

Bartlett—Bell shaped with thin green skin turning yellow when ripe. Red variety available.

Bartlett

Bosc—Symmetrical body with long, tapered neck. Skin is russet brown. Good for poaching and baking.

Bosc

Comice—Squat chubby shape with short neck and stem. Skin is greenish yellow with some red blush. Very juicy when ripe.

Persimmons—Wash before cutting. Round, squat-shaped fruit with green leafy stem. Size of a small baseball. Skin color ranges from pale orange to bright orange-red. Some varieties, such as fuyu, have a crunchy texture and can be eaten raw, sliced into salads, or pureed and used as an ingredient in baked goods. The pulp of the softer variety, hachiya, is best suited for use as an ingredient in baked goods.

Persimmons

Pineapple—Wash before cutting. Characterized by a dry, crisp shell and dark green leaves. Color ranges from greenish-brown to golden-brown. Flesh is firm and light yellow with a sweet to sweet-acidic flavor. Pineapple does not continue to ripen once picked. See Figure 3.14 for instructions on how to clean fresh pineapple.

Pineapple

Plantains—Wash before cutting. Banana-shaped fruit with thick greenish-yellow skin that darkens when ripe. Can be used at various stages of ripeness. In its green stage, the flesh is starchy similar to a potato or squash. When ripe the plantain is sweet and starchy.

Plantains

Plums—Wash before cutting or serving as whole fruit by rinsing in cool water, being careful not to bruise. Range in shape from oblong to round and in flavor from sweet to tart. Common varieties include:

Black Frier—Dark purple with silvery bloom.

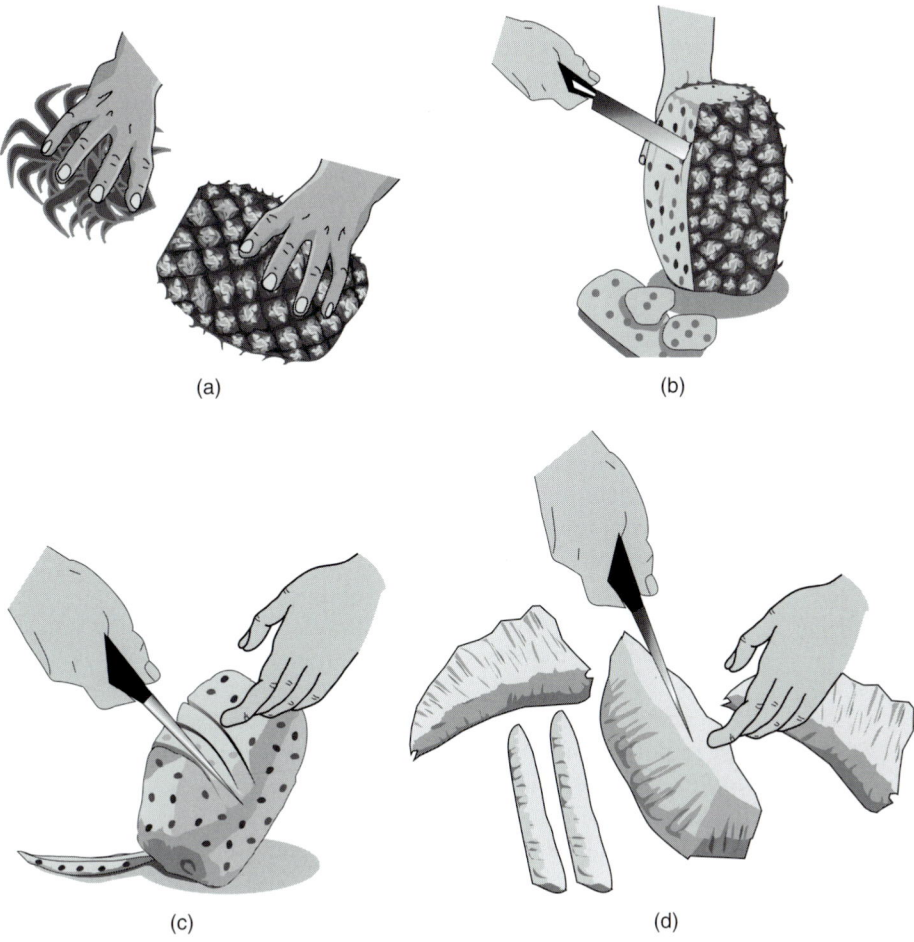

(a)   (b)

(c)   (d)

FIGURE 3.14   Preparing fresh pineapple: (a) Remove crown by holding pineapple in one hand and crown in the other, then twisting in opposite directions. (b) Trim top of pineapple and cut off base. Using a sharp knife, remove peel by using a downward cutting motion. (c) Remove eyes by making narrow wedge-shaped grooves into the pineapple. Cut diagonally around the fruit, following the pattern of the eyes. Cut away as little of the fruit as possible. (d) Cut pineapple vertically into eighths, then cut the hard center core from each spear. To make pineapple chunks, cut each spear into pieces of the desired size.

Damson

Damson—Small with light purple or reddish skin and green flesh. Good for pies.
Greengage—Green skin with yellow-green flesh.
Santa Rosa—Purple-crimson skin with light yellow or amber flesh.

Santa Rosa

FRESH VEGETABLES— PRE-PREPARATION GUIDELINES AND GENERAL INFORMATION

Fresh vegetables add color, flavor, and texture to an array of menu items and must be prepared in a way to enhance their quality attributes. The following information will be useful for production staff when preparing fresh vegetables.

Artichokes—Wash in cool water. Cut 1 inch off tops. Cut off stem and bottom leaves. Trim

Artichokes

the outer leaves, if necessary. With a melon ball cutter or spoon, remove and discard the fuzzy center core (choke). Immediately dip cut flesh into lemon juice to prevent discoloration. Choke can be removed after cooking.

Arugula—Carefully trim tough stems from leaves (leaves bruise easily). Wash leaves by immersing in cool water. Repeat as necessary. Drain. See Table 3.13.

Arugula

Asparagus—Break or cut off tough end of stems. Thoroughly wash remaining portions in cool water. Remove lower scales if they harbor sand. Lower part of stalks may be peeled. For blanched asparagus, immerse in boiling water for 2 minutes. Remove quickly and dip in ice-cold water. Drain. Use blanched asparagus on fresh vegetable platters.

Asparagus

Beans (any tender variety)—Wash in cool water, trim ends by cutting or snapping off. Some varieties have tough strings that should be removed. For blanched beans, immerse in boiling water for 1 1/2–2 minutes. Remove quickly and dip in ice-cold water. Drain.

Green Beans

Beets—Wash in cool water. Trim off leaves, leaving 1 inch of stem and root remaining. Can be peeled before cooking but most often peeled after cooking when the peels slip off easily. Beet tops may be cooked as greens or if small and tender used in salads. Red variety is sweeter and more common than golden variety.

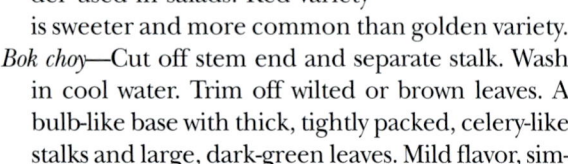

Beets

Bok choy—Cut off stem end and separate stalk. Wash in cool water. Trim off wilted or brown leaves. A bulb-like base with thick, tightly packed, celery-like stalks and large, dark-green leaves. Mild flavor, sim-

ilar to cabbage. Used for stir-fry, in soups, and as a main ingredient in Korean Kimchi.

Bok choy

Broccoli—Wash by immersing in cool water. Trim off blemished outer leaves and woody ends of stalks. For florets, separate florets from stalk. Peel stalks if desired. Split or slice large stalks to help them cook evenly.

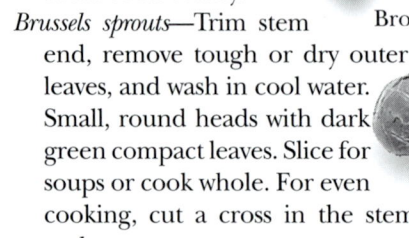

Broccoli

Brussels sprouts—Trim stem end, remove tough or dry outer leaves, and wash in cool water. Small, round heads with dark green compact leaves. Slice for soups or cook whole. For even cooking, cut a cross in the stem end.

Brussels sprouts

Cabbage—Remove tough or dry outer leaves. Wash heads in cool water and cut into 4 to 6 pieces through the stem end. Remove hard, white center core. Shred or cut as desired. Crisp in ice water 15–30 minutes. Drain well. See Table 3.13.

Green Cabbage

Red Cabbage

TABLE 3.13   Descriptions of greens for cooking, salad greens, and lettuces

GREENS USED FOR COOKING

Beet	Thin, deep red stems, flat green leaves, red ribs in leaves. Cook mature tops; use young, tender beet tops in salads.
Collard	Wide, flat, green leaves.
Dandelion	Thin white stems. Dark green, ragged-edged leaves.
Kale	A hardy dark green curly leaf that may be cooked. More often used for decorative purposes as a salad bar garnish. Flowering kale makes a decorative salad bar garnish with its large, ruffle-edged leaves, and attractive color varying from green to cream to violet.
Mustard	Long narrow stems. Large green curly leaves. Slightly bitter and spicy (hot).
Spinach	Dark green, crinkled leaves with a bold flavor. More mature leaves are best when cooked.
Swiss chard (green and red)	Thick white (green chard) or red (red/ruby chard) stems, dark green, large wrinkled leaves, with prominent white or bright red veins.
Turnip	Long, narrow green stems. Flat, green, and slightly fuzzy leaves.

SALAD GREENS AND LETTUCES

Arugula or rocket	Small, narrow, tender, smooth, notched leaves with a dark green color and spicy peppery flavor. Small leaves are the mildest. Combines well with mild-flavored greens. May be considered an herb.
Bibb lettuce or limestone lettuce	Small cup-shaped lettuce with a deep rich green color that blends into whitish green near the core. Flavor is buttery and sweet. Texture delicate and tender. Similar to but smaller and more delicate than Boston lettuce.
Boston lettuce	Soft, pliable, fragile leaf. Delicate sweet flavor. Not as tender or sweet as Bibb lettuce. Deep green outside blending to light yellow to nearly white near the core. Bruises easily and does not keep well.
Cabbage	*Green:* Pale green, tough, crisp leaves generally used in slaws. Round, compact head. *Nappa (Chinese Cabbage):* Pale green to white with tightly packed crinkled leaves. Mild flavor. *Red:* Purple, crisp leaves; may be used with other greens to add color. Round, compact head. Sweeter than green cabbage. *Savoy:* Light green, crinkly leaves with a delicate cabbage flavor. Loosely compact round head. Use sparingly in a tossed salad.
Endive (Belgian) or French endive	Characterized by an elongated stock of narrow, lightly packed leaves, resembling a spearhead (4–6 inches long). Off white or pale green in color. Turns greener when exposed to light. Mild, slightly bitter flavor and waxy texture. Served typically as a small, separate course salad or as a decorative component of an arranged salad.
Endive (curly) or chicory	A bunchy head with narrow, ragged edge leaves. Mild center leaves, bitter outer leaves. Use sparingly in combination salads. Primary use for garnishing or as a base.
Escarole	A variety of endive with broad leaves that do not curl at the tips. Texture is coarse and slightly tough, flavor somewhat bitter. Mix sparingly with other greens.
Frisée	Feathery leaves that are very thin and spiky. Pale yellow interior leaves, green outer leaves. Less bitter than curly endive. Crisp, crunchy, and mildly peppery.
Iceberg (head lettuce)	Firm, round, compact head, bright to light green in color. Crisp leaves with a mild, delicate flavor. Stays crisp longer than most other lettuces. Mixes well with other greens; can be used for an underliner.
Leaf lettuce	Soft, fragile leaves, most with curly edges and crisp delicate texture. Bunched tightly. Red leaf or green leaf. Red leaf is tinged with red along the edges. Mixes well with other greens; used in sandwiches or as an underliner. Wilts easily and does not keep well.
Mâche	Small, round, spoon-shaped leaf with a sweet nutty flavor and delicate texture. Mix with other young tender greens.
Mesclun	Not a leaf but a mixture of tender, small lettuces. Available as a mixture in some markets.
Red oak leaf	Narrow leaves with deep scalloping. Resembles an oak leaf. Very tender with a nutty flavor. Green oak (lime green) red oak (dark red).
Radicchio	Small, round, compact head similar to iceberg lettuce. Maroon-red leaves with white ribs or veins, and with a bitter peppery taste. Combine sparingly with mild, tender greens.
Romaine or cos	Long, loaf-shaped head with long, narrow leaves. Coarse, dark green outer leaves and greenish-yellow to light green inner ones. Very crisp texture, tender and sweet.
Spinach	Dark green, crinkled leaves with a bold flavor. Small, young tender leaves are best for salads. Tougher, more mature leaves can be cooked.
Watercress	Dark green, small, glossy leaves with a pungent, peppery flavor. Use as a garnish, in sandwiches, or mixed with tender leaf greens.

Carrots—Trim top and root end. Wash in cool water; peel off outer skin.

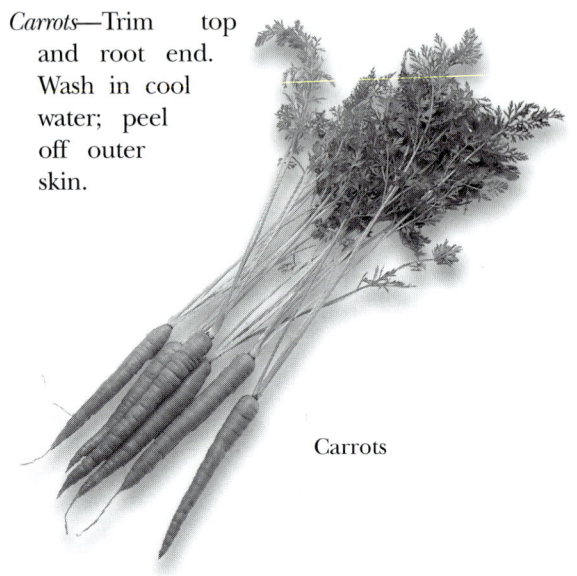

Carrots

Cauliflower—Remove all leaves and cut away dark spots. Wash in cool water. To separate florets, cut around thick white core by using a paring knife to make a circular cut around the core. Separate into florets, using hands to break apart. White is predominant color; also a green and purple variety.

Cauliflower

Celery—Trim any tough or dry portions from both ends of stalk. Separate outer stalks from the heart. Use outer stalks and leaves for stock, soup, mirepoix. Wash in cool water, trim, and remove bruised or blemished parts. If desired, peel to remove strings. To dice, cut lengthwise. Several stalks can be cut at one time. Place on board and cut crosswise with a French knife. For celery *curls* or fans, cut celery into 2½-inch lengths. Make lengthwise cuts ⅛-inch apart about 1-inch in length on one or both ends of celery strips. Place in ice water for about 2 hours before serving. For celery *rings,* cut celery into 2-inch lengths and then into pieces ⅛–inch thick. Place in ice water for several hours. Each strip of celery will form a ring.

Celery

Celery Root (Celeriac)—Wash in cool water and peel. Bulb-shaped root that can be served raw in salads or cooked in soup, stew, and stir-fry. Crisp texture and celery-like flavor.

Celery Root

Chard, Swiss—Use a chef's knife to cut (separate) leaves from stems. Wash both stems and leaves by immersing in cool water. Repeat washing until all grit is gone. Trim any brown or blemished portions. See Table 3.13.

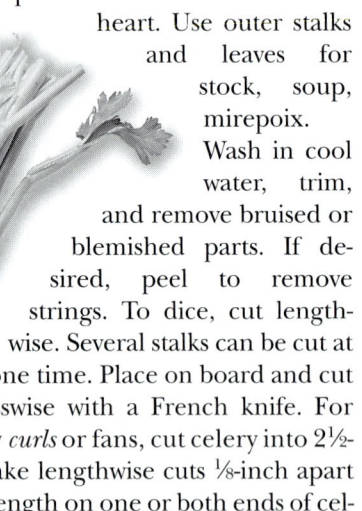

Swiss Chard

Collards—Use a chef's knife to cut stems away from both sides of leaves. Discard tough stems. Wash leaves by immersing in cool water. Chop as desired. See Table 3.13.

Corn—Remove husk and stalk end. Rinse in cool water to remove silk-like fibers that surround ear. Trim ends as required. Grilled corn may be cooked with husk on.

Collard Greens

Corn

Cress—Separate leaves for thorough washing. Wash in a spray of water or by immersing in cool water. Drain thoroughly. If gritty, repeat washing until grit is gone. A hot, peppery leaf that resembles radish leaves.

Cucumbers—Wash in cool water. Peel or score lengthwise with a fork. Peel if cucumbers are waxed. If desired, cut in half lengthwise and scoop out seeds with a spoon. Dice or cut into slices, wedges, or spears. Crisp by placing sliced cucumbers in salted ice water for 30 minutes, drain and rinse.

Pickling

Green

Hothouse

Daikon radish (Japanese or Oriental radish)—Wash in cool water and peel. Long, white, carrot-shaped root that can be served raw in salads or cooked in soups and stir-fries. Hot radish flavor.

Daikon Radish

Eggplant—Wash in cool water and remove stem and green cap. Can be peeled or unpeeled. Slice lengthwise into strips or crosswise into rounds. *Purple* and *white* eggplant are globe or egg-shaped and vary in size. *Japanese* eggplant is small and slender with a light to medium purple color. Good quality eggplants are light in weight in relationship to their size.

Eggplant

Japanese Eggplant

Endive, Belgian or French endive—Trim and discard any decayed or wilted outer leaves. Wash by immersing in cool water very quickly. Drain thoroughly. If served fresh, cut out tough core. See Table 3.13.

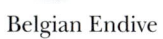

Belgian Endive

Endive (curly)—Separate leaves for thorough washing. Discard any tough or wilted outer leaves and tough stems. Wash in a spray of water or by immersing in cool water. Drain thoroughly. If gritty, repeat washing until grit is gone. See Table 3.13.

Curly Endive

Escarole—Wash as for curly endive. See Table 3.13.

Escarole

Fennel—Trim stalks from bulb and leaves; discard or use in stock. Wash by immersing in cool water. Drain thoroughly. Distinctive anise-like flavor that becomes milder when cooked. *Bulb* is white and round with short celery-like stalks. Bulb can be eaten raw or cooked (baked, grilled, steamed, sautéed). Peel and cut thin slice from root end. Remove core. Cut into thin wedges or long batons. Feathery leaves or fronds are used as an herb and *seeds* for flavoring.

Fennel

Frisée—Wash by immersing in cool water. Drain thoroughly. See Table 3.13.

Garlic—Separate cloves from bulb. Trim root end and peel cloves. Remove and discard any sprouts from the inside of cloves.

Garlic

Greens—Greens should be clean, crisp, chilled, and well drained. It may be necessary to separate leaves for thorough washing. Discard brown or decayed leaves. Wash in a spray of water or by immersing in cool water. Repeat washing if necessary until all grit is gone. Shake off excess water, drain thoroughly, and refrigerate. Draining in a colander or on a rack placed on a baking sheet will keep the greens from standing in water while chilling. Cover with a clean damp cloth or plastic film to prevent dehydration. Table 3.13 describes common greens and lettuces.

Herbs—Rinse in cool water. Discard brown or decayed leaves. Some recipes may require that the stems be removed from the leaves. See Table 3.16 for descriptions of commonly used herbs.

Jicama—Peel and cut into strips, slices, cubes, or batons. Rounded in shape. Light brown skin, ivory flesh with a subtle sweet flavor, and crisp, juicy texture. Serve raw (salads, relish tray) or cooked (stir-fry). Jicama can be substituted for water chestnuts.

Jicama

Kale—Separate leaves for thorough washing. Discard brown or decayed leaves. Wash in a spray of water or by immersing in tepid water. Drain thoroughly. For cooking, use a chef's knife to cut stems away from both sides of leaves. Discard tough stems. Chop as desired. Often used for decorative purposes as a salad bar garnish. Flowering kale makes a decorative salad bar garnish with its large, ruffle-edged leaves, and attractive color varying from green to cream to violet.

Kale

Dandelion

Mustard

Ornamental Kale

Sorrel

Kohlrabi—Trim and discard leaves and stalks. Peel bulb. Wash in cool water. Cut into wedges or slice into very thin rounds. Globe-shaped root with

Turnip Greens

Kohlrabi

green leaves attached by a thick stem. Bulb is similar in flavor to a turnip, and leaves are similar to collard greens or kale. Bulb may be eaten raw; leaves must be cooked.

Leeks—Trim and discard dark green tops, tough outer leaves, and root end. Remove the root. Halve the leek lengthwise and wash thoroughly in running cool water. Leeks may need to be washed several times to remove trapped sand. If particularly sandy, let leeks soak in several changes of water. Characterized by long thick stem and coarse drooping tops. Member of the green onion and shallot family with a mild onion flavor.

Leeks

Lettuce (leaf)—Trim stem and separate leaves for thorough washing. Discard brown or decayed leaves. Wash in a spray of water or by immersing in cool water (Figure 3.15). Drain thoroughly. See Table 3.13.

Red and Green
Leaf Lettuce

Romaine

Boston

Baby Red Oak Leaf

Mâche

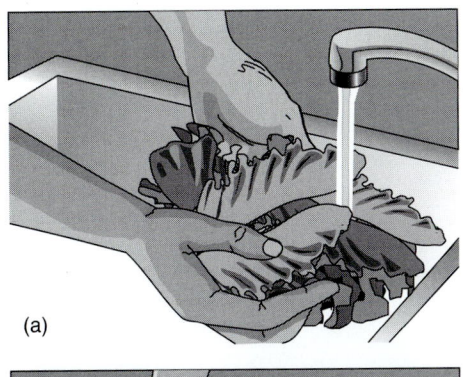

(a)

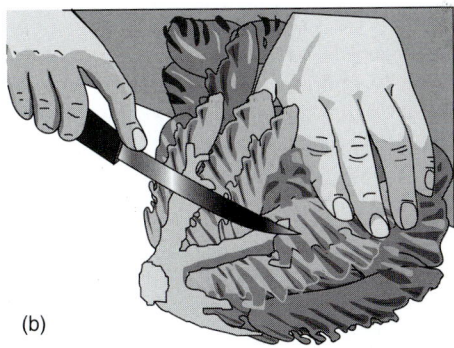

(b)

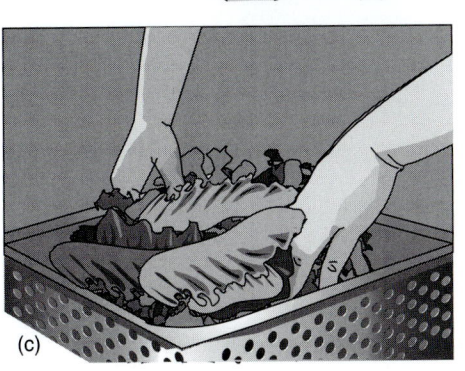

(c)

FIGURE 3.15 Preparing leaf lettuce. (a) Wash lettuce under cold running water. (b) Remove stem end by cutting with a sharp knife. (c) Place leaf end up in a perforated pan to drain. Chill 2 to 3 hours to crisp.

FIGURE 3.16 Coring head lettuce.
(a) Hit stem end of lettuce sharply on
flat surface. (b) Remove loosened core.

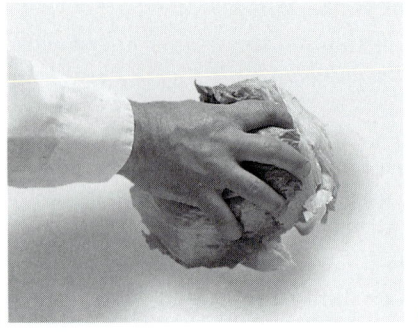

(a)

(b)

Lettuce (head)—Trim stem and remove any outside leaves that are wilted or brown. Immerse in cool water. Position to drain water from inside the head. To core *iceberg lettuce*, hit stem end of lettuce sharply on flat surface and remove loosened core (see Figure 3.16). See Table 3.13.

Mushrooms—Do not soak in water or scrub. Trim bottoms of stems. Wipe clean with a damp paper towel or rinse quickly in cold water just before serving or using in a recipe. Adding a small amount of acid to the water will help keep mushrooms from discoloring. See Table 3.14, page 161 for common types of mushrooms.

Napa (Chinese Cabbage)—Separate leaves for thorough washing. Wash in a spray of water or by immersing in cool water. Drain thoroughly. Oblong shaped with tightly packed, wrinkled leaves ranging in color from pale green to white. Mild cabbage flavor and tender crisp texture. May be eaten cooked or uncooked.

Okra—Wash in cool water and trim stem end. Leave whole or slice. A carrot-shaped pod ranging in length from 2 to 5 inches. Medium to dark green in color with a slight fuzz on exterior.

Onions (green) (Scallions)—Trim root end and green tops. Wash in cool water to remove dirt and sand.

Okra

Scallions

Onions (mature)—Pour water over onions to cover. While submerged remove outer layer of the bulb, firm root end, and all bruised or decayed parts. Peel without immersing in water by making a slit in the onion skin from stem end to root end and peeling away outer layer.

Iceberg

Napa Cabbage

Savoy

Red

White

Yellow

Pearl

TABLE 3.14 Common types of mushroom

AGARICUS

Description: This widely available variety of mushroom varies in color from creamy white to light brown and in size from small to jumbo. It is plump and dome shaped and is also referred to as a "button mushroom."

Flavor/Texture: Pleasing mild woodsy flavor that intensifies when cooked. Those with open veils and darker caps are more mature and have a richer taste. Meat-like texture.

Handling: Refrigerate upon arrival. Leave in shipping container until needed. Shelf life, approximately 5–7 days.

Usage: Very versatile; may be used fresh or cooked. Before use, rinse quickly in cool water.

CRIMINI (ITALIAN BROWN, GOLDEN BROWN)

Description: Naturally dark cap that ranges in color from light tan to rich brown. Similar in appearance to Agaricus.

Flavor/Texture: Meat-like texture and earthy flavor is more intense than the Agaricus.

Handling: Refrigerate upon arrival. Leave in shipping container until needed. Shelf life, approximately 5–7 days.

Usage: Can be substituted in any recipe using white buttons when more full-bodied taste is preferred. Before use, rinse quickly in cold water.

ENOKI

Description: White in color with long stems and tiny white caps. Mushrooms are joined at the base and resemble bean sprouts.

Flavor/Texture: Light, mild sweet flavor with a crisp texture.

Handling: Refrigerate upon arrival. Leave in shipping container until needed. Shelf life, approximately 14 days.

Usage: Used for sandwiches, delicate salads, oriental dishes and soups, and garnishes. Trim base and separate stems. Before use, rinse quickly in cold water.

OYSTER

Description: Fluted cap resembles a fan or oyster shell. Colors range from a soft beige-brown to gray.

Flavor/Texture: Delicate flavor and texture.

Handling: Carefully rotate stocks. Refrigerate in a bowl covered with slightly damp cloth. Shelf life, approximately 5–7 days.

Usage: Sliced raw in salads or cooked in meat dishes. In preparations requiring extended cooking times, add mushrooms toward the end of the cooking period to preserve their delicate texture. Before use, rinse quickly in cool water.

PORTABELLA

Description: A mature crimini mushroom that is the largest of the commercially available mushrooms. May be 6 inches or more across. Large brown cap with dark brown gills.

Flavor/Texture: Meat-like, earthy flavor and meat-like texture.

Handling: Need circulating air to remain fresh. Shelf life, 7–10 days.

Usage: Generally cooked. May be incorporated in a recipe or served as a center of the plate item in a meat-like fashion. Gills may be scraped out using a spoon (optional). Before use, rinse quickly in cool water.

continues

TABLE 3.14 *continued*

SHIITAKE (BLACK FOREST OR GOLDEN OAK)

Description: Broad, umbrella-shaped caps, wide-open veils, and tan gills. Golden brown to dark brown in color.
Flavor/Texture: Rich, full-bodied, meaty, woodsy flavor with a spongy texture when cooked.
Handling: Refrigerate upon arrival. Leave in shipping container until needed. Shelf life, approximately 14 days.
Usage: Generally cooked. Tough stems should be chopped and used in stock or discarded. Before use, rinse quickly in cool water.

Hundreds of varieties of edible mushrooms grow, but only a few are grown and sold commercially year around. When in season, several wild varieties are sold locally at farmers markets and some grocery stores. Because it is difficult to distinguish poisonous mushrooms from edible ones, fresh mushrooms should only be purchased from reputable purveyors. Some wild mushroom varieties include morels and chanterelles.

Morel

Parsnips—Trim tops and root tip. Wash in cool water; peel. If large and woody, split lengthwise and remove core. Slice crosswise, dice, or cut in strips. White smooth skin root with a carrot-like shape. Ranges in length from 5 to 10 inches.

Parsnips

Peas—Wash in cool water. Trim ends. To blanch sugar snap and snow peas immerse in boiling water for 30 seconds or just until peas brighten in color. Remove quickly and dip into ice water. Drain. *Green peas* must be shelled, and the pod is not edible. The edible pods of *sugar snap peas* are similar to but smaller in size than green peas. Sugar snap peas are not shelled and may be eaten raw or cooked. Strings should be removed from the pod. *Snow peas* are flat green edible pods with small immature peas inside. Pods can be eaten fresh or cooked. Snow peas open easily along the side and can be stuffed with a savory filling

Fresh Shell Peas

(leave hinged when opening). Removing the strings from the edge of the pod is optional. *Edamame* are fresh green soybeans. The pods are tough and not eaten. May be served cold on a salad, stir-fried, or heated and served like other green peas or lima beans. Resembles a small lima bean but more rounded.

Peppers (chile)—Wash. Cut off stem end. Halve the peppers from the stem end. Remove seeds and membrane (optional). **Capsaicin,** the chemical that causes the sensory reaction to hot chile peppers is concentrated in the membrane or thin tissue that attaches the seeds to the soft, spongy, inside part of the pepper. When working with hot chiles wear protective food handling gloves and be careful not to touch eyes, lips, or nose. See Table 3.15 for descriptions of common peppers.

Jalapeños

Poblano

Serranos

Anaheim Chiles

California Dried Chiles

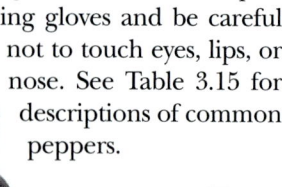

Ancho Dried Chile

Soy Beans (Edamame)

Snow Peas

Habaneros

DeÁrbol Dried Chile

TABLE 3.15   Chile pepper varieties

Name	Description	Uses
Anaheim (also called mild green chile)	Tapered, 6 to 7-inch long pod. Deep green. Mild to medium hot.	Stuffed whole as for Chile Rellenos; chopped for salads and salsas; in tomato-based products.
Ancho	Dried poblano chile. Sweet flavor. Glossy mahogany red-brown in color.	Sauces; moles; chili powders.
Chipotle	Smoked-dried Jalapeno chile. Mottled light and dark brown.	Cooked Mexican products as in chili con carne; barbeque sauces; bean and cheese dishes.
Fresno	Small, tapered pod that is not too thin. Red or green. Very hot.	Chopped and generally used in cooked products. Can be used uncooked.
Habanero (also called Scotch bonnet)	Small, cherry pepper-sized pepper, shaped like a miniature wrinkled bell pepper. Green, orange, or red. Extremely hot, use with caution.	Chopped in hot Mexican and Asian products.
Jalapeño	Small tapered pod, 2 1/2 to 3 1/2-inches long, 1/2 to 3/4-inch wide. Bright green or greenish black. Very hot.	Chopped in cooked and uncooked products.
Poblano	Tapered bell pepper-like shape with a pointed end (3 to 5-inches long, 2 to 3-inches wide). Deep, dark green to almost black. Mild to slightly hot.	Stuffed whole; chopped in tomato-based products.
Serrano	Tiny, very thin, tapering shape 1 1/2 to 2-inches long, 1/2-inch wide. Dark green or red. Very hot.	Chopped in cooked and uncooked products.
Thai	Tiny, extremely thin, tapered shape, 1/2 to 1-inch long, 1/4-inch wide. Green or red. Extremely hot.	Season soups, sauces, and stews.

- Chile pepper's heat is measured in *Scoville Heat Units*. For comparison, the sweet bell pepper has an approximate Scoville rating of 0 units; Poblano, 15,000 units; Jalapeño 25,000 units; Serrano 50,000 units; Cayenne 70,000 units; Habanero and Scotch bonnet (among the hottest peppers) 250,000 to 350,000 units.
- *Capsaicin,* the chemical responsible for the sensory reaction to hot chile peppers, is released when the membrane or thin tissue that attaches the seeds to the soft, spongy, inside part of the pepper is ruptured. To minimize the release of capsaicin, make one cut to divide the chile and remove the ribs and seeds with a spoon. Rinse the chile in cool running water to wash away any capsaicin that spills onto the chile's flesh. Wear protective gloves and be careful not to touch eyes, face, or nose.

Peppers (sweet bell)—Wash. Cut off stem end and remove core, seeds, and membrane. Cut into desired shape. The most abundant colors are green, red, yellow. To make *rings,* cut whole pepper into thin crosswise slices. To make *sticks,* cut peppers lengthwise into narrow strips.

Potatoes—Peel or, if peels are to be left on, scrub clean under cool running water. Remove eyes and blemishes from peeled potatoes. Cut into cubes and cook; or wash, cook with skins on, peel, and dice. The oblong shaped *Russet* potato is a widely used white potato variety. A high starch, dry texture makes them a good choice for baking, roasting, mashing, and frying. Smooth skinned *round red* and *round white* potatoes have a low starch, waxy texture, and are good for potato salads, roasting, boiling, and frying. The *long white* variety is oval shaped with a thin tan colored

Bell Peppers

Fingerlings   Purple Potatoes

skin. Their medium starch, waxy texture makes them a good all-purpose potato suitable for boiling, salads, soups, and roasting. Yellow fleshed potatoes such as *Yukon gold* and *yellow finn* have a buttery golden flesh and are suited for baking, mashing, and roasting. *Blue* and *purple* varieties have a flesh that ranges in color from dark blue or lavender to white and are characterized by a subtle nutty flavor. Color may dissipate some when cooked.

Red Potatoes

Russet Potatoes

White Potatoes

Yukon Gold Potatoes

Radicchio—Separate leaves for thorough washing. Discard brown or decayed leaves. Wash in a spray of water or by immersing in cool water. Drain thoroughly. See Table 3.13.

Radicchio

Radishes—Trim off root and stem end with a sharp knife. Wash. To make radish *accordions,* cut long radishes not quite through into 10–12 narrow slices. Place in ice water. Slices will fan out accordion style. To make *roses,* leave an inch or two of green stem. Cut 4 or 5 petal-shaped slices around the radish from cut tip to center. Place radishes in ice water, and petals will open.

Red Radish

Rutabaga—Trim root and stem end, and peel off thick skin. Cut into cubes for cooking. Round shape similar to a turnip; mild turnip-like flavor with golden yellow flesh.

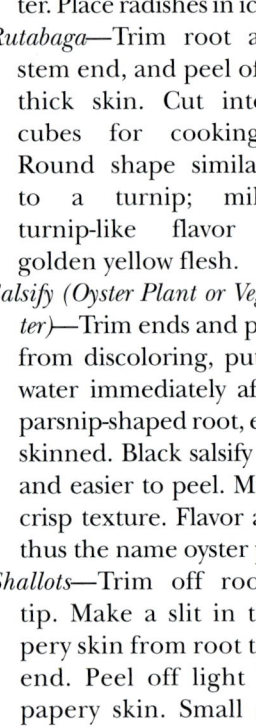

Rutabaga

Salsify (Oyster Plant or Vegetable Oyster)—Trim ends and peel. To keep from discoloring, put peeled root in acidulated water immediately after peeling. Long, slender, parsnip-shaped root, either black skinned or white skinned. Black salsify is fleshier than white salsify and easier to peel. Mild artichoke-like flavor and crisp texture. Flavor also compared to an oyster; thus the name oyster plant.

Shallots—Trim off root and tip. Make a slit in the papery skin from root to stem end. Peel off light brown papery skin. Small onion-like bulb with a mild, sweet onion flavor and golden-purple flesh.

Shallots

Spinach—Separate leaves for thorough washing. Remove coarse stems and damaged leaves. Wash by immersing in cool water, lifting spinach up and down to wash off grit. Lift leaves from water. See Table 3.13.

Spinach

Squash, Winter (hard shell)—Wash before cutting. Cut long squash in half lengthwise and round squash crosswise. Scoop out and discard seeds and fibrous strings. May cook with peel on or off. If squash is baked before cutting, pierce skin in several places to allow steam to escape. Squash should be heavy for their size. Most applicable baking methods:

boiling (soup), braising, and roasting. Common winter squash include:

Acorn—Dark green color sometimes with orange patches. Acorn shaped with yellow-orange flesh. Moderately sweet and sometimes fibrous. Small, 1–2 pounds.

Acorn

Banana—Creamy yellow to pale orange rind. Large, cylinder shape with slightly pointed ends.

Banana

Buttercup—Dark green and round with turban-shaped top. Orange sweet flesh; somewhat dry. Size varies but most weigh about 3 pounds.

Butternut——Light tan or yellow-orange, thin, smooth skin that peels easily. Elongated pear shape with seeds in the bulbous end. Bright orange flesh cooks up creamy and smooth (never stringy).

Butternut

Size varies considerably but ranges from about 2 to 6 pounds.

Hubbard——Bluish-grey or dusty green, thick bumpy skin that is difficult to cut. Smooth, sweet, orange flesh. Old varieties weigh 10 pounds or more; newer variety 3 to 5 pounds.

Spaghetti—Yellow, smooth, semi-hard skin. Oblong shaped. Pale golden flesh with stringy fibers that resemble spaghetti when separated (raked) with a fork. Size ranges from 3 to 5 pounds. Spaghetti squash is cooked without cutting or peeling.

Spaghetti

Squash, Summer (soft shell)—Trim stem and blossom end. Wash to remove all soil that may have adhered to the squash. Summer squash is not usually peeled or seeded and can be eaten raw or cooked. Depending on the variety, summer squash can be cut in many shapes (diced, halves, ribbons, shredded, sticks, coins). Common summer squash include:

Pattypan—Light green, yellow, or white skin. White flesh. Round, squat shape with scalloped edges.

Yellow crookneck—Pale yellow skin. White flesh. Cylinder in shape with a narrower curved neck. Has more seeds than zucchini.

Yellow Crookneck

Yellow zucchini—Deep yellow skin with green at stem end. White flesh. Same cylinder shape as green zucchini.

Zucchini—Dark green, shiny rind with some light speckling. White flesh. Cylinder shaped, thinner when young.

Tomatillo—Botanically a

Zucchini

fruit but treated like a vegetable. Small round fruit covered with a parchment-like, green husk. Remove husk and stem before using. Fruit has a smooth, green skin resembling a green cherry tomato. The green flesh contains tiny edible seeds and a solid texture. Tomatillo has a lemony and acidic flavor. Used cooked

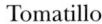

Tomatillo

in stews and casseroles, or uncooked in salads and salsas.

Tomatoes—Botanically a fruit but treated like a vegetable. Wash, remove core, stem, and flower end. If peeling, place in wire basket and dip in boiling water 10–20 seconds or until skins begin to loosen. Dip in ice water immediately and remove skins and core.

Tomatoes

Turnips—Trim root and stem end and peel off thick skin. Cut small turnips into wedges or thin rounds. Dice larger turnips. Creamy white skin with pinkish-red at the stem end. White flesh. For turnip greens see Table 3.13.

Turnips

Watercress

Watercress—Remove thick stems from leaves. Wash by immersing in cool water. Drain thoroughly. See Table 3.13.

FRESH HERBS AND FLOWERS

Herbs are the leaves of aromatic plants that add aroma and a distinctive flavor to foods. Herbs may be used to enhance taste without added calories, fat, or sodium. Table 3.16 describes fresh herbs used in cooking and gives their flavor profile and common use. Most herbs can be purchased as dried leaves, seeds, or ground. The flavor profile may be different, however, between fresh and dried herbs. See Table 3.20, p. 178 for herb and spice usage for different categories of food.

Edible flowers may be added to salads or used as a garnish to add color or flavor. Flowers are perishable and should be held for only a few days. Store flowers in a small amount of water and dry with paper towel before using. Table 3.17 provides a color and taste profile for commonly used flowers. When flowers are used as an ingredient rather than a garnish, sample the flowers first to make sure they complement the other foods used. If using flowers other than those listed in the table, make sure they are not poisonous. For example, lily of the valley and daffodils should not be eaten. Call the local extension office for more information about flower varieties that are safe to eat. Buy flowers from a reputable distributor to make sure they are non-poisonous, free from harmful pesticides, and grown and handled in a safe manner.

Nasturtiums

Calendulas

Pansies

TABLE 3.16   Fresh herb descriptions, flavor, and usage

ARUGULA

Description: Small, narrow, tender, smooth, notched leaves with a dark green color. May also be considered a salad green. Also known as rocket and roquette.

Flavor: Spicy, peppery, pungent. Small leaves are the mildest. Loses flavor when cooked. Add to cooked dishes just before serving.

Usage: Used in Mediterranean cuisine. Use small leaves in salads mixed with other mild-flavored greens. Seasoning for or complement to eggs, lamb, olives, pasta, poultry, salads soufflés, soups, tomatoes.

BASIL

Opal Basil

Description: Slightly crinkled, pointed leaves that range in color from medium or dark green to purple. Sweet basil is the most common variety, but other specialty varieties include cinnamon, lemon, opal, and other flavors. Member of the mint family.

Flavor: Pungent, clove-like aroma and anise-like flavor. Aromatic, warm, and slightly peppery.

Usage: Widely used in Mediterranean cuisines and with poultry, tomato sauces, and many vegetables. Blends well with garlic, lemon, fennel, marjoram, oregano, thyme, and curry. Ingredient in pesto. Seasoning for or complement to eggs, fish, meat, pesto, pizza, poultry, rice, salads, spaghetti sauce, and vegetables, especially beans, cabbage, summer squash, tomatoes.

BAY LEAF (BAY LAUREL)

Description: Long, thick, aromatic, dull green leaves (1/2-inch wide, 1 to 2-inches long). Member of laurel family.

Flavor: Peppery with hint of menthol when cooked. Flavor mellows when products cool.

Usage: Used to add flavor to meat, chicken, seafood dishes, and soups, stews, and casseroles. Usually discarded after cooking and prior to serving. Best if long simmered. Seasoning for or complement to fish, game, marinades, meats, poultry, sauces (especially tomato), soups, stews.

CHERVIL (SWEET CICELY)

Description: Small, fern-like leaves similar in appearance to parsley. Member of parsley family.

Flavor: Delicate parsley flavor with a mild anise flavor and aroma.

Usage: One of the traditional fines herbes. Heat for a short time. Seasoning for or complement to breads, eggs, fish, poultry, salads, salad dressing, shellfish, soups, vegetables.

continues

TABLE 3.16 *continued*

CHIVES

Description: Hollow, round, thin, sturdy stems that resemble young green onions. Bright green with round, purple flowers. Member of onion family.

Flavor: Mild onion or garlic flavor.

Usage: One of the traditional fines herbes. Flavoring for any savory dish or as a garnish. Purple flowers can be used in salads. Heat for a short time. Seasoning for or complement to butters, cheese, eggs, fish, meat, potatoes, poultry, salads, sauces, soups, vegetables (especially beans, carrots, cauliflower, corn, mushrooms, peas, squash).

CILANTRO (CHINESE PARSLEY OR MEXICAN PARSLEY)

Description: The green leafy plant that produces coriander seeds. Resembles flat leaf parsley.

Flavor: Bold sage-citrus flavor that is sometimes characterized as bitter and astringent. Flavor is pronounced and unique.

Usage: Important herb in cooking Mexican and Southwest fare and in Chinese, Indian, and Thai cuisines. Blends well with chiles, curry spices, and garlic. Best used raw or only slightly cooked. Use sparingly. Discard tough stems. Seasoning for or complement to cauliflower, chili, eggplant, fish, guacamole, meat, poultry, salads, salsa, tomatoes.

DILL

Description: Feathery and delicate blue-green leaf. Dill seeds are flattened, oval, and brown.

Flavor: Leaves have an anise-parsley-celery flavor that is pungent and slightly bitter. Seeds have a caraway-like bitter flavor.

Usage: Common in European and Scandinavian cuisines. Flavor of the leaf diminishes with heat, and flavor of the seed increases. Seasoning for or complement to butters, dressings, eggs, fish, meat, potatoes, poultry, salads, sauces, seafood or chicken salads, soups, vegetables.

EPAZOTE

Description: Flat, thin green leaves. Grows wild and is also called wormseed or stinkweed.

Flavor: Strong, kerosene-like aroma and wild flavor.

Usage: Flavoring in Mexican and Southwest cuisine. After drying, can be brewed. Seasoning for or complement to chiles, corn, pork, squash, tomatoes.

TABLE 3.16   *continued*

FENNEL

Description: Feathery leaf attached to a fennel bulb.

Flavor: Mild licorice flavor.

Usage: Chopped and sprinkled as a garnish. Seasoning for or complement to beans, lamb, omelets, pork, salads.

LAVENDER

Description: Thin leaves on long stems bearing a spiked purple flower.

Flavor: Aromatic herb. Flowers have a sweet, lemon-like flavor.

Usage: Used to flavor teas, tisanes, jams, and preserves.

LEMONGRASS (CITRONELLA GRASS)

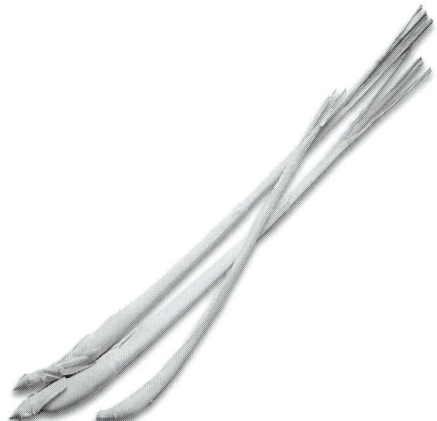

Description: Straw-like stalk similar to green onions in appearance but with a woody texture.

Flavor: Strong aroma and lemon flavor.

Usage: Only the lower portion of the white stalk is used. Used in Southeast Asian cuisine. Seasoning for or complement to curries, fish, salsa, soups, vinaigrettes.

LOVAGE

Description: Tall, celery-like stalks with dark green, celery-like leaves.

Flavor: Celery-like flavor.

Usage: Leaves and stalks used in salads, stews, and as a garnish. Seeds used to flavor cooked savory dishes.

continues

TABLE 3.16   *continued*

MARJORAM

Description: Tiny, rounded, bright green leaves similar to thyme. Member of the mint family.

Flavor: Aromatic, sweet-minty, slightly bitter. Similar to oregano but sweeter, milder, and less earthy.

Usage: Used in Greek, Italian, and Mexican dishes. Heat for a short time. Seasoning for or complement to fish, lamb, meat, omelets, pork, poultry, salads, soups, stews, vegetables (especially brussels sprouts, zucchini, peas, potatoes).

MINT

Peppermint

Spearmint

Description: Pointed, textured leaf. Size depends on variety.

Flavor: Aromatic with a peppery, spicy flavor. Peppermint has a more pronounced menthol and less-sweet flavor than spearmint.

Usage: Used to flavor sweet and savory dishes. Used in Middle Eastern, Thai, and Vietnamese cuisine. Seasoning for or complement to cheeses, curries, fruit, lamb, potatoes, poultry, salads, soups, vegetables (especially green beans, beets, carrots, peas). Used to flavor teas and tisanes.

OREGANO

Description: Thin, woody stalks with small oval leaves that are larger than marjoram. Member of the mint family.

Flavor: Bold, bitter, earthy, clove-like flavor similar to marjoram and thyme.

Usage: Used to season Greek, Italian, Mexican, and Spanish dishes. Seasoning for or complement to beans, fish, lamb, meats, pizza, poultry, salad dressings, shellfish, tomato dishes and sauces, vegetables (especially avocado, broccoli, cabbage, eggplant, peppers, tomatoes).

PARSLEY (CURLY, ITALIAN, OR FLAT LEAF)

Curly

Italian or Flat Leaf

Description: Curly has small, curly, bright green leaves, and Italian has flat, darker green leaves.

Flavor: Grassy, peppery flavor. Curly is sweeter than Italian parsley. Both have a distinctive clean, bitter flavor. Stems have stronger flavor than leaves.

Usage: Italian preferred for cooking. Used in savory dishes and as a garnish (curly). Component of fines herbes and of Bouquet garni. Seasoning for or complement to fish, pasta, potatoes, poultry, rice, vegetables.

TABLE 3.16 *continued*

ROSEMARY

Description: Leaves resemble short, spiky pine needles on a woody stalk. Member of the mint family.

Flavor: Fragrant, spicy, pine-like aroma and flavor.

Usage: Large branches can be soaked in water and used as skewers for grilled foods. Used in Middle Eastern dishes. Flavor is as intense when dried as when fresh. Cook at least 10 minutes to release flavor. Seasoning for or complement to breads, lamb, meat, pizza, pork sausage, potatoes, soup, stews, veal, vegetables (especially cauliflower, eggplant, peas, potatoes).

SAGE

Description: Narrow, oval-shaped, elongated leaves with a gray-green color. Large leaves may be velvety. Member of the mint family.

Flavor: Assertive, slightly bitter, musty flavor.

Usage: May impart a "soapy" flavor when too much is used. Use sparingly. Seasoning for or complement to breads, pork, poultry, sausages, stuffings, vegetables (especially winter squash).

SAVORY (SUMMER SAVORY)

Description: Tiny, narrow green leaves. Member of the mint family. (Winter savory resembles rosemary and has a strong pine flavor.)

Flavor: Sharp, peppery, clove-like and slightly bitter. Subtle thyme flavor.

Usage: Use sparingly. Seasoning for or complement to chowders, eggs, fish, meat, pork, potatoes, poultry, soups, vegetables (especially asparagus, beans, brussels sprouts, carrots, squash, tomatoes).

SORREL

Description: Pale green leaves that resemble spinach.

Flavor: Sharp, sour, lemony flavor.

Usage: Young leaves used as a salad green. Seasoning for or complement to eggs, fish, pork, poultry, salads, soufflés, sauces and soups (especially cream-based).

continues

TABLE 3.16   *continued*

TARRAGON

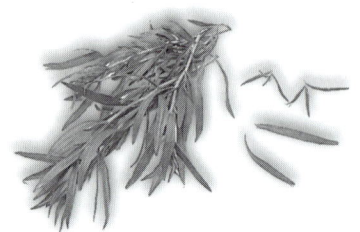

Description: Bushy with narrow, dark green leaves.

Flavor: Spicy and aromatic with a distinctive anise flavor.

Usage: Used in béarnaise sauce. Often used in French cuisine. A component of fines herbes. Use sparingly. Seasoning for or complement to cheese, eggs, fish, meat, poultry, shellfish, vegetables (especially artichokes, asparagus, beets, carrots, mushrooms, potatoes, squash), vinegars.

THYME

Description: Tiny, green-grey leaves on a small, bushy, woody stem. Member of the mint family.

Flavor: Aromatic, biting, spicy, mint or clove-like, lemony taste and aroma. Flavor varies with type of thyme.

Usage: An integral ingredient in bouquet garni. Important spice for Creole and Cajun dishes. Seasoning for or complement to eggplant, meat, peppers, poultry, seafood dishes, soups, sauces, tomatoes, vegetables (especially eggplant, onions, peppers, tomatoes).

Note: Fresh and dried herbs and spices are often combined and tied with twine in a bundle or tied in cheesecloth to provide flavorings, seasonings, and aromatics to sauces, soups, stews, and soups. The spices are removed and discarded after the desired level of flavoring has been achieved. Classic combinations include *Bouquet garni* (1 bay leaf, 2 oz carrot sticks, 4 oz celery stalks and leaves, 1 fresh thyme sprig, 3 leek leafs, 4 parsley stems); *Sachet d'épices* (1 bay leaf, 1 crushed garlic clove, 1/2 teaspoon dried thyme, 4 parsley stems, 1/2 teaspoon cracked peppercorns); and *Oignon Piqué* (1 whole onion studded with 12 cloves and 2 bay leaves that are slid into knife slits made in the onion).

TABLE 3.17   Edible flowers

Flower	*Taste*	*Description*
Bachelor's buttons	Bland	Pink, white, blue, and purple. 1-inch flowers.
Carnations, mini	Bland to bitter	Wide variety of colors.
Chive blossoms	Mild onion	Blue to lavender, ball shaped. 1-inch diameter.
Daisies	Bland	White or yellow petals with a yellow center. 1-inch diameter.
Lavender	Floral, herb	Light to medium purple.
Marigolds	Bland	Saffron-like color. Yellow to deep rust color.
Nasturtiums	Radish/peppery	Orange, yellow, rust, or red flowers. 1-inch diameter.
Pansies	Bland	Flat, multi-colored flowers. 1 to 2-inch diameter.
Roses, mini	Sweet, fruity	Orange, red, pink, yellow.
Snapdragons	Slightly bitter	Yellow, pink, red, orange, white. Peanut shaped.
Squash blossoms	Mild squash-like	Bright yellow.
Violas	Bland	Purple, yellow. Dime sized.
Violets	Slightly sweet, often peppery	Purple, yellow.

CANNED AND FROZEN FRUITS AND VEGETABLES

The canning process changes the character of fruits and vegetables by softening their texture and often changing their color. Canned products are available in standard-sized cans (Table 2.12, p 94). Vegetables may be water packed or packed with a variety of seasonings and sauces. Fruits also may be packed with water or in a sugar syrup (light, medium, or heavy). Solid-pack fruit without added water is available for products such as pies and fillings.

Canned fruits and vegetables will keep for an extended period of time in a cool storage area. Leaking or bulging cans should be discarded. Cans with deep dents or dented on a seam or around the lid should also be discarded.

Freezing is an effective method of preserving fruits and vegetables without causing as much color and texture change as canning. Individually quick frozen

(IQF) fruits and vegetables are easy to use and available in several carton sizes. Because they are frozen very quickly, ice crystals are small. Frozen products should be stored at a constant 0 to −10°F.

The USDA has established grades of quality for many canned and frozen vegetables and fruits. The grades are based on color, uniformity of size, shape, tenderness or degree of ripeness, and lack of blemishes. The label may designate U.S. Grade A (Fancy), U.S. Grade B (Extra-Select or Choice), and U.S. Grade C (Standard). The use of the USDA grades is voluntary and is paid for by the packer.

TOFU AND DRIED BEANS, LENTILS, AND PEAS

Tofu, a curd made from soybeans is bland tasting and can be purchased in a range of textures. Because it absorbs the flavor of other foods, it is extremely versatile and used in a variety of sweet and savory products.

Silken tofu is very soft and often pureed for sauces and dips. Because it falls apart easily, it should not be cooked for a long period of time. Firm and extra-firm tofu holds its shape better than silken or soft tofu and is best used in recipes specifying marinating or stir-frying. Tofu can be pressed to force out some of the water and make it firmer. Press tofu by placing it in a pan between several layers of clean cheesecloth and topping it with a counter pan. Put approximately 5 pounds of weight in the pan above the tofu and, while under refrigeration, allow the weighted pan to press the tofu for several hours. Freezing makes tofu porous and gives it a tougher texture. Fresh tofu is usually packed in water and should be drained before using. Tofu is a potentially hazardous food and must be kept refrigerated.

Among the many kinds of dried legumes available are dried beans, lentils, and peas. High in protein and fiber, legumes are an important component in one's diet. Table 3.18 identifies common varieties of dried beans, lentils, and peas.

TABLE 3.18   Common varieties of dried beans, lentils, and peas

Name	Description
Appaloosa bean	Speckled red, or black and white. Long and thin.
Black bean / turtle bean	Dark black with a white line. Medium-sized and almost round.
Black-eyed pea	Ivory or beige in color with a black spot. Small kidney shapes.
Cannelini bean	White, smooth, long. Looks like and sometimes called a white kidney bean.
Chickpea / garbanzo bean	Beige. Rounded acorn shape with lumps.
Dry split peas	Green or yellow. Skin is removed and pea split in half.
Great northern bean	White. Large oval. Very common white bean.
Kidney bean	Reddish to dark brown. Kidney shaped.
Lentils	Small disk shape about the size of a split pea half. Brown, dark or light green, orange, and yellow.
Lima bean	Broad and flat shape. Ivory color.
Navy / pea bean	White. Small round. Very common white bean.
Pigeon pea	Small, nearly round, ivory colored with orange-brown mottling.
Pinto bean	Medium-sized, kidney-shaped, mottled pink color.

Notes: • Generally beans are kidney shaped, lentils disk shaped, and peas round.
• Other varieties of beans are available. Flavor of beans varies slightly. Cooking times may vary slightly.

Black Beans

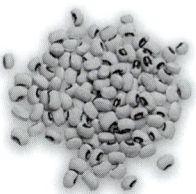

Black-Eyed Peas

Great Northern Beans

Red Kidney Beans

Lentils

Pinto Beans

Food Production and Service Staples

- Coffee and Tea
- Condiments and Vinegars
- Dried Herbs, Spices, and Seasonings
- Nuts and Seeds
- Extracts, Alcohol, and Sweeteners
- Fats

COFFEE AND TEA

Coffee beans are the seeds of a bush grown in many tropical and subtropical regions throughout the world. After harvesting the seeds by hand, they are cleaned, fermented, and dried. The green coffee beans are shipped to processors to be roasted, blended, and ground. Coffee is roasted and blended differently to produce brews with different flavor and color profiles.

High-altitude beans from Central and South America produce lively, light-bodied coffee with high concentrations of natural acids. Coffees made from Central or South American beans pair well with cheeses, vegetables, and hot and spicy foods, and are good for breakfast service. Beans grown in Africa are robust, with fewer natural acids. They are good served with desserts, full-flavored foods, chocolates, and rich desserts, and as an after-dinner coffee. Pacific beans feature moderate acidity and rich, mellow overtones. Pacific beans are good served with Asian foods and rich, creamy foods, and for breakfast.

Light/pale and medium/city roast are all-purpose roasts. Brazilian and Viennese roasts are also all-purpose roasts but are slightly darker than city roast. French/dark and Italian/espresso roasts are especially suited for after-dinner coffee and for serving with desserts and chocolate. Roast terminology may vary among geographic areas and among roasters.

Coffee is judged on four attributes: acidity, aroma, body, and flavor. Some acidity is a positive characteristic and refers to the tartness. The aroma provides the first hint as to the way the coffee will taste. Some coffees are more fragrant than others. Body refers to mouthfeel or how thick or heavy the coffee seems. Terms used to describe flavor include mellow, harsh, and earthy. Flavor is subjective and may be described differently by different tasters.

Specialty coffee refers to coffee made with flavored beans, espresso and espresso-based beverage, or coffee flavored with syrups, liquors, or other post-brew flavorings. Espresso-based drinks include:

Espresso—Espresso is made by forcing superheated water under pressure through a very dark-roasted, finely ground, packed coffee to make a strong, rich, smooth brew. A specially designed machine is necessary to make espresso. The process extracts more of the solids and flavor from the bean than conventional drip brewing. A single serving of espresso uses approximately ¼ ounce of ground coffee to 1½ ounces of water.

Espresso

Cappuccino—Made by using one-third espresso, one-third steamed milk, and one-third foamed milk.

Caffé Latte—Made by using one-third espresso and two-thirds steamed milk.

Cappuccino

Caffé Mocha—One-third espresso, two-thirds steamed milk, and flavored with chocolate syrup. Usually topped with whipped cream and chocolate shavings or cocoa powder.

Caffé Mocha

Flavored syrups are added to individual servings in a proportion of approximately 1 ounce per cup. Popular syrup flavorings include almond, caramel, chocolate, hazelnut, raspberry, strawberry, and vanilla. Shakers for dry flavorings such as allspice, chocolate, cinnamon, malt, nutmeg, and vanilla may be provided for self-service. Other condiments for coffee include brown or raw sugar, chocolate shavings, cinnamon sticks, citrus peel, and whipped cream.

Tea is made from the leaves of a shrub-like tree that grows at high altitudes in tropical regions of the world. Three main types of tea are available and are produced from the same plant by varying the processing. *Black tea* derives its color from a special processing treatment that allows the leaves to ferment and oxidize. The process turns the leaves black and produces an amber-brown and rich-flavored brew. English Breakfast and Orange Pekoe are familiar black teas. *Green tea* is made from leaves that are dried without fermenting. The brew is pale yellow-green in color and has a bitter flavor. Gunpowder is a quality green tea. *Oolong tea* is partially fermented and brews light in color.

CONDIMENTS AND VINEGARS

A condiment is added to a dish during or after cooking to introduce hot, piquant, sharp, spicy, or sweet flavors to foods. Some examples are fermented black bean sauce, fish sauce, hot pepper sauce, jam or jelly, ketchup, prepared mustard, and vinegar. Condiments may also be served on the side as an accompaniment. Accompaniment condiments include salsa, relishes, and pickles.

Vinegar is used as an ingredient or is added to foods as a condiment to impart a clean, sharp flavor. The flavor of vinegar varies depending on the liquid used. White or distilled vinegar is neutral in flavor and only adds sharpness to foods. The degree of a vinegar's tartness depends on the acidity or strength. Most vinegars are about 5 percent acidity but some are as high as 8 percent. Strong vinegars may need to be diluted with water before using in a recipe. Types of vinegars include:

Balsamic—A sweet tart vinegar with a dark reddish-brown color and intense but mellow flavor. This red wine vinegar has been aged in wooden barrels. Long-aged vinegar is extremely expensive and used in very small quantities, often to flavor berries or delicate salad greens. The readily available and inexpensive balsamic vinegars are made using a quick caramelization and flavoring process instead of an aging process. Balsamic vinegar can be reduced (boiled down) to produce an intensely flavored sweet-sour "syrup".

Cider—A pale brown vinegar with mild acidity, fruity aroma, and slightly sweet apple flavor. Made from apple pulp or cider. Cider vinegar is an all purpose vinegar.

Flavored—Another product is added to a vinegar (usually wine or distilled vinegar) to produce a product with the flavor and often the color of the added ingredients. Common products used to infuse vinegar to make a flavored vinegar include garlic, herbs (often tarragon), garlic, fruit (often raspberries).

Malt—A slightly sweet, mild flavored vinegar made from malted barley. Often used as a condiment with fried foods, especially fish.

Rice—A clear, light, slightly sweet vinegar made from fermented rice. Often used to flavor rice used for sushi, pickled ginger, and other Asian dishes.

Wine—A vinegar made from red or white wine, sherry, or champagne. The vinegar's color, flavor, and sharpness will depend on the characteristics of the wine used.

White or Distilled—Sharp, strong, and vinegary with a neutral flavor. General purpose vinegar.

DRIED HERBS, SPICES, AND SEASONINGS

Dried herbs, spices, and seasonings are indispensable kitchen staples necessary for preparing and serving flavorful foods. Herbs are defined as the leaf, stem, and sometimes flower portion of an aromatic plant. Spices are defined as the dried bark, buds, flowers, fruits, roots, and seeds of aromatic plants. Seeds are sometimes classified separately. Table 3.23, p. 184 describes some common seeds used in foods. Both spices and herbs are used to build flavor, and it is difficult to separate the two. Generally herbs and spices impart a new flavor to foods. Seasonings, such as salt, enhance natural flavors without causing a striking change in taste. The terms flavoring and seasoning are often used interchangeably.

Herbs and Spices

Many spices and dried herbs can be purchased whole or ground. Ground products have relatively more surface area than whole products and lose their flavor more quickly. Most ground herbs and spices lose flavor when heated for a long period of time and should be added near the end of the cooking process. Whole spices can be added earlier in the cooking process without losing flavor.

Some flavor differences can be expected when dry herbs are substituted for fresh. A guideline for substituting dried herbs for fresh is to use ⅓ the amount of fresh. For example, if a recipe specifies 1 tablespoon of fresh herbs, the alternative would be to use 1 teaspoon of dried. Table 3.19, p. 176 provides the number of teaspoons per ounce for some commonly used dry herbs and spices.

TABLE 3.19 Teaspoons per ounce for dry herbs and spices

Herb or spice (dry)	Equivalents (tsp per oz) (approx.)	Description
Allspice, ground	15	Flavor resembling blend of cloves, cinnamon, and nutmeg.
Anise seed	15	Warm licorice-like and mildly fennel-like taste.
Basil leaves	40	Anise, clove, and mint-like. Blends well with oregano, parsley, rosemary, thyme, sage, and saffron.
Bay leaf, crumbled	47	Also known as *laurel*. Strong distinctive flavor.
whole	136 (leaves)	
Caraway seed	13	Dill and anise-like flavor.
Cardamom, ground	19	Pungent, lemony flavor. Essential to Indian cookery.
Cayenne (red) pepper	16	Hot. Also known as *red pepper.*
Celery seeds	15	Slightly bitter with a celery-like flavor.
Chervil leaves	90	Delicate flavor of parsley and mild anise.
Chili powder	12	Distinctive flavor in Mexican cookery.
Chives, snipped (freeze-dried)	140	Mild onion and garlic flavor.
Cilantro leaves	45	Assertive sage-citrus flavor. Use sparingly.
Cinnamon, ground	20	Distinctive flavor in baked goods. Essential ingredient in *curry* spice blends, *Chinese five-spice powder.*
Cloves, ground	16 (ground) 17 (whole)	Strong aromatic spice. Commonly found in spice mixtures including *curry* and *bouquet garni.*
Coriander, ground	20	Citrus-like aroma and mild mint flavor. An essential ingredient in *curry, garam masala,* and *pickling spice.*
Cumin	17 (ground) 13 (seed)	Potent spicy flavor that tends to dominate food. Used in Mexican, North African, and Indian dishes. Use sparingly.
Curry Powder	14	Distinctive flavor in Indian cuisine.
Dill	13 (seed) 28 (weed)	Mild anise-parsley flavor.
Fennel, seed	14	Mild licorice flavor. Common in Italian and Swedish cookery.
Ginger, ground	15	Spicy and pungent.
Mace	15	The lacy covering of the nutmeg seed. Flavor more delicate than nutmeg.
Majoram	20 (ground) 57 (leaves)	Subtly minty and sweet, similar to oregano. Essential in Italian cooking.
Mint	50	Popular in Middle Eastern cooking.
Mustard	9 (seed) 16 (ground)	Pungent and slightly bitter.
Nutmeg	14	Warm and spicy. Blends well with mace, cardamom, cinnamon, cloves, and ginger.
Oregano	18 (ground) 45 (leaf)	Minty and sweet.
Paprika	14	Sweet capsicum flavor.
Parsley flakes	95	Mild, sweet in flavor.
Pepper, black	15	
Pepper, red	14 (ground) 16 (crushed)	Used to season Mexican dishes. Add in small quantities.
Pepper, white	13	Comes from the same pod as black pepper but the outer shell is removed. Milder, more delicate flavor than black pepper.
Pickling spice	15	Spice mixture.
Poppy seed	11	Sweet-nut flavor. Best if toasted before use.
Poultry seasoning	14	Herb and spice mixture.
Pumpkin pie spice	16	Spice mixture.
Rosemary	30 (leaves)	Spicy, strong, pine-like. Use sparingly.
Saffron	40	Expensive spice used to impart a golden color and distinctive flavor to foods. Often used in Spanish rice dishes.
Sage, rubbed	23	Strong flavored with a camphor-like taste. Blends well with rosemary, thyme, parsley, oregano, and bay leaf.
Savory	20	Slightly peppery, sharp and clove-like. Use sparingly.

TABLE 3.19   *continued*

Herb or spice (dry)	Equivalents (tsp per oz) (approx.)	Description
Sesame seed	14	Distinctive flavor develops if toasted prior to use. Often used in Middle Eastern and Asian cooking.
Tarragon leaves	50	Spicy, aromatic, and sharp. Essential to French cooking.
Thyme	20 (ground) 40 (leaves)	Spicy and clove-like. Use sparingly.
Tumeric	12	Used in small amounts to add a saffronlike color to foods. Used to flavor many African dishes.

Notes: • Spices should be stored in cool (68°F) and dry (humidity 60% or less) environment. Cool storage (32°–45°F) is recommended for paprika, red pepper, chili powder, allspice, cloves, parsley flakes, dill, marjoram, and cumin. Generally, spices should not be held for longer than 3 months. All spices should be kept tightly closed and measured with dry utensils and away from steam.
  • Spices and herbs can be creatively combined to enhance the flavor of foods. The art of skillfully adding the right amount of seasonings is basic to successful cookery. Both low-sodium and low-calorie foods can be made more interesting by the addition of spices and herbs.

For optimum flavor retention, dried herbs and spices should be stored in a cool, (68°F) dry (humidity 60% or less) environment, and out of direct sunlight. Very cool storage (32°F to 45°F) is recommended for allspice, dill, chili powder, cloves, cumin, marjoram, parsley flakes, paprika, and red pepper. Generally dried herbs and spices should be held for no longer than 3 months in a tightly closed container. Whole spices have relatively less surface area than ground spices and retain their flavor for a longer time. Measure herbs and spices with a dry utensil away from cooking steam.

The same herbs and spices are used to flavor many different food products. Table 3.20, p. 178 provides information about herb and spice usage for different categories of food.

Herbs and spices help to define the ethnic flavors and cuisines of different cultures. Table 3.21 lists spices and herbs that provide the unique flavor profile associated with foods from various countries or geographic regions of the world.

Often spices and dried herbs are combined to make natural spice blends that are associated with different cuisines. Some common natural spice blends with ingredient measurements follow.

Many foodservice operators prefer to mix their own spice blends for signature menu items. See

Natural Spice Blends

Bouquet Garni

Whole Marjoram	4 Tbsp
Whole Thyme	3 Tbsp
Parsley	2 Tbsp
Ground Bay Leaf	¼ tsp

Garam Masala

Ground Coriander	7 Tbsp
Ground Cumin	10 Tbsp
Ground Cinnamon	4 tsp
Ground Cardamon	4 tsp
Ground Black Pepper	2 tsp
Ground Cloves	2 tsp
Ground Mace	2 tsp
Ground Bay Leaf	½ tsp

Quatre-Epices

Black Pepper	7 Tbsp
Ground Nutmeg	8 tsp
Ground Cloves	4 tsp
Ground Ginger	4 tsp

Fines Herbes

Parsley	3 Tbsp
Chives	3 Tbsp
Chervil	1 Tbsp
Tarragon	1 Tbsp

Herbes de Provence

Whole Thyme	4 Tbsp
Whole Marjoram	8 tsp
Basil Leaves	8 tsp
Fennel Seed	4 tsp
Rosemary	4 tsp
Sage Leaves	4 tsp

From McCormick Food Service Division.

TABLE 3.20   Herb and spice usage for different categories of food

Spice	Appetizers	Soups	Meat	Seafood	Poultry	Vegetables
ALLSPICE	Steamed Shrimp, Liver Paté	Cream Soups, Split Pea, Oyster Bisque	Ham, Pork, Gravy, Marinade, Spiced Beef	Oyster Stew, Shellfish, Poached Fish	Quail, Duck, Goose, Pheasant	Squash, Sweet Potatoes, Carrots
ANISE	Oysters Rockefeller	Fish Chowder, Chicken Soup	Veal, Hungarian Goulash, Beef Marinade	Red Snapper, Lobster	Chicken, Duck, Quail	Cabbage, Leeks
BASIL	Cheese, Seafood	Minestrone, Clam Chowder	Beef Stew, Lamb, Spareribs, Beef Marinade	Lobster, Shrimp, Squid, Swordfish	Chicken, Turkey Stuffing, Quiche	Sweet Peppers, Eggplant, Potatoes, Zucchini, Tomatoes
BAY LEAF	Paté de Foie Gras	Onion, Bean, Vegetable, Lobster Bisque	Beef Stew, Broth, Beef Marinade	Seafood Stew, Poached Fish, Bouillabaisse	Chicken Pot Pie, Gravy, Marinade	Pickled Vegetables, Ratatouille, Green Beans
BLACK PEPPER	Paté	Gazpacho, Lentil, Minestrone	Steak, Hamburger, Gravy, Pork, Beef Marinade	Poached Fish, Marinade, Calamary	Fried Chicken Batter, Duck	All Vegetables
CARAWAY	Cheese Spreads, Muenster Cheese	Borscht, Cream Soups	Pork, Meatloaf, Sauerbraten	Shrimp, Crab	Duck, Goose	Cabbage, Carrots, Potatoes, French Fries
CARDAMOM	Pickled Herring	Chicken Soup, Fish Soup	Lamb, Meatloaf, Hamburger	Trout, Mussels	Roast Chicken	Sweet Potatoes, Fried Eggplant
CELERY SEED	Canapés, Cheese Dips, Shrimp Cocktail	Chicken, Potato, Vegetable, Lentil, Fish Chowder	Beef Stew, Pot Roast, Ham, Grilled Beef	Tuna, Shrimp, Oyster Stew	Eggs, Omelettes, Stuffing	Potatoes, Cauliflower, Corn Relish
CHIVES	Cream Cheese, Canapés, Stuffed Mushrooms	Chicken Soup, Vichyssoise	Pork, Gravy, Lamb	Salmon, Oysters	Omelettes, Quiche	Cucumbers, Baked Potatoes, Potato Pancakes
CILANTRO	Ceviche, Guacamole, Salsa	Hot & Sour Soup	Chili con Carne, Beef Stew	Poached Fish, Steamed Fish	Chicken	Onion, Tomatoes, Chili Peppers
CINNAMON	Fresh Fruit	Lamb Soup	Pork, Ham, Beef Stew, Lamb		Fruit Stuffing for Game	Sweet Potatoes, Carrots, Squash
CLOVES	Spiced Fruit	Beef Noodle, Beef Vegetable, Cream of Tomato	Ham Glaze, Beef Stew, Gravy		Cornish Hen, Duck, Gravy, Stock	Boiled Onions, Sweet Potatoes, Carrots
CORIANDER	Corn Pudding	Cream of Chicken, Hot & Sour Soup, Consommé	Pork, Ham, Spareribs, Marinade	Poached Fish, Steamed Fish	Chicken, Duck	Sweet Potatoes, Scalloped Potatoes, Braised Celery
CUMIN	Nachos, Cheese, Salsa	Seafood Gumbo, Chili-Bean	Chili con Carne, Sausage, Pork Stew	Fried Shrimp Batter, Deviled Crab	Chicken Stew, Chicken Crocquettes	Sauerkraut, Chili Peppers, Beans
DILL	Sour Cream Dips, Deviled Eggs, Shrimp Paté	Borscht, Lobster Bisque, Tomato	Veal, Grilled Lamb, Pork	All Seafood	Chicken, Omelettes	Cucumbers, Potatoes, Green Beans, Braised Cabbage
FENNEL	Shrimp Cocktail, Oysters Rockefeller	Creamed Fish Soup, Fish Chowder	Italian Sausage, Pork, Meatloaf	All Seafood (especially grilled)	Stuffing, Chicken Stew	Sautéed Mushrooms, Spinach, Cabbage
GARLIC	Dips, Escargot	Vegetable, Oxtail	Beef, Roast Lamb, Meatballs	All Seafood, Marinade	Chicken, Quail, Pheasant	Green Beans, Zucchini, Potatoes
GINGER	Shrimp, Cheese	Beef Vegetable, Beef Noodle, Hot & Sour Soup	Spareribs, Pork, Marinade	All Seafood	Duck, Poultry Glaze	Sweet Potatoes, Carrots, Stir-Fry Vegetables

TABLE 3.20   *continued*

Sauces	Salads	Dressings	Breads	Pastas & Grains	Desserts	Beverages
Barbecue, Sweet Cream, Creole	Fruit Salad	Fruit Dressing	Pancakes, Waffles, Muffins	Rice	Spice Cake, Angel Food Cake, Pies	Mulled Wine, Tea, Rum Drinks
Tomato		Orange Vinaigrette	Honey Buns, Sweet Rolls, Fritters		Spice Cake, Cookies, Candy	Lemonade, Cordials, Espresso, Hot Milk Punch
Barbecue, Pesto, Tomato	Vegetable Salad, Seafood Salad, Tomato Salad	Italian, Russian, Vinaigrette	Pesto Bread, Zucchini Muffins	Rotini, Rice, Linguini, Spaghetti		Carrot Juice, Tomato Juice
Béchamel, Creole, Tomato, Barbecue		Vinaigrette				
Tomato, Barbecue, Curry	Green Salad	Vinaigrette, Mayonnaise		Carbonara, Fried Rice, Pasta		Tomato Juice
Lemon, Butter, Cream	Coleslaw, Potato Salad	Mayonnaise, Vinaigrette	Biscuits, Rye Bread, Corn Muffins	Risotto	Cookies, Seed Cakes	Kümmel
Curry, Spiced Yogurt	Fruit Salad	Oriental Dressing		Risotto, Rice Pilaf	Ice Cream, Cakes, Pastries, Apple Pie	Coffee, Tea, Glögg, Spiced Wine
Cream, Creole, Tomato	Tuna Salad, Potato Salad, Macaroni Salad	Mayonnaise	Biscuits, Breads, Rolls	Pasta	Pastries	Tomato Juice
Tomato, Cream, Hollandaise	Green Salad, Potato Salad, Macaroni Salad	Green Goddess, Thousand Island	Buttermilk Bread, Bread Spreads, Potato Rolls	Pasta		
Yogurt Sauce, Tomato, Curry		Mexican Dressing	Herb Bread	Lentils, Mexican Green Rice, Chinese Noodles		
Custard Sauce, Yogurt Sauce, Sweet & Sour	Fruit Salad	Fruit Dressing	Rolls, French Toast, Breads	Curried Rice, Risotto	Apple Pie, Chocolate Cakes, Cookies	Coffee, Cider, Mulled Wine, Hot Chocolate
Béchamel, Raisin Sauce, Curry		Fruit Dressing	Cinnamon Bread		Chocolate, Gingerbread, Mincemeat	Fruit Punch, Mulled Wine
Curry, Cream	Potato Salad		Honey-Wheat Bread, Corn Bread	Orzo	Pastries, Cookies, Cakes	Pineapple Juice, Grapefruit Juice
Barbecue, Spiced Yogurt	Bean Salad	Spanish Dressing	Jalapeño Bread, Corn Bread	Rice		Kümmel
Mustard Sauce, Cream, Cucumber Sauce	Macaroni Salad, Potato Salad, Shrimp Salad	Dill Cream, Mayonnaise, Vinaigrette	Rye, Pumpernickel, Bread Spreads	Rice, Pasta		
Cream, Curry	Potato Salad, Shrimp Salad	Mayonnaise, Vinaigrette, Mustard	Cracker, Rolls, Bread Sticks	Risotto Rice	Apple Pie, Candy, Pound Cake	
Tomato, Garlic Butter	Green Salad	Mayonnaise, Vinaigrette, Italian	Garlic Bread, Bread Spreads, Focaccia	Linguini, Spaghetti		
Curry, Soy Sauce, Sweet & Sour			Pastries	Couscous, Rice	Gingerbread, Pudding, Apple Pie	Mulled Wine, Tea, Ginger Beer

continues

TABLE 3.20 *continued*

Spice	Appetizers	Soups	Meat	Seafood	Poultry	Vegetables
MACE	Liver Paté, Cheese	Vichyssoise	Sausage	Potted Shrimp, Oyster Stew	Creamed Chicken, Cornish Hens	Rutabaga, Spinach, Asparagus, Sweet Potatoes
MARJORAM	Fried Cheese, Paté, Anchovies	Consommé, Bean, Corn, Split Pea	Lamb, Hamburger, Pork, Veal	Baked Fish, Seafood Breading	Chicken Stuffing, Eggs	Zucchini, Tomato, Carrots, Peas, Lima Beans
MINT	Cucumber-Yogurt Dip	Fruit Soup, Split Pea	Lamb Stew, Venison		Marinade	Peas, Potatoes, Cucumbers
MUSTARD	Deviled Eggs, Meatballs, Ham Spread	Creamed Seafood	Ham Glaze, Beef, Sausage, Cold Meat	Baked Fish, Crab		Baked-Mashed Potatoes, Cabbage, Sauerkraut
NUTMEG	Fruit	Mushroom Soup	Pot Roast, Meatloaf, Ham		Fried Chicken Batter, Turkey Stuffing	Spinach, Carrots, Sweet Potatoes, Braised Cabbage
OREGANO	Fried Cheese, Paté, Salsa Meatballs	Corn Soup, Vegetable Soup, Consommé	Pork, Veal, Lamb, Hamburger	Seafood Breading, Baked Fish	Chicken Stuffing	Zucchini, Tomatoes, Carrots, Green Beans
PAPRIKA	Deviled Eggs, Nachos, Potted Cheese	Minestrone, Seafood Soup, Chowder	Goulash, Veal, Sausage, Meatloaf	Seafood Breading, Baked Fish, Shellfish	Chicken Stuffing	Potatoes, Cabbage, Mushrooms, Cucumbers
PARSLEY	Canapés, Deviled Eggs	Vegetable Soup, Chicken Soup	Meatballs, Hamburger, Veal	Shellfish, Baked Fish	Chicken	Zucchini, Potatoes, Tomatoes, Green Beans
POPPY SEED	Cheese			Broiled Fish, Tuna Casserole	Turkey Stuffing	Green Beans, Onions, Tomatoes
RED PEPPER	Deviled Eggs	Hot & Sour Soup	Sausage	Crab Cakes, Shrimp	Omelettes, Chicken	
ROSEMARY		Consommé	Lamb, Pork, Venison, Meatballs, Marinade	Baked Fish, Shrimp	Chicken, Quail, Pheasant, Goose, Cornish Hen	Eggplant, Turnips, Squash, Potatoes
SAFFRON		Chicken Soup, Fish Soup	Lamb	All Seafood	Chicken Stew, Scrambled Eggs	
SAGE	Cheese, Country Paté	Consommé, Minestrone	Sausage, Ham, Lamb, Veal, Venison	Seafood Stuffing, Trout	Stuffing, Quail, Duck, Goose, Pheasant	Acorn, Squash
SAVORY	Goat Cheese	Lentil, Bean, Split Pea	Stuffing, Veal, Gravy, Hamburger, Meatloaf	Baked Fish, Sea Bass	Stuffing, Chicken, Turkey, Eggs	Onions, Peas, Green Beans, Navy Beans
SESAME	Hummus Dip		Beef, Pork, Hamburger, Lamb	Baked Fish, Shrimp, Scallops	Chicken	Vegetable Stir-Fry, Green Beans
TARRAGON	Mushroom Caps	Turtle Soup, Fish Chowder	Steak, Beef Stew, Marinade	Lobster, Shrimp	Cornish Hens, Marinade, Chicken, Eggs, Omelettes	Mushrooms, Stuffed Tomatoes
THYME		Oxtail, Consommé	Sauerbraten, Pork, Lamb, Marinade	Baked Fish, Seafood Stuffing	Stuffing, Chicken, Fried Chicken Batter	Potatoes, Tomatoes Zucchini
TURMERIC	Deviled Eggs	Chicken Noodle, Lentil		Shrimp, Scallops	Chicken, Eggs	
WHITE PEPPER	Veal Paté	Consommé, Vichyssoise		Baked Fish	Chicken, Turkey	Potatoes

TABLE 3.20 *continued*

Sauces	Salads	Dressings	Breads	Pastas & Grains	Desserts	Beverages
Chicken Cream, Béchamel					Chocolate, Vanilla Pudding, Gingerbread	Wassail, Chocolate Drinks
Barbecue, Tomato, Butter	Cucumber-Yogurt Salad	Oil & Vinegar, French, Italian	Bread Sticks, Pizza, Herb Bread	Spaghetti, Pasta Orzo		
Sweet Sauce, Yogurt Sauce, Mint Sauce	Cucumber Salad	Fruit Dressing, Yogurt Dressing, Cranberry Dressing	Minted Yogurt Bread	Bulgar, Orzo	Candy, Chocolate	Iced Tea, Mint Julep, Hot Chocolate
Cheese, Sour Cream, Lemon-Mustard Yogurt Sauce	Coleslaw	Vinaigrette, Mayonnaise, Rémoulade				
Cream Mushroom Sauce, Béchamel		Creamy Dressings	Cinnamon Rolls	Tortellini, Ravioli	Rice Pudding, Custard Cakes, Soufflés	Egg Nog, Brandy Alexander, Punch
Barbecue, Tomato, Butter	Tomato & Onion Seafood Salad	Oil & Vinegar, French, Italian	Cheese Bread, Pizza, Bread Sticks	Pasta, Rice, Ravioli		
Barbecue, Cream, Yogurt		French, Russian	Garlic Bread, Muffins	Lasagne, Rice, Orzo		
Tartar Sauce, Béarnaise, Tomato	Tuna or Egg Salad, Macaroni Salad, Green Salad	Mayonnaise, Italian, Ranch, Vinaigrette	Garlic Bread	Pasta, Orzo		
Curry, Butter	Fruit Salad	Oil & Vinegar, Blue Cheese	Rolls, Breads, Crackers	Egg Noodles, Rice	Cakes, Cookies, Pastry Filling, Apple Strudel	
Barbecue, Tomato-Anchovy		Mayonnaise, Thousand Island	Pizza, Corn Muffins	Rice, Tabbouleh		Tomato Juice, Bloody Mary
Tomato, Cheese	Cold Beef Salad	Vinaigrette	Spoon Bread, Herb Bread, Pizza	Pasta, Lentils		
Seafood Saffron, Vegetable Cream, Tomato			Rolls, Biscuits, Sweet Breads	Rice, Risotto, Orzo	Cakes, Rice Pudding, Cookies	
Tomato		Herb Dressing	Sage Bread, Rolls	Risotto, Fetuccine		
Tomato, Horseradish			Savory Rolls, Herb Bread	Lentils, Egg Noodles		
Hoisin Sauce, Peanut Sauce	Green Salad	Mayonnaise, Tahini Dressing	Buns, Rolls, Waffles, Breads	Egg Noodles, Rice, Bulgar	Cookies, Pie, Pastry, Pecan Pie	
Rémoulade, Béarnaise, Tartar, Mustard Sauce	Shrimp Salad, Tomato Salad	Mayonnaise, Vinaigrette, Green Goddess	Herb Bread	Pasta, Orzo	Rhubarb Compote	
Tomato, Thyme Pesto		Vinaigrette	Bread Spreads, Herb Rolls	Pasta, Rice		Mulled Wine
Cream, Yogurt Caper Sauce, Satay	Egg Salad	Mayonnaise, Creamy Dressings	Breads	Rice, Egg Noodles		
Béchamel Cream		Mayonnaise, Vinaigrette		Rice, Egg Noodles		Vegetable Juice

From McCormick Food Service Division.

TABLE 3.21   Regional flavorings

African	Dill seed	Nutmeg	Red pepper
Anise	Nutmeg	Red pepper	Sweet pepper
Cinnamon	Onion		
Coriander	Paprika	**Indonesian**	**Spanish**
Cumin	Rosemary	Caraway	Anise
Mint		Cinnamon	Bay leaf
Saffron	**Greek**	Cloves	Cinnamon
	Bay leaf	Curry	Cumin
Chinese	Cinnamon	Garlic	Garlic
Anise	Fennel	Ginger	Paprika
Cinnamon	Garlic	Nutmeg	Parsley
Cloves	Lemon	Red pepper	Saffron
Fennel	Mint		
Garlic	Oregano	**Italian**	**Swedish**
Ginger		Basil	Allspice
Red Pepper	**Hungarian**	Fennel	Bay leaf
Sesame	Caraway	Garlic	Dill
Soy Sauce	Cinnamon	Marjoram	Cardamom
	Dill	Oregano	Cinnamon
French	Paprika	Pepper	Mustard
Chives	Poppy seed	Sage	Nutmeg
Fines herbes			
Garlic	**Indian**	**Mexican**	**Thai**
Marjoram	Anise	Achiote	Chile Pepper
Rosemary	Cardamom	Chile pepper	Citrus
Shallots	Celery seed	Cilantro	Coriander
Tarragon	Coriander	Coriander	Dill
Thyme	Cumin	Cumin	Garlic
	Curry	Garlic	Mint
German	Garlic	Lime	Turmeric
Caraway seed	Ginger	Oregano	

recipes for dry seasoning blends, pp 781–783. The following spice blends are available commercially.

Chinese five-spice—Equal parts of finely ground Szechuan pepper, star anise, cloves, cinnamon, and fennel seed.

Curry powder—There are many different curry mixtures, some sweet and others hot and pungent. Traditional curry mixtures contain many of the following spices: black pepper, cilantro, cinnamon, cloves, coriander, cumin, ginger, mace, red chiles, and turmeric.

Italian seasoning—Basil, marjoram, oregano, rosemary, sage, savory, and thyme are common spices used in an Italian seasoning blend.

Pickling spice—The blend of spice varies by manufacturer and will include black peppercorns and red chiles with some or all of the following: allspice berries, cinnamon stick, whole cloves, ginger, mustard seeds, coriander seeds, bay leaves, and dill seed.

The aroma and flavor of any whole spice or seed will be enhanced by toasting or dry-frying in a skillet or in the oven. See p. 782 for a procedure to toast spices.

Salt and Pepper

Salt, the most basic seasoning, is used universally in every food production kitchen throughout the world. Salt has the ability to "round out" flavors in foods and provide a desirable flavor balance. While technically a spice, pepper also enhances the flavor of food without altering its flavor appreciably. Table 3.22 identifies and describes the salt and pepper seasonings used most often to enhance the natural flavors of food products.

Monosodium glutamate (MSG) resembles salt in appearance and enhances the natural flavor of food without imparting a distinct flavor of its own. MSG occurs naturally in some foods and is also manufactured commercially. The distinctive taste that MSG produces has been called *umami*. The umami taste is referred to as a "savory" taste, distinct from the four classical tastes of sweet, sour, salty, and bitter. MSG enhances the flavor of low-acid foods (fish, meats, poultry, and vegetables) but has little effect on high-acid foods (fruits) and milk products.

MSG has been designated as safe for consumption by the general population. However, it has been reported to cause a reaction in some people and the FDA

TABLE 3.22   Salt and pepper seasonings

Name	*Description*
SALT	
Curing	A blend of salt and sodium nitrate. Used for curing meats.
Kosher	A purified rock salt without additives. Kosher salt is lighter in weight and flakier than table salt. The lightness varies by brand. Kosher salt dissolves quickly and will not cloud clear food products. It is a cooking salt preferred by most foodservice professionals. To achieve the same level of saltiness that table salt provides, the amount of kosher salt may need to be increased by 1 1/2 to 2 times the volume. Saltiness differs among brands.
Rock	Unrefined salt not used directly in food. Used in some ice cream machines for freezing ice cream.
Table	A salt product that is commonly used for cooking and for adding to foods at the table. Dissolves slowly. Table salt generally has a chemical added to keep it free flowing. Available both with and without added iodine.
Sea	Known also as *fleur de sel* or *sel gris* (French for gray salt). Salt is made from evaporating natural sea water and is available ground or in whole crystals. Because of the presence of other minerals, sea salt has a more complex flavor and often a gray-brown color. The salt's flavor will vary depending on the geographic location of the sea water used. Sea salt is considerably more expensive than other salt and is often used for finishing and as a condiment.
PEPPER	
Peppercorns	*Black peppercorns* are the dried, unripe berry of a climbing vine (piper nigrum) that is unrelated botanically to red peppers, which belong to plants from the genus Capsicum. The green berries become dark brown or black in the drying process. *White peppercorns* are the kernels of the ripe red berry with the skin removed to expose the white interior. White pepper is more intense than black pepper. *Pink peppercorns* are from a South American tree and not the same vine that produces black and white peppercorns. Pink peppercorns are bitter and less spicy than true pepper. *Green peppercorns* are unripe peppercorns that are packed in vinegar or brine, canned, or freeze dried. Freeze-dried peppercorns must be reconstituted before using. They have a strong distinct flavor but are not hot.

Black Pepper   White Pepper

Pink Peppercorns

Green Peppercorns

Other Peppers	Cayenne, chile flakes, and paprika are sometimes used to season food. In addition to seasoning, these peppers are likely to impart their characteristic flavors.

Cayenne Pepper

Crushed Chiles

Paprika

Note: Salt and pepper may be mixed to simplify seasoning of meats and vegetables. A recommended mixture is four parts of table salt to one part of ground black pepper. Kosher and sea salt are less salty and a higher salt ratio is recommended.

requires that it be listed as an ingredient when added to food. Foodservice operators should be aware of products that contain MSG so customers' inquiries about its use can be accurately answered.

NUTS AND SEEDS

Nuts and seeds are used to add both flavor and texture to foods. Nuts have a high fat content and will absorb odors or become rancid if held improperly or for too long a time. Nuts and seeds will retain their freshness for 3 to 6 months if stored tightly covered in a cool, dark, well ventilated area or up to 1 year in a freezer. The aroma and flavor of nuts and seeds will be enhanced by toasting or dry-frying in a skillet or in the oven. Toast nuts and seeds following the procedure on p. 782.

Common nuts and seeds used in the kitchen are described in Table 3.23.

TABLE 3.23   Nuts and seeds

Name	Description
Almond 	Tear-drop shaped. Available whole, sliced, slivered, ground, and as paste. Blanched almonds (brown skin removed) or natural almonds (with skin) may be used interchangeably in recipes if skin color is not undesirable. Main ingredient in marzipan. Used in pastries and candies. Pale-brown woody shell.
Brazil nut 	Large, elongated oval shape and creamy white color. High oil content. Eaten raw and used for bakery and candy products. Hard, dark brown, three-sided shell.
Cashew 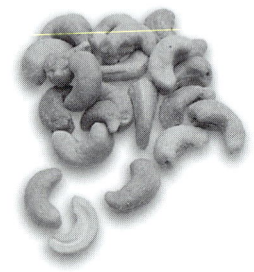	Kidney shaped with a distinct flavor. Eaten raw and used in candies, cookies, and cooking (especially in some Asian dishes). Always sold shelled.
Chestnut 	Large brown tear-shaped nut that must be cooked before using. Can be purchased cooked (boiled, dried, roasted, steamed) and canned, or raw in the shell. Distinctive flavor. High starch content. Used in stuffing, soups, sauces, sweet dishes, and pastries. Glossy dark-brown shell.

TABLE 3.23   *continued*

Name	Description
Coconut 	Large melon-sized nut with white, sweet, nutty flavored meat and a crisp, chewy texture. Can be purchased in the shell or as processed shredded or flaked coconut (sweetened or unsweetened). Requires considerable amount of effort to remove the nutmeat from the shell of a fresh coconut. Used in pastries and candies. Important ingredient in Caribbean and Indian cuisines. Thick, hard, dark-brown shell covered with coarse fibers. *Coconut water* is the thin liquid from inside the raw coconut; it is usually discarded. *Coconut milk* is a liquid made by steeping shredded coconut in boiling water and then separating the "milk" (liquid) from the coconut. *Coconut cream* is made like coconut milk but with less water. Coconut cream is different from *cream of coconut* (a canned commercial product that is a thick, sweetened, coconut-flavored liquid used in baking and for beverages. Cream of coconut is not an acceptable substitute for coconut cream or coconut milk.
Hazelnut 	Small round shape with a rich delicate flavor. Often ground for use in cakes and pastries. Outer bitter skin can be removed by roasting the whole shelled nut in a 275°F oven for 12 to 15 minutes and, while still hot, rubbing the nuts in a dry towel or mesh sifter. Shell is hard and shiny with a lighter color where the cap was attached. The closely related filbert nut is slightly larger than a hazelnut and very similar in appearance and flavor.
Macadamia 	Small, round, creamy white nut with a high fat content. Associated with Hawaiian cuisine. Used in cookies and sweet pastries. Always sold shelled because shelling must be done by machine.
Peanut 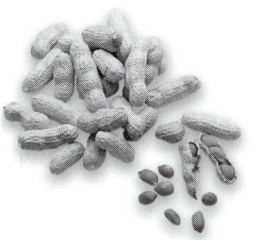	A legume that grows underground along the root of a plant. Available raw or roasted. Shell is light brown and breaks easily.
Pecan 	Medium brown nutmeat with a rich, mapley flavor. Available in halves or various size pieces. Used in breads, pastries, sweets. Shell is medium-brown, smooth, and glossy.

continues

TABLE 3.23   *continued*

Name	*Description*
Pine nut 	Also known as piñon nuts and pignole. Seeds of several species of pine trees. Tiny, cream-colored, elongated kernel. High in fat and becomes rancid quickly. Used in breads, pastries, salads. Essential ingredient in pesto.
Pistachio 	Green colored meat (red pistachios are dyed) with distinctive sweet flavor. Used in pastries, desserts, meat dishes. Hard, light-brown shell that opens at one end when mature.
Poppy seeds 	Tiny, round, blue-black seeds, with a sweet nutty flavor and crunchy texture. Used in pastries, breads, salad dressings.
Pumpkin seeds	Flat, oval, cream colored seed with a mild nutty flavor. Semi-hard hull with soft oiler interior. Eat out of hand or use as garnish.
Sesame seeds 	Small, flat ovals with a creamy-white or black color. Nutty, earthy flavor. Often ground into a paste (known as tahini), or served as a garnish (often toasted) in bread and meat dishes. Popular in Indian and Asian cuisines.
Sunflower seeds	Small, flat, teardrop-shaped. Light tan in color with a nutty flavor. Used as a topping for salads, in cookies, or eaten out of hand. Shell is black and white.
Walnut 	Light brown in color with a mild, sweet flavor and tender texture. General all-purpose nut. Hard, light-brown, rounded shell.

EXTRACTS, ALCOHOL, AND SWEETENERS

Flavorings other than herbs and spices are important kitchen staples necessary for making flavorful dishes. Extracts and essential oils from aromatic plants, dissolved in alcohol, are commonly used in baked products and sauces. Only small amounts of extracts are needed to flavor products and, if feasible, should be added toward the end of the cooking period. For products that are baked, the extracts should be incorporated into the fat to reduce volatilization. Keep alcohol-based extracts tightly closed and in a cool environment.

Liquors, liqueurs, distilled spirits, and wines add a flavor profile to foods that is distinctly different from other flavorings. The common selections for use in food production include ales, beers, brandies, cognacs, champagnes, liqueurs or cordials, red and white wines, ports, sauternes, sherry, and vermouth. Bourbon, rum, and whiskey are also used to flavor foods and beverages.

For flavoring purposes, it is not always necessary to purchase the highest quality of product available. The products should, however, be a quality that is suitable for drinking. The aroma and flavor of delicate foods and sauces will reflect the quality of alcohol used.

Table wines begin to lose their flavor after opening and should be used within a short amount of time. Keeping opened wines tightly closed and refrigerated will help preserve their flavor. Fortified wines (e.g., sherry, port), liqueurs or cordials (e.g., amaretto, crème de cacao, crème de cassis, kirsch, Kahlúa), and brandies (e.g., cognac) keep their quality longer than table wine. Room temperature storage, away from heat and light, is acceptable. Refrigerator storage is recommended if space is available.

Sugars and syrups add flavor to foods when used as an ingredient in recipes or when added to food and beverages after cooking. Sugars and syrups used in kitchens are identified in Table 3.24.

FATS

Fat is the general term that describes a category of kitchen staples used for flavoring, as a cooking medium, and as an ingredient in many recipes. Generally fats can be categorized as solid or liquid. Solid fats include butter, lard, margarine, and shortening.

Butter is the fat portion separated from cow's milk. See p. 119.

Lard is the fat rendered from the fatty tissue of hogs. Because of lard's excellent shortening power it makes flaky pie crusts. Because of the degree of saturation and health concerns, lard is used less today than in the past.

Margarine or oleomargarine can be used in place of butter in most recipes. Some flavor differences may be noticed and some texture changes can be expected

TABLE 3.24   Sugars and syrups

Name	Description
SUGAR	
Brown	Refined sugar that has molasses returned to it and therefore has a slight molasses flavor. Light brown sugar has less molasses added than dark. May be used to flavor cooked cereal.
Turbinado	A partially refined sugar with coarse crystals and a caramel flavor. May be used to flavor beverages.
Granulated	All-purpose sugar also called table sugar. Fine, uniformly shaped crystals. Adds sweetness to any product.
Sanding	Large, coarse crystals that are slow to dissolve. Used primarily for decorating cookies and pastries.
Superfine	Also called castor sugar. Granulated sugar with smaller-sized crystals. Dissolves quickly in liquids.
Powdered	Also called confectioner's sugar. Made by grinding granulated sugar into a fine powder. Cornstarch is added to absorb moisture and prevent lumping. Sprinkled on cookies and pastries as a garnish and in icing, glazes, and for decorating.
SYRUP	
Flavored	A sugar or other syrup with added flavorings. Used to flavor beverages.
Honey	A distinctive sweetener made by honey bees from the flowers of a wide variety of plants. The color and flavor depends on the nectar collected by the bees and the season of the year. Most honey sold commercially is from the nectars of sweet clover and alfalfa. Honey is a flavorful sweetener for hot tea and condiment for baked yeast and quick breads.
Maple	Real maple syrup, made from the sap of maple trees, adds a distinct flavor to pancakes, waffles, and ice cream when used as a topping. An artificial maple syrup is made by adding maple flavoring to corn syrup.
Molasses	A liquid by-product from sugar refining that adds a unique flavor to food products. The amount of refinement determines the color and flavor.

in baked products. Soybean and cottonseed are the primary oils used to make margarine.

Shortening (vegetable) is a product made by hydrogenating vegetable oils into a more solid plastic product. The degree of hydrogenation determines the hardness. Vegetable shortening may be all-purpose or manufactured for a specific purpose such as deep-fat frying or cake making. Shortening not designated as vegetable shortening may contain animal fat.

Oils are fats that are liquid at room temperature and are made by extracting oil from high-oil-content seeds, plants, fruits, and vegetables. Because cost, flavor, and other attributes vary among oils, it is important to select the correct one.

Canola oil is a light golden-colored oil processed from rapeseeds. It is a flavorless, all-purpose oil good for frying and general cooking, and is high in unsaturated fatty acids.

Coconut oil is a heavy oil extracted from coconuts used primarily in processed foods. It has a high proportion of saturated fatty acids.

Corn oil is a medium-yellow oil. It is mildly flavored and a good all-purpose oil.

Cottonseed Oil is a pale-yellow oil processed from the cotton plant. It is a flavorless all-purpose oil often used for frying.

Frying oil is a blend of oils that will remain stable when exposed repeatedly to high heat.

Grapeseed oil is a light medium-yellow oil made from grape seeds. An aromatic oil with a delicate, mild flavor, it is often used for salad dressing.

Olive oil varies from pale yellow to deep green depending on the processing procedures and the variety of olive used. Color is not a good indicator of flavor. The acidity level and extent of processing used to extract the oil is designated by extra virgin, virgin, and pure. *Virgin* oil is from the first cold pressing and has the lowest acidity level and most flavor. *Extra virgin* designates a top grade of virgin olive oil with the lowest acidity level. *Pure* olive oil and oil labeled "olive oil" are made from the pulp left after the first pressing. Olive oil has the least flavor and is suitable for cooking. Heat and chemicals may be used to produce pure olive oil.

Peanut oil is a pale-yellow refined oil with a very subtle scent and flavor. Because of its high smoke point, peanut oil is often used in high-heat Asian cooking.

Safflower oil is a golden-colored oil with a light texture and neutral flavor. It is a good all-purpose oil.

Salad oil is a blend of oils, neutral or mild in flavor, used as an all-purpose oil.

Sesame oil has a pronounced aroma and flavor. The light variety made from untoasted seeds is milder than the darker variety made from toasted seeds. Often used as a flavoring for Asian dishes.

Soybean oil is a light-yellow, relatively heavy oil with a mild flavor. A good frying oil.

Sunflower oil is pale-yellow, light oil with a neutral flavor and no aroma. It is an excellent all-purpose oil.

Vegetable oil is made by blending several oils; it might be a heavy oil. Vegetable oil is blended to have a mild taste and a high smoke point.

Walnut oil is medium yellow in color with a distinct nutty flavor and aroma. With a low smoke point, it is more suited for flavoring than cooking. Other flavorful nut oils are **almond,** and **hazelnut.**

The temperature at which fat begins to break down is called the smoke point. Cooking at high temperatures, such as for deep-fat frying or sautéing, requires a fat with a high smoke point. The smoke point can be low for oils used for flavoring purposes, as in salad dressings. Table 3.25 identifies the smoke point for commonly used frying fats.

TABLE 3.25   Approximate smoke points of selected fats

Fat	Smoke Point
Butter	260°F/127°C
Butter (clarified)	335–380°F/168–193°C
Canola	430–448°F/220–230°C
Corn	410°F/210°C
Cottonseed	450°F/232°C
Margarine	410–430°F/210–221°C
Olive (extra virgin)	250°F/121°C
Olive (pure)	410°F/210°C
Peanut	450°F/232°C
Safflower	510°F/265°C
Shortening (formulated for deep-fat frying)	440°F/227°C
Shortening (vegetable)	410°F/210°C
Soybean	495°F/257°C
Sunflower	440°F/225°C

- Smoke point is the temperature at which a fat's chemical structure is altered, causing it to smoke. When this change occurs, it is often referred to as *breaking down.*
- Fats with a high smoke point should be used for high-heat cooking such as deep-fat frying and sautéing.
- The smoke point temperatures may vary for different brands of the same fat because of a slightly different chemical structure.
- Heating fats repeatedly can cause the smoke point to lower. Some points are lowered also by salt, water, overheating, food particles, and oxygen.
- Fryer fat should be changed when it becomes dark, smokes, foams, or develops off-flavors.

CHAPTER 4

Production Fundamentals

Ian O'Leary © Dorling Kindersley

Organizing the production process and following basic food production principles is fundamental to producing quality food. This chapter describes how to develop a production schedule and complete classic *mise en place* tasks. Basic cooking terms and methods will be explained.

Evaluating food quality at critical points throughout production is elementary to continuous improvement. The information and guides included in this chapter will make the evaluation task easier.

This chapter includes the following topics:

- Production and Kitchen Readiness
- Production Scheduling
- Cooking Methods and Terms
- Evaluating Food for Quality

PRODUCTION AND KITCHEN READINESS

Mise en place—a French term meaning "*everything in its place*"—describes a series of elementary preparations that are essential for producing quality food in an efficient manner. The goal of *mise en place* activities is to complete as much work as possible before the actual food production without detracting from the quality of the final product. The efficiencies achieved will help production staff apply their cooking skills effectively.

The efficiencies will allow for greater attention to be given to preparing and serving quality food without the delays and interruptions that could jeopardize quality. *Mise en place* benefits also include improved sanitation and a professional-looking production area.

The following guidelines represent the advance preparations, organization, and kitchen set-up— *designed to get "everything in its place"*—that should be completed before food production begins. There is no specified order for completing the *mise en place* tasks. Generally, however, it is recommended that the tasks requiring the most time or involving the most functional areas be started first.

Assemble Tools and Equipment

The work space should be organized for convenience and efficiency before cooking begins. Identify, gather, and conveniently store the equipment and tools required to prepare the recipes and to serve and hold food correctly. Equipment will include mixing bowls, sauce pans, cookware, thermometers, serving pans and plates, storage containers, measuring devices, tasting spoons and dishes, and required hand tools. Pre-heat ovens and cooking surfaces and assemble equipment such as choppers and food processors. Set up breading and battering stations. Assemble the correct equipment to complete the tasks to be accomplished. Sharpen knives if needed and store knives and cutting boards in a convenient location. Sharp knives reduce preparation time, reduce injury, and improve quality.

189

See Chapter 5, Knives and Other Equipment, for knife sharpening instructions and information about basic tools and equipment used in food production.

Gather Ingredients

Assemble food products that will be needed and store them in a convenient location and at the correct temperatures if potentially hazardous. Wipe can lids, open packages and cans, wash fruits and vegetables, fill food bins, etc.

Complete Pre-preparation Steps and Prepare Sub-Recipes; Prepare Par Levels of Seasonings and Food Staples

Review recipes and prepare in advance any pre-preparation steps or sub-recipes that can be done without jeopardizing food quality. For example, clarify butter, toast nuts and spices, make bread crumbs, pare and cut fruits and vegetables, make mierpoix (see p. 198), make cold sauces, drain fruit, roast peppers, and zest lemons. The goal is to have all ingredients ready to assemble so the final recipe preparation can be efficient and as close to service time as possible.

Prepare or assemble par levels of frequently used ingredients and products that are needed to produce the recipes. Examples of products that often have par level amounts established include seasoning bundles like bouquet garni or sachet (p. 172 and 460), marinades (pp. 783–787), pastes and rubs (p. 782), spices, and garnishes.

Weigh and Measure Ingredients

Whenever possible, weigh or measure the ingredients that are needed in the recipes. Assemble the ingredients close to the production area.

Clean the Workplace and Keep It Orderly

Work surfaces should be clean and sanitary before starting production and should be kept clean throughout the production period. Place sanitizing solution and clean wipe cloths in an easily accessed location away from food. Designate an area for soiled utensils, dishes, cloths, and trash receptacles.

PRODUCTION SCHEDULING

Production scheduling is a decision making and communication process to establish the time sequence needed to transform raw food into quality menu items for a specific period of time or meal. It requires an understanding of production steps, timing requirements for production processes, food science and food safety principles, and quality standards. Knowledge about production staff's skills and talents and about how to use time, equipment, and space resources efficiently is also needed. Production scheduling is a control in the production process that serves to minimize production problems and delays and maximize food quality. The production controls provided by a well thought out production schedule will help reduce the instances of both over and under production. Producing too much or too little food might introduce food safety risks. In addition, it usually challenges food quality, and often increases both food and labor costs.

Production scheduling includes developing a *production worksheet* (also called a production sheet or production schedule). A production worksheet is a written plan that communicates to production staff the work that is to be accomplished during a specific period of time. Items included on a production worksheet should be individualized to the needs of each organization. The following items are often included on production sheets and discussed at production meetings:

- Calendar date and meal or period of time the production schedule covers.
- Menu items to be produced and recipe name if different from the menu item name.
- Forecast amount and actual yield of recipes produced.
- Names of production staff who are responsible for specific tasks.
- Approximate starting and completion times for menu items.
- Batch cooking instructions and partial or just-in-time assembly expectations.
- Substitutions or back-up items.
- Special instructions and comments.
- Instructions for using pre-served (leftover) foods. (Instructions for safety and for making foods being served a second time look appealing and taste good.) (See also menu planning guidelines for minimizing leftovers, p. 10).
- Instructions for handling anticipated leftover food.
- Pre-preparation tasks and additional assignments.
- Facilities may use the production worksheet to record end-point cooking temperatures and other HACCP information. When used for this purpose, a designated section should be established on the production worksheet so the information can be easily retrieved and reviewed.

COOKING METHODS AND TERMS

Food is cooked when heat is transferred from a heat source (usually gas or electric) to the food by one of three methods: conduction, convection, or radiation. *Conduction* is the transfer of heat via a food's direct contact with a metal pan, liquid, or air. Heat is also transferred when a cooler portion of a food conducts heat from a hotter area. *Convection* heat transfer is achieved by moving heated air, liquid, or steam around food. This can be from the natural movement of hot and cool liquids or gases, or from mechanical means such as fans that circulate air in an oven. *Radiation* heating occurs when waves of either microwave (light waves) or infrared energy (heat waves) are transmitted to the food. In most cooking methods, more than one means of heat transfer occurs. In all cases, heat is disseminated throughout the food by conduction. Table 4.1 identifies the primary method of heat transfer for the basic cooking methods.

Table 5.6 identifies the large equipment requirements for basic cooking methods.

Applying heat to food causes changes in color, texture, flavor, and shape. Understanding the effect of heat on protein, carbohydrates (starches and sugars), water, and fats will facilitate the control of the cooking processes to produce quality food.

Coagulation is the irreversible transformation of protein molecules from a soft to a firm state. Examples that clearly represent the effect of heat on protein can be seen in egg white protein becoming white and solid, meat protein firming up, and gluten (wheat protein) setting up to give bread its characteristic structure. Most proteins complete the coagulation process between 160 and 185°F. Using excessive heat and cooking meat protein beyond the optimum coagulation point will cause excessive loss of moisture and toughening of the meat fibers. When connective tissue is heated with moisture, however, some collagen is softened and tenderization occurs.

When heated, starch granules absorb water and swell. This process, called *gelatinization*, is responsible for the thickening of liquids and for the firming and drying of baked products, such as cakes and breads. The temperature at which starch granules gelatinize varies depending on the specific starch and other ingredients in the product. Generally, however, swelling is usually complete at a temperature of 190 to 195°F. Proper starch gelatinization can be interrupted by such things as excessive and prolonged heat, insufficient heat, failure to disperse dry starch in melted fat or cold water, and excessive agitation after a gel is formed.

Browning and flavor changes occur when sugar is exposed to high heat (sucrose at about 338°F) and is allowed to *caramelize*. The sugars that caramelize may be common table sugar like that used in baked products or sugars that occur naturally in most foods. Excessive caramelization may give the food a burned flavor and an unappealing dark color.

Most food contains water that will turn to steam and *evaporate* when heated to the boiling point. If food is heated for too long a time or at too high a temperature, the excessive moisture loss will cause a dry product. Fat is *melted* when heated and serves to alter the texture and flavor of foods. Melted fat can attain a temperature high enough for browning to occur.

Foods are cooked by either dry or moist heat when they come in contact with hot air, fat, liquid, or steam. *Dry heat methods* are those that use hot air or fat as the cooking media or subject food to direct flame heat. *Moist heat methods* cook by surrounding food with a hot liquid or steam. Moist heat techniques start the cooking process with dry heat and are sometimes referred to as *combination cooking methods*.

Careful selection of the cooking media and heat method is necessary to ensure that quality standards and the desired sensory characteristics are met. The following criteria should be considered when deciding on the cooking methods that are best suited for foods.

- **Texture of the food.** For example, firm, delicate, dense. Foods must be able to withstand the handling required by the cooking method selected.
- **Amount of fat in meat or fish.** For example, highly marbled with fat, lean. Foods that are self-basting (with internal fat) will stay moist without added moisture.

TABLE 4.1   Primary heat transfer for basic cooking methods

Cooking method	Convection	Conduction	Radiation
Barbecuing			X
Boiling	X		
Braising	X	X	
Broiling			X
Deep-fat frying	X	X	
Grilling			X
Oven frying	X		
Panfrying	X	X	
Poaching	X		
Roasting and baking	X		
Sautéing		X	
Simmering	X		
Steaming	X		
Stewing	X	X	
Stir frying		X	

Note: All cooking methods cause a conduction heat transfer within the food once the food or its surface becomes heated. Some cooking methods use more than one method of transferring heat to the food. In this case, both methods are identified in the table. Table 5.6 identifies the large equipment requirements for basic cooking methods.

Table 4.2   Names and suggested cooking methods for beef cuts

Beef cut	Also known as . . .	Stir fry	Sauté	Panbroil	Broil	Grill	Braise
CHUCK							
Top Blade Steak, Boneless	Book Steak, Butler Steak, Lifter Steak, Petite Steak, Top Chuck Steak Boneless	X	X	X	X	X	X
Shoulder Steak, Boneless	Clod Steak, English Steak, London Broil, Shoulder Steak Half Cut		X[a]	X[a]	X[a]	X[a]	X
Chuck Arm Steak	Arm Swiss Steak, Chuck Steak for Swissing, Round Bone Steak						X
Chuck Eye Steak, Boneless	Boneless Chuck Fillet Steak, Boneless Steak Bottom Chuck, Boneless Chuck Slices	X	X	X	X	X	X
Chuck Mock Tender Steak	Chuck Eye Steak, Chuck Fillet Steak, Fish Steak, Chuck Tender Steak						X
Chuck 7-Bone Steak	Center Chuck Steak				X[a]	X[a]	X
RIB							
Rib Steak		X	X	X	X	X	
Rib Eye Steak	Beauty Steak, Delmonico Steak, Fillet Steak, Spencer Steak	X	X	X	X	X	
PLATE							
Skirt Steak	Fajita Meat, Inside Skirt Steak, Outside Skirt Steak, Philadelphia Steak		X[a]	X[a]	X[a]	X[a]	X
SHORT LOIN							
T-bone/Porterhouse Steak			X	X	X	X	
Tenderloin Steak	Filet Mignon, Fillet De Bouef, Fillet Steak, Tender Steak	X	X	X	X	X	
Top Loin Steak, Boneless	Ambassador Steak, Strip Steak, Boneless Club Steak, Hotel Style Steak, Kansas City Steak, New York Strip Steak, Veiny Steak	X	X	X	X	X	
Top Loin Steak, Bone-in	Chip Club Steak, Club Steak, Country Club Steak, Delmonico Steak, Shell Steak, Sirloin Strip Streak, Strip Steak	X	X	X	X	X	

- **Amount of connective tissue in meat.** Moist heat cooking methods soften connective tissue and have a tenderizing effect. Dry heat methods do not.
- **Grade and location of the meat cut.** For example, loin, round, shoulder. Grade and location of the cut will determine the amount of internal fat and connective tissue.
- **Size, shape, and thickness of the food.** The way heat penetrates food varies among cooking methods making the food's physical characteristics an important consideration.
- **Sensory characteristics desired.** For example, color, flavor, texture. The cooking method used will have an impact on the food's color, flavor, and other sensory attributes.

Foods appropriate for the different cooking methods are identified in the discussion of each method. Table 4.2 provides suggested cooking methods for beef cuts.

Table 4.2   *continued*

Beef cut	Also known as . . .	Stir fry	Sauté	Panbroil	Broil	Grill	Braise
SIRLOIN							
Sirloin Steak	Flat Bone Steak, Pin Bone Steak, Round Bone Steak, Wedge Bone Steak	X	X	X	X	X	
Top Sirloin Steak, Boneless	Sirloin Butt Steak, Top Sirloin Butt Center Cut Steak	X	X	X	X	X	
Tri-Tip Steak	Triangle Steak	X	X	X	X	X	
FLANK							
Flank Steak	Flank Steak Fillet, Jiffy Steak, London Broil	X			X[a]	X[a]	X
ROUND							
Round Tip Steak, Thin Cut	Ball Tip Steak, Beef Sirloin Tip Steak, Breakfast Steak, Knuckle Steak, Sandwich Steak, Minute Steak	X	X	X			
Round Steak	Full-cut Round Steak						X
Top Round Steak	Top Round London Broil	X	X[a]	X[a]	X[a]	X[a]	
Eye Round Steak				X[a]		X[a]	X
OTHER CUTS							
Cubed Steak		X	X	X			X
Chopped Steak			X	X	X	X	

From National Cattlemen's Beef Association, *The Complete Take On Steak: The Food Professional's Handbook* (Chicago, 1997).

[a]Marinate before cooking.

Cooking methods for chicken, turkey, duck, and goose are identified in Chapter 13, p. 527.

Dry Heat Cooking Methods

Broiling, Griddle Broiling/Pan Broiling, Grilling, and Barbequing

Broiling, griddle broiling/panbroiling, and *grilling* techniques cook food using direct or radiant heat from either an overhead or underneath heat source. Broiling generally refers to heat from an overhead heat source, grilling from an underneath source, and griddle broiling and panbroiling from a hot flat surface such as a griddle or heavy pan. Broiling and grilling temperatures are regulated by the food's distance from the heat source. *Barbecuing* and grilling differ only in that barbecuing generally means cooking food in an outdoor environment using wood, charcoal, or gas fuel.

Broiled and grilled food have a browned, flavorful exterior and a moist interior. Broiling is suited for foods that are relatively thin and uniform in size, and with enough internal fat or moisture to keep from becoming dry when subjected to high broiling or grilling temperatures. The following are examples of foods typically broiled and grilled:

Meat	Poultry	Fish	Vegetables	Fruit
Tender cuts, e.g., chops, steaks, patties; 1–2 inches thick.	Cook whole birds rotisserie style. Chicken pieces are not usually broiled but may be suitable for grilling if brushed with oil or marinated.	Oily fish, e.g., bass, salmon, swordfish, trout, tuna; 1–2 inches thick. (Brush with oil before broiling or grilling.)	Not usually broiled. Bell peppers, eggplant, mushrooms, onions, squash, are suitable for grilling if brushed with oil.	Bananas, grapefruit halves, pineapple.

Broiling and grilling procedures

1. Preheat broiler or grill. A preheated rack will provide the desired markings on the food.

2. Place food on the rack. Put presentation side on the rack first. When grid marks are desired, halfway through cooking on the first side gently slide a spatula under the food and rotate a quarter turn. A distance of 3 to 5 inches from the heat source is recommended. The distance from the heat source should increase when broiling thick or very cold meat. Brushing lean cuts of meat and other foods with oil will keep them from sticking to the grate.

   Delicate or very tender foods that will be damaged by placing them directly on the broiler rack can be placed on a preheated heat-proof platter and then placed under the broiler. Care should be taken to keep food from cooking in its own juices because if moisture accumulates, the method will change from dry heat to moist heat.

3. Broil or grill meat until the side closest to the heat source is attractively browned and cooked almost halfway through.

4. Turn meat. Turn only once during cooking. To keep from piercing meat, use tongs or a long-handled spatula. Broil second side to desired doneness and season. See tables in Chapter 12, p. 479 for approximate cooking times for meat.

   To keep thick cuts or meat cooked well done from becoming charred on the outside before reaching the desired internal temperature, move the meat farther from the heat source or finish it in the oven.

   For high volume production, it may be necessary to quickly mark the meat on the grill without cooking, chill it quickly, and then place it on a sheet pan to cook in the oven.

Panbroiling and griddle broiling procedures

1. Place food on a preheated ungreased griddle or heavy frying pan.

2. Cook slowly, turning as necessary. Since the meat is in contact with the hot metal of the pan or griddle, turning more than once may be necessary for even cooking. If the meat is thick, reduce the temperature after browning.

3. Cook the meat at a moderate temperature. To keep juices in, care should be taken not to puncture the meat while cooking. Use long-handled tongs or a spatula for turning.

4. Do not add fat or water. Pour off or scrape away any excess fat or juices as they accumulate. If juices accumulate around the food, the method of cooking will change from dry heat to moist heat.

5. Cook meat to the desired degree of doneness. Season. See tables in Chapter 12, p. 479 for approximate cooking times.

Barbequing procedures

1. Light charcoal. When coals are ash covered (in approximately 30 minutes) spread into a single layer.

2. Place seasoned or unseasoned meat on the grill directly over the ash-colored, medium-hot coals. (Coals are medium-hot when a hand can be held at cooking height for 4 seconds before the heat forces it to be pulled away. Extreme care should be taken when measuring the temperature of the coals in this way.)

3. Grill meat uncovered. See tables in Chapter 12, p. 486 for approximate cooking times. If using bamboo skewers, they should be soaked in water for at least 30 minutes to keep them from burning. If using a sauce or glaze, it should be brushed on several times and the product should be turned repeatedly to keep it from burning. Season.

Roasting and Broiling

Roasting and *baking* refer to a cooking process using air heated in an oven. A dry cooking environment is maintained by putting the food in an open pan without adding moisture. Food cooks when hot air is transferred by convection to the food's surface. The term roasting is generally used for meats and poultry, and baking for fish, fruits, pastries, and vegetables. There are exceptions to the terms' use, however, as in baked ham and roasted red-skinned potatoes. Roasting and baking methods are appropriate for a wide variety of foods that vary in size and shape.

Roasted and baked foods have a brown, rich-flavored, caramelized exterior, and a moist interior. The degree of browning and caramelization depends on the cooking time, the oven temperature, and the nature of the product being cooked. Browning and tenderizing occurs when meat is roasted at a low, constant oven temperature. Less tender cuts with considerable connective tissue should be cooked at lower temperatures for a longer time than tender cuts. Moist heat cooking methods will dissolve more connective tissue and are more appropriate than roasting for tough cuts of meat.

Meats may be completely or partially defrosted, or frozen at the time the cooking process is begun. Meat roasted from the frozen state will yield as much meat as roasts partially or completely thawed before cooking. However, when time is a factor, defrosting meat before cooking is the accepted method. The additional cooking time required for frozen roasts is from one-third to one-half again the amount of time recommended for cooking a similar cut from the chilled state. Oven temperature should not change.

Roasting and baking methods are appropriate for a variety of foods with varying sizes and shapes. The recipe sections of this book include information and procedures for baking breads (Chapter 8, p. 263) and desserts (Chapter 9, p. 319), and timetables for roasting meats (Chapter 12, p. 479), chicken (Chapter 13, p. 527), and fish (Chapter 11, p. 457).

The following are examples of foods typically roasted and baked:

Meat	Poultry	Fish	Vegetables	Fruit
Tender, relatively large or thick cuts (standing rib, fillet, leg of lamb)	Whole, quartered, or half birds	Large and medium sized whole fish or thick steaks or fillets	Most vegetables, especially root and starchy vegetables (carrots, beets, eggplant, parsnips, potatoes, turnips, winter squash)	Firm, large fruits (apples, peaches, pears)

Roasting and baking procedures for savory foods

1. Preheat the oven.
2. Prepare the foods to be roasted or baked. Brush with oil or butter, if appropriate (as for roasted potatoes, and some lean meats). Add herbs and other seasonings. Prick whole potatoes to allow steam to escape. Very lean game birds and lean meats will benefit from larding (fat, usually pork, is inserted deep into the flesh). Salt does not penetrate far into a large piece of meat so it makes little difference if a large roast is seasoned at the beginning or end of the roasting time.
3. Place the food on a rack in a pan, or directly in a roasting pan. When cooking meat, place fat side up. As the fat melts and runs down over the meat, it bastes the roast. Basting adds flavor and keeps the surface of the roast from drying out.
4. Roast the food, uncovered, at the appropriate temperature until it reaches the desired doneness. Baste meat with the juices that collect in the pan or with a marinade as necessary to keep it from drying out and to add flavor. Vegetables and cut potatoes should be turned once or twice as they roast.

   Do not add water and do not cover meat. Adding water to the pan changes the cooking method from dry to moist heat.

   Roast at a constant oven temperature. High heat is used for small, very tender cuts of meat that cook quickly, such as beef tenderloin. Meats cooked at high temperatures will have more caramelization and greater shrinkage.
5. Toward the end of the roasting period, insert a meat thermometer so that the tip rests in the center of the roast without touching bone or fat. Vegetable and fruit doneness can be tested by inserting a fork to measure softness or tenderness.

The length of the cooking period depends on several factors: oven temperature, size and shape of the food item, style of cut (bone-in or boneless), proportion of meat to bone, meat quality, oven load, and degree of doneness required. See recipe chapters for timetables for roasting beef, lamb, pork, and veal (Chapter 12, p. 479) and poultry (Chapter 13, p. 527).

Meat should be removed from the oven and allowed to set in a warm place, generally tented with foil, for 15 to 20 minutes or more before being sliced. Roasts will continue to cook during this period as the heat continues to penetrate to the center. Generally a 5 – 10°F rise or **carry over** can be expected. Small roasts lose surface heat rapidly and will have the lowest rise in temperature. During this resting time, the meat will become more firm and easier to slice with minimal juice loss.

6. Season as appropriate.

Frying

Frying is a dry-heat method of cooking and a term used to describe cooking in fat. The amount of fat distinguishes the methods of frying. *Deep-fat frying* uses a large amount of fat; *panfrying* and *griddle frying* (also called *griddling*), a moderate amount of fat; *oven frying*, some fat; and *sautéing* and *stir frying*, a small amount of fat.

Deep-fat frying heats food through conduction and convection by submerging it in hot fat. The high heat causes food to brown and cook quickly. Other frying methods cook foods through contact with fat but also through heat conducted from the pan or griddle. Pan frying and griddle frying are similar to pan and griddle broiling except that both frying methods have fat added. Fat and drippings are not scraped away during griddle frying as they are with griddle broiling. The amount of added fat depends on the food being cooked.

Well prepared deep-fat fried foods will have a crisp, golden-brown exterior, a minimum amount of fat absorption, and no off-flavors imparted by the frying fat. Most deep-fat fried foods have a protective coating of breading or batter to provide color, flavor, and crispness. The color and crispness of pan and griddle-fried foods will depend on whether a coating or breading is used, the length of cooking time, and the nature of the product. Sautéed and stir-fried foods are cooked very quickly at a high temperature in a small amount of fat. They may or may not be browned and crispness is not always an objective. Oven-fried foods are cooked at a high temperature in an oven after first being drizzled with fat. The food resulting from this production method is intended to resemble pan fried and deep-fat fried foods in texture and exterior color. Following are examples of foods typically fried:

	Meat/Poultry/Eggs	Fish	Vegetables/Fruit
DEEP-FAT FRIED	A variety of meat and poultry products, usually battered or breaded; bone-in or bone-out chicken pieces. Large pieces of meat or poultry are usually not deep-fat fried.	A variety of fish and shellfish, usually battered or breaded; shrimp.	A variety of vegetables, usually battered or breaded; mushrooms, okra, onions, potatoes.
PAN FRIED	A variety of meat and poultry products. May be dredged in seasoned flour to form a crisp crust as for fried chicken. Chicken, turkey, veal scallops.	A variety of fish products. May be dredged in seasoned flour to form a crisp crust.	Eggplant, potatoes.
GRIDDLE FRIED	Boneless, thin meat and poultry products; fried eggs; scrambled eggs.	Thin fillets.	Hash browned potatoes.
OVEN FRIED	Meat and poultry with some thickness; chicken pieces, quarters, or halves.	Thick fillets.	Not usually oven fried.
SAUTÉED	Thin pieces of poultry and tender cuts of meat.	Thin fillets.	High moisture vegetables, bell peppers, mushrooms, onions, summer and zucchini squash. Fruits; bananas, pineapple, apples, peaches.
STIR FRIED	Small thin strips of poultry and tender cuts of meat.	Scallops, shrimp.	A variety of vegetables; beans, bell peppers, edamame, greens, mushrooms, onions, peas, other.

Deep-fat frying procedures

1. Prepare the food to be fried—cut, trim, bread, batter. Portioned prebreaded items can be cooked from a frozen state.
2. Heat the fat to approximately 350°F (or per recipe). Foods will absorb some fat during cooking. A cooking temperature that is too low will increase the amount of fat absorbed. Adding 15 to 20 percent fresh fat or oil each day the fryer is in use will extend the life of the fat. Care should be taken not to damage fat. Fat is damaged by prolonged heating, overheating, moisture, salt, and food particles.
3. Submerge food in hot fat by either loading a wire basket with food to be fried and lowering it slowly into the fat or dropping the food directly into the hot fat. If food is crowded, it will not cook evenly and the fat temperature might be reduced too quickly thereby increasing fat absorption and inhibiting browning. When filling a wire basket, do so away from the grease. Particles of food and ice crystals will damage the fat. Stacking an empty basket over a basket with food will help keep it submerged for even cooking.
4. Continue cooking until the outside of the product is browned and crisp and the meat reaches the desired doneness. Internal temperature is the most accurate indicator of doneness. A combination of sensory indicators are helpful in determining doneness: surface color, timing, and sampling for doneness. Cooking time depends on the size of the food item, whether it is frozen or chilled, and whether the food has been precooked.
5. Remove meat from fat and let it drain. Do not shake the basket over the fat if the product is

coated; shaking will cause particles and crumbs to fall into the fat and damage it.

6. Transfer the food to a pan lined with a rack or absorbent paper. Season away from fat. Serve as soon as possible after frying. The crust on fried products softens quickly after cooking.

Pan and griddle frying procedures

1. Prepare the food to be fried—cut, flatten, bread, batter, flour.

2. For pan frying, heat (approximately 325°F) enough fat in a heavy pan or skillet to cover the food to a depth of ⅓ to ½-inch. When using a griddle (solid cooking surface), put some fat at the place the food will be placed. For both pan frying and griddle frying, the amount of fat depends on the food being cooked.

3. Carefully place food in the pan or on the griddle. Take care not to splash hot fat.

4. Cook slowly, uncovered, until the food is brown on one side. Turn and brown on the other side. Generally pan- and griddle-fried foods are done when browned on both sides. Pan- and griddle-fried meats may be browned and removed to a pan and finished in the oven. The pan should not be covered and moisture should not be added. Since food is in contact with the hot metal of the pan or griddle, turning more than once may be necessary for even cooking. If meat is thick, reduce the temperature after browning.

5. Cook meat to the desired degree of doneness. Drain on absorbent paper. Season.

Oven frying procedures

1. Prepare the food to be oven fried—dust with flour if desired, put on a greased baking pan and drizzle food with oil or brush with melted fat. Season. Placing food on silicone paper will make clean-up easier.

2. Preheat oven to 400 to 450°F. Place food in oven. Cook uncovered until the food is brown and cooked to the desired doneness.

3. Do not cover or add moisture.

Sautéing procedures

1. Prepare the food to be sautéed—flatten or cut to an even thickness, dust in flour if desired.

2. Heat a sauté pan and add enough oil or fat (clarified butter, pure olive oil, frying oil) to cover the bottom of the pan. Both the pan and oil should be very hot when the food is added. The amount of oil depends on the food. Meats with considerable internal marbling will require only a small amount of fat.

3. Place the food in the pan, presentation side down. To allow for proper color and flavor development, the food should not be crowded and the pieces should not overlap.

4. Fry the food on one side until browned. Using tongs, turn once and brown the other side. Thin meat used for sautéing is usually done when browned on both sides. When thicker meat is sautéed, the temperature should be lowered after some browning or the food can be finished to the desired doneness in the oven.

5. Remove the food from the pan and make a sauce using the pan drippings. All or some of the fat can be poured off before making a sauce using the pan drippings and the stuck-on bits that are removed in a *deglazing process* (adding a liquid such as broth, cognac, stock, water, or wine and scraping loose any stuck-on pieces of browned food.)

Stir-frying procedures

1. Prepare the food to be stir-fried—cut into small uniform pieces, cut meat into thin slices or strips. Partially freezing meat will facilitate slicing.

2. Heat a wok or other suitable pan and add a small amount of oil to the pan. Both the pan and the oil should be very hot when the food is added.

3. Add the main ingredient or meat and stir-fry quickly, keeping the food moving constantly using a light tossing motion to keep from breaking up the pieces. Stir and cook until the main ingredient is done, pushing it up the sides of the wok away from the most intense heat. Add additional ingredients in sequence (those with the longest cooking time first), cooking and moving them up the sides of the wok. Cook until vegetables are tender-crisp.

4. Add thickening liquid and sauces (see p. 877 for cornstarch and water ratio). Cook just until sauce thickens and ingredients are lightly coated. Serve immediately after cooking.

Moist Heat Cooking Methods

Moist heat cooking methods transfer heat to food through liquid or steam. Food products cooked by moist heat methods have a more subtle flavor, softer texture, and different appearance than those cooked with dry heat. Flavor and color differences are due in part to the absence of surface caramelization that occurs with dry heat.

Blanching and Parboiling

Blanching and *parboiling* are terms to describe the process of submerging food in a hot liquid for a brief time and then quickly chilling it in a cold liquid. The cooking time for parboiling food is longer than for blanching food. Boiling water is generally used to blanch and parboil fruits and vegetables. French fries may be blanched or parboiled in hot oil. Blanching and parboiling fruits and vegetables sets the color, destroys enzymes, and loosens skins for easier peeling. Parboiling softens the food more than blanching and is appropriate for foods that will be finished by sautéing or stewing.

Blanching and parboiling procedures

1. Immerse fruits and vegetables in a large quantity of boiling water. The time depends on the amount of softening desired and the nature of the food. Blanching requires immersion for a few seconds to a minute. Parboiling may require several minutes depending on the food and the degree of cooking desired.

2. After immersing for the desired amount of time, remove the food from the boiling water and plunge it immediately into ice water to stop the cooking process. The process of quickly chilling blanched or parcooked food is referred to as *shocking* or *refreshing*.

Braising

Braising is a cooking process that begins with dry heat and finishes with moist heat. Food is first browned using high heat and a small amount of fat and then liquid is added. The food is covered and cooked slowly over low heat. Fricasseeing is a braising method in which food is simmered in a thickened liquid (gravy) rather than water or other non-thickened liquid. Pot-roasting also applies to this cooking method. Braised foods should have a deep color that is appropriate for the food being prepared and a robust flavor with a full-bodied sauce. Foods should retain their natural shape and be moist and fork-tender. Fork-tender is a term that means a fork will slide out of the food easily after being inserted in the thickest part.

Portion-sized or larger pieces of meat and poultry are most often braised. The method is appropriate but not often used for parboiled vegetables and whole fish.

Braising procedures

1. Prepare the food to be braised—trim meat and poultry and dredge in flour if desired. Dredging in flour increases browning and may be omitted. Parboil vegetables.

2. Sear the food on all sides in a small amount of hot oil. Browning develops aroma, flavor, and color. Large pieces can be browned in a heavy pot on top of the stove, in the oven, or in a steam-jacketed kettle.

3. Remove the food from the pan and add **mirepoix**, if desired. Cook until the desired color. For meats, the mirepoix is usually browned more than for poultry. One ounce of mirepoix for each pound of

meat is a guideline. The standard mirepoix mix of vegetables is chopped onion or leeks (2 parts), chopped carrots (1 part), and chopped celery (1 part). For a white mirepoix, parsnips may be substituted for the carrots. Bacon or ham may be added to give flavor. The vegetables should be larger when the mirepoix will be cooked for an extended time. When a mirepoix is used for moisture and seasoning only, the vegetables can be left unpeeled, except for the onion. If the vegetables will become part of the dish, they should be peeled.

4. Add flour or a roux for thickening if desired. Stir some liquid into the pan to deglaze and to combine with the flour or roux if used.

5. Return the food to the pan and add the cooking liquid. Liquids may be well-seasoned stock, tomato juice, or appropriate jus. Use enough liquid to cover approximately one-third of the food. For tough cuts of meat that will cook for an extended time and have considerable liquid evaporation, use enough liquid to cover up to one-half of the meat. If necessary to keep liquid on the product, add additional liquid during cooking.

6. Cover pan with a tight-fitting lid or aluminum foil. Cook at a low oven temperature (300 to 325°F) until fork-tender or slowly on top of the stove. Steam that condenses on the lid and drops on the food will help keep the food moist. Exposed surfaces can be moistened with the braising liquid by turning the food occasionally.

7. Add aromatics and seasonings at the appropriate times to ensure maximum flavor extraction.

8. Remove the food from the braising liquid when it is fork-tender and hold it in a warm place. See timetable for braising meat (Chapter 12, p. 487). If desired, make a sauce from the braising liquid. A sauce can be made by reducing the liquid and thickening, if desired, using arrowroot, cornstarch, or a roux. Strain the sauce or, if desired, purée the mirepoix and return it to the sauce. Adjust for seasoning and consistency.

Boiling

Boiling refers to cooking food in a liquid that is bubbling rapidly. The water movement and high temperature cooks food quicker than poaching and simmering. Few foods are boiled; most are simmered. Boiling temperatures will toughen meat, fish, and egg protein, and break up delicate foods. Pasta is cooked by boiling. The boiling point of water at sea level is 212°F. For every 1000 feet above sea level, the temperature at which water boils is two degrees less. Because of the lower boiling temperature, food cooks slower at high altitudes. The boiling point of water is lowered slightly by adding alcohol and increased by adding salt or sugar.

Boiling procedures

1. Bring liquid to a boil over high heat. Add seasonings if desired.

2. Add the food carefully to the rapidly boiling water. Bring the liquid back to a boil and adjust the temperature to maintain a boil. The higher the proportion of water to food, the faster the water will return to a boil.

3. Cook until the food reaches the desired doneness (determined by timing or texture). See Chapter 12, p. 479 for timetables for cooking meat.

4. Remove the food from the boiling liquid and serve. Some foods, such as pasta, can be chilled quickly in cold water and reheated by submerging briefly in boiling water.

Poaching

Poaching is a moist-heat cooking method that gently transfers heat from a cooking liquid to food that is completely submerged in the liquid. *Shallow poached* food is cooked in just enough liquid to come approximately halfway up the sides of the food. Poaching produces a product that is moist, plump, and tender. Foods cooked by poaching are delicately flavored and naturally tender, such as out of the shell eggs, fish, poultry, and fruit. Generally there is minimal flavor transfer to the poaching liquid. Foods are cooked within a temperature range of 160 to 180°F and only until they reach a safe internal temperature.

Very delicate foods may be wrapped in cheesecloth and tied to keep them from falling apart. A flavorful cooking liquid that complements the food being poached should be used. Common poaching liquids and aromatics include flavorful broth, stock, court bouillon, wines, herbs, spices, and vegetables. Poached foods are often served with a flavorful sauce prepared separately. Shallow-poached foods often have a sauce made from the poaching liquid. Poached foods may use some of the poaching liquid in a sauce.

Poaching procedure

1. Prepare the food to be poached—trim, wrap in cheesecloth, tie with string.

2. Bring the poaching liquid to the desired temperature. Some foods, such as eggs, are started in water that is close to the poaching temperature. Foods that are generally started in a cold liquid and gradually brought to the poaching temperature include dense fruits such as pears.

3. Add the food to the poaching liquid. It is important to keep the food completely submerged in liquid or half submerged for shallow poaching. Shallow poaching requires that the food be covered with buttered parchment paper or a lid.

4. Poach food in the oven or on the stove top until just set or until the desired internal temperature is reached. Keep the poaching temperature between 160 and 180°F. Skim as necessary to improve the appearance of the final product.

5. Remove the food carefully from the cooking liquid. Moisten hot food with some liquid to keep it from drying while a sauce is being prepared. Foods cooled in the poaching liquid will continue to cook after being removed from the heat source and should be undercooked by one or two degrees. Food safety standards for chilling potentially hazardous foods must be followed.

Simmering

Simmering is a term for cooking foods in a liquid that is held just below the boiling point (185 to 205°F.) The temperature is high enough to soften connective tissue in meats yet gentle enough to keep it from becoming stringy. Simmering is appropriate for meats such as ham and corned beef that need to be tenderized through long, slow, moist cooking. Whole fish and other foods that may fall apart can be wrapped in cheesecloth or tied with twine. Simmered foods will be tender and juicy, and will absorb some flavor from the seasoned cooking liquid.

Simmering procedures

1. Prepare the food to be simmered—trim, tie in cheesecloth or with twine.

2. Bring liquid to a boil over high heat. Add mirepoix and seasonings as desired. (Starting cured smoked meat in cold water without added salt will reduce the saltiness of the final product.)

3. Add the food carefully to boiling water. Adjust the temperature to keep the liquid just below the boiling point, (185 to 205°F.)

4. Cook until the food reaches the desired doneness (determined by timing or tenderness). Skim as necessary. See Chapter 12, p. 487 for timetable for cooking meat in liquid.

5. Remove the food from the simmering liquid and serve or cool quickly in the cooking liquid following HACCP guidelines.

Steaming, en Papillote, and Pan Steaming

Steaming, en papillote, and pan steaming cooks by exposing food directly to steam. Steamed food will be moist, plump, flavorful, and visually appealing. Flavors may be added by wrapping in aromatic leaves, stuffing with flavorful ingredients, or marinating. A wide variety of fish, meat, poultry, and vegetables can be steamed. Steaming keeps foods intact because it cooks without agitation. Good nutrient and color retention is achieved because there is minimal water to leach nutrients and pigment from the food.

Foods may be cooked using low pressure, high pressure, and zero pressure steam equipment. Steaming is also achieved with smaller stove-top pans and with small steamers such as rice cookers. Wrapping food tightly to allow steam to be formed by its own moisture is another a steaming method.

Steaming procedures using commercial steam equipment

1. Place food to be steamed not more than 3 to 4 inches deep in stainless steel inset pans. Perforated pans provide the best circulation but if cooking liquid needs to be retained, solid pans should be used.
2. Steam according to timetables for food items being cooked. See Chapter 19, p. 825 for vegetable timetables.

Steaming procedures using stove-top methods

1. Bring a small amount of liquid to a gentle boil in a covered pan. Use enough liquid to last throughout the entire cooking time.
2. Add the food to be steamed in a single layer on a rack above the boiling liquid. Place the food so steam can circulate easily around the food.
3. Place a tight-fitting lid on top of the pan and allow steam to build up.
4. Steam the food until it reaches the desired doneness. Serve immediately with appropriate sauce.

Pan-steaming procedures

1. Follow the same procedures as for pan poaching except cover with a tight-fitting lid instead of parchment paper.

en Papillote procedures

1. Cut parchment paper in a heart shape large enough so the food being encased will fit without being overcrowded. There should be enough room for the paper to expand during cooking. Butter or oil both sides of the paper to keep it from burning.
2. Place a bed of aromatics, vegetables, or sauce on one half of the paper; then place the main item on top.
3. Fold the empty side of the paper over the filled side. Crimp the edges of the paper to form a tight seal.
4. Place the packet on a pan and into a very hot oven. Bake the encased food until it is puffy and browned and the main ingredient is just done. Timing standards developed through experience is the best way of determining doneness. Controlling the size of the main ingredient and par cooking some foods are important to properly cooking en papillote foods.

Stewing

Stewing is a cooking method similar to braising, but the main item is cut into bite-sized pieces. The main ingredient can be browned in a small amount of oil or blanched in a liquid. Because stewed foods are cut smaller, the cooking time is less than for braising. See recipe chapters for stewing timetables (meat, Chapter 12, p. 479; chicken, Chapter 13, p. 527).

Stewing procedures

1. Follow braising procedures, except cut the main ingredient into smaller pieces.
2. Garnishes and vegetables may be cooked separately and added to the stew toward the end of the stewing process.

EVALUATING FOOD FOR QUALITY

Quality control is achieved by continuous evaluation of food products in accordance with the standards established by the foodservice operation. By knowing the desired characteristics of the final product, checks can be established at critical points in production, holding, and service to assure quality is being achieved. Critical points in food production where quality can be compromised include ingredient weighing and measuring; preparation procedures and techniques; cooking times and temperatures; selection of tools, equipment, and utensils; sanitation; and the physical condition of the product throughout preparation. Holding and service functions share some of the same control points. Chapters 2 through 5 and general information in the recipe chapters provide information that is helpful for preparing quality food products, with good visual appeal and sensory characteristics that are safe.

A quality food standard establishes the basis for judging a product's quality attributes. The quality standard should include attributes such as color, consistency, crumb, crust, density, flavor, form, moistness or juiciness, shape, tenderness, texture, and volume. Descriptors may not be applicable to every product.

Production staff will find it helpful to have quality standards identified on the recipe so they can visualize what a quality product should represent. This is especially important for new menu items or for inexperienced cooks. Standards should be written for the actual recipes being used and should include terminology that considers the recipe's ingredients and food items. Following are examples of quality standards for selected food products.

Bread

- **Banana Bread.** The top should be slightly rounded, pebbly, with a shallow crack down the middle section, and with a medium brown tender crust. The bread should have an even grain, free from tunnels, a light and tender texture with a moist, beige-colored crumb and dark brown banana flecks. The flavor should be sweet and mild with a characteristic banana flavor.

- **Muffins.** The crust should be crisp, shiny, pebbly, and golden brown. The top should be rounded but not peaked. The volume should be large when compared with weight. The crumb should be moist, light, and tender with a slightly coarse, even grain and no tunnels. Flavor should be slightly sweet and characteristic of the nuts, fruit, spices, and other flavorings used.

- **French Bread.** The crust should be crisp, smooth, tender, and relatively thin with an even, golden brown color. The loaf should be symmetrically shaped. The grain should be fine and even with uniform thin cell walls. The crumb color should be creamy white and the texture moist, soft, elastic, and resilient with a nutlike flavor.

Desserts

- **White Cake.** The crust should be thin, soft, and a uniform golden brown. A slightly rounded top should be smooth and free from cracks. The grain should have small, uniform, evenly distributed thin-walled cells. The crumb should be resilient, soft, and velvety. The cake should be light, tender, and moist. The flavor should be delicately sweet and well blended.

- **Cherry Pie Crust.** Texture should be crisp, flaky, tender. Both crusts should be rolled thin. The appearance of the top crust should be blistery with a soft luster. The color should be light and golden, with brown deepening slightly toward the edges. The flavor is pleasantly bland with a characteristic flavor depending on proportion of salt and kind of fat used.

- **Cherry Pie Filling.** Cherries should be a rich, bright, shiny, red color in a transparent, smooth, thickened sauce. Whole cherries should be obvious. Fruit filling should ooze out gently from between the crusts when served. The pie should have a sweet-tart flavor, characteristic of red sour cherries.

Entrees

- **Beef Pot Pie.** The pastry top crust should be golden brown, crisp, and flaky. The vegetables should be bright and colorful and the meat a characteristic brown. Bite-size pieces of meat and vegetables should be tender but not mushy. The vegetables and meat should be evenly distributed in a smooth, medium-thick, beef-flavored sauce that flows slowly when spooned onto a plate. The beef and vegetable flavors should be characteristic and seasonings balanced.

- **Chili.** The color of the ground beef and beans should be a deep red-brown tomato color with the meat and beans mixed evenly throughout the mixture. The meat should be moist, not dry or crumbly, and the beans tender yet firm. The size of the meat pieces should be the same as the beans or a little smaller. The flavor should be distinct with meat, tomatoes, chili powder, and other seasonings well blended. The chili should be a thick sauce consistency that flows easily when ladled into a bowl.

- **Lasagna.** The top should have a tomato red color. The alternating layers of meat mixture, pasta, and cheese should be distinct. The noodles should be tender yet hold their shape. The spicy tomato-beef flavor of the meat mixture should blend well with the cheeses and pasta. Lasagna servings should hold their shape with the layers identifiable.

Soups

- **Beef Rice Soup.** The transparent brown beef broth stock should possess body and may have a slight sheen due to dispersed fat globules from the meat. The browned stew meat should be tender with a distinct beef flavor. The bite-size celery, finely chopped onions, and rice should be tender, yet firm enough to hold their shape. Flavor should be a blend of the characteristic flavors of the ingredients and seasonings.

- **Cream of Vegetable Soup.** The thin white-sauce base should be an off-white opaque color, with the characteristic color of the vegetables distributed throughout. The soup should be smooth, coating a spoon lightly. The vegetables should be finely chopped, retaining a slightly crisp but tender bite. The flavor should be mild with a blend of the characteristic flavors of the ingredients and seasonings.

Vegetables/Starches

- **Scalloped Potatoes.** The potato slices should be uniform in size, about 2 inches in diameter and $\frac{1}{8}$ inch thick. A creamy white sauce that contains tender, very finely chopped onions should cling to the tender yet firm, white, slightly opaque potatoes. The served product should form a barely rounded mass that spreads slightly. The mild potato flavor should be pleasant and blend with the delicate mild cooked flavor of the sauce. Seasonings should enhance the flavor of the potato-sauce mixture.

- **Harvard Beets.** The product should possess a deep-toned red color, with the beet slices having a tender yet firm texture, round shape, and smooth surface. The sauce should be a flowing gelatinous glaze with deep, red translucence. The beets should be evenly glazed and readily discernable. Flavor should be well blended and mildly sweet with a slightly sour sensation.

The forms in Tables 4.3, 4.4, and 4.5 will be useful in evaluating the quality of food products.

Evaluating food products regularly throughout preparation and service, and making adjustments where necessary is important for assuring good quality food and customer satisfaction.

TABLE 4.3   Evaluating food using sensory attributes

PRODUCT _____

Attribute	*Score*
VISUAL APPEARANCE	EXCELLENT 1 --- 2 --- 3 --- 4 --- 5 --- 6 --- 7 POOR
Desirable Characteristics:	
Comments:	
AROMA	EXCELLENT 1 --- 2 --- 3 --- 4 --- 5 --- 6 --- 7 POOR
Desirable Characteristics:	
Comments:	
FLAVOR	EXCELLENT 1 --- 2 --- 3 --- 4 --- 5 --- 6 --- 7 POOR
Desirable Characteristics:	
Comments:	
TEXTURE	EXCELLENT 1 --- 2 --- 3 --- 4 --- 5 --- 6 --- 7 POOR
Desirable Characteristics:	
Comments:	

TOTAL SCORE _____

Notes: • Foods should be evaluated when they are at their ideal serving temperature.
   • To improve objectivity when evaluating a food product, the desirable characteristics may be added to the score sheet in Table 4.3. For example, when evaluating muffins, the texture characteristics might be identified as a light tender crumb and slightly coarse even grain. For meat, the descriptive words for texture would be in regard to tenderness; for French fries, crispness.
   • Descriptive terminology to describe the desirable characteristics of food:
   Visual Appearance may be described in terms of color, form/shape, lumpiness, size, smoothness, and uniformity, and whether the item is bright, coarse, cracked, fine, flat, pale, pebbly, pointed, or rounded. Dullness, gloss, opaqueness, and transparency are also visual characteristics.
   Aroma may be described in terms of characteristic aroma, pleasant, pungent, sour, and sweet.
   Flavor may be described in terms of acidic, balanced, bitter, distinct, mellow, mild, pleasing, salty, sour, spicy, sweet, and unsweet.
   Texture (and mouthfeel, or the texture of food as perceived in the mouth) may be described in terms of coarse, crisp, crumbly, elastic, firm, flaky, gritty, heavy, light, mealy, moist, smooth, soft, tender, tough. Consistency, viscosity, and grain may help describe desirable textures.

TABLE 4.4   Evaluating food products during preparation and service

Evaluation points	Criteria to assess quality
Taste	(a) Seasonings are balanced. (b) Food production methods are appropriate for the product being prepared. (c) Quality of ingredients used are appropriate for the product being prepared. (d) Flavor profile of the finished product is characteristic of ingredients.
Proper Production and Holding	(a) Food production procedures based on food science principles are followed; for example: • Meats, poultry, and fish are cooked just until the optimum end-point temperature is reached. • Vegetables are brightly colored. • Starches are cooked just until done (al dente). • Sauces are smooth and have the correct consistency. (b) Food is served at its optimum quality (generally within a very short time after preparation). (c) HACCP principles are followed.
Presentation	(a) Portion sizes are correct and uniform. (b) Foods are presented or arranged in a manner that enhances their appeal. (c) Foods being served together are complementary in color, consistency, form, and methods of preparation.
Serving Temperature	(a) Hot foods are served hot using warmed plates when possible. (b) Cold foods are served cold using chilled plates/bowls when possible.

Note: Evaluating food products regularly throughout preparation and service, and making adjustments where necessary is important for assuring good quality food and customer satisfaction.

TABLE 4.5   Quality food evaluation form

FOOD PRODUCT _____

DATE AND MEAL SERVED _____

Overall Quality: <u>Excellent</u>   <u>Average</u>   <u>Poor</u>

TASTE   LOW   1 -- 2 -- 3 -- 4 -- 5 -- 6 -- 7   HIGH

[seasonings appropriate and balanced][appropriate food production methods followed][ingredient quality appropriate][flavor profile characteristic of ingredients]

Comments:

FOOD PRODUCTION PROCEDURES   LOW   1 -- 2 -- 3 -- 4 -- 5 -- 6 -- 7   HIGH

[food production procedures based on appropriate food science principles were followed]

Comments:

QUALITY DURING HOLDING/STAGING   LOW   1 -- 2 -- 3 -- 4 -- 5 -- 6 -- 7   HIGH

[food is served at its optimum quality including color, consistency, texture, and form]

Comments:

FOOD PRESENTATION   LOW   1 -- 2 -- 3 -- 4 -- 5 -- 6 -- 7   HIGH

[portion sizes are correct and uniform][foods are presented or arranged in a manner that enhances their appeal][foods are appealing in their color, form, textures, and method of preparation]

Comments:

SERVING TEMPERATURES   LOW   1 -- 2 -- 3 -- 4 -- 5 -- 6 -- 7   HIGH

[hot food served hot and with hot plates if appropriate][cold food served cold and with chilled plates if appropriate]

Comments:

Note: This scorecard is useful when evaluating food being served from a buffet line or hot counter, and for plated meals.

CHAPTER 5

Knives and Other Equipment

Brady / Pearson Education / PH College

Selecting and using the proper equipment is necessary to produce food in an efficient and effective manner. This chapter provides basic information about using and caring for knives and general information about identifying and using other equipment. Tables are included that provide pan capacity guidelines and portioning information.

This chapter includes the following topics:

- Knives—Knife Identification, Knife Care and Safety, Knife Skills
- Equipment

KNIFE IDENTIFICATION, KNIFE CARE AND SAFETY, AND KNIFE SKILLS

Knife Identification

Choosing the correct style and shape of knife for a specific cutting task will save time and will provide the tool necessary to meet the quality standards for the product being produced. Safety is also improved when the knife selected fits its use. The types of knives identified here do not represent all the knives that are available, but they are the basic ones required for general food production.

Boning Knife (rigid)
A thin blade especially suited for separating raw meat and poultry from the bone. A 5- to 7-inch-long blade. A filleting knife is similar but has a flexible blade.

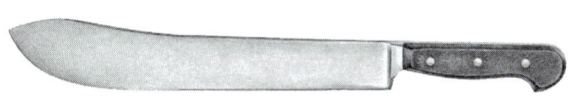

Butcher Knife or Scimitar
A large knife with a rigid 6- to 14-inch-long blade that curves upward at the tip. Designed for breaking down raw meat into smaller cuts.

Chef's or French Knife
An all-purpose knife used for many chopping, dicing, mincing, and slicing tasks. A long, rigid blade in lengths from 8 to 14 inches. Blade is wide at the heel and tapers to a point at the tip.

continues

continued

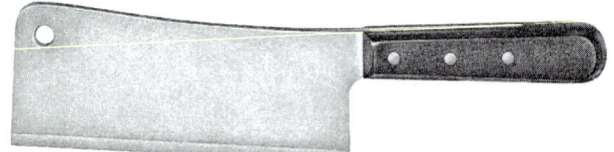

Cleaver

A rectangular-shaped blade in various sizes that is usually heavy enough to cut through bones. Used for chopping.

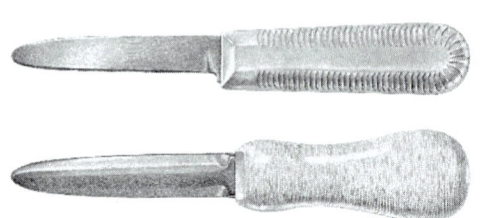

Clam and Oyster Knives

Knives with short rigid blades used for opening clam and oyster shells. Clam knife has a sharp edge.

Paring Knife

A short knife with a 2- to 4-inch-long blade. Used for detail work and for trimming, peeling, and cutting fruits and vegetables.

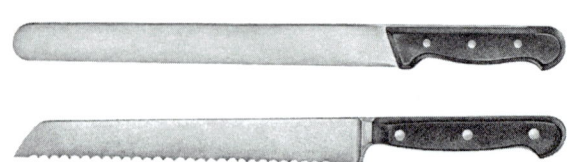

Slicer

A knife with a long, thin, flexible or rigid blade with either a pointed or a rounded tip. May be serrated. Used for slicing cooked meat, poultry, and breads.

Utility Knife

An all-purpose knife used for light cutting or carving tasks. Smaller and lighter than a chef's knife with a blade from 5 to 7 inches long.

Knife Care and Safety

A set of good-quality knives is a costly investment, but properly cared for they will provide many years of safe and efficient service. A good knife-sharpening program is basic to proper knife care. A sharp knife is also more efficient and safer than a dull knife because less pressure is needed to cut foods. The edge of a sharp knife will cut with a minimum amount of pressure and the guiding hand of a skilled user.

Knife care and safety tips:

1. Keep knives sharp.

   A whetstone (or stone) or a good electric sharpener are used to return an edge to a dull knife. Sharpening knives should be considered a daily *mise en place* task for knives that get considerable use. See Figure 5.1 for instructions on how to sharpen a knife using a stone.

   A steel does not sharpen, but it removes or smooths out tiny irregularities in the knife's edge that are caused by normal use. Regular use of a steel maintains the knife's edge and keeps it sharp between sharpenings. See Figure 5.2 for

instructions on how to hone a knife blade using a steel.

2. Keep knives clean.

   Hand wash, sanitize, and dry knives after finishing each task, or more often if necessary for food safety reasons. Soaking knives can damage wooden handles and is a safety hazard if knives are submerged in water and out of sight. Because hot dishmachine temperatures can damage knives, they should always be hand washed in hot soapy water and sanitized using a sanitizing solution.

3. Use a cutting surface that will protect the knife's edge.

   Glass, granite, marble, metal, and other hard surfaces will damage a knife. Wooden or composition cutting boards should always be used.

4. Store knives properly.

   There are many ways to store knives that will protect their edge. Some common methods are knife kit cases, knife rolls, slot racks, and magnet holders mounted near production areas. Knives

(a) Hold the knife at a 20-degree angle to a stone or steel when sharpening.

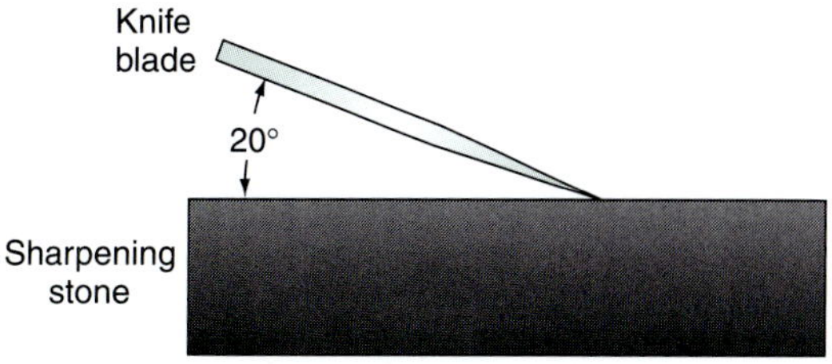

(b) Hold knife handle firmly with one hand and use the other hand to apply steady, even pressure and to guide the knife.

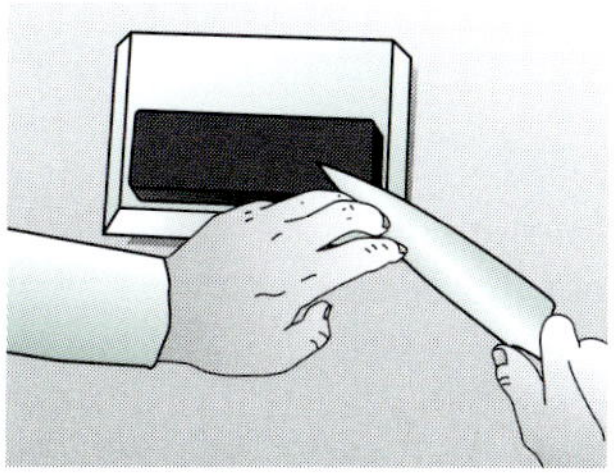

(c) Draw the knife over the stone while applying gentle, even, and light pressure on the blade. Sharpen only in one direction. Repeat on other side of the knife. Use the same number of strokes on each side of the knife.

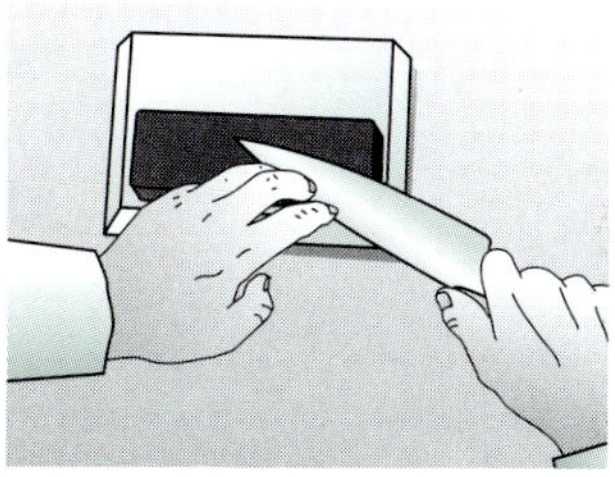

(d) Keep the motion smooth as the knife blade is drawn across the stone all the way to the heel of the knife. Finish by using a steel on the sharpened edge. (See Figure 5.2)

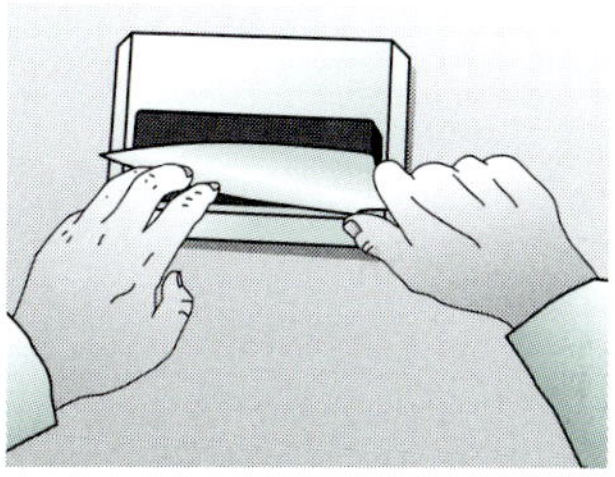

FIGURE 5.1   Sharpening a knife using a stone.

should always be clean and dry before storing. Storage equipment should be kept clean so it does not become a source of contamination and a food safety hazard. For safety reasons, do not store knives on a flat surface covered with a towel or other similar covering.

5. Use safe procedures when handling knives.

- When passing a knife, lay it down on the work surface with the handle closest to the person you are passing it to.

- When walking with a knife, place it in a sheathe or hold it by the handle close to your leg, with the point facing down.

- Use a knife for its intended purpose only, and never to open containers such as cans or boxes.
- Use the correct knife for the task.
- Cut away from yourself.
- Keep knives sharp. Sharp knives are safer because less pressure is needed to make cuts. With less pressure, the chance of the knife or hand slipping is reduced.
- Do not attempt to catch a falling knife.
- Never leave a knife submerged in a sink of water or stored under a towel or similar covering.
- Never cut on a "make-shift" or unstable work surface.

(a) Hold the knife at a constant 20-degree angle to a steel. See Figure 5.1. Hold knife and steel away from you to prevent injury.

Position the knife so the heel of the blade is next to the steel.

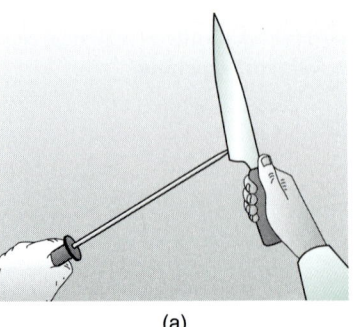

(a)

(b) Lightly and smoothly pass the knife blade along the steel in a movement that makes an arc.

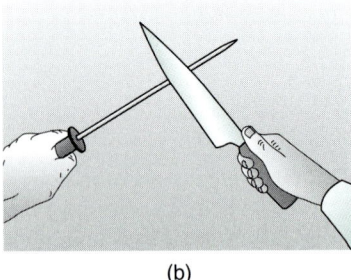

(b)

(c) Continue the stroke until the knife tip passes over the steel. Do not strike the knife edge on the steel guard. Use only 5 or 6 strokes on each side of the blade.

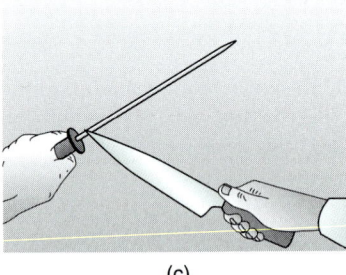

(c)

(d, e, f) Repeat the motion on the other side of the knife.

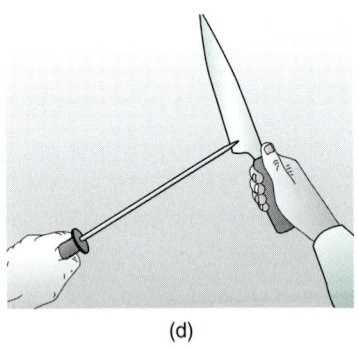

(d)

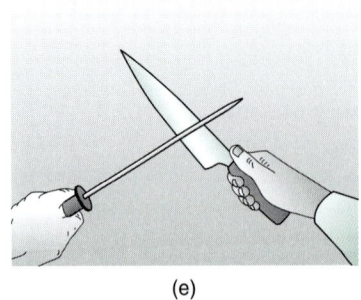

(e)

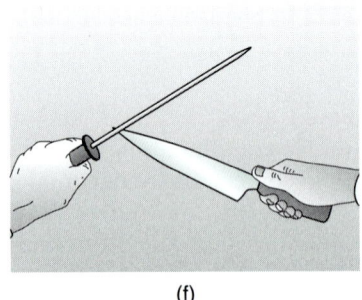

(f)

FIGURE 5.2 Honing a knife using a steel.

Knife Skills—Gripping, Guiding, Cutting

Gripping a knife properly is basic to skillfully and safely using a knife. A grip should be firm and controlling but not so tight that it causes the hand to cramp or tire. Following are three standard grips to use with a chef's or French knife. The parts of a chef's knife are identified in Figure 5.3.

1. Hold the handle with three fingers while gripping the blade between the thumb and index finger. This grip gives the maximum amount of stability and control and is useful for fine cutting.

2. Hold the handle with four fingers and place the thumb against the top of the blade (knife's spine).

3. Hold the handle with four fingers and place the thumb against the side of the blade.

Guiding the knife with one hand while positioning and holding the food being cut with the other hand is a necessary skill for using a knife efficiently and effectively. Following are guidelines for using a chef's or French knife correctly:

1. Hold the food firmly with the finger tips and thumb curled under slightly, away from the cutting edge of the knife blade.

2. Allow the knife blade to sit against the knuckles with the finger tips tucked under.

3. The position of the hand holding the food controls the cut (called the "guiding hand".) As successive cuts are made the fingertips should move back and control the width of each cut that is made.

4. The tip of the knife is used for small items. The center of the blade is for general cutting and the heel (back of blade) is for heavy work when a greater force is needed (for dense rutabagas for example).

5. *Method 1:* With the tip of the knife left on the cutting board, lift the blade, and with a forward and down motion, cut the food. Finish the cut with the knife against the cutting board. For the second slice, lift the heel of the knife backwards, just the opposite of the forward and down motion. The tip of the knife acts as the fulcrum and should not leave the cutting board.

   Method 2: Start the cut with the knife's tip rested on top of the food being cut. Slice downward and forward. Allow the weight of the knife to do most of the work. Repeat action. The wrist acts as the fulcrum for this method.

Cutting food into uniformly shaped pieces is the goal whenever food is cut. Uniformity adds to the visual appeal of food and also helps food cook evenly. Descriptions for the basic vegetable cuts and shapes follow.

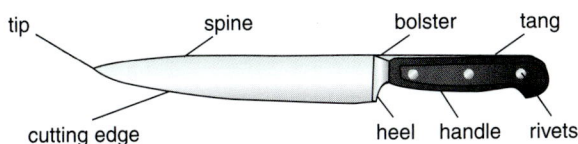

FIGURE 5.3   Identification of the parts of a chef's knife.

Dice	Processing method	Shape
Dicing is a cutting technique that produces a cube shape (six equal sides).	1. Cut a julienne or bâtonnet shaped item with the dimension appropriate for the size of dice desired. For paysanne, use a ½ × ½-inch stick. 2. Gather the stick-shaped vegetables and cut through them crosswise at evenly spaced intervals. For paysanne cut at ¼ or ⅛-inch intervals to make a tile shaped item.	

Brunoise (broo-nwaz) (⅛ × ⅛ × ⅛ inch)
Fine brunoise (1/16 × 1/16 × 1/16)

Small dice (¼ × ¼ × ¼ inch)

Medium dice (½ × ½ × ½ inch)

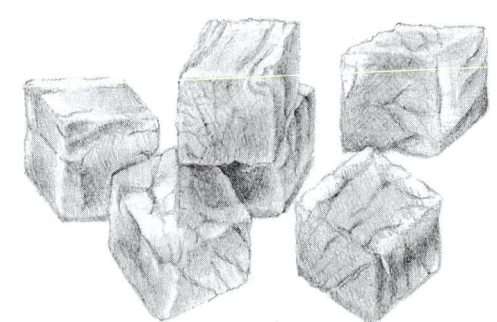

Large dice (¾ × ¾ × ¾ inch)

Paysanne (pahy-sahn) (tile shape)
(½ × ½ × ¼ or ⅛ inch)

Chiffonade (chef-fon-nahd)	*Processing method*	*Shape*
A slicing technique that produces finely sliced or shredded leafy vegetables and herbs.	1. For tight heads such as Belgian endive and cabbage, core and if large cut in half. For herbs, remove stems. For loose leaves, roll large leaves into tight cigar shaped cylinders. For small leaves, stack several leaves on top of one another and roll into cylinders. 2. Use a chef's or French knife to make very fine, parallel cuts. Hard heads such as cabbages or head lettuce can be shredded using a box grater or mandoline.	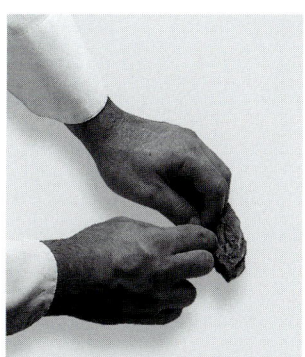 

Coarse chopping	*Processing method*	*Shape*
Slicing or chopping food without emphasizing uniform cuts. Coarse chopped items are generally not served unless strained or puréed. A technique used for making a mirepoix.	1. Chop according to guidelines for using a chef's or French knife, p. 209. 2. Cut into pieces that are not uniform but are similar in size and shape so they cook evenly.	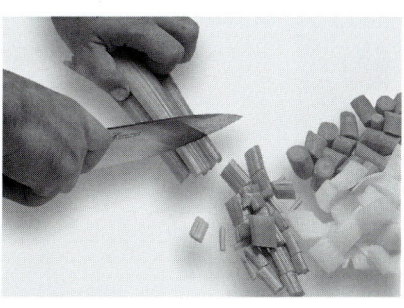

Julienne (ju-lee-en) and Bâtonnet (bah-toh-nah)	*Processing method*	*Shape*
A cutting and dicing technique that produces a stick-shaped item. A julienne shape used for potatoes is often called an allumette (al-yoo-meht) cut.	1. Trim vegetables so that they have straight sides. 2. Slice the vegetable lengthwise into even slices that are the thickness desired (e.g., fine julienne ¹⁄₁₆-inch, julienne or allumette ⅛-inch, bâtonnet ¼-inch). 3. Stack the slices, aligning the edges, and make parallel cuts of the same thickness as in step #2.	 

Mince	*Processing method*	*Shape*
Mincing is a technique for cutting item such as garlic, herbs, and shallots into very small even pieces.	1. Pile coarsely chopped item on a cutting board. 2. With the guiding hand, hold the tip of the knife on the cutting board and rapidly raise and lower the heel of the knife chopping through the vegetable. See method #1, guidelines for using a chef's or French knife, p. 209.	 

Oblique (oh-bleek)	*Processing method*	*Shape*
Also called a roll cut. A slicing technique used with long vegetables such as carrots, celery, and parsnips.	1. Peel vegetable (if desired). Make a 45-degree diagonal cut to remove stem end. 2. Roll the vegetable a half-turn and cut at the same 45-degree angle as the first cut. The resulting piece will have a wedge-shaped cut on each end, oriented in the opposite direction. 3. Repeat half-turn and cut pieces until the entire vegetable has been cut.	

Rondelles (ron-dellz)	*Processing method*	*Shape*
One of the simplest cuts for slicing vegetables such as carrots, cucumbers, and other cylindrical vegetables into disc-shaped or bias disc-shaped pieces.	1. Peel vegetable (if desired). Make uniform slices perpendicular to the item being cut. 2. For diagonal or bias cuts, position knife at the desired angle and cut into uniform slices. For half-moon cuts, cut slices in half.	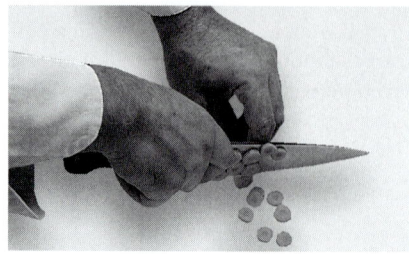 

Tournè (toor-nay)	*Processing method*	*Shape*
A carving technique used for making football- or barrel-shaped vegetables with seven equal sides and flattened ends. A difficult cut requiring practice to carve equal sides. Used for large round or oval vegetables such as beets, large carrots, potatoes, turnips, rutabagas.	1. Peel vegetable (if desired). 2. For large vegetables, cut into smaller pieces approximately 2 inches thick. Cut large carrots into two sections. 3. Use a paring knife to carve seven smooth, even, curved sides with flattened ends. Resulting product should be thick at the center with tapered ends.	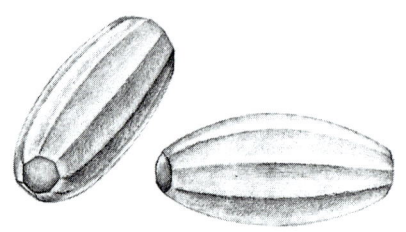 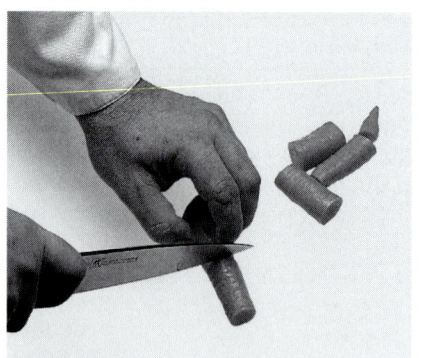 

HAND TOOLS AND SMALL EQUIPMENT

A wide variety of hand tools and small equipment are available that help simplify food production processes.

Following are general categories and visual descriptions of small equipment that should be available to production staff. Knives are identified on p. 205. Tables 5.1, 5.2, 5.3, 5.4, 5.5, and 5.6 provide information about the capacity of selected equipment.

Basic Hand Tools (non-mechanical)

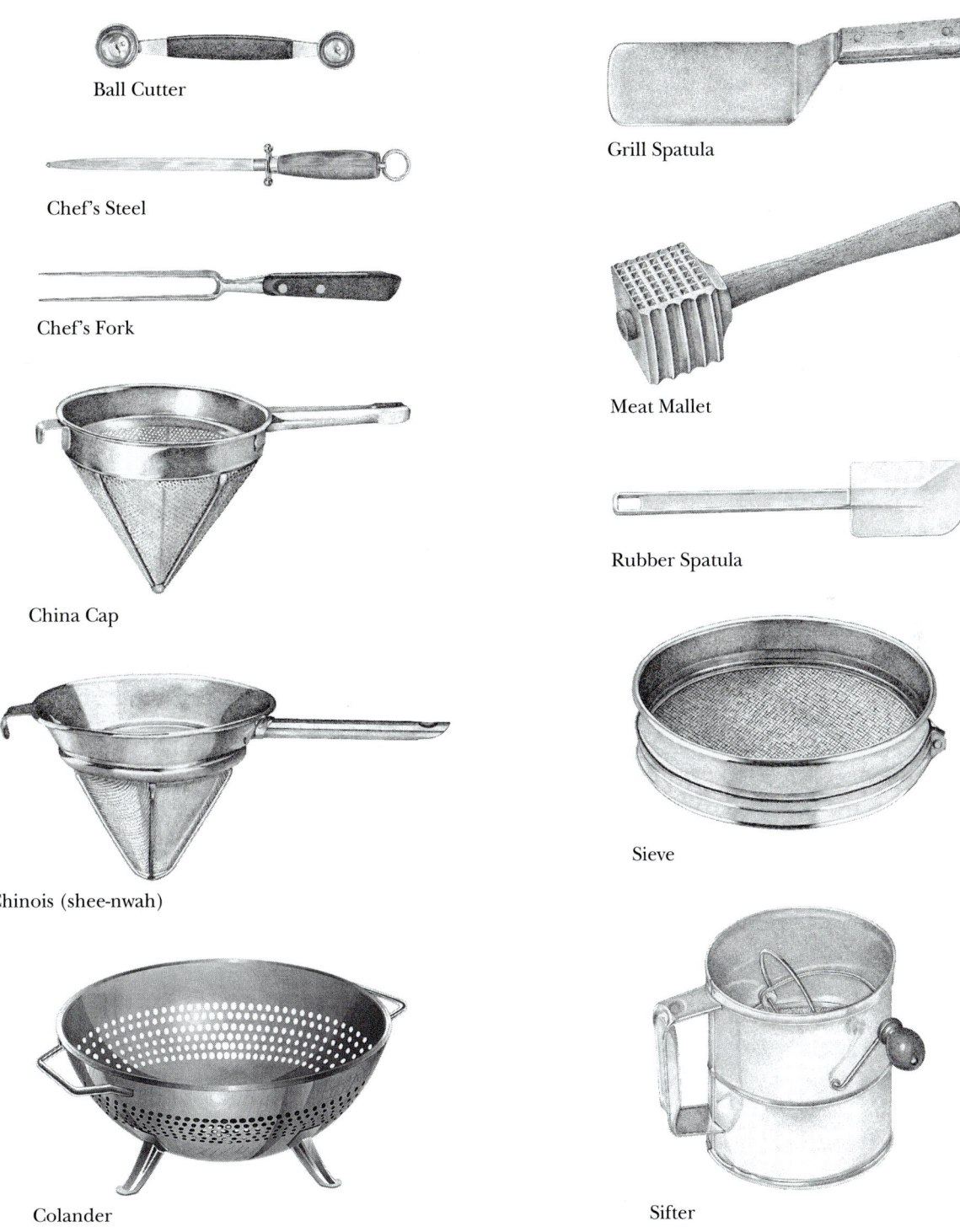

Ball Cutter

Chef's Steel

Chef's Fork

China Cap

Chinois (shee-nwah)

Colander

Grill Spatula

Meat Mallet

Rubber Spatula

Sieve

Sifter

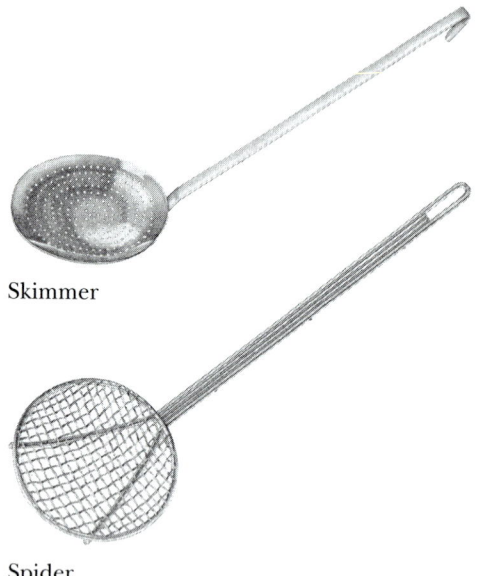

Skimmer

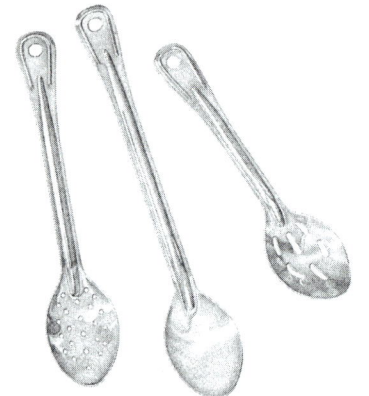

Spider

Spoons (perforated, plain, slotted)

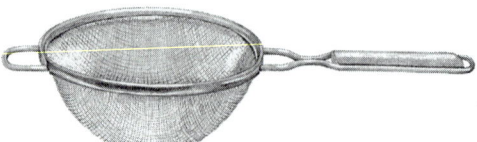

Strainer (round mesh)

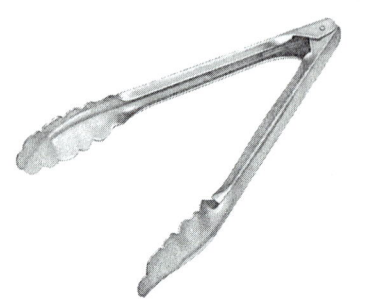

Tongs

Vegetable Peeler

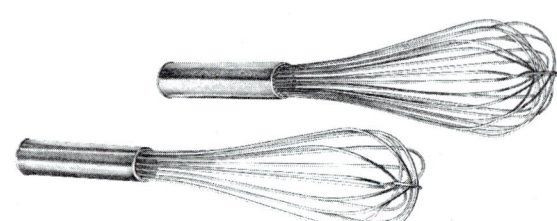

Whisks

Straight Spatula (cake spatula)

Zester

Measuring and Portioning Equipment

Dipper (Other names: Scoop, Disher)
See Table 5.3 for sizes.

Ladles
Available in a variety of sizes. The size, in ounces, is stamped on the handle. See Table 5.4 for sizes.

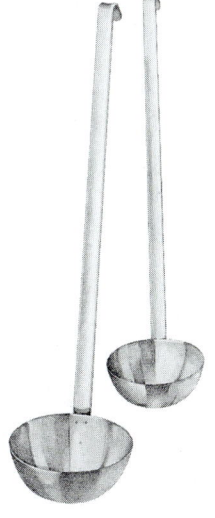

Dry Volume Measuring Cups
Available in ¼-, ⅓-, ½-, and 1-cup units.

Liquid Volume Measure

Gallon	Half-Gallon	Quart	Pint
128 oz	64 oz	32 oz	16 oz

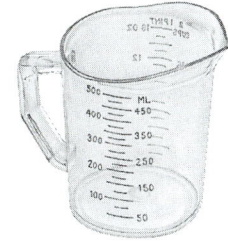

Measuring Spoons
Usually sold in sets of ¼, ½, and 1 tsp, and 1 Tbsp.

Small Processing Equipment (manual)

Food Mill

Mandoline

Pans

Brazier

Hotel Pans (counter pan, steam-table pan)

Saucepan

Sauce Pot

Sautéuse (sloped sides)

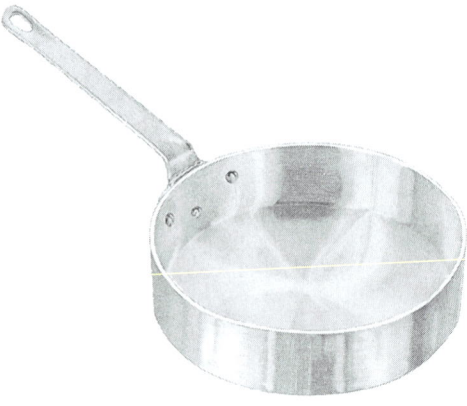

Sautoir (straight sides)

Stockpot (with spigot)

Wok

TABLE 5.1   Pan capacities for baked products

Pan size	Maximum capacity	Portion	Suggested use
18 × 26 × 2 inches (cake pan)	8–10 lb	Cut 6 × 10 (3 × 2½ inches)	Cakes
18 × 26 × 1 inch (sheet pan)	4–6 lb	Cut 6 × 10 (3 × 2½ inches)	Sheet cakes, bar cookies
		Panned 8 × 12	Dinner rolls
		Dropped 3 × 5	Cookies
13 × 18 × 1 inch (half sheet pan)	2–3 lb	Cut 5 × 6 (2½ × 3 inches)	Sheet cakes, bar cookies
12 × 18 × 2 inches	4–5 lb	Cut 5 × 6 (2½ × 3 inches)	Cakes
10-inch tube	2–2½ lb	Cut $\frac{1}{14}$	Chiffon cakes
9-inch round (cake)	1½ lb	Cut $\frac{1}{16}$	Layer cakes, corn bread
8-inch round (cake)	1¼ lb	Cut $\frac{1}{12}$–$\frac{1}{14}$	Layer cakes
9-inch round (pie)	1½ lb	Cut $\frac{1}{8}$	Pies
8-inch round (pie)	1 lb	Cut $\frac{1}{6}$	Pies
5 × 16 × 4 inches (loaf)	3–5 lb	Cut $\frac{1}{24}$–$\frac{1}{32}$	Quick breads, yeast breads
		Cut $\frac{1}{24}$	Cakes
5 × 8 × 4 inches (loaf)	1½–2½ lb	Cut $\frac{1}{12}$–$\frac{1}{16}$	Quick breads, yeast breads
		Cut $\frac{1}{12}$	Cakes
5 × 9 × 2¾ inches (loaf)	1½–2 lb	Cut $\frac{1}{16}$	Quick breads, yeast breads, cakes

Notes: • The product volume/weight ratio will dictate the weight per pan.
 • See recipes for specific instruction.
 • A formula for determining scaling weight of cakes is given on p. 320.

TABLE 5.2 Counter pan capacities

		Maximum capacity		*Number of portions*					
Pan size	*Depth (in inches)*	*lb*	*qt*	*Cut*	*1 oz*	*2 oz*	*4 oz*	*8 oz*	*Suggested use*
Full size 20 × 12 inches	2	12–15	8	48 (3 × 2½ inches)			67	33	Baked entrees Baked desserts
	4	24–30	14	24 (3 × 3⅓ inches) 32 (3 × 2½ inches)			113	56	Baked entrees
Half size 10 × 12 inches	2½	6–7	4	12 (3 × 3 inches)			34	17	Baked entrees
				16 (3 × 2½ inches)			34	17	Baked entrees
	4	12–15	6½				53	27	Baked entrees
	6		10				80	40	Vegetables
One-third size 6⅞ × 12¾ inches	2				85	42			Salad bar items
	4				134	67			Condiments
	6				197	98			Sauces
One-fourth size 6⅜ × 10⅜ inches	2				60	30			Salad bar items
	4				96	48			Condiments
	6				146	73			Sauces

TABLE 5.3 Dipper equivalents

Dipper number[a]	*Approximate measure*	*Approximate weight*	*Suggested use*
6	10 Tbsp (⅔ cup)	6 oz	Entree salads
8	8 Tbsp (½ cup)	4–5 oz	Entrees
10	6 Tbsp (⅜ cup)	3–4 oz	Desserts, meat patties
12	5 Tbsp (⅓ cup)	2½–3 oz	Croquettes, vegetables, muffins, desserts, salads
16	4 Tbsp (¼ cup)	2–2¼ oz	Muffins, desserts, croquettes
20	3⅕ Tbsp	1¾–2 oz	Muffins, cupcakes, sauces, sandwich fillings
24	2⅔ Tbsp	1½–1¾ oz	Cream puffs
30	2⅕ Tbsp	1–1½ oz	Large drop cookies
40	1½ Tbsp	¾ oz	Drop cookies
60	1 Tbsp	½ oz	Small drop cookies, garnishes
100	Scant 2 tsp		Tea cookies

[a] Portions per quart.

Notes:
- These measurements are based on food leveled off in the dipper. If food is left rounded in the dipper, the measure and weight are closer to those of the next-larger dipper.
- *Scoop* and *disher* are terms often used synonymously with *dipper*.

TABLE 5.4   Ladle equivalents

Approximate weight	Approximate measure	Approximate portions per quart	Suggested use
1 oz	⅛ cup	32	Sauces, salad dressings
2 oz	¼ cup	16	Gravies, some sauces
4 oz	½ cup	8	Stews, creamed dishes
6 oz	¾ cup	5	Stews, creamed dishes, soup
8 oz	1 cup	4	Soup

Note: • These measurements are based on food leveled off in the ladle. If food is left rounded in the ladle, the measure and weight are closer to those of the next-larger ladle.

TABLE 5.5   Recommended mixer bowl and steam-jacketed kettle sizes for selected products

	50 portions	100 portions	200 portions	500 portions
Breads, yeast	7 lb/12 qt MB[a]	14 lb/12 qt MB	28 lb/20 qt MB	70 lb/60 qt MB
Quick	10 lb/12 qt MB	20 lb/20 qt MB	40 lb/60 qt MB	100 lb/80 qt MB
Cakes, angel food	6 lb/12 qt MB	12 lb/30 qt MB	24 lb/60 qt MB	60 lb/2 batch sizes, 60 qt MB
Other	8 lb/12 qt MB	16 lb/20 qt MB	32 lb/30 qt MB	80 lb/80 qt MB
Cookies	5 lb/5 qt MB	10 lb/12 qt MB	20 lb/30 qt MB	50 lb/60 qt MB
Pastry	7 lb/12 qt MB	14 lb/20 qt MB	28 lb/30 qt MB	70 lb/80 qt MB
Pie fillings				
Fruit	12 lb/10 qt SJK 10 qt SP	24 lb/20 qt SJK 20 qt SP	48 lb/20 gal SJK	120 lb/20 gal SJK
Frozen/chiffon	12 lb/20 qt MB	24 lb/60 qt MB	48 lb/80 qt MB	120 lb/2 batch sizes, 80 qt MB
Puddings/pie fillings	12 lb/10 qt SJK 10 qt SP	24 lb/20 qt SJK 10 qt SP	48 lb/20 gal SJK	120 lb/20 gal SJK
Scrambled eggs	10 lb/12 qt MB	20 lb/20 qt MB	40 lb/60 qt MB	100 lb/2 batch sizes, 60 qt MB
Cheese soufflé	14 lb/30 qt MB	28 lb/60 qt MB	56 lb/2 batch sizes, 60 qt MB	140 lb/3 batch sizes, 80 qt MB
Meat loaf	12 lb/20 qt MB	24 lb/30 qt MB	48 lb/60 qt MB	120 lb/2 batch sizes, 80 qt MB
Spaghetti sauce	19 lb/20 qt SJK 15 qt SP	38 lb/20 gal SJK 20 qt SP	76 lb/20 gal SJK	190 lb/40 gal SJK
Pasta (and cooking water)	45 lb/20 gal SJK 25 qt SP	90 lb/20 gal SJK	180 lb/40 gal SJK	450 lb/80 gal SJK
Salad dressing	8 lb/12 qt MB	16 lb/20 qt MB	32 lb/60 qt MB	80 lb/80 qt MB
Soups/stews	25 lb/20 qt SJK 15 qt SP	50 lb/20 gal SJK 25 qt SP	100 lb/20 gal SJK	250 lb/40 gal SJK
Mashed potatoes	15 lb/20 qt MB	30 lb/30 qt MB	60 lb/80 qt MB	150 lb/3 batch sizes, 80 qt MB
Whipped cream or topping	1½ qt/5 qt MB	3 qt/12 qt MB	6 qt/30 qt MB	15 qt/60 qt MB

[a] Abbreviations used: MB = mixer bowl; SJK = steam-jacketed kettle; SP = stock pot.

TABLE 5.6 Large-equipment requirements for basic cooking methods

Cooking method	Equipment
Baking	Oven: Deck; Convection[*]; Conveyor; Range
Blanching	Steam-jacketed kettle; Range and stockpot or other pan
Boiling	Steam-jacketed kettle; Range and stockpot or other pan
Braising	Tilting fry pan; Steam-jacketed kettle; Range and fry pan
Broiling	Broiler
Deep-fat frying	Deep-fat fryer; Pressure fryer
Frying	Tilting fry pan; Range and fry pan
Griddling	Griddle
Grilling	Grill
Oven frying	Oven: Deck; Convection[*]; Conveyor; Range
Panfrying	Tilting fry pan; Range and skillet
Poaching	Tilting fry pan; Steamer; Range and shallow pan
Roasting	Oven: Deck; Convection[*]; Conveyor; Range
Sautéing	Tilting fry pan; Range and sauté pan
Searing	Tilting fry pan; Range and skillet
Simmering	Steam-jacketed kettle; Range and stockpot or other pan
Steaming	Steamer: High pressure; Low pressure; Zero pressure; Range
Stewing	Steam-jacketed kettle; Tilting fry pan; Range and stockpot
Stir frying	Tilting fry pan; Range and skillet; Griddle; Wok

[*]A convection oven cooks faster than a conventional oven. Reduce cooking time by 10 to 15 percent and the temperature by 25 to 50°F.

PART III

Recipes

Chapter 6	Appetizers, Hors d'oeuvres, and Special Event Foods	227
Chapter 7	Beverages	245
Chapter 8	Breads	263
Chapter 9	Desserts	319
Chapter 10	Eggs and Cheese	437
Chapter 11	Fish and Shellfish	457
Chapter 12	Meat	479
Chapter 13	Poultry	527
Chapter 14	Pasta, Rice, Cereals, and Foods with Grains, Beans, and Tofu	559
Chapter 15	Salads and Salad Dressings	639
Chapter 16	Sandwiches	713
Chapter 17	Sauces, Marinades, Rubs, and Seasonings	747
Chapter 18	Soups	789
Chapter 19	Vegetables	823

RECIPE INFORMATION

Yield

The recipes in this book produce servings for 50 people unless otherwise stated. Factors that may affect yield include portioning, ingredient weighing error, mistakes in calculating increased or decreased quantities, abnormal handling loss, and variation in the edible portion (EP) and as purchased (AP) factors for food products such as fresh produce and meats.

A standard counter pan 12×20 inches has been indicated for many recipes. For baked desserts and some bread products, either a 12×18-inch or 18×26-inch pan is specified, as they are standard bakeware sizes. Weight of product per pan may need to be changed if pans other than those specified in the recipe are used. Care should be taken to scale products so that portion weight will be accurate and recipe yield remains correct. Tables 5.1 and 5.2 give capacities of baking and counter pans.

The number of servings per pan will depend on the portion size desired. Many standard-sized baking or counter pans will yield from 24 to 32 servings per pan, and where these size pans are indicated, the recipes generally are calculated for 48 or 64 servings. Yield adjustments may be made by cutting the servings into sizes that will yield the desired number of portions. Portion size is included in each recipe, and the yield is given in number of portions, volume produced, and/or number of pans. Some foodservices may wish to adjust the yield based on the clientele to be served.

Ingredients

In most cases, the type of ingredient used in testing the recipes has been specified; for example, granulated, brown, or powdered sugar; and all-purpose or cake flour. High-ratio and/or hydrogenated shortenings were used in cake and pastry recipes; margarine or butter in cookies, some quick breads, and most sauce recipes. Solid fats such as margarine, butter, and hydrogenated fats were used interchangeably in recipes that specify "shortening." Corn, soybean, or cottonseed oil was used in recipes that specify salad or vegetable oil. Sodium aluminum sulfate-type baking powder (double acting) and active dry yeast were used for leavening.

Fresh eggs, large size, weighing approximately 2 ounces unshelled ($1\frac{3}{4}$ oz shelled) were used in the preparation of the recipes. Eggs are specified by both number and weight. In many foodservices, frozen eggs are used, in which case the eggs are weighed or measured. If the eggs are to be measured, the number and weight may easily be converted to volume by referring to Table 2.5.

Nonfat dry milk is indicated in some recipes, but in those specifying fluid milk, dry milk may be substituted. Table 2.6 gives a formula for conversion. In most cases, it is not necessary to rehydrate the dry milk, since it is mixed with other dry ingredients, and water is added in place of the fluid milk. The amount of fat in the recipe may need to be increased slightly.

Nutritional values are identified for most *Food for Fifty* recipes. Unless stated otherwise, values are for the portion listed at the top of each recipe. Percent Daily Values (%DV) are based on a 2000-calorie diet. Individuals' daily values may be higher or lower depending on calorie need. FDA guidelines for Recommended Daily Intakes (RDIs) and the Daily Reference Values (DRVs) follow.

Recommended Daily Intakes (RDIs)

Vitamin A	5000 IU
Vitamin C	60 mg
Thiamin	1.5 mg
Riboflavin	1.7 mg
Niacin	20 mg
Calcium	1 g
Iron	18 mg
Vitamin D	400 IU
Vitamin E	30 IU
Vitamin B	2 mg
Folic acid	0.4 mg
Vitamin B12	6 microg
Phosphorous	1 g
Iodine	150 microg
Magnesium	400 mg
Zinc	15 mg
Copper	2 mg
Biotin	0.3 mg
Pantothenic acid	10 mg

Daily Reference Values (DRVs) based on a 2000-calorie diet

Fat	65 g
Saturated Fat	20 g
Cholesterol	300 mg
Total Carbohydrates	300 g
Fiber	25 g
Potassium	3500 mg
Protein	50 g
Sodium	2400 mg

Nutrient values for *Food for Fifty* recipes are approximate and are intended to be used as general guidelines. Values identified for recipes may vary from actual values if substitute ingredients are used. Differences may occur also if ingredient amounts are adjusted, portion sizes are altered, or production procedures are changed.

Weights and Measures

Quantities of dry ingredients weighing more than 1 ounce are given by weight in ounces (oz) and pounds (lb). Weights are for foods as purchased (AP) unless otherwise stated. Liquid ingredients are indicated by measure: teaspoons (tsp), tablespoons (Tbsp), cups (cups), quarts (qt), and gallons (gal).

Accurate weighing and measuring of ingredients are essential for a satisfactory product. Weighing is more accurate than measuring and is recommended whenever possible, but reliable scales are essential. A table model scale with a 15- to 20-pound capacity and ¼- to ½-ounce graduations (or an electronic digital readout scale with a 15- to 20-pound capacity) is suitable for weighing ingredients for 50 portions.

Standard measuring equipment should be used to ensure accuracy, and measurements should be level. Use the largest appropriate measure to reduce the possibility of error and to save time. For example, use a one-gallon measure once instead of a one-quart measure four times. Flour is the exception: Use measures no larger than one quart for flour.

Cooking Time and Temperature

The cooking time given in each recipe is based on the size of pan and the amount of food in the pan. If a smaller or larger pan is used, an adjustment in cooking time may be necessary. The number of pans placed in the oven at one time also may affect the length of baking time; the larger the number of pans or the colder a product, the longer the cooking time. In convection ovens, the temperature as specified for a conventional oven should be reduced by 25–50°F and the total bake/roast time by 10 to 15 percent.

Critical Control Points

Monitoring cooking time and food temperature are important steps in the food production process because of their relationship to food contamination and foodborne illness. Time and temperatures are designated as critical control points (CCPs) in all Hazard Analysis Critical Control Point (HACCP) plans. Recipes in this book provide production, service, and storage procedures that can prevent or reduce food safety hazards of potentially hazardous foods. Standards for reducing food safety hazards may be found in Tables 2.18 and 2.26 (p. 100–106). Safe temperatures for cooked foods are shown in Table 2.23 (p. 103). Cooling procedures for hot foods are shown in Table 2.25 (p. 105). Examples of potentially hazardous foods can be found on p. 107. Recipes that contain potentially hazardous foods are identified in the recipe notes.

Abbreviations Used in Recipes

AP	as purchased
EP	edible portion
°F	degrees Fahrenheit
fl oz	fluid ounce
gal	gallon
g	gram
lb	pound
mg	milligram
oz	ounce
psi	pounds per square inch
pt	pint
qt	quart
tsp	teaspoon
Tbsp	tablespoon

Basic Recipes

Food for Fifty recipes are written to provide step-by-step guidelines for producing standard quality products. Many recipes printed in trade and popular magazines can be produced by adapting recipes in *Food for Fifty*, rather than standardizing new recipes. Adapting a *Food for Fifty* recipe may include only changing spices or adding a sauce. Creative presentations may be gleaned from trendy cookbooks and publications and with some modifications applied to the basic recipes in *Food for Fifty*.

CHAPTER 6

Appetizers, Hors d'oeuvres, and Special Event Foods

David Murray and Jules Selmes © Dorling Kindersley

ppetizers are foods served as a hot or cold first course before a meal and should complement the menu items that follow without duplicating flavors. Seafood cocktail (crab, lobster, oyster, shrimp), chunked fresh fruit cocktail, or soup is often served for an appetizer. *Hors d'oeuvres* may be served before a meal or may be the only food provided. They should be small (one or two bites), flavorful, and attractive. The style of service—whether buffet, served, or a combination of the two—will depend on the event and the expectations of the client or guest. Hors d'oeuvres and appetizers are similar and the terms are often used interchangeably.

Cold hors d'oeuvres may be canapés, crudités, or dips. *Canapés* are tiny sandwiches made by spreading a well-seasoned mixture on a bread or vegetable base. Canapé bases include toasted or untoasted bread slices cut into various shapes, crackers, quick breads, melba toast, tiny biscuits, puff pastry rounds, and small shells made from pastry or savory dough. Vegetable bases may be slices of cucumber, summer squash, or other vegetables that will support the weight of the spread. Spreads are the primary flavor ingredient. Flavorful spreads include mixtures made from flavored butters or cream cheese. A salad mixture made from eggs, fish, cheese, or meat is often used for a canapé spread. All canapés should be artfully garnished. Some canapés are made by holding an attractive garnish in place with a small amount of spread. Making canapés close to serving time will help keep the bases from becoming soggy. *Crudités* are raw or slightly blanched vegetables,

cut into attractive shapes and artfully displayed and garnished. They are usually served with one or more dips. Presentation is important. Broad flat dishes, baskets, silver trays, and shallow decorative pans may be used for the container. Vegetables are arranged with consideration for shape, color, balance, and overall decorative appeal. *Dips* are accompaniments to chips, crackers, fruits, toasts, or vegetables. They should complement the foods being served with them. Dips may be served in attractive serving bowls or hollowed out vegetables, such as cabbages or squash. Hot dips are often served in chafing pans.

Hot hors d'oeuvres are especially good for late afternoon or evening events when a full meal is not served. Filled pastry or savory dough shells, skewered pieces of meat or vegetables, and chicken wings or small meatballs are popular hot hors d'oeuvres. Hot and cold hors d'oeuvres are usually served at the same event.

Table 6.1 is a general guideline for quantities of appetizers or hors d'oeuvres needed to serve 50 people. Table 6.2 suggests the number of appetizers or hors d'oeuvres needed per person during a reception or predinner cocktail hour. Entree and vegetable tray guidelines may be found in Table 6.3. The characteristics of the group being served, time of day, type and duration of event, and number of different items offered may require increasing or decreasing the amount of food recommended. Historical data from similar events will be useful in planning food quantities. Table 6.4 suggests names for hors d'oeuvres and appetizers.

TABLE 6.1   Suggestions for appetizers

Food item	Guide to serving quantities for 50
BEVERAGES	
Punch	2–2½ gal, recipes pp. 251–260
Wine	See Tables 1.11 and 1.12, pp. 24–26
CANAPÉ SPREADS AND FILLINGS	
Chicken salad spread	Recipe p. 720, prepare ¼ recipe
Ham salad spread	Recipe p. 719, prepare ¼ recipe
Tuna salad spread	Recipe p. 721, prepare ¼ recipe
Miniature puffs	Recipe p. 426, prepare ½ recipe
COCKTAILS	
Broiled grapefruit	25 fruit
Fruit cup	10 lb
Melon balls or cubes	10 lb
Punch	2 gal, recipes pp. 251–260
Shrimp cocktail	Recipe for sauce p. 764
DIPS	
Artichoke, hot	Recipe p. 232
Artichoke and crab, hot	Recipe p. 232
Baba Ghanoush	Recipe p. 238
Basic, and variations	Recipe p. 232–233
Garden dressing (dip)	Recipe p. 700
Guacamole	Recipe p. 235
Hummus	Recipe p. 244
Layered Mexican	Recipe p. 234
Nacho	Recipe p. 236
Salsa	Recipe p. 756
Summer fruit	Recipe p. 233
Vegetable	Recipe p. 711
Yogurt	Recipes p. 710
HORS D'OEUVRES	
Apple and cheese wedges	1½ lb cheese, 8 apples, cut in wedges
Carrot curls	3–4 lb
Celery sticks	3–4 lb
Cheese ball with crackers	Recipe p. 237; 125–150 crackers
Cheese balls, hot	Recipe p. 451, prepare ½ recipe, use No. 40 dipper
Cheese cubes	5 lb
Cheese olive puffs	Recipe p. 239
Cherry tomatoes	2 lb
Chicken wings	Recipe p. 240
Chips	5 lb
Cocktail sausages	3–5 lb
Crudités	12–15 lb assorted vegetables p. 230
Deviled eggs	Recipe p. 450, prepare ½ recipe
Fruit chunks	8 lb
Marinated mushrooms	Recipe p. 652
Meatballs in barbecue sauce	Recipe p. 498, prepare ⅓ recipe, use No. 70 dipper
Mixed nuts	1–1½ lb
Party mix	3 lb
Pinwheels	Recipe p. 242
Quesadillas	Recipe p. 744
Sausage balls	100, recipe p. 239
Shrimp	Recipe p. 241
Caribbean shrimp	Recipe p. 474
Vegetable relishes	See p. 230 for ideas
Whole shrimp, with cocktail sauce	3–5 lb shrimp, recipe for sauce p. 764, prepare ½ recipe

TABLE 6.1   *continued*

Food item	Guide to serving quantities for 50
SOUPS	
Bouillon	Recipe p. 792, prepare ½ recipe for 4-oz portion
French onion	Recipe p. 809, prepare ½ recipe for 4-oz portion
Gazpacho	Recipe p. 821
Vichyssoise	Recipe p. 822, prepare ½ recipe for 4-oz portion
OTHER FINGER FOODS	
Cheese ball and crackers	4 lb cheese, 40 oz crackers
Cheese block and crackers	4 lb cheese, 40 oz crackers
Fresh fruit platter	8–10 lb fruit
Fresh vegetables and dip	8–10 lb vegetables, 1 qt dip
Nut bread tea sandwiches	50–75 sandwiches
Tea sandwiches	40–60 tuna, ham, or chicken salad sandwiches
Petite rolls and cold cuts	40–60 petite rolls served with 5 lb of assorted cold cuts and 2–3 lb of cheese slices

Notes:
- The quantity of appetizers needed for 50 portions will depend on the group being served, the type of function, and the number of different items offered. If food items are served in combination with other foods, adjust the amounts to yield the approximate total weight or total number recommended. Example: Carrot curls, in combination with celery sticks, require a total weight of 3–4 lb.
- Preparing appetizers for an attractive buffet requires careful planning. Choosing foods that need last-minute preparation, along with those that can be produced in advance, is suggested. Following are useful guidelines for production planning:

  Canapés, spreads, and fillings: Highly perishable fillings should be made shortly before serving.
  Cocktails: Prepare fruit a day in advance. Cook and chill shrimp a day in advance. Make and chill beverages 1 to 3 days in advance.
  Dips: Prepare and chill 1 to 3 days in advance. Store in glass or other inert-material container.
  Hors d'oeuvres: Prepare vegetable relishes a day in advance; store in cold water. To freshen, cover with ice for 30 minutes before serving. Marinate vegetables a day in advance. Prepare cheese balls 1 to 5 days in advance; cover tightly. Cut cheese cubes no more than a day in advance; cover tightly.
  Soups: Prepare cold soups 1 to 2 days in advance, hot soups just before serving.

TABLE 6.2   Number of hors d'oeuvres and appetizers to prepare per person

	½ Hour		1 Hour		2–3 Hours	
	Hot	Cold	Hot	Cold	Hot	Cold
Men only	6	4	8	6	10	8
Women only	3	2	5	4	6	5

Notes:
- When serving shrimp, prepare five pieces per ½ hour per person for cold shrimp and four pieces per ½ hour per person for hot shrimp.
- If a dinner will follow, reduce by one-third the amount of appetizers suggested.

TABLE 6.3   **Meat, cheese, and vegetable trays**

Meat and cheese trays (approximate amount to serve 50)			
Meat (shaved or thinly sliced)	*Cheese (thinly sliced)*	*Bread (thinly sliced bread or buns)*	*Spreads/other*
Choose 10 lb (total):	Choose 3 lb (total):	Choose 125 small slices or 75 buns:	Use suggested amount:
Cold cuts	American	Small buns	Margarine or butter, softened, 1 lb
Corned beef	Cheddar	Sliced bread	Mayonnaise or salad dressing, 1½ cups
Roast beef	Edam	Pumpernickel	
Ham	Gouda	Rye	Prepared mustard, 1 cup
Pastrami	Monterey Jack	White	Horseradish, 1 cup
Turkey	Muenster	Whole wheat	Leaf lettuce, 3 lb
	Provolone		Alfalfa sprouts, 1 lb
	Swiss		Tomatoes, sliced, 7 lb
	See p. 111 for additional cheeses		Onions, sliced, 2 lb

Vegetable trays and dips (approximate amount to serve 50; see Notes)		
Vegetables	*Relishes*	*Dips*
Choose 5 lb (total):	Choose 3 lb (total):	Choose 1–1½ qt (total):
Asparagus spears	Black or green olives	Hot artichoke
Broccoli florets	Dill spears	Blue cheese
Baby carrots	Pickled beets	Creamy herb
Carrot sticks or slices	Pickled eggs	Creamy onion
Cauliflower florets	Pickled vegetables	Dill
Celery sticks	Sweet pickles	Garden (prepare ½ recipe)
Cherry tomatoes	Garnishes (p. 891)	Italian
Cucumber spears or circles	Chives	Picante
Green beans	Flowers	Seafood
Green onions	Herbs	Summer fruit
Jicama	Scallions	Yogurt
Kohlrabi		
Mushrooms		
Pea pods		
Radish roses		
Red, green, or yellow bell peppers		
Zucchini spears		

Notes:
- Meat and cheese may be rolled, folded, or stacked and garnished with leaf lettuce, parsley, and colorful vegetables. Vegetables look appealing when cut in creative shapes and garnished with crisp greens.
- Arranging food neatly so the tray will remain attractive is important. Including larger quantities of more-popular items will make food trays appear well supplied throughout the serving period. Color and flavor combinations also should be considerations for determining placement of food items.
- Crudité trays may require two or three times the amount of vegetables for an attractive display to be arranged and garnished.
- Blanching asparagus, broccoli, cauliflower, and green beans heightens their flavor and appearance (p. 198).

TABLE 6.4   Name suggestions for hors d'oeuvres and appetizers

CHEESE

Assorted domestic cheese and crackers
Assorted imported cheese and
  crackers
Cheese ball with crackers
Cheese block and crackers
Nacho dip and tortilla chips

FRUIT

Fresh fruit platter
Fresh fruit platter with domestic or
  imported cheese
Fresh berries and dip
Carved melon basket with summer
  fruits

Imported cheese and fruit tray with
  sweet crackers and hot fudge dip
Fresh seasonal melon

SEAFOOD

Shrimp peel with cocktail sauce
Iced peeled shrimp
Hot spiced shrimp peel
Smoked salmon with lavosh cracker
  bread
Whole poached salmon

VEGETABLES

Assorted fresh vegetables and dip
Fresh raw vegetable tray with dip
Open-faced vegetable canapés
Belgian endive with herbed cheese

MEAT/POULTRY

Chicken tenders with sauce
Prosciutto-wrapped melon
Sliced meat and cheese tray
Roast tenderloin of beef and
  cocktail rolls
Mini puffs with white chicken salad
Assorted decorated canapés
Stuffed pita pockets

Note: • *Food for Fifty* recipes will provide guidelines for making hors d'oeuvres and appetizer suggestions.

APPETIZER RECIPES

HOT ARTICHOKE DIP

Yield: 50 portions   *Portion:* 1½ oz
Oven: 350°F   *Bake:* 20–25 minutes

Ingredient	Amount	Procedure
Artichoke hearts, canned	2 lb 10 oz	Drain and chop artichoke hearts.
Garlic clove, mashed	3 cloves	Stir remaining ingredients into artichoke hearts.
Mayonnaise	2 cups	
Worcestershire sauce	1½ tsp	
Parmesan cheese, grated	3 cups	
Pepper, white	¼ tsp	
		Pour into 2 one-quart ovenproof bowls or pans. Bake at 350°F until mixture reaches 165°F (20–25 minutes). Serve warm (above 140°F) with chips or crackers.

Approximate nutritive values per portion   **Calories** 92

Amount/portion	%DV	Amount/portion	%DV	Amount/portion	%DV		%DV		%DV
Total Fat 7 g	11%	**Cholest.** 4 mg	1%	**Total Carb.** 5 g	2%	**Vitamin A**	1%	**Calcium**	1%
Sat. Fat 1 g	4%	**Sodium** 148 mg	6%	Fiber 1 g	5%	**Vitamin C**	4%	**Iron**	2%
Protein 2 g				Sugars 0.3 g					

Percent Daily Values (%DV) are based on a 2000-calorie diet.

Note: • Potentially hazardous food. *Food Safety Standards:* Hold food for service at an internal temperature above 140°F. Do not mix old product with new. Cool leftover product quickly (within 4 hours) to below 41°F. See p. 105 for cooling procedures. Reheat leftover product quickly (within 2 hours) to 165°F. Reheat product only once, discard if not used.

Variation   • **Hot Crab and Artichoke Dip.** Add 1 lb chopped crabmeat before baking.

BASIC DIP

Yield: 50 portions

Ingredient	Amount	Procedure
Cream cheese	8 oz	Mix cream cheese until softened, using flat beater.
Sour cream	1 lb 8 oz	Add sour cream. Mix until smooth. Add ingredients for variations from following chart. Mix until evenly distributed. Chill quickly (within 4 hours) to below 41°F.

Note   • Dip may be thinned by adding a small quantity of buttermilk or milk.

VARIATIONS TO BASIC DIP RECIPE

Variation	Ingredients added to basic dip	Serve with
Avocado (guacamole) (see Notes)	(Delete cream cheese from Basic Dip; reduce sour cream to 8 oz) 1 lb 8 oz avocado pulp 1 Tbsp lemon juice 3 oz onion, finely chopped 2 Tbsp fresh cilantro, finely chopped ¼ tsp garlic powder 8 oz fresh tomatoes, diced	Tortilla chips Nacho chips
Blue Cheese	8 oz blue cheese, crumbled 1½ tsp lemon juice 1 Tbsp onion, finely chopped ½ cup buttermilk or milk	Crackers Fresh vegetables Chips
Creamy Herb	¼ cup fresh onion, finely chopped ¼ cup snipped fresh parsley ¼ cup chives, chopped 1 Tbsp Worcestershire sauce ¼ tsp garlic powder	Fresh vegetables
Creamy Onion	2 oz dry onion soup mix ½ oz snipped fresh parsley or chives	Chips
Dill	1½ Tbsp chopped onion 1 Tbsp dill weed 1½ tsp Beau Monde seasoning	Fresh vegetables
Italian	1½ oz dry Italian salad dressing mix ½ oz snipped fresh parsley	Fresh vegetables
Picante	(Delete sour cream; increase cream cheese to 2 lb) 8 oz salsa (see Notes) ¼ cup fresh cilantro, chopped 1 oz stuffed olives, chopped	Tortilla chips Nacho chips Fresh vegetables Spread for canapés
Seafood	8 oz cooked shrimp, clam, or crab, finely chopped 1 oz dry onion soup mix 2 oz chili sauce 1½ Tbsp horseradish	Crackers Toasted party bread
Summer Fruit	(Delete cream cheese) 8 oz brown sugar or honey 1½ tsp vanilla	Fresh fruit
Yogurt, Vegetable Yogurt, Fruit	see p. 711 see p. 710	Fresh vegetables Fresh fruit

Notes
- Chunky avocado dip may be made by deleting sour cream and using 2 lb cubed fresh avocados.
- More salsa may be added to Picante for a thinner dip.

LAYERED MEXICAN DIP

Yield: 50 portions or 3 14-inch platters   *Portion:* 4 oz

Ingredient	Amount	Procedure
Bean dip	4 lb (6 10½-oz cans)	
Avocado pulp	3 lb	Blend. Save for later step.
Lemon juice	6 Tbsp	
Salt	1 tsp	
Pepper, black	1½ tsp	
Sour cream	1 lb 8 oz	Blend. Save for later step.
Mayonnaise	1½ cups	
Taco seasoning	3¾ oz	
Tomatoes, fresh, diced	3 lb	
Green onions, sliced	9 oz	
Ripe olives, sliced	1 lb 4 oz	
Cheddar cheese, shredded	12 oz	

1. Spread 1 lb 5 oz bean dip on each of 3 14-inch round platters.
2. Spread 1 lb avocado mixture over bean dip layer.
3. Spread 12 oz sour cream mixture over avocado layer.
4. Sprinkle remaining ingredients over each platter in the following order: tomatoes, green onions, olives, and cheese. Chill quickly (within 4 hours) to below 41°F.
5. Serve with tortilla or nacho chips.

Approximate nutritive values per portion   **Calories** 212

Amount/portion	%DV	Amount/portion	%DV	Amount/portion	%DV		%DV		%DV
Total Fat 18 g	28%	**Cholest.** 14 mg	5%	**Total Carb.** 8 g	3%	**Vitamin A**	12%	**Calcium**	10%
Sat. Fat 5 g	24%	**Sodium** 787 mg	33%	Fiber 4 g	15%	**Vitamin C**	13%	**Iron**	6%
Protein 5 g				Sugars 1 g					

Percent Daily Values (%DV) are based on a 2000-calorie diet.

Notes
- Potentially hazardous food. Hold for service below 41°F. Discard partially used platters. Dip may be made a day ahead and kept below 41°F.
- Refried beans (½ recipe, p. 834) may be substituted for purchased bean dip.
- Salsa may be substituted for diced tomatoes, taco seasoning, and mayonnaise. Use 7½ cups salsa (2½ cups on each tray).

GUACAMOLE

Yield: 50 portions   *Portion:* 2 oz

Ingredient	Amount	Procedure
Avocado	12 (6 lb)	Peel, pit, and dice avocados.
Lime juice, freshly squeezed	½ cup	Sprinkle lime juice on avocados. Stir lightly to mix.
Plain yogurt	1 cup	Mix yogurt and spices into avocado until well mixed.
Ground cumin	1 tsp	
Hot pepper sauce	1 tsp	
Salt	½ tsp	
Pepper, ground black	½ tsp	
Plum tomatoes, seeded and diced to ¼ inch	2 lb (EP)	Stir tomatoes, onion, and cilantro into avocado mixture.
Red onion, diced	6 oz (EP)	
Fresh cilantro, chopped	1 oz (EP)	
		Serve with tortilla chips or as a condiment.

Approximate nutritive values per portion   **Calories** 100

Amount/portion	%DV	Amount/portion	%DV	Amount/portion	%DV		%DV		%DV
Total Fat 8 g	13%	**Cholest.** 0 mg	0%	**Total Carb.** 6g	2%	**Vitamin A**	5%	**Calcium**	2%
Sat. Fat 1 g	7%	**Sodium** 38 mg	2%	Fiber 3 g	12%	**Vitamin C**	15%	**Iron**	4%
Protein 1.5 g				Sugars 1g					

Percent Daily Values (%DV) are based on a 2000-calorie diet.

Note   ● Potentially hazardous food. *Food Safety Standards:* Hold food for service at an internal temperature below 41°F. Do not mix old product with new.

NACHOS

Yield: 50 portions   *Portion:* 3½ oz sauce + 1 oz chips

Ingredient	Amount	Procedure
Shortening	1 oz	Sauté onions in shortening until tender.
Onions, chopped	3 oz	
Green chili peppers, chopped	6 oz	Add chilies and tomatoes to onions. Simmer for 15 minutes.
Tomatoes, diced, canned	1 lb 8 oz	
Chicken Stock (p. 790)	2 qt	Add stock and seasonings. Bring to a boil. Reduce heat to medium.
Cumin, ground	1 Tbsp	
Garlic powder	2 tsp	
Processed cheese, shredded	6 lb 10 oz	Add cheese to hot mixture. Stir until melted.
Cornstarch	3 oz	Combine cornstarch and water to make a smooth paste. Add slowly to cheese mixture, stirring constantly.
Water	½ cup	Cook and stir until mixture thickens. Turn heat to low.
Nacho chips	4 lb	Place 12 nacho chips on dinner plate.
Jalapeño peppers, sliced	8 oz	Using a 4-oz ladle, pour 3½ oz of sauce over chips. Garnish with sliced jalapeño peppers.

Approximate nutritive values per portion   **Calories** 424

Amount/portion	%DV	Amount/portion	%DV	Amount/portion	%DV		%DV		%DV
Total Fat 29 g	44%	**Cholest.** 58 mg	19%	**Total Carb.** 26 g	9%	**Vitamin A**	24%	**Calcium**	42%
Sat. Fat 14 g	69%	**Sodium** 1138 mg	47%	Fiber 3 g	10%	**Vitamin C**	18%	**Iron**	5%
Protein 16 g				Sugars 1 g					

Percent Daily Values (%DV) are based on a 2000-calorie diet.

Notes
- Potentially hazardous food. *Food Safety Standards:* Hold food for service at an internal temperature above 140°F. Do not mix old product with new. Cool leftover product quickly (within 4 hours) to below 41°F. See p. 105 for cooling procedures. Reheat leftover product quickly (within 2 hours) to 165°F. Reheat product only once; discard if not used.
- The sauce may be thinned with chicken broth.
- Canned cheese sauce may be substituted for scratch prepared cheese sauce. Add green chili peppers and diced tomatoes if desired.

Variation
- **Quick Nacho Sauce.** In a steam-jacketed kettle combine 2 oz chopped onion, 4 oz canned green chilies (diced), 1½ cups diced tomatoes, 1 qt water, 2 tsp ground cumin, 2 tsp garlic powder, ½ tsp dried cilantro. Bring to boil, reduce heat and simmer 15–20 min. Stir in 3 lb 12 oz shredded processed cheese. Stir until melted. Return temperature to 150°F.

CHEESE BALL

Yield: 50 portions   *Portion:* 1½ oz

Ingredient	*Amount*	*Procedure*
Cream cheese, softened	1 lb	Mix all ingredients until smooth, using flat beater. Shape into two balls, 2 lb 4 oz each. Chill quickly (within 4 hours) to below 41°F.
Blue cheese, crumbled	1 lb 8 oz	
Sharp cheddar cheese, shredded	2 lb	
Onion, finely minced	3 oz	
Worcestershire sauce	1 tsp	

Approximate nutritive values per portion   **Calories** 154

Amount/portion	%DV	Amount/portion	%DV	Amount/portion	%DV		%DV		%DV
Total Fat 13 g	20%	**Cholest.** 39 mg	13%	**Total Carb.** 1 g	0.3%	**Vitamin A**	12%	**Calcium**	21%
Sat. Fat 8 g	42%	**Sodium** 331 mg	14%	Fiber 0 g	0%	**Vitamin C**	0%	**Iron**	1%
Protein 8 g				Sugars 0.5 g					

Percent Daily Values (%DV) are based on a 2000-calorie diet.

Notes
- Potentially hazardous food. Hold for service below 41°F. Discard partially used cheese balls.
- Ball may be rolled in chopped pecans, snipped fresh parsley, or paprika.
- Cheese mixture may be shaped into a long roll. After chilling, slice and serve on crackers or other canapé base.

BABA GHANOUSH

Yield: 50 portions   *Portion:* 3 oz
Oven: 425°F

Ingredient	Amount	Procedure
Eggplant	10 lb 12 oz AP	Cut eggplant in half. Place cut side down on greased or silicone-paper lined bun sheet. Bake until soft. Cool, peel, chop, and mix until smooth.
Onions, chopped	12 oz EP	Add onions, parsley, and garlic to eggplant.
Parsley, chopped (fresh)	3 Tbsp EP	Mix well.
Garlic, minced	3 oz EP	
Lemon juice (fresh)	4 oz	Mix lemon juice, oil, tahini paste, and spices with vegetables.
Olive oil	2 oz	Hold for service at or below 41°F.
Tahini paste	3 oz	Serve as a dip with pita points or as a Middle Eastern spread.
Red pepper flakes	1¼ tsp	
Cumin (ground)	1 Tbsp	
Salt	¼ tsp	

Approximate nutritive values per portion   **Calories** 50

Amount/portion	%DV	Amount/portion	%DV	Amount/portion	%DV		%DV		%DV
Total Fat 2.2 g	3%	**Cholest.** 0 mg	0%	**Total Carb.** 7 g	2%	**Vitamin A**	2%	**Calcium**	1%
Sat. Fat .3 g	2%	**Sodium** 18.3 mg	1%	Fiber 2.5 g	10%	**Vitamin C**	6%	**Iron**	2%
Protein 1.5 g				Sugars 3.4 g					

Percent Daily Values (%DV) are based on a 2000-calorie diet.

Note   • Potentially hazardous food. *Food Safety Standards:* Hold food for service at an internal temperature below 41°F. Do not mix old product with new.

SAUSAGE BALLS

Yield: 50 portions   *Portion:* 2 balls
Oven: 350°F   *Bake:* 20–25 minutes, both steps

Ingredient	Amount	Procedure
Pork sausage, bulk	2 lb	Form sausage into 100 1-inch balls, using a No. 70 dipper. Place on baking sheet. Bake at 350°F for 15 minutes. Drain on paper towels.
Cheddar cheese, grated	1 lb	Combine cheese, margarine, flour, and seasonings in mixer bowl, using flat beater.
Margarine, softened	8 oz	
Flour, all-purpose	12 oz	
Salt	½ tsp	
Paprika	2 tsp	
		Wrap 2 Tbsp (No. 70 dipper) of dough around each sausage ball. Place on ungreased baking sheet. Bake at 350°F for 8–10 minutes. Serve hot, above 140°F.

Approximate nutritive values per portion **Calories** 145

Amount/portion	%DV	Amount/portion	%DV	Amount/portion	%DV		%DV		%DV
Total Fat 11 g	17%	**Cholest.** 21 mg	7%	**Total Carb.** 6 g	2%	**Vitamin A**	4%	**Calcium**	7%
Sat. Fat 4 g	21%	**Sodium** 296 mg	12%	Fiber 0.2 g	1%	**Vitamin C**	0%	**Iron**	3%
Protein 6 g				Sugars 0.3 g					

Percent Daily Values (%DV) are based on a 2000-calorie diet.

Notes
- Potentially hazardous food. *Food Safety Standards:* Hold food for service at an internal temperature above 140°F. Cool leftover product quickly (within 4 hours) to below 41°F. See p. 105 for cooling procedures. Reheat leftover product quickly (within 2 hours) to 165°F. Reheat product only once; discard if not used.
- Balls may be frozen after wrapping with dough. Bake while still frozen at 400°F for 12–15 minutes.

Variation
- **Cheese Olive Puffs.** Wrap dough around large stuffed green olives. Bake same as for Sausage Balls.

HOT BARBECUED WINGS

Yield: 50 portions   *Portion:* 6 wing pieces
Oven: 400°F   *Bake:* 20–25 minutes

Ingredient	Amount	Procedure
Barbecue Sauce (p. 755) Pepper, red, crushed	1¼ qt 1 tsp	Mix barbecue sauce and crushed red pepper.
Chicken wings, split, tip removed	20 lb	Pour barbecue sauce over chicken wings and stir to coat evenly. Place chicken wings on a lightly greased rack that is set inside a baking pan. (Wings should not touch.) Bake at 400°F for 10 minutes. Remove from oven and brush with barbecue sauce. Bake another 10–15 minutes until browned and internal temperature is 170°F. Remove from oven and serve. Additional heated barbecue sauce may be poured on wings before service. (Do not use the barbecue sauce that was used to sauce the raw wings.)

Approximate nutritive values per portion   **Calories** 384

Amount/portion	%DV	Amount/portion	%DV	Amount/portion	%DV		%DV		%DV
Total Fat 15 g	23%	**Cholest.** 156 mg	52%	**Total Carb.** 3 g	1%	**Vitamin A**	5%	**Calcium**	2%
Sat. Fat 4 g	20%	**Sodium** 316 mg	13%	Fiber 0.2 g	1%	**Vitamin C**	3%	**Iron**	12%
Protein 55 g				Sugars 2 g					

Percent Daily Values (%DV) are based on a 2000-calorie diet.

Notes
- Always wash hands and wash and sanitize countertops, utensils, and containers between production steps when preparing raw poultry.
- Potentially hazardous food. *Food Safety Standards:* Hold food for service at an internal temperature above 140°F. Do not mix old product with new. Cool leftover product quickly (within 4 hours) to below 41°F. See p. 105 for cooling procedures. Reheat leftover product quickly (within 2 hours) to 165°F. Reheat product only once; discard if not used.

Variations
- **Cajun Wings.** Season chicken wings with Cajun Seasoning (p. 782). Serve with a Blue Cheese or Barbecue Sauce (p. 755) or bottled hot pepper sauces.
- **Sweet and Sour Wings.** Substitute Sweet and Sour Sauce (p. 766) for Barbecue Sauce.

SHRIMP PEEL

Yield: 50 portions   *Portion:* 2 oz

Ingredient	Amount	Procedure
Water	3¾ qt	Bring water, lemon juice, lemons, and seasonings to a rolling boil in steam-jacketed or large kettle.
Lemon juice	½ cup	
Lemons, quartered	2 lemons	
Allspice, whole	1 Tbsp	
Bay leaves	8 leaves	
Pepper, cayenne	2 tsp	
Cloves, whole	1 Tbsp	
Coriander, ground	1 tsp	
Dill weed	2 tsp	
Mustard seed	2 tsp	
Parsley, dried	3 Tbsp	
Salt	1 Tbsp	
Shrimp, thawed (medium to medium large)	7 lb	Add shrimp and bring to a full rolling boil. Cook only until shrimp turn pink, approximately 3 minutes. Remove from heat and drain immediately. Chill quickly (4 hours or less) to below 41°F. (See p. 105 for cooling procedures.) To serve, arrange shrimp on top of shaved ice. Serve with Cocktail Sauce on p. 764. Garnish with lemon wedges and fresh herbs.

Approximate nutritive values per portion   **Calories** 71

Amount/portion	%DV	Amount/portion	%DV	Amount/portion	%DV		%DV		%DV
Total Fat 1 g	2%	**Cholest.** 96 mg	32%	**Total Carb.** 1 g	1%	**Vitamin A**	3%	**Calcium**	4%
Sat. Fat 0 g	0%	**Sodium** 225 mg	9%	Fiber 0 g	0%	**Vitamin C**	6%	**Iron**	9%
Protein 13 g				Sugars 0 g					

Percent Daily Values (%DV) are based on a 2000-calorie diet.

Notes
- Potentially hazardous food. *Food Safety Standards:* Hold food for service at an internal temperature below 41°F.
- Frozen unthawed shrimp may be used. Stir after adding to boiling water.
- Shrimp may be served hot.
- A commercial shrimp boil may be substituted for spices.

TOMATO, BASIL, AND CHEESE PINWHEELS

Yield: 50 portions   *Portion:* 2 pinwheels

Ingredient	Amount	Procedure
Cream cheese	3 lb	Soften cream cheese to room temperature. Place in mixer bowl.
Parsley, minced	4 oz	Add fresh herbs, garlic, tomatoes, pimento,
Basil, minced	2 oz	and black olives to softened cream cheese.
Thyme, minced	½ oz	Mix until well blended.
Rosemary, finely minced	½ oz	
Garlic, minced	1 Tbsp	
Rehydrated dried tomatoes, minced	6 oz	
Pimento, diced (well drained)	4 oz	
Black olives, coarsely chopped or thinly sliced (well drained)	4 oz	
Flour tortillas, 12 inch	10	Place tortillas on work surface. Smooth 6 oz cream cheese mixture over tortillas. Roll very tightly (as for a jelly roll) to create a pinwheel effect. Cover and refrigerate until well chilled, 4–6 hours.
		Cut off ends of tortilla roll and discard. Portion remaining roll into 10 slices per roll.

Approximate nutritive values per portion   **Calories** 150

Amount/portion	%DV	Amount/portion	%DV	Amount/portion	%DV		%DV		%DV
Total Fat 11 g	17%	**Cholest.** 30 mg	10%	**Total Carb.** 10 g	3%	**Vitamin A**	13%	**Calcium**	5%
Sat. Fat 6 g	31%	**Sodium** 208 mg	9%	Fiber 1 g	4%	**Vitamin C**	11%	**Iron**	7%
Protein 3.6 g				Sugars .5g					

Percent Daily Values (%DV) are based on a 2000-calorie diet.

Note   ● Potentially hazardous food. *Food Safety Standards:* Hold food for service at an internal temperature below 41°F.

FOCACCIA WITH HERB CHEESE SPREAD

Yield: 4 Focaccia rounds with spread

Ingredient	Amount	Procedure
Focaccia	Recipe p. 305	Prepare Focaccia.
Nonfat cream cheese, softened	2 cups	Combine cream cheese, sour cream, and mayonnaise in a mixer bowl. Beat on low speed until smooth.
Low-fat sour cream	1½ cups	
Low-fat mayonnaise	¼ cup	
Parmesan cheese, freshly grated	3 oz	Add cheese, herbs, and pepper. Mix until just combined.
Basil, fresh, chopped	⅓ cup	
Chives, fresh, minced	⅓ cup	
Garlic, minced	½ tsp	
Pepper, black	½ tsp	
		Spread 6–8 oz of spread on top of Focaccia rounds and broil 6 inches from heat until spread melts (1–2 minutes). Cut into narrow strips or wedges. Serve warm.

Approximate nutritive values per portion **Calories** 2158

Amount/portion	%DV	Amount/portion	%DV	Amount/portion	%DV		%DV		%DV
Total Fat 100 g	154%	**Cholest.** 50 mg	17%	**Total Carb.** 242 g	81%	Vitamin A	70%	Calcium	88%
Sat. Fat 12 g	59%	**Sodium** 2759 mg	115%	Fiber 9 g	35%	Vitamin C	4%	Iron	74%
Protein 61 g				Sugars 0 g					

Percent Daily Values (%DV) are based on a 2000-calorie diet.

Notes
- Potentially hazardous food. Serve within 2 hours after heating cheese topping. If not used within 2 hours, refrigerate at below 41°F, or discard.
- Serve as an appetizer or as an accompaniment to soup or salad.

RED PEPPER HUMMUS ON PITA POINTS

Yield: 50 portions   *Portion:* 3 oz hummus

Ingredient	Amount	Procedure
Garbanzo beans, drained and rinsed (canned)	6 lb EP	Place drained garbanzo beans, minced garlic, tahini paste, and lime juice in food processor.
Garlic, minced	7 oz	Process until smooth.
Tahini paste	1 lb 5 oz	
Lime juice (fresh)	2⅔ cups	
Roasted red peppers (p. 854)	2 lbs	Add peppers and seasonings to food processor. Process only until peppers are finely chopped.
Basil leaves (dried, crumbled)	2¼ tsp	
Salt	3¾ tsp	
Red pepper flakes	1¼ tsp	
Black pepper	¼ tsp	
Pita or Gyro bread	4 lb 8 oz	Cut pita or gyro bread into pie shaped pieces.
Cucumbers, peeled, sliced	7 lb 8 oz	Serve hummus on bread points with slices of cucumber.

Approximate nutritive values per portion of Hummus   **Calories** 126

Amount/portion	%DV	Amount/portion	%DV	Amount/portion	%DV		%DV		%DV
Total Fat 6 g	9%	**Cholest.** 0 mg	0%	**Total Carb.** 15.3 g	5%	**Vitamin A**	15%	**Calcium**	4%
Sat. Fat .8 g	4%	**Sodium** 307 mg	13%	Fiber 2.9 g	11%	**Vitamin C**	25%	**Iron**	7%
Protein 4.5 g				Sugars 0.1 g					

Percent Daily Values (%DV) are based on a 2000-calorie diet.

Note   • Potentially hazardous food. *Food Safety Standards:* Hold food for service at an internal temperature below 41°F. Do not mix old product with new.

CHAPTER 7

Beverages

Ian O'Leary © Dorling Kindersley

COFFEE

The type of coffee-making equipment used in a food-service determines the method of preparation and the grind of coffee. Urns or modular brewers are used when large quantities of coffee are required, as on a rapidly moving cafeteria line or for a large catered function. Where the service is spread over a longer period, coffee may be prepared in small batches in a drip coffee maker, or for single servings in an espresso machine.

The equipment selected should make a clear, rich brew, hold the coffee at a consistent temperature, and provide the quantity needed at an appropriate speed with minimal labor. Regardless of the method used, certain guidelines should be observed:

1. Select a grind that is designed for the brewing equipment. Fine or vacuum grind is suitable for equipment that brews in 1–4 minutes (espresso machines), medium grind for drip makers that brew in 4–6 minutes, and coarse grind for urns that brew in 6–8 minutes.

2. Use fresh coffee. Coffee loses its strength and flavor rapidly after it is ground and exposed to air. Large amounts should not be stored. To maintain good coffee flavor, store ground coffee or whole beans in an airtight container at cool room temperature. To keep coffee for more than 2–3 weeks, store in the freezer in an airtight container.

3. Use a proportion of fresh, cold water to coffee that makes a brew of the strength preferred by the clientele. A proportion of 2½ gal of water per pound of coffee (20 oz of water to 1 oz of coffee) makes a commonly accepted brew. See p. 247 for coffee recipes. For a stronger brew, use 1 lb of coffee per 2 gal of water.

4. Have the water cold, freshly drawn, accurately measured, and brought to a temperature of 195–200°F. Water that is too hot will extract bitter solids. Water that is too cold will not extract enough color or flavor. Bottled or filtered water may be used to brew coffee.

5. Hold brewed coffee at 185°F. Urn coffee can be held for up to 1 hour. Coffee brewed in small pots and kept warm by a heat source under the pot should be served within 20 minutes of brewing. Carafes that hold brewed coffee in an insulated serving decanter will hold the coffee for 2 hours or more. Reheating coffee results in a bitter brew.

6. Clean the coffee-making equipment after each use, following instructions that come with the equipment.

Specialty coffee refers to coffee made from flavored beans, espresso, and espresso-based drinks, or coffee flavored with syrups or other post-brew flavorings. See p. 174 for espresso-based drinks.

TEA

Tea is brewed by the process of infusion, in which boiling water is poured over tea leaves or bags. The following brewing guidelines should be followed.

- Start with fresh, high-quality tea.
- Start with fresh, cold water and bring it to a rolling boil. Do not boil the water for a long period of time.
- Use a stainless steel, earthenware, or porcelainlike pot that has been preheated with a small amount of hot water.
- Add tea bags or loose tea (in a strainer or infuser) to the pot. A generally acceptable brew is made by using 1 Tbsp of loose tea or one tea bag per cup of water.
- Pour boiling water directly over the tea and allow to steep 3–5 minutes. Remove the tea bag or leaves from the water after the tea has steeped or it becomes bitter.

For iced tea, make the brew stronger than for hot tea to compensate for the ice that melts. Pour tea over ice just before serving.

A suggested selection of teas includes a black, green, and Oolong variety, and a specialty or flavored tea such as black currant or raspberry. Caffeine-free and herbal tea selections also should be available. See p. 174 for descriptions of teas.

PUNCH

Punch may be made easily from frozen or canned juices in various combinations. Lemonade (p. 000) or Basic Fruit Punch (p. 252) make good bases for many other fruit drinks when combined with fresh, frozen, canned, or powdered juices of the desired flavor.

The amount of sugar needed varies with the sugar concentration of the juices and individual preference. A recipe for Simple Syrup for sweetening punch is given on p. 252. If time does not allow making the syrup, the sugar may be added directly to the punch and stirred until the sugar is dissolved.

For punch that is to be served iced, the ingredients should be refrigerated. The chilled ingredients may be combined several hours in advance of service. If ginger ale or other carbonated beverage is to be used, however, it should be chilled and added just before serving. Hot punch should be served at 180°F. If wine or other liquor is an ingredient in hot punch recipes, the temperature should not exceed 180°F.

Punch may be served from a bowl and kept cold by adding ice cubes, or it may be poured over an ice mold (p. 251). It may also be served as a nonalcoholic cocktail in appropriate glassware and garnished. See p. 261 for a few suggestions for nonalcoholic cocktails that use recipes in this book. Hot punch may be served from a punch bowl or hot-holding equipment. Preheat a glass punch bowl with a small amount of hot water before filling with hot punch.

The amount of punch or iced beverage to prepare depends on the size of the punch cup or glass, the number of guests to be served, and whether second servings will be offered. Service from a punch bowl requires slightly more punch than if it is to be poured from a pitcher for individual service. It is always desirable to have extra chilled, unopened cans of the main punch ingredients to facilitate serving a larger crowd than anticipated.

Most recipes in this book were developed for 2–2½ gallons of punch. Each gallon will yield 32½-cup portions. Punch cups vary in size from 3–6 oz, so it is important that the size be considered in determining the correct amount of punch to prepare.

WINE

Pairing wine with food is a matter of individual preference and usually requires some experimentation. Table 1.11 (p. 24) provides guidelines helpful for selecting wine. The amount of wine to serve depends on glass size and the type of meal or event. The volumes of different-sized wine bottles are located in Table 1.12 (p. 26).

BEVERAGE RECIPES

COFFEE

Yield: 50 portions or 2½ gal   *Portion:* 6 oz (¾ cup)

Ingredient	Amount	Procedure
Coffee	1 lb	Use proper blend and grind for the coffee maker used.
Water, cold	2½ gal	Use method recommended by the manufacturer of the coffee maker.

Note • The amount of water will vary with the brand of coffee and the strength preferred.

Variations • **Iced Coffee.** Increase coffee to 2 lb. Pour over ice in glasses. Coffee may be cooled to room temperature but should not be refrigerated. Flavorings (e.g., vanilla or almond) may be added for variety.

• **Instant Coffee.** Use 3 oz instant coffee or 2 oz freeze-dried to 2½ gal boiling water. Dissolve the coffee in a small amount of boiling water and add to the remaining hot water. Keep hot just below the boiling point, 185°–190°F.

• **Steeped Coffee.** Tie regular grind coffee loosely in a cloth bag. Immerse bag in cold water, which has been measured into a stainless steel kettle or stock pot. Heat to boiling point. Boil 3 minutes or until of desired strength. Remove coffee bag. Cover container and hold over low heat to keep at serving temperature.

HOT TEA

Yield: 50 portions or 2½ gal   *Portion:* 6 oz (¾ cup)

Ingredient	Amount	Procedure
Tea bags, 1oz	2	Place tea bags in a stainless steel, enamel, or earthenware container.
Water, cold	2½ gal	Bring water to a boil; pour over tea. Steep for 3 minutes. Remove bags.

Notes • If bulk tea is used, tie loosely in a bag.

• The amount of tea to be used will vary with the quality.

• Instant tea (¾–1 oz) may be used in place of the tea bags. The exact amount will vary according to the strength desired.

SPICED TEA

Yield: 48 portions or 1½ gal   *Portion:* 4 oz (½ cup)

Ingredient	Amount	Procedure
Water, boiling	1½ gal	Mix all ingredients except tea.
Sugar, granulated	1 lb 8 oz	Simmer 20 minutes.
Lemon juice	¼ cup	Strain.
Lemon peel, grated	1 lemon	
Orange juice	1 cup	
Orange peel, grated	1 orange	
Cloves, whole	4 tsp	
Cinnamon sticks	8	
Tea bag, 1oz	1	Add tea bag to hot liquid. Steep for 5 minutes. Remove tea bag. Serve hot.

Approximate nutritive values per portion   **Calories** 60

Amount/portion	%DV	Amount/portion	%DV	Amount/portion	%DV		%DV		%DV
Total Fat 0 g	0%	**Cholest.** 0 mg	0%	**Total Carb.** 16 g	5%	**Vitamin A**	0%	**Calcium**	0%
Sat. Fat 0 g	0%	**Sodium** 7 mg	0.3%	Fiber 0 g	0%	**Vitamin C**	8%	**Iron**	0%
Protein 0.1 g				Sugars 14 g					

Percent Daily Values (%DV) are based on a 2000-calorie diet.

Variation   • **Russian Tea.** Use only 1¼ gal water. Add 1 qt grape juice when adding other juice.

ICED TEA

Yield: 48 portions or 3 gal   *Portion:* 8 oz (1 cup)

Ingredient	Amount	Procedure
Tea bags, 1 oz	6	Place tea bags in enamel, stainless steel, or earthenware container.
Water, boiling	1 gal	Pour boiling water over tea bags. Steep 4–6 minutes. Remove bags.
Water, cold	2 gal	Pour hot tea into cold water.
Ice, chipped or cubed	10–15 lb	Fill 12 oz glasses with ice. Pour tea over ice just before serving.

Notes   • Always pour the hot tea concentrate into the cold water. Do not refrigerate or ice the tea prior to service. Cloudiness develops in tea that has been refrigerated.

• Instant tea (1–1½ oz) may be used in place of the tea bags.

• Six to seven lemons, cut in eighths, may be served with the tea.

• Iced tea may be garnished with lemon or orange slices or mint leaves.

COCOA

Yield: 50 portions or 2½ gal   *Portion:* 6 oz (¾ cup)

Ingredient	Amount	Procedure
Sugar, granulated	1 lb 8 oz	Mix sugar, cocoa, and salt.
Cocoa	8 oz	
Salt	½ tsp	
Water	1 qt	Add water and mix until smooth.
		Boil approximately 3 minutes or to form a thin syrup.
Milk	2½ gal	Heat milk to scalding. Stir in syrup.
Vanilla	1 tsp	Just before serving, add vanilla and stir until well mixed.

Approximate nutritive values per portion   **Calories** 182

Amount/portion	%DV	Amount/portion	%DV	Amount/portion	%DV		%DV		%DV
Total Fat 7 g	11%	**Cholest.** 26 mg	9%	**Total Carb.** 25 g	8%	**Vitamin A**	7%	**Calcium**	24%
Sat. Fat 4 g	21%	**Sodium** 121 mg	5%	Fiber 0 g	0%	**Vitamin C**	3%	**Iron**	9%
Protein 7 g				Sugars 23 g					

Percent Daily Values (%DV) are based on a 2000-calorie diet.

Notes
- Potentially hazardous food. *Food Safety Standards:* Hold for service at 185°F. Cool leftover product quickly (within 4 hours) to below 41°F. See p. 105 for cooling procedures. Reheat leftover product quickly (within 2 hours) to 185°F. Reheat product only once; discard if not used.

- A marshmallow or 1 tsp whipped cream may be added to each cup if desired.

- Cocoa syrup may be made in amounts larger than this recipe and stored in the refrigerator for 3 or 4 days. To serve, add 1 qt cocoa syrup to each 2 gal hot milk.

Variations
- **Hot Chocolate.** Substitute 10 oz unsweetened baking chocolate for cocoa. Add to water and stir until melted.

- **Instant Hot Cocoa.** Dissolve 2½ lb instant cocoa powder in 2 gal boiling water.

- **Mexican Chocolate.** Follow hot chocolate recipe. Substitute 1 gal of hot coffee for 1 gal of milk. Add 1 oz (¼ cup) ground cinnamon.

- **Amaretto Cocoa.** Add ¾ cup amaretto along with the milk. Delete vanilla. For a nonalcoholic version, substitute 1½ Tbsp of almond extract for the amaretto.

FRENCH CHOCOLATE

Yield: 64 portions or 3 gal   *Portion:* 6 oz (¾ cup)

Ingredient	Amount	Procedure
Unsweetened chocolate	1 lb 2 oz	Combine chocolate and water. Cook over direct heat, stirring constantly, for 5 minutes or until chocolate is melted.
Water, cold	3 cups	Remove from heat. Beat with a wire whip until smooth.
Sugar, granulated	2 lb 8 oz	Add sugar and salt to chocolate mixture.
Salt	½ tsp	Return to heat. Cook over hot water 20–30 minutes or until thick. Chill.
Whipping cream	3½ cups	Whip cream. Fold into cold chocolate mixture.
Milk	2½ gal	Heat milk to scalding. To serve, place 1 Tbsp (rounded) chocolate mixture in each serving cup. Add hot milk to fill cup. Stir until well blended. Serve immediately.

Approximate nutritive values per portion   **Calories** 247

Amount/portion	%DV	Amount/portion	%DV	Amount/portion	%DV		%DV		%DV
Total Fat 14 g	22%	**Cholest.** 38 mg	13%	**Total Carb.** 28 g	9%	**Vitamin A**	11%	**Calcium**	19%
Sat. Fat 8 g	39%	**Sodium** 97 mg	4%	Fiber 1 g	2%	**Vitamin C**	2%	**Iron**	3%
Protein 6 g				Sugars 26 g					

Percent Daily Values (%DV) are based on a 2000-calorie diet.

Notes

- Potentially hazardous food. *Food Safety Standards:* Hold for service at 185°F. Cool leftover product quickly (within 4 hours) to below 41°F. See p. 105 for cooling procedures. Reheat leftover product quickly (within 2 hours) to 185°F. Reheat product only once; discard if not used.
- The milk must be kept at 185°F during the serving period.
- The chocolate mixture may be stored for 24 hours in the refrigerator.
- To make in quantity, prepare chocolate syrup and add hot milk. Whip cream to soft peaks and fold into hot chocolate. Keep hot.

BASIC FRUIT PUNCH

Yield: 80 portions or 2½ gal   *Portion:* 4 oz (½ cup)

Ingredient	Amount	Procedure
Sugar, granulated	2 lb 8 oz	Mix sugar and water.
Water	1 qt	Bring to boil. Cool.
Orange juice, frozen, undiluted	3 cups (2 12-oz cans)	Combine juices and water.
Lemon juice, frozen, undiluted	3 cups (2 12-oz cans)	Add sugar syrup and stir until mixed. Chill.
Water, cold	1½ gal	

Approximate nutritive values per portion   **Calories** 74

Amount/portion	%DV	Amount/portion	%DV	Amount/portion	%DV		%DV		%DV
Total Fat 0.1 g	0.1%	**Cholest.** 0 mg	0%	**Total Carb.** 19 g	6%	Vitamin A	0%	Calcium	0%
Sat. Fat 0 g	0%	**Sodium** 3 mg	0.1%	Fiber 0 g	0%	Vitamin C	31%	Iron	0%
Protein 0.3 g				Sugars 14 g					

Percent Daily Values (%DV) are based on a 2000-calorie diet.

Notes
- If time does not allow making and cooling syrup, the sugar may be added to the cold punch and stirred until dissolved. Increase cold water to 1¾ gal.
- Ginger ale may be substituted for part or all of the water. Chill and add just before serving.

Variations
- **Golden Punch.** Reduce orange and lemon juice to one 12-oz can each. Add two 46-oz cans pineapple juice.
- **Ginger Ale Fruit Punch.** Use 1½ qt lemon juice, 1½ qt orange juice, 1 qt pineapple juice, and 1 gal water. Increase sugar to 3 lb. Add 2 qt ginger ale just before serving. Lime, orange, lemon, or raspberry sherbet may be added to punch just before serving.
- **Sparkling Grape Punch.** Reduce orange and lemon juice to one 12-oz can each. Add two 12-oz cans frozen grape juice. Just before serving, add two 20-oz bottles of ginger ale.

ICE MOLD

Yield: 1 mold

Ingredient	Amount	Procedure
Ice mold	1	Select mold that will fit in punch bowl.
Punch, juice, lemonade		Fill mold with liquid, half to two-thirds full. Freeze.
Garnishes	See Notes	Add garnishes and enough liquid to partially cover garnishes. Freeze.
		After thin layer of liquid and fruit are frozen, fill mold with liquid and freeze until firm.
		To unmold ice ring, dip the mold in warm water until the ice slips out easily. Place the ring in very cold punch, garnished side up. Replace mold as necessary.

Notes
- Some attractive garnishes include strawberries, cherries, pineapple, grapes, orange or lemon or lime slices, mint, ivy, and fresh flowers. (See p. 172 for flower garnishes.)
- If water is the liquid, use distilled or boiled tap water. Allow boiled water to sit and de-aerate about 15 minutes.
- For a decorative ice mold, use two or three layers of garnish between layers of ice. Freeze the garnish in place before adding the layers of liquid.

SIMPLE SYRUP

Yield: 2 qt

Ingredient	Amount	Procedure
Sugar, granulated	2 lb	Mix sugar and water.
Water	1 qt	Boil for 3 minutes.
		Chill before using in punch.

Notes
- For a thicker syrup, increase sugar to 2 lb 8 oz and add 1 Tbsp corn syrup.
- May be stored in the refrigerator for use in beverages or where recipe specifies Simple Syrup.

LEMONADE

Yield: 48 portions or 3 gal   *Portion:* 8 oz (1 cup)

Ingredient	Amount	Procedure
Lemon juice	1¼ qt (approximately 30 lemons)	Mix lemon juice and sugar.
Sugar, granulated	2 lb 8 oz	
Water, cold	2¼ gal	Add water. Stir until sugar is dissolved. Chill.

Approximate nutritive values per portion   **Calories** 97

Amount/portion	%DV	Amount/portion	%DV	Amount/portion	%DV		%DV		%DV
Total Fat 0 g	0%	**Cholest.** 0 mg	0%	**Total Carb.** 25 g	8%	**Vitamin A**	0%	**Calcium**	0%
Sat. Fat 0 g	0%	**Sodium** 11 mg	0.5%	Fiber 0 g	0%	**Vitamin C**	10%	**Iron**	0%
Protein 0 g				Sugars 24 g					

Percent Daily Values (%DV) are based on a 2000-calorie diet.

Notes
- Three 6-oz cans undiluted frozen lemon juice may be substituted for fresh lemon juice. Increase water to 2½ gal.
- Three 32-oz cans frozen lemonade concentrate, diluted 1:4 parts water, will yield 60 1-cup portions.
- Lemonade makes a good base for fruit punch.

BANANA PUNCH

Yield: 64 portions or 2 gal   *Portion:* 4 oz (½ cup)

Ingredient	Amount	Procedure
Sugar, granulated	2 lb	Mix sugar and water.
Water, hot	1½ qt	Boil for 3 minutes. Cool.
Orange juice, frozen, undiluted	1½ cups (1 12-oz can)	Combine juices, fruits, and water.
Lemon juice, frozen, undiluted	¾ cup (1 6-oz can)	Add cooled sugar syrup. Chill.
Water, cold	1 qt	
Pineapple, crushed	3 qt (1 No. 10 can)	
Bananas, ripe, mashed	6 medium	
Ginger ale, chilled	1 qt	Add ginger ale just before serving.

Approximate nutritive values per portion   **Calories** 105

Amount/portion	%DV	Amount/portion	%DV	Amount/portion	%DV		%DV		%DV
Total Fat 0 g	0%	**Cholest.** 0 mg	0%	**Total Carb.** 27 g	9%	Vitamin A	0%	Calcium	1%
Sat. Fat 0 g	0%	**Sodium** 3 mg	0.1%	Fiber 1 g	2%	Vitamin C	25%	Iron	1%
Protein 1 g				Sugars 27 g					

Percent Daily Values (%DV) are based on a 2000-calorie diet.

Notes
- Mixture may be frozen before ginger ale is added and held for use later.
- Two 46-oz cans of unsweetened pineapple juice and one 12-oz can lemonade may be substituted for the crushed pineapple and lemon juice.

Variation
- **Banana Slush Punch.** Mix and freeze juices, syrup, and mashed bananas. To serve, fill glass about half full of partially frozen slush and add chilled ginger ale.

CRANBERRY PUNCH

Yield: 80 portions or 2½ gal   *Portion:* 4 oz (½ cup)

Ingredient	Amount	Procedure
Cranberry juice	3 qt	Mix juices and water. Chill.
Pineapple juice	3 qt (2 46-oz cans)	
Lemonade, frozen, undiluted	1 qt (1 32-oz can)	
Water, cold	1 qt	
Ginger ale, chilled	3 28-oz bottles	Add ginger ale just before serving.

Approximate nutritive values per portion   **Calories** 76

Amount/portion	%DV	Amount/portion	%DV	Amount/portion	%DV		%DV		%DV
Total Fat 0 g	0%	**Cholest.** 0 mg	0%	**Total Carb.** 19 g	6%	Vitamin A	0%	Calcium	0%
Sat. Fat 0 g	0%	**Sodium** 5 mg	0.2%	Fiber 0.3 g	1%	Vitamin C	34%	Iron	1%
Protein 0 g				Sugars 17 g					

Percent Daily Values (%DV) are based on a 2000-calorie diet.

SANGRIA SIPPER

Yield: 80 portions or 3¾ gal   *Portion:* 6 oz

Ingredient	Amount	Procedure
Grape juice, frozen, undiluted	3 12-oz cans	Combine juices and water. Stir well.
Orange juice, frozen, undiluted	3 12-oz cans	Refrigerate until time of service.
Lemonade, frozen, undiluted	3 12-oz cans	
Water	5 qt	
Club soda	7 qt	Just before service, combine juice mixture, club soda, and sliced fruit.
Oranges, thinly sliced	10	
Lemons, thinly sliced	9	
Limes, thinly sliced	6	
		Serve punch and sliced fruit in a stemmed goblet.

Approximate nutritive values per portion   **Calories** 80

Amount/portion	%DV	Amount/portion	%DV	Amount/portion	%DV		%DV		%DV
Total Fat 0 g	0%	**Cholest.** 0 mg	0%	**Total Carb.** 21 g	7%	**Vitamin A**	0%	**Calcium**	2%
Sat. Fat 0 g	0%	**Sodium** 21 mg	1%	Fiber 1 g	4%	**Vitamin C**	85%	**Iron**	1%
Protein 0.7 g				Sugars 12 g					

Percent Daily Values (%DV) are based on a 2000-calorie diet.

Note   • May be garnished with skewered fruit.

WHITE WINE SANGRIA

Yield: 80 portions or 3¾ gal   *Portion:* 6 oz

Ingredient	Amount	Procedure
White wine	2 gal	Mix until sugar dissolves.
Orange juice	1½ qt	
Sugar	1 lb	
Oranges, thinly sliced	3 lb	Mix fruit with wine-juice mixture.
Peaches, peeled, thinly sliced (See note)	4 lb	Let stand at room temperature for 3 hours, then refrigerate until cold.
Apples, thinly sliced	3 lb	
Limes, thinly sliced	1 lb	
		Pour 6 oz of sangria (liquid and fruit) over ice in a stemmed goblet.

Approximate nutritive values per portion   **Calories** 95

Amount/portion	%DV	Amount/portion	%DV	Amount/portion	%DV		%DV		%DV
Total Fat 0 g	0%	**Cholest.** 0 mg	0%	**Total Carb.** 8 g	3%	**Vitamin A**	0%	**Calcium**	1%
Sat. Fat 0 g	0%	**Sodium** 5 mg	0%	Fiber 0 g	0%	**Vitamin C**	16%	**Iron**	2%
Protein 0 g				Sugars 8 g					

Percent Daily Values (%DV) are based on a 2000-calorie diet.

Note   • Mango and kiwi can be substituted for some or all of the peaches.

SPARKLING APRICOT–PINEAPPLE PUNCH

Yield: 80 portions or 2½ gal   *Portion:* 4 oz (½ cup)

Ingredient	Amount	Procedure
Apricot nectar	3 qt (2 46-oz cans)	Combine juices and water.
Pineapple juice, unsweetened	3 qt (2 46-oz cans)	Chill.
Lemon or lime juice, frozen, undiluted	1½ cups	
Water, cold	2 qt	
Ginger ale, chilled	2 qt	Add ginger ale just before serving.

Approximate nutritive values per portion   **Calories** 55

Amount/portion	%DV	Amount/portion	%DV	Amount/portion	%DV		%DV		%DV
Total Fat 0 g	0%	**Cholest.** 0 mg	0%	**Total Carb.** 14 g	5%	**Vitamin A**	4%	**Calcium**	1%
Sat. Fat 0 g	0%	**Sodium** 4 mg	0.2%	Fiber 0.3 g	1%	**Vitamin C**	16%	**Iron**	1%
Protein 0.3 g				Sugars 7 g					

Percent Daily Values (%DV) are based on a 2000-calorie diet.

MOCK PIÑA COLADA

Yield: 96 portions or 3 gal   *Portion:* 4 oz (½ cup)

Ingredient	Amount	Procedure
Vanilla ice cream mix, liquid, unfrozen	2 gal	Combine, using wire whip.
Milk	3 qt	Place in punch bowl.
Coconut extract	½ cup	
Rum extract	5 Tbsp	
Pineapple juice	1 qt	
Maraschino cherries, with stems	50	Serve in punch cup or stemmed glass. Garnish with maraschino cherry.

Approximate nutritive values per portion   **Calories** 200

Amount/portion	%DV	Amount/portion	%DV	Amount/portion	%DV		%DV		%DV
Total Fat 12 g	18%	**Cholest.** 77 mg	26%	**Total Carb.** 21 g	7%	**Vitamin A**	13%	**Calcium**	14%
Sat. Fat 7 g	33%	**Sodium** 64 mg	3%	Fiber 0 g	0%	**Vitamin C**	3%	**Iron**	1%
Protein 4 g				Sugars 3 g					

Percent Daily Values (%DV) are based on a 2000-calorie diet.

Note   • Softened vanilla ice cream may be substituted for ice cream mix.

PINK CHAMPAGNE-STYLE PUNCH

Yield: 96 portions or 3 gal   *Portion:* 4 oz (½ cup)

Ingredient	Amount	Procedure
Water	2 qt	Heat water and sugar until sugar dissolves.
Sugar	1 lb 4 oz	Remove from heat and cool.
Unsweetened red grapefruit juice	2 qt	Mix juices and grenadine syrup with water-sugar mixture. Refrigerate until ready to serve.
Fresh lemon juice	½ cup	
Grenadine syrup	1¼ cups	
Ginger ale	7 qt	Just before service, combine chilled juice mixture with chilled ginger ale. Ladle the punch into champagne glasses. Garnish with a strip of lemon peel.

Approximate nutritive values per portion   **Calories** 65

Amount/portion	%DV	Amount/portion	%DV	Amount/portion	%DV		%DV		%DV
Total Fat 0 g	0%	**Cholest.** 0 mg	0%	**Total Carb.** 17 g	6%	**Vitamin A**	0%	**Calcium**	0%
Sat. Fat 0 g	0%	**Sodium** 0 mg	0.2%	Fiber 0 g	0%	**Vitamin C**	10%	**Iron**	1%
Protein 0 g				Sugars 16 g					

Percent Daily Values (%DV) are based on a 2000-calorie diet.

BLUSHING PINEAPPLE PUNCH

Yield: 50 portions or 1¾ gal   *Portion:* 4 oz (½ cup)

Ingredient	Amount	Procedure
Sugar, granulated	6 oz	Cook sugar, water, and cinnamon candies over low heat, stirring until candies are dissolved.
Water	1½ cups	
Cinnamon candies (red hots)	6 oz	
Pineapple juice	1 gal	Combine pineapple juice and cinnamon candy syrup.
Ginger ale	2 qt	Add ginger ale and ice just before serving.
Ice	8 oz	

Approximate nutritive values per portion   **Calories** 84

Amount/portion	%DV	Amount/portion	%DV	Amount/portion	%DV		%DV		%DV
Total Fat 0 g	0%	**Cholest.** 0 mg	0%	**Total Carb.** 21 g	7%	**Vitamin A**	0%	**Calcium**	1%
Sat. Fat 0 g	0%	**Sodium** 4 mg	0.2%	Fiber 0 g	1%	**Vitamin C**	14%	**Iron**	1%
Protein 0.3 g				Sugars 20 g					

Percent Daily Values (%DV) are based on a 2000-calorie diet.

Variation   • **Red-Hot Tea.** Use following ingredients in place of those in recipe: 12 oz cinnamon candies dissolved in 5½ qt hot water. Add 16 oz concentrated orange juice and lemon juice to taste. Serve hot.

WASSAIL

Yield: 80 portions or 2½ gal   *Portion:* 4 oz (½ cup)

Ingredient	Amount	Procedure
Sugar, granulated	2 lb 8 oz	Mix sugar, water, and spices.
Water	2½ qt	Boil 10 minutes.
Cloves, whole	1½ tsp	Cover and let stand 1 hour in a warm place.
Cinnamon sticks	10	Strain.
Allspice berries	10	
Crystallized ginger, chopped	2 oz	
Orange juice, strained	2 qt	When ready to serve, add juices and cider.
Lemon juice, strained	1¼ qt	Heat quickly to boiling point.
Apple cider	5 qt	
Crabapples or small oranges	6–10	To serve, pour hot mixture over fruit, studded with cloves, in a punch bowl.
Cloves, whole		If using a glass bowl, temper by filling with warm water to prevent cracking when hot punch is poured in.

Approximate nutritive values per portion   **Calories** 105

Amount/portion	%DV	Amount/portion	%DV	Amount/portion	%DV		%DV		%DV
Total Fat 0 g	0%	**Cholest.** 0 mg	0%	**Total Carb.** 27 g	9%	**Vitamin A**	0%	**Calcium**	1%
Sat. Fat 0 g	0%	**Sodium** 3 mg	0.1%	Fiber 0.5 g	0%	**Vitamin C**	36%	**Iron**	1%
Protein 0.4 g				Sugars 24 g					

Percent Daily Values (%DV) are based on a 2000-calorie diet.

TOMATO JUICE COCKTAIL

Yield: 72 portions or 2¼ gal   *Portion:* 4 oz (½ cup)

Ingredient	Amount	Procedure
Tomato juice	8½ qt (6 46-oz cans)	Mix all ingredients. Chill.
Lemon juice	¾ cup	
Worcestershire sauce	3 Tbsp	
Hot pepper sauce	½ tsp	
Celery salt	3 Tbsp	

Approximate nutritive values per portion   **Calories** 21

Amount/portion	%DV	Amount/portion	%DV	Amount/portion	%DV		%DV		%DV
Total Fat 0 g	0%	**Cholest.** 0 mg	0%	**Total Carb.** 5 g	2%	**Vitamin A**	6%	**Calcium**	1%
Sat. Fat 0 g	0%	**Sodium** 644 mg	27%	Fiber 1 g	6%	**Vitamin C**	38%	**Iron**	3%
Protein 0.9 g				Sugars 4 g					

Percent Daily Values (%DV) are based on a 2000-calorie diet.

HOT SPICED TOMATO JUICE

Yield: 64 portions or 2 gal   *Portion:* 4 oz (½ cup)

Ingredient	Amount	Procedure
Tomato juice	4¼ qt (3 46-oz cans)	Add onions, celery, and seasonings to tomato juice. Simmer for about 15 minutes.
Onions, chopped	8 oz	Strain.
Celery stalks, cut in 1-inch pieces	6	
Bay leaves	3	
Cloves, whole	12	
Salt	1 tsp	
Dry mustard	1 Tbsp	
Consommé	1 gal	Add consommé to tomato mixture and reheat. Serve hot.

Approximate nutritive values per portion   **Calories** 21

Amount/portion	%DV	Amount/portion	%DV	Amount/portion	%DV		%DV		%DV
Total Fat 0 g	0%	**Cholest.** 0 mg	0%	**Total Carb.** 4 g	1%	**Vitamin A**	3%	**Calcium**	1%
Sat. Fat 0 g	0%	**Sodium** 430 mg	18%	Fiber 1 g	4%	**Vitamin C**	21%	**Iron**	3%
Protein 2 g				Sugars 2 g					

Percent Daily Values (%DV) are based on a 2000-calorie diet.

Note   • Two 50-oz cans condensed beef or chicken consommé, diluted with 2 qt water, may be used.

FRESH CRANBERRY WARMER

Yield: 50 portions or 3 gal   *Portion:* 8 oz

Ingredient	Amount	Procedure
Cranberries, fresh	2 lb 4 oz (3 12-oz pkgs)	Cook cranberries until soft. Strain, forcing pulp through sieve. Reserve strained liquid for next step.
Water	2 qt	
Water	2 qt	Combine. Cook until red hots dissolve.
Sugar, granulated	1 lb	Remove cloves and add liquid strained from cooked cranberries.
Red hots (cinnamon candies)	1 lb	
Cloves, whole	24	
Orange juice, frozen, undiluted	12 oz	Add undiluted concentrate and water. Strain and heat before serving.
Lemonade frozen, undiluted	12 oz	
Water	1½ gal	
Red food coloring	few drops	

Approximate nutritive values per portion   **Calories** 93

Amount/portion	%DV	Amount/portion	%DV	Amount/portion	%DV		%DV		%DV
Total Fat 0 g	0%	**Cholest.** 0 mg	0%	**Total Carb.** 24 g	8%	**Vitamin A**	0%	**Calcium**	0%
Sat. Fat 0 g	0%	**Sodium** 0 mg	0%	Fiber 1 g	4%	**Vitamin C**	39%	**Iron**	0%
Protein 0 g				Sugars 15 g					

Percent Daily Values (%DV) are based on a 2000-calorie diet.

SPICED CIDER

Yield: 80 portions or 2½ gal   *Portion:* 4 oz (½ cup)

Ingredient	Amount	Procedure
Cinnamon sticks	10	Tie cinnamon, cloves, and allspice loosely in a clean white cloth to make a spice bag.
Cloves, whole	2½ Tbsp	
Allspice berries	2½ Tbsp	
Apple cider	2½ gal	Add spice bag, sugar, and mace to cider.
Sugar, brown (see Note)	12 oz	Bring slowly to the boiling point. Simmer for about 15 minutes.
Mace	½ tsp	Remove spices. Serve hot or chilled.

Approximate nutritive values per portion   **Calories** 75

Amount/portion	%DV	Amount/portion	%DV	Amount/portion	%DV		%DV		%DV
Total Fat 0 g	0%	**Cholest.** 0 mg	0%	**Total Carb.** 19 g	6%	**Vitamin A**	0%	**Calcium**	1%
Sat. Fat 0 g	0%	**Sodium** 5 mg	0.2%	Fiber 0.3 g	1%	**Vitamin C**	2%	**Iron**	3%
Protein 0 g				Sugars 14 g					

Percent Daily Values (%DV) are based on a 2000-calorie diet.

Note
- If a very sweet cider is used, omit or reduce brown sugar.

Variations
- **Cider Punch.** Omit spices. Substitute 1 qt reconstituted frozen orange juice and 1 qt pineapple juice for an equal amount of cider. Garnish with thin slices of orange.

- **Hot Mulled Orange Cider.** Combine 2 gal apple cider, 1½ qt reconstituted frozen orange juice, and 1 cup reconstituted frozen lemon juice. Add 2 sticks cinnamon, 1½ tsp ground cinnamon, 1½ tsp whole cloves, and 10 oz sliced fresh orange peels, which have been tied in a clean white cloth. Bring to a boil. Reduce heat and simmer for 15 minutes. Remove spice bag.

- **Spiced Cranberry Juice.** Substitute cranberry juice for apple cider. Reduce brown sugar to 4 oz.

SPICED ROSÉ WARMER

Yield: 80 portions or 2½ gal   *Portion:* 4 oz

Ingredient	Amount	Procedure
Apple juice	2 qt	Combine juices, lemon peel, water, sugar, and spices in a steam-jacketed or other kettle. Stir to dissolve sugar.
Cranberry juice	2 qt	
Lemon peel strips (fresh)	2 lemons	Bring to a boil. Reduce heat and simmer for 10 minutes. Remove and discard lemon peel.
Water	2 qt	
Sugar	1 lb 12 oz	
Cinnamon sticks	12 inches	
Cloves, whole	½ tsp	
Rosé wine	1 gal	Add wine and lemon juice to juice mixture. Heat to 180°F. Garnish with lemon slices.
Lemon juice (fresh)	1 cup	

Approximate nutritive values per portion   **Calories** 99

Amount/portion	%DV	Amount/portion	%DV	Amount/portion	%DV		%DV		%DV
Total Fat 0 g	0%	**Cholest.** 0 mg	0%	**Total Carb.** 17 g	6%	**Vitamin A**	0%	**Calcium**	0%
Sat. Fat 0 g	0%	**Sodium** 0 mg	0%	Fiber 0 g	0%	**Vitamin C**	28%	**Iron**	1%
Protein 0 g				Sugars 17 g					

Percent Daily Values (%DV) are based on a 2000-calorie diet.

Note   • Care should be taken when pouring hot liquid into a glass punch bowl. Heat punch bowl first with warm water, then pour hot beverage slowly into warm bowl.

RUBY WINE PUNCH

Yield: 80 portions or 2½ gal   *Portion:* 4 oz

Ingredient	Amount	Procedure
Water	1 qt	Combine water, sugar, and spices in a steam-jacketed or other kettle.
Sugar	1 lb 12 oz	Bring to a boil. Reduce heat and simmer for 10 minutes. Discard spices. (Chill water-sugar mixture if using for cold punch.)
Cinnamon sticks	15 inches	
Cloves, whole	1 Tbsp	
Cran-Raspberry juice	1½ gal	Combine water-sugar mixture with juice and wine. Heat to 180°F.
Burgundy wine	3 qt	

Approximate nutritive values per portion   **Calories** 106

Amount/portion	%DV	Amount/portion	%DV	Amount/portion	%DV		%DV		%DV
Total Fat 0 g	0%	**Cholest.** 0 mg	0%	**Total Carb.** 21 g	7%	**Vitamin A**	0%	**Calcium**	0%
Sat. Fat 0 g	0%	**Sodium** 34 mg	34%	Fiber 0 g	0%	**Vitamin C**	1%	**Iron**	1%
Protein 0 g				Sugars 10 g					

Percent Daily Values (%DV) are based on a 2000-calorie diet.

Notes   • For cold wine punch, heat water, sugar, and spices. Chill. Combine with cold juice and wine.

• Care should be taken when pouring hot liquid into a glass punch bowl. Heat punch bowl first with warm water, then pour hot beverage slowly into warm bowl.

NONALCOHOLIC COCKTAILS

Cocktail	Beverage to use	Garnish	Glassware
Apple Cooler	Spiced Cider, Chilled (p. 259)	Apple on a skewer	Goblet
Citrus Spritzer	Ginger Ale Fruit Punch (p. 251)	Orange and lemon on skewer with maraschino cherry	Stemmed glass
Champale Punch	Pink Champagne-Style Punch (p. 256)	Lemon peel strip	Stemmed glass
Chocolate Mint Warmer	French Chocolate (p. 250)	Crème de menthe syrup Mint leaf	Cup or mug
Hot Apple Toddy	Spiced Cider, hot (p. 259)	Cinnamon stick	Mug
Piña Colada	Mock Piña Colada (p. 255)	Pineapple and maraschino cherry on skewer	Stemmed glass
Sangria Sipper	Sangria Sipper (p. 254)	Sliced fruit	Stemmed goblet
Tomato Juice Cocktail	Tomato Juice Cocktail (p. 257)	Celery stalk	Tumbler

Note • Recipe yields may need to be adjusted, depending on the size of glassware used.

Breads

QUICK BREADS

Basic ingredients in all quick breads are flour, liquid, a leavening agent, and flavorings. Fat and eggs are usually included also. The type and quantity of each of these ingredients and their interaction affect the characteristics of the finished product. They may be classified, according to the proportion of flour to liquid, as:

- *pour batter:* pancakes, waffles, popovers, crepes
- *drop batter:* muffins, pan breads, drop biscuits
- *soft dough:* rolled and cut biscuits

Quick breads are leavened by baking powder, baking soda, or steam, which act quickly, requiring them to be baked at once. If a double-acting baking powder is used, quick breads may be mixed, panned, refrigerated, and then baked as needed during the serving period, although they will have slightly decreased volume. A variety of sweet and savory quick breads may be made from basic biscuit and muffin recipes by adding fruits, nuts, and other flavorings.

Quick-bread mixes may be prepared by sifting together the dry ingredients, which generally include nonfat dry milk, and then cutting in the shortening. Such a mix may be made on days when the work load is light and stored for periods up to 6 weeks without refrigeration, or longer if refrigerated. Many food-services use some type of commercial mix. The decision to purchase a mix or to prepare from scratch depends on the amount of time and skilled labor

available, food inventories, and the cost and quality of the mix.

Pans for quick breads should be greased on the bottoms only. A coating mixture may be prepared and brushed on (p. 328), or the pans may be coated with a vegetable spray. Muffin pans with paper baking cups are often used. See p. 265 for quality standards for quick breads.

Methods of Mixing

Ingredients for most quick breads are combined by the muffin or biscuit method, although the conventional cake method, described on p. 319, is used for some loaf breads. Most quick-bread ingredients should be mixed only to blend, with as little handling as possible.

Muffin Method

The muffin method is used for muffins, pancakes, waffles, and popovers.

1. Mix the dry ingredients in a mixer bowl. If dry milk is used, add it to the other dry ingredients.

2. Combine beaten eggs, milk, and melted or liquid fat and add to the dry ingredients all at once.

3. Mix at low speed only enough to dampen the dry ingredients.

The mixture should be slightly lumpy and appear undermixed when put into the pan. Excess mixing causes gluten to develop and carbon dioxide to be lost, resulting in the formation of long "tunnels" in the baked product. Effects of overmixing are less evident in rich muffins and loaf breads that contain a high proportion of fat and sugar, or when the batter is made with cake or pastry flour. The batter should be dipped into pans carefully to avoid additional mixing.

Biscuit Method

The biscuit method is used mainly for baking powder biscuits.

1. Combine dry ingredients in a mixer bowl.
2. Cut fat into the flour with a flat beater or pastry knife.
3. Add liquid and mix to form a soft dough.
4. Knead dough on low speed for 15–30 seconds (or on a lightly floured board for 15–20 strokes) to develop the gluten. Kneading contributes to making a good volume biscuit with a crumb that peels off in flakes. Overkneading or working in extra flour when kneading by hand may result in a biscuit that is compact and less tender. The volume can be affected also by the temperature of the liquid used and the amount of standing time before baking.

Conventional Cake Method

The conventional method, described on p. 319, may be used for coffee cakes, loaf breads, and rich muffins.

YEAST BREADS

Ingredients

An understanding of the functions of the main ingredients in yeast-raised doughs is essential to the production of good bread and rolls.

Flour

Flour used for baked products must contain enough protein to make an elastic framework of gluten that will stretch and hold the air bubbles of carbon dioxide gas formed as the dough ferments. *Bread flour* is made from hard wheat and contains more protein than other flour. It is used for making breads and pasta when strength and elasticity are required. *All-purpose flour* is milled from a blend of hard and soft wheats and contains enough protein to provide the gluten that is essential to making good rolls and yeast breads. An all-purpose flour, unless otherwise noted, was used in testing the recipes in this book. *Whole wheat, rye,* and *specialty flours* add variety to breads. These flours should be combined with a high-protein flour because they do not have enough protein to effect proper gluten formation.

Yeast

Yeast is added to dough for its leavening effect, as well as to enhance the flavor and texture of the finished product. In the fermentation process, sugar in the dough is fermented, and carbon dioxide, ethanol, and other by-products such as lactic acid and acetic acid are released. Fermentation is controlled very carefully by monitoring time, temperature, and humidity throughout the mixing and rising process. When the yeast cells reach about 140°F, as they do soon after baking begins, the cells are destroyed and fermentation ceases. The continued rising is a result of heat expanding the gases trapped within the gluten structure.

The three types of yeast used for yeast bread doughs are compressed, active dry, and instant active dry. *Compressed yeast,* often referred to as fresh yeast, may be purchased in 1-lb cakes or 0.6 oz cubes. It is highly perishable and may be held under refrigeration (30–40°F) for 2 to 3 weeks. The longer the storage time, the more the yeast activity is lost. Compressed yeast is softened in lukewarm water (95°F) before it is added to the other ingredients.

Active dry yeast differs from compressed yeast in that the moisture is removed by dehydrating at a low temperature. The yeast does not require refrigeration and can be stored for several months in a cool, dry environment. It is recommended that yeast be stored for as short a time as possible because some yeast activity is lost during storage. Active dry yeast must be rehydrated before using in water that ranges in temperature between 105 and 115°F. When substituting active dry yeast for compressed yeast, use 60 percent of the compressed yeast weight plus enough water to make up the difference.

Instant or *quick-rise dry yeast* differs from active dry yeast in its genetics and method of processing. Instant dry yeast is less sensitive to temperature extremes than active dry yeast and can be added to the dry ingredients without first reconstituting. Water at 125°F is recommended for hydrating the yeast and other dry ingredients. Water above about 138°F will destroy the living yeast organism. Instant dry yeast is vacuum packed and can be stored unopened for several months.

Liquid

The amount of liquid necessary to produce an optimum dough varies with the flour and generally is related to the flour's protein content. Flours with high protein values absorb more water than low-protein flour.

The liquid used for yeast breads generally is milk or water, although potato water and fruit juice may be used. Milk improves the browning and nutritive value of the bread and tends to delay staling. If fresh milk is used, it is scaled to stop enzyme action that may produce undesirable characteristics, then cooled to the appropriate temperature. Nonfat dry milk may be mixed with the dry ingredients or reconstituted and used in liquid form. The nutritive value of bread may be increased by the addition of extra quantities of dry milk.

The temperature of the liquid used has an effect on the end-point dough temperature after mixing. When using high-speed mixers or making large quantities, it is necessary to calculate the water temperature based on factors such as friction heat generated by the equipment, flour temperature, and room temperature. For quantities used in this book, however, the following guidelines for water temperature are recommended: lukewarm (95°F) for compressed yeast, warm (105–115°F) for active dry yeast, and very warm (125°F) for instant active dry yeast that is mixed with flour and other ingredients.

Other Ingredients

Although used in small quantities, other ingredients influence the quality of the finished product. Salt is added for flavor and also helps to control the rate of fermentation. Sugar, a ready source of food for the yeast, accelerates the action of the yeast. Although the addition of a small amount of sugar makes the dough rise faster, too much sugar inhibits yeast activity. Granulated sugar generally is used for bread making, but honey, corn syrup, brown sugar, and molasses are also used, especially in dark whole-grain bread, sweet rolls, or coffee cake. Fat is added to improve flavor, tenderness, browning, and keeping quality. Fat in large amounts, or fat added directly to the yeast, will slow its action. Eggs affect flavor, richness, tenderness, and color.

Bread Bases

Commercially available bread bases may include ingredients for dough conditioning, flavoring, and coloring, as well as flour, salt, eggs, and seeds or nuts. These bases generally require mixing with flour, yeast, and liquid. Mixing and proofing time and techniques may differ from standard procedures, so the manufacturer's instructions should be followed.

Mixing the Dough

Mixing and kneading of dough has three important functions: to uniformly distribute the ingredients into a homogeneous mass, develop the gluten structure that will entrap the carbon dioxide gas, and develop the dough into a continuous gluten network that will have maximum gas-holding capacity. A repeated

---

QUALITY STANDARDS FOR QUICK BREADS

Quality standard: Golden brown color, slightly rounded with pebbly top, well-proportioned shape; tender crust, even grain, with no tunnels; moist crumb, breaks easily without crumbling; light and tender; good flavor.

Deviation	Possible Cause
Pale color	Overmixing, oven temperature too low
Rough surface	Undermixing, too much flour
Peaked shape	Wrong size pans, overmixing, incorrect liquid measurement, oven temperature too high
Undersized	Incorrect proportion of ingredients, inaccurate measurements, improper mixing, too hot water (leavening gone), oven temperature too low, too large a proportion of acidic ingredients (blueberries, oranges, etc.) or dough held too long before baking when using acidic ingredients, too much flour used when rolling biscuits
Texture coarse, tunneled	Incorrect proportion of ingredients, inaccurate measurements, overmixing
Dry	Too much flour or too little liquid, oven temperature too low, overbaking
Tough, elastic	Overmixing, too little liquid
Unpleasant flavor	Not enough salt, too much baking powder or soda, poor-quality fat or flavorings

stretching-and-folding motion, performed always in the same direction, is the most effective way to produce quality bread with high volume; a soft, silky, uniform grain and texture; and good keeping quality. Dividing, rounding, sheeting, and shaping all have a beneficial effect on bread quality because they too contribute to the mixing functions.

The mixing speed and length of time will vary with the size of mixer and amount of dough. Overmixing and allowing the dough temperature to get too high will produce a product with a dense texture and low volume. Generally dough is mixed only until it leaves the sides and bottom of the bowl. When mixed adequately, a small piece of dough may be stretched, without tearing, to resemble a membrane (sometimes referred to as the membrane test).

Moisture content of the flour may vary, making it necessary to adjust slightly the amount of flour called for in the recipe. Reserving some of the flour specified and adding it as needed toward the end of the mixing process is suggested. Enough flour should be added to produce a soft—but not sticky—dough. Dough for rolls is usually softer than for loaf bread.

Fermentation of Dough

The flavor and texture of the bread depend on the fermentation process. Fermentation begins when the dough is mixed and continues until the yeast is killed by the heat of the oven (approximately 140°F). After mixing is completed, the dough should be set in a warm place (80–85°F), with a relative humidity near 75 percent. The length of the fermentation period depends on the type of product, amount of yeast, strength of the flour, amount of sugar, and temperature of the dough and proofing area. Usually 1 to 1½ hours are required for the dough to double in bulk for the first time.

After the dough has doubled, air must be forced out and the dough returned to its original bulk. This may be done with a mixer using a dough arm or by hand for small amounts of dough. This process continues to decrease the size of the air bubbles and helps form a good grain and texture in the finished product. Dough at this stage may be retarded by chilling and held in a refrigerator for use at a later time. It is important to cover the dough tightly so that moisture is not lost and a dry, tough skin does not develop on the surface.

Shaping, Proofing, and Baking

After the dough has fermented until double and the air bubbles are forced out, it is time to form it into the desired shape. A rest period of 10–15 minutes allows the gluten structure to relax and makes shaping easier (see p. 300 for recipes and directions for shaping). When panning rolls or bread, the distance between pieces will affect the shape, size, and amount of crust in the final product. Individual preference should be considered.

Panned bread or rolls should rise (proof) at 90–100°F and 80 to 85 percent humidity until double in bulk. A general test for assessing how long to proof is to press the dough lightly with a finger. When proofed for the correct length of time, a slight indentation remains. When not proofed long enough, the dough will spring back, leaving no indentation. Overproofed dough will collapse when pressed with a finger. Too short a proofing period will produce a dense, undersized product with a tough crust; too long a proofing period will cause an open, crumbly, texture with low volume and unpleasant flavor.

Crust texture may be determined partly by the treatment applied both prior to baking and during the early stages in the oven. For a crisp crust, spray loaves or rolls with cold water before baking and again after about 10 minutes in the oven. An egg-white glaze (one slightly beaten egg white with 1 tsp water) also may be used to produce a crisp crust. For a shiny, golden crust, brush loaves or rolls with egg or egg-yolk glaze (one slightly beaten egg or egg yolk with 1 Tbsp water or milk) prior to baking. For a soft or tender crust, brush with melted butter or margarine immediately after baking; and to give baked sweet rolls a shiny, glossy appearance brush with simple syrup, then glaze as usual.

Most bread is baked at 375–400°F. Rich and sweet doughs may overbrown quickly and may need to be baked at a slightly lower temperature, 350°F. Generally, small rolls, spaced apart, are baked at a higher temperature than larger loaves so that they become browned in the short time it takes to bake them. For best volume and texture, preheat the oven before baking yeast breads. The final expansion of the dough, called "oven spring," occurs in the first 10–15 minutes of baking in a hot oven. The bread is usually done when tapping the crust produces a hollow sound and the sides, bottom, and top are golden brown. Remove bread from the pans immediately and place on a wire rack to prevent steaming and softening of the crust. Cool the loaves uncovered.

Freezing Yeast Doughs and Breads

Yeast doughs can be frozen up to 6 weeks before or after shaping. Sugar and yeast are usually increased slightly. It is important that the dough be frozen quickly and covered tightly. Some quality loss can be expected when freezing dough using techniques available in most bakeries. Commercial processors are able to achieve better results.

To freeze baked bread and rolls, allow to cool to room temperature, then wrap and freeze. Frozen baked products should be allowed to return to room temperature before being warmed or used.

BREADS

Exhibit I Bread Loaves

Well-shaped and nicely browned bread loaves. (Photos courtesy of the Kansas Wheat Commission)

Exhibit IV   Yeast Bread Variations

Yeast bread variations may be made by adding toppings either before or after baking or by making decorative cuts before baking. (Photos courtesy of Fleischmann's Yeast, Inc.)

Yeast bread dough may be made into a variety of shapes. (Photos courtesy of the Wheat Foods Council)

(Focaccia photo courtesy of Fleischmann's Yeast, Inc.)

Exhibit V   Quick Breads

Scones and biscuits add variety to quick bread selections. (Photos courtesy of the Wheat Foods Council)

QUALITY STANDARDS FOR YEAST BREADS

Quality standard: Symmetrical, uniform shape, rounded top, good volume; smooth, tender crust; golden brown color; fine, even grain, free from large air bubbles, thin cell walls; moist, silky, elastic crumb; nutlike flavor.

Deviation	*Possible Cause*
Excessive volume	Too much yeast, too little salt, oven temperature too low, protein content of flour too high, overproofing
Poor volume	Protein content of flour too low, not enough yeast, over- or underdeveloped gluten, over- or underproofing, too much salt
Pale color	Not enough sugar, overfermented dough, oven temperature too low, crust formed before baking
Dark color	Excessive sugar or milk, oven temperature too high, baking time too long
Cracked	Overmixing, improper shaping, formation of dried crust before baking, cooling too fast
Coarse texture	Not enough flour, slack dough, underkneading, proofing period too long or at too high a temperature, oven temperature too low, temperature of dough out of mixer too high
Heavy texture	Yeast partially killed, not enough yeast, underkneading, poor distribution of ingredients, too-cool proofing temperature, too-short proofing period, excessive dough in pan, too much salt
Crumbly, dry	Too-stiff dough, oven temperature too low, underkneading
Poor flavor	Flat: too little salt
	Yeasty: too-long proofing period, proofing temperature too warm
	Sour: too-long proofing period, poor-quality ingredients

QUICK BREAD RECIPES

BAKING POWDER BISCUITS

Yield: 100 2½-inch biscuits or 130 2-inch biscuits
Oven: 425°F   *Bake:* 15 minutes

Ingredient	Amount	Procedure
Flour, all-purpose Baking powder Salt	5 lb 5 oz 2 Tbsp	Combine flour, baking powder, and salt in mixer bowl. Mix on low speed until blended, approximately 10 seconds, using flat beater.
Shortening, hydrogenated	1 lb 4 oz	Add shortening to flour mixture. Mix on low speed for 1 minute. Stop and scrape sides and bottom of bowl. Mix 1 minute longer. The mixture will be crumbly.

Milk	1¾ qt	Add milk. Mix on low speed to form a soft dough, about 30
		  seconds. Do not overmix. Dough should be as soft as can
		  be handled.

1. Place one-half of dough on lightly floured board or table. Knead lightly 15–20 times.
2. Roll to ¾-inch thickness. Biscuits will approximately double in height during baking. Cut with a 2½-inch (or 2-inch) cutter; or cut into 2-inch squares with a knife. When using round hand cutters, cut straight down and do not twist to produce the best shape. Space the cuts close together to minimize scraps. Use of a roller cutter or cutting the dough into squares eliminates or reduces scraps. The scraps can be rerolled, but the biscuits may not be as tender.
3. Place on ungreased baking sheets ½ inch apart for crusty biscuits, just touching for softer biscuits. Repeat, using remaining dough.
4. Bake at 425°F for 15 minutes, or until golden brown. (See Exhibit V in the color insert.)
5. Biscuits may be held 2–3 hours in the refrigerator until time to bake.

Approximate nutritive values per portion   **Calories** 145

Amount/portion	%DV	Amount/portion	%DV	Amount/portion	%DV		%DV		%DV
Total fat 6 g	10%	**Cholest.** 2 mg	1%	**Total Carb.** 18 g	6%	**Vitamin A**	0%	**Calcium**	11%
Sat. Fat 2 g	9%	**Sodium** 278 mg	12%	Fiber 1 g	2%	**Vitamin C**	0%	**Iron**	5%
Protein 3 g				Sugars 1 g					

Percent Daily Values (%DV) are based on a 2000-calorie diet.

Note
- 7 oz nonfat dry milk and 1¾ qt water may be substituted for fluid milk. Combine dry milk with other dry ingredients. Increase shortening to 1 lb 6 oz.

Variations
- **Buttermilk Biscuits.** Substitute cultured buttermilk (or 7 oz dry buttermilk and 1¾ qt water) for milk. Add 1 Tbsp baking soda to dry ingredients.
- **Butterscotch Biscuits.** Divide dough into eight parts. Roll each part into a rectangle ¼ inch thick. Spread with melted margarine or butter and brown sugar. Roll the dough as for jelly roll. Cut off slices ¾ inch thick. Bake at 375°F for 15 minutes.
- **Cheese Biscuits.** Reduce shortening to 1 lb and add 1 lb grated cheddar cheese.
- **Cinnamon Raisin Biscuits.** Substitute 2 lb 8 oz margarine for shortening. Combine 8 oz sugar and 2½ Tbsp cinnamon with dry ingredients. Add 1 lb 12 oz raisins to mixture after margarine has been mixed in. When baked, ice with Powdered Sugar Glaze (p. 359).
- **Drop Biscuits.** Increase milk to 2 qt. Drop by spoon or No. 30 dipper onto greased baking sheets.
- **Orange Biscuits.** Proceed as for Butterscotch Biscuits. Spread with orange marmalade.

- **Raisin Biscuits.** Reduce shortening to 14 oz and use ½ cup less milk; add 4 whole eggs, beaten, 3 Tbsp grated orange rind, 8 oz sugar, and 8 oz chopped raisins.
- **Scotch Scones.** Add 10 oz sugar and 7 oz currants to dry ingredients. Add 5 eggs, beaten, mixed with the milk. Cut dough in squares and then cut diagonally to form triangles. Brush lightly with milk before baking. (See Exhibit V in the color insert.)
- **Shortcake.** Increase shortening to 1 lb 12 oz. Add 8 oz sugar.
- **Whole Wheat Biscuits.** Substitute 2 lb whole wheat flour for 2 lb all-purpose flour.

BASIC MUFFINS (CAKE METHOD)

Yield: 50 3-oz muffins or 70 2¼-oz muffins
Oven: 350°F   *Bake:* 18–20 minutes

Ingredient	Amount	Procedure
Sugar, granulated	1 lb 3 oz	Cream sugar and shortening until fluffy, about 10 minutes, using flat beater.
Shortening	14 oz	
Eggs	5 (9 oz)	Add eggs slowly to creamed mixture. Mix until blended. Scrape sides of bowl.
Flour, all-purpose	3 lb 3 oz	Combine dry ingredients.
Baking powder	3 oz	
Salt	1 Tbsp	
Milk	1½ qt	Add milk and vanilla alternately with dry ingredients to creamed mixture. Do not overmix.
Vanilla	1 Tbsp	
		Grease bottoms of muffin pans or line with paper baking cups. Portion batter into pans with No. 12 dipper for 3-oz muffins or No. 16 dipper for 2¼-oz muffins. Bake at 350°F for 18–20 minutes.

Approximate nutritive values per portion   **Calories** 245

Amount/portion	%DV	Amount/portion	%DV	Amount/portion	%DV		%DV		%DV
Total fat 10 g	15%	**Cholest.** 26 mg	9%	**Total Carb.** 35 g	12%	Vitamin A	2%	Calcium	14%
Sat. Fat 3 g	14%	**Sodium** 320 mg	13%	Fiber 1 g	3%	Vitamin C	0%	Iron	7%
Protein 5 g				Sugars 12 g					

Percent Daily Values (%DV) are based on a 2000-calorie diet.

Note
- 6 oz nonfat dry milk and 1½ qt water may be substituted for fluid milk. Combine dry milk with flour.

Variations
- **Chocolate Chip Muffins.** Add 1 lb chocolate chips to batter.
- **Coconut Muffins.** Add 1 lb flaked coconut to batter.
- **Honey Streusel Topping for Muffins.** Combine 8 oz brown sugar, 8 oz margarine or butter, 2 Tbsp honey, and ¼ tsp salt. Stir in 1 lb all-purpose flour. Sprinkle on top of muffins before baking.
- For other variations, see Basic Muffins (Muffin method), p. 270.

BASIC MUFFINS (MUFFIN METHOD)

Yield: 50 muffins   *Portion:* 2¼ oz
Oven: 400°F   *Bake:* 20–25 minutes

Ingredient	Amount	Procedure
Flour, all-purpose	2 lb 8 oz	Combine dry ingredients in mixer bowl.
Baking powder	2 oz	Blend on low speed for 10 seconds, using flat beater.
Salt	1 Tbsp	
Sugar, granulated	6 oz	
Eggs, beaten	4 (7 oz)	Combine eggs, milk, and melted shortening.
Milk	1½ qt	Add to dry ingredients. Mix on low speed only long enough
Oil or melted shortening	8 oz (1 cup)	to blend, about 15 seconds. Batter will still be lumpy.
		Portion batter with No. 16 dipper into greased muffin pans, about ⅔ full. Batter should be dipped all at once with as little handling as possible. The dipped muffin batter may be refrigerated for up to 24 hours and baked as needed. See Notes. Bake at 400°F for 20–25 minutes, or until golden brown. Remove muffins from pans as soon as baked.

Approximate nutritive values per portion   **Calories** 161

Amount/portion	%DV	Amount/portion	%DV	Amount/portion	%DV		%DV		%DV
Total fat 6 g	9%	**Cholest.** 21 mg	7%	**Total Carb.** 22 g	7%	**Vitamin A**	1%	**Calcium**	11%
Sat. Fat 2 g	10%	**Sodium** 261 mg	11%	Fiber 1 g	2%	**Vitamin C**	0%	**Iron**	6%
Protein 4 g				Sugars 5 g					

Percent Daily Values (%DV) are based on a 2000-calorie diet.

Notes
- 6 oz nonfat dry milk and 1½ qt water may be substituted for fluid milk. Combine dry milk with other dry ingredients. Increase fat to 9 oz.
- No. 24 dipper yields 6½ dozen muffins.
- For best results, bake muffins immediately. If refrigerated, let come to room temperature before baking or they will have peaks or exploding tops.
- If adding acidic fruits, bake immediately. Acidic fruits will affect the leavening action.

Variations
- **Apple Muffins.** Add 1 lb chopped, peeled apples. Fold into batter.
- **Apricot Muffins.** Add 1 lb cooked apricots, drained and chopped. Fold into batter.
- **Blueberry Muffins.** Carefully fold 1 lb well-drained blueberries into the batter. Increase sugar to 10 oz. Bake immediately.
- **Cherry Muffins.** Add 1 lb well-drained, cooked cherries. Fold into batter.
- **Cornmeal Muffins.** Substitute 1 lb white cornmeal for 1 lb flour.
- **Cranberry Muffins.** Sprinkle 4 oz granulated sugar over 1 lb chopped raw cranberries. Fold into batter. Bake immediately.
- **Currant Muffins.** Add 8 oz chopped currants. Fold into batter.
- **Date Muffins.** Add 1 lb chopped dates. Fold into batter.
- **Jelly Muffins.** Drop ¼–½ tsp jelly on top of each muffin just before placing in the oven.
- **Nut Muffins.** Add 10 oz chopped nuts. Fold into batter.
- **Raisin Nut Muffins.** Add 6 oz chopped nuts and 6 oz chopped raisins. Fold into batter.
- **Spiced Muffins.** Add 1½ tsp cinnamon, 1 tsp ginger, and ½ tsp allspice to dry ingredients.
- **Whole Wheat Muffins.** Substitute 12 oz whole wheat flour for 12 oz white flour. Add ¼ cup molasses with liquid ingredients.

BANANA WHOLE WHEAT MUFFINS

Yield: 50 muffins   *Portion:* 2¼ oz.
Oven: 350°F   *Bake:* 35–40 minutes

Ingredient	Amount	Procedure
Sugar, granulated	1 lb 9 oz	Cream sugar and shortening on medium speed until fluffy, using flat beater.
Shortening	13 oz	
Eggs	7 (12 oz)	Add eggs and vanilla to creamed mixture and mix thoroughly. Scrape sides of bowl.
Vanilla	1 Tbsp	
Bananas, mashed	2 lb 11 oz	Add bananas. Mix on medium speed for 10 minutes.
Flour, whole wheat	10 oz	Combine dry ingredients.
Flour, all-purpose	1 lb 8 oz	Add to banana mixture.
Baking soda	3½ tsp	Mix on low speed only until blended. Scrape sides of bowl as needed.
Salt	1½ tsp	Portion batter into greased muffin pans with No. 16 dipper. Bake at 350°F for 35–40 minutes.

Approximate nutritive values per portion   **Calories** 224

Amount/portion	%DV	Amount/portion	%DV	Amount/portion	%DV		%DV		%DV
Total fat 8 g	13%	**Cholest.** 29 mg	10%	**Total Carb.** 35 g	12%	**Vitamin A**	1%	**Calcium**	0%
Sat. Fat 2 g	11%	**Sodium** 161 mg	7%	Fiber 1 g	4%	**Vitamin C**	3%	**Iron**	5%
Protein 3 g				Sugars 18 g					

Percent Daily Values (%DV) are based on a 2000-calorie diet.

Variation   • **Banana Muffins.** Delete whole wheat flour. Increase all-purpose flour to 2 lb 2 oz.

OATMEAL MUFFINS

Yield: 50 muffins   *Portion:* 2¼ oz
Oven: 400°F   *Bake:* 15–20 minutes

Ingredient	Amount	Procedure
Rolled oats	14 oz	Combine rolled oats and buttermilk in mixer bowl. Let
Buttermilk	1¼ qt	stand 1 hour.
Eggs, beaten	5 (9 oz)	Combine eggs, sugar, and shortening.
Sugar, brown	1 lb 4 oz	Add to rolled-oat mixture. Mix 30 seconds.
Oil or melted shortening	1 lb	Scrape sides of bowl.
Flour, all-pupose	1 lb 4 oz	Combine dry ingredients.
Baking powder	5 tsp	Add to rolled-oat mixture. Mix on low speed only until dry
Salt	2½ tsp	ingredients are moistened, about 15 seconds.
Baking soda	2½ tsp	
		Portion batter with No. 16 dipper into greased muffin pans (⅔ full). Bake at 400°F for 15–20 minutes. Remove from pans as soon as baked.

Approximate nutritive values per portion   **Calories** 213

Amount/portion	%DV	Amount/portion	%DV	Amount/portion	%DV		%DV		%DV
Total fat 10 g	16%	**Cholest.** 23 mg	8%	**Total Carb.** 26 g	9%	**Vitamin A**	1%	**Calcium**	6%
Sat. Fat 3 g	13%	**Sodium** 236 mg	10%	Fiber 0.3 g	1%	**Vitamin C**	0%	**Iron**	6%
Protein 4 g				Sugars 1 g					

Percent Daily Values (%DV) are based on a 2000-calorie diet.

Notes
- 4 oz dry buttermilk and 1¼ qt water may be substituted for liquid buttermilk.
- Flavor may be varied by the addition of 1 tsp cinnamon to the dry ingredients.
- No. 24 dipper yields 7 dozen muffins.

Variation
- **Oatmeal Fruit Muffins.** Add 1 lb raisins, chopped dates, or other fruit. Fold into batter.

POPPY SEED–YOGURT MUFFINS

Yield: 50 muffins   *Portion:* 2¼ oz
Oven: 400°F   *Bake:* 18–22 minutes

Ingredient	Amount	Procedure
Flour, all-purpose	2 lb 8 oz	Blend. Set aside for later step.
Poppy seeds	¼ cup	
Salt	2 tsp	
Baking soda	3½ tsp	
Sugar, granulated	1 lb 12 oz	Cream sugar and margarine on medium speed until light
Margarine	12 oz	and fluffy, using flat beater.
Eggs	(9) 1 lb	Combine and add gradually to creamed mixture.
Vanilla	4 tsp	Mix until smooth.
Lemon juice	1½ tsp	
Yogurt, plain	2 lb 3 oz	Add yogurt alternately with dry ingredients from first step, blending after each addition.
		Portion into prepared muffin pans, using No. 16 dipper.
		Bake at 400°F for 18–22 minutes.
		Cool briefly before removing from pans.

Approximate nutritive values per portion   **Calories** 222

Amount/portion	%DV	Amount/portion	%DV	Amount/portion	%DV		%DV		%DV
Total fat 7 g	11%	**Cholest.** 38 mg	13%	**Total Carb.** 35 g	12%	**Vitamin A**	8%	Calcium	5%
Sat. Fat 1 g	7%	**Sodium** 273 mg	11%	Fiber 1 g	3%	**Vitamin C**	0%	Iron	6%
Protein 5 g				Sugars 16 g					

Percent Daily Values (%DV) are based on a 2000-calorie diet.

Variation   • **Glazed Poppy Seed–Yogurt Muffins.** Combine ¾ cup lemon juice and 2 Tbsp granulated sugar. Brush on baked muffins.

FRESH CRANBERRY SCONES

Yield: 50 portions *Portion:* 1 scone
Oven: 400°F *Bake:* 10–12 minutes

Ingredient	Amount	Procedure
Flour Baking powder Salt	3 lb 3 oz 3 oz 1 Tbsp	Combine dry ingredients in mixer bowl.
Butter (very cold)	1 lb 3 oz	Cut cold butter into small cubes. Add to dry ingredients. Cut butter into dry ingredients until mixture resembles coarse crumbs. Set aside.
Eggs Honey Whipping cream	1 lb 6 oz 10 oz 3 cups	Mix eggs, honey, and cream until well blended.
Cranberries (fresh), coarsely chopped	12 oz	Add chopped cranberries to egg-cream mixture. Add egg-cream mixture to dry ingredients. Mix on low speed only until dry ingredients are moistened. Do not overmix. Dough should be as soft as can be handled. Scale dough into 1 lb rounds onto floured table. Pat or roll dough into a circle ½-inch thick. Lightly dust tops with flour. Cut each circle using a floured knife into 6 wedges. Place wedges 4 × 6 onto greased or silicone-paper-lined 18 × 13 × 1-inch baking pan. Bake 400°F for 10–12 minutes or until golden brown.
Orange marmalade or apricot jam	1 lb	Melt marmalade or jam. Brush lightly over warm scones after removing from the oven. Serve scones warm with butter.

Approximate nutritive values per portion **Calories** 290

Amount/portion	%DV	Amount/portion	%DV	Amount/portion	%DV		%DV		%DV
Total fat 15 g	24%	**Cholest.** 88 mg	29%	**Total Carb.** 34 g	11%	**Vitamin A**	13%	**Calcium**	13%
Sat. Fat 9 g	46%	**Sodium** 425 mg	18%	Fiber 1.1 g	4%	**Vitamin C**	2%	**Iron**	9%
Protein 5 g				Sugars 5.5 g					

Percent Daily Values (%DV) are based on a 2000-calorie diet.

Note ● 6 oz sliced almonds can be folded into the dough along with the cranberries.

FRENCH BREAKFAST PUFFS

Yield: 50 puffs   *Portion:* 2¼ oz
Oven: 350°F   *Bake:* 20–25 minutes

Ingredient	Amount	Procedure
Margarine	1 lb 2 oz	Cream margarine and sugar on medium speed until light
Sugar, granulated	1 lb 10 oz	and fluffy, using flat beater.
Eggs	6 (10 oz)	Add eggs to creamed mixture. Blend on low speed, then beat on medium speed for 3–5 minutes.
Flour, all-purpose	2 lb 8 oz	Combine dry ingredients.
Baking powder	2½ Tbsp	
Salt	1 Tbsp	
Nutmeg, ground	1½ tsp	
Nonfat dry milk	3 oz	
Water	3⅓ cups	Add dry ingredients and water alternately, on low speed, to creamed mixture.
		Portion batter into greased muffin pans with No. 16 dipper. Bake at 350°F for 20–25 minutes.
Sugar, granulated	1 lb 10 oz	Mix sugar and cinnamon.
Cinnamon, ground	2 Tbsp	
Margarine, melted	1 lb 4 oz	When muffins are baked, remove from pans. Roll in melted margarine, then in sugar-cinnamon mixture.

Approximate nutritive values per portion   **Calories** 368

Amount/portion	%DV	Amount/portion	%DV	Amount/portion	%DV		%DV		%DV
Total fat 18 g	**28%**	**Cholest.** 24 mg	**8%**	**Total Carb.** 48 g	**16%**	**Vitamin A**	8%	**Calcium**	6%
Sat. Fat 4 g	18%	**Sodium** 393 mg	16%	Fiber 1 g	2%	**Vitamin C**	0%	**Iron**	7%
Protein 4 g				Sugars 30 g					

Percent Daily Values (%DV) are based on a 2000-calorie diet.

Notes
- 3½ cups fluid milk may be used in place of the nonfat dry milk and water.
- For small, tea-sized muffins, dip batter with No. 40 dipper into small (1½-inch) muffin pans.

Variations
- **Apple Nut Muffins.** Add 1 lb chopped apples and 8 oz chopped nuts.
- **Plain Cake Muffins.** Delete nutmeg. Do not roll in sugar and cinnamon.

BISHOP'S BREAD

Yield: 64 portions or 2 pans 12 × 18 × 2 inches   *Portion:* 3 × 2¼ inches
Oven: 365°F   *Bake:* 35–45 minutes

Ingredient	Amount	Procedure
Shortening	1 lb	Cream shortening and sugar on medium speed for
Sugar, brown	3 lb 2 oz	5 minutes, using flat beater.
Flour, all-purpose	2 lb 14 oz	Combine flour, salt, and cinnamon.
Salt	2 tsp	Add to creamed mixture and mix until well blended.
Cinnamon, ground	1 Tbsp	Remove 1 lb 12 oz of the mixture to sprinkle on top later.
Flour, all-purpose	1 lb 2 oz	Combine flour, baking powder, and soda.
Baking powder	5 tsp	
Baking soda	1½ tsp	
Eggs, beaten	5 (9 oz)	Combine eggs and buttermilk.
Buttermilk	1½ qt	Add alternately with dry ingredients to creamed mixture.
		Scrape sides of bowl.
		Mix on low speed about 30 seconds. (Batter will not be smooth.)
		Scale batter into two greased 12 × 18 × 2-inch baking pans, 5 lb per pan.
		Sprinkle 14 oz of the reserved topping over batter in each pan.
		Bake at 365°F for 35–45 minutes.
		Cut 4 × 8.

Approximate nutritive values per portion   **Calories** 265

Amount/portion	%DV	Amount/portion	%DV	Amount/portion	%DV		%DV		%DV
Total fat 8 g	12%	**Cholest.** 18 mg	6%	**Total Carb.** 44 g	15%	**Vitamin A**	0%	**Calcium**	6%
Sat. Fat 2 g	10%	**Sodium** 157 mg	7%	Fiber 1 g	3%	**Vitamin C**	0%	**Iron**	10%
Protein 4 g				Sugars 2 g					

Percent Daily Values (%DV) are based on a 2000-calorie diet.

Notes
- May be baked in one 18 × 26 × 2-inch pan. Cut 6 × 10 for 60 portions 3 × 2½ inches.
- 4 oz dry buttermilk and 1 qt water may be substituted for fluid buttermilk.

BLUEBERRY COFFEE CAKE

Yield: 64 portions or 2 pans 12 × 18 × 2 inches   *Portion:* 3 × 2¼ inches
Oven: 350°F   *Bake:* 45 minutes

Ingredient	Amount	Procedure
Sugar, brown	12 oz	Combine sugars, flour, cinnamon, and margarine.
Sugar, granulated	4 oz	Mix on low speed to a coarse crumb consistency, about
Flour, all-purpose	4 oz	5 minutes, using flat beater.
Cinnamon, ground	2 tsp	Set aside for final step.
Margarine, soft	4 oz	
Shortening	14 oz	Cream shortening and sugar on medium speed for about
Sugar, granulated	2 lb 10 oz	10 minutes.
Eggs	7 (12 oz)	Add eggs to creamed mixture and continue mixing, 3–5 minutes.
Flour, all-purpose	3 lb 6 oz	Combine flour, baking powder, and salt.
Baking powder	2 oz	
Salt	1 Tbsp	
Milk	3½ cups	Add dry ingredients and milk alternately to creamed mixture. Mix on low speed for 3 minutes. Scrape sides of bowl. Mix on medium speed 10 seconds.
Blueberries, frozen or canned (well-drained and rinsed)	2 lb	Carefully fold blueberries into batter. (Berries may be sprinkled on top of batter.)
		Scale into two greased 12 × 18 × 2-inch baking pans, 4 lb 12 oz per pan. Crumble topping mixture evenly over top of batter, 10 oz per pan. Bake at 350°F for 45 minutes. Cut 4 × 8.

Approximate nutritive values per portion   **Calories** 220

Amount/portion	%DV	Amount/portion	%DV	Amount/portion	%DV		%DV		%DV
Total fat 9 g	14%	**Cholest.** 24 mg	8%	**Total Carb.** 31 g	10%	**Vitamin A**	2%	Calcium	8%
Sat. Fat 2 g	12%	**Sodium** 222 mg	9%	Fiber 1 g	3%	**Vitamin C**	0%	Iron	8%
Protein 4 g				Sugars 3 g					

Percent Daily Values (%DV) are based on a 2000-calorie diet.

Notes
- May be baked in one 18 × 26 × 2-inch pan. Cut 6 × 10 for 60 portions 3 × 2½ inches.
- 3 oz nonfat dry milk and 3½ cups water may be substituted for fluid milk. Add dry milk to other dry ingredients. Increase shortening to 15 oz.
- After cake is baked, thin Powdered Sugar Glaze (p. 359) may be drizzled in a fine stream over the top to form an irregular design.
- Recipe can be used for blueberry muffins. Sprinkle blueberries on top.

DUTCH APPLE COFFEE CAKE

Yield: 64 portions or 2 pans 12 × 20 × 2-inch   *Portion:* 3 × 2½ inches
Oven: 365°F   *Bake:* 50–60 minutes

Ingredient	Amount	Procedure
Sugar, granulated	2 lb 8 oz	Cream sugar, shortening, and eggs on medium speed for 10 minutes, using flat beater.
Shortening	12 oz	
Eggs	8 (14 oz)	
Flour, all-purpose	2 lb 8 oz	Combine dry ingredients and mix until well blended.
Baking powder	2 oz	
Salt	2 tsp	
Milk	1 qt	Add milk and dry ingredients alternately to creamed mixture. Mix on low speed for 3 minutes. Scrape sides of bowl. Mix on medium speed for 10 seconds.
Apples, frozen or canned	2 lb 8 oz	Drain apples and chop.
Margarine, melted	2 oz	Combine with margarine, sugar, and cinnamon.
Sugar, granulated	1 lb 2 oz	
Cinnamon, ground	2 Tbsp	
		Scale batter into two greased 12 × 20 × 2-inch baking pans, 4 lb 6 oz per pan. Spread 1 lb 14 oz apple mixture over batter in each pan. Bake at 365°F for 50–60 minutes. Cut 4 × 8.

Approximate nutritive values per portion   **Calories** 246

Amount/portion	%DV	Amount/portion	%DV	Amount/portion	%DV		%DV		%DV
Total fat 7 g	11%	**Cholest.** 28 mg	9%	**Total Carb.** 43 g	14%	**Vitamin A**	2%	**Calcium**	8%
Sat. Fat 2 g	10%	**Sodium** 180 mg	8%	Fiber 1 g	3%	**Vitamin C**	0%	**Iron**	5%
Protein 3 g				Sugars 26 g					

Percent Daily Values (%DV) are based on a 2000-calorie diet.

Notes   • Cake batter may be mixed and panned the day before using. Refrigerate overnight, then add topping and bake.

• 4 oz nonfat dry milk and 1 qt water may be substituted for fluid milk.

COFFEE CAKE

Yield: 64 portions or 2 pans 12 × 18 × 2 inches   *Portion:* 3 × 2¼ inches
Oven: 350°F   *Bake:* 25 minutes

Ingredient	Amount	Procedure
Margarine	10 oz	Place margarine, sugar, flour, cinnamon, and salt in mixer bowl.
Sugar, granulated	1 lb 4 oz	
Flour, all-purpose	3 oz	Mix on low speed until crumbly, using flat beater. Set aside, to be used later as topping.
Cinnamon, ground	1 oz	
Salt	1½ tsp	
Flour, all-purpose	3 lb 6 oz	Combine dry ingredients in mixer bowl.
Baking powder	2 oz	
Sugar, granulated	2 lb	
Salt	1⅔ Tbsp	
Eggs, beaten	6 (10 oz)	Combine eggs and milk.
Milk	1¼ qt	Add to dry ingredients.
		Mix on low speed until dry ingredients are just moistened.
Shortening, melted and cooled	1 lb 10 oz	Add shortening and mix on low speed for 1 minute.
		Scale dough into two greased 12 × 18 × 2-inch baking pans, 4 lb 2 oz per pan.
		Sprinkle with reserved topping mixture, 1 lb per pan.
		Bake at 350°F for 25 minutes or until done.
		Cut 4 × 8.

Approximate nutritive values per portion   **Calories** 335

Amount/portion	%DV	Amount/portion	%DV	Amount/portion	%DV		%DV		%DV
Total fat 16 g	25%	**Cholest.** 21 mg	7%	**Total Carb.** 44 g	15%	**Vitamin A**	2%	**Calcium**	9%
Sat. Fat 4 g	21%	**Sodium** 363 mg	15%	Fiber 1 g	3%	**Vitamin C**	0%	**Iron**	7%
Protein 4 g				Sugars 24 g					

Percent Daily Values (%DV) are based on a 2000-calorie diet.

Notes
- 5 oz nonfat dry milk and 1¼ qt water may be substituted for the fluid milk. Combine dry milk with other dry ingredients. Increase shortening to 1 lb 12 oz.
- May be baked in one 18 × 26 × 2-inch pan. Cut 6 × 10 for 60 portions 3 × 2½ inches.
- If used for breakfast, may be mixed and panned the day before. Refrigerate until morning, then bake. Allow 5–10 minutes extra time because batter will be cold.

WALNUT COFFEE CAKE

Yield: 4 cakes   *Portion:* 16 slices per cake
Oven: 350°F   *Bake:* 45–50 minutes

Ingredient	Amount	Procedure
Sugar, granulated	3 lb	Cream sugar and margarine on medium speed until light
Margarine	1 lb	and fluffy, using flat beater.
Eggs	16 (1 lb 12 oz)	Add eggs slowly to creamed mixture, beating well after each
Vanilla	1 Tbsp	addition. Add vanilla.
Flour, all-purpose	3 lb	Mix flour, baking powder, and salt together.
Baking powder	4 Tbsp	
Salt	2 tsp	
Milk	1 qt	Add milk alternately with dry ingredients to creamed mixture. Combine thoroughly after each addition.
Sugar, brown	2 lb	Combine brown sugar, margarine, flour, cinnamon, and
Margarine	4 oz	walnuts for crumb mixture.
Flour, all-purpose	2 oz	
Cinnamon, ground	1 Tbsp	
Walnuts, chopped	1 lb	
		Scale 1 lb 4 oz batter into each of 4 greased 10-inch tube pans. Sprinkle 6 oz crumb mixture over batter. Spread with 1 lb 4 oz batter. Top with 6 oz crumb mixture. Bake at 350°F for 45–50 minutes. Cool slightly. Remove from pans. Ice with Powdered Sugar Glaze (p. 359) if desired. Slice 16 servings per cake.

Approximate nutritive values per portion   **Calories** 350

Amount/portion	%DV	Amount/portion	%DV	Amount/portion	%DV		%DV		%DV
Total fat 13 g	20%	**Cholest.** 54 mg	18%	**Total Carb.** 54 g	18%	**Vitamin A**	12%	**Calcium**	8%
Sat. Fat 2 g	11%	**Sodium** 193 mg	8%	Fiber 1 g	4%	**Vitamin C**	0%	**Iron**	9%
Protein 6 g				Sugars 21 g					

Percent Daily Values (%DV) are based on a 2000-calorie diet.

Note   • 4 oz nonfat dry milk and 1 qt water may be substituted for the fluid milk.

CORN BREAD

Yield: 64 portions or 2 pans 12 × 18 × 2 inches   *Portion:* 3 × 2¼ inches
Oven: 350°F   *Bake:* 35 minutes

Ingredient	Amount	Procedure
Cornmeal, yellow	2 lb 3 oz	Combine dry ingredients in mixer bowl.
Flour, all-purpose	2 lb 5 oz	Blend on low speed, using flat beater.
Baking powder	3½ oz	
Salt	2½ Tbsp	
Sugar, granulated	10 oz	
Eggs, beaten	9 (1 lb)	Combine eggs, milk, and shortening.
Milk	1¾ qt	Add to dry ingredients. Mix on low speed only until dry
Shortening, melted and cooled	10 oz	ingredients are moistened.
		Scale batter into two greased 12 × 18 × 2-inch baking pans, 5 lb per pan. Bake at 350°F for 35 minutes. Cut 4 × 8.

Approximate nutritive values per portion   **Calories** 196

Amount/portion	%DV	Amount/portion	%DV	Amount/portion	%DV		%DV		%DV
Total fat 7 g	10%	**Cholest.** 34 mg	11%	**Total Carb.** 30 g	10%	**Vitamin A**	3%	**Calcium**	13%
Sat. Fat 2 g	10%	**Sodium** 432 mg	18%	Fiber 3 g	11%	**Vitamin C**	0%	**Iron**	7%
Protein 5 g				Sugars 6 g					

Percent Daily Values (%DV) are based on a 2000-calorie diet.

Notes
- 7 oz nonfat dry milk and 1¾ qt water may be substituted for fluid milk. Mix dry milk with other dry ingredients. Increase shortening to 11 oz.
- May be baked in one 18 × 26 × 2-inch pan. Cut 6 × 10 for 60 portions 3 × 3½ inches.
- May be baked in corn stick or muffin pans. Reduce baking time to 15–20 minutes.
- White cornmeal may be used.

SPOON BREAD

Yield: 50 portions or 2 pans 12 × 20 × 2 inches   *Portion:* 4 oz
Oven: 350°F   *Bake:* 45–60 minutes

Ingredient	Amount	Procedure
Milk	5¾ qt	Scald milk by heating to point just below boiling.
Cornmeal, yellow Salt	1 lb 12 oz 1 oz (1½ Tbsp)	Add cornmeal and salt to milk, stirring briskly with a wire whip. Cook 10 minutes, or until thick.
Eggs, beaten Margarine, melted Baking powder	25 (2 lb 12 oz) 6 oz 2 oz	Add eggs slowly to cornmeal mixture, while stirring. Add margarine and baking powder to cornmeal mixture. Stir to blend.
		Pour batter into two greased 12 × 20 × 2-inch baking pans, 8 lb per pan. Place in pans of hot water. Bake at 250°F for 45–60 minutes or until set.

Approximate nutritive values per portion   **Calories** 190

Amount/portion	%DV	Amount/portion	%DV	Amount/portion	%DV		%DV		%DV
Total fat 10g	15%	**Cholest.** 122 mg	41%	**Total Carb.** 18 g	6%	**Vitamin A**	10%	**Calcium**	22%
Sat. Fat 4 g	19%	**Sodium** 430 mg	18%	Fiber 2 g	10%	**Vitamin C**	1%	**Iron**	5%
Protein 8 g				Sugars 6 g					

Percent Daily Values (%DV) are based on a 2000-calorie diet.

Note   ● Serve with crisp bacon, Creamed Chicken (p. 545), or Creamed Ham (p. 521).

BOSTON BROWN BREAD

Yield: 64 portions or 8 round loaves, 3¼ × 4½ inches   *Portion:* ½-inch slice
Steam Pressure: 5 lb   *Steam:* 1¼–1½ hours

Ingredient	Amount	Procedure
Cornmeal, yellow	1 lb	Combine dry ingredients in mixer bowl.
Flour, whole wheat	12 oz	Blend on low speed for 10 seconds, using flat beater.
Flour, all-purpose	12 oz	
Salt	1 oz (1½ Tbsp)	
Baking soda	1½ Tbsp	
Buttermilk	1½ qt	Blend buttermilk and molasses.
Molasses	2¼ cups	Add all at once to dry ingredients.
		Mix on low speed only until ingredients are blended.
		Fill eight greased 3¼ × 4½-inch cans ¾ full.
		Cover tightly with aluminum foil.
		Steam for 1¼–1½ hours.
		Cut eight slices per loaf.

Approximate nutritive values per portion   **Calories** 99

Amount/portion	%DV	Amount/portion	%DV	Amount/portion	%DV		%DV		%DV
Total fat 1 g	1%	**Cholest.** 1 mg	0.3%	**Total Carb.** 21 g	7%	Vitamin A	0%	Calcium	10%
Sat. Fat 0.2 g	0.9%	**Sodium** 275 mg	11%	Fiber 1 g	6%	Vitamin C	0%	Iron	14%
Protein 2 g				Sugars 6 g					

Percent Daily Values (%DV) are based on a 2000-calorie diet.

Notes
- 12 oz raisins may be added.
- May be baked as loaves. Add 3 Tbsp melted fat. Scale into three 5 × 9-inch loaf pans, 2 lb 8 oz per pan. Bake at 375°F for 1 hour.

NUT BREAD

Yield: 80 portions or 5 loaves 5 × 9 inches   *Portion:* ½-inch slice
Oven: 350°F   *Bake:* 50 minutes

Ingredient	Amount	Procedure
Flour, all-purpose	3 lb	Combine dry ingredients and nuts in mixer bowl.
Baking powder	1 oz	Mix on low speed until blended, using flat beater.
Salt	1 Tbsp	
Sugar, granulated	1 lb 8 oz	
Pecans or walnuts, chopped	1 lb	
Eggs, beaten	6 (10 oz)	Combine eggs, milk, and shortening.
Milk	1½ qt	Add to dry ingredients.
Oil or melted shortening	4 oz	Mix on low speed only until blended.
		Scale batter into five greased loaf pans (5 × 9 × 2¾ inches), approximately 1 lb 14 oz per pan.
		Bake at 350°F for about 50 minutes. Cut 16 slices per loaf.

Approximate nutritive values per portion

Calories 159

Amount/portion	%DV	Amount/portion	%DV	Amount/portion	%DV		%DV		%DV
Total fat 6 g	9%	**Cholest.** 18 mg	6%	**Total Carb.** 23 g	8%	Vitamin A	1%	Calcium	5%
Sat. Fat 1 g	5%	**Sodium** 129 mg	5%	Fiber 1 g	3%	Vitamin C	0%	Iron	5%
Protein 4 g				Sugars 10 g					

Percent Daily Values (%DV) are based on a 2000-calorie diet.

Note   • 5 oz nonfat dry milk and 1½ qt water may be substituted for fluid milk. Combine dry milk with other dry ingredients. Increase shortening to 6 oz.

DATE NUT BREAD

Yield: 64 portions or 4 loaves 5 × 9 inches   *Portion:* ½-inch slice
Oven: 350°F   *Bake:* 50 minutes

Ingredient	Amount	Procedure
Dates, chopped	1 lb 8 oz	Add water and soda to dates. Let stand 20 minutes.
Baking soda	1½ Tbsp	
Water, boiling	3¼ cups	
Shortening	3 oz	Cream shortening and sugar on medium speed for 5 minutes, using flat beater.
Sugar, granulated	1 lb 12 oz	
Eggs	4 (7 oz)	Add eggs and vanilla to creamed mixture. Mix on medium speed for 2 minutes.
Vanilla	1½ Tbsp	
Flour, all-purpose	2 lb	Combine flour, salt, and nuts.
Salt	1½ tsp	Add alternately with dates to creamed mixture.
Pecans or walnuts, chopped	8 oz	Scale batter into four greased loaf pans (5 × 9 × 2¾ inches), approximately 2 lb per pan.
		Bake at 350°F for about 50 minutes. Cut 16 slices per loaf.

Approximate nutritive values per portion   **Calories** 168

Amount/portion	%DV	Amount/portion	%DV	Amount/portion	%DV		%DV		%DV
Total fat 4 g	6%	**Cholest.** 13 mg	4%	**Total Carb.** 32 g	11%	**Vitamin A**	0%	Calcium	0%
Sat. Fat 1 g	3%	**Sodium** 144 mg	6%	Fiber 1 g	6%	**Vitamin C**	0%	Iron	5%
Protein 3 g				Sugars 19 g					

Percent Daily Values (%DV) are based on a 2000-calorie diet.

BANANA NUT BREAD

Yield: 64 portions or 4 loaves 5 × 9 inches   *Portion:* ½-inch slice
Oven: 350°F   *Bake:* 50 minutes

Ingredient	Amount	Procedure
Margarine Sugar, granulated	10 oz 1 lb 10 oz	Cream margarine and sugar on medium speed for 5 minutes, using flat beater.
Eggs	5 (9 oz)	Add eggs to creamed mixture. Beat 2 minutes.
Bananas, mashed	1 lb 10 oz	Add bananas. Beat 1 minute.
Flour, all-purpose Baking powder Salt Baking soda Pecans or walnuts, chopped	2 lb 4 Tbsp 2 tsp ½ tsp 8 oz	Combine dry ingredients and nuts.
Milk	¾ cup	Add dry ingredients and milk to creamed mixture. Mix on low speed for 1 minute.
		Scale batter into four greased loaf pans (5 × 9 × 2¾ inches), approximately 2 lb per pan. Bake at 350°F for 50 minutes. Cut 16 slices per loaf.

Approximate nutritive values per portion   **Calories** 171

Amount/portion	%DV	Amount/portion	%DV	Amount/portion	%DV		%DV		%DV
Total fat 7 g	10%	**Cholest.** 17 mg	6%	**Total Carb.** 26 g	9%	**Vitamin A**	2%	**Calcium**	4%
Sat. Fat 1 g	6%	**Sodium** 175 mg	7%	Fiber 1 g	3%	**Vitamin C**	1%	**Iron**	4%
Protein 2 g				Sugars 14 g					

Percent Daily Values (%DV) are based on a 2000-calorie diet.

CRANBERRY NUT BREAD

Yield: 80 portions or 5 loaves 5 × 9 inches   *Portion:* ½-inch slice
Oven: 350°F   *Bake:* 50 minutes

Ingredient	Amount	Procedure
Cranberries, raw	1 lb 4 oz	Wash and sort cranberries.
Orange peel	7 oz	Coarsely grind cranberries and orange peel.
Flour, all-purpose	2 lb 8 oz	Combine dry ingredients in mixer bowl.
Sugar, granulated	2 lb 4 oz	Blend on low speed for 10 seconds or until mixed, using
Baking powder	1 oz	flat beater.
Salt	2 tsp	
Baking soda	2 tsp	
Eggs, beaten	5 (9 oz)	Combine and add to dry ingredients.
Orange juice	1½ cups	Mix on low speed, only until dry ingredients are moistened.
Water	3¾ cups	
Vegetable oil	½ cup	
Pecans or walnuts, chopped	1 lb	Add nuts and cranberry mixture to batter. Mix on low speed until blended. Batter may be lumpy.
		Scale batter into five greased loaf pans (5 × 9 × 2¾ inches), approximately 2 lb per pan. Bake at 350°F for about 50 minutes. Cut 16 slices per loaf.

Approximate nutritive values per portion   **Calories** 164

Amount/portion	%DV	Amount/portion	%DV	Amount/portion	%DV		%DV		%DV
Total fat 6 g	9%	**Cholest.** 14 mg	5%	**Total Carb.** 27 g	9%	**Vitamin A**	0%	**Calcium**	3%
Sat. Fat 1 g	4%	**Sodium** 125 mg	5%	Fiber 1 g	5%	**Vitamin C**	10%	**Iron**	4%
Protein 2 g				Sugars 13 g					

Percent Daily Values (%DV) are based on a 2000-calorie diet.

PUMPKIN BREAD

Yield: 80 portions or 5 loaves 5 × 9 inches   *Portion:* ½-inch slice
Oven: 350°F   *Bake:* 50 minutes

Ingredient	Amount	Procedure
Sugar, granulated	2 lb 12 oz	Combine sugar, oil, pumpkin, and eggs in mixer bowl.
Vegetable oil	2 cups	Cream on medium speed for 10 minues, using flat beater.
Pumpkin, canned	2 lb 6 oz	Scrape sides of bowl and beater.
Eggs	9 (15 oz)	
Flour, all-purpose	2 lb 2 oz	Combine dry ingredients.
Baking soda	4 tsp	
Baking powder	2 tsp	
Salt	1 Tbsp	
Cinnamon, ground	1 Tbsp	
Nutmeg, ground	1 tsp	
Water	1¼ cups	Add dry ingredients and water alternately to creamed mixture. Mix 3 minutes on low speed. Scrape sides of bowl.
		Scale batter into five greased loaf pans (5 × 9 × 2¾ inches), approximately 1 lb 15 oz per pan. Bake at 350°F for 50 minutes or until done. Cool 30 minutes before removing from pans. Cut 16 slices per loaf.

Approximate nutritive values per portion   **Calories** 165

Amount/portion	%DV	Amount/portion	%DV	Amount/portion	%DV		%DV		%DV
Total fat 6 g	9%	**Cholest.** 23 mg	8%	**Total Carb.** 26 g	9%	**Vitamin A**	30%	**Calcium**	1%
Sat. Fat 2 g	8%	**Sodium** 158 mg	7%	Fiber 1 g	3%	**Vitamin C**	0%	**Iron**	4%
Protein 2 g				Sugars 15 g					

Percent Daily Values (%DV) are based on a 2000-calorie diet.

Note   • 8 oz raisins or chopped nuts may be added.

PANCAKES

Yield: 7 qt batter or 100 cakes (50 portions)   *Portion:* 2 4-inch cakes

Ingredient	Amount	Procedure
Flour, all-purpose	4 lb 8 oz	Place dry ingredients in mixer bowl.
Baking powder	4 oz	Mix on low speed until well blended, using flat beater.
Salt	2 Tbsp	
Sugar, granulated	12 oz	
Eggs	12 (1 lb 5 oz)	In another bowl, beat eggs until light.
Milk	3½ qt	Add milk and melted shortening to eggs.
Shortening, melted and cooled, or vegetable oil	12 oz	Add to dry ingredients. Mix on low speed for 30 seconds. If necessary, thin with milk. Refrigerate batter, removing from refrigerator small amounts as needed. Use No. 16 dipper to place batter on griddle, which has been preheated to 350°F. Cook until surface of cake is full of bubbles and golden brown. Turn pancake and finish cooking.

Approximate nutritive values per portion   **Calories** 297

Amount/portion	%DV	Amount/portion	%DV	Amount/portion	%DV		%DV		%DV
Total fat 11 g	16%	**Cholest.** 60 mg	20%	**Total Carb.** 42 g	14%	**Vitamin A**	4%	**Calcium**	23%
Sat. Fat 4 g	18%	**Sodium** 532 mg	22%	Fiber 1 g	4%	**Vitamin C**	1%	**Iron**	11%
Protein 8 g				Sugars 11 g					

Percent Daily Values (%DV) are based on a 2000-calorie diet.

Notes
- Potentially hazardous food. Keep batter at an internal temperature below 41°F.
- 14 oz nonfat dry milk and 3½ qt water may be substituted for the fluid milk. Add dry milk to other dry ingredients. Increase shortening to 1 lb.

Variations
- **Apple Pancakes.** Add 1 lb chopped cooked apples and 1 tsp cinnamon or nutmeg.
- **Blueberry Pancakes.** Fold 1 lb individually quick frozen (IQF) blueberries or well-drained and rinsed canned blueberries carefully into batter after cakes are mixed. Handle carefully to avoid mashing berries. If a large batch is being prepared, add berries to a small portion of the batter at one time. Serve with Blueberry Syrup, p. 778.
- **Buttermilk Pancakes.** Substitute buttermilk for milk. Add 1 Tbsp baking soda to dry ingredients; 14 oz dry buttermilk and 3½ qt water may be substituted for fluid buttermilk. Add dry buttermilk and soda to other dry ingredients. Increase shortening to 1 lb.
- **Pecan Pancakes.** Add 1 lb chopped pecans.
- **Silver Dollar Pancakes.** Portion 1–2 Tbsp of batter onto hot grill and cook as directed previously. Garnish with powdered sugar sprinkled on top of pancakes and fresh blueberries or raspberries.

WHOLE WHEAT PANCAKES

Yield: 2½ gal batter or 100 cakes (50 portions)   *Portion:* 2 cakes
Griddle: 350°F

Ingredient	Amount	Procedure
Flour, whole wheat	3 lb	Combine dry ingredients in mixer bowl. Mix, using flat beater, until blended.
Flour, all-purpose	2 lb 12 oz	
Sugar, granulated	8 oz	
Salt	2 oz (3 Tbsp)	
Baking powder	4 oz	
Baking soda	5½ tsp	
Nonfat dry milk	1 lb 2 oz	
Vegetable oil	3 cups	Add to dry ingredients, mixing just until large lumps disappear.
Water	1 gal + 2 cups	Refrigerate batter, removing small amounts from refrigerator as needed.
Eggs	2 lb (18 eggs)	Portion batter with No. 12 dipper onto greased preheated griddle.
		Bake until edges start to dry and bubbles appear on top surface.
		Flip and bake other side.

Approximate nutritive values per portion   **Calories** 383

Amount/portion	%DV	Amount/portion	%DV	Amount/portion	%DV		%DV		%DV
Total fat 16 g	24%	**Cholest.** 79 mg	26%	**Total Carb.** 49 g	16%	**Vitamin A**	10%	**Calcium**	29%
Sat. Fat 4 g	21%	**Sodium** 832 mg	35%	Fiber 4 g	16%	**Vitamin C**	0%	**Iron**	13%
Protein 12 g				Sugars 11 g					

Percent Daily Values (%DV) are based on a 2000-calorie diet.

Notes
- Potentially hazardous food. Keep batter at an internal temperature below 41°F.
- 1¼ gal fluid milk may be substituted for nonfat dry milk and water. Add milk along with vegetable oil and eggs.

PANCAKE MIX

Yield: 12 lb mix

Ingredient	Amount	Procedure
Flour, all-purpose	9 lb	Combine ingredients in mixer bowl.
Baking powder	8 oz	Blend well, using flat beater or whip.
Salt	¼ cup	Store in covered container.
Sugar, granulated	1 lb 8 oz	
Nonfat dry milk	1 lb 8 oz	

Variation
- **Buttermilk Pancake Mix.** Substitute 1 lb 8 oz dry buttermilk for nonfat dry milk and add 2 Tbsp baking soda.

PANCAKES FROM MIX

Ingredient	30 cakes	50 cakes	100 cakes	200 cakes
Pancake mix	2 lb	3 lb	6 lb	12 lb
Eggs, beaten	4 (7 oz)	6 (10 oz)	12 (1 lb 5 oz)	24 (2 lb 10 oz)
Water	1 qt	1½ qt	3 qt	1½ gal
Oil or melted shortening	4 oz	6 oz	12 oz	1 lb 8 oz

To use mix:

1. Weigh appropriate amount of mix (p. 290) as given in the table.
2. Add beaten eggs, water, and cooled melted fat.
3. Stir only until mix is dampened.
4. Place on hot griddle with No. 16 dipper.
5. Cook until cake is full of bubbles. Turn and finish cooking.

WAFFLES

Yield: 6 qt batter or 50–60 waffles   *Portion:* 1 waffle

Ingredient	Amount	Procedure
Flour, all-purpose	3 lb	Combine dry ingredients in mixer bowl.
Baking powder	3 oz	Blend on low speed for 10 seconds, using flat beater.
Salt	2 Tbsp	
Sugar, granulated	4 oz	
Egg yolks	18 (11 oz)	Combine egg yolks, milk, and melted shortening.
Milk	2¼ qt	Add to dry ingredients.
Oil or melted shortening	1 lb (2 cups)	Mix on low speed just enough to moisten dry ingredients.
Egg whites	18 (1 lb 5 oz)	Beat egg whites until stiff but not dry. Fold into batter.
		Refrigerate batter, removing from refrigerator small amounts as needed.
		Use No. 10 dipper to place batter on preheated waffle iron.
		Bake about 4 minutes.

Approximate nutritive values per portion   **Calories** 223

Amount/portion	%DV	Amount/portion	%DV	Amount/portion	%DV		%DV		%DV
Total fat 12 g	18%	**Cholest.** 78 mg	26%	**Total Carb.** 23 g	8%	Vitamin A	12%	Calcium	15%
Sat. Fat 3 g	17%	**Sodium** 428 mg	18%	Fiber 1 g	3%	Vitamin C	0%	Iron	7%
Protein 6 g				Sugars 4 g					

Percent Daily Values (%DV) are based on a 2000-calorie diet.

Notes
- Potentially hazardous food. Keep batter at an internal temperature below 41°F.
- 9 oz nonfat dry milk and 2¼ qt water may be substituted for fluid milk. Mix dry milk with dry ingredients. Increase shortening to 1 lb 2 oz.

Variation
- **Pecan Waffles.** Add 6 oz chopped pecans.

CREPES

Yield: 50 portions or 5 qt batter   *Portion:* 2 crepes

Ingredient	Amount	Procedure
Flour, all purpose Salt	2 lb 8 oz 1 oz (1½ Tbsp)	Combine flour and salt in mixer bowl.
Eggs	24 (2 lb 10 oz)	Beat eggs until fluffy.
Milk Margarine, melted	2¾ qt 6 oz	Add milk and margarine to eggs. Add to flour and mix until smooth. Batter will be thinner than pancake batter.
		Refrigerate batter, removing from refrigerator small amounts as needed. Portion batter with No. 20 (1¾ oz) dipper onto lightly greased hot griddle. Brown lightly on both sides. Crepes will roll best if they are not overbrowned. Stack, layered with waxed paper, until ready to use.

Approximate nutritive values per portion   **Calories** 176

Amount/portion	%DV	Amount/portion	%DV	Amount/portion	%DV		%DV		%DV
Total fat 7 g	11%	**Cholest.** 109 mg	36%	**Total Carb.** 20 g	7%	Vitamin A	7%	Calcium	8%
Sat. Fat 2 g	12%	**Sodium** 281 mg	12%	Fiber 1 g	2%	Vitamin C	0%	Iron	7%
Protein 7 g				Sugars 3 g					

Percent Daily Values (%DV) are based on a 2000-calorie diet.

Notes
- Potentially hazardous food. Keep batter at an internal temperature below 41°F.
- Crepes may be folded or rolled around desired filling. (See recipe for Chicken Crepes, p. 544).
- If used for dessert crepes, add 3 Tbsp sugar to dry ingredients. Fill with fruit filling.

ZUCCHINI CORN CAKES

Yield: 50 portions   *Portion:* 3 pancakes

Ingredient	Amount	Procedure
Water	1 gal	Combine water and dry buttermilk in mixer bowl.
Dry buttermilk	1 lb 3 oz	
Eggs	2 lb 3 oz	Add eggs. Mix until combined, approximately 3 minutes.
Flour	6 lb	Combine dry ingredients in baker's bowl.
Salt	2½ Tbsp	Add dry ingredients to buttermilk mixture. Mix only until barely mixed. (Overmixing will cause cakes to be tough.)
Baking soda	1 tsp	
Baking powder	1 oz (2¼ Tbsp)	
Granulated sugar	6 oz	
Black pepper	1½ Tbsp	
Vegetable oil	2 lb 3 oz	Add to flour mixture and mix lightly.
Zucchini squash, shredded	6 lb 3 oz EP	Fold zucchini squash and corn into batter just before cooking cakes.
Corn, defrosted (whole kernel frozen)	3 lb 10 oz EP	Preheat grill to 325–350°F. Lightly grease grill. Using a No. 12 dipper, portion cakes onto hot grill. Flip cakes when browned and small bubbles appear on the top side. Brown second side of cakes. Remove from grill and shingle stack into 2-inch counter pans. Cover with waxed paper and serve soon after cooking. Serve with salsa and sour cream or other toppings.

Approximate nutritive values per portion   **Calories** 450

Amount/portion	%DV	Amount/portion	%DV	Amount/portion	%DV		%DV		%DV
Total fat 23 g	35%	**Cholest.** 79 mg	26%	**Total Carb.** 51 g	17%	**Vitamin A**	3%	**Calcium**	18%
Sat. Fat 3 g	16%	**Sodium** 514 mg	21%	Fiber 1.5 g	6%	**Vitamin C**	1%	**Iron**	16%
Protein 12 g				Sugars 4.2 g					

Percent Daily Values (%DV) are based on a 2000-calorie diet.

Note • Potentially hazardous food. *Food Safety Standards:* Hold food for service at an internal temperature above 140°F. Do not mix old product with new. Cool leftover product quickly (within 2 hours)to 70°F and then (within an additional 4 hours) to 41°F. See p. 105 for cooling procedures. Reheat leftover product quickly (within 2 hours) to 165°F. Reheat product only once; discard if not used.

CAKE DOUGHNUTS

Yield: 8 dozen doughnuts   *Portion:* 1 doughnut
Deep-fat fryer: 375°F   *Fry:* 3–4 minutes

Ingredient	Amount	Procedure
Eggs	6 (10 oz)	Beat eggs until light.
Sugar, granulated	1 lb 4 oz	Add sugar and melted shortening to eggs.
Oil or melted shortening	3 oz	Mix on medium speed about 10 minutes.
Flour, all-purpose	3 lb 4 oz	Combine dry ingredients.
Baking powder	3 oz	
Salt	2½ tsp	
Nutmeg, ground	2 tsp	
Ginger, ground	¼ tsp	
Orange peel, grated	1 Tbsp	
Milk	1 qt	Add dry ingredients and milk alternately to egg mixture. Mix to form a soft dough. Add more flour if dough is too soft to handle. Chill.
		Roll dough to ⅜-inch thickness on floured board or table. Cut with floured 2½-inch doughnut cutter. Fry in deep fat for 3–4 minutes.
Sugar, granulated	8 oz	Sprinkle with sugar when partially cool.

Approximate nutritive values per portion (plus frying fat)   **Calories** 176

Amount/portion	%DV	Amount/portion	%DV	Amount/portion	%DV		%DV		%DV
Total fat 2 g	3%	**Cholest.** 14 mg	5%	**Total Carb.** 21 g	7%	**Vitamin A**	0%	**Calcium**	7%
Sat. Fat 1 g	3%	**Sodium** 153 mg	6%	Fiber 0.4 g	2%	**Vitamin C**	0%	**Iron**	4%
Protein 2 g				Sugars 9 g					

Percent Daily Values (%DV) are based on a 2000-calorie diet.

Note
- 4 oz nonfat dry milk and 1 qt water may be substituted for fluid milk. Mix dry milk with the dry ingredients. Increase shortening to 4 oz.

Variation
- **Chocolate doughnuts.** Substitute 2 oz cocoa for 2 oz flour.

DUMPLINGS

Yield: 50 portions   *Portion:* 2 dumplings
Steam pressure: 5 lb   *Steam:* 12–15 minutes

Ingredient	Amount	Procedure
Flour, all-purpose Baking powder Salt	2 lb 8 oz 3 oz (6 Tbsp) 2 Tbsp	Combine dry ingredients in mixer bowl. Mix on low speed until blended, using flat beater.
Eggs, beaten Milk	6 (10 oz) 5½ cups	Combine eggs and milk. Add to dry ingredients. Mix on low speed, only until blended.
		Portion batter with No. 24 dipper onto trays. Do not cover trays. Steam for 12–15 minutes.

Approximate nutritive values per portion   **Calories** 109

Amount/portion	%DV	Amount/portion	%DV	Amount/portion	%DV		%DV		%DV
Total fat 2 g	3%	**Cholest.** 28 mg	9%	**Total Carb.** 19 g	6%	Vitamin A	2%	Calcium	10%
Sat. Fat 1 g	4%	**Sodium** 381 mg	16%	Fiber 1 g	2%	Vitamin C	0%	Iron	6%
Protein 4 g				Sugars 2 g					

Percent Daily Values (%DV) are based on a 2000-calorie diet.

Notes
- 5 oz nonfat dry milk and 5½ cups water may be substituted for the fluid milk. Add dry milk to other dry ingredients.
- Serve with meat stew or stewed chicken. Mixture may be dropped onto hot meat mixture in counter pans and steamed.

Variation
- **Spaetzles (Egg Dumplings).** Use 1 lb 4 oz flour, 1 tsp baking powder, 1½ tsp salt, 6 eggs, and 3 cups milk. Mix as above. Drop small bits of dough or press through a colander into 3 gal simmering soup. Cook approximately 5 minutes. Soup must be very hot to cook dumplings.

FRENCH TOAST

Yield: 50 slices   *Portion:* 1 slice

Ingredient	Amount	Procedure
Eggs	24 (2 lb 10 oz)	Beat eggs.
Milk	1½ qt	Add milk, salt, and sugar to eggs. Mix well.
Salt	1 Tbsp	Refrigerate batter, removing from refrigerator small amounts
Sugar, granulated	4 oz	as needed.
Bread slices, day old	50	Dip bread into egg mixture. Do not let bread soak. (Care should be taken to avoid getting raw eggs on the cooked food.) Fry on a well-greased griddle or in deep fat at 360°F until golden brown. Serve sprinkled with powdered sugar.

Approximate nutritive values per portion (plus frying fat)   **Calories** 124

Amount/portion	%DV	Amount/portion	%DV	Amount/portion	%DV		%DV		%DV
Total fat 4 g	7%	**Cholest.** 105 mg	35%	**Total Carb.** 15 g	5%	**Vitamin A**	5%	**Calcium**	6%
Sat. Fat 1 g	7%	**Sodium** 331 mg	14%	Fiber 3 g	11%	**Vitamin C**	0%	**Iron**	6%
Protein 6 g				Sugars 5 g					

Percent Daily Values (%DV) are based on a 2000-calorie diet.

Note ● Potentially hazardous food. Keep batter at an internal temperature below 41°F.

Variations ● **Batter-Fried French Toast.** Use 1-inch-thick bread slices. Cut into triangles or leave whole. Dip in mixture made from 18 eggs (2 lb), 1¼ qt milk, ⅓ cup vegetable oil, 2 lb 8 oz all-purpose flour, 1 oz (1½ Tbsp) salt, and 1 oz (2⅓ Tbsp) baking powder. Fry in deep fat at 350–375°F until golden brown. Dredge in powdered sugar. Serve with warm maple syrup.

● **Cinnamon French Toast.** Add 1 tsp cinnamon to egg mixture.

FRITTERS

Yield: 50 portions   *Portion:* 2 fritters
Deep-fat fryer: 375°F   *Fry:* 4–6 minutes

Ingredient	Amount	Procedure
Flour, all-purpose	4 lb	Combine dry ingredients in mixer bowl.
Baking powder	4 oz	Mix on low speed for 10 seconds or until mixed, using flat
Salt	1 Tbsp	beater.
Sugar, granulated	2 oz	
Eggs, beaten	12 (1 lb 5 oz)	Combine eggs, milk, and melted shortening.
Milk	2 qt	Add to dry ingredients. Mix only enough to moisten dry
Oil or melted shortening	6 oz (¾ cup)	ingredients.
		Portion batter with No. 30 dipper into hot deep fat. Fry at 375°F for 4–6 minutes. Serve with syrup.

Approximate nutritive values per portion (plus frying fat)   **Calories** 211

Amount/portion	%DV	Amount/portion	%DV	Amount/portion	%DV		%DV		%DV
Total fat 6 g	10%	**Cholest.** 56 mg	19%	**Total Carb.** 31 g	10%	**Vitamin A**	3%	**Calcium**	20%
Sat. Fat 2 g	10%	**Sodium** 390 mg	16%	Fiber 1 g	4%	**Vitamin C**	0%	**Iron**	10%
Protein 7 g				Sugars 4 g					

Percent Daily Values (%DV) are based on a 2000-calorie diet.

Notes
- Potentially hazardous food. Keep batter at an internal temperature below 41°F.
- 8 oz nonfat dry milk and 2 qt water may be substituted for fluid milk. Add dry milk to other dry ingredients.

Variations
- **Apple Fritters.** Add 3 lb tart raw apple, peeled and finely chopped, and 1 tsp cinnamon (optional).
- **Banana Fritters.** Add 3 lb bananas, mashed.
- **Corn Fritters.** Add 2 qt whole kernel corn, drained.
- **Fruit Fritters.** Add 1 qt drained fruit: peach, pineapple, or other fruit.
- **Green Chili Fritters.** Add 2 lb 8 oz chopped green chilis, drained. Serve with nacho sauce (Nachos, p. 236). Make ¼ recipe.

CHEESE STRAWS

Yield: 6 dozen 4 × 1-inch straws
Oven: 350°F   *Bake:* 10–15 minutes

Ingredient	Amount	Procedure
Butter or margarine	6 oz	Cream butter on medium speed until soft.
Cheddar cheese, sharp, shredded	8 oz	Blend in cheese.
Flour, all-purpose	8 oz	Combine dry ingredients and add to cheese mixture on low speed.
Baking powder	2 tsp	
Salt	1 tsp	
Pepper, cayenne	¼ tsp	
Eggs, beaten	3	Add eggs and water, combined.
Water	2 Tbsp	Mix on low speed to form a stiff dough. Chill.
		Roll ¼ inch thick and cut into strips 4 inches long and 1 inch wide. Place on ungreased baking sheet. Bake at 350°F for 10–15 minutes.

Approximate nutritive values per portion   **Calories** 44

Amount/portion	%DV	Amount/portion	%DV	Amount/portion	%DV		%DV		%DV
Total fat 3 g	5%	**Cholest.** 17 mg	6%	**Total Carb.** 3 g	0.9%	**Vitamin A**	3%	**Calcium**	3%
Sat. Fat 2 g	10%	**Sodium** 71 mg	3%	Fiber 0 g	0%	**Vitamin C**	0%	**Iron**	1%
Protein 1 g				Sugars 0 g					

Percent Daily Values (%DV) are based on a 2000-calorie diet.

Variations   ● **Caraway Cheese Straws.** Add 2 tsp caraway seeds to flour before mixing.

YEAST BREAD RECIPES

WHITE BREAD

Yield: 16 1½-lb loaves
Oven: 400°F   *Bake:* 30–40 minutes

Ingredient	Amount	Procedure
Yeast, active dry	5 oz	Soften yeast in warm water.
Water, warm (110°F)	3 cups	Let stand 10 minutes.
Sugar, granulated	10 oz	Combine sugar, salt, dry milk, water, and shortening.
Salt	5 oz	Add softened yeast.
Nonfat dry milk	14 oz	Mix on medium speed until blended, using dough arm.
Water, lukewarm	1 gal	
Shortening, melted	12 oz	
Flour, all-purpose	15 lb	Add flour. Mix on low speed about 10 minutes or until dough is smooth and elastic and small blisters appear on the surface.

1. Let dough rise in a warm place (80°F) approximately 2 hours, or until double in bulk.
2. Punch down dough by pulling the dough up on all sides, folding it over the center, and pressing down, then turning over in the bowl. Shape into 16 loaves, 1 lb 8 oz each (Figure 8.1). Place in greased 5 × 9 × 2¾-inch loaf pans.
3. Let rise approximately 1½ hours, or until double in bulk.
4. Bake at 400°F for 30–40 minutes or until loaves are golden brown and sound hollow when tapped (Exhibit I in the color insert).
5. Brush tops of loaves with melted margarine or butter.

Approximate nutritive values per loaf   **Calories** 1918

Amount/portion	%DV	Amount/portion	%DV	Amount/portion	%DV		%DV		%DV
Total fat 26 g	39%	**Cholest.** 4 mg	1%	**Total Carb.** 359 g	120%	Vitamin A	17%	Calcium	39%
Sat. Fat 6 g	30%	Sodium 3586 mg	149%	Fiber 14 g	57%	Vitamin C	2%	Iron	117%
Protein 56 g				Sugars 37 g					

Percent Daily Values (%DV) are based on a 2000-calorie diet.

Notes
- 1¼ gal fresh milk may be substituted for the water and dry milk. Scald milk, combine with sugar, salt, and shortening. Cool to lukewarm before adding to other ingredients.
- The dough temperature should be about 80°F when mixed.
- Mixing may be simplified by combining dry yeast with sugar, salt, dry milk, and 2 lb of the flour. Mix thoroughly. In mixer bowl, combine very warm water (120°F) and shortening. Blend on low speed. Add yeast-flour mixture while mixing on low speed. Add remaining flour gradually, mixing until a smooth, elastic dough is formed.
- Shortening may be increased to 1 lb and sugar to 12 oz if a richer dough is desired.
- A variety of shapes may be made from the dough (Exhibits II, III, and IV in the color insert).

Variations
- **Buffet Submarine Buns.** Scale dough into 1-lb portions. Shape into 18-inch-long loaves. (See Figure 8.1 for shaping instructions.) Use for Submarine Sandwiches (p. 724).
- **Cinnamon Bread.** After dough has been divided and scaled into loaves, roll each into a rectangular sheet. Brush with melted margarine or shortening; sprinkle generously with cinnamon and sugar. Roll as for jelly roll. Seal edge of dough and place in greased loaf pans sealed edge down. Sprinkle top with cinnamon and sugar.

- **Raisin Bread.** Add 3 lb raisins to dough after mixing.
- **Sandwich Ring Bread.** Scale fermented dough into 11-oz balls and shape each ball into a 16-inch rope. Braid three ropes together and pinch ends to seal. Shape braided ropes into a 15-inch circle with a 5-inch center hole (work ends together to form a smooth ring). Proof ring in a warm place until double in bulk (30–40 minutes). Bake at 375°F until done (about 20 minutes).
- **Whole Wheat Bread.** Substitute whole wheat flour for half of the all-purpose flour.

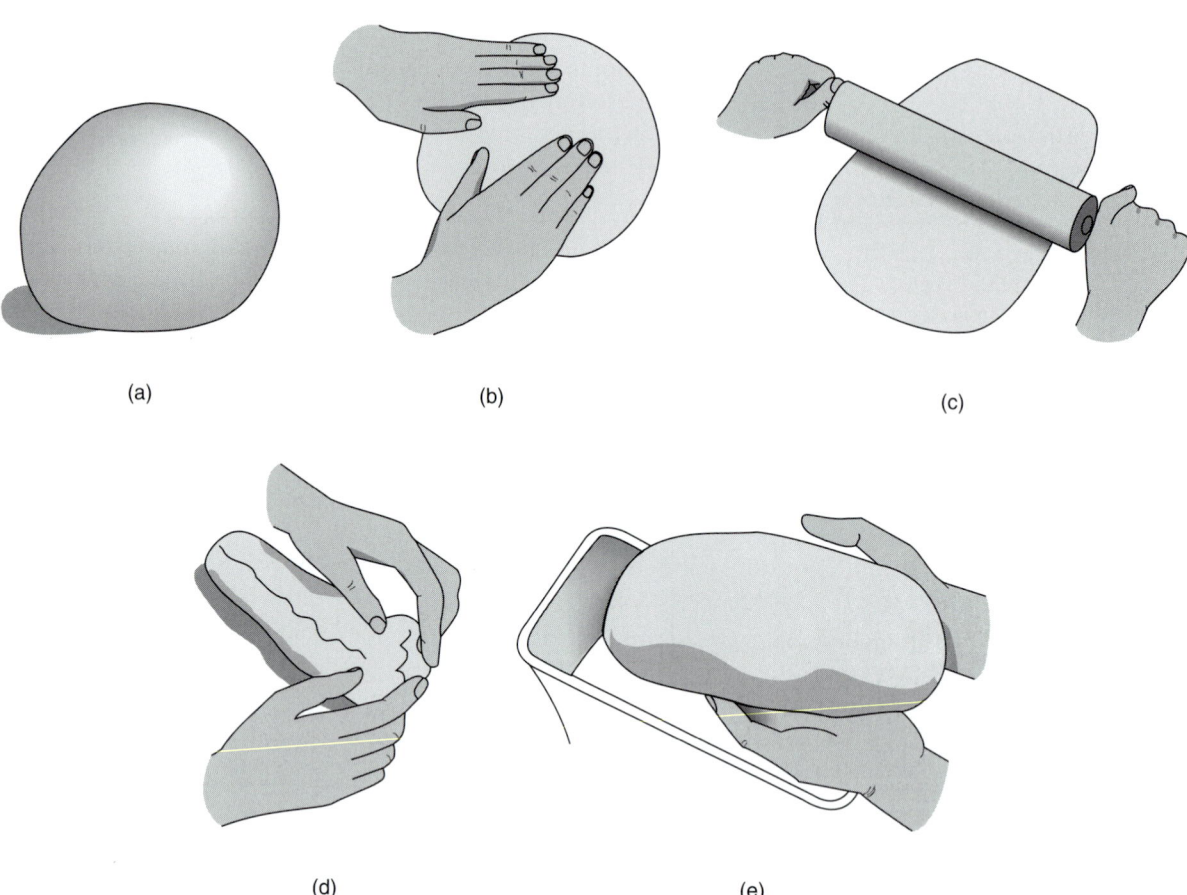

FIGURE 8.1 Shaping bread loaves: (a)Lightly flour the work surface. Divide the dough into 1 lb 8 oz, smooth balls. (b) Press dough by hand to force out air bubbles. (c) Use a rolling pin to form a rectangle. (d) Begin at the short end of the rectangle and roll the dough tightly to make a loaf shape. Seal by pinching ends together. (e) Place dough, seam-side down, in greased pan.

WHOLE WHEAT BREAD

Yield: 5 1½-lb loaves
Oven: 365°F   *Bake:* 30–35 minutes

Ingredient	*Amount*	*Procedure*
Yeast, active dry	1¼ oz	Combine yeast, water, and sugar.
Water, warm (110°F)	1¾ cup	Let stand 10 minutes.
Sugar, granulated	1 Tbsp	
Water, hot	1 qt	Combine water, milk, sugar, salt, and shortening in mixer
Nonfat dry milk	5 oz	bowl, using dough arm.
Sugar, granulated	5 oz	Mix until shortening is softened.
Salt	1½ oz	
Shortening	6 oz	
Flour, all-purpose	3 lb	Add enough flour to mixture in mixer bowl to make a thin, smooth batter. Add yeast mixture. Mix 15 minutes on medium speed.
Flour, whole wheat	1 lb	Add remaining all-purpose flour and whole wheat flour in small amounts to make a soft dough that pulls itself from side of bowl. Mix on low speed about 10 minutes or until dough is smooth and elastic and small blisters appear on the surface.

1. Let dough rise (proof) in warm place for about 2 hours or until double in bulk.

2. Punch down dough. Scale into five portions 1 lb 8 oz each.

3. Shape into loaves. Place in greased 5 × 9 × 2¾-inch loaf pans. Let rise until double in size.

4. Bake at 365°F for 30–35 minutes.

5. Remove bread from oven. Brush with melted margarine.

Approximate nutritive values per loaf   **Calories** 1862

Amount/portion	%DV	Amount/portion	%DV	Amount/portion	%DV		%DV		%DV
Total fat 38 g	**58%**	**Cholest.** 5 mg	**2%**	**Total Carb.** 326 g	**109%**	**Vitamin A**	**20%**	**Calcium**	**43%**
Sat. Fat 9 g	**46%**	**Sodium** 3467 mg	**144%**	Fiber 12 g	**48%**	**Vitamin C**	**2%**	**Iron**	**100%**
Protein 50 g				Sugars 50 g					

Percent Daily Values (%DV) are based on a 2000-calorie diet.

Note   ● Recipe may be used for Whole Wheat Rolls. See p. 310 for procedure. Recipe makes approximately 100 1½-oz rolls. Bake at 375°F for 20–25 minutes.

Variations   ● **Cornmeal Bread.** Delete whole wheat flour. Add 1 lb cornmeal.

● **Egg Bread.** Delete whole wheat flour. Increase all-purpose flour to 3 lb 12 oz. Add 5 eggs (8 oz), beaten.

● **Jalapeño Cheese Bread.** Delete whole wheat flour. Increase all-purpose flour to 4 lb. Increase yeast to 1½ oz. Reduce nonfat dry milk to 1 oz. Add 3 oz seeded jalapeño peppers, finely chopped; 8 oz green chilis, chopped; 10 oz shredded cheddar cheese; and 8 oz shredded processed cheese.

● **White Loaves.** Delete whole wheat flour. Increase all-purpose flour to 4 lb.

FRENCH BREAD

Yield: 5 loaves 1 lb 12 oz
Oven: 425°F   *Bake:* 25–30 minutes

Ingredient	*Amount*	*Procedure*
Yeast, active dry	1½ oz	Combine yeast, water, and sugar.
Water, warm (110°F)	2 cups	Stir to dissolve yeast. Let stand 10 minutes.
Sugar, granulated	2 oz	
Water, warm	3 cups	Add to yeast mixture. Mix until blended, using dough arm.
Shortening	3 oz	
Salt	1¾ oz	
Flour, all-purpose	5 lb	Add flour all at once. Mix on low speed to blend. Mix on medium speed for 7–10 minutes, or until sides of bowl are clean and dough makes a rhythmic slapping sound against side of bowl.

1. Let dough rise (proof) in a warm place for about 2 hours, or until double in bulk.
2. Punch down dough by pulling the dough up on all sides, folding it over the center and pressing down, then turning over in the bowl.
3. Divide into five portions, 1 lb 12 oz each. On lightly floured surface, roll or pat dough to a 12 × 6-inch rectangle.
4. Starting with longer side, roll up tightly, pressing dough into roll with each turn. Pinch edges and ends to seal.
5. Place on greased baking sheet sprinkled with cornmeal.
6. Proof until double in bulk.
7. With sharp knife, make two or three diagonal slashes across top of loaf.
8. Spray or brush with cold water.
9. Bake at 425°F for 25–30 minutes until golden brown. Spray or brush loaf with cold water several times during baking for a crisp crust.

Approximate nutritive values per loaf   **Calories** 1869

Amount/portion	%DV	Amount/portion	%DV	Amount/portion	%DV		%DV		%DV
Total fat 21 g	33%	**Cholest.** 0 mg	0%	**Total Carb.** 361 g	120%	**Vitamin A**	0%	**Calcium**	9%
Sat. Fat 5 g	25%	**Sodium** 3861 mg	161%	Fiber 15 g	60%	**Vitamin C**	0%	**Iron**	124%
Protein 50 g				Sugars 19 g					

Percent Daily Values (%DV) are based on a 2000-calorie diet.

Notes
- For a shiny, golden crust, brush loaves before baking with an egg glaze made from one slightly beaten egg and 1 Tbsp of water or milk.
- After baking, leave uncovered at room temperature to keep the crust crisp.

DILLY BREAD

Yield: 5 1½-lb loaves
Oven: 375°F   *Bake:* 30–35 minutes

Ingredient	Amount	Procedure
Yeast, active dry	1¼ oz	Combine yeast, water, and sugar.
Water, warm (110°F)	½ cup	Stir to dissolve yeast.
Sugar, granulated	3 oz	Let stand for later step.
Cottage cheese, cream style	1 lb 12 oz	Combine cottage cheese and water in mixer bowl.
Water, warm	1¼ cups	
Vegetable oil	¼ cup	Add oil, onion, dill weed, and eggs to cottage cheese mixture. Mix to blend, using dough arm.
Dehydrated chopped onion	½ oz	Add yeast mixture.
Dill weed	1 Tbsp	
Eggs, whole	3 (6 oz)	
Flour, all-purpose	4 lb 2 oz	Combine dry ingredients. Add enough to cottage cheese mixture to make a smooth batter. Scrape sides of bowl occasionally.
Salt	1 Tbsp	Add remaining flour gradually until dough pulls itself from sides of bowl. Dough will be sticky.
Baking soda	½ tsp	Proof until double in bulk.
		Scale dough into five portions, 1 lb 8 oz each. Shape into loaves.
		Place in greased 5 × 9 × 2¾-inch loaf pans.
		Proof until double in size.
		Bake at 375°F for 30–35 minutes.
		Brush with melted margarine.

Approximate nutritive values per loaf   **Calories** 1770

Amount/portion	%DV	Amount/portion	%DV	Amount/portion	%DV		%DV		%DV
Total fat 25 g	39%	**Cholest.** 169 mg	56%	**Total Carb.** 313 g	104%	**Vitamin A**	14%	**Calcium**	19%
Sat. Fat 9 g	45%	**Sodium** 2102 mg	88%	Fiber 13 g	50%	**Vitamin C**	3%	**Iron**	108%
Protein 66 g				Sugars 24 g					

Percent Daily Values (%DV) are based on a 2000-calorie diet.

ENGLISH MUFFIN BREAD

Yield: 5 1½-lb loaves
Oven: 375°F   *Bake:* 40–50 minutes

Ingredient	Amount	Procedure
Water, hot	2 cups	Combine water and oil in mixer bowl.
Vegetable oil	1½ cups	
Flour, all-purpose	2 lb	Add flour, sugar, salt, and eggs to water-oil mixture.
Sugar, granulated	6 oz	
Salt	2 oz	
Eggs, beaten	6 (10 oz)	
Yeast, active dry	1¼ oz	Dissolve yeast in warm water.
Water, warm (110°F)	1½ cups	Add to flour mixture. Mix on medium speed for 2 minutes, using dough arm.
Flour, all-purpose	2 lb	Add enough remaining flour to make a stiff batter. Cover and let rise until light and double in bulk. Punch down dough.
Cornmeal	2 oz	Grease five loaf pans (5 × 9 × 2¾ inches). Sprinkle with cornmeal. Scale 1 lb 8 oz dough per pan. Shape and place in pans. Sprinkle with cornmeal. Cover. Let rise until double in bulk. Bake at 375°F for 40–50 minutes or until loaf sounds hollow when tapped lightly.

Approximate nutritive values per loaf   **Calories** 2176

Amount/portion	%DV	Amount/portion	%DV	Amount/portion	%DV		%DV		%DV
Total fat 75 g	115%	**Cholest.** 242 mg	81%	**Total Carb.** 323 g	108%	**Vitamin A**	11%	**Calcium**	11%
Sat. Fat 19 g	97%	**Sodium** 4483 mg	187%	Fiber 14 g	55%	**Vitamin C**	0%	**Iron**	106%
Protein 49 g				Sugars 39 g					

Percent Daily Values (%DV) are based on a 2000-calorie diet.

FOCACCIA

Yield: 4 loaves
Oven: 450°F   *Bake:* 15–20 minutes

Ingredient	Amount	Procedure
Yeast, active dry	1 oz	Combine yeast, water, and sugar. Stir to dissolve yeast. Let stand for later step.
Water, warm (110°F)	2 cups	
Sugar, granulated	¼ tsp	
Olive oil	1½ cups	Add to yeast mixture. Mix until blended using dough arm.
Water, warm	2 cups	
Salt	1 Tbsp	
Flour, all-purpose	2 lb 10 oz	Add flour. Mix on low speed for about 10 minutes until dough is smooth and satiny.

1. Turn into lightly greased bowl, then turn over to grease top. Cover. Let rise in warm place (80°F) until double in bulk (30–40 minutes).

2. Shape with a rolling pin into four 1 lb 5 oz ovals, circles, or rectangles about ½–⅔-inch thick. See Exhibit IV in the color insert.

3. Make several very shallow parallel or fan-shaped cuts in center of bread, then gently pull the edges of the dough to slightly open the shallow cuts.

4. Put rounds on lightly greased pans.

5. Brush rounds with olive oil and sprinkle lightly with coarse sea salt and coarse ground pepper. Let rise 20 minutes.

6. Bake at 450°F for approximately 15 minutes, until golden brown. Serve warm.

Approximate nutritive values per loaf   **Calories** 1819

Amount/portion	%DV	Amount/portion	%DV	Amount/portion	%DV		%DV		%DV
Total fat 84 g	130%	**Cholest.** 0 mg	0%	**Total Carb.** 230 g	77%	**Vitamin A**	0%	**Calcium**	6%
Sat. Fat 11 g	57%	**Sodium** 1611 mg	67%	Fiber 9 g	34%	**Vitamin C**	0%	**Iron**	73%
Protein 33 g				Sugars 0 g					

Percent Daily Values (%DV) are based on a 2000-calorie diet.

Note • Focaccia may be split and filled with a sandwich filling or served unsplit as an accompaniment to soup or salad.

Variation • **Focaccia with Onions.** Toss 1 lb of thinly sliced onions with ¼ cup olive oil, ½ tsp salt, and ½ tsp pepper. Distribute approximately 4 oz of onion mixture on Focaccia after shaping. Let rise 20–30 minutes and bake as directed.

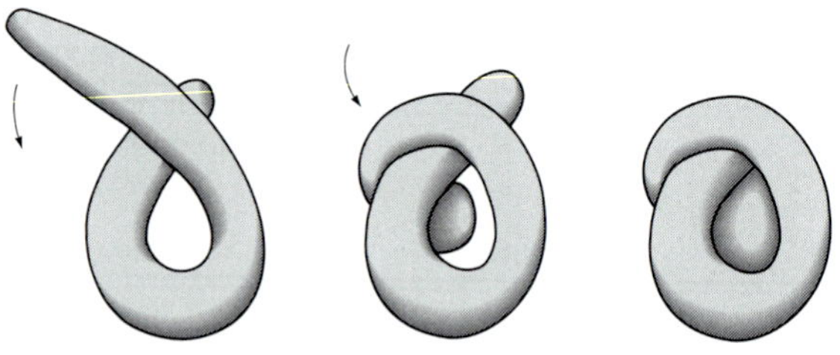

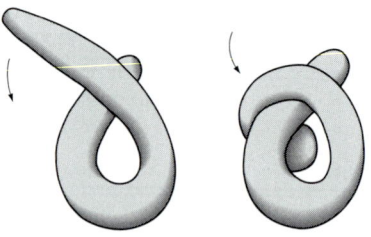

FIGURE 8.2   Shaping bowknot rolls

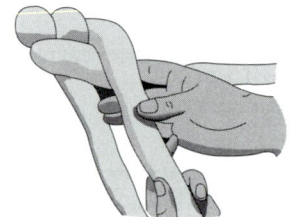

FIGURE 8.3   Braiding yeast dough

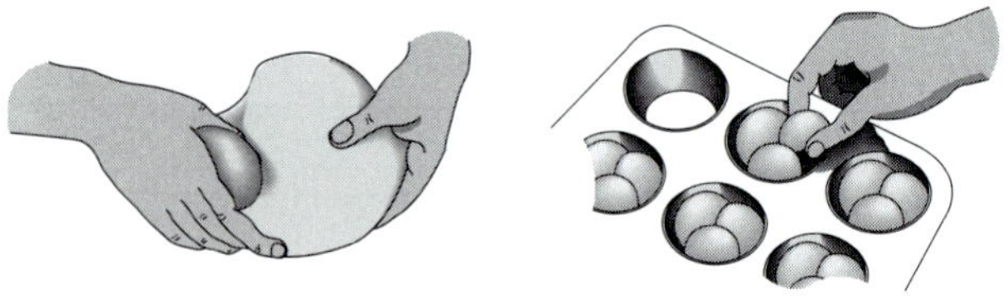

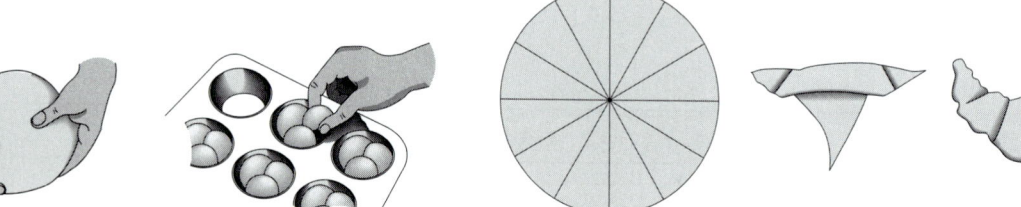

FIGURE 8.4   Shaping and panning cloverleaf rolls

FIGURE 8.5   Shaping crescent rolls

Immediately loosen from pan with a spatula. Invert pans to remove. Cool. Serve irregular side up to resemble a crown. Garnish with maraschino cherries.

- **Cloverleaf Rolls.** Pinch off 1-oz pieces of dough and roll into smooth balls. Fit into greased muffin pans, three balls per cup (see Figure 8.4).

- **Crescents.** Weigh dough into 12-oz portions. Roll each into a circle ⅛ inch thick and 8 inches in diameter. Cut into 12 triangles and brush top with melted margarine or butter. Beginning at base, roll each triangle, keeping point in middle of roll and bringing ends toward each other to form a crescent shape. Place on greased baking sheets 1½ inches apart (see Figure 8.5).

- **Dinner or Pan Rolls.** Shape dough into 1½-oz balls and place on well-greased baking sheets. Cover. Let rise until light. Brush with mixture made of egg yolk and milk—1 egg yolk to 1 Tbsp milk.

- **Fan Tan or Butterflake Rolls.** Weigh dough into 12-oz portions. Roll out into very thin rectangular sheet. Brush with melted margarine or butter. Cut in strips about 1 inch wide. Pile 6–7 strips together. Cut 1½-inch pieces and place on end in greased muffin pans.

- **Gooey Buns.** Grease sides of one 18 × 26 × 2-inch baking sheet. Combine in kettle or saucepan 8 oz margarine, 1 lb 8 oz brown sugar, and ¾ cup corn syrup. Cook until sugar is dissolved. Pour into prepared pan. Cool. If desired, sprinkle 1 lb pecans over mixture. Place 1½-oz portions of dough 8 × 12 on sugar mixture. Let rise. Bake at 375°F for 20–25 minutes. Remove from oven and turn upside down onto 18 × 26 × 1-inch baking sheet.

- **Half-and-Half Rolls.** Proceed as for Twin Rolls. Use one round plain dough and one round whole wheat dough for each roll.

- **Hamburger Buns.** Divide dough into two portions. Roll each piece of dough into a strip 1½ inches in diameter. Cut strips into pieces approximately 2½ oz each. Round the pieces into balls. Place balls in rows on greased baking sheets 1½–2 inches apart. Let stand 10–15 minutes, then flatten to desired thickness with finger, rolling pin, or another baking sheet.

- **Hot Cross Buns.** Divide dough into thirds. Roll ½ inch thick. Cut rounds 3 inches in diameter. Brush tops with beaten egg. Score top of bun to make a cross before baking, or make a cross on top with frosting after baking. (See p. 315 for variation.)

- **Hot Dog Buns.** Divide dough into two portions. Roll each piece of dough into a strip 1½ inches in diameter. Cut strips of dough into pieces approximately 2½ oz each. Round pieces of dough; roll into pieces approximately 4½ inches long. Place in rows on greased baking sheets ½ inch apart.

- **Parker House Rolls.** Divide dough into thirds. Roll dough to ⅓ inch thickness. Cut rounds 2–2½ inches in diameter with a biscuit cutter. Let dough rest a few minutes after cutting. Brush with melted butter or margarine. Crease the rolls across the center with the dull edge of a table knife. Fold over and press down on the folded edge (see Figure 8.6), and Exhibit II in the color insert.
- **Popcorn Rolls.** Shape dough into 1½-oz balls. Place on greased baking sheets. Snip top of each ball twice with scissors.
- **Poppy Seed Rolls.** (a) Proceed as for Twists. Substitute poppy seed for sugar and cinnamon. (b) Proceed as for Cinnamon Rolls (p. 316). Substitute poppy seed for sugar, cinnamon, and raisins.
- **Ribbon Rolls.** Weigh dough into 12-oz pieces. Roll ¼ inch thick. Spread with melted margarine. Place on top of this a layer of whole wheat dough rolled to the same thickness. Repeat, using the contrasting dough until five layers thick. Cut with a 1½-inch cutter. Place in greased muffin pans with cut surface down.
- **Rosettes.** Follow directions for Bowknots. After tying, bring one end through center and the other over the side.
- **Sesame Rolls.** Proceed as for Twin Rolls (below). Brush tops with melted margarine and sprinkle with sesame seeds.
- **Twin Rolls.** Weigh dough into 12-oz pieces. Roll ⅝ inch thick. Cut rounds 1 inch in diameter. Brush with melted margarine. Place on end in well-greased muffin pans, allowing two rounds for each roll.
- **Twists.** Weigh dough into 12-oz pieces. Roll ⅓ inch thick and spread with melted margarine, sugar, and cinnamon. Cut into strips ⅓ × 8 inches, bring both ends together, and twist dough.
- **Whole Wheat Rolls.** Substitute 2 lb 6 oz whole wheat flour for 2 lb 6 oz of the all-purpose flour. Proceed as for Basic Roll Dough.

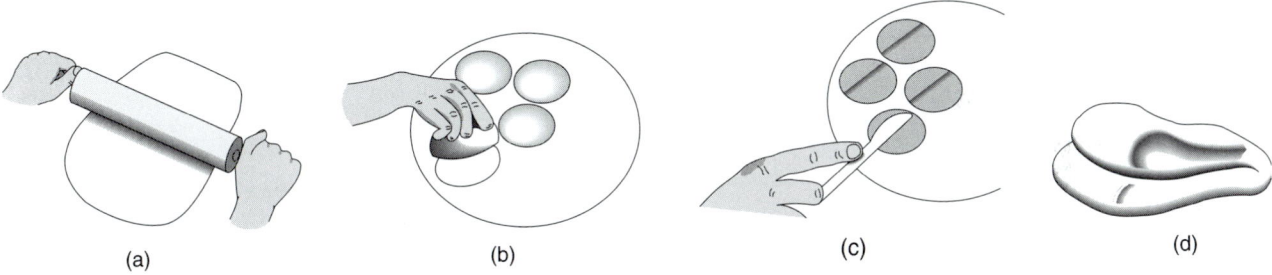

(a)   (b)   (c)   (d)

FIGURE 8.6 Shaping Parker House rolls. (a) Divide dough into thirds. Roll to 1/3 inch thickness and brush with melted margarine. (b) Cut into circles with cutter. (c) Crease rolls with back of a table knife. (d) Fold over and press down on folded edge.

BUTTER BUNS

Yield: 9–10 dozen buns   *Portion:* 1¾ oz
Oven: 400°F   *Bake:* 15–20 minutes

Ingredient	Amount	Procedure
Sugar, granulated Salt Margarine or butter	1 lb 1 oz 1 lb 8 oz	Place sugar, salt, and margarine in mixer bowl.
Milk	3 cups	Scald milk by heating to a point just below boiling. Add to ingredients in mixer bowl and mix. Cool to lukewarm.
Yeast, active dry Water, warm (110°F)	2 oz 1 cup	Soften yeast in warm water.

Eggs
Egg yolks
Lemon extract
  (optional)
	12 (1 lb 5 oz)
	16 (10 oz)
	4 tsp
		Beat eggs and yolks.
		Add eggs, lemon extract, and yeast to milk mixture. Mix
		  until blended.

Flour, all-purpose	4 lb 8 oz	Add flour and mix thoroughly, using dough arm. Let dough rise until double in bulk. Portion with No. 30 dipper into greased muffin pans. Let rise 1 hour. Bake at 400°F for 15–20 minutes.

Approximate nutritive values per portion

Calories 146

Amount/portion	%DV	Amount/portion	%DV	Amount/portion	%DV		%DV		%DV
Total fat 6 g	10%	**Cholest.** 55 mg	18%	**Total Carb.** 18 g	6%	**Vitamin A**	7%	**Calcium**	1%
Sat. Fat 2 g	8%	**Sodium** 164 mg	7%	Fiber 1 g	3%	**Vitamin C**	0%	**Iron**	6%
Protein 4 g				Sugars 4 g					

Percent Daily Values (%DV) are based on a 2000-calorie diet.

Note   • 3 oz nonfat dry milk and 3 cups water may be substituted for the fluid milk. Combine dry milk with flour. Increase margarine to 1 lb 9 oz.

RAISED MUFFINS

Yield: 8 dozen muffins *Portion:* 2 oz
Oven: 350°F *Bake:* 20 minutes

Ingredient	Amount	Procedure
Sugar, granulated Salt Shortening	12 oz 2 oz 9 oz	Place sugar, salt, and shortening in mixer bowl.
Milk	1½ qt	Scald milk by heating to point just below boiling. Add to mixture in mixing bowl. Cool to lukewarm.
Yeast, active dry Water, warm (110°F)	1½ oz 1½ cups	Soften yeast in warm water.
Eggs, beaten	12 (1 lb 5 oz)	Add eggs and softened yeast to milk mixture.
Flour, all-purpose	2 lb	Add flour. Beat on medium speed for 10 minutes, using flat beater. Let rise in warm place for 1½ hours.
Flour, all-purpose	2 lb 12 oz (variable)	Add remaining flour. Beat until batter is smooth. Portion with No. 20 dipper into greased muffin pans. Let rise until double in bulk (about 1 hour). Bake at 350°F for 20 minutes.

Approximate nutritive values per portion   **Calories** 139

Amount/portion	%DV	Amount/portion	%DV	Amount/portion	%DV		%DV		%DV
Total fat 4 g	6%	**Cholest.** 28 mg	10%	**Total Carb.** 22 g	7%	**Vitamin A**	1%	**Calcium**	2%
Sat. Fat 1 g	6%	**Sodium** 245 mg	10%	Fiber 1 g	3%	**Vitamin C**	0%	**Iron**	6%
Protein 4 g				Sugars 5 g					

Percent Daily Values (%DV) are based on a 2000-calorie diet.

Note   ● 6 oz nonfat dry milk and 1½ qt water may be substituted for the fluid milk. Combine dry milk with the first portion of flour.

BASIC SWEET ROLL DOUGH

Yield: 8 dozen rolls   *Portion:* 2 oz
Oven: 375°F   *Bake:* 20–25 minutes

Ingredient	Amount	Procedure
Yeast, active dry	2 oz	Soften yeast in warm water.
Water, warm (110°F)	1½ cups	
Water, hot	3 cups	Combine hot water, dry milk, sugar, shortening, and salt in mixer bowl.
Nonfat dry milk	3 oz	
Sugar, granulated	1 lb	Mix until shortening is softened, using dough arm. Cool to lukewarm.
Shortening	1 lb	
Salt	1¾ oz	
Eggs, beaten	9 (1 lb)	Add eggs and yeast to mixture in bowl. Blend.
Flour, all-purpose	5–6 lb (variable)	Add flour gradually on low speed. Mix on medium speed to a smooth dough, 5–6 minutes. Do not overmix. Dough should be moderately soft.

1. The dough temperature just after mixing should be 78–82°F.
2. Place dough in lightly greased bowl. Grease top of dough, cover, and let rise in warm place until double in bulk, about 2 hours.
3. Punch down and let rise again, about 1 hour.
4. Punch down and divide into portions for rolls. Let rest for 10 minutes.
5. Scale 2 oz per roll. Shape (see Variations) and let rise until rolls are almost double in bulk, about 45 minutes.
6. Bake at 375°F for 20–25 minutes.

Approximate nutritive values per portion   **Calories** 167

Amount/portion	%DV	Amount/portion	%DV	Amount/portion	%DV		%DV		%DV
Total fat 5 g	8%	**Cholest.** 20 mg	7%	**Total Carb.** 25 g	8%	Vitamin A	1%	Calcium	1%
Sat. Fat 1 g	7%	**Sodium** 212 mg	9%	Fiber 1 g	4%	Vitamin C	0%	Iron	7%
Protein 4 g				Sugars 5 g					

Percent Daily Values (%DV) are based on a 2000-calorie diet.

Notes
- Mixing may be simplified by combining dry yeast with sugar, salt, dry milk, and 2 lb of the flour. Mix thoroughly. Combine eggs, very warm water (120°F), and melted shortening. Add yeast-flour mixture on low speed. Add remaining flour gradually, mixing until a smooth, elastic dough is formed.
- 3 cups fluid milk may be used in place of nonfat dry milk and hot water. Scald milk, then add sugar, salt, and shortening, and cool to lukewarm.
- For a quicker rising dough, increase yeast to 3 oz.

Variations
- **Cherry Nut Rolls.** Add 1 tsp nutmeg, ½ tsp almond or lemon extract, 1 lb chopped glacé cherries, and 1 lb chopped pecans to dough. Shape into 1-oz balls. When baked, cover with glaze made of orange juice and powdered sugar.
- **Cinnamon Twists.** Combine 1 lb granulated sugar and 1 Tbsp cinnamon. Melt 4 oz margarine. Dip 2-oz portions of dough into melted margarine, then roll in sugar-cinnamon mixture. Elongate and twist dough portions into 3-inch-long rolls. Place side by side in two 13 × 18-inch baking pans. Bake at 375°F for 20–25 minutes.
- **Coffee Cake.** Scale 4 lb dough and roll out to size of 18 × 26 × 1-inch baking sheet. Cover top of dough with melted margarine or butter and topping (see p. 317). Fruit fillings may be used also.

- **Crullers.** Roll dough ⅓ inch thick. Cut into strips ½ × 8 inches. Bring two ends together and twist dough. Let rise, then fry in deep fat. Ice with Powdered Sugar Glaze (p. 359) or dip in fine granulated sugar.

- **Danish Pastry.** Roll a 5-lb piece of dough into a rectangular shape about ¼ inch thick. Start at one edge and cover completely ⅔ of the dough with small pieces of hard butter, margarine, or special Danish pastry shortening. The latter is stable at bakeshop temperature and is easier to use than butter or margarine. Use 2–5 oz per lb of dough.

  Fold the unbuttered ⅓ portion of dough over an equal portion of buttered dough. Fold the remaining ⅓ buttered dough over the top to make three layers of dough separated by a layer of fat. Roll out dough ¼ inch thick. This completes the first roll. Repeat folding and rolling two or more times. Do not allow the fat to become soft while working with the dough. Let dough rest 45 minutes. Make into desired shapes.

- **Hot Cross Buns.** Add to dough 8 oz chopped glacé cherries, 8 oz raisins, 2 Tbsp cinnamon, ¼ tsp cloves, and ¼ tsp nutmeg. Shape into round buns, 1 oz per bun. When baked, make a cross on top with Powdered Sugar Glaze (p. 359).

- **Kolaches.** Add 2 Tbsp freshly grated lemon peel to dough. Shape dough into 1-oz balls. Place on lightly greased baking sheet. Let rise until light. Press down center to make cavity and fill with 1 tsp filling. Brush with melted margarine or butter and sprinkle with chopped nuts. Suggested fillings: chopped cooked prunes and dried apricots cooked with sugar and cinnamon; poppy seed mixed with sugar and milk; apricot or peach marmalade.

- **Long Johns.** Roll out dough to a thickness of ½ inch. Cut dough into rectangular pieces ½ × 4 inches. Let rise until double in bulk. Fry in deep fat.

- **Swedish Braids.** Add to dough 1 lb chopped candied fruit, 8 oz pecans, and ½ tsp cardamom seed. Weigh dough into 1¾-lb portions and braid. Place on greased 18 × 26 × 1-inch baking sheets, four per pan. When baked, brush with Powdered Sugar Glaze (p. 359) made with milk in place of water.

FRUIT COFFEE RINGS

Yield: 8 rings
Oven: 350°F   *Bake:* 25–30 minutes

Ingredient	Amount	Procedure
Basic Roll Dough (p. 309) or Basic Sweet Roll Dough (p. 314)	10 lb (1 recipe)	Let dough rise until double in bulk. Divide dough into 1½-lb portions. Roll out each portion into a rectangular strip 9 × 14 × ⅓ inches.
Filling (see Suggested Fillings)	2 qt	Spread each strip with 1 cup filling. Roll as for Cinnamon Rolls. Arrange in ring mold or 10-inch tube pan. Cut slashes in dough with scissors about 1 inch apart Let rise until double in bulk. Bake at 350°F for 25–30 minutes. Brush with Powdered Sugar Glaze (p. 359).

Suggested Fillings

- Use 2 qt Apricot Filling (p. 360) or apricot preserves, Fig Filling (p. 360), Prune-Date Filling (p. 360), orange marmalade, or a mixture of 1 lb margarine or butter and 1 lb honey whipped together until light and fluffy. Dough may be shaped in a twist.

CINNAMON ROLLS

Yield: 5 dozen rolls   *Portion:* 3 oz
Oven: 375°F   *Bake:* 20–25 minutes

Ingredient	Amount	Procedure
Basic Roll Dough (p. 309) or Basic Sweet Roll Dough (p. 314)	10 lb (1 recipe)	Let dough rise until double in bulk. Divide dough into eight portions, 1 lb 4 oz each. Roll each portion into rectangular sheet 9 × 14 × ⅓ inches.
Margarine or butter, melted	12 oz	Spread each sheet with melted margarine.
Sugar, granulated Cinnamon, ground	2 lb 1 oz (4 Tbsp)	Combine sugar and cinnamon. Sprinkle 6 oz over each sheet. Roll as for Cinnamon Roll (see Figure 8.7). Cut into 1-inch slices. Place cut side down on greased baking sheets, in muffin pans, or round pans. Let rise until double in bulk, about 45 minutes. Bake at 375°F for 20–25 minutes. After removing from oven, spread tops with Powdered Sugar Glaze (p. 359) made with milk in place of water, Peanut Butter Glaze (p. 358), or Chocolate Glaze (p. 358).

Approximate nutritive values per portion   **Calories** 353

Amount/portion	%DV	Amount/portion	%DV	Amount/portion	%DV		%DV		%DV
Total fat 13 g	20%	**Cholest.** 32 mg	11%	**Total Carb.** 53 g	18%	Vitamin A	4%	Calcium	3%
Sat. Fat 3 g	15%	**Sodium** 393 mg	16%	Fiber 1 g	5%	Vitamin C	0%	Iron	12%
Protein 6 g				Sugars 23 g					

Percent Daily Values (%DV) are based on a 2000-calorie diet.

Note   • 8 oz brown sugar may be substituted for part of granulated sugar.

Variations   • **Butterfly Rolls.** Cut rolled dough into 2-inch slices. Press each roll across center parallel to the cut side, with the back of a large knife handle. Press or flatten out the folds of each end. Place on greased baking sheets 1½ inches apart.

• **Butterscotch Rolls.** Use brown sugar and omit cinnamon, if desired. Cream 8 oz margarine or butter, 1 lb 8 oz brown sugar, and 1 tsp salt. Gradually add 1 cup water, blending thoroughly. Spread 10 oz of mixture over each of four greased 18 × 26 × 1-inch baking sheets or place 1 Tbsp mixture into each greased muffin pan cup. Place rolls cut side down in pans.

FIGURE 8.7 Preparing cinnamon rolls. (a) Roll dough into rectangular sheets, brush with melted margarine or butter, and sprinkle with sugar-cinnamon mixture. (b) Roll up as for jelly roll. (c) Cut into 1-inch slices and place in individual muffin cups or in a pan.

- **Caramel Pecan Rolls.** Melt 12 oz margarine. Add 1 lb chopped pecans, 2 lb 6 oz brown sugar, and 12 oz light corn syrup. Stir to mix. Scale 1 lb 10 oz into each 12 × 18 × 2-inch pan. Place rolls cut side down onto caramel mixture.

- **Cinnamon Raisin Rolls.** Use brown sugar in place of granulated sugar and add 8 oz raisins to filling.

- **Double Cinnamon Buns.** Proceed as for Butterfly Rolls. Roll sheet of dough from both sides to form a double roll.

- **Glazed Marmalade Rolls.** Omit cinnamon. Dip cut slices in additional melted margarine or butter and granulated sugar. When baked, glaze with orange marmalade mixed with powdered sugar until of a consistency to spread. Apricot marmalade, strawberry jam, or other preserves may be used for the glaze.

- **Honey Rolls.** Substitute honey filling for sugar and cinnamon. Whip 1 lb margarine or butter and 1 lb honey until light and fluffy.

- **Jumbo Cinnamon Rolls.** Use 24 lb dough, 3 lb granulated sugar mixed with 5 Tbsp cinnamon, and 1 lb margarine or butter. Divide dough into four 6-lb portions. Roll each portion into approximately a 26 × 26-inch square. Spread with 4 oz softened margarine and sprinkle with 1½ cups sugar-cinnamon mixture. Roll into a 26-inch-long roll. Cut into 12 slices 2 inches thick. Pan 2 × 4 in 12 × 18-inch baking pans. Proof until double in bulk. Bake at 350°F for 25 minutes or until done. Ice with Powdered Sugar Glaze (p. 359).

- **Orange Rolls.** Omit cinnamon. Spread with mixture of 1 lb 8 oz granulated sugar and 1 cup fresh grated orange peel. When baked, brush with a glaze made of powdered sugar and orange juice. If desired, use a filling made by creaming 1 lb margarine or butter, 2 Tbsp fresh grated orange peel, 2 lb granulated sugar, and ¾ cup undiluted frozen orange juice concentrate. Spread on dough.

- **Pecan Rolls.** Coarsely chop 1 lb 8 oz pecans. Sprinkle 8 oz over bottom of each of three 12 × 18 × 2-inch baking pans. Combine 2 lb margarine or butter, 2 Tbsp cinnamon, ⅓ cup corn syrup, ⅓ cup water, and 2 lb 8 oz brown sugar. Cook over medium heat until margarine melts. Pour over chopped nuts, 1 lb 12 oz per pan. Place rolls cut side down on mixture.

- **Sugared Snails.** Proceed as for Butterfly Rolls, rolling dough thinner before adding sugar filling. Cut rolled dough into slices ¾ inch thick. Dip cut surface of each roll in granulated sugar. Place on greased baking sheets ½ inch apart, with sugared side up. Allow to stand 10–15 minutes, then flatten before baking.

FILLINGS OR TOPPINGS FOR COFFEE CAKE AND SWEET ROLLS

1. *Almond Filling.* Mix 1 lb almond paste, 1 lb granulated sugar, 12 oz margarine or butter, and 4 oz flour. Add 2 eggs and beat until smooth.

2. *Butter Cinnamon Topping.* Cream 8 oz margarine or butter, 1 lb granulated sugar, 3 Tbsp cinnamon, and 1/2 tsp salt. Add 4 beaten eggs and 3 oz flour and blend.

3. *Butter Crunch Topping.* Blend 1 lb granulated sugar, 1 lb margarine or butter, 1/2 tsp salt, 3 oz honey, and 2 lb flour together to form a crumbly mixture.

4. *Crumb Topping.* Mix 8 oz margarine or butter, 12 oz granulated sugar, 1/2 tsp cinnamon, and 12 oz flour until crumbly. Add 4 oz chopped nuts if desired.

CHAPTER 9

Desserts

David King © Dorling Kindersley

CAKES AND ICINGS

Cakes may be classified according to two major types: butter or shortened cakes and foam or sponge cakes. Butter cakes contain butter, margarine, or other shortening and usually are leavened with baking powder or with baking soda and an acid. True sponge cakes are leavened chiefly by air incorporated into beaten eggs, although modified sponge cakes may have baking powder added.

A properly balanced formula, correct temperature of ingredients, accurate measurements, controlled mixing of ingredients, proper relationship of batter to pan, and correct oven temperature and baking time are essential to good cake making. Cake flour yields better volume and finer texture than all-purpose flour and was used in testing recipes in this section, unless otherwise specified. If all-purpose flour is used, see Table 2.6 for substitution guidelines.

Methods of Mixing Butter or Shortened Cakes

For all methods of mixing, weigh or measure ingredients accurately and have them at room temperature (75–80°F).

Conventional Method

1. Cream shortening and sugar on medium speed, using flat beater, for about 10 minutes or until light and fluffy.

2. Add eggs and beat 3–5 minutes on high speed. Stop mixer and scrape sides and bottom of bowl and beater. Removing the beater to make sure bottom of bowl is scraped is recommended.

3. Combine flour, leavening, and other dry ingredients. Add alternately with the liquid to the creamed mixture.

4. Mix on low speed until thoroughly blended. Scrape sides of bowl and beater occasionally for even mixing.

Dough-Batter Method

1. Cream flour, baking powder, and shortening on low speed for 2 minutes, using flat beater. Scrape sides of bowl and beater. Mix for 3 minutes.

2. Add sugar, salt, and half the milk. Mix 2 minutes. Scrape bowl and beater. Mix 3 minutes.

3. Combine egg, flavoring, and remaining milk. Add half to flour mixture. Mix 30 seconds. Scrape bowl and beater. Mix 1 minute.

4. Add remaining egg mixture. Mix 1 minute. Scrape bowl and beater. Mix 2½ minutes.

This method requires less time and fewer utensils than the conventional method and yields a good product. See p. 333 for White Cake made by the dough-batter method.

Dry Blending and Wetting Method

1. Blend dry ingredients in mixer bowl and mix on low speed for 1 minute, using flat beater.

2. Add 60 percent of the water to the dry ingredients. Mix slightly; flour is not completely hydrated.

3. Add fat and mix on low speed for 1 minute, then on medium speed for 4 minutes.

4. Add 10 percent of the water. Mix 1 minute on low speed, then 3 minutes on medium speed.

5. Add remainder of water (30 percent), eggs, and flavoring. Mix 3 minutes on low speed.

This method of mixing produces a cake with good volume and fine texture. Converting water from weight to liquid measurements may produce awkward numbers. A small adjustment of the three liquid additions may need to be made for easy measurement, but the total weight of water should be the same as the amount specified in the recipe. See p. 332 for White Cake made by the dry blending and wetting method of mixing.

Muffin Method

1. Mix dry ingredients, including dry milk if used, in a mixer bowl.

2. Combine liquids (beaten eggs, milk or water, and melted shortening or oil).

3. Add liquids all at once to dry ingredients. Mix at low speed only enough to combine ingredients.

This method is quick and most successful when the cake is used soon after baking.

Methods of Mixing Foam or Sponge Cakes

Angel Food Cakes

1. Sift the flour with part of the sugar. This step helps the flour mix more evenly with the foam.

2. Beat the egg whites, using the whip attachment, until they form soft peaks. Egg whites should be at room temperature and all utensils used for whipping must be dry and free from fat or grease. Salt and cream of tartar are added near the beginning of the beating process.

3. Gradually beat in the sugar that was not mixed with the flour. Continue to beat until the egg whites form stiff, glossy peaks. Do not overbeat.

4. Fold in the flour/sugar mixture carefully to minimize loss of air from the foam. Fold until it is absorbed, but no longer.

5. Place in ungreased tube, loaf, or sheet pans and bake immediately.

Sponge Cakes

All egg-foam cakes are similar in that they contain little or no shortening and depend for most or all of their leavening on the air trapped in beaten eggs. However, the whole-egg foams and egg-yolk foams are handled differently from those made with egg whites alone. In sponge cakes, the sugar and liquid are added to the eggs or egg yolks and beaten until light. Dry ingredients are folded in. Chiffon cakes contain baking powder, which is mixed with the flour, and a small amount of fat in the form of vegetable oil that is added to the egg yolks and liquid. The beaten egg whites are folded into the batter.

Cake Mixes

Prepared cake mixes offer the foodservice a wide variety of products that can be produced with fewer and less-skilled employees than cakes prepared from scratch. However, care should be given to the selection of the mix, and the instructions for preparation should be followed carefully to ensure high-quality products. The formulas in commercial mixes are balanced, and deviations such as the substitution of milk for water or the addition of eggs may change the finished product.

Scaling Batter

Pan Preparation

Prepare pans before mixing cake batters, so that cakes can be baked without delay as soon as they are mixed.

1. For butter cakes, grease pans and line with parchment cake liners or grease and dust with flour. For best results, use a solid shortening. Oil will cause the cake to stick to the pan. A commercial vegetable spray may be used, or a coating mixture may be prepared and brushed on the pans (p. 328). Sides of the pan should be left ungreased unless cakes are to be removed from the pan for layers.

2. For angel food cakes and other foam cakes, do not grease the pan. The batter must be able to cling to the sides to rise.

Scaling

Butter or other shortened cakes usually are baked as sheet cakes for ease of preparation and serving but may be baked in layers or as cupcakes. Layer cakes may be made by cutting 18 × 26-inch sheet cakes in half or layering two 13 × 18-inch sheet cakes. (See Figure 9.1 for layering and icing a sheet cake.)

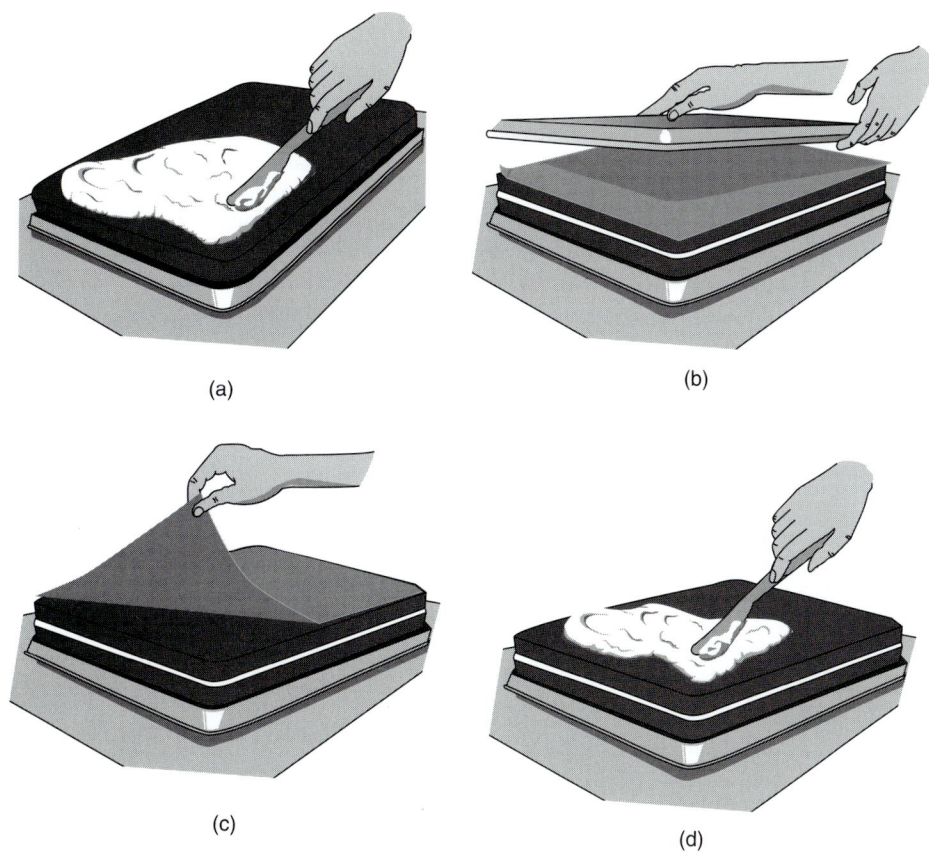

(a)

(b)

(c)

(d)

FIGURE 9.1   Layering and icing a sheet cake. (a) Remove sheet cake from pan after loosening sides. Place top side down on inverted baking sheet. Spread icing evenly over cake. (b) Carefully turn second cake onto iced layer. (c) Remove cake liner if used. (d) Ice top and sides of cake.

The correct amount of cake batter per pan is important in producing a cake with consistently high quality and volume. Table 9.1 gives approximate weights of batter for selected pan sizes. The proper scaling weight for different batters, however, can be determined by actual baking tests and experimentation. Once it has been determined, scaling weights for all pan sizes using the same batter can be calculated mathematically. The formula follows.

Step 1   Experiment, using any pan, to determine the proper scaling weight.

Step 2   Determine the volume of the pan used, expressed as cubic inches.

$$\text{square or rectangular pan volume} = \text{length} \times \text{width} \times \text{height}$$

$$\text{round pan volume} = 3.14 \times \text{radius squared} \times \text{height}$$

Step 3   Determine the cubic inches per ounce of batter (factor) by dividing the cubic inches (as found in Step 2) by the ounces of batter determined to be correct by experimentation in Step 1.

$$\text{factor} = \frac{\text{cubic inches in pan}}{\text{correct scaling weight per pan}}$$

Step 4   Find the proper scaling weight of the particular batter calculated for any pan by dividing the known factor into the pan volume.

$$\frac{\text{volume of cake pan to be used}}{\text{factor}} = \frac{\text{proper scaling}}{\text{weight of batter}}$$

The following example illustrates the procedure for calculating proper scaling weight for a cake. The proper scaling weight of a 6 × 1½-inch round chocolate cake was determined to be 8 ounces. What would be the scaling weight for the same batter in a 10 × 1½-inch round pan?

Step 1   Through experimentation, it was determined that 8 oz in a 6 × 1½-inch pan was correct.

Step 2   Volume = $3.14 \times 3^2 \times 1.5 = 42$ cubic inches

TABLE 9.1   Approximate scaling weights and yields for cakes

Pan size	Approximate weight per pan	Yield	Type of cake
12 × 18 × 2 inches	4–5 lb	30 portions (5 × 6) 32 portions (4 × 8)	Butter, sheet
13 × 18 × 1 inches (half-size baking sheet)	2–2½ lb	48 portions (6 × 8)	Butter, layer
18 × 26 × 2 inches	8–10 lb	60 portions (6 × 10) 64 portions (8 × 8)	Butter, sheet
8-inch round	16–20 oz per layer	16 portions (2 layers)	Butter, layer
9-inch round	20–24 oz per layer	16 portions (2 layers)	Butter, layer
10-inch tube	28–40 oz	14–16 portions	Foam, sponge
Cupcakes	1¾ oz each		Butter

Notes: • See p. 323 for scaling weights for icings and fillings.

Step 3   42 cubic inches ÷ 8 ounces = 5.25 cubic inches per ounce = factor

Step 4   10-inch pan volume = $3.14 \times 5^2 \times 1.5 = 118$ cubic inches. 118 cubic inches ÷ 5.25 (factor) = 22.5 ounces scaling weight

Baking

Cake structure is fragile, so proper baking conditions are essential for quality products. The following are guidelines for producing quality cakes.

1. Preheat the oven.

2. Make sure oven and shelves are level.

3. Make sure batter is level in the pan and pan is filled in corners.

4. Do not let pans touch each other in the oven. If pans touch, air circulation is inhibited and the cakes rise unevenly.

5. Bake at correct temperature. A too high temperature can cause tunneling in the cakes, cakes with a cracked top crust, or excessively high peaks. A too low oven temperature can cause a pale top crust, a sticky top crust, or low volume.

6. Do not open ovens or disturb cakes until they have finished rising and are partially browned. In a convection oven, sheet cakes should be turned halfway through the baking time to ensure uniform baking and symmetry.

7. Test for doneness. Cakes are fully baked when cake center springs back when touched lightly. A cake tester inserted near the center of the cake will come out clean. Shortened cakes will shrink away from sides of pan slightly.

Cooling and Removing from Pans

1. Cool butter layer cakes 10–15 minutes before removing from pans. Cool cakes completely before icing.

2. Sheet cakes may be left in the pans and iced when cool or removed from the pan and layered (Figure 9.1).

3. Invert pans of angel food cakes or sponge cakes and cool completely. Be sure the edges of the pan are supported so that the top of the cake does not rest on the table. When cool, loosen cake from sides of pan with spatula or knife and pull out carefully.

Icings and Fillings

The presentation of cakes may be varied by the use of different icings and fillings. The amount to use will depend on the kind of cake to be iced and the individual preference of the patrons. Table 9.2 may serve as a guide. Sheet cakes usually are iced in their baking pans. Layered sheet cakes should be removed from the pans before icing (Figure 9.1). If possible, cakes should be iced as soon as they have cooled to help prevent drying. If uniced cakes will not be used within a short time, they should be covered and kept in a closed cabinet or freezer. To freeze cakes, cover with plastic wrap or put in an airtight container. It is best to freeze cakes uniced. Figure 9.2 suggests cutting configurations for cakes.

TABLE 9.2 Approximate scaling weights for icings and fillings

Pan size	Approximate weight per pan
13 × 18 × 2 inch	1 lb 8 oz (3 cups)
18 × 26 × 2 inch	3 lb (1½ qt)
9-inch layer	1 lb (2 cups)
	⅔ cup in the middle
	1¼ cups top and sides
10-inch tube	12 oz (1½ cups)

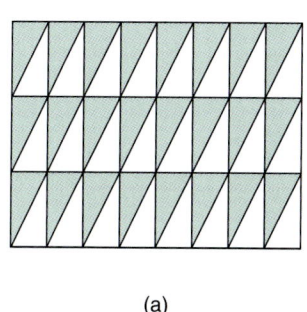

(a)

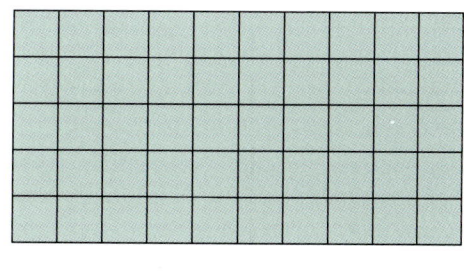

(b)

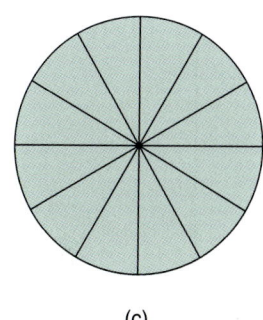

(c)

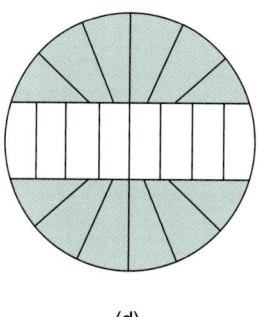

(d)

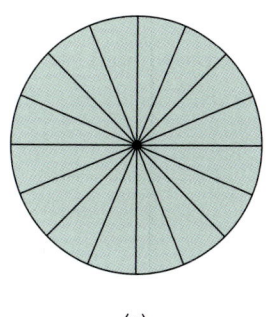

(e)

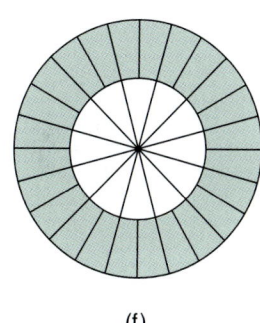

(f)

FIGURE 9.2 Suggested cutting configurations for cakes. (a) 18 × 26-inch baking sheet, 48 portions; (b) 18 × 26-inch baking sheet, 50 portions; (c) 8- to 12-inch round, 12 portions; (d) 10- to 12-inch round, 20 portions; (e) 8- to 12-inch round, 16 portions; (f) 10- to 12-inch round, 36 portions.

QUALITY STANDARDS FOR CAKES

Quality standards for butter cakes: Smooth surface, slightly rounded top, high volume; fine-grained, small, evenly distributed cell walls, light but not crumbly; soft texture, velvety, moist, light, tender crumb; delicate, sweet, well-blended flavor. Cakes other than chocolate should be a golden brown color.

Deviation	Possible Cause
Peaked or cracked	Too much flour, too little liquid, overmixing, oven temperature too high
Flat top	Oven temperature too low (Some cakes used for layering are formulated for a flat top.)
Pale color	Too little sugar, too much liquid, wrong type pan, underbaking, oven temperature too low
Too dark color	Too much sugar, oven temperature too high, overbaking
Low volume	Too much shortening, too much liquid, insufficient leavening, undermixing, wrong size pan, too long standing time before baking or holding too long in a warm room, oven temperature too high
Large cells	Too little liquid, too much shortening, under- or overmixing, oven temperature too low
Compact texture	Overbeating
Crumbly texture	Too much shortening or sugar, too little liquid, insufficient mixing
Tunnels	Too much egg, too little sugar, overmixing, oven temperature too high, excessive bottom heat
Dry	Too little sugar, too much leavening, overbaking
Soggy	Too much shortening, undermixing, underbaking, improper cooling before covering
Tough	Too much shortening, protein content of flour too high, improper balance of ingredients, overmixing, overbaking, oven temperature too high
Unpleasant flavor	Flat, too little salt, rancid fat
Shrinkage	Oven temperature too low, overbaking

Quality standards for angel, sponge, or chiffon cakes: Thin, golden brown crust, rounded top, slightly split in the middle; fine texture, with thin cell walls, light in weight in proportion to size; moist, tender crumb; delicate flavor.

Deviation	Possible Cause
Thick, hard crust	Oven temperature too low, overbaked
Sticky crust	Too much sugar, insufficient baking
Large cracks	Mixture too stiff, overbeating eggs, oven temperature too high
Undersized, heavy	Grease on equipment or bowl, overbeating or underbeating egg whites, overmixing, improper balance of ingredients, oven temperature too high, cakes removed from pan too soon after baking, underbaking
Dry	Overbeating egg whites, too much flour, too little sugar, overbaking, oven temperature too low
Tough	Oven temperature too high, overmixing, sugar content too high, too much flour or wrong type used
Coarse	Overbeating egg whites, insufficient mixing, oven temperature too low

COOKIES

Cookies are made in a variety of shapes, sizes, and textures. They may be crisp, soft, or chewy, depending on the proportion of ingredients, the method of mixing, and the baking time and temperature.

Proportion of Ingredients

Crisp cookies generally have a low proportion of liquid and a high sugar and fat content. Soft cookies have a high proportion of liquid and are lower in fat and sugar. Chewy cookies have high sugar and liquid content but are low in fat and have a high proportion of eggs. Some cookies are best when the dough spreads some during baking, while others must hold their shape. A high sugar or liquid content may increase cookie spread during baking.

Methods of Mixing

Most cookies are prepared by one of the following methods:

Creaming method—Cream shortening, sugar, and flavorings at low speed until blended. The amount of creaming can affect the texture of the cookies. A short creaming time is used for a chewy cookie; for a cookie with cake-like texture, the shortening and sugar are creamed until light and fluffy. The amount of creaming may also affect the spread of the cookie while it is baking. After the creaming is completed, blend in the eggs and liquid, then the flour and leavening. Mix the dough only until ingredients are combined.

One-stage method—Place all ingredients in the mixer and mix at low speed until blended.

Sponge method—Beat eggs (white, yolks, or whole) until light. Add the remaining ingredients and blend, being careful not to overmix or deflate the eggs.

Shaping

Drop cookies are made from a soft dough, which is portioned onto prepared baking sheets with a dipper. A No. 40 dipper, which was used for most of the recipes in this book, makes a medium-size cookie, approximately 2½–3 inches in diameter and weighing about ¾ ounce. Larger cookies may be made by using a No. 20 or No. 30 dipper, while Nos. 60 or 70 make tea cookies. If using the recipe for larger or smaller cookies, the yield may need to be adjusted by using the procedure on p. 45.

Bar cookies are made from a soft dough or batter that is spread evenly on prepared baking pans. Most recipes in this section suggest using two 13 × 18 × 1-inch pans (half baking sheet) or one 18 × 26 × 1-inch pan (baking sheet). The 13 × 18-inch pan will yield 30 2½ × 3-inch bars by cutting 5 × 6. An 18 × 26-inch pan may be cut 6 × 10 to yield 60 bars 3 × 2½ inches or 8 × 12 for 96 cookies.

Rolled cookies are made from a stiff dough that has been chilled thoroughly. The dough is rolled out to ⅛–inch thickness on a lightly floured board and cut with a cookie cutter.

Refrigerator cookies are made by shaping dough into rolls of uniform size (1–2 inches in diameter) and chilling, then cutting into slices. Using a slicing machine ensures uniform thickness. The dough may be made into rolls, wrapped in waxed or parchment paper, refrigerated or frozen, and baked as needed.

Molded or pressed cookies are made by shaping dough into small balls, which are then flattened by pressing with a mold or other flat utensil dipped in sugar. Cookies may be shaped also with a cookie press or, if using a soft dough, with a pastry bag.

Baking

Pans are prepared by lightly greasing or lining with baking pan liners. A heavily greased pan increases the spread of the cookie. Some high-fat cookies can be baked on ungreased pans. Most cookies are baked at a relatively high temperature. A too low temperature increases spreading and may produce dry, pale cookies. A too high temperature decreases spreading and may burn the edges or bottoms.

Cookies should be watched carefully to prevent overbaking or burning. To test for doneness, touch the center of the cookie lightly with a finger. If almost no imprint remains and the cookie is browned, it is done. Fudge-type bars will be done when the top has a dull crust; and cake-like bars, when a pick inserted in the center comes out clean. Soft cookies should be removed from the oven when they are still soft to the touch.

In most cases, to prevent sticking, the cookies should be removed from pans while they are still warm. If baking pan liners are used, the cookies may be left on the pan to cool. Very soft cookies, however, should not be removed until they are cool and firm enough to handle. Cookies should be completely cooled before storing.

Storing

Proper storage is important to maintain the quality and freshness of cookies. Crisp cookies may become soft if they absorb moisture, so they should be stored loosely covered away from moisture. Soft cookies should be stored tightly covered because they will become dry if allowed to lose moisture. All cookies are best if served soon after baking.

QUALITY STANDARDS FOR COOKIES

Quality standards for drop cookies: Uniform shape and color; good flavor; crisp or chewy texture (true to type of cookie).

Deviation	Possible Cause
Misshapen	Improper dropping of dough, oven temperature too high or too low, improper mixing
Excessive spreading	Too much liquid, too much fat and sugar, liquid fat substituted for solid fat, overcreaming, dough too warm, incorrect oven temperature, not peaked when dropped, cookies panned too close together
Dry, crumbly texture	Incorrect proportion of ingredients, inaccurate measuring, poor mixing or baking techniques, incorrect oven temperature

Quality standards for bar cookies: Uniform, well-cut shape; rich, moist eating quality; thin, delicate crust; appealing flavor.

Deviation	Possible Cause
Crumbles when cut	Cut while too warm
Dry, crumbly texture	Overbaking, improper proportion of ingredients
Hard, crusty top	Overmixed, overbaked

Quality standards for rolled cookies: Retain shape of cutter; lightly browned surface; crisp or soft texture, depending on thickness.

Deviation	Possible Cause
Tough	Excessive rerolling
Dry	Rolling in too much flour or rerolling

Quality standards for pressed and molded cookies: Well-defined pattern and shape; tender, crisp texture; rich, buttery flavor; delicately browned color.

Deviation	Possible Cause
Misshapen	Improper use of cookie press or poor molding, dough too cold or too warm, dough placed on hot baking sheet, oven temperature too low
Crumbly, dry	Incorrect proportion of ingredients, insufficient shaping

Quality standards for refrigerator cookies: Uniform thin slices, lightly browned surface, crisp and crunchy texture, rich flavor.

Deviation	Possible Cause
Irregular shape	Improper molding of dough roll, dough not chilled before slicing, improper slicing technique
Too soft	Cut too thick

QUALITY STANDARDS FOR PASTRY

Quality standards: Golden brown color, blistery surface, uniform, attractive edges, fits pan well; flaky or mealy texture, cuts easily, pleasant bland flavor.

Deviation	*Possible Cause*
Smooth surface	Overhandling, too much flour when rolling
Shrunken	Stretched crust when easing into pan, overmixing, protein content of flour too high, too much water
Tough	Too much water, overmixing, overhandling, protein content of flour too high
Not flaky	Temperature of dough too high, shortening too soft, overmixing
Too tender	Undermixing, not enough liquid, too much shortening
Soggy bottom crust	Baked too short a time, too much fat in crust, oven temperature too low or not enough bottom heat, using a filling that is too hot
Compact	Underbaking, too much liquid
Dry	Shortening cut in too finely, not enough liquid

PIES

A good pie has a tender crust that cuts easily and a filling that will hold its shape when cut. Pie crust is an uncomplicated mixture, consisting of four ingredients: flour, shortening, water, and salt. The quality of the crust depends on the mixing technique as well as the type and proportion of ingredients.

Ingredients

Tenderness depends largely on the kind of flour, the amount of fat and water used, and the amount of mixing. Choice of flour is important in pastry making. Gluten is developed from the protein present in wheat flours and gives structure and strength to baked goods. Pastry flour, which is made from soft wheat, has enough protein to produce the desired structure and flakiness, yet is low enough in protein to yield a tender product if handled properly. All-purpose flour, which is a blend of soft and hard wheats, contains enough protein to provide the gluten essential to make good pastry and is the type of flour used in recipes in this book.

Regular hydrogenated shortening is the fat used most often for pie crusts because it has the right plasticity to produce a flaky crust. It is firm and moldable enough to make a workable dough. The tenderness of pastry increases with the proportion of fat, but excess fat may cause the crust to be too tender to remove from

the pan. Shortening should be cool when added to the flour. If it is warm, it blends too quickly with the flour.

Addition of a liquid, generally water, develops some gluten in the flour and gives structure and flakiness to the dough. Excess water gives a less tender product, but if not enough water is used, the crust will not hold together. The water should be cold (35–40°F) when added to the flour/fat mixture.

Salt, which is added mainly for flavor, is dissolved in the water before adding to the mix in order to ensure even distribution.

Mixing

Pastry is mixed by cutting the fat into the flour, then adding water and salt. The type of crust produced is partially determined by the method of combining the fat and flour. For a *flaky* crust, the fat and flour are mixed until small lumps are formed throughout the mixture. A *mealy* crust results when the fat and flour are thoroughly mixed until the mixture resembles cornmeal. Overmixing after the water has been added or using too much flour when rolling toughens pastry.

Pie dough should be kept cool during mixing and makeup. Chilling the dough for several hours, or until 50–60°F, allows the water to become distributed better throughout the dough and hardens the shortening so that it is less likely to soften during handling and shaping operations.

A pie crust mix, made by cutting the fat into the flour and salt mixture, may be stored in the refrigerator for 4–6 weeks and used as needed by adding water to make fresh pie crusts. If freezer storage is adequate, crusts may be made and frozen unbaked until needed.

OTHER DESSERTS

Although cakes, cookies, and pies remain popular, today's foodservices offer a wide variety of other desserts, such as fruit cobblers and crisps, cheesecake, frozen yogurt and ice cream, and fresh fruits in a variety of presentations. Recipes for many of these desserts are included in this section, as are the time-tested custards and other puddings, gelatin desserts, and refrigerator desserts used in many foodservices.

Basic custard consists of milk, sugar, eggs, and flavoring and may be of two types. Soft or stirred custard is cooked slowly over low heat, while stirring, until it is slightly thickened. It remains pourable when cooked. Baked custard, which is not stirred, is baked until it sets and becomes firm. Custards should be cooked to an internal temperature of 181–185°F. If heated beyond this point, the custard may curdle and become watery. Cooking baked custards in a water bath, in which the custard cups or baking pan are placed in a pan of hot water, helps prevent curdling.

Cream puddings contain starch thickeners and eggs, resulting in a thicker, more stable product. The thickener may be cornstarch, flour, tapioca, or a cereal product. These desserts require sweetening, usually sugar. Too much sugar interferes with the thickening of the eggs and the starch; therefore, a properly balanced formula is important. To make a cream pudding, the milk is added slowly to the combined dry ingredients, while stirring with a wire whip. The mixture is stirred occasionally and cooked until thickened in a steam-jacketed or other kettle over low heat to prevent scorching. The method of adding the eggs is also important to a smooth pudding. To avoid curdling when the eggs are added, a small amount of the hot mixture is first added to the beaten eggs, then this mixture is stirred into the rest of the pudding. Cream puddings should be smooth and creamy.

Gelatin desserts, usually in the form of a fruit gelatin or Bavarian cream, are served as dessert choices in many institutions. A basic recipe for Fruit Gelatin Salad on p. 667 gives proportions for gelatin and fruit and instructions for preparing gelatin mixtures. Bavarian cream has whipped cream folded in.

Fruit offers a wide range of dessert possibilities and may be served fresh, poached, baked, as a sauce, or combined with other ingredients to make a baked dessert such as strawberry shortcake, fruit cobbler, or fruit crisp. A fresh-fruit and cheese plate, with in-season fresh fruit and cheese attractively displayed, is a popular dessert. Suggestions for a fruit and cheese dessert are given on p. 436.

CAKE RECIPES

COATING FOR BAKING PANS

Yield: 2 lb 12 oz

Ingredient	Amount	Procedure
Shortening	1 lb	Mix shortening until creamy.
Flour, all-purpose	12 oz	Add flour gradually, whipping until smooth. Start on low mixer speed, then move to medium.
Vegetable oil	2 cups	Add oil very slowly and whip until light and frothy. Store at room temperature in tightly closed containers. Apply to pans with pastry brush. Use to grease cake pans or cookie sheets.

ANGEL FOOD CAKE

Yield: 42 portions or 3 10-inch cakes   *Portion:* 14 slices per cake
Oven: 350°F   *Bake:* 50–55 minutes

Ingredient	*Amount*	*Procedure*
Egg whites, fresh or frozen	2 lb 8 oz (5 cups)	Beat egg whites on high speed for 1 minute, using whip attachment. Be sure utensils are free from grease.
Salt Cream of tartar	1 tsp 2 Tbsp	Add salt and cream of tartar. Continue beating until egg whites are just stiff enough to hold their shape.
Sugar, granulated	1 lb 8 oz	Add sugar slowly while beating on medium speed.
Vanilla Almond extract (optional)	1 Tbsp 1 tsp	Add flavorings. Continue beating on high speed for 2 minutes, or until mixture will stand in stiff peaks.
Sugar, granulated Flour, cake	12 oz 12 oz	Mix sugar and flour. Sift three times. Gradually add to egg . whites on low speed Continue folding 2 minutes after last addition. Scale into three ungreased tube cake pans, 1 lb 12 oz per pan. Bake at 350°F for 50–55 minutes or at 400°F for 35 minutes. Invert cakes to cool.

Approximate nutritive values per portion   **Calories** 138

Amount/portion	%DV	Amount/portion	%DV	Amount/portion	%DV		%DV		%DV
Total Fat 0 g	0%	**Cholest.** 0 mg	0%	**Total Carb.** 31 g	10%	**Vitamin A**	0%	**Calcium**	0%
Sat. Fat 0 g	0%	**Sodium** 96 mg	4%	Fiber 0 g	0%	**Vitamin C**	0%	**Iron**	3%
Protein 4 g				Sugars 24 g					

Percent Daily Values (%DV) are based on a 2000-calorie diet.

Note
- To add sugar-flour mixture by hand, remove bowl from machine and fold mixture into meringue, using wire whip or spatula, adding 1 cup at a time. Mix about five strokes after each addition.

Variations
- **Chocolate Angel Food Cake.** Substitute 1½ oz cocoa for 1½ oz flour.

- **Frozen-Filled Angel Food Cake.** Cut each cake crosswise into three slices. Spread 1 pt softened strawberry ice cream on first layer and cover with cake slice. Spread second slice with 1 pt softened pistachio ice cream. Top with remaining slice. Frost top and sides with sweetened whipped cream (1 cup cream, 2 Tbsp powdered sugar, and ½ tsp vanilla per cake). Cover with toasted coconut. Freeze. Remove from freezer 1 hour before serving. Other ice cream or sherbet may be used.

- **Orange-Filled Angel Food Cake.** Cut each cake crosswise into three slices. Spread Orange Filling (p. 362) between layers, and ice top and sides with Orange Butter Icing (p. 355).

YELLOW ANGEL FOOD (SPONGE) CAKE

Yield: 42 portions or 3 10-inch cakes   *Portion:* 14 slices per cake
Oven: 350°F   *Bake:* 30–45 minutes

Ingredient	Amount	Procedure
Egg yolks	1 lb 8 oz (3 cups)	Beat egg yolks on medium speed, using whip attachment.
Water, boiling	2 cups	Add water to egg yolks. Beat on high speed until light, about 5 minutes.
Sugar, granulated	1 lb	Sift sugar. Add to egg mixture gradually, beating on high speed while adding.
Flour, cake Sugar, granulated	12 oz 12 oz	Combine flour and sugar. Add on low speed to egg mixture.
Flour, cake Baking powder Salt	10 oz 4½ tsp 1 tsp	Mix flour, baking powder, and salt.
Lemon juice Fresh lemon peel, grated	3 Tbsp 1 Tbsp	On low speed, gradually add flour alternately with lemon juice and peel to egg mixture.
Vanilla Lemon extract	1 Tbsp 1½ tsp	Add flavoring and continue mixing on low speed for 2 minutes.
		Scale into three ungreased tube cake pans, 1 lb 14 oz per pan. Bake at 350°F for 30–45 minutes. Immediately upon removal from oven, invert cakes to cool.

Approximate nutritive values per portion   **Calories** 186

Amount/portion	%DV	Amount/portion	%DV	Amount/portion	%DV		%DV		%DV
Total Fat 5 g	8%	**Cholest.** 208 mg	69%	**Total Carb.** 31 g	10%	Vitamin A	31%	Calcium	4%
Sat. Fat 2 g	8%	**Sodium** 90 mg	4%	Fiber 0 g	0%	Vitamin C	0%	Iron	9%
Protein 4 g				Sugars 19 g					

Percent Daily Values (%DV) are based on a 2000-calorie diet.

ORANGE CHIFFON CAKE

Yield: 42 portions or 3 10-inch cakes   *Portion:* 14 slices per cake
Oven: 350°F   *Bake:* 45–50 minutes

Ingredient	Amount	Procedure
Flour, cake Baking powder Salt Sugar, granulated	1 lb 8 oz 1½ oz (3 Tbsp) 2 tsp 1 lb 3 oz	Combine dry ingredients in mixer bowl. Mix on low speed for about 10 seconds, or until blended, using flat beater.
Egg yolks, beaten Vegetable oil Water	1 lb (2 cups) 1½ cups 1½ cups	Combine egg yolks, salad oil, and water. Add to dry ingredients. Mix on medium speed until smooth.
Orange juice Orange peel, grated	1 cup 2 Tbsp	Add orange juice and peel gradually. Mix well after each addition, but avoid overmixing.
Egg whites Cream of tartar	1 lb 4 oz (2½ cups) 2 tsp	Whip egg whites until foamy. Add cream of tartar and continue beating until egg whites form soft peaks.
Sugar, granulated	1 lb 2 oz	Add sugar gradually and continue beating until very stiff. Fold gently into batter. Scale into three ungreased tube cake pans, 2 lb 12 oz per pan. Bake at 350°F for 45–50 minutes. Immediately on removal from oven, invert cakes to cool.
Orange Butter Icing (p. 355)	1½ qt	When cake has cooled, remove from pan and ice.

Approximate nutritive values per portion   **Calories** 418

Amount/portion	%DV	Amount/portion	%DV	Amount/portion	%DV		%DV		%DV
Total Fat 16 g	24%	**Cholest.** 139 mg	46%	**Total Carb.** 66 g	22%	**Vitamin A**	22%	**Calcium**	6%
Sat. Fat 4 g	20%	**Sodium** 268 mg	11%	Fiber 0 g	0%	**Vitamin C**	5%	**Iron**	9%
Protein 5 g				Sugars 50 g					

Percent Daily Values (%DV) are based on a 2000-calorie diet.

Variations
- **Cocoa Chiffon Cake.** Omit orange juice and peel. Add 5 oz cocoa to dry ingredients. Increase water to 2⅓ cups. Add 1 Tbsp vanilla.
- **Walnut Chiffon Cake.** Omit orange juice and peel. Increase water to 2⅓ cups. Add 2 Tbsp vanilla and 12 oz finely chopped walnuts. Ice with Burnt Butter Icing (p. 352).

WHITE CAKE (DRY BLENDING METHOD)

Yield: 60 portions or 2 pans 12 × 18 × 2 inches   *Portion:* 2½ × 3 inches
Oven: 350°F   *Bake:* 25–30 minutes

Ingredient	Amount	Procedure
Flour, cake	1 lb 13 oz	Combine dry ingredients in mixer bowl. Mix on low speed for 1 minute.
Sugar, granulated	2 lb 5 oz	
Nonfat dry milk	3 oz	
Salt	4 tsp	
Baking powder	1¾ oz	
Water	1¾ cups	Add water. Mix slightly.
Shortening	1 lb	Add shortening. Mix 1 minute on low speed. Mix 4 minutes on medium speed.
Water	½ cup	Add water. Mix 1 minute on low speed. Scrape bowl. Mix 3 minutes on medium speed. Scrape bowl and beater.
Egg whites	1 lb	Add eggs, water, and vanilla. Mix 3 minutes on low speed.
Eggs, whole	3 oz	
Water	1 cup	
Vanilla	2 Tbsp	
		Scale batter into two greased 12 × 18 × 2-inch pans, 4 lb per pan. Bake at 350°F for 25–30 minutes. Cool and frost.

Approximate nutritive values per portion   **Calories** 132

Amount/portion	%DV	Amount/portion	%DV	Amount/portion	%DV		%DV		%DV
Total Fat 8 g	12%	**Cholest.** 6 mg	2%	**Total Carb.** 12 g	4%	**Vitamin A**	1%	**Calcium**	7%
Sat. Fat 2 g	10%	**Sodium** 248 mg	10%	Fiber 0 g	0%	**Vitamin C**	0%	**Iron**	5%
Protein 3 g				Sugars 1 g					

Percent Daily Values (%DV) are based on a 2000-calorie diet.

Note • May be baked in one 18 × 26 × 2-inch pan. Cut 6 × 10 for 60 portions.
Variations • See p. 333.

WHITE CAKE (DOUGH-BATTER METHOD)

Yield: 60 portions or 2 pans 12 × 18 × 2 inches   *Portion:* 2½ × 3 inches
Oven: 350°F   *Bake:* 35–40 minutes

Ingredient	Amount	Procedure
Flour, cake Baking powder Shortening, hydrogenated	2 lb 4 oz 1½ oz 1 lb 2 oz	Place flour, baking powder, and shortening in mixer bowl. Mix on low speed for 2 minutes, using flat beater. Scrape sides of bowl. Mix 3 minutes.
Sugar, granulated Salt Milk	2 lb 4 oz 1 Tbsp 2 cups	Combine sugar, salt, and milk. Add to flour mixture. Mix on low speed 2 minutes. Scrape sides of bowl. Mix 3 minutes.
Egg whites Milk Vanilla	12 (14 oz) 1⅓ cups 2 Tbsp	Combine egg whites, milk, and vanilla. Add half to mixture in bowl. Mix on low speed for 30 seconds. Scrape sides of bowl. Mix 1 minute. Add remaining egg-milk mixture. Mix on low speed for 1 minute. Scrape sides of bowl. Mix 2½ minutes.
		Scale batter into two greased 12 × 18 × 2-inch pans, 5 lb 7 oz per pan. Bake at 350°F for 35–40 minutes. Cool and ice. Cut 5 × 6.

Approximate nutritive values per portion   **Calories** 216

Amount/portion	%DV	Amount/portion	%DV	Amount/portion	%DV		%DV		%DV

Total Fat 9 g
  Sat. Fat 2 g
Protein 3 g
	14%
	12%
		Cholest. 2 mg
		Sodium 196 mg
			1%
			8%
				Total Carb. 31 g
				  Fiber 0 g
				  Sugars 17 g
					10%
					0%
						Vitamin A
						Vitamin C
							0%
							0%
								Calcium
								Iron
									6%
									7%

Percent Daily Values (%DV) are based on a 2000-calorie diet.

Notes
- 3 oz nonfat dry milk and 3⅓ cups water may be substituted for fluid milk. Increase shortening to 1 lb 3 oz. Mix dry milk with flour.
- May be baked in one 18 × 26 × 2-inch pan. Cut 6 × 10 for 60 portions.
- For six 9-inch layer pans, scale 1 lb 6 oz per pan.

Variations
- **Chocolate Chip Cake.** Add 12 oz chocolate chips to batter.
- **Coconut Lime Cake.** Scale into six 9-inch layer cake pans. When baked, cool, then spread Lime Filling (p. 362) between layers. Ice with Ice Cream Icing (p. 353). Sprinkle with toasted flaked coconut.
- **Cupcakes.** Portion batter with No. 20 dipper into muffin pans or paper baking cups. Yield: 7 dozen.
- **Lady Baltimore Cake.** Bake cake in layers. Prepare one recipe Ice Cream Icing (p. 353). To 1½ qt icing, add 1 tsp orange juice, 4 oz macaroon crumbs, 5 oz chopped almonds, and 6 oz chopped raisins. Spread on bottom layers; place second layers on top and spread with filling. Ice tops and sides with remaining frosting.
- **Poppy Seed Cake.** Add 6 oz poppy seeds that have been soaked in part of the milk. Ice with Chocolate Butter Cream Icing (p. 354).
- **Silver White Cake.** Scale batter into six 9-inch layer cake pans. When baked, cool and then spread Lemon Filling (p. 362) between layers. Ice with Ice Cream Icing (p. 353).
- **Starburst Cake.** Bake in two 12 × 18 × 2-inch pans. While cake is warm, perforate top with a meat fork every half inch. Prepare 2 qt flavored gelatin, and while still liquid slowly pour 1 qt over each cake. Cool and ice with Ice Cream Icing (p. 353) or other white icing.

CARROT CAKE

Yield: 60 portions or 2 pans 12 × 18 × 2 inches   *Portion:* 2½ × 3 inches
Oven: 325°F   *Bake:* 40–45 minutes

Ingredient	Amount	Procedure
Sugar, granulated	2 lb 6 oz	Combine sugar, oil, and eggs.
Vegetable oil	2½ cups	Beat 2 minutes on medium speed, using flat beater.
Eggs	9 (1 lb)	
Flour, all-purpose	1 lb 12 oz	Combine dry ingredients.
Salt	1 oz (1½ Tbsp)	Add to oil mixture and beat 1 minute.
Baking soda	⅔ oz (5 tsp)	
Cinnamon, ground	⅔ oz (3 Tbsp)	
Carrots, raw, grated	2 lb 8 oz	Add carrots and nuts. Mix until blended.
Nuts, chopped	1 lb	
		Scale batter into two greased 12 × 18 × 2-inch pans, 5 lb per pan.
		Bake at 325°F for 40–45 minutes.
		Ice with Cream Cheese Icing (p. 355)
		Cut 5 × 6.

Approximate nutritive values per portion   **Calories** 263

Amount/portion	%DV	Amount/portion	%DV	Amount/portion	%DV		%DV		%DV
Total Fat 14 g	21%	**Cholest.** 32 mg	11%	**Total Carb.** 32 g	11%	**Vitamin A**	54%	**Calcium**	3%
Sat. Fat 3 g	15%	**Sodium** 282 mg	12%	Fiber 2 g	7%	**Vitamin C**	3%	**Iron**	6%
Protein 4 g				Sugars 19 g					

Percent Daily Values (%DV) are based on a 2000-calorie diet.

Note   ● May be baked in one 18 × 26 × 2-inch pan cut 6 × 10 for 60 portions.

YELLOW CAKE

Yield: 60 portions or 2 pans 12 × 18 × 2 inches   *Portion:* 2½ × 3 inches
Oven: 350°F   *Bake:* 35–40 minutes

Ingredient	Amount	Procedure
Flour, cake	2 lb 5 oz	Place flour, baking powder, and shortening in mixer bowl.
Baking powder	3¾ Tbsp	Mix on low speed for 2 minutes, using flat beater.
Shortening, hydrogenated	1 lb	Scrape sides of bowl. Mix 3 minutes.
Sugar, granulated	2 lb 13 oz	Combine sugar, salt, and milk. Add to flour mixture.
Salt	2 tsp	Mix on low speed 2 minutes.
Milk	2 cups	Scrape sides of bowl. Mix 3 minutes.
Eggs	8 (14 oz)	Combine eggs, milk, and vanilla.
Milk	2½ cups	Add half to flour mixture. Mix on low speed 30 seconds.
Vanilla	2 Tbsp	Scrape sides of bowl. Mix 1 minute.
		Add remaining egg mixture. Mix 1 minute.
		Scrape sides of bowl. Mix 2½ minutes.
		Scale batter into two greased 12 × 18 × 2-inch baking pans 4 lb 10 oz per pan. Bake at 350°F for 35–40 minutes. Cut 5 × 6.

Approximate nutritive values per portion   **Calories** 232

Amount/portion	%DV	Amount/portion	%DV	Amount/portion	%DV		%DV		%DV
Total Fat 9 g	13%	**Cholest.** 29 mg	10%	**Total Carb.** 36 g	12%	**Vitamin A**	2%	**Calcium**	6%
Sat. Fat 2 g	10%	**Sodium** 90 mg	4%	Fiber 0 g	0%	**Vitamin C**	0%	**Iron**	7%
Protein 3 g				Sugars 21 g					

Percent Daily Values (%DV) are based on a 2000-calorie diet.

Notes
- 4 oz nonfat dry milk and 4½ cups water may be substituted for fluid milk. Add dry milk to flour mixture. Divide water as stated in recipe.
- May be baked in one 18 × 26 × 2-inch pan. Cut 6 × 10 for 60 portions.
- For layer cakes, scale 1 lb 9 oz batter into each of six 9-inch layer cake pans.
- For cupcakes, portion with No. 30 dipper into muffin pan. Yield: 8½ dozen.

Variations
- **Boston Cream Pie.** For two 12 × 18-inch pies, scale batter into four pans, 2 lb 5 oz each. When baked, spread Custard Filling (p. 361) on two cakes, 3 lb 3 oz each. Place other cakes on top. Cover with Chocolate Glaze (p. 358), 1 lb per cake. Cut 5 × 6.

  For two 18 × 26-inch pies, scale 4 lb 10 oz into each of two pans. Use 6 lb 6 oz Custard Filling and 2 lb Chocolate Glaze. Cut 6 × 10.

  For 9-inch layers, scale batter into eight pans, 1 lb 2 oz per pan. Use ½ recipe Custard Filling. Spread 1½ cups on each of four layers. Use ½ recipe Chocolate Glaze, spreading ½ cup on each pie.

  Powdered sugar sifted over top of pies may be substituted for Chocolate Glaze.
- **Cottage Pudding.** Cut cake into squares and serve with No. 20 dipper of fruit, lemon, nutmeg, or other sauce.
- **Dutch Apple Cake.** After the cake batter is poured into baking pans, arrange 2 lb 8 oz peeled sliced apples in rows over each pan. Sprinkle over top of each pan 4 oz granulated sugar and 1 tsp cinnamon, mixed.
- **Lazy Daisy Cake.** Mix 1 lb 2 oz melted margarine or butter, 2 lb brown sugar, 2 lb coconut, and 1½ cups half and half, or enough to moisten to consistency for spreading. Spread over baked cake, 3 lb per pan, and brown under the broiler or in the oven.

- **Marble Cake.** Divide batter into two portions after mixing. To one portion add 3 Tbsp cocoa, 1 Tbsp cinnamon, and 1 tsp nutmeg. Place batters alternately in cake pans; swirl with knife.
- **Pineapple Upside-Down Cake.** Mix one No. 10 can drained crushed pineapple (or tidbits), 8 oz melted margarine or butter, 12 oz brown sugar, and 8 oz chopped nuts. Pour 4 lb 3 oz in each 12 × 18-inch baking pan. Pour cake batter over mixture. Apricots or peaches may be substituted for pineapple.
- **Praline Cake.** Substitute chopped pecans for coconut in Lazy Daisy Cake.

APPLESAUCE CAKE

Yield: 60 portions or 2 pans 12 × 18 × 2 inches   *Portion:* 2½ × 3 inches
Oven: 350°F   *Bake:* 40–45 minutes

Ingredient	Amount	Procedure
Shortening, hydrogenated	1 lb	Cream shortening and sugar on medium speed for 10 minutes, using flat beater.
Sugar, granulated	1 lb 14 oz	
Eggs	8 (14 oz)	Add eggs to creamed mixture. Mix on medium speed for 5 minutes.
Flour, cake	1 lb 12 oz	Combine dry ingredients.
Baking powder	2½ Tbsp	
Salt	1¾ tsp	
Baking soda	½ tsp	
Cinnamon, ground	2½ tsp	
Cloves, ground	1 tsp	
Nutmeg, ground	1 tsp	
Water	2½ cups	Add dry ingredients alternately with water on low speed to creamed mixture, ending with dry ingredients.
Applesauce	2½ cups	Add remaining ingredients.
Raisins	1 lb 4 oz	Mix on low speed only to blend.
Nuts, chopped	10 oz	
		Scale batter into two greased 12 × 18 × 2-inch baking pans, 5 lb per pan. Bake at 350°F for 40–45 minutes. Cool and ice. See Notes for suggested icings. Cut 5 × 6.

Approximate nutritive values per portion   **Calories** 245

Amount/portion	%DV	Amount/portion	%DV	Amount/portion	%DV		%DV		%DV
Total Fat 11 g	17%	**Cholest.** 28 mg	9%	**Total Carb.** 35 g	12%	**Vitamin A**	1%	**Calcium**	4%
Sat. Fat 2 g	12%	**Sodium** 120 mg	5%	Fiber 1 g	4%	**Vitamin C**	0%	**Iron**	8%
Protein 3 g				Sugars 22 g					

Percent Daily Values (%DV) are based on a 2000-calorie diet.

Notes
- May be baked in one 18 × 26 × 2-inch pan. Cut 6 × 10 for 60 portions.
- This cake is too tender to bake in layers.
- Suggested icings: Ice Cream Icing (p. 353) or Cream Cheese Icing (p. 355)

BANANA CAKE

Yield: 48 portions or 3 2-layer cakes (9 inch)   *Portion:* 16 slices per cake
Oven: 350°F   *Bake:* 25–30 minutes

Ingredient	Amount	Procedure
Shortening, hydrogenated	1 lb	Cream shortening, sugar, and vanilla on medium speed for 10 minutes, using flat beater.
Sugar, granulated	2 lb	
Vanilla	1 Tbsp	
Eggs	8 (14 oz)	Add eggs to creamed mixture and mix on medium speed for 3 minutes, then add bananas and mix for an additional 2 minutes.
Bananas, mashed	2 lb (4 cups)	
Flour, cake	2 lb	Combine dry ingredients.
Salt	1¼ tsp	
Baking powder	3⅓ Tbsp	
Baking soda	2 tsp	
Buttermilk	1 cup	Add dry ingredients alternately with buttermilk on low speed. Mix on medium speed 2–3 minutes.
		Scale batter into six greased 9-inch layer cake pans, 1 lb 6 oz per pan. Bake at 350°F for 25–30 minutes. Cool. Remove from pans and ice. See Notes for suggested icings.

Approximate nutritive values per portion   **Calories** 254

Amount/portion	%DV	Amount/portion	%DV	Amount/portion	%DV		%DV		%DV
Total Fat 11 g	16%	**Cholest.** 35 mg	12%	**Total Carb.** 39 g	13%	**Vitamin A**	1%	**Calcium**	5%
Sat. Fat 3 g	14%	**Sodium** 185 mg	8%	Fiber 1 g	3%	**Vitamin C**	2%	**Iron**	8%
Protein 3 g				Sugars 22 g					

Percent Daily Values (%DV) are based on a 2000-calorie diet.

Notes
- May be baked in two 12 × 18 × 2-inch pans, scaled 4 lb 3 oz per pan. Cut 5 × 6 for 30 portions per pan.
- For sheet cake, bake in one 18 × 26 × 2-inch pan. Cut 6 × 10 for 60 portions.
- Suggested icings: Creamy Icing (p. 355) or Cream Cheese Icing (p. 355).

BURNT SUGAR CAKE

Yield: 60 portions or 2 pans 12 × 18 × 2 inches   *Portion:* 2½ × 3 inches
Oven: 375°F   *Bake:* 35–40 minutes

Ingredient	Amount	Procedure

Sugar, granulated
Shortening,
  hydrogenated
	2 lb 11 oz
	1 lb
		Cream shortening and sugar on medium speed for
		  10 minutes, using flat beater.

Egg yolks	8 (5 oz)	Add egg yolks to creamed mixture and mix on medium speed for 5 minutes.
Milk Water Burnt sugar syrup (see Notes) Vanilla	2 cups 2 cups ⅔ cup 4 tsp	Combine liquids.
Flour, cake Baking powder Salt	2 lb 2 oz 2⅔ Tbsp 1¼ tsp	Combine dry ingredients. On low speed, add to creamed mixture alternately with liquids. Scrape sides of bowl. Mix 2 minutes.
Egg whites	8 (9 oz)	Beat egg whites until they form soft peaks. Fold into batter on low speed.
		Scale batter into two greased 12 × 18 × 2-inch baking pans, 4 lb 8 oz per pan. Bake at 375°F for 35–40 minutes. Cool and ice. See Notes for suggested icings. Cut 5 × 6.

Approximate nutritive values per portion   **Calories** 232

Amount/portion	%DV	Amount/portion	%DV	Amount/portion	%DV		%DV		%DV
Total Fat 9 g	13%	**Cholest.** 31 mg	10%	**Total Carb.** 36 g	12%	**Vitamin A**	4%	**Calcium**	4%
Sat. Fat 2 g	12%	**Sodium** 98 mg	4%	Fiber 0.4 g	2%	**Vitamin C**	0%	**Iron**	7%
Protein 2 g				Sugars 22 g					

Percent Daily Values (%DV) are based on a 2000-calorie diet.

Notes

- **Burnt Sugar Syrup.** Place ⅓ cup granulated sugar in pan and melt slowly, stirring constantly. Cook until light brown (caramelized), being careful not to scorch. Add ⅓ cup boiling water. Cook slowly until a syrup is formed. For larger amounts, use 1 lb sugar and 2 cups boiling water.

- May be baked in one 18 × 26 × 2-inch pan cut 6 × 10; or in eight 9-inch layers, scaled 1 lb 2 oz per pan.

- Suggested icings: Burnt Butter Icing (p. 352), Creamy Icing (p. 355), Cream Cheese Icing (p. 355), or Ice Cream Icing (p. 353).

CHOCOLATE CAKE

Yield: 60 portions or 2 pans 12 × 18 × 2 inches   *Portion:* 2½ × 3 inches
Oven: 350°F   *Bake:* 25–30 minutes

Ingredient	Amount	Procedure
Flour, cake	1 lb 8 oz	Combine dry ingredients in mixer bowl.
Cocoa	5 oz	Mix on low speed for 1 minute, using flat beater.
Sugar, granulated	2 lb 5 oz	
Nonfat dry milk	2½ oz	
Salt	1 Tbsp	
Baking powder	1 oz	
Baking soda	3½ tsp	
Water	1½ cups	Add to dry ingredients.
Shortening	1 lb	Mix on low speed for 1 minute.
		Mix on medium speed for 3 minutes.
		Scrape sides of bowl and beater.
Water	1½ cups	Add and mix on low speed for 1 minute.
		Mix on medium speed for 2 minutes.
Eggs	10 (1 lb 2 oz)	Blend in eggs. Mix on low speed for 2 minutes.
Water	1 cup	
Vanilla	¼ cup	
		Scale batter into two greased 12 × 18 × 2-inch baking pans, 4 lb 2 oz per pan.
		Bake at 350°F for 25–30 minutes.
		Cool and ice. See Notes for suggested icings.
		Cut 5 × 6.

Approximate nutritive values per portion   **Calories** 200

Amount/portion	%DV	Amount/portion	%DV	Amount/portion	%DV		%DV		%DV
Total Fat 9 g	13%	**Cholest.** 36 mg	12%	**Total Carb.** 29 g	10%	**Vitamin A**	2%	**Calcium**	5%
Sat. Fat 2 g	11%	**Sodium** 247 mg	10%	Fiber 0.3 g	1%	**Vitamin C**	0%	**Iron**	9%
Protein 3 g				Sugars 18 g					

Percent Daily Values (%DV) are based on a 2000-calorie diet.

Notes
- Cake may be baked in one 18 × 26 × 2-inch pan. Cut 6 × 10 for 60 servings.
- Suggested icings: Chocolate Butter Cream Icing (p. 354), Mocha Icing (p. 357), or Ice Cream Icing (p. 353).

FUDGE CAKE

Yield: 48 portions or 3 2-layer cakes (9 inch)   *Portion:* 16 slices per cake
Oven: 350°F   *Bake:* 25–30 minutes

Ingredient	Amount	Procedure
Shortening, hydrogenated	12 oz	Cream shortening, sugar, and vanilla on medium speed for 10 minutes, using flat beater.
Sugar, granulated	2 lb	
Vanilla	1 Tbsp	
Eggs	6 (10 oz)	Add eggs and mix on medium speed for 5 minutes.
Cocoa	5 oz	Mix cocoa and hot water.
Water, hot	1½ cups	
Flour, cake	1 lb 12 oz	Combine flour, salt, and soda.
Salt	1 tsp	
Baking soda	1½ Tbsp	
Buttermilk	3 cups	Add dry ingredients alternately with buttermilk and cocoa to creamed mixture on low speed. Scrape sides of bowl and beater. Continue mixing until smooth and ingredients are mixed.
		Scale batter into six greased 9-inch layer cake pans, 1 lb 4 oz per pan. Bake at 350°F for 25–30 minutes. Cool. Remove from pans and ice. See Notes.

Approximate nutritive values per portion   **Calories** 217

Amount/portion	%DV	Amount/portion	%DV	Amount/portion	%DV		%DV		%DV
Total Fat 8 g	13%	**Cholest.** 26 mg	9%	**Total Carb.** 34 g	11%	**Vitamin A**	1%	**Calcium**	2%
Sat. Fat 2 g	11%	**Sodium** 189 mg	8%	Fiber 0.4 g	2%	**Vitamin C**	0%	**Iron**	12%
Protein 3 g				Sugars 19 g					

Percent Daily Values (%DV) are based on a 2000-calorie diet.

Notes
- For 12 × 18-inch layer cake, scale into two 12 × 18 × 2-inch or two 13 × 18 × 1-inch pans, 3 lb 13 oz per pan. When baked and cooled, ice one cake, then remove cake from pan and place on top (see Figure 9.1). Ice top and sides.
- Suggested icings: Chocolate Butter Cream Icing (p. 354), Ice Cream Icing (p. 353), or Mocha Icing (p. 357).

Variations
- **Chocolate Cupcakes.** Portion with No. 20 dipper into muffin pans or paper liners. Yield: 5 dozen.
- **Chocolate Sheet Cake.** Bake in one 18 × 26 × 2-inch baking pan. Cut 6 × 10 for 60 portions.

GERMAN SWEET CHOCOLATE CAKE

Yield: 60 portions or 2 pans 12 × 18 × 2 inches   *Portion:* 2½ × 3 inches
Oven: 350°F   *Bake:* 40–45 minutes

Ingredient	Amount	Procedure
German sweet chocolate	10 oz	Melt chocolate in water. Cool. Add vanilla. Set aside.
Water, boiling	1¼ cups	
Vanilla	2½ tsp	
Shortening, hydrogenated	1 lb 4 oz	Cream shortening and sugar on medium speed for 10 minutes, using flat beater.
Sugar, granulated	2 lb 8 oz	
Egg yolks	10 (6 oz)	Add egg yolks one at a time. Beat well after each addition. Add chocolate mixture and blend.
Flour, cake	1 lb 9 oz	Combine flour, salt, and soda.
Salt	1¼ tsp	
Baking soda	2½ tsp	
Buttermilk	2½ cups	Add dry ingredients alternately with buttermilk to creamed mixture. Mix on low speed until smooth. Scrape sides of bowl.
Egg whites	10 (11 oz)	Beat egg whites until stiff peaks form. Fold into batter on low speed. Do not overmix. Scale batter into two greased 12 × 18 × 2-inch baking pans, 4 lb 7 oz per pan. Bake at 350°F for 40–45 minutes.
Coconut Pecan Icing (p. 354)	2 qt	When cool, ice with Coconut Pecan Icing. Cut 5 × 6.

Approximate nutritive values per portion   **Calories** 378

Amount/portion	%DV	Amount/portion	%DV	Amount/portion	%DV		%DV		%DV
Total Fat 22 g	34%	**Cholest.** 63 mg	21%	**Total Carb.** 43 g	14%	**Vitamin A**	10%	**Calcium**	4%
Sat. Fat 7 g	34%	**Sodium** 165 mg	7%	Fiber 1 g	5%	**Vitamin C**	0%	**Iron**	7%
Protein 4 g				Sugars 31 g					

Percent Daily Values (%DV) are based on a 2000-calorie diet.

Notes
- May be baked in one 18 × 26 × 2-inch pan. Cut 6 × 10 for 60 portions.
- For four 2-layer cakes, scale into eight 9-inch layer cake pans, 1 lb 1 oz per pan. Cut 16 slices per cake for 64 portions.

PEANUT BUTTER CAKE

Yield: 60 portions or 1 pan 18 × 26 × 2 inches   *Portion:* 2½ × 3 inches
Oven: 350°F   *Bake:* 30–35 minutes

Ingredient	Amount	Procedure
Margarine	9 oz	Cream margarine, peanut butter, and sugar for 15 minutes, using flat beater. Scrape bottom and sides of bowl after each 5 minutes.
Peanut butter, creamy	12 oz	
Sugar, granulated	2 lb 2 oz	
Eggs	(5) 8 oz	Add to creamed mixture.
Vanilla	2 Tbsp	
Flour, all-purpose	1 lb 12 oz	Combine flour, baking powder, and salt.
Baking powder	½ oz (3½ tsp)	
Baking soda	1 oz (2⅓ Tbsp)	
Buttermilk	4⅔ cups	Add dry ingredients and buttermilk alternately to creamed mixture. Scrape bottom and sides of bowl after each addition.
		Scale 8 lb batter into one 18 × 26 × 2-inch baking pan. Bake at 350°F for 30–35 minutes or until cake springs back when lightly depressed in the center.
Peanut Butter Icing (p. 356)	2 qt	Ice with Peanut Butter Icing.

Approximate nutritive values per portion   **Calories** 333

Amount/portion	%DV	Amount/portion	%DV	Amount/portion	%DV		%DV		%DV
Total Fat 13 g	20%	**Cholest.** 17 mg	6%	**Total Carb.** 52 g	17%	**Vitamin A**	2%	**Calcium**	4%
Sat. Fat 3 g	14%	**Sodium** 257 mg	11%	Fiber 1 g	3%	**Vitamin C**	0%	**Iron**	4%
Protein 4 g				Sugars 38 g					

Percent Daily Values (%DV) are based on a 2000-calorie diet.

Notes
- ½ oz (1 Tbsp) caramel food color may be added for a darker color.
- May be baked in two 12 × 18 × 2-inch pans. Scale 4 lb batter per pan.

GINGERB

Yield: 60 port
Oven: 350°F

Ingredient

Shortening,
  hydrogen
Sugar, gran

Molasses

Flour, cake
Baking soda
Salt
Cinnamon,
Cloves, gro
Ginger, gro

Water, hot

Eggs, beate

Approximate

Amount/port

Total Fat 7 g
  Sat. Fat 2 g
Protein 2 g

Percent Daily

Note

Variations

PINEAPPLE CASHEW CAKE

Yield: 48 portions or 3 2-layer cakes (9 inch)   *Portion:* 16 slices per cake
Oven: 350°F   *Bake:* 25–30 minutes

Ingredient	Amount	Procedure
Margarine or butter	1 lb 2 oz	Cream margarine, sugar, and vanilla on medium speed for 10 minutes, using flat beater.
Sugar, granulated	1 lb 14 oz	
Vanilla	1 Tbsp	
Egg yolks	10 (6 oz)	Add egg yolks in three portions, while creaming. Mix 2 minutes.
Flour, cake	1 lb 14 oz	Combine flour, baking powder, and salt.
Baking powder	1½ oz	
Salt	1½ tsp	
Milk	2¼ cups	Add dry ingredients alternately with milk on low speed to creamed mixture.
Crushed pineapple, drained	1 lb	Add pineapple to batter. Mix on low speed only to blend.
Egg whites	10 (11 oz)	Beat egg whites on high speed until stiff but not dry. Fold into batter on low speed. Scale batter into six greased 9-inch layer cake pans, 1 lb 5 oz per pan. Bake at 350°F for 25–30 minutes.
Pineapple Icing (p. 357)	2 qt	When cool, remove cake from pans. Cover with icing and sprinkle with toasted cashews.
Cashew nuts, toasted, coarsely chopped	8 oz	

Approximate nutritive values per portion

Calories 517

Amount/portion	%DV	Amount/portion	%DV	Amount/portion	%DV		%DV		%DV
Total Fat 24 g	37%	**Cholest.** 56 mg	19%	**Total Carb.** 73 g	24%	**Vitamin A**	16%	**Calcium**	10%
Sat. Fat 5 g	25%	**Sodium** 450 mg	19%	Fiber 1 g	4%	**Vitamin C**	4%	**Iron**	12%
Protein 5 g				Sugars 52 g					

Percent Daily Values (%DV) are based on a 2000-calorie diet.

Note   • May be baked in one 18 × 26 × 2-inch pan, cut 6 × 10 for 60 portions, or in two 12 × 18 × 2-inch pans, scaled 4 lb per pan, and cut 5 × 6 for 30 portions per pan.

FRUIT

Yield: 64

Oven: 3(

Ingredi

Shorter
  hydr
Sugar,

Eggs

Jelly
Cinnan
Cloves,
Raisins
Curran
Dates,
Nuts
Flour,

Baking
Coffee

Approx

Amoun

Total F:
  Sat. F
Protein

Percen

Notes

CHOCOLATE ROLL

Yield: 48 portions or 4 pans 12 × 18 × 2 inches   *Portion:* 1-inch slice
Oven: 325°F   *Bake:* 20 minutes

Ingredient	Amount	Procedure
Egg yolks	24 (14 oz)	Beat egg yolks on high speed, using flat beater.
Sugar, granulated	2 lb 4 oz	Add sugar and continue beating until mixture is lemon colored, thick, and fluffy.
Unsweetened chocolate, melted	12 oz	Add chocolate and vanilla. Blend on low speed.
Vanilla	2 Tbsp	
Flour, cake	9 oz	Combine flour, baking powder, and salt. Add to creamed mixture on low speed.
Baking powder	1 Tbsp	
Salt	1½ tsp	
Egg whites	24 (1 lb 11 oz)	Beat egg whites on high speed until they form rounded peaks. Fold into cake mixture on low speed. Scale batter, 1 lb 7 oz per pan, into four greased 12 × 18 × 2-inch pans lined with baking liners. Bake at 325°F for 20 minutes.
		When baked, remove from pans and quickly remove baking liner. Trim edges if hard. Roll (Figure 9.3) and let stand a few minutes. Unroll and spread with one of the fillings suggested (see Note). Roll up securely. Cover with a thin layer of Chocolate Icing (p. 353).

Approximate nutritive values per portion   **Calories** 159

Amount/portion	%DV	Amount/portion	%DV	Amount/portion	%DV		%DV		%DV
Total Fat 5 g	7%	**Cholest.** 35 mg	12%	**Total Carb.** 28 g	9%	Vitamin A	1%	Calcium	2%
Sat. Fat 2 g	9%	**Sodium** 122 mg	5%	Fiber 0.6 g	2%	Vitamin C	0%	Iron	5%
Protein 4 g				Sugars 22 g					

Percent Daily Values (%DV) are based on a 2000-calorie diet.

Note   • Suggested fillings: Custard Filling (p. 361) or whipped cream, plain or flavored with peppermint.

Variation • **Ice Cream Roll.** Spread with a thick layer of softened vanilla ice cream. Roll up securely and wrap in waxed paper. Place in freezer for several hours before serving.

JELLY ROLL

Yield: 48 portions or 4 pans 12 × 18 × 2 inches   *Portion:* 1-inch slice
Oven: 375°F   *Bake:* 12 minutes

Ingredient	Amount	Procedure
Eggs	27 (3 lb)	Beat eggs on high speed for 1–2 minutes, using flat beater.
Sugar, granulated Vanilla	3 lb 1 Tbsp	Add sugar and vanilla to eggs. Beat 10–15 minutes.
Flour, cake Cream of tartar Baking powder Salt	1 lb 8 oz 2 Tbsp 2 Tbsp 2 tsp	Mix dry ingredients. Fold on low speed into egg-sugar mixture.
		Scale batter, 1 lb 14 oz per pan, into four greased 12 × 18 × 2-inch baking pans lined with baking liners. Bake at 375°F for 12 minutes.
		When baked, turn onto a cloth or heavy paper covered with powdered sugar (Figure 9.3). Quickly remove baking liners and trim edges if hard. Immediately roll cakes tightly.
Jelly or Custard Filling (p. 361)	1 qt	When cooled but not cold, unroll, spread with jelly or Custard Filling, 1 cup per roll. Roll firmly and wrap with waxed paper.
Sugar, powdered	1 lb	Sprinkle top of each roll with 4 oz powdered sugar. Slice each roll into 12 portions.

Approximate nutritive values per portion   **Calories** 311

Amount/portion	%DV	Amount/portion	%DV	Amount/portion	%DV		%DV		%DV
Total Fat 3 g	5%	**Cholest.** 121 mg	40%	**Total Carb.** 67 g	22%	**Vitamin A**	5%	**Calcium**	4%
Sat. Fat 1 g	5%	**Sodium** 170 mg	7%	Fiber 0.3 g	1%	**Vitamin C**	2%	**Iron**	10%
Protein 5 g				Sugars 49 g					

Percent Daily Values (%DV) are based on a 2000-calorie diet.

Note   • May be baked in two 18 × 26 × 1-inch pans, scaled 3 lb 12 oz per pan.

Variation   • **Apricot Roll.** Cover cakes with Apricot Filling (p. 360) and roll. Cover outside with sweetened whipped cream or whipped topping and toasted coconut.

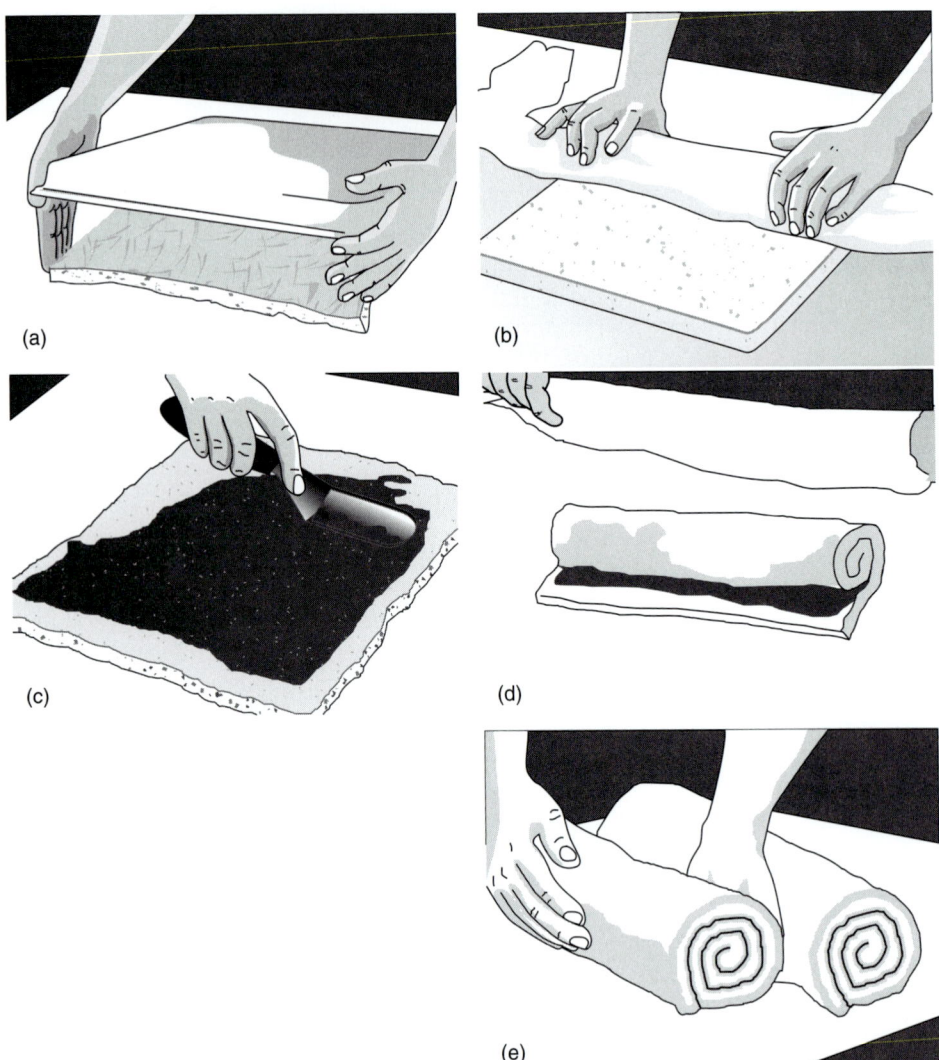

FIGURE 9.3 Rolling and filling a jelly roll. (a) Turn baked cake onto a cloth sprinkled with powdered sugar. Remove waxed or parchment paper. (b) While still warm, roll tightly. (c) When cooled but not cold, unroll and spread with filling. (d) Roll firmly. (e) Sprinkle finished jelly roll with powdered sugar.

PUMPKIN CAKE ROLL

Yield: 50 portions or 2 rolls   *Portion:* 25 slices per roll
Oven: 375°F   *Bake:* 15 minutes

Ingredient	Amount	Procedure
Eggs	18 (2 lb)	Whip eggs on high speed until thick and lemon colored, using flat beater.
Sugar, granulated	2 lb 13 oz	Add sugar gradually while mixing on medium speed.
Pumpkin, canned Lemon juice	2 lb 3 oz 2 Tbsp	Add pumpkin and lemon juice to egg mixture, mixing until blended.
Flour, all-purpose Baking powder Salt Cinnamon, ground Ginger, ground Nutmeg, ground	1 lb 2 oz 1 oz 1 Tbsp 1 oz 4 tsp 1 Tbsp	Combine dry ingredients in a bowl. Fold into pumpkin mixture. Scale batter, 4 lb per pan, into two greased 28 × 26 × 1-inch baking pans lined with baking liners. Bake at 375°F for 15 minutes or until cake tests done.
Sugar, powdered	6 oz	Sift powdered sugar generously onto a large white cloth. Loosen edges of cake and turn onto cloth. Remove paper (Figure 9.3). Roll cake and cloth up jelly-roll fashion. Cool.
Cream cheese, softened Margarine	2 lb 10 oz	Beat cream cheese and margarine until creamy, using flat beater.
Sugar, powdered Vanilla	1 lb 6 oz 1 Tbsp	Add sugar and vanilla to cream cheese mixture. Beat until smooth and creamy. Unroll cooled cake. Spread cream cheese filling over unrolled cakes, 2 lb per cake. Reroll cake.
Nuts, chopped	2 cups	Garnish with 1 cup nuts sprinkled over each roll. Chill. Cut each roll into 25 portions.

Approximate nutritive values per portion   **Calories** 370

Amount/portion	%DV	Amount/portion	%DV	Amount/portion	%DV		%DV		%DV
Total Fat 16 g	24%	**Cholest.** 97 mg	32%	**Total Carb.** 53 g	18%	**Vitamin A**	56%	Calcium	9%
Sat. Fat 6 g	29%	**Sodium** 318 mg	13%	Fiber 1 g	5%	**Vitamin C**	1%	Iron	9%
Protein 6 g				Sugars 40 g					

Percent Daily Values (%DV) are based on a 2000-calorie diet.

Note   • If needed, sift additional powdered sugar over top of rolled cake.

ICING RECIPES

BOILED ICING

Yield: 2 qt

Ingredient	Amount	Procedure
Sugar, granulated Water, hot	2 lb 1¼ cups	Combine sugar and water. Stir until sugar is dissolved. Boil without stirring to soft ball stage (238°F).
Egg whites	4 (4 oz)	Beat egg whites on high speed until stiff but not dry, using wire whip attachment. Gradually pour syrup over egg whites while beating. Continue beating until icing is of consistency to spread.
Vanilla	1 Tbsp	Add vanilla. Spread on cake at once.

Approximate nutritive values per cup   **Calories** 451

Amount/portion	%DV	Amount/portion	%DV	Amount/portion	%DV		%DV		%DV
Total Fat 0 g	**0%**	**Cholest.** 0 mg	**0%**	**Total Carb.** 114 g	**38%**	**Vitamin A**	**0%**	**Calcium**	**0%**
Sat. Fat 0 g	0%	**Sodium** 26 mg	1%	Fiber 0 g	0%	**Vitamin C**	0%	**Iron**	0%
Protein 1 g				Sugars 110 g					

Percent Daily Values (%DV) are based on a 2000-calorie diet.

Variation   ● See variations of Ice Cream Icing (p. 353).

BURNT BUTTER ICING

Yield: 1¼ qt

Ingredient	Amount	Procedure
Butter or margarine	9 oz	Heat butter in saucepan until golden brown.
Sugar, powdered, sifted	1 lb 8 oz	Add sugar to butter and blend.
Vanilla Water, hot	1 Tbsp ½ cup	Add vanilla and water. Beat until of spreading consistency. Add more water if necessary.

Approximate nutritive values per cup   **Calories** 899

Amount/portion	%DV	Amount/portion	%DV	Amount/portion	%DV		%DV		%DV
Total Fat 41 g	**63%**	**Cholest.** 0 mg	**0%**	**Total Carb.** 137 g	**46%**	**Vitamin A**	**15%**	**Calcium**	**1%**
Sat. Fat 8 g	40%	**Sodium** 483 mg	20%	Fiber 0 g	0%	**Vitamin C**	0%	**Iron**	0%
Protein 1 g				Sugars 127 g					

Percent Daily Values (%DV) are based on a 2000-calorie diet.

Note   ● This amount will ice 8 dozen 1½-inch cookies. If used for cake, increase by one-fourth.

ICE CREAM ICING

Yield: 2½ qt

Ingredient	Amount	Procedure
Sugar, granulated Water, hot	1 lb 8 oz 1 cup	Combine sugar and water. Boil without stirring to soft ball stage (238°F).
Pasteurized egg whites	9 (10 oz)	Beat egg whites until frothy, using wire whip attachment.
Sugar, powdered, sifted	3 oz	Add powdered sugar to egg whites and beat on high speed to consistency of meringue. Add hot syrup slowly and continue beating until mixture is thick and creamy.
Sugar, powdered, sifted Vanilla	8 oz 1 Tbsp	Add powdered sugar and vanilla. Beat until smooth. Add more sugar if necessary to make icing hold its shape when spread.

Approximate nutritive values per cup   **Calories** 402

Amount/portion	%DV	Amount/portion	%DV	Amount/portion	%DV		%DV		%DV
Total Fat 0 g	0%	**Cholest.** 0 mg	0%	**Total Carb.** 100 g	33%	**Vitamin A**	0%	Calcium	0%
Sat. Fat 0 g	0%	**Sodium** 49 mg	2%	Fiber 0 g	0%	**Vitamin C**	0%	Iron	0%
Protein 3 g				Sugars 95 g					

Percent Daily Values (%DV) are based on a 2000-calorie diet.

Note
- This icing can be kept 2–3 days in a covered container in the refrigerator.

Variations
- **Bittersweet Icing.** Melt 8 oz unsweetened chocolate over hot water. Gradually stir in 1½ oz margarine or butter. When slightly cool, pour over white icing to form a design.
- **Candied Fruit Icing.** Add 8 oz chopped candied fruit.
- **Chocolate Icing.** Add 8 oz melted chocolate.
- **Coconut Icing.** Frost cake. Sprinkle with 4 oz dry shredded coconut.
- **Maple Nut Icing.** Delete vanilla. Flavor with 1½ tsp maple flavoring. Add 6 oz chopped nuts.
- **Maraschino Cherry Icing.** Delete vanilla. Add ½ tsp almond extract and 8 oz chopped maraschino cherries.
- **Peppermint Icing.** Add 8 oz finely crushed peppermint candy.

CHOCOLATE BUTTER CREAM ICING

Yield: 2 qt

Ingredient	Amount	Procedure
Margarine or butter	1 lb 8 oz	Cream margarine on medium speed until fluffy.
Evaporated milk	½ cup	Add milk and blend.
Sugar, powdered, sifted	1 lb 8 oz	Add sugar gradually. Mix on medium speed until smooth.
Unsweetened chocolate, melted	6 oz	Add chocolate and vanilla. Beat on high speed until light and fluffy.
Vanilla	1 tsp	

Approximate nutritive values per cup **Calories** 1067

Amount/portion	%DV	Amount/portion	%DV	Amount/portion	%DV		%DV		%DV
Total Fat 81 g	124%	**Cholest.** 5 mg	2%	**Total Carb.** 94 g	31%	**Vitamin A**	26%	**Calcium**	8%
Sat. Fat 19 g	93%	**Sodium** 821 mg	34%	Fiber 1 g	6%	**Vitamin C**	0%	**Iron**	9%
Protein 4 g				Sugars 82 g					

Percent Daily Values (%DV) are based on a 2000-calorie diet.

Note   • Milk may be substituted for evaporated milk.

COCONUT PECAN ICING

Yield: 2 qt

Ingredient	Amount	Procedure
Evaporated milk	2 cups	Combine milk, egg yolks, sugar, and margarine.
Egg yolks, beaten	6 (4 oz)	Cook in steam-jacketed kettle or over hot water until
Sugar, granulated	1 lb	thickened.
Margarine	8 oz	
Pecans, finely chopped	12 oz	Add pecans, coconut, and vanilla.
Coconut, flaked	12 oz	Cool, then beat well until thick enough to spread.
Vanilla	2 tsp	

Approximate nutritive values per cup **Calories** 1033

Amount/portion	%DV	Amount/portion	%DV	Amount/portion	%DV		%DV		%DV
Total Fat 74 g	114%	**Cholest.** 200 mg	67%	**Total Carb.** 89 g	30%	**Vitamin A**	40%	**Calcium**	21%
Sat. Fat 23 g	115%	**Sodium** 350 mg	15%	Fiber 5 g	21%	**Vitamin C**	3%	**Iron**	13%
Protein 12 g				Sugars 71 g					

Percent Daily Values (%DV) are based on a 2000-calorie diet.

CREAM CHEESE ICING

Yield: 1¾ qt

Ingredient	Amount	Procedure
Cream cheese, softened	12 oz	Blend cream cheese, margarine, and milk on medium speed
Margarine, softened	2 oz	until smooth.
Milk	¼ cup	
Sugar, powdered, sifted	2 lb 12 oz	Add sugar gradually to cheese-margarine mixture.
Vanilla	1 Tbsp	Add vanilla and beat until smooth and of spreading consistency.

Approximate nutritive values per cup   **Calories** 927

Amount/portion	%DV	Amount/portion	%DV	Amount/portion	%DV		%DV		%DV
Total Fat 24 g	37%	**Cholest.** 55 mg	18%	**Total Carb.** 181 g	60%	**Vitamin A**	23%	**Calcium**	5%
Sat. Fat 12 g	61%	**Sodium** 228 mg	10%	Fiber 0 g	0%	**Vitamin C**	0%	**Iron**	4%
Protein 4 g				Sugars 167 g					

Percent Daily Values (%DV) are based on a 2000-calorie diet.

Variation   • **Orange Cheese Icing.** Substitute 1 Tbsp orange juice and 1 Tbsp grated orange peel for vanilla.

CREAMY ICING

Yield: 1½ qt

Ingredient	Amount	Procedure
Margarine	12 oz	Cream margarine on medium speed for 1 minute or until soft.
Evaporated milk	½ cup	Add milk and vanilla. Mix until blended.
Vanilla	1 Tbsp	
Sugar, powdered, sifted	2 lb	Add sugar gradually. Whip on medium speed until mixture is smooth and creamy.

Approximate nutritive values per cup   **Calories** 1024

Amount/portion	%DV	Amount/portion	%DV	Amount/portion	%DV		%DV		%DV
Total Fat 47 g	73%	**Cholest.** 6 mg	2%	**Total Carb.** 155 g	52%	**Vitamin A**	18%	**Calcium**	7%
Sat. Fat 10 g	50%	**Sodium** 558 mg	23%	Fiber 0 g	0%	**Vitamin C**	0%	**Iron**	1%
Protein 2 g				Sugars 141 g					

Percent Daily Values (%DV) are based on a 2000-calorie diet.

Note   • Milk or cream may be substituted for evaporated milk.

Variations   • **Cocoa Icing.** Increase liquid to 1¼ cups. Add 6 oz cocoa sifted with the sugar.

   • **Lemon Butter Icing.** Substitute ¼ cup lemon juice for an equal amount of milk, and 1½ Tbsp fresh grated lemon peel for the vanilla.

   • **Orange Butter Icing.** Substitute ½ cup orange juice for an equal amount of milk, and 1 Tbsp fresh grated orange peel for the vanilla.

ORANGE ICING

Yield: 1½ qt

Ingredient	Amount	Procedure
Margarine	8 oz	Cream margarine until fluffy.
Sugar, powdered, sifted	2 lb 8 oz	Add sugar gradually on medium speed. Mix until creamy.
Vanilla	2 Tbsp	Add remaining ingredients. Blend until smooth.
Salt	½ tsp	
Orange juice	¼ cup	
Lemon juice	¼ cup	
Orange peel, grated	1 tsp	

Approximate nutritive values per cup   **Calories** 1020

Amount/portion	%DV	Amount/portion	%DV	Amount/portion	%DV		%DV		%DV
Total Fat 30 g	47%	**Cholest.** 0 mg	0%	**Total Carb.** 193 g	64%	**Vitamin A**	11%	**Calcium**	1%
Sat. Fat 6 g	30%	**Sodium** 538 mg	22%	Fiber 0 g	0%	**Vitamin C**	11%	**Iron**	1%
Protein 0 g				Sugars 177 g					

Percent Daily Values (%DV) are based on a 2000-calorie diet.

PEANUT BUTTER ICING

Yield: 2 qt

Ingredient	Amount	Procedure
Sugar, powdered, sifted	3 lb	Cream powdered sugar and shortening for 5 minutes.
Margarine	10 oz	
Peanut butter, creamy	5 oz	Add to creamed mixture. Cream until fluffy. Spread on Peanut Butter Cake (p. 342).
Water, warm	¾ cup	
Vanilla	1 Tbsp	

Approximate nutritive values per cup   **Calories** 1018

Amount/portion	%DV	Amount/portion	%DV	Amount/portion	%DV		%DV		%DV
Total Fat 38 g	58%	**Cholest.** 0 mg	0%	**Total Carb.** 174 g	58%	**Vitamin A**	35%	**Calcium**	1%
Sat. Fat 7 g	35%	**Sodium** 469 mg	20%	Fiber 1 g	4%	**Vitamin C**	0%	**Iron**	2%
Protein 4 g				Sugars 160 g					

Percent Daily Values (%DV) are based on a 2000-calorie diet.

Note   • ½ oz (1 Tbsp) caramel food color may be added for a darker color.

PINEAPPLE ICING (FOR PINEAPPLE CASHEW CAKE)

Yield: 2 qt

Ingredient	Amount	Procedure
Margarine	1 lb	Blend in mixer bowl, using flat beater.
Sugar, powdered	1 lb 4 oz	
Salt	¼ tsp	
Pineapple juice	¾ cup	Add pineapple juice. Mix to blend.
Sugar, powdered	1 lb 6 oz	Add sugar in three additions. Beat on medium speed until light and of the desired consistency.

Approximate nutritive values per cup   **Calories** 1048

Amount/portion	%DV	Amount/portion	%DV	Amount/portion	%DV		%DV		%DV
Total Fat 46 g	70%	**Cholest.** 0 mg	0%	**Total Carb.** 167 g	56%	Vitamin A	16%	Calcium	2%
Sat. Fat 9 g	45%	**Sodium** 603 mg	25%	Fiber 0 g	0%	Vitamin C	4%	Iron	1%
Protein 1 g				Sugars 155 g					

Percent Daily Values (%DV) are based on a 2000-calorie diet.

Note   • Crushed pineapple may be substituted for pineapple juice. Add additional juice in small quantities until icing is of spreading consistency.

MOCHA ICING

Yield: 2 qt

Ingredient	Amount	Procedure
Hot coffee, strong	1½ cups	Add coffee to margarine and cocoa.
Margarine, softened	3 oz	Mix on medium speed until blended.
Cocoa	4 oz	
Sugar, powdered, sifted	3 lb	Add sugar, salt, and vanilla. Mix until smooth. Add more sugar if necessary to make icing hold its shape when spread.
Salt	¼ tsp	
Vanilla	½ tsp	

Approximate nutritive values per cup   **Calories** 761

Amount/portion	%DV	Amount/portion	%DV	Amount/portion	%DV		%DV		%DV
Total Fat 10 g	15%	**Cholest.** 0 mg	0%	**Total Carb.** 179 g	60%	Vitamin A	3%	Calcium	2%
Sat. Fat 2 g	10%	**Sodium** 178 mg	7%	Fiber 0.2 g	1%	Vitamin C	0%	Iron	28%
Protein 3 g				Sugars 158 g					

Percent Daily Values (%DV) are based on a 2000-calorie diet.

Note   • Instant coffee, 2 Tbsp dissolved in 1½ cups hot water, may be used in place of brewed coffee.

CHOCOLATE GLAZE

Yield: 1 qt

Ingredient	Amount	Procedure
Unsweetened chocolate	4 oz	Melt chocolate and margarine over low heat.
Margarine	3 oz	
Sugar, powdered, sifted	1 lb 5 oz	Add sugar, vanilla, and water gradually.
Vanilla	1 Tbsp	Beat until smooth. If needed, add boiling water, a few drops at
Water, boiling	½ cup	a time, to make spreading consistency.

Approximate nutritive values per cup   **Calories** 877

Amount/portion	%DV	Amount/portion	%DV	Amount/portion	%DV		%DV		%DV
Total Fat 32 g	49%	**Cholest.** 0 mg	0%	**Total Carb.** 159 g	53%	**Vitamin A**	6%	**Calcium**	2%
Sat. Fat 9 g	46%	**Sodium** 204 mg	8%	Fiber 2 g	7%	**Vitamin C**	0%	**Iron**	11%
Protein 3 g				Sugars 143 g					

Percent Daily Values (%DV) are based on a 2000-calorie diet.

PEANUT BUTTER GLAZE

Yield: 5½ cups

Ingredient	Amount	Procedure
Margarine, melted	3 oz	Cream margarine and peanut butter.
Peanut butter	8 oz	
Sugar, powdered, sifted	1 lb 10 oz	Add sugar and milk alternately to make spreading consistency.
Milk	1 cup	Spread over rolls.

Approximate nutritive values per cup   **Calories** 822

Amount/portion	%DV	Amount/portion	%DV	Amount/portion	%DV		%DV		%DV
Total Fat 32 g	49%	**Cholest.** 5 mg	2%	**Total Carb.** 133 g	44%	**Vitamin A**	5%	**Calcium**	6%
Sat. Fat 7 g	34%	**Sodium** 336 mg	14%	Fiber 2 g	9%	**Vitamin C**	0%	**Iron**	4%
Protein 11 g				Sugars 119 g					

Percent Daily Values (%DV) are based on a 2000-calorie diet.

POWDERED SUGAR GLAZE

Yield: 5 cups

Ingredient	Amount	Procedure
Sugar, powdered	2 lb	Mix until smooth, adding more water if necessary.
Corn syrup, white	½ cup	Cover tightly until needed. Stir before using.
Water, warm	¾ cup	
Vanilla	2 tsp	

Approximate nutritive values per cup   **Calories** 791

Amount/portion	%DV	Amount/portion	%DV	Amount/portion	%DV		%DV		%DV
Total Fat 0 g	0%	**Cholest.** 0 mg	0%	**Total Carb.** 206 g	69%	**Vitamin A**	0%	Calcium	0%
Sat. Fat 0 g	0%	**Sodium** 0 mg	0%	Fiber 0 g	0%	**Vitamin C**	0%	Iron	1%
Protein 0 g				Sugars 192 g					

Percent Daily Values (%DV) are based on a 2000-calorie diet.

Notes
- Use for icing baked rolls or products requiring a thin icing.
- Thin, if necessary, to spread.

FILLING RECIPES

CHOCOLATE CREAM FILLING

Yield: 3 qt

Ingredient	Amount	Procedure
Chocolate chips	2 lb 4 oz (3 12-oz pkgs)	Combine chocolate chips, orange juice, and sugar. Melt over hot water. Cool.
Orange juice or water	1 cup	
Sugar, granulated	8 oz	
Cream, whipping	1½ qt	Whip cream until stiff. Fold into chocolate mixture.

Approximate nutritive values per cup   **Calories** 827

Amount/portion	%DV	Amount/portion	%DV	Amount/portion	%DV		%DV		%DV
Total Fat 61 g	94%	**Cholest.** 133 mg	44%	**Total Carb.** 81 g	27%	**Vitamin A**	42%	Calcium	10%
Sat. Fat 23 g	116%	**Sodium** 44 mg	2%	Fiber 0 g	0%	**Vitamin C**	13%	Iron	12%
Protein 7 g				Sugars 72 g					

Percent Daily Values (%DV) are based on a 2000-calorie diet.

Note
- Use as filling for Orange Cream Puffs (p. 426).

Variation
- **Chocolate Mousse.** Whip 1½ cup (12 oz) pasteurized egg whites to a soft peak and fold into chocolate whipped cream mixture. Chill. May be frozen.

DATE FILLING

Yield: 1½ qt

Ingredient	Amount	Procedure
Dates, pitted, chopped	2 lb	Combine dates, water, and sugar.
Water	2¼ cups	Cook until mixture is thick. Cool.
Sugar, granulated	12 oz	

Approximate nutritive values per cup   **Calories** 635

Amount/portion	%DV	Amount/portion	%DV	Amount/portion	%DV		%DV		%DV
Total Fat 1 g	1%	**Cholest.** 0 mg	0%	**Total Carb.** 168 g	56%	**Vitamin A**	0%	**Calcium**	5%
Sat. Fat 0 g	0%	**Sodium** 8 mg	1%	Fiber 13 g	53%	**Vitamin C**	0%	**Iron**	9%
Protein 3 g				Sugars 152 g					

Percent Daily Values (%DV) are based on a 2000-calorie diet.

Notes
- Use as cake or cookie filling.
- To add flavor, 6 oz jelly or ¼ cup orange juice may be used in place of ¼ cup of the water.

APRICOT FILLING

Yield: 2 qt

Ingredient	Amount	Procedure
Apricots, dried	2 lb	Cook apricots and water together until soft.
Water	2 cups	When cooked, chop apricots.
Sugar, granulated	1 lb	Add sugar, flour, salt, and lemon juice to apricots. Cook to a
Flour, all-purpose	4 oz	paste.
Salt	½ tsp	
Lemon juice	½ cup	
Margarine	1 lb	Blend margarine into hot mixture.

Approximate nutritive values per cup   **Calories** 951

Amount/portion	%DV	Amount/portion	%DV	Amount/portion	%DV		%DV		%DV
Total Fat 46 g	71%	**Cholest.** 0 mg	0%	**Total Carb.** 139 g	46%	**Vitamin A**	99%	**Calcium**	7%
Sat. Fat 9 g	45%	**Sodium** 686 mg	29%	Fiber 9 g	37%	**Vitamin C**	10%	**Iron**	33%
Protein 6 g				Sugars 100 g					

Percent Daily Values (%DV) are based on a 2000-calorie diet.

Variations
- **Fig Filling.** Substitute 2 lb dried figs, cooked and chopped, for the apricots. Increase lemon juice to 1 cup.
- **Prune–Date Filling.** Substitute 1 lb cooked, pitted, and chopped prunes and 1 lb chopped dates for the apricots.

CUSTARD FILLING

Yield: 4 qt

Ingredient	Amount	Procedure
Cornstarch Sugar, granulated Salt	6 oz 1 lb ½ tsp	Combine dry ingredients.
Milk, cold	2 cups	Add cold milk to dry ingredients and stir until smooth.
Milk, hot	2½ qt	Add cold mixture to hot milk, stirring constantly with wire whip. Cook over hot water until thick.
Eggs, beaten	10 (1 lb)	Add, while stirring, a small amount of hot mixture to the beaten eggs. Add to remainder of hot mixture, stirring constantly. Cook 7 minutes.
Vanilla	2 tsp	Remove from heat. Add vanilla. Cool quickly (within 4 hours) to below 41°F.

Approximate nutritive values per cup   **Calories** 307

Amount/portion	%DV	Amount/portion	%DV	Amount/portion	%DV		%DV		%DV
Total Fat 9 g	14%	**Cholest.** 146 mg	49%	**Total Carb.** 47 g	16%	**Vitamin A**	12%	**Calcium**	23%
Sat. Fat 5 g	23%	**Sodium** 194 mg	8%	Fiber 0 g	0%	**Vitamin C**	2%	**Iron**	3%
Protein 10 g				Sugars 37 g					

Percent Daily Values (%DV) are based on a 2000-calorie diet.

Notes
- Potentially hazardous food. *Food Safety Standard:* Store at an internal temperature below 41°F. See p. 105 for recommended cooling procedures.
- Use as a filling for cakes, Cream Puffs (p. 426), Chocolate Roll (p. 348), and Eclairs (p. 426).
- To fill three 9-inch layer cakes, use ⅓ recipe.

LEMON FILLING

Yield: 1¾ qt

Ingredient	Amount	Procedure
Sugar, granulated	1 lb	Heat sugar and water to boiling point.
Water	3 cups	
Cornstarch	2½ oz	Blend cornstarch and cold water.
Water, cold	¾ cup	Gradually add to boiling sugar and water while stirring with a wire whip.
		Cook until thickened and clear, stirring constantly.
Egg yolks, beaten	4 (3 oz)	Stir a small amount of hot mixture into egg yolks, then blend egg yolks into hot mixture with wire whip.
		Cook 5–8 minutes while stirring.
Salt	¾ tsp	Add remaining ingredients. Stir to blend.
Lemon juice	½ cup	Cool quickly (within 4 hours) to below 41°F.
Fresh lemon peel, grated	2 tsp	
Margarine	1 oz (2 Tbsp)	

Approximate nutritive values per cup   **Calories** 365

Amount/portion	%DV	Amount/portion	%DV	Amount/portion	%DV		%DV		%DV
Total Fat 7 g	11%	**Cholest.** 156 mg	52%	**Total Carb.** 76 g	25%	**Vitamin A**	24%	**Calcium**	2%
Sat. Fat 2 g	9%	**Sodium** 281 mg	12%	Fiber 0.2 g	1%	**Vitamin C**	8%	**Iron**	3%
Protein 2 g				Sugars 63 g					

Percent Daily Values (%DV) are based on a 2000-calorie diet.

Note
- Potentially hazardous food. *Food Safety Standard:* Store at an internal temperature below 41°F. See p. 105 for recommended cooling procedures.

Variations
- **Lime Filling.** Substitute fresh lime for the lemon. Add a few drops of green food coloring.
- **Orange Filling.** Substitute orange juice for the water and fresh orange peel for the lemon peel. Reduce lemon juice to 3 Tbsp.

MARMALADE NUT FILLING

Yield: 1 qt

Ingredient	Amount	Procedure
Margarine	2 oz	Melt margarine.
Walnuts, pieces	1 lb	Add nuts. Cook and stir until nuts are toasted.
Sugar, brown	6 oz	Add sugar and cinnamon. Cook until heated through.
Cinnamon, ground	1 tsp	
Orange marmalade	1 lb	Add marmalade. Mix well.

Approximate nutritive values per cup   **Calories** 1052

Amount/portion	%DV	Amount/portion	%DV	Amount/portion	%DV		%DV		%DV
Total Fat 76 g	**116%**	**Cholest.** 0 mg	**0%**	**Total Carb.** 79 g	**26%**	**Vitamin A**	8%	**Calcium**	12%
Sat. Fat 6 g	**32%**	**Sodium** 156 mg	**6%**	Fiber 4 g	**17%**	**Vitamin C**	63%	**Iron**	27%
Protein 30 g				Sugars 2 g					

Percent Daily Values (%DV) are based on a 2000-calorie diet.

Note   • Use for filling in fruit ring or sweet rolls.

PRUNE FILLING

Yield: 1½ qt

Ingredient	Amount	Procedure
Prunes, pitted, cooked and chopped	2 cups	Add cream, margarine, and eggs to prunes. Heat over hot water.
Sour cream	1 cup	
Margarine	2 oz	
Eggs, beaten	4 (7 oz)	
Sugar, granulated	1 lb	Mix dry ingredients. Add to prune mixture.
Salt	½ tsp	Cook and stir over hot water until thick. Cool.
Flour, all-purpose	1 oz (¼ cup)	

Approximate nutritive values per cup   **Calories** 587

Amount/portion	%DV	Amount/portion	%DV	Amount/portion	%DV		%DV		%DV
Total Fat 19 g	**29%**	**Cholest.** 158 mg	**53%**	**Total Carb.** 102 g	**34%**	**Vitamin A**	20%	**Calcium**	8%
Sat. Fat 8 g	**38%**	**Sodium** 332 mg	**14%**	Fiber 3 g	**11%**	**Vitamin C**	4%	**Iron**	8%
Protein 7 g				Sugars 90 g					

Percent Daily Values (%DV) are based on a 2000-calorie diet.

Note   • 8 oz chopped nuts may be added.

Variation   • **Apricot Filling.** Substitute dried apricots for prunes.

DROP COOKIE RECIPES

BUTTERSCOTCH DROP COOKIES

Yield: 8 dozen cookies   *Portion:* ¾ oz per cookie
Oven: 375°F   *Bake:* 10–15 minutes

Ingredient	Amount	Procedure
Margarine Sugar, brown	8 oz 1 lb	Cream margarine and brown sugar on medium speed for 5 minutes, using flat beater.
Eggs Vanilla	4 (7 oz) 2 tsp	Add eggs and vanilla to creamed mixture. Mix on medium speed until well blended.
Flour, all-purpose Baking powder Baking soda Salt	1 lb 4 oz 1 tsp 2 tsp 1 tsp	Combine dry ingredients.
Sour cream	1 lb	Add dry ingredients alternately with sour cream to dough. Mix on low speed until blended.
Walnuts, chopped	8 oz	Add nuts. Mix until blended. Chill dough until firm.
		Portion with No. 40 dipper 3 × 5 onto lightly greased or parchment-paper-lined 18 × 26-inch baking sheets. Bake at 375°F for 10–15 minutes. Cover with Burnt Butter Icing (p. 352) while cookies are still warm.

Approximate nutritive values per cookie   **Calories** 84

Amount/portion	%DV	Amount/portion	%DV	Amount/portion	%DV		%DV		%DV
Total Fat 4 g	7%	**Cholest.** 11 mg	4%	**Total Carb.** 10 g	3%	**Vitamin A**	2%	**Calcium**	1%
Sat. Fat 1 g	6%	**Sodium** 81 mg	3%	Fiber 0 g	0%	**Vitamin C**	0%	**Iron**	2%
Protein 2 g				Sugars 1 g					

Percent Daily Values (%DV) are based on a 2000-calorie diet.

Variations
- **Butterscotch Squares.** Spread batter in 12 × 18 × 2-inch baking pan. Bake at 325°F for 25 minutes.
- **Chocolate Drop Cookies.** Add 4 oz unsweetened chocolate, melted, to creamed mixture.

COCONUT MACAROONS

Yield: 9 dozen cookies   *Portion:* ½ oz per cookie
Oven: 325°F   *Bake:* 15 minutes

Ingredient	Amount	Procedure
Egg whites Salt	8 (9 oz) ⅛ tsp	Beat egg whites and salt on high speed until frothy, using whip attachment.
Sugar, granulated Sugar, powdered	12 oz 12 oz	Combine sugars and add gradually to egg whites.
Vanilla	2 tsp	Add vanilla. Continue beating on high speed until stiff.
Coconut, shredded	1 lb 6 oz	Carefully fold in coconut on low speed. Portion with No. 60 dipper 4 × 6 onto lightly greased or parchment-paper-lined 18 × 26-inch baking sheets. Bake at 325°F for 15 minutes.

Approximate nutritive values per cookie   **Calories** 53

Amount/portion	%DV	Amount/portion	%DV	Amount/portion	%DV		%DV		%DV
Total Fat 2 g	3%	**Cholest.** 0 mg	0%	**Total Carb.** 9 g	3%	**Vitamin A**	0%	**Calcium**	0%
Sat. Fat 2 g	8%	**Sodium** 24 mg	1%	Fiber 0 g	0%	**Vitamin C**	0%	**Iron**	0%
Protein 1 g				Sugars 8 g					

Percent Daily Values (%DV) are based on a 2000-calorie diet.

CHOCOLATE CHIP COOKIES

Yield: 10 dozen cookies   *Portion:* ¾ oz per cookie
Oven: 375°F   *Bake:* 8–10 minutes

Ingredient	Amount	Procedure
Margarine Sugar, granulated Sugar, brown	12 oz 8 oz 8 oz	Cream margarine and sugars on medium speed for 5 minutes, using flat beater.
Eggs Vanilla	4 (7 oz) 2 tsp	Add eggs and vanilla to creamed mixture and beat until light and fluffy.
Flour, all-purpose Salt Baking soda	1 lb 4 oz 1 tsp 2 tsp	Combine dry ingredients. Add on low speed to creamed mixture.
Nuts, coarsely chopped Chocolate chips	1 lb 1 lb 8 oz	Add nuts and chocolate chips. Mix until blended.
		Portion with No. 40 dipper 3 × 5 onto lightly greased or parchment-paper-lined 18 × 26-inch baking sheets. Bake at 375°F for 8–10 minutes.

Approximate nutritive values per cookie   **Calories** 103

Amount/portion	%DV	Amount/portion	%DV	Amount/portion	%DV		%DV		%DV
Total Fat 6 g	9%	**Cholest.** 7 mg	2%	**Total Carb.** 12 g	4%	**Vitamin A**	1%	**Calcium**	1%
Sat. Fat 1 g	3%	**Sodium** 69 mg	3%	Fiber 1 g	2%	**Vitamin C**	0%	**Iron**	3%
Protein 2 g				Sugars 5 g					

Percent Daily Values (%DV) are based on a 2000-calorie diet.

Note   • For jumbo cookies, use No. 20 dipper. Bake at 365°F for 12–15 minutes

BUTTERSCOTCH PECAN COOKIES

Yield: 10 dozen cookies   *Portion:* ³⁄₄ oz per cookie
Oven: 375°F   *Bake:* 10–12 minutes

Ingredient	Amount	Procedure
Margarine Sugar, brown	1 lb 2 lb	Cream margarine and sugar on medium speed for 5 minutes, using flat beater.
Eggs Vanilla	4 (7 oz) 1 Tbsp	Add eggs and vanilla to creamed mixture. Mix on low speed until blended.
Flour, all-purpose Pecans, chopped	1 lb 8 oz 1 lb	Add flour and pecans. Mix on low speed until blended.
		Portion with No. 40 dipper 3 × 5 onto lightly greased or parchment-paper-lined 18 × 26-inch baking sheets. Bake at 375°F for 10–12 minutes.

Approximate nutritive values per cookie   **Calories** 104

Amount/portion	%DV	Amount/portion	%DV	Amount/portion	%DV		%DV		%DV
Total Fat 6 g	9%	**Cholest.** 7 mg	2%	**Total Carb.** 12 g	4%	**Vitamin A**	1%	**Calcium**	1%
Sat. Fat 1 g	4%	**Sodium** 41 mg	2%	Fiber 0.4 g	2%	**Vitamin C**	0%	**Iron**	2%
Protein 1 g				Sugars 1 g					

Percent Daily Values (%DV) are based on a 2000-calorie diet.

OATMEAL COOKIES

Yield: 8 dozen cookies   *Portion:* ¾ oz per cookie
Oven: 375°F   *Bake:* 8–11 minutes

Ingredient	Amount	Procedure
Margarine	1 lb 4 oz	Cream margarine and sugars on medium speed for 5 minutes, using flat beater.
Sugar, brown	8 oz	
Sugar, granulated	8 oz	
Eggs	2 (4 oz)	Add eggs and vanilla to creamed mixture. Continue to cream until well mixed.
Vanilla	2 tsp	
Flour, all-purpose	12 oz	Combine dry ingredients. Add to creamed mixture.
Salt	1 tsp	
Baking soda	2 tsp	
Rolled oats, uncooked	1 lb	Add oats. Mix on low speed until blended.
Raisins, softened	12 oz	Add raisins. Mix only to blend. Portion with No. 40 dipper 3 × 5 onto lightly greased or parchment-paper-lined 18 × 26-inch baking sheets. Flatten slightly. Bake at 375°F for 8–9 minutes for a chewy cookie, 10–11 minutes for a crisp cookie.

Approximate nutritive values per cookie   **Calories** 104

Amount/portion	%DV	Amount/portion	%DV	Amount/portion	%DV		%DV		%DV
Total Fat 5 g	8%	**Cholest.** 5 mg	2%	**Total Carb.** 14 g	5%	**Vitamin A**	1%	**Calcium**	0%
Sat. Fat 1 g	5%	**Sodium** 95 mg	4%	Fiber 0.3 g	1%	**Vitamin C**	0%	**Iron**	2%
Protein 1 g				Sugars 5 g					

Percent Daily Values (%DV) are based on a 2000-calorie diet.

Notes
- For variety, add 8 oz chopped nuts, chocolate chips, or coconut.
- 2 tsp cinnamon may be added.

PEANUT BUTTER COOKIES

Yield: 9 dozen cookies *Portion:* ¾ oz per cookie
Oven: 375°F *Bake:* 8 minutes

Ingredient	Amount	Procedure
Margarine	1 lb	Cream margarine and sugars on medium speed for 5 minutes using flat beater.
Sugar, granulated	1 lb	
Sugar, brown	10 oz	
Eggs	4 (7 oz)	Add eggs and vanilla.
Vanilla	2 tsp	Continue beating until blended.
Peanut butter, creamy	1 lb 2 oz	Add peanut butter to creamed mixture. Blend on low speed.
Flour, all-purpose	1 lb	Combine dry ingredients.
Baking soda	2 tsp	Add to creamed mixture. Mix on low speed until well blended.
Salt	1 tsp	
		Portion dough with No. 40 dipper 3 × 5 onto lightly greased or parchment-paper-lined 18 × 26-inch baking sheets. Flatten with tines of a fork. Bake at 375°F for 8 minutes.

Approximate nutritive values per cookie **Calories** 102

Amount/portion	%DV	Amount/portion	%DV	Amount/portion	%DV		%DV		%DV
Total Fat 6 g	9%	**Cholest.** 8 mg	3%	**Total Carb.** 11 g	4%	Vitamin A	1%	Calcium	0%
Sat. Fat 1 g	6%	**Sodium** 109 mg	5%	Fiber 0.4 g	2%	Vitamin C	0%	Iron	1%
Protein 2 g				Sugars 5 g					

Percent Daily Values (%DV) are based on a 2000-calorie diet.

Variations
- **Chocolate Chip Peanut Butter Cookies.** Add 1 lb chocolate chips.
- **Chunky Peanut Butter Cookies.** Use chunky peanut butter or add 12 oz chopped peanuts.

JUMBO CHUNK CHOCOLATE COOKIES

Yield: 5 dozen cookies   *Portion:* $3\frac{1}{2}$ oz per cookie
Oven: 350°F   *Bake:* 10–12 minutes

Ingredient	Amount	Procedure
Sugar, brown	1 lb 8 oz	Cream sugars and shortening on medium speed for 5 minutes using flat beater.
Sugar, granulated	1 lb	
Shortening	2 lb	
Eggs, beaten	9 (1 lb)	Add eggs and vanilla to creamed mixture.
Vanilla	$1\frac{1}{2}$ Tbsp	
Flour, all-purpose	2 lb 8 oz	Combine dry ingredients and add to creamed mixture. Mix thoroughly.
Baking soda	4 tsp	
Salt	4 tsp	
Semisweet chocolate chunks	4 lb 12 oz	Add chocolate and nuts.
Nuts, chopped	1 lb	
		Portion with No. 20 dipper 3 × 5 onto lightly greased or parchment-paper-lined 18 × 26-inch baking sheets. Flatten slightly. Bake at 350°F for 10–12 minutes.

Approximate nutritive values per cookie   **Calories** 502

Amount/portion	%DV	Amount/portion	%DV	Amount/portion	%DV		%DV		%DV
Total Fat 31 g	**48%**	**Cholest.** 32 mg	**11%**	**Total Carb.** 56 g	**19%**	**Vitamin A**	1%	**Calcium**	5%
Sat. Fat 12 g	**58%**	**Sodium** 243 mg	**10%**	Fiber 4 g	**14%**	**Vitamin C**	0%	**Iron**	15%
Protein 7 g				Sugars 24 g					

Percent Daily Values (%DV) are based on a 2000-calorie diet.

Note   • These cookies are best when served the same day they are baked.

DROP MOLASSES COOKIES

Yield: 8 dozen cookies   *Portion:* ¾ oz per cookie
Oven: 350°F   *Bake:* 8–10 minutes

Ingredient	Amount	Procedure
Flour, all-purpose	2 lb	Stir together flour, soda, and spices.
Baking soda	2⅔ Tbsp	Set aside.
Cinnamon, ground	¼ cup	
Cloves, ground	1 tsp	
Nutmeg, ground	1 tsp	
Ginger, ground	2 tsp	
Salt	2 tsp	
Oil or melted shortening	1 lb 8 oz	Combine shortening and sugar in mixer bowl. Beat on medium speed for 5 minutes, using flat beater.
Sugar, granulated	2 lb	
Eggs	4 (7 oz)	Add eggs, one at a time, beating well after each addition.
Molasses	1 cup	Add molasses gradually to egg mixture. Add dry ingredients gradually on low speed and mix well.
		Portion with No. 40 dipper 3 × 5 onto lightly greased or parchment-paper-lined 18 × 26-inch baking sheets. Bake at 350°F for 8–10 minutes.

Approximate nutritive values per cookie   **Calories** 146

Amount/portion	%DV	Amount/portion	%DV	Amount/portion	%DV		%DV		%DV
Total Fat 7 g	11%	**Cholest.** 9 mg	3%	**Total Carb.** 19 g	6%	**Vitamin A**	0%	**Calcium**	1%
Sat. Fat 2 g	9%	**Sodium** 153 mg	6%	Fiber 0.3 g	1%	**Vitamin C**	0%	**Iron**	4%
Protein 1 g				Sugars 11 g					

Percent Daily Values (%DV) are based on a 2000-calorie diet.

Note   ● Cookies will be soft in center.

GINGERSNAPS

Yield: 8 dozen cookies   *Portion:* ⅔ oz per cookie
Oven: 375°F   *Bake:* 10–12 minutes

Ingredient	Amount	Procedure
Shortening	1 lb	Cream shortening and brown sugar until light and fluffy.
Sugar, brown	1 lb 4 oz	
Eggs	3 (5 oz)	Add eggs and molasses. Mix well.
Molasses	⅔ cup	
Flour	1 lb 6 oz	Combine dry ingredients. Add gradually to creamed mixture.
Baking soda	1⅔ Tbsp	Blend well.
Cinnamon	2½ tsp	
Ginger, ground	2½ tsp	
Cloves	1¼ tsp	
Salt	¾ tsp	
Sugar, granulated	8 oz	Portion with a No. 60 dipper. Roll dough in sugar and place 4 × 5 onto lightly greased or parchment-paper-lined 18 × 26-inch baking sheets. Bake at 375°F for 10–12 minutes.

Approximate nutritive values per cookie   **Calories** 105

Amount/portion	%DV	Amount/portion	%DV	Amount/portion	%DV		%DV		%DV
Total Fat 5 g	8%	**Cholest.** 7 mg	2%	**Total Carb.** 15 g	5%	**Vitamin A**	0%	Calcium	1%
Sat. Fat 2 g	7%	**Sodium** 87 mg	4%	Fiber 0.2 g	1%	**Vitamin C**	0%	Iron	2%
Protein 1 g				Sugars 4 g					

Percent Daily Values (%DV) are based on a 2000-calorie diet.

PEANUT COOKIES

Yield: 9 dozen cookies   *Portion:* ¾ oz per cookie
Oven: 350°F   *Bake:* 10–12 minutes

Ingredient	Amount	Procedure
Margarine	12 oz	Cream margarine and sugars on medium speed for 5 minutes, using flat beater.
Sugar, granulated	8 oz	
Sugar, brown	1 lb	
Eggs	4 (7 oz)	Add eggs and vanilla. Mix for 5 minutes.
Vanilla	2 tsp	
Flour, all-purpose	12 oz	Combine dry ingredients.
Baking soda	1 tsp	Add to creamed mixture.
Salt	1 tsp	
Rolled oats, quick, uncooked	10 oz	Add rolled oats and peanuts. Mix until blended.
Peanuts, salted	1 lb	
		Portion dough with No. 40 dipper 3 × 5 onto lightly greased or parchment-paper-lined 18 × 26-inch baking sheets. Bake at 350°F for 10–12 minutes.

Approximate nutritive values per cookie   **Calories 96**

Amount/portion	%DV	Amount/portion	%DV	Amount/portion	%DV		%DV		%DV
Total Fat 5 g	8%	**Cholest.** 8 mg	3%	**Total Carb.** 11 g	4%	**Vitamin A**	1%	**Calcium**	0%
Sat. Fat 1 g	5%	**Sodium** 66 mg	3%	Fiber 0.4 g	1%	**Vitamin C**	0%	**Iron**	2%
Protein 2 g				Sugars 2 g					

Percent Daily Values (%DV) are based on a 2000-calorie diet.

PEANUT BUTTER CHOCOLATE CHIP COOKIES

Yield: 8 dozen cookies   *Portion:* ¾ oz per cookie
Oven: 350°F   *Bake:* 10–12 minutes

Ingredient	Amount	Procedure
Chunky peanut butter	1 lb 8 oz	Cream peanut butter, sugar, and margarine on medium
Brown sugar	1 lb 8 oz	speed for 5 minutes.
Margarine	12 oz	
Eggs	3 (5 oz)	Add eggs, honey, and vanilla.
Honey	¾ cup	Mix well.
Vanilla	1 Tbsp	
Flour, all-purpose	1 lb	Combine dry ingredients.
Rolled oats	3 oz	Add gradually to creamed mixture. Blend well.
Baking soda	1 Tbsp	
Salt	¾ tsp	
Semi sweet chocolate chips	1 lb	Stir chocolate chips into batter. Refrigerate until dough is firm and not sticky.
		Portion dough with No. 40 dipper 3 × 5 onto lightly greased or parchment-paper-lined 18 × 26-inch baking sheets. Bake 350°F for 10–12 minutes.

Approximate nutritive values per cookie   **Calories** 150

Amount/portion	%DV	Amount/portion	%DV	Amount/portion	%DV		%DV		%DV
Total Fat 8 g	12%	**Cholest.** 6.5 mg	2%	**Total Carb.** 18 g	6%	Vitamin A	3%	Calcium	1%
Sat. Fat 2 g	11%	**Sodium** 130 mg	5%	Fiber 1 g	4%	Vitamin C	0%	Iron	4%
Protein 3 g				Sugars 12 g					

Percent Daily Values (%DV) are based on a 2000-calorie diet.

SNICKERDOODLES

Yield: 8 dozen cookies *Portion:* ¾ oz per cookie
Oven: 375°F *Bake:* 8–10 minutes

Ingredient	Amount	Procedure
Margarine	1 lb	Cream margarine and sugar on medium speed for 5 minutes, using flat beater.
Sugar, granulated	1 lb 8 oz	
Eggs	4 (7 oz)	Add eggs to creamed mixture. Mix thoroughly.
Flour, all-purpose	1 lb 6 oz	Mix dry ingredients. Add to creamed mixture.
Cream of tartar	4 tsp	Mix on low speed until well-blended.
Baking soda	2 tsp	
Salt	½ tsp	
Sugar, granulated	8 oz	Combine sugar and cinnamon.
Cinnamon	5 Tbsp	Portion dough with No. 40 dipper. Roll in sugar-cinnamon mixture.
		Place 3 × 5 onto lightly greased or parchment-paper-lined 18 × 26-inch baking sheets.
		Bake at 375°F for 8–10 minutes or until lightly browned but still soft. These cookies puff up at first, then flatten out with crinkled tops.

Approximate nutritive values per cookie   **Calories** 99

Amount/portion	%DV	Amount/portion	%DV	Amount/portion	%DV		%DV		%DV
Total Fat 4 g	6%	**Cholest.** 9 mg	3%	**Total Carb.** 15 g	5%	**Vitamin A**	1%	**Calcium**	0%
Sat. Fat 1 g	4%	**Sodium** 86 mg	4%	Fiber 0 g	0%	**Vitamin C**	0%	**Iron**	2%
Protein 1 g				Sugars 9 g					

Percent Daily Values (%DV) are based on a 2000-calorie diet.

DROP SUGAR COOKIES

Yield: 8 dozen cookies   *Portion:* ¾ oz per cookie
Oven: 375°F   *Bake:* 8–10 minutes

Ingredient	Amount	Procedure
Shortening	1 lb	Cream fats and sugar, starting on low speed, progressing to medium, then high speed for 5 minutes. Use flat beater.
Margarine or butter	1 lb 2 oz	
Sugar, granulated	2 lb	
Eggs	3 (5 oz)	Add eggs and vanilla to creamed mixture and mix thoroughly.
Vanilla	4 tsp	
Flour, all-purpose	1 lb 14 oz	Combine dry ingredients.
Cream of tartar	2 tsp	Add gradually to creamed mixture.
Baking soda	2½ tsp	Blend well.
Salt	½ tsp	
		Portion with No. 40 dipper 3 × 5 onto lightly greased or parchment-paper-lined 18 × 26-inch baking sheets. Bake at 375°F for 8–10 minutes.

Approximate nutritive values per cookie   **Calories** 152

Amount/portion	%DV	Amount/portion	%DV	Amount/portion	%DV		%DV		%DV
Total Fat 9 g	14%	**Cholest.** 6 mg	2%	**Total Carb.** 16 g	5%	**Vitamin A**	1%	**Calcium**	0%
Sat. Fat 2 g	10%	**Sodium** 97 mg	4%	Fiber 0.2 g	1%	**Vitamin C**	0%	**Iron**	2%
Protein 1 g				Sugars 9 g					

Percent Daily Values (%DV) are based on a 2000-calorie diet.

Notes
- Cookies will be soft in center.
- For jumbo cookies, use No. 20 dipper.

WHOLE WHEAT SUGAR COOKIES

Yield: 8 dozen cookies   *Portion:* ¾ oz per cookie
Oven: 375°F   *Bake:* 8–10 minutes

Ingredient	Amount	Procedure
Margarine	1 lb	Cream margarine and sugar for 5 minutes or until light and fluffy, using flat beater.
Sugar, granulated	2 lb	
Eggs	4 (7 oz)	Add eggs, vanilla, and milk. Mix well.
Vanilla	4 tsp	
Milk	½ cup	
Flour, whole wheat	2 lb	Combine dry ingredients.
Baking powder	4 tsp	Add gradually to creamed mixture.
Baking soda	2 tsp	Blend well.
Salt	2 tsp	
Nutmeg, ground	2 tsp	
Orange peel, grated	4 Tbsp	
Sugar, granulated	4 oz	Combine sugar and cinnamon.
Cinnamon, ground	2 tsp	
		Portion with No. 40 dipper 3 × 5 onto lightly greased or parchment-paper-lined 18 × 26-inch baking sheets. Flatten slightly and sprinkle with sugar and cinnamon mixture. Bake at 375°F for 8–10 minutes.

Approximate nutritive values per cookie   **Calories** 106

Amount/portion	%DV	Amount/portion	%DV	Amount/portion	%DV		%DV		%DV
Total Fat 4 g	6%	**Cholest.** 9 mg	3%	**Total Carb.** 16 g	5%	**Vitamin A**	1%	**Calcium**	1%
Sat. Fat 1 g	4%	**Sodium** 131 mg	5%	Fiber 0 g	0%	**Vitamin C**	0%	**Iron**	2%
Protein 1 g				Sugars 11 g					

Percent Daily Values (%DV) are based on a 2000-calorie diet.

Note   • Cookies will be soft in center.

BAR COOKIE RECIPES

BROWNIES

Yield: 60 portions or 2 pans 12 × 18 × 1 inch   *Portion:* 2½ × 3 inches
Oven: 325°F   *Bake:* 20 minutes

Ingredient	Amount	Procedure
Eggs	15 (1 lb 10 oz)	Beat eggs on high speed for 5 minutes, using flat beater.
Sugar, granulated	2 lb 4 oz	Add sugar, fats, and vanilla to eggs.
Shortening, melted	10 oz	Mix on medium speed for 5 minutes.
Margarine, melted	8 oz	
Vanilla	2 Tbsp	
Flour, cake	14 oz	Combine dry ingredients.
Cocoa	10 oz	Add to creamed mixture. Mix on low speed about 5 minutes.
Baking powder	2 tsp	
Salt	½ tsp	
Nuts, chopped	12 oz	Add nuts to batter. Mix to blend.
		Scale batter into two lightly greased 12 × 18 × 1-inch baking pans, 3 lb 8 oz per pan. Bake at 325°F for 20 minutes. Do not overbake. Should be soft to touch when done. While warm, sprinkle with powdered sugar, or cool and cover with a thin layer of mocha or chocolate frosting if desired.

Approximate nutritive values per cookie   **Calories** 221

Amount/portion	%DV	Amount/portion	%DV	Amount/portion	%DV		%DV		%DV
Total Fat 12 g	19%	**Cholest.** 52 mg	17%	**Total Carb.** 26 g	9%	**Vitamin A**	3%	**Calcium**	3%
Sat. Fat 3 g	13%	**Sodium** 82 mg	3%	Fiber 0.7 g	3%	**Vitamin C**	0%	**Iron**	13%
Protein 4 g				Sugars 17 g					

Percent Daily Values (%DV) are based on a 2000-calorie diet.

Notes
- 12 oz unsweetened chocolate may be substituted for the cocoa. Melt and add to the fat-sugar-egg mixture.
- 13 oz all-purpose flour may be substituted for cake flour.
- 2 lb chopped dates may be added.
- May be baked in one 18 × 26 × 1-inch baking sheet.

FUDGE BROWNIES

Yield: 60 portions or 1 pan 18 × 26 × 1 inch   *Portion:* 2½ × 3 inches
Oven: 325°F   *Bake:* 20–25 minutes

Ingredient	Amount	Procedure
Bitter chocolate	1 lb	Melt chocolate and shortening.
Shortening	1 lb 4 oz	
Flour, cake	10 oz	Combine dry ingredients in mixer bowl.
Flour, all-purpose	10 oz	
Baking powder	5½ tsp	
Salt	2¼ tsp	
Eggs	15 (1 lb 10 oz)	Combine eggs, sugar, and vanilla in mixer bowl. Beat well.
Sugar, granulated	3 lb	Blend chocolate mixture into egg-sugar mixture.
Vanilla	1 Tbsp	Add dry ingredients, beating only until blended.
		Scale 8 lb of batter into greased 18 × 26 × 2-inch pan. Smooth batter. Bake at 325°F for 20–25 minutes or until edges shrink slightly from edge of pan. Cool. Cut 6 × 10.

Approximate nutritive values per cookie   **Calories** 260

Amount/portion	%DV	Amount/portion	%DV	Amount/portion	%DV		%DV		%DV
Total Fat 15 g	23%	**Cholest.** 52 mg	17%	**Total Carb.** 32 g	11%	Vitamin A	2%	Calcium	2%
Sat. Fat 5 g	26%	**Sodium** 140 mg	6%	Fiber 1 g	5%	Vitamin C	0%	Iron	7%
Protein 3 g				Sugars 22 g					

Percent Daily Values (%DV) are based on a 2000-calorie diet.

Variation   ● **Fudge Nut Brownies.** Add 10 oz chopped walnuts to batter.

COCONUT PECAN BARS

Yield: 96 portions or 2 pans 12 × 18 × 1 inch   *Portion:* 2 × 2¼ inches
Oven: 350°F   *Bake:* 15–20 minutes, first layer; 20–25 minutes, second layer

Ingredient	Amount	Procedure
Margarine	1 lb 8 oz	Blend margarine, brown sugar, and flour on low speed until mixture resembles coarse meal, using flat beater.
Sugar, brown	12 oz	Press even layer of mixture into two 12 × 18 × 1-inch baking pans, 1 lb 12 oz per pan.
Flour, all-purpose	1 lb 4 oz	Bake at 350°F until light brown, 15–20 minutes.
Eggs, beaten	8 (14 oz)	Combine remaining ingredients to form topping.
Flour, all-purpose	4 oz	
Baking powder	1 Tbsp	
Salt	2 tsp	
Sugar, brown	2 lb 8 oz	
Vanilla	1 Tbsp	
Coconut, shredded or flaked	8 oz	
Pecans, chopped	12 oz	
		Spread topping over baked crust, 3 lb per pan. Bake 20–25 minutes. Ice with Orange Icing (p. 356) if desired. Cut 6 × 8.

Approximate nutritive values per cookie   **Calories** 179

Amount/portion	%DV	Amount/portion	%DV	Amount/portion	%DV		%DV		%DV
Total Fat 10 g	15%	**Cholest.** 18 mg	6%	**Total Carb.** 22 g	7%	**Vitamin A**	2%	**Calcium**	2%
Sat. Fat 1 g	7%	**Sodium** 137 mg	6%	Fiber 0.4 g	2%	**Vitamin C**	0%	**Iron**	4%
Protein 2 g				Sugars 1 g					

Percent Daily Values (%DV) are based on a 2000-calorie diet.

Note   ● May be baked in one 18 × 26 × 1-inch baking sheet.

Variation   ● **Dreamland Bars.** Reduce coconut to 4 oz. Increase pecans to 1 lb. Add 12 oz chopped maraschino cherries and 1 lb chopped dates. Combine 2 oz margarine or butter and 8 oz powdered sugar. Spread over top. Bake.

DATE BARS

Yield: 60 portions or 2 pans 12 × 18 × 1 inch   *Portion:* 2½ × 3 inches
Oven: 350°F   *Bake:* 25–30 minutes

Ingredient	Amount	Procedure
Egg yolks	12 (7 oz)	Beat egg yolks on high speed until lemon colored, using flat beater.
Sugar, granulated	2 lb	Add sugar to yolks gradually and continue beating after each addition.
Flour, all-purpose Baking powder Salt	1 lb 1½ Tbsp ½ tsp	Combine flour, baking powder, and salt.
Dates, chopped Nuts, chopped	3 lb 1 lb	Add dates and nuts to flour mixture. Combine with egg-sugar mixture.
Egg whites	12 (14 oz)	Beat egg whites on high speed until they form soft peaks, using wire whip attachment. Fold into batter.
		Spread batter evenly into two lightly greased 12 × 18 × 1-inch baking pans, 4 lb 3 oz per pan. Bake at 350°F for 25–30 minutes.
Sugar, powdered	6 oz	Sift powdered sugar over top of warm baked bars. Cut 5 × 6.

Approximate nutritive values per cookie   **Calories** 219

Amount/portion	%DV	Amount/portion	%DV	Amount/portion	%DV		%DV		%DV
Total Fat 5 g	8%	**Cholest.** 42 mg	14%	**Total Carb.** 42 g	14%	Vitamin A	6%	Calcium	4%
Sat. Fat 1 g	4%	**Sodium** 54 mg	2%	Fiber 3 g	11%	Vitamin C	0%	Iron	5%
Protein 4 g				Sugars 32 g					

Percent Daily Values (%DV) are based on a 2000-calorie diet.

Note   • May be baked in one 18 × 26 × 1-inch baking sheet. Cut 6 × 10.

BUTTERSCOTCH SQUARES

Yield: 60 portions or 2 pans 12 × 18 × 1 inch   *Portion:* 2½ × 3 inches
Oven: 325°F   *Bake:* 25 minutes

Ingredient	Amount	Procedure
Margarine	1 lb	Cream margarine and sugar on medium speed for 5 minutes, using flat beater.
Sugar, brown	2 lb 8 oz	
Eggs	10 (1 lb)	Add eggs, one at a time, and vanilla. Mix on low speed until blended.
Vanilla	1 Tbsp	
Flour, all-purpose	1 lb 8 oz	Combine dry ingredients.
Baking powder	2 Tbsp	Add to creamed mixture. Mix on low speed until blended.
Salt	1 tsp	
Nuts, chopped (optional)	12 oz	Add nuts to batter. Mix to blend.
		Spread batter evenly in two lightly greased 12 × 18 × 1-inch baking pans, 3 lb 6 oz per pan. Bake at 325°F for 25 minutes. Cut 5 × 6.

Approximate nutritive values per cookie   **Calories** 213

Amount/portion	%DV	Amount/portion	%DV	Amount/portion	%DV		%DV		%DV
Total Fat 10 g	15%	**Cholest.** 32 mg	11%	**Total Carb.** 29 g	10%	Vitamin A	3%	Calcium	5%
Sat. Fat 2 g	9%	**Sodium** 154 mg	6%	Fiber 0.8 g	3%	Vitamin C	0%	Iron	6%
Protein 3 g				Sugars 1 g					

Percent Daily Values (%DV) are based on a 2000-calorie diet.

Note ● May be baked in one 18 × 26 × 1-inch baking sheet. Cut 6 × 10.

Variation ● **Butterscotch Chocolate Chip Brownies.** Add 1 lb chocolate chips.

OATMEAL DATE BARS

Yield: 96 portions or 2 pans 12 × 18 × 1 inch   *Portion:* 2 × 2¼ inches
Oven: 325°F   *Bake:* 45 minutes

Ingredient	Amount	Procedure
Margarine Sugar, brown	1 lb 10 oz 2 lb 12 oz	Cream margarine and sugar on medium speed for 5 minutes, using flat beater.
Flour, all-purpose Rolled oats, quick, uncooked Baking soda	2 lb 1 lb 8 oz 2⅔ Tbsp	Combine dry ingredients. Add to creamed mixture. Mix on low speed until crumbly. Spread 2 lb 10 oz prepared mixture into both 12 × 18 × 1-inch baking pans. Flatten to an even layer.
Date Filling (p. 360)	3 qt	Spread date filling over oatmeal mixture, 1½ qt per pan. Cover with remainder of dough, 1 lb 4 oz per pan. Bake at 325°F for 45 minutes. Cut 6 × 8 into bars.

Approximate nutritive values per cookie   **Calories** 245

Amount/portion	%DV	Amount/portion	%DV	Amount/portion	%DV		%DV		%DV
Total Fat 7 g	10%	**Cholest.** 0 mg	0%	**Total Carb.** 46 g	15%	**Vitamin A**	2%	**Calcium**	2%
Sat. Fat 1 g	7%	**Sodium** 184 mg	8%	Fiber 2 g	8%	**Vitamin C**	0%	**Iron**	6%
Protein 3 g				Sugars 19 g					

Percent Daily Values (%DV) are based on a 2000-calorie diet.

Notes
- May be baked in one 18 × 26 × 1-inch baking sheet. Cut 8 × 12.
- Crushed pineapple or cooked dried apricots may be used in place of dates in the filling.

MARSHMALLOW KRISPIE SQUARES

Yield: 60 portions or 2 pans 12 × 18 × 1 inch   *Portion:* 2½ × 3 inches

Ingredient	Amount	Procedure
Margarine Marshmallows Vanilla	1 lb 4 lb 1 Tbsp	Melt margarine. Add marshmallows and vanilla. Stir until completely melted. Cook over low heat 3 minutes longer, stirring constantly. Remove from heat.
Crisp rice cereal	2 lb 8 oz	Stir crisp rice cereal into marshmallow mixture until well-coated. Using buttered spatula, press mixture evenly into two lightly greased 12 × 18 × 1-inch baking pans, 3 lb per pan. Cut while warm, 5 × 6.

Approximate nutritive values per cookie   **Calories** 225

Amount/portion	%DV	Amount/portion	%DV	Amount/portion	%DV		%DV		%DV
Total Fat 6 g	10%	**Cholest.** 0 mg	0%	**Total Carb.** 41 g	14%	**Vitamin A**	27%	**Calcium**	1%
Sat. Fat 1 g	6%	**Sodium** 309 mg	13%	Fiber 0.4 g	1%	**Vitamin C**	16%	**Iron**	9%
Protein 2 g				Sugars 15 g					

Percent Daily Values (%DV) are based on a 2000-calorie diet.

Note
- May be made in one 18 × 26 × 1-inch baking sheet. Cut 6 × 10.

Variations
- **Chocolate Marshmallow Squares.** Cover squares with a thin, rich chocolate icing.
- **Peanut Butter Squares.** Add 1 lb 2 oz peanut butter to marshmallow mixture. Proceed as indicated. Frost with Chocolate Glaze (p. 358).

PRESSED, MOLDED, AND ROLLED COOKIE RECIPES

BUTTER TEA COOKIES

Yield: 10 dozen cookies
Oven: 375°F   *Bake:* 10–12 minutes

Ingredient	*Amount*	*Procedure*
Butter Sugar, granulated	1 lb 9 oz	Cream butter and sugar on medium speed for 5 minutes, using flat beater.
Eggs yolks Vanilla	6 (4 oz) 1 tsp	Add egg yolks and vanilla to creamed mixture. Mix on medium speed until blended.
Flour, all-purpose	1 lb 4 oz	Add flour and mix on low speed. Chill dough.
		Shape with cookie press onto ungreased baking sheets. Bake at 375°F for 10–12 minutes.

Approximate nutritive values per cookie   **Calories** 56

Amount/portion	%DV	Amount/portion	%DV	Amount/portion	%DV		%DV		%DV
Total Fat 3 g	5%	**Cholest.** 20 mg	7%	**Total Carb.** 6 g	2%	**Vitamin A**	4%	**Calcium**	0%
Sat. Fat 2 g	10%	**Sodium** 32 mg	1%	Fiber 0 g	0%	**Vitamin C**	0%	**Iron**	1%
Protein 1 g				Sugars 2 g					

Percent Daily Values (%DV) are based on a 2000-calorie diet.

Variation   ● **Thimble Cookies.** Roll dough into 1-inch balls. Dip in egg white and roll in finely chopped pecans. Bake 3 minutes at 325°F, then make indentation in center of cookies and fill with jelly. Bake 10–12 minutes longer.

CHOCOLATE TEA COOKIES

Yield: 10 dozen cookies
Oven: 350°F   *Bake:* 6–10 minutes

Ingredient	*Amount*	*Procedure*
Margarine Sugar, granulated	1 lb 12 oz	Cream margarine and sugar on medium speed for 5 minutes, using flat beater.
Eggs Vanilla	2 (4 oz) 1 Tbsp	Add eggs and vanilla to creamed mixture. Blend on medium speed for 5 minutes.
Flour, all-purpose Baking powder Salt Cocoa	1 lb 2 oz 1 tsp ¼ tsp 1 oz (¼ cup)	Combine dry ingredients. Add to creamed mixture and mix on low speed until blended. Chill dough. Shape dough with cookie press onto ungreased baking sheets. Bake at 350°F for 6–10 minutes.

Approximate nutritive values per cookie   **Calories** 56

Amount/portion	%DV	Amount/portion	%DV	Amount/portion	%DV		%DV		%DV
Total Fat 3 g	5%	**Cholest.** 4 mg	1%	**Total Carb.** 6 g	2%	**Vitamin A**	1%	**Calcium**	0%
Sat. Fat 1 g	3%	**Sodium** 44 mg	2%	Fiber 0 g	0%	**Vitamin C**	0%	**Iron**	1%
Protein 1 g				Sugars 3 g					

Percent Daily Values (%DV) are based on a 2000-calorie diet.

SANDIES

Yield: 8 dozen cookies
Oven: 325°F   *Bake:* 20 minutes

Ingredient	Amount	Procedure
Margarine or butter Sugar, granulated Vanilla	12 oz 3 oz 1 tsp	Cream margarine, sugar, and vanilla on medium speed for 5 minutes, using flat beater.
Flour, all-purpose Salt	1 lb 2 oz 1 tsp	Add flour and salt to creamed mixture. Mix on low speed until blended.
Water Pecans, finely chopped	1 Tbsp 8 oz	Add water and pecans and blend. Chill dough.
		Shape dough into small balls ¾ inch in diameter. If mixture crumbles so it will not stick together, add a small amount of melted margarine. Place on lightly greased or parchment-paper-lined baking sheets. Bake at 325°F until lightly browned, about 20 minutes.
Sugar, powdered, sifted	8 oz (approximate)	Roll in powdered sugar while still hot.

Approximate nutritive values per cookie   **Calories** 73

Amount/portion	%DV	Amount/portion	%DV	Amount/portion	%DV		%DV		%DV
Total Fat 5 g	7%	**Cholest.** 0 mg	0%	**Total Carb.** 8 g	3%	Vitamin A	1%	Calcium	0%
Sat. Fat 1 g	3%	**Sodium** 56 mg	2%	Fiber 0.3 g	1%	Vitamin C	0%	Iron	1%
Protein 1 g				Sugars 3 g					

Percent Daily Values (%DV) are based on a 2000-calorie diet.

Variation   • **Frosty Date Balls.** Add 1 lb chopped pitted dates.

BUTTERSCOTCH REFRIGERATOR COOKIES

Yield: 8 dozen cookies
Oven: 375°F   *Bake:* 8–10 minutes

Ingredient	Amount	Procedure
Margarine	8 oz	Cream fats and sugars on medium speed for 5 minutes, using flat beater.
Shortening	8 oz	
Sugar, granulated	12 oz	
Sugar, brown	1 lb	
Eggs	4 (7 oz)	Add eggs and vanilla to creamed mixture. Mix on medium speed for 5 minutes.
Vanilla	2 tsp	
Flour, all-purpose	2 lb	Combine dry ingredients.
Cream of tartar	2 tsp	
Baking soda	2 tsp	
Dates, finely chopped	8 oz	Add dry ingredients, dates, and nuts to dough. Mix on low speed until well blended.
Nuts, chopped	8 oz	
		Form dough into three 2-lb rolls, 2 inches in diameter. Wrap in waxed paper. Chill several hours. Slice cookies ⅛ inch thick. Place on ungreased baking sheets. Bake at 375°F for 8–10 minutes.

Approximate nutritive values per cookie   **Calories** 128

Amount/portion	%DV	Amount/portion	%DV	Amount/portion	%DV		%DV		%DV
Total Fat 6 g	9%	**Cholest.** 9 mg	3%	**Total Carb.** 18 g	6%	Vitamin A	1%	Calcium	1%
Sat. Fat 1 g	6%	**Sodium** 54 mg	2%	Fiber 1 g	3%	Vitamin C	0%	Iron	3%
Protein 2 g				Sugars 5 g					

Percent Daily Values (%DV) are based on a 2000-calorie diet.

CRISP GINGER COOKIES

Yield: 8 dozen cookies
Oven: 375°F   *Bake:* 8–10 minutes

Ingredient	*Amount*	*Procedure*
Molasses Sugar, granulated	1 cup 8 oz	Combine molasses and sugar. Boil 1 minute. Cool.
Shortening	8 oz	Place shortening and molasses in mixer bowl. Blend on medium speed, using flat beater.
Eggs	2 (4 oz)	Add eggs and mix thoroughly.
Flour, all-purpose Salt Baking soda Ginger, ground	1 lb 12 oz (or more) ½ tsp 1 tsp 2 tsp	Combine dry ingredients. Add to molasses-egg mixture. Mix on low speed until well blended.
		Form dough into two rolls 2 inches in diameter. Wrap in waxed paper. Chill thoroughly. Cut into ⅛-inch slices. Place on lightly greased baking sheets. Bake at 375°F for 8–10 minutes.

Approximate nutritive values per cookie   **Calories** 70

Amount/portion	%DV	Amount/portion	%DV	Amount/portion	%DV		%DV		%DV
Total Fat 3 g	4%	**Cholest.** 5 mg	2%	**Total Carb.** 11 g	4%	**Vitamin A**	0%	**Calcium**	0%
Sat. Fat 1 g	3%	**Sodium** 26 mg	1%	Fiber 0.2 g	1%	**Vitamin C**	0%	**Iron**	3%
Protein 1 g				Sugars 4 g					

Percent Daily Values (%DV) are based on a 2000-calorie diet.

Note   • Dough may be rolled and cut with cookie cutter.

OATMEAL CRISPIES

Yield: 8 dozen cookies
Oven: 350°F   *Bake:* 12–15 minutes

Ingredient	Amount	Procedure
Flour, all-purpose	12 oz	Combine flour, salt, and soda in mixer bowl.
Salt	2 tsp	
Baking soda	2 tsp	
Shortening	1 lb	Add shortening, sugar, eggs, and vanilla to flour mixture.
Sugar, granulated	1 lb	Mix on low speed about 5 minutes, using flat beater.
Sugar, brown	1 lb	
Eggs	4 (7 oz)	
Vanilla	2 tsp	
Rolled oats, quick, uncooked	1 lb	Add rolled oats and nuts. Mix on low speed to blend. Shape dough into three 2-lb rolls, 2 inches in diameter. Wrap in waxed paper and chill.
Nuts, chopped	8 oz	
		Cut dough into slices ¼ inch thick. Place 2 inches apart on ungreased baking sheets. Bake at 350°F for 12–15 minutes.

Approximate nutritive values per cookie   **Calories** 126

Amount/portion	%DV	Amount/portion	%DV	Amount/portion	%DV		%DV		%DV
Total Fat 6 g	10%	**Cholest.** 9 mg	3%	**Total Carb.** 16 g	5%	**Vitamin A**	0%	**Calcium**	1%
Sat. Fat 1 g	7%	**Sodium** 76 mg	3%	Fiber 0.3 g	1%	**Vitamin C**	0%	**Iron**	3%
Protein 2 g				Sugars 5 g					

Percent Daily Values (%DV) are based on a 2000-calorie diet.

Note   ● For smaller cookies, form into four 1½-inch rolls and slice ⅛ inch thick. Yield: approximately 25 dozen.

Variation   ● **Oatmeal Coconut Crispies.** Add 1 cup flaked coconut.

ROLLED SUGAR COOKIES

Yield: 10 dozen cookies   *Portion:* 2-inch cookie
Oven: 375°F   *Bake:* 7 minutes

Ingredient	Amount	Procedure
Margarine or butter Sugar, granulated	1 lb 1 lb	Cream margarine and sugar on medium speed for 5 minutes, using flat beater.
Eggs Vanilla	4 (7 oz) 1 Tbsp	Add eggs and vanilla to creamed mixture. Blend on medium speed for 2 minutes.
Flour, all-purpose Salt Baking powder	1 lb 8 oz 2 tsp 2 tsp	Combine dry ingredients. Add to creamed mixture. Mix on low speed until blended.
Flour, all-purpose Sugar, granulated	4 oz 2 oz	Mix flour and sugar. Roll dough ⅛ inch thick on a surface that has been lightly dusted with flour-sugar mixture. Cut into desired shapes. Place on ungreased baking sheets. Bake at 375°F for 7 minutes or until lightly browned.

Approximate nutritive values per cookie   **Calories** 71

Amount/portion	%DV	Amount/portion	%DV	Amount/portion	%DV		%DV		%DV
Total Fat 3 g	5%	**Cholest.** 7 mg	2%	**Total Carb.** 9 g	3%	**Vitamin A**	1%	**Calcium**	0%
Sat. Fat 1 g	3%	**Sodium** 78 mg	3%	Fiber 0.2 g	1%	**Vitamin C**	0%	**Iron**	1%
Protein 1 g				Sugars 4 g					

Percent Daily Values (%DV) are based on a 2000-calorie diet.

Variations

- **Christmas Wreath Cookies.** Cut rolled dough with doughnut cutter. Brush with beaten egg and sprinkle with chopped nuts. Decorate with candied cherry rings and pieces of citron arranged to represent holly.

- **Coconut Cookies.** Cut rolled dough with round cookie cutter. Brush with melted margarine or butter and sprinkle with shredded coconut, plain or tinted with food coloring.

- **Filled Cookies.** Cut dough with round cutter. Cover half with Fig or Date Filling (p. 360). Brush edges with milk and cover with remaining cookies. Press edges together with tines of fork.

- **Pinwheel Cookies.** Divide dough into two portions. Add 2 oz melted unsweetened chocolate to one portion. Roll each portion into the same size sheet, ⅛ inch thick. Place chocolate dough over the white dough and press together. Roll as for jelly roll. Chill thoroughly. Cut into thin slices.

PIE RECIPES

PASTRY

Yield: 50 lb dough

Ingredient	Amount	Procedure
Flour, all-purpose	25 lb	Mix flour and shortening on low speed, using flat beater.
Shortening, hydrogenated	18 lb	Mix until fat particles are the size of small peas for a flaky crust. For a mealy crust, mixture should resemble cornmeal.
Ice water	3¾ qt	Add water and salt to flour-fat mixture.
Salt	12 oz	Mix on low speed only until dough will hold together.

Approximate nutritive values per pound　　　　　　　　　　**Calories** 2268

Amount/portion	%DV	Amount/portion	%DV	Amount/portion	%DV		%DV		%DV
Total Fat 166 g	255%	**Cholest.** 0 mg	0%	**Total Carb.** 173 g	58%	Vitamin A	0%	Calcium	5%
Sat. Fat 41 g	206%	**Sodium** 2643 mg	110%	Fiber 6 g	25%	Vitamin C	0%	Iron	58%
Protein 23 g				Sugars 4 g					

Percent Daily Values (%DV) are based on a 2000-calorie diet.

Notes
- For seven 9-inch one-crust pies, use 4 lb; for seven 9-inch two-crust pies, use 7 lb. See pp. 390–392 for directions for preparation.
- For eight 8-inch one-crust pies, use 2 lb 8 oz; for eight 8-inch two-crust pies, use 4 lb 8 oz. See pp. 390–392 for directions for preparation.

PASTRY FOR ONE-CRUST PIES

Yield: 56 portions or 4 lb dough or 7 9-inch pies   *Portion:* 8 pieces per pie

Ingredient	Amount	Procedure

Flour, all-purpose
Shortening,
  hydrogenated
	2 lb
	1 lb 6 oz
		Mix flour and shortening on low speed for 1 minute, using
		  pastry knife or flat beater.
		Scrape sides of bowl and continue mixing until shortening is
		  evenly distributed, 1 to 2 minutes.

Ice water
Salt
	1–1¼ cups
	1 oz (1½ Tbsp)
		Dissolve salt in smaller amount of water (use reserved amount
		  of water if needed).
		Add to flour mixture. Mix on low speed only until dough is
		  formed, about 40 seconds.
		Portion into 9-oz balls for 9-inch pies. See Note for 8-inch pies.

To Make a One-Crust Pie:

1. Roll dough into a circle 2 inches larger than pie pan.

2. Fit pastry loosely into pan so there are no air spaces between the crust and pan (Figure 9.4).

3. Trim, allowing ½ inch extra to build up edge.

4. For custard-type pie, crimp edge, add filling, and bake according to the recipe.

5. For cream or chiffon pies, crimp edge (Figure 9.4) and prick crust with fork. Bake according to directions that follow.

6. Bake in a hot oven (425°F) for 10 minutes or until light brown. Cool. A second pan may be placed over the crust for the first part of baking, then removed and the crust allowed to brown. The second pan helps to keep the crust in shape.

7. Fill baked crust with desired filling.

Approximate nutritive values per portion   **Calories** 157

Amount/portion	%DV	Amount/portion	%DV	Amount/portion	%DV		%DV		%DV
Total Fat 11 g	17%	**Cholest.** 0 mg	0%	**Total Carb.** 12 g	4%	Vitamin A	0%	Calcium	0%
Sat. Fat 3 g	14%	**Sodium** 172 mg	7%	Fiber 0.4 g	2%	Vitamin C	0%	Iron	4%
Protein 2 g				Sugars 0 g					

Percent Daily Values (%DV) are based on a 2000-calorie diet.

Note   • For eight 8-inch pies, use 1 lb 3 oz flour, 13 oz shortening, 1 cup water, and 2½ tsp salt. Scale
              5 oz for each crust. To serve, cut pies in six portions.

FIGURE 9.4 Preparing
pastry for a baked pie shell.
Holes are made in shells to
keep them flat during baking.

PASTRY FOR TWO-CRUST PIES

Yield: 56 portions or 7 lb dough or 7 9-inch pies   *Portion:* 8 pieces per pie

Ingredient	Amount	Procedure
Flour, all-purpose Shortening, hydrogenated	3 lb 6 oz 2 lb 7 oz	Mix flour and shortening on low speed for 1 minute, using pastry knife or flat beater. Scrape sides of bowl and continue mixing until shortening is evenly distributed, 1–2 minutes.
Ice water Salt	1¾–2 cups 1¾ oz (2½ Tbsp)	Dissolve salt in smaller amount of water (use reserved amount of water if needed). Add to flour mixture. Mix on low speed only until dough is formed, about 40 seconds. Portion into 9-oz balls for bottom crust and 7-oz for top crust. See Notes for 8-inch pies.

TO MAKE A TWO-CRUST PIE:

1. Roll each ball of dough into a circle. Place pastry for bottom crust in pie pan, easing into pan without stretching the dough.

2. Trim off overhanging dough. If desired, leave ½ inch extra pastry around the edge and fold over to make a pocket of pastry to prevent fruit juices from running out.

3. Add desired filling.

4. Moisten edge of bottom crust with water (Figure 9.5).

5. Cover with top crust, in which slits or vents have been cut near the center to allow steam to escape.

6. Trim top pastry to extend ½ inch beyond edge of pan.

7. Fold edge of top pastry under edge of lower pastry, then seal by pressing the two crusts together and fluting with fingertips.

8. If desired, brush top crusts with milk and sprinkle with sugar.

9. Bake as directed in the recipe.

Approximate nutritive values per portion   **Calories** 275

Amount/portion	%DV	Amount/portion	%DV	Amount/portion	%DV		%DV		%DV
Total Fat 20 g	31%	**Cholest.** 0 mg	0%	**Total Carb.** 21 g	7%	**Vitamin A**	0%	**Calcium**	0%
Sat. Fat 5 g	25%	**Sodium** 286 mg	12%	Fiber 1 g	3%	**Vitamin C**	0%	**Iron**	7%
Protein 3 g				Sugars 0 g					

Percent Daily Values (%DV) are based on a 2000-calorie diet.

Notes
- For eight 8-inch pies, use 2 lb flour, 1 lb 8 oz shortening, 1½–1¾ cups water, and 1 oz (1½ Tbsp) salt. Scale 5 oz for bottom crust and 4 oz for top crust. To serve, cut into six portions.
- Using scrap dough is often necessary. Using no more than 50 percent of scrap dough and restricting its use to bottom crusts is recommended. Care must be taken to handle the dough as little as possible.

Variation
- **Cheddar Cheese Pastry.** Use 2 lb 8 oz flour, 1 lb 13 oz shortening, 1 lb 14 oz shredded cheddar cheese, ¾ cup water, and 1½ oz salt. Add cheese after flour and shortening have been mixed.

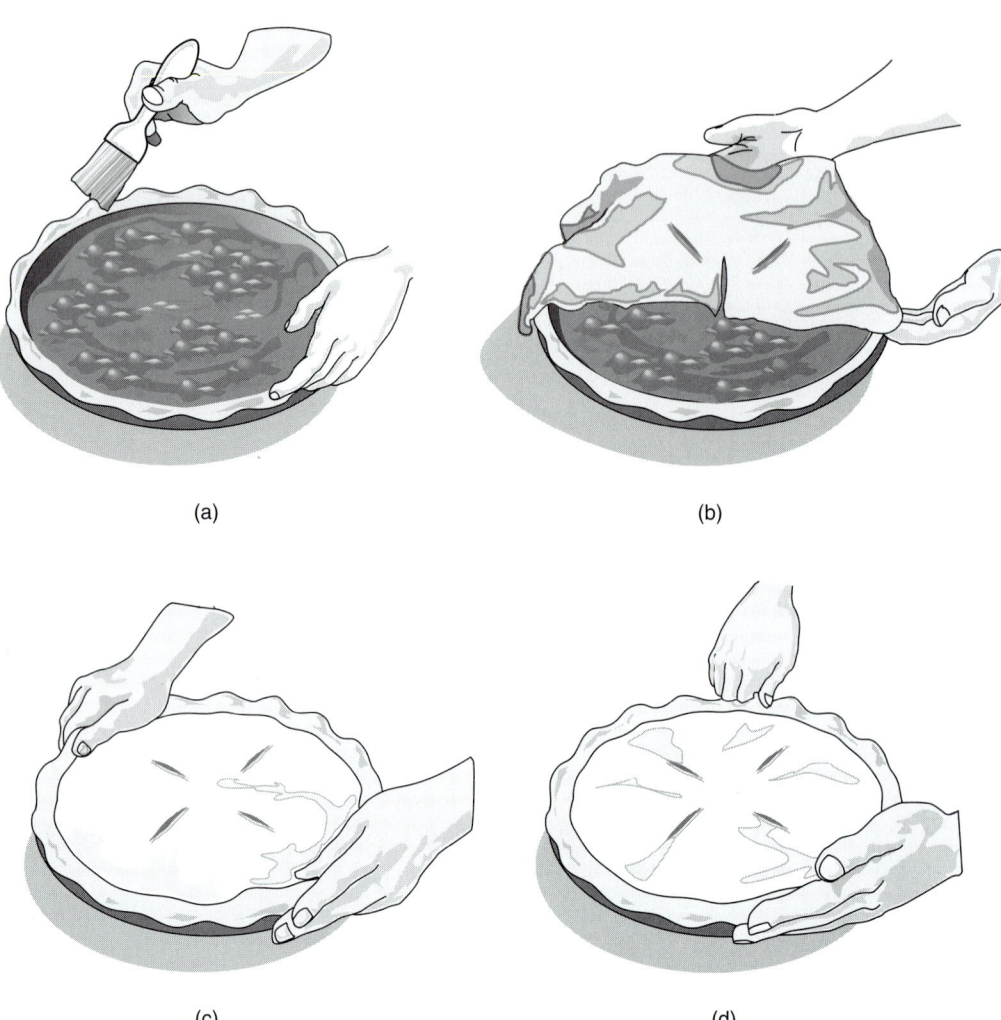

(a)

(b)

(c)

(d)

FIGURE 9.5 Preparing pastry for a two-crust pie. (a) Moistening edge of crust. (b) Placing top crust on filled pie. (c) Pressing top crust to seal tightly. (d) Fluting edge of pie.

GRAHAM CRACKER CRUST

Yield: 56 portions or 7 9-inch pies   *Portion:* 8 pieces per pie
Oven: 375°F   *Bake:* 5 minutes

Ingredient	Amount	Procedure
Graham cracker crumbs	2 lb	Mix all ingredients.
Sugar, granulated	15 oz	Pat 9 oz crumb mixture evenly into each pie pan. For 8-inch crusts, see Notes.
Margarine, melted	15 oz	Bake at 375°F for about 5 minutes.

Approximate nutritive values per portion   **Calories** 155

Amount/portion	%DV	Amount/portion	%DV	Amount/portion	%DV		%DV		%DV
Total Fat 8 g	12%	**Cholest.** 0 mg	0%	**Total Carb.** 20 g	7%	**Vitamin A**	7%	**Calcium**	0%
Sat. Fat 1 g	6%	**Sodium** 169 mg	7%	Fiber 0 g	0%	**Vitamin C**	0%	**Iron**	2%
Protein 1 g				Sugars 7 g					

Percent Daily Values (%DV) are based on a 2000-calorie diet.

Notes
- For eight 8-inch shells, use 1 lb 5 oz crumbs, 10 oz sugar, and 10 oz melted margarine. Portion 5 oz per shell.
- Vanilla wafer crumbs or chocolate cookie crumbs may be substituted for graham cracker crumbs.
- Crusts may be refrigerated several hours instead of baking.

Variation
- **Chocolate Crumb Crust.** Add 6 oz cocoa to graham cracker crumbs and sugar. Mix, then add melted margarine.

MERINGUE FOR PIES

Yield: 56 portions or meringue for 7 9-inch pies   *Portion:* 8 pieces per pie
Oven: 375°F   *Bake:* 10–12 minutes

Ingredient	Amount	Procedure
Pasteurized egg whites, at room temperature	16 (2 cups/1 lb)	Add salt and cream of tartar to egg whites. Whip past frothy stage, on high speed, approximately 1½ minutes, using wire whip attachment.
Salt	½ tsp	
Cream of tartar	½ tsp	
Sugar, granulated	1 lb	Add sugar gradually while beating. Beat until sugar has dissolved. The meringue should be stiff enough to hold peaks but not dry.
		Spread meringue on filled pies while filling is hot, 5–6 oz per pie. The meringue should touch all edges of the crust. Brown in oven at 375°F for 10–12 minutes or until golden brown.

Approximate nutritive values per portion   **Calories** 36

Amount/portion	%DV	Amount/portion	%DV	Amount/portion	%DV		%DV		%DV
Total Fat 0 g	0%	**Cholest.** 0 mg	0%	**Total Carb.** 8 g	3%	**Vitamin A**	0%	**Calcium**	0%
Sat. Fat 0 g	0%	**Sodium** 33 mg	1%	Fiber 0 g	0%	**Vitamin C**	0%	**Iron**	0%
Protein 1 g				Sugars 8 g					

Percent Daily Values (%DV) are based on a 2000-calorie diet.

Notes
- For 8-inch pies, use 4 oz per pie.
- For proper volume, egg whites must have no yolk mixed in them, and the beater and bowl must be free of any trace of fat. Even a small trace of fat will prevent the whites from foaming properly.
- Egg whites should be at room temperature before beating. The meringue will be higher and lighter.
- For food safety reasons, pasteurized egg whites are recommended.

MERINGUE SHELLS

Yield: 50 shells   *Portion:* 3 oz
Oven: 275°F   *Bake:* 1 hour

Ingredient	Amount	Procedure
Egg whites	28 (3 cups/1 lb 8 oz)	Add salt and cream of tartar to egg whites. Beat on high speed until frothy, using wire whip attachment.
Salt	1 tsp	
Cream of tartar	1 tsp	
Sugar, granulated	3 lb	Add sugar ½ cup at a time, beating on high speed between each addition until sugar is dissolved and mixture will hold its shape, 20–30 minutes.
		Place mixture on greased and floured baking sheets with No. 10 dipper and shape into nests with spoon; or place on pans with pastry tube. Bake at 275°F for about 1 hour. Watch carefully the last 15–20 minutes to avoid overcooking. Meringues should be white, not brown. If overcooked, they are too brittle. Serve ice cream or fruit in the center.

Approximate nutritive values per portion   **Calories** 112

Amount/portion	%DV	Amount/portion	%DV	Amount/portion	%DV		%DV		%DV
Total Fat 0 g	0%	**Cholest.** 0 mg	0%	**Total Carb.** 27g	9%	**Vitamin A**	0%	**Calcium**	0%
Sat. Fat 0 g	0%	**Sodium** 65 mg	3%	Fiber 0 g	0%	**Vitamin C**	0%	**Iron**	0%
Protein 1 g				Sugars 26 g					

Percent Daily Values (%DV) are based on a 2000-calorie diet.

Variations

- **Angel Pie.** Place meringue in well-greased and floured pie pans, about 1¼ qt per pan. Use spoon to build up sides. After baking, fill each shell with 3 cups Cream Pie filling (p. 404), Lemon Pie filling (p. 406), or Chocolate Cream Pie filling (p. 404). Then top with a thin layer of whipped cream.

- **Meringue Sticks.** Force mixture through pastry tube to form sticks. Sprinkle with chopped nuts. Bake.

PIES MADE WITH CANNED FRUIT

Yield: 56 portions or 7 9-inch pies   *Portion:* 8 pieces per pie
Oven: 400°F   *Bake:* 30 minutes

Ingredient	Amount	Procedure
Pastry for Two-Crust Pies (p. 391)	7 lb	Make pastry. Divide into 9-oz balls for bottom crusts and 7-oz balls for top crusts. Roll and place bottom crusts in seven 9-inch pie pans. For 8-inch pies, see Notes.
Fruit, pie pack	2 No. 10 cans	Drain fruit. Measure liquid and add water to make 2 qt. Bring 1½ qt of the liquid to boiling point.
Cornstarch	8 oz	Mix remaining liquid with cornstarch and add gradually to hot liquid, while stirring with a wire whip. Cook until thick and clear.
Sugar, granulated Salt	3 lb 8 oz 2 tsp	While still hot, add sugar and salt. Mix thoroughly and bring to boiling point. Add drained fruit and mix carefully to avoid breaking or mashing fruit. Cool slightly.
		Scale 1 lb 12 oz–2 lb (3½–4 cups) filling into each unbaked pie shell. Moisten edge of bottom crust with water. Cover with top crust. Seal edge, trim, and flute edges (Figure 9.5). Bake at 400°F for 30 minutes or until crust is browned.

Notes

- For eight 8-inch pies, make 4 lb 8 oz dough for crusts and portion into 5 oz for bottom crust and 4 oz for top crust. For filling, use 1½ No. 10 cans fruit, 3 lb sugar (variable), 6 oz cornstarch, and 1½ tsp salt. Drain liquid from fruit and add water to make 1½ qt liquid. Scale 1 lb–1 lb 8 oz (approximately 3 cups) filling per pie.

- Suggested fillings: apple, apricot, blackberry, cherry, gooseberry, or peach.

- Other thickening agents may be used, such as waxy maize (6 oz total for 9-inch or 4½ oz total for 8-inch pies) or tapioca (9 oz total for 9-inch or 7½ oz total for 8-inch pies).

PIES MADE WITH FROZEN FRUIT

Yield: 56 portions or 7 9-inch pies   *Portion:* 8 pieces per pie
Oven: 400°F   *Bake:* 30–40 minutes

Ingredient	Amount	Procedure
Pastry for Two-Crust Pies (p. 391)	7 lb	Make pastry. Divide into 9-oz balls for bottom crusts, 7-oz balls for top crusts. Roll and place bottom crusts in seven 9-inch pie pans. For 8-inch pies, see Notes.
Fruit, frozen	10 lb	Thaw fruit. Measure juice. If necessary, add water to bring total liquid to 1½–2 qt according to consistency desired.
Sugar, granulated Cornstarch or waxy maize (see Notes)	See Table 9.3 See Table 9.3	Combine sugar and starch. Add to hot liquid, stirring with wire whip.
Seasonings	See Table 9.3	Add seasonings to thickened liquid and pour over fruit. Mix carefully to avoid breaking or mashing fruit.
		Scale 1 lb 12 oz–2 lb (3½–4 cups) filling into each unbaked pie shell. Moisten edge of bottom crust with water. Cover with top crust in which slits have been made for steam to escape. Seal edge, trim and flute edges (see Figure 9.5). Bake at 400°F for 30–40 minutes or until fruit is done and crust is golden brown.

Notes

- Allow 2–3 oz cornstarch or 2–2½ oz waxy maize per qt of liquid. Use of waxy maize or other waxy starch products results in a translucent soft gel through which the fruit shows clearly. The color is brighter and the gel is less opaque and less rigid, making it ideal for thickening fruit fillings. It is important to use a waxy starch if the pies are to be frozen.

- For eight 8-inch pies, use 4 lb 8 oz pastry, portioned 5 oz for bottom crust and 4 oz for top crust. Portion 1 lb–1 lb 8 oz (approximately 3 cups) filling per pie.

TABLE 9.3   Guide for using frozen fruit in pies or cobblers (seven 9-inch pies)

| Fruit 10 lb | Sugar* | Thickening | | Seasonings |
		Cornstarch*	Waxy maize*	
Apples	1 lb 8 oz	3 oz	2½ oz	Salt, 1 tsp; nutmeg, 1 tsp; cinnamon, 1 Tbsp; butter, 2 oz
Apricots	2 lb	5½ oz	4 oz	Cinnamon, 2 tsp
Berries	2½–3½ lb	6½ oz	5 oz	Lemon juice, 2 Tbsp; salt, 1 tsp
Blueberries	3 lb	8 oz	6 oz	Salt, 1 tsp; butter, 2 oz; lemon juice, 1½ cups; cinnamon, 1 tsp
Blue plums	2–2½ lb	5½ oz	4 oz	Salt, 1 tsp; butter, 2 oz
Cherries	1 lb 12 oz	7 oz	5 oz	Salt, 1 tsp
Gooseberries	6 lb	14 oz	10 oz	Salt, ½ tsp
Peaches	1 lb 6 oz	5½ oz	4 oz	Butter, 1 oz; salt, 1 tsp; almond extract, ¼ tsp; cinnamon, 1 tsp; nutmeg, 1 tsp
Pineapple	2 lb	5½ oz	4 oz	Salt, 1 tsp
Rhubarb	5 lb	7 oz	5 oz	Salt, 1 tsp
Strawberries	2 lb	12 oz	8½ oz	Lemon juice, ¾ cup; red color, ¾ tsp

*The amount of sugar and cornstarch or waxy maize added to the fruit will vary according to the pack of the fruit and individual preferences of flavor and consistency. Frozen fruits packed without the addition of sugar are known as "dry pack." When sugar is added during the freezing process, the ratio is usually 3, 4, or 5 parts by weight of fruit to 1 part by weight of sugar. Use less thickening for cobblers. Some fruits are available individually quick frozen (IQF) without added sugar.

FRESH APPLE PIE

Yield: 56 portions or 7 9-inch pies   *Portion:* 8 pieces per pie
Oven: 400°F   *Bake:* 45 minutes

Ingredient	Amount	Procedure
Pastry for Two-Crust Pies (p. 391)	7 lb	Make pastry. Divide into 9-oz balls for bottom crusts, 7-oz balls for top crusts. Roll and place bottom crusts in seven 9-inch pie pans. For 8-inch pies, see Notes.
Apples, tart, fresh	12 lb (EP) 15 lb (AP)	Peel, core, and slice apples.
Sugar, granulated Flour, all-purpose Cinnamon	3 lb 4 oz 1 Tbsp	Combine sugar, fruit, and cinnamon. Add to apples and mix carefully.
Margarine	8 oz	Portion 2 lb 4 oz filling into each unbaked crust. Add 1 oz margarine to each pie. Moisten edge of bottom crust. Cover with perforated top crust. Seal edge, trim excess dough, and flute edges (see Figure 9.5). Bake at 400°F for 45 minutes or until apples are tender.

Approximate nutritive values per portion   **Calories** 462

Amount/portion	%DV	Amount/portion	%DV	Amount/portion	%DV		%DV		%DV
Total Fat 24 g	**36%**	**Cholest.** 0 mg	**0%**	**Total Carb.** 62 g	**21%**	Vitamin A	1%	Calcium	1%
Sat. Fat 6 g	**28%**	**Sodium** 326 mg	**14%**	Fiber 3 g	**12%**	Vitamin C	9%	Iron	8%
Protein 3 g				Sugars 37 g					

Percent Daily Values (%DV) are based on a 2000-calorie diet.

Notes
- For eight 8-inch pies, use 4 lb 8 oz dough for crust and portion 5 oz for bottom crust and 4 oz for top crust. Portion filling, 2 lb per pie.
- Suggested apples are Jonathan, Granny Smith, and Winesap. Frozen (IQF) apples may be substituted for fresh apples.

Variation
- **Apple Crumb Pie.** Omit top crust. Sprinkle apples with **Streusel Topping:** Mix 1 lb flour, 1 lb 10 oz sugar, 2 oz nonfat dry milk, and 1 tsp salt. Cut in 10 oz margarine or butter and add 6 oz chopped pecans. Use 1 cup per pie. Bake until apples are tender and topping is brown.

SOUR CREAM APPLE NUT PIE

Yield: 56 portions or 7 9-inch pies   *Portion:* 8 pieces per pie
Oven: 450°F, 350°F   *Bake:* 10 minutes, 55 minutes

Ingredient	Amount	Procedure
Pastry for One-Crust Pies (p. 390)	4 lb	Make pastry. Line seven 9-inch pie pans, 9 oz per pan. For 8-inch pies, see Note.
Sour cream	3 lb	Combine and mix until thoroughly blended.
Sugar, granulated	8 oz	
Flour, all-purpose	6 oz	
Eggs	4 (6 oz)	
Vanilla	2 Tbsp	
Salt	1 tsp	
Frozen sliced apples	8 lb 8 oz	Combine apples and sour cream mixture, being careful not to break apples.
		Scale 1 lb 12 oz filling into each unbaked crust. Bake at 450°F for 10 minutes. Reduce temperature to 350°F and continue baking until filling is slightly puffed and golden brown, about 40 minutes.

TOPPING

Ingredient	Amount	Procedure
Flour, all-purpose	5 oz	Combine flour, sugars, and cinnamon.
Sugar, brown	4 oz	
Sugar, granulated	5 oz	
Cinnamon	2 Tbsp	
Margarine	5 oz	Add margarine to dry ingredients. Mix until crumbly.
Walnuts, coarsely chopped	8 oz	Add nuts. Mix in. Scale 3½ oz topping over each pie and bake for 15 minutes.

Approximate nutritive values per portion   **Calories** 345

Amount/portion	%DV	Amount/portion	%DV	Amount/portion	%DV		%DV		%DV
Total Fat 21 g	**33%**	**Cholest.** 24 mg	**8%**	**Total Carb.** 36 g	**12%**	**Vitamin A**	7%	**Calcium**	4%
Sat. Fat 7 g	**33%**	**Sodium** 254 mg	**11%**	Fiber 2 g	**9%**	**Vitamin C**	0%	**Iron**	8%
Protein 5 g				Sugars 7 g					

Percent Daily Values (%DV) are based on a 2000-calorie diet.

Note   • For eight 8-inch pies, use 2 lb 8 oz dough portioned 5 oz per pie. For filling, scale apple mixture 1 lb 8 oz per pie and topping 3 oz per pie.

RAISIN PIE

Yield: 56 portions or 7 9-inch pies   *Portion:* 8 pieces per pie
Oven: 400°F   *Bake:* 30 minutes

Ingredient	Amount	Procedure
Pastry for Two-Crust Pies (p. 391)	7 lb	Make pastry. Divide into 9-oz balls for bottom crusts, 7-oz balls for top crusts. Roll and place bottom crusts in seven 9-inch pie pans. For 8-inch pies, see Note.
Raisins Water, hot	4 lb 4½ qt	Simmer raisins in water until plump. Cool slightly.
Sugar, granulated Cornstarch Salt	2 lb 4 oz 6 oz 2 tsp	Combine sugar, cornstarch, and salt. Add to raisins and cook until thickened. Remove from heat.
Lemon juice Margarine	6 Tbsp 3 oz	Add lemon juice and margarine to raisin mixture. Cool slightly.
		Portion 2 lb 4 oz (3½–4 cups) filling into each unbaked crust. Moisten edge of bottom crust. Cover with perforated top crust. Seal edge, trim excess dough, and flute edges (see Figure 9.5). Bake at 400°F for 30 minutes or until crust is golden brown.

Approximate nutritive values per portion   **Calories** 465

Amount/portion	%DV	Amount/portion	%DV	Amount/portion	%DV		%DV		%DV
Total Fat 21 g	33%	**Cholest.** 0 mg	0%	**Total Carb.** 68 g	23%	**Vitamin A**	0%	**Calcium**	2%
Sat. Fat 5 g	26%	**Sodium** 384 mg	16%	Fiber 2 g	10%	**Vitamin C**	2%	**Iron**	10%
Protein 4 g				Sugars 39 g					

Percent Daily Values (%DV) are based on a 2000-calorie diet.

Note ● For eight 8-inch pies, use 4 lb 8 oz dough, portioned 5 oz for bottom crust and 4 oz for top crust. For filling, portion 1 lb 14 oz (3–3½ cups) filling per pie.

Variation ● **Dried Apricot Pie.** Use 5 lb dried apricots. Cover with hot water; let stand 1 hour. Cook slowly without stirring until tender. Combine 4 lb granulated sugar and 2½ oz cornstarch. Mix with ½ cup cold water. Add to fruit a few minutes before it is done. Continue cooking until juice is clear. Proceed as for Raisin Pie.

RHUBARB PIE

Yield: 56 portions or 7 9-inch pies   *Portion:* 8 pieces per pie
Oven: 400°F   *Bake:* 35 minutes

Ingredient	Amount	Procedure
Rhubarb, fresh or frozen	10 lb (EP)	If fresh rhubarb is used, wash and trim. Do not peel. Cut in 1-inch pieces.
Sugar, granulated Tapioca, quick-cooking Salt Orange peel, grated	5 lb 8 oz 6 oz 2 tsp 3 Tbsp	Combine and stir into rhubarb. Let stand 30 minutes.
Pastry for Two-Crust Pies (p. 391)	7 lb	Make pastry. Divide into 9-oz balls for bottom crusts, 7-oz balls for top crusts. Roll and place bottom crusts in seven 9-inch pie pans, 9 oz per pan. For 8-inch pies, see Notes.
Margarine, melted	5 oz	Portion 2 lb 4 oz filling into each unbaked crust. Distribute margarine over filling in each pie. Moisten edges with cold water. Cover with top crust or pastry strips. Press edges together. Bake at 400°F for 35 minutes or until crust is golden brown and fruit is tender.

Approximate nutritive values per portion   **Calories** 494

Amount/portion	%DV	Amount/portion	%DV	Amount/portion	%DV		%DV		%DV
Total Fat 22 g	34%	**Cholest.** 0 mg	0%	**Total Carb.** 72 g	24%	**Vitamin A**	1%	**Calcium**	7%
Sat. Fat 5 g	27%	**Sodium** 391 mg	16%	Fiber 2 g	9%	**Vitamin C**	11%	**Iron**	8%
Protein 4 g				Sugars 44 g					

Percent Daily Values (%DV) are based on a 2000-calorie diet.

Notes
- For eight 8-inch pies, use 4 lb 8 oz dough portioned 5 oz for bottom crust and 4 oz for top crust. Scale 1 lb 14 oz filling per pie.
- 8 oz cornstarch or 5 oz waxy maize starch may be substituted for the tapioca.

RHUBARB CUSTARD PIE

Yield: 56 portions or 7 9-inch pies   *Portion:* 8 pieces per pie
Oven: 375°F   *Bake:* 45–50 minutes

Ingredient	*Amount*	*Procedure*
Pastry for One-Crust Pies (p. 390)	4 lb	Make pastry. Line seven 9-inch pie pans, 9 oz per pan. Flute edges. For 8-inch pies, see Notes.
Rhubarb, fresh or frozen	8 lb (EP)	If fresh rhubarb is used, wash and trim. Do not peel. Cut into ¼-inch pieces.
Eggs, beaten	12 (1 lb 5 oz)	Add eggs to rhubarb.
Sugar, granulated Flour, all-purpose Salt Lemon peel, grated	4 lb 8 oz 9 oz 1 tsp 1 tsp	Mix dry ingredients. Add to rhubarb mixture. Scale 2 lb (4½ cups) filling into each unbaked crust. Bake at 375°F for 45–50 minutes or until custard is set. Cool. Refrigerate if not served within 4 hours.

Approximate nutritive values per portion   **Calories** 345

Amount/portion	%DV	Amount/portion	%DV	Amount/portion	%DV		%DV		%DV
Total Fat 13 g	19%	**Cholest.** 45 mg	15%	**Total Carb.** 55 g	18%	Vitamin A	2%	Calcium	6%
Sat. Fat 3 g	16%	**Sodium** 227 mg	9%	Fiber 2 g	7%	Vitamin C	8%	Iron	7%
Protein 4 g				Sugars 36 g					

Percent Daily Values (%DV) are based on a 2000-calorie diet.

Notes
- Potentially hazardous food. Store at temperature below 41°F.
- For eight 8-inch pies, use 2 lb 8 oz dough, portioned 5 oz per pie. Use 1 lb 12 oz filling per pie.
- May be topped with Meringue (p. 394).
- Unbaked pie may be covered with a top crust or a latticed top made of ⅛-inch pastry strips.

CREAM PIE

Yield: 56 portions or 7 9-inch pies   *Portion:* 8 pieces per pie
Oven: 425°F for pastry, 375°F for meringue   *Bake:* 10 minutes, 12 minutes

Ingredient	Amount	Procedure
Pastry for One-Crust Pies (p. 390)	4 lb	Make pastry. Line seven 9-inch pie pans, 9 oz per pan. For 8-inch pies, see Note. Flute edges and prick crust with fork (Figure 9.4). Bake at 425°F for 10 minutes or until light brown. Cool.
Milk	3¾ qt	Heat milk to boiling point in a steam-jacketed or other large kettle.
Sugar, granulated Cornstarch Salt Milk, cold	2 lb 12 oz 13 oz 2½ tsp 1¼ qt	Mix sugar, cornstarch, and salt. Add cold milk and stir until smooth. Add to hot milk gradually, stirring briskly with a wire whip. Cook until smooth and thick, approximately 10 minutes.
Egg yolks, beaten	20 (13 oz)	Add, while stirring, a small amount of hot mixture to the egg yolks. Add to remaining hot mixture, stirring constantly. Stir slowly and cook 5–10 minutes. Remove from heat.
Margarine Vanilla	5 oz 2½ Tbsp	Stir in margarine and vanilla. Pour 2 lb (4 cups) filling into each baked pie shell.
Egg whites Salt Sugar, granulated Cream of tartar	20 (1 lb 6 oz) ½ tsp 1 lb 4 oz ½ tsp	Prepare Meringue (p. 394). Cover each filled pie with 5 oz meringue. Bake at 375°F for 10–12 minutes or until meringue is golden brown. Cool quickly (within 4 hours) to below 41°F. Refrigerate until served.

Approximate nutritive values per portion   **Calories** 397

Amount/portion	%DV	Amount/portion	%DV	Amount/portion	%DV		%DV		%DV
Total Fat 17 g	26%	**Cholest.** 40 mg	13%	**Total Carb.** 55 g	18%	**Vitamin A**	5%	**Calcium**	11%
Sat. Fat 5 g	26%	**Sodium** 380 mg	16%	Fiber 0.5 g	2%	**Vitamin C**	1%	**Iron**	5%
Protein 7 g				Sugars 36 g					

Percent Daily Values (%DV) are based on a 2000-calorie diet.

Notes
- Potentially hazardous food. Store at temperature below 41°F.
- For eight 8-inch pies, use 2 lb 8 oz dough, portioned 5 oz per pie. Use 1 lb 12 oz (3½ cups) filling per pie.

Variations
- **Banana Cream Pie.** Slice 1 large banana into each pie shell before adding cream filling.
- **Chocolate Cream Pie.** Add 6 oz cocoa or 8 oz unsweetened chocolate. Increase sugar to 3 lb. If using cocoa, mix with cornstarch and sugar. If using chocolate, melt and add to hot milk.
- **Coconut Cream Pie.** Add 10 oz toasted coconut to filling and sprinkle 2 oz coconut over meringue.
- **Date Cream Pie.** Add 3 lb chopped, pitted dates to cooked filling.
- **Fruit Glazed Pie.** Use frozen blueberries, strawberries, or cherries. Thaw 6 lb frozen fruit and drain. Measure 1 qt fruit syrup, adding water if needed to make that amount. Add slowly to a mixture of 6 oz sugar, 4 oz cornstarch, and ¾ cup lemon juice if using blueberries, strawberries or sweet cherries or ¾ cup additional water if using sour cherries. Cook until thick and clear. Cool slightly. Add drained fruit. Spread over cream pies.
- **Nut Cream Pie.** Add ½ cup chopped pecans or other nuts.
- **Pineapple Cream Pie.** Add 3½ cups crushed pineapple, drained, to cooked filling.

BUTTERSCOTCH CREAM PIE

Yield: 56 portions or 7 9-inch pies   *Portion:* 8 pieces per pie
Oven: 425°F for pastry, 375°F for meringue   *Bake:* 10 minutes, 12 minutes

Ingredient	Amount	Procedure
Pastry for One-Crust Pies (p. 390)	4 lb	Make pastry. Line seven 9-inch pie pans, 9 oz per pan. For 8-inch pies, see Notes. Flute edges and prick crust with fork (Figure 9.4). Bake at 425°F for 10 minutes or until light brown.
Margarine Sugar, brown	1 lb 2 lb 8 oz	Melt margarine. Stir in sugar. Cook over low heat to 220°F, stirring occasionally.
Milk	3 qt	Add milk slowly to margarine-sugar mixture while stirring with wire whip. Stir until all sugar is dissolved. Heat mixture to boiling.
Cornstarch Flour, all-purpose Salt	6 oz 6 oz 1 Tbsp	Combine cornstarch, flour, and salt.
Milk, warm Eggs, whole Egg yolks	1 qt 5 (9 oz) 10 (6 oz)	Combine milk and eggs. Add to cornstarch and flour mixture and mix. Add to the hot mixture while stirring. Cook until thick. Remove from heat.
Margarine Vanilla	4 oz 2 Tbsp	Add margarine and vanilla. Cool partially. Fill baked pie shells, 1 lb 12 oz (3½ cups) per pie.
Egg whites Salt Sugar, granulated Cream of tartar	16 (1 lb 2 oz) ½ tsp 1 lb ½ tsp	Prepare Meringue (p. 394). Cover each filled pie with 5 oz meringue. Bake at 375°F for 10–12 minutes, or until meringue is golden brown. Cool quickly (within 4 hours) to temperature below 41°F. Refrigerate until served.

Approximate nutritive values per portion   **Calories** 427

Amount/portion	%DV	Amount/portion	%DV	Amount/portion	%DV		%DV		%DV
Total Fat 23 g	36%	**Cholest.** 68 mg	23%	**Total Carb.** 49 g	16%	**Vitamin A**	12%	**Calcium**	11%
Sat. Fat 6 g	31%	**Sodium** 465 mg	19%	Fiber 0.5 g	2%	**Vitamin C**	1%	**Iron**	8%
Protein 6 g				Sugars 12 g					

Percent Daily Values (%DV) are based on a 2000-calorie diet.

Notes
- Potentially hazardous food. Store at temperature below 41°F.
- For eight 8-inch pies, use 2 lb 8 oz dough portioned 5 oz per pie. Use 1 lb 8 oz (3 cups) filling per pie.

LEMON PIE

Yield: 56 portions or 7 9-inch pies *Portion:* 8 pieces per pie
Oven: 425°F pastry, 375°F meringue *Bake:* 10 minutes, 12 minutes

Ingredient	Amount	Procedure
Pastry for One-Crust Pies (p. 390)	4 lb	Make pastry. Line seven 9-inch pie pans, 9 oz per pan. For 8-inch pies, see Note. Flute edges and prick bottom and sides of crust with fork. Bake at 425°F for 10 minutes or until light brown.
Water Salt Lemon rinds, grated	2¼ qt 2 tsp 3	Heat water, salt, and lemon peel to boiling point.
Sugar, granulated Cornstarch Water, cold	3 lb 8 oz 12 oz 3 cups	Mix sugar and cornstarch. Add cold water and stir until mixed. Add slowly to boiling water, stirring constantly with wire whip. Cook until thickened and clear. Remove from heat.
Egg yolks, beaten	16 (1½ cups)	Add, while stirring, a small amount of hot mixture to egg yolks. Add to remaining hot mixture, stirring constantly. Return to heat and cook about 5 minutes. Remove from heat.
Margarine Lemon juice	3 oz 1½ cups	Add margarine and lemon juice. Blend. Scale into baked pie shells, 1 lb 10 oz (3½ cups) per pie.
Egg whites Salt Sugar, granulated Cream of tartar	16 (1 lb 2 oz) ½ tsp 1 lb ½ tsp	Prepare Meringue (p. 394). Cover each pie with 5 oz meringue. Bake at 375°F for 10–12 minutes, or until meringue is golden brown. Cool quickly (within 4 hours) to temperature below 41°F. Refrigerate until served.

Approximate nutritive values per portion **Calories** 355

Amount/portion	%DV	Amount/portion	%DV	Amount/portion	%DV		%DV		%DV
Total Fat 14 g	**22%**	**Cholest.** 61 mg	**20%**	**Total Carb.** 55 g	**18%**	Vitamin A	9%	Calcium	1%
Sat. Fat 4 g	**18%**	**Sodium** 302 mg	**13%**	Fiber 0.5 g	**2%**	Vitamin C	3%	Iron	5%
Protein 3 g				Sugars 36 g					

Percent Daily Values (%DV) are based on a 2000-calorie diet.

Notes
- Potentially hazardous food. Store at temperature below 41°F.
- For eight 8-inch pies, use 2 lb 8 oz dough portioned 5 oz per pie. Use 3 cups filling per pie.

CUSTARD PIE

Yield: 56 portions or 7 9-inch pies   *Portion:* 8 pieces per pie
Oven: 450°F, 350°F   *Bake:* 15 minutes, 20 minutes

Ingredient	Amount	Procedure
Pastry for One-Crust Pies (p. 390)	4 lb	Make pastry. Line seven 9-inch pie pans, 9 oz per pan. For 8-inch pies, see Notes. Flute edges.
Eggs Sugar, granulated Salt Vanilla	30 (3 lb 4 oz) 1 lb 14 oz 1¼ tsp 2½ Tbsp	Beat eggs slightly. Add sugar, salt, and vanilla. Mix.
Milk, scalded	1¼ gal	Add hot milk, slowly at first, then more rapidly. Pour into unbaked pie shells, 1 qt per pie.
Nutmeg, ground	2 tsp	Sprinkle nutmeg over top of pies. Bake at 450°F for 15 minutes. Reduce heat to 350°F and bake for 20 minutes, or until a knife inserted halfway between the edge and center comes out clean. Cool quickly (within 4 hours) to below 41°F. Refrigerate until served.

Approximate nutritive values per portion　　　　　　　　　　　　　　　　**Calories** 312

Amount/portion	%DV	Amount/portion	%DV	Amount/portion	%DV		%DV		%DV
Total Fat 17 g	26%	**Cholest.** 124 mg	41%	**Total Carb.** 32 g	11%	**Vitamin A**	8%	**Calcium**	12%
Sat. Fat 5 g	27%	**Sodium** 296 mg	12%	Fiber 0.4 g	2%	**Vitamin C**	1%	**Iron**	6%
Protein 8 g				Sugars 19 g					

Percent Daily Values (%DV) are based on a 2000-calorie diet.

Notes
- Potentially hazardous food. Store at temperature below 41°F.
- For eight 8-inch pies, use 2 lb 8 oz dough portioned 5 oz per pie. For filling, use 24 (2 lb 8 oz) eggs, 1 lb 8 oz sugar, 1 tsp salt, 2 Tbsp vanilla, and 1 gal milk, portioned 3 cups per pie.

Variation
- **Coconut Custard Pie.** Add 1 lb flaked coconut. Omit nutmeg.

PUMPKIN PIE

Yield: 56 portions or 7 9-inch pies   *Portion:* 8 pieces per pie
Oven: 450°F, 350°F   *Bake:* 15 minutes, 30 minutes

Ingredient	Amount	Procedure
Pastry for One-Crust Pies (p. 390)	4 lb	Make pastry. Line seven 9-inch pie pans, 9 oz per pan. For 8-inch pies, see Notes. Flute edges.
Eggs, beaten Pumpkin	14 (1 lb 8 oz) 2½ qt (3 No. 2½ cans)	Combine eggs and pumpkin in mixer bowl.
Sugar, granulated Sugar, brown Ginger, ground Cinnamon, ground Salt	1 lb 12 oz 10 oz 1½ tsp 1½ Tbsp 1 Tbsp	Combine sugars and seasonings. Add to pumpkin mixture.
Milk, hot	2¾ qt	Add milk to pumpkin mixture. Mix. Pour into unbaked pie shells, 1 qt per pie. Bake at 450°F for 15 minutes. Reduce heat to 350°F and bake for 30 minutes, or until a knife inserted halfway between the edge and center comes out clean. Cool quickly (within 4 hours) to below 41°F. Refrigerate until served.

Approximate nutritive values per portion   **Calories** 295

Amount/portion	%DV	Amount/portion	%DV	Amount/portion	%DV		%DV		%DV
Total Fat 14 g	22%	**Cholest.** 58 mg	19%	**Total Carb.** 38 g	13%	**Vitamin A**	100%	**Calcium**	8%
Sat. Fat 4 g	21%	**Sodium** 329 mg	14%	Fiber 2 g	7%	**Vitamin C**	3%	**Iron**	9%
Protein 5 g				Sugars 16 g					

Percent Daily Values (%DV) are based on a 2000-calorie diet.

Notes
- Potentially hazardous food. Store at temperature below 41°F.
- For eight 8-inch pies, use 2 lb 8 oz pastry portioned 5 oz per pie. Use 3½ cups filling per pie.
- Undiluted evaporated milk may be substituted for fresh milk.
- One pound chopped pecans may be sprinkled over tops of pies after 15 minutes of baking. Continue baking.

Variation
- **Praline Pumpkin Pie.** Mix 12 oz finely chopped pecans, 14 oz brown sugar, and 8 oz margarine or butter. Pat 4 oz of mixture into each unbaked pie shell before pouring in filling.

PECAN PIE

Yield: 56 portions or 7 9-inch pies   *Portion:* 8 pieces per pie
Oven: 350°F   *Bake:* 40 minutes

Ingredient	Amount	Procedure
Pastry for One-Crust Pies (p. 390)	4 lb	Make pastry. Line seven 9-inch pie pans, 9 oz per pan. For 8-inch pies, see Note. Flute edges.
Sugar, granulated Margarine Salt	5 lb 5 oz 1 Tbsp	Cream sugar, margarine, and salt on medium speed until fluffy, using flat beater.
Eggs, beaten	30 (3 lb 4 oz)	Add eggs to creamed mixture and mix well.
Corn syrup, white Vanilla	1¼ qt 3 Tbsp	Add corn syrup and vanilla. Blend thoroughly.
Pecan halves or pieces	2 lb	Place 4½ oz pecans in each unbaked pie shell. Pour 1 lb 8 oz (3 cups) egg-sugar mixture over pecans. Bake at 350°F for 40 minutes, or until filling is set.

Approximate nutritive values per portion   **Calories** 568

Amount/portion	%DV	Amount/portion	%DV	Amount/portion	%DV		%DV		%DV
Total Fat 27 g	**41%**	**Cholest.** 112 mg	**37%**	**Total Carb.** 78 g	**26%**	**Vitamin A**	5%	**Calcium**	3%
Sat. Fat 5 g	**25%**	**Sodium** 365 mg	**15%**	Fiber 1.5 g	6%	**Vitamin C**	0%	**Iron**	14%
Protein 6 g				Sugars 54 g					

Percent Daily Values (%DV) are based on a 2000-calorie diet.

Note   ● For eight 8-inch pies, use 2 lb 8 oz pastry portioned 5 oz per pie. Use 2½ cups filling and 4 oz pecans per pie.

PECAN CREAM CHEESE PIE

Yield: 56 portions or 7 9-inch pies *Portion:* 8 pieces per pie
Oven: 375°F, 350°F *Bake:* 10 minutes, 40–45 minutes

Ingredient	Amount	Procedure
Pastry for One-Crust Pies (p. 390)	4 lb	Make pastry. Line seven 9-inch pie pans, 5 oz per pan. For 8-inch pies, see Notes. Flute edges and prick crust with fork (Figure 9.4). Bake at 375°F for 10 minutes or until set. Cool.
Cream cheese, softened Sugar, granulated	3 lb 12 oz 1 lb	Combine cream cheese and sugar in mixer bowl. Beat on medium until smooth, using flat beater.
Eggs Salt Vanilla	7 (12 oz) 1 tsp 2 Tbsp	Add eggs, salt, and vanilla to creamed mixture. Beat until smooth. Spread 12 oz filling into each pie shell.
Pecan pieces	2 lb 3 oz	Sprinkle 5 oz pecans over cream cheese layer.
Eggs Sugar, brown Corn syrup Vanilla	11 (1 lb 4 oz) 8 oz 2 lb 8 oz 1 Tbsp	Combine eggs, sugar, corn syrup, and vanilla in mixer bowl. Mix until blended. Scale 10 oz (approximately 1 cup) over pecans. Bake at 350°F for 40–45 minutes. Cool. Refrigerate 6–8 hours before serving.

Approximate nutritive values per portion

Calories 514

Amount/portion	%DV	Amount/portion	%DV	Amount/portion	%DV		%DV		%DV
Total Fat 36 g	55%	**Cholest.** 103 mg	34%	**Total Carb.** 43 g	14%	Vitamin A	16%	Calcium	5%
Sat. Fat 11 g	55%	**Sodium** 337 mg	14%	Fiber 2 g	6%	Vitamin C	0%	Iron	14%
Protein 7 g				Sugars 19 g					

Percent Daily Values (%DV) are based on a 2000-calorie diet.

Notes
- Potentially hazardous food. Store at temperature below 41°F.
- For eight 8-inch pies, use 2 lb 8 oz pastry portioned 5 oz per pie. For the filling, portion 11 oz cream cheese filling, 8 oz (1 cup) syrup mixture, and 4 oz pecans per pie.

CHOCOLATE CHIFFON PIE

Yield: 56 portions or 7 9-inch pies   *Portion:* 8 pieces per pie
Oven: 425°F pastry   *Bake:* 10 minutes

Ingredient	Amount	Procedure
Pastry for One-Crust Pies (p. 390)	4 lb	Make pastry. Line seven 9-inch pie pans, 9 oz per pan. For 8-inch pies, see Notes. Flute edges and prick crust with a fork (Figure 9.4). Bake at 425°F for 10 minutes or until light brown.
Gelatin, unflavored Water, cold	1½ oz 1½ cups	Sprinkle gelatin over water. Let stand 10 minutes.
Unsweetened chocolate Water, boiling	8 oz 3 cups	Melt chocolate. Add hot water slowly. Stir until mixed. Add gelatin and stir until dissolved.
Egg yolks, beaten Sugar, granulated Salt	24 (1 lb) 1 lb 8 oz 1½ tsp	Combine egg yolks, sugar, and salt. Cook until mixture begins to thicken.
Vanilla	2 Tbsp	Add vanilla and chocolate to egg mixture. Chill until mixture begins to congeal.
Egg whites (see Notes) Sugar, granulated	24 (1 lb 12 oz) 1 lb 8 oz	Beat egg whites until frothy. Gradually add sugar and beat at high speed until meringue can be formed into soft peaks. Fold into chocolate mixture. Scale into baked pie shells, 1 lb (4 cups) per pie. Cool quickly (within 4 hours) to below 41°F. Refrigerate until served.
Cream, whipping Sugar, granulated	1 qt ¼ cup	Just before serving, whip cream. Add sugar. Spread 1 cup whipped cream over each pie.

Approximate nutritive values per portion   **Calories** 365

Amount/portion	%DV	Amount/portion	%DV	Amount/portion	%DV		%DV		%DV
Total Fat 21 g	33%	**Cholest.** 123 mg	41%	**Total Carb.** 40 g	13%	Vitamin A	21%	Calcium	3%
Sat. Fat 8 g	39%	**Sodium** 263 mg	11%	Fiber 1 g	3%	Vitamin C	0%	Iron	7%
Protein 6 g				Sugars 26 g					

Percent Daily Values (%DV) are based on a 2000-calorie diet.

Notes
- Potentially hazardous food. Store at temperature below 41°F.
- Use of pasteurized frozen egg yolks and whites is recommended.
- For eight 8-inch pies, use 2 lb 8 oz pastry portioned 5 oz per pie. For filling, use 12 oz (3 cups) per pie.
- Graham Cracker Crust (p. 393) may be used in place of pastry.

Variations
- **Chocolate Peppermint Chiffon Pie.** Cover pie with whipped cream to which 1 lb crushed peppermint candy sticks has been added.
- **Chocolate Refrigerator Dessert.** Use ⅔ recipe Chocolate Chiffon Pie. Spread 12 oz vanilla wafer crumbs over bottom of 12 × 20 × 2-inch pan. Pour in chocolate chiffon mixture and cover with 1 lb 12 oz crumbs.
- **Frozen Chocolate Chiffon Pie.** Fold in 3 cups cream, whipped. Pile into pastry or graham cracker crust. Spread over tops of pies 1½ cups cream, whipped and sweetened with 3 Tbsp sugar. Freeze. Serve frozen.

STRAWBERRY CHIFFON PIE

Yield: 56 portions or 7 9-inch pies   *Portion:* 8 pieces per pie
Oven: 425°F pastry   *Bake:* 10 minutes

Ingredient	Amount	Procedure
Pastry for One-Crust Pies (p. 390)	4 lb	Make pastry. Line seven 9-inch pie pans, 9 oz per pan. For 8 inch pies, see Notes. Flute edges and prick crust with fork (Figure 9.4). Bake at 425°F for 10 minutes or until light brown.
Strawberries, sliced frozen	3 lb 12 oz	Drain strawberries. Reserve juice.
Strawberry gelatin Water, boiling	1 lb 4 oz 1¼ qt	Dissolve gelatin in boiling water.
Strawberry juice drained from berries Lemon juice	2 lb (1 qt) ⅔ cup	Add enough water to reserved juice to make 1 qt. Combine lemon and strawberry juices. Add to gelatin mixture. Chill until partially set. Stir occasionally.
Whipped topping	3 cups	Whip topping stiff but not dry. Whip gelatin mixture until soft peaks form. Fold in whipped topping.
Egg whites (see Notes) Salt Sugar, granulated	10 (12 oz) 1 tsp 12 oz	Add salt to egg whites. Beat until soft peaks form. Gradually add sugar. Beat until stiff peaks form. Fold in gelatin mixture. Fold strawberries into mixture. Portion 1 lb 4 oz filling into each baked pie shell. Cool quickly (within 4 hours) to below 41°F. Refrigerate until served.

Approximate nutritive values per portion   **Calories** 295

Amount/portion	%DV	Amount/portion	%DV	Amount/portion	%DV		%DV		%DV
Total Fat 15 g	24%	**Cholest.** 14 mg	5%	**Total Carb.** 29 g	10%	**Vitamin A**	4%	**Calcium**	1%
Sat. Fat 5 g	26%	**Sodium** 472 mg	20%	Fiber 1.3 g	5%	**Vitamin C**	27%	**Iron**	5%
Protein 7 g				Sugars 9 g					

Percent Daily Values (%DV) are based on a 2000-calorie diet.

Notes
- Potentially hazardous food. Store at internal temperature below 41°F.
- Use of pasteurized frozen egg whites is recommended.
- For eight 8-inch pies, use 2 lb 8 oz pastry portioned 5 oz per pie. For the filling, use 1 lb per pie.

LEMON CHIFFON PIE

Yield: 56 portions or 7 9-inch pies   *Portion:* 8 pieces per pie
Oven: 425°F pastry   *Bake:* 10 minutes

Ingredient	Amount	Procedure
Pastry for One-Crust Pies (p. 390)	4 lb	Make pastry. Line seven 9-inch pie pans, 9 oz per pan. For 8-inch pies, see Notes. Flute edges and prick crust with fork (Figure 9.4). Bake at 425°F for 10 minutes or until light brown.
Gelatin, unflavored Water, cold	1½ oz 1¾ cups	Sprinkle gelatin over water. Let stand 10 minutes.
Egg yolks, beaten Sugar, granulated Salt Lemon juice	21 (13 oz) 1 lb 8 oz 2 tsp 2½ cups	Add sugar, salt, and lemon juice to egg yolks. Cook in steam-jacketed kettle or over hot water until consistency of custard. Remove from heat. Add softened gelatin. Stir until dissolved.
Lemon peel, grated	2 Tbsp	Add lemon peel. Chill until mixture begins to congeal.
Egg whites (see Notes) Sugar, granulated	21 (1 lb 8 oz) 1 lb 2 oz	Beat egg whites until frothy. Gradually add sugar and beat until meringue will form soft peaks. Fold into lemon mixture. Scale into baked pie shells, 1 lb (4 cups) per pie. Cool quickly (within 4 hours) to below 41°F. Refrigerate until served.
Cream, whipping Sugar, granulated	1 qt ½ cup	Just before serving, whip cream. Spread 1 cup cream over each pie.

Approximate nutritive values per portion   **Calories** 331

Amount/portion	%DV	Amount/portion	%DV	Amount/portion	%DV		%DV		%DV
Total Fat 19 g	29%	**Cholest.** 103 mg	34%	**Total Carb.** 37 g	12%	**Vitamin A**	18%	**Calcium**	2%
Sat. Fat 7 g	34%	**Sodium** 280 mg	12%	Fiber 0.5 g	2%	**Vitamin C**	5%	**Iron**	5%
Protein 5 g				Sugars 23 g					

Percent Daily Values (%DV) are based on a 2000-calorie diet.

Notes
- Potentially hazardous food. Store at temperature below 41°F.
- Use of pasteurized frozen egg yolks and whites is recommended.
- For eight 8-inch pies, use 2 lb 8 oz pastry portioned 5 oz per pie. For the filling, use 12 oz (3 cups) per pie.
- Graham Cracker Crust (p. 393) may be used in place of pastry.

Variations
- **Frozen Lemon Pie.** Increase sugar in custard to 2 lb. Delete sugar from meringue. Beat egg whites and fold into 2 qt cream, whipped. Fold into chilled lemon mixture. Pour into Graham Cracker Crust (p. 393). Freeze. Serve frozen.
- **Lemon Refrigerator Dessert.** Crush 3 lb 8 oz vanilla wafers. Spread half of crumbs in bottom of 12 × 20 × 2-inch pan. Pour chiffon pie mixture over crumbs and cover with remaining crumbs.
- **Orange Chiffon Pie.** Substitute 2 cups orange juice for 2 cups lemon juice. Substitute grated orange peel for lemon peel.

ICE CREAM PIE

Yield: 56 portions or 7 9-inch pies   *Portion:* 8 pieces per pie
Oven: 500°F   *Bake:* 2–3 minutes

Ingredient	Amount	Procedure
Graham Cracker Crust (p. 393)	1 recipe	Prepare seven 9-inch crusts. For 8-inch pies, see Notes.
Vanilla ice cream	2 gal	Soften ice cream. Dip into prepared crusts, using 4½ cups per pie. Freeze several hours.
Egg whites (see Notes) Salt Sugar, granulated Vanilla	24 (2 lb 10 oz) ¾ tsp 1 lb 8 oz 1½ tsp	Add salt to egg whites. Beat until frothy, using whip attachment. Add sugar gradually, beating at high speed until sugar has dissolved. Add vanilla. Cover pies with meringue, 9 oz per pie. Brown quickly (2–3 minutes) in oven at 500°F. Return to freezer if not served immediately.
Chocolate Sauce (p. 774)	1½ qt	Serve with chocolate sauce or fresh strawberries.

Approximate nutritive values per portion   **Calories** 467

Amount/portion	%DV	Amount/portion	%DV	Amount/portion	%DV		%DV		%DV
Total Fat 22 g	**34%**	**Cholest.** 35 mg	**12%**	**Total Carb.** 64 g	**21%**	Vitamin A	12%	Calcium	12%
Sat. Fat 9 g	**43%**	**Sodium** 339 mg	**14%**	Fiber 0.3 g	**1%**	Vitamin C	0%	Iron	5%
Protein 7 g				Sugars 31 g					

Percent Daily Values (%DV) are based on a 2000-calorie diet.

Notes
- Use of pasteurized frozen egg whites is recommended.
- For eight 8-inch pies, portion 1 qt ice cream per pie. Cover with 8 oz meringue.
- Pastry crust, baked, may be used in place of graham cracker crust.
- Other flavors of ice cream may be used.

Variation
- **Raspberry Alaska Pie.** Thicken three 40-oz packages frozen red raspberries with 2 oz cornstarch. Make thin layers of thickened berries and ice cream in graham cracker crusts, using about half of the berries. Proceed as for Ice Cream Pie. Spoon remaining berries over individual servings of pie.

FROZEN MOCHA ALMOND PIE

Yield: 56 portions or 7 9-inch pies   *Portion:* 8 pieces per pie

Ingredient	Amount	Procedure
Graham Cracker Crust (p. 393)	1 recipe	Prepare seven 9-inch crusts. For 8-inch pies, see Notes.
Gelatin, unflavored Water, cold	1½ oz 1 cup	Sprinkle gelatin over water. Let stand 10 minutes.
Egg yolks, beaten Sugar, granulated Salt Coffee, hot	18 (11 oz) 1 lb 8 oz 1 Tbsp 2 qt	Add sugar, salt, and coffee to egg yolks. Cook in steam-jacketed kettle or over hot water until mixture coats spoon. Remove from heat. Add softened gelatin. Stir until dissolved. Chill until mixture is consistency of unbeaten egg whites.
Egg whites (see Notes) Cream of tartar Sugar, granulated	18 (1 lb 5 oz) 1½ tsp 1 lb 8 oz	Add cream of tartar to egg whites. Beat until frothy. Add sugar gradually and beat on high speed until consistency of meringue. Fold into gelatin mixture.
Cream, whipping Sugar, granulated	1 qt ¼ cup	Whip cream. Add sugar to one-third of the whipped cream. Save for topping.
Almonds, toasted Vanilla	1 lb 2 Tbsp	Add almonds and vanilla to remaining whipped cream. Fold into gelatin mixture. Pour into prepared crusts. Spread remaining whipped cream over pies and freeze. Remove from freezer 15–20 minutes before serving.

Approximate nutritive values per portion   **Calories** 378

Amount/portion	%DV	Amount/portion	%DV	Amount/portion	%DV		%DV		%DV
Total Fat 19 g	**29%**	**Cholest.** 90 mg	**30%**	**Total Carb.** 48 g	**16%**	Vitamin A	18%	Calcium	5%
Sat. Fat 6 g	**29%**	**Sodium** 312 mg	**13%**	Fiber 0.7 g	**3%**	Vitamin C	0%	Iron	6%
Protein 6 g				Sugars 33 g					

Percent Daily Values (%DV) are based on a 2000-calorie diet.

Notes
- Use of pasteurized frozen egg yolks and whites is recommended.
- For eight 8-inch pies, use 2 lb 8 oz pastry, portioned 5 oz per pie. Portion filling 3 cups per pie.

OTHER DESSERT RECIPES

BUTTERSCOTCH PUDDING

Yield: 50 portions or 6 qt   *Portion:* ½ cup

Ingredient	Amount	Procedure
Margarine Sugar, brown	10 oz 3 lb 4 oz	Cook margarine and sugar in steam-jacketed kettle until sugar starts to dissolve.
Water, warm	1 qt	Add water slowly, while stirring. Turn off heat.
Milk	2½ qt	Add milk to warm mixture.
Cornstarch Flour, all-purpose Salt Milk	6 oz 2½ oz ½ tsp 3 cups	Combine dry ingredients in mixer bowl. Add milk to make a smooth paste. Slowly add to warm sugar-milk mixture, stirring constantly. Cook until mixture thickens. Turn off heat.
Eggs	8 (14 oz)	Beat eggs on medium speed for 3 minutes. Add some of the hot mixture to the beaten eggs while still beating. Gradually add egg mixture to hot mixture. Turn on heat. Cook to 185°F.
Vanilla	2 Tbsp	Stir in vanilla. Cool quickly (within 4 hours) to temperature below 41°F. Cover with plastic wrap or waxed paper while cooling to prevent formation of film (see Notes). Serve cold with No. 10 dipper (rounded).

Approximate nutritive values per portion   **Calories** 222

Amount/portion	%DV	Amount/portion	%DV	Amount/portion	%DV		%DV		%DV
Total Fat 7 g	12%	**Cholest.** 42 mg	14%	**Total Carb.** 36 g	12%	**Vitamin A**	5%	**Calcium**	10%
Sat. Fat 2 g	12%	**Sodium** 128 mg	5%	Fiber 0 g	0%	**Vitamin C**	1%	**Iron**	4%
Protein 3 g				Sugars 3 g					

Percent Daily Values (%DV) are based on a 2000-calorie diet

Notes
- Potentially hazardous food. Store at internal temperature below 41°F.
- See p. 105 for recommended cooling procedures.

CHOCOLATE PUDDING

Yield: 50 portions or 6 qt   *Portion:* ½ cup

Ingredient	*Amount*	*Procedure*
Sugar, granulated	2 lb 6 oz	Combine dry ingredients.
Flour, all-purpose	6 oz	
Cornstarch	3 oz	
Salt	1 tsp	
Cocoa	8 oz	
Milk	1 gal	Pour milk into steam-jacketed kettle or stock pot.
		Gradually add dry ingredients while stirring briskly with a wire whip.
		Heat to boiling point, then cook until thickened, about 20 minutes. Stir occasionally.
		Remove from heat.
Margarine	8 oz	Add margarine and vanilla. Blend.
Vanilla	2 Tbsp	Cool quickly (within 4 hours) to temperature below 41°F.
		Cover with plastic wrap or waxed paper while cooling to prevent formation of film (see Notes).
		Serve cold with No. 10 dipper (rounded).

Approximate nutritive values per portion   **Calories** 193

Amount/portion	%DV	Amount/portion	%DV	Amount/portion	%DV		%DV		%DV
Total Fat 7 g	10%	**Cholest.** 11 mg	4%	**Total Carb.** 32 g	11%	Vitamin A	4%	Calcium	10%
Sat. Fat 2 g	12%	**Sodium** 127 mg	5%	Fiber 0 g	0%	Vitamin C	1%	Iron	9%
Protein 4 g				Sugars 25 g					

Percent Daily Values (%DV) are based on a 2000-calorie diet.

Notes
- Potentially hazardous food. Store at internal temperature below 41°F.
- See p. 105 for recommended cooling procedures.

Variations
- **Chocolate Banana Pudding.** Slice 12 bananas into cooled pudding.
- **Chocolate Pudding with Chips.** Stir 8 oz peanut butter, butterscotch, or chocolate chips into cooled pudding.

TAPIOCA CREAM PUDDING

Yield: 50 portions or 6 qt   *Portion:* ½ cup

Ingredient	Amount	Procedure
Milk	1 gal	Heat milk to boiling point in a steam-jacketed kettle or stock pot.
Tapioca, quick-cooking	9 oz	Add tapioca gradually while stirring with a wire whip. Cook until clear, stirring frequently.
Egg yolks, beaten Sugar, granulated Salt	10 (6 oz) 1 lb 2 tsp	Mix egg yolks, sugar, and salt. Add slowly to hot mixture while stirring. Cook about 10 minutes. Remove from heat.
Egg whites (see Notes) Sugar, granulated	10 (12 oz) 4 oz	Beat egg whites until frothy. Add sugar and beat on high speed to form a meringue.
Vanilla	2 Tbsp	Fold egg whites and vanilla into tapioca mixture. Cool quickly (within 4 hours) to temperature below 41°F. Serve cold with No. 10 dipper (rounded).

Approximate nutritive values per portion   **Calories** 129

Amount/portion	%DV	Amount/portion	%DV	Amount/portion	%DV		%DV		%DV
Total Fat 4 g	6%	**Cholest.** 54 mg	18%	**Total Carb.** 20 g	7%	Vitamin A	9%	Calcium	9%
Sat. Fat 2 g	10%	**Sodium** 137 mg	6%	Fiber 0 g	0%	Vitamin C	1%	Iron	1%
Protein 4 g				Sugars 15 g					

Percent Daily Values (%DV) are based on a 2000-calorie diet.

Notes
- Use of pasteurized frozen egg whites is recommended.
- Potentially hazardous food. Store at internal temperature below 41°F.
- See p. 105 for recommended cooling procedures.

Variation
- **Fruit Tapioca Cream.** Add 1 qt chopped canned peaches or crushed pineapple, drained. Add ½ tsp almond extract for peach tapioca.

VANILLA CREAM PUDDING

Yield: 50 portions or 6 qt   *Portion:* ½ cup

Ingredient	Amount	Procedure
Milk Sugar, granulated	3 qt 1 lb	Heat milk and sugar in steam-jacketed kettle.
Sugar, granulated Cornstarch Salt Milk, cold	1 lb 4 oz 6 oz 1½ tsp 2¼ qt	Combine dry ingredients with cold milk in mixer bowl. Whip until smooth. Add to hot milk mixture slowly, stirring constantly with a wire whip. Cook mixture until it is thickened and there is no starch taste, approximately 10 minutes.
Egg yolks, beaten	20 (12 oz)	Add, while stirring, a small amount of hot mixture to the beaten eggs. Add to remainder of hot mixture in kettle, stirring constantly. Stir slowly and cook about 2 minutes. Remove from heat.
Margarine Vanilla	4 oz 2 Tbsp	Stir in margarine and vanilla. Cool quickly (within 4 hours) to temperature below 41°F. Cover with waxed paper while cooling to prevent formation of film (see Notes). Serve cold with No. 10 dipper (rounded).

Approximate nutritive values per portion   **Calories** 197

Amount/portion	%DV	Amount/portion	%DV	Amount/portion	%DV		%DV		%DV
Total Fat 7 g	11%	**Cholest.** 101 mg	34%	**Total Carb.** 29 g	10%	**Vitamin A**	17%	**Calcium**	13%
Sat. Fat 3 g	16%	**Sodium** 139 mg	6%	Fiber 0 g	0%	**Vitamin C**	1%	**Iron**	1%
Protein 5 g				Sugars 25 g					

Percent Daily Values (%DV) are based on a 2000-calorie diet.

Notes
- Potentially hazardous food. Store at internal temperature below 41°F.
- See p. 105 for recommended cooling procedures.

Variations
- **Banana Cream Pudding.** Add 12 bananas, sliced, to cooled pudding.
- **Chocolate Cream Pudding.** Add 6 oz sugar and 8 oz cocoa.
- **Coconut Cream Pudding.** Add 8 oz shredded coconut just before serving.
- **Pineapple Cream Pudding.** Add 1 qt crushed pineapple, well drained.

BAKED DATE PUDDING

Yield: 54 portions or 1 pan 12 × 20 × 2 inches   *Portion:* 3 oz
Oven: 350°F   *Bake:* 45 minutes

Ingredient	Amount	Procedure
Dates	2 lb 4 oz	Pour hot water over dates in mixer bowl. Cover and let dates steam for 15 minutes.
Water, hot	2½ cups	Mix on low speed and then on medium speed until dates are broken into small pieces.
Sugar, granulated	1 lb	Combine dry ingredients in bowl and stir until blended.
Flour, all-purpose	1 lb	Add to date mixture. Mix on low speed only until blended.
Baking powder	1½ oz	Scale into well-greased 12 × 20 × 2-inch baking pan.
Nonfat dry milk	2 oz	
Salt	1½ tsp	
Walnuts, coarsely chopped	12 oz	
Sugar, brown	1 lb 4 oz	Mix sugar, margarine, and water. Heat to boiling point.
Margarine	2 oz	Pour hot sauce over batter in pan. Do not stir.
Water, boiling	1½ qt	Bake at 350°F for 45 minutes. Cool.
		Cut 6 × 9 for 54 portions or 6 × 8 for 48 portions. Serve with whipped cream or whipped topping.

Approximate nutritive values per portion   **Calories** 205

Amount/portion	%DV	Amount/portion	%DV	Amount/portion	%DV		%DV		%DV
Total Fat 5 g	7%	**Cholest.** 0 mg	0%	**Total Carb.** 40 g	13%	**Vitamin A**	1%	**Calcium**	8%
Sat. Fat 0 g	0%	**Sodium** 160 mg	7%	Fiber 2 g	8%	**Vitamin C**	0%	**Iron**	5%
Protein 3 g				Sugars 21 g					

Percent Daily Values (%DV) are based on a 2000-calorie diet.

LEMON CAKE PUDDING

Yield: 60 portions or 2 pans 12 × 20 × 2 inches   *Portion:* 2½ × 3 inches
Oven: 350°F   *Bake:* 1 hour

Ingredient	Amount	Procedure
Egg yolks	35 (1 lb 6 oz)	Beat egg yolks, lemon juice, and margarine together until lemon colored.
Lemon juice	5 cups	
Margarine, softened	3 oz	
Sugar, granulated	6 lb	Combine sugar, flour, and salt.
Flour, all-purpose	1 lb 3 oz	
Salt	1 oz (1½ Tbsp)	
Milk	3 qt	Add dry ingredients and milk alternately to egg mixture on low speed, ending with dry ingredients.
Egg whites	27 (2 lb)	Beat egg whites on high speed, until stiff, using wire whip attachment. Blend into egg mixture on low speed.
		Pour pudding into two 12 × 20 × 2-inch counter pans, 9 lb 8 oz per pan. Set filled pans in two other counter pans that have been filled half full with boiling water. Bake at 350°F for 1 hour. Cut 5 × 6.

Approximate nutritive values per portion   **Calories** 297

Amount/portion	%DV	Amount/portion	%DV	Amount/portion	%DV		%DV		%DV
Total Fat 6 g	9%	**Cholest.** 140 mg	47%	**Total Carb.** 56 g	19%	**Vitamin A**	22%	**Calcium**	7%
Sat. Fat 2 g	11%	**Sodium** 232 mg	10%	Fiber 0.3 g	1%	**Vitamin C**	9%	**Iron**	4%
Protein 6 g				Sugars 47 g					

Percent Daily Values (%DV) are based on a 2000-calorie diet.

Note   ● Potentially hazardous food. Store at internal temperature below 41°F.

CHEESECAKE

Yield: 48 portions or 6 8-inch cakes   *Portion:* cut 8 per cake
Oven: 350°F   *Bake:* 45 minutes

Ingredient	Amount	Procedure
Graham cracker crumbs	1 lb 8 oz	Combine crumbs, sugar, and melted margarine. Place 1 cup crumb mixture into each of six 8-inch pie pans or six 6 × 6-inch square cake pans. Press crumbs to sides and bottom of pans.
Sugar, granulated	12 oz	
Margarine, melted	12 oz	
Cream cheese	4 lb 8 oz	Let cheese stand until it reaches room temperature. Cream until smooth, using flat beater.
Eggs	11 (1 lb 3 oz)	Add eggs slowly to cream cheese while beating.
Sugar, granulated	1 lb 2 oz	Add sugar and vanilla to cheese mixture. Beat on high speed for about 5 minutes. Place about 3 cups filling in each shell. Bake at 350°F for 30–35 minutes or until set. Do not overbake.
Vanilla	2 Tbsp	
Sour cream	1¼ qt	Mix sour cream, sugar, and vanilla. Spread 1 cup topping on each cake.
Sugar, granulated	4 oz	
Vanilla	1½ tsp	
Graham cracker crumbs	4 oz	Sprinkle with a few graham cracker crumbs. Bake 10 minutes.

Approximate nutritive values per portion   **Calories** 420

Amount/portion	%DV	Amount/portion	%DV	Amount/portion	%DV		%DV		%DV
Total Fat 28 g	44%	**Cholest.** 106 mg	35%	**Total Carb.** 35 g	12%	**Vitamin A**	28%	**Calcium**	7%
Sat. Fat 14 g	72%	**Sodium** 321 mg	13%	Fiber 0 g	0%	**Vitamin C**	0%	**Iron**	7%
Protein 7 g				Sugars 20 g					

Percent Daily Values (%DV) are based on a 2000-calorie diet.

Note • Potentially hazardous food. Store below 41°F.

Variation • **Cheesecake with Fruit Glaze.** Cover baked cheesecake with the following glaze: Thaw and drain 6 lb frozen strawberries, raspberries, or cherries. Measure 1 qt fruit syrup, adding water if needed to make that amount. Add slowly to mixture of 4 oz cornstarch, 6 oz granulated sugar, and ¾ cup lemon juice if using berries or sweet cherries or ¾ cup additional water if using sour cherries. Cook until thick and clear. Cool slightly. Add drained fruit. Spread over cheesecakes. Canned fruit pie fillings may be used for the glaze.

BAKED CUSTARD

Yield: 50 custards   *Portion:* 4 oz
Oven: 325°F   *Bake:* 40–45 minutes

Ingredient	Amount	Procedure
Eggs	20 (2 lb 3 oz)	Beat eggs slightly, using wire whip attachment.
Sugar, granulated	1 lb 4 oz	Add sugar, salt, cold milk, and vanilla.
Salt	½ tsp	Mix on low speed only until blended.
Milk, cold	1 qt	
Vanilla	2 Tbsp	
Milk	1 gal	Scald milk by bringing to point just below boiling. Add to egg mixture and blend.
Nutmeg	2 tsp	Pour mixture into custard cups that have been arranged in baking pans. Sprinkle nutmeg over tops. Pour hot water around cups. Bake at 325°F for 40–45 minutes or until a knife inserted in custard comes out clean (180°F). Cool quickly (within 4 hours) to below 41°F.

Approximate nutritive values per portion   **Calories** 136

Amount/portion	%DV	Amount/portion	%DV	Amount/portion	%DV		%DV		%DV
Total Fat 5 g	8%	**Cholest.** 98 mg	33%	**Total Carb.** 16 g	5%	**Vitamin A**	7%	**Calcium**	12%
Sat. Fat 3 g	13%	**Sodium** 95 mg	4%	Fiber 0 g	0%	**Vitamin C**	1%	**Iron**	1%
Protein 6 g				Sugars 16 g					

Percent Daily Values (%DV) are based on a 2000-calorie diet.

Notes
- Potentially hazardous food. Store at internal temperature below 41°F.
- Custard may be baked in a 12 × 20 × 2-inch pan set in a pan of hot water. Cut 5 × 8 for 40 portions.

Variations
- **Bread Pudding.** Pour liquid mixture over 1 lb dry bread cubes and let stand until bread is softened. Add 1 lb raisins if desired. Bake. Day-old sweet rolls may be substituted for bread.
- **Caramel Custard.** Add 1 cup Burnt Sugar Syrup (p. 338) slowly to scalded milk and stir carefully until melted.
- **Rice Custard.** Use ½ Baked Custard recipe, adding 1 lb rice (AP) cooked, 1 lb raisins, and 3 oz melted margarine or butter.

FLOATING ISLAND

Yield: 50 portions or 6 qt   *Portion:* ½ cup (4 oz)

Ingredient	Amount	Procedure
Milk	4½ qt	Heat milk to boiling point.
Sugar, granulated Cornstarch Salt	1 lb 4 oz ½ tsp	Combine sugar, cornstarch, and salt. Add gradually to hot milk, stirring briskly with wire whip. Cook over hot water or in steam-jacketed kettle until slightly thickened.
Egg yolks, beaten Vanilla	27 (1 lb 2 oz) 2 Tbsp	Gradually stir egg yolks and vanilla into hot mixture. Continue cooking until thickened, about 5 minutes.
Egg whites Sugar, granulated	27 (1 lb 14 oz) 12 oz	Beat egg whites on high speed past the frothy stage, approximately 1½ minutes, using wire whip attachment. Add sugar gradually, while beating. Beat until sugar has dissolved and mixture resembles meringue. Drop by spoonfuls onto hot water and bake at 375°F until set.
		Cool custard slightly and pour into sherbet dishes; or dip, using a No. 10 dipper. Lift meringues from water with a fork and place on top of portioned custards. Add dash of nutmeg. Chill quickly before serving (below 41°F within 4 hours).

Approximate nutritive values per portion   **Calories** 164

Amount/portion	%DV	Amount/portion	%DV	Amount/portion	%DV		%DV		%DV
Total Fat 6 g	9%	**Cholest.** 121 mg	40%	**Total Carb.** 23 g	8%	**Vitamin A**	19%	**Calcium**	11%
Sat. Fat 3 g	13%	**Sodium** 95 mg	4%	Fiber 0 g	0%	**Vitamin C**	1%	**Iron**	2%
Protein 6 g				Sugars 20 g					

Percent Daily Values (%DV) are based on a 2000-calorie diet.

Notes
- Potentially hazardous food. Store at an internal temperature below 41°F.
- See p. 105 for recommended cooling procedures.

Variation
- **Creamy Custard Sauce with Fruit.** Ladle 3 oz custard over fresh fruit. Suggested combinations are sliced bananas, blueberries, and sliced peaches; or cubed pineapple, raspberries, and sliced peaches.

CHRISTMAS PUDDING

Yield: 48 portions   *Portion:* 3 oz
Steam pressure: 5–6 lb   *Steam:* 40–45 minutes

Ingredient	Amount	Procedure
Carrots, raw, peeled	1 lb 4 oz (EP)	Peel and grate carrots and potatoes.
Potatoes, raw, peeled	1 lb 11 oz (EP)	
Sugar, granulated	2 lb	Cream sugar and margarine on medium speed, using flat beater.
Margarine	1 lb	
Raisins	1 lb 4 oz	Add raisins, dates, and nuts to creamed mixture.
Dates, chopped	1 lb 4 oz	Add carrots and potatoes.
Nuts, chopped	12 oz	Mix on low speed until blended.
Flour, all-purpose	1 lb	Combine dry ingredients.
Baking soda	4 tsp	Add to fruit mixture. Mix on low speed until blended.
Cinnamon	1 Tbsp	
Cloves	1 Tbsp	
Nutmeg	1 Tbsp	
Salt	¼ tsp	
		Portion mixture with No. 16 dipper into greased muffin pans. Cover each filled pan with an inverted empty muffin pan. Steam for 40–45 minutes. Serve warm with Vanilla Sauce (p. 776), Hard Sauce (p. 776), or Nutmeg Sauce (p. 776). Garnish with holly leaf and whole cranberries for Christmas.

Approximate nutritive values per portion   **Calories** 304

Amount/portion	%DV	Amount/portion	%DV	Amount/portion	%DV		%DV		%DV
Total Fat 12 g	18%	**Cholest.** 0 mg	0%	**Total Carb.** 50 g	17%	**Vitamin A**	36%	**Calcium**	3%
Sat. Fat 2 g	10%	**Sodium** 213 mg	9%	Fiber 3 g	11%	**Vitamin C**	4%	**Iron**	7%
Protein 3 g				Sugars 35 g					

Percent Daily Values (%DV) are based on a 2000-calorie diet.

Variation   • **Flaming Pudding.** Dip sugar cube in lemon extract. Place on hot pudding and light just before serving.

CREAM PUFFS

Yield: 50 portions   *Portion:* 1 puff
Oven: 425°F, 325°F   *Bake:* 15 minutes, 30 minutes

Ingredient	Amount	Procedure
Margarine or butter Water, boiling	1 lb 1 qt	Melt margarine in boiling water.
Flour, all-purpose Salt	1 lb 3 oz 1 tsp	Add flour and salt all at once to boiling mixture. Beat vigorously. Remove from heat as soon as mixture leaves sides of pan. Transfer to mixer bowl. Cool slightly.
Eggs	16 (1 lb 12 oz)	Add eggs one at a time, beating on high speed after each addition.
		Drop batter with No. 24 dipper onto greased baking sheets. Bake at 425°F for 15 minutes. Reduce heat to 325°F and bake 30 minutes longer.
		When ready to use, make a cut in top of each puff with a sharp knife. Fill with Custard Filling (p. 361), using a No. 16 dipper. Top with Chocolate Sauce (p. 774) if desired.

Approximate nutritive values per portion plus filling   **Calories** 128

Amount/portion	%DV	Amount/portion	%DV	Amount/portion	%DV		%DV		%DV
Total Fat 9 g	14%	**Cholest.** 68 mg	23%	**Total Carb.** 9 g	3%	**Vitamin A**	5%	**Calcium**	1%
Sat. Fat 2 g	10%	**Sodium** 149 mg	6%	Fiber 0.3 g	1%	**Vitamin C**	0%	**Iron**	4%
Protein 3 g				Sugars 0 g					

Percent Daily Values (%DV) are based on a 2000-calorie diet.

Note
- Potentially hazardous food. Hold for service at below 41°F internal temperature when filled.

Variations
- **Butterscotch Cream Puffs.** Fill cream puffs with Butterscotch Pudding (p. 416). Top with Butterscotch Sauce (p. 773) if desired.
- **Eclairs.** Shape cream puff mixture by piping with a pastry tube, ¾ inch wide and 4 inches long. Bake. Split lengthwise. Proceed as for Cream Puffs. When filled, ice with Chocolate Glaze (p. 358).
- **Ice Cream Puffs.** Fill puffs with vanilla ice cream and serve with Chocolate Sauce (p. 774).
- **Orange Cream Puffs with Chocolate Filling.** Add ½ cup grated orange peel and 10 oz chopped almonds to cream puff mixture. Bake. Fill with Chocolate Cream Filling (p. 359) or Chocolate Pudding (p. 417).
- **Puff Shells.** Make bite-size shells with pastry tube or No. 100 dipper. Bake. Fill with chicken, fish, or ham salad. Yield: approximately 200 puffs.

PINEAPPLE BAVARIAN CREAM

Yield: 60 portions or 2 pans 12 × 20 × 2 inches   *Portion:* 2½ × 3 inches

Ingredient	Amount	Procedure
Gelatin, unflavored Water, cold	3 oz 1 qt	Sprinkle gelatin over water. Let stand 10 minutes.
Crushed pineapple Sugar, granulated	1 No. 10 can 1 lb 12 oz	Heat pineapple and sugar to boiling point.
Lemon juice	¼ cup	Add gelatin to pineapple mixture. Stir until dissolved. Add lemon juice. Chill until mixture begins to congeal.
Whipping cream	1 qt	Whip cream and fold into pineapple mixture. Pour into 50 individual molds or two 12 × 20 × 2-inch pans. Cut 5 × 6.

Approximate nutritive values per portion   **Calories** 129

Amount/portion	%DV	Amount/portion	%DV	Amount/portion	%DV		%DV		%DV
Total Fat 5 g	8%	**Cholest.** 18 mg	6%	**Total Carb.** 20 g	7%	**Vitamin A**	5%	**Calcium**	1%
Sat. Fat 3 g	15%	**Sodium** 9 mg	1%	Fiber 0.4 g	2%	**Vitamin C**	8%	**Iron**	1%
Protein 2 g				Sugars 22 g					

Percent Daily Values (%DV) are based on a 2000-calorie diet.

Note   • May be used for pie filling.

Variations • **Apricot Bavarian Cream.** Substitute 3 lb dried apricots, cooked, or 6 lb canned apricots, sieved, for the crushed pineapple.

• **Strawberry Bavarian Cream.** Substitute 6 lb fresh or frozen sliced strawberries for pineapple.

BAKED APPLES

Yield: 50 portions   *Portion:* 1 apple
Oven: 375°F   *Bake:* 45 minutes

Ingredient	Amount	Procedure
Apples	50	Wash and core apples. Peel down about one-fourth of the way from the top. Place in baking pans, peeled-side up.
Sugar, granulated Water, hot Salt Cinnamon, ground	3 lb 3 cups 1 tsp 1 Tbsp	Mix sugar, water, salt, and cinnamon. Pour over apples. Bake at 375°F until tender, about 45 minutes, basting occasionally while cooking to glaze. Test for doneness with a pointed knife inserted in the apple.

Approximate nutritive values per portion   **Calories** 187

Amount/portion	%DV	Amount/portion	%DV	Amount/portion	%DV		%DV		%DV
Total Fat 0 g	0%	**Cholest.** 0 mg	0%	**Total Carb.** 48 g	16%	**Vitamin A**	0%	**Calcium**	1%
Sat. Fat 0 g	0%	**Sodium** 45 mg	2%	Fiber 3 g	12%	**Vitamin C**	13%	**Iron**	1%
Protein 0 g				Sugars 45 g					

Percent Daily Values (%DV) are based on a 2000-calorie diet.

Notes
- Use apples of uniform size, suitable for baking, such as Rome Beauty or Jonathan.
- Amount of sugar will vary with tartness of apples.
- ½ cup red cinnamon candies may be substituted for cinnamon.
- Apple centers may be filled with chopped dates, raisins, nuts, or mincemeat.
- 3 oz margarine or butter may be added to the syrup for flavor.

APPLE DUMPLINGS

Yield: 50 dumplings   *Portion:* 1 dumpling
Oven: 350°F   *Bake:* 25–30 minutes

Ingredient	Amount	Procedure
Pastry for Two-Crust Pies (p. 391)	7 lb	Make pastry. Scale into 10-oz balls. Chill for 10 minutes or more.
Flour, all-purpose Sugar, granulated Salt Cinnamon, ground	10 oz 6 lb 1 Tbsp 1 Tbsp	Make sauce. Combine flour, sugar, salt, and cinnamon.
Water, hot	1½ gal	Add dry ingredients to water while stirring with a wire whip. Cook until thickened.
Margarine	1 lb	Add margarine and stir until margarine is melted. Remove from heat.
Vanilla	2 Tbsp	Add vanilla.
Apples, medium size	50	Wash, core, and peel apples.
Margarine	1 lb 8 oz	Roll pastry to ⅛-inch thickness. Position apple on dough and cut a circle approximately 7 inches in diameter around it. Insert 1 Tbsp margarine into center of each apple. Push toward center of apple.
Sugar, granulated Cinnamon, ground Nutmeg, ground	1 lb 5 oz 1½ Tbsp 2 tsp	Combine sugar, cinnamon, and nutmeg. Use mixture to fill centers of apples. Enclose the apple in the cut dough, pinching to seal the edges. Turn the apple over so that the bottom is the top and make three slashes in the top of the apple. Place in lightly greased baking pans. Bake for 15 minutes at 350°F. Baste dumplings with one-half of the sauce and bake 10–15 minutes longer or until golden brown. Serve dumplings with additional warm sauce as desired.

Approximate nutritive values per portion   **Calories** 831

Amount/portion	%DV	Amount/portion	%DV	Amount/portion	%DV		%DV		%DV
Total Fat 41 g	63%	**Cholest.** 0 mg	0%	**Total Carb.** 116 g	39%	**Vitamin A**	7%	**Calcium**	3%
Sat. Fat 9 g	46%	**Sodium** 668 mg	28%	Fiber 4 g	16%	**Vitamin C**	13%	**Iron**	11%
Protein 4 g				Sugars 83 g					

Percent Daily Values (%DV) are based on a 2000-calorie diet.

Notes
- Apples may be wrapped with dough and frozen for later use. To serve, make sauce and bake as directed but allow 15–20 minutes longer baking time.
- Sliced apples, frozen or fresh, may be used in place of whole apples. Cut pastry into 6-inch squares. Place No. 10 dipper of fruit in the center and sprinkle with sugar-cinnamon mixture. Fold corners of pastry to the center and on top of fruit and seal edges together. Bake as directed for Apple Dumplings.

APPLESAUCE

Yield: 50 portions   *Portion:* ½ cup (4 oz)

Ingredient	Amount	Procedure
Apples, tart	15 lb (AP)	Wash, peel, and core apples. Cut into quarters.
Water	1 qt	Add water to apples. Cook slowly until soft.
Sugar, granulated	3 lb	Add sugar and stir until dissolved. Serve with No. 10 dipper (rounded).

Approximate nutritive values per portion   **Calories** 185

Amount/portion	%DV	Amount/portion	%DV	Amount/portion	%DV		%DV		%DV
Total Fat 0 g	0%	**Cholest.** 0 mg	0%	**Total Carb.** 48 g	16%	**Vitamin A**	0%	**Calcium**	1%
Sat. Fat 0 g	0%	**Sodium** 2 mg	0%	Fiber 3 g	12%	**Vitamin C**	12%	**Iron**	1%
Protein 0 g				Sugars 45 g					

Percent Daily Values (%DV) are based on a 2000-calorie diet.

Notes
- Thin slices of lemon, lemon juice, or 1 tsp cinnamon may be added.
- Peaches or pears may be substituted for apples.
- Apples may be cooked unpeeled.
- Amount of sugar will vary with tartness of apples.

Variation
- **Apple Compote.** Combine sugar and water and heat to boiling point. Add apples and cook until transparent.

FRUIT COBBLER

Yield: 64 portions or 2 pans 12 × 20 × 2 inches   *Portion:* 3 × 2½ inches
Oven: 425°F   *Bake:* 30 minutes

Ingredient	Amount	Procedure
Fruit, frozen	10 lb	Drain fruit. Reserve juice.
Juice drained from fruit, plus water to make total amount needed	2 qt	Heat juice and water to boiling point.
Sugar, granulated Cornstarch Seasonings	1–2 lb (see Table 9.3, p. 398) 6 oz See Table 9.3, p. 398	Mix sugar, cornstarch, salt, and seasonings, if any.
Water, cold	2 cups	Add cold water to dry ingredients and stir until smooth. Add to hot juice while stirring briskly with a wire whip. Cook until thickened.
		Add cooked, drained fruit to thickened juice. Mix carefully to prevent breaking or mashing fruit. Cool. Pour into two 12 × 20 × 2-inch baking pans, 9 lb 6 oz per pan.
Pastry (p. 389) or Biscuit Topping for Fruit Cobbler (p. 434)	3 lb	Roll pastry or topping to fit pans. Place on top of fruit. Seal edges to sides of pan. Perforate top. Bake at 425°F for 30 minutes or until top is browned. Cut 4 × 8.

Approximate nutritive values per portion   **Calories** 193

Amount/portion	%DV	Amount/portion	%DV	Amount/portion	%DV		%DV		%DV
Total Fat 3.7 g	6%	**Cholest.** 5 mg	2%	**Total Carb.** 32 g	11%	**Vitamin A (see note)**		**Calcium**	2%
Sat. Fat 1 g	5%	**Sodium** 80 mg	3%	Fiber 1.6 g	3%	**Vitamin C (see note)**		**Iron**	4%
Protein 1.4 g				Sugars 14 g					

Percent Daily Values (%DV) are based on a 2000-calorie diet.

Note: Amounts of Vitamin A and Ce depends on fruit used.

Notes
- Use cherries, berries, peaches, apricots, apples, plums, or other fruits.
- The amount of sugar will vary with the tartness of the fruit.
- For canned fruit, see p. 396.

Variations
- **Fruit Slices.** Use 2 lb 12 oz pastry. Line an 18 × 26 × 2-inch baking pan with 1 lb 8 oz of the pastry. Add fruit filling prepared as for cobbler. Moisten edges of dough and cover with crust made of remaining pastry. Trim and seal edges and perforate top. Bake at 400°F for 1–1¼ hours.
- **Peach Cobbler with Hard Sauce.** Use 10 lb frozen sliced peaches, thawed, and mixed with 1 lb sugar, 1 tsp nutmeg, 4 oz flour, and 6 oz margarine, melted. Top with pastry crust and bake. Serve warm with Hard Sauce (p. 776) or ice cream.

BISCUIT TOPPING FOR FRUIT COBBLER

Yield: topping for two 12 × 20-inch pans or 64 portions

Ingredient	Amount	Procedure
Flour, all-purpose	1 lb 6 oz	Blend dry ingredients in mixer bowl.
Baking powder	1 oz	
Salt	1 tsp	
Sugar, granulated	3 oz	
Nonfat dry milk	2 tsp	
Shortening	8 oz	Cut shortening into dry ingredients on low speed until it appears as coarse as cornmeal.
Eggs	2 (4 oz)	Beat eggs. Add water and blend.
Water	1¼ cups	Add to flour-shortening mixture.
		Blend on low speed until a soft dough is formed.
		Scale 1 lb 8 oz dough per pan. Roll to fit 12 × 20-inch pan.
		Roll onto rolling pin. Place over filling in pan, allowing dough to extend up edge of pan, about 1 inch all around (to allow for shrinkage).
		Cut several slits in dough.
Milk	¼ cup	Brush top of each pan with 2 Tbsp milk and 2 Tbsp sugar.
Sugar, granulated	2 oz	

Approximate nutritive values per portion   **Calories** 79

Amount/portion	%DV	Amount/portion	%DV	Amount/portion	%DV		%DV		%DV
Total Fat 4 g	6%	**Cholest.** 8 mg	3%	**Total Carb.** 10 g	3%	Vitamin A	0%	**Calcium**	3%
Sat. Fat 1 g	5%	**Sodium** 81 mg	3%	Fiber 0.3 g	1%	Vitamin C	0%	**Iron**	2%
Protein 1 g				Sugars 2 g					

Percent Daily Values (%DV) are based on a 2000-calorie diet.

OLD-FASHIONED STRAWBERRY SHORTCAKE

Yield: 50 individual shortcakes   *Portion:* 1 shortcake + ¾ cup (6 oz) strawberries
Oven: 375°F   *Bake:* 15 minutes

Ingredient	Amount	Procedure
Strawberries, fresh Sugar, granulated	9 qt 2 lb (variable)	Wash, drain, and stem strawberries. Slice and sweeten. Adjust sugar according to sweetness of berries.
Flour, all-purpose Baking powder Salt Sugar	4 lb 5 oz 1 Tbsp 1 lb 5 oz	Mix dry ingredients in mixer bowl.
Margarine or butter	2 lb	Cut margarine into dry ingredients, using pastry blender or flat beater. Mixture should have coarse, mealy consistency.
Milk	1½ qt	Stir milk quickly into flour mixture. Mix just enough to moisten.
		Portion dough with No. 20 dipper onto ungreased baking sheets. Place about 2 inches apart to allow for spreading. Bake at 375°F for 12–15 minutes or until golden brown.
Cream, half-and-half, or whipping	1½ qt (3 qt if whipped)	To serve, dip ¾ cup (6 oz) strawberries over shortcake. Serve with cream or top with whipped cream.

Approximate nutritive values per portion   **Calories** 470

Amount/portion	%DV	Amount/portion	%DV	Amount/portion	%DV		%DV		%DV
Total Fat 20 g	30%	**Cholest.** 15 mg	5%	**Total Carb.** 69 g	23%	**Vitamin A**	10%	**Calcium**	27%
Sat. Fat 6 g	28%	**Sodium** 611 mg	25%	Fiber 3 g	12%	**Vitamin C**	102%	**Iron**	11%
Protein 6 g				Sugars 37 g					

Percent Daily Values (%DV) are based on a 2000-calorie diet.

Note   ● For frozen strawberries, use 12 lb. Portion ½ cup over shortcake.

Notes

- Hard-cooked eggs will peel easier if the raw eggs have been held in the refrigerator for 24 hours before cooking. A greenish color may appear on the yolks of hard-cooked eggs when the eggs have been overcooked or allowed to cool slowly in the cooking water. Cooking the eggs for the minimum length of time required to make them solid and cooling them in cold running water or ice water help to prevent this color formation.

- Cook scrambled eggs in small batches (no larger than 3 quarts) until no visible liquid egg remains. Do not combine raw egg mixture with cooked scrambled eggs. Keep scrambled egg mixture below 41°F.

- Do not combine eggs that have been held in a steam table pan with a fresh batch of eggs. Always use a fresh steam table pan.

- The practice of breaking large quantities of eggs together and holding for a period of time greatly increases the risk of bacterial contamination.

- Never leave eggs or egg-containing products at temperatures between 41°F and 140°F (room temperature) for more than 1 hour (including preparation and service).

- Hold cold egg dishes below 41°F.

- Hold hot egg dishes above 140°F. Do not hold hot foods on buffet line for longer than 30 minutes.

- When refrigerating a large quantity of a hot egg-rich dish or leftover, divide into several shallow containers so it will cool quickly. See p. 105 for recommended cooling procedures.

SCRAMBLED EGGS

Yield: 50 portions   *Portion:* 3 oz

Ingredient	Amount	Procedure
Eggs (see Notes)	75 (8 lb 3 oz)	Break eggs into mixer bowl. If using frozen eggs, defrost. Beat slightly on medium speed, using wire whip attachment.
Milk Salt	1½ qt 2 Tbsp	Add milk and salt to eggs. Beat until blended. Refrigerate mixture, removing small amounts as needed.
Margarine	8 oz	Melt margarine in fry pan, griddle, or steam-jacketed kettle. Pour in egg mixture (see Notes). Cook over low heat, stirring occasionally, until of desired consistency. Eggs should be glossy and 165°F. Serve with No. 10 dipper.

Approximate nutritive values per portion   **Calories** 162

Amount/portion	%DV	Amount/portion	%DV	Amount/portion	%DV		%DV		%DV
Total Fat 12 g	19%	**Cholest.** 320 mg	107%	**Total Carb.** 2 g	1%	**Vitamin A**	16%	**Calcium**	7%
Sat. Fat 4 g	18%	**Sodium** 407 mg	17%	Fiber 0 g	0%	**Vitamin C**	0%	**Iron**	6%
Protein 10 g				Sugars 1 g					

Percent Daily Values (%DV) are based on a 2000-calorie diet.

Notes
- Potentially hazardous food. Hold uncooked mixture below 41°F and cooked eggs above 140°F.
- Breaking and pooling large quantities of shell eggs is not recommended.
- Recommend using pasteurized eggs when scrambled egg mixture must be held longer than 2 hours.
- The type of equipment used will determine batch size. Eggs should be cooked in small batches and held for a minimum amount of time before serving.
- **Steamer method.** Melt 4 oz margarine in each of two steamer or counter pans. Pour egg mixture into pans. Steam for 6–8 minutes at 5 lb pressure until desired degree of hardness is reached.
- **Oven method.** Melt 4 oz margarine in each of two counter or baking pans. Pour egg mixture into pans. Bake approximately 20 minutes at 350°F, stirring once after 10 minutes of baking.
- For lower cholesterol, egg whites may be substituted for half of the whole eggs.

Variations
- **Scrambled Eggs and Cheese.** Add 1 lb grated cheddar cheese.
- **Scrambled Eggs and Chipped Beef.** Add 1 lb chopped chipped beef. Reduce salt to 1 Tbsp or less.
- **Scrambled Eggs and Ham.** Add 1 lb 4 oz chopped cooked ham. Reduce salt to 1 Tbsp or less.

CREAMED EGGS

Yield: 50 portion   *Portion:* 5 oz

Ingredient	Amount	Procedure
Eggs, hard cooked (p. 439)	75	Peel eggs. Set aside for later step. Refrigerate if not using immediately.
Margarine Flour, all-purpose Salt Pepper, white	1 lb 8 oz 1 oz (1½ Tbsp) ¼ tsp	Melt margarine. Add flour, salt, and pepper. Stir until smooth. Cook for 5 minutes.
Milk	1 gal	Add milk gradually, stirring constantly with wire whip. Cook until thickened.
		Slice or quarter hard-cooked eggs. Refrigerate if not using immediately. When ready to serve, pour hot sauce over eggs. Mix carefully. Reheat if necessary to 165°F.

Approximate nutritive values per portion   **Calories** 242

Amount/portion	%DV	Amount/portion	%DV	Amount/portion	%DV		%DV		%DV
Total Fat 17 g	27%	**Cholest.** 330 mg	110%	**Total Carb.** 8 g	3%	**Vitamin A**	19%	**Calcium**	13%
Sat. Fat 5 g	27%	**Sodium** 410 mg	17%	Fiber 0 g	0%	**Vitamin C**	1%	**Iron**	7%
Protein 13 g				Sugars 4 g					

Percent Daily Values (%DV) are based on a 2000-calorie diet.

Note
- Potentially hazardous food. *Food Safety Standard:* Hold food for service at an internal temperature above 140°F. Do not mix old product with new. Cool leftover product quickly (within 4 hours) to below 41°F. See p. 105 for cooling procedures. Reheat leftover product quickly (within 2 hours) to 165°F. Reheat product only once; discard if not used.

Variations
- **Curried Eggs.** Substitute chicken broth for 2 qt of the milk. Add 2 Tbsp curry powder. May be served with steamed rice or chow mein noodles.
- **Eggs à la King.** Substitute Chicken Stock for 2 qt of the milk. Add 1 lb mushrooms that have been sautéed, 12 oz chopped green peppers, and 8 oz chopped pimiento.
- **Goldenrod Eggs.** Mash or rice egg yolks. Add sliced whites to sauce. Serve on toast. Sprinkle mashed yolks over the top.
- **Scotch Woodcock.** Add 1 lb sharp cheddar cheese to sauce. Cut eggs in half lengthwise and place in pans. Pour sauce over eggs. Cover with buttered crumbs. Bake until heated through and crumbs are brown.

BAKED OMELET

Yield: 48 portions or 2 pans 12 × 20 × 2 inches   *Portion:* 3 oz
Oven: 325°F   *Bake:* 45 minutes

Ingredient	Amount	Procedure
Margarine Flour, all-purpose Salt Pepper, white	12 oz 8 oz 2 Tbsp ½ tsp	Melt margarine. Add flour and seasonings. Stir until smooth. Cook 5 minutes.
Milk	3 qt	Add milk gradually, stirring constantly with a wire whip. Cook until thick.
Egg yolks, beaten	24 (15 oz)	Add egg yolks and mix well with wire whip.
Egg whites	24 (1 lb 12 oz)	Beat egg whites until they form rounded peaks. Fold into egg yolk mixture.
		Pour mixture into two greased 12 × 20 × 2-inch baking pans, 5 lb per pan. Set pans in counter pans with 3 cups of hot water in each. Bake at 325°F for approximately 45 minutes or until set, 180°F internal end-point temperature. Cut 4 × 6.

Approximate nutritive values per portion   **Calories** 146

Amount/portion	%DV	Amount/portion	%DV	Amount/portion	%DV		%DV		%DV
Total Fat 11 g	16%	**Cholest.** 122 mg	41%	**Total Carb.** 7 g	2%	Vitamin A	21%	Calcium	9%
Sat. Fat 3 g	16%	**Sodium** 394 mg	16%	Fiber 0 g	0%	Vitamin C	0%	Iron	3%
Protein 6 g				Sugars 3 g					

Percent Daily Values (%DV) are based on a 2000-calorie diet.

Note
- Potentially hazardous food. Hold at internal temperature above 140°F.

Variations
- **Bacon Omelet.** Fry 1 lb 8 oz diced bacon; substitute bacon fat for margarine in white sauce. Add diced bacon to egg mixture.
- **Cheese Omelet.** Add 12 oz grated cheese before placing pans in ovens.
- **Cheese and Bacon Omelet.** Combine 8 lb eggs, 1 Tbsp (¾ oz) salt, and 1 Tbsp white pepper and mix on low speed just until blended. Portion with No. 12 dipper onto lightly greased preheated grill. Cook until set. Portion 1 oz shredded processed cheese and ½ oz cooked crumbled bacon over each omelet. Fold omelet with spatula. Place in 12 × 20 × 2-inch pans. Cover and keep hot. Prepare 3 lb cheese and 1 lb 8 oz bacon for 50 omelets.
- **Grilled Cheese Omelet.** Combine 11 lb eggs, 1½ Tbsp (1 oz) salt, and 1 Tbsp white pepper and mix on low speed just until blended. Portion with No. 8 dipper onto lightly greased preheated grill. As omelet begins to set, portion 1½ oz shredded processed cheese over each (4 lb 8 oz for 50 omelets). Fold omelet with spatula and place in 12 × 20 × 2-inch pans. Cover and keep hot.
- **Ham Omelet.** Add 3 lb finely diced cooked ham. Reduce salt to 1 Tbsp or less.
- **Jelly Omelet.** Spread 1 lb tart jelly over cooked omelet.
- **Mushroom and Cheese Omelet.** Add 8 oz grated cheese and 6 oz sliced mushrooms.
- **Spanish Omelet.** Add 8 oz chopped green chilies to egg mixture. Serve with Spanish Sauce (p. 763).

POTATO OMELET

Yield: 56 portions or 2 pans 12 × 20 × 2 inches   *Portion:* 6 oz
Oven: 325°F   *Bake:* 1 hour

Ingredient	Amount	Procedure
Bacon slices	50	Arrange bacon, slightly overlapping, in baking pans. Cook in oven at 400°F until crisp. Remove from pans. Place on paper towels to absorb fat.
Potatoes, cooked, diced	9 lb (EP)	Brown potatoes slightly in bacon fat. Remove to two greased 12 × 20 × 2-inch baking pans, 4 lb 8 oz per pan.
Eggs, beaten Salt Pepper, white Pepper, cayenne Milk, hot	36 (3 lb 15 oz) 2 oz 1 tsp few grains 3 qt	Combine eggs, milk, and seasonings. Pour over potatoes.
		Bake at 325°F for approximately 1 hour, or until set, 180°F internal end-point temperature. Serve as soon as removed from oven. Cut 4 × 7. Place a slice of crisp bacon on top of each serving.

Approximate nutritive values per portion   **Calories** 180

Amount/portion	%DV	Amount/portion	%DV	Amount/portion	%DV		%DV		%DV
Total Fat 8 g	12%	**Cholest.** 148 mg	49%	**Total Carb.** 19 g	6%	**Vitamin A**	8%	**Calcium**	8%
Sat. Fat 3 g	15%	**Sodium** 552 mg	23%	Fiber 2 g	7%	**Vitamin C**	19%	**Iron**	4%
Protein 9 g				Sugars 4 g					

Percent Daily Values (%DV) are based on a 2000-calorie diet.

Notes
- Potentially hazardous food. Hold at internal temperature above 140°F.
- 4 oz chopped green pepper and 4 oz chopped onion may be added.

Variation
- **Potato-Ham Omelet.** Omit bacon. Add 4 lb diced cooked ham to potatoes. Reduce salt to 1 Tbsp.

CHINESE OMELET

Yield: 48 portions or 2 pans 12 × 20 × 2 inches   *Portion:* 4 oz
Oven: 325°F   *Bake:* 45 minutes

Ingredient	Amount	Procedure
Rice, long-grain	2 lb (AP)	Cook rice according to directions on p. 594.
Water	2½ qt	
Salt	1 Tbsp	
Margarine or vegetable oil	1 Tbsp	
Margarine	4 oz	Melt margarine. Add flour and salt. Stir until smooth.
Flour, all-purpose	2 oz	Cook 5 minutes.
Salt	1 tsp	
Milk	1 qt	Add milk gradually, stirring constantly with wire whip. Cook until thickened.
Cheddar cheese, sharp, shredded	1 lb	Add cheese to white sauce. Stir until cheese is melted.
Egg yolks	24 (15 oz)	Beat egg yolks until light and fluffy. Add seasonings.
Mustard, dry	1 tsp	Add to cheese sauce. Stir until smooth.
Salt	2 Tbsp	Add rice and mix to blend
Paprika	1 tsp	
Egg whites	24 (1 lb 12 oz)	Beat egg whites until they form soft peaks. Fold into rice mixture.
		Pour into two greased 12 × 20 × 2-inch pans, 7 lb per pan. Bake at 325°F for approximately 45 minutes or until set, 180°F internal end-point temperature. Cut 4 × 6. Serve with Cheese Sauce (p. 749), Italian Tomato Sauce (p. 762), or Mushroom Sauce (p. 750).

Approximate nutritive values per portion   **Calories** 185

Amount/portion	%DV	Amount/portion	%DV	Amount/portion	%DV		%DV		%DV
Total Fat 9 g	14%	**Cholest.** 126 mg	42%	**Total Carb.** 18 g	6%	Vitamin A	21%	Calcium	12%
Sat. Fat 4 g	19%	**Sodium** 614 mg	26%	Fiber 0.4 g	1%	Vitamin C	0%	Iron	6%
Protein 8 g				Sugars 1 g					

Percent Daily Values (%DV) are based on a 2000-calorie diet.

Note • Potentially hazardous food. *Food Safety Standard:* Hold food for service at an internal temperature above 140°F. Do not mix old product with new. Cool leftover product quickly (within 4 hours) to below 41°F. See p. 105 for cooling procedures. Reheat leftover product quickly (within 2 hours) to 165°F. Reheat product only once; discard if not used.

EGG AND SAUSAGE BAKE

Yield: 48 portions or 2 pans 12 × 20 × 2 inches   *Portion:* 6 oz
Oven: 325°F   *Bake:* 1 hour

Ingredient	Amount	Procedure
Bread, sliced	2 lb 8 oz	Cut bread in cubes. Cover bottoms of two greased 12 × 20 × 2-inch baking pans with bread cubes. Pans should be well covered.
Sausage, bulk	9 lb	Brown sausage. Drain well.
Cheddar cheese, shredded	2 lb 8 oz	Spread cheese and sausage over bread cubes.
Eggs, beaten Milk Mustard, dry	42 (4 lb 8 oz) 3 qt 1½ Tbsp	Combine eggs, milk, and mustard. Pour over mixture in pans, 2½ qt per pan. May be mixed, covered, and refrigerated overnight.
		Bake uncovered at 325°F for approximately 1 hour or until set, 180°F internal end-point temperature. If browning too fast, cover with foil. Cut 4 × 6.

Approximate nutritive values per portion   **Calories** 568

Amount/portion	%DV	Amount/portion	%DV	Amount/portion	%DV		%DV		%DV
Total Fat 42 g	64%	**Cholest.** 286 mg	95%	**Total Carb.** 15 g	5%	Vitamin A	17%	Calcium	30%
Sat. Fat 17 g	84%	**Sodium** 1483 mg	62%	Fiber 3 g	11%	Vitamin C	3%	Iron	14%
Protein 32 g				Sugars 4 g					

Percent Daily Values (%DV) are based on a 2000-calorie diet.

Notes
- Potentially hazardous food. *Food Safety Standard:* Hold food for service at an internal temperature above 140°F. Do not mix old product with new. Cool leftover product quickly (within 4 hours) to below 41°F. See p. 105 for cooling procedures. Reheat leftover product quickly (within 2 hours) to 165°F. Reheat product only once; discard if not used.
- Chopped ham or bacon may be substituted for sausage.

Variations
- **Sausage-Potato Bake.** Substitute frozen hashed brown potatoes for bread cubes.
- **Egg-Potato Bake.** Delete sausage. Substitute frozen hashed brown potatoes for bread cubes.

ROASTED PEPPER AND BASIL FRITTATA

Yield: 48 portions   *Portion:* 4½ oz (1 wedge)
Oven: 350°F   *Bake:* 17–20 minutes

Ingredient	Amount	Procedure
Onions, thinly sliced Olive oil	12 lb (EP) 2½ cups	Using a covered pan, fry onions in oil on low heat, 200°F, until reduced in bulk. Uncover and continue cooking on very low heat until onions are browned and dry (12 lb fresh sliced onions will yield approximately 4 lb after cooking).

Roasted red bell
  peppers, diced
  (p. 854) (see Notes)
Salt
	1 lb (EP)
	
	1 oz
		Stir peppers and salt into cooked onion.

Eggs	60 (6 lb 12 oz)	Break eggs into bowl. Beat until blended.
Parmesan cheese, shredded Black pepper	6 oz 2 tsp	Add onion mixture, cheese, and pepper into eggs. Stir to mix.
Fresh basil, torn into small pieces	4 oz	Add basil to egg mixture. Mix lightly.
Butter, melted	12 oz	Pour 2 oz butter into six 13-inch round pizza pans. Scale 2 lb 4 oz of egg mixture into each pan. (Stir often while scaling in pans to keep the vegetables evenly distributed.) Bake at 350°F for approximately 20 minutes or until eggs are set and top has some brown speckling beginning to occur. Cut into eight wedges.

Approximate nutritive values per portion

Calories 250

Amount/portion	%DV	Amount/portion	%DV	Amount/portion	%DV		%DV		%DV
Total Fat 19 g	29%	**Cholest.** 270 mg	90%	**Total Carb.** 11 g	4%	**Vitamin A**	19%	**Calcium**	9%
Sat. Fat 4 g	21%	**Sodium** 350 mg	15%	Fiber 2.3 g	9%	**Vitamin C**	43%	**Iron**	7%
Protein 10 g				Sugars 3 g					

Percent Daily Values (%DV) are based on a 2000-calorie diet.

Notes
- Potentially hazardous food. *Food Safety Standard:* Hold food for service at an internal temperature above 140°F. Do not mix old product with new. Cool leftover product quickly (within 4 hours) to below 41°F. See p. 105 for cooling procedures. Reheat leftover product quickly (within 2 hours) to 165°F. Reheat product only once; discard if not used.
- Use freshly shredded Parmesan cheese.
- Frozen roasted peppers may be substituted for freshly roasted peppers. When using frozen roasted peppers, place in a single layer on a baking sheet and heat in a 375°F oven until heated through (discard liquid that accumulates).
- 6 oz reconstituted sun-dried tomatoes can be substituted for 6 oz of the roasted red peppers.
- Frittata can be cooked in an ovenproof 10-inch sauté pan. Melt 2 Tbsp butter in pan. When butter begins to foam, pour 1 lb 3 oz of egg mixture into pan. Turn heat to very low and cook until eggs are set on the bottom and only slightly runny on the surface. Put pan under broiler until eggs become set but not browned. Cut into four wedges.

CHEESE SOUFFLÉ

Yield: 48 portions or 2 pans 12 × 20 × 2 inches   *Portion:* 4 oz
Oven: 300°F   *Bake:* 55–60 minutes

Ingredient	Amount	Procedure
Margarine Flour, all-purpose Salt	1 lb 4 oz 10 oz 1 tsp	Melt margarine. Add flour and salt. Stir until smooth. Cook 5 minutes.
Milk	3 qt	Add milk gradually, stirring constantly with wire whip. Cook until thick.
Egg yolks, beaten	38 (1 lb 8 oz)	Add egg yolks to white sauce, stirring constantly. Cook for 2 minutes.
Cheddar cheese, shredded	1 lb 8 oz	Add cheese to sauce and stir until cheese is melted. Remove from heat.
Egg whites Cream of tartar	38 (2 lb 12 oz) 2 tsp	Add cream of tartar to egg whites. Beat until stiff, but not dry. Fold into cheese mixture.
		Scale mixture into two 12 × 20 × 2-inch baking pans, greased only on the bottoms, 6 lb 12 oz per pan. Bake at 300°F for 55–60 minutes or until set. Cut 4 × 6.

Approximate nutritive values per portion   **Calories** 265

Amount/portion	%DV	Amount/portion	%DV	Amount/portion	%DV		%DV		%DV
Total Fat 21 g	32%	**Cholest.** 205 mg	68%	**Total Carb.** 8 g	3%	Vitamin A	37%	Calcium	20%
Sat. Fat 7 g	37%	**Sodium** 323 mg	13%	Fiber 0.2 g	1%	Vitamin C	0%	Iron	5%
Protein 11 g				Sugars 3 g					

Percent Daily Values (%DV) are based on a 2000-calorie diet.

Notes
- Potentially hazardous food. *Food Safety Standard:* Hold food for service at an internal temperature above 140°F. Do not mix old product with new. Cool leftover product quickly (within 4 hours) to below 41°F. See p. 105 for cooling procedures. Reheat leftover product quickly (within 2 hours) to 165°F. Reheat product only once; discard if not used.
- Serve with Cheese Sauce (p. 749), Fresh Mushroom Sauce (p. 754), or Shrimp Sauce (p. 750).

Variation
- **Mushroom Soufflé.** Add 1 lb chopped mushrooms and 5 oz chopped green peppers to uncooked mixture. Serve with Béchamel Sauce (p. 750).

CHEESE AND BROCCOLI STRATA

Yield: 56 portions or 2 pans 12 × 20 × 2 inches   *Portion:* 8 oz
Oven: 325°F   *Bake:* 1–1½ hours

Ingredient	Amount	Procedure
Bread slices, dry	2 lb	Cut bread into 1½-inch cubes. Set aside.
Broccoli cuts, frozen	5 lb	Cook broccoli until tender.

Cheddar cheese, shredded	2 lb	Layer as follows in each pan:
		    8 oz bread cubes
		    2 lb 8 oz broccoli
		    1 lb cheese
		    8 oz bread cubes

Eggs, beaten Milk Salt Prepared mustard Hot pepper sauce	9 doz (12 lb) 1 gal 2 oz 3 oz (6 Tbsp) 1½ tsp	Combine eggs, milk, and seasonings. Pour 1¼ gal into each pan. Smooth down evenly.
Paprika	½ tsp	Sprinkle with paprika, ¼ tsp per pan. Set each pan in another counter pan containing 3 cups hot water. Baked uncovered at 325°F until custard sets, approximately 1–1½ hours, 180°F internal end-point temperature. Cut 4 × 7.

Approximate nutritive values per portion   **Calories** 307

Amount/portion	%DV	Amount/portion	%DV	Amount/portion	%DV		%DV		%DV
Total Fat 18 g	28%	**Cholest.** 441 mg	147%	**Total Carb.** 14 g	5%	**Vitamin A**	34%	**Calcium**	28%
Sat. Fat 8 g	40%	**Sodium** 784 mg	33%	Fiber 2 g	7%	**Vitamin C**	28%	**Iron**	13%
Protein 21 g				Sugars 4 g					

Percent Daily Values (%DV) are based on a 2000-calorie diet.

Notes

- Potentially hazardous food. *Food Safety Standard:* Hold food for service at an internal temperature above 140°F. Do not mix old product with new. Cool leftover product quickly (within 4 hours) to below 41°F. See p. 105 for cooling procedures. Reheat leftover product quickly (within 2 hours) to 165°F. Reheat product only once; discard if not used.
- Baking time may be reduced if milk mixture is warmed to 140°F before baking.
- May be served with 1 oz Cheese Sauce (p. 749).
- **Asparagus Cheese Strata.** Substitute asparagus for broccoli. Frozen asparagus cuts (thawed and drained) may be used. Serve with Cheese Sause (p. 749).

BROCCOLI AND CHEESE CASSEROLE

Yield: 48 portions or 4 pans 12 × 10 × 2 inches   *Portion:* 8 oz
Oven: 350°F   *Bake:* 1 hour 15 minutes

Ingredient	Amount	Procedure
Eggs	27 (3 lb)	Beat eggs and flour together, using a wire whip, until smooth.
Flour, all-purpose	12 oz	
Broccoli cuts, thawed, drained	6 lb 4 oz	Drain, then weigh. Fold into the egg-flour mixture.
Cottage cheese, low fat, drained	10 lb	Drain cottage cheese, then weigh. Add cheeses and salt to eggs.
Cheddar cheese, shredded	5 lb 6 oz	
Salt	2 Tbsp	
		Scale mixture into four greased 10 × 12 × 2-inch pans, 6 lb per pan. Bake at 350°F for approximately 1 hour 15 minutes or until a knife inserted near the center comes out clean, 180°F internal end-point temperature. Let stand 15 minutes. Cut 3 × 4.

Approximate nutritive values per portion   **Calories** 372

Amount/portion	%DV	Amount/portion	%DV	Amount/portion	%DV		%DV		%DV
Total Fat 22 g	33%	**Cholest.** 182 mg	61%	**Total Carb.** 12 g	4%	**Vitamin A**	30%	**Calcium**	47%
Sat. Fat 13 g	64%	**Sodium** 1014 mg	42%	Fiber 0.2 g	1%	**Vitamin C**	62%	**Iron**	9%
Protein 31 g				Sugars 4 g					

Percent Daily Values (%DV) are based on a 2000-calorie diet.

Notes

- Potentially hazardous food. *Food Safety Standard:* Hold food for service at an internal temperature above 140°F. Do not mix old product with new. Cool leftover product quickly (within 4 hours) to below 41°F. See p. 105 for cooling procedures. Reheat leftover product quickly (within 2 hours) to 165°F. Reheat product only once; discard if not used.

- May add topping of 3 cups bread crumbs mixed with ⅓ cup melted margarine and 6 oz Parmesan cheese. Add during last 15 minutes of cooking.

- May be garnished with fresh broccoli florets.

- For a vegetable, serve 4 oz portion.

WELSH RAREBIT

Yield: 50 portions or 6½ qt   *Portion:* ½ cup (4 oz)

Ingredient	Amount	Procedure
Margarine	10 oz	Melt margarine. Add flour and salt. Stir until smooth. Cook 5 minutes.
Flour, all-purpose	8 oz	
Salt	1 oz (1½ Tbsp)	
Milk	1 gal	Add milk gradually, stirring constantly with wire whip. Cook until thickened.
Cheddar cheese, shredded	5 lb	Add cheese and seasonings to sauce. Cook over hot water until cheese is melted. Serve on toast or toasted buns.
Dry mustard	2 Tbsp	
Worcestershire sauce	2 Tbsp	
Pepper, white	½ tsp	

Approximate nutritive values per portion   **Calories** 290

Amount/portion	%DV	Amount/portion	%DV	Amount/portion	%DV		%DV		%DV
Total Fat 22 g	34%	**Cholest.** 58 mg	19%	**Total Carb.** 8 g	3%	**Vitamin A**	19%	**Calcium**	42%
Sat. Fat 12 g	60%	**Sodium** 571 mg	24%	Fiber 0 g	0%	**Vitamin C**	3%	**Iron**	3%
Protein 14 g				Sugars 5 g					

Percent Daily Values (%DV) are based on a 2000-calorie diet.

Notes
- Potentially hazardous food. *Food Safety Standard:* Hold food for service at an internal temperature above 140°F. Do not mix old product with new. Cool leftover product quickly (within 4 hours) to below 41°F. See p. 105 for cooling procedures. Reheat leftover product quickly (within 2 hours) to 165°F. Reheat product only once; discard if not used.

Variation
- **Welsh Rarebit with Bacon.** Serve rarebit over toast, with two slices cooked bacon and two slices fresh tomato.

TABLE 11.2   Methods of cooking fin fish and shellfish

Type	Baking Temperature (°F)	Baking Time (minutes)	Broiling (3–4 inches from heat) Time (minutes)	Deep-fat frying (350°–375°F) Time (minutes)	Pan frying (moderate heat) Time (minutes)
Fin Fish					
Dressed, 3–4 lb	350–400	40–60			
Pan-dressed, ½–1 lb	350–400	25–30	5–15	4–5	15–20
Steaks, ½–1¼ inch	350–400	25–35	5–15	4–5	15–25
Fillets	350–400	25–35	5–15	4–5	8–10
Portions, 1–6 oz	350–400	30–40		4–5	8–10
Sticks, ¾–1¼ oz	400	15–20		3–5	
Shellfish					
Clams, live, shucked	450	12–15	5–8	2–3	4–5
Crabs, live, soft shell			8–10	2–4	
Lobsters, live, ¾–1 lb	400	15–20	12–15	2–4	8–10
Spiny lobster tails, frozen, ¼–½ lb	450	20–30	8–12	3–5	8–10
Oysters, live, shucked	450	12–15	5–8	2–3	4–5
Scallops, ocean	350	15–20	6–8	2–3	4–6
Shrimp, headless, raw, peeled	350	15–20	5–8	2–3	8–10

Adapted from *How to Eye and Buy Seafood*, National Marine Fisheries Service, U.S. Department of Commerce; *Seafood, Foodservice Training*, U.S. Department of Commerce, Chicago, Ill.; and *Seafood, Foodservice Training Manual*, the National Fisheries Institute.

Notes: • See p. 459 for microwave cooking methods.
  • A basic guide is to bake or pan fry fish for 20–25 minutes (350°–400°F) per inch of thickness for frozen fish; 10–15 minutes per inch of thickness for thawed or fresh fish.
  • For steaming fish or shellfish, see Table 11.2
  • End-point internal temperature must be 145°F.

Whole Fish for Buffet Display

Rinse and dry fish, then salt inside and out. Bake at 325°F until fish flakes easily, about 2 hours for a 12-pound fish and approximately 3 hours for a 20–24-pound fish. When done, gently remove skin, then garnish, being careful to arrange garnish so that fish can be cut and served easily. See p. 467 for Baked Whole Salmon.

Broiling

Fish fillets or steaks should be as dry as possible and at least 1 inch thick. Brush both sides with melted margarine or basting sauce, then season. See p. 781 for Lemon Herb Seasoning. Place frozen fish on greased broiler rack or pan. If the skin is on, place skin side down. Broil 2–4 inches from preheated heating unit. Broiling time will range from 5 to 20 minutes. Thicker fillets may need to be turned once, halfway through cooking time.

En Papillote

Cooking en papillote is similar to steaming in that fish, vegetables, herbs, and spices are encased in parchment paper and cooked at a high enough temperature to cause steam to build up inside the bag. See p. 200 for procedure for en papillote cooking.

Frying

Pan Frying and Sautéing

To pan fry, season fillets, steaks, or small whole fish with salt and pepper. Dip in milk and roll in flour or cornmeal or a combination of both. To sauté, lightly dust thawed, dry fish with seasoned flour. Cook in a small amount of fat at 360–375°F. Turn halfway through cooking time to brown each side.

Deep-Fat Frying

Dip frozen fish fillets, steaks, or small whole fish in milk or egg mixture and seasoned crumbs; or purchase breaded or battered product. Fry 4–5 minutes at 360–375°F (thicker whole fish will require more time).

Oven Frying

Dip frozen fillets or steaks in seasoned milk; drain, then coat with fine bread crumbs. Place in greased shallow pan or pan lined with parchment paper or aluminum foil. Do not cover. Drizzle melted fat over fish. Bake at 400°F.

Microwave

Primary Cooking Guidelines

The source for the following microwave cooking directions is the *Seafood Foodservice Training Manual,* published by the National Fisheries Institute, Washington, D.C.:

1. Maximum moisture retention and even cooking can be achieved by generously brushing the fish and seafood item with margarine and tightly covering or wrapping the item before cooking. Fish Marinade, p. 784, may be used.

2. If the item is to be browned under a broiler after microwave cooking, it should be cooked to only 75–80 percent doneness in the microwave. Fish will not yet be flaky, and shellfish will be slightly translucent.

3. Microwave individual portions on medium-high setting to retain juices and flavor.

4. Let fish or seafood stand 2–3 minutes prior to serving.

5. Test for doneness: Fish is flaky when lifted gently with a fork near the center. It should be opaque in color; bones should be easily removed from meat. Shellfish will be slightly translucent in center. Let stand for a short period to finish cooking.

Oven Steaming

Place frozen fish on greased aluminum foil. Season and flavor with lemon juice, spices, and thinly sliced vegetables. Wrap securely. Place in shallow baking pan. Bake at 400°F for 20–25 minutes per inch of thickness.

Poaching

Prepare poaching liquid: acidulated water, court bouillon, bouquet garni liquid, fish stock, milk, or milk and water. Place fish fillets or thick steaks in a flat, shallow baking pan. Barely cover fish with boiling liquid, then cover with parchment paper or a lid. Cook in a 350°F oven or in a steamer until fish loses its translucent appearance or until fish flakes easily when tested with a fork (see Table 11.3). Remove fish from liquid and serve with a sauce or garnish.

TABLE 11.3   Timetable for steaming fish and shellfish

Type	Amount per pan	Pan size solid	Procedure	Time (minutes) 5 PSI	15 PSI	Pressureless
Clams, soft shell	8–10 servings	12 × 20 × 2½ inches Perforated	Place washed clams in a 2½-inch perforated pan inside a 4-inch solid pan with 2–3 qt water.	6–8	4–6	6–8
Clams, hard shell	12 each 3 lb	12 × 20 × 2½ inches	As above.	6–8	4–6	6–8
Crabs	10–16 each	12 × 20 × 2½ inches Perforated	Put live crabs in perforated pan. Steam cook.	16–18	14–16	16–18
Fish fillets (haddock, sole, cod)	5 lb	12 × 20 × 2½ inches	Place preportioned fresh or defrosted fish in pan, skin-side down. Season as desired. Time depends on thickness of fish.	4–12	2–8	4–12
Fish steaks	5 lb	12 × 20 × 2½ inches	Place steaks, fresh or defrosted, in shallow pan. Season if desired. Cooking time dependent on thickness.	6–12	4–8	6–12
Lobster (1–1½ lb each)	4–5 each	12 × 20 × 2½ inches Perforated	Put lobsters in perforated pan. Steam cook.	6–8	4½–6	6–8
Lobster (1½–2 lb each)	4 each	12 × 20 × 2½ inches Perforated	Put lobsters in perforated pan. Steam cook.	8–10	7–9	8–10
Oysters	12 each 3 lb	12 × 20 × 2½ inches Perforated	Put oysters in perforated pan. Steam cook.	4–6	3–4	5–7
Shrimp, cooked and deveined (12–15), frozen	5 lb	12 × 20 × 2½ inches	Place shrimp in solid pan. Add 1 quart water and seasonings if desired.	4–8	3–6	4–8
Shrimp, raw	10 lb	12 × 20 × 2½ inches Perforated	Place shrimp in perforated pans, being careful not to overcrowd. Steam cook.	7–9	4–5	8–11

Acidulated Water

Use 1 Tbsp salt and 3 Tbsp lemon juice or vinegar for each quart of water.

Court Bouillon

Add to 1 gal water, ¾ cup each of chopped carrots, chopped onion, and chopped celery; 3 Tbsp salt; ½ cup vinegar; 2 or 3 bay leaves; 6 peppercorns; 9 cloves; and 3 Tbsp margarine or butter. Boil gently for 20–30 minutes. Strain to remove spices and vegetables.

Bouquet garni

Place in cheesecloth tied into a bag: 6 parsley sprigs; 2 celery tops; 3 bay leaves; 1 tsp thyme leaves (dried); 1 tsp peppercorns. Makes enough to season 1 gal of liquid.

FISH AND SHELLFISH RECIPES

BAKED FISH FILLETS

Yield: 50 portions   *Portion:* 5 oz
Oven: 375°F   *Bake:* 25–35 minutes

Ingredient	Amount	Procedure
Fish fillets, 5 oz	50	Dip fish in margarine (see Notes).
Margarine, melted	1 lb	
Bread crumbs	1 lb 12 oz	Combine bread crumbs, flour, and seasonings.
Flour, all-purpose	12 oz	
Salt	1 Tbsp	
Paprika	1½ Tbsp	
Seasoned salt	1 Tbsp	
Marjoram	1 tsp	
Grated lemon peel, fresh	1 tsp	
		Dredge fish with crumb mixture and place on greased baking pans. Bake at 375°F for approximately 10 minutes for each inch of thickness, or until fish flakes easily when tested with a fork at thickest part and internal temperature is 145°F.

Approximate nutritive values per portion   **Calories** 281

Amount/portion	%DV	Amount/portion	%DV	Amount/portion	%DV		%DV		%DV
Total Fat 13 g	19%	**Cholest.** 49 mg	16%	**Total Carb.** 25 g	8%	**Vitamin A**	12%	**Calcium**	9%
Sat. Fat 3 g	17%	**Sodium** 832 mg	35%	Fiber 1 g	3%	**Vitamin C**	0%	**Iron**	6%
Protein 17 g				Sugars 1 g					

Percent Daily Values (%DV) are based on a 2000-calorie diet.

Notes
- Potentially hazardous food. *Food Safety Standard:* Hold food for service at an internal temperature above 140°F. Do not mix old product with new. Cool leftover product quickly (within 4 hours) to below 41°F. See p. 105 for cooling procedures. Reheat leftover product quickly (within 2 hours) to 165°F. Reheat product only once; discard if not used.
- Double the cooking time for frozen fish that has not been defrosted.
- Fish portions or steaks may be substituted for fish fillets.
- Refrigerate all fish not currently being prepared or cooked.

Variation
- **Herbed Marinated Fish Steak.** Make Fish Marinade (p. 784). Marinate steaks for 3 hours. Grill or broil according to Table 11.2.

FAJITA-SPICED TROUT

Yield: 50 portions   *Portion:* 6 oz fillet

Ingredient	Amount	Procedure
Boneless trout fillet, 6 oz	50 fillets	Pat trout fillets dry.
Potato flakes (dry) Cornstarch Flour Fajita seasoning Salt	1 lb 8 oz 10 oz 4 oz 10 oz 4 oz	Mix potato flakes, cornstarch, flour, and seasonings to make a breading. Coat each fillet with breading mixture.
Vegetable oil	4 cups	Heat oil in fry pan. Place breaded trout into hot oil, presentation side down. Cook until browned. Turn and cook other side. Remove from skillet and drain. If necessary continue cooking in a 350°F oven until done.

Approximate nutritive values per portion   **Calories** 350

Amount/portion	%DV	Amount/portion	%DV	Amount/portion	%DV		%DV		%DV
Total Fat 11 g	17%	**Cholest.** 100 mg	33%	**Total Carb.** 22 g	7%	**Vitamin A**	9%	**Calcium**	12%
Sat. Fat 3 g	14%	**Sodium** 1331 mg	55%	Fiber 1 g	4%	**Vitamin C**	27%	**Iron**	4%
Protein 37 g				Sugars 1 g					

Percent Daily Values (%DV) are based on a 2000-calorie diet.

Notes
- Potentially hazardous food. *Food Safety Standards:* Hold food for service at an internal temperature above 140°F. Do not mix old product with new. Cool leftover product quickly (within 2 hours) to 70°F and then within an additional 4 hours to 41°F. See p. 105 for cooling procedures. Reheat leftover product quickly (within 2 hours) to 165°F. Reheat product only once; discard if not used.

Variation
- **Fajita Spiced Catfish with Asian Rice and Chile-Cilantro Dipping Sauce.** Substitute U.S Farm-Raised Catfish for trout. To serve: Portion 2 cups Asian Fried Rice (p. 598) in large deep bowl. Lay prepared catfish fillet over top of rice and ladle ⅓ cup Chile Cilantro Sauce (p. 722) over top. Garnish with leaves of fresh herbs. Note: increase rice recipe on p. 594 to yield a 2-cup serving.

LEMON BAKED FISH

Yield: 50 portions   *Portion:* 5 oz
Oven: 375°F   *Bake:* 25–35 minutes

Ingredient	Amount	Procedure
Fish fillets, 5 oz	50	Thaw fish (if frozen) and bake, using either Method 1 or Method 2.

METHOD 1

Margarine	1 lb 8 oz	Place 16 thawed fillets onto each 18 × 26-inch sheet pan.
Salt	1 oz (1½ Tbsp)	Melt margarine. Mix with lemon juice and seasonings.
Paprika	3 Tbsp	Brush generously on each piece of fish.
Lemon juice	⅓ cup	Bake at 375°F for approximately 10 minutes for each inch of thickness or until fish flakes easily with a fork when tested at the thickest part and internal temperature is 145°F. Transfer to 12 × 10 × 2-inch pans.

METHOD 2

Shortening, melted	1 lb	Mix shortening, salt, pepper, and lemon juice.
Salt	1 Tbsp	Dip each piece of fish into seasoned fat.
Pepper, white	1 tsp	
Lemon juice	½ cup	
Flour, all-purpose	1 lb	Dredge fish with flour. Place close together in single layer in greased baking pans.
Margarine, melted	2 oz	Mix margarine and milk and drizzle over fish.
Milk	¾ cup	Bake at 375°F for approximately 10 minutes for each inch of thickness or until fish flakes easily when tested with a fork at thickest part and internal temperature is 145°F. Sprinkle with chopped parsley before serving.

Approximate nutritive values per portion—Method 1   **Calories** 228

Amount/portion	%DV	Amount/portion	%DV	Amount/portion	%DV		%DV		%DV
Total Fat 13 g	20%	**Cholest.** 75 mg	25%	**Total Carb.** 0 g	0%	**Vitamin A**	7%	**Calcium**	2%
Sat. Fat 3 g	13%	**Sodium** 464 mg	19%	Fiber 0 g	0%	**Vitamin C**	1%	**Iron**	2%
Protein 27 g				Sugars 0 g					

Percent Daily Values (%DV) are based on a 2000-calorie diet.

Approximate nutritive values per portion—Method 2   **Calories** 253

Amount/portion	%DV	Amount/portion	%DV	Amount/portion	%DV		%DV		%DV
Total Fat 12 g	18%	**Cholest.** 75 mg	25%	**Total Carb.** 7 g	2%	**Vitamin A**	1%	**Calcium**	2%
Sat. Fat 3 g	15%	**Sodium** 257 mg	11%	Fiber 0.3 g	1%	**Vitamin C**	1%	**Iron**	4%
Protein 28 g				Sugars 0 g					

Percent Daily Values (%DV) are based on a 2000-calorie diet.

Notes
- Potentially hazardous food. *Food Safety Standard:* Hold food for service at an internal temperature above 140°F. Do not mix old product with new. Cool leftover product quickly (within 4 hours) to below 41°F. See p. 105 for cooling procedures. Reheat leftover product quickly (within 2 hours) to 165°F. Reheat product only once; discard if not used.
- Double the cooking time for frozen fish that has not been defrosted.
- Refrigerate all fish not in the preparation process or being cooked.

Variation
- **Creole Baked Fish.** Make spice mixture of 1 cup dried parsley flakes, ½ cup red pepper flakes, ½ cup black pepper, ½ cup paprika, ¼ cup crushed thyme leaves, ¼ cup crumbled rosemary, 2 Tbsp crumbled oregano, 2 Tbsp crumbled basil. Brush fish fillets with melted margarine. Sprinkle generously with spice mixture. Follow baking directions for Lemon Baked Fish—Method 1.

BREADED FISH FILLETS

Yield: 50 portions   *Portion:* 5 oz
Deep-fat fryer: 360°F   *Fry:* 4–5 minutes

Ingredient	Amount	Procedure
Frozen fish fillets, 5 oz	50	Dredge fish in mixture of flour, salt, and pepper (see Notes).
Flour, all-purpose	8 oz	
Salt	1 Tbsp	
Pepper, white	1 tsp	
Eggs, beaten	6 (11 oz)	Combine eggs and milk.
Milk	2 cups	
Bread crumbs	1 lb 4 oz	Dip fish in egg mixture, then in crumbs. Fry in deep fat at 360°F for 4–5 minutes or until fish is golden brown and internal temperature is 145°F. Serve at once or place for a short time in uncovered counter pans in 250°F oven until service.

Approximate nutritive values per portion   **Calories** 205

Amount/portion	%DV	Amount/portion	%DV	Amount/portion	%DV		%DV		%DV
Total Fat 3 g	5%	**Cholest.** 103 mg	34%	**Total Carb.** 12 g	4%	Vitamin A	2%	Calcium	5%
Sat. Fat 1 g	5%	**Sodium** 340 mg	14%	Fiber 1 g	2%	Vitamin C	0%	Iron	6%
Protein 30 g				Sugars 1 g					

Percent Daily Values (%DV) are based on a 2000-calorie diet.

Notes
- Potentially hazardous food. *Food Safety Standard:* Hold food for service at an internal temperature above 140°F. Do not mix old product with new. Cool leftover product quickly (within 4 hours) to below 41°F. See p. 105 for cooling procedures. Reheat leftover product quickly (within 2 hours) to 165°F. Reheat product only once; discard if not used.
- Keep refrigerated all fish not being prepared or cooked.
- Suggested fish: flounder, sole, haddock, perch, grouper.

Variation
- **Cornmeal-Breaded Fish Fillets.** Delete eggs, milk, and bread crumbs. Increase flour to 1 lb. Mix flour, 2 lb 8 oz cornmeal, salt, and pepper. Dip fish fillets into cornmeal-flour mixture, thoroughly coating each piece. Fry according to directions.

FILLET OF SOLE AMANDINE

Yield: 50 portions   *Portion:* 5 oz
Oven: 375°F   *Bake:* 15–20 minutes

Ingredient	Amount	Procedure
Fillet of sole, 3 per lb	17 lb	Dredge fish in mixture of flour, salt, and pepper.
Flour, all-purpose	8 oz	Place in greased counter pans in single layers (see Notes).
Salt	1 Tbsp	
Pepper, white	1 tsp	
Margarine	1 lb 8 oz	Sauté onion and garlic in margarine.
Onion, finely chopped	4 oz	
Garlic, minced	1 clove	
Water	2 cups	Combine water, lemon juice, and seasonings. Add onions and garlic.
Lemon juice	1½ cups	
Salt	1 Tbsp	Heat, but do not boil.
Pepper, white	1 tsp	Just before baking, pour sauce over fish, 1 cup per pan.
Almonds, slivered	8 oz	Sprinkle almonds over fish.
		Bake at 375°F for approximately 10 minutes for each inch of thickness or until fish flakes easily when tested with a fork at thickest part and internal temperature is 145°F.

Approximate nutritive values per portion   **Calories 324**

Amount/portion	%DV	Amount/portion	%DV	Amount/portion	%DV		%DV		%DV
Total Fat 16 g	24%	**Cholest.** 104 mg	35%	**Total Carb.** 5 g	2%	**Vitamin A**	5%	**Calcium**	4%
Sat. Fat 3 g	15%	**Sodium** 548 mg	23%	Fiber 1 g	2%	**Vitamin C**	12%	**Iron**	5%
Protein 39 g				Sugars 1 g					

Percent Daily Values (%DV) are based on a 2000-calorie diet.

Notes

- Keep refrigerated all fish not being prepared or cooked.
- Other white fish, such as halibut, haddock, cod, or flounder, may be used. Baking time on thicker fillets or steaks will be 25–35 minutes.
- Potentially hazardous food. *Food Safety Standards:* Hold food for service at an internal temperature above 140°F. Do not mix old product with new. Cool leftover product quickly (within 4 hours) to below 41°F. See p. 105 for cooling procedures. Reheat leftover product quickly (within 2 hours) to 165°F. Reheat product only once; discard if not used.

BROILED TUNA WITH WHITE BEANS AND TOMATO SAUCE

Yield: 50 portions   *Portion:* 6 oz tuna, 3 oz sauce
Broiler: 400°F   *Broil:* 10 minutes

Ingredient	Amount	Procedure
Red wine vinegar	¾ cup	Combine vinegar, oil, and spices.
Olive oil	½ cup	
Pepper	1½ tsp	
Salt	2 tsp	
Tuna steaks, 6 oz (approximately 1-inch thick)	50 steaks	Brush oil mixture evenly over both sides of tuna steaks. Arrange tuna on oiled sheet pans. Place pans in preheated 400°F broiler. Cook approximately 5 minutes on each side, until fish flakes easily and reaches 145°F.
White Bean and Tomato Sauce	recipe p. 760	Serve tuna over a 3 oz bed of White Bean and Tomato Sauce. Garnish plate with fresh basil or thyme.

Approximate nutritive values per portion   **Calories** 401

Amount/portion	%DV	Amount/portion	%DV	Amount/portion	%DV		%DV		%DV
Total Fat 7 g	11%	**Cholest.** 74 mg	25%	**Total Carb.** 33 g	11%	**Vitamin A**	6%	**Calcium**	16%
Sat. Fat 1 g	6%	**Sodium** 245 mg	10%	Fiber 1 g	2%	**Vitamin C**	7%	**Iron**	37%
Protein 51 g				Sugars 1 g					

Percent Daily Values (%DV) are based on a 2000-calorie diet.

Note • Potentially hazardous food. *Food Safety Standard:* Hold food for service at an internal temperature above 140°F. Cool leftover product quickly (within 4 hours) to below 41°F. See p. 105 for cooling procedures. Reheat leftover product quickly (within 2 hours) to 165°F. Reheat product only once; discard if not used.

Variation • **Broiled Halibut with Black Bean Sauce.** Substitute halibut steaks for tuna. Substitute Black Bean and Tomato Sauce (p. 760) for White Bean and Tomato Sauce.

LEMON RICE-STUFFED COD

Yield: 50 portions   *Portion:* 6 oz cod, 2¼ oz rice
Oven: 350°F   *Bake:* 25–30 minutes

Ingredient	Amount	Procedure
Cod fillets, 6 oz	50	Cut cod portions to open like a wallet, hinged in center.
Margarine Celery, diced Onion, chopped	4 oz 12 oz 6 oz	Sauté celery and onions in margarine in steam-jacketed kettle or other large pan.
Water, hot Salt Thyme	1½ qt 1 Tbsp 1 tsp	Add water and seasonings to vegetable mixture.
Rice, uncooked	1 lb 4 oz	Stir in raw rice. Cover and simmer until rice is tender and liquid is absorbed, approximately 15 minutes.
Yogurt, plain Lemon, peeled and diced	1 lb 4 oz	Stir in yogurt and lemon.
		Place No. 16 dipper (2¼ oz) of rice mixture on one side of fish fillet. Fold other half over top to close like a wallet. Place on greased baking sheets or 12 × 20-inch counter pans. Bake uncovered at 350°F for approximately 25–30 minutes or until fish flakes easily when tested with a fork at thickest part and internal temperature reaches 145°F. Serve garnished with a slice of lemon.

Approximate nutritive values per portion   **Calories** 207

Amount/portion	%DV	Amount/portion	%DV	Amount/portion	%DV		%DV		%DV
Total Fat 3 g	5%	**Cholest.** 75 mg	25%	**Total Carb.** 10 g	3%	**Vitamin A**	3%	**Calcium**	5%
Sat. Fat 1 g	4%	**Sodium** 253 mg	11%	Fiber 0.2 g	1%	**Vitamin C**	5%	**Iron**	6%
Protein 31 g				Sugars 1 g					

Percent Daily Values (%DV) are based on a 2000-calorie diet.

Notes
- Potentially hazardous food. *Food Safety Standard:* Hold food for service at an internal temperature above 140°F. Do not mix old product with new. Cool leftover product quickly (within 4 hours) to below 41°F. See p. 105 for cooling procedures. Reheat leftover product quickly (within 2 hours) to 165°F. Reheat product only once; discard if not used.
- Keep refrigerated all fish not being prepared or cooked.
- Brown rice or a brown and wild rice mixture may be substituted for white rice.
- Any firm fish may be substituted for cod: orange roughy, perch, pollack.

BAKED WHOLE SALMON, CHILLED

Yield: 1 salmon or 50 portions
Oven: 350°F   *Bake:* 2 hours

Ingredient	Amount	Procedure
Whole salmon, thawed	1 (approx. 10 lb)	Thoroughly wash fish. Rub inside and outside of fish while running cool, clear water over. Place fish on 12 × 20-inch sheet pan that has been sprayed with vegetable spray or lined with parchment paper. Bake at 350°F for approximately 1 hour.
		Remove from oven and skin fish. Cut skin behind head, down the length of back and halfway down across belly. Remove cut skin. Leave head, fins, and tail on.
Margarine or butter, melted	4 oz	Combine melted butter or margarine and lemon juice. Use to baste fish.
Lemon juice	½ cup (4 oz)	Return fish to oven and bake approximately 1 hour or until fish flakes easily when tested with a fork at thickest part and internal temperature reaches 145°F.
		Remove fish from oven. Cool quickly (within 4 hours) to below 41°F. Fish should be cooked 1 day in advance to be served on cold buffet.

To Serve Whole Baked Salmon:

1. Place fish on attractive tray.
2. Garnish with orange, lemon, and cucumber slices; carrot curls, ripe olives, and shredded cabbage. If mouth is large and open, a fluted orange can be inserted.

Approximate nutritive values per portion   **Calories** 148

Amount/portion	%DV	Amount/portion	%DV	Amount/portion	%DV		%DV		%DV
Total Fat 7 g	11%	**Cholest.** 35 mg	12%	**Total Carb.** 0 g	0%	**Vitamin A**	0%	**Calcium**	0%
Sat. Fat 1 g	7%	**Sodium** 64 mg	3%	Fiber 0 g	0%	**Vitamin C**	2%	**Iron**	3%
Protein 19 g				Sugars 0 g					

Percent Daily Values (%DV) are based on a 2000-calorie diet.

Notes
- Potentially hazardous food. Store at an internal temperature below 41°F. See p. 105 for recommended cooling procedures.
- Thaw fish in refrigerator for 1–2 days.

POACHED SALMON

Yield: 50 portions   *Portion:* 5 oz
Oven: 350°F   *Bake:* 10-15 minutes

Ingredient	Amount	Procedure
Onion, coarsely chopped	4 oz	Put vegetables, spices, and lemon into a cheesecloth bag.
Parsley sprigs	2 oz	
Celery tops, coarsely chopped	4 oz	
Bay leaves	8	
Thyme, dried leaves	4 tsp	
Peppercorns, black	2 tsp	
Salt	4 tsp	
Lemons, thickly sliced	2	
Water	2 gal	Combine water and wine. Cover and simmer seasoning bag with liquid for 15 minutes.
White wine	1 qt	Discard seasoning bag.
Salmon fillets, 5 oz (fresh or thawed)	50 fillets	Lightly grease four 12 × 20 × 4-inch pans. Divide salmon evenly into pans. Carefully pour approximately 2 qt of simmering hot liquid over salmon. (Fish should be just covered with liquid.) Bake uncovered at 350°F for 10-15 minutes or until fish flakes easily and reaches a temperature of 145°F. Remove salmon carefully from liquid. Serve with Horseradish Caper Sauce (p. 765) or Fruit Salsa (p. 759).

Approximate nutritive values per portion   **Calories** 190

Amount/portion	%DV	Amount/portion	%DV	Amount/portion	%DV		%DV		%DV
Total Fat 11 g	16%	**Cholest.** 0 mg	0%	**Total Carb.** 4 g	1%	**Vitamin A**	24%	**Calcium**	1%
Sat. Fat 0 g	0%	**Sodium** 179 mg	7%	Fiber 0 g	0%	**Vitamin C**	5%	**Iron**	1%
Protein 16 g				Sugars 0 g					

Percent Daily Values (%DV) are based on a 2000-calorie diet.

Notes
- Potentially hazardous food. *Food Safety Standard:* Hold food for service at an internal temperature above 140°F. Do not mix old product with new. Cool leftover product quickly (within 4 hours) to below 41°F. See p. 105 for cooling procedures. Reheat leftover product quickly (within 2 hours) to 165°F. Reheat product only once; discard if not used.

- Thermometer or thermocouple probe must be inserted in the fish without first passing through the poaching liquid.

- Salmon may be served hot or cold. If served cold, chill quickly (within 4 hours) to 41°F or below.

SALMON LOAF

Yield: 50 portions or 5 loaves 5 × 9 inches   *Portion:* 4½ oz
Oven: 325°F   *Bake:* 1–1½ hours

Ingredient	Amount	Procedure
Milk, scalded	3¾ cups	Mix milk and bread cubes.
Bread cubes, soft	1 lb 4 oz	
Eggs, beaten	18 (2 lb)	Add eggs to milk and bread mixture.
Salmon, flaked	10 lb	Add salmon and other ingredients.
Salt	1 oz (1½ Tbsp)	Mix lightly.
Paprika	1 tsp	Scale salmon mixture into five greased 5 × 9-inch loaf pans,
Pepper, white	1 tsp	2 lb 14 oz per pan.
Onions, chopped	3 oz	Bake at 325°F for 1–1½ hours or until internal temperature
Lemon juice	½ cup	reaches 180°F.

Approximate nutritive values per portion   **Calories** 196

Amount/portion	%DV	Amount/portion	%DV	Amount/portion	%DV		%DV		%DV
Total Fat 8 g	13%	**Cholest.** 130 mg	43%	**Total Carb.** 7 g	2%	**Vitamin A**	5%	Calcium	24%
Sat. Fat 2 g	12%	**Sodium** 785 mg	33%	Fiber 0.3 g	1%	**Vitamin C**	1%	Iron	7%
Protein 22 g				Sugars 1 g					

Percent Daily Values (%DV) are based on a 2000-calorie diet.

Notes
- Potentially hazardous food. *Food Safety Standard:* Hold food for service at an internal temperature above 140°F. Do not mix old product with new. Cool leftover product quickly (within 4 hours) to below 41°F. See p. 105 for cooling procedures. Reheat leftover product quickly (within 2 hours) to 165°F. Reheat product only once; discard if not used.
- For a lighter textured product, beat egg whites separately and fold into salmon mixture.

Variation
- **Tuna Loaf.** Substitute drained tuna for salmon.

TUNA AND NOODLES

Yield: 48 portions or 2 pans 12 × 20 × 2 inches   *Portion:* 8 oz
Oven: 350°F   *Bake:* 30–45 minutes

Ingredient	Amount	Procedure
Noodles Water, boiling Salt Vegetable oil	3 lb AP 3 gal 2 oz (3 Tbsp) 2 Tbsp	Cook noodles according to direction on p. 561. Drain. (Should yield 9 lb cooked.)
Tuna	5 lb 8 oz	Flake tuna and add to noodles.
Margarine Onions, chopped Celery, chopped	8 oz 1 lb 8 oz 1 lb 8 oz	Melt margarine in steam-jacketed or other kettle. Add onions and celery. Sauté until tender.
Flour, all-purpose Pepper, black	6 oz ½ tsp	Add flour and pepper to onion mixture. Stir until blended. Cook 5–10 minutes.
Chicken base Water	3 oz 1 gal	Stir in chicken base. Add water gradually, stirring constantly with wire whip. Cook until thickened. Add tuna and noodles to sauce. Stir gently until well blended.
Processed cheese, shredded Paprika	8 oz ½ tsp	Scale noodle mixture into two greased 12 × 20 × 2-inch baking pans, 13 lb per pan. Sprinkle with cheese, 4 oz per pan. Sprinkle lightly with paprika. Bake at 350°F until mixture is heated to 180°F and cheese is melted, 30–45 minutes.

Approximate nutritive values per portion   **Calories** 251

Amount/portion	%DV	Amount/portion	%DV	Amount/portion	%DV		%DV		%DV
Total Fat 8 g	12%	**Cholest.** 47 mg	16%	**Total Carb.** 25 g	8%	**Vitamin A**	4%	**Calcium**	6%
Sat. Fat 2 g	11%	**Sodium** 1044 mg	44%	Fiber 1 g	2%	**Vitamin C**	3%	**Iron**	13%
Protein 19 g				Sugars 2 g					

Percent Daily Values (%DV) are based on a 2000-calorie diet.

Notes
- Potentially hazardous food. *Food Safety Standard:* Hold food for service at an internal temperature above 140°F. Do not mix old product with new. Cool leftover product quickly (within 4 hours) to below 41°F. See p. 105 for cooling procedures. Reheat leftover product quickly (within 2 hours) to 165°F. Reheat product only once; discard if not used.
- Two 46-oz cans cream of mushroom or cream of celery soup and 1 qt milk may be substituted for the sauce made from margarine, flour, chicken base, and water.

Variations
- **Tuna Macaroni Casserole.** Substitute macaroni for noodles.
- **Tuna and Rice.** Substitute 1 lb 8 oz rice for the noodles. Cook rice according to directions on p. 594.

SCALLOPE

Yield: 50 portio
Oven: 400°F

Ingredient

Oysters

Cracker crum
Margarine, m
Salt
Paprika
Pepper, white

Milk
Oyster liquor

Approximate n

Amount/portio

Total Fat 11 g
  Sat. Fat 3 g
Protein 3 g

Percent Daily V

Notes

CREAMED TUNA

Yield: 50 portions or 7½ qt   *Portion:* 4 oz

Ingredient	*Amount*	*Procedure*
Eggs, hard cooked (p. 439)	9	Peel eggs and chop coarsely, reserve for later step.
Margarine	12 oz	Melt margarine in steam-jacketed or other kettle.
Flour, all-purpose	6 oz	Add flour and salt. Stir until smooth.
Salt	1 Tbsp	Cook 5 minutes.
Milk	1 gal	Add milk gradually, stirring constantly with a wire whip. Cook until thickened.
Green pepper, chopped	6 oz	Add green pepper, pimiento, and seasonings to sauce.
Pimiento, chopped	6 oz	
Worcestershire sauce (optional)	6 Tbsp	
Pepper, cayenne	¼ tsp	
Tuna, flaked	5 lb	Add tuna and eggs to sauce. Heat to 180°F. Serve with 4-oz ladle on toast, biscuits, or corn bread.

Approximate nutritive values per portion   **Calories** 179

Amount/portion	%DV	Amount/portion	%DV	Amount/portion	%DV		%DV		%DV
Total Fat 9 g	15%	**Cholest.** 62 mg	21%	**Total Carb.** 7 g	2%	**Vitamin A**	10%	**Calcium**	13%
Sat. Fat 3 g	16%	**Sodium** 413 mg	17%	Fiber 0.2 g	1%	**Vitamin C**	16%	**Iron**	7%
Protein 16 g				Sugars 4 g					

Percent Daily Values (%DV) are based on a 2000-calorie diet.

Notes
- Potentially hazardous food. *Food Safety Standard:* Hold food for service at an internal temperature above 140°F. Do not mix old product with new. Cool leftover product quickly (within 4 hours) to below 41°F. See p. 105 for cooling procedures. Reheat leftover product quickly (within 2 hours) to 165°F. Reheat product only once; discard if not used.
- Other cooked fish may be substituted for tuna.

Variations
- **Creamed Salmon.** Substitute salmon for tuna.
- **Creamed Tuna and Celery.** Delete hard-cooked eggs and green pepper. Add 1 lb diced cooked celery, 3 oz chopped onion sautéed in margarine, and 3 oz chopped pimiento.
- **Creamed Tuna and Peas.** Delete hard-cooked eggs and green pepper. Add 3 lb frozen peas, cooked until just tender and drained.
- **Tuna Rarebit.** Delete hard-cooked eggs. Add 1 lb 8 oz shredded cheddar cheese.

DEVILI

Yield: 50
Oven: 400

Ingredie

Crabme

Eggs, be
Lemon
Salt
Pepper
Pepper,
Worcest
Onion j

Margari
Flour, a

Milk

Prepar

Bread
Margar

Approx

Amount

Total Fa
Sat. Fa
Protein

Percent

Notes

Meat

David Murray and Jules Selmes
© Dorling Kindersley

TIME AND TEMPERATURE TIMETABLES AND GUIDELINES

Cooking meat to the correct doneness requires that cooking times and temperatures be followed carefully. The timetables in this chapter (Tables 12.1 through 12.9) will be helpful for producing quality meat products. Meat cooking methods are described in Chapter 4.

DEGREE OF DONENESS

Proper cooking is one of the most effective ways to kill harmful bacteria and maintain quality standards. The time required to reach the optimum degree of doneness will vary depending on such things as the equipment, product temperature, product size, and quantity being cooked at one time. Exhibit VI provides color descriptions for beef steaks cooked at varying degrees of doneness. For steaks that are broiled, pan broiled, or grilled, the easiest way to determine doneness is by cutting a small slit and checking the color of the meat near the bone, or near the center of a boneless cut. Ground beef should always be cooked to 155°F or above for 15 seconds. Cooking to 160°F, which is often recommended, provides a safety factor because the time variable is removed.

Color is not always an accurate predictor for end temperature, because of the meat pH or the interaction of beef with other ingredients. End temperatures should be verified with a sanitized thermometer or thermocouple.

TABLE 12.1   Timetable for roasting beef

Beef cut	Oven temperature (preheated)	Weight (pounds)	Approx. total cooking time (based on meat removed directly from refrigerator)		Remove roast from oven when internal temperature reaches (F°):
Rib Eye Roast, small end	350°F	3 to 4	Medium rare:	1½–1¾ hr	135
			Medium:	1¾–2 hr	150
		4 to 6	Medium rare:	1¾–2 hr	135
			Medium:	2–2½ hr	150
		6 to 8	Medium rare:	2–2¼ hr	135
			Medium:	2½–2¾ hr	150
	325°F	8* to 10*	Medium rare:	2½–3¼ hr	135
			Medium:	3–3¾ hr	145
Rib Eye Roast, large end	350°F	3 to 4	Medium rare:	1¾–2¼ hr	135
			Medium:	2–2½ hr	150
		4 to 6	Medium rare:	2–2½ hr	135
			Medium:	2½–3 hr	150
		6 to 8	Medium rare:	2¼–2½ hr	135
			Medium:	2¾–3 hr	150
Rib Roast, chine bone removed	350°F	4 to 6 (2 ribs)	Medium rare:	1¾–2¼ hr	135
			Medium:	2¼–2¾ hr	150
		6 to 8 (2 to 4 ribs)	Medium rare:	2¼–2½ hr	135
			Medium:	2¾–3 hr	150
		8 to 10 (4 to 5 ribs)	Medium rare:	2½–3 hr	135
			Medium:	3–3½ hr	150
Tenderloin Roast, well trimmed	425°F	2 to 3 (center cut)	Medium rare:	35–40 min	135
			Medium:	45–50 min	150
		4 to 5 (whole)	Medium rare:	50–60 min	135
			Medium:	60–70 min	150
Round Tip Roast, cap off	325°F	3 to 4	Medium rare:	1¾–2 hr	140
			Medium:	2¼–2½ hr	155
		4 to 6	Medium rare:	2–2½ hr	140
			Medium:	2½–3 hr	155
		6 to 8	Medium rare:	2½–3 hr	140
			Medium:	3–3½ hr	155
		8* to 10*	Medium rare:	3–3¾ hr	135
			Medium:	3¾–4½ hr	150
Top Round Roast	325°F	6* to 8*	Medium rare:	2½–3 hr	135
		8* to 10*	Medium rare:	3–3¾ hr	135
Eye Round Roast	325°F	2 to 3	Medium rare:	1½–1¾ hr	135
Tri-Tip Roast	425°F	1½ to 2	Medium rare:	30–40 min	135
			Medium:	40–45 min	150

Medium rare doneness = 145°F final internal temperature after 15 to 20 minutes standing time.
Medium doneness = 160°F final internal temperature after 15 to 20 minutes standing time.

From the National Cattlemen's Beef Association.

Information based on consumer roasting data. Cooking times and temperatures for quantity production may vary depending on the roast size, number of roasts in the oven, temperature of roast before cooking, and equipment.

During standing time, roasts will continue to rise 5°–10°F.

*Tent loosely with aluminum foil halfway through roasting time.

TABLE 12.2   Timetable for roasting lamb and veal

Cut	Approximate weight (pounds)	Oven temperature (°F)	Interior temperature of roast when removed from oven (°F)[a][b]	Minutes per pound based on one roast	Approximate total cooking time (hours)
LAMB					
Leg, shank off, No. 233C	5–7	325	140 (rare)	15–20	1¾–2½
			145 (medium rare)	20–25	1¾–3
			155 (medium)	25–30	3–3½
Leg, shank off, boneless, No. 233D	4–7	325	140 (rare)	20	1½–2½
			145 (medium rare)	25	1¾–3
			155 (medium)	25–30	2–3½
Shoulder, boneless and tied, No. 208	3½–6	325	140 (rare)	30	2–2½
			145 (medium rare)	35	2¼–3
			155 (medium)	40	2½–3½
Rib rack, No. 204	1½–2½	375	140 (rare)	30	¾–1
			145 (medium rare)	35	1–1¼
			155 (medium)	40	1–1½
Rib rack, No. 204	2–3	375	140 (rare)	25	1–1¼
			145 (medium rare)	30	1¼–1½
			155 (medium)	35	1½–1¾
VEAL					
Loin roast	3–4	300–325	155 (medium)	34–36	1¾–2⅓
			165 (well)	38–40	2–2⅔
Loin roast, boneless	2–3	300–325	155 (medium)	18–20	¾–1
			165 (well)	22–24	¾–1¼
Rib roast	4–5	300–325	155 (medium)	25–27	1⅔–2¼
			165 (well)	29–31	2–2½
Crown roast (12–14 ribs)	7½–9½	300–325	155 (medium)	19–21	2¼–3¼
			165 (well)	21–23	2½–3½
Rib Eye roast	2–3	300–325	155 (medium)	26–28	1–1½
			165 (well)	30–33	1–1⅔
Rump roast, boneless	2–3	300–325	155 (medium)	33–35	1–1¾
			165 (well)	37–40	1¼–2
Shoulder roast, boneless	2¼–3	300–325	155 (medium)	31–34	1¼–1½
			165 (well)	34–37	1¼–1¾

Compiled from materials by National Cattlemen's Beef Association, Veal Committee, and American Lamb Council materials.

[a] For safety, lamb and veal must reach a temperature of 145°F or above for 15 seconds.

[b] During the required 15–20 minute standing time, temperature will rise 5°F.

KABOBS

Yield: 50 portions   *Portion:* 1 kabob
Oven: 400°F   *Bake:* 15–20 minutes

Ingredient	Amount	Procedure
Beef (tender), cut in 1½-inch cubes	20 lb	Place beef in stainless steel baker's bowl.
Salad oil	2 lb	Combine oil and seasonings.
Soy sauce	2½ cups	Pour over beef cubes to cover completely.
Lemon juice	2 cups	Refrigerate for 24–36 hours.
Worcestershire sauce	1 cup	Drain well. Discard marinade.
Prepared mustard	1 cup	
Garlic, fresh, minced	½ oz	
Pepper, black	1 oz (4 Tbsp)	
Green peppers, fresh	1 lb 6 oz	Cut peppers into ¾-inch squares.
Onions, whole, canned	4 lb	Thread beef cubes (5 oz), green pepper, onions, and pineapple alternately on skewer. Do not crowd.
Pineapple, fresh or fresh frozen chunks	2 lb	Place on oiled 18 × 26 × 1-inch baking sheets. Bake at 400°F for approximately 8–10 minutes.
Skewers, bamboo	50	Turn. Continue baking for 5–10 minutes more; total 15–20 minutes, depending on degree of doneness desired (must reach at least 140°F).
Cherry tomatoes	1 lb 10 oz	Place a cherry tomato on tip of each skewer. Place in 12 × 20 × 2-inch pans with liners. Keep hot.

Approximate nutritive values per portion   **Calories** 484

Amount/portion	%DV	Amount/portion	%DV	Amount/portion	%DV		%DV		%DV
Total Fat 30 g	47%	**Cholest.** 91 mg	30%	**Total Carb.** 7 g	2%	**Vitamin A**	14%	**Calcium**	4%
Sat. Fat 9 g	45%	**Sodium** 1056 mg	44%	Fiber 0.4 g	2%	**Vitamin C**	48%	**Iron**	25%
Protein 44 g				Sugars 4 g					

Percent Daily Values (%DV) are based on a 2000-calorie diet.

Notes
- Potentially hazardous food. *Food Safety Standards:* Hold food for service at an internal temperature above 140°F. Cool leftover product quickly (within 4 hours) to below 41°F. See p. 105 for cooling procedures. Reheat leftover product quickly (within 2 hours) to 165°F. Reheat product only once; discard if not used.

- Other garnishes may be substituted for those listed in recipe: tomato quarters, mandarin orange sections, carrot chunks (slightly cooked), stuffed olives, button mushrooms. Poultry or shellfish may be substituted for the beef. Marinate only 12–24 hours.

BEEF LIVER WITH SPANISH SAUCE

Yield: 50 portions   *Portion:* 4 oz
Oven: 350°F   *Bake:* 1 hour

Ingredient	Amount	Procedure
Beef liver, sliced, cut 5 per lb	10 lb	Dredge liver with seasoned flour.
Flour, all-purpose	8 oz	
Salt	2 oz (3 Tbsp)	
Pepper, black	2 tsp	
Shortening	1 lb 8 oz	Brown liver in hot shortening. Place in two 12 × 20 × 2-inch baking pans.
Spanish Sauce (p. 763)	1 recipe	Pour sauce over liver, 5 cups per pan. Cover with aluminum foil. Bake at 350°F until tender, about 1 hour depending on the degree of doneness desired. Internal temperature of liver must reach at least 145°F.

Approximate nutritive values per portion   **Calories** 273

Amount/portion	%DV	Amount/portion	%DV	Amount/portion	%DV		%DV		%DV
Total Fat 18 g	28%	**Cholest.** 284 mg	95%	**Total Carb.** 10 g	3%	Vitamin A	634%	Calcium	1%
Sat. Fat 5 g	25%	**Sodium** 562 mg	23%	Fiber 1 g	2%	Vitamin C	26%	Iron	26%
Protein 17 g				Sugars 0 g					

Percent Daily Values (%DV) are based on a 2000-calorie diet.

Notes
- Potentially hazardous food. *Food Safety Standards:* Hold food for service at an internal temperature above 140°F. Do not mix old product with new. Cool leftover product quickly (within 4 hours) to below 41°F. See p. 105 for cooling procedures. Reheat leftover product quickly (within 2 hours) to 165°F. Reheat product only once; discard if not used.
- Liver may be soaked in milk before cooking.

Variations
- **Baked Liver and Onions.** Brown liver as above. Sauté 5 lb sliced onions in 8 oz shortening. Arrange liver in two counter pans. Spread onions over liver. Cover pans with aluminum foil. Bake 30–40 minutes.
- **Braised Liver.** Brown liver as above. Cover with sauce made of 10 oz shortening, 5 oz flour, 3 qt beef stock, 2 oz salt, and 2 tsp pepper.
- **Grilled Liver and Onions.** Have liver cut ⅜ inch thick. Preheat grill to 350°F. Oil grill slightly. Cook liver quickly, browning on one side, then turning and browning on the other side. Serve immediately with steamed or grilled sliced onions.
- **Liver and Bacon.** Dredge liver with seasoned flour and fry in bacon fat. Top each serving with one slice of crisp bacon.

MEAT LOAF

Yield: 50 portions or 5 loaves 5 × 9 inches   *Portion:* 4 oz
Oven: 325°F   *Bake:* 1½ hours

Ingredient	Amount	Procedure
Ground beef	10 lb	Mix all ingredients on low speed until blended, using flat beater. Do not overmix.
Ground pork	2 lb	Press meat mixture into five 5 × 9-inch pans, 3 lb 4 oz per pan.
Bread crumbs, soft	12 oz	Bake at 325°F for approximately 1½ hours, or until internal temperature reaches 180°F.
Milk	1 qt	Meat loaf may also be made in a 12 × 20 × 4-inch counter pan.
Eggs	12 (1 lb 5 oz)	Press mixture into pan. Divide into two loaves (Figure 12.1). Increase baking time to 2 hours.
Onion, finely chopped	4 oz	
Salt	2 Tbsp	
Pepper, black	1 tsp	
Pepper, cayenne	few grains	

Approximate nutritive values per portion   **Calories** 276

Amount/portion	%DV	Amount/portion	%DV	Amount/portion	%DV		%DV		%DV
Total Fat 18 g	28%	**Cholest.** 120 mg	40%	**Total Carb.** 6 g	2%	Vitamin A	3%	Calcium	5%
Sat. Fat 7 g	36%	**Sodium** 376 mg	16%	Fiber 0.3 g	1%	Vitamin C	0%	Iron	15%
Protein 21 g				Sugars 1 g					

Percent Daily Values (%DV) are based on a 2000-calorie diet.

Notes
- Potentially hazardous food. *Food Safety Standards:* Hold food for service at an internal temperature above 140°F. Cool leftover product quickly (within 4 hours) to below 41°F. See p. 105 for cooling procedures. Reheat leftover product quickly (within 2 hours) to 165°F. Reheat product only once; discard if not used.
- Ground pork may be omitted. Increase ground beef to 12 lb.
- Topping of 8 oz brown sugar, 2 Tbsp dry mustard, 1¼ cups catsup, and 1 Tbsp nutmeg may be spread over loaves the last ½ hour of cooking.
- ½ oz (¼ cup) dehydrated onions, rehydrated in ½ cup water, may be substituted for fresh onions.

Variations
- **Barbecued Meatballs.** Measure with No. 8 dipper and shape into balls. Cover with 1 gal Barbecue Sauce (p. 755).
- **Italian Meatballs.** Omit cayenne pepper. Increase onion to 8 oz. Add ¼ cup minced garlic, 1 cup grated Parmesan cheese, 1 cup grated Romano cheese, 1½ cups chopped fresh parsley, and 4 tsp dried oregano leaves. Proceed as for Swedish Meatballs, p. 500. If adding to Italian Tomato Sauce, cook until partially done. Add to sauce and continue cooking until done.
- **Meatballs.** Measure with No. 8 dipper and shape into balls. Proceed as for Swedish Meatballs (p. 500) or Spaghetti with Meatballs (p. 588).
- **Vegetable Meat Loaf.** Add 2 cups catsup; 8 oz each raw carrots, onions, and celery; and 4 oz green peppers. Grind vegetables. Pour a small amount of tomato juice over loaves before baking.

FIGURE 12.1 Shaping meat loaf.
(a) Press mixture into counter pans, then smooth top. (b) Form into two loaves.

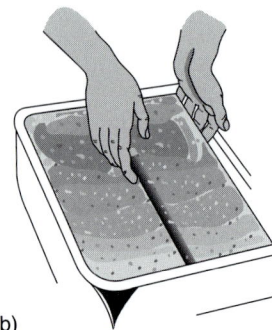

(a)   (b)

SPANISH MEATBALLS

Yield: 50 portions   *Portion:* 2 3-oz meatballs
Oven: 325°F   *Bake:* 1½ hours

Ingredient	Amount	Procedure
Rice, converted	1 lb 2 oz	Cook rice (p. 594) until slightly underdone.
Water	1¼ qt	Drain off excess liquid.
Salt	1 tsp	
Ground beef	12 lb	Place ground beef in mixer bowl.
Eggs	12 (1 lb 5 oz)	Add cooked rice and other ingredients.
Potatoes, cooked and mashed	1 lb	Mix until blended, using flat beater. Do not overmix.
Onion, grated	4 oz	
Green peppers, chopped	4 oz	
Salt	2 oz (3 Tbsp)	
Pepper, black	1½ Tbsp	
		Form meatballs, using a No. 12 dipper. Place in a single layer on two 12 × 20 × 2-inch baking pans.
		Bake at 325°F for 1½ hours, or until internal temperature of meatballs reaches 180°F.
		Drain off fat.
Chili sauce	3 qt	Mix chili sauce and water.
Water	2 qt	Pour over meatballs.
		Cover tightly and bake an additional 30 minutes. Add more liquid if necessary.

Approximate nutritive values per portion   **Calories** 348

Amount/portion	%DV	Amount/portion	%DV	Amount/portion	%DV		%DV		%DV
Total Fat 18 g	27%	**Cholest.** 117 mg	39%	**Total Carb.** 25 g	8%	**Vitamin A**	10%	**Calcium**	3%
Sat. Fat 7 g	34%	**Sodium** 1344 mg	56%	Fiber 0.4 g	2%	**Vitamin C**	17%	**Iron**	15%
Protein 22 g				Sugars 7 g					

Percent Daily Values (%DV) are based on a 2000-calorie diet.

Notes
- Potentially hazardous food. *Food Safety Standards:* Hold food for service at an internal temperature above 140°F. Cool leftover product quickly (within 4 hours) to below 41°F. See p. 105 for cooling procedures. Reheat leftover product quickly (within 2 hours) to 165°F. Reheat product only once; discard if not used.
- Spanish Sauce (p. 763) or tomato puree may be substituted for chili sauce.
- ½ oz (¼ cup) dehydrated onions, rehydrated in ½ cup water, may be substituted for fresh onions.

SWEDISH MEATBALLS

Yield: 50 portions   *Portion:* 2 2½-oz meatballs
Oven: 300°F   *Bake:* 1 hour

Ingredient	Amount	Procedure
Bread, cubed	2 lb 8 oz	Soak bread in milk for 1 hour.
Milk	1½ qt	
Ground beef	5 lb	Combine meat, potato, onion, and seasonings in mixer bowl.
Ground pork	3 lb	Add bread. Mix to blend, using flat beater. Do not overmix.
Potatoes, raw, grated	1 lb 4 oz	
Onions, minced	12 oz	
Salt	2 oz	
Pepper, black	2 tsp	
		Form meatballs, using a No. 16 dipper. Place in a single layer on baking pans.
		Brown in hot oven (400°F).
		Transfer to two 12 × 20 × 2-inch counter pans.
Meat drippings	6 oz	Add flour and seasonings to meat drippings and blend.
Flour, all-purpose	6 oz	Add milk gradually, stirring constantly with a wire whip.
Salt	2 tsp	Cook until smooth and thickened.
Pepper, black	¾ tsp	Pour over meatballs.
Milk	3 qt	Bake at 300°F for 1 hour, or until internal temperature of meatballs reaches 180°F.

Approximate nutritive values per portion   **Calories** 292

Amount/portion	%DV	Amount/portion	%DV	Amount/portion	%DV		%DV		%DV
Total Fat 15 g	23%	**Cholest.** 56 mg	19%	**Total Carb.** 20 g	7%	Vitamin A	4%	Calcium	16%
Sat. Fat 6 g	30%	**Sodium** 768 mg	32%	Fiber 3 g	11%	Vitamin C	3%	Iron	15%
Protein 20 g				Sugars 5 g					

Percent Daily Values (%DV) are based on a 2000-calorie diet.

Notes

- Potentially hazardous food. *Food Safety Standards:* Hold food for service at an internal temperature above 140°F. Cool leftover product quickly (within 4 hours) to below 41°F. See p. 105 for cooling procedures. Reheat leftover product quickly (within 2 hours) to 165°F. Reheat product only once; discard if not used.

- Veal or ground turkey may be substituted for part of beef.

- 1½ oz (¾ cup) dehydrated onions, rehydrated in 1 cup water, may be substituted for fresh onions.

BEEF STEW

Yield: 50 portions   *Portion:* 7 oz

Ingredient	Amount	Procedure
Beef, 1-inch cubes	15 lb AP (10 lb EP)	Brown beef in kettle or oven.
Water	2 qt	Add water and seasonings to meat.
Salt	2 oz (3 Tbsp)	Cover and simmer 2 hours. Add more water as necessary.
Pepper, black	2 tsp	
Worcestershire sauce	¾ cup	
Potatoes, cubed	4 lb	Cook vegetables in steamer or in small amount of water in kettle or oven.
Carrots, sliced or cubed	3 lb	
Onion, cubed	1 lb	
Celery, diced	12 oz	
Flour, all-purpose	12 oz	Mix flour and water until smooth.
Water	1 qt	Add to meat and cook until thickened. Add vegetables and, if necessary, return heat to 180°F.

Approximate nutritive values per portion   **Calories** 236

Amount/portion	%DV	Amount/portion	%DV	Amount/portion	%DV		%DV		%DV
Total Fat 6 g	10%	**Cholest.** 77 mg	26%	**Total Carb.** 16 g	5%	**Vitamin A**	65%	**Calcium**	2%
Sat. Fat 2 g	10%	**Sodium** 543 mg	23%	Fiber 1 g	2%	**Vitamin C**	17%	**Iron**	20%
Protein 27 g				Sugars 0 g					

Percent Daily Values (%DV) are based on a 2000-calorie diet.

Notes
- Potentially hazardous food. *Food Safety Standards:* Hold food for service at an internal temperature above 140°F. Do not mix old product with new. Cool leftover product quickly (within 4 hours) to below 41°F. See p. 105 for cooling procedures. Reheat leftover product quickly (within 2 hours) to 165°F. Reheat product only once; discard if not used.
- One 40-oz package of frozen green peas may be added just before serving. Reheat to serving temperature.

Variations
- **Beef Pot Pie.** Add one 40-oz package of frozen peas. Place cooked stew in two 12 × 20 × 2-inch counter pans, 13 lb per pan. Make Pastry for One-Crust Pies (p. 390). Roll out 2 lb per pan and place on stew. Bake at 425°F for 20–25 minutes.
- **Beef Stew with Biscuits.** Place hot stew in two 12 × 20 × 2-inch counter pans. Prepare ½ recipe of Baking Powder Biscuits (p. 268). Cut into 48 2½-inch biscuits. Place on hot stew, 24 per pan. Bake at 425°F for 15–20 minutes.
- **Beef Stew with Dumplings.** Drop Dumplings (p. 295) on meat mixture and steam 15–18 minutes.
- **Beef Stew with Tomatoes.** Delete carrots and celery. Add 4 lb diced canned tomatoes and 1 lb 8 oz green pepper strips the last 5 minutes of cooking.

GREEN CHILI STEW AND CORN BREAD

Yield: 50 portions   *Portion:* 8 oz

Ingredient	Amount	Procedure
Beef, strips or cubes	5 lb	Brown beef in steam-jacketed or other large kettle.
Water	1 gal	Add water. Cover and simmer until tender.
Green chili peppers, canned	5 lb	Add vegetables and spices. Cover and simmer until onion is cooked (approximately 30 minutes).
Pinto beans, canned, drained	3 lb 8 oz	
Tomatoes, canned, diced	2 qt	
Onions, chopped	2 lb	
Garlic, minced	1 oz	
Salt	2½ Tbsp	
Cumin	1 Tbsp	
Oregano leaves, dried	1 Tbsp	
Corn Bread (p. 281)	1 recipe	Serve 8 oz of stew in a bowl with a wedge of Corn Bread alongside.

Approximate nutritive values per portion   **Calories** 323

Amount/portion	%DV	Amount/portion	%DV	Amount/portion	%DV		%DV		%DV
Total Fat 10 g	15%	**Cholest.** 56 mg	19%	**Total Carb.** 41 g	14%	**Vitamin A**	32%	**Calcium**	17%
Sat. Fat 3 g	15%	**Sodium** 1014 mg	42%	Fiber 5 g	18%	**Vitamin C**	58%	**Iron**	17%
Protein 18 g				Sugars 8 g					

Percent Daily Values (%DV) are based on a 2000-calorie diet.

Note • Potentially hazardous food. *Food Safety Standards:* Hold food for service at an internal temperature above 140°F. Do not mix old product with new. Cool leftover product quickly (within 4 hours) to below 41°F. See p. 105 for cooling procedures. Reheat leftover product quickly (within 2 hours) to 165°F. Reheat product only once; discard if not used.

BEEF STROGANOFF

Yield: 50 portions or 2 gal   *Portion:* 6 oz Stroganoff + 4 oz noodles

Ingredient	Amount	Procedure
Beef round, cut in ¼-inch strips	12 lb	Brown meat in shortening.
Shortening	8 oz	Add onion and seasonings.
Onion, chopped	1 lb 4 oz	
Salt	1 Tbsp	
Pepper, black	1 tsp	
Beef Stock (p. 791)	2½ qt	Add stock to meat and simmer 35–40 minutes or until meat is tender.
Flour, all-purpose	8 oz	Mix flour, water, and Worcestershire sauce and stir until smooth.
Water, cold	2 cups	Add to meat while stirring and cook until thickened.
Worcestershire sauce	¾ cup	
Mushrooms, fresh, sliced	2 lb 8 oz	Sauté mushrooms in margarine.
Margarine, melted	4 oz	
Sour cream	1 qt	Add sour cream to meat mixture, stirring constantly. Add mushrooms. Heat to 180°F.
Noodles	4 lb 8 oz	Cook noodles according to directions on p. 561.
Water	4½ gal	Serve 6 oz Stroganoff over 4 oz noodles.
Salt	2 oz	
Vegetable oil	3 Tbsp	

Approximate nutritive values per portion   **Calories** 597

Amount/portion	%DV	Amount/portion	%DV	Amount/portion	%DV		%DV		%DV
Total Fat 17 g	26%	**Cholest.** 92 mg	31%	**Total Carb.** 50 g	17%	**Vitamin A**	6%	**Calcium**	7%
Sat. Fat 6 g	29%	**Sodium** 1180 mg	49%	Fiber 3 g	11%	**Vitamin C**	15%	**Iron**	26%
Protein 61 g				Sugars 3 g					

Percent Daily Values (%DV) are based on a 2000-calorie diet.

Notes
- Potentially hazardous food. *Food Safety Standards:* Hold food for service at an internal temperature above 140°F. Do not mix old product with new. Cool leftover product quickly (within 4 hours) to below 41°F. See p. 105 for cooling procedures. Reheat leftover product quickly (within 2 hours) to 165°F. Reheat product only once; discard if not used.
- May be served over rice. Cook 3 lb 8 oz rice in 4¼ qt water, 2 Tbsp salt, and 2 Tbsp oil. See p. 594.

Variation
- **Ground-Beef Stroganoff.** Substitute ground beef for beef round. Add 1 lb 8 oz chopped celery, ¼ cup paprika, ¼ cup Worcestershire sauce, and 2 tsp dry mustard.

CHOP SUEY

Yield: 50 portions   *Portion:* 5 oz chop suey + 4 oz rice

Ingredient	Amount	Procedure
Beef, julienne strips	5 lb	Brown meat in steam-jacketed or other kettle.
Pork, julienne strips	2 lb	
Water	2 qt	Add water and salt to meat.
Salt	2 tsp	Simmer until tender.
Cornstarch	8 oz	Make a smooth paste of cornstarch and water.
Water, cold	1¼ cups	Pour slowly into meat and broth, stirring constantly while pouring.
		Cook until thickened.
Soy sauce	1 cup	Add soy sauce and Worcestershire sauce. Stir to blend.
Worcestershire sauce	1 cup	
Green peppers, sliced	4 oz	Steam vegetables until tender crisp.
Onions, sliced	1 lb	
Celery, diagonally sliced	2 lb	
Bean sprouts, canned, undrained	3 lb	Add bean sprouts and vegetables to meat mixture just before serving.
Rice, converted	3 lb 8 oz	Cook rice according to directions on p. 594.
Water	4¼ qt	Serve 5 oz chop suey over 4 oz rice.
Salt	2 Tbsp	
Margarine or vegetable oil	2 Tbsp	

Approximate nutritive values per portion   **Calories** 247

Amount/portion	%DV	Amount/portion	%DV	Amount/portion	%DV		%DV		%DV
Total Fat 5 g	**7%**	**Cholest.** 34 mg	**11%**	**Total Carb.** 34 g	**11%**	**Vitamin A**	**2%**	**Calcium**	**6%**
Sat. Fat 1 g	**7%**	**Sodium** 746 mg	**31%**	Fiber 1 g	**4%**	**Vitamin C**	**30%**	**Iron**	**16%**
Protein 16 g				Sugars 0 g					

Percent Daily Values (%DV) are based on a 2000-calorie diet.

Notes

- Potentially hazardous food. *Food Safety Standards:* Hold food for service at an internal temperature above 140°F. Do not mix old product with new. Cool leftover product quickly (within 4 hours) to below 41°F. See p. 105 for cooling procedures. Reheat leftover product quickly (within 2 hours) to 165°F. Reheat product only once; discard if not used.

- 8 oz water chestnuts may be added.

- May be served over 2 oz chow mein noodles (6 lb) instead of rice.

Variation

- **Chicken Chow Mein.** Substitute cubed, cooked chicken or turkey for beef and pork; chicken stock for water. Delete green peppers and add 1 lb sliced mushrooms. Serve over rice or chow mein noodles.

VEGETABLE CHOW MEIN

Yield: 50 portions   *Portion:* 6 oz chow mein + 2 oz noodles

Ingredient	Amount	Procedure
Water	5¼ qt	Combine in steam-jacketed kettle.
Sugar, granulated	2 oz	Heat to a simmer.
Salt	2¼ tsp	
Pepper, white	1 tsp	
Ginger, ground	1 tsp	
Garlic powder	1 tsp	
Soy sauce	1¼ cups	
Cornstarch	10 oz	Blend cornstarch, water, and soup base to a smooth paste.
Water	2¼ cups	Add slowly to broth, stirring constantly.
Chicken base	¾ oz	Cook until thickened and clear.
Bamboo shoots, canned	12 oz	Drain vegetables. Rinse and drain again.
Bean sprouts, canned	1 lb 4 oz	Add to mixture in kettle.
Water chestnuts, canned, sliced	1 lb	
Celery	12 oz	Cut celery into diagonal slices.
Onions	8 oz	Dice onions into ½-inch cubes.
Carrots	1 lb 4 oz	Cut carrots into matchsticks.
		Steam vegetables until tender-crisp.
		Add to mixture.
Pimiento, canned, chopped, drained	4 oz	Add to mixture.
Mushrooms, canned, drained	1 lb	
Broccoli, fresh	1 lb 8 oz	Divide broccoli tops into florets. Cut stalks into ¼-inch slices.
Green peppers	4 oz	Cut green peppers into ½-inch squares.
		Steam until tender-crisp.
		Scale sauce into two 12 × 10 × 6-inch pans, approximately 9 lb per pan.
		Stir 12 oz broccoli and 2 oz peppers into each pan.
Chow mein noodles	6 lb	Ladle 6 oz Chow Mein over 2 oz chow mein noodles.

Approximate nutritive values per portion   **Calories** 346

Amount/portion	%DV	Amount/portion	%DV	Amount/portion	%DV		%DV		%DV
Total Fat 17 g	27%	**Cholest.** 0 mg	0%	**Total Carb.** 43 g	15%	**Vitamin A**	34%	**Calcium**	3%
Sat. Fat 2 g	12%	**Sodium** 883 mg	37%	Fiber 3 g	12%	**Vitamin C**	25%	**Iron**	18%
Protein 7 g				Sugars 3 g					

Percent Daily Values (%DV) are based on a 2000-calorie diet.

Notes
- Potentially hazardous food. *Food Safety Standards:* Hold food for service at an internal temperature above 140°F. Do not mix old product with new. Cool leftover product quickly (within 4 hours) to below 41°F. See p. 105 for cooling procedures. Reheat leftover product quickly (within 2 hours) to 165°F. Reheat product only once; discard if not used.
- May be served over rice instead of chow mein noodles. Cook 3 lb 8 oz rice according to directions on p. 594.

PIZZA

Yield: 48 portions or 3 pans 18 × 26 × 1 inches or 6 round 14-inch pans   *Portion:* 7 oz

Oven: Baking sheet, 475°F for 10–12 minutes; round, 500°F for 5–8 minutes

Ingredient	Amount	Procedure
DOUGH		
Flour, all-purpose	5 lb	Place flour, salt, sugar, and dry milk in mixer bowl. Mix on low speed, using dough hook.
Salt	1½ oz	
Sugar, granulated	4 oz	
Nonfat dry milk	2 oz	
Yeast, active dry (see Notes)	1½ oz	Soften yeast in warm water.
Water, warm (110°F)	1½ qt	
Shortening	4 oz	Add softened yeast and shortening to dry ingredients. Mix on low speed to form dough. Continue kneading until smooth and elastic. Cover and let rise until double in bulk, about 2 hours.
		Punch down dough according to directions on p. 300 and let rest 45 minutes.
PIZZA SAUCE		
Onions, chopped	12 oz	Cook onions in fat until transparent.
Shortening or oil	1 oz	Add tomatoes, sugar, and seasonings.
Tomato juice	2 qt	Heat to boiling. Reduce heat and simmer 30–45 minutes. Cool.
Tomato paste	1 qt	Remove bay leaves.
Sugar, granulated	2 oz	Spread sauce over dough, 1 qt per 18 × 26-inch pan or 1-1¼ cups per 14-inch round pan. (See Table 12.10 for portioning guidelines.)
Oregano, dried, crumbled	1 Tbsp	
Basil, dried, crumbled	2 Tbsp	
Garlic powder	1 tsp	
Pepper, black	1 tsp	
Bay leaves	3 leaves	
SEASONED BEEF		
Ground beef	9 lb	Brown beef in steam-jacketed kettle or pan until internal temperature reads 155°F for 15 seconds. Drain well.
Salt	1 Tbsp	Add seasonings, stirring to distribute.
Fennel seed	1 tsp	Sprinkle evenly over tomato sauce, approximately 1 lb 8 oz per 18 × 26 × 1-inch pan, 8 oz per 14-inch round pan.
Paprika	1 tsp	
Pepper, cayenne	½ tsp	
Oregano, dried, crumbled	1 tsp	
Basil, dried, crumbled	1 Tbsp	

TABLE 12.10 Portioning guidelines for pizza

Size (round) (in)	Sauce (oz)	Cheese (oz)	Dough (oz)
7	1½	2	4–6
10	3	3½	12–14
12	4	6	16–20
14	6	8	16–22
16	8	12	26

Note: • Amount of dough will vary depending on whether a thin, medium, or thick crust is desired.

Notes
- Active dry yeast may be mixed with dry ingredients. See p. 299 for procedure.
- Sausage (4 lb 8 oz) may be substituted for 4 lb 8 oz ground beef. Omit fennel, paprika, cayenne pepper, and garlic.
- Dough may be mixed and refrigerated for use up to 24 hours later. Remove dough from refrigerator and let sit at room temperature for 1–1½ hours before shaping. Shape into dough rounds and let rise 1 hour before topping.
- Bake within 30 minutes after topping to prevent a doughy layer. Once the doughy layer has formed, it cannot be reversed.

Variations for Making 14" Round Pizzas
- **Ground Beef and Mushroom Pizza.** Layer in the following order: 10 oz sauce; 8 oz shredded mozzarella cheese; 8 oz seasoned ground beef; 3 oz canned sliced mushrooms, drained; and 3 oz shredded mozzarella cheese.
- **Ground-Beef Pizza Supreme.** Layer in the following order: 10 oz sauce; 8 oz shredded mozzarella cheese; 8 oz seasoned beef; 1 oz each of diced onions, chopped green peppers, and sliced ripe olives; and 3 oz shredded mozzarella cheese.
- **Pepperoni Pizza.** Layer in the following order: 10 oz sauce, 8 oz shredded mozzarella cheese, 2 oz sliced pepperoni (arranged evenly over the top), and 3 oz mozzarella cheese.
- **Triple Cheese Pizza.** Layer in the following order: 10 oz sauce, 8 oz shredded mozzarella cheese, 4 oz shredded Monterey Jack cheese, and 4 oz shredded cheddar cheese.
- **Garden Pizza.** Layer in the following order: 10 oz sauce; 6 oz shredded mozzarella cheese; 2 oz shredded cheddar cheese; 1 oz each of diced green peppers, sliced canned mushrooms, diced onion, and sliced ripe olives.

ASSEMBLY AND BAKING

If using 18 × 26 × 1-inch baking sheet:

1. Divide dough into three portions, 2 lb 8 oz each. Roll out very thin, stretching to fit three 18 × 26 × 1-inch baking sheets. Allow 1¼ inches to extend up sides of pan.
2. Spread 1 qt sauce over dough.
3. Sprinkle 1 lb 8 oz seasoned beef over sauce.
4. Top each pan with 1 lb 4 oz mozzarella cheese.
5. Bake at 475°F for 10–12 minutes in a conventional oven.
6. Cut each pan 2 × 4 and then each of the 8 pieces diagonally, yielding 16 pie-shaped portions per pan (48 slices).

If using 14-inch round pans:

1. Prepare six 14-inch pans by spraying lightly with vegetable spray.
2. Press 1 lb 6 oz dough into pans, allowing 1 inch to extend up sides.
3. Perforate dough with fork or dough docker.
4. Choose pizza topping from Variations and layer in the order given.
5. Bake until crust is browned, sauce is bubbly, and cheese is melted. (See Table 12.11 for time and temperature guidelines.)
6. Cut each pizza into 8 slices, yielding 8 portions per pan (48 slices).

Approximate nutritive values per portion　　　　　　　　　　　　　　　　　**Calories** 502

Amount/portion	%DV	Amount/portion	%DV	Amount/portion	%DV		%DV		%DV
Total Fat 21 g	33%	**Cholest.** 72 mg	24%	**Total Carb.** 50 g	17%	Vitamin A	21%	Calcium	23%
Sat. Fat 9 g	47%	**Sodium** 958 mg	40%	Fiber 4 g	15%	Vitamin C	42%	Iron	27%
Protein 28 g				Sugars 5 g					

Percent Daily Values (%DV) are based on a 2000-calorie diet.

TABLE 12.11   **Approximate temperatures and times for cooking pizza**

Oven type	Temp. (°F)	6–8 in (min)	10–12 in (min)	14–17 in (min)
Convection	325	10–12	12–15	16–20
Conveyor	500	5–7	5–7	5–7
Conventional	450	13–15	15–18	18–22
Deck	450	13–15	15–18	18–22
Pizza Deck	500	8–10	10–12	10–14

TACO SALAD CASSEROLE

Yield: 48 portions or 3 pans 12 × 20 × 2 inches   *Portion:* 8 oz

Ingredient	Amount	Procedure
Corn chips	2 lb 8 oz	Spread corn chips in bottoms of three 12 × 20 × 2-inch counter pans, 14 oz per pan.
Ground beef	8 lb AP	Brown meat in steam-jacketed kettle until internal temperature reaches 155°F for 15 seconds. Drain off fat.
Onions, minced Garlic, minced	8 oz 3 cloves	Add onions and garlic to meat. Cook until tender.
Flour, all-purpose Tomato juice	3 oz 1¼ qt	Combine flour and tomato juice and add to meat mixture.
Vinegar, cider Catsup Chili sauce Sugar, granulated Salt Pepper, black Chili powder Pepper, cayenne Hot pepper sauce Worcestershire sauce Red beans, canned	2 Tbsp 1½ cups 1 cup 2 Tbsp 2 Tbsp ½ tsp 2 tsp ¼ tsp ¾ tsp 1 tsp 3 lb 12 oz	Add to meat mixture. Blend. Heat until very hot. Scale 4 lb 5 oz meat sauce over each pan of chips. Keep warm and serve soon after vegetables are layered on top. (See Notes for an alternate assembly method.)
Lettuce, chopped Green peppers, chopped Onions, finely chopped Tomatoes, fresh, diced	4 lb 12 oz 12 oz 2 lb 10 oz	Combine vegetables. Mix gently. Sprinkle over hot meat mixture, 2 lb 8 oz per pan.
Processed cheese, shredded	2 lb 10 oz	Sprinkle 14 oz cheese over each pan. Cut 4 × 4. Serve immediately.

Approximate nutritive values per portion   **Calories** 422

Amount/portion	%DV	Amount/portion	%DV	Amount/portion	%DV		%DV		%DV
Total Fat 24 g	37%	**Cholest.** 60 mg	20%	**Total Carb.** 30 g	10%	**Vitamin A**	20%	**Calcium**	27%
Sat. Fat 10 g	48%	**Sodium** 1183 mg	49%	Fiber 5 g	18%	**Vitamin C**	34%	**Iron**	18%
Protein 22 g				Sugars 6 g					

Percent Daily Values (%DV) are based on a 2000-calorie diet.

Notes

- Potentially hazardous food. Serve within 30 minutes after preparation. *Food Safety Standards:* Hold food for service at an internal temperature above 140°F. Do not mix old product with new. Cool leftover product quickly (within 4 hours) to below 41°F. See p. 105 for cooling procedures.
- Chips will become soggy if held for very long. Spread meat on chips only as needed.
- Casserole may be assembled on each plate individually. Place ¾ oz taco chips on plate. Ladle 4 oz hot meat mixture over chips and top with 2½ oz salad mixture and ¾ oz shredded cheese.
- Serve with Salsa (p. 756) or commercial salsa.
- 1 oz (½ cup) dehydrated onion, rehydrated in ¾ cup water, may be substituted for the fresh onions that are added to the ground beef.

SPANISH RICE

Yield: 50 portions or 2 pans 12 × 20 × 2 inches   *Portion:* 8 oz
Oven: 350°F   *Bake:* 1 hour

Ingredient	Amount	Procedure
Rice, converted	2 lb 8 oz	Cook rice according to directions on p. 594
Water, boiling	3 qt	
Salt	1 oz (1½ Tbsp)	
Vegetable oil	2 Tbsp	
Ground beef	7 lb	Cook beef until internal temperature reaches 155°F.
Onions, chopped	1 lb 8 oz	Add onion, peppers, and celery to meat.
Green peppers, chopped	8 oz	Cook about 10 minutes.
Celery, chopped	8 oz	
Tomatoes, canned, diced	1 No. 10 can	Add remaining ingredients to meat mixture.
Chili sauce	3 cups	Combine with cooked rice.
Tomato paste	3 cups	Scale into two 12 × 20 × 2-inch pans, 15 lb per pan.
Salt	2 oz (3 Tbsp)	Bake at 350°F for 1 hour.
Pepper, black	¼ tsp	
Pepper, cayenne	few grains	
Sugar, granulated	2 Tbsp	
Water	2 cups	

Approximate nutritive values per portion   **Calories** 260

Amount/portion	%DV	Amount/portion	%DV	Amount/portion	%DV		%DV		%DV
Total Fat 10 g	15%	**Cholest.** 38 mg	13%	**Total Carb.** 30 g	10%	Vitamin A	9%	Calcium	5%
Sat. Fat 4 g	18%	**Sodium** 1115 mg	46%	Fiber 2 g	7%	Vitamin C	37%	Iron	15%
Protein 14 g				Sugars 4 g					

Percent Daily Values (%DV) are based on a 2000-calorie diet.

Notes
- Potentially hazardous food. *Food Safety Standards:* Hold food for service at an internal temperature above 140°F. Do not mix old product with new. Cool leftover product quickly (within 4 hours) to below 41°F. See p. 105 for cooling procedures. Reheat leftover product quickly (within 2 hours) to 165°F. Reheat product only once; discard if not used.
- 3 lb bacon, diced and cooked, may be substituted for the ground beef.
- 3 oz (1½ cups) dehydrated onions, rehydrated in 2 cups water, may be substituted for fresh onions.

Variation
- **Stuffed Peppers.** Wash 25 large green peppers and remove stem end. Cut peppers in half lengthwise. Remove seeds and tough white portion. Place in baking pans and steam or parboil for 3–5 minutes. Place No. 8 dipper of Spanish Rice in each pepper half. Combine 2 50-oz cans tomato soup and 2 qt tomato sauce. Ladle 2 oz over each pepper. Bake at 350°F for 45–60 minutes. Ladle extra sauce over peppers during baking.

CHEESEBURGER PIE

Yield: 48 portions or 2 pans 12 × 20 × 2 inches   *Portion:* 8 oz (6 oz meat)
Oven: 400°F   *Bake:* 30–35 minutes

Ingredient	Amount	Procedure
Ground beef	12 lb AP (8 lb EP)	Brown beef in steam-jacketed or other kettle until internal temperature reaches 155°F. Drain off fat.
Onions, chopped	1 lb 4 oz	Add onions and green peppers to meat. Cook until vegetables are tender.
Green peppers, chopped	1 lb 4 oz	
Garlic powder	1 tsp	Add seasonings and tomatoes.
Salt	1 oz (1½ Tbsp)	Simmer 30 minutes or until thick.
Chili powder	3 oz	Scale meat mixture into two 12 × 20 × 2-inch pans, 9 lb
Cumin, ground	1 tsp	per pan.
Pepper, cayenne	¼ tsp	
Sugar, brown	1 oz	
Tomatoes, diced, canned	7 lb 12 oz	

CHEESE BISCUIT TOPPING

Flour, all-purpose	2 lb 14 oz	Combine dry ingredients in mixer bowl on low speed for
Baking powder	2¾ oz (6 Tbsp)	1 minute, using flat beater.
Salt	2 Tbsp	
Dry mustard	1 tsp	
Nonfat dry milk	7 oz	
Shortening	12 oz	Cut shortening and cheese into flour on low speed for
Processed cheese, shredded	10 oz	1–1½ minutes.
Water	1½ qt	Add water to make a thick batter. Mix only until flour is moistened.
		With No. 20 dipper, place topping 4 × 6 over meat mixture just before baking. Bake at 400°F for 30–35 minutes. Cut 4 × 6.

Approximate nutritive values per portion   **Calories** 432

Amount/portion	%DV	Amount/portion	%DV	Amount/portion	%DV		%DV		%DV
Total Fat 24 g	36%	**Cholest.** 65 mg	22%	**Total Carb.** 30 g	10%	Vitamin A	20%	Calcium	24%
Sat. Fat 8 g	42%	**Sodium** 892 mg	37%	Fiber 2 g	9%	Vitamin C	39%	Iron	24%
Protein 25 g				Sugars 5 g					

Percent Daily Values (%DV) are based on a 2000-calorie diet.

Notes
- Potentially hazardous food. *Food Safety Standards:* Hold food for service at an internal temperature above 140°F. Do not mix old product with new. Cool leftover product quickly (within 4 hours) to below 41°F. See p. 105 for cooling procedures. Reheat leftover product quickly (within 2 hours) to 165°F. Reheat product only once; discard if not used.
- 2½ oz (1¼ cups) dehydrated onions, rehydrated in 2 cups water, may be substituted for fresh onions.

VEAL RECIPES

VEAL BIRDS

Yield: 50 portions   *Portion:* 4 oz
Oven: 300°F   *Bake:* 2 hours

Ingredient	Amount	Procedure
Margarine	8 oz	Sauté onion and celery in margarine.
Onions, finely chopped	8 oz	
Celery, finely chopped	8 oz	
Beef base	1½ oz	Combine beef base, seasonings, and water. Add to sautéed vegetables.
Salt	1 tsp (see Notes)	
Pepper, black	1½ tsp	
Sage, ground	1 Tbsp	
Water	2 qt	
Bread, dry, cubed	2 lb	Add bread gradually to vegetable mixture, tossing lightly until thoroughly mixed.
Veal cutlets, 4 oz	50	Place No. 16 dipper of bread mixture on each piece of meat. Roll and fasten with a pick.
Flour, all-purpose	8 oz	Combine flour and salt.
Salt	2 oz	Roll each "bird" in flour and brown in hot shortening.
Shortening	1 lb 8 oz	Place in two 12 × 20 × 2-inch counter pans.
Water	1 qt	Add 2 cups water to each pan. Cover with aluminum foil. Bake at 300°F for 1½–2 hours. (Internal temperature 165°F.)

Approximate nutritive values per portion   **Calories** 414

Amount/portion	%DV	Amount/portion	%DV	Amount/portion	%DV		%DV		%DV
Total Fat 19 g	29%	**Cholest.** 128 mg	43%	**Total Carb.** 17 g	6%	**Vitamin A**	1%	**Calcium**	5%
Sat. Fat 5 g	23%	**Sodium** 759 mg	32%	Fiber 1 g	4%	**Vitamin C**	1%	**Iron**	12%
Protein 42 g				Sugars 1 g					

Percent Daily Values (%DV) are based on a 2000-calorie diet.

Notes
- Potentially hazardous food. *Food Safety Standards:* Hold food for service at an internal temperature above 140°F. Do not mix old product with new. Cool leftover product quickly (within 4 hours) to below 41°F. See p. 105 for cooling procedures. Reheat leftover product quickly (within 2 hours) to 165°F. Reheat product only once; discard if not used.
- Veal round, ¼-inch thick, cut into 4-oz pieces, may be substituted for the cutlets.
- 1 oz (½ cup) dehydrated onion, rehydrated in ¾ cup water, may be substituted for fresh onion.
- If beef base is highly salted, reduce or delete salt in recipe.

Variations
- **Beef Birds.** Make with beef cubed steaks or flank steaks.
- **Pork Birds.** Make with pork cutlets.
- **Veal Birds with Sausage Stuffing.** Reduce bread to 2 lb 8 oz. Reduce salt to 1 tsp and sage to 1 Tbsp. Add 2 lb 8 oz sausage, cooked and drained.

BREADED VEAL CUTLETS

Yield: 50 portions   *Portion:* 4 oz
Oven: 325°F   *Bake:* 45–60 minutes

Ingredient	Amount	Procedure
Veal cutlets, 4 oz	12 lb 8 oz	Dredge cutlets with seasoned flour.
Flour, all-purpose	8 oz	
Salt	1 oz (1½ Tbsp)	
Pepper, black	¼ tsp	
Eggs, beaten	7 (12 oz)	Combine eggs and milk.
Milk	1½ cups	Dip cutlets in egg mixture, then roll in crumbs.
Bread crumbs, fine	1 lb	
Shortening	1 lb 8 oz	Brown meat in hot fat. Place, slightly overlapping, in two 12 × 20 × 2-inch counter pans. Add 2 cups water to each pan. Cover with aluminum foil. Bake at 325°F for 45–60 minutes.

Approximate nutritive values per portion   **Calories** 378

Amount/portion	%DV	Amount/portion	%DV	Amount/portion	%DV		%DV		%DV
Total Fat 18 g	**28%**	**Cholest.** 159 mg	**53%**	**Total Carb.** 11 g	**4%**	**Vitamin A**	**1%**	**Calcium**	**4%**
Sat. Fat 5 g	**24%**	**Sodium** 363 mg	**15%**	Fiber 0.5 g	**2%**	**Vitamin C**	**0%**	**Iron**	**11%**
Protein 41 g				Sugars 1 g					

Percent Daily Values (%DV) are based on a 2000-calorie diet.

Notes
- Potentially hazardous food. *Food Safety Standards:* Hold food for service at an internal temperature above 140°F. Do not mix old product with new. Cool leftover product quickly (within 4 hours) to below 41°F. See p. 105 for cooling procedures. Reheat leftover product quickly (within 2 hours) to 165°F. Reheat product only once; discard if not used.
- Veal round, sliced ¼ inch thick and cut into 5-oz portions, may be used.

Variations
- **Veal Cacciatore.** Dredge cutlets with flour. Brown in fat and place in baking pans. Pour over sauce made of 1 lb chopped peppers, 1 lb chopped onions, and ⅛ tsp minced garlic, simmered in margarine or butter for 10 minutes; 1 lb 8 oz sautéed sliced mushrooms; 1½ qt canned tomatoes; ¼ cup vinegar; 2 qt Chicken Stock (p. 790); 1 oz salt; and 1 tsp pepper. Bake 45 minutes.
- **Veal New Orleans.** To 2 qt medium White Sauce (p. 749), add 8 oz chopped onions, 12 oz sliced mushrooms, 2 Tbsp Worcestershire sauce, ¼ tsp salt, ¼ tsp pepper, ¼ tsp paprika, and 3½ cups tomato soup. Arrange browned breaded cutlets in two 12 × 20 × 2-inch counter pans. Pour 1¾ qt sauce over each pan. Cover with aluminum foil and bake at 325°F for 1 hour.
- **Veal Parmesan.** Add 8 oz grated Parmesan cheese to bread crumbs. After cutlets are browned and arranged in baking pans, pour 2 qt Italian Tomato Sauce (p. 762) over them. Top with 1 lb 8 oz grated mozzarella cheese. Bake at 325°F for 1 hour.
- **Veal Piccata.** Flour cutlets and brown in hot shortening. Arrange in two 12 × 20 × 2-inch counter pans. Sauté 1 lb sliced mushrooms and 2 cloves garlic, minced, in 2 Tbsp margarine. Add 2½ cups Beef Stock (p. 791) and 2 Tbsp lemon juice. Bring to a boil. Pour 2 cups over each pan. Sprinkle ¼ cup Parmesan cheese over each pan. Cover with aluminum foil. Bake at 325°F for 1 hour.
- **Veal Scallopini.** Dredge cutlets with seasoned flour and sauté in hot shortening. Arrange in baking pans. Sauté 3 lb fresh mushrooms, sliced, and 1 lb chopped onion in 8 oz margarine. Add 2 qt Chicken Stock (p. 790), 1½ cups lemon juice or vinegar, and 1 tsp each of parsley, rosemary, and oregano or marjoram. Pour over cutlets. Bake at 325°F for 1 hour.

PORK RECIPES

JEWELED PORK LOIN

Yield: 50 portions   *Portion:* 4 oz
Oven: 325°F   *Bake:* Approx. 2–3 hours

Ingredient	Amount	Procedure
Boneless pork loin Pepper, black	20 lb 1 Tbsp	Rub pepper over all sides of loin. Cut vertical slits 1 inch deep along top of roasts.
Prunes, pitted, dried Apricots, dried	8 oz 8 oz	Cut dried fruit into medium-size pieces. Push into the slits on top of the loin. Roast, uncovered, at 325°F until meat thermometer registers 155°F. Remove from oven and cover loosely with aluminum foil. Let stand about 15 minutes before slicing.

Approximate nutritive values per portion   **Calories** 240

Amount/portion	%DV	Amount/portion	%DV	Amount/portion	%DV		%DV		%DV
Total Fat 6 g	10%	**Cholest.** 105 mg	35%	**Total Carb.** 6 g	2%	Vitamin A	4%	Calcium	1%
Sat. Fat 2 g	11%	**Sodium** 75 mg	3%	Fiber 1 g	3%	Vitamin C	1%	Iron	12%
Protein 38 g				Sugars 4 g					

Percent Daily Values (%DV) are based on a 2000-calorie diet.

Note
- Potentially hazardous food. *Food Safety Standards:* Hold food for service at an internal temperature above 140°F. Do not mix old product with new. Cool leftover product quickly (within 4 hours) to below 41°F. See p. 105 for cooling procedures. Reheat leftover product quickly (within 2 hours) to 165°F. Reheat product only once; discard if not used.

Variations
- **Garlic and Peppercorn Pork Loin.** Brush pork loins with olive oil. Cover with approximately 1 cup crushed peppercorns and approximately ¾ cup chopped garlic. Roast as for Jeweled Pork Loin.

- **Herbed Pork Loin.** Combine 1½ oz salt, 2 Tbsp dried whole rosemary, 2 Tbsp dried whole thyme, 3 Tbsp coarse cracked black pepper, ½ cup crushed garlic, ¾ cup fresh lemon juice, and ¾ cup vegetable oil. Rub paste over roasts. Refrigerate for several hours or overnight. Roast as for Jeweled Pork Loin.

- **Rosemary Pork Loin.** Combine ½ cup dried whole rosemary, 1 Tbsp garlic powder, 1 Tbsp cumin, and 2 tsp salt. Sprinkle over pork before roasting.

- **Teriyaki-Glazed Pork Loin.** Omit pepper and dried fruit. Make marinade by combining 2 cups soy sauce, 1 cup cooking sherry, ¼ cup sugar, 3 Tbsp black pepper, ¼ cup minced garlic, 1½ cup oil. Pour over pork loin roasts. Turn to cover all sides. Marinate in refrigerator a minimum of 8 hours or overnight. Drain marinade. Roast as for Jeweled Pork Loin.

BREADED PORK CHOPS

Yield: 50 chops   *Portion:* 5 oz
Oven: 400°F, 325°F   *Bake:* 10 minutes, 1 hour

Ingredient	Amount	Procedure
Pork chops, cut 3 per lb	17 lb	Dredge chops with seasoned flour.
Flour, all-purpose	12 oz	
Salt	3 oz	
Pepper, black	2 Tbsp	
Eggs, beaten	6 (10 oz)	Combine eggs and milk.
Milk	3½ cups	Dip chops in egg mixture, then roll in crumbs.
Bread crumbs	1 lb 4 oz	Place in single layer on greased sheet pans.
		Bake at 400°F until browned, about 10 minutes.
Water	1 qt	Remove chops from oven and arrange in partially overlapping rows in two 12 × 20 × 2-inch counter pans.
		Add 2 cups water to each pan. Cover pans.
		Bake at 325°F, approximately 1 hour, until internal temperature reaches 160°F.

Approximate nutritive values per portion   **Calories** 239

Amount/portion	%DV	Amount/portion	%DV	Amount/portion	%DV		%DV		%DV
Total Fat 11 g	**16%**	**Cholest.** 81 mg	**27%**	**Total Carb.** 15 g	**5%**	**Vitamin A**	**2%**	**Calcium**	**7%**
Sat. Fat 4 g	**20%**	**Sodium** 810 mg	**34%**	Fiber 1 g	**3%**	**Vitamin C**	**1%**	**Iron**	**10%**
Protein 20 g				Sugars 2 g					

Percent Daily Values (%DV) are based on a 2000-calorie diet.

Note
- Potentially hazardous food. *Food Safety Standards:* Hold food for service at an internal temperature above 140°F. Do not mix old product with new. Cool leftover product quickly (within 4 hours) to below 41°F. See p. 105 for cooling procedures. Reheat leftover product quickly (within 2 hours) to 165°F. Reheat product only once; discard if not used.

Variations
- **Baked Pork Chops.** Dredge chops with 1 lb flour, ¼ cup vegetable oil, 2 oz salt, and 1 tsp black pepper, mixed. Place on well-greased sheet pans. Bake at 350°F until thoroughly cooked and browned, approximately 1¼ hours.

- **Baked Pork Chops and Apples.** Brown chops as for Breaded Pork Chops. Place in two greased 12 × 20 × 2-inch baking pans. Pour over 1 qt apple juice, 2 cups per pan. Bake at 350°F for 1 hour. Serve with Buttered Apples (p. 693).

- **Pork Chops and Dressing.** Serve chops with No. 16 dipper of Bread Dressing (p. 557) and ladle of gravy dipped over.

- **Stuffed Pork Chops.** Use 6-oz pork chops and cut a pocket in each chop. Fill with Bread Dressing (use ¼ recipe, p. 557) or Apple Stuffing (p. 000, ½ recipe). Brown chops and place in baking pans. Pour 2 cups water or chicken broth in each pan. Cover and bake at 350°F for 1½ hours. Internal temperature must reach 165°F for 15 seconds.

DEVILED PORK CHOPS

Yield: 50 chops   *Portion:* 5 oz
Oven: 350°F   *Bake:* 1½ hours

Ingredient	Amount	Procedure
Chili sauce	1½ qt	Combine into a sauce.
Water	3 cups	
Dry mustard	1 tsp	
Worcestershire sauce	3 Tbsp	
Lemon juice	3 Tbsp	
Onion, grated	2 tsp	
Pork chops, cut 3 per lb	17 lb	Dip each chop in sauce. Place in single layer on greased sheet pans. Bake at 350°F for 1–1½ hours, or until internal temperature reaches 160°F.

Approximate nutritive values per portion   **Calories** 182

Amount/portion	%DV	Amount/portion	%DV	Amount/portion	%DV		%DV		%DV
Total Fat 9 g	14%	**Cholest.** 54 mg	18%	**Total Carb.** 7 g	2%	**Vitamin A**	4%	**Calcium**	2%
Sat. Fat 3 g	16%	**Sodium** 446 mg	19%	Fiber 0 g	0%	**Vitamin C**	10%	**Iron**	5%
Protein 17 g				Sugars 3 g					

Percent Daily Values (%DV) are based on a 2000-calorie diet.

Note
- Potentially hazardous food. *Food Safety Standards:* Hold food for service at an internal temperature above 140°F. Do not mix old product with new. Cool leftover product quickly (within 4 hours) to below 41°F. See p. 105 for cooling procedures. Reheat leftover product quickly (within 2 hours) to 165°F. Reheat product only once; discard if not used.

Variations
- **Barbecued Pork Chops.** Place chops on greased baking sheets. Brush with melted fat. Sprinkle with salt. Brown chops in 450°F oven for 12–15 minutes. Transfer to counter pans. Pour Barbecue Sauce (p. 755) over chops. Bake at 325°F for 1½ hours or until chops are tender.

- **Chili-Seasoned Pork Chops.** Prepare a spice blend by combining 6 Tbsp chili powder, 2 Tbsp ground cumin, 2 tsp garlic powder, 1 Tbsp onion powder, 1 tsp salt, and 2 tsp black pepper. Mix 1 Tbsp of the spice mixture with 1 cup vegetable oil. Cover and store for several hours to blend seasonings with oil. Save the remaining dry spice mixture to sprinkle on top of the chops. To cook chops, oil griddle with seasoned oil, heat to 350°F. Place chops on griddle and cook until browned, turn and brown other side. Sprinkle remaining seasonings lightly over chops. Place in 12 × 10 × 2-inch counter pans. Cover with foil and bake at 350°F for 1 hour.

- **Honey-Glazed Pork Chops.** Marinate pork chops for 4 hours in a mixture of 2 cups soy sauce, 6 oz honey, 1 cup applesauce, 1 oz salt, and 4 oz sugar. Place in single layer on greased baking sheets. Bake at 350°F for 1 hour. Turn and brush with marinade as needed.

- **Pork Chops Supreme.** Arrange chops in single layer in baking pans. Sprinkle with salt. Combine 1 lb brown sugar, 3 cups catsup, and 1 cup lemon juice. Place about 2 Tbsp, No. 30 dipper, on each chop. Cut 4 medium-size onions into thin slices. Place 1 slice on top of each chop. Cover and bake at 350°F for 45 minutes. Uncover and bake 30 minutes longer.

BARBECUED SPARERIBS

Yield: 50 portions   *Portion:* 8 oz
Oven: 350°F   *Bake:* 2½ hours

Ingredient	Amount	Procedure
Pork spareribs or loin back ribs	25 lb	Separate ribs into 8 oz portions. Place in roasting pans. Brown uncovered in oven at 350°F until browned lightly, about 30 minutes. Pour off fat.
Barbecue Sauce (p. 755)	3 qt	Pour sauce over ribs. Cover with aluminum foil. Bake at 350°F until meat is tender, about 1½ hours. Uncover and bake an additional 20–30 minutes.

Approximate nutritive values per portion   **Calories** 590

Amount/portion	%DV	Amount/portion	%DV	Amount/portion	%DV		%DV		%DV
Total Fat 31 g	47%	**Cholest.** 206 mg	69%	**Total Carb.** 8 g	3%	**Vitamin A**	5%	**Calcium**	2%
Sat. Fat 10 g	52%	**Sodium** 644 mg	27%	Fiber 1 g	2%	**Vitamin C**	8%	**Iron**	16%
Protein 66 g				Sugars 7 g					

Percent Daily Values (%DV) are based on a 2000-calorie diet.

Notes
- Potentially hazardous food. *Food Safety Standards:* Hold food for service at an internal temperature above 140°F. Do not mix old product with new. Cool leftover product quickly (within 4 hours) to below 41°F. See p. 105 for cooling procedures. Reheat leftover product quickly (within 2 hours) to 165°F. Reheat product only once; discard if not used.
- For larger portions, use 40 lb spareribs and 1 gal Barbecue Sauce.

Variations
- **Baked Spareribs with Dressing.** Brown ribs as for Barbecued Spareribs. Pour off fat. Spread with mixture of 2 oz salt, 2 tsp pepper, 1½ tsp ground sage, 1 lb chopped apples, 2 tsp caraway seeds, 1 tsp ground cloves, and 12 oz brown sugar. Bake 1½ hours until tender. Baste to keep moist. Serve with Bread Dressing (p. 557).
- **Baked Spareribs with Sauerkraut.** Sprinkle ribs with 2 oz seasoned salt. Brown lightly. Pour off fat. Remove ribs from pan. Add 2 No. 10 cans sauerkraut to baking pan and place ribs on top. Bake for 1 hour.
- **Barbecued Short Ribs.** Substitute beef short ribs for spareribs.
- **Sweet-Sour Spareribs.** Brown spareribs for 30 minutes in 400°F oven, or simmer in water for 1 hour. Drain and cover with Sweet-Sour Sauce (p. 766). Bake at 350°F until meat is done. Serve with Steamed Rice (p. 594) or Fried Rice with Almonds (p. 597).

SWEET-SOUR PORK

Yield: 50 portions   *Portion:* 5 oz pork + 4 oz rice

Ingredient	Amount	Procedure
Pork strips, julienne	10 lb AP (7 lb EP)	Brown pork in steam-jacketed kettle.
Water	2 qt	Add water to pork and simmer until meat is tender.
Vinegar	1¼ qt	Combine and add to pork.
Soy sauce	1½ cups	Simmer until sugar is dissolved and pineapple is hot,
Catsup	1½ cups	10–15 minutes.
Sugar, granulated	2 lb	
Pineapple juice	1 qt	
Pineapple chunks	1 lb	
Cornstarch	8 oz	Combine to make a smooth paste.
Water	2 cups	Pour slowly into pork mixture, stirring constantly.
Ginger, ground	1½ tsp	Cook until thickened and clear.
Garlic powder	½ tsp	
Carrots, fresh, sliced	1 lb 12 oz	Steam carrots until tender-crisp. Add to mixture.
Snow peas	1 lb	Stir in just before serving.
Rice, converted	3 lb 8 oz	Cook rice according to directions on p. 594.
Water, boiling	4¼ qt	Serve 5 oz pork over 4 oz rice.
Salt	2 Tbsp	
Margarine or vegetable oil	2 Tbsp	

Approximate nutritive values per portion   **Calories** 350

Amount/portion	%DV	Amount/portion	%DV	Amount/portion	%DV		%DV		%DV
Total Fat 6 g	9%	**Cholest.** 40 mg	13%	**Total Carb.** 59 g	20%	**Vitamin A**	45%	**Calcium**	4%
Sat. Fat 2 g	10%	**Sodium** 862 mg	36%	Fiber 1 g	5%	**Vitamin C**	17%	**Iron**	13%
Protein 17 g				Sugars 23 g					

Percent Daily Values (%DV) are based on a 2000-calorie diet.

Note
- Potentially hazardous food. *Food Safety Standards:* Hold food for service at an internal temperature above 140°F. Do not mix old product with new. Cool leftover product quickly (within 4 hours) to below 41°F. See p. 105 for cooling procedures. Reheat leftover product quickly (within 2 hours) to 165°F. Reheat product only once; discard if not used.

Variations
- **Sweet-Sour Beef.** Substitute beef strips for pork.
- **Sweet-Sour Chicken.** Substitute cooked chicken or turkey for the pork. Do not brown.

GLAZED BAKED HAM

Yield: 50 portions   *Portion:* 3 oz
Oven: 325°F   *Bake:* 2–2½ hours

Ingredient	Amount	Procedure
Ham, boneless, fully cooked	15 lb	Place ham fat side up on a rack in roasting pan. Do not cover. Bake at 325°F for approximately 2–2½ hours.
Cloves, whole	3 Tbsp	Remove ham from oven about 30 minutes before it is done. Drain off drippings. Score ham ¼ inch deep in diamond pattern. Stud with whole cloves. Cover with glaze.

HAM GLAZE

Sugar, brown	8 oz	Combine ingredients for glaze.
Cornstarch	2 Tbsp	Spoon over ham. Repeat if heavier glaze is desired.
Corn syrup	¼ cup	Return ham to oven and bake until internal temperature
Pineapple juice	2 Tbsp	reaches 155°F (see Table 12.3).

Approximate nutritive values per portion   **Calories** 160

Amount/portion	%DV	Amount/portion	%DV	Amount/portion	%DV		%DV		%DV
Total Fat 11 g	17%	**Cholest.** 57 mg	19%	**Total Carb.** 17 g	6%	**Vitamin A**	0%	**Calcium**	1%
Sat. Fat 4 g	18%	**Sodium** 1931 mg	80%	Fiber 0 g	0%	**Vitamin C**	61%	**Iron**	7%
Protein 23 g				Sugars 2 g					

Percent Daily Values (%DV) are based on a 2000-calorie diet.

Notes

- Potentially hazardous food. *Food Safety Standards:* Hold food for service at an internal temperature above 140°F. Do not mix old product with new. Cool leftover product quickly (within 4 hours) to below 41°F. See p. 105 for cooling procedures. Reheat leftover product quickly (within 2 hours) to 165°F. Reheat product only once; discard if not used.

- If using a whole cured ham, not precooked, increase cooking time to 4–4½ hours; or simmer 3–4 hours in a kettle, then trim, glaze, and complete cooking in the oven.

Glaze Variations

- **Apricot Glaze.** 1 cup apricot jam and ¼ cup fruit juice or enough to cover ham.
- **Brown Sugar Glaze.** 6 oz brown sugar, 1½ tsp dry mustard (or 3 Tbsp prepared mustard), and ¼ cup vinegar.
- **Cranberry Glaze.** 1¼ cups strained cranberry sauce, or enough to cover.
- **Honey Glaze.** 1 cup honey, ½ cup brown sugar, and ¼ cup fruit juice. Baste with fruit juice or ginger ale.
- **Orange Glaze.** 1 cup orange marmalade and ¼ cup orange juice.

HAM LOAF

Yield: 50 portions or 5 pans 5 × 9 inches *Portion:* 4 oz
Oven: 350°F *Bake:* 1–1½ hours

Ingredient	Amount	Procedure
Ground cured ham	7 lb	Combine all ingredients in mixer bowl. Mix on low speed, using flat beater, only until ingredients are blended. *Do not overmix.*
Ground fresh lean pork	7 lb	
Onion, finely chopped	4 oz	
Milk	1 qt	
Eggs, beaten	14 (1 lb 8 oz)	
Pepper, black	1 tsp	
Bread crumbs	1 lb	
		Press meat mixture into five 5 × 9-inch loaf pans, 3 lb 8 oz per pan.
		Bake at 350°F for 1–1½ hours, or until internal temperature reaches 180°F.
		If desired, cover tops of loaves with glaze (see Variations) during last 30 minutes of cooking.
		Cut 10 slices per pan.

Approximate nutritive values per portion   **Calories** 208

Amount/portion	%DV	Amount/portion	%DV	Amount/portion	%DV		%DV		%DV
Total Fat 10 g	15%	**Cholest.** 124 mg	41%	**Total Carb.** 13 g	4%	**Vitamin A**	3%	**Calcium**	4%
Sat. Fat 3 g	17%	**Sodium** 1019 mg	42%	Fiber 0.3 g	1%	**Vitamin C**	29%	**Iron**	10%
Protein 27 g				Sugars 2 g					

Percent Daily Values (%DV) are based on a 2000-calorie diet.

Notes
- Potentially hazardous food. *Food Safety Standards:* Hold food for service at an internal temperature above 140°F. Do not mix old product with new. Cool leftover product quickly (within 4 hours) to below 41°F. See p. 105 for cooling procedures. Reheat leftover product quickly (within 2 hours) to 165°F. Reheat product only once; discard if not used.
- Meat may be baked in 12 × 20 × 4-inch baking or counter pan. Press mixture into pan and divide into two loaves. Increase baking time to 1½–2 hours.
- 4 lb ground beef may be substituted for 4 lb fresh pork.
- ½ oz (¼ cup) dehydrated onion, rehydrated in ½ cup water, may be substituted for fresh onion.

Variations
- **Glazed Ham Balls.** Measure with No. 8 dipper and shape into balls. Place on baking sheets. Brush with glaze (following) and bake 1 hour.
- **Glazed Ham Loaf.** Cover tops of loaves with a mixture of 1 lb 8 oz brown sugar, 1 cup vinegar, and 1½ Tbsp dry mustard.
- **Ham Patties with Cranberries.** Measure with No. 8 dipper and shape into patties. Spread pan with Cranberry Sauce (p. 695). Place ham patties on sauce and bake 1 hour.
- **Ham Patties with Pineapple.** Measure with No. 8 dipper and shape into patties. Top each with slice of pineapple and a clove. Pour pineapple juice over patties and bake 1 hour.

CREAMED HAM

Yield: 50 portions or 6¼ qt   *Portion:* 4 oz (½ cup)

Ingredient	Amount	Procedure
Margarine	1 lb	Melt margarine. Add flour and stir until smooth.
Flour, all-purpose	6 oz	Cook 5 minutes.
Milk	1 gal	Add milk gradually, stirring constantly with wire whip. Cook until thickened.
Ham, cooked	6 lb	Cut ham in cubes or grind coarsely.
Salt	To taste	Add to sauce and heat slowly for about 20 minutes, or until internal temperature reaches serving temperature (170–180°F).
Pepper, white	½ tsp	Add salt, if needed, and pepper.
		Serve 4 oz ham over biscuits, toast, spoon bread, corn bread, or baked potato.

Approximate nutritive values per portion   **Calories** 180

Amount/portion	%DV	Amount/portion	%DV	Amount/portion	%DV		%DV		%DV
Total Fat 14 g	22%	**Cholest.** 33 mg	11%	**Total Carb.** 11 g	4%	**Vitamin A**	5%	**Calcium**	10%
Sat. Fat 5 g	23%	**Sodium** 938 mg	39%	Fiber 0 g	0%	**Vitamin C**	25%	**Iron**	3%
Protein 12 g				Sugars 4 g					

Percent Daily Values (%DV) are based on a 2000-calorie diet.

Notes
- Potentially hazardous food. *Food Safety Standards:* Hold food for service at an internal temperature above 140°F. Do not mix old product with new. Cool leftover product quickly (within 4 hours) to below 41°F. See p. 105 for cooling procedures. Reheat leftover product quickly (within 2 hours) to 165°F. Reheat product only once; discard if not used.
- 1 lb chopped celery or sliced mushrooms or 1 dozen chopped hard-cooked eggs may be added. Reduce ham to 5 lb.

Variation
- **Plantation Shortcake.** Substitute 3 lb cooked turkey for 3 lb cooked ham. Substitute Chicken Stock (p. 790) for half of milk in sauce. Add 1 lb grated cheddar cheese. Serve over hot corn bread.

OVEN-FRIED BACON

Yield: 50 portions   *Portion:* 2 slices
Oven: 400°F; convection, 325°F   *Bake:* 6–10 minutes; convection 4–6 minutes

Ingredient	Amount	Procedure
Bacon, 17–20 slices per lb	100 slices (5–6 lb)	Arrange bacon slices on baking sheets. Bake at 400°F, without turning, until crisp, about 6–10 minutes. In convection oven, cook at 325°F for 4–6 minutes. Pour off accumulating fat as necessary. Drain on paper towels or place in perforated pans for serving.

Approximate nutritive values per portion   **Calories** 73

Amount/portion	%DV	Amount/portion	%DV	Amount/portion	%DV		%DV		%DV
Total Fat 6 g	10%	**Cholest.** 11 mg	4%	**Total Carb.** 0 g	0%	**Vitamin A**	0%	**Calcium**	0%
Sat. Fat 2 g	11%	**Sodium** 202 mg	8%	Fiber 0 g	0%	**Vitamin C**	7%	**Iron**	1%
Protein 4 g				Sugars 0 g					

Percent Daily Values (%DV) are based on a 2000-calorie diet.

Note • Bacon may be purchased separated and arranged on parchment paper, ready to be placed on baking sheets and baked.

Variation • **Oven-Fried Sausage.** Arrange 1-oz sausage patties or links on baking sheets. In conventional oven, bake at 400°F for 15–20 minutes. In convection oven, bake at 325°F for 10–12 minutes.

MEATS

Exhibit VI   Beef Steak Color Guide

(Photo courtesy of the National Cattleman's Beef Association, Chicago, IL)

Exhibit IX   Sandwich Presentations

(Photo courtesy of the National Cattleman's
Beef Association, Chicago, IL)

(Photo copyright: The Norwegian Seafood Export Council)

SCRAPPLE

Yield: 50 portions or 5 loaf pans 5 × 9 inches   *Portion:* 2 slices

Ingredient	Amount	Procedure
Sausage, bulk	8 lb AP	Crumble sausage and cook until internal temperature reaches 160°F. Do not overbrown. Drain off fat.
Water Salt	1½ gal 1 oz (1½ Tbsp)	Add salt to water. Bring to a boil.
Cornmeal Water, cold	3 lb 2 qt	Mix cornmeal with cold water. Pour gradually into boiling water, stirring constantly. Cook until very thick, 10–15 minutes.
		Add cooked sausage to cornmeal mixture. Scale into five greased 5 × 9-inch loaf pans, 4 lb 5 oz per pan. Cover with waxed paper to prevent formation of crust. Chill for 24 hours.
		Cut into ½-inch slices. Cook on greased grill preheated to 350°F. Grill until browned and crisp on both sides. Serve with warm syrup.

Approximate nutritive values per portion   **Calories** 266

Amount/portion	%DV	Amount/portion	%DV	Amount/portion	%DV		%DV		%DV
Total Fat 15 g	23%	**Cholest.** 38 mg	13%	**Total Carb.** 21 g	7%	Vitamin A	1%	Calcium	2%
Sat. Fat 5 g	25%	**Sodium** 792 mg	33%	Fiber 4 g	17%	Vitamin C	1%	Iron	10%
Protein 11 g				Sugars 0 g					

Percent Daily Values (%DV) are based on a 2000-calorie diet.

Notes
- Potentially hazardous food. *Food Safety Standards:* Hold food for service at an internal temperature above 140°F. Do not mix old product with new. Cool leftover product quickly (within 4 hours) to below 41°F. See p. 105 for cooling procedures. Reheat leftover product quickly (within 2 hours) to 165°F. Reheat product only once; discard if not used.
- 8 lb fresh pork, simmered until done and chopped finely, may be used in place of the sausage. Increase salt to 2 oz and add 1 Tbsp ground sage.

Variation
- **Fried Cornmeal Mush.** Delete sausage. Increase cornmeal to 4 lb, salt to 2 oz, boiling water to 2 gal, and cold water to 2½ qt. Proceed as for Scrapple.

CHEESE-STUFFED FRANKFURTERS

Yield: 50 portions   *Portion:* 2 frankfurters
Oven: 350°F   *Bake:* 30 minutes

Ingredient	Amount	Procedure
Frankfurters, 10 per lb	10 lb	Split frankfurters lengthwise, but do not cut completely through.
Cheddar cheese	3 lb	Cut cheese into strips about 3½ inches long.
Pickle relish	1 qt	Place a strip of cheese and ½ Tbsp relish in each frankfurter.
Bacon, 24–26 slices per lb	100 slices (4–5 lb)	Wrap a slice of bacon around each frankfurter. Secure with a pick. Place on greased baking sheets. Bake at 350°F for 30 minutes.

Approximate nutritive values per portion   **Calories** 497

Amount/portion	%DV	Amount/portion	%DV	Amount/portion	%DV		%DV		%DV
Total Fat 42 g	64%	**Cholest.** 86 mg	29%	**Total Carb.** 9 g	3%	**Vitamin A**	11%	**Calcium**	25%
Sat. Fat 18 g	89%	**Sodium** 1543 mg	64%	Fiber 0 g	0%	**Vitamin C**	47%	**Iron**	10%
Protein 21 g				Sugars 2 g					

Percent Daily Values (%DV) are based on a 2000-calorie diet.

Notes

- Potentially hazardous food. *Food Safety Standards:* Hold food for service at an internal temperature above 140°F. Do not mix old product with new. Cool leftover product quickly (within 4 hours) to below 41°F. See p. 105 for cooling procedures. Reheat leftover product quickly (within 2 hours) to 165°F. Reheat product only once; discard if not used.

- The names wieners, hot dogs, and frankfurters are often used interchangeably. Beef, pork, or poultry wieners are available.

Variations

- **Barbecued Frankfurters.** Place frankfurters in counter pans. Cover with Barbecue Sauce (p. 755). Bake at 400°F for about 30 minutes. Add more sauce if necessary.

- **Chili Dog.** Serve 2 oz Chili Con Carne (p. 800) over a frankfurter or wiener in a hot dog bun. Chili may be made with or without beans.

- **Frankfurters and Sauerkraut.** Steam frankfurters or cook in boiling water. Serve with sauerkraut (2 No. 10 cans) that has been heated.

- **Nacho Dog.** Serve 2 oz Nacho Sauce (p. 236) over a frankfurter or wiener in a hot dog bun. Sprinkle over the top one or more of the following: chopped green chilies or jalapeño peppers, chopped tomatoes, chopped black olives, or chopped onion.

CREAMED SAUSAGE AND BISCUITS

Yield: 50 portions   *Portion:* 4 oz gravy over 2 biscuits

Ingredient	Amount	Procedure
Baking Powder Biscuits (p. 268)	100	Prepare biscuits according to recipe.
Ground sausage	7 lb 8 oz AP (5 lb EP)	Cook raw sausage in tilting or large fry pan until browned and 155°F. Weight after browning should be 5 lb. Drain well. Reserve sausage for later step.
Margarine Flour	1 lb 1 lb 6 oz	Mix margarine and flour in a steam-jacketed or other large kettle. Stir with wire whip. Cook for 10–15 minutes, stirring often.
Milk	1¾ gal	Stir milk into margarine-flour mixture, stirring constantly with a wire whip. Cook until mixture thickens.
Salt Black pepper	2 tsp 1 tsp	Add salt and pepper to creamed mixture. Stir in cooked sausage reserved from earlier step. Heat to 180°–190°F.
		Serve two biscuits split in half with 4 oz gravy.

Approximate nutritive values per portion   **Calories** 425

Amount/portion	%DV	Amount/portion	%DV	Amount/portion	%DV		%DV		%DV
Total Fat 31 g	**48%**	**Cholest.** 57 mg	**19%**	**Total Carb.** 17 g	6%	**Vitamin A**	11%	**Calcium**	18%
Sat. Fat 12 g	**61%**	**Sodium** 586 mg	**24%**	Fiber 0.4 g	1%	**Vitamin C**	3%	**Iron**	6%
Protein 14 g				Sugars 7 g					

Percent Daily Value (%DV) are based on a 2000-calorie diet.

Note
- Potentially hazardous food. *Food Safety Standards:* Hold food for service at an internal temperature above 140°F. Do not mix old product with new. Cool leftover product quickly (within 4 hours) to below 41°F. See p. 105 for cooling procedures. Reheat leftover product quickly (within 2 hours) to 165°F. Reheat product only once; discard if not used.

SAUSAGE ROLLS

Yield: 50 rolls   *Portion:* 1 roll, 2 oz gravy
Oven: 400°F   *Bake:* 20 minutes

Ingredient	*Amount*	*Procedure*
Sausages, link	12 lb 8 oz	Partially cook sausages. Remove from fat.
Flour, all-purpose	3 lb	Make into biscuit dough, according to directions on p. 268.
Baking powder	3 oz	
Salt	3½ tsp	
Shortening	12 oz	
Milk	1 qt	
		Divide biscuit dough into two portions.
		Roll each portion to ½-inch thickness and cut into 3 × 4-inch rectangles.
		Place two sausages in the center of each piece of dough and fold over.
		Place seam side down on greased baking sheets.
		Bake at 400°F for 20 minutes, until bread is browned and sausage temperature is at least 170°F.
Margarine	6 oz	Melt margarine, add flour, and blend. Add salt and pepper. Cook for 5 minutes.
Flour, all-purpose	6 oz	Add water or stock gradually, stirring constantly. Cook until smooth and thickened.
Salt	2 tsp	
Pepper, black	½ tsp	Ladle 2 oz gravy over each sausage roll.
Water or chicken broth	3 qt	

Approximate nutritive values per portion   **Calories** 478

Amount/portion	%DV	Amount/portion	%DV	Amount/portion	%DV		%DV		%DV
Total Fat 33 g	51%	**Cholest.** 64 mg	21%	**Total Carb.** 26 g	9%	**Vitamin A**	5%	**Calcium**	20%
Sat. Fat 10 g	52%	**Sodium** 1360 mg	57%	Fiber 1 g	3%	**Vitamin C**	2%	**Iron**	15%
Protein 18 g				Sugars 1 g					

Percent Daily Values (%DV) are based on a 2000-calorie diet.

Note   • Potentially hazardous food. *Food Safety Standards:* Hold food for service at an internal temperature above 140°F. Do not mix old product with new. Cool leftover product quickly (within 4 hours) to below 41°F. See p. 105 for cooling procedures. Reheat leftover product quickly (within 2 hours) to 165°F. Reheat product only once; discard if not used.

Variations   • **Italian Sausage Sandwich.** Grill fifty 5- to 6-inch-long Italian sausages. Serve one sausage in a long bun with 1 oz Sandwich Tomato Sauce (p. 580) ladled on top. Serve with sautéed green peppers and onions. May be sprinkled with 1 oz shredded mozzarella cheese

   • **Pigs in Blankets.** Substitute 50 wieners for link sausages. Place each wiener diagonally on dough portion and roll up. Delete gravy. May serve with Cheese Sandwich Sauce (p. 749).

   • **Pigs in Blankets with Cheese.** Wrap 1 oz cheese around each wiener. Proceed as for Pigs in Blankets.

CHAPTER 13

Poultry

Simon Smith © Dorling Kindersley

HANDLING POULTRY SAFELY

Poultry is perishable and a potential carrier of illness-causing microorganisms. It should be handled with care to ensure food safety. Good handling practices include:

- Keeping fresh poultry refrigerated in the coldest part of the refrigerator (28–32°F). Limit the time during production that poultry is at room temperature to 30 minutes to 1 hour.

- Thawing poultry in the refrigerator. (See Table 2.21 for approximate thawing times for poultry.)

- Keeping raw poultry and raw poultry juices separate from other foods.

- Washing hands frequently and washing and sanitizing countertops, cutting boards, knives, and other utensils used in preparing raw poultry before they come in contact with other raw or cooked foods.

COOKING METHODS

Chapter 4 describes the various moist and dry heat cooking methods that are appropriate for cooking poultry and other meat products. Cooking methods specific to poultry are included in this chapter. Information from both chapters will be useful for producing quality poultry products.

Most frozen poultry, except breaded and precooked products, is thawed prior to cooking. If frozen poultry is cooked, it will take approximately 1½ times longer than thawed poultry.

Poultry should be cooked at moderate heat (325–350°F) for optimum tenderness and juiciness. Recommended cooking methods for various classes of poultry are given in Table 13.1.

Poultry is easily flavored by imaginative use of herbs and spices. Possible spice choices for poultry include celery salt, curry, dillweed, fennel seed, garlic, marjoram, ground mustard, oregano, paprika, parsley, poultry seasoning, rosemary, saffron, sage, savory, sesame seed, sweet basil, tarragon, and thyme. A recipe for a salt-free Lemon–Herb Seasoning appears on p. 781.

Whole chickens can easily be cut into pieces suitable for a variety of cooking processes. Figure 13.1 identifies procedures for dividing whole chicken into smaller pieces.

Broiling or Grilling

Most cuts of chicken and some turkey products may be cooked by broiling or grilling. Choose from half and quarter chickens, bone-in parts, and boneless chicken or turkey cuts such as breasts, breast or thigh steaks, and tenderloins. The procedure for broiling poultry follows:

- Use poultry that has been marinated, or brush with melted fat. Season as appropriate.

TABLE 13.1 Cooking methods for poultry

Kind of poultry	Class	Average ready-to-cook weight (pounds)	Cookery method	Per-person allowance, ready-to-cook weight (ounces)
Chicken	Broiler-fryer	3–4½	Fry, broil, grill, roast	¼–½ bird
	Roaster	5–8	Roast	12–16
	Breast, boneless		Grill, broil	5–6
Turkey	Whole	8–24	Roast	12–16
	Roast, boned and tied	12	Roast	5–6
	Roll, ready to cook	3–6	Roast	5–6
	Cutlet		Grill, broil	
	Steaks	¼–½	Grill, broil	
	Tenderloin		Grill, broil	
	Wings		Roast, broil	
	Drumsticks		Roast, broil	
Duck		3–7	Roast	12–16
Goose		6–12	Roast	12–16

Notes: • For cooked yields for chicken and turkey, see p. 71.
        • For additional information on amounts of poultry to purchase, see Table 2.4
        • For roasting times see Table 13.2. For broiling and grilling times, see Broiling or Grilling, p. 527.

• Place lightly greased rack 6–8 inches from heat source. Place poultry on broiler, skin side down if skin is left on. Turn larger pieces often so they cook and brown evenly. Thin steaks and breasts should be turned only once. For chicken breasts or turkey breast steaks, cook 4–7 minutes per side; for cutlets, 2–3 minutes per side; and 8–12 minutes per side for turkey tenderloin. Cook until poultry reaches an internal temperature of 170°F for bone-in pieces or 165°F for boneless pieces.

Poultry browns very quickly and larger pieces may become too dark before they are cooked through. If the poultry is browning too quickly, it may be placed in an oven on sheet pans or racks to complete cooking.

Deep-Fat Frying

Broiler-fryer pieces and many breaded patties, cutlets, and steaks may be cooked by submerging them in hot fat—deep-fat frying. Pressure frying (deep-fat frying in a covered fryer that allows steam to build up and cook the product under pressure) is also a common way to cook poultry.

    Poultry products usually are breaded before deep-fat frying or are purchased with a batter or breaded coating. The recipe for coating chicken is on p. 99. Figure 13.2 shows the technique for breading. Guidelines for deep-fat frying raw broiler fryer pieces are as follows:

• Fry at 350–375°F for regular deep-fat frying, 345–350°F for pressure frying.

• Fill baskets so that hot fat can circulate around pieces. Do not overload.

• Use a good-quality fat with a high smoke point.

• 15–20 percent fresh fat should be added after each daily use. Old fat should be discarded.

• Cook until chicken reaches an internal temperature of 170°F for bone-in pieces or 165°F for boneless pieces.

Cooking time will vary because of size differences. Approximate frying times for raw chicken pieces are 15–20 minutes for regular deep-fat frying and 14–18 minutes for pressure frying. If cooked or partially cooked pieces are being used, refer to manufacturer's directions.

Pan Frying

Pan-fried chicken pieces are usually coated with flour or breading before cooking. See recipe on p. 538 and breading techniques in Figure 13.2. Chicken may be purchased breaded and ready to pan fry. Follow these guidelines for pan frying raw chicken pieces:

• Heat ½ inch of fat to 350°F. Arrange breaded chicken in hot fat, skin side down. Brown on all sides.

• Reduce temperature to 325°F and cook slowly until tender, usually 40–60 minutes, or until internal temperature reaches 170°F for bone-in pieces or 165°F for boneless pieces. Cooking time depends on size of pieces. Turn as necessary to assure even browning and doneness.

1. Place chicken, breast-side up, on cutting board. Cut skin between thigh and body, near the thigh joint.
2. Bend back legs backward until bones break at hip joints. Remove leg-thigh from carcass by cutting between the joints.
3. Separate thighs and drumsticks. Locate knee joint by bending thigh and leg together. With skin side down, cut through joints at each leg.
4. With chicken on back, remove wings by cutting inside of wing just over joint. Pull wing away from body and cut top down through joint.
5. Separate breast and back by placing chicken on its breast and cutting along backbone from bird's tail to head. (Pictures (5) and (6) show splitting a chicken with wings and legs intact. Remove legs and wings as described in steps above when cutting a chicken in pieces. Leave wings and legs on when splitting a chicken in half.)
6. Lay bird flat and remove backbone by cutting through ribs connecting it to breast. May also separate breast and back by placing chicken on back and cutting (toward board) through joints along each side of rib cage.
7. Split the breast by putting skin side down and cutting in half. May cut wishbone from the breast.

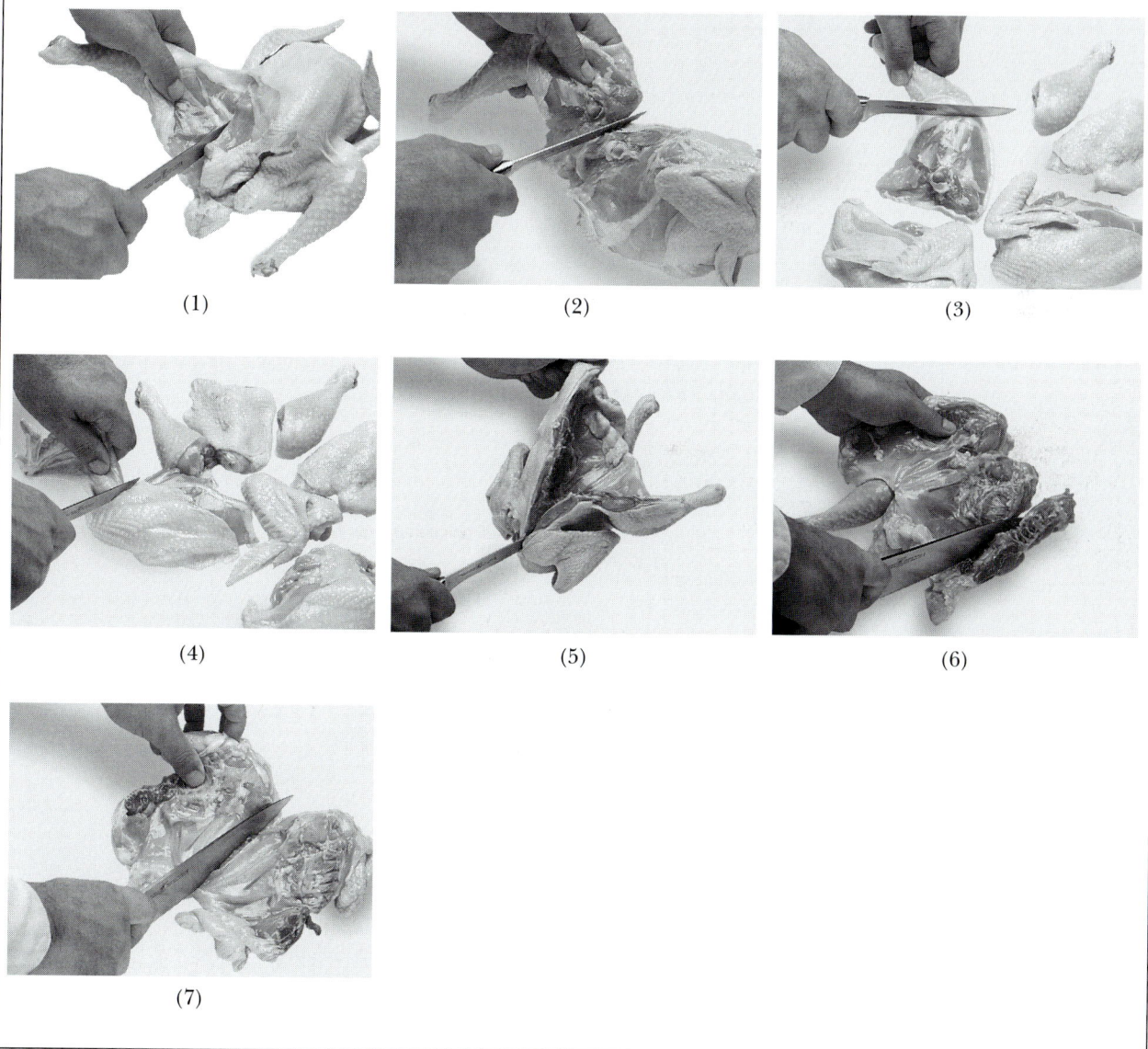

FIGURE 13.1   Cutting up a whole chicken.

Arrange work station in the order shown in the diagram.

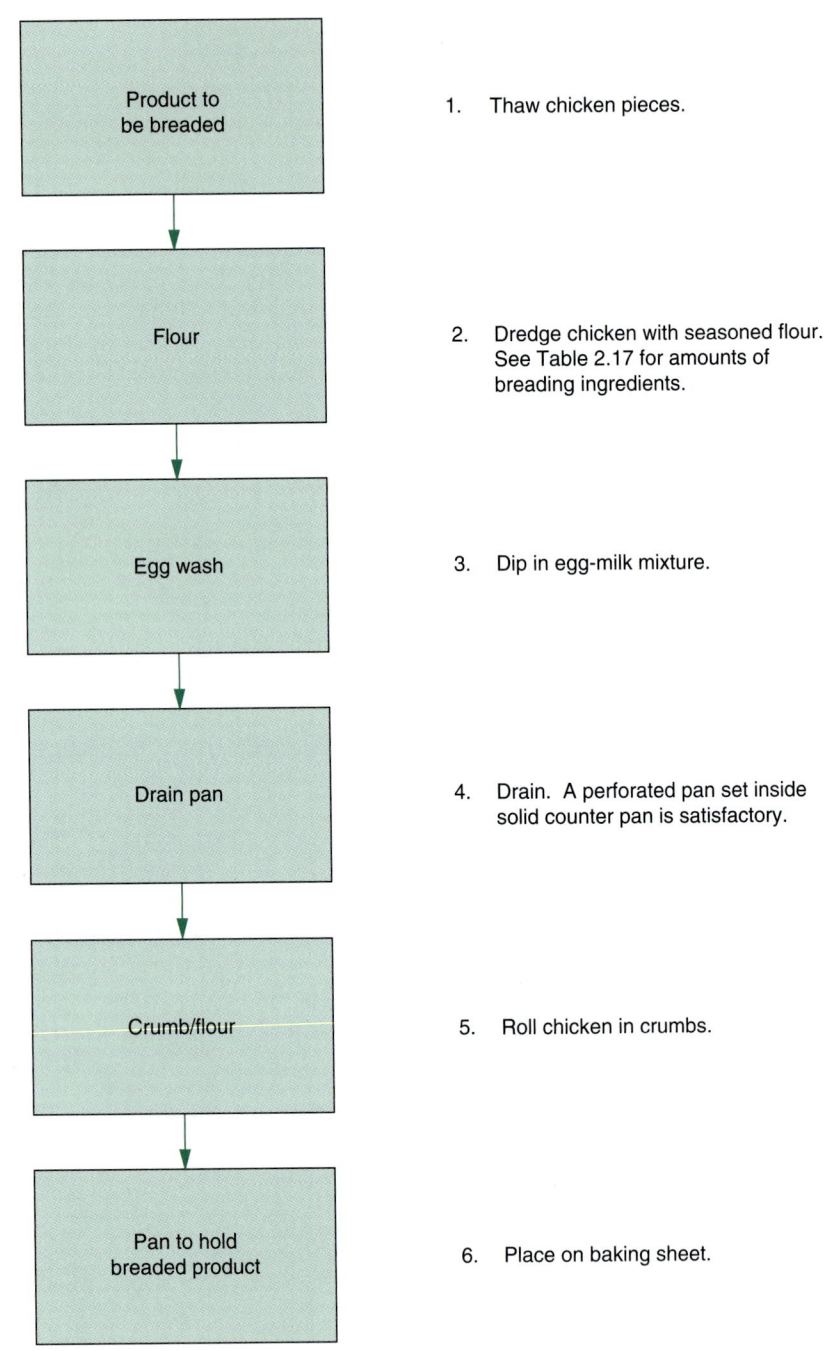

1. Thaw chicken pieces.

2. Dredge chicken with seasoned flour. See Table 2.17 for amounts of breading ingredients.

3. Dip in egg-milk mixture.

4. Drain. A perforated pan set inside solid counter pan is satisfactory.

5. Roll chicken in crumbs.

6. Place on baking sheet.

FIGURE 13.2   Breading techniques for poultry.

Notes: • Always wash hands and wash and sanitize countertops, utensils, and containers between production steps to prevent cross-contamination.
• Keep chicken refrigerated, removing small quantities as needed.
• Breading ingredients in all steps should be kept below 41°F whenever possible and discarded after being held above 41°F for 2 hours.

Sautéing thin slices of poultry in a small amount of fat is popular for many poultry dishes. Large pieces may require pan sautéing for browning, then finishing by another method, such as braising or baking.

Oven Frying

Oven frying is a satisfactory method for producing fried chicken without large quantities of fat. When properly cooked, the finished product is tender, moist, and crispy. The following guidelines are for oven frying chicken:

- Dredge chicken pieces in seasoned flour, then roll in melted fat.
- Place on sheet pans and bake approximately 1 hour at 350–375°F or until internal temperature reaches 170°F for bone-in pieces or 165°F for boneless pieces.

This method of cooking chicken should result in a nicely browned product with no turning. See recipe on p. 539. Turkey drumsticks and drumettes may be oven fried using the same procedure. Cooking time will vary depending on the size.

Braising

Braising—cooking meat slowly in a closely covered pan with a small amount of moisture—is often required for mature, less tender poultry. Guidelines for braising whole and cut-up poultry follow:

Braising Whole Poultry

- Preheat oven to 450°F for young poultry, 325°F for more mature birds.
- Season and brush ready-to-cook poultry with fat.
- Place poultry in a heavy pan and cover tightly.
- Poultry is done when internal temperature reaches 180°F, 1–2 hours. Uncovering the poultry for the last 30 minutes of cooking will allow it to brown.

Braising Cut-up Poultry

- Roll serving-size pieces of poultry in seasoned flour, then brown in fat in a heavy fry pan. Drain off fat. Place chicken in a baking pan.
- Add a small amount of hot water. Cover tightly and cook in a 325°F oven. Add more water as necessary to prevent sticking.
- Remove cover during the final 30 minutes of cooking to brown. Total cooking time will be 1½–2½ hours, depending on size of the pieces and maturity of the bird. Poultry is done when internal tempera-

ture reaches 170°F for bone-in pieces or 165°F for boneless pieces.

Stewing or Simmering and Poaching

Stewing or simmering and poaching refers to cooking in a liquid. Stewing or simmering requires that the temperature be kept just below the boiling point, bubbling very gently. Poaching temperature is slightly lower and less liquid is used. This moist heat method of stewing and simmering is used for larger, older, and tougher birds that require longer cooking times to soften. Poaching is used to gently cook tender poultry and develop a delicate subtle flavor. Guidelines are as follows:

Stewing or Simmering

- Barely cover poultry with seasoned boiling water.
- Simmer until tender, approximately 2½ hours.
- For cooking in a steamer, place whole or parts of birds in a solid steamer pan. Cook until tender. Internal temperature must reach 180°F for whole birds, 170°F for bone-in pieces, and 165°F for boneless pieces.

Poaching

Poaching is a technique that uses either liquid or steam and liquid to cook the food items. In addition to chicken, poaching is used for tender cuts of meat, fish, eggs, fruits, and vegetables. Items can be partially covered with liquid or fully submerged. The temperature of the poaching liquid should be approximately 185°F.

Procedures for poaching in a small amount of liquid (usually single-serving portions) are as follows:

- Heat a small amount of butter in a shallow poaching pan. Add vegetables, spices, and herbs. Arrange the food to be poached in the pan.
- Pour cold poaching liquid into the pan. Liquid should cover the product ⅓ to ½ inch deep. Bring the liquid to a simmer and cover with a lid or parchment paper. Finish cooking over direct heat or in an oven until done (for chicken: 170°F for bone-in pieces, 165°F for boneless pieces). Remove the chicken from the poaching liquid, cover, and keep warm.
- If desired, reduce the poaching liquid and use as a sauce.

Procedures for poaching in a large amount of liquid (usually for larger items) are as follows:

- Bring the liquid to a simmer and add the item being poached. The food should be fully submerged. Cook over direct heat without covering.

• The food item may be removed from the poaching liquid or cooled in the liquid. The liquid is generally not used as a sauce.

When stewed or simmered poultry meat is to be used in salads or creamed dishes, the following may be added to the cooking water for additional flavor: 1 carrot, 1 medium onion, 1 celery stalk, and 2 whole peppercorns for each bird.

Cooked poultry must be cooled immediately if prepared for use at a later time. Remove from broth and place on sheet pans. When poultry is cool enough to handle, remove meat from bones, place in shallow pans, and store in the refrigerator at 38°F or below. Broth should be cooled rapidly by stirring frequently during cooling.

Roasting

For large-quantity cookery, it is recommended that poultry be roasted unstuffed and that dressing be baked separately. If turkey is to be stuffed, mix the stuffing just before it is needed. Do not prepare the dressing or stuff the bird in advance. Follow this order of procedure in roasting poultry:

1. Prepare bird. Remove giblets and neck from body and neck cavities. Rinse bird well inside and out. Tuck wing tips under back of bird. Add ½ cup water to pan.

2. Season inside and outside of bird.

3. Brush with vegetable oil or soft fat (optional).

4. Place bird on rack in shallow baking pan, breast up. If bird will not be carved for show, bake breast side down. In the beginning, a tent of aluminum foil may be placed over the poultry, then removed for browning.

5. Baste with pan drippings or vegetable oil (optional).

6. Roast at 325°F to an internal temperature of 180°F. Insert thermometer in center of inside thigh muscle, being careful not to touch the bone with the stem (see Table 13.2 for roasting guide). If thermometer is not available, test doneness by moving drumstick. It moves easily at the thigh joint when done. Juices should be clear when meat is pierced in the deepest part with a long-tined fork.

7. Whole turkeys and larger roasts should be allowed to stand 20 minutes before carving. See Figure 13.3 for carving instructions. Figure 13.4 describes a procedure for skinning and boning a turkey breast.

The yield of cooked meat from poultry is influenced by the size of the bird, the amount of bone, the method of preparation and service, and the size of portions desired. Whole, ready-to-cook turkey will yield approximately 47 percent edible cooked meat without skin, neck meat, or giblets; turkey roast or roll will yield about 66 percent. Large fryers will yield approximately 35–40 percent usable cooked meat.

TABLE 13.2   Roasting guide for poultry (defrosted)

Kind of poultry	Ready-to-cook weight (pounds)	Approximate total roasting time at 325°F	Internal temperature of poultry when done (°F)
Chicken, whole roasters	2½–4	1–1½ hr	180
Ducks	3–7	1–2 hr	180
Geese	6–8	2½–3½ hr	180
	8–12	3½–4½ hr	180
Turkeys, whole, thawed	8–12	2¾–3 hr	180
	12–16	3–3¾ hr	180
	16–20	3¾–4¼ hr	180
	18–20	4¼–4½ hr	180
	20–24	4½–5 hr	180
Turkey, breast and breast portions	4–6	1½–2¼ hr	170
	6–8	2¼–3¼ hr	170
Turkey roast, boneless	3–10	35–45 min per pound	170
Turkey tenderloin		18–30 min at 400°F	170
Turkey wings, drumsticks, wing drumettes, thigh		1–1¾ hr	180

Note: • Thermometer is inserted in thigh muscle of whole turkeys and in center of turkey roasts. The thermometer should not touch bone.

Carving Dark Meat

1

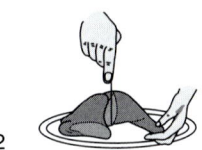

2

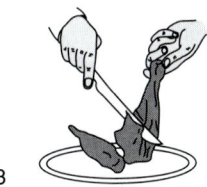

3

4

1. Remove drumstick and thigh by pulling leg away from body. Joint connecting leg to backbone will often snap free or may be severed easily with knife point. Cut dark meat from body by following body contour carefully with knife.
2. Place drumstick and thigh on cutting surface and cut through connecting joint.
3. Tilt drumstick to convenient angle, slicing down toward cutting surface.
4. Hold thigh firmly on cutting surface with fork. Cut slices evenly and parallel to bone.

Carving White Meat

1

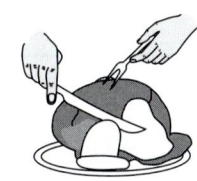

2

Traditional Method
1. Hold turkey breast firmly on cutting surface with fork. Place knife parallel and as close to wing as possible. Make deep cut into breast cutting toward ribs. This makes a base cut. Each breast slice will stop at this horizontal base cut.
2. Slice breast by carving downward, ending at base cut. Keep slices thin and even.

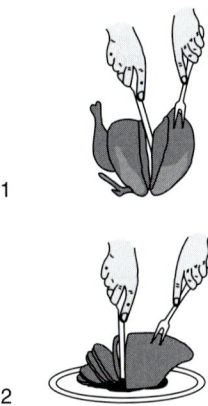

1

2

Kitchen Method
1. Hold turkey breast firmly on cutting surface with fork. Using a sharp knife, carve each breast half away from ribs by cutting along keel bone and rib cage.
2. On cutting surface, carve each breast half into thin, even slices against grain of meat.

FIGURE 13.3 Carving a turkey. Courtesy of National Turkey Federation.

ORAN

Yield: 50
Oven: 32

Ingredie

Cornish

Butter o
   melte

Orange
   undilu
Corn syr
Orange

Approxim

Amount/p

Total Fat
   Sat. Fat
Protein   5

Percent Da

Notes

CHICKEN WITH NOODLES ON WHIPPED POTATOES

Yield: 50 portions   *Portion:* 5 oz Chicken and Noodles, 4 oz Whipped Potatoes

Ingredient	Amount	Procedure
Water	5½ qt	Mix water and chicken base in a steam-jacketed kettle.
Chicken base (see Note)	3 oz	
Onions, chopped	8 oz	Add vegetables and spices. Bring to a rolling boil.
Celery, chopped	8 oz	
Black pepper (cracked)	¾ tsp	
Sage (rubbed)	½ tsp	
Rosemary (dried)	½ tsp	
Parsley flakes (dried)	1 Tbsp	
Egg noodles, ¼-inch (frozen)	2 lb	Stir noodles into boiling liquid mixture. Reduce heat and simmer for 35–45 minutes. Stir often to keep noodles separated.
Cooked chicken, diced	2 lb 12 oz	Add chicken to noodle mixture. Stir carefully to prevent breaking up chicken.
Water (cold)	1 lb 8 oz	In a separate bowl blend cold water and flour together using a wire whip.
Flour	1½ oz	Add water-flour slurry to the broth, pouring through a strainer if not smooth. Stir constantly but gently while adding to prevent lumps from forming. Simmer until mixture reaches 200°F and sauce thickens.
Whipped Potatoes (p. 856)	13 lb	Prepare whipped potatoes according to recipe. Serve 5 oz of chicken and noodles over 4 oz whipped potatoes.

Approximate nutritive values per portion   **Calories** 266

Amount/portion	%DV	Amount/portion	%DV	Amount/portion	%DV		%DV		%DV
Total Fat 7 g	11%	**Cholest.** 56 mg	19%	**Total Carb.** 33 g	11%	**Vitamin A**	2%	**Calcium**	5%
Sat. Fat 1.6 g	8%	**Sodium** 1243 mg	52%	Fiber 2.5 g	10%	**Vitamin C**	22%	**Iron**	9%
Protein 18 g				Sugars 3.4 g					

Percent Daily Values (%DV) are based on a 2000-calorie diet.

Notes
- Potentially hazardous food. Food Safety Standards: Hold food for service at an internal temperature above 140°F. Do not mix old product with new. Cool leftover product quickly (within 2 hours) to 70°F and then (within an additional 4 hours) to 41°F. See p. 105 for cooling procedures. Reheat leftover product quickly (within 2 hours) to 165°F. Reheat product only once; discard if not used.
- Use a high-quality chicken base. The salt concentration of bases varies by brand. Check for salt and adjust as necessary.

CHICKEN AND RICE CASSEROLE

Yield: 50 portions or 2 pans 12 × 20 × 2 inches   *Portion:* 8 oz
Oven: 350°F   *Bake:* 1 hour

Ingredient	Amount	Procedure
Cooked chicken	6 lb	Dice chicken.
Rice, converted Water, boiling Salt Margarine or vegetable oil	2 lb 8 oz 2 qt 2 Tbsp 2 Tbsp	Cook rice according to directions on p. 594.
Margarine, melted Onion, chopped Celery, chopped Mushrooms, sliced	6 oz 3 oz 8 oz 1 lb	Sauté onion, celery, and mushrooms in margarine.
Flour, all-purpose	8 oz	Add flour to vegetables and stir to blend.
Milk Chicken Stock (p. 790) Pepper, white	1½ qt 2 qt ¼ tsp	Add milk and stock, stirring constantly with wire whip. Cook until thickened. Add pepper. Add salt if needed.

Almonds, slivered
Pimento, chopped
	6 oz
	3 oz
		Add almonds, pimento, and chicken to sauce. Combine
		  carefully.
		Scale into two lightly greased 12 × 20 × 2-inch baking pans,
		  10 lb 8 oz per pan.

Bread crumbs
Margarine, melted
Cheddar cheese,
  shredded
	9 oz
	3 oz
	6 oz
		Combine bread crumbs, margarine, and cheese.
		Sprinkle over mixture in pans, 9 oz per pan.
		Bake at 350°F for 1 hour or until internal temperature
		  reaches 180°F.

Approximate nutritive values per portion   **Calories** 320

Amount/portion	%DV	Amount/portion	%DV	Amount/portion	%DV		%DV		%DV
Total Fat 13 g	**20%**	**Cholest.** 53 mg	**18%**	**Total Carb.** 29 g	**10%**	Vitamin A	5%	Calcium	10%
Sat. Fat 4 g	**18%**	**Sodium** 585 mg	**24%**	Fiber 1 g	**5%**	Vitamin C	3%	Iron	12%
Protein 21 g				Sugars 2 g					

Percent Daily Values (%DV) are based on a 2000-calorie diet.

Notes
- Potentially hazardous food. *Food Safety Standards:* Hold food for service at an internal temperature above 140°F. Do not mix old product with new. Cool leftover product quickly (within 4 hours) to below 41°F. See p. 105 for cooling procedures. Reheat leftover product quickly (within 2 hours) to 165°F. Reheat product only once; discard if not used.
- 18–20 lb chicken AP will yield approximately 6 lb cooked meat.
- Sliced water chestnuts may be substituted for almonds.
- Chopped parsley may be sprinkled over the baked product just before serving.
- ¼ oz (2 Tbsp) dehydrated onions, rehydrated in ¼ cup water, may be substituted for fresh onions.

TURKEY AND DUMPLINGS

Yield: 48 portions or 2 pans 12 × 20 × 2 inches   *Portion:* 8 oz

Ingredient	Amount	Procedure
Margarine Onions, chopped	14 oz 1 lb	Melt margarine in steam-jacketed or other kettle. Sauté onions until tender.
Flour, all-purpose Pepper, black	1 lb 8 oz 1½ tsp	Stir flour and pepper into onions. Cook 5–10 minutes, stirring often.
Water Chicken base	1½ gal 6 oz	Add water and chicken base to mixture in kettle. Cook until thickened, stirring often.
Turkey, cooked	6 lb 10 oz	Cut turkey into ½-inch cubes. Add to sauce.
Celery, chopped Carrots, sliced	1 lb 10 oz 2 lb 4 oz	Steam celery and carrots until tender-crisp. Fold into turkey mixture. Scale into two 12 × 20 × 2-inch pans, 13 lb per pan.

STEAMED DUMPLINGS

Ingredient	Amount	Procedure
Flour, all-purpose Baking powder Salt	2 lb 4 oz 3 oz 2 Tbsp	Combine flour, baking powder, and salt in mixer bowl. Mix until blended.
Eggs, beaten Milk Parsley, fresh, chopped Poultry seasoning	5 (9 oz) 1½ qt 1 oz 2 tsp	Combine eggs, milk, and seasonings. Add to dry ingredients and mix only until blended. Portion 4 × 6 with No. 24 dipper onto turkey and gravy. Steam until dumplings are done, approximately 20 minutes.

Approximate nutritive values per portion   **Calories 336**

Amount/portion	%DV	Amount/portion	%DV	Amount/portion	%DV		%DV		%DV
Total Fat 14 g	21%	**Cholest.** 62 mg	21%	**Total Carb.** 35 g	12%	**Vitamin A**	64%	**Calcium**	20%
Sat. Fat 4 g	18%	**Sodium** 1593 mg	66%	Fiber 2 g	8%	**Vitamin C**	8%	**Iron**	16%
Protein 18 g				Sugars 5 g					

Percent Daily Values (%DV) are based on a 2000-calorie diet.

Notes

- Potentially hazardous food. *Food Safety Standards:* Hold food for service at an internal temperature above 140°F. Do not mix old product with new. Cool leftover product quickly (within 4 hours) to below 41°F. See p. 105 for cooling procedures. Reheat leftover product quickly (within 2 hours) to 165°F. Reheat product only once; discard if not used.

- Steam as soon as dumplings are portioned onto gravy. Product holds well after cooking.

- 2 oz (1 cup) dehydrated onions, rehydrated in 1½ cups water, may be substituted for fresh onions.

LIME TARRAGON TURKEY STEAK

Yield: 50 steaks   *Portion:* 6 oz
Grill: 350°F   *Grill:* 4–7 minutes per side

Ingredient	Amount	Procedure
Turkey steaks, 6 oz	50	
Vegetable oil	3½ cups	Combine oil, liquids, and spices in stainless steel container.
Lime juice, frozen, reconstituted	1 qt	Pour over turkey steaks and refrigerate for several hours or overnight. Turn if necessary to make sure both sides of turkey are coated.
Cooking sherry	2 cups	
Garlic cloves, minced	4 oz	
Chives, chopped	3 oz	
Tarragon, dried whole leaves	½ cup	
Salt	2½ oz	
Pepper, black	5 tsp	
Dry mustard	1 tsp	
Worcestershire sauce	¼ cup	
Water	2 cups	
		Drain marinade from turkey steaks. Preheat grill to 350°F. Grill steaks approximately 4–7 minutes per side until internal temperature reaches 165°F.

Approximate nutritive values per portion   **Calories** 240

Amount/portion	%DV	Amount/portion	%DV	Amount/portion	%DV		%DV		%DV
Total Fat 11 g	17%	**Cholest.** 66 mg	22%	**Total Carb.** 3 g	1%	**Vitamin A**	1%	**Calcium**	4%
Sat. Fat 2 g	10%	**Sodium** 630 mg	26%	Fiber 0 g	0%	**Vitamin C**	9%	**Iron**	10%
Protein 30 g				Sugars 0 g					

Percent Daily Values (%DV) are based on a 2000-calorie diet.

Notes

- Potentially hazardous food. *Food Safety Standards:* Hold food for service at an internal temperature above 140°F. Do not mix old product with new. Cool leftover product quickly (within 4 hours) to below 41°F. See p. 105 for cooling procedures. Reheat leftover product quickly (within 2 hours) to 165°F. Reheat product only once; discard if not used.

- Always wash hands and wash and sanitize countertops, utensils, and containers between production steps when preparing raw poultry.

Variation

- **Creole Turkey Steaks.** Prepare Creole Spice Mixture, p. 462 (Creole Baked Fish). Dip turkey steaks in melted margarine, then sprinkle generously with spice mixture. Grill steaks until done, 4–7 minutes per side.

CORN BREAD DRESSING

Yield: 50 portions or 1 pan 12 × 20 × 2 inches   *Portion:* 4 oz
Oven: 375°F   *Bake:* 20–30 minutes

Ingredient	Amount	Procedure
Corn Bread (p. 281) ⅓ recipe	3 lb 10 oz	Prepare Corn Bread. Crumble.
Bread, cubed or torn	1 lb 12 oz	Crumble bread. Add to Corn Bread.
Margarine	4 oz	Melt margarine in steam-jacketed or other kettle.
Onions, chopped	1 lb	Add onions and celery. Sauté until vegetables are tender.
Celery, chopped	1 lb 8 oz	Add bread.
Chicken base	2 oz	Combine chicken base, water, and seasonings. Pour over
Water, hot	3 qt	bread mixture. Stir to moisten.
Salt (see Notes)	1 tsp	
Poultry seasoning	1 Tbsp	
Pepper, black	1 tsp	
		Scale mixture (12 lb) into lightly greased 12 × 20 × 2-inch pan. Bake at 375°F for 20–30 minutes or until 180°F. Serve with No. 12 dipper.

Approximate nutritive values per portion   **Calories** 157

Amount/portion	%DV	Amount/portion	%DV	Amount/portion	%DV		%DV		%DV
Total Fat 6 g	9%	**Cholest.** 15 mg	5%	**Total Carb.** 23 g	8%	**Vitamin A**	2%	**Calcium**	8%
Sat. Fat 1 g	7%	**Sodium** 546 mg	23%	Fiber 2 g	8%	**Vitamin C**	2%	**Iron**	6%
Protein 4 g				Sugars 4 g					

Percent Daily Values (%DV) are based on a 2000-calorie diet.

Notes
- Potentially hazardous food. *Food Safety Standards:* Hold food for service at an internal temperature above 140°F. Do not mix old product with new. Cool leftover product quickly (within 4 hours) to below 41°F. See p. 105 for cooling procedures. Reheat leftover product quickly (within 2 hours) to 165°F. Reheat product only once; discard if not used.
- If chicken base is highly salted, reduce or delete salt in recipe.

BREAD DRESSING (OR STUFFING)

Yield: 50 portions or 1 pan 12 × 20 × 2 inches   *Portion:* 4½ oz
Oven: 325°F   *Bake:* 1 hour 15 minutes

Ingredient	Amount	Procedure
Onion, chopped	1 lb	Sauté onion and celery in margarine until lightly browned.
Celery, chopped (optional)	1 lb	
Margarine	1 lb	
Water (see Notes)	1 gal	Add water, chicken base, and seasonings to sautéed vegetables. Heat until hot.
Chicken base	3 oz	
Salt (see Notes)	1 Tbsp	
Pepper, black	1 Tbsp	
Poultry seasoning (see Notes)	1 Tbsp	
Thyme, ground	1 Tbsp	
Dry bread, cubed	3 lb 12 oz	Add bread gradually to vegetable mixture, tossing lightly until thoroughly mixed. Avoid overmixing, which causes dressing to be soggy and compact.
		Scale dressing (15 lb) into lightly greased 12 × 20 × 2-inch pan. Bake at 325°F for approximately 1 hour 15 minutes, internal temperature 180°F. Serve with No. 10 dipper.

Approximate nutritive values per portion   **Calories** 159

Amount/portion	%DV	Amount/portion	%DV	Amount/portion	%DV		%DV		%DV
Total Fat 9 g	14%	**Cholest.** 0 mg	0%	**Total Carb.** 17 g	6%	**Vitamin A**	2%	**Calcium**	4%
Sat. Fat 2 g	8%	**Sodium** 757 mg	32%	Fiber 4 g	17%	**Vitamin C**	2%	**Iron**	7%
Protein 4 g				Sugars 2 g					

Percent Daily Values (%DV) are based on a 2000-calorie diet.

Notes
- Potentially hazardous food. *Food Safety Standards:* Hold food for service at an internal temperature above 140°F. Do not mix old product with new. Cool leftover product quickly (within 4 hours) to below 41°F. See p. 105 for cooling procedures. Reheat leftover product quickly (within 2 hours) to 165°F. Reheat product only once; discard if not used.
- The amount of liquid will depend on the dryness of the bread.
- If chicken base is highly salted, reduce or delete salt in recipe.
- Sage may be used for part or all of the poultry seasoning.

Variations
- **Apple Stuffing.** Add 1 lb finely chopped apples. Reduce bread cubes to 3 lb 4 oz.
- **Chestnut Stuffing.** Add 1 lb 4 oz cooked chestnuts, chopped. Reduce bread to 3 lb 8 oz. Substitute 2 qt milk for 2 qt water.
- **Mushroom Stuffing.** Reduce celery and onions to 8 oz each. Sauté 2 lb fresh mushrooms with the vegetables.
- **Nut Stuffing.** Add 2 cups chopped almonds or pecans that have been browned lightly in 4 oz melted margarine. Substitute 1 qt milk for 1 qt water.
- **Oyster Stuffing.** Add 1 lb 8 oz oysters.
- **Raisin Stuffing.** Add 1 lb seedless raisins.
- **Sausage Stuffing.** Reduce bread cubes to 3 lb 4 oz. Add 2 lb sausage, cooked and drained, and 1 lb tart apples, peeled and chopped.

CHAPTER 14

Pasta, Rice, Cereals, and Foods with Grains, Beans and Tofu

Ian O'Leary © Dorling Kindersley

The cooking of pasta, rice, cereals, and grains is similar. Water is added, heat is applied, and cooking is continued until the starch granules gelatinize. Dry beans are cooked in a liquid (generally water or stock) until softened. Tofu (bean curd) does not need to be cooked prior to being incorporated in a recipe.

PASTA

Most dry pasta will approximately double in *volume* after cooking (egg noodle volume remains about the same). Thickness varies among pasta shapes, and the volume increase is directly related to this variation. Certain shapes such as ziti, lasagna, and rigatoni have more fluctuation in their volume increase than do spaghetti and macaroni. The *weight* of dry pasta increases, but the amount depends on the type of pasta. See p. 561 for the weight increase of selected pastas.

Pasta is best if cooked uncovered at a fast boil, using plenty of water. A general rule is to allow 1 gallon of water, 1 ounce (1½ tablespoons) salt, and 1½ teaspoons cooking oil for every pound of pasta. Directions for cooking are given on p. 561. Pasta should be cooked until it is tender but firm (*al dente*), then drained to stop the cooking. Overcooking produces a soft, pasty product that breaks easily when combined with sauces or other ingredients.

RICE

Long-grain rice is cooked until all water is absorbed, so the key to properly cooked rice is the proportion of rice to water and the correct cooking time. Converted (parboiled) long-grain white rice requires slightly more water and a longer cooking time than regular long-grain or medium-grain rice. Table 14.1 gives basic proportions and yields for converted rice. The cooking time for brown rice is almost double that of the white rice. Rice may be cooked in a kettle, steamer, or oven. See p. 594 for cooking directions. Cooked rice is a potentially hazardous food and should be stored outside the temperature danger zone.

CEREALS

Cereals may be whole, cracked, flaked or rolled, or granular. The amount of water used for cooking determines the volume of the finished product. Cereal swells until all water has been absorbed or until the limit of the grain is reached. As a rule, granular cereals absorb more water than whole or flaked. The fineness of grind of the cereal and the amount of bran or cellulose are factors that determine the length of time a cereal needs to be cooked. Cereals cooked in quantity usually are prepared in a steam-jacketed kettle or steamer but may be cooked in a heavy kettle on top of the range. Directions for cooking breakfast cereals are given on p. 611.

559

TABLE 14.1   Basic proportions and yields for converted rice

Rice	Water[a]	Salt	Approximate volume yield	Approximate number of 4-oz servings
1 lb	1¼ qt	1 Tbsp	2 qt	16
2 lb	2½ qt	2 Tbsp	1 gal	32
3 lb	3¾ qt	3 Tbsp (2 oz)	6¼ qt	50
4 lb	5 qt	¼ cup (2½ oz)	8½ qt	68
5 lb	6¼ qt	⅓ cup (3½ oz)	11 qt	88
8 lb	10 qt	½ cup (5 oz)	18½ qt	148
10 lb	12½ qt	¾ cup (8 oz)	24 qt	192

[a] Liquids other than water that can be used include: chicken, beef or vegetable stock or base, tomato or vegetable juice, diluted orange or apple juice.

BEANS

Many varieties of dry beans are available. Some commonly used ones are described on p. 173.

Most dry beans will double to triple in bulk during cooking. Because sorting machines may mistake rocks or other debris for dry beans, it is recommended that beans be sorted before rinsing and cooking.

Some general cooking guidelines:

1. Place beans in a large pot or steam jacketed kettle and cover with water. Bring the water to a boil and skim foam if necessary. Cover loosely and reduce heat so beans simmer slowly.

2. Cook until beans are slightly tender. Stir very carefully as the beans become tender so they are not broken and do not become mushy.

3. Season as desired. A general rule is to add 2 tsp salt to 1 lb of beans. Other seasonings may be added.

4. Cook, stirring very carefully, until the beans are tender. Add additional water if necessary. Drain and serve or store in refrigerator until needed. Cooked beans are a potentially hazardous food. Follow cooling guidelines on p. 105.

Soaking beans prior to cooking will reduce the cooking time by about 25%.

PASTA RECIPES

COOKING PASTA

Yield: 50 portions   *Portion:* 4 oz

Ingredient	Amount	Procedure
Pasta	5 lb	Bring water to a rapid boil. Add salt and oil.
Water	5 gal	Add pasta gradually while stirring.
Salt	5 oz	Return to boiling. Cook uncovered at a fast boil until tender
Vegetable oil (optional)	3 Tbsp	but firm (*al dente*), 5–10 minutes (see Cooking Times table). Stir occasionally to prevent sticking.
		Test for doneness. Drain.

Notes
- Weight of cooked pasta will vary, depending on length of time cooked.
- Addition of oil is optional. It helps prevent foaming and sticking.
- If pasta is to be used as an ingredient in a recipe requiring further cooking, undercook slightly.
- If product is not to be served immediately, drain and rinse quickly with cold water. To keep pasta from becoming sticky or drying out, toss lightly with a little vegetable oil. Cover tightly and store in the refrigerator. To reheat, put pasta in a colander and immerse in rapidly boiling water just long enough to heat through. *Do not continue to cook.* Or, reheat in a microwave oven.
- Pasta can be covered tightly and refrigerated or frozen. Reheat to serving temperature.

APPROXIMATE YIELD AND COOKING TIMES FOR SELECTED PASTAS

Type of pasta	Approximate cooking time (al dente) (min)	Yield of cooked pasta from 1 lb dry pasta
Acini di pepe	8	3 lb 4 oz
Bow ties	11	2 lb
Fettuccine	8	2 lb 12 oz
Kluski	15	2 lb 12 oz
Lasagna noodles	15	2 lb
Linguine	10	2 lb 8 oz
Elbow macaroni	6	2 lb 12 oz
Mostaccioli	10	2 lb 4 oz
Noodles	6	2 lb 12 oz
Orzo	6	2 lb 8 oz
Rigatoni	10	2 lb
Rotini	8	2 lb
Shells	9	2 lb 8 oz
Spaghetti	10	2 lb 8 oz
Vermicelli	7	2 lb 8 oz
Wheels	11	2 lb
Ziti	10	2 lb 4 oz

ORZO PILAF

Yield: 50 portions   *Portion:* 4 oz

Ingredient	Amount	Procedure
Orzo	3 lb 8 oz	Cook orzo according to directions on p. 561. Do not overcook. Drain and keep hot. Save for later step.
Water, boiling	3½ gal	
Salt	2 Tbsp	
Vegetable oil	2 Tbsp	
Olive oil	1 cup	Sauté onions, garlic, mushrooms, and almonds in oil until onions and mushrooms are just tender.
Green onions, thinly sliced	1 lb 4 oz	
Garlic, minced	2 oz	
Mushrooms, fresh, sliced	1 lb 12 oz	
Almonds	12 oz	
Parsley, minced	2 oz	Stir parsley, juice, and spices into vegetable mixture. Mix with cooked orzo. Heat if necessary to 165°F. Serve immediately.
Lemon juice	2 Tbsp	
Rosemary leaves, dried	2 Tbsp	
Pepper, black	1 tsp	
Salt	1 tsp	

Approximate nutritive values per portion   **Calories** 208

Amount/portion	%DV	Amount/portion	%DV	Amount/portion	%DV		%DV		%DV
Total Fat 9 g	13%	**Cholest.** 0 mg	0%	**Total Carb.** 28 g	9%	**Vitamin A**	6%	**Calcium**	4%
Sat. Fat 1 g	5%	**Sodium** 311 mg	13%	Fiber 1 g	6%	**Vitamin C**	7%	**Iron**	12%
Protein 6 g				Sugars 2 g					

Percent Daily Values (%DV) are based on a 2000-calorie diet.

Note ● Potentially hazardous food. *Food Safety Standards:* Hold food for service at an internal temperature above 140°F. Do not mix old product with new. Cool leftover product quickly (within 4 hours) to below 41°F. See p. 105 for cooling procedures. Reheat leftover product quickly (within 2 hours) to 165°F. Reheat product only once; discard if not used.

Variations ● **Orzo and Feta.** Make the following changes to the Orzo Pilaf recipe. Delete 1 tsp salt (not the salt from the pasta cooking water). Stir in 1 lb 10 oz crumbled feta cheese along with the parsley, juice, and rosemary.

● **Rosemary Orzo Amandine.** Make the following changes to the Orzo Pilaf recipe. Soak 2 oz sun-dried tomatoes in 8 oz hot water for 2 hours or more. Drain and coarsely chop tomatoes. Toast slivered almonds (see toasting instructions below). Reduce mushrooms to 8 oz. Stir in 12 oz sliced ripe olives and the rehydrated tomatoes. (To toast almonds: spread in single layer on half-sized bun sheet. Toast in oven at 300°F for 15–20 min or until nuts turn golden and become fragrant. Turn two or three times during toasting to prevent burning.)

HERBED [

Yield: 50 port[

Ingredient

Margarine
Garlic, min[

Cream chee[
softened

Parsley, fres[
minced
Basil, dried
crumble[
Pepper, bla[
Salt

Water, boili[

Fettuccine
Water, boili[
Salt
Vegetable [

Approximat[

Amount/por[

Total Fat 23 [
Sat. Fat 9 g
Protein 5 g

Percent Dail[

Notes

LEMON ORZO

Yield: 50 portions   *Portion:* 4 oz

Ingredient	*Amount*	*Procedure*
Orzo	5 lb	Cook according to directions on p. 561.
Water	5 gal	Drain.
Salt	5 oz	
Chives, finely sliced	3 oz (EP)	Combine chives, lemon, pepper, and oil.
Lemon zest	1 Tbsp	Stir into pasta. Serve hot, above 140°F.
Lemon juice	1 cup	
Pepper, black	1 tsp	
Olive oil	2 cups	

Approximate nutritive values per portion

Calories 250

Amount/portion	%DV	Amount/portion	%DV	Amount/portion	%DV		%DV		%DV
Total Fat 9g	14%	**Cholest.** 0 mg	0%	**Total Carb.** 34 g	11%	**Vitamin A**	1%	Calcium	2%
Sat. Fat 1 g	6%	**Sodium** 290 mg	12%	Fiber 1 g	5%	**Vitamin C**	5%	Iron	10%
Protein 6 g				Sugars 1.6 g					

Percent Daily Values (%DV) are based on a 2000-calorie diet.

Notes

- Potentially hazardous food. *Food Safety Standards:* Hold food for service at an internal temperature above 140°F. Do not mix old product with new. Cool leftover product quickly (within 4 hours) to below 41°F. See p. 105 for cooling procedures. Reheat leftover product quickly (within 2 hours) to 165°F. Reheat product only once; discard if not used.

- Other pasta shapes may be substituted for the orzo.

MACA

Yield: 48
Oven: 35(

Ingredie

Macaro
Water, b
Salt
Vegetab

Margar
Flour, a
Salt
Dry mu
Worces

Milk

Chedda
  sharp

Bread
Margar

Approx

Amount

Total Fa
  Sat. F.
Protein

Percent

Notes

Variatio

CREOLE SPAGHETTI

Yield: 50 portions or 2 pans 12 × 20 × 2 inches   *Portion:* 8 oz
Oven: 325°F   *Bake:* 20–30 minutes

Ingredient	Amount	Procedure
Ground beef	7 lb (AP) (4 lb 10 oz EP)	Cook beef in steam-jacketed or other kettle until meat reaches 155°F. Drain off fat.
Onion, chopped	8 oz	Add onion and green pepper to meat.
Green pepper, chopped	5 oz	Cook until vegetables are tender.
Water	2 qt	Add water, tomatoes, sauce, and puree to meat.
Tomatoes, canned, diced	2 qt	
Tomato puree	2 qt	
Tomato paste	1 qt	
Salt	2 Tbsp	Add seasonings to meat mixture. Stir to blend.
Sugar, granulated	1 Tbsp	Simmer for 15 minutes.
Pepper, cayenne	1 tsp	Remove bay leaves.
Garlic, fresh, minced	2 cloves	
Worcestershire sauce	¼ cup	
Bay leaves	4	
Thyme, ground	1 tsp	
Oregano, crumbled, dried	1 Tbsp	
Spaghetti	2 lb (AP) (6 lb cooked)	Cook spaghetti according to directions on p. 561. Do not overcook.
Water, boiling	3 gal	
Salt	3 oz	
Vegetable oil (optional)	2 Tbsp	
Cheddar cheese, shredded	1 lb 4 oz	Combine hot sauce and hot cooked spaghetti. Pour into two 12 × 20 × 2-inch baking pans, 13 lb 12 oz per pan. Sprinkle cheese over top. Bake at 325°F for 20–30 minutes, 180°F internal temperature.

Approximate nutritive values per portion   **Calories** 273

Amount/portion	%DV	Amount/portion	%DV	Amount/portion	%DV		%DV		%DV
Total Fat 12 g	19%	**Cholest.** 53 mg	18%	**Total Carb.** 23 g	8%	**Vitamin A**	16%	**Calcium**	12%
Sat. Fat 6 g	28%	**Sodium** 767 mg	32%	Fiber 3 g	12%	**Vitamin C**	56%	**Iron**	17%
Protein 18 g				Sugars 3 g					

Percent Daily Values (%DV) are based on a 2000-calorie diet.

Notes   • Potentially hazardous food. *Food Safety Standards:* Hold food for service at an internal temperature above 140°F. Do not mix old product with new. Cool leftover product quickly (within 4 hours) to below 41°F. See p. 105 for cooling procedures. Reheat leftover product quickly (within 2 hours) to 165°F. Reheat product only once; discard if not used.

• 1 oz (½ cup) dehydrated onions, rehydrated in ¾ cup water, may be substituted for fresh onions.

VEGETARIAN SPAGHETTI

Yield: 50 portions or 1 pan 12 × 20 × 4 inches   *Portion:* 8 oz

Ingredient	Amount	Procedure
Margarine, melted Flour, all-purpose	1 lb 12 oz	Combine margarine and flour in steam-jacketed kettle. Cook and stir until smooth. Cook 5 minutes, stirring frequently.
Milk	1 gal	Add milk gradually. Cook over low heat until thickened, stirring constantly. Turn off heat.
Salt American cheese, shredded	1 Tbsp 1 lb 6 oz	Add salt and cheese to sauce. Stir until cheese melts.
Carrots, sliced Green peppers, chopped Celery, chopped Broccoli, cut	1 lb 12 oz 8 oz 1 lb 1 lb	Steam vegetables until tender. Drain. Combine with cheese sauce.
Mushrooms, pieces and stems, canned	3 lb	Add mushrooms to sauce. Keep hot, 180°F.
Spaghetti Water, boiling Salt Vegetable oil	2 lb 12 oz 2¾ gal 3 oz 2 Tbsp	Cook spaghetti according to directions on p. 561. Drain. Combine cooked spaghetti gently with cheese sauce.

Approximate nutritive values per portion   **Calories** 296

Amount/portion	%DV	Amount/portion	%DV	Amount/portion	%DV		%DV		%DV
Total Fat 15 g	22%	**Cholest.** 22 mg	7%	**Total Carb.** 32 g	11%	**Vitamin A**	63%	**Calcium**	24%
Sat. Fat 6 g	28%	**Sodium** 684 mg	29%	Fiber 3 g	10%	**Vitamin C**	23%	**Iron**	13%
Protein 10 g				Sugars 6 g					

Percent Daily Values (%DV) are based on a 2000-calorie diet.

Note   • Potentially hazardous food. *Food Safety Standards:* Hold food for service at an internal temperature above 140°F. Do not mix old product with new. Cool leftover product quickly (within 4 hours) to below 41°F. See p. 105 for cooling procedures. Reheat leftover product quickly (within 2 hours) to 165°F. Reheat product only once; discard if not used.

Variations   • **Garden Pasta.** Substitute 3 lb rotini for spaghetti. Omit green peppers and salt. Reduce mushrooms to 2 lb. Increase milk to 1¼ gal and cheese to 2 lb. Add 4 oz chicken base. Add 1 lb 8 oz cauliflower florets, steamed only until tender-crisp.

• **Spaghetti with Vegetarian Sauce.** Ladle 4 oz of sauce over 4 oz cooked spaghetti. Increase spaghetti to 5 lb AP for 50 servings.

SPAGHETTI WITH CHICKEN SAUCE

Yield: 50 portions   *Portion:* 6 oz sauce + 4 oz spaghetti

Ingredient	Amount	Procedure
Margarine	7 oz	Sauté vegetables in margarine until tender-crisp.
Celery, chopped	1 lb 8 oz	
Onions, chopped	1 lb 8 oz	
Green peppers, chopped	2 oz	
Flour, all-purpose	10 oz	Stir in flour. Cook over low heat for 10 minutes.
Chicken stock (p. 000)	4¾ qt	Add stock to vegetable mixture, stirring constantly. Cook until thickened.
Salt	2 tsp	Season with salt and pepper.
Pepper, white	1 tsp	
Chicken, cooked, cubed	7 lb	Fold in chicken and pimiento. Keep hot, 180°F.
Pimiento, chopped	2 oz	
Spaghetti	5 lb	Cook spaghetti according to directions on p. 561.
Water, boiling	5 gal	Serve 6 oz sauce over 4 oz spaghetti.
Salt	5 oz	
Vegetable oil (optional)	3 Tbsp	

Approximate nutritive values per portion   **Calories 366**

Amount/portion	%DV	Amount/portion	%DV	Amount/portion	%DV		%DV		%DV
Total Fat 10 g	15%	**Cholest.** 54 mg	18%	**Total Carb.** 40 g	13%	**Vitamin A**	4%	**Calcium**	5%
Sat. Fat 2 g	12%	**Sodium** 709 mg	30%	Fiber 2 g	7%	**Vitamin C**	6%	**Iron**	22%
Protein 27 g				Sugars 2 g					

Percent Daily Values (%DV) are based on a 2000-calorie diet.

Notes

- Potentially hazardous food. *Food Safety Standards:* Hold food for service at an internal temperature above 140°F. Do not mix old product with new. Cool leftover product quickly (within 4 hours) to below 41°F. See p. 105 for cooling procedures. Reheat leftover product quickly (within 2 hours) to 165°F. Reheat product only once; discard if not used.

- Sauce may be combined with spaghetti and served as a casserole.

- 3 oz (1½ cups) dehydrated onions, rehydrated in 2¼ cups water, may be substituted for fresh onions.

SPAGHETTI WITH MEAT SAUCE

Yield: 50 portions   *Portion:* 6 oz sauce + 4 oz spaghetti

Ingredient	Amount	Procedure
Ground beef	8 lb AP	Brown beef until internal temperature reaches 155°F. Drain off fat.
Tomato puree (or tomatoes)	5 qt	Add remaining sauce ingredients to cooked beef.
Water	1 qt	Cook slowly, stirring frequently, until thickened, approximately ½ hour.
Tomato sauce	1¾ qt	Remove bay leaves before serving.
Onions, chopped	1 lb	Keep hot, 190°F.
Bay leaves	2	
Thyme, ground	1 tsp	
Garlic, minced	1 clove	
Oregano, dried, crumbled	1 Tbsp	
Basil, dried, crumbled	1 Tbsp	
Sugar, granulated	1 oz (2 Tbsp)	
Worcestershire sauce	¼ cup	
Pepper, cayenne	1 tsp	
Salt	1 oz (1½ Tbsp)	
Spaghetti	5 lb	Cook spaghetti according to directions on p. 561.
Water, boiling	5 gal	Serve 6 oz sauce over 4 oz spaghetti.
Salt	5 oz	
Vegetable oil	3 Tbsp	

Approximate nutritive values per portion   **Calories** 371

Amount/portion	%DV	Amount/portion	%DV	Amount/portion	%DV		%DV		%DV
Total Fat 11 g	17%	**Cholest.** 47 mg	16%	**Total Carb.** 48 g	16%	**Vitamin A**	21%	**Calcium**	6%
Sat. Fat 4 g	20%	**Sodium** 1090 mg	45%	Fiber 4 g	16%	**Vitamin C**	71%	**Iron**	32%
Protein 21 g				Sugars 2 g					

Percent Daily Values (%DV) are based on a 2000-calorie diet.

Notes
- Potentially hazardous food. *Food Safety Standards:* Hold food for service at an internal temperature above 140°F. Do not mix old product with new. Cool leftover product quickly (within 4 hours) to below 41°F. See p. 105 for cooling procedures. Reheat leftover product quickly (within 2 hours) to 165°F. Reheat product only once; discard if not used.
- Grated Parmesan cheese may be sprinkled over top of each serving.
- 2 oz (1 cup) dehydrated onions, rehydrated in 1½ cups water, may be substituted for fresh onions.

SPAGHETTI WITH MEATBALLS

Yield: 50 portions   *Portion:* 3 2-oz or 2 3-oz meatballs + 4 oz spaghetti
Oven: 400°F, 350°F   *Bake:* 15, 30 minutes

Ingredient	Amount	Procedure
MEATBALLS		
Ground beef	15 lb (AP)	Mix meat, bread crumbs, eggs, milk, and seasonings on low
Bread crumbs, dry	8 oz	speed. Do not overmix.
Eggs	16 (1lb 10 oz)	Portion meat with No. 20 dipper onto baking sheets for
Milk	3¾ cups	150 2-oz balls; use No. 12 dipper for 100 3-oz balls.
Salt	3 oz	Brown in 400°F oven for 15–20 minutes, or until internal
		temperature reaches 155°F.
Pepper, black	4 tsp	Remove to 12 × 20 × 4-inch counter pan or roasting pan.
Basil, dried, crumbled	4 Tbsp	
Garlic, minced	6 cloves	
Parsley, fresh chopped (optional)	3 cups	
SAUCE		
Italian Tomato Sauce p. 762	2 gal (1 recipe)	Make sauce according to directions.
		Pour over browned meatballs.
		Cover and cook in 350°F oven for about 30 minutes.
PASTA		
Spaghetti	5 lb	Cook spaghetti according to directions on p. 561.
Water, boiling	5 gal	Serve 2 or 3 meatballs and 5 oz sauce over 4 oz spaghetti.
Salt	5 oz	
Vegetable oil	3 Tbsp	

Approximate nutritive values per portion   **Calories** 550

Amount/portion	%DV	Amount/portion	%DV	Amount/portion	%DV		%DV		%DV
Total Fat 24 g	37%	**Cholest.** 148 mg	49%	**Total Carb.** 50 g	17%	**Vitamin A**	26%	**Calcium**	12%
Sat. Fat 9 g	45%	**Sodium** 1962 mg	82%	Fiber 4 g	15%	**Vitamin C**	43%	**Iron**	43%
Protein 33 g				Sugars 3 g					

Percent Daily Values (%DV) are based on a 2000-calorie diet.

Notes
- Potentially hazardous food. *Food Safety Standards:* Hold food for service at an internal temperature above 140°F. Do not mix old product with new. Cool leftover product quickly (within 4 hours) to below 41°F. See p. 105 for cooling procedures. Reheat leftover product quickly (within 2 hours) to 165°F. Reheat product only once; discard if not used.
- If desired, mix the cooked spaghetti with the tomato sauce. Place in two counter pans, arrange meatballs over top, and bake at 375°F for 20–30 minutes.

HUNGARIAN GOULASH

Yield: 50 portions   *Portion:* 6 oz goulash + 4 oz noodles

Ingredient	Amount	Procedure
Beef, cubed	10 lb (AP)	Brown beef and vegetables in shortening in steam-jacketed
Onion, chopped	1 lb 8 oz	kettle or tilting fry pan.
Garlic, finely chopped	1 clove	
Shortening	8 oz	
Sugar, brown	5 oz	Combine sugar, seasonings, and liquid ingredients.
Mustard, dry	1 Tbsp	Add to browned meat.
Paprika	1 oz (¼ cup)	Cover container and simmer 1–2 hours or until meat is tender.
Pepper, cayenne	⅛ tsp	
Salt	2½ oz	
Worcestershire sauce	1½ cups	
Vinegar, cider	2 Tbsp	
Catsup	1 qt	
Water	3 qt	
Flour, all-purpose	1 lb 4 oz	Mix flour and water until smooth.
Water, cold	1 qt	Add gradually to hot mixture and cook until thickened. Keep hot, 190°F.
Noodles	4 lb 8 oz	Cook noodles according to directions on p. 561.
Water, boiling	4½ gal	Serve 6 oz goulash over 4 oz noodles.
Salt	2 oz	
Vegetable oil	3 Tbsp	

Approximate nutritive values per portion   **Calories** 390

Amount/portion	%DV	Amount/portion	%DV	Amount/portion	%DV		%DV		%DV
Total Fat 11 g	16%	**Cholest.** 90 mg	30%	**Total Carb.** 48 g	16%	**Vitamin A**	8%	**Calcium**	6%
Sat. Fat 3 g	15%	**Sodium** 1093 mg	46%	Fiber 2 g	8%	**Vitamin C**	27%	**Iron**	33%
Protein 24 g				Sugars 4 g					

Percent Daily Values (%DV) are based on a 2000-calorie diet.

Notes
- Potentially hazardous food. *Food Safety Standards:* Hold food for service at an internal temperature above 140°F. Do not mix old product with new. Cool leftover product quickly (within 4 hours) to below 41°F. See p. 105 for cooling procedures. Reheat leftover product quickly (within 2 hours) to 165°F. Reheat product only once; discard if not used.
- Beef may be browned in a roasting pan in 450°F oven.
- 3 lb 8 oz dry rice, cooked, may be substitued for the noodles. See p. 594 for directions for cooking.
- 3 oz (1½ cups) dehydrated onions, rehydrated in 2¼ cups water, may be substituted for fresh onions.

CHICKEN TETRAZZINI

Yield: 50 portions or 2 pans 12 × 20 × 2 inches   *Portion:* 8 oz
Oven: 350°F   *Bake:* 30–40 minutes

Ingredient	Amount	Procedure
Cooked chicken	6 lb	Dice chicken.
Pimiento, chopped	4 oz	Add pimiento and parsley.
Parsley, chopped	2 Tbsp	
Spaghetti	3 lb (AP) (9 lb cooked)	Cook spaghetti according to directions on p. 561 Drain.
Water, boiling	3 gal	
Salt	1 oz (1½ Tbsp)	
Vegetable oil (optional)	2 Tbsp	
Margarine	6 oz	Sauté vegetables in margarine.
Onion, finely chopped	1 lb	
Green peppers, chopped	4 oz	
Mushrooms, sliced	1 lb 8 oz	
Flour, all-purpose	9 oz	Blend flour and seasonings into sautéed vegetables.
Salt	1 tsp	Stir in chicken base. Cook 5 minutes.
Pepper, black	1 tsp	
Chicken base	3 oz	
Water	1 gal	Add water, stirring constantly. Cook until thickened. Combine cooked spaghetti, chicken, and sauce. Scale into two greased 12 × 20 × 2-inch baking pans, 10 lb per pan.
Processed cheese, shredded	1 lb	Sprinkle 8 oz cheese over top of each pan. Bake at 350°F for 30-40 minutes or until internal temperature reaches 180°F and cheese is bubbly.

Approximate nutritive values per portion   **Calories 284**

Amount/portion	%DV	Amount/portion	%DV	Amount/portion	%DV		%DV		%DV
Total Fat 10 g	16%	**Cholest.** 54 mg	18%	**Total Carb.** 25 g	8%	**Vitamin A**	5%	**Calcium**	8%
Sat. Fat 3 g	17%	**Sodium** 500 mg	21%	Fiber 2 g	7%	**Vitamin C**	8%	**Iron**	11%
Protein 22 g				Sugars 2 g					

Percent Daily Values (%DV) are based on a 2000-calorie diet.

Notes

- Potentially hazardous food. *Food Safety Standards:* Hold food for service at an internal temperature above 140°F. Do not mix old product with new. Cool leftover product quickly (within 4 hours) to below 41°F. See p. 105 for cooling procedures. Reheat leftover product quickly (within 2 hours) to 165°F. Reheat product only once; discard if not used.
- 18–20 lb chickens AP will yield approximately 6 lb cooked meat.
- 2 oz (1 cup) dehydrated onions, rehydrated in 1½ cups water, may be substituted for fresh onions.

Variations

- **Tuna Tetrazzini.** Substitute tuna for chicken.
- **Turkey Tetrazzini.** Substitute turkey for chicken.

PASTA, BEEF, AND TOMATO CASSEROLE

Yield: 50 portions   *Portion:* 8 oz

Ingredient	Amount	Procedure
Ground beef	10 lb (AP) (7 lb EP)	Cook meat in kettle until internal temperature reaches 155°F. Stir often to prevent lumps from forming. Drain off fat.
Onions, chopped Celery, chopped	6 oz 3 oz	Add onions and celery to meat. Cook until tender.
Tomatoes, canned, diced Tomato puree Chili sauce Salt Pepper, black Sugar, granulated	1½ gal 2 cups 3 cups 2 oz (3 Tbsp) 1½ tsp 2 Tbsp	Add tomatoes and seasonings to meat mixture. Simmer 45–60 minutes.
Macaroni, elbow Water, boiling Salt Vegetable oil	2 lb 8 oz 2½ gal 2 oz 2 Tbsp	Cook macaroni according to directions on p. 561. Fold into tomato-meat mixture. Keep hot, 180°F.

Approximate nutritive values per portion   **Calories** 313

Amount/portion	%DV	Amount/portion	%DV	Amount/portion	%DV		%DV		%DV
Total Fat 13 g	20%	**Cholest.** 62 mg	21%	**Total Carb.** 27 g	9%	**Vitamin A**	12%	**Calcium**	6%
Sat. Fat 5 g	24%	**Sodium** 982 mg	41%	Fiber 1 g	5%	**Vitamin C**	38%	**Iron**	23%
Protein 22 g				Sugars 6 g					

Percent Daily Values (%DV) are based on a 2000-calorie diet.

Notes

- Potentially hazardous food. *Food Safety Standards:* Hold food for service at an internal temperature above 140°F. Do not mix old product with new. Cool leftover product quickly (within 4 hours) to below 41°F. See p. 105 for cooling procedures. Reheat leftover product quickly (within 2 hours) to 165°F. Reheat product only once; discard if not used.

- Other pasta shapes may be substituted for macaroni.

- ¾ oz (⅓ cup) dehydrated onions, rehydrated in ¾ cup water, may be substituted for fresh onions.

BEEF, PORK, AND NOODLE CASSEROLE

Yield: 50 portions or 2 pans 12 × 20 × 2 inches   *Portion:* 6 oz
Oven: 325°F   *Bake:* 30 minutes

Ingredient	Amount	Procedure
Ground beef	4 lb (AP)	Brown meat and onion until internal temperature
Ground pork	4 lb (AP)	reaches 155°F.
Onion, finely chopped	1 lb	Drain off fat.
Tomato soup	1½ qt	Mix soup, water, and seasonings. Add to meat and simmer
Water	1½ qt	for 10 minutes.
Salt	1 Tbsp	
Pepper, black	1 tsp	
Noodles	1 lb 12 oz	Cook noodles according to directions on p. 561. Drain.
Water, boiling	1¼ gal	
Salt	2 Tbsp	
Vegetable oil (optional)	1 Tbsp	
Cheddar cheese, grated or ground	2 lb	Combine noodles, meat mixture, and cheese. Scale into two 12 × 20 × 2-inch pans, 8 lb 4 oz per pan.
Bread crumbs	1 lb 2 oz	Combine crumbs and margarine.
Margarine, melted	5 oz	Sprinkle over meat and noodle mixture, 10 oz per pan. Bake at 325°F for 30 minutes. Keep hot, 180°F.

Approximate nutritive values per portion   **Calories** 332

Amount/portion	%DV	Amount/portion	%DV	Amount/portion	%DV		%DV		%DV
Total Fat 18 g	**28%**	**Cholest.** 77 mg	**26%**	**Total Carb.** 21 g	**7%**	**Vitamin A**	**9%**	**Calcium**	**20%**
Sat. Fat 8 g	**40%**	**Sodium** 581 mg	**24%**	Fiber 1 g	**2%**	**Vitamin C**	**14%**	**Iron**	**17%**
Protein 20 g				Sugars 0 g					

Percent Daily Values (%DV) are based on a 2000-calorie diet.

Notes
- Potentially hazardous food. *Food Safety Standards:* Hold food for service at an internal temperature above 140°F. Do not mix old product with new. Cool leftover product quickly (within 4 hours) to below 41°F. See p. 105 for cooling procedures. Reheat leftover product quickly (within 2 hours) to 165°F. Reheat product only once; discard if not used.
- 2 oz (1 cup) dehydrated onions, rehydrated in 1½ cups water, may be substituted for fresh onions.

BEEF ON NOODLES

Yield: 50 portions   *Portion:* 6 oz meat and sauce + 4 oz noodles

Ingredient	Amount	Procedure
Beef, cubed	15 lb (AP) (10 lb EP)	Brown beef in steam-jacketed or other kettle.
Onions, chopped Celery, chopped	2 lb 8 oz 1 lb 8 oz	Add onions and celery to meat. Sauté until vegetables are tender.
Water Pepper, black Worcestershire sauce	2 qt 1 Tbsp ½ cup	Add water and seasonings to meat-vegetable mixture. Simmer until beef is tender.
Flour, all-purpose Water Beef base	12 oz 1½ qt 5 oz	Make a smooth paste of flour, water, and beef base. Add to meat mixture to make a gravy. Cook until thickened. Keep hot, 180°F.
Noodles Water, boiling Salt Vegetable oil	4 lb (AP) (12 lb cooked) 4 gal 4 oz 2 Tbsp	Cook noodles according to directions on p. 561. Drain. Serve 6 oz beef and sauce over 4 oz cooked noodles.

Approximate nutritive values per portion   **Calories** 381

Amount/portion	%DV	Amount/portion	%DV	Amount/portion	%DV		%DV		%DV
Total Fat 11 g	16%	**Cholest.** 122 mg	41%	**Total Carb.** 34 g	11%	**Vitamin A**	1%	**Calcium**	4%
Sat. Fat 4 g	18%	**Sodium** 237 mg	10%	Fiber 2 g	7%	**Vitamin C**	11%	**Iron**	36%
Protein 35 g				Sugars 2 g					

Percent Daily Values (%DV) are based on a 2000-calorie diet.

Notes
- Potentially hazardous food. *Food Safety Standards:* Hold food for service at an internal temperature above 140°F. Do not mix old product with new. Cool leftover product quickly (within 4 hours) to below 41°F. See p. 105 for cooling procedures. Reheat leftover product quickly (within 2 hours) to 165°F. Reheat product only once; discard if not used.
- 5 oz (2½ cups) dehydrated onions, rehydrated in 3¼ cups water, may be substituted for fresh onions.

RICE RECIPES

COOKING RICE

Yield: 50 portions   *Portion:* 4 oz

Ingredient	Amount	Procedure
Rice, converted	3 lb 8 oz	Cook in steamer, oven, or a stockpot or steam-jacketed
Salt	2 Tbsp	kettle, according to directions that follow.
Margarine or vegetable oil	2 Tbsp	
Water, hot	4¼ qt	

STEAMER

Weigh rice into a 12 × 20 × 2-inch counter pan. Add salt and margarine.
Pour boiling water over rice. Stir.
Steam uncovered for 30–40 minutes.
Fluff with fork.

OVEN

Weigh rice into a 12 × 20 × 2-inch counter pan. Add salt and margarine.
Pour boiling water over rice. Stir.
Cover pans tightly with aluminum foil.
Bake at 350°F for 1 hour.
Remove from oven and let stand covered for 5 minutes.
Fluff with fork.

STOCKPOT OR STEAM-JACKETED KETTLE (BOILED RICE)

Bring water to a boil in steam-jacketed kettle or other large kettle.
Add salt, rice, and margarine. Stir. Cover tightly.
Cook on low heat until rice is tender and all water is absorbed, about 15–20 minutes.
Remove from heat and let stand covered 5–10 minutes.
Fluff with fork.

Approximate nutritive values per portion   **Calories** 118

Amount/portion	%DV	Amount/portion	%DV	Amount/portion	%DV		%DV		%DV
Total Fat 1 g	1%	**Cholest.** 0 mg	0%	**Total Carb.** 25 g	8%	**Vitamin A**	0%	**Calcium**	0%
Sat. Fat 0 g	0%	**Sodium** 265 mg	11%	Fiber 0 g	0%	**Vitamin C**	0%	**Iron**	7%
Protein 2 g				Sugars 0 g					

Percent Daily Values (%DV) are based on a 2000-calorie diet.

Notes
- If using regular white rice in place of converted rice, the cooking time may need to be reduced.
- For brown rice, increase cooking time to 50–60 minutes for steamed rice, to 1½ hours for baked rice, and to 40–50 minutes for boiled rice.
- For buttered rice, add 5 oz butter or margarine. Add to dry rice in counter pan. Add salt and hot water.
- 1 lb uncooked rice yields 2 qt cooked rice.
- Suggested spices to use with rice: allspice, basil, coriander, curry powder, ginger, marjoram, mint, oregano, rosemary, tarragon, thyme.

GINGER RICE

Yield: 50 portions   *Portion:* 4 oz
Oven: 350°F   *Bake:* 45 minutes

Ingredient	Amount	Procedure
Margarine	½ cup	Sauté vegetables and cinnamon in oil until vegetables begin to soften, 10–15 minutes.
Oil	½ cup	
Onion, diced	1 lb (EP)	
Garlic, minced	4 oz (EP)	
Fresh ginger, peeled and minced	4 oz (EP)	
Carrots, peeled and diced	8 oz (EP)	
Cinnamon	1 tsp	
Rice, converted	3 lb	Add uncooked rice to vegetables and stir over heat until completely coated with margarine and oil.
Salt	1 tsp	Place rice-vegetable mixture in a 12 × 20 × 4-inch counter pan.
Pepper, black	¼ tsp	Add seasonings and chicken stock. Stir to combine. Cover tightly with aluminum foil.
Chicken stock (p. 790)	1 gal	
		Bake at 350°F for 45 minutes; or steam uncovered 30 minutes. Stir before serving.

Approximate nutritive values per portion   **Calories** 160

Amount/portion	%DV	Amount/portion	%DV	Amount/portion	%DV		%DV		%DV
Total Fat 4.7 g	7%	**Cholest.** 0 mg	0%	**Total Carb.** 24.5 g	8%	**Vitamin A**	15%	**Calcium**	2%
Sat. Fat .8 g	4%	**Sodium** 320 mg	13%	Fiber .8 g	3%	**Vitamin C**	3%	**Iron**	8%
Protein 3.8 g				Sugars .7 g					

Percent Daily Values (%DV) are based on a 2000-calorie diet.

Note • Potentially hazardous food. *Food Safety Standards:* Hold food for service at an internal temperature above 140°F. Do not mix old product with new. Cool leftover product quickly (within 4 hours) to below 41°F. See p. 105 for cooling procedures. Reheat leftover product quickly (within 2 hours) to 165°F. Reheat product only once; discard if not used.

GINGER RICE STIR-FRY

Yield: 50 portions   *Portion:* 3 oz
Griddle: 300°F

Ingredient	Amount	Procedure

Rice, converted
Water
	3 lb 4 oz
	3⅓ cups
		Place 1 lb 10 oz rice and 1⅔ cups water in each of two
		    12 × 4 × 10-inch pans.
		Steam uncovered for 15 minutes or until all of the liquid
		    has been absorbed. Rice will be firm.

Soy sauce Sugar, granulated Garlic powder Pepper, white Ginger, ground	1 cup 1 Tbsp 1 tsp 1 tsp 1 tsp	Mix together soy sauce and spices. Set aside.

Eggs
Green onions,
    chopped
	1 lb 12 oz
	1 lb 8 oz
		Grease griddle lightly with cooking oil. Preheat to 300°F.
		Place eggs on griddle. Spread thin, scramble, and chop
		    into small pieces.
		Add chopped onions and continue to cook 3–4 minutes
		    until onions are tender.
		Add steamed rice and blend well.
		Drizzle soy sauce mixture over rice.
		Cook, turning frequently until mixture reaches 160°F.
		Place in 12 × 10 × 4-inch pan. Serve 3 oz with No. 12 dipper.

Approximate nutritive values per portion   **Calories** 141

Amount/portion	%DV	Amount/portion	%DV	Amount/portion	%DV		%DV		%DV
Total Fat 2 g	3%	**Cholest.** 68 mg	23%	**Total Carb.** 26 g	9%	**Vitamin A**	3%	**Calcium**	2%
Sat. Fat 1 g	3%	**Sodium** 353 mg	15%	Fiber 1 g	2%	**Vitamin C**	0%	**Iron**	8%
Protein 4 g				Sugars 0 g					

Percent Daily Values (%DV) are based on a 2000-calorie diet.

Notes
- Potentially hazardous food. *Food Safety Standards:* Hold food for service at an internal temperature above 140°F. Do not mix old product with new. Cool leftover product quickly (within 4 hours) to below 41°F. See p. 105 for cooling procedures. Reheat leftover product quickly (within 2 hours) to 165°F. Reheat product only once; discard if not used.
- If griddle is small, prepare in two batches. Use ½ cup soy sauce, 14 oz eggs, and 12 oz green onions for each pan of cooked rice.

FRIED RICE

Yield: 50 portions   *Portion:* 3 oz

Ingredient	Amount	Procedure
Rice	2 lb 8 oz	Cook rice according to directions on p. 594.
Water	3 qt	Do not overcook. Let cool.
Salt	2 tsp	
Peas, frozen	1 lb 8 oz	Cook peas and drain. Set aside.
Eggs	6 (11 oz)	Break eggs into bowl and stir until yolks and whites are
Salt	2 tsp	mixed. Add salt.
Vegetable oil	2 Tbsp	Cook eggs in oil, stirring to break into small pieces. Set aside.
Onions, chopped	1 lb	Sauté onions and carrots in oil until tender.
Carrots, shredded	8 oz	Add rice and cook until heated.
Vegetable oil	¾ cup	
Soy sauce	1 cup	Add soy sauce to rice mixture, stirring to mix evenly. Stir in peas and eggs. Serve at once.

Approximate nutritive values per portion   **Calories** 147

Amount/portion	%DV	Amount/portion	%DV	Amount/portion	%DV		%DV		%DV
Total Fat 5 g	7%	**Cholest.** 27 mg	9%	**Total Carb.** 22 g	7%	**Vitamin A**	14%	**Calcium**	2%
Sat. Fat 1 g	6%	**Sodium** 513 mg	21%	Fiber 1 g	3%	**Vitamin C**	4%	**Iron**	6%
Protein 3 g				Sugars 1 g					

Percent Daily Values (%DV) are based on a 2000-calorie diet.

Note
- Potentially hazardous food. *Food Safety Standards:* Hold food for service at an internal temperature above 140°F. Do not mix old product with new. Cool leftover product quickly (within 4 hours) to below 41°F. See p. 105 for cooling procedures. Reheat leftover product quickly (within 2 hours) to 165°F. Reheat product only once; discard if not used.

Variations
- **Confetti Rice.** Delete peas, eggs, carrots, and soy sauce. Cook rice until almost done. Heat oil in fry pan. Sauté for 2 minutes 12 oz sliced green peppers, 12 oz sliced mushrooms, 4 oz chopped scallions. Stir vegetables into cooked rice. Add 8 oz chopped pimientos.
- **Fried Rice with Almonds.** Cook 3 lb rice according to directions on p. 594. Sauté 4 oz chopped onions and 4 oz chopped green peppers in 1 cup vegetable oil. Add cooked rice, 1 Tbsp pepper, 1 tsp garlic salt, ½ cup soy sauce, and 2 lb slivered almonds. Add salt if needed. Bake until heated.
- **Fried Rice with Ham.** Delete peas. Reduce chopped onions to 4 oz. Increase carrots to 12 oz. Add 4 oz sliced green onions, 12 oz sliced celery, and 1 lb chopped ham.
- **Plain Fried Rice.** Heat a small amount of vegetable oil in tilting fry pan. Sauté 12 oz sliced celery and 4 oz onion until tender-crisp. Stir 10 lb cooked, cold rice into vegetable. Reduce heat and cover. Cook for 15–20 minutes. Pour 1 cup eggs over surface of hot rice, stir to mix. Cover and cook for 5 minutes. Stir in 1 cup soy sauce, 12 oz finely shredded carrots, and 6 oz thinly sliced green onion. Cover for 5 minutes. Take up in serving pans. Recipe portion, 4 oz.
- **Pork Fried Rice.** Delete peas. Add 4 lb cubed, cooked pork. Fry 1 lb bacon. Use bacon fat for sautéing vegetables and rice. Crumble bacon and add.
- **Rice and Black-Eyed Peas.** Cook 1 lb rice according to directions on p. 594. Cook 3 lb 8 oz frozen black-eyed peas according to directions on p. 852. Sauté 8 oz onion in ¼ cup vegetable oil. Add hot rice and black-eyed peas. Stir to combine. Add 1 tsp ground allspice, 1 Tbsp dried whole thyme, and 2 tsp coarse ground black pepper. Heat until very hot. Stir in 4 lb fresh tomatoes (peeled, seeded, and diced), 2 cups chopped fresh parsley, and 1 lb shredded cheddar cheese.
- **Shrimp Fried Rice.** Add 1 lb 8 oz cooked shrimp.

ASIAN FRIED RICE

Yield: 50 portions   *Portion*: 4 oz

Ingredient	Amount	Procedure
Jasmine rice	3 lb 8 oz	Cook rice according to directions on p. 594.
Water	4¼ qt	Chill rice and reserve for later step.
Margarine	2 Tbsp	
Salt	2 Tbsp	
Butter (not salted)	4 oz	Heat butter in tilting fry pan.
Onion, chopped (sweet)	8 oz	Add onion, ginger, garlic, and toasted and ground cumin. Sauté until fragrant, about 4 minutes.
Ginger root, minced	2½ oz	
Garlic, minced	2 Tbsp	
Whole cumin, toasted then ground (see Note)	1½ Tbsp	
Catsup	½ cup	Add catsup, fish sauce, sugar, and salt to sautéed vegetables. Simmer until the sauce is slightly thickened, about 5 minutes.
Fish sauce	2 Tbsp	
Sugar, granulated	2 tsp	Add rice reserved from earlier step. Stir-fry rice until thoroughly mixed and hot.
Salt, kosher	1½ tsp	
Green onions, thinly sliced	4 oz	Stir in green onions and mix well. Take up in 12 × 10 × 4-inch pans.

Approximate nutritive values per portion   **Calories** 135

Amount/portion	%DV	Amount/portion	%DV	Amount/portion	%DV		%DV		%DV
Total Fat 2.6 g	4%	**Cholest.** 4.7 mg	2%	**Total Carb.** 26.5 g	9%	**Vitamin A**	2%	**Calcium**	2%
Sat. Fat 1.2 g	6%	**Sodium** 410 mg	17%	Fiber .2 g	1%	**Vitamin C**	2%	**Iron**	7%
Protein 1.9 g				Sugars .6 g					

Percent Daily Values (%DV) are based on a 2000-calorie diet.

Notes
- Potentially hazardous food. *Food Safety Standards*: Hold food for service at an internal temperature above 140°F. Do not mix old product with new. Cool leftover product quickly (within 2 hours) to 70°F and then (within an additional 4 hours) 41°F. See p. 105 for cooling procedures. Reheat leftover product quickly (within 2 hours) to 165°F. Reheat product only once; discard if not used.
- See p. 782 for spice toasting instructions.

HOPPING JOHN

Yield: 50 portions   *Portion:* 4 oz

Ingredient	Amount	Procedure
Rice, converted	1 lb	Cook rice according to directions on p. 594. Rice should yield 3 lb cooked rice. Save cooked rice for later step.
Vegetable oil Onions, chopped Garlic, minced	¼ cup 1 lb 6 oz (EP) 2 oz (EP)	Heat oil in steam-jacketed kettle. Add onions and garlic and cook until transparent.
Black-eye peas, frozen or fresh Water Salt Vegetable base Parsley, dried Thyme, dried Liquid smoke Pepper, black Red pepper sauce	4 lb 5½ qt 1 Tbsp 1½ oz 3 Tbsp 1 tsp ½ tsp ½ tsp ¼ tsp	Add peas, water, and seasonings to vegetables. Bring to a boil, reduce heat, and simmer until peas are tender, 40–50 minutes. If peas become dry, add a small amount of water. Most of the water should be evaporated when peas are done.
Red wine vinegar Green onions, sliced	¾ cup 1 oz (EP)	Stir vinegar and rice into black-eye peas. Take up into 12 × 10 × 4-inch pan. Garnish with sliced green onions.

Approximate nutritive values per portion   **Calories** 100

Amount/portion	%DV	Amount/portion	%DV	Amount/portion	%DV		%DV		%DV
Total Fat 1.8 g	3%	**Cholest.** 0 mg	0%	**Total Carb.** 18 g	6%	**Vitamin A**	0%	**Calcium**	2%
Sat. Fat 0.1 g	1%	**Sodium** 264 mg	11%	Fiber 2.2 g	9%	**Vitamin C**	3%	**Iron**	6%
Protein 4 g				Sugars 0.8 g					

Percent Daily Values (%DV) are based on a 2000-calorie diet.

Note
- Potentially hazardous food. *Food Safety Standards:* Hold food for service at an internal temperature above 140°F. Do not mix old product with new. Cool leftover product quickly (within 4 hours) to below 41°F. See p. 105 for cooling procedures. Reheat leftover product quickly (within 2 hours) to 165°F. Reheat product only once; discard if not used.

RISOTTO

Yield: 50 portions   *Portion:* 4 oz

Ingredient	Amount	Procedure

Water
Vegetable base
  (see Notes)
	1 gal
	2 oz
		Mix vegetarian base and water in a steam-jacketed kettle.
		   Bring to boil, then reduce heat to low.
		Cover and keep hot. Reserve broth for later step.

Olive oil Onion, finely chopped Garlic, minced	3 oz 12 oz (EP) 1 oz	Heat oil to 350°F in fry pan. Sauté onion and garlic in oil until translucent, about 4 minutes.
Arborio rice	2 lb 4 oz	Add rice to onion. Stir and cook 3 minutes.

Water	1½ cups	Add water and cook until water evaporates.
		Reduce temperature and add broth slowly, 2 cups at a time
		   (broth reserved from earlier step). Stir very often but not
		   constantly. Do not let the pan become dry before adding
		   more broth.
		Cook and stir rice until rice is *al dente* and mixture is creamy
		   (about 20 minutes).
		Turn off heat.

Butter Parmesan cheese, freshly shredded	12 oz 12 oz	Add butter and Parmesan cheese. Stir until incorporated.
		Pan Risotto into 12 × 10 × 2-inch pans. Cover. Hold for service above 140°F. Prepare close to serving time.

Approximate nutritive values per portion   **Calories** 190

Amount/portion	%DV	Amount/portion	%DV	Amount/portion	%DV		%DV		%DV
Total Fat 9 g	14%	**Cholest.** 21 mg	7%	**Total Carb.** 22 g	7%	Vitamin A	8%	Calcium	7%
Sat. Fat 4.8 g	24%	**Sodium** 190 mg	8%	Fiber 0.6 g	2%	Vitamin C	1%	Iron	1%
Protein 4 g				Sugars 0.4 g					

Percent Daily Values (%DV) are based on a 2000-calorie diet.

Notes

- Potentially hazardous food. *Food Safety Standards:* Hold food for service at an internal temperature above 140°F. Do not mix old product with new. Cool leftover product quickly (within 4 hours) to below 41°F. See p. 105 for cooling procedures. Reheat leftover product quickly (within 2 hours) to 165°F. Reheat product only once; discard if not used.

- When extending recipe, add broth to rice at a rate of 1 cup per pound of rice.

- Parmesan cheese can be stirred into the rice after it has been put in a pan. Add Parmesan cheese in a ratio of 1 oz cheese to 1 lb rice mixture.

- Risotto should be soft and creamy, but not runny. The product will stiffen during holding and may require additional small amounts of hot broth.

- Chicken broth may be substituted for vegetarian broth. Adjust salt as necessary.

TOMATO CILANTRO RICE

Yield: 50 portions   *Portion:* 4 oz

Ingredient	Amount	Procedure
Vegetable oil	½ cup	Heat oil to 350°F in tilting or other large fry pan.
Rice, converted Garlic, minced Onion, chopped	3 lb 2 Tbsp 1 lb (EP)	Add rice and vegetables to hot oil. Stir and cook until rice is slightly browned.
Diced tomatoes (canned) Vegetable base (see Notes) Water	2 lb 5 oz 3 qt	Add tomatoes, base, and water to rice mixture. Bring to boil. Reduce heat to low. Cover and simmer until rice is tender and liquids are absorbed, 25–30 minutes.
Fresh cilantro leaves, minced	1 oz	Fold cilantro into rice mixture. Take up into serving pans.

Approximate nutritive values per portion   **Calories** 135

Amount/portion	%DV	Amount/portion	%DV	Amount/portion	%DV		%DV		%DV
Total Fat 2.5 g	4%	**Cholest.** 0 mg	0%	**Total Carb.** 25 g	8%	**Vitamin A**	3%	**Calcium**	2%
Sat. Fat 0.3 g	1%	**Sodium** 220 mg	9%	Fiber 0.7 g	3%	**Vitamin C**	6%	**Iron**	3%
Protein 2 g				Sugars 1 g					

Percent Daily Values (%DV) are based on a 2000-calorie diet.

Notes
- Potentially hazardous food. *Food Safety Standards:* Hold food for service at an internal temperature above 140°F. Do not mix old product with new. Cool leftover product quickly (within 4 hours) to below 41°F. See p. 105 for cooling procedures. Reheat leftover product quickly (within 2 hours) to 165°F. Reheat product only once; discard if not used.
- Chicken base can be substituted for the vegetable base. Adjust salt if necessary.

VEGETABLE PAELLA

Yield: 50 portions *Portion:* 8 oz

Ingredient	*Amount*	*Procedure*
Vegetable oil	½ cup	Lightly coat bottom of fry pan with oil. Heat to 375°F.
Onion, diced ½ inch	1 lb 12 oz	Add onion and garlic. Sauté 3 minutes or until garlic is
Garlic, fresh, minced	1 oz	fragrant.
Water	3½ qt	Add water and vegetable base. Bring to a boil.
Vegetable base (see Notes)	4 oz	
Rice	3 lb	Stir in rice and spices. Cover. Reduce heat and simmer
Salt	3½ tsp	15 minutes.
Paprika	1 Tbsp	
Turmeric	1 Tbsp	
Pepper, black, ground	4 tsp	
Red bell pepper, cut in strips	1 lb 8 oz	Add peppers and vegetables. Cover and cook 10 minutes or until liquid is absorbed and end-point temperature is 170°F.
Yellow bell pepper, cut in strips	1 lb 8 oz	Scale into 12 × 10 × 4-inch pans.
Green peas, frozen	1 lb 12 oz	
Artichoke quarters, canned, drained	4 lb	
Kidney beans, canned, drained	2 lb	
Baby corn, frozen	2 lb	

Approximate nutritive values per portion   **Calories** 202

Amount/portion	%DV	Amount/portion	%DV	Amount/portion	%DV		%DV		%DV
Total Fat 5 g	8%	**Cholest.** 0 mg	0%	**Total Carb.** 36 g	12%	**Vitamin A**	2%	**Calcium**	2%
Sat. Fat 1 g	2%	**Sodium** 341 mg	14%	Fiber 4 g	15%	**Vitamin C**	111%	**Iron**	10%
Protein 5 g				Sugars 1 g					

Percent Daily Values (%DV) are based on a 2000-calorie diet.

Notes
- Potentially hazardous food. *Food Safety Standards:* Hold food for service at an internal temperature above 140°F. Do not mix old product with new. Cool leftover product quickly (within 4 hours) to below 41°F. See p. 105 for cooling procedures. Reheat leftover product quickly (within 2 hours) to 165°F. Reheat product only once; discard if not used.
- Recipe is calculated for an entree portion. For 50 4-oz side dish portions, reduce the amount of ingredients by one-half.
- Chicken base may be substituted for the vegetable base in the recipe. Adjust salt if base is highly salted.

RICE PILAF

Yield: 50 portions or 1 pan 12 × 20 × 4 inches   *Portion:* 4 oz
Oven: 350°F   *Bake:* 45 minutes

Ingredient	Amount	Procedure
Onions, finely chopped	1 lb 8 oz	Sauté onion in margarine until it begins to soften. Do not brown.
Margarine, melted	8 oz	
Rice, converted	3 lb	Add uncooked rice to onions and stir over heat until completely coated with the margarine.
Salt	1 tsp	Place rice in a 12 × 20 × 4-inch counter pan.
Pepper, white	¼ tsp	Add seasonings and Chicken Stock.
Bay leaf	1	Stir to combine.
Chicken Stock (p. 790)	1 gal	Cover tightly with aluminum foil. Bake at 350°F for 45 minutes; or steam uncovered for 30 minutes. Stir before serving.

Approximate nutritive values per portion   **Calories** 151

Amount/portion	%DV	Amount/portion	%DV	Amount/portion	%DV		%DV		%DV
Total Fat 4 g	7%	**Cholest.** 0 mg	0%	**Total Carb.** 24 g	8%	**Vitamin A**	1%	Calcium	2%
Sat. Fat 1 g	4%	**Sodium** 336 mg	14%	Fiber 1 g	3%	**Vitamin C**	1%	Iron	6%
Protein 4 g				Sugars 0 g					

Percent Daily Values (%DV) are based on a 2000-calorie diet.

Notes
- Potentially hazardous food. *Food Safety Standards:* Hold food for service at an internal temperature above 140°F. Do not mix old product with new. Cool leftover product quickly (within 4 hours) to below 41°F. See p. 105 for cooling procedures. Reheat leftover product quickly (within 2 hours) to 165°F. Reheat product only once; discard if not used.
- Suggested additions for variety: chopped green pepper, pimiento, tomato, or nuts; sliced mushrooms or water chestnuts; ground or diced ham.
- 3 oz (1½ cups) dehydrated onions, rehydrated in 2¼ cups water, may be substituted for fresh onions.

Variations
- **Curried Rice.** Add 3 Tbsp curry powder.
- **Mexican Rice.** Sauté 14 oz chopped onion, 10 oz chopped green pepper, and 3 oz chopped celery in ⅓ cup vegetable oil. Add uncooked rice and stir 2–3 minutes until grains are coated with oil. Stir in 3 Tbsp salt, 2 oz chili powder, and 1 tsp garlic powder. Place in a 12 × 20 × 4-inch counter pan. Pour a mixture of 2½ qt tomato juice and 1¾ qt Beef Stock (p. 791) over rice. Steam 25–35 minutes. Stir before serving.
- **Mushroom Rice Pilaf.** Reduce rice to 1 lb 12 oz and Chicken Stock to 2½ qt. Delete bay leaf and add 1½ tsp thyme. Add 2 lb mushroom pieces and stems and 1 lb 8 oz chopped celery.
- **Toasted Herb Rice.** Measure uncooked rice into 12 × 2 × 4-inch pan. Bake at 325°F for 20 minutes or until rice is toasted and golden. Proceed as for Rice Pilaf. Add 2 Tbsp crumbled dried basil or tarragon.

BASMATI RICE AND LENTIL PILAF

Yield: 50 portions   *Portion*: 4 oz

Ingredient	Amount	Procedure
Lentils (dried)	10 oz	Combine water and lentils in a steam jacketed kettle.
Water	3 qt	Bring to a boil, then reduce heat and simmer for 25–30 minutes until just tender. Drain and save for later step.
Margarine	10 oz	Heat margarine in tilting fry pan.
Onions, chopped	1 lb EP	Sauté onions and rice until onions are fragrant and rice
Basmati rice	3 lb	begins to turn brown. Stir often.
Water	1½ qt	Add water, base, and spices to rice mixture. Stir to blend.
Vegetable base (see Note)	2 oz	Bring to a boil. Reduce heat, cover, and simmer 10 minutes. Add cooked lentils reserved from earlier step. Continue
Salt (see Note)	4 tsp	cooking until rice is tender and water is absorbed,
Black pepper	½ tsp	approximately 10–15 minutes.
Cumin, ground	2½ Tbsp	Scale into 12 × 10 × 2-inch pans (6 lb/pan).
Tumeric	1 tsp	
Lemon juice, fresh	2½ Tbsp	

Approximate nutritive values per portion   **Calories** 165

Amount/portion	%DV	Amount/portion	%DV	Amount/portion	%DV		%DV		%DV
Total Fat 5.7 g	9%	**Cholest.** 0 mg	0%	**Total Carb.** 2.5 g	8%	**Vitamin A**	4%	**Calcium**	2%
Sat. Fat 1 g	5%	**Sodium** 350 mg	15%	Fiber 3.2 g	13%	**Vitamin C**	2%	**Iron**	6%
Protein 3.8 g				Sugars .6 g					

Percent Daily Values (%DV) are based on a 2000-calorie diet.

Notes

- Potentially hazardous food. *Food Safety Standards*: Hold food for service at an internal temperature above 140°F. Do not mix old product with new. Cool leftover product quickly (within 2 hours) to 70°F and then (within an additional 4 hours) to 41°F. See p. 105 for cooling procedures. Reheat leftover product quickly (within 2 hours) to 165°F. Reheat product only once; discard if not used.

- Double the recipe for an 8 oz entree-size portion.

- Chicken base can be substituted for vegetable base. Taste before adding salt. Salt concentration varies among brands of bases.

SICILIAN RICE AND VEGETABLES

Yield: 48 portions   *Portion:* 8 oz
Oven: 325°F   *Bake:* 10–15 minutes

Ingredient	Amount	Procedure
Brown rice	1 lb 4 oz	Cook rice according to directions on p. 594. Should yield
Water	1½ qt	4 lb 8 oz cooked rice. Save for later step.
Salt	1 Tbsp	
Onions, sliced	1 lb	Sauté onions and garlic in oil until tender.
Garlic, minced	4 cloves	
Olive oil	½ cup	
Oregano, dried, crumbled	2 Tbsp	Add seasonings and brown sugar to onion. Mix well.
Sweet basil, dried, crumbled	3 Tbsp	
Salt	2 Tbsp (3 oz)	
Pepper, black	1 tsp	
Bay leaves	4	
Parsley, fresh, chopped	2 cups	
Sugar, brown	¼ cup (1½ oz)	
Tomato juice	3 qt (2 46-oz cans)	Combine tomatoes, paste, and juice with spices and onion. Reduce heat and simmer uncovered for 15–20 minutes.
Tomato paste	12 oz	Remove bay leaves.
Diced tomatoes, canned	1½ qt	Add cooked rice from first step.
Broccoli stalks, sliced	2 lb	Add broccoli, carrots, and mushrooms to sauce and cook for 5 minutes.
Carrots, julienne cut	1 lb	
Mushrooms, fresh, sliced	1 lb 8 oz	
Squash, yellow summer	3 lb	Quarter squash lengthwise, then slice ½ inch thick. Carefully stir squash into sauce. Cook for 5 minutes. Scale into four 12 × 10 × 2-inch pans, 6 lb per pan.
Squash, zucchini	3 lb	
Mozzarella cheese, shredded	2 lb	Sprinkle 8 oz cheese over each pan. Place in 325°F oven to melt cheese.

Approximate nutritive values per portion   **Calories** 170

Amount/portion	%DV	Amount/portion	%DV	Amount/portion	%DV		%DV		%DV
Total Fat 7 g	11%	**Cholest.** 15 mg	5%	**Total Carb.** 22 g	7%	Vitamin A	43%	Calcium	15%
Sat. Fat 3 g	15%	**Sodium** 808 mg	34%	Fiber 2 g	7%	Vitamin C	64%	Iron	11%
Protein 7 g				Sugars 4 g					

Percent Daily Values (%DV) are based on a 2000-calorie diet.

Notes

- Potentially hazardous food. *Food Safety Standards:* Hold food for service at an internal temperature above 140°F. Do not mix old product with new. Cool leftover product quickly (within 4 hours) to below 41°F. See p. 105 for cooling procedures. Reheat leftover product quickly (within 2 hours) to 165°F. Reheat product only once; discard if not used.

- Mixture may be scaled into pan after the raw vegetables are added, then baked at 350°F for approximately 30 minutes. Sprinkle with cheese the last 2–3 minutes of baking.

- Other vegetables may be substituted, or the ratio of vegetables changed, for those listed in the recipe. Use a total of 10 lb 8 oz vegetables for 50 servings. Suggested substitutes: eggplant, Japanese eggplant, celery, onion, frozen green beans, peas.

BARLEY CASSEROLE

Yield: 50 portions or 1 pan 12 × 20 × 2 inches   *Portion:* 4 oz
Oven: 350°F   *Bake:* 1½ hours

Ingredient	Amount	Procedure
Margarine	6 oz	Sauté barley and vegetables in margarine.
Pearl barley	2 lb 6 oz	
Onions, chopped	1 lb 4 oz	
Mushroom pieces and stems, canned	1 lb 11 oz	
Chicken Stock (p. 790)	3½ qt	Add chicken stock to barley mixture. Pour into a 12 × 20 × 2-inch counter pan. Bake at 350°F for 1½ hours. Serve with No. 10 dipper.

Approximate nutritive values per portion   **Calories** 119

Amount/portion	%DV	Amount/portion	%DV	Amount/portion	%DV		%DV		%DV
Total Fat 3 g	5%	**Cholest.** 0 mg	0%	**Total Carb.** 19 g	6%	**Vitamin A**	1%	**Calcium**	1%
Sat. Fat 1 g	4%	**Sodium** 317 mg	13%	Fiber 4 g	16%	**Vitamin C**	1%	**Iron**	4%
Protein 4 g				Sugars 1 g					

Percent Daily Values (%DV) are based on a 2000-calorie diet.

Notes
- Potentially hazardous food. *Food Safety Standards:* Hold food for service at an internal temperature above 140°F. Do not mix old product with new. Cool leftover product quickly (within 4 hours) to below 41°F. See p. 105 for cooling procedures. Reheat leftover product quickly (within 2 hours) to 165°F. Reheat product only once; discard if not used.
- 2½ oz (1¼ cups) dehydrated onions, rehydrated in 2 cups water, may be substituted for fresh onions.

Variations
- **Chicken Barley Casserole.** Increase chicken stock to 1 gal. Stir in 6 lb cooked cubed chicken. Turkey may be substituted for chicken.
- **Mediterranean Barley Pilaf.** Add 1 lb 8 oz golden raisins, 1 lb chopped pecans, and 1 tsp dried thyme.

BARLEY AND VEGETABLE MEDLEY

Yield: 50 portions   *Portion:* 4 oz

Ingredient	Amount	Procedure
Olive oil	3 oz	Heat oil to 350°F in tilting fry pan or steam-jacketed kettle.
Onions, sliced into thin half-rings	1 lb 8 oz (EP)	Sauté onions, garlic, and barley in hot oil until onions and barley are golden brown, about 5 minutes.
Garlic, minced	1 Tbsp	
Barley	1 lb	
Water	1¼ qt	Mix base with part of the water. Add water and base to vegetable-barley mixture.
Vegetable base (see Notes)	1 oz	Heat to boiling. Reduce heat and simmer until barley is almost tender, about 30 minutes. Stir occasionally.
Carrots, peeled, sliced	1 lb 6 oz (EP)	Add carrots, cauliflower, broccoli, herbs, and spices to barley mixture.
Cauliflower, small florets	10 oz (EP)	Cover and simmer for 12–15 minutes.
Broccoli, small florets	8 oz (EP)	
Basil leaves, dried	1 Tbsp	
Thyme leaves, dried	1 Tbsp	
Salt	2 tsp	
Pepper, black	½ tsp	
Tomatoes, diced (fresh)	2 lb (EP)	Add tomatoes, squash, green peppers, and peas to barley mixture. Cook 5–10 minutes until vegetables are tender.
Zucchini squash, sliced	1 lb (EP)	
Green peppers, diced	10 oz (EP)	
Peas, frozen	1 lb 8 oz	

Approximate nutritive values per portion   **Calories** 80

Amount/portion	%DV	Amount/portion	%DV	Amount/portion	%DV		%DV		%DV
Total Fat 2 g	3%	**Cholest.** 0 mg	0%	**Total Carb.** 13 g	4%	**Vitamin A**	38%	**Calcium**	2%
Sat. Fat 0.3 g	1%	**Sodium** 198 mg	8%	Fiber 3.4 g	14%	**Vitamin C**	26%	**Iron**	4%
Protein 2.6 g				Sugars 3 g					

Percent Daily Values (%DV) are based on a 2000-calorie diet.

Notes
- Potentially hazardous food. *Food Safety Standards:* Hold food for service at an internal temperature above 140°F. Do not mix old product with new. Cool leftover product quickly (within 4 hours) to below 41°F. See p. 105 for cooling procedures. Reheat leftover product quickly (within 2 hours) to 165°F. Reheat product only once; discard if not used.
- Chicken base can be substituted for the vegetable base. Adjust salt if necessary.

BARLEY TOMATO RISOTTO

Yield: 40 portions   *Portion:* 4 oz

Ingredient	Amount	Procedure
Butter Onions, chopped Garlic, minced	3 oz 6 oz (EP) 1 oz (EP)	Heat butter in tilting or other large fry pan. Sauté onions and garlic until barely tender.
Barley	1 lb 4 oz	Add barley. Cook 2–3 minutes until barley is coated with butter and slightly toasted.
Water	10 oz	Add water. Slowly cook uncovered until water is absorbed, 15–30 minutes.
Water Chicken base	1 gal 4 oz	Mix base with water to make a stock. Heat stock and keep hot. Add stock (1 qt at a time) to barley mixture while cooking over medium heat. Add additional stock only after liquid from previous addition is absorbed. Stir very often but not necessarily continuously throughout the liquid-adding step.
Whipping cream Tomatoes, fresh, diced ¼ inch Parmesan cheese, freshly shredded	8 oz 2 lb (EP) 6 oz	Stir in cream, tomatoes, and cheese. Stir until cheese melts.
Green onions, sliced thin Flat leaf parsley, chopped	4 oz (EP) 1 oz	Stir green onions and parsley into barley mixture.

Approximate nutritive values per portion

Calories 95

Amount/portion	%DV	Amount/portion	%DV	Amount/portion	%DV		%DV		%DV
Total Fat 4.5 g	7%	**Cholest.** 13 mg	4%	**Total Carb.** 11 g	4%	**Vitamin A**	6%	**Calcium**	4%
Sat. Fat 2.5 g	13%	**Sodium** 266 mg	15%	Fiber 2 g	8%	**Vitamin C**	8%	**Iron**	3%
Protein 3 g				Sugars 0.8 g					

Percent Daily Values (%DV) are based on a 2000-calorie diet.

Notes
- Potentially hazardous food. *Food Safety Standards:* Hold food for service at an internal temperature above 140°F. Do not mix old product with new. Cool leftover product quickly (within 4 hours) to below 41°F. See p. 105 for cooling procedures. Reheat leftover product quickly (within 2 hours) to 165°F. Reheat product only once; discard if not used.
- Vegetable base can be substituted for chicken base. Adjust salt as necessary.

Variation
- **Southwest Barley Risotto.** Substitute vegetable base for chicken base. Add 1 oz fresh squeezed lime juice to vegetable base. Stir in 1½ oz chopped canned jalapeño peppers. Substitute ½ oz fresh chopped cilantro for the parsley.

GINGER VEGETABLES AND BARLEY

Yield: 50 entree portions   *Portion*: 8 oz (for 4 oz side portions, decrease recipe by one half)

Ingredient	Amount	Procedure
Water	3¾ gal	Bring water to boil in steam-jacketed kettle.
Salt	5 oz (7½ Tbsp)	Stir barley into boiling water. Cook about 50 minutes or until
Barley	5 lb	tender. Stir occasionally.
		Drain and save for later step. (Yield 13 lb 12 oz cooked barley.)
Olive oil	6 oz	Heat oil to 325°F in a tilting fry pan.
Ginger root, minced	4 oz EP	Add ginger and carrots to oil. Sauté until fragrant,
Carrots, ½-inch dice	3 lb 6 oz EP	approximately 1 minute.
Red bell peppers, ½-inch dice	1 lb EP	Add peppers. Sauté to heat through, approximately 1 minute.
Yellow bell peppers, ½-inch dice	1 lb EP	
Green bell peppers, ½-inch dice	12 oz EP	
Corn, defrosted (whole kernel frozen)	2 lb 12 oz	Add corn, peas, and seasonings. Sauté for 1 minute. Add 13 lb 12 oz cooked barley (reserved from earlier step) to bell pepper mixture.
Peas, defrosted (frozen)	3 lb	Heat through to 165–170°F.
Salt	2¼ oz (3½ Tbsp)	
Black pepper		
Sliced green onions	1 lb 5 oz	Stir in onions and mint.
Mint leaves, finely chopped (see Note)	3 oz	Take up in 12 × 10 × 2-inch pans. Cover.

Approximate nutritive values per portion   **Calories** 250

Amount/portion	%DV	Amount/portion	%DV	Amount/portion	%DV		%DV		%DV
Total Fat 4.4 g	7%	**Cholest.** 0 mg	0%	**Total Carb.** 48 g	16%	**Vitamin A**	177%	**Calcium**	4%
Sat. Fat .6 g	3%	**Sodium** 1620 mg	68%	Fiber 10 g	40%	**Vitamin C**	48%	**Iron**	10%
Protein 7.6 g				Sugars 6.1 g					

Percent Daily Values (%DV) are based on a 2000-calorie diet.

Notes
- Potentially hazardous food. *Food Safety Standards*: Hold food for service at an internal temperature above 140°F. Do not mix old product with new. Cool leftover product quickly (within 2 hours) to 70°F and then (within an additional 4 hours) to 41°F. See p. 105 for cooling procedures. Reheat leftover product quickly (within 2 hours) to 165°F. Reheat product only once; discard if not used.
- 1 oz dried crushed mint leaves may be substituted for fresh mint.

SPICY BARLEY WITH CONFETTI VEGETABLES

Yield: 50 entree portions   *Portions:* 8 oz (for 4 oz side portions, decrease recipe by one half)

Ingredient	Amount	Procedure
Water	3¾ gal	Bring water to boil in steam-jacketed kettle.
Salt	5 oz (7½ Tbsp)	Stir barley into boiling water. Cook about 50 minutes or until
Barley	5 lb	tender. Stir occasionally.
		Drain and save for later step. (Yield 13 lb 12 oz cooked barley.)
Olive oil	1 lb 5 oz	Heat oil and base to 350°F in a tilting fry pan.
Vegetable base (see Note)	2 oz	
Carrots, fine julienne cut	2 lb 4 oz EP	Add carrots to oil and sauté 1 minute.
Roasted red peppers, chopped (p. 854)	4 lb 4 oz	Add roasted peppers and seasonings to carrots. Sauté just until peppers are soft.
Salt (see Note)	2 oz	Add 13 lb 12 oz cooked barley reserved from earlier step.
Black pepper	3 Tbsp	Heat through, 165–170°F.
Red pepper flakes	5 tsp	
Green onions, sliced	3 lb 4 oz EP	Add onions, peas, and thyme.
Peas, thawed	3 lb	Mix gently to distribute.
Dried thyme leaves	4 Tbsp	Take up in 12 × 10 × 2-inch pans. Cover.

Approximate nutritive values per portion   **Calories 285**

Amount/portion	%DV	Amount/portion	%DV	Amount/portion	%DV		%DV		%DV
Total Fat 13 g	20%	**Cholest.** 0 mg	0%	**Total Carb.** 38 g	13%	**Vitamin A**	52%	**Calcium**	4%
Sat. Fat 1.7 g	9%	**Sodium** 1450 mg	60%	Fiber 8.7 g	35%	**Vitamin C**	129%	**Iron**	11%
Protein 6 g				Sugars 2.4 g					

Percent Daily Values (%DV) are based on a 2000-calorie diet.

Notes
- Potentially hazardous food. *Food Safety Standards:* Hold food for service at an internal temperature above 140°F. Do not mix old product with new. Cool leftover product quickly (within 2 hours) to 70°F and then within an additional 4 hours to 41°F. See p. 105 for cooling procedures. Reheat leftover product quickly (within 2 hours) to 165°F. Reheat product only once; discard if not used.
- Chicken base can be substituted for vegetable base. Taste before adding salt. Salt concentration varies among brands of bases.

BARLEY AND VEGETABLES

Yield: 50 entree portions   *Portion:* 8 oz (for 4 oz side portions, decrease recipe by one half)

Ingredient	Amount	Procedure
Water Salt Barley	2½ gal 3 oz (4⅔ Tbsp) 3 lb 6 oz	Bring water to boil in steam-jacketed kettle. Stir barley into boiling water. Cook about 50 minutes or until tender. Stir occasionally. Drain and save for later step. (Yield 9 lb 6 oz cooked barley.)
Olive oil Ranchero sauce concentrate (see Note)	2¾ cup 2½ oz	Heat oil and Ranchero concentrate to 350°F in a tilting fry pan.
Pecan halves	1 lb 5 oz	Add pecans to hot oil and cook until golden brown.
Carrot coins (fresh) Red bell peppers, ½-inch dice Yellow bell peppers, ½-inch dice Green bell peppers, ½-inch dice Celery, ¼-inch slice Salt Black pepper	2 lb EP 2 lb EP 2 lb EP 2 lb EP 2 lb EP 1½ oz (2⅓ Tbsp) 1 Tbsp	Add vegetables and seasoning to pecans and sauté until tender crisp, approximately 5 minutes.
Garlic, minced Black beans (drained, rinsed) Mint leaves, finely chopped (fresh)	4 oz EP 5 lb 4 oz EP 1 oz	Add garlic, beans, and 9 lb 6 oz cooked barley reserved from earlier step. Heat until hot, 165–170°F. Add mint and toss lightly to distribute. Take up in 12 × 10 × 2-inch pans. Cover.

Approximate nutritive values per portion   **Calories** 350

Amount/portion	%DV	Amount/portion	%DV	Amount/portion	%DV		%DV		%DV
Total Fat 20 g Sat. Fat 2.5 g **Protein** 8 g	31% 13%	**Cholest.** 0 mg **Sodium** 1150 mg	0% 48%	**Total Carb.** 38 g Fiber 9.4 g Sugars 5.1 g	13% 38%	**Vitamin A** **Vitamin C**	97% 69%	**Calcium** **Iron**	6% 13%

Percent Daily Values (%DV) are based on a 2000-calorie diet.

Notes
- Potentially hazardous food. *Food Safety Standards:* Hold food for service at an internal temperature above 140°F. Do not mix old product with new. Cool leftover product quickly (within 2 hours) to 70°F and then (within an additional 4 hours) to 41°F. See p. 105 for cooling procedures. Reheat leftover product quickly (within 2 hours) to 165°F. Reheat product only once; discard if not used.
- Ranchero sauce concentrate, a highly spiced paste, is a Minor's® product manufactured by Nestle® and available through most distributors.

BULGUR WITH CRANBERRIES AND TOASTED ALMONDS

Yield: 50 entree portions   *Portion:* 4 oz

Ingredient	Amount	Procedure
Margarine	6 oz	Heat margarine in steam-jacketed kettle.
Leeks, sliced (white and light green parts only)	1 lb 8 oz EP	Sauté leeks until tender, approximately 12 minutes.
Vegetable base (see Note)	5 oz	Add base and water to sautéed leeks. Bring to a boil.
Water	6 qt	
Bulgur	2 lb 10 oz	Stir in bulgur and seasonings.
Salt (see Note)	1 oz (1½ Tbsp)	Cover and reduce heat to simmer for about 20 minutes or
Black pepper	1 tsp	until bulgur is tender and liquid has been absorbed.
Dried cranberries	8 oz	Add dried cranberries. Cover and let stand for 15 minutes.
Toasted slivered almonds	12 oz	Stir in toasted almonds. Fluff with a fork before serving.

Approximate nutritive values per portion   **Calories** 130

Amount/portion	%DV	Amount/portion	%DV	Amount/portion	%DV		%DV		%DV
Total Fat 5.2 g	8%	**Cholest.** 0 mg	0%	**Total Carb.** 19 g	6%	**Vitamin A**	5%	**Calcium**	3%
Sat. Fat .7 g	3%	**Sodium** 390 mg	16%	Fiber 3.9 g	16%	**Vitamin C**	2%	**Iron**	6%
Protein 3.6 g				Sugars 2.8 g					

Percent Daily Values (%DV) are based on a 2000-calorie diet.

Notes
- Potentially hazardous food. *Food Safety Standards:* Hold food for service at an internal temperature above 140°F. Do not mix old product with new. Cool leftover product quickly (within 2 hours) to 70°F and then (within an additional 4 hours) to 41°F. See p. 105 for cooling procedures. Reheat leftover product quickly (within 2 hours) to 165°F. Reheat product only once; discard if not used.

- Chicken base can be substituted for vegetable base. Taste before adding salt. Salt concentration varies among brands of bases.

VEGETABLE COUSCOUS

Yield: 50 portions   *Portion:* 4 oz

Ingredient	Amount	Procedure
Margarine, melted	8 oz	Sauté vegetables in margarine in steam-jacketed kettle or stock
Zucchini, julienne	1 lb 12 oz	pot until tender-crisp.
Green onions, sliced	4 oz	
Carrots, julienne	12 oz	
Chicken base	3 oz	Mix chicken base with water. Add to vegetables. Bring to a
Water	3 qt	rolling boil.
Couscous, quick cooking	3 lb	Add couscous to vegetables and stir. Cover. Turn off heat. Let stand 5 minutes. Stir to fluff. Place in 12 × 10 × 4-inch pans. Cover tightly and keep hot.

Approximate nutritive values per portion   **Calories** 145

Amount/portion	%DV	Amount/portion	%DV	Amount/portion	%DV		%DV		%DV
Total Fat 4 g	6%	**Cholest.** 0 mg	0%	**Total Carb.** 23 g	8%	**Vitamin A**	18%	**Calcium**	1%
Sat. Fat 1 g	4%	**Sodium** 368 mg	15%	Fiber 4 g	17%	**Vitamin C**	1%	**Iron**	2%
Protein 4 g				Sugars 0 g					

Percent Daily Values (%DV) are based on a 2000-calorie diet.

Notes
- Potentially hazardous food. *Food Safety Standards:* Hold food for service at an internal temperature above 140°F. Do not mix old product with new. Cool leftover product quickly (within 4 hours) to below 41°F. See p. 105 for cooling procedures. Reheat leftover product quickly (within 2 hours) to 165°F. Reheat product only once; discard if not used.
- Vegetable base may be substituted for chicken base. Add salt if vegetable base is unsalted.
- Salt may need to be added if the chicken base is low in salt.

ISRAELI COUSCOUS WITH OLIVES AND ROASTED TOMATOES

Yield: 50 portions   *Portion:* 8 oz
Oven: 250°F (conventional); 200°F (convection).

Ingredient	Amount	Procedure
Cherry tomatoes	10 lb 8 oz	Place tomatoes in single layer on silicone paper lined 18 × 26 × 1-inch pans. Roast at 250°F (conventional oven); 200°F (convection oven) for about 1 hour or until slightly shriveled. Hold warm to combine with cooked couscous in a later step.
Garlic cloves	4 oz	Mix garlic with oil and stir to coat.
Olive oil	1½ Tbsp	Place tomatoes and garlic on silicone-paper-lined pans.
Cherry tomatoes	2 lb	Roast tomatoes and garlic at 250°F (conventional oven); 200°F (convection oven) for about 1 hour or until slightly shriveled. Cool slightly before processing into a tomato-garlic dressing in the next step.
Olive oil	2 cups	Make tomato-garlic dressing by putting cooled tomatoes and garlic, oil, liquids, and seasonings in a food processor.
Warm water	2 cups	Process until smooth. (Process in batches if using a small food processor.)
Lemon juice (fresh)	3 Tbsp	Save tomato-garlic dressing for later step.
Salt	2½ Tbsp	
Black pepper	1 Tbsp	
Vegetable base (see Note)	4 oz	
Water	3½ gal	Bring water and salt to a rolling boil in steam-jacketed or other kettle.
Salt	1 oz (1½ Tbsp)	Add couscous while stirring.
Middle Eastern couscous (see Note)	4 lb 6 oz	Return water to boil. Reduce heat and simmer 10–12 min until couscous is al dente. Stir occasionally. Drain and hold warm. (Yield 13 lb cooked couscous.)
Olive oil	4 oz	To 13 lb cooked couscous add oil, olive pesto, herbs, and spices.
Kalamata Olive Pesto (see Note)	10 oz	Add tomato-garlic dressing reserved from earlier step.
Parsley, minced	2½ oz EP	Add roasted tomatoes reserved from earlier step.
Thyme (dried leaves)	1 Tbsp	Toss gently to distribute ingredients.
Salt	2 tsp	Take up in 12 × 10 × 2-inch pans. Serve warm.
Black pepper	1 Tbsp	

Approximate nutritive values per portion   **Calories** 260

Amount/portion	%DV	Amount/portion	%DV	Amount/portion	%DV		%DV		%DV
Total Fat 11.7 g	18%	**Cholest.** 1.2 mg	0%	**Total Carb.** 33.8 g	11%	**Vitamin A**	18%	**Calcium**	4%
Sat. Fat 1.7 g	8%	**Sodium** 817 mg	34%	Fiber 3.2 g	%	**Vitamin C**	36%	**Iron**	6%
Protein 6 g				Sugars 3 g					

Percent Daily Values (%DV) are based on a 2000-calorie diet.

Notes
- Potentially hazardous food. *Food Safety Standards:* Hold food for service at an internal temperature above 140°F. Do not mix old product with new. Cool leftover product quickly (within 2 hours) to 70°F and then (within an additional 4 hours) to 41°F. See p. 105 for cooling procedures. Reheat leftover product quickly (within 2 hours) to 165°F. Reheat product only once; discard if not used.
- Kalamata Olive Pesto is a Minor's® product manufactured by Nestle® and available through most distributors. If unavailable, substitute sliced or pureed kalamata olives. The amount of salt may need to be adjusted when substituting kalamata olives for the pesto.
- The salt concentration of vegetable bases varies by brand. Add less salt if a highly salted base is used.

RED PEPPER COUSCOUS

Yield: 50 portions   *Portion:* 4 oz

Ingredient	Amount	Procedure
Olive oil	½ cup	Sauté vegetables in oil in a steam-jacketed kettle or stockpot until tender-crisp.
Green onion, sliced	1 lb	
Red bell pepper, julienne	6 oz	
Garlic, minced	2 Tbsp	
Paprika	2 Tbsp	Add paprika and cook for 1 minute.
Water	3 qt	Add water, juice, tomato paste, pimiento, and spices to sautéed vegetable mixture.
Lemon juice	¼ cup	Bring to a rolling boil.
Tomato paste	8 oz	
Pimiento, chopped	8 oz	
Red pepper, crushed	½ tsp	
Salt	1 Tbsp	
Couscous, quick cooking	3 lb	Add couscous to mixture and stir. Cover, turn off heat. Let stand 5 minutes. Stir to fluff.

Approximate nutritive values per portion   **Calories** 141

Amount/portion	%DV	Amount/portion	%DV	Amount/portion	%DV		%DV		%DV
Total Fat 3 g	4%	**Cholest.** 0 mg	0%	**Total Carb.** 26 g	9%	**Vitamin A**	23%	**Calcium**	2%
Sat. Fat 1 g	2%	**Sodium** 141 mg	6%	Fiber 5 g	20%	**Vitamin C**	129%	**Iron**	61%
Protein 4 g				Sugars 0 g					

Percent Daily Values (%DV) are based on a 2000-calorie diet.

Note   • Potentially hazardous food. *Food Safety Standards:* Hold food for service at an internal temperature above 140°F. Do not mix old product with new. Cool leftover product quickly (within 4 hours) to below 41°F. See p. 105 for cooling procedures. Reheat leftover product quickly (within 2 hours) to 165°F. Reheat product only once; discard if not used.

QUINOA PILAF

Yield: 50 portions   *Portion:* 4 oz

Ingredient	Amount	Procedure
Olive oil	1 cup	Sauté vegetables in olive oil until tender-crisp.
Green onion, sliced	1 lb 8 oz	
Celery	1 lb	
Mushrooms, fresh, sliced	1 lb 8 oz	
Garlic	1 Tbsp	
Chicken base	3 oz	Mix chicken base with water. Add to vegetables. Bring to a rolling boil.
Water	3½ qt	
Quinoa, rinsed and drained	3 lb 8 oz	Add quinoa to vegetables and stir. Cover and reduce heat to low. Simmer until all liquid is absorbed and the grains are translucent, 10–15 minutes.

Approximate nutritive values per portion **Calories** 166

Amount/portion	%DV	Amount/portion	%DV	Amount/portion	%DV		%DV		%DV
Total Fat 6 g	10%	**Cholest.** 0 mg	0%	**Total Carb.** 24 g	8%	**Vitamin A**	6%	**Calcium**	3%
Sat. Fat 1 g	4%	**Sodium** 18 mg	1%	Fiber 2 g	9%	**Vitamin C**	6%	**Iron**	18%
Protein 5 g				Sugars 1 g					

Percent Daily Values (%DV) are based on a 2000-calorie diet.

Notes

- Potentially hazardous food. *Food Safety Standards:* Hold food for service at an internal temperature above 140°F. Do not mix old product with new. Cool leftover product quickly (within 4 hours) to below 41°F. See p. 105 for cooling procedures. Reheat leftover product quickly (within 2 hours) to 165°F. Reheat product only once; discard if not used.
- A vegetable base may be substituted for the chicken base. If vegetable base is lightly salted or unsalted, add salt.
- Quinoa must be rinsed to remove the bitter coating on the grain.
- Quinoa may be toasted prior to cooking. Toast as for a dry spice, p. 782.

SOFT POLENTA

Yield: 50 portions   *Portion:* 4 oz

Ingredient	*Amount*	*Procedure*
Oil	5 oz	Heat oil in steam-jacketed kettle.
Onion, chopped	12 oz EP	Sauté onion and garlic until fragrant.
Garlic, minced	1 Tbsp EP	
Water	4½ qt	Add water and base to sautéed onions and garlic. Stir to dissolve base.
Vegetable base (see Note)	4 oz	Bring water mixture to a boil. Turn off heat.
Cornmeal	1 lb 12 oz	Pour cornmeal in a very slow stream into water. Stir constantly with a wire whip while pouring to prevent lumping. Turn heat on medium low and simmer until mixture thickens (becomes the consistency of thick pudding).
Milk (see Note)	2 qt	Stir in milk, chives, salt, and pepper.
Chives (dried)	3 Tbsp	Take up in 12 × 10 × 4-inch pans.
Salt	1½ tsp	Cover. Serve hot.
Black pepper	1 tsp	If polenta thickens during service, stir in warm milk to return to the correct consistency.

Approximate nutritive values per portion   **Calories** 105

Amount/portion	%DV	Amount/portion	%DV	Amount/portion	%DV		%DV		%DV
Total Fat 4.2 g	6%	**Cholest.** 5 mg	2%	**Total Carb.** 4.5 g	5%	**Vitamin A**	1%	**Calcium**	1%
Sat. Fat 1.1 g	5%	**Sodium** 268 mg	11%	Fiber 1.2 g	5%	**Vitamin C**	1%	**Iron**	1%
Protein 2.7 g				Sugars 1.9 g					

Percent Daily Values (%DV) are based on a 2000-calorie diet.

Notes

- Potentially hazardous food. *Food Safety Standards:* Hold food for service at an internal temperature above 140°F. Do not mix old product with new. Cool leftover product quickly (within 2 hours) to 70°F and then (within an additional 4 hours) to 41°F. See p. 105 for cooling procedures. Reheat leftover product quickly (within 2 hours) to 165°F. Reheat product only once; discard if not used.
- Serve as an accompaniment or under meat or grilled/roasted vegetable entrees.
- Chicken base can be substituted for vegetable base. Taste before adding salt. Salt concentration varies among brands of bases.
- For a vegan polenta, substitute soy milk for cow's milk.

PARMESAN POLENTA

Yield: 48 portions   *Portion:* 2 triangles

Ingredient	Amount	Procedure
Butter Onions, finely chopped Garlic, minced	1 lb 2 lb 10 oz (EP) 2 oz (EP)	Sauté onions and garlic in butter, using stock pot or steam-jacketed kettle.
Water Vegetable base (see Notes)	3½ gal 12 oz	Add water and base to onion mixture. Bring to a boil and turn off heat.
Cornmeal	5 lb 8 oz	Stir into water very quickly, blending with a wire whisk. Turn heat on medium low and simmer 10 minutes stirring often to prevent sticking and burning. Turn off heat.
Parmesan cheese, shredded Milk Chives, freeze dried Salt Pepper, black	1 lb 2 cups ¼ oz 1 oz 1 Tbsp	Stir cheese, milk, chives, and seasonings into cornmeal mixture. Scale 7 lb 3 oz into four 12 × 20 × 2-inch pans that have been oiled or sprayed with a food release spray. Chill at or below 40°F until polenta sets up, at least 6 hours.
		Cut pan 4 × 3. Cut each square in half diagonally to make two triangles.
Vegetable oil	1 cup	Lightly coat grill with oil. Heat to 325°–350°F. Cook polenta until lightly browned on both sides, approximately 180°F. Turn only once during cooking.

Approximate nutritive values per portion   **Calories 365**

Amount/portion	%DV	Amount/portion	%DV	Amount/portion	%DV		%DV		%DV
Total Fat 16 g	25%	**Cholest.** 31 mg	10%	**Total Carb.** 46 g	15%	**Vitamin A**	21%	**Calcium**	12%
Sat. Fat 7 g	37%	**Sodium** 785 mg	33%	Fiber 4 g	18%	**Vitamin C**	5%	**Iron**	13%
Protein 8.3 g				Sugars 2.5 g					

Percent Daily Values (%DV) are based on a 2000-calorie diet.

Notes
- Potentially hazardous food. *Food Safety Standards:* Hold food for service at an internal temperature above 140°F. Do not mix old product with new. Cool leftover product quickly (within 4 hours) to below 41°F. See p. 105 for cooling procedures. Reheat leftover product quickly (within 2 hours) to 165°F. Reheat product only once, discard if not used.
- Chicken base may be substituted for vegetable base. Adjust salt as necessary.

Variation
- **Polenta Cups with Marinara Sauce.** Mix 1 lb 13 oz yellow cornmeal with 5¼ qt water in a steam-jacketed kettle. Cook, stirring constantly, until mixture thickens and boils. Reduce heat, cover, and simmer, stirring occasionally, for about 10 minutes. Turn off heat and stir in 1 lb 8 oz Parmesan cheese. Portion 3 oz (use no. 12 disher) into greased muffin tins. Bake at 375°F until brown and crusty (approximately 60 minutes). Cool in pans. Remove carefully after loosening sides with a sharp-pointed knife. Reheat in low oven to 165°F. Serve one per serving with marinara sauce.

BEAN AND TOFU RECIPES

BEAN RAGOUT OVER GRILLED PARMESAN POLENTA

Yield: 50 portions   *Portion:* 4 oz ragout + 2 polenta triangles

Ingredient	*Amount*	*Procedure*
Vegetable oil Onions, chopped Garlic, minced	⅓ cup 1 lb 12 oz (EP) 2 oz (EP)	Sauté onions and garlic in oil, using stock pot or steam-jacketed kettle.

Green chilies
  (canned) diced
Red bell peppers,
  ¼-inch dice
	6 oz
	
	1 lb 4 oz (EP)
		Add chilies and peppers to sautéed vegetables. Cook
		  1–2 minutes.

Chili powder Cumin, ground Oregano leaves, dried Pepper, black	2 oz 2 Tbsp 2 tsp 1 tsp	Add spices and continue to cook 1–2 minutes.

Diced tomatoes (canned)
Zucchini, coarsely
  chopped
Pinto beans, drained
  and rinsed (canned)
Black beans, drained
  and rinsed (canned)
	4 lb 12 oz
	1 lb 12 oz (EP)
	
	2 lb 12 oz (EP)
	
	2 lb 12 oz (EP)
		Add vegetables and beans to sautéed mixture. Bring to
		  a boil.
		Reduce heat and simmer until zucchini is tender-crisp.

Parmesan Polenta (p. 626)		Serve 4 oz ragout over two polenta triangles. Garnish with fresh shredded Parmesan cheese if desired.

Approximate nutritive values per portion of Bean Ragout   **Calories** 80

Amount/portion	%DV	Amount/portion	%DV	Amount/portion	%DV		%DV		%DV
Total Fat 2 g	**3%**	**Cholest.** 0 mg	**0%**	**Total Carb.** 12 g	**4%**	Vitamin A	12%	Calcium	3%
Sat. Fat 0.2 g	**1%**	**Sodium** 348 mg	**15%**	Fiber 4 g	**17%**	Vitamin C	55%	Iron	7%
Protein 3.6 g				Sugars 0.8 g					

Percent Daily Values (%DV) are based on a 2000-calorie diet.

Note
- Potentially hazardous food. *Food Safety Standards:* Hold food for service at an internal temperature above 140°F. Do not mix old product with new. Cool leftover product quickly (within 4 hours) to below 41°F. See p. 105 for cooling procedures. Reheat leftover product quickly (within 2 hours) to 165°F. Reheat product only once; discard if not used.

Variation
- **Bean Ragout on Pasta.** Cook 5–6 lb pasta according to directions on p. 561. Prepare 1½ recipes of Bean Ragout. Serve 6 oz Bean Ragout over 4 oz pasta.

BLACK BEANS AND COUSCOUS

Yield: 50 entrees or 100 accompaniment portions   *Portion:* 8 oz (entree) or 4 oz (accompaniment)

Ingredient	Amount	Procedure
Margarine	1 lb	Sauté onion and bell pepper just until soft, using a stock pot or steam-jacketed kettle.
Green onions, cut into 1-inch lengths	12 oz (EP)	
Red bell peppers, ¼-inch dice	3 lb 8 oz (EP)	
Black beans, drained and rinsed (canned)	5 lb 8 oz (EP)	Stir beans, water, vegetable base, and lime juice into sautéd vegetables.
Water	4¾ qt	Bring to a rolling boil.
Vegetable base (see Notes)	5 oz	
Lime juice, fresh	1½ cup	
Instant couscous	5 lb	Add couscous to liquid and stir. Turn off heat. Cover and let stand 5 minutes. Stir to fluff.
Parsley, chopped	1 oz	Sprinkle parsley over each pan or stir into couscous.

Approximate nutritive values per portion (Entree Portion)   **Calories** 295

Amount/portion	%DV	Amount/portion	%DV	Amount/portion	%DV		%DV		%DV
Total Fat 8 g	12%	**Cholest.** 0 mg	0%	**Total Carb.** 45 g	15%	**Vitamin A**	29%	**Calcium**	4%
Sat. Fat 1.5 g	7%	**Sodium** 393 mg	16%	Fiber 5.8 g	23%	**Vitamin C**	108%	**Iron**	10%
Protein 9 g				Sugars 0.8 g					

Percent Daily Values (%DV) are based on a 2000-calorie diet.

Notes
- Potentially hazardous food. *Food Safety Standards:* Hold food for service at an internal temperature above 140°F. Do not mix old product with new. Cool leftover product quickly (within 4 hours) to below 41°F. See p. 105 for cooling procedures. Reheat leftover product quickly (within 2 hours) to 165°F. Reheat product only once; discard if not used.
- Chicken base can be substituted for vegetable base. Depending on the base used, salt may need to be added.

CUBAN BLACK BEANS AND RICE

Yield: 50 entrees or 100 accompaniment portions   *Portion:* 8 oz (entree) or 4 oz (accompaniment)

Ingredient	Amount	Procedure
Black beans (canned)	6 lb 4 oz	Drain beans and reserve juice. Save both beans and juice for later step.
Vegetable oil	6 oz	Heat oil to 350°F in tilting or other large fry pan.
Onions, chopped Garlic, minced Rice, converted	1 lb 8 oz (EP) 1 oz (EP) 4 lb	Add vegetables and rice to hot oil. Stir and cook until rice is browned.
Black bean juice plus water	4¾ qt	Weigh bean juice reserved from earlier step. Add enough water to equal the required volume. Pour juice-water mixture over the rice.
Chipotle base (see Notes) Vegetable base (see Notes) Oregano leaves, dried Cumin, ground Cilantro, dried	4 oz 4 oz 1 tsp 1 Tbsp 1 Tbsp	Stir bases and spices into rice mixture. Reduce heat and simmer covered for 15 minutes.
Green bell peppers, cut in 1-inch-long thin strips Red bell peppers, cut in 1-inch-long thin strips Yellow bell peppers, cut in 1-inch-long thin strips	1 lb (EP) 12 oz (EP) 12 oz (EP)	Stir peppers and beans reserved from earlier step to the rice mixture. Cover and simmer 10–15 minutes or until liquid is absorbed and rice is tender.

Take up in 12 × 10 × 2-inch pans. Cover.

Approximate nutritive values per portion (Entree Portion)   **Calories** 235

Amount/portion	%DV	Amount/portion	%DV	Amount/portion	%DV		%DV		%DV
Total Fat 4.5 g	7%	**Cholest.** 0 mg	0%	**Total Carb.** 41 g	14%	**Vitamin A**	7%	**Calcium**	5%
Sat. Fat 0 4 g	2%	**Sodium** 603 mg	25%	Fiber 4 g	17%	**Vitamin C**	58%	**Iron**	11%
Protein 6.3 g				Sugars 1.4 g					

Percent Daily Values (%DV) are based on a 2000-calorie diet.

Notes
- Potentially hazardous food. *Food Safety Standards:* Hold food for service at an internal temperature above 140°F. Do not mix old product with new. Cool leftover product quickly (within 4 hours) to below 41°F. See p. 105 for cooling procedures. Reheat leftover product quickly (within 2 hours) to 165°F. Reheat product only once; discard if not used.
- A frozen pepper blend can be substituted for the bell peppers.
- Chipotle base is available commercially. Chipotles are dried jalapeño peppers that have been slow roasted to give them a smokey flavor. To use dried chipotles, cover with boiling water and let set for 30 minutes. Remove from the water and drain. Using a sharp knife, split chipotles open and remove seeds before chopping. If using canned chipotles, drain and chop.
- Chicken base can be substituted for the vegetable base. Adjust salt as required.

BLACK BEANS AND HAM ON RICE

Yield: 50 portions   *Portion:* 6 oz ham and beans + 4 oz rice

Ingredient	Amount	Procedure
Black turtle beans Water	3 lb 1¼ gal	Rinse beans with cold running water. Discard any stones and other foreign material or shriveled beans. Add water and bring to a boil. Boil for 2 minutes. Cover. Turn off heat and allow to stand for 1 hour.
Cumin, ground Hot pepper sauce Pepper, black Thyme, crumbled, dried Oregano, crumbled, dried	1 Tbsp 1½ tsp 1 tsp 1 Tbsp 1 Tbsp	Add seasonings to beans. Simmer until almost tender, about 45 minutes. If beans become too thick, add some tomato juice drained from the diced tomatoes used in a later step.
Onions, chopped Garlic cloves, minced Salt Ham, diced	12 oz 3 1½ oz 2 lb 8 oz	Add to beans. Simmer until beans are tender, about 30 minutes. Add tomato juice from later step or a small amount of water if necessary to keep beans from becoming too thick.
Tomatoes, diced, canned Green peppers, ¾-inch chunks	3 lb 8 oz 12 oz	Add tomatoes with juice and peppers. Simmer for 15 minutes.
Rice, converted Water, boiling Salt Vegetable oil	3 lb 8 oz 4½ qt 2 Tbsp 2 Tbsp	Cook rice according to directions on p. 594.
Parsley, fresh, chopped	4 oz	Serve 6 oz ham and beans over 4 oz cooked rice. Garnish plate by sprinkling with 1 Tbsp chopped parsley.

Approximate nutritive values per portion   **Calories** 212

Amount/portion	%DV	Amount/portion	%DV	Amount/portion	%DV		%DV		%DV
Total Fat 3 g	5%	**Cholest.** 13 mg	4%	**Total Carb.** 35 g	12%	**Vitamin A**	3%	**Calcium**	5%
Sat. Fat 1 g	5%	**Sodium** 987 mg	41%	Fiber 2 g	9%	**Vitamin C**	32%	**Iron**	14%
Protein 10 g				Sugars 1 g					

Percent Daily Values (%DV) are based on a 2000-calorie diet.

Notes

- Potentially hazardous food. *Food Safety Standards:* Hold food for service at an internal temperature above 140°F. Do not mix old product with new. Cool leftover product quickly (within 4 hours) to below 41°F. See p. 105 for cooling procedures. Reheat leftover product quickly (within 2 hours) to 165°F. Reheat product only once; discard if not used.
- Anaheim chilies may be substituted for green peppers.
- 6 lb 8 oz canned black beans (rinsed) may be substituted for dried beans and water. Add beans toward the end of the cooking period. Serving temperature 180–190°F.

Variations

- **Black Beans and Andouille Sausage.** Reduce hot sauce to ½ tsp. Omit ham. Add 3 lb cooked andouille sausage cut diagonally into ¾-inch pieces.
- **Black Beans over Rice.** Delete ham. Increase salt to 2 oz. Chicken broth may be substituted for the water to enhance flavor.
- **Black Bean Soup.** Follow recipe for Black Beans and Ham on Rice but make the following changes: Increase beans to 4 lb, water to 2¼ gal, onions to 1 lb, and salt to 2 oz. Decrease ham to 2 lb, tomatoes to 2 lb, and green pepper to 6 oz. Delete rice.

BLACK BEAN AND TORTILLA CASSEROLE

Yield: 48 portions   *Portion:* 8 oz

Ingredient	Amount	Procedure
Onions, chopped	2 lb 10 oz	Combine onions, peppers, tomatoes, picante sauce, and spices in steam-jacketed kettle.
Green peppers, chopped	2 lb 4 oz	
Tomatoes, diced, canned	2¼ qt	Bring to boil. Reduce heat and simmer uncovered for 15–20 minutes.
Picante sauce	1 qt	
Garlic, fresh, minced	6 cloves	
Cumin, ground	3 Tbsp	
Black beans, canned, drained, rinsed	10 lb	Stir beans into tomato mixture. Turn off heat. Spread 2 lb 6 oz of bean mixture in 12 × 10 × 2-inch pan.
Tortillas, corn	64	Top bean mixture with 8 corn tortillas, overlapping as necessary.
Monterey Jack cheese, shredded	3 lb	Sprinkle 6 oz cheese over tortillas. Spread 2 lb 6 oz bean mixture over cheese. Top with 8 corn tortillas, overlapping as necessary. Sprinkle 6 oz cheese over tortillas. Cover and bake at 350°F for 30–35 minutes or to 165°F. Cut 4 × 3.
Tomatoes, fresh, finely diced	1 lb	Sprinkle 4 oz tomatoes and 1 Tbsp sliced onions over each pan. Keep hot (above 140°F).
Green onions, thinly sliced	2 oz	
Picante sauce	6 lb	Serve immediately with picante sauce as a condiment.

Approximate nutritive values per portion   **Calories** 379

Amount/portion	%DV	Amount/portion	%DV	Amount/portion	%DV		%DV		%DV
Total Fat 12 g	19%	**Cholest.** 25 mg	8%	**Total Carb.** 54 g	18%	**Vitamin A**	27%	**Calcium**	34%
Sat. Fat 6 g	28%	**Sodium** 1261 mg	53%	Fiber 6 g	23%	**Vitamin C**	102%	**Iron**	21%
Protein 20 g				Sugars 4 g					

Percent Daily Values (%DV) are based on a 2000-calorie diet.

Note   • Potentially hazardous food. *Food Safety Standards:* Hold food for service at an internal temperature above 140°F. Do not mix old product with new. Cool leftover product quickly (within 4 hours) to below 41°F. See p. 105 for cooling procedures. Reheat leftover product quickly (within 2 hours) to 165°F. Reheat product only once; discard if not used.

RED BEANS AND RICE

Yield: 50 portions   *Portion:* 6 oz red beans + 4 oz rice

Ingredient	Amount	Procedure
Vegetable oil	4 oz	Sauté vegetables in steam-jacketed or large kettle until softened.
Celery, chopped	2 lb (EP)	
Onions, chopped	2 lb (EP)	
Green bell peppers, chopped	1 lb 6 oz (EP)	
Garlic, finely chopped	1 oz (EP)	
Red beans (canned, undrained)	14 lb	Add beans, water, and spices to vegetables. Bring to a boil. Reduce heat.
Water	1 qt	Cover and simmer for approximately 1 hour, until bean mixture is thickened slightly. Stir often.
Liquid smoke	2 tsp	
Red pepper sauce	2 Tbsp	
Salt	1 tsp	
Pepper, black	1 tsp	
Ground red pepper	2 tsp	
Thyme leaves, dried	1 tsp	
Oregano leaves, dried	2 tsp	
Bay leaves, dried	5 leaves	
Rice, converted	3 lb 8 oz	Cook rice according to directions on p. 594.
Water, boiling	4½ qt	Serve 6 oz red beans over 4 oz cooked rice.
Salt	2 Tbsp	
Vegetable oil	2 Tbsp	

Approximate nutritive values per portion

Calories 265

Amount/portion	%DV	Amount/portion	%DV	Amount/portion	%DV		%DV		%DV
Total Fat 3.5 g	5%	**Cholest.** 0 mg	0%	**Total Carb.** 49 g	16%	**Vitamin A**	2%	**Calcium**	6%
Sat. Fat 0.5 g	2%	**Sodium** 784 mg	33%	Fiber 10 g	38%	**Vitamin C**	25%	**Iron**	18%
Protein 10 g				Sugars 4 g					

Percent Daily Values (%DV) are based on a 2000-calorie diet.

Note
- Potentially hazardous food. *Food Safety Standards:* Hold food for service at an internal temperature above 140°F. Do not mix old product with new. Cool leftover product quickly (within 4 hours) to below 41°F. See p. 105 for cooling procedures. Reheat leftover product quickly (within 2 hours) to 165°F. Reheat product only once; discard if not used.

SWEET AND SOUR TOFU

Yield: 50 portions   *Portion:* 6 oz tofu + 4 oz rice
Oven: 350°F

Ingredient	Amount	Procedure
Tofu	5 lb	Drain tofu and dice into ½-inch cubes.
Water	1 cup	Mix water, garlic powder, and soy sauce.
Garlic powder	2 tsp	Dip cubed tofu in liquid, then roll in bread crumbs.
Soy sauce	¼ cup	Place breaded tofu on silicone-paper-lined or lightly greased
Dry bread crumbs	1 lb	baking sheet.
		Bake tofu until brown and crisp. Hold for later step at above 140°F.
Drained pineapple chunks (reserve juice)	2 lb 4 oz	Reserve drained pineapple tidbits for later step. Mix cornstarch with pineapple juice and water.
Pineapple juice (reserved juice from draining pineapple plus water to make up the difference)	2 qt	In steam-jacketed or other large kettle, mix pineapple juice–cornstarch mixture with tomato puree, vinegar, soy sauce, brown sugar, and granulated sugar (use wire whip). Bring to a boil. Boil until mixture thickens.
Cornstarch	2 oz	
Tomato puree	1 qt	
Cider vinegar	1½ cups	
Soy sauce	1½ cups	
Sugar, brown	4 oz	
Sugar, granulated	10 oz	
Onions, ½-inch dice	1 lb (EP)	Stir in pineapple reserved from earlier step, onions, mushrooms, and peppers into thickened mixture. Return to boil.
Mushrooms, quartered (fresh)	8 oz (EP)	
Green peppers, ½-inch dice	1 lb (EP)	Just prior to serving, gently stir in baked tofu reserved from earlier step.
Rice, converted	3 lb 8 oz	Cook rice according to directions on p. 594.
Water, boiling	4½ qt	Serve 6 oz sweet and sour tofu on 4 oz rice.
Salt	2 Tbsp	
Vegetable oil	2 Tbsp	

Approximate nutritive values per portion   **Calories** 395

Amount/portion	%DV	Amount/portion	%DV	Amount/portion	%DV		%DV		%DV
Total Fat 3.6 g	6%	**Cholest.** 0 mg	0%	**Total Carb.** 80 g	26%	**Vitamin A**	3%	**Calcium**	15%
Sat. Fat 0.6 g	3%	**Sodium** 976 mg	41%	Fiber 2.5 g	10%	**Vitamin C**	21%	**Iron**	16%
Protein 10 g				Sugars 14 g					

Percent Daily Values (%DV) are based on a 2000-calorie diet.

Note
- Potentially hazardous food. *Food Safety Standards:* Hold food for service at an internal temperature above 140°F. Do not mix old product with new. Cool leftover product quickly (within 4 hours) to below 41°F. See p. 105 for cooling procedures. Reheat leftover product quickly (within 2 hours) to 165°F. Reheat product only once; discard if not used.

BROWN BEAN SALAD

Yield: 50 portions or 6 qt   *Portion:* ½ cup (4 oz)

Ingredient	Amount	Procedure
Eggs, hard-cooked (p. 439)	12	Peel and dice eggs.
Brown or kidney beans	1½ No. 10 cans	Rinse beans with cold water. Drain.
Celery, diced	12 oz	Combine with beans. Add eggs.
Green pepper, chopped	3 oz	
Onion, minced	3 oz	
Pickle relish	10 oz	
Salad dressing or mayonnaise	3 cups	Combine and add to bean mixture. Mix lightly.
Salt	2 Tbsp	
Vinegar, cider	¾ cup	

Approximate nutritive values per portion   **Calories** 197

Amount/portion	%DV	Amount/portion	%DV	Amount/portion	%DV		%DV		%DV
Total Fat 12 g	19%	**Cholest.** 59 mg	20%	**Total Carb.** 17 g	6%	**Vitamin A**	3%	**Calcium**	3%
Sat. Fat 2 g	10%	**Sodium** 665 mg	28%	Fiber 4 g	17%	**Vitamin C**	7%	**Iron**	10%
Protein 7 g				Sugars 2 g					

Percent Daily Values (%DV) are based on a 2000-calorie diet.

Notes
- Potentially hazardous food. Store for service at an internal temperature below 41°F. Keep leftover product chilled below 41°F. See p. 105 for cooling procedures.
- 4 lb dried beans, cooked according to directions on p. 826, may be substituted for canned beans.
- Great Northern or pinto beans may be substituted for half of the kidney beans.

GARBANZO BEAN SALAD

Yield: 50 portions or 4½ qt   *Portion:* ⅓ cup (3 oz)

Ingredient	Amount	Procedure
Garbanzo beans, canned	2 lb 8 oz	Rinse beans with cold water. Drain.
Red beans, canned	1 lb 8 oz	
Pinto beans, canned	2 lb	
Celery, sliced	1 lb	Combine with beans.
Cucumbers, peeled and sliced	12 oz	
Green onions, sliced	5 oz	
Radishes, sliced	8 oz	
Black olives, sliced	4 oz	
French Dressing (p. 703)	1 cup	Pour dressing over bean mixture. Toss lightly. Marinate for 2 hours.

Approximate nutritive values per portion   **Calories** 80

Amount/portion	%DV	Amount/portion	%DV	Amount/portion	%DV		%DV		%DV
Total Fat 4 g	6%	**Cholest.** 0 mg	0%	**Total Carb.** 10 g	3%	**Vitamin A**	1%	**Calcium**	2%
Sat. Fat 1 g	4%	**Sodium** 260 mg	11%	Fiber 2 g	8%	**Vitamin C**	7%	**Iron**	7%
Protein 3 g				Sugars 1 g					

Percent Daily Values (%DV) are based on a 2000-calorie diet.

Notes
- Potentially hazardous food. Store for service at an internal temperature below 41°F. Keep leftover product chilled below 41°F. See p. 105 for cooling procedures.
- Cooked Great Northern beans may be substituted for garbanzo beans.
- Vegetable Marinade (p. 784) may be substituted for French Dressing.

Variation
- **Garbanzo Pasta Salad.** Delete pinto beans. Cook 8 oz shell macaroni to the *al dente* stage. Combine with other ingredients.

BARLEY AND BLACK BEAN SALAD

Yield: 50 portions   *Portion:* 4 oz

Ingredient	Amount	Procedure
Water	1¼ gal	Bring water to boil in steam-jacketed kettle.
Salt	1½ oz (2⅓ Tbsp)	Stir barley into boiling water. Cook about 50 minutes or until tender. Stir occasionally.
Barley	1 lb 10 oz	Drain, cool, and save for later step. (Yield 4 lb 8 oz cooked barley.)
Black beans, drained, rinsed (canned)	2 lb 12 oz EP	Add drained and rinsed beans, vinegar, and pepper to 4 lb 8 oz cooked and cooled barley reserved from earlier step.
Red wine vinegar	3 oz	
Black pepper	¾ tsp	
Corn, defrosted (whole kernel frozen)	2 lb 5 oz	Add vegetables. Toss to combine.
Green peppers, chopped	1 lb 3 oz EP	
Red jalapeno peppers, chopped (canned)	4 oz	
Cilantro, chopped (fresh)	1½ oz (2½ cups)	
Lime juice (fresh)	6 oz	Whisk lime juice and spices together in a bowl.
Salt	5 tsp	
Cumin (ground)	3½ Tbsp	
Ancho chili powder	4 Tbsp	
Olive oil	12 oz	Whisk oil into lime juice while pouring in a slow stream. Drizzle dressing over salad and toss to combine.

Approximate nutritive values per portion   **Calories** 150

Amount/portion	%DV	Amount/portion	%DV	Amount/portion	%DV		%DV		%DV
Total Fat 7.4 g	11%	**Cholest.** 0 mg	0%	**Total Carb.** 17 g	6%	**Vitamin A**	7%	**Calcium**	2%
Sat. Fat 1 g	5%	**Sodium** 652 mg	27%	Fiber 4.5 g	18%	**Vitamin C**	19%	**Iron**	8%
Protein 4 g				Sugars 1.4 g					

Percent Daily Values (%DV) are based on a 2000-calorie diet.

Note   ● Potentially hazardous food. *Food Safety Standards:* Hold food for service at an internal temperature below 41°F. Do not mix old product with new. See p. 105 for cooling procedures.

COLESLAW

Yield: 50 portions or 4½ qt   *Portion:* ⅓ cup (2½ oz)

Ingredient	Amount	Procedure
Cabbage	7 lb EP (9 lb AP)	Shred or chop cabbage.
Vinegar, cider Sugar, granulated Salt Celery seed	3 cups 1 lb 8 oz 1 oz (1½ Tbsp) 1 Tbsp	Combine vinegar, sugar, and seasonings. Add to cabbage. Mix lightly.

Approximate nutritive values per portion   **Calories** 68

Amount/portion	%DV	Amount/portion	%DV	Amount/portion	%DV		%DV		%DV
Total Fat 0 g	0%	**Cholest.** 0 mg	0%	**Total Carb.** 18 g	6%	Vitamin A	0%	Calcium	3%
Sat. Fat 0 g	0%	**Sodium** 204 mg	8%	Fiber 1 g	4%	Vitamin C	50%	Iron	2%
Protein 1 g				Sugars 15 g					

Percent Daily Values (%DV) are based on a 2000-calorie diet.

Note   ● Red cabbage may be substituted for part or all of green cabbage.

Variations   ● **Cauliflower Broccoli Salad.** Substitute 3 lb 8 oz EP each of cauliflower and broccoli florets for the cabbage. Add 3 oz chopped onion. Serve soon after preparing.

● **Green Pepper Slaw.** Add 4 oz chopped green pepper, 2 oz chopped onion, and 4 Tbsp celery seed.

● **Oriental Coleslaw.** Substitute ⅓ recipe Sesame Seed Dressing (p. 703) for dressing given in recipe.

CREAMY COLESLAW

Yield: 50 portions or 4¼ qt   *Portion:* ⅓ cup (2½ oz)

Ingredient	Amount	Procedure
Cabbage	7 lb EP (9 lb AP)	Shred or chop cabbage.
Mayonnaise or salad dressing	2 cups	Combine and add to cabbage. Mix lightly. Serve with No. 12 dipper.
Light cream, half-and-half	2 cups	
Vinegar, cider	½ cup	
Sugar, granulated	4 oz	
Salt	1 oz (1½ Tbsp)	
Pepper, white	½ tsp	

Approximate nutritive values per portion   **Calories 100**

Amount/portion	%DV	Amount/portion	%DV	Amount/portion	%DV		%DV		%DV
Total Fat 8 g	13%	**Cholest.** 9 mg	3%	**Total Carb.** 7 g	2%	**Vitamin A**	2%	**Calcium**	4%
Sat. Fat 2 g	9%	**Sodium** 258 mg	11%	Fiber 1 g	4%	**Vitamin C**	50%	**Iron**	2%
Protein 1 g				Sugars 4 g					

Percent Daily Values (%DV) are based on a 2000-calorie diet.

Note
- Potentially hazardous food. Store for service at an internal temperature below 41°F. Keep leftover product chilled below 41°F. See p. 105 for cooling procedures.

Variations
- **Apple Cabbage Salad.** See p. 670.
- **Cabbage Carrot Slaw.** Reduce cabbage to 5 lb. Add 1 lb shredded or chopped carrots, 8 oz chopped green pepper, and 4 oz chopped onion.
- **Cabbage-Pineapple-Marshmallow Salad.** To 4 lb shredded or chopped cabbage, add 2 lb pineapple tidbits, drained, 1 lb miniature marshmallows, and a dressing made of 2 cups mayonnaise or salad dressing and 2 cups cream, whipped.
- **Creamy Cauliflower-Broccoli Salad.** Substitute 3 lb 8 oz EP each of cauliflower and broccoli for the cabbage. Add 3 oz chopped green onion. Garnish with cherry tomatoes.

SLICED CUCUMBER AND ONION IN SOUR CREAM

Yield: 50 portions or 4¼ qt   *Portion:* ⅓ cup (2½ oz)

Ingredient	Amount	Procedure
Cucumbers	5 lb	Cut cucumbers and onions in thin slices.
Onions	8 oz	
Sour cream	3 cups	Blend rest of ingredients to form a thin cream dressing.
Mayonnaise	3 cups	Pour over cucumbers and onions. Mix lightly.
Salt	1½ tsp	
Sugar, granulated	3 Tbsp	
Vinegar, cider	¾ cup	

Approximate nutritive values per portion   **Calories** 135

Amount/portion	%DV	Amount/portion	%DV	Amount/portion	%DV		%DV		%DV
Total Fat 14 g	21%	**Cholest.** 14 mg	5%	**Total Carb.** 4 g	1%	Vitamin A	5%	Calcium	2%
Sat. Fat 3 g	17%	**Sodium** 148 mg	6%	Fiber 0 g	0%	Vitamin C	4%	Iron	1%
Protein 1 g				Sugars 1 g					

Percent Daily Values (%DV) are based on a 2000-calorie diet.

Notes
- Potentially hazardous food. Store for service at an internal temperature below 41°F. Keep leftover product chilled below 41°F. See p. 105 for cooling procedures.
- This cream dressing may be used as a dressing for lettuce.

Variation
- **German Cucumbers.** Reduce onions to 4 oz. Delete cream dressing. Pour mixture of 1 cup vinegar, ½ cup water, 1 Tbsp salt, and 8 oz sugar over cucumbers and onions. Marinate at least 1 hour.

MARINATED MUSHROOMS

Yield: 50 portions   *Portion:* 2¾ oz

Ingredient	Amount	Procedure
Mushrooms, fresh, small	6 lb	Clean mushrooms and trim ends. Leave whole.
Water	1 qt	Combine water and lemon juice.
Lemon juice	½ cup	Bring to a boil. Add mushrooms and blanch for 1–3 minutes. Drain and immerse in cold water. Drain.
Vegetable Marinade (p. 784)	1½ qt	Pour marinade over mushrooms. Refrigerate for 2–3 hours. Drain off most of the marinade before serving.

Approximate nutritive values per portion   **Calories** 37

Amount/portion	%DV	Amount/portion	%DV	Amount/portion	%DV		%DV		%DV
Total Fat 3 g	4%	**Cholest.** 0 mg	0%	**Total Carb.** 3 g	1%	**Vitamin A**	0%	**Calcium**	0%
Sat. Fat 1 g	3%	**Sodium** 110 mg	5%	Fiber 1 g	3%	**Vitamin C**	6%	**Iron**	4%
Protein 1 g				Sugars 1 g					

Percent Daily Values (%DV) are based on a 2000-calorie diet.

Note
- Before serving, mushrooms may be tossed with fresh minced parsley or other fresh herb.

Variations
- **Marinated Asparagus.** Blanch fresh asparagus spears (see instructions for mushrooms). Marinate. To serve, drain and arrange 3–5 spears on plate with Bibb lettuce liner. Garnish with lemon twist or pimiento strip.
- **Marinated Green Beans.** Cover whole green beans with marinade. If fresh green beans are used, cook until tender-crisp.
- **Vegetable Collage.** Pour 3 cups Italian Dressing (p. 703) or Vegetable Marinade (p. 784) over: 2 lb broccoli florets, 2 lb cauliflower florets, 12 oz sliced celery, 1 lb 8 oz cherry tomatoes cut in half, 2 lb sliced zucchini, 1 lb sliced green onions, 6 oz sliced carrots, and 1 lb 8 oz sliced black olives. Marinate in refrigerator for 4 hours, but if salad is to be held longer than 4 hours, add broccoli shortly before serving. Add 1 lb cooked crumbled bacon and toss.

TOMATO BASIL SALAD

Yield: 50 portions   *Portion:* ½ cup

Ingredient	Amount	Procedure
Tomatoes	15 lb (AP)	Peel and seed tomatoes (see Notes). Cut tomatoes into bite-size pieces. Put in baker's bowl.
Basil leaves, fresh	1 oz	Cut or tear basil into small pieces. Gently stir into tomatoes.
Red wine vinegar Sugar, granulated Salt Pepper, cracked black	1½ cups 1½ cups 2 tsp ½ tsp	Mix vinegar, sugar, and spices. Pour over tomatoes. Let stand 30 minutes.
		Serve tomatoes in a bowl with some of the vinegar dressing. Garnish with fresh basil leaves.

Approximate nutritive values per portion   **Calories** 50

Amount/portion	%DV	Amount/portion	%DV	Amount/portion	%DV		%DV		%DV
Total Fat 0.4 g	1%	**Cholest.** 0 mg	0%	**Total Carb.** 12 g	4%	**Vitamin A**	8%	**Calcium**	1%
Sat. Fat 0 g	0%	**Sodium** 104 mg	4%	Fiber 1.4 g	6%	**Vitamin C**	40%	**Iron**	3%
Protein 1 g				Sugars 9 g					

Percent Daily Values (%DV) are based on a 2000-calorie diet.

Notes
- Use very ripe, bright red tomatoes.
- Procedure for seeding tomatoes: Cut the tomato in half horizontally. Gently squeeze each half of the tomato to push out the seeds.

Variation
- **Tomato Basil and Romaine Salad.** Cut or tear 10 lb romaine lettuce into bite-size pieces. Portion 3 oz lettuce onto individual salad plates. Using a No. 12 dipper, portion tomatoes on top of greens (being careful not to use too much vinegar dressing). Sprinkle 1 tsp freshly grated Parmesan cheese on top of each salad. Drizzle a small amount of the vinegar on top, if desired. Garnish with whole basil leaves. May substitute slices of fresh mozzarella cheese for the Parmesan cheese.

MARINATED TOMATOES

Yield: 50 portions   *Portion:* 2 slices

Ingredient	Amount	Procedure
Tomatoes, fresh, peeled	6 lb	Cut peeled tomatoes into ½-inch slices. Place in bottom of 12 × 20 × 2-inch pan.
Onion, chopped	¾ cup	Combine. Pour over tomato slices.
Garlic, minced	3 cloves	Cover tightly. Refrigerate if storing for later use.
Parsley, chopped	⅓ cup	
Basil, crumbled, dried	1 Tbsp	
Sugar, granulated	1 Tbsp	
Salt	2 tsp	
Pepper, black	1½ tsp	
Olive oil	2 cups	
Vinegar, red wine or balsamic	1½ cups	

Approximate nutritive values per portion   **Calories** 99

Amount/portion	%DV	Amount/portion	%DV	Amount/portion	%DV		%DV		%DV
Total Fat 9 g	13%	**Cholest.** 0 mg	0%	**Total Carb.** 4 g	1%	**Vitamin A**	5%	**Calcium**	1%
Sat. Fat 1 g	6%	**Sodium** 203 mg	8%	Fiber 1 g	2%	**Vitamin C**	9%	**Iron**	2%
Protein 1 g				Sugars 2 g					

Percent Daily Values (%DV) are based on a 2000-calorie diet.

Notes
- ⅓ cup fresh basil may be substituted for dried.
- Salad oil may be substituted for olive oil.
- Refrigerator storage causes tomatoes to lose some flavor.

Variation
- **Fresh Tomato Relish.** Cut peeled tomatoes in half and gently squeeze out most of the seeds. Chop coarsely and stir into the marinade.

FRESH SLICED TOMATOES AND CUCUMBERS

Yield: 50 portions   *Portion:* 2 tomato and 2 cucumber slices

Ingredient	Amount	Procedure
Tomatoes	8 lb	Slice tomatoes and cucumbers ¼ inch thick.
Cucumbers	5 lb	Alternate tomatoes and cucumbers, slightly overlapping, on a serving platter.
Basil, fresh, chopped	½ cup	Sprinkle basil and parsley over tomatoes and cucumbers.
Parsley, fresh, chopped	½ cup	
Italian salad dressing	2½ cups	Drizzle evenly over tomatoes and cucumbers.
Basil, fresh, whole leaves	for garnish	Garnish with fresh basil leaves and serve immediately.

Approximate nutritive values per portion   **Calories** 79

Amount/portion	%DV	Amount/portion	%DV	Amount/portion	%DV		%DV		%DV
Total Fat 6 g	9%	**Cholest.** 0 mg	0%	**Total Carb.** 5 g	2%	**Vitamin A**	8%	**Calcium**	2%
Sat. Fat 1 g	4%	**Sodium** 249 mg	10%	Fiber 1 g	3%	**Vitamin C**	13%	**Iron**	1%
Protein 1 g				Sugars 2 g					

Percent Daily Values (%DV) are based on a 2000-calorie diet.

Note
- Cucumbers may be scored with tines of a fork before slicing. Cucumbers may be peeled or unpeeled.

Variation
- **Sliced Tomato and Mozzarella Salad.** Substitute 4 lb low-fat mozzarella cheese slices for cucumbers.

MARINATED CARROTS

Yield: 50 portions *Portion:* ⅓ cup (3 oz)

Ingredient	Amount	Procedure
Carrots, fresh, cut in ¼-inch slices	5 lb	Cook carrots until tender-crisp. Drain.
Tomato soup	2 cups	Combine and heat to boiling point.
Sugar, granulated	1 lb	Pour over warm carrots.
Salad oil	½ cup	Marinate for at least 4 hours.
Vinegar, cider	1½ cups	
Salt	2 tsp	
Pepper, black	1 tsp	
Prepared mustard	1 Tbsp	
Worcestershire sauce	1 Tbsp	
Onions, chopped	12 oz	
Green pepper, chopped	3 oz	

Approximate nutritive values per portion   **Calories** 81

Amount/portion	%DV	Amount/portion	%DV	Amount/portion	%DV		%DV		%DV
Total Fat 2 g	4%	**Cholest.** 0 mg	0%	**Total Carb.** 16 g	5%	**Vitamin A**	127%	**Calcium**	1%
Sat. Fat 1 g	3%	**Sodium** 143 mg	6%	Fiber 1 g	5%	**Vitamin C**	15%	**Iron**	2%
Protein 1 g				Sugars 12 g					

Percent Daily Values (%DV) are based on a 2000-calorie diet.

Notes
- Frozen crinkle-sliced carrots, cooked until tender-crisp, may be substituted for fresh carrots.
- Marinated carrots will keep in the refrigerator for a week.

MARINATED GARDEN SALAD

Yield: 50 portions or 8 lb   *Portion:* ⅓ cup (2½ oz)

Ingredient	Amount	Procedure
Carrots, sliced	1 lb (EP)	Steam carrots just until tender-crisp. Drain.
Cauliflower, fresh	2 lb (EP)	Cut cauliflower into florets.
Broccoli spears	2 lb (EP)	Cut broccoli into florets and slice stems.
Mushrooms, fresh	1 lb	Clean mushrooms. Cut large mushrooms in half. Combine all vegetables.
French Dressing (p. 703) Dill weed Basil, dried, crumbled Oregano, dried, crumbled	1½ qt ¼ oz 1 Tbsp 1 tsp	Combine dressing and seasonings. Pour over vegetables. Marinate at least 2 hours.

Approximate nutritive values per portion   **Calories** 145

Amount/portion	%DV	Amount/portion	%DV	Amount/portion	%DV		%DV		%DV
Total Fat 12 g	19%	**Cholest.** 4 mg	1%	**Total Carb.** 9 g	3%	**Vitamin A**	36%	**Calcium**	3%
Sat. Fat 3 g	15%	**Sodium** 463 mg	19%	Fiber 1 g	5%	**Vitamin C**	43%	**Iron**	4%
Protein 1 g				Sugars 5 g					

Percent Daily Values (%DV) are based on a 2000-calorie diet.

Note   • Peel broccoli stems before slicing if they appear tough.

SPINACH CHEESE SALAD

Yield: 50 portions   *Portion:* 3 oz

Ingredient	Amount	Procedure
Spinach, chopped, frozen	3 lb	Thaw spinach. Squeeze out excess moisture and drain.
Eggs, hard-cooked (p. 439)	10	Peel and chop eggs coarsely.
Onion, chopped Celery, chopped Cheddar cheese, shredded	6 oz 8 oz 1 lb	Add onion, celery, cheese, and eggs to spinach. Mix lightly.
Mayonnaise or salad dressing Salt Hot pepper sauce Vinegar, cider Horseradish	1¼ qt 2 tsp 2 tsp 2 Tbsp ⅔ cup	Combine mayonnaise and seasonings. Pour over spinach mixture. Mix lightly. Refrigerate for 2 hours. Serve with No. 12 dipper.

Approximate nutritive values per portion   **Calories** 221

Amount/portion	%DV	Amount/portion	%DV	Amount/portion	%DV		%DV		%DV
Total Fat 22 g	33%	**Cholest.** 65 mg	22%	**Total Carb.** 3 g	1%	Vitamin A	27%	Calcium	11%
Sat. Fat 5 g	24%	**Sodium** 343 mg	14%	Fiber 1 g	3%	Vitamin C	7%	Iron	14%
Protein 5 g				Sugars 0 g					

Percent Daily Values (%DV) are based on a 2000-calorie diet.

Note   • Potentially hazardous food. Store for service at an internal temperature below 41°F. Keep leftover product chilled below 41°F. See p. 105 for cooling procedures.

BASIC PASTA SALAD

Yield: 50 portions   *Portion:* 4 oz

Ingredient	Amount	Procedure
Pasta Water, boiling Salt Vegetable oil	3 lb 8 oz (AP) 3½ gal 3 oz 2 Tbsp	Cook pasta according to directions on p. 561. Do not overcook. Pasta should be *al dente*. There should be approximately 9 lb cooked pasta. Information on cooked weights of pasta is given on p. 561.
Dressing	1½–1¾ qt	Add dressing and toss gently to mix.
Vegetables and/or other ingredients	1 lb 8 oz–2 lb	Fold in other ingredients. Chill.

Suggested Ingredients

- **Pasta:** Rotini, rigatoni, shell macaroni, elbow macaroni, radiatore, wheels. See Figure 3.2 for other pasta choices.

- **Dressing:** Vinaigrette and variations (p. 706), Lemon Basil (p. 706), Lime Salad Dressing (p. 706), Green Peppercorn Cream (p. 700), Thousand Island (p. 700), Italian (p. 703), Sour Cream Basil (p. 700).

- **Vegetables (cooked until tender-crisp):** Asparagus cuts, broccoli florets, carrot coins, Italian green beans, snow peas, sugar snap peas.

- **Vegetables (raw):** Avocado slices or chunks, broccoli, cauliflower, chives, cucumbers, green peppers, red onion rings, parsley, radishes, summer squash slices, tomatoes, water chestnuts, zucchini slices or strips.

- **Other:** Chicken strips, beef strips, pepperoni slices, ham, crabmeat, scallops, shrimp, turkey, olives, pickles, cheese.

Note

- Yield for this recipe may vary, depending on the shape of the pasta used and the amount of vegetables and other ingredients added.

MACARONI SALAD

Yield: 50 portions or 6 qt   *Portion:* ½ cup (4 oz)

Ingredient	Amount	Procedure
Elbow macaroni	2 lb 8 oz	Cook macaroni according to directions on p. 561.
Water, boiling	2½ gal	Rinse in cold water. Drain well after rinsing.
Salt	2 Tbsp	(Should be 6 lb 10 oz cooked macaroni.)
Vegetable oil	1 Tbsp	
French Dressing (p. 703)	2 cups	Combine. Pour over macaroni and let marinate overnight.
Salt	¾ tsp	
Vinegar, cider	½ cup	
Eggs, hard-cooked (p. 439)	12	Peel and coarsely chop eggs.
Green peppers, chopped	6 oz	Add vegetables, cheese, and eggs to marinated macaroni.
Celery, chopped	1 lb 4 oz	
Onions, chopped	6 oz	
Pimiento, chopped and drained	3 oz	
Cheddar cheese, diced or shredded	1 lb	
Salad dressing	1 lb	Combine dressing and relish.
Sweet pickle relish, drained	10 oz	Pour over macaroni mixture. Mix carefully to combine. Serve with No. 10 dipper.

Approximate nutritive values per portion   **Calories** 260

Amount/portion	%DV	Amount/portion	%DV	Amount/portion	%DV		%DV		%DV
Total Fat 16 g	25%	**Cholest.** 67 mg	22%	**Total Carb.** 22 g	7%	**Vitamin A**	6%	**Calcium**	8%
Sat. Fat 4 g	22%	**Sodium** 610 mg	25%	Fiber 0.3 g	1%	**Vitamin C**	9%	**Iron**	7%
Protein 7 g				Sugars 3 g					

Percent Daily Values (%DV) are based on a 2000-calorie diet.

Notes
- Potentially hazardous food. Store for service at an internal temperature below 41°F. Keep leftover product chilled below 41°F. See p. 105 for cooling procedures.
- Other types of pasta may be substituted for elbow macaroni. (See Figure 3.2.)

Variations
- **Chicken and Pasta Salad.** Delete cheese, pickle relish, and eggs. Cook 2 lb 8 oz fettuccine or other type of pasta according to directions on p. 561. Add 3 lb cooked chicken, diced.
- **Ham and Pasta Salad.** Delete eggs. Add 2 lb cooked ham, diced.

ISRAELI COUSCOUS SALAD

Yield: 50 portions   *Portion:* 4 oz

Ingredient	Amount	Procedure
Water	2 gal	Bring water and salt to a rolling boil in steam-jacketed or
Salt	2 tsp	other kettle.
Middle Eastern couscous (see Note)	2 lb 6 oz	Add couscous while stirring. Return water to boil. Reduce heat and simmer 10–12 min until couscous is *al dente.* Stir occasionally. Drain, cool, and save for later step. (Yield 7 lb 3 oz cooked couscous.)
Cucumbers, diced (not peeled)	1 lb 12 oz EP	Add vegetables, oil, vinegar, juice, and seasonings to cooled couscous reserved from earlier step.
Red onions, chopped	1 lb	Toss well to distribute ingredients.
Parsley, minced	2¾ oz EP	
Mint, finely chopped (fresh)	6 Tbsp	
Olive oil	1½ cups	
Red wine vinegar	2 cups	
Lemon juice (fresh)	2 oz (¼ cup)	
Salt	2¾ oz (4 Tbsp)	
Black pepper	2 Tbsp	

Approximate nutritive values per portion   **Calories** 145

Amount/portion	%DV	Amount/portion	%DV	Amount/portion	%DV		%DV		%DV
Total Fat 6.8 g	10%	**Cholest.** 0 mg	0%	**Total Carb.** 17.5 g	6%	**Vitamin A**	2%	**Calcium**	2%
Sat. Fat .9 g	5%	**Sodium** 693 mg	29%	Fiber .9 g	4%	**Vitamin C**	7%	**Iron**	6%
Protein 3 g				Sugars 1 g					

Percent Daily Values (%DV) are based on a 2000-calorie diet.

Notes
- Potentially hazardous food. *Food Safety Standards:* Hold food for service at an internal temperature below 41°F. Do not mix old product with new.
- Middle Eastern couscous is the size of a small pea and resembles pearl tapioca.

CITRUS COUSCOUS SALAD

Yield: 50   *Portions:* 4 oz

Ingredient	Amount	Procedure

Water
Salt
Middle Eastern
  couscous
  (see Note)
	1¾ gal
	1 tsp
	2 lb
		Bring water and salt to a rolling boil in steam-jacketed or
		  other kettle.
		Add couscous while stirring.
		Return water to boil. Reduce heat and simmer 10–12 min
		  until couscous is *al dente*. Stir occasionally.
		Drain, cool, and save for later step. (Yield 6 lb 5 oz cooked
		  couscous.)

Slivered almonds,
  toasted
	8 oz	Spread almonds in a single layer on bun sheet.
		Toast at 300°F for 15–20 minutes until almonds turn golden
		  and become fragrant. (Watch carefully so they do not
		  burn.)
		Turn two or three times during toasting. Cool almonds on
		  bun sheet. Save for later step.

Olive oil
Lemon juice, fresh
Orange juice
Garlic, minced
Green onions,
  sliced thin
Ginger root,
  finely minced
Raisins
Salt
Black pepper
	6 oz
	6 oz
	1¼ cup
	2 oz EP
	8 oz EP
	
	1 oz
	
	8 oz
	1½ tsp
	1¾ tsp
		Combine liquids, vegetables, and seasoning in baker's bowl.

Mandarin oranges,
  drained
	3 lb EP	Stir 6 lb 5 oz cooled couscous, reserved from earlier step,
		  into vegetable dressing mixture.
		Gently stir in mandarin oranges and 8 oz toasted almonds
		  reserved from earlier step.

Approximate nutritive values per portion

Calories 150

Amount/portion	%DV	Amount/portion	%DV	Amount/portion	%DV		%DV		%DV
Total Fat 5.6 g	9%	**Cholest.** 0 mg	0%	**Total Carb.** 21.6 g	7%	Vitamin A	5%	Calcium	3%
Sat. Fat .6 g	3%	**Sodium** 118 mg	5%	Fiber 1.9 g	8%	Vitamin C	24%	Iron	4%
Protein 3.6 g				Sugars 3.8 g					

Percent Daily Values (%DV) are based on a 2000-calorie diet.

Notes
- Potentially hazardous food. *Food Safety Standards:* Hold food for service at an internal temperature below 41°F. Do not mix old product with new.
- Middle Eastern couscous is the size of a small pea and resembles pearl tapioca.

ITALIAN PASTA SALAD

Yield: 50 portions   *Portion:* ½ cup (4 oz)

Ingredient	Amount	Procedure
Rotini or other pasta	2 lb 8 oz	Cook pasta according to directions on p. 561.
Water, boiling	2½ gal	Rinse in cold water. Drain.
Salt	2 Tbsp	
Vegetable oil	1 Tbsp	
Thousand Island Dressing (p. 700)	1¾ qt	Combine dressing and seasonings. Pour over pasta. Mix gently.
Basil, dried, crumbled	1 Tbsp	Chill.
Salt	1 Tbsp	
Garbanzo beans, canned	8 oz	Drain and rinse beans. Add to pasta mixture.
Tomatoes, fresh, cut in wedges	1 lb 8 oz	Add vegetables and olives to pasta mixture. Toss gently. Refrigerate until served.
Cucumbers, peeled and sliced	1 lb	
Cauliflower, fresh, sliced	8 oz	
Black olives, large, pitted	4 oz	

Approximate nutritive values per portion   **Calories** 229

Amount/portion	%DV	Amount/portion	%DV	Amount/portion	%DV		%DV		%DV
Total Fat 13 g	20%	**Cholest.** 11 mg	4%	**Total Carb.** 24 g	8%	**Vitamin A**	5%	**Calcium**	2%
Sat. Fat 2 g	11%	**Sodium** 484 mg	20%	Fiber 2 g	7%	**Vitamin C**	9%	**Iron**	9%
Protein 3 g				Sugars 1 g					

Percent Daily Values (%DV) are based on a 2000-calorie diet.

Notes
- Potentially hazardous food. Store for service at an internal temperature below 41°F. Keep leftover product chilled below 41°F. See p. 105 for cooling procedures.
- An oil-base dressing may be substituted for Thousand Island Dressing.

CHILLED FETTUCCINE VINAIGRETTE

Yield: 50 portions   *Portion:* 5 oz

Ingredient	Amount	Procedure
Fettuccine	3 lb 6 oz	Cook fettuccine according to directions on p. 561. Drain.
Water	3½ gal	There should be 10 lb cooked fettuccine.
Salt	2 Tbsp	
Vegetable oil	2 Tbsp	
Yogurt, plain, nonfat	2 lb	Blend yogurt and vinaigrette well.
Vinaigrette Dressing (p. 706)	2 qt	Pour over hot fettuccine. Toss, using tongs, until all pasta is coated with dressing. Cover and chill until service.

Approximate nutritive values per portion   **Calories** 331

Amount/portion	%DV	Amount/portion	%DV	Amount/portion	%DV		%DV		%DV
Total Fat 24 g	37%	**Cholest.** 0 mg	0%	**Total Carb.** 25 g	8%	**Vitamin A**	0%	**Calcium**	5%
Sat. Fat 6 g	31%	**Sodium** 610 mg	25%	Fiber 0 g	0%	**Vitamin C**	2%	**Iron**	7%
Protein 5 g				Sugars 2 g					

Percent Daily Values (%DV) are based on a 2000-calorie diet.

Notes
- Potentially hazardous food. Store for service at an internal temperature below 41°F. Keep leftover product chilled below 41°F. See p. 105 for cooling procedures.
- Serve Fettuccine Vinaigrette as an accompaniment to a chilled poultry breast. Add a colorful fruit garnish.
- Bottled Italian salad dressing may be substituted for Vinaigrette Dressing.

Variation
- **Marinated Fettuccine.** Prepare as for Chilled Fettuccine Vinaigrette. After the yogurt and dressing are added, heat in oven. Serve hot.

POTATO SALAD

Yield: 50 portions or 7 qt   *Portion:* ½ cup (4 oz)

Ingredient	Amount	Procedure
Potatoes, peeled	10 lb (EP) (12 lb AP)	Cook potatoes until tender. Dice while warm.
Salad oil Vinegar, cider Lemon juice Prepared mustard Sugar, granulated Salt Hot pepper sauce	½ cup ½ cup 1 Tbsp 2 Tbsp 3 oz 1 Tbsp Few drops	Make a marinade of oil, vinegar, lemon juice, and seasonings. Add to warm potatoes and mix gently. Marinate until cold.
Eggs, hard-cooked (p. 439), diced Celery, diced Onion, finely chopped Pepper, black	12 1 lb 8 oz ½ tsp	Add eggs, celery, onion, and pepper to marinated potatoes. Mix lightly.
Mayonnaise	2 cups	Add mayonnaise. Mix carefully to blend. Chill at least 1 hour before serving. Serve with No. 10 dipper.

Approximate nutritive values per portion   **Calories** 190

Amount/portion	%DV	Amount/portion	%DV	Amount/portion	%DV		%DV		%DV
Total Fat 11 g	16%	**Cholest.** 56 mg	19%	**Total Carb.** 21 g	7%	**Vitamin A**	2%	**Calcium**	2%
Sat. Fat 2 g	10%	**Sodium** 214 mg	9%	Fiber 1 g	6%	**Vitamin C**	12%	**Iron**	3%
Protein 3 g				Sugars 3 g					

Percent Daily Values (%DV) are based on a 2000-calorie diet.

Notes
- Potentially hazardous food. Store for service at an internal temperature below 41°F. Keep leftover product chilled below 41°F. See p. 105 for cooling procedures.
- 2 cups French Dressing may be substituted for the marinade given in the recipe.
- Sour cream or yogurt may be substituted for half of the mayonnaise.
- Potatoes may be cooked with skins on, then peeled. Use 12 lb AP.
- 4 oz pickle relish, chopped pimiento, or chopped green pepper may be added.

Variation
- **Sour Cream Potato Salad.** Reduce eggs to 8 and mayonnaise to 1 cup. Add 2 cups sour cream, 1 tsp celery seed, and 12 oz peeled, sliced cucumbers.

HOT POTATO SALAD

Yield: 50 portions   *Portion:* ⅔ cup (6 oz)

Ingredient	Amount	Procedure
Potatoes	12 lb (EP) (15 lb AP)	Wash potatoes and trim as necessary. Steam until just tender, about 30 minutes. Peel and slice.
Bacon	1 lb	Dice bacon, cook until crisp. Drain. Reserve fat.
Onion, chopped	8 oz	Sauté onion in bacon fat.
Flour, all-purpose	4 oz	Add flour to onion and stir until well mixed. Cook 5 minutes.
Sugar, granulated Salt Pepper, black Celery seed Vinegar, cider Water	1 lb 2½ oz 2 tsp 1 Tbsp 3 cups 1 qt	Mix sugar, spices, vinegar, and water. Boil 1 minute. Add to fat-flour mixture gradually while stirring. Cook until slightly thickened.
		Add hot dressing to warm potatoes and bacon. Mix lightly. Serve hot.

Approximate nutritive values per portion

Calories 205

Amount/portion	%DV	Amount/portion	%DV	Amount/portion	%DV		%DV		%DV
Total Fat 7 g	11%	**Cholest.** 8 mg	3%	**Total Carb.** 34 g	11%	**Vitamin A**	0%	**Calcium**	1%
Sat. Fat 3 g	14%	**Sodium** 597 mg	25%	Fiber 2 g	6%	**Vitamin C**	15%	**Iron**	3%
Protein 3 g				Sugars 11 g					

Percent Daily Values (%DV) are based on a 2000-calorie diet.

Notes

- Potentially hazardous food. *Food Safety Standards:* Hold food for service at an internal temperature above 140°F. Do not mix old product with new. Cool leftover product quickly (within 4 hours) to below 41°F. See p. 105 for cooling procedures. Reheat leftover product quickly (within 2 hours) to 165°F. Reheat product only once; discard if not used.
- 12 hard-cooked eggs, sliced or diced, may be added.
- Mayonnaise or a combination of mayonnaise and salad dressing may be used in place of the hot vinegar dressing. Add to potato mixture and heat to serving temperature.

GELATIN SALAD RECIPES

FRUIT GELATIN SALAD

Yield: 40 or 48 portions or 1 pan 12 × 20 × 2 inches   *Portion:* $2\frac{1}{4}$ × $2\frac{1}{2}$ or 2 × $2\frac{1}{2}$ inches

Ingredient	Amount	Procedure
Gelatin, flavored	1 lb 8 oz	Pour boiling water over gelatin.
Water, boiling	2 qt	Stir until dissolved.
Fruit juice or water, cold	2 qt	Add to hot liquid. Chill.
Fruit, drained	4 lb	Place fruit in counter pan. When gelatin begins to congeal, pour over fruit. Place in refrigerator to congeal. Cut 5 × 8 for 40 portions. Cut 6 × 8 for 48 portions.

Approximate nutritive values per portion (cut 48)   **Calories** 91

Amount/portion	%DV	Amount/portion	%DV	Amount/portion	%DV		%DV		%DV
Total Fat 0 g	0%	**Cholest.** 0 mg	0%	**Total Carb.** 10 g	3%	**Vitamin A**	0%	**Calcium**	0%
Sat. Fat 0 g	0%	**Sodium** 20 mg	1%	Fiber 1 g	3%	**Vitamin C**	40%	**Iron**	5%
Protein 13 g				Sugars 9 g					

Percent Daily Values (%DV) are based on a 2000-calorie diet.

Notes
- For quick preparation, dissolve 1 lb 8 oz flavored gelatin in $1\frac{1}{2}$ qt boiling water. Measure $2\frac{1}{2}$ qt chipped or finely crushed ice, then add enough cold water or fruit juice to cover ice. Add to gelatin and stir constantly until ice is melted. Gelatin will begin to congeal at once. Speed of congealing depends on proportion of ice to water and size of ice particles.
- One or more canned, frozen, or fresh fruits, cut into desired shapes and sizes, may be used. Fresh or frozen pineapple must be cooked before adding to gelatin salad.
- Fruit juice may be used for part or all of the liquid. Not more than 50 percent of heavy syrup, however, should be substituted for water.
- If unflavored granulated gelatin is used, sprinkle $2\frac{1}{2}$ oz over 2 cups cold water and let stand for 10 minutes. Add $3\frac{1}{2}$ qt boiling fruit juice and 1 lb sugar.

Variations
- **Apple Cinnamon Swirl.** Heat $1\frac{1}{4}$ qt water to boiling. Add 1 lb lemon gelatin and 10 oz cinnamon candies (red-hots). Stir until dissolved. Stir in 3 lb ($1\frac{1}{2}$ qt) applesauce, $\frac{1}{4}$ cup lemon juice, and 1 Tbsp salt. Pour into a 12 × 20 × 2-inch pan and chill until partially set. Fold in 8 oz coarsely chopped walnuts. Beat 10 oz cream cheese, $\frac{1}{2}$ cup milk, $\frac{1}{4}$ cup mayonnaise until smooth. Spoon mixture (2 cups) on top of gelatin. Swirl through gelatin with rubber spatula to marble.
- **Applesauce Gelatin Salad.** Heat 6 lb 10 oz (1 No. 10 can) applesauce, 8 oz granulated sugar, 1 Tbsp ground cinnamon, and 2 tsp ground nutmeg, stirring frequently. Add 1 lb 8 oz strawberry gelatin and stir until dissolved. Add 2 qt cold water and $\frac{1}{3}$ cup lemon juice.
- **Arabian Peach Salad.** Drain 1 No. 10 can sliced peaches, saving juice. Combine peach juice, $1\frac{1}{2}$ cups white vinegar, 1 lb 12 oz granulated sugar, 1 oz stick cinnamon, and 2 tsp whole cloves. Simmer 10 minutes. Strain, and add enough hot water to make 1 gal liquid. Add to 1 lb 8 oz orange gelatin and stir until dissolved. When slightly thickened, add peaches. Apricot halves may be substituted for peaches.
- **Autumn Salad.** Dissolve 1 lb 8 oz orange gelatin in 2 qt boiling water. Add 2 qt cold liquid, 2 lb 8 oz sliced fresh peaches, and 3 lb 8 oz fresh pears.
- **Blueberry Gelatin Salad.** Make in two layers. First layer: Drain 1 No. 10 can blueberries. Add water to juice if necessary to make 1 qt and heat to boiling. Add 12 oz raspberry gelatin and stir until

dissolved. Pour into 12 × 20 × 2-inch pan and chill. Second layer: Drain 1 No. 10 can crushed pineapple. Add water if necessary to make 1 qt liquid. Heat to boiling and add 12 oz lemon gelatin. Stir until dissolved. Stir in the crushed pineapple and 1 qt sour cream. Cool. Pour over first layer and chill.

- **Boysenberry Mold.** Thaw 2 lb 12 oz frozen boysenberries in a colander. Reserve juice. Heat juice plus water if needed to make 2 qt. Add 1 lb 8 oz raspberry gelatin and stir until dissolved. Stir in 1½ cups cold water. Chill until gelatin is the consistency of egg whites. Whip 1¼ qt whipped topping until soft peaks form. Fold in the thickened gelatin mixture and boysenberries. Pour into molds and refrigerate until firm.

- **Cranberry Apple Salad.** Dissolve 1 lb 8 oz cherry or raspberry gelatin in 2 qt boiling water. Add 3 lb fresh or frozen cranberry relish, 1 lb chopped apples, and 1 lb crushed pineapple. One No. 10 can whole cranberry sauce and 4 oranges, ground, may be used in place of the relish. Delete pineapple.

- **Cranberry Mold.** Drain 3½ cups crushed pineapple (2½ cups drained). Heat juice, plus enough water to make 3¼ cups, to boiling. Add 1 lb raspberry gelatin and stir until dissolved. Stir in 1½ qt cranberry relish. Chill until consistency of unbeaten egg whites. Fold in 3 cups mandarin oranges, drained and chopped, and 3¼ cups whipped topping whipped until stiff (6½ cups whipped). Spread in oiled gelatin molds.

- **Cucumber Soufflé Salad.** Dissolve 1 lb 8 oz lime or lemon gelatin in 1½ qt boiling water. Add 2 qt ice and cold water. Chill until partially set. Whip until fluffy. Add 3 cups mayonnaise and ⅓ cup lemon juice. Fold in 5 lb cucumbers, chopped.

- **Frosted Cherry Salad.** Dissolve 1 lb 8 oz cherry gelatin in 2 qt boiling water. Add 2 qt cold fruit juice, 2 lb drained, pitted red cherries, and 2 lb crushed pineapple. When congealed, frost with whipped cream cheese and chopped toasted almonds.

- **Frosted Lime Salad.** Dissolve 1 lb 8 oz lime gelatin in 2 qt boiling water. Add 2 qt cold fruit juice and, when mixture begins to congeal, add 4 lb crushed pineapple, drained, 2 lb 8 oz cottage cheese, 8 oz diced celery, 4 oz chopped pimiento, and 4 oz chopped nuts. When congealed, frost with mixture of 4 lb cream cheese blended with ½ cup mayonnaise.

- **Jellied Waldorf Salad.** Dissolve 1 lb 8 oz raspberry or cherry gelatin in 2 qt boiling water. Add 1 cup red cinnamon candies (red-hots) and stir until dissolved. Add 2 qt cold water or fruit juice. When mixture begins to congeal, add 2 lb diced apple, 12 oz finely diced celery, and 8 oz chopped pecans or walnuts.

- **Lemon Cream Mold.** Dissolve 1 lb 8 oz lemon gelatin in 1 qt boiling water. Stir in 1 qt cold water, ¾ cup vinegar, and ¼ tsp salt. Cool to room temperature. Add to 3 lb 12 oz sour cream and mix until smooth. Garnish with very thin slices of lemon and cucumber.

- **Molded Pineapple Cheese Salad.** Dissolve 1 lb 8 oz lemon gelatin in 2 qt boiling water. Add 2 qt cold fruit juice, 1 lb grated cheddar cheese, 3 lb drained crushed pineapple, 3 oz chopped green pepper or pimiento, and 4 oz finely chopped celery.

- **Ribbon Gelatin Salad.** Dissolve 1 lb 8 oz raspberry gelatin in 1 gal boiling water. Divide into three equal parts. Pour one-third into one 12 × 20 × 2-inch pan and chill. Add 1 lb cream cheese to another third and whip to blend; pour on the first part when it is congealed. Return it to the refrigerator until it, too, is congealed, then top with remaining portion.

- **Sunshine Salad.** Dissolve 1 lb 8 oz lemon gelatin in 2 qt boiling water. Add 2 qt cold fruit juice, 3 lb drained crushed pineapple, and 8 oz grated raw carrot.

- **Swedish Green-Top Salad.** Dissolve 12 oz lime gelatin in 2 qt boiling water. Pour into a 12 × 10 × 2-inch pan. Dissolve 12 oz orange gelatin in 2 qt boiling water. While still hot, add 1 lb 8 oz marshmallows and stir until melted. When cool, add 12 oz cream cheese, 1½ cups mayonnaise, and ½ tsp salt, blended together. Fold in 1 pt cream, whipped. Pour over congealed lime gelatin and return to the refrigerator to chill. To serve, invert so that green portion is on top.

- **Under-the-Sea Salad.** Dissolve 1 lb 8 oz lime gelatin in 1 gal boiling water. Divide into two parts. Pour one part into a 12 × 20 × 2-inch pan and chill. When it begins to congeal, add 12 oz drained crushed pineapple or sliced pears. To the remaining gelatin mixture, add 1 lb cream cheese and whip until smooth. Pour over first portion.

PERFECTION SALAD

Yield: 40 or 48 portions or 1 pan 12 × 20 × 2 inches   *Portion:* 2¼ × 2½ or 2 × 2½ inches

Ingredient	Amount	Procedure
Gelatin, unflavored	3 oz	Sprinkle gelatin over cold water.
Water, cold	2 cups	Let stand 10 minutes.
Water, boiling	3 qt	Add boiling water to gelatin. Stir until gelatin is dissolved.
Vinegar, cider	1 cup	Add to gelatin mixture. Stir until sugar is dissolved.
Lemon juice	1 cup	Chill.
Salt	1 oz (1½ Tbsp)	
Sugar, granulated	1 lb	
Cabbage, chopped	1 lb 8 oz	When liquid begins to congeal, add vegetables.
Celery, chopped	10 oz	Pour into a 12 × 20 × 2-inch counter pan. Place in the
Pimiento, chopped	4 oz	refrigerator to congeal.
Green pepper, chopped	4 oz	Cut 5 × 8 for 40 portions. Cut 6 × 8 for 48 portions.
Paprika	1 Tbsp	

Approximate nutritive values per portion (cut 48)   **Calories** 50

Amount/portion	%DV	Amount/portion	%DV	Amount/portion	%DV		%DV		%DV
Total Fat 0 g	0%	**Cholest.** 0 mg	0%	**Total Carb.** 11 g	4%	**Vitamin A**	1%	**Calcium**	1%
Sat. Fat 0 g	0%	**Sodium** 213 mg	9%	Fiber 0.4 g	2%	**Vitamin C**	22%	**Iron**	1%
Protein 2 g				Sugars 10 g					

Percent Daily Values (%DV) are based on a 2000-calorie diet.

TOMATO ASPIC

Yield: 40 or 48 portions or 1 pan 12 × 20 × 2 inches   *Portion:* 2¼ × 2½ or 2 × 2½ inches

Ingredient	Amount	Procedure
Gelatin, unflavored	4 oz	Sprinkle gelatin over cold water.
Water, cold	1 qt	Let stand 10 minutes.
Tomato juice	1 gal	Combine tomato juice and seasonings.
Onions, small, sliced	2	Boil 5 minutes. Strain.
Bay leaf	1	Add gelatin. Stir until dissolved.
Celery stalks	4	
Cloves, whole	8	
Dry mustard	2 tsp	
Sugar, granulated	14 oz	
Salt	1 Tbsp	
Vinegar or lemon juice	2 cups	Add vinegar or lemon juice.
		Pour into a 12 × 20 × 2-inch counter pan.
		Place in refrigerator to congeal.
		Cut 5 × 8 for 40 portions. Cut 6 × 8 for 48 portions.

Approximate nutritive values per portion (cut 48)   **Calories** 58

Amount/portion	%DV	Amount/portion	%DV	Amount/portion	%DV		%DV		%DV
Total Fat 0 g	0%	**Cholest.** 0 mg	0%	**Total Carb.** 13 g	4%	**Vitamin A**	4%	**Calcium**	1%
Sat. Fat 0 g	0%	**Sodium** 435 mg	18%	Fiber 1 g	4%	**Vitamin C**	31%	**Iron**	3%
Protein 3 g				Sugars 11 g					

Percent Daily Values (%DV) are based on a 2000-calorie diet.

FRUIT SALAD RECIPES

WALDORF SALAD

Yield: 50 portions or 6 qt   *Portion:* ⅓ cup (3 oz)

Ingredient	Amount	Procedure
Cream, whipping (optional)	½ cup	Whip cream. Combine with mayonnaise.
Mayonnaise or salad dressing	2 cups	
Apples, tart (peeled or unpeeled)	8 lb EP	Dice apples into fruit juice to prevent apples from turning dark. Drain and stir into salad dressing.
Celery, chopped	2 lb EP	Add celery, seasonings, and nuts to apples.
Salt	1 oz (1½ Tbsp)	Mix lightly until all ingredients are coated with dressing.
Sugar, granulated (optional)	6 oz	Serve with No. 12 dipper.
Walnuts, coarsely chopped	8 oz	

Approximate nutritive values per portion   **Calories 158**

Amount/portion	%DV	Amount/portion	%DV	Amount/portion	%DV		%DV		%DV
Total Fat 11 g	17%	**Cholest.** 8 mg	3%	**Total Carb.** 16 g	5%	**Vitamin A**	2%	**Calcium**	2%
Sat. Fat 2 g	9%	**Sodium** 260 mg	11%	Fiber 2 g	8%	**Vitamin C**	9%	**Iron**	2%
Protein 1 g				Sugars 13 g					

Percent Daily Values (%DV) are based on a 2000-calorie diet.

Notes
- Add walnuts only to salad that will be used immediately, as nuts will cause the salad to become gray.
- Fruit Salad Dressing (p. 709) may be substituted for mayonnaise.

Variations
- **Apple Cabbage Salad.** Use 6 lb diced apples and 4 lb crisp shredded cabbage. Omit celery. Sour cream or plain yogurt may be substituted for half the mayonnaise.
- **Apple Carrot Salad.** Use 6 lb diced apples, 3 lb shredded carrots, and only 1 lb chopped celery.
- **Apple Celery Salad.** Delete walnuts. Add 8 oz marshmallows.
- **Apple Date Salad.** Substitute 2 lb cut dates for celery.
- **Apple Fruit Salad.** Substitute 4 lb fresh fruit in season for half the apples.

APPLE PEAR SALAD

Yield: 50 plated salads

Ingredient	Amount	Procedure
Apples, red delicious Pears, Anjou	8–10 lb 8–10	Core and section fruit according to directions on pp. 146, 151. Section each pear and apple into 6–8 slices. Dip in diluted lemon juice to reduce discoloration.
Leaf lettuce Blue cheese, crumbled Apple Cider Dressing (p. 708)	50 leaves 3 lb 1 qt	Line salad plate with lettuce leaf. Alternate 3–4 sections of each fruit in a pinwheel-like arrangement on top of lettuce leaf. Sprinkle with 1 oz blue cheese. Drizzle with 1–2 Tbsp Apple Cider Dressing.

Approximate nutritive values per portion   **Calories** 250

Amount/portion	%DV	Amount/portion	%DV	Amount/portion	%DV		%DV		%DV
Total Fat 11 g	17%	**Cholest.** 20 mg	7%	**Total Carb.** 35 g	12%	**Vitamin A**	10%	**Calcium**	17%
Sat. Fat 5.5 g	27%	**Sodium** 407 mg	17%	Fiber 4 g	16%	**Vitamin C**	16%	**Iron**	6%
Protein 6.6 g				Sugars 20 g					

Percent Daily Values (%DV) are based on a 2000-calorie diet.

ACINI DE PEPE FRUIT SALAD

Yield: 50 portions   *Portion:* 4 oz

Ingredient	Amount	Procedure
Acini de pepe (see Note)	2 lb 6 oz (AP)	Cook pasta according to directions on p. 561.
Water, boiling	2 gal	Drain and cool slightly. There should be 7 lb 8 oz cooked
Salt	1 oz (1½ Tbsp)	product. Save for later step.
Sugar, granulated	7 oz	Combine sugar, flour, and salt in steam-jacketed kettle.
Flour, all-purpose	2 Tbsp	
Salt	1 tsp	
Pineapple juice drained from pineapple	1½ cups	Pour juice slowly into mixture while stirring with wire whip. Cook over moderate heat, stirring until slightly thickened.
Eggs, beaten	2 (3 oz)	Stir a small amount of the hot mixture into eggs, then stir eggs into the hot mixture. Cook and stir until thickened, 190°F.
Lemon juice	1 Tbsp	Add lemon juice. Cool to room temperature. Combine with cooked pasta. Mix lightly. Chill.
Mandarin oranges, drained	1 lb	Add fruit to pasta mixture. Mix lightly but thoroughly.
Crushed pineapple, drained	1 lb 12 oz	
Pineapple tidbits, drained	1 lb 12 oz	
Whipped topping	1¼ cups	Whip topping to stiff peaks. There should be 2½ cups whipped. Fold into salad. Chill until served. Serve with No. 8 dipper.

Approximate nutritive values per portion   **Calories** 144

Amount/portion	%DV	Amount/portion	%DV	Amount/portion	%DV		%DV		%DV
Total Fat 2 g	4%	**Cholest.** 14 mg	5%	**Total Carb.** 28 g	9%	**Vitamin A**	2%	**Calcium**	2%
Sat. Fat 1 g	6%	**Sodium** 246 mg	10%	Fiber 0.4 g	2%	**Vitamin C**	14%	**Iron**	5%
Protein 3 g				Sugars 11 g					

Percent Daily Values (%DV) are based on a 2000-calorie diet.

Note   ● Acini de pepe is a small round pasta resembling bb shot (p. 125).

AMBROSIA FRUIT SALAD

Yield: 50 portions   *Portion:* 2½ oz

Ingredient	Amount	Procedure
Mandarin oranges, canned, drained	3 lb	Combine fruits, marshmallows, and coconut.
Pineapple tidbits, canned, drained	3 lb 8 oz	
Miniature marsh-mallows	12 oz	
Shredded coconut	6 oz	
Sour cream	12 oz	Add sour cream to fruit. Toss lightly to combine. Serve with No. 12 dipper.

Approximate nutritive values per portion   **Calories** 82

Amount/portion	%DV	Amount/portion	%DV	Amount/portion	%DV		%DV		%DV
Total Fat 3 g	4%	**Cholest.** 3 mg	1%	**Total Carb.** 15 g	5%	Vitamin A	2%	Calcium	2%
Sat. Fat 2 g	9%	**Sodium** 17 mg	1%	Fiber 1 g	4%	Vitamin C	28%	Iron	1%
Protein 1 g				Sugars 12 g					

Percent Daily Values (%DV) are based on a 2000-calorie diet.

Notes
- Salad does not hold well and is best when served soon after mixing.
- Plain unflavored yogurt may be substituted for sour cream.

GRAPEFRUIT ORANGE SALAD

Yield: 50 portions   *Portion:* 2 orange, 3 grapefruit sections

Ingredient	Amount	Procedure
Grapefruit, medium	16	Peel and section fruit according to directions on p. 148
Oranges, large	17	For each salad, arrange 3 grapefruit sections and 2 orange sections, alternately on lettuce or other salad greens. Serve with Celery Seed Fruit Dressing (p. 709) or Honey French Dressing (p. 704).

Approximate nutritive values per portion   **Calories** 45

Amount/portion	%DV	Amount/portion	%DV	Amount/portion	%DV		%DV		%DV
Total Fat 0 g	0%	**Cholest.** 0 mg	0%	**Total Carb.** 11 g	4%	**Vitamin A**	2%	**Calcium**	2%
Sat. Fat 0 g	0%	**Sodium** 0 mg	0%	Fiber 2 g	9%	**Vitamin C**	88%	**Iron**	0%
Protein 1 g				Sugars 9 g					

Percent Daily Values (%DV) are based on a 2000-calorie diet.

Variations

- **Citrus Pomegranate Salad.**   Arrange grapefruit and orange sections on curly endive. Sprinkle pomegranate seeds over fruit. Serve with Celery Seed Dressing (pp. 702, 709).

- **Fresh Fruit Salad Bowl.**   Place chopped lettuce or other salad greens in individual salad bowls, 2 oz per bowl. Arrange wedges of cantaloupe, honeydew melon, and avocado, and sections of orange or grapefruit on the lettuce. Garnish with green grapes, Bing cherries, or fresh strawberries. Fresh pineapple, peaches, or apricots also are good in this salad. Serve with Celery Seed Fruit Dressing (p. 709) or Honey French Dressing (p. 704).

- **Grapefruit Apple Salad.**   Substitute wedges of unpeeled red apples for oranges.

- **Grapefruit-Orange-Avocado Salad.**   Place avocado wedges between grapefruit and orange sections. Garnish with fresh strawberries.

- **Grapefruit-Orange-Pear Salad.**   Alternate slices of fresh pear with grapefruit and orange sections.

SPICED APPLE SALAD

Yield: 50 portions   *Portion:* 1 apple

Ingredient	Amount	Procedure
Sugar, granulated	6 lb	Combine sugar, water, and flavorings.
Water	2 qt	Boil for about 5 minutes to form a thin syrup.
Vinegar, cider	1 cup	Set aside for next step.
Red coloring	½ tsp	
Cloves, whole	1 oz	
Cinnamon sticks	1 oz	
Apples, fresh	50	Core and peel apples. Leave apples whole unless they are large; then cut in half crosswise. Place apples in a flat pan. Pour syrup over apples. Cook on top of range or in oven until tender. Turn while cooking. Cool.
Celery, chopped	8 oz	Combine celery and nuts.
Nuts, chopped	4 oz	Add mayonnaise and salt.
Mayonnaise	¾ cup	Fill centers of cooked apples with this mixture.
Salt	½ tsp	

Approximate nutritive values per portion   **Calories** 165

Amount/portion	%DV	Amount/portion	%DV	Amount/portion	%DV		%DV		%DV
Total Fat 4 g	7%	**Cholest.** 0 mg	0%	**Total Carb.** 34 g	11%	**Vitamin A**	0%	**Calcium**	1%
Sat. Fat 1 g	4%	**Sodium** 61 mg	3%	Fiber 2 g	9%	**Vitamin C**	9%	**Iron**	2%
Protein 1 g				Sugars 29 g					

Percent Daily Values (%DV) are based on a 2000-calorie diet.

Notes
- Select apples that will hold their shape when cooked, such as Jonathan, Rome Beauty, or Winesap. Approximately 12 lb will be needed.
- 8 oz softened cream cheese may be substituted for mayonnaise.

FROZEN FRUIT SALAD

Yield: 48 portions or 1 pan 12 × 20 × 2 inches   *Portion:* 4 oz

Ingredient	Amount	Procedure
Gelatin, unflavored Water, cold	1 oz ½ cup	Sprinkle gelatin over cold water. Let stand 10 minutes.
Orange juice Pineapple juice	1¾ cups 1¾ cups	Combine juices and heat to boiling point. Add gelatin and stir to dissolve. Cool until slightly congealed.
Cream, whipping Mayonnaise	2 cups 1 cup	Whip cream. Combine with mayonnaise. Fold into the slightly congealed gelatin mixture.
Pineapple chunks, drained Orange sections, cut in halves Peaches, sliced, drained Bananas, diced Pecans, chopped Maraschino cherries Miniature marsh-mallows	1 lb 12 oz 1 lb 8 oz 1 lb 8 oz 2 lb 12 oz 8 oz 8 oz	Fold fruit into gelatin mixture. Pour into a 12 × 20 × 2-inch counter pan or into molds. Freeze. Cut 6 × 8.

Approximate nutritive values per portion   **Calories** 178

Amount/portion	%DV	Amount/portion	%DV	Amount/portion	%DV		%DV		%DV
Total Fat 12 g	18%	**Cholest.** 14 mg	5%	**Total Carb.** 19 g	6%	**Vitamin A**	5%	**Calcium**	2%
Sat. Fat 3 g	14%	**Sodium** 33 mg	1%	Fiber 2 g	6%	**Vitamin C**	27%	**Iron**	2%
Protein 2 g				Sugars 14 g					

Percent Daily Values (%DV) are based on a 2000-calorie diet.

Notes
- Whipped topping may be used in place of whipped cream.
- Other combinations of fruit (a total of 8 lb) may be used.

ENTREE SALAD RECIPES

CHEF'S SALAD BOWL

Yield: 50 portions   *Portion:* 7 oz

Ingredient	Amount	Procedure
Head lettuce or mixed greens	12 lb	Cut or tear lettuce into bite-size pieces. Portion into individual salad bowls, 4 oz per bowl.
Cooked turkey Cooked ham Cheddar cheese or Swiss cheese	6 lb 3 lb 3 lb	Cut meat and cheese into thin strips. Arrange on top of lettuce, 2 oz turkey, 1 oz ham, 1 oz cheese per bowl.
Green pepper rings Tomatoes, cut into wedges Eggs, hard-cooked, quartered (p. 439)	50 (8 lb AP) 6 lb (AP) 25	Garnish with 1 green pepper ring, 2 tomato wedges, and 2 egg quarters.
Salad dressing (see Notes)	1½–2 qt	Serve salad with choice of dressings.

Approximate nutritive values per portion   **Calories** 457

Amount/portion	%DV	Amount/portion	%DV	Amount/portion	%DV		%DV		%DV
Total Fat 29 g	44%	**Cholest.** 200 mg	67%	**Total Carb.** 15 g	5%	**Vitamin A**	28%	**Calcium**	26%
Sat. Fat 10 g	50%	**Sodium** 987 mg	41%	Fiber 4 g	16%	**Vitamin C**	139%	**Iron**	17%
Protein 35 g				Sugars 6 g					

Percent Daily Values (%DV) are based on a 2000-calorie diet.

Notes
- Potentially hazardous food. Store for service at an internal temperature below 41°F. Keep leftover product chilled below 41°F. See p. 105 for cooling procedures.
- Suggested salad dressings: Mayonnaise, Thousand Island, Roquefort, Creamy French, or Ranch.

Variations
- **Chicken and Bacon Salad.** Delete ham and turkey. Cut 6 lb cooked chicken into strips or cubes and mix with salad greens. Sprinkle 4 lb chopped, crisply cooked bacon over top of salads, 1 oz per salad.
- **Seafood Chef Salad.** Delete turkey and ham. Substitute 1 oz salmon, drained and broken into small chunks, 1 oz shrimp pieces or 2 whole shrimp for each salad.
- **Taco Salad.** Fry 50 10-inch flour tortillas by forming in basket shape around a large dipper or can. Submerge tortillas in hot fat, while still formed around dipper or can, for 20–30 seconds. Remove from fat and drain on paper towel. Prepare ground beef mixture (p. 509). Chill. Prepare lettuce mixture (p. 509). In bottom of shell basket, place 2½ oz lettuce mixture, then 4 oz cold ground beef mixture on top of lettuce. Sprinkle with sliced black olives and Cheddar cheese. Serve with Salsa (p. 756).

CHICKEN SALAD

Yield: 50 portions or 6¼ qt   *Portion:* ½ cup (4 oz)

Ingredient	Amount	Procedure
Cooked chicken	8 lb	Cut chicken into ½-inch cubes.
Eggs, hard-cooked (p. 439)	12	Peel and dice eggs.
Celery, diced	3 lb	Combine all ingredients. Mix lightly. Chill quickly to below 41°F.
Onion, minced	2 Tbsp	Serve with No. 8 dipper.
Salt	2 Tbsp	
Pepper, white	1 tsp	
Mayonnaise	1 qt	
Lemon juice	4 tsp	

Approximate nutritive values per portion   **Calories** 227

Amount/portion	%DV	Amount/portion	%DV	Amount/portion	%DV		%DV		%DV
Total Fat 21 g	32%	**Cholest.** 122 mg	41%	**Total Carb.** 2 g	1%	**Vitamin A**	6%	**Calcium**	3%
Sat. Fat 4 g	20%	**Sodium** 446 mg	19%	Fiber 0.4 g	2%	**Vitamin C**	3%	**Iron**	6%
Protein 23 g				Sugars 0 g					

Percent Daily Values (%DV) are based on a 2000-calorie diet.

Notes

- Potentially hazardous food. Store for service at an internal temperature below 41°F. Keep leftover product chilled below 41°F. See p. 105 for cooling procedures.
- Chilling the ingredients before combining shortens the amount of time product is in the temperature danger zone (above 41°F).
- 24–25 lb chicken AP will yield approximately 8 lb cooked meat.
- Cubed chicken may be marinated for 2 hours in ⅔ cup French Dressing (p. 703).

Variations

- **Chicken-Avocado-Orange Salad.**   Delete eggs. Gently stir into chicken mixture 1 qt diced orange segments, drained, 12 oz broken or slivered toasted almonds, and 6 oz chopped pimiento. Just before serving, add 6 avocados, diced.
- **Crunchy Chicken Salad.**   Add 8 oz sliced water chestnuts or toasted slivered almonds or walnuts.
- **Curried Chicken Salad.**   Add 1 Tbsp curry powder to mayonnaise.
- **Fruited Chicken Salad.**   Just before serving, add 2 lb 8 oz seedless grapes or pineapple chunks, drained, and 8 oz sunflower seeds.
- **Mandarin Chicken Salad.**   Delete eggs and pepper. Reduce mayonnaise to 2 cups. Add 2 cups sour cream. Substitute 2 Tbsp lime juice for lemon juice. Gently fold in 1 No. 10 can mandarin oranges and 1 No. 10 can pineapple tidbits, well drained.
- **Turkey Salad.**   Substitute turkey for chicken.

MARINATED CHICKEN AND FRESH FRUIT SALAD

Yield: 50 portions   *Portion:* 3 oz chicken + 3 oz greens + 3 oz fruit + 2 oz dressing

Ingredient	Amount	Procedure
Chicken breasts, 3 oz	50	Prepare and grill chicken according to Tarragon Chicken recipe, p. 536. Chill quickly to below 41°F.
Head lettuce (iceberg)	7 lb	Cut or tear lettuce into bite-size pieces.
Leaf lettuce, Bibb or romaine	3 lb	
Fresh fruit in season (see Notes)	10–12 lb	Prepare fruit. Peel if necessary and cut into wedges, medium-size chunks, or clusters.
Leaf lettuce	2 lb	For plate liners.
Golden Fruit Dressing (p. 709)	3 qt	Serve to the side.

To Assemble:

1. Line 50 9-inch luncheon plates with leaf lettuce.
2. Arrange 3 oz greens on each plate.
3. Place 3 oz grilled chicken strips in center of plate.
4. Arrange 3 oz fruit around the chicken.
5. In a side dish, serve Golden Fruit Dressing, p. 709.

Approximate nutritive values per portion   **Calories** 462

Amount/portion	%DV	Amount/portion	%DV	Amount/portion	%DV		%DV		%DV
Total Fat 31 g	47%	**Cholest.** 39 mg	13%	**Total Carb.** 34 g	11%	**Vitamin A**	29%	**Calcium**	6%
Sat. Fat 8 g	39%	**Sodium** 431 mg	18%	Fiber 2 g	10%	**Vitamin C**	86%	**Iron**	11%
Protein 16 g				Sugars 30 g					

Percent Daily Values (%DV) are based on a 2000-calorie diet.

Notes
- Potentially hazardous food. Store for service at an internal temperature below 41°F. Keep leftover product chilled below 41°F. See p. 105 for cooling procedures.
- Choose at least three kinds of fruit that complement each other. Suggested fruits: cantaloupe wedges, watermelon chunks, fresh pineapple spears or chunks, whole fresh strawberries, papaya pieces, mango slices, green or red grapes.

Variation
- **Blackened Chicken Salad.**   Season 25 chicken breasts with Cajun Seasoning (p. 782). Cook following Grilled Chicken Breast directions. Increase lettuce to 13 lb. Arrange 4 oz lettuce on plate and top with one-half sliced chicken breast. Garnish with chopped tomato and yellow bell pepper. Dress as desired.

CHICKEN AND PASTA SALAD PLATE

Yield: 50 portions   *Portion:* 7 oz

Ingredient	Amount	Procedure
Rotini	1 lb 2 oz (AP) (2 lb 8 oz cooked)	Cook according to direction on p. 561. Drain.
Water, boiling	1 gal	
Salt	1 Tbsp	
Vinegar, cider	2¾ cups	Combine in mixing bowl.
Lemon juice	⅓ cup	
Prepared mustard	3 Tbsp	
Garlic, minced	3 cloves	
Salt	2 Tbsp	
Oregano, dried, crumbled	1 tsp	
Pepper, black	2 tsp	
Sugar, granulated	2 tsp	
Salad oil	3½ cups	Add oil very gradually while mixing on medium speed with wire whip attachment.
Cooked chicken, cut in 1-inch pieces	8 lb 8 oz	Add chicken to dressing. Toss to coat well. Add cooked rotini and mix well. Chill quickly to 41°F.
Broccoli florets	1 lb 4 oz	Steam broccoli until tender-crisp. Add to marinated mixture shortly before serving.
Cherry tomatoes, cut in half	3 lb	Add to marinated mixture shortly before serving.
Zucchini, fresh, cut in julienne strips	2 lb 4 oz	
Carrots, shredded	10 oz	
Green onions, chopped	8 oz	
Leaf lettuce	2 lb	Cover plate with leaf lettuce.
Hard rolls	50	Portion 7 oz salad onto lettuce. Place one hard roll on each salad plate shortly before service.

Approximate nutritive values per portion   **Calories** 498

Amount/portion	%DV	Amount/portion	%DV	Amount/portion	%DV		%DV		%DV
Total Fat 23 g	36%	**Cholest.** 64 mg	21%	**Total Carb.** 43 g	14%	**Vitamin A**	26%	**Calcium**	10%
Sat. Fat 6 g	29%	**Sodium** 837 mg	35%	Fiber 1 g	6%	**Vitamin C**	37%	**Iron**	22%
Protein 29 g				Sugars 3 g					

Percent Daily Values (%DV) are based on a 2000-calorie diet.

Notes
- Potentially hazardous food. Store for service at an internal temperature below 41°F. Keep leftover product chilled below 41°F. See p. 105 for cooling procedures.
- Chilling ingredients before combining shortens the time product is in the temperature danger zone (above 40°F).
- Salad may be served in a bowl or on a plate with a bed of shredded lettuce.

SHRIMP TORTELLINI SALAD PLATE

Yield: 50 portions   *Portion:* 6 oz salad mixture

Ingredient	*Amount*	*Procedure*
Spinach tortellini, cheese-stuffed, frozen	4 lb (AP) (6 lb cooked)	Cook tortellini in boiling water for 3–5 minutes. Drain. Place in bowl.
Italian Dressing (p. 703)	2¼ qt	Pour dressing over pasta and toss gently to coat. Chill quickly to 41°F or less.
Salad shrimp, cooked, frozen	5 lb	Thaw shrimp under cold running water. Drain well and add to cold pasta.
Celery, thinly sliced	1 lb 10 oz	Add to pasta mixture. Toss well. Cover. Refrigerate until chilled to 41°F or less.
Carrots, cut into ¾-inch-long thin julienne strips	12 oz	
Green onions, thinly sliced	10 oz	
Water chestnuts, sliced, drained	1 lb 6 oz	
Leaf lettuce	2 lb 12 oz	Cover plate with leaf lettuce. Portion 6 oz salad onto lettuce.
Black olives	1 lb	Garnish plate with 3 black olives and 1 cherry tomato. Serve with 2 breadsticks.
Cherry tomatoes	1 lb	
Bread sticks	100	

Approximate nutritive values per portion   **Calories** 704

Amount/portion	%DV	Amount/portion	%DV	Amount/portion	%DV		%DV		%DV
Total Fat 28 g	43%	**Cholest.** 89 mg	30%	**Total Carb.** 88 g	29%	**Vitamin A**	31%	**Calcium**	12%
Sat. Fat 3 g	16%	**Sodium** 2465 mg	103%	Fiber 3 g	13%	**Vitamin C**	16%	**Iron**	27%
Protein 24 g				Sugars 3 g					

Percent Daily Values (%DV) are based on a 2000-calorie diet.

Notes
- Potentially hazardous food. Store for service at an internal temperature below 41°F. Keep leftover product chilled below 41°F. See p. 105 for cooling procedures.
- Chilling ingredients before combining shortens the time product is in the temperature danger zone (above 41°F).

POACHED SALMON ON FIELD GREENS

Yield: 50 portions   *Portion:* 4 oz salmon fillet, 4 oz greens, 1–2 oz dressing

Ingredient	Amount	Procedure
Salmon, poached (4 oz fillets)	50 fillets	Poach salmon according to directions on p. 468.
Lettuce assortment (see Notes)	12 lb 8 oz	Place 4 oz lettuce on plate. Drizzle with ½–1 oz of Vinaigrette Dressing.
Vinaigrette Dressing (p. 706)	2 qt	Carefully place salmon fillet on top of greens. Drizzle with ½–1 oz of Vinaigrette Dressing. Garnish with fresh herbs or edible flowers. (See p. 166 for suggestions.)

Notes
- Potentially hazardous food. *Food Safety Standards:* Hold for service at a temperature below 41°F.
- One of several commercial lettuce assortments may be used or an assortment made using several different salad greens (p. 155).
- Horseradish Caper Sauce (p. 765) may be ladled over salmon fillet in place of Vinaigrette Dressing.

CRAB SALAD

Yield: 50 portions or 6 qt   *Portion:* ½ cup (4 oz)

Ingredient	Amount	Procedure
Eggs, hard-cooked (p. 439)	30	Peel and chop eggs coarsely.
Crabmeat, flaked	5 lb	Add eggs and other ingredients to crabmeat.
Almonds, blanched, slivered (optional)	1 lb	Mix lightly. Chill quickly to below 41°F. Serve with No. 10 dipper.
Black olives, sliced	1 lb	
Lemon juice	⅓ cup	
Mayonnaise	1 qt	

Approximate nutritive values per portion   **Calories** 281

Amount/portion	%DV	Amount/portion	%DV	Amount/portion	%DV		%DV		%DV
Total Fat 24 g	37%	**Cholest.** 183 mg	61%	**Total Carb.** 4 g	1%	**Vitamin A**	7%	**Calcium**	7%
Sat. Fat 4 g	19%	**Sodium** 445 mg	19%	Fiber 1 g	4%	**Vitamin C**	0%	**Iron**	8%
Protein 14 g				Sugars 1 g					

Percent Daily Values (%DV) are based on a 2000-calorie diet.

Notes
- Potentially hazardous food. Store for service at an internal temperature below 41°F. Keep leftover product chilled below 41°F. See p. 105 for cooling procedures.
- Chilling ingredients before combining shortens the time product is in the temperature danger zone (above 41°F).
- Olives may be deleted and 1 lb diced cucumbers added.
- If desired, omit mayonnaise and marinate with French Dressing (p. 703).

Variation
- **Lobster Salad.**   Substitute lobster for crab.

Exhibit X Entree Salads

(Photos courtesy of Tyson Foods)

Exhibit XIII Fruit and Vegetable Garnishes

(Photo courtesy of Tyson Foods)

PASTA AND CRAB SALAD

Yield: 50 portions   *Portion:* 2½ oz

Ingredient	Amount	Procedure
Radiatore	1 lb 8 oz	Cook pasta according to directions on p. 561.
Water	1½ gal	Drain. Yield should be 3 lb cooked radiatore.
Salt	1 oz (1½ Tbsp)	
Lemon Basil Dressing (p. 706)	3¾ cups	Add dressing. Toss to coat pasta. Chill to below 41°F.
Onions, green, finely chopped	2 oz	Add onions and snow peas. Toss.
Snow peas, thawed, uncooked	1 lb 4 oz	
Crabmeat, diced	2 lb	Add crabmeat. Toss. Keep chilled below 41°F.

Approximate nutritive values per portion   **Calories** 139

Amount/portion	%DV	Amount/portion	%DV	Amount/portion	%DV		%DV		%DV
Total Fat 7 g	11%	**Cholest.** 18 mg	6%	**Total Carb.** 14 g	5%	**Vitamin A**	0%	**Calcium**	2%
Sat. Fat 2 g	9%	**Sodium** 416 mg	17%	Fiber 0.3 g	1%	**Vitamin C**	12%	**Iron**	5%
Protein 5 g				Sugars 2 g					

Percent Daily Values (%DV) are based on a 2000-calorie diet.

Notes
- Potentially hazardous food. Store for service at an internal temperature below 41°F. Keep leftover product chilled below 41°F. See p. 105 for cooling procedures.
- Chilling ingredients before combining shortens the time product is in the temperature danger zone (above 41°F).
- Cooked shrimp, cooked scallops, or lobster may be substituted for crabmeat.

SHRIMP SALAD

Yield: 50 portions or 6¼ qt   *Portion:* ½ cup (4 oz)

Ingredient	Amount	Procedure
Cooked shrimp (see Notes)	6 lb	Cut shrimp into ½-inch pieces. Place in bowl.
Celery, diced	2 lb	Add vegetables to shrimp.
Cucumber, diced	1 lb	
Lettuce, chopped (optional)	1 head	
Mayonnaise	1 qt	Combine mayonnaise and seasonings.
Lemon juice	2 Tbsp	Add to shrimp mixture. Mix lightly. Chill quickly to below 41°F.
Salt	2 tsp	Serve with No. 10 dipper.
Paprika	1 tsp	
Prepared mustard	2 tsp	

Approximate nutritive values per portion   **Calories** 187

Amount/portion	%DV	Amount/portion	%DV	Amount/portion	%DV		%DV		%DV
Total Fat 15 g	23%	**Cholest.** 117 mg	39%	**Total Carb.** 2 g	1%	Vitamin A	6%	Calcium	3%
Sat. Fat 2 g	11%	**Sodium** 327 mg	14%	Fiber 0.4 g	2%	Vitamin C	5%	Iron	10%
Protein 12 g				Sugars 0 g					

Percent Daily Values (%DV) are based on a 2000-calorie diet.

Notes

- Potentially hazardous food. Store for service at an internal temperature below 41°F. Keep leftover product chilled below 41°F. See p. 105 for cooling procedures.
- Chilling ingredients before combining shortens the time product is in the temperature danger zone (above 41°F).
- 12 lb raw shrimp in shell or 10 lb raw, peeled, and deveined shrimp will yield the 6 lb cooked shrimp needed. Cook according to directions on p. 458.
- 1 dozen hard-cooked eggs (p. 439), coarsely chopped, may be added. Reduce shrimp to 5 lb.
- Salad may be garnished with tomato wedges or served in a tomato cup.

SHRIMP RICE SALAD

Yield: 50 portions   *Portion:* ½ cup (4 oz)

Ingredient	Amount	Procedure
Rice, converted	1 lb	Cook rice according to directions on p. 594.
Water	1¼ qt	Chill.
Salt	1 Tbsp	
Margarine or vegetable oil	1 Tbsp	
Celery	1 lb 8 oz	Cut celery in thin slices crosswise.
Green peppers	1 lb	Slice green peppers in thin strips.
Cooked shrimp, chilled	5 lb	Combine shrimp, rice, and vegetables.
Vinegar, cider	1 cup	Combine and pour over shrimp-rice mixture.
Salad oil	½ cup	Marinate in refrigerator at least 3 hours.
Worcestershire sauce	2 Tbsp	
Sugar, granulated	2 Tbsp	
Salt	1 Tbsp	
Curry powder	2 tsp	
Ginger, ground	¾ tsp	
Pepper, black	½ tsp	
Pineapple chunks, canned or frozen, drained	3 lb	Just before serving, add pineapple. Serve with No. 8 dipper.

Approximate nutritive values per portion   **Calories** 122

Amount/portion	%DV	Amount/portion	%DV	Amount/portion	%DV		%DV		%DV
Total Fat 3 g	5%	**Cholest.** 89 mg	30%	**Total Carb.** 13 g	4%	**Vitamin A**	3%	**Calcium**	3%
Sat. Fat 1 g	4%	**Sodium** 377 mg	16%	Fiber 1 g	3%	**Vitamin C**	22%	**Iron**	11%
Protein 10 g				Sugars 5 g					

Percent Daily Values (%DV) are based on a 2000-calorie diet.

Notes
- Potentially hazardous food. Store for service at an internal temperature below 41°F. Keep leftover product chilled below 41°F. See p. 105 for cooling procedures.
- Chilling ingredients before combining shortens time the product is in the temperature danger zone (above 41°F).

TUNA PASTA SALAD PLATE

Yield: 50 portions   *Portion:* 3½ oz salad mixture

Ingredient	Amount	Procedure
Shell macaroni	2 lb (AP) (6 lb cooked)	Cook macaroni according to directions on p. 561. Drain. Place in bowl.
Water, boiling	2 gal	
Salt	2 oz	
Vegetable oil	2 Tbsp	
Italian Dressing (p. 703)	1 qt	Pour dressing over cooked macaroni. Stir to coat evenly. Cover and refrigerate 6–8 hours.
Canned tuna	2 lb	Drain tuna. Carefully fold into macaroni.
Green peppers	1 lb 6 oz	Cut peppers into strips approximately 1-inch long. Add to macaroni mixture.
Stuffed green olives, chopped	4 oz	Add chopped olives to macaroni mixture.
Lettuce leaves	1 lb 8 oz	Place 1 lettuce leaf off center on dinner plate. Place 3½ oz (¾ cup) salad on lettuce.
Eggs, hard-cooked (p. 439)	25	Place half an egg on one side of macaroni salad.
Fresh tomatoes	6 lb	Cut each tomato into 8 wedges. Place 2 wedges on other side of salad. Place one hard roll on plate shortly before serving.
Hard rolls	50	

Approximate nutritive values per portion   **Calories** 402

Amount/portion	%DV	Amount/portion	%DV	Amount/portion	%DV		%DV		%DV
Total Fat 15 g	23%	**Cholest.** 112 mg	37%	**Total Carb.** 50 g	17%	Vitamin A	11%	Calcium	9%
Sat. Fat 3 g	13%	**Sodium** 651 mg	27%	Fiber 1 g	5%	Vitamin C	39%	Iron	20%
Protein 17 g				Sugars 3 g					

Percent Daily Values (%DV) are based on a 2000-calorie diet.

Notes
- Potentially hazardous food. Store for service at an internal temperature below 41°F. Keep leftover product chilled below 41°F. See p. 105 for cooling procedures.
- Chilling ingredients before combining shortens time product is in the temperature danger zone (above 41°F).

TUNA SALAD

Yield: 50 portions or 6¼ qt   *Portion:* ½ cup (4 oz)

Ingredient	Amount	Procedure
Eggs, hard-cooked (p. 439)	12	Peel and dice eggs.
Tuna, flaked	7 lb	Add vegetables, relish, and eggs to tuna. Mix lightly.
Celery, chopped	1 lb	
Cucumber, diced	1 lb	
Onion, minced	2 oz	
Pickle relish, drained	8 oz	
Mayonnaise	1 qt	Add mayonnaise to tuna mixture. Mix lightly to blend. Chill quickly to below 41°F. Serve with No. 8 dipper.

Approximate nutritive values per portion   **Calories** 228

Amount/portion	%DV	Amount/portion	%DV	Amount/portion	%DV		%DV		%DV
Total Fat 16 g	24%	**Cholest.** 80 mg	27%	**Total Carb.** 3 g	1%	Vitamin A	4%	Calcium	2%
Sat. Fat 3 g	13%	**Sodium** 374 mg	16%	Fiber 0.2 g	1%	Vitamin C	2%	Iron	7%
Protein 18 g				Sugars 0 g					

Percent Daily Values (%DV) are based on a 2000-calorie diet.

Notes
- Potentially hazardous food. Store for service at an internal temperature below 41°F. Keep leftover product chilled below 41°F. See p. 105 for cooling procedures.
- Chilling ingredients before combining shortens time product is in the temperature danger zone (above 41°F).

Variations
- **Salmon Salad.** Substitute salmon for tuna.
- **Tuna Apple Salad.** Substitute tart, diced apples for cucumbers. Omit pickle relish.
- **Tuna Pea Salad.** Delete eggs and minced onion. Substitute 5 cups sour cream mixed with ½ cup lemon juice for the mayonnaise. Add 2 lb frozen green peas, thawed, 8 oz green pepper, and 8 oz sliced green onions.

STUFFED TOMATO SALAD

Yield: 50 portions *Portion:* 1 tomato

Ingredient	Amount	Procedure
Tomatoes, medium size	50	Place tomatoes in a wire basket and dip in boiling water. Let stand for 1 minute. Dip in cold water. Remove skins.
Chicken, crab, shrimp, tuna, or egg salad (chilled)	10 lb	Turn tomato stem end down. Cut, not quite through, into fourths. Fill with No. 12 dipper of salad.

Approximate nutritive values per portion   **Calories** 248

Amount/portion	%DV	Amount/portion	%DV	Amount/portion	%DV		%DV		%DV
Total Fat 16 g	25%	**Cholest.** 30 mg	10%	**Total Carb.** 13 g	4%	**Vitamin A**	8%	**Calcium**	6%
Sat. Fat 2 g	10%	**Sodium** 628 mg	26%	Fiber 3 g	10%	**Vitamin C**	40%	**Iron**	12%
Protein 13 g				Sugars 3 g					

Percent Daily Values (%DV) are based on a 2000-calorie diet.

Notes
- Potentially hazardous food. Store for service at an internal temperature below 41°F. Keep leftover product chilled below 41°F. See p. 105 for cooling procedures.
- 50 medium-size tomatoes will weigh approximately 12 lb.

Variations
- **Tomato Cabbage Salad.**   Combine 1 lb cabbage and 1 lb. celery, finely chopped, 1 Tbsp salt, and 1 cup mayonnaise for salad mixture. Fill tomato cups, using No. 40 dipper.
- **Tomato Cottage Cheese Salad.**   Substitute 6 lb cottage cheese for salad mixture. Fill tomato cups, using No. 20 dipper.

COTTAGE CHEESE SALAD

Yield: 50 portions or 6 qt   *Portion:* ½ cup (4 oz)

Ingredient	Amount	Procedure
Tomatoes, fresh, peeled and diced	3 lb	Prepare vegetables.
Green peppers, chopped	4 oz	
Celery, diced	1 lb	
Cucumber, diced	1 lb	
Radishes, sliced	8 oz	
Cottage cheese, dry curd (see Notes)	6 lb	Just before serving, add vegetables and mix all ingredients gently.
Salt	1 oz (1½ Tbsp)	
Mayonnaise	3 cups	

Approximate nutritive values per portion   **Calories** 150

Amount/portion	%DV	Amount/portion	%DV	Amount/portion	%DV		%DV		%DV
Total Fat 11 g	17%	**Cholest.** 11 mg	4%	**Total Carb.** 3 g	1%	**Vitamin A**	3%	**Calcium**	3%
Sat. Fat 2 g	9%	**Sodium** 328 mg	14%	Fiber 0.4 g	2%	**Vitamin C**	13%	**Iron**	2%
Protein 10 g				Sugars 1 g					

Percent Daily Values (%DV) are based on a 2000-calorie diet.

Notes
- Potentially hazardous food. Store for service at an internal temperature below 41°F. Keep leftover product chilled below 41°F. See p. 105 for cooling procedures.
- Chilling ingredients before combining shortens time product is in the temperature danger zone (above 41° F).
- If creamed cottage cheese is used, reduce mayonnaise to 1 cup and omit salt.

DELI PLATE

Yield: 50 portions   *Portion:* 2½ oz salad + 2 oz meat and cheese

Ingredient	Amount	Procedure
Pasta Salad (p. 659) or Potato Salad (p. 665) or Macaroni Salad (p. 660)	9 lb	Prepare salad.
Pastrami, corned beef, or other cold cuts	3 lb	Wafer slice meat.
Lettuce leaves Swiss cheese, sliced	1 lb 8 oz 3 lb	Place lettuce leaf on dinner plate. Place one 1-oz cheese slice on lettuce. Portion 1 oz pastrami on cheese. Place No. 16 dipper pasta, potato, or macaroni salad on plate.

Tomatoes, sliced
Dill pickle spears, drained
Black olives
	6 lb 8 oz (EP)
	1 lb 8 oz
	
	6 oz
		Arrange on plate:
		    2 tomato slices
		    1 dill pickle spear
		    1 black olive

Rye bread	100 slices	Place alongside meat on plates.

Note   • Potentially hazardous food. Store for service at an internal temperature below 41°F. Keep leftover product chilled below 41°F. See p. 105 for cooling procedures.

Variation   • Ham rolls or slices, sliced turkey, deviled or hard-cooked eggs, green pepper rings, green onions, cucumber slices, onion slices, cherry tomatoes, or marinated mushrooms may be used.

TURKEY CROISSANT SALAD PLATE

Yield: 50 portions   *Portion:* 2½ oz turkey

Ingredient	Amount	Procedure
Spinach, fresh, raw	2 lb (EP)	Prepare vegetables and fruits.
Tomatoes, fresh sliced	7 lb	
Oranges, navel, fresh, unpeeled, sliced	3 lb 3 oz	
Grapes, red seedless	6 lb	
Alfalfa sprouts	2 oz	
Smoked turkey, wafer-sliced	8 lb	
Croissants	50 (2½-oz size)	Assemble plates according to directions given below.

TO ASSEMBLE TURKEY CROISSANT PLATES:

1. Line three-fourths of plate with ¾ oz spinach.
2. Place 2 tomato slices on spinach leaves.
3. Cut orange slices in half. Place beside tomato slices.
4. Place 2½ oz turkey beside orange slices.
5. Place 1 Tbsp alfalfa sprouts beside turkey.
6. Place a 2-oz cluster of grapes beside sprouts.
7. Place 1 croissant on plate.

Approximate nutritive values per portion   **Calories** 304

Amount/portion	%DV	Amount/portion	%DV	Amount/portion	%DV		%DV		%DV
Total Fat 14 g	22%	**Cholest.** 88 mg	29%	**Total Carb.** 31 g	11%	**Vitamin A**	18%	**Calcium**	16%
Sat. Fat 6 g	28%	**Sodium** 885 mg	37%	Fiber 3 g	14%	**Vitamin C**	72%	**Iron**	17%
Protein 17 g				Sugars 19 g					

Percent Daily Values (%DV) are based on a 2000-calorie diet.

Notes
- Potentially hazardous food. Store for service at an internal temperature below 41°F. Keep leftover product chilled below 41°F. See p. 105 for cooling procedures.
- Chicken salad, crab salad, shrimp salad, or other wafer-sliced deli meats may be substituted for smoked turkey. If substituting salad meat for solid meat, omit tomato slices and add another fruit (e.g., apples or plums).

FRUIT SALAD PLATE

Yield: 50 portions   *Portion:* 6 oz fruit + 4 oz salad or sherbet

Ingredient	Amount	Procedure
Fruit in season (3–4 selections from fruits listed in Note)	20 lb (EP)	Prepare fruit.
Cottage cheese, Chicken Salad (p. 678), or sherbet	12 lb	Prepare salad according to recipe.
Nut bread sand-wiches or muffins	50–100	
Lettuce	1 lb 8 oz	Prepare lettuce. Place lettuce leaf on dinner plate. Arrange fruit, salad, and bread on lettuce.

Note   • Choose a combination that offers contrast in shape, color, and flavor from the following lists:

Fruit suggestions

Apple wedges
Avocado wedges, slices, or halves
Bananas, cut in strips or chunks, rolled in chopped nuts
Cherries, sweet
Grape clusters, red or green
Grapefruit sections
Kiwi fruit
Mangoes
Melon: cantaloupe, honeydew, watermelon; cut in wedges, rings, or balls
Orange slices, half slices, sections
Papayas
Peach halves or slices: cream cheese filling, cranberry sauce, or cottage cheese in halves
Pear halves, filled, or slices
Pineapple chunks, spears, rings
Plums
Strawberries

Salad suggestions

Cheese strips or slices
Cottage cheese
Chicken salad
Sliced chicken or turkey
Ham roll

Bread suggestions

Hard roll
Muffin
Finger sandwich: chicken, tuna
Nut bread sandwich
Raisin bread–cream cheese sandwich

Garnishes (See p. 891 for additional garnish suggestions.)

Coconut
Lemon or lime wedge
Pomegranate seeds
Stuffed prune

RELISH RECIPES

BUTTERED APPLES

Yield: 50 portions or 7 qt   *Portion:* ½ cup (4 oz)

Ingredient	*Amount*	*Procedure*
Apples, fresh	13 lb (EP) (16 lb AP)	Wash apples and cut into sections. Remove cores. Arrange in pan.
Margarine, melted Water, hot Sugar, granulated Salt	8 oz 2 cups 1 lb 8 oz 1 Tbsp	Mix remaining ingredients and pour over apples. Cover and simmer until apples are tender, approximately 1 hour.

Approximate nutritive values per portion   **Calories** 155

Amount/portion	%DV	Amount/portion	%DV	Amount/portion	%DV		%DV		%DV
Total Fat 4 g	6%	**Cholest.** 0 mg	0%	**Total Carb.** 32 g	11%	**Vitamin A**	1%	**Calcium**	1%
Sat. Fat 1 g	4%	**Sodium** 171 mg	7%	Fiber 3 g	10%	**Vitamin C**	11%	**Iron**	1%
Protein 0 g				Sugars 29 g					

Percent Daily Values (%DV) are based on a 2000-calorie diet.

Notes
- Select apples that will hold their shape when cooked, such as Jonathan, Rome Beauty, or Winesap.
- Apple sections may be arranged in a counter pan and steamed until tender. Sprinkle margarine and sugar over the top and bake for 15–20 minutes.
- Hot buttered apples often are served in place of a vegetable.
- Frozen or canned apples may be used.

Variations
- **Apple Rings.**   Cut rings of unpared apples, steam until tender. Add sugar and margarine and bake 15 minutes.
- **Cinnamon Apples.**   Cut pared apples into rings. Add cinnamon drops (red-hots) for flavor and color. Proceed as for Buttered Apples but reduce sugar to 12 oz.
- **Fried Apples**   Melt 1 lb margarine or butter in frying pan. Add sliced apples. Add 8 oz brown sugar, 1 tsp salt, and 1 tsp cinnamon. Cook apples, turning occasionally, until apples are lightly browned and just tender. Frozen apple slices, thawed and drained, may be used.

CRANBERRY RELISH (RAW)

Yield: 50 portions or 5 qt   *Portion:* ⅓ cup (3 oz)

Ingredient	Amount	Procedure
Oranges, unpeeled	3 (size 72)	Wash and quarter oranges and apples.
Apples, cored	5 lb	Sort and wash cranberries.
Cranberries, raw	3 lb	Put fruit through chopper or grinder.
Sugar, granulated	2 lb 4 oz	Add sugar to fruit and blend.
		Chill for 24 hours.
		Serve with No. 16 dipper as a relish or salad.

Approximate nutritive values per portion   **Calories** 123

Amount/portion	%DV	Amount/portion	%DV	Amount/portion	%DV		%DV		%DV
Total Fat 0 g	0%	**Cholest.** 0 mg	0%	**Total Carb.** 32 g	11%	**Vitamin A**	0%	**Calcium**	0%
Sat. Fat 0 g	0%	**Sodium** 0 mg	0%	Fiber 2 g	9%	**Vitamin C**	17%	**Iron**	0%
Protein 0 g				Sugars 27 g					

Percent Daily Values (%DV) are based on a 2000-calorie diet.

Variation   • **Cranberry Orange Relish.** Delete apples. Increase oranges to 6 and sugar to 3 lb. Add ¼ cup lemon juice.

CRANBERRY SAUCE

Yield: 50 portions or 5 qt　　　　*Portion:* ⅓ cup

Ingredient	Amount	Procedure
Cranberries	4 lb (AP)	Wash cranberries. Discard soft berries.
Sugar, granulated Water	4 lb 1 qt	Combine sugar and water. Bring to a boil. Add cranberries and boil gently until skins burst. Do not overcook. Chill. Serve with No. 12 dipper.

Approximate nutritive values per portion　　　　　　　　　　　　　　**Calories** 158

Amount/portion	%DV	Amount/portion	%DV	Amount/portion	%DV		%DV		%DV
Total Fat 0 g	0%	**Cholest.** 0 mg	0%	**Total Carb.** 41 g	14%	**Vitamin A**	0%	Calcium	0%
Sat. Fat 0 g	0%	**Sodium** 0 mg	0%	Fiber 2 g	6%	**Vitamin C**	8%	Iron	0%
Protein 0 g				Sugars 35 g					

Percent Daily Values (%DV) are based on a 2000-calorie diet.

Note
- Make sauce at least 24 hours before using.

Variations
- **Baked Cranberry Relish.**　Wash and drain 4 lb cranberries. Stir in 2 lb 12 oz granulated sugar, ⅓ cup water, and 1 tsp cinnamon. Place berries in glass chafing dishes or other baking pan suitable for serving. Mix together 2½ cups chopped pecans, ½ cup grated fresh lemon rind, and 4 cups orange marmalade. Spread on top of berries. Bake at 350°F for 45 minutes. Serve warm.
- **Pureed Cranberry Sauce.**　Add water to cranberries and cook until skins burst. Puree cranberries and add sugar. Cook until sugar is dissolved.
- **Royal Cranberry Sauce.**　Make half of cranberry sauce recipe. When cool add 3 oranges, chopped; 1 lb apples, chopped; 1 lb white grapes, seeded; 1 lb pineapple, diced; and 4 oz coarsely chopped pecans. Serve with No. 24 dipper as a relish. Yield: 1 gal.

CORN RELISH

Yield: 50 portions   *Portion:* 3 oz

Ingredient	Amount	Procedure
Sugar, granulated	1 lb	Mix sugar, flour, and salt in steam-jacketed kettle or stockpot until well blended.
Flour, all-purpose	2 oz (½ cup)	
Salt	1 oz	
Water	1½ cups	Add to dry ingredients in kettle. Stir until smooth. Cook until thickened, stirring constantly.
Vinegar, cider	1⅔ cups	
Prepared mustard	6 Tbsp	
Corn, whole kernel, frozen, thawed	6 lb	Place corn and seasonings in baker's bowl. Pour hot dressing over corn and mix lightly. Serve chilled.
Celery seed	1½ tsp	
Pimiento, chopped, drained	3 oz	
Onions, fresh, finely chopped	2 oz	
Green peppers, chopped	3 oz	

Approximate nutritive values per portion   **Calories 84**

Amount/portion	%DV	Amount/portion	%DV	Amount/portion	%DV		%DV		%DV
Total Fat 0 g	0%	**Cholest.** 0 mg	0%	**Total Carb.** 21 g	7%	**Vitamin A**	1%	**Calcium**	0%
Sat. Fat 0 g	0%	**Sodium** 247 mg	10%	Fiber 0 g	0%	**Vitamin C**	7%	**Iron**	2%
Protein 2 g				Sugars 9 g					

Percent Daily Values (%DV) are based on a 2000-calorie diet.

Variation   • **Black Bean and Corn Relish.**   Substitute 2 lb cooked black beans for 2 lb corn.

SAUERKRAUT RELISH

Yield: 50 portions   *Portion:* ⅓ cup (3 oz)

Ingredient	Amount	Procedure
Sauerkraut	1 No. 10 can	Combine all ingredients.
Carrots, shredded	1 lb	Refrigerate for at least 12 hours.
Celery, chopped	12 oz	
Onion, chopped	8 oz	
Green pepper, chopped	1 lb	
Sugar, granulated	1 lb 8 oz	

Approximate nutritive values per portion   **Calories** 73

Amount/portion	%DV	Amount/portion	%DV	Amount/portion	%DV		%DV		%DV
Total Fat 0 g	0%	**Cholest.** 0 mg	0%	**Total Carb.** 18 g	6%	**Vitamin A**	26%	**Calcium**	2%
Sat. Fat 0 g	0%	**Sodium** 399 mg	17%	Fiber 2 g	8%	**Vitamin C**	30%	**Iron**	5%
Protein 1 g				Sugars 14 g					

Percent Daily Values (%DV) are based on a 2000-calorie diet.

Note   • Sauerkraut may be chopped before combining with other ingredients.

PICKLED BEETS

Yield: 50 portions or 2 gal   *Portion:* 3 oz

Ingredient	Amount	Procedure
Beets, canned, sliced or whole	2 No. 10 cans	Drain beets. Reserve 1 cup juice for next step.
Vinegar, cider	2 qt	Mix vinegar, sugars, spices, and liquid from beets.
Sugar, brown	1 lb	Heat to boiling point. Boil 5 minutes.
Sugar, granulated	8 oz	Pour hot mixture over beets.
Salt	1 tsp	Chill 24 hours before serving.
Pepper, black	½ tsp	
Cinnamon sticks	2	
Cloves, whole	1 tsp	
Allspice, whole	1 tsp	

Approximate nutritive values per portion   **Calories** 74

Amount/portion	%DV	Amount/portion	%DV	Amount/portion	%DV		%DV		%DV
Total Fat 0 g	0%	**Cholest.** 0 mg	0%	**Total Carb.** 21 g	7%	**Vitamin A**	0%	**Calcium**	2%
Sat. Fat 0 g	0%	**Sodium** 246 mg	10%	Fiber 1 g	5%	**Vitamin C**	5%	**Iron**	9%
Protein 1 g				Sugars 8 g					

Percent Daily Values (%DV) are based on a 2000-calorie diet.

Notes   • If using fresh beets, cook 14 lb AP according to directions on p. 825. Peel and slice, then proceed as in the recipe. Substitute 1 cup water for beet juice.

• Sliced onions, separated into rings, may be added.

• Granulated sugar may be substituted for brown sugar.

MINTED TABOULI

Yield: 50 portions   *Portion:* 2 oz

Ingredient	Amount	Procedure
Bulgur	8 oz	Combine bulgar and water in large mixing bowl. Let stand at least 2 hours.
Water	1¼ qt	Drain well.
Tomatoes, fresh, seeded and diced	1 lb	Add to bulgur.
Cucumbers, peeled and chopped	6 oz	
Red onions, finely chopped	6 oz	
Parsley, fresh, chopped	2 oz	
Mint leaves, coarsely chopped	½ oz	
Lemon juice, fresh	1¼ cups	Blend lemon juice, oil, and spices.
Olive oil	½ cup	Pour over bulgur mixture. Toss to blend. Cover.
Salt	2¼ tsp	Refrigerate for at least 12 hours before serving. Keeps well.
Pepper, black	1 tsp	
Sugar, granulated	1½ tsp	

Approximate nutritive values per portion   **Calories** 41

Amount/portion	%DV	Amount/portion	%DV	Amount/portion	%DV		%DV		%DV
Total Fat 2 g	4%	**Cholest.** 0 mg	0%	**Total Carb.** 5 g	2%	**Vitamin A**	1%	**Calcium**	0%
Sat. Fat 1 g	2%	**Sodium** 100 mg	4%	Fiber 1 g	5%	**Vitamin C**	8%	**Iron**	1%
Protein 1 g				Sugars 1 g					

Percent Daily Values (%DV) are based on a 2000-calorie diet.

Note   • Salad oil may be substituted for olive oil. Mint leaves may be omitted for plain Tabouli.

SALAD DRESSING RECIPES

MAYONNAISE

Yield: 1 gal

Ingredient	Amount	Procedure
Egg yolks (see Notes) Salt Paprika Dry mustard	8 (5 oz) 2 oz (3 Tbsp) 2 tsp 2 Tbsp	Place egg yolks and seasonings in mixer bowl. Mix thoroughly, using wire whip attachment.
Vinegar, cider	¼ cup	Add vinegar and blend.
Salad oil	2 qt	Add oil very slowly, beating steadily on high speed until an emulsion is formed. Oil may then be added, ½ cup at a time and later 1 cup at a time, beating well after each addition.
Vinegar, cider	¼ cup	Add vinegar. Beat well.
Salad oil	2 qt	Continue beating and adding oil until all oil has been added and emulsified.

Approximate nutritive values per ounce　　　　　　　　　　　　　　　　　　　　　**Calories** 246

Amount/portion	%DV	Amount/portion	%DV	Amount/portion	%DV		%DV		%DV
Total Fat 28 g	43%	**Cholest.** 14 mg	5%	**Total Carb.** 0 g	0%	**Vitamin A**	2%	Calcium	0%
Sat. Fat 7 g	36%	**Sodium** 150 mg	6%	Fiber 0 g	0%	**Vitamin C**	0%	Iron	0%
Protein 0 g				Sugars 0 g					

Percent Daily Values (%DV) are based on a 2000-calorie diet.

Notes
- Potentially hazardous food. Store for service at an internal temperature below 41°F. Keep leftover product chilled below 41°F. See p. 105 for cooling procedures.
- For safety reasons, the use of pasteurized frozen egg yolks is recommended.
- The addition of oil too rapidly or insufficient beating may cause the oil to separate from the other ingredients, resulting in a curdled appearance. Curdled or broken mayonnaise may be reformed by adding it (a small amount at a time) to 2 well-beaten egg yolks or eggs and beating well after each addition. It also may be reformed by adding it to a small portion of uncurdled mayonnaise.

Variations　　**To make approximately 2 qt dressing:**
- **Buttermilk Dressing.**   To 1 qt mayonnaise, add 1 qt buttermilk; 2 tsp basil; ½ tsp oregano; 1 Tbsp finely chopped fresh parsley; 1 clove garlic, minced; 2 tsp black pepper; 2 oz chopped onion; and 1 tsp tarragon.
- **Campus Dressing.**   To 2 qt mayonnaise, add ⅓ cup fresh parsley, ¼ cup chopped green pepper, and ½ cup finely chopped celery.
- **Chantilly Dressing.**   To 1½ qt mayonnaise, fold in 1½ cups cream, whipped.
- **Creamy Blue Cheese Dressing.**   To 1 qt mayonnaise, add 2 cups (1 lb) sour cream, ¼ cup lemon juice, 1 Tbsp grated onion, 1 tsp salt, and 8 oz finely crumbled blue cheese.
- **Dilly Dressing.**   To 1½ qt mayonnaise, add 2 cups evaporated milk or buttermilk, 1 Tbsp seasoned salt, 1 tsp garlic powder, and ¼ cup chopped dill weed.
- **Egg and Green Pepper Dressing.**   To 1¾ qt mayonnaise, add 12 chopped hard-cooked eggs, ¼ cup finely chopped green pepper, 2 Tbsp onion juice, and a few grains cayenne pepper.

- **Garden Dressing.** Combine 3 cups mayonnaise and 1½ qt (3 lb) sour cream. Add 3 oz granulated sugar, 2 tsp salt, and 1 tsp black pepper. Fold in 12 oz thinly sliced green onions, 8 oz thinly sliced radishes, 8 oz chopped cucumbers, and 8 oz minced green pepper. This may be used for a vegetable dip also.

- **Green Peppercorn Cream Dressing.** To 1 cup mayonnaise, add 1¼ qt (2 lb 8 oz) sour cream, 1 cup Dijon-style mustard, ⅓ cup finely crushed and drained green peppercorns, ¼ cup white wine vinegar, and ⅔ cup chopped parsley (optional).

- **Honey Cream Dressing.** Blend together 4 oz cream cheese, 1⅓ cups honey, 1 cup lemon or pineapple juice, and ¼ tsp salt; then fold into 1½ qt mayonnaise.

- **Honey Yogurt Dressing.** To 1 cup mayonnaise, add 1½ qt unflavored yogurt, ⅓ cup honey, ¼ cup raspberry vinegar, 2 Tbsp lemon juice, and 1 Tbsp grated fresh orange peel.

- **Horseradish Cream Dressing.** To 1 cup mayonnaise, add 1½ qt (3 lb) sour cream, 2 Tbsp lemon juice, 2 tsp curry powder, 5 oz horseradish, 1 tsp salt, and 1 tsp paprika.

- **Roquefort Dressing.** To 1½ qt mayonnaise, add 2 cups French dressing, 8 oz crumbled Roquefort cheese, and 2 tsp Worcestershire sauce.

- **Russian Dressing.** To 2 qt mayonnaise, add 2 cups chili sauce, 2 Tbsp Worcestershire sauce, 2 tsp onion juice, and a few grains of cayenne.

- **Sour Cream Basil Dressing.** To 1 cup mayonnaise, add ¾ cup vinegar, 1½ qt (3 lb) sour cream, 1 oz granulated sugar, 1½ oz salt, 1½ Tbsp celery seed, and 2 Tbsp basil leaves.

- **Thousand Island Dressing.** To 1½ qt mayonnaise, add 1½ oz minced onion, 3 oz chopped pimiento, 1 cup chili sauce, 8 chopped hard-cooked eggs, 1 tsp salt, ¼ cup pickle relish, and a few grains of cayenne.

COOKED SALAD DRESSING

Yield: 3 gal

Ingredient	Amount	Procedure
Sugar, granulated	3 lb	Combine dry ingredients in a steam-jacketed kettle or stockpot.
Flour, all-purpose	1 lb 8 oz	
Salt	6 oz	
Dry mustard	3 oz	
Water, cold	1 qt	Add water to dry ingredients and stir with wire whip until a smooth paste is formed.
Milk, hot	1 gal	Add hot milk and water, stirring continuously while adding. Cook 20 minutes, or until thickened.
Water, hot	2 qt	
Margarine	1 lb	Stir in margarine and vinegar.
Vinegar, cider, hot	3 qt	
Egg yolks, beaten (see Notes)	50 (2 lb)	Add cooked mixture slowly to egg yolks, stirring briskly. Cook 7–10 minutes. Remove from heat and cool quickly to below 41°F.

Approximate nutritive values per ounce — **Calories 44**

Amount/portion	%DV	Amount/portion	%DV	Amount/portion	%DV		%DV		%DV
Total Fat 2 g	3%	**Cholest.** 32 mg	11%	**Total Carb.** 6 g	2%	**Vitamin A**	5%	Calcium	1%
Sat. Fat 1 g	3%	**Sodium** 189 mg	8%	Fiber 0 g	0%	**Vitamin C**	0%	Iron	1%
Protein 1 g				Sugars 4 g					

Percent Daily Values (%DV) are based on a 2000-calorie diet.

Notes
- Potentially hazardous food. Store for service at an internal temperature below 41°F.
- 25 whole eggs may be substituted for egg yolks, and hot water for hot milk.

Variation
- **Combination Dressing.** Combine 1 qt Cooked Salad Dressing and 1 qt mayonnaise.

CHILEAN DRESSING

Yield: 1½ qt

Ingredient	Amount	Procedure
Salad oil	2 cups	Combine all ingredients.
Vinegar, cider	1 cup	Beat on low speed until well blended.
Sugar, granulated	4 oz	Store in covered container.
Salt	2 tsp	Shake or beat well before serving.
Onion, finely chopped	2 oz	
Chili sauce	2 cups	
Catsup	1 cup	

Approximate nutritive values per ounce   **Calories** 106

Amount/portion	%DV	Amount/portion	%DV	Amount/portion	%DV		%DV		%DV
Total Fat 9 g	14%	**Cholest.** 0 mg	0%	**Total Carb.** 7 g	2%	**Vitamin A**	2%	**Calcium**	0%
Sat. Fat 2 g	12%	**Sodium** 275 mg	11%	Fiber 0 g	0%	**Vitamin C**	3%	**Iron**	0%
Protein 0 g				Sugars 4 g					

Percent Daily Values (%DV) are based on a 2000-calorie diet.

BACON DRESSING

Yield: 2 qt

Ingredient	Amount	Procedure
Bacon, sliced, cut into 1-inch pieces	12 oz	Fry bacon until crisp. Remove from fat.
Onions, finely chopped	4 oz	Sauté onions in bacon fat.
Sugar, granulated	8 oz	Add sugar, vinegar, and water to sautéed onions.
Vinegar, cider	¼ cup	Bring to boiling point.
Water	1½ cups	Cool.
Mayonnaise (p. 699)	3 cups	Place Mayonnaise in mixer bowl. Add cooled onion-vinegar mixture slowly, beating on low speed until smooth. Stir in bacon pieces. Serve with tossed green salad.

Approximate nutritive values per ounce   **Calories** 97

Amount/portion	%DV	Amount/portion	%DV	Amount/portion	%DV		%DV		%DV
Total Fat 9 g	14%	**Cholest.** 7 mg	2%	**Total Carb.** 4 g	1%	**Vitamin A**	0%	**Calcium**	0%
Sat. Fat 1 g	7%	**Sodium** 83 mg	3%	Fiber 0 g	0%	**Vitamin C**	1%	**Iron**	0%
Protein 1 g				Sugars 3 g					

Percent Daily Values (%DV) are based on a 2000-calorie diet.

Note   • Potentially hazardous food. Store for service at an internal temperature below 41°F.

SOUR CREAM DRESSING

Yield: 3 qt

Ingredient	Amount	Procedure
Eggs, beaten	16 (1 lb 12 oz)	Mix eggs and sour cream.
Sour cream	1 qt	
Sugar, granulated	2 lb	Combine sugar and flour.
Flour, all-purpose	1½ oz	Add water and mix only until smooth.
Water, cold	1 cup	Add to the cream and egg mixture.
Vinegar, cider	2 cups	Add vinegar and cook until thick.
		Stir as necessary. Chill quickly to below 41°F.

Approximate nutritive values per ounce   **Calories 107**

Amount/portion	%DV	Amount/portion	%DV	Amount/portion	%DV		%DV		%DV
Total Fat 4 g	7%	**Cholest.** 59 mg	20%	**Total Carb.** 16 g	5%	**Vitamin A**	5%	**Calcium**	2%
Sat. Fat 2 g	11%	**Sodium** 24 mg	1%	Fiber 0 g	0%	**Vitamin C**	0%	**Iron**	1%
Protein 2 g				Sugars 14 g					

Percent Daily Values (%DV) are based on a 2000-calorie diet.

Notes
- Potentially hazardous food. Store for service at an internal temperature below 41°F.
- 2 cups cream, whipped, may be added before serving.

FRENCH DRESSING (THICK)

Yield: 2 qts

Ingredient	Amount	Procedure
Sugar, granulated	2 lb	Combine sugar and seasonings in mixer bowl, using wire whip
Paprika	2 Tbsp	attachment.
Dry mustard	4 tsp	
Salt	2 Tbsp	
Onion juice	1½ tsp	
Vinegar, cider	1½ cups	Add vinegar. Mix well.
Salad oil	1 qt	Add oil gradually in small amounts.
		Beat well after each addition.

Approximate nutritive values per ounce   **Calories 235**

Amount/portion	%DV	Amount/portion	%DV	Amount/portion	%DV		%DV		%DV
Total Fat 18 g	28%	**Cholest.** 0 mg	0%	**Total Carb.** 20 g	7%	**Vitamin A**	1%	**Calcium**	0%
Sat. Fat 5 g	24%	**Sodium** 267 mg	11%	Fiber 0 g	0%	**Vitamin C**	0%	**Iron**	0%
Protein 0 g				Sugars 18 g					

Percent Daily Values (%DV) are based on a 2000-calorie diet.

Note
- If a French Dressing of usual consistency is desired, use only 8 oz of sugar.

Variations
- **Celery Seed Dressing.** Add 2 oz celery seed.
- **Poppy Seed Dressing.** Add 1 oz poppy seed.

FRENCH DRESSING

Yield: 3 qt

Ingredient	Amount	Procedure
Salt	2 oz (3 Tbsp)	Combine dry ingredients in mixer bowl.
Dry mustard	2 Tbsp	
Paprika	2 Tbsp	
Pepper, black	1 Tbsp	
Vinegar, cider	1 qt	Add vinegar and onion juice to dry ingredients.
Onion juice	4 tsp	Add salad oil slowly. Beat on high speed until thick and blended.
Salad oil	2 qt	This is a temporary emulsion that separates rapidly. Beat well or pour into a jar and shake vigorously just before serving.

Approximate nutritive values per ounce   **Calories** 161

Amount/portion	%DV	Amount/portion	%DV	Amount/portion	%DV		%DV		%DV
Total Fat 18 g	**28%**	**Cholest.** 0 mg	**0%**	**Total Carb.** 0 g	**0%**	**Vitamin A**	0%	**Calcium**	0%
Sat. Fat 5 g	**24%**	**Sodium** 204 mg	**9%**	Fiber 0 g	**0%**	**Vitamin C**	0%	**Iron**	0%
Protein 0 g				Sugars 0 g					

Percent Daily Values (%DV) are based on a 2000-calorie diet.

Variations Prepare by adding the following to 3 qt (1 recipe) French Dressing:

- **Chiffonade Dressing.** Add ⅓ cup chopped fresh parsley, 4 oz chopped onion, 6 oz chopped green pepper, 4 oz chopped red pepper or pimiento, and 16 chopped hard-cooked eggs.
- **Italian Dressing.** Delete paprika. Add 2 tsp oregano, ¼ tsp garlic powder, and 1 Tbsp basil.
- **Mexican Dressing.** Add 3 cups chili sauce, 10 oz chopped green pepper, 2 oz chopped onion, and 1 Tbsp cilantro.
- **Oil and Vinegar.** Delete mustard, paprika, and onion juice.
- **Roquefort Cheese Dressing.** Add French Dressing slowly, while whipping, to 1 lb finely crumbled Roquefort cheese. 1 qt cream may be mixed with cheese before it is added to the dressing.
- **Sesame Seed Dressing.** Delete salt, paprika, pepper, and onion juice. Increase mustard to ¼ cup and vinegar to 5½ cups. Add 3½ cups granulated sugar, 1¼ cups soy sauce, and ½ cup toasted sesame seeds.
- **Tarragon Dressing.** Use tarragon vinegar in place of cider vinegar.
- **Tomato Dressing.** Add 1 lb granulated sugar, 1½ qt tomato soup, and ¼ cup celery or poppy seeds. Increase onion juice to 2 Tbsp.

HONEY FRENCH DRESSING

Yield: 2 qt

Ingredient	Amount	Procedure
Dry mustard	4 tsp	Mix mustard, salt, and celery seed in large mixing bowl.
Salt	1 tsp	
Celery seed or poppy seed	4 tsp	
Honey	2 cups	While mixing, add remaining ingredients in order listed.
Vinegar, cider	1¼ cups	
Lemon juice	¼ cup	
Onion, grated	1 Tbsp	
Salad oil	1 qt	

Approximate nutritive values per ounce   **Calories** 155

Amount/portion	%DV	Amount/portion	%DV	Amount/portion	%DV		%DV		%DV
Total Fat 14 g	21%	**Cholest.** 0 mg	0%	**Total Carb.** 9 g	3%	Vitamin A	0%	Calcium	0%
Sat. Fat 4 g	18%	**Sodium** 34 mg	1%	Fiber 0 g	0%	Vitamin C	0%	Iron	0%
Protein 0 g				Sugars 9 g					

Percent Daily Values (%DV) are based on a 2000-calorie diet.

HONEY LIME DRESSING

Yield: 3 qt

Ingredient	Amount	Procedure
Mayonnaise, low fat	1 qt	Measure all ingredients into mixer bowl. Blend together, using wire whip.
Yogurt, plain	1 qt	
Honey	2 cups	Cover and refrigerate. Store (below 41°F).
Lime juice, fresh	2 cups	
Celery seed	1 Tbsp	

Approximate nutritive values per ounce   **Calories** 45

Amount/portion	%DV	Amount/portion	%DV	Amount/portion	%DV		%DV		%DV
Total Fat 0.8 g	1%	**Cholest.** .6 mg	0%	**Total Carb.** 10 g	3%	Vitamin A	7%	Calcium	2%
Sat. Fat 0.1 g	1%	**Sodium** 100 mg	4%	Fiber 0 g	0%	Vitamin C	2%	Iron	0%
Protein 0.6 g				Sugars 8 g					

Percent Daily Values (%DV) are based on a 2000-calorie diet.

Note • Potentially hazardous food. *Food Safety Standard:* Hold food for service at an internal temperature below 41°F. Do not mix old product with new.

BASIL VINAIGRETTE DRESSING

Yield: 1½ qt

Ingredient	Amount	Procedure
Vinegar, cider	2 cups	Combine in mixer bowl, using wire whip.
Water	¾ cup	
Sugar, granulated	2 oz	
Garlic, fresh, minced	1½ Tbsp	
Salt	2 oz	
Basil, dried, crumbled	⅔ cup	
Salad oil	2 cups	Add oil very gradually while mixing.
Olive oil	½ cup	Store covered in the refrigerator. Stir before serving.

Approximate nutritive values per ounce **Calories** 108

Amount/portion	%DV	Amount/portion	%DV	Amount/portion	%DV		%DV		%DV
Total Fat 12 g	18%	**Cholest.** 0 mg	0%	**Total Carb.** 2 g	1%	**Vitamin A**	0%	**Calcium**	0%
Sat. Fat 3 g	14%	**Sodium** 468 mg	20%	Fiber 0 g	0%	**Vitamin C**	0%	**Iron**	0%
Protein 0 g				Sugars 1 g					

Percent Daily Values (%DV) are based on a 2000-calorie diet.

CHAPTER 16

Sandwiches

Norman Hollands © Dorling Kindersley

Sandwiches continue to be favorite choices for the noon and evening meals. They have become popular, too, at breakfast or any meal throughout the day where a fast, flavorful meal is desired. Sandwiches are also popular as hors d'oeuvres or buffet foods. Sandwiches may be closed or open faced and may be served hot or cold. Nutritional requirements are easily satisfied by choosing breads and fillings that are high in fiber, low in fat, and low in cholesterol.

PREPARATION OF INGREDIENTS

Sandwich ingredients include bread, spread, filling, and vegetable accompaniments. Many ingredient variations are possible, but the basic procedures for preparing ingredients are the same.

Breads

Different breads and rolls add variety in flavor, texture, size, and shape. In addition to the traditional loaves, foccacia, pita, tortillas, quick breads, and flavored speciality breads may be used for sandwiches.

Bread should be kept fresh during and after preparation. Keep bread tightly wrapped until used. French bread or other crusty breads, however, should not be wrapped because the crust will soften. They should be used the day they are baked. Bread should not be refrigerated, because it will become stale faster than if kept at room temperature. If bread must be kept longer than 1–2 days, it may be frozen. Defrost frozen bread without unwrapping.

Spreads

Bread for sandwiches is first spread with plain or seasoned margarine or butter, mayonnaise, mustard, olive paste, pesto, chutney, or a Sandwich Spread (p. 716). Covering bread evenly with a spread helps keep the sandwich from becoming soggy. Margarine or butter may be softened by letting it stand at room temperature, or it may be whipped for easy spreading (see p. 716). Allow 1 tsp of spread per slice of bread.

Fillings

Slice meat and cheese into even slices. Tender meats may be sliced thicker than less tender ones. A serving of thinly sliced or wafer-sliced meats usually appears larger than an equal weight of thicker slices. Since sliced meats and cheese dry out quickly, they should be sliced only as needed and kept covered. Mixed fillings should be prepared the day they are served and kept chilled. Nonmeat fillings in addition to cheese may include salads and grilled or fresh vegetables.

Vegetable Accompaniments

Prepare greens, tomato and onion slices, and pickles or other vegetable accompaniments. Ingredients should be fresh, crisp, and attractive. See pp. 153-166 for preparing vegetable accompaniments.

PREPARATION OF SANDWICHES

Closed Sandwiches

1. Prepare filling and spread.
2. Arrange fresh bread in rows on a baking sheet or a worktable. Four rows of 10 slices each is a manageable number.
3. Spread all bread slices to the edges with softened margarine or butter or other spread.
4. Portion filling with dipper or spoon on alternate rows of bread and spread to the edges, or arrange sliced filling to fit the sandwich.
5. If lettuce or other vegetable accompaniment is used, arrange on filling. If sandwiches are to be held for some time, vegetable accompaniments should be omitted.
6. Place plain buttered (or spread) slices of bread on the filled slices.
7. If the sandwiches are to be cut in half or in fourths, stack two or three together and cut with a sharp knife, being careful not to mash bread.
8. To keep sandwiches fresh, place in sandwich bags or plastic wrap. Avoid stacking sandwiches more than three high, because stacking insulates the filling and prevents it from reaching the desired temperature as quickly as it should.
9. Refrigerate until served. If freezing sandwiches for later use, see precautions on p. 715.
10. Handle bread and fillings as little as possible during preparation. Use plastic gloves or tongs when picking up food.

Grilled and Toasted Sandwiches

1. For a grilled sandwich, place filling between two slices of bread. Fillings may be sliced cheese, meat, or poultry; chopped fillings as in salads; or a combination of fillings as in a Reuben Sandwich (p. 739).
2. Brush the outside with melted margarine or butter. For large quantities, a brush or roller dipped in the melted spread may be used. The steps for this method are: (a) Place parchment paper in bottom of baking sheet. (b) Place bread slices directly on coated paper. Add filling to all slices in pan. (c) Top with slices of bread.
3. Brown sandwich on a griddle, in a hot oven, or under a broiler.
4. For a toasted sandwich, toast the bread before filling.

Open-Faced Hot Sandwiches

1. Place buttered or unbuttered bread on a serving plate.
2. Cover with hot meat or other filling.
3. Top with gravy, sauce, or other topping.
4. For a hot sandwich that is to be broiled, arrange slices of bread on a baking sheet. Cover with slices of cheese or other topping. Broil just before serving.

Canapés

1. Remove crusts from bread.
2. Cut into desired shapes.
3. Spread with softened margarine or butter.
4. Cover with filling.
5. Decorate with parsley, sliced olives, sliced radishes, pimiento pieces, chopped hard-cooked eggs, or other garnish.

Ribbon Sandwiches

1. Remove crusts from two kinds of bread, being careful to have all slices the same size.
2. Spread one or more fillings on slices of breads.
3. Make stacks of five slices of bread, alternating kinds of bread.
4. Press together firmly.
5. Arrange stacks in shallow pan; cover with plastic wrap, plastic bag, or waxed paper.
6. Chill for several hours.
7. To serve, cut each slice into thirds, halves, or triangles.

Checkerboard Sandwiches

1. Spread slices of white and whole wheat bread with desired filling.
2. Make stacks of ribbon sandwiches by alternating two slices of white and two slices of whole wheat bread. Trim and cut each stack into ½-inch slices.

3. Using butter or smooth spread as a filling, stack three slices together so that white and whole wheat squares alternate to give a checkerboard effect.

4. Chill for several hours.

5. Remove from refrigerator and, with sharp knife, slice into checkerboard slices, ½ inch thick.

Rolled Sandwiches

1. Remove crusts from three sides of a loaf of unsliced bread.

2. With crust at left, cut loaf into lengthwise slices ⅛–¼ inch thick.

3. Run rolling pin the length of each slice to make it easier to handle.

4. Spread with softened margarine or butter.

5. Spread with desired smooth filling.

6. Place olives, watercress, or other foods across the end.

7. Starting at end with garnish, roll tightly, being careful to keep sides straight. Tight rolling makes for easier slicing.

8. Wrap rolls individually in waxed paper or aluminum foil, twisting ends securely.

9. Chill several hours or overnight. Rolls may be made ahead of time, then wrapped and frozen. Let thaw about 45 minutes before slicing.

10. Cut chilled rolls into ¼–⅓ inch slices.

FREEZING SANDWICHES

When making sandwiches to be frozen for later use, certain precautions should be taken.

1. Spread bread with margarine or butter instead of mayonnaise or salad dressing.

2. Do not use fillings containing mayonnaise, egg white, or some vegetables such as tomatoes and parsley. Chicken, meat, fish, cheese, and peanut butter freeze well.

3. Place large closed sandwiches individually in a sandwich bag or wrap individually in plastic wrap.

4. Pack tea-sized closed sandwiches in layers, separated by waxed paper or plastic wrap, in freezer boxes; or place in any suitable box and overwrap with moisture-proof material.

5. Place open-faced sandwiches on trays, wrap as for closed sandwiches.

6. Wrap ribbon, closed, or other loaf sandwiches uncut.

7. Allow 1–2 hours for sandwiches to defrost. Do not remove outer wrapping until sandwiches are partly thawed.

8. If sandwiches are not served immediately after thawing, refrigerate until serving time.

SANDWICH RECIPES

WHIPPED MARGARINE OR BUTTER

Yield: spread for 50 sandwiches   *Portion:* 1 tsp per slice

Ingredient	Amount	Procedure
Margarine or butter	1 lb	Place in mixer bowl. Let stand at room temperature until soft enough to mix.
Milk or boiling water (optional)	½ cup	Add milk or water while whipping. Mix on low speed, gradually increasing to high speed. Whip until fluffy.

Variations

- **Honey Butter.**   Cream 1 lb butter or margarine until light and fluffy. Add 8 oz honey gradually, beating on medium speed until mixture is light. Serve with hot biscuits or other hot bread.

- **Savory Spread.**   Add minced cucumber, onion, or pimiento; chopped chives or parsley; horseradish; or prepared mustard to whipped butter or margarine.

SANDWICH SPREAD

Yield: spread for 100 sandwiches   *Portion:* 1 tsp per slice

Ingredient	Amount	Procedure
Margarine or butter	8 oz	Whip margarine on high speed until light and fluffy.
Light cream (half-and-half)	¼ cup	Add cream and mix.
Prepared mustard	1½ tsp	Fold in remaining ingredients.
Mayonnaise	3 cups	Use as a spread for meat or cheese sandwiches.
Pickle relish	½ cup	

CHEESE SALAD SANDWICH

Yield: 50 sandwiches

Ingredient	Amount	Procedure
Cheddar cheese	3 lb 8 oz	Grind or shred cheese.
Salad dressing or cream	2 cups	Combine with cheese. Refrigerate and remove small amounts of filling as necessary for production.
Salt	2 tsp	
Pepper, cayenne	Few grains	
Margarine, softened	4 oz	
Bread	100 slices	Assemble filling and bread (p. 714). Portion filling with No. 20 dipper.

Approximate nutritive values per portion   **Calories** 318

Amount/portion	%DV	Amount/portion	%DV	Amount/portion	%DV		%DV		%DV
Total Fat 18 g	28%	**Cholest.** 36 mg	12%	**Total Carb.** 28 g	9%	Vitamin A	11%	Calcium	27%
Sat. Fat 7 g	37%	**Sodium** 726 mg	30%	Fiber 6 g	25%	Vitamin C	0%	Iron	11%
Protein 13 g				Sugars 3 g					

Percent Daily Values (%DV) are based on a 2000-calorie diet.

Note ● Potentially hazardous food. Store filling at an internal temperature below 41°F.

Variation ● **Pimiento Cheese Sandwich.**   Add 6 oz chopped pimiento.

EGG SALAD SANDWICH

Yield: 50 sandwiches   *Portion:* 2 oz filling

Ingredient	Amount	Procedure
Eggs, hard-cooked (p. 439)	36	Peel eggs and chop coarsely.
Mayonnaise or salad dressing	2½ cups	Combine and add to eggs. Mix lightly.
Pickle relish	1 cup	Refrigerate and remove small amounts of filling as necessary
Salt	2 tsp	for production.
Pepper, white	¼ tsp	
Onion juice	1 tsp	
Pimiento, chopped	4 oz	
Bread	100 slices	Assemble filling, bread, and lettuce (p. 714).
Lettuce, iceberg or leaf	2–3 heads	Portion filling with No. 20 dipper.

Approximate nutritive values per portion   **Calories** 248

Amount/portion	%DV	Amount/portion	%DV	Amount/portion	%DV		%DV		%DV
Total Fat 10 g	16%	**Cholest.** 157 mg	52%	**Total Carb.** 31 g	10%	**Vitamin A**	8%	**Calcium**	6%
Sat. Fat 2 g	8%	**Sodium** 611 mg	25%	Fiber 7 g	26%	**Vitamin C**	4%	**Iron**	14%
Protein 10 g				Sugars 3 g					

Percent Daily Values (%DV) are based on a 2000-calorie diet.

Notes
- Potentially hazardous food. Store filling at an internal temperature below 41°F.
- Chilling ingredients before combining shortens the time product is in the temperature danger zone (above 41°F).
- 1 lb chopped celery may be substituted for pickle relish.
- 2 Tbsp prepared mustard may be added.

HAM SALAD SANDWICH

Yield: 50 sandwiches   *Portion:* 2 oz filling

Ingredient	Amount	Procedure
Cooked ham	4 lb	Grind ham coarsely.
Eggs, hard-cooked (p. 439)	6	Peel eggs and chop coarsely.
Onion, finely chopped	4 oz	Combine all ingredients. Mix lightly.
Pickle relish	8 oz	Refrigerate and remove small amounts of filling as necessary for production.
Mayonnaise or salad dressing	2–2½ cups	
Bread	100 slices	Assemble filling, bread, and lettuce (p. 714).
Lettuce, iceberg or leaf	2–3 heads	Portion filling with No. 20 dipper.

Approximate nutritive values per portion   **Calories** 257

Amount/portion	%DV	Amount/portion	%DV	Amount/portion	%DV		%DV		%DV
Total Fat 10 g	15%	**Cholest.** 50 mg	17%	**Total Carb.** 30 g	10%	Vitamin A	2%	Calcium	5%
Sat. Fat 2 g	9%	**Sodium** 1013 mg	42%	Fiber 7 g	26%	Vitamin C	15%	Iron	14%
Protein 15 g				Sugars 3 g					

Percent Daily Values (%DV) are based on a 2000-calorie diet.

Notes
- Potentially hazardous food. Store filling at an internal temperature below 41°F.
- Chilling ingredients before combining shortens the time product is in the temperature danger zone (above 41°F).

Variations
- **Ham and Cheese Sandwich.** Delete eggs. Reduce ham to 3 lb. Add 1 lb 8 oz cheddar or Swiss cheese, ground.
- **Meat Salad Sandwich.** Substitute ground cooked beef or pork for ham. Add 4 oz finely chopped celery. Check for seasoning and add salt and pepper if needed.

CHICKEN SALAD SANDWICH

Yield: 50 sandwiches   *Portion:* 2 oz filling

Ingredient	Amount	Procedure
Cooked chicken	5 lb	Chop chicken coarsely.
Salt	2 tsp	Add remaining ingredients. Mix to blend.
Pepper, white	½ tsp	Refrigerate and remove small amounts of filling as necessary
Celery, finely chopped	8 oz	for production.
Lemon juice or cider vinegar	¼ cup	
Mayonnaise or salad dressing	2–2½ cups	
Bread	100 slices	Assemble filling, bread, and lettuce (p. 714).
Lettuce, iceberg or leaf	2–3 heads	Portion filling with No. 20 dipper.

Approximate nutritive values per portion   **Calories** 258

Amount/portion	%DV	Amount/portion	%DV	Amount/portion	%DV		%DV		%DV
Total Fat 9 g	13%	**Cholest.** 40 mg	13%	**Total Carb.** 28 g	9%	**Vitamin A**	2%	**Calcium**	5%
Sat. Fat 1 g	6%	**Sodium** 546 mg	23%	Fiber 7 g	27%	**Vitamin C**	2%	**Iron**	14%
Protein 18 g				Sugars 3 g					

Percent Daily Values (%DV) are based on a 2000-calorie diet.

Notes
- Potentially hazardous food. Store filling at an internal temperature below 41°F.
- Chilling ingredients before combining shortens the time product is in the temperature danger zone (above 41°F).
- 4 oz chopped, toasted almonds may be added.
- Alfalfa sprouts may be placed on top of filling for variety.

TUNA SALAD SANDWICH

Yield: 50 sandwiches   *Portion:* 2 oz filling

Ingredient	Amount	Procedure
Eggs, hard-cooked (p. 439)	7	Peel eggs and chop coarsely.
Tuna, flaked	4 lb	Combine all filling ingredients.
Celery, chopped	4 oz	Refrigerate and remove small amounts of filling as necessary
Lemon juice	¼ cup	for production.
Onion juice	1 tsp	
Mayonnaise or salad dressing	1½ cups	
Bread	100 slices	Assemble filling, bread, and lettuce (p. 714).
Lettuce, iceberg or leaf	2–3 heads	Portion filling with No. 20 dipper.

Approximate nutritive values per portion   **Calories** 251

Amount/portion	%DV	Amount/portion	%DV	Amount/portion	%DV		%DV		%DV
Total Fat 9 g	13%	**Cholest.** 38 mg	13%	**Total Carb.** 28 g	9%	**Vitamin A**	3%	**Calcium**	5%
Sat. Fat 1 g	6%	**Sodium** 547 mg	23%	Fiber 7 g	26%	**Vitamin C**	2%	**Iron**	14%
Protein 17 g				Sugars 3 g					

Percent Daily Values (%DV) are based on a 2000-calorie diet.

Notes
- Potentially hazardous food. Store filling at an internal temperature below 41°F.
- Chilling ingredients before combining shortens the time product is in the temperature danger zone (above 41°F).
- 1 cup pickle relish may be substituted for celery.

Variations
- **Grilled Tuna Salad Sandwich.** Brush both sides of sandwiches with melted margarine or butter. Grill until golden brown.
- **Salmon Salad Sandwich.** Substitute salmon for tuna.

BACON, LETTUCE, AND TOMATO SANDWICH

Yield: 50 sandwiches

Ingredient	Amount	Procedure
Tomatoes, fresh	7 lb	Wash tomatoes. Peel, if desired, and cut into thin slices.
Lettuce, iceberg or leaf	2–3 heads or 2 lb leaf	Wash lettuce and separate leaves. Drain.
Bacon	150 slices (7 lbs)	Cook bacon according to directions on p. 522. Drain.
Bread (white or whole wheat) Mayonnaise Whipped Margarine or Butter (p. 716)	100 slices 1 cup 8 oz	Spread 50 slices of bread with mayonnaise. Place 3 cooked bacon slices, 2 tomato slices, and a lettuce leaf on each. Top with remaining 50 slices of bread, which have been spread with Whipped Margarine or Butter.

Approximate nutritive values per portion   **Calories 287**

Amount/portion	%DV	Amount/portion	%DV	Amount/portion	%DV		%DV		%DV
Total Fat 15 g	23%	**Cholest.** 18 mg	6%	**Total Carb.** 29 g	10%	**Vitamin A**	4%	**Calcium**	6%
Sat. Fat 4 g	18%	**Sodium** 770 mg	32%	Fiber 7 g	28%	**Vitamin C**	27%	**Iron**	15%
Protein 12 g				Sugars 4 g					

Percent Daily Values (%DV) are based on a 2000-calorie diet.

Variations
- **Club Sandwich.** Use 150 thin-sliced white bread, toasted. Spread with mayonnaise. Place on first slice 1 lettuce leaf, 2 tomato slices, and 2 strips of bacon. Place second slice of toast on top, spread side down. Spread top with mayonnaise, then add 2 oz thinly sliced turkey or chicken breast and lettuce leaf. Top with third slice of toast, spread side down. Secure with 4 picks. Cut into quarters to serve.

- **Sliced Ham and Cheese Sandwiches.** Substitute 6 lb 8 oz wafer-sliced ham and 3 lb 2 oz (1 oz slices) cheese for bacon.

- **Turkey Club Hoagie.** Reduce bacon to 2 lb. Substitute 7-inch hoagie buns for sliced bread. Use 6 lb 8 oz cooked turkey breast (approximately 10 lb AP), wafer sliced. Each sandwich includes choice of sandwich spread, 2 oz sliced turkey, 1 bacon slice, 1 lettuce leaf, and 2 tomato slices. Garnish plate with dill pickle spear.

CHICKEN POCKET SANDWICH

Yield: 50 sandwiches   *Portion:* 1 sandwich

Ingredient	*Amount*	*Procedure*
Pita pockets, 6 inch	50	Open pita pockets carefully.
Leaf lettuce leaves	2 lb	Just prior to service fill each pocket in the order below:
Tomato slices	3 lb	1 leaf lettuce
Alfalfa sprouts	1 lb 8 oz	2 tomato slices
Chicken Salad (p. 720)	1 recipe	3 oz Chicken Salad
		½ oz alfalfa sprouts
		Serve soon after filling.

Approximate nutritive values per portion   **Calories** 480

Amount/portion	%DV	Amount/portion	%DV	Amount/portion	%DV		%DV		%DV
Total Fat 32 g	49%	**Cholest.** 95 mg	32%	**Total Carb.** 29 g	10%	**Vitamin A**	10%	**Calcium**	5%
Sat. Fat 6 g	29%	**Sodium** 990 mg	41%	Fiber 2 g	9%	**Vitamin C**	17%	**Iron**	15%
Protein 19 g				Sugars 1 g					

Percent Daily Values (%DV) are based on a 2000-calorie diet.

Note   ● Potentially hazardous food. Keep chilled to below 41°F.

Variation   ● **Vegetarian Pocket.** Delete Chicken Salad. In addition to the lettuce, tomato, and alfalfa sprouts, stuff each pita pocket with 1 oz cucumber slices, ½ oz slice of Swiss cheese, and 1 oz avocado slices. Drizzle sandwich with ½ oz Italian salad dressing.

SPICY PORK LOIN SANDWICH WITH SOUTHWEST PEACH SALSA

Yield: 50 sandwiches   *Portion:* 1 sandwich (4 oz meat, 2 oz salsa, 1 bun)

Ingredient	*Amount*	*Procedure*
Garlic and Peppercorn Pork Loin (p. 514)	20 lb EP	Prepare pork loin according to recipe. Chill. Slice thinly.
Southwest Peach Salsa (p. 759)	1 recipe	
Kaiser bun	50	To serve, place open bun on plate. Portion on bottom half of bun, 4 oz thinly sliced pork garnished on top with 2 oz salsa.

Approximate nutritive values per portion   **Calories** 512

Amount/portion	%DV	Amount/portion	%DV	Amount/portion	%DV		%DV		%DV
Total Fat 11 g	17%	**Cholest.** 125 mg	42%	**Total Carb.** 41 g	14%	**Vitamin A**	37%	**Calcium**	8%
Sat. Fat 3 g	17%	**Sodium** 474 mg	20%	Fiber 2 g	7%	**Vitamin C**	278%	**Iron**	155%
Protein 59 g				Sugars 3 g					

Percent Daily Values (%DV) are based on a 2000-calorie diet.

Note   ● Potentially hazardous food. *Food Safety Standard:* Hold food for service at an internal temperature below 41°F.

SUBMARINE SANDWICH

Yield: 50 sandwiches   *Portion:* 3 oz meat + 1 oz cheese

Ingredient	Amount	Procedure
Buns, submarine or hoagie, 4–5 inches	50	Slice buns in half lengthwise.
Sandwich Spread (p. 716)	½ recipe	Spread both sides of bun with Sandwich Spread.
Salami, 1-oz slices	3 lb 2 oz	Cut slices of meat and cheese in half.
Luncheon meat, 1-oz slices	3 lb 2 oz	Arrange 1 oz of each kind of meat and 1 oz cheese on bottom half of each bun.
Ham, pullman, 1-oz slices	3 lb 2 oz	Alternate meat and cheese and arrange so that full length of each bun is covered.
Cheese, processed, American or Swiss, 1-oz slices	3 lb 2 oz	
Tomatoes, fresh, sliced	24	Place 2 slices tomato, ½ oz shredded lettuce, and 2 dill pickle slices on each sandwich.
Dill pickle slices, well drained (optional)	1 qt	Cover with top half of bun.
Shredded head lettuce	1 lb 9 oz	To serve, cut each sandwich in half.

Approximate nutritive values per portion   **Calories** 789

Amount/portion	%DV	Amount/portion	%DV	Amount/portion	%DV		%DV		%DV
Total Fat 37 g	57%	**Cholest.** 80 mg	27%	**Total Carb.** 81 g	27%	**Vitamin A**	15%	**Calcium**	25%
Sat. Fat 14 g	70%	**Sodium** 2557 mg	107%	Fiber 5 g	20%	**Vitamin C**	46%	**Iron**	26%
Protein 32 g				Sugars 13 g					

Percent Daily Values (%DV) are based on a 2000-calorie diet.

Notes
- Potentially hazardous food. Store meats at an internal temperature below 41°F.
- Other meats such as turkey, corned beef, pastrami, or roast beef may be used.
- Shredded red or green cabbage, alfalfa sprouts, or leaf lettuce may be substituted for shredded head lettuce.
- Mayonnaise or Italian dressing may be substituted for sandwich spread.

Variations
- **Buffet Submarine.** Use 12 long, thin buns, approximately 18 inches. Arrange 4 oz each of meats and cheese on each bun. Garnish with 2 tomatoes, sliced, ⅓ cup pickle slices, and 1–2 oz shredded lettuce. Secure with long picks. Portion as served into 4–5-inch sections.
- **Ring Submarine.** Use bread shaped in a ring. See p. 300 for Sandwich Ring recipe.

DELI WRAP

Yield: 50 portions   *Portion:* 1 wrap (2 halves)

Ingredient	Amount	Procedure
Wraps, 12 inch	50 wraps	If frozen, thaw under refrigeration.
Honey mustard Mayonnaise	1 lb 1 lb 8 oz	Mix mustard and mayonnaise. Place wraps flat on baking sheet. Spread 2 Tbsp of mustard-mayonnaise mixture over each wrap, leaving a 1-inch border.
Deli turkey, wafer sliced Deli ham, wafer sliced	3 lb 3 lb	Portion 1 oz each of turkey and ham over dressing.
Fresh salsa (see Notes) Lettuce, shredded Cheddar cheese, shredded	3 qt 3 lb (EP) 1 lb 8 oz	Portion 2 oz salsa, 1 oz lettuce, and ½ oz cheese over meat. To roll sandwich: (a) Fold 2 sides of wrap 2 inches over filling. (b) Roll tightly as for jelly roll, starting to roll from side not over filling. Cut wrap in half diagonally. One portion is two halves. Keep cold, below 41°F.

Notes

- Potentially hazardous food. *Food Safety Standards:* Hold food for service at an internal temperature above 140°F. Do not mix old product with new. Cool leftover product quickly (within 4 hours) to below 41°F. See p. 105 for cooling procedures. Reheat leftover product quickly (within 2 hours) to 165°F. Reheat produce only once, discard if not used.

- Use any fresh fruit or fresh vegetable salsa. See Cucumber and Melon Salsa (p. 757).

Variation

- **Southwestern-Style Steak Wrap.** Brown 5 lb seasoned fajita meat in hot oil. Add 3 lb 8 oz fresh mushrooms and sauté until tender. In separate bowl, combine 2 lb 8 oz diced tomatoes, 1 lb 4 oz chopped red onions, and 3 oz fresh chopped cilantro. Mix together 3 lb 4 oz shredded cheddar cheese and 2 lb 8 oz shredded Monterey jack cheese. Place 12-inch wrap on plate. Portion 2 oz mixed cheeses onto center of wrap, leaving a 1-inch border. Sprinkle 1 oz of tomato mixture over cheese. Portion 2 oz of beef-mushroom mixture over vegetables. Fold two sides over filling and roll.

ASIAN ORANGE GINGER BEEF WRAP

Yield: 50 portions   *Portion:* 1 wrap

Ingredient	Amount	Procedure
Sushi Style Rice (p. 610)	12 lb 8 oz	Prepare rice according to directions on p. 594. Reserve for later step.
Ginger Orange Beef (p. 491)	12 lb	Prepare ginger beef according to directions on p. 491. Reserve for later step.
Asian Sesame Sauce (p. 754)	3½ cups	Prepare sauce according to directions on p. 754. Reserve for later step.
Wraps, 12-inch Lettuce leaves	50 wraps 2 lb 12 oz	*Wrapping Procedure* 1. Place one wrap on flat surface. 2. Place lettuce leaf on half of the wrap extending to the edge of the wrap. 3. Portion 4 oz Sushi Rice on wrap. Distribute rice on the side of the wrap opposite the lettuce leaf in approximately a 3 × 8-inch shape from the top of the wrap to the bottom. Stop 1½ inches on the wrap's edge. 4. Portion 4 oz Ginger Beef over rice. 5. Pour 1 Tbsp Asian Sesame Sauce over beef. 6. Fold border edge of wrap (1½ inch without filling) over fillings. Roll wrap tightly. Cut in half diagonally and serve with Asian Sesame Sauce.

Note
- Potentially hazardous food. *Food Safety Standards:* Hold food for service at an internal temperature above 41°F. Do not mix old product with new.

PACK-A-PITA PLATE

Yield: 50 portions   *Portion:* one plate = 3 oz filling, 2 pita halves

Ingredient	Amount	Procedure
Leaf lettuce	1 lb 8 oz (EP)	Place one large leaf on dinner plate, leaving room for the pita bread.
Pita filling (see Notes)	9 lb 8 oz	Place 3 oz filling on top of lettuce leaf.
Tomatoes, thinly sliced	12 lb (EP)	Place 4 slices of tomato beside filling.
Alfalfa sprouts (see Notes)	8 oz	Place a small amount of sprouts on top of tomatoes.
Sweet pickles, sliced Olives, black	4 lb 8 oz	Garnish plate with 6 pickle slices and 2 black olives.
Pita bread	50 rounds	Just before service, place 2 pita halves on plate.

Notes
- Potentially hazardous food. *Food Safety Standards:* Hold food for service at an internal temperature below 41°F.
- Alfalfa sprouts may be potentially hazardous. Purchase sprouts from a reputable source and follow carefully all food safety standards.
- Filling choices may include egg salad, tuna salad, ham salad, sliced meats, sliced cheese, or chilled grilled vegetables. Small, thin portions of cooked and chilled solid meats may be used; for example, chicken breast, baked salmon.

MARINATED VEGETABLE PITA

Yield: 50 portions   *Portion:* one-half pita, 2 oz vegetables, 1 oz cheese

Ingredient	Amount	Procedure
Herb and Garlic Marinade (p. 787)	1 qt	Prepare marinade.
Eggplant, ½-inch dice	1 lb 4 oz (EP)	Pour marinade over vegetables. Toss to coat.
Summer squash, ½-inch dice	1 lb (EP)	Let stand 30 minutes, drain well.
Zucchini squash, ½-inch dice	1 lb (EP)	Heat fry pan. Stir-fry vegetables 8–10 minutes until vegetables are tender-crisp.
Red bell pepper, ¼ × 1-inch strips	8 oz (EP)	
Green bell pepper, ¼ × 1-inch strips	8 oz (EP)	
Onion, sliced (rings separated)	8 oz (EP)	
Mushrooms, sliced	1 lb 12 oz (EP)	
Pita bread (see Notes)	25 rounds	Cut pita bread into halves.
Mozzarella cheese, shredded	3 lb	Open pita and stuff with 2 oz vegetables. Sprinkle 1 oz cheese over filling.

Approximate nutritive values per portion   **Calories** 300

Amount/portion	%DV	Amount/portion	%DV	Amount/portion	%DV		%DV		%DV
Total Fat 21 g	32%	**Cholest.** 21 mg	7%	**Total Carb.** 20 g	7%	**Vitamin A**	10%	**Calcium**	17%
Sat. Fat 5.5 g	28%	**Sodium** 412 mg	17%	Fiber 1.6 g	6%	**Vitamin C**	23%	**Iron**	6%
Protein 9 g				Sugars 3 g					

Percent Daily Values (%DV) are based on a 2000-calorie diet.

Notes
- Potentially hazardous food. *Food Safety Standards:* Hold food for service at an internal temperature above 140°F. Do not mix old product with new. Cool leftover product quickly (within 4 hours) to below 41°F. See p. 105 for cooling procedures. Reheat leftover product quickly (within 2 hours) to 165°F. Reheat product only once, discard if not used.
- Gyro bread may be substituted for the pita bread. Serve by placing one warmed gyro-style bread on a plate. Portion 2 oz filling onto center of bread. Sprinkle with 1 oz cheese. Fold over and serve immediately.

Variation
- **Marinated Vegetable Fajita.** Substitute flour tortillas for pita bread. Serve with Mexican condiments.

GRILLED SANDWICHES

Yield: 50 portions   *Portion:* 1 sandwich

Ingredient	Amount	Procedure
Bread (white, whole wheat, or rye)	100 slices	See following procedures for preparing sandwiches.
Meat and/or cheese	6 lb 4 oz	
Margarine	1 lb	Grill sandwiches at 350°F on griddle until both sides are delicately brown.

PROCEDURE NO. 1

1. Melt margarine. Pour into 2-inch counter pan.
2. Pick up two slices of bread, one in each hand. Dip one side of one slice in melted margarine. Press dipped slice against second slice.
3. Place buttered side of one slice on 18 × 26-inch baking sheet lined with parchment or waxed paper. Place 24 slices 4 × 6.
4. Top each slice with 2 oz meat and/or cheese.
5. Top meat and/or cheese with buttered bread (from Step 2), buttered side up.
6. Cover layer with parchment or waxed paper.
7. Repeat for a second layer or use another baking sheet. Cover tightly with plastic wrap if the sandwiches are not to be grilled immediately.

PROCEDURE NO. 2

1. Place meat and/or cheese between two slices of bread.
2. Brush sandwiches with melted margarine; or in large quantities, use a roller dipped in melted margarine.
3. Place sandwiches on baking sheet and cover with plastic wrap until grilled.

Note
- Potentially hazardous food. *Food Safety Standards:* Hold food for service at an internal temperature above 140°F. Cool leftover product quickly (within 4 hours) to below 41°F. See p. 105 for cooling procedures. Reheat leftover product quickly (within 2 hours) to 165°F. Reheat product only once; discard if not used.

Variations
- **Grilled Cheese.** Use processed American cheese, 2 1-oz slices per sandwich.
- **Grilled Corned Beef and Swiss on Rye.** Substitute corned beef for ham in variation No. 3. Use Swiss cheese and rye bread.
- **Grilled Ham and Cheese.** Use 1½ oz ham and 1 oz cheese per sandwich, 4 lb 12 oz wafer-sliced ham and 3 lb 2 oz (1-oz slices) will be needed.
- **Grilled Turkey and Swiss on Whole Wheat.** Use 1½ oz turkey and 1 oz Swiss cheese per sandwich. 4 lb 12 oz wafer-sliced turkey and 3 lb 2 oz cheese (1-oz slices) will be needed.
- **Hot Tuna Grill.** Use No. 10 dipper of Tuna Salad Sandwich filling (p. 721) for each sandwich. Other salad sandwich fillings may be used.

BIEROCKS

Yield: 50 sandwiches
Oven: 400°F   *Bake:* 25–30 minutes, 5 minutes

Ingredient	Amount	Procedure
DOUGH		
Yeast, active dry	1¼ oz	Sprinkle yeast over water. Let stand 5 minutes.
Water, warm (110°F)	2 qt	
Sugar, granulated	14 oz	Add sugar, salt, and flour to yeast.
Salt	1 oz (1½ Tbsp)	Mix on medium speed, until mixture is smooth, using dough
Flour, all-purpose	2 lb 6 oz	arm or flat beater.
Eggs	8 (14 oz)	Add eggs and shortening. Continue beating.
Shortening, melted	5 oz	
Flour, all-purpose	5 lb 8 oz	Add flour on low speed to make a soft dough. Knead 5 minutes. Cover and let rise until double in bulk.
		When dough has doubled, punch down and divide into 4 or 5 portions. Roll dough to ¼-inch thickness. Cut into 4 × 6-inch rectangles. Place on each piece of dough a No. 8 dipper of filling (recipe follows). Fold lengthwise and pinch edges of dough securely to seal. Place on baking sheets with sealed edges down. Bake at 400°F for 25–30 minutes.
Egg, yolk	1	Brush with egg and water mixture.
Water	2 Tbsp	Return to oven for 5 minutes.
FILLING		
Ground beef	10 lb AP (7 lb EP)	Cook beef to an internal temperature of 155°F. Drain.
Cabbage, chopped	2 lb 8 oz	Steam cabbage and onion until slightly underdone.
Onion, chopped	3 lb	
Worcestershire sauce	⅓ cup	Add seasonings and vegetables to beef.
Salt	2½ oz	If not used immediately, cool quickly to below 41°F. See p. 105
Pepper, black	1½ tsp	for cooling procedures.
Savory, ground	1 tsp	
Chili powder	1½ tsp	

Approximate nutritive values per portion   **Calories** 530

Amount/portion	%DV	Amount/portion	%DV	Amount/portion	%DV		%DV		%DV
Total Fat 17 g	25%	**Cholest.** 100 mg	33%	**Total Carb.** 67 g	22%	**Vitamin A**	2%	**Calcium**	4%
Sat. Fat 6 g	29%	**Sodium** 834 mg	35%	Fiber 3 g	12%	**Vitamin C**	25%	**Iron**	31%
Protein 27 g				Sugars 10 g					

Percent Daily Values (%DV) are based on a 2000-calorie diet.

Note
- Potentially hazardous food. *Food Safety Standards:* Hold food for service at an internal temperature above 140°F. Cool leftover product quickly (within 4 hours) to below 41°F. See p. 105 for cooling procedures. Reheat leftover product quickly (within 2 hours) to 165°F. Reheat product only once; discard if not used.

Variation
- **Bierock Pockets.** Scale 3 lb dough onto 18 × 26 × 1-inch greased pans. Cut dough in half lengthwise. Spread 2 lb beef mixture evenly onto each strip of dough. Roll jelly roll fashion and seal tightly. Place seam side down on greased 18 × 26 × 1-inch pan. Bake at 350°F for 30–35 minutes or until done. Cut each roll into 8 portions, 16 per pan.

HOT MEAT AND CHEESE SANDWICH

Yield: 50 sandwiches   *Portion:* 2½ oz meat + 1½ oz sauce

Ingredient	Amount	Procedure
Ham, roast beef, or corned beef	8 lb	Wafer-slice meat into 12 × 10 × 2-inch pans. Cover and heat to 165°F.
Hamburger buns	50	To serve, place open bun on plate. Portion 2½ oz meat on bottom half of bun.
Cheese Sandwich Sauce, American or Cheddar (p. 749) or Swiss (p. 749)	3 qt	Ladle 1½ oz (No. 30 dipper) sauce over meat.

Approximate nutritive values per portion   **Calories** 458

Amount/portion	%DV	Amount/portion	%DV	Amount/portion	%DV		%DV		%DV
Total Fat 24 g	37%	**Cholest.** 80 mg	27%	**Total Carb.** 29 g	10%	**Vitamin A**	12%	**Calcium**	34%
Sat. Fat 11 g	53%	**Sodium** 1740 mg	73%	Fiber 0 g	0%	**Vitamin C**	28%	**Iron**	16%
Protein 30 g				Sugars 3 g					

Percent Daily Values (%DV) are based on a 2000-calorie diet.

Note   • Potentially hazardous food. *Food Safety Standards:* Hold food for service at an internal temperature above 140°F. Cool leftover product quickly (within 4 hours) to below 41°F. See p. 105 for cooling procedures. Reheat leftover product quickly (within 2 hours) to 165°F. Reheat product only once; discard if not used.

TUNA MELT

Yield: 50   *Portion:* 1 sandwich
Griddle: 350°F

Ingredient	Amount	Procedure
Tuna, drained	3 lb 4 oz	Mix drained tuna and drained pickle with celery and salad dressing.
Pickle relish, drained	12 oz	
Celery, finely chopped	1 lb	Refrigerate filling, removing small amounts as needed for production.
Salad dressing	1 lb 8 oz	
Wheat bread, pullman	100 slices	Assemble and cook sandwiches as described next.
Swiss cheese, ½ oz slices	3 lb 2 oz	
Margarine, melted	1 lb	

To Assemble:

1. Preheat griddle to 350°F.

2. Assemble sandwiches on greased griddle as follows:
   1 slice wheat bread
   1 slice Swiss cheese
   1 No. 24 (2 oz) dipper tuna mixture (preceding recipe)
   1 slice Swiss cheese
   1 slice wheat bread

3. When bread has browned (approximately 10 minutes), pour small amount of melted margarine on empty portion of grill.

4. Flip the sandwiches onto empty portion of grill. Cook until browned.

5. Place cooked sandwiches in 12 × 20 × 2-inch pans. Serve within 15 minutes.

6. Serve cut in half diagonally and garnish with tomato wedge on parsley sprig.

Approximate nutritive values per portion   **Calories** 411

Amount/portion	%DV	Amount/portion	%DV	Amount/portion	%DV		%DV		%DV
Total Fat 22 g	34%	**Cholest.** 30 mg	10%	**Total Carb.** 32 g	11%	**Vitamin A**	10%	**Calcium**	32%
Sat. Fat 7 g	36%	**Sodium** 780 mg	32%	Fiber 6 g	25%	**Vitamin C**	0%	**Iron**	16%
Protein 22 g				Sugars 2 g					

Percent Daily Values (%DV) are based on a 2000-calorie diet.

Note
- Potentially hazardous food. *Food Safety Standards:* Hold food for service at an internal temperature above 140°F. Cool leftover product quickly (within 4 hours) to below 41°F. See p. 105 for cooling procedures. Reheat leftover product quickly (within 2 hours) to 165°F. Reheat product only once; discard if not used.

Variation
- **Patty Melt.** Substitute grilled ground beef patty for tuna mixture. Place 1 oz grilled onions on top of patty before last slice of cheese is added. Rye bread may be substituted for wheat bread and cheddar or American cheese for Swiss cheese.

HOT ROAST BEEF SANDWICH

Yield: 50 sandwiches   *Portion:* 3 oz meat + ¼ cup gravy

Ingredient	Amount	Procedure
Beef roast	10 lb EP (15 lb AP)	Roast beef according to directions on pp. 195, 480. Slice into 3-oz portions. Place in two 12 × 20 × 2-inch counter pans.
Beef Stock (p. 791)	1½ qt	Heat stock to 190°F. Pour over meat. Cover with aluminum foil and place in oven to keep warm.
Bread	50 slices	Place 3 oz meat on each slice of bread.
Mashed Potatoes (p. 856)	12 lb 8 oz	Serve No. 12 dipper of Mashed Potatoes on the plate beside the bread.
Pan Gravy (p. 752)	1 gal	Cover meat and potato with Pan Gravy, using 2-oz ladle.

Approximate nutritive values per portion   **Calories** 417

Amount/portion	%DV	Amount/portion	%DV	Amount/portion	%DV		%DV		%DV
Total Fat 17 g	26%	**Cholest.** 84 mg	28%	**Total Carb.** 35 g	12%	**Vitamin A**	2%	**Calcium**	6%
Sat. Fat 6 g	28%	**Sodium** 1025 mg	43%	Fiber 5 g	20%	**Vitamin C**	11%	**Iron**	24%
Protein 32 g				Sugars 6 g					

Percent Daily Values (%DV) are based on a 2000-calorie diet.

Notes
- Potentially hazardous food. *Food Safety Standards:* Hold food for service at an internal temperature above 140°F. Do not mix old product with new. Cool leftover product quickly (within 4 hours) to below 41°F. See p. 105 for cooling procedures. Reheat leftover product quickly (within 2 hours) to 165°F. Reheat product only once; discard if not used.
- A tender cut of meat should be used.
- Meat may be covered with additional slice of bread if desired. Omit mashed potatoes. Cover entire sandwich with gravy.

Variations
- **Barbecued Beef Sandwich.** Place thinly sliced beef roast in two counter pans and keep warm. Heat 1½ qt Barbecue Sauce (p. 755) and pour 3 cups over each pan of meat. Toss together until sauce is evenly distributed. Serve in warm hamburger buns.
- **French Dip Sandwich.** Slice roast beef wafer thin. Place in 12 × 20 × 2-inch counter pan. Pour 1 cup Beef Stock (p. 791) over meat. Cover with aluminum foil and keep warm. To serve, place 3 oz beef on hard roll. Serve with side cup of hot seasoned broth for dipping.
- **Hot Roast Pork Sandwich.** Substitute roast pork for beef.
- **Hot Turkey Dip.** Follow directions for French Dip Sandwich, but substitute wafer-sliced turkey for beef and chicken broth for beef broth. Season chicken stock with poultry seasoning.
- **Hot Turkey Sandwich.** Substitute roast turkey or turkey roll for beef. Use Chicken Stock (p. 790) in place of Beef Stock.
- **Meat Loaf Sandwich.** Prepare Meat Loaf (p. 498). Substitute Meat Loaf for roast beef.

BROCCOLI AND RICOTTA CALZONE

Yield: 50 portions   *Portion:* 1 calzone
Oven: 350°F

Ingredient	Amount	Procedure
Broccoli cuts, frozen	6 lb (AP)	Thaw broccoli cuts in a colander or perforated pan. Drained EP yield should equal 5 lb 8 oz. Save drained broccoli for later step.
Pizza dough	50 dough balls (5 oz)	If using frozen dough balls, cover and let thaw to 65°F, 2–3 hours. Working with a small number of dough balls at a time, flatten into rounds.
Ricotta cheese	6 lb 6 oz	Blend cheeses and spices together.
Parmesan cheese, shredded	10 oz	Portion 2 oz (No. 16 dipper) of cheese mixture onto one-half of flattened dough ball. Smooth filling slightly, leaving ½-inch border.
Pepper, black	1 Tbsp	Distribute ½ cup (1¾ oz) of thawed broccoli (reserved from earlier step) over cheese.
Garlic powder	½ tsp	Brush edges of dough with water. Fold dough over filling and crimp edges to seal tightly.
Eggs, whole	1 oz	Mix eggs and water. Brush over tops of calzones.
Water	2 oz	Sprinkle with herbs.
Italian herbs	3 Tbsp	Bake at 350°F for 18–25 minutes in a conventional oven until the calzone registers 185°F. Follow the manufacturers' directions when using a conveyor-type pizza oven.
Marinara sauce	3 qt	Serve 2 oz warm marinara sauce ladled on top of calzone.
Parmesan cheese, shredded	1 lb	Serve with Parmesan cheese.

Approximate nutritive values per portion   **Calories** 520

Amount/portion	%DV	Amount/portion	%DV	Amount/portion	%DV		%DV		%DV
Total Fat 14 g	21%	**Cholest.** 45 mg	15%	**Total Carb.** 7 g	24%	**Vitamin A**	21%	**Calcium**	29%
Sat. Fat 8 g	39%	**Sodium** 471 mg	20%	Fiber 4.3 g	18%	**Vitamin C**	46%	**Iron**	26%
Protein 24 g				Sugars 3 g					

Percent Daily Values (%DV) are based on a 2000-calorie diet.

Note
- Potentially hazardous food. *Food Safety Standards:* Hold food for service at an internal temperature above 140°F. Do not mix old product with new. Cool leftover product quickly (within 4 hours) to below 41°F. See p. 105 for cooling procedures. Reheat leftover product quickly (within 2 hours) to 165°F. Reheat product only once; discard if not used.

Variations
- **Roasted Vegetable and Ricotta Calzone.** Heat 3 lb frozen roasted peppers and onions (available commercially) with 6 oz sliced black olives. In a bowl, mix 6 lb 12 oz ricotta cheese, 1 lb 8 oz freshly grated Parmesan cheese, ¾ oz dried parsley, 3 Tbsp dried basil, 5 tsp black pepper, 4 tsp crushed red pepper, and 1 oz salt. Portion 1½ oz vegetables and 2 oz ricotta cheese mixture (approximately No. 16 dipper) on dough. Follow makeup and service procedures as for Broccoli and Ricotta Calzone.
- **Ham and Swiss Florentine Calzone.** Steam 2 lb fresh spinach for 1 minute. Drain well and reserve for later step. Blend together 6 lb 6 oz ricotta cheese, 10 oz freshly grated parmesan cheese, and 1 Tbsp black pepper. Portion 2 oz cheese mixture and ¾ oz (No. 30 dipper) drained spinach on dough. Portion ¾ oz of wafer-sliced ham over spinach. Follow makeup and service procedures as for Broccoli and Ricotta Calzone.
- **Pepperoni Calzone.** Omit broccoli from Broccoli and Ricotta Calzone. Use 1 lb 4 oz of thily sliced pepperoni and 2 lb shredded mozzarella cheese. Place six slices of pepperoni on filling and ¾ oz shredded mozzeralla over pepperoni before folding and sealing.

GRILLED CORN AND ROASTED PEPPER QUESADILLAS

Yield: 50 portions   *Portion:* 2 quesadillas

Ingredient	Amount	Procedure
Vegetable oil	4 oz	Mix oil and chipotle base. Heat in a tilting fry pan, or on a griddle.
Chipotle base (see Notes)	2 oz	
Corn, frozen (see Notes)	5 lb 4 oz	Sauté corn and onion in flavored oil until onion is translucent and corn is slightly browned.
Onion, chopped	2 lb (EP)	Add roasted peppers and crushed red pepper.
Roasted Red Bell Peppers, diced (p. 854) (see Notes)	3 lb 4 oz	Heat through. Save for later step.
Red pepper, crushed	¾ tsp	
Flour tortillas (6 inch)	100 tortillas	Place flat on 18 × 26 × 1-inch pans.
Cojack cheese, shredded	6 lb 4 oz	Distribute 1 oz shredded cheese on one-half of tortilla, leave ½-inch border without cheese.
		Distribute 1¾ oz corn-pepper blend over cheese (reserved from earlier step).
		Place open tortilla on oiled, 300°F griddle.
		Cook until cheese begins to melt and tortilla is soft.
		Fold empty half of tortilla over filled half, press slightly with spatula. Turn and grill until slightly brown.
		Serve immediately. May serve with salsa, guacamole, and sour cream.

Approximate nutritive values per portion   **Calories** 525

Amount/portion	%DV	Amount/portion	%DV	Amount/portion	%DV		%DV		%DV
Total Fat 27 g	42%	**Cholest.** 51 mg	17%	**Total Carb.** 50 g	17%	Vitamin A	33%	Calcium	49%
Sat. Fat 14 g	69%	**Sodium** 847 mg	35%	Fiber 4 g	17%	Vitamin C	112%	Iron	14%
Protein 20 g				Sugars 3 g					

Percent Daily Values (%DV) are based on a 2000-calorie diet.

Notes
- Potentially hazardous food. *Food Safety Standards:* Hold food for service at an internal temperature above 140°F. Do not mix old product with new. Cool leftover product quickly (within 4 hours) to below 41°F. See p. 105 for cooling procedures. Reheat leftover product quickly (within 2 hours) to 165°F. Reheat product only once; discard if not used.

- Chipotle base is available commercially.

- Roasted corn and roasted peppers may be purchased frozen and substituted for the corn and peppers in the recipe. When using frozen roasted peppers, place in a single layer on a baking sheet and heat in a 375°F oven until heated through (discard liquid that accumulates).

Variation
- **Cheese Quesadillas.** Mix together 6 lb shredded Monterey Jack cheese, 6 lb shredded cheddar cheese, 3 lb 8 oz canned green chiles, drained, and 4 Tbsp dried cilantro. Scale 2½ oz cheese mixture onto each 6-inch or 8-inch tortilla. Proceed as for Grilled Corn and Roasted Pepper Quesadillas.

CHICKEN FAJITAS

Yield: 50 fajitas   *Portion:* 4 oz meat mixture (two 6-inch fajitas or one 10-inch fajita)

Ingredient	*Amount*	*Procedure*
Vegetable oil	¼ cup	Heat oil to 350°F in tilting or large fry pan.
Chicken white meat, cut into strips	10 lb (EP)	Add chicken and garlic. Stir-fry until chicken begins to brown.
Garlic, minced	3 oz (EP)	
Lime juice	1 qt	Add liquids, herbs, and spices to chicken. Cook until liquid evaporates and chicken is done, above 165°F.
Water	2 cups	
Chicken base	2 oz	
Cilantro leaves, finely chopped (see Notes)	¾ oz	
Pepper, black	1 Tbsp	
Red pepper, crushed	1 tsp	
Salt	1½ Tbsp	
Onions, sliced	2 lb 6 oz (EP)	Add onions and peppers. Stir-fry until tender-crisp.
Green bell peppers, cut in 1-inch long strips	12 oz (EP)	
Red bell peppers, cut in 1-inch long strips	8 oz (EP)	
Yellow bell peppers, cut in 1-inch long strips	8 oz (EP)	
Flour tortillas	50 10-inch or 100 6-inch	Heat tortillas to soften. Keep covered. Do not allow to dry out.
		Serve 4 oz meat mixture on one 10-inch or two 6-inch tortillas.
		Serve with condiments: Guacamole (pp. 235), shredded Monterey Jack cheese, shredded lettuce, sour cream, Salsa (p. 756), sliced black olives, sliced jalapeños.

Approximate nutritive values per portion   **Calories** 350

Amount/portion	%DV	Amount/portion	%DV	Amount/portion	%DV		%DV		%DV
Total Fat 7g	11%	**Cholest.** 53 mg	18%	**Total Carb.** 41 g	14%	**Vitamin A**	4%	**Calcium**	10%
Sat. Fat 1.6 g	8%	**Sodium** 733 mg	31%	Fiber 3 g	12%	**Vitamin C**	53%	**Iron**	17%
Protein 27 g				Sugars 1 g					

Percent Daily Values (%DV) are based on a 2000-calorie diet.

Notes

- Potentially hazardous food. *Food Safety Standards:* Hold food for service at an internal temperature above 140°F. Do not mix old product with new. Cool leftover product quickly (within 4 hours) to below 41°F. See p. 105 for cooling procedures. Reheat leftover product quickly (within 2 hours) to 165°F. Reheat product only once; discard if not used.

- 3 Tbsp of dried cilantro leaves can be substituted for fresh cilantro.

- Ranchero Base (commercial product) can be substituted for chicken base. Adjust seasonings as necessary.

BEEF FAJITAS

Yield: 50 sandwiches   *Portion:* 1 fajita, 2 oz meat + 2 oz vegetable

Ingredient	Amount	Procedure
Pureed jalapeño peppers, with juice	4 oz	Combine in bowl to make a marinade.
Lemon juice	1½ cups	
Pineapple juice	1½ cups	
Salt	1 Tbsp	
Pepper, black	2 Tbsp	
Meat tenderizer	2 oz	
Water	3 cups	
Beef, round or flank steak	10 lb AP	Cut beef into 1 × 5-inch strips, ¼ inch thick (see Notes). Pour marinade over meat. Stir to coat meat. Cover and marinate for 24 hours.
		Drain meat in colander. Discard marinade. Stir-fry in frying pan with a small amount of oil until cooked.
Onions, sliced, separated in rings	2 lb 8 oz	Add onions and green peppers to meat. Stir-fry until tender-crisp.
Green pepper strips	1 lb 8 oz	Transfer to 12 × 10 × 4-inch pan.
Tomatoes, fresh	2 lb 8 oz	Cut tomatoes into thin wedges. Combine carefully with beef. Gently lift beef and vegetables from juice into 12 × 20 × 2-inch counter pan.
Tortillas, flour 10-inch	50	Heat tortillas to soften. Keep covered. Do not allow to dry out. Serve 1 tortilla on plate and 4 oz beef and vegetables in center of tortilla. Tortilla may be rolled or folded in half.
		Serve with condiments: Guacamole (pp. 235), shredded Monterey Jack cheese, shredded lettuce, sour cream, Salsa (p. 756), sliced black olives, sliced jalapeños.

Approximate nutritive values per portion   **Calories** 246

Amount/portion	%DV	Amount/portion	%DV	Amount/portion	%DV		%DV		%DV
Total Fat 7 g	10%	**Cholest.** 51 mg	17%	**Total Carb.** 25 g	8%	**Vitamin A**	2%	**Calcium**	5%
Sat. Fat 2 g	9%	**Sodium** 360 mg	15%	Fiber 1 g	4%	**Vitamin C**	35%	**Iron**	18%
Protein 21 g				Sugars 3 g					

Percent Daily Values (%DV) are based on a 2000-calorie diet.

Notes
- Potentially hazardous food. *Food Safety Standards:* Hold food for service at an internal temperature above 140°F. Do not mix old product with new. Cool leftover product quickly (within 4 hours) to below 41°F. See p. 105 for cooling procedures. Reheat leftover product quickly (within 2 hours) to 165°F. Reheat product only once; discard if not used.
- Meat will slice more easily if it is partially frozen.
- Fajita meat can be made spicier by substituting additional pureed jalapeños for equal parts of water. More water in proportion to less jalapeños may be used for a less spicy Fajita.
- Beef strips may be purchased frozen, seasoned, or unseasoned.
- Commercial Fajita marinade mix may be substituted for marinade in the recipe.
- May serve beef separate from onions, peppers, tomatoes.

Variation
- **Chicken Fajitas.** Delete meat tenderizer. Increase salt to 2 Tbsp. Substitute chicken breasts for beef.

WESTERN SANDWICH

Yield: 50 sandwiches   *Portion:* 3 oz

Ingredient	Amount	Procedure
Ground beef	10 lb AP	Brown beef and onion until internal temperature reaches
Onion, chopped	1 lb	155°F. Drain off fat.
Tomato puree	3 cups	Add remaining filling ingredients to meat.
Catsup	3 cups	Simmer 15–20 minutes.
Water	1 cup	
Salt	1 Tbsp	
Paprika	2 tsp	
Dry mustard	2 tsp	
Worcestershire sauce	2 Tbsp	
Chili powder	1 Tbsp	
Hamburger buns	50	Serve with No. 12 dipper of filling on buns.

Approximate nutritive values per portion   **Calories** 330

Amount/portion	%DV	Amount/portion	%DV	Amount/portion	%DV		%DV		%DV
Total Fat 14 g	**22%**	**Cholest.** 62 mg	**21%**	**Total Carb.** 28 g	9%	**Vitamin A**	5%	**Calcium**	7%
Sat. Fat 5 g	**26%**	**Sodium** 646 mg	**27%**	Fiber 1 g	3%	**Vitamin C**	15%	**Iron**	19%
Protein 21 g				Sugars 2 g					

Percent Daily Values (%DV) are based on a 2000-calorie diet.

Notes
- Potentially hazardous food. *Food Safety Standards:* Hold food for service at an internal temperature above 140°F. Do not mix old product with new. Cool leftover product quickly (within 4 hours) to below 41°F. See p. 105 for cooling procedures. Reheat leftover product quickly (within 2 hours) to 165°F. Reheat product only once; discard if not used.

- If mixture becomes dry, add a small amount of water.

- 2 oz (1 cup) dehydrated onions, rehydrated in 1½ cups water, may be substituted for fresh onions.

Variations
- **Pizzaburger.** Delete paprika and chili powder. Add 1 Tbsp oregano, 1½ tsp basil, and 8 oz sliced mushrooms. Serve meat on bun and sprinkle with 1 lb 8 oz grated mozzarella cheese, ½ oz per serving.

- **Sloppy Joe.** Reduce ground beef to 8 lb. Sauté 2 lb chopped onions, 1 lb chopped celery, and 1 lb chopped green peppers with ground beef. Add 1½ oz flour to beef-vegetable mixture; mix to combine. Cook 10 minutes. Add 2¾ cups tomato puree, 2¾ cups catsup, ⅓ cup water, ⅔ cup Worcestershire sauce, 1 Tbsp red pepper sauce, 1 Tbsp dry mustard, 2 Tbsp paprika, 3 Tbsp chili powder, 3 Tbsp sugar, ¾ oz beef base. Stir to mix. Cover and simmer for 15–20 minutes. Stir occasionally.

- **Beanie Joe.** Drain and rinse enough canned red beans to equal 6 lb. Lightly coat bottom of fry pan with vegetable oil. Sauté 2½ Tbsp minced garlic, 1 lb chopped onion, and 1 lb 5 oz chopped green pepper until fragrant. Add rinsed and drained beans to vegetables and mix. Heat while stirring and lightly breaking up the beans. In a baker's bowl, combine 1½ qt tomatoe paste, 4¼ cups water, 1 cup catsup, 1 Tbsp soy sauce, 4 tsp honey, 3 tsp dried oregano leaves, 1 tsp ground red papper, 2 tsp salt (see Note), 6 Tbsp Southwest seasoning blend. Mix liquids and spices with bean mixture. Heat to 180–190°F. Serve 4 oz bean mixture on a hamburger bun. (Note: Use any Southwest seasoning blend with paprika, cumin, and garlic. Seasoning blends vary in the amount of salt. Taste product before adding additional salt.)

TACOS

Yield: 50 sandwiches   *Portion:* 2 tacos

Ingredient	Amount	Procedure
Ground beef, round	13 lb AP (9 lb EP)	Brown beef in steam-jacketed or other kettle until internal temperature reaches 155°F. Drain off fat.
Onions, chopped	1 lb	Add onions and cook until softened.
Cornstarch	3 Tbsp	Combine cornstarch and seasonings in a bowl.
Chili powder	½ cup	Add to ground beef and onions. Mix well.
Garlic powder	1¾ Tbsp	
Salt	3 Tbsp	
Oregano, leaf	1 Tbsp	
Cumin, ground	2 Tbsp	
Pepper, cayenne	1 Tbsp	
Water	1½ qt	Add water to meat mixture. Mix. Simmer 45 minutes, stirring frequently.
Taco shells	100	Place shells in counter pans. Heat in oven until warm and crisp. To serve, fill each taco shell with No. 24 dipper of meat mixture, 1½ oz each.
TOPPING		
Head lettuce, chopped	4 lb EP	Cover meat mixture with lettuce, then tomato, and then shredded cheese.
Tomatoes, fresh diced	3 lb EP	Serve with Salsa (p. 756) to spoon on top.
Processed cheese, shredded	2 lb	

Approximate nutritive values per portion   **Calories** 447

Amount/portion	%DV	Amount/portion	%DV	Amount/portion	%DV		%DV		%DV
Total Fat 26 g	40%	**Cholest.** 64 mg	21%	**Total Carb.** 29 g	10%	**Vitamin A**	10%	**Calcium**	33%
Sat. Fat 9 g	47%	**Sodium** 1171 mg	49%	Fiber 4 g	15%	**Vitamin C**	7%	**Iron**	14%
Protein 24 g				Sugars 6 g					

Percent Daily Values (%DV) are based on a 2000-calorie diet.

Notes
- Potentially hazardous food. *Food Safety Standards:* Hold food for service at an internal temperature above 140°F. Do not mix old product with new. Cool leftover product quickly (within 4 hours) to below 41°F. See p. 105 for cooling procedures. Reheat leftover product quickly (within 2 hours) to 165°F. Reheat product only once; discard if not used.
- Commercial salsa may be substituted for Salsa recipe.
- Commercial taco seasoning mix may be substituted for spices. Follow manufacturer's directions for amount to use.
- 2 oz (1 cup) dehydrated onions, rehydrated in 1½ cups water, may be substituted for fresh onions.

Variations
- **Nacho Tostados.** Place ¾ oz (about 6 large) round unsalted nacho chips on serving plate. Place No. 12 dipper (3 oz) taco meat on top of chips. Ladle 2 oz Nacho Sauce (p. 236) over meat. Place approximately 1½ oz shredded head lettuce and ¾ oz diced fresh tomatoes on top of meat. Serve with condiments: Guacamole (pp. 235), sour cream, and Salsa (p. 756).
- **Tostados.** Fry 50 10-inch flour or corn tortillas in hot oil, 20–30 seconds on each side, until crisp and golden brown. Drain on paper towel. Keep warm. To serve, spread each tortilla with No. 20 dipper Refried Beans (p. 834), then one No. 12 dipper of meat (3 oz). Top with 1½ oz chopped head lettuce, ¾ oz chopped fresh tomatoes, and 1 oz shredded cheese. Serve with condiments: Guacamole (p. 235), sour cream, Salsa (p. 756), chopped green onions, chopped green chiles, and sliced ripe olives.
- **Turkey Tacos.** Substitute ground turkey for ground beef.

REUBEN SANDWICH

Yield: 50 sandwiches   *Portion:* 3 oz

Ingredient	Amount	Procedure
Cooked corned beef	4 lb 8 oz	Cut corned beef into very thin slices.

Rye bread
Mayonnaise or
  Sandwich Spread
  (p. 716)
	100 slices
	2 cups
		Spread No. 100 dipper (scant 2 tsp) dressing on bread.

Sauerkraut, well
  drained
Swiss cheese, 1-oz
  slices
	1½ qt
	
	3 lb 2 oz
		Place filling on bread, in order given:
		  1½ oz corned beef
		  2 Tbsp sauerkraut
		  1 oz cheese
		Cover with top slice of bread.

Margarine, melted	1 lb	Brush sandwiches with melted margarine. Preheat grill to 325°F. Grill sandwiches on both sides until delicately browned.

Approximate nutritive values per portion   **Calories** 447

Amount/portion	%DV	Amount/portion	%DV	Amount/portion	%DV		%DV		%DV
Total Fat 26 g	40%	**Cholest.** 64 mg	21%	**Total Carb.** 29 g	10%	**Vitamin A**	10%	**Calcium**	33%
Sat. Fat 9 g	47%	**Sodium** 1171 mg	49%	Fiber 4 g	15%	**Vitamin C**	7%	**Iron**	14%
Protein 24 g				Sugars 6 g					

Percent Daily Values (%DV) are based on a 2000-calorie diet.

Note   • Potentially hazardous food. *Food Safety Standards:* Hold food for service at an internal temperature above 140°F. Cool leftover product quickly (within 4 hours) to below 41°F. See p. 105 for cooling procedures. Reheat leftover product quickly (within 2 hours) to 165°F. Reheat product only once; discard if not used.

CHIMICHANGA

Yield: 50 portions   *Portion:* 4 oz
Deep-Fat Fryer: 350°F

Ingredient	Amount	Procedure
Ground beef	10 lb 12 oz AP	Brown meat in steam-jacketed kettle until internal temperature reaches 155°F. Drain.
Onions, chopped	1 lb 10 oz	Add onions and chile peppers to meat.
Green chile peppers, chopped	8 oz	Cook until tender.
Flour, all-purpose	4 oz	Stir flour and seasonings into meat mixture.
Garlic powder	½ tsp	
Cumin, ground	2 tsp	
Chili powder	1 Tbsp	
Salsa (see Notes)	1 lb 14 oz	Add Salsa, beef base, and water. Cook 15–20 minutes or until very thick.
Beef base	¾ oz	
Water	1 qt	The filling may be prepared the day before and refrigerated.
Flour tortillas, 10 inch	5 lb 8 oz	Separate tortillas and place slightly overlapping in counter pans. Cover tightly and heat a few at a time for about 5 minutes or just until soft.
Water, cold	2¼ cups	Mix water and cornstarch.
Cornstarch	2 oz	

To Assemble:

1. Brush edges of tortillas with water-cornstarch mixture.
2. Place No. 12 dipper or 4 oz meat mixture slightly below center of each tortilla.
3. Fold bottom edge over filling.
4. Fold sides in, then roll into a cylinder. If necessary, brush on more water-cornstarch mixture to help seal edges.
5. Place seam side down on baking sheets until ready to fry. Cover.
6. Fry at 350°F until golden brown and crisp. Internal temperature should be 165°F.
7. Place in counter pans with liners. Do not cover.
8. Serve with topping (recipe follows).

Topping

Lettuce, shredded	3 lb 8 oz	Serve each Chimichanga with 1 oz each of shredded lettuce, chopped onion, Guacamole, sour cream, and olives; and 2 oz Salsa. See Notes.
Tomato, chopped	3 lb 8 oz	
Guacamole (pp. 235)	3 lb 8 oz	
Sour cream	3 lb 8 oz	
Black olives, chopped	3 lb 8 oz	
Salsa (p. 756) or Spanish Sauce (p. 763)	3 qt	

Approximate nutritive values per portion									Calories 581	
Amount/portion	%DV	Amount/portion	%DV	Amount/portion	%DV		%DV			%DV
Total Fat 36 g	55%	Cholest. 76 mg	25%	Total Carb. 46 g	15%	Vitamin A	24%	Calcium		16%
Sat. Fat 10 g	51%	Sodium 1148 mg	48%	Fiber 2 g	9%	Vitamin C	77%	Iron		28%
Protein 27 g				Sugars 2 g						

Percent Daily Values (%DV) are based on a 2000-calorie diet.

Notes

- Potentially hazardous food. *Food Safety Standards:* Hold food for service at an internal temperature above 140°F. Cool leftover product quickly (within 4 hours) to below 41°F. See p. 105 for cooling procedures. Reheat leftover product quickly (within 2 hours) to 165°F. Reheat product only once; discard if not used.

- Salsa (p. 756) or commercial salsa may be used.

- 7 lb shredded cooked beef may be substituted for ground beef. Omit browning the beef and sauté onions and peppers in a little shortening.

- 3 oz (1½ cups) dehydrated onions, rehydrated in 2½ cups water, may be substituted for fresh onions.

OVEN-BAKED HAMBURGERS

Yield: 50 sandwiches   *Portion:* 4 oz
Oven: 400°F   *Bake:* 15–20 minutes

Ingredient	Amount	Procedure
Ground beef	12 lb AP	Place meat in mixer bowl.
Eggs, beaten Milk	3 (5 oz) 2 cups	Combine eggs and milk and add to meat.
Bread crumbs, soft Onion, chopped Salt Pepper, black	4 oz 4 oz 2 Tbsp 2 tsp	Add crumbs and seasonings. Blend on low speed for approximately 1 minute, using flat beater.
		Portion meat mixture with No. 10 dipper onto lightly greased baking sheets. Flatten into patties. Bake at 400°F for 15–20 minutes or until internal temperature reaches 155°F.
Hamburger buns	50	Serve patties on warm buns.

Approximate nutritive values per portion **Calories** 348

Amount/portion	%DV	Amount/portion	%DV	Amount/portion	%DV		%DV		%DV
Total Fat 17 g	**26%**	**Cholest.** 84 mg	**28%**	**Total Carb.** 23 g	**8%**	Vitamin A	0%	Calcium	8%
Sat. Fat 6 g	**31%**	**Sodium** 584 mg	**24%**	Fiber 0 g	**0%**	Vitamin C	0%	Iron	19%
Protein 24 g				Sugars 1 g					

Percent Daily Values (%DV) are based on a 2000-calorie diet.

Notes
- Potentially hazardous food. *Food Safety Standards:* Hold food for service at an internal temperature above 140°F. Cool leftover product quickly (within 4 hours) to below 41°F. See p. 105 for cooling procedures. Reheat leftover product quickly (within 2 hours) to 165°F. Reheat product only once; discard if not used.
- ½ oz (¼ cup) dehydrated onions, rehydrated in ½ cup water, may be substituted for fresh onions.

Variations
- **Barbecued Hamburgers.**   Place browned hamburgers in baking pans. Pour Barbecue Sauce (p. 755) over patties. Cover with aluminum foil and bake at 325°F until hot, about 10–20 minutes.
- **Grilled Hamburgers and Accompaniments.**   Cook 4-oz hamburger patties on the grill only until they are no longer pink. Place on bun and serve with accompaniments: mayonnaise, mustard, catsup, sliced dill pickles, sliced or chopped onions, sliced tomato, and leaf lettuce.

CROISSANT WITH SAUTÉED GARDEN VEGETABLES

Yield: 50   *Portion:* 1 sandwich
Oven: 350°F   *Heat:* 5–10 minutes

Ingredient	Amount	Procedure
Green peppers, sliced	2 lb 6 oz	Toss together.
Onions, sliced	2 lb 6 oz	
Mushrooms, fresh, sliced	2 lb 6 oz	
Margarine	14 oz	Melt margarine in steam-jacketed kettle. Add vegetables. Sauté until tender-crisp. Drain.
Croissants, cut in half lengthwise	50 (2½-oz size)	Assemble sandwiches in 12 × 20 × 2-inch pans:
Swiss cheese, ⅔ oz slices	4 lb 3 oz (100 slices)	1. Bottom of croissant 2. ⅔ oz Swiss cheese slice 3. 2 oz sautéed vegetables
Ripe olives, sliced, drained	1 lb 6 oz	4. ½ oz sliced olives 5. 2 tomato slices
Tomatoes, sliced	2 lb	6. ⅔ oz Swiss cheese slice 7. Top of croissant

Heat at 350°F just long enough to melt cheese, 5–10 minutes. Do not hold over 15 minutes before serving.

Approximate nutritive values per portion   **Calories** 346

Amount/portion	%DV	Amount/portion	%DV	Amount/portion	%DV		%DV		%DV
Total Fat 24 g	**38%**	**Cholest.** 64 mg	**21%**	**Total Carb.** 18 g	**6%**	Vitamin A	15%	Calcium	40%
Sat. Fat 11 g	**57%**	**Sodium** 544 mg	**23%**	Fiber 2 g	**9%**	Vitamin C	38%	Iron	10%
Protein 14 g				Sugars 5 g					

Percent Daily Values (%DV) are based on a 2000-calorie diet.

TAHINI AND YOGURT SPREAD

Yield: 50 portions   *Portion:* 1½ oz

Ingredient	Amount	Procedure
Minced garlic	1 oz	Blend garlic and tahini together in a bowl.
Tahini	12 oz	
Yogurt (unflavored)	3 lb 4 oz	Add yogurt, lemon juice, and spices to garlic-tahini mixture
Lemon juice (fresh)	1 cup	and mix well.
Paprika	1 tsp	
Salt	1 tsp	

Approximate nutritive values per portion   **Calories 65**

Amount/portion	%DV	Amount/portion	%DV	Amount/portion	%DV		%DV		%DV
Total Fat 5 g	8%	**Cholest.** 3.8 mg	1%	**Total Carb.** 2.8 g	1%	Vitamin A	1%	Calcium	4%
Sat. Fat 1.2 g	6%	**Sodium** 7.8 mg	3%	Fiber .3 g	1%	Vitamin C	4%	Iron	0%
Protein 2.8 g				Sugars 2.1 g					

Percent Daily Values (%DV) are based on a 2000-calorie diet.

Note • Potentially hazardous food. *Food Safety Standards:* Hold food for service at an internal temperature below 41°F. Do not mix old product with new.

CHAPTER 17

Sauces, Marinades, Rubs, and Seasonings

Jerry Young © Dorling Kindersley

A sauce serves to complement an entree, vegetable, or dessert. It may be used as a binding agent to hold foods together or as a topping. Sauces add richness, moistness, color, and form to foods and may enhance or offer contrast in flavor or color to foods they accompany. Marinades, rubs, and seasoning blends add flavor to entrees and vegetables. They may be used also to tenderize.

ENTREE AND VEGETABLE SAUCES

Basic to many sauces is a roux, which is a cooked mixture of fat and flour, usually equal parts by weight. A roux may range from white, in which the fat and flour are cooked only for a short time, to brown, cooked until it is light brown in color and has a nutty aroma. The amount of browning will influence both the flavor and color characteristics of the sauce. Calories may be lowered by eliminating the fat and making the sauce with a starch thickener, such as flour or cornstarch, mixed with a cold liquid (stock or milk).

Other starch thickening agents commonly used in sauces are arrowroot, cornstarch, pregelatinized or instant starch, and waxy maize. Waxy maize is preferred for sauces that will be frozen because it will not break and separate as easily as other starches. When re-

heated, products containing waxy maize are smoother than those with cornstarch. Egg yolks have a slight thickening power and are used for some sauces. When egg yolks are cooked to too high a temperature, or held too long, the egg protein will coagulate and cause a curdled effect.

Most meat and vegetable sauces are modifications of the basic recipes: white sauce, blond sauce, brown sauce, red sauce, and butter sauces.

- **White Sauce** (p. 749), made with a roux of fat and flour and with milk as the liquid, has many uses in quantity food preparation, as a sauce with vegetables, eggs, and fish and as an ingredient in many casseroles. A White Sauce Mix (p. 748), combining flour, fat, and nonfat dry milk, may be made and stored in the refrigerator until needed. Water and seasonings are added when the mixture is to be used. Béchamel Sauce (p. 750) is a white sauce that uses milk and chicken stock as the liquid and, with its variations, usually is served with poultry, seafood, eggs, or vegetables.

- **Blond sauces** are made from a roux that is cooked a little longer than the white sauce, just until the roux begins to brown. Velouté Sauce (p. 750) is a blond sauce that uses chicken, veal, or fish broth as its liquid.

- **Brown Sauce** (p. 753) is made with a well-browned roux, and beef stock as the liquid. Brown Sauce is used with meat.

PAN GRAVY

Yield: 1 gal   *Portion:* ⅓ cup (2½ oz)

Ingredient	Amount	Procedure
Fat, hot (meat drippings)	8 oz	Add flour to fat and blend.
Flour, all-purpose	8 oz	
Salt	1 Tbsp	Stir in salt and pepper. Cook 5 minutes.
Pepper, black	1 tsp	
Chicken or Meat Stock (pp. 790, 791)	1 gal	Add stock gradually. Cook, stirring constantly with wire whip. Cook until smooth and thickened.

Approximate nutritive values per ounce   **Calories 25**

Amount/portion	%DV	Amount/portion	%DV	Amount/portion	%DV		%DV		%DV
Total Fat 2 g	3%	**Cholest.** 2 mg	1%	**Total Carb.** 0 g	0%	**Vitamin A**	0%	**Calcium**	0%
Sat. Fat 1 g	5%	**Sodium** 148 mg	6%	Fiber 0 g	0%	**Vitamin C**	0%	**Iron**	0%
Protein 1 g				Sugars 0 g					

Percent Daily Values (%DV) are based on a 2000-calorie diet.

Notes
- Potentially hazardous food. *Food Safety Standards:* Hold food for service at an internal temperature above 140°F. Do not mix old product with new. Cool leftover product quickly (within 4 hours) to below 41°F. See p. 105 for cooling procedures. Reheat leftover product quickly (within 2 hours) to 165°F. Reheat product only once; discard if not used.
- If beef or chicken base is used for stock, delete or reduce salt.

Variations
- **Brown Gravy.** Use 10 oz flour and brown in the fat.
- **Chicken Gravy.** Use chicken drippings for fat and chicken stock for liquid.
- **Chicken or Turkey Gravy (using base).** In steam-jacketed kettle melt 12 oz margarine. Using a wire whip, stir in 14 oz flour. Cook 30 minutes, stirring often. Add 3½ qt water and 3 oz chicken base. Cook until thickened and no starchy flavor remains, 190°F. Add 1 tsp black pepper, ½ tsp poultry seasoning, and 1 tsp caramel coloring (kitchen bouquet) (optional). Makes 1 gal. Salt may need to be adjusted depending on the amount of salt in the chicken base.
- **Cream Gravy.** Substitute milk for water or stock.
- **Giblet Gravy.** Use chicken drippings for fat and chicken stock for liquid. Add 1 qt cooked giblets, chopped.
- **Onion Gravy.** Lightly brown 1 lb thinly sliced onions in fat before adding flour.
- **Vegetable Gravy.** Add 1 lb diced carrots, 4 oz chopped celery, and 12 oz chopped onion, cooked in water, meat, or vegetable stock.

BROWN SAUCE

Yield: 2 qt   *Portion:* 3 Tbsp (1½ oz)

Ingredient	Amount	Procedure
Beef Stock (p. 791)	2 qt	Add onions and seasonings to meat stock. If soup base has
Onion, thinly sliced	4 oz	been used to make stock, taste before adding salt.
Salt	2 tsp	Simmer about 10 minutes.
Pepper, black	¼ tsp	Strain.
Shortening	8 oz	Heat shortening and blend with flour. Cook about
Flour, all-purpose	5 oz	10 minutes until it becomes uniformly brown in color. Add hot stock while stirring with wire whip. Cook until thickened.

Approximate nutritive values per ounce   **Calories** 39

Amount/portion	%DV	Amount/portion	%DV	Amount/portion	%DV		%DV		%DV
Total Fat 3 g	5%	**Cholest.** 0 mg	0%	**Total Carb.** 2 g	1%	**Vitamin A**	0%	**Calcium**	0%
Sat. Fat 1 g	4%	**Sodium** 150 mg	6%	Fiber 0 g	0%	**Vitamin C**	0%	**Iron**	0%
Protein 1 g				Sugars 0 g					

Percent Daily Values (%DV) are based on a 2000-calorie diet.

Note
- Potentially hazardous food. *Food Safety Standards:* Hold food for service at an internal temperature above 140°F. Do not mix old product with new. Cool leftover product quickly (within 4 hours) to below 41°F. See p. 105 for cooling procedures. Reheat leftover product quickly (within 2 hours) to 165°F. Reheat product only once; discard if not used.

Variations
- **Jelly Sauce.** Add 2 cups currant jelly, beaten until soft, 2 Tbsp tarragon vinegar, and 4 oz sautéed minced onions. Serve with lamb or game.
- **Mushroom Sauce.** Add 1 lb sliced mushrooms and 2 oz minced onions, sautéed. Serve with steak.
- **Olive Sauce.** Add 6 oz chopped stuffed olives. Serve with meat or duck.
- **Piquant Sauce.** Add 2 oz minced onions, 2 oz capers, ½ cup vinegar, 4 oz sugar, ¼ tsp salt, ¼ tsp paprika, and ½ cup chili sauce or chopped sweet pickle. Serve with meats.
- **Savory Mustard Sauce.** Add ½ cup prepared mustard and ½ cup horseradish. Serve with meats.

SALSA

Yield: 1 gal

Ingredient	Amount	Procedure
Tomatoes, canned, crushed	3 lb 10 oz	Combine all ingredients in stainless steel or glass container. Mix well.
Tomato juice	3 lb 6 oz	Store covered in refrigerator.
Green pepper, dried, chopped	1 oz	May be heated before service.
Onion, fresh, chopped	8 oz	
Garlic powder	¼ tsp	
Peppers, green chilies	8 oz	
Peppers, jalapeño, canned, chopped	10 oz	
Vinegar, cider	¾ cup	
Salt	2 tsp	
Sugar, granulated	1 Tbsp	
Hot pepper sauce	1 Tbsp	
Oregano, dried, crumbled	½ tsp	
Pepper, cayenne	¾ tsp	
Cumin, ground	¾ tsp	

Approximate nutritive values per ounce

Calories 6

Amount/portion	%DV	Amount/portion	%DV	Amount/portion	%DV		%DV		%DV
Total Fat 0 g	0%	**Cholest.** 0 mg	0%	**Total Carb.** 0 g	0%	Vitamin A	1%	Calcium	0%
Sat. Fat 0 g	0%	**Sodium** 134 mg	6%	Fiber 0.3 g	1%	Vitamin C	8%	Iron	1%
Protein 0 g				Sugars 1 g					

Percent Daily Values (%DV) are based on a 2000-calorie diet.

Note   • May be served as a condiment with tacos, tostadas, chimichangas, or other Mexican entrees.

SUMMER CUCUMBER AND MELON SALSA

Yield: 50 portions   *Portion:* 4 oz

Ingredient	Amount	Procedure
Cucumber, diced ¼ inch (peeled)	4 lb (EP)	Gently mix all ingredients being careful not to mash fruit and vegetables.
Red bell pepper, chopped	1 lb 8 oz (EP)	Cover and refrigerate up to 6 hours.
Red onion, finely chopped	1 lb 8 oz (EP)	
Cilantro leaves, chopped fresh	4 oz	
Cantaloupe, ½-inch dice (peeled)	4 lb 8 oz (EP)	
Olive oil	¾ cup	
Lime juice, fresh	¾ cup	
Red wine vinegar	¾ cup	
Sugar, granulated	2 tsp	
Salt	½ tsp	
Pepper, black	⅛ tsp	

Serve as a side accompaniment with chicken or fish.
Keep cold, below 41°F.

Approximate nutritive values per portion   **Calories** 55

Amount/portion	%DV	Amount/portion	%DV	Amount/portion	%DV		%DV		%DV
Total Fat 3.4 g	5%	**Cholest.** 0 mg	0%	**Total Carb.** 7 g	2%	**Vitamin A**	25%	**Calcium**	2%
Sat. Fat 0 .5 g	2%	**Sodium** 34 mg	1%	Fiber 1 g	5%	**Vitamin C**	75%	**Iron**	2%
Protein 0.9 g				Sugars 5 g					

Percent Daily Values (%DV) are based on a 2000-calorie diet.

BLACK EYED PEA AND CORN SALSA

Yield: 50 portions   *Portion:* 3 oz

Ingredient	Amount	Procedure
Tomatoes, ¼-inch dice	2 lb 10 oz EP	Combine in stainless steel bowl being careful to not mash tomatoes.
Roasted red bell peppers, ¼-inch dice (p. 854)	10 oz	
Seasoned Black Eyed Peas (p. 852)	2 lb 4 oz	Drain well and add to pepper and tomato mixture.
Green onions, thinly sliced	7 oz EP	Add vegetables and seasonings. Stir lightly being careful to not over-mix.
Garlic, finely chopped	2 Tbsp EP	Cover and refrigerate for 6–8 hours, stirring occasionally.
Whole kernel corn, thawed	2 lb 4 oz	
Picante sauce	1 qt	
Cilantro (fresh), chopped	1 oz EP (1½ cups)	
Lime juice (fresh)	¼ cup	
Salt	2 tsp	

Approximate nutritive values per ounce   **Calories** 50

Amount/portion	%DV	Amount/portion	%DV	Amount/portion	%DV		%DV		%DV
Total Fat .4 g	1%	**Cholest.** 0 mg	0%	**Total Carb.** 10 g	3%	**Vitamin A**	7%	**Calcium**	1%
Sat. Fat 0 g	0%	**Sodium** 295 mg	12%	Fiber 1.2 g	5%	**Vitamin C**	8%	**Iron**	2%
Protein 1.8 g				Sugars 3.1 g					

Percent Daily Values (%DV) are based on a 2000-calorie diet.

Note   • Serve with nacho chips or as a plate garnish for Southwest seasoned pork or chicken.

FRUIT SALSA

Yield: 50 portions   *Portion:* 2 oz

Ingredient	Amount	Procedure
Fresh fruit (see suggestions below)	3 lb 12 oz (EP)	Prepare fruit as required (peel, seed, etc.). Slice or cut into ¼-inch cubes.
Red bell peppers Anaheim chili peppers Jalapeño peppers	1 lb 4 oz (EP) 6 oz (EP) 6 oz (EP)	Remove stem end and seed pod from peppers. Dice bell peppers into ¼-inch cubes. Slice Anaheim and jalapeño peppers into thin slices. Stir carefully into fruit.
Onions, red	6 oz	Dice onions into ¼-inch cubes. Stir carefully into fruit.
Red pepper flakes Lime juice, fresh Cilantro, fresh, chopped	1 tsp 1 cup 1 oz (¾ cup)	Stir carefully into fruit mixture. Cover and chill.

Fruit suggestions

Tropical fruit: papaya or papaya and mango
Sunburst: papaya and orange
Southwest peach: fresh peaches
Fruit and cucumber: papaya and cucumber

Approximate nutritive values per portion   **Calories** 65

Amount/portion	%DV	Amount/portion	%DV	Amount/portion	%DV		%DV		%DV
Total Fat 0 g	0%	**Cholest.** 0 mg	0%	**Total Carb.** 16 g	5%	**Vitamin A**	54%	**Calcium**	2%
Sat. Fat 0 g	0%	**Sodium** 62 mg	3%	Fiber 2 g	10%	**Vitamin C**	410%	**Iron**	190%
Protein 2 g				Sugars 5 g					

Percent Daily Values (%DV) are based on a 2000-calorie diet.

Notes
- Canned jalapeño peppers, drained and chopped, can be substituted for fresh jalapeño peppers.
- Reconstituted frozen lime juice may be substituted for fresh lime juice.

WHITE BEAN AND TOMATO SAUCE

Yield: 50 portions *Portion:* 3 oz
Oven: 425°F *Bake:* 15–20 minutes plus 15 minutes

Ingredient	Amount	Procedure
Tomatoes, diced, canned	3 lb 12 oz	Combine tomato, onion, garlic, and oil. Put mixture into one 12 × 20 × 4-inch pan and bake at 425°F until most of the tomato liquid evaporates and onion is tender (approximately 20 minutes).
Onion, chopped coarsely	1 lb 8 oz	
Garlic, minced	3 oz	
Olive oil	1 cup	
White beans, canned	9 lb	Carefully combine undrained beans (see Notes), vinegar, herbs, and spices with tomato mixture.
Red wine vinegar	⅓ cup	Cover and bake until heated to 165°F (approximately 15 minutes).
Parsley, fresh, chopped	2 cups	Remove from oven and keep warm, above 140°F.
Basil, fresh, chopped	¼ cup	Serve as a base under fish or poultry.
Thyme, fresh, chopped	2 Tbsp	
Pepper, black	1 Tbsp	
Salt	1½ tsp	

Approximate nutritive values per portion **Calories** 122

Amount/portion	%DV	Amount/portion	%DV	Amount/portion	%DV		%DV		%DV
Total Fat 5 g	7%	**Cholest.** 0 mg	0%	**Total Carb.** 16 g	5%	**Vitamin A**	5%	**Calcium**	5%
Sat. Fat 1 g	3%	**Sodium** 489 mg	20%	Fiber 1 g	3%	**Vitamin C**	12%	**Iron**	10%
Protein 5 g				Sugars 2 g					

Percent Daily Values (%DV) are based on a 2000-calorie diet.

Notes
- Potentially hazardous food. *Food Safety Standards:* Hold food for service at an internal temperature above 140°F. Do not mix old product with new. Cool leftover product quickly (within 4 hours) to below 41°F. See p. 105 for cooling procedures. Reheat leftover product quickly (within 2 hours) to 165°F. Reheat product only once; discard if not used.
- If canned beans have a large amount of liquid, partially drain and carefully stir in reserved liquid until the desired consistency is achieved.
- Fresh tomatoes may be substituted for canned. Peel and remove seeds before coarsely chopping.
- ¼ cup fresh cilantro may be substituted for the parsley.

Variation
- **Black Bean and Tomato Sauce.** Substitute canned black beans for the white beans.

MARINARA SAUCE

Yield: 2 gal   *Portion:* 4 oz

Ingredient	Amount	Procedure
Onion, chopped	1 lb	Sauté onion and garlic in oil until tender and golden in color.
Garlic, minced	8 cloves	
Olive oil	¾ cup	
Plum tomatoes, canned, undrained	20 lb (2½ gal)	Add tomatoes to onion-garlic mixture. Break tomatoes into small pieces.
Parsley, fresh, chopped	3 oz	Stir in seasonings. Cover and simmer for 2 hours, stirring occasionally. Cook until sauce reaches desired consistency.
Basil, dried, crumbled	3 Tbsp	
Salt	2 Tbsp	
Pepper, black	1½ tsp	

Approximate nutritive values per ounce   **Calories** 14

Amount/portion	%DV	Amount/portion	%DV	Amount/portion	%DV		%DV		%DV
Total Fat 1 g	1%	**Cholest.** 0 mg	0%	**Total Carb.** 2 g	1%	**Vitamin A**	2%	**Calcium**	1%
Sat. Fat 0 g	0%	**Sodium** 108 mg	5%	Fiber 0.3 g	1%	**Vitamin C**	9%	**Iron**	1%
Protein 0 g				Sugars 1g					

Percent Daily Values (%DV) are based on a 2000-calorie diet.

Notes

- Potentially hazardous food. *Food Safety Standards:* Hold food for service at an internal temperature above 140°F. Do not mix old product with new. Cool leftover product quickly (within 4 hours) to below 41°F. See p. 105 for cooling procedures. Reheat leftover product quickly (within 2 hours) to 165°F. Reheat product only once; discard if not used.

- Serve over pasta, meats, or poultry. Sprinkle with Parmesan cheese.

- 3 Tbsp brown sugar may be added for a sweeter sauce.

- Vegetable oil may be substituted for olive oil.

- 2 oz finely chopped sweet red bell pepper may be added along with parsley and spices.

- Diced tomatoes may be substituted for plum tomatoes. Drain some of the juice before adding or cook longer until the liquid evaporates and sauce thickens.

- To make a thicker sauce requiring less cooking time substitute 6 lb tomato puree for 6 lb tomatoes.

Variations

- **Marinara Sauce with Olives.** Add to sauce 2 lb 8 oz sliced black olives, drained; 2 Tbsp oregano, dried, leaf; and 2 tsp red pepper flakes. Small whole olives may be substituted for sliced olives. 8 oz capers may be added.

- **Tomato Zucchini Sauce.** Follow recipe for Marinara Sauce with Olives. Add 3 lb sliced zucchini just before serving and heat to serving temperature. Serve with grated Romano or Parmesan cheese.

ITALIAN TOMATO SAUCE

Yield: 1½ gal   *Portion:* 4 oz

Ingredient	Amount	Procedure
Olive oil	3 oz	In steam-jacketed kettle or large pan, sauté onions, garlic, and peppers until onions are transparent.
Onions, finely chopped	1 lb 6 oz (EP)	
Garlic, minced	2 oz (EP)	
Green peppers, finely chopped	6 oz (EP)	
Tomato juice	2½ qt	Add liquids and spices. Stir well to combine.
Tomato puree	3 cups	Heat to boiling. Reduce heat and simmer for 20–30 minutes.
Tomato paste	3½ cups	For a thicker sauce, increase cooking time.
Water	2 qt	Remove bay leaves before serving.
Oregano leaves, dried	1 Tbsp	
Thyme leaves, dried	1 tsp	
Basil leaves, dried	¼ cup	
Red pepper, crushed	1 tsp	
Parsley, dried	¼ cup	
Bay leaves	4 leaves	
Pepper, black	1 Tbsp	
Salt	1 oz	
Sugar, granulated (see Notes)	2 Tbsp	

Approximate nutritive values per portion

Calories 60

Amount/portion	%DV	Amount/portion	%DV	Amount/portion	%DV		%DV		%DV
Total Fat 2 g	3%	**Cholest.** 0 mg	0%	**Total Carb.** 10 g	3%	**Vitamin A**	7%	**Calcium**	3%
Sat. Fat 0.3 g	1%	**Sodium** 472 mg		Fiber 2 g	9%	**Vitamin C**	32%	**Iron**	7%
Protein 1.6 g				Sugars 6 g					

Percent Daily Values (%DV) are based on a 2000-calorie diet.

Notes

- Potentially hazardous food. *Food Safety Standards:* Hold food for service at an internal temperature above 140°F. Do not mix old product with new. Cool leftover product quickly (within 4 hours) to below 41°F. See p. 105 for cooling procedures. Reheat leftover product quickly (within 2 hours) to 165°F. Reheat product only once; discard if not used.

- For a less sweet sauce, omit sugar. For a sweeter sauce, increase sugar to 3 Tbsp.

- Serve over pasta or as a base for Italian sauces with meat or shellfish.

- The names Marinara and Italian Tomato Sauce may be used interchangeably.

SPANISH SAUCE

Yield: 3 qt   *Portion:* 3 Tbsp (2 oz)

Ingredient	Amount	Procedure
Onion, chopped	4 oz	Sauté onion in shortening.
Shortening	4 oz	
Tomatoes, canned, diced	2 qt	Add remaining ingredients. Simmer until vegetables are tender.
Celery, diced	1 lb	
Green pepper, chopped	8 oz	
Pimiento, chopped	6 oz	
Salt	1 Tbsp	
Pepper, black	½ tsp	
Pepper, cayenne	Few grains	

Approximate nutritive values per ounce   **Calories** 17

Amount/portion	%DV	Amount/portion	%DV	Amount/portion	%DV		%DV		%DV
Total Fat 1 g	2%	**Cholest.** 0 mg	0%	**Total Carb.** 1 g	1%	**Vitamin A**	1%	**Calcium**	0%
Sat. Fat 1 g	2%	**Sodium** 104 mg	4%	Fiber 0.3 g	1%	**Vitamin C**	11%	**Iron**	1%
Protein 0 g				Sugars 1 g					

Percent Daily Values (%DV) are based on a 2000-calorie diet.

Notes
- Potentially hazardous food. *Food Safety Standards:* Hold food for service at an internal temperature above 140°F. Do not mix old product with new. Cool leftover product quickly (within 4 hours) to below 41°F. See p. 105 for cooling procedures. Reheat leftover product quickly (within 2 hours) to 165°F. Reheat product only once; discard if not used.
- Serve with meat, fish, cheese, or Mexican entrees.
- ½ oz (¼ cup) dehydrated onions, rehydrated in ½ cup water, may be substituted for fresh onions.
- 1 tsp cilantro may be added.

HORSERADISH SAUCE

Yield: 5 cups   *Portion:* 1½ Tbsp (½ oz)

Ingredient	Amount	Procedure
Horseradish, drained	8 oz	Combine.
Prepared mustard	2 Tbsp	
Salt	½ tsp	
Paprika	¼ tsp	
Pepper, cayenne	⅛ tsp	
Vinegar, cider	⅓ cup	
Cream, whipping	2 cups	Whip cream. Fold in horseradish mixture. Chill.

Approximate nutritive values per ounce   **Calories** 54

Amount/portion	%DV	Amount/portion	%DV	Amount/portion	%DV		%DV		%DV
Total Fat 5 g	8%	**Cholest.** 19 mg	6%	**Total Carb.** 1 g	1%	**Vitamin A**	5%	**Calcium**	1%
Sat. Fat 3 g	17%	**Sodium** 61 mg	3%	Fiber 0.4 g	1%	**Vitamin C**	0%	**Iron**	0%
Protein 1 g				Sugars 0 g					

Percent Daily Values (%DV) are based on a 2000-calorie diet.

Notes
- Potentially hazardous food. Store for service at an internal temperature below 41°F.
- Serve with ham or roast beef.

COCKTAIL SAUCE

Yield: 2 qt   *Portion:* 2½ Tbsp (1½ oz)

Ingredient	Amount	Procedure
Chili sauce	1 qt	Mix all ingredients. Chill.
Catsup	2 cups	
Lemon juice	1 cup	
Onion juice	2 Tbsp	
Celery, finely chopped	10 oz	
Worcestershire sauce	5 tsp	
Horseradish	3 oz	
Hot pepper sauce	Few drops	

Approximate nutritive values per ounce   **Calories** 26

Amount/portion	%DV	Amount/portion	%DV	Amount/portion	%DV		%DV		%DV
Total Fat 0 g	0%	**Cholest.** 0 mg	0%	**Total Carb.** 6 g	2%	**Vitamin A**	3%	**Calcium**	0%
Sat. Fat 0 g	0%	**Sodium** 288 mg	12%	Fiber 0.3 g	1%	**Vitamin C**	8%	**Iron**	1%
Protein 0 g				Sugars 3 g					

Percent Daily Values (%DV) are based on a 2000-calorie diet.

Note
- Serve as a condiment for clam, crab, lobster, oyster, or shrimp.

HORSERADISH CAPER SAUCE

Yield: 50 portions   *Portion:* 1 oz

Ingredient	*Amount*	*Procedure*
Nonfat sour cream	3 cups	Combine all ingredients in a mixer bowl. Mix until combined. Chill quickly (within 4 hours) to below 41°F.
Buttermilk	2 cups	
Chives, minced, fresh	¾ cup	
Capers, small	½ cup	
Horseradish, prepared	⅓ cup	
Pepper, black	¼ tsp	

Approximate nutritive values per portion   Calories 13

Amount/portion	%DV	Amount/portion	%DV	Amount/portion	%DV		%DV		%DV
Total Fat 0 g	0%	**Cholest.** 0 mg	0%	**Total Carb.** 2 g	1%	**Vitamin A**	5%	**Calcium**	3%
Sat. Fat 0 g	0%	**Sodium** 21 mg	1%	Fiber 0 g	0%	**Vitamin C**	0%	**Iron**	0%
Protein 1 g				Sugars 0 g					

Percent Daily Values (%DV) are based on a 2000-calorie diet.

Notes
- Potentially hazardous food. Hold for service at a temperature below 41°F.
- Serve with fish.

Variation
- **Horseradish–Dill Sauce.** Delete capers. Add ⅓ cup fresh dill weed.

MUSTARD SAUCE (COLD)

Yield: 3 cups   *Portion:* 1 Tbsp

Ingredient	*Amount*	*Procedure*
Sugar, granulated	2 Tbsp	Mix dry ingredients.
Salt	½ tsp	
Dry mustard	2 tsp	
Water	2 Tbsp	Add water, vinegar, and eggs to dry ingredients. Cook until thick.
Vinegar, cider	¼ cup	
Eggs, beaten	2 (3 oz)	
Margarine	1 oz	Add margarine. Stir until melted. Cool quickly to below 41°F.
Cream, whipping	2 cups	Whip cream and fold into cooked mixture.

Approximate nutritive values per ounce   Calories 77

Amount/portion	%DV	Amount/portion	%DV	Amount/portion	%DV		%DV		%DV
Total Fat 7 g	12%	**Cholest.** 37 mg	12%	**Total Carb.** 2 g	1%	**Vitamin A**	7%	**Calcium**	1%
Sat. Fat 4 g	21%	**Sodium** 72 mg	3%	Fiber 0 g	0%	**Vitamin C**	0%	**Iron**	0%
Protein 1 g				Sugars 2 g					

Percent Daily Values (%DV) are based on a 2000-calorie diet.

Notes
- Potentially hazardous food. Store for service at an internal temperature below 41°F.
- Serve cold with ham, pork, or beef roast.

Variation
- **Hot Chinese Mustard.** Combine 8 oz dry mustard, ⅓ cup salad oil, and 1 oz (1½ Tbsp) salt. Add 2 cups boiling water. Stir until smooth. Serve with egg rolls.

MUSTARD SAUCE (HOT)

Yield: 2 qt   *Portion:* 2 Tbsp (1 oz)

Ingredient	Amount	Procedure
Beef Stock (p. 791)	2 qt	Heat stock to boiling point.
Cornstarch	5 oz	Blend dry ingredients with cold water.
Sugar, granulated	2 Tbsp	Add gradually to hot stock. Cook and stir until thickened.
Salt	2 tsp	
Pepper, white	½ tsp	
Water, cold	½ cup	
Prepared mustard	2 oz	Add remaining ingredients.
Horseradish	4 oz	Stir until blended.
Vinegar, cider	2 Tbsp	
Margarine	1 oz	

Approximate nutritive values per ounce   **Calories** 14

Amount/portion	%DV	Amount/portion	%DV	Amount/portion	%DV		%DV		%DV
Total Fat 0 g	0%	**Cholest.** 0 mg	0%	**Total Carb.** 2 g	1%	**Vitamin A**	0%	**Calcium**	0%
Sat. Fat 0 g	0%	**Sodium** 155 mg	6%	Fiber 0 g	0%	**Vitamin C**	0%	**Iron**	0%
Protein 0 g				Sugars 0 g					

Percent Daily Values (%DV) are based on a 2000-calorie diet.

Notes
- Potentially hazardous food. *Food Safety Standards:* Hold food for service at an internal temperature above 140°F. Do not mix old product with new. Cool leftover product quickly (within 4 hours) to below 41°F. See p. 105 for cooling procedures. Reheat leftover product quickly (within 2 hours) to 165°F. Reheat product only once; discard if not used.
- Serve hot with fresh or cured ham or fish.

SWEET-SOUR SAUCE

Yield: 1¼ qt   *Portion:* 1½ Tbsp

Ingredient	Amount	Procedure
Sugar, granulated	10 oz	Combine sugar and cornstarch in kettle.
Cornstarch	¼ cup	
Vinegar, cider	1 cup	Add vinegar, water, and soy sauce to dry ingredients and stir until smooth.
Water	2½ cups	
Soy sauce	¼ cup	
Catsup	¾ cup	Stir catsup into mixture in kettle. Cook until translucent, stirring constantly. Serve as a condiment with egg rolls or chicken nuggets.

Approximate nutritive values per ounce   **Calories** 24

Amount/portion	%DV	Amount/portion	%DV	Amount/portion	%DV		%DV		%DV
Total Fat 0 g	0%	**Cholest.** 0 mg	0%	**Total Carb.** 7 g	2%	**Vitamin A**	0%	**Calcium**	0%
Sat. Fat 0 g	0%	**Sodium** 106 mg	4%	Fiber 0 g	0%	**Vitamin C**	0%	**Iron**	0%
Protein 0 g				Sugars 5 g					

Percent Daily Values (%DV) are based on a 2000-calorie diet.

RAISIN SAUCE

Yield: 1½ qt   *Portion:* 2 Tbsp

Ingredient	Amount	Procedure
Raisins, seedless	1 lb	Steam raisins or simmer in small amount of water for 3–5 minutes.
Sugar, granulated Water	4 oz 2 cups	Mix sugar and water, and heat to boiling point.
Currant jelly Vinegar, cider Margarine Worcestershire sauce Salt Pepper, white Cloves, ground Mace Red food coloring (optional)	1 lb ⅓ cup 2 oz 1 Tbsp 1 tsp ¼ tsp ½ tsp ⅛ tsp Few drops	Add cooked raisins, currant jelly, and remaining ingredients. Simmer 5 minutes or until jelly is melted.

Approximate nutritive values per ounce   **Calories** 66

Amount/portion	%DV	Amount/portion	%DV	Amount/portion	%DV		%DV		%DV
Total Fat 1 g	1%	**Cholest.** 0 mg	0%	**Total Carb.** 15 g	5%	**Vitamin A**	0%	**Calcium**	0%
Sat. Fat 0 g	0%	**Sodium** 56 mg	2%	Fiber 0.4 g	1%	**Vitamin C**	2%	**Iron**	1%
Protein 0 g				Sugars 12 g					

Percent Daily Values (%DV) are based on a 2000-calorie diet.

Note   • Serve with baked ham.

CUCUMBER SAUCE

Yield: 3 cups   *Portion:* 1 Tbsp (½ oz)

Ingredient	Amount	Procedure
Cucumbers	1 lb	Peel cucumbers; remove seeds. Grate or chop finely.
Sour cream Onion, grated Vinegar, cider Lemon juice Salt Pepper, cayenne	1 cup 1 Tbsp 1 Tbsp 1½ Tbsp ½ tsp Few grains	Combine remaining ingredients and add to cucumber. Chill.

Approximate nutritive values per ounce   **Calories** 23

Amount/portion	%DV	Amount/portion	%DV	Amount/portion	%DV		%DV		%DV
Total Fat 2 g	3%	**Cholest.** 4 mg	1%	**Total Carb.** 0 g	0%	**Vitamin A**	2%	**Calcium**	1%
Sat. Fat 1 g	6%	**Sodium** 50 mg	2%	Fiber 0 g	0%	**Vitamin C**	2%	**Iron**	0%
Protein 0 g				Sugars 0 g					

Percent Daily Values (%DV) are based on a 2000-calorie diet.

Notes   • Potentially hazardous food. Store for service at an internal temperature below 41°F.

• Serve with fish.

TARTAR SAUCE

Yield: 1¾ qt   *Portion:* 2 Tbsp (1 oz)

Ingredient	Amount	Procedure
Mayonnaise	1 qt	Mix all ingredients.
Pickle relish	6 oz	
Green pepper, chopped	¼ cup	
Parsley, chopped	¼ cup	
Green olives, chopped	6 oz	
Onion, minced	1 Tbsp	
Pimiento, chopped	2 oz	
Vinegar or lemon juice	½ cup	
Worcestershire sauce	Few drops	
Hot pepper sauce	Few drops	

Approximate nutritive values per ounce   **Calories** 135

Amount/portion	%DV	Amount/portion	%DV	Amount/portion	%DV		%DV		%DV
Total Fat 15 g	22%	**Cholest.** 10 mg	3%	**Total Carb.** 2 g	1%	Vitamin A	2%	Calcium	0%
Sat. Fat 2 g	10%	**Sodium** 198 mg	8%	Fiber 0 g	0%	Vitamin C	4%	Iron	1%
Protein 0 g				Sugars 0 g					

Percent Daily Values (%DV) are based on a 2000-calorie diet.

Note   • Serve with fish.

HOLLANDAISE SAUCE

Yield: 12 portions   *Portion:* 1½ Tbsp (¾ oz)

Ingredient	Amount	Procedure
Butter	2 oz	Place butter, lemon juice, and egg yolks over hot (not boiling) water.
Lemon juice	1½ Tbsp	
Egg yolks (see Notes)	3 (2 oz)	Cook slowly, beating constantly.
Butter	2 oz	When first portion of butter is melted, add second portion and beat until mixture thickens.
Butter	2 oz	Add third portion of butter and seasonings.
Salt	Few grains	Beat until thickened.
Pepper, cayenne	Few grains	Serve immediately. Discard any unused sauce.

Approximate nutritive values per ounce   **Calories** 176

Amount/portion	%DV	Amount/portion	%DV	Amount/portion	%DV		%DV		%DV
Total Fat 19 g	30%	**Cholest.** 127 mg	42%	**Total Carb.** 0 g	0%	**Vitamin A**	28%	Calcium	1%
Sat. Fat 11 g	57%	**Sodium** 180 mg	8%	Fiber 0 g	0%	**Vitamin C**	0%	Iron	1%
Protein 1 g				Sugars 0 g					

Percent Daily Values (%DV) are based on a 2000-calorie diet.

Notes
- Potentially hazardous food.
- Serve with fish or green vegetables such as asparagus or broccoli.
- If sauce tends to curdle, add hot water, a teaspoon at a time, stirring vigorously.
- For safety and quality reasons, it is recommended that this sauce be made only in small quantity.
- Pasteurized eggs are recommended.

MOCK HOLLANDAISE SAUCE

Yield: 2 qt   *Portion:* 2½ Tbsp (1½ oz)

Ingredient	Amount	Procedure
Butter or margarine	6 oz	Melt butter. Add flour and stir until smooth.
Flour, all-purpose	3 oz	Cook 3–5 minutes.
Milk	1½ qt	Add milk gradually, stirring constantly with wire whip. Cook until smooth and thickened.
Salt	1 tsp	Add seasonings.
Pepper, white	½ tsp	
Pepper, cayenne	Few grains	
Egg yolks, unbeaten (see Notes)	12 (8 oz)	Add a little egg yolk at a time, a little butter, and a little lemon juice until all are added.
Butter, cut in pieces	1 lb	Beat well.
Lemon juice	½ cup	Serve immediately. Discard any unused sauce.

Approximate nutritive values per ounce   **Calories** 82

Amount/portion	%DV	Amount/portion	%DV	Amount/portion	%DV		%DV		%DV
Total Fat 8 g	**12%**	**Cholest.** 51 mg	**17%**	**Total Carb.** 2 g	**1%**	**Vitamin A**	**11%**	**Calcium**	**2%**
Sat. Fat 4 g	**19%**	**Sodium** 104 mg	**4%**	Fiber 0 g	**0%**	**Vitamin C**	**0%**	**Iron**	**0%**
Protein 1 g				Sugars 1 g					

Percent Daily Values (%DV) are based on a 2000-calorie diet.

Notes
- Potentially hazardous food.
- Pasteurized eggs are recommended.

MEUNIÈRE SAUCE

Yield: 3 cups

Ingredient	Amount	Procedure
Margarine	1 lb 4 oz	Heat margarine until lightly browned.
Onion, minced	2 oz	Add onion and brown slightly.
Lemon juice	½ cup	Add juice and seasonings.
Worcestershire sauce	1 Tbsp	Serve hot over broccoli, brussels sprouts, green beans, spinach,
Lemon peel, grated	1 Tbsp	or cabbage.
Salt	1 tsp	

Approximate nutritive values per ounce   **Calories** 180

Amount/portion	%DV	Amount/portion	%DV	Amount/portion	%DV		%DV		%DV
Total Fat 20 g	**31%**	**Cholest.** 0 mg	**0%**	**Total Carb.** 0 g	**0%**	**Vitamin A**	**7%**	**Calcium**	**1%**
Sat. Fat 4 g	**20%**	**Sodium** 333 mg	**14%**	Fiber 0 g	**0%**	**Vitamin C**	**5%**	**Iron**	**0%**
Protein 0 g				Sugars 0 g					

Percent Daily Values (%DV) are based on a 2000-calorie diet.

Note
- 3 oz toasted sliced almonds may be sprinkled over top of vegetable.

HOT BACON SAUCE

Yield: 2½ qt

Ingredient	Amount	Procedure
Bacon	1 lb	Dice bacon. Fry until crisp.
Flour, all-purpose	4 oz	Add flour and stir until smooth.
Sugar, granulated Salt Vinegar, cider Water	1 lb 4 oz ¼ cup 3 cups 3 cups	Mix sugar, salt, vinegar, and water. Boil 1 minute. Add to fat-flour mixture gradually while stirring. Cook until slightly thickened.

Approximate nutritive values per ounce   **Calories** 65

Amount/portion	%DV	Amount/portion	%DV	Amount/portion	%DV		%DV		%DV
Total Fat 3 g	4%	**Cholest.** 5 mg	2%	**Total Carb.** 9 g	3%	**Vitamin A**	0%	**Calcium**	0%
Sat. Fat 1 g	5%	**Sodium** 411 mg	17%	Fiber 0 g	0%	**Vitamin C**	3%	**Iron**	1%
Protein 2 g				Sugars 7 g					

Percent Daily Values (%DV) are based on a 2000-calorie diet.

Note   • Use to wilt lettuce or spinach; or with hot potato salad or shredded cabbage.

DRAWN BUTTER SAUCE

Yield: 2 qt   *Portion:* 3 Tbsp (1½ oz)

Ingredient	Amount	Procedure
Butter Flour, all-purpose	2 oz 4 oz	Melt butter. Add flour and blend.
Water, hot	2 qt	Gradually add hot water, while stirring with wire whip. Cook 5 minutes until thickened.
Salt Butter, cut into pieces	1 tsp 6 oz	When ready to serve, add salt and butter. Beat until blended.

Approximate nutritive values per ounce   **Calories** 29

Amount/portion	%DV	Amount/portion	%DV	Amount/portion	%DV		%DV		%DV
Total Fat 3 g	4%	**Cholest.** 7 mg	2%	**Total Carb.** 1 g	1%	**Vitamin A**	2%	**Calcium**	0%
Sat. Fat 2 g	8%	**Sodium** 58 mg	2%	Fiber 0 g	0%	**Vitamin C**	0%	**Iron**	0%
Protein 0 g				Sugars 0 g					

Percent Daily Values (%DV) are based on a 2000-calorie diet.

Note   • Serve with green vegetables, fried or broiled fish, or egg dishes.

Variations   • **Almond Butter Sauce.** Add ¼ cup lemon juice and 6 oz toasted slivered almonds just before serving.

• **Lemon Butter Sauce.** Add 1 Tbsp grated lemon peel and ¼ cup lemon juice just before serving. Serve with fish, new potatoes, broccoli, or asparagus.

• **Maître d'Hôtel Sauce.** Add ¼ cup lemon juice, ¼ cup chopped parsley, and 6 oz pasteurized egg yolks, well beaten.

• **Parsley Butter Sauce.** Add 1½ cups minced parsley just before serving. Serve with fish, potatoes, or other vegetables.

CHILE CILANTRO SAUCE

Yield: 1 gal   *Portion:* 3 oz

Ingredient	Amount	Procedure
Granulated sugar	1 lb 8 oz	Put sugar, ginger root, cilantro, garlic, and chiles in the bowl
Ginger root, chopped (fresh)	10 oz EP	of a food processor.
Cilantro leaves (fresh)	2 oz	Process until finely chopped.
Garlic cloves	4 oz	
Chiles, seeded and chopped (small hot chiles)	½ oz EP (see Note)	
Rice wine vinegar	2⅔ cups	Add vinegar and process until smooth.
Fish sauce	4 cups	Put processed mixture in a non-reactive container. Stir in fish
Water	3 cups	sauce, water, juice, and soy sauce.
Lime juice (fresh)	3 cups	Cover tightly and refrigerate until ready to serve.
Soy sauce	1⅓ cups	Serve as a dipping sauce or condiment for rice.

Approximate nutritive values per ounce   **Calories** 70

Amount/portion	%DV	Amount/portion	%DV	Amount/portion	%DV		%DV		%DV
Total Fat .1 g	0%	**Cholest.** 0 mg	0%	**Total Carb.** 16.2 g	5%	**Vitamin A**	1%	**Calcium**	2%
Sat. Fat 0 g	0%	**Sodium** 1977 mg	82%	Fiber .3 g	1%	**Vitamin C**	9%	**Iron**	2%
Protein 1.9 g				Sugars 12.5 g					

Percent Daily Values (%DV) are based on a 2000-calorie diet.

Notes
- Potentially hazardous food. *Food Safety Standards:* Hold food for service at an internal temperature below 41°F. Do not mix old product with new.
- Use 12–20 hot peppers depending on the degree of hotness desired. The hotness of chile peppers varies among varieties. Thai bird chile peppers are suggested.

DESSERT SAUCE RECIPES

BUTTERSCOTCH SAUCE

Yield: 1¼ qt   *Portion:* 1½ Tbsp (1 oz)

Ingredient	Amount	Procedure
Sugar, brown	1 lb	Combine and cook to soft-ball stage (240°F).
Corn syrup, light	1⅓ cups	Remove from heat.
Water	⅔ cup	
Margarine	6 oz	Add margarine and marshmallows.
Marshmallows	2 oz	Stir until melted. Cool.
Evaporated milk	1⅓ cups	When cool, add milk.

Approximate nutritive values per ounce   **Calories** 97

Amount/portion	%DV	Amount/portion	%DV	Amount/portion	%DV		%DV		%DV
Total Fat 3 g	5%	**Cholest.** 2 mg	1%	**Total Carb.** 17 g	6%	Vitamin A	1%	Calcium	3%
Sat. Fat 1 g	4%	**Sodium** 50 mg	2%	Fiber 0 g	0%	Vitamin C	0%	Iron	3%
Protein 1 g				Sugars 5 g					

Percent Daily Values (%DV) are based on a 2000-calorie diet.

CARAMEL SAUCE

Yield: 2 qt   *Portion:* 2½ Tbsp (1½ oz)

Ingredient	Amount	Procedure
Sugar, brown	1 lb	Mix sugars and flour. Stir in water.
Sugar, granulated	1 lb	Boil until thickened.
Flour, all-purpose	2 oz	
Water	1 qt	
Margarine	8 oz	Stir in margarine and vanilla.
Vanilla	1 Tbsp	

Approximate nutritive values per ounce   **Calories** 82

Amount/portion	%DV	Amount/portion	%DV	Amount/portion	%DV		%DV		%DV
Total Fat 3 g	4%	**Cholest.** 0 mg	0%	**Total Carb.** 15 g	5%	Vitamin A	1%	Calcium	0%
Sat. Fat 1 g	3%	**Sodium** 36 mg	2%	Fiber 0 g	0%	Vitamin C	0%	Iron	1%
Protein 0 g				Sugars 7 g					

Percent Daily Values (%DV) are based on a 2000-calorie diet.

Note   • Serve warm or cold over ice cream or apple desserts.

CHOCOLATE SAUCE

Yield: 1½ qt   *Portion:* 2 Tbsp (1 oz)

Ingredient	Amount	Procedure
Sugar, granulated	12 oz	Mix dry ingredients.
Cornstarch	2 oz	
Salt	1 tsp	
Cocoa	3 oz	
Water, cold	1 cup	Add cold water gradually to form a smooth paste.
Water, boiling	3½ cups	Add boiling water slowly while stirring. Boil for 5 minutes or until thickened. Remove from heat.
Margarine	6 oz	Add margarine and vanilla. Stir to blend.
Vanilla	1 tsp	

Approximate nutritive values per ounce   **Calories** 59

Amount/portion	%DV	Amount/portion	%DV	Amount/portion	%DV		%DV		%DV
Total Fat 3 g	4%	**Cholest.** 0 mg	0%	**Total Carb.** 9 g	3%	**Vitamin A**	1%	**Calcium**	0%
Sat. Fat 1 g	3%	**Sodium** 77 mg	3%	Fiber 0 g	0%	**Vitamin C**	0%	**Iron**	3%
Protein 0 g				Sugars 7 g					

Percent Daily Values (%DV) are based on a 2000-calorie diet.

Note   • Serve warm or cold on puddings, cake, cream puffs, or ice cream.

HOT FUDGE SAUCE

Yield: 1½ qt   *Portion:* 2 Tbsp (1 oz)

Ingredient	Amount	Procedure
Margarine, soft	8 oz	Combine margarine, sugar, and milk over hot water.
Sugar, powdered	1 lb 8 oz	Stir and cook slowly for 30 minutes.
Evaporated milk	1 13-oz can	
Unsweetened chocolate, chipped or melted	8 oz	Add chocolate and stir until blended.

Approximate nutritive values per ounce   **Calories** 133

Amount/portion	%DV	Amount/portion	%DV	Amount/portion	%DV		%DV		%DV
Total Fat 8 g	12%	**Cholest.** 2 mg	1%	**Total Carb.** 18 g	6%	**Vitamin A**	2%	**Calcium**	2%
Sat. Fat 2 g	11%	**Sodium** 58 mg	2%	Fiber 0.3 g	1%	**Vitamin C**	0%	**Iron**	2%
Protein 1 g				Sugars 15 g					

Percent Daily Values (%DV) are based on a 2000-calorie diet.

Notes   • Serve hot over ice cream.

• This sauce may be stored in the refrigerator. Heat over hot water before serving. If too thick or grainy, add evaporated milk before heating.

CUSTARD SAUCE

Yield: 1 gal   *Portion:* ⅓ cup (2½ oz)

Ingredient	Amount	Procedure
Sugar, granulated	14 oz	Mix dry ingredients.
Cornstarch	2 oz	
Salt	½ tsp	
Milk, cold	2 cups	Add cold milk and mix until smooth.
Milk, hot	3 qt	Add cold mixture to hot milk gradually while stirring.
Egg yolks, beaten	10 (6 oz)	Stir in egg yolks gradually. Cook over hot water until thickened, about 5 minutes.
Vanilla	2 Tbsp	Remove from heat and add vanilla. Cool.

Approximate nutritive values per ounce   **Calories** 35

Amount/portion	%DV	Amount/portion	%DV	Amount/portion	%DV		%DV		%DV
Total Fat 1 g	2%	**Cholest.** 21 mg	7%	**Total Carb.** 5 g	2%	Vitamin A	3%	Calcium	3%
Sat. Fat 1 g	3%	**Sodium** 22 mg	1%	Fiber 0 g	0%	Vitamin C	0%	Iron	0%
Protein 1 g				Sugars 4 g					

Percent Daily Values (%DV) are based on a 2000-calorie diet.

Notes
- Potentially hazardous food. Store at an internal temperature below 41°F. Keep leftover product below 41°F. See p. 105 for cooling procedures.
- Serve over cake-type puddings.

FLUFFY ORANGE SAUCE

Yield: 3 qt   *Portion:* 3 Tbsp (1½ oz)

Ingredient	Amount	Procedure
Margarine	1 lb 5 oz	Melt margarine. Gradually add sugar.
Sugar, powdered	2 lb 2 oz	Beat with wire whip until it resembles whipped cream.
Eggs, beaten	10 (1 lb 2 oz)	Add eggs slowly, beating constantly.
Orange juice	1¾ cup	Slowly blend in orange juice and peel. Heat 10–15 minutes.
Orange peel, grated	1½ Tbsp	Beat again.

Approximate nutritive values per ounce   **Calories** 109

Amount/portion	%DV	Amount/portion	%DV	Amount/portion	%DV		%DV		%DV
Total Fat 6 g	10%	**Cholest.** 27 mg	9%	**Total Carb.** 12 g	4%	Vitamin A	3%	Calcium	0%
Sat. Fat 1 g	7%	**Sodium** 77 mg	3%	Fiber 0 g	0%	Vitamin C	3%	Iron	0%
Protein 1 g				Sugars 12 g					

Percent Daily Values (%DV) are based on a 2000-calorie diet.

LEMON SAUCE

Yield: 3 qt   *Portion:* 3 Tbsp (2 oz)

Ingredient	Amount	Procedure
Sugar, granulated	2 lb	Mix dry ingredients.
Cornstarch	3 oz	
Salt	½ tsp	
Water, boiling	2 qt	Add boiling water. Cook until clear.
Lemon juice	⅔ cup	Add lemon juice and margarine.
Margarine	1 oz (2 Tbsp)	

Approximate nutritive values per ounce   **Calories** 48

Amount/portion	%DV	Amount/portion	%DV	Amount/portion	%DV		%DV		%DV
Total Fat 0 g	0%	**Cholest.** 0 mg	0%	**Total Carb.** 12 g	4%	**Vitamin A**	0%	**Calcium**	0%
Sat. Fat 0 g	0%	**Sodium** 17 mg	1%	Fiber 0 g	0%	**Vitamin C**	0%	**Iron**	0%
Protein 0 g				Sugars 10 g					

Percent Daily Values (%DV) are based on a 2000-calorie diet.

Note   • Serve hot with Christmas Pudding (p. 425), Bread Pudding (p. 423), or Rice Custard (p. 423).

Variations • **Nutmeg Sauce.** Omit lemon juice. Add 1 tsp nutmeg. Increase margarine to 4 oz.

 • **Orange Sauce.** Substitute orange juice for lemon juice. Add 1 tsp freshly grated orange peel.

 • **Vanilla Sauce.** Omit lemon juice and reduce sugar to 1 lb 4 oz. Add 2 Tbsp vanilla.

HARD SAUCE

Yield: 3⅓ cups   *Portion:* 1 Tbsp (½ oz)

Ingredient	Amount	Procedure
Butter	8 oz	Cream butter on medium speed until soft and fluffy.
Water, boiling	2 Tbsp	Add water and continue to cream until very light.
Sugar, powdered	1 lb 3 oz	Add sugar gradually. Continue creaming.
Lemon juice	½ tsp	Add lemon juice.
		Place in refrigerator to harden.

Approximate nutritive values per ounce   **Calories** 143

Amount/portion	%DV	Amount/portion	%DV	Amount/portion	%DV		%DV		%DV
Total Fat 7 g	11%	**Cholest.** 19 mg	6%	**Total Carb.** 21 g	7%	**Vitamin A**	6%	**Calcium**	0%
Sat. Fat 4 g	22%	**Sodium** 73 mg	3%	Fiber 0 g	0%	**Vitamin C**	0%	**Iron**	0%
Protein 0 g				Sugars 19 g					

Percent Daily Values (%DV) are based on a 2000-calorie diet.

Note   • Serve with Christmas Pudding (p. 425), Baked Apples (p. 430), or Peach Cobbler (p. 433).

Variations • **Cherry Hard Sauce.** Add ½ cup chopped maraschino cherries.

 • **Strawberry Hard Sauce.** Omit lemon juice and water. Add ¾ cup fresh or frozen strawberries, chopped.

BROWN SUGAR HARD SAUCE

Yield: 1 qt   *Portion:* 1 Tbsp ($\frac{1}{2}$ oz)

Ingredient	*Amount*	*Procedure*
Butter	12 oz	Cream butter on medium speed until light.
Sugar, light brown Vanilla	1 lb 4 oz 2 tsp	Add sugar gradually while creaming. Add vanilla. Cream until fluffy.
Cream, whipping	$\frac{3}{4}$ cup	Whip cream. Fold into sugar mixture. Chill.

Approximate nutritive values per ounce   **Calories** 160

Amount/portion	%DV	Amount/portion	%DV	Amount/portion	%DV		%DV		%DV
Total Fat 10 g	**16%**	**Cholest.** 30 mg	**10%**	**Total Carb.** 18 g	**6%**	**Vitamin A**	**9%**	**Calcium**	**2%**
Sat. Fat 6 g	**32%**	**Sodium** 97 mg	**4%**	Fiber 0 g	**0%**	**Vitamin C**	**0%**	**Iron**	**1%**
Protein 0 g				Sugars 0 g					

Percent Daily Values (%DV) are based on a 2000-calorie diet.

Note   • Serve with Christmas Pudding (p. 425).

PEANUT BUTTER SAUCE

Yield: 2 qt   *Portion:* $2\frac{1}{2}$ Tbsp ($1\frac{1}{2}$ oz)

Ingredient	*Amount*	*Procedure*
Sugar, granulated Corn syrup, light Water, hot	12 oz $1\frac{1}{3}$ cups $\frac{3}{4}$ cup	Combine sugar, syrup, and water. Cook to 228°F and turn off heat or remove from burner.
Margarine Marshmallows, miniature	6 oz 3 oz	Add margarine and marshmallows. Stir until melted. Cool. Place in mixer bowl.
Evaporated milk Peanut butter	12 oz 8 oz	Add milk and peanut butter. Beat until well blended. Refrigerate.

Approximate nutritive values per ounce   **Calories** 109

Amount/portion	%DV	Amount/portion	%DV	Amount/portion	%DV		%DV		%DV
Total Fat 5 g	**8%**	**Cholest.** 2 mg	**1%**	**Total Carb.** 15 g	**5%**	**Vitamin A**	**1%**	**Calcium**	**1%**
Sat. Fat 1 g	**6%**	**Sodium** 59 mg	**2%**	Fiber 0.3 g	**1%**	**Vitamin C**	**0%**	**Iron**	**0%**
Protein 2 g				Sugars 13 g					

Percent Daily Values (%DV) are based on a 2000-calorie diet.

Note   • Serve over ice cream.

RASPBERRY SAUCE

Yield: 3 qt   *Portion:* 3 Tbsp (2 oz)

Ingredient	Amount	Procedure
Red raspberries, frozen	5 lb	Defrost berries. Do not drain.
Sugar, granulated	2 oz	Combine sugar and cornstarch and add to berries.
Cornstarch	1 oz	Cook until clear.
Currant jelly	1 lb 8 oz	Add jelly. Stir until melted. Cool.

Approximate nutritive values per ounce   **Calories 47**

Amount/portion	%DV	Amount/portion	%DV	Amount/portion	%DV		%DV		%DV
Total Fat 0 g	0%	**Cholest.** 0 mg	0%	**Total Carb.** 12 g	4%	**Vitamin A**	0%	**Calcium**	0%
Sat. Fat 0 g	0%	**Sodium** 0 mg	0%	Fiber 1 g	4%	**Vitamin C**	7%	**Iron**	1%
Protein 0 g				Sugars 9 g					

Percent Daily Values (%DV) are based on a 2000-calorie diet.

Notes
- Serve over vanilla ice cream or raspberry, lemon, or lime sherbet.
- Raspberries may be strained before thickening.

Variations
- **Fresh Strawberry Sauce.** Substitute 5 lb fresh strawberries, cleaned and hulled, for raspberries. Mash berries, add 2½ cups water, and strain to remove seeds. Combine 1¼ cups sugar and ⅓ cup cornstarch with juice. Heat to boiling, stirring constantly. Cook until thickened and clear. Chill. Serve over ice cream or other desserts.
- **Peach Melba.** Pour 3 Tbsp Raspberry Sauce over a scoop of vanilla ice cream placed in the center of a canned, fresh, or frozen peach half.

BROWN SUGAR SYRUP

Yield: 2 gal

Ingredient	Amount	Procedure
Sugar, brown	5 lb	Combine all ingredients.
Sugar, granulated	5 lb 8 oz	Stir and heat until sugar is dissolved.
Corn syrup	1 cup	
Water	2½ qt	
Margarine	4 oz	

Approximate nutritive values per ounce   **Calories 80**

Amount/portion	%DV	Amount/portion	%DV	Amount/portion	%DV		%DV		%DV
Total Fat 0 g	0%	**Cholest.** 0 mg	0%	**Total Carb.** 20 g	7%	**Vitamin A**	0%	**Calcium**	0%
Sat. Fat 0 g	0%	**Sodium** 9 mg	1%	Fiber 0 g	0%	**Vitamin C**	0%	**Iron**	1%
Protein 0 g				Sugars 10 g					

Percent Daily Values (%DV) are based on a 2000-calorie diet.

Notes
- Serve warm or cold on pancakes, fritters, or waffles.
- ½ tsp maple flavoring may be added.

Variation
- **Blueberry Syrup.** Combine 1½ qt water, 12 oz granulated sugar, 1 tsp salt, and ⅓ cup lemon juice. Heat to boiling. Mix 4 oz waxy maize starch and 1½ cups cold water to make a paste. Add slowly to sugar mixture, stirring constantly. Cook until thickened and clear. Fold in 3 lb 8 oz individually quick frozen (IQF) blueberries. Serve warm over pancakes, French toast, or ice cream.

MARINADE, RUB, AND SEASONING RECIPES

COMPOUND BUTTERS

Yield: 2 lb

Ingredient	Amount	Procedure
Butter, unsalted, softened	2 lb	Mix flavoring with softened butter. Form into ¾-inch-diameter logs or cube.
Flavoring	See Variations	Refrigerate until firm enough to slice. Use for meats, pasta, rice, vegetables, and breads. A ¼-inch slice equals 1 tsp; a ¾-inch slice equals 1 Tbsp.

Note
- Compound butter may be tightly wrapped in foil and frozen. Freeze for no more than 1 month.

Variations
- **Basil Butter.** Add 4 cups fresh basil leaves; 3 cloves garlic, minced; and ¼ cup lemon juice.
- **Dill Butter.** Add 2 cups minced dill or ½ cup dried dill weed and ¼ cup lemon juice. Use on potatoes and other cooked vegetables, rice, and fish.
- **Garlic Butter.** Add 16 cloves garlic, crushed. Use on potatoes and other cooked vegetables, pasta, and pasta sauce.
- **Herb Butter.** Add 1 cup finely chopped chives, 1 cup finely chopped fresh parsley, ¼ cup fresh tarragon, and 1 tsp lemon juice.
- **Lemon Butter.** Add 1 cup lemon juice, 2 tsp lemon zest, and ¼ cup Dijon-style mustard (optional).
- **Mustard Butter.** Add 10 oz minced scallions, 8 oz whole grain mustard, 1 oz chopped fresh parsley, ¼ cup lemon juice, and ½ tsp ground red pepper.
- **Parsley Butter.** Add 2 cups finely chopped fresh parsley. Use on potatoes and other vegetables, rice, fish, soups, and sauces.
- **Parsley Lemon Butter.** Add 2 cups finely chopped fresh parsley and ¾ cup fresh lemon juice.
- **Red Pepper Butter.** Add 1 cup sweet red pepper, finely chopped; 1 cup yellow onion, finely chopped; and 8 cloves garlic, finely minced.

HERB BUTTER SEASONING

Yield: 1 qt

Ingredient	Amount	Procedure
Butter	2 lb	Place butter in mixer bowl. Let stand at room temperature until soft enough to mix.
Lemon juice Seasonings	2 tsp See next step	Add lemon juice and seasonings to butter. Mix on low speed, using flat beater, until all ingredients are mixed thoroughly.
For vegetables:		
Basil leaves, dried, crushed	1 Tbsp	
Marjoram, ground	2 tsp	
Savory leaves, dried, crushed	1 Tbsp	
For meats:		
Marjoram, ground	2 tsp	
Dry mustard	4 tsp	
Tarragon leaves, dried, crushed	1 Tbsp	
Rosemary leaves, dried, crushed	1 Tbsp	

Notes
- Other spices and herbs may be substituted for those listed in the recipe. See p. 178 for use of herbs and spices in cooking.
- White, cider, or wine vinegar may be substituted for part or all of the lemon juice.
- Unsalted butter may be substituted for salted butter.

Variations
- **Curry Butter.** Omit seasonings. Add 1 Tbsp curry powder.
- **Dill Butter.** Omit seasonings. Add 1 Tbsp dill weed.
- **Lemon Butter.** Omit seasonings. Increase lemon juice to 1 cup and add 3 Tbsp freshly grated lemon peel.
- **Onion Butter.** Omit seasonings and lemon juice. Blend in 2 oz onion soup mix.
- **Tarragon Butter.** Omit seasonings. Add 4 Tbsp tarragon leaves.

LEMON HERB SEASONING

Yield: approximately 2 cups

Ingredient	Amount	Procedure
Lemons	8	Finely shred lemon peel. Spread on baking pan. Dry in 300°F oven for about 10 minutes. Stir occasionally. Cool.
Basil, dried, leaves	5 Tbsp	Crush herbs. Mix with dry lemon peel.
Marjoram, dried, leaves	5 Tbsp	Store in airtight container.
Sage, dried, leaves	2 Tbsp	
Savory, dried, leaves	5 Tbsp	
Parsley, dried, leaves	3 Tbsp	
Thyme, dried, leaves	5 Tbsp	

Notes
- Use sparingly to season soups, stews, meats, fish, poultry, and vegetables.
- To substitute fresh herbs for dried herbs, use three times more fresh than dried. If using ground herbs, use only one-fourth as much as dried.
- Variations in flavor may be made by using different combinations of herbs. The following herbs may be substituted for those in the recipe: celery flakes, cilantro, dill weed, oregano, rosemary, or tarragon.

SEASONED SALT

Yield: approximately 2 cups

Ingredient	Amount	Procedure
Salt	1 lb	Mix all ingredients together thoroughly.
Celery salt	2 oz	Store covered.
Onion powder	2 oz	
Garlic powder	1 oz	
Paprika	1 Tbsp	
Chili powder	4 Tbsp	

Note
- Can be used to season meats, salads, or vegetables.

TOASTED SPICE BLEND

Yield: 1 cup
Oven: 375°F

Ingredient	Amount	Procedure
Allspice, ground	1 Tbsp	Combine spices. Spread in a thin, even layer in a dry skillet or baking pan.
Cardamom, ground	2 tsp	
Cinnamon, ground	1 Tbsp	Cook over medium heat (375°F oven) for approximately 1–2 minutes, until fragrant and just beginning to smoke.
Cumin, ground	2 Tbsp	
Ginger, ground	4 Tbsp	Shake the pan throughout cooking to prevent burning. Cool.
Mace, ground	1 tsp	Store in airtight container for up to 2 weeks.
Dry mustard	2 Tbsp	
Pepper, coarse ground, black	1 Tbsp	
Pepper, cayenne	2 Tbsp	
Tumeric, ground	2 Tbsp	

Notes

- Use sparingly to season soups, stews, and meats. The flavor profile complements Moroccan and African dishes.
- Spice flavors intensify when toasted.
- Other spices may be toasted. Follow procedure as for Toasted Spice Blend.
- When toasting seeds, cover loosely with a lid to prevent seeds from popping out of the pan. Increase cooking time to 2–3 minutes, or until seeds begin to pop and are fragrant.
- When toasting nuts, heat until the nuts begin to darken in color, 3–4 minutes.

CAJUN SEASONING

Yield: approximately 1½ cups

Ingredient	Amount	Procedure
Paprika	2 oz	Combine spices and store in airtight container.
Garlic powder	2 oz	
Onion powder	1 oz	
Marjoram, dried	4 Tbsp	
Thyme, dried	4 Tbsp	
Pepper, cayenne	3 Tbsp	
Pepper, black	4 Tbsp	
Salt	4 Tbsp	

Note

- Use to season poultry and fish. For blackened chicken or fish, rub with Cajun Seasoning before browning in a heavy pan.

DRY MARINADE FOR MEAT OR POULTRY

Yield: 10 oz dry spice

Ingredient	Amount	Procedure
Salt	2 oz	Mix spices. Store in sealed glass jar.
Pepper, cracked, black	1 Tbsp	Use as needed for marinade (follows).
Paprika	4 oz	
Oregano, dried, crumbled	1 oz	
Thyme, dried, crumbled	2 oz	
Cumin, ground	2 Tbsp	

MARINADE FOR 20 LB MEAT:

Ingredient	Amount	Procedure
Spice blend (above)	4 oz (1 cup)	Mix spices with onion, garlic, oil, and lemon juice. May be prepared in food processor.
Onion, very finely chopped	1 lb	Rub over meat or poultry. Marinate several hours or over night in the refrigerator.
Garlic cloves, minced	2 oz	Grill or roast meat or poultry as per recipe instructions.
Vegetable oil	½ cup	
Lemon juice	½ cup	

MEAT MARINADE

Yield: 2 qt

Ingredient	Amount	Procedure
Salad oil	1 qt	Combine ingredients, mixing well.
Worcestershire sauce	¼ cup	Pour over meat. Marinate in the refrigerator 6 hours or longer.
Liquid smoke	¼ cup	
Soy sauce	2 cups	
Vinegar, cider	¼ cup	
Garlic, minced	4 cloves	
Celery salt	¼ cup	
Dry mustard	¼ cup	
Ginger, ground	¼ cup	
Sugar, brown	1 cup	

Note   • Pour over pork or beef.

FISH MARINADE

Yield: 2½ qt

Ingredient	Amount	Procedure
Vegetable oil	1 qt	Combine ingredients, mixing well.
Olive oil	3 cups	Place fish in marinade.
Lemon juice, fresh	3 cups	Refrigerate for 3 hours. Remove fish from marinade and grill
Oregano, dried, crumbled	¼ cup	or broil.
Parsley, dried	¼ cup	
Basil, dried, crumbled	¼ cup	
Garlic powder	1 Tbsp	
Salt	1 Tbsp	
Pepper, black	1 tsp	

VEGETABLE MARINADE

Yield: 1½ qt

Ingredient	Amount	Procedure
Lemon juice	2½ Tbsp	Combine.
Vinegar, white	⅓ cup	
Salad oil	1 cup	
Worcestershire sauce	1 Tbsp	
Water	⅓ cup	
Onion, finely chopped	3 oz	Add and mix.
Garlic, crushed	2 cloves	
Pimiento, chopped	¼ cup	
Parsley, finely chopped	¼ cup	
Salt	1½ Tbsp	Blend in and mix.
Sugar, granulated	1 Tbsp	Pour over fresh vegetables and marinate 6 hours or longer.
Pepper, black	⅛ tsp	
Tarragon	1 Tbsp	

Note • Pour over fresh mushrooms or other fresh vegetables or pasta.

ASIAN MARINADE

Yield: 2 qt

Ingredient	Amount	Procedure
Soy sauce	3 cups	Combine all ingredients in stainless steel container. Mix well.
Granulated sugar	11 oz	
Toasted sesame seed oil	1¼ cups	
White pepper	5 tsp	
Green onions, finely chopped	1 lb EP	
Garlic, minced	5 oz EP	
Sesame seeds	2 Tbsp	Toast sesame seeds: • Spread in a thin, even layer in a dry skillet or baking pan. • Cook over medium heat (375°F) until seeds become golden brown and just begin to smoke (3–5 min). Shake pan once or twice and watch carefully so seeds do not burn. Add seeds to soy sauce mixture. Stir to distribute.

Notes   • Use to marinate ribs, poultry, and pork loin or chops.

GRILLED VEGETABLE MARINADE

Yield: 3½ cups

Ingredient	Amount	Procedure
Olive oil	1 lb 5 oz	Combine ingredients. Use as a vegetable marinade.
Balsamic vinegar	8 oz	
Garlic, minced	1½ Tbsp	
Thyme leaves (dried)	1 tsp	
Basil leaves (dried)	½ tsp	
Parsley leaves (dried)	1 tsp	
Red pepper flakes	½ tsp	
Black pepper	¾ tsp	
Salt	1 Tbsp	

BALSAMIC VINEGAR MARINADE FOR VEGETABLES

Yield: 1¼ qt

Ingredient	Amount	Procedure
Balsamic vinegar	¾ cup	Mix vinegars, onion, garlic, and spices using a wire whip.
Sherry wine vinegar	¼ cup	
Onion, finely minced	3 oz	
Garlic, finely minced	3 cloves	
Salt	½ tsp	
Pepper, black	½ tsp	
Vegetable oil	1½ cups	Whisk in oils.
Olive oil	2 cups	Store in a covered container in refrigerator for up to 1 week. Stir before using.

HONEY-BALSAMIC MARINADE

Yield: 5½ cups

Ingredient	Amount	Procedure
Honey	2 cups	Mix all ingredients.
Olive oil	2 Tbsp	Brush on fish or chicken before grilling or baking.
Dijon mustard	2 cups	
Balsamic vinegar	1¼ cups	
Pepper, coarse ground, black	1 Tbsp	
Garlic salt	1 Tbsp	

HERB MARINADE FOR POULTRY OR FISH

Yield: For approximately 50 portions of poultry or fish

Ingredient	Amount	Procedure
White wine	¾ cup	Combine all ingredients.
Lemon juice, fresh squeezed	1½ cups	Rub on both sides of chicken or fish portions.
Garlic cloves, minced	2 oz (EP)	Marinate in refrigerator for 30 minutes.
Parsley, minced	2 oz	Follow recipe instructions for grilling, broiling, or roasting.
Dijon mustard	¼ cup	
Red pepper flakes	2 Tbsp	
Fennel seeds, crushed	1 Tbsp	
Tarragon leaves, dried	1 Tbsp	
Salt	1 tsp	

HERB AND GARLIC MARINADE FOR VEGETABLES

Yield: 1½ qt

Ingredient	Amount	Procedure
Olive oil	1¼ qt	Combine all ingredients and stir to combine.
Red wine vinegar	1 cup	Stir before using.
Garlic, minced	2 oz (EP)	
Salt	1 oz	
Pepper, black	1½ tsp	
Thyme leaves, dried	1 tsp	
Basil leaves, dried	1 tsp	
Parsley, dried	1 tsp	
Red pepper, crushed	2 tsp	

VINAIGRETTE MARINADE

Yield: 3 qt

Ingredient	Amount	Procedure
Vegetable oil	1 qt	Using a wire whip, whisk together all ingredients.
Olive oil	1 qt	Use to marinate vegetables before roasting or to season
Cider vinegar	2½ cups	steamed vegetables.
Lemon juice (fresh)	1¼ cups	
Soy sauce	¼ cup	
Garlic, finely minced	4 oz (EP)	
Tarragon, dried	2 oz	
Dijon mustard	⅓ cup	
Salt	2 tsp	
Pepper, black	1 tsp	

Notes   ● Use marinade within 1 week. Keep refrigerated.

CHAPTER 18

Soups

Simon Smith © Dorling Kindersley

Homemade soups are popular and versatile menu items that may be served as an appetizer or as a center-of-the-plate entree. The type of soup served should complement the other menu items or be hearty enough for the entree. Hot soups should be heated to 180°F and cold soups should be served below 41°F.

TYPES OF SOUPS

Soups may be clear and thin or thick and hearty. Stock or broth, the basic ingredient of many soups, is made by simmering meat and/or meat, fish, or poultry bones, and/or vegetables in water to extract their flavor. The most frequently used stocks are brown (made from beef that has been browned before simmering) and white or light (made from veal and/or chicken). See pp. 790–793 for stock recipes.

Mirepoix, a mixture of chopped vegetables—usually in the proportion of 50 percent onions, 25 percent carrots, and 25 percent celery—is used in flavoring soup stock. Flavorings commonly used are bay leaves, peppercorns, whole cloves, and parsley stems.

For a clear soup, the stock should be clarified. Clarifying removes flecks that are too small to be strained out with cheesecloth, but that will cloud a soup's appearance. Stock is highly perishable. If it is not to be used immediately, it may be reduced in volume by boiling to one-half or one-fourth its volume and frozen for later use. Recipes for beef, chicken, and vegetable stocks and directions for clarifying stock are given on pp. 790–793.

Clear soups are made from a clear, seasoned stock or broth and include:

- **Bouillon,** made from beef broth that may or may not be clarified.

- **Consommé,** a strong, concentrated stock or broth.

- **Vegetable soup,** a clear seasoned stock or broth, with vegetables and sometimes meat or poultry products added.

Thick soups are opaque rather than transparent. They are thickened either by a roux, which is a mixture of melted fat and flour slightly browned, or a puree of one of the ingredients. Examples are:

- **Cream soups,** made with a thin or medium white sauce combined with either mashed, strained, or finely chopped vegetables or meat, chicken, or fish. Chicken stock may be used to replace part of the milk in the sauce to enhance the flavor. If a stock base is used, it may be added to the margarine-flour roux or may be added to water and used as part of the liquid.

- **Chowders,** unstrained, chunky, hearty soups prepared from meat, poultry, seafood, and/or vegetables. Most chowders contain potatoes and milk or cream.

- **Purees,** thick soups made by pressing cooked vegetables or fish through a sieve into their own stock.

COMMERCIAL SOUP BASES

Because preparation of soups, especially those made from stock, is time-consuming, commercial food or soup bases are often used. The amount of meat concentrate in commercial soup bases varies, so the choice of base should be made carefully to ensure a desirable, full-flavored stock. A high-quality base is a concentrate of cooked meat, poultry, seafood, or vegetables that includes the concentrated cooking juices and seasonings. It has a puree or pastelike consistency and may require refrigeration. One pound of soup base produces an average of 5 gallons of ready-to-use stock. Most granulated soup bases and many paste products are highly salted. When using these products, the salt listed in the recipe should be deleted or reduced. Soup bases also can be used to prepare sauces, gravies, and stuffings.

SERVING AND HOLDING SOUPS

Hot soup cools off quickly in serving bowls. It is important that soup be very hot when served. Using a heated bowl helps hot soups retain their heat. Soups should be prepared in batches small enough for ingredients to retain their texture throughout the serving period. Cream soups will curdle if kept at too high a temperature or held for too long a time. For this reason, the milk may be added just before serving and the mixture reheated to serving temperature (180°F). Cold soups should be served in chilled bowls at 41°F.

STOCK SOUP RECIPES

CHICKEN STOCK

Yield: 3 gal

Ingredient	Amount	Procedure
Chicken bones	24 lbs	Rinse chicken bones and place in steam-jacketed or large stock pot.
Water, cold	5 gal	Add water. Simmer 3–4 hours. Skim as necessary.
Onions, quartered	1 lb 8 oz	Add vegetables and seasonings. Bring to boiling point.
Celery, with leaves, chopped	12 oz	Reduce heat and simmer 1 hour longer.
Carrots, chopped	12 oz	
Salt	3 oz	
Peppercorns, cracked	1 Tbsp	
Bay leaves	4 leaves	
Thyme, dried	2 tsp	
		Remove bones from broth. Strain and refrigerate. When broth is cold, fat will congeal on top; skim off.

Notes
- Potentially hazardous food. *Food Safety Standards:* Hold food for service at an internal temperature above 140°F. Do not mix old product with new. Cool leftover product quickly (within 4 hours) to below 41°F. See p. 105 for cooling procedures. Reheat leftover product quickly (within 2 hours) to 165°F. Reheat product only once; discard if not used.

- If a clear broth is desired, clarify by adding egg shells and whites to broth. Bring stock to boiling point and simmer for 15 minutes. Strain through a fine strainer.

Variations
- **Chicken Stock with Soup Base.** Add 8 oz concentrated chicken base to 2½ gal water. Exact proportion of base and water may vary among manufacturers. Chicken base is often highly salted. When using chicken base for making stock, taste recipes before adding salt. The flavor of chicken stock made with base can be enhanced by simmering 12 oz clean vegetable trimmings (or vegetables listed above) with 2½ gal stock for approximately 15 minutes. Strain before using.

- **White Stock.** Substitute knuckle of veal for part of chicken bones.

BEEF STOCK

Yield: 3 gal

Ingredient	Amount	Procedure
Beef shank, lean	20 lb	Pour water over beef shanks in steam-jacketed kettle or
Water, cold	5 gal	large stock pot.
		Bring water to boiling point. Reduce heat and simmer until
		meat leaves bone, about 3 hours.
Onions, quartered	1 lb 8 oz	Add vegetables and seasonings. Simmer 1 hour.
Celery, with leaves, chopped	12 oz	Remove meat, strain broth.
		Refrigerate for several hours.
Carrots, chopped	12 oz	Skim congealed fat off top.
Peppercorns, cracked	1 Tbsp	
Bay leaves	2 leaves	
Salt	3 oz	

Notes
- Potentially hazardous food. *Food Safety Standards:* Hold food for service at an internal temperature above 140°F. Do not mix old product with new. Cool leftover product quickly (within 4 hours) to below 41°F. See p. 105 for cooling procedures. Reheat leftover product quickly (within 2 hours) to 165°F. Reheat product only once; discard if not used.

Variations
- **Beef Stock with Soup Base.** Add 8 oz concentrated beef base to 2½ gal water. Exact proportions may vary with different manufacturers. Beef base is often highly salted. When using beef base for making stock, taste recipes before adding salt. The flavor of beef stock made with base can be enhanced by simmering 12 oz clean vegetable trimmings (or the vegetables listed above) with 2½ gal stock for approximately 15 minutes. Strain before using.
- **Brown Stock.** Roast beef bones in hot oven until they are a rich brown color. Brown or caramelize vegetables before adding to the water. Proceed as for Beef Stock.

BOUILLON

Yield: 3 gal   *Portion:* 1 cup (8 oz)

Ingredient	Amount	Procedure
Beef, lean	8 lb	Sear beef. Add bone and water.
Beef bone, cracked	4 lb	Simmer for 3–4 hours. Replace water as necessary.
Water, cold	4 gal	
Carrots, diced	8 oz	Add vegetables and seasonings.
Celery, chopped	8 oz	Cook 1 hour. Strain.
Onions, quartered	8 oz	Chill overnight.
Bay leaves	4	Remove congealed fat from broth.
Peppercorns	1 Tbsp	
Salt	¼ cup	
To clarify:		Add egg shells and whites to clarify the broth.
Egg shells, washed and crushed	3	Bring slowly to boiling point, stirring constantly. Boil 15–20 minutes without stirring.
Egg whites, beaten	3	Strain through a fine strainer.

Note
- Potentially hazardous food. *Food Safety Standards:* Hold food for service at an internal temperature above 140°F. Do not mix old product with new. Cool leftover product quickly (within 4 hours) to below 41°F. See p. 105 for cooling procedures. Reheat leftover product quickly (within 2 hours) to 165°F. Reheat product only once; discard if not used.

Variations
- **Chicken Bouillon.** Substitute 20 lb chicken, cut up, for the beef and bone. Do not sear chicken.
- **Tomato Bouillon.** To 1½ gal Bouillon, add four 46-oz cans tomato juice, 2 oz chopped onion, 2 oz sugar, 2 oz salt (amount will vary), ½ tsp pepper, and 2 bay leaves.

VEGETABLE STOCK

Yield: 3 gal

Ingredient	Amount	Procedure
Vegetable oil	6 oz	Heat oil in steam-jacketed kettle or large stock pot.
Green cabbage, coarsely chopped	12 oz	Add vegetables to oil. Cover and cook until softened and moisture is released, 3–5 minutes.
Carrots, coarsely chopped	1 lb 8 oz	
Celery, coarsely chopped	1 lb 8 oz	
Celery leaves, coarsely chopped	1 lb	
Garlic cloves, crushed	8 cloves	
Onions, quartered	2 lb 8 oz	
Parsley stems, chopped	3 oz	
Parsnips, peeled	1 lb	
Tomato, chopped	1 lb	
Turnips, chopped	12 oz	
Water	5 gal	Add water and spices.
Salt	3 oz	Simmer for 40–50 minutes.
Peppercorns, cracked	1 Tbsp	Strain stock and cool.
Bay leaves	6 leaves	
Thyme, dried	2 tsp	

Notes
- Potentially hazardous food. *Food Safety Standards:* Cool product quickly (within 4 hours) to below 41°F. See p. 105 for cooling procedures.
- Clean vegetable trimmings may be substituted for part of the vegetables specified.

Variation
- **Vegetable Stock with Base.** Exact proportions of base and water differ among brands. Follow manufacturers' directions. Vegetable base is often highly salted. When using vegetable base for making stock, taste recipes before adding salt. The flavor of vegetable stock made with base can be enhanced by simmering 2 lb clean vegetable trimmings (or the soft or leafy vegetables listed above) with 3 gal stock for approximately 15 minutes. Strain before using.

BEEF BARLEY SOUP

Yield: 50 portions or 3 gal   *Portion:* 1 cup (8 oz)

Ingredient	Amount	Procedure
Beef, cubed	3 lb	Brown beef cubes in kettle. Drain off fat.
Celery, chopped	1 lb 6 oz	Add celery and onions. Sauté until tender.
Onions, chopped	1 lb 6 oz	
Beef Stock (p. 791)	3 gal	Add remaining ingredients. Bring to a boil.
Pepper, black	1 tsp	Lower heat and simmer for 1 hour.
Salt	1 tsp	Taste for seasoning and add salt if needed.
Bay leaf	1	
Carrots, diced	1 lb 6 oz	
Pearl barley	10 oz	

Approximate nutritive values per portion   **Calories** 81

Amount/portion	%DV	Amount/portion	%DV	Amount/portion	%DV		%DV		%DV
Total Fat 2 g	3%	**Cholest.** 15 mg	5%	**Total Carb.** 7 g	2%	**Vitamin A**	35%	**Calcium**	2%
Sat. Fat 1 g	3%	**Sodium** 818 mg	34%	Fiber 2 g	6%	**Vitamin C**	4%	**Iron**	6%
Protein 9 g				Sugars 1 g					

Percent Daily Values (%DV) are based on a 2000-calorie diet.

Notes
- Potentially hazardous food. *Food Safety Standards:* Hold food for service at an internal temperature above 140°F. Do not mix old product with new. Cool leftover product quickly (within 4 hours) to below 41°F. See p. 105 for cooling procedures. Reheat leftover product quickly (within 2 hours) to 165°F. Reheat product only once; discard if not used.
- 2¾ oz (1⅓ cups) dehydrated onions may be substituted for fresh onions.

VEGETABLE BEEF SOUP

Yield: 50 portions or 3 gal   *Portion:* 1 cup (8 oz)

Ingredient	Amount	Procedure
Beef Stock (p. 791)	2 gal	Heat stock in kettle.
Carrots, cubed	8 oz	Add vegetables and seasonings.
Celery, chopped	1 lb	Cover and simmer about an hour. Replace water as necessary.
Onions, chopped	1 lb 8 oz	Taste for seasoning. Add additional salt if needed.
Potatoes, cubed	1 lb	
Salt	1 Tbsp	
Pepper, black	1 tsp	
Tomatoes, diced, canned	1 No. 10 can	
Cooked beef, chopped	2 lb	Add chopped beef. Heat to serving temperature, 180°F.

Approximate nutritive values per portion   **Calories** 80

Amount/portion	%DV	Amount/portion	%DV	Amount/portion	%DV		%DV		%DV
Total Fat 2 g	4%	**Cholest.** 18 mg	6%	**Total Carb.** 6 g	2%	Vitamin A	14%	Calcium	3%
Sat. Fat 1 g	4%	**Sodium** 748 mg	31%	Fiber 0.4 g	2%	Vitamin C	17%	Iron	7%
Protein 9 g				Sugars 1 g					

Percent Daily Values (%DV) are based on a 2000-calorie diet.

Notes
- Potentially hazardous food. *Food Safety Standards:* Hold food for service at an internal temperature above 140°F. Do not mix old product with new. Cool leftover product quickly (within 4 hours) to below 41°F. See p. 105 for cooling procedures. Reheat leftover product quickly (within 2 hours) to 165°F. Reheat product only once; discard if not used.
- 8 oz uncooked rice or 4 oz dry noodles may be substituted for the potatoes.
- Browned beef cubes may be substituted for cooked beef. Brown in kettle before stock is added.
- 3 oz (1½ cups) dehydrated onions may be substituted for fresh onions.

Variations
- **Julienne Soup.** Cut carrots, celery, and potatoes in long, thin strips.
- **Mexican Beef Soup.** Omit carrots and celery. Add 12 oz whole-kernel corn; 4 oz green peppers, chopped; 1 lb 8 oz sliced zucchini; and 3 Tbsp ground cumin.
- **Vegetable Soup.** Delete beef. Increase carrots and celery to 1 lb 8 oz each.

HEARTY BEEF VEGETABLE SOUP

Yield: 50 portions or 3 gal   *Portion:* 1 cup (8 oz)

Ingredient	Amount	Procedure
Ground beef	8 lb (AP)	Brown meat. Drain off fat.
Onions, chopped	1 lb	Add onions to meat and cook until tender.
Margarine	9 oz	Melt margarine and stir in flour.
Flour, all-purpose	9 oz	Cook for 5 minutes.
Beef Stock (p. 791)	1¼ gal	Add stock and seasonings, stirring constantly. Cook until
Salt	1 Tbsp	mixture boils and has thickened.
Pepper, black	½ tsp	Add browned meat and onions.
Carrots, fresh, diced	12 oz	Cook vegetables until barely tender. Drain. (Vegetables
Celery, sliced	10 oz	should be crunchy.)
Mixed vegetables, frozen	4 lb	Cook mixed vegetables until partially done. Add, with other vegetables, to the soup. Stir carefully to blend.
Tomatoes, diced, canned	2 lb 8 oz	Add tomatoes. Heat to serving temperature, 180°F.

Approximate nutritive values per portion   **Calories** 228

Amount/portion	%DV	Amount/portion	%DV	Amount/portion	%DV		%DV		%DV
Total Fat 14 g	21%	**Cholest.** 48 mg	16%	**Total Carb.** 11 g	4%	**Vitamin A**	34%	**Calcium**	3%
Sat. Fat 4 g	22%	**Sodium** 281 mg	12%	Fiber 2 g	7%	**Vitamin C**	9%	**Iron**	11%
Protein 15 g				Sugars 2 g					

Percent Daily Values (%DV) are based on a 2000-calorie diet.

Notes
- Potentially hazardous food. *Food Safety Standards:* Hold food for service at an internal temperature above 140°F. Do not mix old product with new. Cool leftover product quickly (within 4 hours) to below 41°F. See p. 105 for cooling procedures. Reheat leftover product quickly (within 2 hours) to 165°F. Reheat product only once; discard if not used.
- 2 oz (1 cup) dehydrated onions may be substituted for fresh onions.

BEEF NOODLE SOUP

Yield: 50 portions or 3 gal   *Portion:* 1 cup (8 oz)

Ingredient	Amount	Procedure
Vegetable oil	½ cup	Heat oil in kettle. Add beef cubes and seasonings and cook until lightly browned.
Beef, fresh, cubed	2 lb	
Salt	2 tsp	Drain off fat.
Pepper, black	½ tsp	
Onions, chopped	8 oz	Add onions and celery, and sauté.
Celery, chopped	12 oz	
Beef Stock (p. 791)	2¾ gal	Add stock. Simmer for 1 hour.
Noodles	12 oz	Add noodles and simmer until tender, 5–10 minutes. Add salt if needed.

Approximate nutritive values per portion   **Calories** 85

Amount/portion	%DV	Amount/portion	%DV	Amount/portion	%DV		%DV		%DV
Total Fat 4 g	6%	**Cholest.** 17 mg	6%	**Total Carb.** 6 g	2%	**Vitamin A**	0%	**Calcium**	1%
Sat. Fat 1 g	6%	**Sodium** 786 mg	33%	Fiber 0 g	0%	**Vitamin C**	1%	**Iron**	5%
Protein 7 g				Sugars 0 g					

Percent Daily Values (%DV) are based on a 2000-calorie diet.

Notes
- Potentially hazardous food. *Food Safety Standards:* Hold food for service at an internal temperature above 140°F. Do not mix old product with new. Cool leftover product quickly (within 4 hours) to below 41°F. See p. 105 for cooling procedures. Reheat leftover product quickly (within 2 hours) to 165°F. Reheat product only once; discard if not used.
- 1 oz (½ cup) dehydrated onions may be substituted for fresh onions.

Variations
- **Alphabet Soup.** Use alphabet noodles.
- **Beef Rice Soup.** Substitute 1 lb 8 oz rice for noodles.
- **Creole Soup.** Reduce Beef Stock to 2¼ gal. Add 1 No. 10 can tomatoes, 8 oz shredded green peppers, 1 lb sliced okra, and 4 bay leaves. Substitute rice for noodles.

CHICKEN NOODLE SOUP

Yield: 50 portions or 3 gal   *Portion:* 1 cup (8 oz)

Ingredient	Amount	Procedure
Chicken Stock (p. 790)	3 gal	Bring stock to a boil. Add onion and celery. Cook until tender.
Onion, chopped	8 oz	
Celery, chopped	8 oz	
Noodles	1 lb	Add noodles. Cook for about 15 minutes or until noodles are tender.
Margarine, melted	8 oz	Blend margarine and flour.
Flour, all-purpose	4 oz	Add to soup, stirring until slightly thickened.
Salt	1 tsp	Add seasonings.
Pepper, white	½ tsp	
Cooked chicken, diced	1 lb 8 oz	Add chicken and simmer for 5 minutes.

Approximate nutritive values per portion   **Calories** 140

Amount/portion	%DV	Amount/portion	%DV	Amount/portion	%DV		%DV		%DV
Total Fat 6 g	10%	**Cholest.** 21 mg	7%	**Total Carb.** 10 g	3%	**Vitamin A**	1%	**Calcium**	1%
Sat. Fat 1 g	7%	**Sodium** 846 mg	35%	Fiber 0 g	0%	**Vitamin C**	0%	**Iron**	6%
Protein 10 g				Sugars 0 g					

Percent Daily Values (%DV) are based on a 2000-calorie diet.

Notes
- Potentially hazardous food. *Food Safety Standards:* Hold food for service at an internal temperature above 140°F. Do not mix old product with new. Cool leftover product quickly (within 4 hours) to below 41°F. See p. 105 for cooling procedures. Reheat leftover product quickly (within 2 hours) to 165°F. Reheat product only once; discard if not used.
- 1 oz (½ cup) dehydrated onions may be substituted for fresh onions.

Variation
- **Chicken Rice Soup.** Substitute 12 oz rice for the noodles.

TURKEY VEGETABLE SOUP

Yield: 50 portions   *Portion:* 1 cup (8 oz)

Ingredient	Amount	Procedure
Carrots, fresh	1 lb	Cut carrots into thin julienne strips.
Potatoes, red	2 lb	Do not peel potatoes. Dice into ½-inch cubes.
Onions, minced	12 oz	Combine in steam-jacketed kettle.
Celery, chopped	10 oz	Add carrots and potatoes.
Mushrooms, sliced	8 oz	Simmer 20 minutes or until vegetables are tender.
Chicken Stock (p. 790)	2½ gal	
Sage, rubbed	⅛ tsp	Add seasonings to soup.
Thyme, ground	¼ tsp	
Pepper, black	¼ tsp	
Cooked turkey, chopped	2 lb	Add turkey and parsley. Heat to 180°F.
Parsley, fresh, chopped	2 oz	

Approximate nutritive values per portion   **Calories 87**

Amount/portion	%DV	Amount/portion	%DV	Amount/portion	%DV		%DV		%DV
Total Fat 2 g	3%	**Cholest.** 15 mg	5%	**Total Carb.** 6 g	2%	**Vitamin A**	36%	**Calcium**	2%
Sat. Fat 1 g	3%	**Sodium** 645 mg	27%	Fiber 0 g	0%	**Vitamin C**	5%	**Iron**	5%
Protein 10 g				Sugars 0 g					

Percent Daily Values (%DV) are based on a 2000-calorie diet.

Notes

- Potentially hazardous food. *Food Safety Standards:* Hold food for service at an internal temperature above 140°F. Do not mix old product with new. Cool leftover product quickly (within 4 hours) to below 41°F. See p. 105 for cooling procedures. Reheat leftover product quickly (within 2 hours) to 165°F. Reheat product only once; discard if not used.

- 1½ oz (¾ cup) dehydrated onions may be substituted for fresh onions.

CHILI CON CARNE

Yield: 3 gal   *Portion:* 1 cup (8 oz)

Ingredient	Amount	Procedure
Ground beef	10 lb (AP)	Cook beef, onions, and garlic in steam-jacketed kettle until meat loses pink color.
Onions, chopped	8 oz	
Garlic, minced	1 clove	
Tomatoes, canned, diced	2½ qt	Mix tomato and seasonings. Add to beef. Cook until blended.
Tomato puree	2 qt	
Water	1 qt	
Chili powder	3 oz	
Cumin seed, ground	1½ Tbsp	
Salt	1 oz (1½ Tbsp)	
Pepper, black	½ tsp	
Sugar, granulated	2 oz	
Beans, pinto, kidney, or red, canned	9 lb 8 oz	Add beans to meat mixture. Cover and simmer for 1 hour. Add water if chili becomes too thick.

Approximate nutritive values per portion   **Calories** 293

Amount/portion	%DV	Amount/portion	%DV	Amount/portion	%DV		%DV		%DV
Total Fat 13 g	**20%**	**Cholest.** 51 mg	**17%**	**Total Carb.** 23 g	**8%**	**Vitamin A**	**18%**	**Calcium**	**7%**
Sat. Fat 5 g	**24%**	**Sodium** 791 mg	**33%**	Fiber 2 g	**10%**	**Vitamin C**	**33%**	**Iron**	**20%**
Protein 22 g				Sugars 4 g					

Percent Daily Values (%DV) are based on a 2000-calorie diet.

Notes

- Potentially hazardous food. *Food Safety Standards:* Hold food for service at an internal temperature above 140°F. Do not mix old product with new. Cool leftover product quickly (within 4 hours) to below 41°F. See p. 105 for cooling procedures. Reheat leftover product quickly (within 2 hours) to 165°F. Reheat product only once; discard if not used.

- If dried beans are used, substitute 3 lb for canned beans. Wash and prepare according to directions on p. 826.

- If desired, thicken chili by mixing 5 oz flour and 2 cups cold water. Add to chili mixture and heat until flour is cooked.

- 1 oz (½ cup) dehydrated onions, rehydrated in ¾ cup water, may be substituted for fresh onions.

Variations

- **Chili and Cheese.** Sprinkle grated cheddar or Monterey Jack cheese over chili, 1 Tbsp per bowl.

- **Chili Buffet.** Serve chili with accompaniments: chopped onions, tomatoes, and green peppers; sliced black olives; shredded cheese; and sliced jalapeño peppers.

- **Chili Spaghetti.** Use only 7 lb ground beef. Cook 1 lb 8 oz spaghetti according to directions on p. 561. Add to chili mixture just before serving. Macaroni or other pasta shapes may be used also.

- **Turkey Chili.** Substitute 8 lb ground turkey for ground beef.

GARDEN CHILI

Yield: 50 portions   *Portion:* 8 oz

Ingredient	Amount	Procedure
Vegetable oil	¾ cup	Heat oil. Add onions and garlic and sauté until transparent.
Onions, chopped	3 lb 12 oz	
Garlic, minced	1½ Tbsp	
Celery, chopped	2 lb 4 oz	Add celery, carrots, and seasonings to onions.
Carrots, chopped finely	1 lb	Cook until tender-crisp.
Oregano, dried, crumbled	2 tsp	
Cumin, ground	2 Tbsp	
Chili powder	2 Tbsp	
Salt	1 oz (1½ Tbsp)	
Pepper, black	1 Tbsp	
Green peppers, chopped	1 lb	Add to onion mixture.
Zucchini, chopped	2 lb	Heat to 180° F.
Mushrooms and stems, canned	1 lb 8 oz	
Tomatoes, diced, canned	5 lb 6 oz	
Water	1 qt	
Red beans, canned	5 lb 6 oz	
Lemon juice, frozen, reconstituted	⅓ cup	
Cheddar cheese, shredded	1 lb 8 oz	To serve, ladle chili into soup bowls. Sprinkle ½ oz cheese over each portion.

Approximate nutritive values per portion   **Calories** 169

Amount/portion	%DV	Amount/portion	%DV	Amount/portion	%DV		%DV		%DV
Total Fat 8 g	13%	**Cholest.** 14 mg	5%	**Total Carb.** 17 g	6%	**Vitamin A**	35%	**Calcium**	15%
Sat. Fat 4 g	19%	**Sodium** 600 mg	25%	Fiber 5 g	18%	**Vitamin C**	38%	**Iron**	10%
Protein 8 g				Sugars 5 g					

Percent Daily Values (%DV) are based on a 2000-calorie diet.

Note   • Potentially hazardous food. *Food Safety Standards:* Hold food for service at an internal temperature above 140°F. Do not mix old product with new. Cool leftover product quickly (within 4 hours) to below 41°F. See p. 105 for cooling procedures. Reheat leftover product quickly (within 2 hours) to 165°F. Reheat product only once; discard if not used.

WHITE CHILI

Yield: 50 portions   *Portion:* 8 oz

Ingredient	Amount	Procedure
Great Northern beans	3 lb	Sort and wash beans. Cover with water to 2 inches above beans. Let soak overnight.
		Drain beans. Place in steam-jacketed kettle.
Water	2 gal	Add to beans. Bring to a boil. Cover.
Chicken soup base	6 oz	Reduce heat and simmer for 2 hours, stirring occasionally.
Onion, chopped	2 lb	
Garlic, minced	1 oz	
Salt	1½ tsp	
Chicken or turkey, white meat, diced	3 lb	Add to beans. Cover and simmer 30 minutes.
Green chilies, canned, diced	1 lb 8 oz	
Cumin, ground	2 Tbsp	
Oregano, dried, crumbled	1½ Tbsp	
Pepper, cayenne	1½ tsp	
Cloves, ground	½ tsp	
Cilantro, dried, crumbled	1 Tbsp	
Monterey Jack cheese, shredded (optional)	1 lb 12 oz	Sprinkle ½ oz cheese over each portion as it is served.

Approximate nutritive values per portion   **Calories** 210

Amount/portion	%DV	Amount/portion	%DV	Amount/portion	%DV		%DV		%DV
Total Fat 7 g	10%	**Cholest.** 35 mg	12%	**Total Carb.** 20 g	7%	Vitamin A	5%	Calcium	18%
Sat. Fat 3 g	17%	**Sodium** 859 mg	36%	Fiber 0.4 g	1%	Vitamin C	4%	Iron	12%
Protein 18g				Sugars 1 g					

Percent Daily Values (%DV) are based on a 2000-calorie diet.

Notes

- Potentially hazardous food. *Food Safety Standards:* Hold food for service at an internal temperature above 140°F. Do not mix old product with new. Cool leftover product quickly (within 4 hours) to below 41°F. See p. 105 for cooling procedures. Reheat leftover product quickly (within 2 hours) to 165°F. Reheat product only once; discard if not used.

- If a highly salted chicken base is used, check for seasoning before adding salt.

MINESTRONE SOUP

Yield: 50 portions or 3 gal   *Portion:* 1 cup (8 oz)

Ingredient	Amount	Procedure
Bacon, diced	1 lb	Fry bacon until crisp. Drain.
Onions, chopped Garlic, minced	12 oz 2 cloves	Sauté onion and garlic in a little bacon fat until tender. Place, with bacon, in a large kettle.
Beef Stock (p. 791) Bay leaves Pepper, black	2 gal 2 1 tsp	Add stock and seasonings. Heat to boiling.
Cabbage, chopped Carrots, fresh, diced Potatoes, raw, chopped Celery, chopped Spinach, fresh, chopped Green beans, cut, canned Tomatoes, canned, diced Red beans, canned Spaghetti, long	12 oz 12 oz 12 oz 12 oz 3 oz 12 oz 2 lb 1 lb 12 oz 2 oz	Add vegetables and spaghetti. Simmer 45 minutes.
Flour, all-purpose Water, cold	3 oz 1 cup	Make a smooth paste of the flour and water. Stir into soup. Cook 10 minutes longer.
Parsley, chopped	¼ cup	Add parsley just before serving.

Approximate nutritive values per portion   **Calories** 69

Amount/portion	%DV	Amount/portion	%DV	Amount/portion	%DV		%DV		%DV
Total Fat 2 g	3%	**Cholest.** 2 mg	1%	**Total Carb.** 9 g	3%	**Vitamin A**	21%	**Calcium**	3%
Sat. Fat 1 g	3%	**Sodium** 634 mg	26%	Fiber 2 g	7%	**Vitamin C**	17%	**Iron**	6%
Protein 4 g				Sugars 2 g					

Percent Daily Values (%DV) are based on a 2000-calorie diet.

Notes
- Potentially hazardous food. *Food Safety Standards:* Hold food for service at an internal temperature above 140°F. Do not mix old product with new. Cool leftover product quickly (within 4 hours) to below 41°F. See p. 105 for cooling procedures. Reheat leftover product quickly (within 2 hours) to 165°F. Reheat product only once; discard if not used.
- 1½ oz (¾ cup) dehydrated onions may be substituted for fresh onions.

LENTIL AND BLACK BEAN SOUP

Yield: 50 portions   *Portion:* 1 cup (8 oz)

Ingredient	Amount	Procedure
Onions, chopped	3 lb	In a steam-jacketed or other large kettle, sauté onions, garlic, and carrots in oil until just tender.
Garlic, minced	2 cloves	
Carrots, chopped	1 lb 12 oz	
Vegetable oil	1 cup	
Lentils, dry, rinsed	2 lb 8 oz	Add water and rinsed lentils to vegetables. Bring to a boil and simmer for 25 minutes.
Water	1½ gal	
Black beans, canned, drained	4 lb	Add beans, tomatoes, and spices. Cover and simmer until lentils are tender, but not mushy, approximately 20–30 minutes.
Tomatoes, canned, diced	3 qt	Serve hot, 180°F.
Thyme, dried	2 tsp	
Marjoram, dried	1½ tsp	
Parsley, fresh	1 oz	
Salt	1 oz	
Pepper	1 Tbsp	
Cumin	½ tsp	
Tortillas, 6-inch	50	Serve garnished with a warm, rolled tortilla on the side of the plate.

Approximate nutritive values per portion   **Calories** 233

Amount/portion	%DV	Amount/portion	%DV	Amount/portion	%DV		%DV		%DV
Total Fat 5 g	8%	**Cholest.** 0 mg	0%	**Total Carb.** 38 g	13%	**Vitamin A**	54%	**Calcium**	11%
Sat. Fat 1 g	3%	**Sodium** 547 mg	23%	Fiber 5 g	21%	**Vitamin C**	14%	**Iron**	16%
Protein 9 g				Sugars 6 g					

Percent Daily Values (%DV) are based on a 2000-calorie diet.

Notes
- Potentially hazardous food. *Food Safety Standards:* Hold food for service at an internal temperature above 140°F. Do not mix old product with new. Cool leftover product quickly (within 4 hours) to below 41°F. See p. 105 for cooling procedures. Reheat leftover product quickly (within 2 hours) to 165°F. Reheat product only once; discard if not used.
- If soup becomes too thick, add hot water to bring to desired consistency.
- Chicken broth may be substituted for water. Reduce salt if a salted chicken base is used.

Variation
- **Split Pea and Black Bean Soup.** Substitute dried split peas for lentils.

NAVY BEAN SOUP

Yield: 50 portions or 3 gal   *Portion:* 1 cup (8 oz)

Ingredient	Amount	Procedure
Navy beans, dry Water, boiling	4 lb 3 gal	Wash beans. Add boiling water. Cover and let stand 1 hour or longer. Simmer beans for about 1 hour.
Ham cubes Onion, chopped Celery, diced Pepper, black Water	3 lb 12 oz 8 oz 1 Tbsp (see Procedure)	Add ham and seasonings to beans. Cook until beans are tender, 1–1½ hours. Add water to make volume of 3¼ gal. Check seasoning. Add salt if needed. Heat to 180°F.

Approximate nutritive values per portion   **Calories** 93

Amount/portion	%DV	Amount/portion	%DV	Amount/portion	%DV		%DV		%DV
Total Fat 3 g	4%	**Cholest.** 16 mg	5%	**Total Carb.** 8 g	3%	**Vitamin A**	0%	**Calcium**	2%
Sat. Fat 1 g	4%	**Sodium** 582 mg	24%	Fiber 0.2 g	1%	**Vitamin C**	12%	**Iron**	6%
Protein 9 g				Sugars 0 g					

Percent Daily Values (%DV) are based on a 2000-calorie diet.

Notes
- Potentially hazardous food. *Food Safety Standards:* Hold food for service at an internal temperature above 140°F. Do not mix old product with new. Cool leftover product quickly (within 4 hours) to below 41°F. See p. 105 for cooling procedures. Reheat leftover product quickly (within 2 hours) to 165°F. Reheat product only once; discard if not used.
- Great Northern beans may be substituted for navy beans.
- Ham base may be added for additional flavor.
- 1½ oz (¾ cup) dehydrated onions may be substituted for fresh onions.

SPLIT PEA SOUP

Yield: 50 portions or 3 gal   *Portion:* 1 cup (8 oz)

Ingredient	Amount	Procedure
Split peas	3 lb	Wash peas. Add water and bring to a boil.
Water	2 gal	Boil for 2 minutes, then turn off heat. Cover and let stand for 1 hour.
Ham cubes	2 lb	Add ham, onions, carrots, and potatoes.
Onions, chopped	1 lb	Cook for 1 hour or until peas are soft.
Carrots, fresh, chopped	1 lb 8 oz	
Potatoes, raw, chopped	2 lb	
Margarine	4 oz	Melt margarine and add flour. Stir until smooth. Cook 5 minutes.
Flour, all-purpose	2 oz	
Chicken Stock (p. 790)	2 qt	Add stock, while stirring, and cook until thickened. Add to peas.
Pepper, black	1 tsp	Taste for seasoning. Add pepper and salt if needed.

Approximate nutritive values per portion   **Calories** 175

Amount/portion	%DV	Amount/portion	%DV	Amount/portion	%DV		%DV		%DV
Total Fat 4 g	6%	**Cholest.** 11 mg	4%	**Total Carb.** 23 g	8%	**Vitamin A**	39%	**Calcium**	2%
Sat. Fat 1 g	5%	**Sodium** 432 mg	18%	Fiber 2 g	7%	**Vitamin C**	12%	**Iron**	9%
Protein 12 g				Sugars 3 g					

Percent Daily Values (%DV) are based on a 2000-calorie diet.

Notes

- Potentially hazardous food. *Food Safety Standards:* Hold food for service at an internal temperature above 140°F. Do not mix old product with new. Cool leftover product quickly (within 4 hours) to below 41°F. See p. 105 for cooling procedures. Reheat leftover product quickly (within 2 hours) to 165°F. Reheat product only once; discard if not used.

- If soup becomes too thick, add hot water to bring to desired consistency. If a smoother soup is desired, cook and puree peas before adding ham and vegetables.

- 1 lb chopped celery may be substituted for 1 lb potatoes.

- 3 lb sliced Polish sausage may be added to soup before serving. Reduce ham to 1 lb.

- 2 oz (1 cup) dehydrated onions may be substituted for fresh onion.

Variations

- **Lentil Soup.** Substitute lentils for split peas.
- **Yellow Split Pea Soup.** Substitute yellow split peas for green split peas.

TOMATO RICE SOUP

Yield: 50 portions or 3 gal   *Portion:* 1 cup (8 oz)

Ingredient	Amount	Procedure
Chicken or Beef Stock (pp. 790, 791)	2 gal	Heat stock and puree to boiling point.
Tomato puree	1 gal	
Onion, chopped	2 oz	Add vegetables and rice. Cook until rice is tender.
Green pepper, chopped	4 oz	
Rice, converted	8 oz	
Margarine	6 oz	Melt margarine and add flour. Mix until smooth. Add to soup while stirring. Add salt to taste.
Flour, all-purpose	3 oz	

Approximate nutritive values per portion   **Calories** 92

Amount/portion	%DV	Amount/portion	%DV	Amount/portion	%DV		%DV		%DV
Total Fat 3 g	5%	**Cholest.** 0 mg	0%	**Total Carb.** 13 g	4%	**Vitamin A**	12%	**Calcium**	2%
Sat. Fat 1 g	4%	**Sodium** 852 mg	36%	Fiber 2 g	8%	**Vitamin C**	50%	**Iron**	7%
Protein 4 g				Sugars 0 g					

Percent Daily Values (%DV) are based on a 2000-calorie diet.

Notes
- Potentially hazardous food. *Food Safety Standards:* Hold food for service at an internal temperature above 140°F. Do not mix old product with new. Cool leftover product quickly (within 4 hours) to below 41°F. See p. 105 for cooling procedures. Reheat leftover product quickly (within 2 hours) to 165°F. Reheat product only once; discard if not used.
- ¼ oz (2 Tbsp) dehydrated onions may be substituted for fresh onions.

Variation
- **Tomato Barley Soup.** Add 1 lb barley in place of rice.

PEPPER POT SOUP

Yield: 50 portions or 3 gal   *Portion:* 1 cup (8 oz)

Ingredient	Amount	Procedure
Margarine	12 oz	Sauté vegetables in margarine until lightly browned, about
Onion, finely chopped	8 oz	15 minutes.
Green peppers, finely chopped	8 oz	
Celery, thinly sliced	6 oz	
Potatoes, diced	3 lb 8 oz	
Flour, all-purpose	5 oz	Add flour to vegetables and stir until well blended.
Chicken or Beef Stock (pp. 790, 791)	2¼ gal	Combine stock and milk.
Milk, hot	1 qt	Add to vegetable mixture, while stirring.
Salt	1 oz (1½ Tbsp)	If soup base is used for the stock, taste before adding salt.
Pimiento, chopped	2 Tbsp	Add pimiento. Keep just below boiling point for 30 minutes, stirring frequently.

Approximate nutritive values per portion   **Calories** 115

Amount/portion	%DV	Amount/portion	%DV	Amount/portion	%DV		%DV		%DV
Total Fat 7 g	10%	**Cholest.** 3 mg	1%	**Total Carb.** 11 g	4%	**Vitamin A**	3%	**Calcium**	4%
Sat. Fat 2 g	8%	**Sodium** 834 mg	35%	Fiber 1 g	4%	**Vitamin C**	15%	**Iron**	3%
Protein 4 g				Sugars 2 g					

Percent Daily Values (%DV) are based on a 2000-calorie diet.

Notes
- Potentially hazardous food. *Food Safety Standards:* Hold food for service at an internal temperature above 140°F. Do not mix old product with new. Cool leftover product quickly (within 4 hours) to below 41°F. See p. 105 for cooling procedures. Reheat leftover product quickly (within 2 hours) to 165°F. Reheat product only once; discard if not used.
- This soup is good served with Spaetzles (p. 295). Prepare 1 recipe for 50 servings.
- 1 oz (½ cup) dehydrated onions may be substituted for fresh onions.

FRENCH ONION SOUP

Yield: 50 portions or 3 gal   *Portion:* 1 cup (8 oz)

Ingredient	Amount	Procedure
Onions, fresh	8 lb	Cut onions in thin slices.
Margarine or shortening	12 oz	Sauté in margarine in large kettle.
Flour, all-purpose	3 oz	Add flour and pepper. Cook for 10 minutes.
Pepper, black	1 tsp	
Beef Stock (p. 791)	3 gal	Add stock and Worcestershire sauce.
Worcestershire sauce	3 Tbsp	Cook until onions are tender and temperature is 190°F.
Salt	1 tsp (if needed)	
Croutons	12 oz	To serve, ladle soup over croutons or toasted bread.
Parmesan cheese, grated, or Swiss cheese, shredded	2 oz	Sprinkle with cheese.

Approximate nutritive values per portion **Calories** 128

Amount/portion	%DV	Amount/portion	%DV	Amount/portion	%DV		%DV		%DV
Total Fat 6 g	10%	**Cholest.** 0 mg	0%	**Total Carb.** 12 g	4%	**Vitamin A**	2%	**Calcium**	5%
Sat. Fat 2 g	8%	**Sodium** 974 mg	41%	Fiber 2 g	6%	**Vitamin C**	10%	**Iron**	5%
Protein 5 g				Sugars 2 g					

Percent Daily Values (%DV) are based on a 2000-calorie diet.

Note
- Potentially hazardous food. *Food Safety Standards:* Hold food for service at an internal temperature above 140°F. Do not mix old product with new. Cool leftover product quickly (within 4 hours) to below 41°F. See p. 105 for cooling procedures. Reheat leftover product quickly (within 2 hours) to 165°F. Reheat product only once; discard if not used.

CREAM SOUP RECIPES

BASIC SAUCE FOR CREAM SOUP

Yield: 2½ gal basic sauce

Ingredient	Amount	Procedure
Margarine	8 oz	Melt margarine. Add onions and sauté until tender.
Onions, finely chopped	2 oz	
Flour, all-purpose	12 oz	Add flour, chicken base, and pepper to onions. Stir until blended.
Chicken base	3 oz	
Pepper, white	½ tsp	Cook for 5 minutes.
Water	2 qt	Add water and stir until mixture thickens. Add vegetables and seasonings as suggested in Variations to make a variety of cream soups.
Milk, hot	2 gal	Stir in milk. Heat to 180°F.

Notes

- Potentially hazardous food. *Food Safety Standards:* Hold food for service at an internal temperature above 140°F. Do not mix old product with new. Cool leftover product quickly (within 4 hours) to below 41°F. See p. 105 for cooling procedures. Reheat leftover product quickly (within 2 hours) to 165°F. Reheat product only once; discard if not used.

- Chicken base may be omitted. Omit the water and use 2½ gal milk. Add 2 oz salt.

- ¼ oz (2 Tbsp) dehydrated onions, rehydrated in ¼ cup water, may be substituted for fresh onions.

- A reduced-fat milk may be substituted for whole milk. Reduced-fat milk is less stable (curdles more easily) than whole milk.

Variations

- To make 3 gallons of soup (50–60 1-cup, 8-oz portions), use 1 recipe Basic Sauce for Cream Soup plus suggested additions that follow.

- **Cream of Asparagus Soup.** Add 6 lb cooked, chopped (or pureed) asparagus.

- **Cream of Broccoli Soup.** Add 6 lb cooked, chopped broccoli.

- **Cream of Cauliflower Soup.** Increase onion to 1 lb 8 oz and water to 1 gal. Reduce milk to 1½ gal. Add 6 lb cauliflower, cut into small florets, and 1 Tbsp Worcestershire sauce. Stir in 1 lb 8 oz processed American cheese, shredded. Stir until melted. Sprinkle with chopped chives.

- **Cream of Celery Soup.** Increase onions to 8 oz. Add 2 lb 8 oz cooked chopped celery and 1 lb cooked diced carrots.

- **Cream of Mushroom Soup.** Increase onion to 8 oz. Add 3 lb mushrooms, sliced or chopped, sautéed with the onion in margarine.

- **Cream of Potato Soup.** Increase onions to 12 oz. Add 8 lb cooked diced potatoes and 1 lb cooked chopped celery. Increase chicken base to 5 oz. Potatoes may be mashed or pureed if desired.

- **Cream of Spinach Soup.** Increase onion to 8 oz. Add 3 lb chopped spinach, cooked.

- **Cream of Vegetable Soup.** Increase onion to 1 lb. Add 1 lb cooked chopped celery, 1 lb 8 oz cooked diced carrots, and 2 lb cooked diced potatoes.

- **Mushroom Barley Soup.** Reduce milk to 3 qt and increase water to 1¾ gal. Increase margarine to 1 lb, onions to 1 lb, and chicken base to 8 oz. Add 3 lb sliced mushrooms, ½ tsp garlic powder, and 1 lb barley after water has been added. Simmer about 30 minutes, then add milk slowly and heat to 180°F. Sprinkle with chopped parsley.

CREAM OF CHICKEN SOUP

Yield: 50 portions or 3 gal   *Portion:* 1 cup (8 oz)

Ingredient	Amount	Procedure
Margarine Celery, chopped	8 oz 1 lb	Melt margarine. Sauté celery until tender.
Flour, all-purpose Salt	8 oz 1 oz (1½ Tbsp)	Add flour and salt. Stir until blended. Cook for 5 minutes.
Chicken Stock (p. 790) Celery salt Pepper, white	2 gal 2 tsp ½ tsp	Add stock and seasonings. Cook over low heat until it has the consistency of thin white sauce. If chicken base is used for stock, taste before adding celery salt.
Milk Cooked chicken, chopped	1 gal 3 lb	Add milk while stirring. Add chicken. Heat to 180°F.

Approximate nutritive values per portion   **Calories** 172

Amount/portion	%DV	Amount/portion	%DV	Amount/portion	%DV		%DV		%DV
Total Fat 9 g	14%	**Cholest.** 34 mg	11%	**Total Carb.** 8 g	3%	**Vitamin A**	4%	Calcium	11%
Sat. Fat 3 g	16%	**Sodium** 839 mg	35%	Fiber 0.3 g	1%	**Vitamin C**	2%	Iron	5%
Protein 14 g				Sugars 4 g					

Percent Daily Values (%DV) are based on a 2000-calorie diet.

Notes
- Potentially hazardous food. *Food Safety Standards:* Hold food for service at an internal temperature above 140°F. Do not mix old product with new. Cool leftover product quickly (within 4 hours) to below 41°F. See p. 105 for cooling procedures. Reheat leftover product quickly (within 2 hours) to 165°F. Reheat product only once; discard if not used.
- 1 lb cooked rice or noodles may be added. Reduce margarine and flour to 4 oz each.

Variation
- **Chicken Velvet Soup.** Substitute 2 qt light cream (half-and-half) for 2 qt milk. Increase flour to 12 oz.

CHEESE SOUP

Yield: 50 portions or 3 gal   *Portion:* 1 cup (8 oz)

Ingredient	Amount	Procedure
Margarine Onions, chopped	8 oz 8 oz	Sauté onion in margarine until lightly browned.
Flour, all-purpose Cornstarch	4 oz 2 oz	Add flour and cornstarch. Blend. Cook for 5 minutes.
Paprika Salt Pepper, white Milk Chicken Stock (p. 790)	1 tsp 2 Tbsp 1 tsp 1 gal 1½ gal	Add seasonings and blend. Add milk and stock slowly, while stirring. Cook until thickened.
Carrots, finely diced Celery, finely diced	1 lb 12 oz	Cook carrots and celery until tender but slightly crisp. Add to soup.
Cheddar cheese, sharp, shredded	1 lb	Add cheese and stir until melted.
Parsley, fresh, chopped	½ cup	Garnish with chopped parsley.

Approximate nutritive values per portion   **Calories** 156

Amount/portion	%DV	Amount/portion	%DV	Amount/portion	%DV		%DV		%DV
Total Fat 10 g	15%	**Cholest.** 21 mg	7%	**Total Carb.** 9 g	3%	**Vitamin A**	33%	**Calcium**	17%
Sat. Fat 4 g	22%	**Sodium** 776 mg	32%	Fiber 0.5 g	2%	**Vitamin C**	5%	**Iron**	3%
Protein 8 g				Sugars 5 g					

Percent Daily Values (%DV) are based on a 2000-calorie diet.

Notes
- Potentially hazardous food. *Food Safety Standards:* Hold food for service at an internal temperature above 140°F. Do not mix old product with new. Cool leftover product quickly (within 4 hours) to below 41°F. See p. 105 for cooling procedures. Reheat leftover product quickly (within 2 hours) to 165°F. Reheat product only once; discard if not used.
- 1 oz (½ cup) dehydrated onions, rehydrated in ¾ cup water, may be substituted for fresh onions.
- Vegetable base and water may be substituted for Chicken Stock.

BROCCOLI AND CHEESE SOUP

Yield: 50 portions or 3 gal   *Portion:* 1 cup (8 oz)

Ingredient	Amount	Procedure
Margarine	10 oz	Melt margarine in steam-jacketed or other large kettle.
Onions, finely chopped	10 oz	Add onions and sauté until tender.
Flour, all-purpose	12 oz	Add flour and seasonings. Stir until blended.
Salt	1 Tbsp	Cook for 5 minutes, stirring often.
Pepper, black	1 tsp	
Chicken base	3 oz	Stir in chicken base, then add water and milk, stirring constantly.
Water	3 qt	Reduce heat and cook until thickened, stirring often.
Milk	1½ gal	
Processed cheese, coarsely shredded	2 lb 8 oz	Add cheese and stir until melted.
Broccoli cuts, frozen	4 lb	Steam broccoli until just tender. Chop, if necessary. Add to cheese mixture and heat to 180°F.

Approximate nutritive values per portion   **Calories** 239

Amount/portion	%DV	Amount/portion	%DV	Amount/portion	%DV		%DV		%DV
Total Fat 16 g	24%	**Cholest.** 38 mg	13%	**Total Carb.** 14 g	5%	**Vitamin A**	21%	**Calcium**	30%
Sat. Fat 8 g	39%	**Sodium** 890 mg	37%	Fiber 2 g	7%	**Vitamin C**	26%	**Iron**	4%
Protein 11 g				Sugars 7 g					

Percent Daily Values (%DV) are based on a 2000-calorie diet.

Notes
- Potentially hazardous food. *Food Safety Standards:* Hold food for service at an internal temperature above 140°F. Do not mix old product with new. Cool leftover product quickly (within 4 hours) to below 41°F. See p. 105 for cooling procedures. Reheat leftover product quickly (within 2 hours) to 165°F. Reheat product only once; discard if not used.
- 1¼ oz (⅔ cup) dehydrated onions, rehydrated in 1 cup water, may be substituted for fresh onions.
- Vegetable base may be substituted for chicken base.

Variation
- **Broccoli Swiss Soup.** In a steam-jacketed kettle, combine 1 lb chopped onions, 10 oz chopped celery, and 10 oz margarine. Sauté vegetables until tender. Stir in 10 oz flour, 1 tsp white pepper, and 2 tsp salt. Cook 5–10 minutes, stirring often. Using a wire whip, gradually stir in 1½ gal milk, 1¾ qt water, and 4 oz vegetable or chicken base. Reduce heat and cook until thickened, stirring constantly. Add 2 lb 12 oz shredded processed Swiss cheese. Stir until cheese melts. Add 5 lb 8 oz frozen broccoli cuts that have been steamed only until beginning to soften. Heat to 180°F. Makes 3 gal. Salt may need to be adjusted depending on the amount of salt in the vegetable or chicken base.

BAKED POTATO SOUP

Yield: 50 portions   *Portion:* 1 cup (8 oz)

Ingredient	Amount	Procedure
Baking potatoes	11 lb 10 oz	Bake and cool potatoes before dicing. Following cooling procedures on p. 855. After potatoes cool, dice into ½-inch cubes. Do not peel. Reserve for later step.
Margarine Green onions, finely chopped	4 oz 16 oz EP	Heat margarine in steam-jacketed kettle. Add onions. Sauté until fragrant.
Flour	2 oz	Stir flour into margarine and onions. Stir and cook for 10–15 minutes to make roux.
Chicken Stock (p. 790) (see Note)	5 qt	Add stock to roux stirring constantly with a wire whip. Bring to a boil. Reduce heat and simmer 15–20 minutes. Add diced potatoes reserved from earlier step.
Milk Cooked Bacon, crumbled	1¾ qt 6 oz	Add milk and bacon. Bring to 180–190°F.
Cheddar cheese, shredded Green onions, sliced thin Black pepper	12 oz 4 oz EP 3½ tsp	Add cheese, onions, and pepper. Stir until cheese is melted. Taste for salt and adjust as needed.

Approximate nutritive values per portion   **Calories** 180

Amount/portion	%DV	Amount/portion	%DV	Amount/portion	%DV		%DV		%DV
Total Fat 6.3 g	10%	**Cholest.** 11.1 mg	4%	**Total Carb.** 25 g	8%	**Vitamin A**	4%	**Calcium**	9%
Sat. Fat 2.6 g	13%	**Sodium** 347 mg	14%	Fiber 2.5 g	10%	**Vitamin C**	18%	**Iron**	7%
Protein 6.2 g				Sugars 2.4 g					

Percent Daily Values (%DV) are based on a 2000-calorie diet.

Notes
- Potentially hazardous food. *Food Safety Standards:* Hold food for service at an internal temperature above 140°F. Do not mix old product with new. Cool leftover product quickly (within 2 hours) to 70°F and then (within an additional 4 hours) to 41°F. See p. 105 for cooling procedures. Reheat leftover product quickly (within 2 hours) to 165°F. Reheat product only once; discard if not used.
- 4 oz of chicken soup base and 4 3/4 qt water can be substituted for the Chicken Stock.

CHOWDER RECIPES

CORN CHOWDER

Yield: 50 portions or 3 gal   *Portion:* 1 cup (8 oz)

Ingredient	Amount	Procedure
Potatoes, diced	2 lb	Cook potatoes. Drain. Save for later step.
Margarine, melted Onions, finely chopped Celery, chopped	8 oz 4 oz 6 oz	Sauté onions and celery in margarine until tender.
Flour, all-purpose Pepper, white Chicken base	12 oz 1 tsp 3 oz	Add flour, pepper, and chicken base to onions. Stir until well blended. Cook for 5 minutes.
Water	1½ gal	Add water, stirring constantly. Cook until mixture thickens.
Corn, cream style Chives, frozen	1 No. 10 can 1 cup	Add corn, chives, and potatoes. Heat until hot.
Milk	2½ qt	Stir milk into soup. Heat to 180°F.

Approximate nutritive values per portion   **Calories** 153

Amount/portion	%DV	Amount/portion	%DV	Amount/portion	%DV		%DV		%DV
Total Fat 6 g	9%	**Cholest.** 7 mg	2%	**Total Carb.** 23 g	8%	**Vitamin A**	4%	**Calcium**	7%
Sat. Fat 2 g	9%	**Sodium** 392 mg	16%	Fiber 1 g	6%	**Vitamin C**	10%	**Iron**	3%
Protein 4 g				Sugars 3 g					

Percent Daily Values (%DV) are based on a 2000-calorie diet.

Notes
- Potentially hazardous food. *Food Safety Standards:* Hold food for service at an internal temperature above 140°F. Do not mix old product with new. Cool leftover product quickly (within 4 hours) to below 41°F. See p. 105 for cooling procedures. Reheat leftover product quickly (within 2 hours) to 165°F. Reheat product only once; discard if not used.
- Vegetable base may be substituted for chicken base.
- ½ oz (¼ cup) dehydrated onions, rehydrated in ½ cup water, may be substituted for fresh onions.
- 1 lb bacon, diced and cooked until crisp, may be added before serving.

Variations
- **Potato Chowder.** Omit corn and increase potatoes to 8 lb.
- **Vegetable Chowder.** Substitute 3 lb whole kernel corn for cream style corn. Add 4 oz chopped green pepper and 1 lb cooked, diced carrots.

NEW ENGLAND CLAM CHOWDER

Yield: 50 portions or 3 gal   *Portion:* 1 cup (8 oz)

Ingredient	Amount	Procedure
Potatoes, cubed	6 lb	Cook potatoes until tender. Drain.
Water	1 qt	Reserve potatoes to add in last step.
Salt	1 Tbsp	
Bacon, finely diced	4 oz	Sauté bacon, onion, and celery in steam-jacketed or other
Onion, chopped	8 oz	large kettle for 5 minutes, or until lightly browned.
Celery, chopped	12 oz	
Margarine	8 oz	Add margarine to onion and stir until melted.
Flour, all-purpose	8 oz	Add flour, seasonings, and chicken base. Stir until blended.
Pepper, white	1 tsp	Cook for 5 minutes.
Chicken base (see Notes)	4 oz	
Milk	2 gal	Add milk gradually while stirring. Cook until thickened.
Minced clams, undrained	4 lb	Add clams and potatoes. Heat to 180°F.

Approximate nutritive values per portion   **Calories** 235

Amount/portion	%DV	Amount/portion	%DV	Amount/portion	%DV		%DV		%DV
Total Fat 10 g	15%	**Cholest.** 34 mg	11%	**Total Carb.** 25 g	8%	**Vitamin A**	10%	**Calcium**	21%
Sat. Fat 4 g	21%	**Sodium** 709 mg	30%	Fiber 2 g	6%	**Vitamin C**	15%	**Iron**	32%
Protein 12 g				Sugars 9 g					

Percent Daily Values (%DV) are based on a 2000-calorie diet.

Notes
- Potentially hazardous food. *Food Safety Standards:* Hold food for service at an internal temperature above 140°F. Do not mix old product with new. Cool leftover product quickly (within 4 hours) to below 41°F. See p. 105 for cooling procedures. Reheat leftover product quickly (within 2 hours) to 165°F. Reheat product only once; discard if not used.
- 1 gal fresh clams may be used. Clean and steam until tender. Drain and chop. Save juice.
- Garnish with fresh or frozen chives, chopped.
- 1 oz (½ cup) dehydrated onions, rehydrated in ¾ cup water, may be substituted for fresh onions.
- Clam base may be substituted for chicken base.

Variation
- **Fish Chowder.** Delete clams. Add 1 tsp thyme, 1 tsp crushed rosemary, 2 tsp Worcestershire sauce, ½ tsp hot pepper sauce, and 3 lb flaked white fish, or 1 lb shrimp and 2 lb minced clams.

POTATO AND ROASTED RED PEPPER SOUP

Yield: 50 portions   *Portion:* 8 oz

Ingredient	Amount	Procedure
Potatoes, medium diced	6 lb 4 oz	Using a steamer or other steam equipment, steam potatoes until tender. Hold for later step.
Margarine	8 oz	In a steam-jacketed kettle or large stockpot, sauté vegetables until tender.
Onions, finely chopped	1 lb (EP)	
Celery, chopped	1 lb (EP)	
Flour	10 oz	Add flour to vegetables. Stir with wire whip to combine. Cook for 5–10 minutes. Turn off heat.
Water	2 qt	Add water, base, and seasonings to roux, stirring constantly. Cook until mixture thickens.
Chicken base	4 oz	
Pepper, white	1 tsp	
Salt	1½ oz	
Roasted Red Peppers, cut into ¼ × ½-inch strips (p. 854)	1 lb	Add steamed potatoes (from earlier step) and Roasted Red Peppers to onion, celery, and water mixture. Heat to 185°F.
Milk	5 qt	Add milk slowly to potato mixture. Stir constantly to combine. Heat to 180°F.

Approximate nutritive values per portion   **Calories** 170

Amount/portion	%DV	Amount/portion	%DV	Amount/portion	%DV		%DV		%DV
Total Fat 7.5 g	11%	**Cholest.** 13 mg	4%	**Total Carb.** 20 g	7%	**Vitamin A**	12%	**Calcium**	13%
Sat. Fat 2.8 g	14%	**Sodium** 739 mg	31%	Fiber 1.7 g	7%	**Vitamin C**	49%	**Iron**	5%
Protein 5.8 g				Sugars 5 g					

Percent Daily Values (%DV) are based on a 2000-calorie diet.

Notes

- Potentially hazardous food. *Food Safety Standards:* Hold food for service at an internal temperature above 140°F. Do not mix old product with new. Cool leftover product quickly (within 4 hours) to below 41°F. See p. 105 for cooling procedures. Reheat leftover product quickly (within 2 hours) to 165°F. Reheat product only once, discard if not used.

- A frozen roasted pepper blend can be substituted for the Roasted Red Peppers. When using frozen roasted vegetables, place in a single layer on a baking sheet and heat in a 375°F oven until heated through (discard liquid that accumulates).

- Green, orange, or yellow bell peppers can be substituted for some or all of the red bell peppers.

- Vegetable base can be substituted for the chicken base. Adjust salt as required.

HEARTY POTATO HAM CHOWDER

Yield: 50 portions or 3 gal   *Portion:* 1 cup (8 oz)

Ingredient	Amount	Procedure
Margarine	3 oz	Melt margarine in steam-jacketed or other large kettle.
Onion, green, finely chopped	8 oz	Add onion and green pepper and sauté until tender.
Green pepper, chopped	12 oz	
Flour, all-purpose	3 oz	Add flour and seasonings. Stir until blended.
Pepper, white	½ tsp	Cook for 5 minutes, stirring often.
Paprika	1 tsp	
Chicken Stock (p. 790)	3 qt	Add stock and stir until smooth. Cook until mixture begins to thicken.
Ham, coarsely chopped	2 lb 8 oz	Add ham, potatoes, and corn. Heat to 180°F.
Potatoes, cooked, cubed	5 lb 8 oz	
Corn, whole kernel	3 lb 12 oz	
Milk	2¾ qt	Add milk and mix well. Heat to 180°F.
Parsley, fresh, chopped	½ cup	Sprinkle parsley over chowder before serving.

Approximate nutritive values per portion   **Calories** 276

Amount/portion	%DV	Amount/portion	%DV	Amount/portion	%DV		%DV		%DV
Total Fat 7 g	11%	**Cholest.** 21 mg	7%	**Total Carb.** 41 g	14%	**Vitamin A**	5%	**Calcium**	7%
Sat. Fat 2 g	12%	**Sodium** 584 mg	24%	Fiber 5 g	21%	**Vitamin C**	32%	**Iron**	9%
Protein 13 g				Sugars 4 g					

Percent Daily Values (%DV) are based on a 2000-calorie diet.

Notes
- Potentially hazardous food. *Food Safety Standards:* Hold food for service at an internal temperature above 140°F. Do not mix old product with new. Cool leftover product quickly (within 4 hours) to below 41°F. See p. 105 for cooling procedures. Reheat leftover product quickly (within 2 hours) to 165°F. Reheat product only once; discard if not used.
- 1 oz (½ cup) dehydrated onions, rehydrated in ¾ cup water, may be substituted for fresh onions.

OYSTER STEW

Yield: 50 portions or 3 gal   *Portion:* 1 cup (8 oz)

Ingredient	Amount	Procedure
Milk	2½ gal	Scald milk by heating to point just below boiling.
Oysters Butter or margarine	2½ qt 8 oz	Heat undrained oysters and butter only until edges of oysters begin to curl.
Salt Pepper	2 oz (3 Tbsp) ½ tsp	About 10 minutes before serving, add hot oysters, with the oyster liquid, and seasonings to scalded milk. Serve immediately to avoid curdling.

Approximate nutritive values per portion   **Calories** 203

Amount/portion	%DV	Amount/portion	%DV	Amount/portion	%DV		%DV		%DV
Total Fat 12 g	18%	**Cholest.** 76 mg	25%	**Total Carb.** 12 g	4%	Vitamin A	18%	Calcium	26%
Sat. Fat 7 g	34%	**Sodium** 599 mg	25%	Fiber 0 g	0%	Vitamin C	9%	Iron	27%
Protein 12 g				Sugars 10 g					

Percent Daily Values (%DV) are based on a 2000-calorie diet.

Note   • Potentially hazardous food. *Food Safety Standards:* Hold food for service at an internal temperature above 140°F. Do not mix old product with new. Cool leftover product quickly (within 4 hours) to below 41°F. See p. 105 for cooling procedures. Reheat leftover product quickly (within 2 hours) to 165°F. Reheat product only once; discard if not used.

MANHATTAN FISH OR CLAM CHOWDER

Yield: 50 portions or 3 gal   *Portion:* 1 cup (8 oz)

Ingredient	Amount	Procedure
Bacon, diced	1 lb	Cook bacon until crisp. Drain off excess fat.
Onion, chopped	1 lb 6 oz	Add onion and sauté until tender. Place onion and bacon in large kettle.
Water	3 qt	Add water, vegetables, and spices. Bring to a boil.
Tomatoes, diced, canned	1 No. 10 can	Reduce heat. Simmer 40–45 minutes or until vegetables are tender.
Potatoes, chopped	3 lb	Remove bay leaves before serving.
Carrots, fresh, diced	1 lb 4 oz	
Celery, chopped	1 lb 4 oz	
Catsup	2 cups	
Worcestershire sauce	⅓ cup	
Salt	2 Tbsp	
Pepper, black	1 tsp	
Bay leaves	2	
Thyme, ground	1 tsp	
Fish, boneless, cooked and flaked, or minced clams	3 lb 8 oz	Add fish. Cover and simmer 5–10 minutes.
Parsley, fresh, chopped	¼ cup	Sprinkle parsley over soup before serving.

Approximate nutritive values per portion   **Calories** 98

Amount/portion	%DV	Amount/portion	%DV	Amount/portion	%DV		%DV		%DV
Total Fat 2 g	3%	**Cholest.** 13 mg	4%	**Total Carb.** 15 g	5%	**Vitamin A**	40%	**Calcium**	4%
Sat. Fat 1 g	3%	**Sodium** 543 mg	23%	Fiber 2 g	8%	**Vitamin C**	41%	**Iron**	29%
Protein 6 g				Sugars 4 g					

Percent Daily Values (%DV) are based on a 2000-calorie diet.

Notes
- Potentially hazardous food. *Food Safety Standards:* Hold food for service at an internal temperature above 140°F. Do not mix old product with new. Cool leftover product quickly (within 4 hours) to below 41°F. See p. 105 for cooling procedures. Reheat leftover product quickly (within 2 hours) to 165°F. Reheat product only once; discard if not used.
- 2¾ oz (1½ cups) dehydrated onions, rehydrated in 2¼ cups water, may be substituted for fresh onions.

CHILLED SOUP RECIPES

GAZPACHO (SPANISH CHILLED SOUP)

Yield: 50 portions or 1¾ gal   *Portion:* ½ cup (4 oz)

Ingredient	Amount	Procedure
Mushrooms, fresh, chopped	4 oz	Sauté mushrooms in olive oil until light brown.
Olive oil	½ cup	
Garlic	3 cloves	Crush garlic in salt.
Salt	2 Tbsp	
Tomatoes, fresh, finely chopped	3 lb	Combine remaining ingredients in a stainless steel or glass container.
Green peppers, finely chopped	1 lb 4 oz	Add mushrooms and garlic.
Celery, finely chopped	12 oz	If too thick, add more tomato juice.
		Cover and chill quickly to below 41°F.
Cucumbers, finely chopped	1 lb	
Onion, finely chopped	1 lb 8 oz	
Chives, chopped	2 Tbsp	
Parsley, chopped	3 Tbsp	
Pepper, black	1 Tbsp	
Worcestershire sauce	1 Tbsp	
Tarragon vinegar	1½ cups	
Hot pepper sauce	1 tsp	
Tomato juice	2½ qt	

Approximate nutritive values per portion

Calories 45

Amount/portion	%DV	Amount/portion	%DV	Amount/portion	%DV		%DV		%DV
Total Fat 2 g	**4%**	**Cholest.** 0 mg	**0%**	**Total Carb.** 6 g	**2%**	Vitamin A	5%	Calcium	2%
Sat. Fat 1 g	**3%**	**Sodium** 487 mg	**20%**	Fiber 1 g	**5%**	Vitamin C	43%	Iron	4%
Protein 1 g				Sugars 3 g					

Percent Daily Values (%DV) are based on a 2000-calorie diet.

Note   • Potentially hazardous food. Store for service at an internal temperature below 41°F.

food services can be met by the continuous cooking of vegetables in small quantities (batch cooking). Vegetables should be served as soon as possible after cooking for optimum quality and should be handled carefully to prevent breaking or mashing. Vegetables that have been cooked and held for any period of time should not be combined with freshly prepared batches. Appearance is most important to customer acceptance of vegetables, as is the seasoning. Individual recipes recommend the amount of salt for 50 portions and suggest seasonings appropriate to that vegetable.

Directions for Boiling

1. Prepare vegetables. See pp. 823–824 for directions for preparing fresh vegetables. Frozen vegetables should not be thawed before cooking except for solid pack frozen vegetables, which should be thawed only long enough to break apart easily.

2. Add prepared vegetables to boiling salted water in steam-jacketed kettle or stockpot. Cook in lots no larger than 10 lb. Use 1 oz (1½ Tbsp) salt to the amount of water specified in Table 19.1, except for corn. Add salt and/or sugar after cooking to prevent toughening and discoloring of corn kernels.

    The amount of water used in cooking all vegetables is important for retention of nutrients. The less water used, the more nutrients retained. Addition of baking soda to the water also causes loss of vitamins. Mature root vegetables that need longer cooking require more water than young, tender vegetables. Spinach and other greens need only the water clinging to their leaves from washing.

3. Cover and bring water quickly back to the boiling point. Green vegetables retain their color better if the lid is removed just before boiling begins; strong-flavored vegetables, such as cabbage, cauliflower, and brussels sprouts, should be cooked uncovered to prevent development of unpleasant flavors.

4. Start timing when water returns to the boiling point. Use Table 19.1 as a guide. Stir greens occasionally while boiling.

5. Drain cooked vegetables and place in serving pans. Add 4–8 oz melted margarine or butter to each 50 portions.

6. Adjust seasonings.

Directions for Steaming

1. Place prepared vegetables not more than 3–4 inches deep in stainless steel inset pans. Perforated pans provide the best circulation, but if cooking liquid needs to be retained, use solid pans. When cooking winter squash or sweet potatoes, cover with a lid or aluminum foil to prevent water from accumulating in the pan.

2. Steam, using Table 19.1 as a guide. Begin timing when steamer reaches proper cooking pressure.

3. Add 2–4 oz melted margarine or butter and 2 tsp salt to each 5 lb drained vegetables.

Directions for Stir-Frying

1. Select vegetables for color, texture, shape, and flavor.

2. Cut or dice diagonally into small uniform pieces (see p. 210 for dicing instructions.)

3. Heat a small amount of oil or seasoned oil in a pan, steam-jacketed kettle, or tilting fry pan. Prepare seasoned oil for stir-frying by adding ½ oz sliced ginger root and ½ oz fresh peeled garlic to 2 cups salad oil. Refrigerate 8 hours. For safety reasons, use within 24 hours. Strain before using (see p. 574 for Basil Oil recipe).

4. Stir in vegetables, starting with those that take longer to cook (carrots, onions, turnips). Continue to stir for 1 minute until vegetables are coated with oil.

5. Add liquid (water or broth) and seasonings to vegetables. Cover and steam for 3 minutes or until vegetables are tender-crisp.

6. Add cornstarch mixed with a small amount of cold water. (See recipe on p. 877.) Cook and stir just until the sauce thickens and vegetables are glazed.

CANNED VEGETABLES

Heating of canned vegetables should be scheduled so they will be served soon after heating. Prepare 1 or 2 No. 10 cans at a time, with approximately 25 portions in each can.

Directions for Heating

Stockpot or Steam-Jacketed Kettle

1. Drain off half the liquid; use for soups, gravies, and sauces.

2. Heat vegetables and remaining liquid in a stockpot or steam-jacketed kettle. Heat only long enough to bring to 160°F.

3. Drain vegetables and place in counter pans. Add 4–8 oz melted margarine or butter.

TABLE 19.1   Timetable for boiling or steaming fresh and frozen vegetables

	Boiling— approximate cooking time[a,b] (minutes)	Steaming—Approximate cooking time[c,d] for 1–3 pans (minutes)		
		5–6 psi[e]	12–15 psi[e]	Zero pressure
Asparagus, fresh, frozen	10–12	10–12	4–8	6–13
Beans, black-eyed beans or peas, frozen	30–45	20–25	10–20	25–35
Beans, green or wax, fresh	15–25	15–20	4–10	10–15
Beans, green or wax, frozen	10–12	10–12	7–11	6–13
Beans, lima, frozen	10–15	10–12	6–10	6–13
Beets, whole, fresh	40–50	40–50	25–35	40–50
Broccoli, cuts or spears, fresh, frozen	10–12	10–15	4–8	5–10
Brussels sprouts, fresh, frozen	10–15	10–12	6–10	9–14
Cabbage, cored, cut	10–12	14–16	7–14	14–18
Carrots, fresh	10–20	18–20	6–15	18–20
Carrots, frozen	10–20	9–10	5–9	7–12
Cauliflower, fresh, frozen	10–12	10–15	5–10	7–15
Celery, fresh	10–12	10–15	5–10	10–15
Corn, whole kernel, frozen	6–8	9–10	5–9	5–10
Corn on the cob, fresh, frozen	5–15	10–12	5–10	8–12
Eggplant, fresh	15–20	10–15	4–8	5–15
Greens, collard, fresh	25–35	10–15	8–10	12–15
Kale, fresh	15–20	10–15	8–10	12–15
Okra, fresh, frozen	8–15	10–12	6–10	10–12
Onions, fresh	20–30	15–20	5–10	10–15
Parsnips, fresh	20–40	15–20	6–15	18–20
Peas, green, fresh, frozen	8–12	8–10	3–4	5–6
Potatoes, fresh, whole, small	25–40	20–25	13–25	35–40
Rutabagas, fresh	20–35	25–30	10–20	25–30
Spinach, fresh	3–5	3–5	1–3	3–5
Spinach, frozen, thawed	3–5	8–10	4–8	8–10
Squash, summer, fresh, frozen	5–10	8–12	5–8	7–10
Squash, winter, fresh, diced	30–40	15–20	7–9	15–20
Sweet potatoes, fresh	30–40	20–30	13–25	30–40
Turnips, fresh	20–40	25–30	10–20	25–30
Vegetables, mixed, frozen	10–15	10	5–9	5–10

[a] Cook vegetables at a slow boil.
[b] Figures calculated for boiling 10–12 lb of vegetables in 1–3 qt. water. Greens do not require the addition of extra water; the water clinging to their leaves is sufficient.
[c] Figures calculated for steaming 5–6 lb vegetables per batch. A steamer filled to less than capacity will need the cooking time reduced slightly. An overloaded steamer may require a longer cooking time.
[d] When posssible, use 2 ½-inch-deep perforated steamer pans. For best results, break up frozen vegetables to speed cooking.
[e] Pounds per square inch.
Note • Canned vegetables require the following cooking times: 5 psi, 3–5 minutes; 15 psi, 3–4 minutes; 0 psi, 5–10 minutes.

Steamer or Oven

1. Drain off half the liquid; use for soups, gravies, and sauces.

2. Transfer vegetables and remaining liquid to steamer pans and cover. A 12 × 20 × 2-inch pan will hold contents of 2 No. 10 cans, or 50 portions of most vegetables.

3. Heat in steamer at 5–6 lb pressure for 1 minute, or in a 350°F oven until 160°F is reached.

4. Drain vegetables and add 4–8 oz melted margarine or butter for each lot of vegetables.

DRIED VEGETABLES

Among the many kinds of dried legumes available today are dried peas (whole green or split green, yellow split, and black-eyed); beans (navy, black, fava, red kidney, brown, pinto, butter beans, and garbanzo, also known as chick peas); and lentils (brown and red). High in protein and fiber, legumes are an important factor in meatless dishes and health-conscious menus.

Directions for Cooking

1. Sort, discarding any stones or other foreign material and shriveled vegetables. Rinse with cold water.

2. Heat water to boiling in steam-jacketed or other kettle.

3. Add vegetables and boil for 3 minutes.

4. Turn off steam and allow to stand for 1 hour.

5. Add salt and cook slowly until vegetables are tender (1–1½ hours). Add more water if needed.

6. Vegetables may be covered with cold water and soaked overnight, drained, fresh water added, then cooked.

VEGETABLE RECIPES

SEASONED FRESH ASPARAGUS

Yield: 50 portions   *Portion:* 3 oz

Ingredient	Amount	Procedure
Asparagus, fresh	18–20 lb (AP) (10 lb EP)	Break or cut off tough stems. Wash and thoroughly clean remaining portions. Arrange spears in steamer pans with tips in one direction. Sprinkle with salt. Steam (p. 825). Asparagus may be cut into 1-inch pieces and steamed or placed in a kettle and boiled (p. 825).
Margarine, melted Salt	4 oz 1 oz (1½ Tbsp)	Pour margarine over cooked asparagus. If boiling asparagus, add salt to cooking water.

Approximate nutritive values per portion   **Calories** 59

Amount/portion	%DV	Amount/portion	%DV	Amount/portion	%DV		%DV		%DV
Total Fat 2 g	4%	**Cholest.** 0 mg	0%	**Total Carb.** 8 g	3%	Vitamin A	14%	Calcium	4%
Sat. Fat 1 g	2%	**Sodium** 220 mg	9%	Fiber 3 g	13%	Vitamin C	77%	Iron	6%
Protein 4 g				Sugars 3 g					

Percent Daily Values (%DV) are based on a 2000-calorie diet.

Notes
- For frozen asparagus, use 10 lb. See p. 825 for cooking instructions.
- Seasonings for asparagus: sesame seeds, lemon juice, browned butter, crumb butter, basil, chives, tarragon.

Variations
- **Asparagus with Cheese Sauce.** Serve 5–6 stalks of cooked asparagus with 2 Tbsp Cheese Sauce (p. 749). Make 2 qt sauce.
- **Asparagus Vinaigrette.** Blanch asparagus (see p. 198). Marinate in 1½ qt Vinaigrette Dressing (p. 706) or Vegetable Marinade (pp. 785–787).
- **Creamed Asparagus.** Add 1 gal Medium White Sauce (p. 749) to 10 lb asparagus cut in 2-inch lengths and cooked.
- **Fresh Asparagus with Hollandaise Sauce.** Serve 1 Tbsp Hollandaise Sauce (p. 769) over cooked asparagus spears.

SEASONED FRESH GREEN OR WAX BEANS

Yield: 50 portions   *Portion:* 3 oz

Ingredient	Amount	Procedure
Green or wax beans, fresh	11–12 lb (AP) (10 lb EP)	Wash beans. Trim ends. Cut or break into 1-inch pieces. Steam or boil (p. 825).
Margarine, melted Salt	4 oz 1 oz (1½ Tbsp)	Pour margarine over cooked beans and sprinkle with salt. If boiling the beans, add salt to cooking water.

Approximate nutritive values per portion   **Calories** 51

Amount/portion	%DV	Amount/portion	%DV	Amount/portion	%DV		%DV		%DV
Total Fat 2 g	3%	**Cholest.** 0 mg	0%	**Total Carb.** 8 g	3%	**Vitamin A**	7%	**Calcium**	4%
Sat. Fat 1 g	2%	**Sodium** 216 mg	9%	Fiber 2 g	7%	**Vitamin C**	16%	**Iron**	7%
Protein 2 g				Sugars 2 g					

Percent Daily Values (%DV) are based on a 2000-calorie diet.

Notes
- For frozen beans, use 10 lb. See p. 825 for cooking.
- For canned beans, use 2 No. 10 cans. See p. 824 for heating.
- Seasonings for green beans: basil, dill, marjoram, oregano, rosemary, savory, tarragon, thyme, onion, chives, mushrooms, bacon.

Variations
- **French Green Beans.** Cook 10 lb frozen French cut green beans. Drain and season with 1 cup mayonnaise, ¾ cup sour cream, 2 Tbsp vinegar, 2 oz chopped onion sautéed in 2 oz margarine, and salt and pepper to taste.
- **Green Beans Amandine.** Add 8 oz slivered almonds lightly browned in 8 oz margarine.
- **Green Beans and Mushrooms.** Add 2 lb sliced mushrooms that have been sautéed in 8 oz margarine.
- **Green Beans Provincial.** Season green beans with 8 oz Onion Butter (p. 780), 2 cloves garlic, minced, 3 Tbsp chopped parsley, and 2 tsp dried crumbled thyme.
- **Herbed Green Beans.** Season 10 lb frozen green beans, cooked, or 2 No. 10 cans green beans with 1 lb chopped onions, 8 oz chopped celery, and 1 tsp minced garlic sautéed in 8 oz margarine, 2 tsp dried crumbled basil, and 2 tsp dried rosemary.
- **Southern-Style Green Beans.** Cut 1 lb 8 oz bacon into small pieces. Add 6 oz chopped onion and sauté until onion is lightly browned. Add to hot, drained green beans. Good served with ham and Corn Bread (p. 281).

GREEN BEAN CASSEROLE

Yield: 50 portions or 1 pan 12 × 20 × 2 inches   *Portion:* 4 oz
Oven: 350°F   *Bake:* 30–40 minutes

Ingredient	Amount	Procedure
Green beans, frozen, French cut or cut	7 lb 8 oz	Cook green beans (p. 825). Drain.
Mushrooms, fresh Margarine, melted	10 oz 3 oz	Clean mushrooms and slice. Sauté in margarine.
Cream of mushroom soup, undiluted Milk Pepper, black Onion powder Soy sauce	1 qt 1 cup ½ tsp 1 tsp 1 Tbsp	Blend soup, milk, and seasonings.
Water chestnuts, sliced, drained	1 lb	Combine soup mixture, mushrooms, and water chestnuts. Add to green beans. Mix lightly. Pour into one 12 × 20 × 2-inch pan.
Swiss cheese, shredded	8 oz	Sprinkle cheese over beans. Bake at 350°F for 25 minutes.
Bread crumbs Margarine, melted	4 oz 4 oz	Combine crumbs and margarine and sprinkle over bean mixture. Bake 5–10 minutes.

Approximate nutritive values per portion   **Calories** 107

Amount/portion	%DV	Amount/portion	%DV	Amount/portion	%DV		%DV		%DV
Total Fat 6 g	10%	**Cholest.** 5 mg	2%	**Total Carb.** 10 g	3%	**Vitamin A**	6%	**Calcium**	9%
Sat. Fat 2 g	10%	**Sodium** 262 mg	11%	Fiber 1 g	5%	**Vitamin C**	10%	**Iron**	4%
Protein 3 g				Sugars 3 g					

Percent Daily Values (%DV) are based on a 2000-calorie diet.

Notes
- Two No. 10 cans cut green beans may be substituted for frozen beans. Drain before using.
- 8 oz crumbled French fried onion rings (canned) may be sprinkled over the top during the last 10 minutes of baking.

SPANISH GREEN BEANS

Yield: 50 portions   *Portion:* 3 oz

Ingredient	Amount	Procedure
Bacon, diced	8 oz	Sauté bacon, onion, and green pepper until lightly browned.
Onion, chopped	6 oz	
Green pepper, chopped	4 oz	
Flour, all-purpose	4 oz	Add flour and stir until smooth.
Tomatoes, canned	2 qt	Chop tomatoes and heat. Add salt.
Salt	1 Tbsp	Add gradually to bacon-vegetable mixture. Stir and cook until thickened.
Green beans, drained	2 No. 10 cans	Gently stir tomato sauce into the green beans. Simmer 15–20 minutes or until beans are heated to 160°F.

Approximate nutritive values per portion   **Calories** 48

Amount/portion	%DV	Amount/portion	%DV	Amount/portion	%DV		%DV		%DV
Total Fat 1 g	1%	**Cholest.** 0 mg	0%	**Total Carb.** 9 g	3%	**Vitamin A**	2%	Calcium	3%
Sat. Fat 0 g	0%	**Sodium** 213 mg	9%	Fiber 3 g	11%	**Vitamin C**	23%	Iron	7%
Protein 2 g				Sugars 3 g					

Percent Daily Values (%DV) are based on a 2000-calorie diet.

Note
- 8 lb fresh or frozen green beans may be substituted for canned beans. Cook before combining with tomato sauce.

Variations
- **Creole Green Beans.** Omit bacon. Sauté onion, green pepper, and 8 oz chopped celery in 2 oz margarine. Add 2 oz sugar to tomatoes.
- **Green Beans with Dill.** Delete bacon and onion. Sauté the green pepper in 5 oz margarine. Add 1 tsp pepper and 1 Tbsp dill seeds. Simmer slowly for 10–15 minutes. Tomato may be increased to one No. 10 can.
- **Hacienda Green Beans.** Add 1 oz sugar, 1½ Tbsp chili powder, and ½ tsp garlic powder.

SEASONED LIMA BEANS

Yield: 50 portions   *Portion:* 3 oz

Ingredient	Amount	Procedure
Lima beans, baby or fordhook, frozen	10 lb	Steam or boil beans (p. 825).
Margarine, melted Salt	4 oz 1 oz (1½ Tbsp)	Pour margarine over beans and sprinkle with salt. If boiling the beans, add salt to cooking water.

Approximate nutritive values per portion   **Calories** 130

Amount/portion	%DV	Amount/portion	%DV	Amount/portion	%DV		%DV		%DV
Total Fat 2 g	3%	**Cholest.** 0 mg	0%	**Total Carb.** 21 g	7%	Vitamin A	0%	Calcium	2%
Sat. Fat 1 g	2%	**Sodium** 216 mg	9%	Fiber 6 g	25%	Vitamin C	0%	Iron	12%
Protein 7 g				Sugars 3 g					

Percent Daily Values (%DV) are based on a 2000-calorie diet.

Note
- Seasonings for lima beans: basil, chives, dill, marjoram, oregano, sage, savory, tarragon, thyme, pimiento, mushrooms, onion butter, sour cream.

Variations
- **Baked Lima Beans and Peas.** Thaw 5 lb frozen baby lima beans and 5 lb frozen peas. Combine with 2 Tbsp dried basil, 1 oz (1½ Tbsp) salt, ½ tsp cracked black pepper, and 16 green onions, sliced. Place in baking pan. Sprinkle with 1 cup water and dot with 4–6 oz margarine. Cover and bake at 325°F for 45 minutes. Stir occasionally.
- **Succotash.** Use 5 lb lima beans and 5 lb frozen or canned whole kernel corn. Season with 4 oz margarine.

BAKED LIMA BEANS

Yield: 50 portions or 2 pans 12 × 20 × 2 inches   *Portion:* 5 oz
Oven: 350°F   *Bake:* 1 hour

Ingredient	Amount	Procedure
Lima beans, dry, large Water, boiling	6 lb (AP) 1 gal	Wash beans (p. 826). Add boiling water. Cover. Let stand 1 hour or longer. Cook beans in the same water until tender, about 1 hour.
Pimiento, chopped Salt Molasses	4 oz 1 oz (1½ Tbsp) 1 cup	Add seasonings to beans. Scale into two 12 × 20 × 2-inch pans, 8 lb 6 oz per pan.
Bacon, sliced	1 lb 8 oz	Place bacon on top of beans. Bake at 350°F until top is brown, about 1 hour.

Approximate nutritive values per portion   **Calories** 80

Amount/portion	%DV	Amount/portion	%DV	Amount/portion	%DV		%DV		%DV
Total Fat 2 g	3%	**Cholest.** 3 mg	1%	**Total Carb.** 12 g	4%	Vitamin A	0%	Calcium	5%
Sat. Fat 1 g	3%	**Sodium** 444 mg	18%	Fiber 0 g	0%	Vitamin C	5%	Iron	11%
Protein 4 g				Sugars 4 g					

Percent Daily Values (%DV) are based on a 2000-calorie diet.

Variations
- **Baked Lima Beans and Sausage.** Omit bacon. Place 6 lb link sausages on top of beans.
- **Boiled Lima Beans and Ham.** Omit bacon and seasonings. Add 5 lb diced ham to beans and simmer until tender.

RANCH-STYLE BEANS

Yield: 50 portions or 1 pan 12 × 20 × 4 inches   *Portion:* 5 oz
Oven: 300°F   *Bake:* 3–4 hours

Ingredient	Amount	Procedure
Beans, red or pinto, dried	5 lb	Wash beans (p. 826). Add boiling water. Cover and let stand for 1 hour or longer.
Water, boiling	1½ gal	
Bacon, 1-inch cubes	2 lb 8 oz	Add bacon to beans.
Water, cold	to cover	Add water to cover. Cook slowly until tender, about 1 hour.
Chile peppers	3–4 pods	Soak chile peppers in warm water. Remove and discard seeds. Add pods to beans.
Tomatoes, canned	2 qt	Add tomatoes and other seasonings.
Onions, sliced	8 oz	Cook slowly in kettle an additional 2 hours, or pour into a
Garlic, chopped	2 cloves	12 × 20 × 4-inch baking pan and bake at 300°F for
Salt	1 oz (1½ Tbsp)	2–3 hours.
Pepper, black	1 Tbsp	
Pepper, cayenne	Few grains	

Approximate nutritive values per portion   **Calories** 200

Amount/portion	%DV	Amount/portion	%DV	Amount/portion	%DV		%DV		%DV
Total Fat 4 g	6%	**Cholest.** 5 mg	2%	**Total Carb.** 31 g	10%	**Vitamin A**	2%	**Calcium**	7%
Sat. Fat 1 g	6%	**Sodium** 364 mg	15%	Fiber 0.4 g	2%	**Vitamin C**	19%	**Iron**	16%
Protein 12 g				Sugars 1 g					

Percent Daily Values (%DV) are based on a 2000-calorie diet.

Notes
- If chile peppers are not available, 1 oz chili powder may be substituted.
- Two No. 10 cans red beans may be substituted for dry beans. Reduce baking time to 1–2 hours.

BAKED BEANS

Yield: 50 portions or 1 pan 12 × 20 × 4 inches   *Portion:* 5 oz
Oven: 350°F   *Bake:* 3–4 hours

Ingredient	Amount	Procedure
Beans, navy or Great Northern, dried	5 lb (AP)	Wash beans (p. 826). Add boiling water and let stand 1 hour. Cook in same water until tender, about 1 hour. Add more water as necessary.
Water, boiling	1½ gal	
Salt	4 oz	Add remaining ingredients to beans.
Sugar, brown	6 oz	Pour into one 12 × 20 × 4-inch baking pan.
Dry mustard	1 tsp	Cover and bake at 350°F for 3–4 hours. Add more if needed during baking.
Vinegar, cider	2 Tbsp	during baking.
Molasses	1 cup	Uncover during last half hour of baking.
Catsup	2½ cups	
Bacon, cubed	1 lb	
Onion, chopped	3 oz	

Approximate nutritive values per portion   **Calories** 108

Amount/portion	%DV	Amount/portion	%DV	Amount/portion	%DV		%DV		%DV
Total Fat 1 g	2%	**Cholest.** 2 mg	1%	**Total Carb.** 20 g	7%	**Vitamin A**	1%	**Calcium**	8%
Sat. Fat 1 g	2%	**Sodium** 1059 mg	44%	Fiber 2 g	10%	**Vitamin C**	4%	**Iron**	13%
Protein 4 g				Sugars 5 g					

Percent Daily Values (%DV) are based on a 2000-calorie diet.

Variations
- **Baked Pork and Beans.** Use 2 No. 10 cans pork and beans. Fry 1 lb diced bacon until partially cooked. Add 4 oz chopped onion and cook until onions are tender. Pour off fat. Add bacon and onions to pork and beans. Stir in 1 cup catsup, ¼ cup vinegar, 4 oz brown sugar, and 1 Tbsp prepared mustard. Bake at 350°F for 1–2 hours.

- **Boston Baked Beans.** Omit catsup.

- **Trio Baked Beans.** Fry 2 lb diced bacon until partially cooked. Drain. Steam 1 lb 12 oz frozen lima beans. Add to bacon. Add 8 oz chopped onion, 2 lb 8 oz canned red beans, 2 lb 12 oz pork and beans, ½ cup molasses, 6 oz brown sugar, 3 cups catsup, ¼ cup vinegar, 1 Tbsp liquid smoke. Mix to blend. Scale into two 12 × 10 × 2-inch counter pans. Bake at 225°F for 3½ hours.

REFRIED BEANS

Yield: 50 portions   *Portion:* 4 oz

Ingredient	Amount	Procedure
Beans, pinto, dried Water, boiling	5 lb 1 gal	Wash beans. Add boiling water. Cover and let stand 1 hour or longer. Cook beans in the same water until tender, about 1 hour. Add more water if necessary. When beans are done, drain, reserving liquid for later step. Place cooked beans in mixer bowl and mash thoroughly.
Vegetable oil Onions, chopped	1½ cups 6 oz	Heat oil in frying pan. Add chopped onion. Cook until tender.
Chili powder Garlic powder Salt Hot pepper sauce Beef Stock (p. 791)	2 Tbsp 1 tsp 2 tsp Few drops 1 qt	Add seasonings to onion and mix thoroughly. Add beef stock and mix well. Add mashed beans, mixing until well blended. Turn mixture constantly to keep from burning. Bean liquid in small amounts may be added if mixture becomes too thick. Cook bean mixture for 45–60 minutes or until dry.

Approximate nutritive values per portion   **Calories** 132

Amount/portion	%DV	Amount/portion	%DV	Amount/portion	%DV		%DV		%DV
Total Fat 7 g	11%	**Cholest.** 0 mg	0%	**Total Carb.** 14 g	4%	**Vitamin A**	1%	**Calcium**	3%
Sat. Fat 2 g	9%	**Sodium** 528 mg	22%	Fiber 0.2 g	1%	**Vitamin C**	1%	**Iron**	8%
Protein 4 g				Sugars 0 g					

Percent Daily Values (%DV) are based on a 2000-calorie diet.

Notes
- Potentially hazardous food. *Food Safety Standards:* Hold food for service at an internal temperature above 140°F. Do not mix old product with new. Cool leftover product quickly (within 4 hours) to below 41°F. See p. 105 for cooling procedures. Reheat leftover product quickly (within 2 hours) to 165°F. Reheat product only once; discard if not used.
- 10 lb canned pinto beans may be substituted for dried beans. Drain beans and reserve liquid.

Variation
- **Spicy Black Beans.** Use 3 lb dried black beans. Combine 1½ lb beans and 1½ qt water in each of two 12 × 10 × 4-inch pans. Into each pan measure 1 Tbsp cumin, 1 tsp garlic powder, 1 tsp salt, and 1½ Tbsp chili powder. Stir into the beans. Steam for 50–60 minutes or until beans are tender but not mushy. Beans may also be cooked with seasonings in steam-jacketed kettle.

SEASONED FRESH BEETS

Yield: 50 portions   *Portion:* 3 oz

Ingredient	Amount	Procedure
Beets, fresh	14 lb (AP) (11 lb EP)	Cut off all but 2 inches of the beet tops. Wash beets and leave whole, with root ends attached. Boil or steam until tender (p. 825). Drain. Run cold water over beets. Slip off skins and remove root ends. Slice, dice, or cut into shoestring pieces.
Margarine, melted Salt	4 oz 1 oz (1½ Tbsp)	Pour margarine over cooked beets and sprinkle with salt. Heat to serving temperature.

Approximate nutritive values per portion   **Calories** 61

Amount/portion	%DV	Amount/portion	%DV	Amount/portion	%DV		%DV		%DV
Total Fat 2 g	3%	**Cholest.** 0 mg	0%	**Total Carb.** 10 g	3%	**Vitamin A**	1%	**Calcium**	1%
Sat. Fat 1 g	2%	**Sodium** 290 mg	12%	Fiber 0 g	0%	**Vitamin C**	5%	**Iron**	4%
Protein 2 g				Sugars 0 g					

Percent Daily Values (%DV) are based on a 2000-calorie diet.

Notes
- For canned beets, use two No. 10 cans. See p. 824 for heating directions.
- Seasonings for beets: allspice, bay leaves, caraway seed, cloves, dill, ginger, mint, marjoram, mustard seed, basil, nutmeg, onion, orange, sour cream, vinegar.

Variations
- **Beets in Sour Cream.** Grate fresh cooked beets and season with a mixture of 1½ cups lemon juice, 1½ Tbsp onion juice, 2 tsp salt, and 10 oz sugar. Toss lightly. Serve with a spoonful of sour cream on each portion.
- **Julienne Beets.** Cut 8 lb cooked beets into julienne strips. Season with a mixture of 4 oz margarine, 4 oz sugar, 4 tsp salt, and 1 cup lemon juice.
- **Pickled Beets.** See p. 697.
- **Roasted Beets.** Choose small beets. Preheat oven to 400°F. Trim off beet tops, leaving 1 inch of stem. Scrub beets to remove dirt. Put beets on a baking pan in a single layer. Roast until tender, approximately 1 hour. Remove beets from oven. Cool 30 minutes. Cut off top and root end. Peel. Heat before serving. Season with plain or flavored butter.

PARSLEY BUTTERED CARROTS

Yield: 50 portions   *Portion:* 3 oz

Ingredient	Amount	Procedure
Carrots, fresh	14 lb (AP) (10 lb EP)	Wash, trim, and peel carrots. Cut into desired shapes (slices, strips, cubes, or quarters). Steam or boil until just tender (p. 825).
Margarine, melted Salt Parsley, chopped	4 oz 1 oz (1½ Tbsp) 1 oz	Pour margarine over carrots and sprinkle with salt and parsley. If boiling carrots, add salt to the cooking water.

Approximate nutritive values per portion   **Calories** 56

Amount/portion	%DV	Amount/portion	%DV	Amount/portion	%DV		%DV		%DV
Total Fat 2 g	3%	**Cholest.** 0 mg	0%	**Total Carb.** 9 g	3%	**Vitamin A**	256%	**Calcium**	2%
Sat. Fat 1 g	2%	**Sodium** 245 mg	10%	Fiber 2 g	9%	**Vitamin C**	15%	**Iron**	2%
Protein 1 g				Sugars 6 g					

Percent Daily Values (%DV) are based on a 2000-calorie diet.

Note
- Seasonings for carrots: allspice, basil, caraway seed, cloves, cumin, curry powder, dill, fennel, ginger, mace, marjoram, mint, nutmeg, thyme, parsley.

Variations
- **Candied Carrots.** Cut carrots into 1-inch pieces. Cook until tender but not soft. Melt 8 oz margarine. Add 8 oz sugar and 1½ tsp salt. Add to carrots. Bake at 400°F for 15–20 minutes. Turn frequently. Carrots may be prepared, using a skillet instead of the oven. Melt butter, sugar, and salt in a skillet. Add carrots and cook until slightly browned and glazed.
- **Candied Carrots and Parsnips.** Use half carrots and half parsnips. Cook as for Candied Carrots. Season lightly with ground ginger.
- **Glazed Parsnips.** Peel parsnips. If parsnip cores are hard and woody, remove the core. Cut in strips and proceed as for Candied Carrots.
- **Lyonnaise Carrots.** Arrange cooked carrot strips in baking pan. Add 3 lb chopped onion that has been cooked until tender in 4 oz margarine. Bake at 350°F for 10–15 minutes or until vegetables are lightly browned. Just before serving, sprinkle with chopped parsley.
- **Marinated Carrots.** See p. 656.
- **Mint-Glazed Carrots.** Cut carrots into quarters lengthwise. Cook until almost tender. Drain. Melt 8 oz margarine, 8 oz sugar, 1½ tsp salt, and 1 cup mint jelly. Blend. Add carrots and simmer 5–10 minutes.
- **Savory Carrots.** Cook carrots in beef or chicken stock. When done, season with 4 oz melted margarine, salt and pepper, and ¼ cup lemon juice. Sprinkle with chopped parsley.
- **Sweet-Sour Carrots.** Add to cooked carrots a sauce made of 1½ qt vinegar, 2 lb 4 oz sugar, 2 Tbsp salt, and 12 oz melted margarine. Bake at 350°F for 15–20 minutes, or simmer until carrots and sauce are thoroughly heated.

CELERY AND CARROTS AMANDINE

Yield: 50 portions   *Portion:* 3 oz

Ingredient	Amount	Procedure
Celery	7 lb (AP) (5 lb EP)	Wash and trim celery. Cut into diagonal slices. Steam or boil (p. 825).
Salt	2 tsp	Sprinkle with salt. If boiling the celery, add salt to cooking water.
Carrots, fresh	7 lb (AP) (5 lb EP)	Wash and peel carrots. Cut into strips. Steam or boil until tender-crisp. Drain.
Salt	2 tsp	Sprinkle with salt. If boiling the carrots, add salt to the cooking water.
Margarine	8 oz	Heat margarine in frying pan.
Almonds, blanched, slivered	8 oz	Add almonds and brown lightly.
Lemon juice	⅓ cup	Remove almonds from heat. Add lemon juice. Combine vegetables. Pour almond mixture over and stir carefully to mix seasoning with vegetables.

Approximate nutritive values per portion   **Calories** 86

Amount/portion	%DV	Amount/portion	%DV	Amount/portion	%DV		%DV		%DV
Total Fat 6 g	10%	**Cholest.** 0 mg	0%	**Total Carb.** 7 g	2%	**Vitamin A**	129%	**Calcium**	4%
Sat. Fat 1 g	5%	**Sodium** 269 mg	11%	Fiber 2 g	9%	**Vitamin C**	13%	**Iron**	3%
Protein 2 g				Sugars 4 g					

Percent Daily Values (%DV) are based on a 2000-calorie diet.

Note   • Seasonings for celery: fresh basil, parsley, thyme.

Variation   • **Creole Celery.** Cook 5 lb diced celery until partially done. Add 1 lb chopped onions and 4 oz chopped green pepper that have been sautéed in 6 oz margarine. Add 2 No. 10 cans tomatoes and 1½ tsp salt. Cook until tender.

SEASONED CAULIFLOWER

Yield: 50 portions   *Portion:* 3 oz

Ingredient	Amount	Procedure
Cauliflower, fresh	16 lb (AP) (10 lb EP)	Wash cauliflower. Remove outer leaves and woody stem. Break into florets. Steam or boil cauliflower (p. 825).
Margarine, melted Salt	4 oz 1 oz (1½ Tbsp)	Pour margarine over cooked cauliflower and sprinkle with salt. If boiling the cauliflower, add salt to the cooking water.

Approximate nutritive values per portion   **Calories** 49

Amount/portion	%DV	Amount/portion	%DV	Amount/portion	%DV		%DV		%DV
Total Fat 2 g	4%	**Cholest.** 0 mg	0%	**Total Carb.** 6 g	2%	**Vitamin A**	0%	**Calcium**	2%
Sat. Fat 1 g	2%	**Sodium** 234 mg	10%	Fiber 0 g	0%	**Vitamin C**	107%	**Iron**	2%
Protein 3 g				Sugars 0 g					

Percent Daily Values (%DV) are based on a 2000-calorie diet.

Note
- Seasonings for cauliflower: caraway seed, celery salt, dill, mace, tarragon, buttered crumbs, cheese, lemon juice.

Variations
- **Cauliflower with Almond Butter.** Season freshly cooked cauliflower with 12 oz slivered almonds that have been browned in 8 oz margarine.
- **Cauliflower with Cheese Sauce.** Pour 3 qt Cheese Sauce (p. 749) over cooked fresh cauliflower.
- **Cauliflower with Peas.** Combine 6 lb freshly cooked cauliflower with 4 lb cooked frozen peas. Season with 4 oz melted margarine.
- **Creamed Cauliflower.** Pour 3 qt white sauce over cooked cauliflower.
- **French Fried Cauliflower.** See p. 851.

SEASONED WHOLE KERNEL CORN

Yield: 50 portions   *Portion:* 3 oz

Ingredient	Amount	Procedure
Whole kernel corn, frozen	10 lb	Steam or boil corn (p. 825). Do not add salt until after cooking to prevent toughening and discoloring of corn kernels.
Margarine, melted Salt	4 oz 1 oz (1½ Tbsp)	Pour margarine over corn. Stir in salt.

Approximate nutritive values per portion   **Calories** 90

Amount/portion	%DV	Amount/portion	%DV	Amount/portion	%DV		%DV		%DV
Total Fat 2 g	3%	**Cholest.** 0 mg	0%	**Total Carb.** 19 g	6%	**Vitamin A**	2%	**Calcium**	0%
Sat. Fat 0 g	0%	**Sodium** 218 mg	9%	Fiber 2 g	8%	**Vitamin C**	3%	**Iron**	1%
Protein 3 g				Sugars 2 g					

Percent Daily Values (%DV) are based on a 2000-calorie diet.

Notes
- Seasonings for corn: cilantro, curry, green pepper, rosemary, savory, thyme.
- For canned corn, use two No. 10 cans. See p. 824 for heating instructions.

Variations
- **Corn in Cream.** Add 1¼ qt light cream (half-and-half), 6 oz margarine or butter, 1½ Tbsp salt, and 1 Tbsp white pepper to cooked corn. Bring just to boiling point and serve immediately.
- **Corn O'Brien.** Add 1 lb chopped bacon, 12 oz chopped green pepper, and 12 oz chopped onion that have been cooked together. Just before serving, add 3 oz chopped pimiento, salt, and pepper.
- **Creamed Whole Kernel Corn.** Combine 2 cups whipping cream, 2 oz granulated sugar, and 1 oz (1½ Tbsp) salt. Bring to a boil. Add 1 cup whipping cream and 1½ oz cornstarch, which have been mixed with a wire whip until smooth. Stir and cook until thick and bubbly. Cook 2 minutes longer. Stir into 10 lb cooked frozen whole kernel corn.

SCALLOPED CORN

Yield: 50 portions or 2 pans 12 × 20 × 2 inches   *Portion:* 4 oz
Oven: 350°F   *Bake:* 35–40 minutes

Ingredient	Amount	Procedure
Corn, cream style Milk Salt Pepper, black	2 No. 10 cans 1 qt 1 Tbsp ½ tsp	Mix corn, milk, and seasonings.
Cracker crumbs Margarine, melted	14 oz 12 oz	Combine crumbs and margarine. Place alternate layers of buttered crumbs and corn mixture in two 12 × 20 × 2-inch baking pans. Bake at 350°F for 35–40 minutes.

Approximate nutritive values per portion   **Calories** 180

Amount/portion	%DV	Amount/portion	%DV	Amount/portion	%DV		%DV		%DV
Total Fat 8 g	12%	**Cholest.** 3 mg	1%	**Total Carb.** 28 g	9%	**Vitamin A**	3%	**Calcium**	4%
Sat. Fat 2 g	9%	**Sodium** 641 mg	27%	Fiber 1 g	6%	**Vitamin C**	9%	**Iron**	4%
Protein 4 g				Sugars 1 g					

Percent Daily Values (%DV) are based on a 2000-calorie diet.

Note
- 6 oz chopped green pepper and 6 oz chopped pimiento may be added.

CORN PUDDING

Yield: 50 portions or 2 pans 12 × 20 × 2 inches   *Portion:* 5 oz
Oven: 325°F   *Bake:* 40–45 minutes

Ingredient	Amount	Procedure
Corn, whole kernel, frozen	9 lb	Thaw corn.
Egg yolks, beaten Milk Margarine, melted Salt Pepper, white	24 (1 lb) 3 qt 6 oz 2 Tbsp 1 tsp	Combine corn and all ingredients except egg whites.
Egg whites	24 (1 lb 10 oz)	Beat egg whites until stiff but not dry. Fold into corn mixture. Pour into two 12 × 20 × 2-inch baking pans. Place in pans of hot water. Bake at 325°F for approximately 40–45 minutes or until internal temperature reaches 180°F.

Approximate nutritive values per portion   **Calories** 398

Amount/portion	%DV	Amount/portion	%DV	Amount/portion	%DV		%DV		%DV
Total Fat 11 g	17%	**Cholest.** 124 mg	41%	**Total Carb.** 64 g	21%	**Vitamin A**	24%	**Calcium**	9%
Sat. Fat 3 g	16%	**Sodium** 373 mg	16%	Fiber 9 g	36%	**Vitamin C**	0%	**Iron**	14%
Protein 13 g				Sugars 3 g					

Percent Daily Values (%DV) are based on a 2000-calorie diet.

Note   ● Potentially hazardous food. *Food Safety Standards:* Hold food for service at an internal temperature above 140°F. Do not mix old product with new. Cool leftover product quickly (within 4 hours) to below 41°F. See p. 105 for cooling procedures. Reheat leftover product quickly (within 2 hours) to 165°F. Reheat product only once; discard if not used.

BAKED EGGPLANT

Yield: 50 portions   *Portion:* 3 oz
Oven: 375°F   *Bake:* 30 minutes

Ingredient	Amount	Procedure
Eggplant	12 lb (AP) (10 lb EP)	Peel eggplant and cut into ½-inch slices. Sprinkle with salt and let stand for 30 minutes. Rinse, drain, and pat dry with paper towels.
Eggs, beaten Milk	6 (10 oz) 2 cups	Combine beaten eggs and milk.
Flour, all-purpose Bread crumbs	1 lb 1 lb 8 oz	Dip eggplant slices in flour, then in egg mixture. Roll in crumbs.
Margarine, melted	8 oz	Place on greased baking sheets. Sprinkle with melted margarine. Bake at 375°F for 30 minutes.

Approximate nutritive values per portion   **Calories** 157

Amount/portion	%DV	Amount/portion	%DV	Amount/portion	%DV		%DV		%DV
Total Fat 6 g	8%	**Cholest.** 25 mg	8%	**Total Carb.** 23 g	8%	**Vitamin A**	3%	**Calcium**	3%
Sat. Fat 1 g	6%	**Sodium** 158 mg	7%	Fiber 1 g	3%	**Vitamin C**	2%	**Iron**	7%
Protein 4 g				Sugars 1 g					

Percent Daily Values (%DV) are based on a 2000-calorie diet.

Note
- Seasonings for eggplant: basil, garlic, marjoram, onion, oregano, cheese, tomato, parsley.

Variations
- **Eggplant Parmesan.** Prepare Italian Tomato Sauce (p. 762). Prepare 10 lb AP eggplant (yield 8 lb EP) and cook as directed for Baked Eggplant. (Frozen eggplant cutlets may be substituted for fresh eggplant.) Cheeses needed: 5 lb shredded mozzarella and 1 lb 4 oz grated Parmesan. Layer eggplant, sauce, and cheeses as follows into each of four 12 × 10 × 2-inch baking pans:

  1½ cups sauce

  1 lb cooked eggplant cutlets

  8 oz shredded mozzarella cheese

  2 oz Parmesan cheese

  2½ cups sauce

  1 lb cooked eggplant cutlets

  8 oz shredded mozzarella cheese

  3 oz Parmesan cheese

  2½ cups sauce

  4 oz shredded mozzarella cheese

  Bake at 350°F for 25–30 minutes or until heated through. To serve, cut 4 × 3.

- **Sautéed Eggplant.** Prepare eggplant as in recipe. Sauté in margarine until tender.

GRILLED EGGPLANT PEPERONATA ON GARLIC BASIL FUSILLI

Yield: 50 portions   *Portion:* 2 slices eggplant, 6 oz pasta

Ingredient	Amount	Procedure
Peperonata (p. 854)	50 portions	Prepare peperonata according to recipe on p. 854. Reserve for later step.
Eggplant, sliced ¾-inch thick (peeled or unpeeled) Salt Black pepper	14 lbs EP 1 Tbsp 2 tsp	Salt and pepper each side of eggplant slices. Lightly grease tilting or other fry pan. (See note for Seasoned Oil) Heat fry pan and place eggplant slices in single layer into pan. Cook 8–10 minutes until tender but not mushy. Turn once during cooking. Add more oil as needed. Place eggplant in a single layer in a lightly oiled 12 × 20 × 2-inch pan. Portion 1–2 oz peperonata (reserved from earlier step) onto each eggplant slice. Cover and keep warm.
Fusilli Water Salt	5 lbs 5 gal 5 oz	Cook pasta according to directions on p. 561. Drain. Pan in 10 × 12 × 4-inch counter pans (6 lb/pan).
Olive oil Garlic, minced Basil, minced (fresh)	¾ cup 1 tsp 2 tsp	Mix olive oil, garlic, and basil. Drizzle pasta lightly with seasoned oil (2 oz/pan). Toss lightly to coat. Keep hot.
Parmesan cheese, freshly grated	2 lb	Serve 4 oz pasta on plate with two slices of eggplant on top. When serving eggplant, take care to keep peperonata topping on top of eggplant. Serve eggplant topped with grated cheese.

Approximate nutritive values per portion   **Calories** 370

Amount/portion	%DV	Amount/portion	%DV	Amount/portion	%DV		%DV		%DV
Total Fat 14.3 g	**22%**	**Cholest.** 14.3 mg	**5%**	**Total Carb.** 46 g	**15%**	**Vitamin A**	**25%**	**Calcium**	**28%**
Sat. Fat 4.7 g	**23%**	**Sodium** 1670 mg	**70%**	Fiber 5.1 g	**20%**	**Vitamin C**	**108%**	**Iron**	**15%**
Protein 15.3 g				Sugars 5.3 g					

Percent Daily Values (%DV) are based on a 2000-calorie diet.

Notes

- Potentially hazardous food. *Food Safety Standards:* Hold food for service at an internal temperature above 140°F. Do not mix old product with new. Cool leftover product quickly (within 2 hours) to 70°F and then (within an additional 4 hours) to 41°F. See p. 105 for cooling procedures. Reheat leftover product quickly (within 2 hours) to 165°F. Reheat product only once; discard if not used.

- **Seasoned Oil:** Mix equal parts of Garlic Oil, Olive Oil, and Salad Oil. Add a small amount of dried basil leaves if desired.

CREOLE EGGPLANT

Yield: 50 portions or 2 pans 12 × 20 × 2 inches   *Portion:* 3 oz
Oven: 350°F   *Bake:* 30 minutes

Ingredient	Amount	Procedure
Eggplant	10 lb (AP) (8 lb EP)	Peel eggplant and cut into 1-inch cubes. Sprinkle with salt and let stand for 30 minutes.
Water, boiling	1½ gal	Rinse and drain.
Salt	2 Tbsp	Steam or boil (p. 825).
Margarine, melted	1 lb	Cook onion, green pepper, and celery in margarine until tender.
Onion, chopped	1 lb 8 oz	
Green pepper, coarsely chopped	12 oz	
Celery, coarsely chopped	1 lb	
Tomatoes, diced, canned	1 No. 10 can	Combine tomatoes and seasonings with eggplant and other ingredients.
Salt	2 Tbsp	Pour into two 12 × 20 × 2-inch baking pans.
Pepper, black	2 tsp	
Sugar, granulated	2 Tbsp	
Bread crumbs	12 oz	Top with buttered crumbs.
Margarine, melted	8 oz	Bake at 350°F for 30 minutes.

Approximate nutritive values per portion   **Calories** 166

Amount/portion	%DV	Amount/portion	%DV	Amount/portion	%DV		%DV		%DV
Total Fat 12 g	18%	**Cholest.** 0 mg	0%	**Total Carb.** 15 g	5%	**Vitamin A**	8%	**Calcium**	4%
Sat. Fat 2 g	11%	**Sodium** 800 mg	33%	Fiber 1 g	5%	**Vitamin C**	29%	**Iron**	5%
Protein 2 g				Sugars 3 g					

Percent Daily Values (%DV) are based on a 2000-calorie diet.

Variation • **Eggplant Tomato Bake.** Peel eggplant and slice 1 inch thick. Steam or parboil until fork-tender. Place on baking sheets in a single layer. Sprinkle with salt and pepper. Cook 1 lb 8 oz chopped onion and 3 cloves garlic, minced, in 1½ cups vegetable oil and 12 oz margarine. Add to 5 lb peeled chopped fresh tomatoes, 1 cup chopped parsley, ¼ tsp oregano, ½ tsp thyme, 1 tsp basil, and 1 lb bread crumbs. Pile mixture on individual slices of eggplant. Sprinkle grated Swiss cheese (2 lb) over top. Bake at 350°F until eggplant is hot and cheese is melted.

ROASTED PORTABELLA MUSHROOM

Yield: 50 portions   *Portion:* 1 mushroom
Oven: 375°F

Ingredient	Amount	Procedure
Portabella mushroom (see Notes)	50 mushrooms (approx. 18 lb)	Clean mushrooms. Dry well.
Balsamic Vinegar Marinade (p. 786)	1 gal	Brush both sides of mushrooms with Balsamic Vinegar Marinade.
		Place mushrooms gill side down on lightly oiled baking pan.
		Roast for 10–12 minutes, until tender.
		After baking, brush mushrooms with marinade.

Notes
- Potentially hazardous food. *Food Safety Standards:* Hold food for service at an internal temperature above 140°F. Do not mix old product with new. Cool leftover product quickly (within 4 hours) to below 41°F. See p. 105 for cooling procedures. Reheat leftover product quickly (within 2 hours) to 165°F. Reheat product only once, discard if not used.

- The gills from the under side of the mushroom cap may be removed before baking.

Variations
- **Portabella Peperonata on Orzo Pilaf.** Prepare Orzo Pilaf (p. 562) (delete mushrooms). Prepare Peperonata (p. 854). Serve one Portabella Mushroom on a bed of Orzo Pilaf topped with 2 oz Peperonata.

BAKED ONIONS

Yield: 50 portions   *Portion:* 1 4-oz onion
Oven: 400°F   *Bake:* 20–30 minutes

Ingredient	Amount	Procedure
Onions, 4 oz, Bermuda or Spanish	50 (15 lb AP)	Peel onions and steam (p. 825) until tender. Place in greased baking pans.
Salt	1 Tbsp	Sprinkle salt and buttered crumbs on onions.
Bread crumbs	8 oz	
Margarine, melted	8 oz	
Chicken or Beef Stock (pp. 790, 791)	1 qt	Pour stock around onions. Bake at 400°F for 20–30 minutes.

Approximate nutritive values per portion   **Calories** 103

Amount/portion	%DV	Amount/portion	%DV	Amount/portion	%DV		%DV		%DV
Total Fat 4 g	6%	**Cholest.** 0 mg	0%	**Total Carb.** 15 g	5%	**Vitamin A**	1%	**Calcium**	3%
Sat. Fat 1 g	4%	**Sodium** 271 mg	11%	Fiber 2 g	10%	**Vitamin C**	14%	**Iron**	2%
Protein 2 g				Sugars 3 g					

Percent Daily Values (%DV) are based on a 2000-calorie diet.

Notes

- Potentially hazardous food. *Food Safety Standards:* Hold food for service at an internal temperature above 140°F. Do not mix old product with new. Cool leftover product quickly (within 4 hours) to below 41°F. See p. 105 for cooling procedures. Reheat leftover product quickly (within 2 hours) to 165°F. Reheat product only once; discard if not used.

- Onions may be cut into thick slices.

- Seasonings for onions: basil, caraway seed, marjoram, oregano, rosemary, sage, or thyme.

Variations

- **Creamed Pearl Onions.** Cook 12 lb 8 oz small unpeeled white onions (p. 825), then peel. Add 2 qt Medium White Sauce (p. 749) to which 4 oz additional margarine has been added. Garnish with paprika.

- **Glazed Onions.** Mix 1 lb 12 oz brown sugar, 2 cups water, 8 oz margarine, and ½ tsp salt. Pour over cooked onions and bake.

- **Onion Casserole.** Cook 10 lb small pearl onions (p. 825). Combine with 10 oz chopped walnuts, 8 oz pimiento strips, and eight 10½-oz cans cream of mushroom or cream of chicken soup. Cover with 6 oz shredded cheddar or Swiss cheese. Bake at 400°F for approximately 30 minutes.

PORTABELLA PEPPER STEAK OVER SOFT POLENTA

Yield: 50 portions   *Portion:* 5 oz mushrooms, 4 oz soft polenta

Ingredient	Amount	Procedure
Portabella mushrooms, stem trimmed (see Note)	3 lb 8 oz	Slice mushrooms into ⅓-inch slices and set aside for a later step.
Olive Oil	5 oz	Heat oil to 350°F in a tilting fry pan.
Onions, ½ inch dice	4 lb 5 oz EP	Sauté onions for approximately 2 min until translucent.
Green peppers, 1 inch squares	3 lb EP	Add peppers and garlic. Sauté 3–5 minutes or until peppers just begin to soften.
Garlic, minced	8 oz EP	
Soy sauce	10 oz	Add sauces, vinegar, tomatoes, black pepper, and roasted peppers. Mix and heat to 170°F.
Red pepper sauce	4½ tsp	Add mushrooms reserved from earlier step. Heat to 170 °F.
Black pepper	2¾ tsp	
Balsamic vinegar	4 Tbsp	Take up into 12 × 10 × 4-inch pans.
Roma tomatoes, chopped (fresh)	3 lb EP	
Roasted red peppers (p. 854)	2 lb	
Soft polenta	Recipe p. 625	Serve mushroom mixture over soft polenta. (see Note)

Approximate nutritive values per portion   **Calories** 170

Amount/portion	%DV	Amount/portion	%DV	Amount/portion	%DV		%DV		%DV
Total Fat 7.9 g	12%	**Cholest.** 0 mg	0%	**Total Carb.** 21.5 g	7%	**Vitamin A**	32%	**Calcium**	3%
Sat. Fat 1 g	5%	**Sodium** 535 mg	22%	Fiber 3.7 g	15%	**Vitamin C**	111%	**Iron**	7%
Protein 5 g				Sugars 3.1 g					

Percent Daily Values (%DV) are based on a 2000-calorie diet.

Notes

- Potentially hazardous food. *Food Safety Standards:* Hold food for service at an internal temperature above 140 °F. Do not mix old product with new. Cool leftover product quickly (within 2 hours) to 70 °F and then (within an additional 4 hours) to 41 °F. See p. 105 for cooling procedures. Reheat leftover product quickly (within 2 hours) to 165 °F. Reheat product only once; discard if not used.
- Increase mushrooms to 4 lb if brown gills are removed.
- Mushroom Pepper Steak may be served over a string pasta, rice, or grilled/baked polenta.

FRENCH FRIED ONION RINGS

Yield: 50 portions   *Portion:* 3 oz
Deep-fat fryer: 350°F   *Fry:* 3–4 minutes

Ingredient	Amount	Procedure
Onions, large round	10 lb (AP) (8 lb EP)	Peel onions and cut crosswise into ¼-inch slices. Separate into rings.
Eggs, beaten Milk	6 (10 oz) 2 cups	Combine eggs and milk.
Flour, all-purpose Baking powder Salt	12 oz 2 tsp 1½ tsp	Combine dry ingredients. Add to egg-milk mixture to make a batter. Dip onion rings in batter and fry in deep fat for 3–4 minutes. Drain.

Approximate nutritive values per portion plus frying oil   **Calories** 67

Amount/portion	%DV	Amount/portion	%DV	Amount/portion	%DV		%DV		%DV
Total Fat 1 g	2%	**Cholest.** 25 mg	8%	**Total Carb.** 12 g	4%	**Vitamin A**	1%	**Calcium**	3%
Sat. Fat 1 g	2%	**Sodium** 90 mg	4%	Fiber 1 g	6%	**Vitamin C**	7%	**Iron**	3%
Protein 3 g				Sugars 2 g					

Percent Daily Values (%DV) are based on a 2000-calorie diet.

Variations

- **Deep-Fat Fried Bananas.** Cut peeled bananas into 2-inch pieces. Sprinkle with lemon juice and powdered sugar. Let stand 30 minutes. Dip in batter and fry at 370°F for 1–3 minutes.

- **French Fried Cauliflower.** Dip 10 lb cold cooked cauliflower into batter and fry at 370°F for 3–4 minutes.

- **French Fried Eggplant.** Peel and cut 13 lb AP eggplant as for French Fried Potatoes (p. 857). Dip in batter and fry at 370°F for 5–7 minutes. Eggplant may be dipped in egg and crumb mixture (p. 99) and fried. Eggplant discolors quickly, so it should be placed in cold water if not breaded immediately.

- **French Fried Mushrooms.** Clean small, uniform-size mushrooms by brushing or rinsing. Do not soak. Dip in batter and fry at 370°F for 4–6 minutes.

- **French Fried Zucchini Sticks.** Cut unpeeled zucchini lengthwise into strips about ½ inch thick. Dip in batter and fry at 370°F for 4–6 minutes.

SEASONED BLACK-EYED PEAS

Yield: 50 portions   *Portion:* 4 oz

Ingredient	Amount	Procedure
Bacon	12 oz	Cut bacon into 1-inch pieces. Cook in a steam-jacketed kettle until crisp.
Onions, chopped	5 oz	Add vegetables and seasonings to bacon. Sauté until onions and garlic are fragrant.
Garlic, minced	1 tsp	
Parsley (fresh), chopped	1 cup	
Bay leaf	4 leaves	
Salt	1⅓ Tbsp	
Black pepper	½ tsp	
Black-eyed peas (frozen)	12 lb	Add peas to vegetable mixture
Water	3½ quart	Add water to barely cover peas. Simmer peas until tender (45–50 min) adding water as necessary.

Approximate nutritive values per portion   **Calories** 135

Amount/portion	%DV	Amount/portion	%DV	Amount/portion	%DV		%DV		%DV
Total Fat 4.2 g	6%	**Cholest.** 4.4 mg	1%	**Total Carb.** 20.4 g	7%	**Vitamin A**	19%	**Calcium**	14%
Sat. Fat 1.5 g	8%	**Sodium** 232 mg	10%	Fiber 5.4 g	22%	**Vitamin C**	7%	**Iron**	7%
Protein 3.8 g				Sugars .1 g					

Percent Daily Values (%DV) are based on a 2000-calorie diet.

Notes

- Potentially hazardous food. *Food Safety Standards:* Hold food for service at an internal temperature above 140°F. Do not mix old product with new. Cool leftover product quickly (within 2 hours) to 70°F and then (within an additional 4 hours) to 41°F. See p. 105 for cooling procedures. Reheat leftover product quickly (within 2 hours) to 165°F. Reheat product only once; discard if not used.

SEASONED PEAS

Yield: 50 portions   *Portion:* 3 oz

Ingredient	Amount	Procedure
Peas, frozen	10 lb	Steam or boil peas (p. 825).
Margarine, melted Salt	4 oz 1 oz (1½ Tbsp)	Pour margarine over cooked peas and sprinkle with salt. If boiling the peas, add salt to the cooking water.

Approximate nutritive values per portion   **Calories** 87

Amount/portion	%DV	Amount/portion	%DV	Amount/portion	%DV		%DV		%DV
Total Fat 2 g	3%	**Cholest.** 0 mg	0%	**Total Carb.** 13 g	4%	**Vitamin A**	6%	**Calcium**	2%
Sat. Fat 1 g	2%	**Sodium** 292 mg	12%	Fiber 3 g	14%	**Vitamin C**	14%	**Iron**	7%
Protein 5 g				Sugars 5 g					

Percent Daily Values (%DV) are based on a 2000-calorie diet.

Notes
- If using canned peas, heat 2 No. 10 cans. See p. 824.
- For fresh peas, use 25 lb AP. Shell and rinse. Steam or boil (p. 825).
- Seasonings for peas: basil, dill, marjoram, mint, oregano, rosemary, sage, savory, mushrooms, water chestnuts, onions.

Variations
- **Creamed Peas with New Potatoes.** Combine 7 lb freshly cooked new potatoes and 5 lb cooked frozen peas with 3 qt Medium White Sauce (p. 749).
- **Green Peas and Sliced New Turnips.** Combine 5 lb frozen peas, cooked, with 3 lb new turnips, sliced and cooked. Add 4 oz melted margarine and salt to taste.
- **Green Peas with Pearl Onions.** Combine 7 lb 8 oz frozen peas, cooked, and 3 lb pearl onions, cooked. Add 4 oz melted margarine or 2 qt Medium White Sauce (p. 749).
- **Green Peas with Mushrooms.** Add 2 lb fresh mushrooms, sliced and sautéed in 8 oz margarine, to 10 lb cooked frozen peas.
- **Green Peas with Lemon-Mint Butter.** Cream 1 lb butter or margarine, ¼ cup lemon juice, and 1 tsp grated lemon peel. Add ½ cup finely chopped fresh mint. The lemon-mint butter can be made ahead and stored in the refrigerator. When ready to use, melt and pour over hot peas.

ROASTED BELL PEPPERS

Yield: 1 lb

Ingredient	Amount	Procedure
Bell peppers (see Notes)	4 large	Stem peppers and remove seeds and ribs. Cut in half lengthwise. Flatten peppers slightly. Lay peppers skin side up on foil-lined baking sheet. Broil 4 inches from heat until skins are charred black, 12–15 minutes. Place peppers in a bowl and cover tightly with plastic wrap. Let steam for 15–20 minutes. Peel off charred skin.
Olive oil (optional) Lemon juice (optional)	2 Tbsp 2 tsp	Drizzle oil and lemon juice over peppers. Use immediately or refrigerate.
		Serve on sandwiches, in sauces, as a topping for focaccia, etc.

Notes
- All colors of bell peppers may be roasted. Red, yellow, and orange are often specified in recipes because they remain colorful after roasting.
- Roasted peppers may be kept frozen, and thawed as needed.

PEPERONATA

Yield: 50 portions   *Portion:* 2 oz

Ingredient	Amount	Procedure
Olive oil Onion, sliced Garlic, minced	8 oz 1 lb (EP) 4 cloves	Heat olive oil in fry pan or steam-jacketed kettle. Sauté onions until golden and translucent. Add garlic and cook until tender, about 3 minutes.
Red bell peppers, julienne strips	1 lb 12 oz (EP)	Add bell peppers and cook until just beginning to soften.
Yellow bell peppers, julienne strips	1 lb 12 oz (EP)	
Tomatoes, chopped (canned) Red wine vinegar Salt Pepper, black Red pepper, crushed Parsley, coarsely chopped (fresh)	1 lb 8 oz ½ cup 1 tsp 1 Tbsp ¼ tsp 1 oz	Add tomatoes, vinegar, spices, and parsley. Cook only until juices evaporate, to 150–160°F. (Note: Peppers should be tender-crisp and brightly colored.) Serve as an accompaniment to sandwiches, with pasta, or as a garnish.

Approximate nutritive values per portion   **Calories** 55

Amount/portion	%DV	Amount/portion	%DV	Amount/portion	%DV		%DV		%DV
Total Fat 5 g	7%	**Cholest.** 0 mg	0%	**Total Carb.** 3.5 g	1%	**Vitamin A**	10%	**Calcium**	1%
Sat. Fat 0.6 g	3%	**Sodium** 76 mg	3%	Fiber 0.8 g	3%	**Vitamin C**	100%	**Iron**	2%
Protein 0.7 g				Sugars 1 g					

Percent Daily Values (%DV) are based on a 2000-calorie diet.

Notes
- Potentially hazardous food. *Food Safety Standards:* Hold food for service at an internal temperature above 140°F. Do not mix old product with new. Cool leftover product quickly (within 4 hours) to below 41°F. See p. 105 for cooling procedures. Reheat leftover product quickly (within 2 hours) to 165°F. Reheat product only once, discard if not used.

BAKED POTATOES

Yield: 50 portions   *Portion:* 1 potato
Oven: 400°F   *Bake:* 1–1½ hours

Ingredient	Amount	Procedure
Baking potatoes, uniform size	50	Scrub potatoes and remove blemishes.
Shortening	4 oz	Rub or brush lightly with shortening. Place on baking sheets. Bake at 400°F for 1–1½ hours or until tender.

Approximate nutritive values per portion   **Calories** 165

Amount/portion	%DV	Amount/portion	%DV	Amount/portion	%DV		%DV		%DV
Total Fat 2 g	4%	**Cholest.** 0 mg	0%	**Total Carb.** 34 g	11%	**Vitamin A**	0%	**Calcium**	0%
Sat. Fat 1 g	3%	**Sodium** 8 mg	1%	Fiber 4 g	15%	**Vitamin C**	33%	**Iron**	3%
Protein 3 g				Sugars 3 g					

Percent Daily Values (%DV) are based on a 2000-calorie diet.

Notes
- Potentially hazardous food. *Food Safety Standards:* Hold food for service at an internal temperature above 140°F. Do not mix old product with new. Cool leftover product quickly (within 4 hours) to below 41°F. See p. 105 for cooling procedures. Reheat leftover product quickly (within 2 hours) to 165°F. Reheat product only once; discard if not used.
- Select a long, mealy-type potato, such as russet.

Variations
- **Baked Potato with Toppings.** Prepare potatoes and bake (see recipe). Serve with one of the following toppings and one or more of the accompaniments: *Toppings* include Cheese Sauce (p. 749), 3 oz; Chili con Carne (p. 800), 3 oz; Creamed Chicken (p. 545), Ham (p. 521), or Sausage (p. 525), 3 oz; Nacho Sauce (p. 236), 3 oz; sour cream, 1 oz. *Accompaniments* include Guacamole (p. 235), chopped broccoli, shredded cheese, sliced mushrooms, chopped green onions, chopped chives, sliced black olives, chopped ham or chicken, chopped lettuce, chopped tomatoes, crumbled cooked bacon, slivered almonds.
- **Broccoli Cheese-Topped Potato.** See p. 749 for Cheese Broccoli Sauce. Serve over baked potato.
- **Cheese-Topped Potato.** Whip 1 lb softened margarine. Add 2 lb sour cream and mix thoroughly. Fold in 1 lb finely shredded American cheese and 6 oz finely chopped green onions. Serve over baked potato.
- **Stuffed Baked Potato.** Cut hot baked potatoes into halves lengthwise. If potatoes are small, cut a slice from one side. Scoop out contents. Mash, season with 2 Tbsp salt, 1 tsp white pepper, 8 oz melted margarine, and 3–4 cups hot milk. Beat until light and fluffy. Pile lightly into shells, leaving tops rough. Sprinkle with paprika or Parmesan cheese, if desired. Bake at 425°F until potatoes are hot and lightly browned, about 30 minutes.

MASHED POTATOES

Yield: 50 portions   *Portion:* 5 oz

Ingredient	Amount	Procedure
Potatoes	15 lb (AP) (12 lb EP)	Peel and eye potatoes. Cut into uniform-size pieces. Steam or boil (p. 825). When done, drain and place in mixer bowl. Mash, using wire whip attachment, on low speed until there are no lumps. Whip on high speed about 2 minutes.
Milk, hot Margarine Salt	2–2½ qt 8 oz 2 oz (3 Tbsp)	Add hot milk, margarine, and salt. Whip on high speed until light and creamy.

Approximate nutritive values per portion   **Calories** 158

Amount/portion	%DV	Amount/portion	%DV	Amount/portion	%DV		%DV		%DV
Total Fat 5 g	8%	**Cholest.** 5 mg	2%	**Total Carb.** 25 g	8%	**Vitamin A**	2%	**Calcium**	5%
Sat. Fat 2 g	8%	**Sodium** 451 mg	19%	Fiber 3 g	10%	**Vitamin C**	23%	**Iron**	2%
Protein 3 g				Sugars 4 g					

Percent Daily Values (%DV) are based on a 2000-calorie diet.

Notes
- Potentially hazardous food. *Food Safety Standards:* Hold food for service at an internal temperature above 140°F. Do not mix old product with new. Cool leftover product quickly (within 4 hours) to below 41°F. See p. 105 for cooling procedures. Reheat leftover product quickly (within 2 hours) to 165°F. Reheat product only once; discard if not used.
- A low-moisture white potato must be used to produce a fluffy product.
- Potato water may be substituted for part of the milk.
- 8 oz nonfat dry milk powder and 2–2½ qt water may be substituted for the liquid milk. Sprinkle dry milk over potatoes before mashing.
- Dehydrated potatoes (2–2½ lb) may be substituted for the raw potatoes. Follow processor's instructions for preparation.
- Seasonings for mashed potatoes: chives, dill, garlic, ground horseradish, nutmeg.

Variations
- **Duchess Potatoes.** Add 18 eggs (2 lb), beaten, to mashed potatoes. Add additional milk if necessary. Pile lightly into baking pans. Bake at 350°F for 20–30 minutes, or until set.
- **Roasted Garlic Mashed Potatoes.** Add 8 oz roasted garlic (p. 856) along with the milk and margarine. **Roasted Garlic:** Preheat oven to 350°F. Remove the loose outside skins of the garlic heads by rolling them back and forth on cutting board, being careful not to loosen the cloves. Place garlic heads on a baking sheet. Drizzle ½ tsp olive oil over each head to coat. Roast until tender, about 1 hour. Cool. Cut garlic head horizontally, exposing the soft flesh. Using a table knife, press the softened cloves out of their skins. Drizzle baked garlic pulp with olive oil. Store covered in refrigerator. Use within 48 hours.
- **Mashed Potato Casserole.** Add ½ cup chopped chives; ½ cup crisp, cooked, crumbled bacon; 12 oz cream cheese; 1 tsp white pepper; and ¼ tsp garlic powder. Mix until blended. Place in baking pans. Sprinkle lightly with grated Parmesan cheese and paprika. Brush lightly with melted margarine. Bake at 375°F for 30 minutes or until light brown.
- **Potato Croquettes.** Add 18 egg yolks, well beaten. Shape into croquettes and dip in egg-milk mixture and crumbs (p. 99). Chill. Fry in deep fat at 360°F for 5–8 minutes.
- **Potato Rosettes.** Force Duchess Potatoes through a pastry tube, forming rosettes. Bake at 350°F until lightly browned. Use as a garnish for planked steak.
- **Whipped Rutabagas and Potatoes.** Peel 10 lb (AP) rutabagas and 5 lb potatoes. Cut into uniform-size pieces and steam or boil (p. 825). Mash and season as for potatoes. 1 tsp nutmeg may be added.

FRENCH FRIED POTATOES

Yield: 50 portions   *Portion:* 3 oz
Deep-fat fryer: 365°F   *Fry:* 6–8 minutes

Ingredient	Amount	Procedure
Potatoes, white	18 lb (AP) (15 lb EP)	Peel and cut potatoes into uniform strips ¼–⅜ inch thick. Cover with cold water to keep potatoes from darkening.
		Just before frying, drain potatoes and dry with paper towels. Fill fryer basket about one-third full of potatoes. Fry according to Method 1 or 2.

METHOD 1

Half fill fryer with fat. Preheat to 365°F. Fry potatoes for 6–8 minutes. Drain. Sprinkle with salt. Serve immediately.

METHOD 2

Blanching: Heat fat to 360°F. Place drained potato strips in hot fat, using an 8 to 1 ratio of fat to potatoes, by weight, as a guide for filling fryer basket. Fry 3–5 minutes depending on thickness of potato. (The potatoes should not brown.) Drain. Turn out on sheet pans. Refrigerate for later browning.

Browning: Reheat fat to 375°F. Place about twice as many potato strips in the kettle as for first-stage frying. Fry 2–3 minutes or until golden brown. Drain. Sprinkle with salt if desired. Serve immediately.

Approximate nutritive values per portion   **Calories** 269

Amount/portion	%DV	Amount/portion	%DV	Amount/portion	%DV		%DV		%DV
Total Fat 14 g	22%	**Cholest.** 0 mg	0%	**Total Carb.** 34 g	11%	**Vitamin A**	0%	**Calcium**	1%
Sat. Fat 4 g	21%	**Sodium** 184 mg	8%	Fiber 0 g	0%	**Vitamin C**	14%	**Iron**	3%
Protein 3 g				Sugars 0 g					

Percent Daily Values (%DV) are based on a 2000-calorie diet.

Notes
- Select a long, mealy potato, such as a russet.
- To cook frozen French Fried Potatoes, use 12 lb for 50 3-oz portions. Fry at 375°F for 3–5 minutes or until golden brown.

Variations
- **Deep-Fat Browned Potatoes.** Partially cook peeled whole or half potatoes. Fry in deep fat at 365°F for 5–7 minutes. Transfer to serving pan. Sprinkle with salt.
- **Lattice Potatoes.** Cut potatoes with lattice slicer. Fry at 365°F for 3–6 minutes. Transfer to serving pan. Sprinkle with salt.
- **Potato Chips.** Cut potatoes into very thin slices. Fry at 365°F for 3–6 minutes. Transfer to serving pan. Sprinkle with salt.
- **Shoestring Potatoes.** Cut potatoes into ⅛-inch strips. Fry at 365°F for 3–6 minutes. Transfer to serving pan. Sprinkle with salt.

PARSLEY BUTTERED NEW POTATOES

Yield: 50 portions   *Portion:* 3 oz

Ingredient	Amount	Procedure
New potatoes	15 lb (AP) (10 lb EP)	Wash and peel potatoes, removing eyes (see Note). Cut potatoes into 1½-inch cubes, or leave whole. If whole potatoes, cut as necessary to be of uniform size. Sprinkle with salt. If boiling the potatoes, add salt to the cooking water. Steam or boil (p. 825) until tender.
Salt	1 oz (1½ Tbsp)	
Margarine, melted	8 oz	Distribute margarine uniformly over cooked potatoes. Sprinkle with parsley.
Fresh parsley, chopped	1 oz	

Approximate nutritive values per portion   **Calories** 104

Amount/portion	%DV	Amount/portion	%DV	Amount/portion	%DV		%DV		%DV
Total Fat 4 g	6%	**Cholest.** 0 mg	0%	**Total Carb.** 17 g	6%	**Vitamin A**	1%	**Calcium**	0%
Sat. Fat 1 g	4%	**Sodium** 239 mg	10%	Fiber 0 g	0%	**Vitamin C**	11%	**Iron**	1%
Protein 1 g				Sugars 0 g					

Percent Daily Values (%DV) are based on a 2000-calorie diet.

Note • New potatoes may be peeled after cooking. If skins are thin they may be served unpeeled.

Variations • **Creamed New Potatoes.** Add 3 qt Medium White Sauce (p. 749) to cooked potatoes.

• **Creamed New Potatoes and Peas.** See p. 853.

• **Lemon-Seasoned New Potatoes.** Peel and cook uniform, small new potatoes. Pour a mixture of ¼ cup lemon juice and 8 oz melted margarine over them; then roll in minced parsley.

• **New Potatoes in Mustard.** Add ¾ cup Dijon mustard and 2 Tbsp dried chervil to the melted margarine.

• **New Potatoes Parmesan.** Scrub small uniform-size new potatoes. Remove 1 inch of peeling from around the center of each potato. Steam or boil (p. 825) until just done. Roll potatoes in melted margarine. Place in baking pans. Sprinkle with Parmesan cheese. Bake at 350°F for 20–25 minutes. Canned small whole potatoes may be substituted for fresh potatoes.

• **Paprika-Seasoned New Potatoes.** Delete parsley. Sprinkle potatoes with 1 Tbsp paprika. Stir lightly to mix seasoning.

ROASTED RED-SKINNED POTATOES

Yield: 50 portions   *Portion:* 5 oz
Oven: 400°F

Ingredient	Amount	Procedure
Potatoes, red-skinned unpeeled, cut into irregular 2-inch chunks, or left whole if small	17 lb (EP)	Place potatoes in large bowl.
Olive oil	1 lb 8 oz	Pour olive oil over potatoes. Stir to coat. Drain excess oil from potatoes.
Salt Pepper, cracked black Garlic, minced (optional)	2 oz 1 Tbsp 1 oz (EP)	Sprinkle salt, pepper, and garlic over potatoes. Stir to coat. Spread potatoes in a single layer on oiled baking sheets. Roast potatoes at 400°F until tender and golden brown, 30–35 minutes.

Approximate nutritive values per portion   **Calories** 230

Amount/portion	%DV	Amount/portion	%DV	Amount/portion	%DV		%DV		%DV
Total Fat 14 g	21%	**Cholest.** 0 mg	0%	**Total Carb.** 28 g	9%	**Vitamin A**	0%	**Calcium**	0%
Sat. Fat 1.8 g	9%	**Sodium** 495 mg	21%	Fiber 1.9 g	7%	**Vitamin C**	8%	**Iron**	0%
Protein 1.9 g				Sugars 0 g					

Percent Daily Values (%DV) are based on a 2000-calorie diet.

Notes
- Potentially hazardous food. *Food Safety Standards:* Hold food for service at an internal temperature above 140°F. Do not mix old product with new. Cool leftover product quickly (within 4 hours) to below 41°F. See p. 105 for cooling procedures. Reheat leftover product quickly (within 2 hours) to 165°F. Reheat product only once; discard if not used.
- Sliced potatoes (⅜ inch) may be used. Reduce cooking time to 20–25 minutes.

Variations
- **Rosemary Roasted Potatoes.** Delete garlic if desired. Sprinkle ½ oz finely minced fresh rosemary on potatoes along with the salt and pepper. Garnish with fresh sprigs of rosemary. May substitute Yukon Gold or other yellow potato.
- **Oven Roasted Sweet Potatoes with Soy Sauce.** Substitute peanut oil for olive oil and sweet potatoes for red potatoes. Delete garlic. Take sweet potatoes out of the oven after 30 minutes and drizzle with ⅓ cup soy sauce. Roast for an additional 5 minutes or until tender. Serve sprinkled with 8 oz toasted almonds and 1 oz coarsely chopped fresh parsley.

AU GRATIN POTATOES

Yield: 50 portions or 2 pans 12 × 10 × 2 inches   *Portion:* 5 oz
Oven: 350°F   *Bake:* 25–30 minutes

Ingredient	Amount	Procedure
Potatoes Salt	10 lb (AP) (8 lb EP) 1 Tbsp	Peel and dice potatoes (or dice before cooking). Steam or boil (p. 825) until just tender. Sprinkle with salt. If boiling the potatoes, add salt to the cooking water.
Margarine Flour, all-purpose Salt	12 oz 6 oz 1 Tbsp	Melt margarine. Add flour and salt. Stir until smooth. Cook 5–10 minutes.
Milk	3 qt	Add milk gradually while stirring. Cook until thickened.
Cheddar cheese, shredded	1 lb 8 oz	Add cheese to sauce and stir until cheese is melted. Pour over potatoes. Scale into two 12 × 20 × 2-inch baking pans, 8 lb per pan.
Bread crumbs Margarine, melted	12 oz 8 oz	Combine crumbs and margarine. Sprinkle over top of potatoes, 10 oz per pan. Bake at 350°F for 25–30 minutes.

Approximate nutritive values per portion   **Calories** 279

Amount/portion	%DV	Amount/portion	%DV	Amount/portion	%DV		%DV		%DV
Total Fat 16 g	25%	**Cholest.** 22 mg	7%	**Total Carb.** 26 g	9%	**Vitamin A**	9%	**Calcium**	18%
Sat. Fat 6 g	30%	**Sodium** 530 mg	22%	Fiber 2 g	8%	**Vitamin C**	16%	**Iron**	4%
Protein 8 g				Sugars 5 g					

Percent Daily Values (%DV) are based on a 2000-calorie diet.

Notes
- Potentially hazardous food. *Food Safety Standards:* Hold food for service at an internal temperature above 140°F. Do not mix old product with new. Cool leftover product quickly (within 4 hours) to below 41°F. See p. 105 for cooling procedures. Reheat leftover product quickly (within 2 hours) to 165°F. Reheat product only once; discard if not used.

- 1 lb 10 oz sliced dehydrated potatoes, reconstituted in 5 qt boiling water, and 1½ oz salt may be substituted for fresh potatoes.

COTTAGE FRIED POTATOES

Yield: 50 portions   *Portion:* 4 oz

Ingredient	Amount	Procedure
Potatoes	18 lb (AP) (15 lb EP)	Peel potatoes. Steam or boil until tender (p. 825).
Fat, hot Salt Pepper, black	As needed 1 oz (1½ Tbsp) 1 tsp	Slice cooked potatoes. Add to hot fat in frying pan. Add salt and pepper. Turn potatoes as needed and fry until browned.

Approximate nutritive values per portion   **Calories** 192

Amount/portion	%DV	Amount/portion	%DV	Amount/portion	%DV		%DV		%DV
Total Fat 7 g	11%	**Cholest.** 0 mg	0%	**Total Carb.** 29 g	10%	Vitamin A	2%	Calcium	1%
Sat. Fat 2 g	7%	**Sodium** 285 mg	12%	Fiber 3 g	13%	Vitamin C	29%	Iron	2%
Protein 3 g				Sugars 2 g					

Percent Daily Values (%DV) are based on a 2000-calorie diet.

Variations

- **American Fried Potatoes.** Add raw sliced potatoes to hot fat. Fry until potatoes are brown and tender. Add additional fat as needed.
- **Hashed Brown Potatoes.** Add finely chopped boiled potatoes to hot fat in frying pan. Add salt and pepper. Stir occasionally and fry until browned.
- **Lyonnaise Potatoes.** Cook 2 lb chopped onion slowly in fat without browning. Add seasoned cut, boiled potatoes and cook until browned.
- **O'Brien Potatoes.** Cook cubed potatoes in a small amount of fat with chopped onion and pimiento.
- **Oven-Fried Potatoes.** Prepare potatoes as for French Fried Potatoes. Place in greased shallow pans in a thin layer and brush with melted fat, turning to cover all sides. Bake at 450°F for 20–30 minutes, or until browned, turning occasionally. Drain on absorbent paper and sprinkle with salt.

POTATO PANCAKES

Yield: 50 portions or 100 cakes   *Portion:* 2 2-oz cakes

Ingredient	Amount	Procedure
Potatoes Onions	15 lb (AP) (12 lb EP) 1 lb 8 oz	Peel potatoes and onions. Grind. Drain.
Eggs, beaten Flour, all-purpose Salt Baking powder Milk	8 (14 oz) 8 oz 2 oz (3 Tbsp) 1 tsp ¾ cup	Combine and add to potatoes and onion. Refrigerate batter, removing small quantities as needed for production.
		Drop potato mixture with No. 20 dipper on hot greased griddle. Fry, turning once, until golden brown on both sides. Serve with warm applesauce.

Approximate nutritive values per portion   **Calories** 121

Amount/portion	%DV	Amount/portion	%DV	Amount/portion	%DV		%DV		%DV
Total Fat 1 g	2%	**Cholest.** 34 mg	11%	**Total Carb.** 25 g	8%	Vitamin A	1%	Calcium	2%
Sat. Fat 1 g	2%	**Sodium** 407 mg	17%	Fiber 0.4 g	1%	Vitamin C	13%	Iron	3%
Protein 3 g				Sugars 1 g					

Percent Daily Values (%DV) are based on a 2000-calorie diet.

SCALLOPED POTATOES

Yield: 50 portions or 2 pans 12 × 20 × 2 inches *Portion:* 6 oz
Oven: 350°F   *Bake:* 1½–2 hours

Ingredient	Amount	Procedure
Potatoes	15 lb (AP)	Peel and eye potatoes.
	(12 lb EP)	Slice and place in two greased 12 × 20 × 2-inch baking
Salt	2 oz (3 Tbsp)	pans, 6 lb per pan.
		Sprinkle with salt.
Margarine	8 oz	Melt margarine. Add flour and salt.
Flour, all-purpose	4 oz	Stir until smooth. Cook 5 minutes.
Salt	1 oz (1½ Tbsp)	
Milk	1 gal	Add milk gradually, stirring with wire whip. Cook until thickened.
		Pour over potatoes.
Bread crumbs	6 oz	Combine crumbs and margarine.
Margarine, melted	2 oz	Sprinkle over potatoes.
		Bake at 350°F for 1½–2 hours.

Approximate nutritive values per portion   **Calories** 212

Amount/portion	%DV	Amount/portion	%DV	Amount/portion	%DV		%DV		%DV
Total Fat 7 g	12%	**Cholest.** 11 mg	4%	**Total Carb.** 31 g	10%	**Vitamin A**	4%	**Calcium**	10%
Sat. Fat 3 g	13%	**Sodium** 698 mg	29%	Fiber 3 g	11%	**Vitamin C**	24%	**Iron**	3%
Protein 5 g				Sugars 6 g					

Percent Daily Values (%DV) are based on a 2000-calorie diet.

Notes
- Potentially hazardous food. *Food Safety Standards:* Hold food for service at an internal temperature above 140°F. Do not mix old product with new. Cool leftover product quickly (within 4 hours) to below 41°F. See p. 105 for cooling procedures. Reheat leftover product quickly (within 2 hours) to 165°F. Reheat product only once; discard if not used.
- Potatoes may be partially cooked and hot White Sauce (p. 749) added to shorten baking time.
- Dehydrated sliced potatoes may be substituted for fresh. Reconstitute according to package directions.

Variations
- **Scalloped Potatoes with Ham.** Add 5 lb cubed ham to White Sauce (p. 749). Reduce salt to 1 Tbsp.
- **Scalloped Potatoes with Onions.** Before baking, cover potatoes with onion rings. About 5 minutes before removing from oven, cover potatoes with shredded cheese.

SOUR CREAM POTATOES

Yield: 50 portions or 3 pans 12 × 10 × 2 inches   *Portion:* 5 oz
Oven: 350°F   *Bake:* 35–45 minutes

Ingredient	Amount	Procedure
Frozen hashed brown potatoes	10 lb	Thaw potatoes. Steam for 10–15 minutes. Hold for later step.
Margarine Onions, chopped	4 oz 1 lb	Melt margarine in steam-jacketed or other kettle. Add onions and sauté until transparent.
Sour cream Salt (see Notes) Pepper, black Eggs, beaten slightly Chicken base Water	2 lb 12 oz 1 oz 1 Tbsp 6 (10 oz) 1 Tbsp 2 cups	Add to onions and mix well.
		Add potatoes to onion mixture. Mix lightly. Scale into three greased 12 × 10 × 2-inch pans, 5 lb 5 oz per pan.
Cornflake crumbs Margarine, melted	3 oz ⅓ cup	Combine crumbs and margarine in mixer bowl, using flat paddle. Mix until crumbly. Sprinkle 2 oz over each pan of potatoes. Bake at 350°F for 35–45 minutes. To serve, spoon into 50 5-oz portions or cut each pan 4 × 4 for 48 servings.

Approximate nutritive values per portion   **Calories** 297

Amount/portion	%DV	Amount/portion	%DV	Amount/portion	%DV		%DV		%DV
Total Fat 19 g	**30%**	**Cholest.** 35 mg	**12%**	**Total Carb.** 29 g	**10%**	**Vitamin A**	**10%**	**Calcium**	**5%**
Sat. Fat 8 g	**41%**	**Sodium** 381 mg	**16%**	Fiber 1 g	**5%**	**Vitamin C**	**12%**	**Iron**	**9%**
Protein 5 g				Sugars 0 g					

Percent Daily Values (%DV) are based on a 2000-calorie diet.

Notes

- Potentially hazardous food. *Food Safety Standards:* Hold food for service at an internal temperature above 140°F. Do not mix old product with new. Cool leftover product quickly (within 4 hours) to below 41°F. See p. 105 for cooling procedures. Reheat leftover product quickly (within 2 hours) to 165°F. Reheat product only once; discard if not used.

- Undiluted cream of mushroom, cream of celery, or cream of chicken soup may be substituted for sour cream. Delete salt and chicken base.

- If a highly salted chicken base is used, delete or reduce salt.

- 2 oz (1 cup) dehydrated onions, rehydrated in 1½ cups water, may be substituted for fresh onions.

POTATOES ROMANOFF

Yield: 60 portions or 2 pans 12 × 20 × 2 inches   *Portion:* 6 oz
Oven: 350°F   *Bake:* 35–45 minutes

Ingredient	Amount	Procedure
Frozen hashed brown potatoes	16 lb	Thaw potatoes. Steam for 15 minutes.
Sour cream	4 lb 4 oz	Combine in mixer bowl and blend on low speed.
Green onions, sliced	6 oz	
Salt	1½ oz	
Pepper, black	1 Tbsp	
Cheddar cheese, shredded	12 oz	
Paprika	½ tsp	Add cooked potatoes to sour cream mixture. Mix well. Scale into two greased 12 × 20 × 2-inch pans, 10 lb per pan. Sprinkle lightly with paprika. Bake uncovered at 350°F for 35–45 minutes. Cut 6 × 5.

Approximate nutritive values per portion   **Calories** 356

Amount/portion	%DV	Amount/portion	%DV	Amount/portion	%DV		%DV		%DV
Total Fat 23 g	35%	**Cholest.** 20 mg	7%	**Total Carb.** 36 g	12%	**Vitamin A**	9%	**Calcium**	9%
Sat. Fat 11 g	54%	**Sodium** 369 mg	15%	Fiber 1 g	5%	**Vitamin C**	13%	**Iron**	10%
Protein 6 g				Sugars 0 g					

Percent Daily Values (%DV) are based on a 2000-calorie diet.

Note   • Potentially hazardous food. *Food Safety Standards:* Hold food for service at an internal temperature above 140°F. Do not mix old product with new. Cool leftover product quickly (within 4 hours) to below 41°F. See p. 105 for cooling procedures. Reheat leftover product quickly (within 2 hours) to 165°F. Reheat product only once; discard if not used.

OVEN-BROWNED OR RISSOLÉ POTATOES

Yield: 50 portions   *Portion:* 1 potato
Oven: 450°F   *Bake:* 1 hour

Ingredient	Amount	Procedure
Potatoes, baking variety	50	Peel potatoes and partially cook by boiling or steaming, about 10 minutes.
Margarine, melted Salt	1 lb 1 oz (1½ Tbsp)	Place potatoes on well-greased baking sheets. Pour melted margarine over potatoes. Sprinkle with salt. Bake at 450°F for 1 hour or until tender. Baste every 15 minutes with margarine from pan. Turn potatoes once during baking to ensure uniform browning.

Approximate nutritive values per portion   **Calories** 210

Amount/portion	%DV	Amount/portion	%DV	Amount/portion	%DV		%DV		%DV
Total Fat 7 g	11%	**Cholest.** 0 mg	0%	**Total Carb.** 34 g	11%	**Vitamin A**	2%	**Calcium**	1%
Sat. Fat 2 g	7%	**Sodium** 286 mg	12%	Fiber 4 g	15%	**Vitamin C**	33%	**Iron**	3%
Protein 3 g				Sugars 3 g					

Percent Daily Values (%DV) are based on a 2000-calorie diet.

Variations

- **Franconia Potatoes.** Cook peeled uniform-size potatoes approximately 15 minutes. Drain and place in pan in which meat is roasting. Bake approximately 40 minutes or until tender and lightly browned, basting with drippings in pan or turning occasionally to brown all sides. Serve with roast.

- **French Baked Potatoes.** Select small, uniform potatoes and peel. Roll potatoes in melted margarine or shortening, then in cracker crumbs or crushed cornflakes. Place in shallow pans and bake.

- **Herbed Potato Bake.** Peel baking potatoes and cut into ½-inch slices. Place in greased baking pans. Combine 1½ cups melted margarine, 3½ oz dehydrated onion soup mix, and 2 Tbsp rosemary. Sprinkle over potatoes and toss lightly. Bake at 325°F for 1½ hours or until potatoes are tender.

GLAZED OR CANDIED SWEET POTATOES

Yield: 50 portions   *Portion:* 4 oz
Oven: 400°F   *Bake:* 20–30 minutes

Ingredient	Amount	Procedure
Sweet potatoes or yams	16 lb (AP) (13 lb EP)	Scrub potatoes. Steam or boil in skins until tender (p. 825). When potatoes are cool enough to handle, peel and cut into halves lengthwise. Arrange in shallow pans.
Sugar, brown	1 lb 12 oz	Mix sugar, water, margarine, and salt. Heat to boiling point.
Water	2 cups	Pour over potatoes.
Margarine	8 oz	Bake at 400°F for 20–30 minutes.
Salt	½ tsp	

Approximate nutritive values per portion   **Calories** 213

Amount/portion	%DV	Amount/portion	%DV	Amount/portion	%DV		%DV		%DV
Total Fat 4 g	6%	**Cholest.** 0 mg	0%	**Total Carb.** 44 g	15%	**Vitamin A**	258%	**Calcium**	4%
Sat. Fat 1 g	4%	**Sodium** 82 mg	3%	Fiber 4 g	14%	**Vitamin C**	48%	**Iron**	4%
Protein 2 g				Sugars 13 g					

Percent Daily Values (%DV) are based on a 2000-calorie diet.

Notes
- Three No. 10 cans of sweet potatoes may be substituted for fresh sweet potatoes.
- Seasonings for sweet potatoes: allspice, cardamom, cinnamon, cloves, or nutmeg.

Variations
- **Baked Sweet Potatoes.** Select small even-size sweet potatoes or yams. Scrub. Bake at 425°F for 40–50 minutes, or until tender.
- **Candied Sweet Potatoes with Almonds.** Proceed as for Glazed Sweet Potatoes. Increase margarine to 12 oz and reduce brown sugar to 1 lb 8 oz. Add 1 cup dark corn syrup and 2 tsp mace. When partially glazed, sprinkle top with chopped almonds and continue cooking until almonds are toasted.
- **Glazed Sweet Potatoes with Orange Slices.** Add ¼ cup grated orange peel to syrup. Cut 5 oranges into thin slices; add to sweet potatoes when syrup is added.
- **Mashed Sweet Potatoes.** Cook and mash sweet potatoes or yams (p. 825), following procedure on p. 000. Add 1½ oz salt; ⅓ tsp nutmeg; 1 oz margarine, melted; and 1¼ qt hot milk.
- **Sweet Potatoes and Apples.** Reduce sweet potatoes to 9 lb, cooked, peeled, and sliced. Peel and slice 5 lb tart apples. Place alternate layers of sweet potatoes and apples in baking pans. Pour hot syrup (see recipe for Glazed Sweet Potatoes) over potatoes and apples. Bake at 350°F for 45 minutes.

SWEET POTATO SOUFFLÉ

Yield: 50 portions or 1 pan 12 × 20 × 2 inches   *Portion:* 4 oz
Oven: 375°F   *Bake:* 30 minutes

Ingredient	Amount	Procedure
Frozen sweet potatoes	8 lb	Steam potatoes for 25 minutes. Place in mixer bowl and whip on low, medium, and high speeds for 1 minute each, or until smooth.
Margarine, melted Sugar, brown Cinnamon, ground Mace, ground Ginger, ground Cloves, ground Milk Eggs	12 oz 1 lb 8 oz 1 Tbsp 1 Tbsp 1 tsp ¼ tsp 1 cup 9 (1 lb)	Add to sweet potatoes. Mix until thoroughly blended. Begin on low speed and progress to high speed for a total of approximately 5 minutes or until mixture is fluffy.
Miniature marsh- mallows	6 oz	Fold marshmallows into potato mixture. Scale into greased 12 × 20 × 2-inch pan. Bake at 375°F for 30 minutes or until hot.

Miniature marsh-
   mallows
	4 oz	Sprinkle marshmallows over sweet potatoes.
		 Return to oven long enough for marshmallows to puff
		   and brown slightly.

Approximate nutritive values per portion   **Calories** 212

Amount/portion	%DV	Amount/portion	%DV	Amount/portion	%DV		%DV		%DV
Total Fat 7 g	10%	**Cholest.** 39 mg	13%	**Total Carb.** 36 g	12%	**Vitamin A**	127%	**Calcium**	4%
Sat. Fat 2 g	8%	**Sodium** 95 mg	4%	Fiber 2 g	9%	**Vitamin C**	20%	**Iron**	5%
Protein 3 g				Sugars 6 g					

Percent Daily Values (%DV) are based on a 2000-calorie diet.

Notes
- Potentially hazardous food. *Food Safety Standards:* Hold food for service at an internal temperature above 140°F. Do not mix old product with new. Cool leftover product quickly (within 4 hours) to below 41°F. See p. 105 for cooling procedures. Reheat leftover product quickly (within 2 hours) to 165°F. Reheat product only once; discard if not used.
- Fresh boiled or steamed sweet potatoes may be substituted for frozen sweet potatoes.

SEASONED FRESH SPINACH AND OTHER GREENS

Yield: 50 portions   *Portion:* 3 oz

Ingredient	Amount	Procedure
Spinach or other greens, fresh	12 lb (AP) (10 lb EP)	Sort and trim greens. Remove veins, coarse stems, and roots. Wash leaves thoroughly, lifting out of water after each washing. Steam or boil (p. 825).
Margarine, melted Salt	4 oz 1 oz (1½ Tbsp)	Pour margarine over greens and sprinkle with salt. If boiling the greens, add salt to the cooking water.

Approximate nutritive values per portion   **Calories** 36

Amount/portion	%DV	Amount/portion	%DV	Amount/portion	%DV		%DV		%DV
Total Fat 2 g	3%	**Cholest.** 0 mg	0%	**Total Carb.** 3 g	1%	**Vitamin A**	61%	**Calcium**	9%
Sat. Fat 1 g	2%	**Sodium** 285 mg	12%	Fiber 2 g	9%	**Vitamin C**	42%	**Iron**	13%
Protein 3 g				Sugars 0 g					

Percent Daily Values (%DV) are based on a 2000-calorie diet.

Notes
- Beet greens, chard, collards, kale, mustard greens, or turnip greens may be used. For kale, strip leaves from coarse stems.
- For frozen spinach, use 10 lb. See p. 825 for cooking.
- Greens may be garnished with 12 hard-cooked eggs, chopped, and 1 lb 8 oz crisp-cooked bacon, crumbled.
- Seasonings for spinach: basil, garlic, mace, marjoram, nutmeg, oregano, mushrooms, bacon, cheese, hard-cooked eggs, vinegar.

Variations
- **Creamed Spinach.** Cook spinach. Drain. Chop coarsely. Add 2 qt White Sauce (p. 749). Season with salt, pepper, and nutmeg.
- **Wilted Spinach or Lettuce.** To 10 lb chopped raw spinach or lettuce, or a combination of the two, add 2 qt Hot Bacon Sauce (p. 771) just before serving.

SPINACH SOUFFLÉ

Yield: 48 portions or 2 pans 12 × 20 × 2 inches   *Portion:* 4 oz
Oven: 350°F   *Bake:* 40 minutes

Ingredient	Amount	Procedure
Margarine Flour, all-purpose Salt	1 lb 4 oz 8 oz 2½ Tbsp	Melt margarine. Add flour and salt. Stir until smooth and cook 5 minutes.
Milk Sour cream	1¼ qt 1¼ qt	Add milk and sour cream. Blend over low heat until smooth, stirring constantly. Remove from heat.
Spinach, chopped frozen	6 lb	Thaw spinach. Drain.
Onion, finely chopped Nutmeg Egg yolks, beaten	8 oz 1½ Tbsp 18 (12 oz)	Add spinach, onion, nutmeg, and egg yolks to sauce. Mix.
Egg whites	18 (1 lb 5 oz)	Beat egg whites until stiff. Fold into spinach mixture.
		Lightly grease two 12 × 20 × 2-inch counter pans on the bottom only. Scale 7 lb 8 oz of the mixture into each pan. Set in pans of hot water. Bake at 350°F for 40 minutes or until soufflé is set. Cut 4 × 6.

Approximate nutritive values per portion   **Calories** 219

Amount/portion	%DV	Amount/portion	%DV	Amount/portion	%DV		%DV		%DV
Total Fat 18 g	27%	**Cholest.** 105 mg	35%	**Total Carb.** 10 g	3%	**Vitamin A**	68%	**Calcium**	15%
Sat. Fat 6 g	31%	**Sodium** 542 mg	23%	Fiber 2 g	6%	**Vitamin C**	12%	**Iron**	7%
Protein 7 g				Sugars 1 g					

Percent Daily Values (%DV) are based on a 2000-calorie diet.

Notes
- Potentially hazardous food. *Food Safety Standards:* Hold food for service at an internal temperature above 140°F. Do not mix old product with new. Cool leftover product quickly (within 4 hours) to below 41°F. See p. 105 for cooling procedures. Reheat leftover product quickly (within 2 hours) to 165°F. Reheat product only once; discard if not used.
- 1 oz (½ cup) dehydrated onions, rehydrated in 1½ cups water, may be substituted for fresh onions.

BAKED ACORN SQUASH

Yield: 50 portions   *Portion:* ½ squash
Oven: 350°F   *Bake:* 30–40 minutes

Ingredient	Amount	Procedure
Acorn squash	25	Wash squash and cut in half lengthwise. Scrape out seeds. Place cut side down in shallow pans with a small amount of water. Bake at 350°F for 20–25 minutes, or until just tender. (Squash may be steamed for 20 minutes.)
Margarine, melted	8 oz	Place squash hollow side up.
Salt	1 oz (1½ Tbsp)	Sprinkle cavities with margarine, salt, and brown sugar.
Sugar, brown	12 oz	Bake until sugar is melted, about 10–15 minutes.

Approximate nutritive values per portion **Calories** 115

Amount/portion	%DV	Amount/portion	%DV	Amount/portion	%DV		%DV		%DV
Total Fat 4 g	6%	**Cholest.** 0 mg	0%	**Total Carb.** 21 g	7%	**Vitamin A**	5%	**Calcium**	5%
Sat. Fat 1 g	2%	**Sodium** 242 mg	10%	Fiber 2 g	9%	**Vitamin C**	18%	**Iron**	6%
Protein 1 g				Sugars 4 g					

Percent Daily Values (%DV) are based on a 2000-calorie diet.

Variations

- **Acorn Squash with Sausage.** Place 4-oz sausage patty or 2 link sausages, partially cooked, in each cooked squash half. Continue baking until meat is done.

- **Stuffed Acorn Squash.** Fill cooked squash with No. 12 dipper of the following mixture: 5 qt cooked rice, 4 lb chopped cooked meat, and 4 oz minced onion, sautéed in margarine and moistened with meat stock.

SPAGHETTI SQUASH

Yield: 50 portions   *Portion:* 6 oz
Oven: 350°F   *Bake:* 45–60 minutes

Ingredient	Amount	Procedure
Spaghetti squash	15 (approximately 3 lb each)	Wash squash and cut in half lengthwise. Scrape out seeds. Place cut side down in shallow pans with ½ inch water. Bake at 350°F for 45–60 minutes, or until squash is just tender when pricked with a fork. Remove squash from water and cool slightly. With a fork, scrape the soft flesh (lengthwise) into pastalike strands. Serve with melted butter or margarine or top with sauce.

Approximate nutritive values per portion

Calories 91

Amount/portion	%DV	Amount/portion	%DV	Amount/portion	%DV		%DV		%DV
Total Fat 0 g	0%	**Cholest.** 0 mg	0%	**Total Carb.** 24 g	8%	Vitamin A	158%	Calcium	9%
Sat. Fat 0 g	0%	**Sodium** 9 mg	1%	Fiber 4 g	15%	Vitamin C	56%	Iron	7%
Protein 2 g				Sugars 9 g					

Percent Daily Values (%DV) are based on a 2000-calorie diet.

Note
- Potentially hazardous food. *Food Safety Standards:* Hold food for service at an internal temperature above 140°F. Do not mix old product with new. Cool leftover product quickly (within 4 hours) to below 41°F. See p. 105 for cooling procedures. Reheat leftover product quickly (within 2 hours) to 165°F. Reheat product only once; discard if not used.

Variations
- **Spaghetti Squash with Clam Sauce.** Prepare Clam Sauce (p. 567) and serve over squash.
- **Spaghetti Squash with Vegetable Sauce.** Prepare Vegetable Sauce (p. 580) and serve over squash.

BAKED TOMATOES

Yield: 50 portions   *Portion:* ½ tomato
Oven: 400°F   *Bake:* 10–12 minutes

Ingredient	Amount	Procedure
Tomatoes, fresh (5 oz each)	25	Wash tomatoes. Cut in halves. Sprinkle each tomato with salt and pepper or seasoned salt.
Salt	1 tsp	
Pepper, black	1 tsp	
Margarine, melted	6 oz	Combine margarine, bread crumbs, and onion.
Bread crumbs	2 oz	Place 2 tsp mixture on each tomato half.
Onion, finely chopped	6 oz	Bake at 400°F for 10–12 minutes.

Approximate nutritive values per portion   **Calories** 45

Amount/portion	%DV	Amount/portion	%DV	Amount/portion	%DV		%DV		%DV
Total Fat 3 g	5%	**Cholest.** 0 mg	0%	**Total Carb.** 4 g	1%	Vitamin A	5%	Calcium	0%
Sat. Fat 1 g	3%	**Sodium** 90 mg	4%	Fiber 1 g	4%	Vitamin C	23%	Iron	2%
Protein 1 g				Sugars 2 g					

Percent Daily Values (%DV) are based on a 2000-calorie diet.

Note
- Seasonings for tomatoes: basil, bay leaf, chili powder, garlic, marjoram, oregano, rosemary, tarragon, thyme.

Variations
- **Mushroom-Stuffed Tomatoes.** Add 2 lb sautéed mushrooms, sliced or chopped, to crumb mixture.
- **Broiled Tomato Slices.** Cut tomatoes in ½-inch slices. Salt, dot with margarine, and broil.
- **Spinach-Stuffed Tomatoes.** Wash medium-size fresh tomatoes. Remove core and part of the tomato pulp. Fill center with 2 oz Spinach Soufflé (p. 869). Sprinkle with buttered crumbs and Parmesan cheese. Bake at 350°F for about 1 hour.

HERB ROASTED TOMATOES

Yield: 50 portions   *Portion:* 3 halves
Oven: 350°F

Ingredient	Amount	Procedure
Plum tomatoes, halved lengthwise (stem and blossom blemish removed)	14 lb	Place tomatoes cut side up in a 12 × 20 × 2-inch pan. Brush with olive oil.
Olive oil	8 oz	
Salt	1 Tbsp	Sprinkle tomatoes lightly with salt and pepper.
Pepper, black	1½ tsp	
Parsley, chopped fresh	8 Tbsp (½ cup)	Mix herbs. Sprinkle half of herb mixture over tomatoes. Save remainder of herb mixture for garnish.
Basil, chopped fresh	8 Tbsp (½ cup)	
Rosemary, finely chopped fresh	4 Tbsp (¼ cup)	
Thyme, chopped fresh	4 Tbsp (¼ cup)	
		Bake tomatoes at 350°F until tender and slightly browned around the edges, 50–60 minutes.
Parmesan cheese, freshly grated (optional)	1 cup	Garnish tomatoes with remaining herbs and parmesan cheese.

Approximate nutritive values per portion   **Calories** 77

Amount/portion	%DV	Amount/portion	%DV	Amount/portion	%DV		%DV		%DV
Total Fat 5.6 g	9%	**Cholest.** 1.6 mg	1%	**Total Carb.** 6 g	2%	**Vitamin A**	9%	**Calcium**	4%
Sat. Fat 1 g	5%	**Sodium** 189 mg	8%	Fiber 1.5 g	6%	**Vitamin C**	43%	**Iron**	4%
Protein 2 g				Sugars 3.5 g					

Percent Daily Values (%DV) are based on a 2000-calorie diet.

Notes
- Other herbs may be substituted for those in the recipe.
- A vegetable marinade may be substituted for the olive oil.
- If substituting dried herbs, reduce amount by two-thirds.

BAKED ITALIAN TOMATOES AND ZUCCHINI

Yield: 50 portions   *Portion:* 4 oz
Oven: 325°F

Ingredient	Amount	Procedure
Plum tomatoes (small size)	3 lb 12 oz (AP)	Submerge tomatoes in boiling water for a few seconds to loosen skins. Peel tomatoes and core. Cut tomatoes in half, from stem to flower end (long way). Save for layering step.
Marinara Sauce (p. 761) Zucchini, ½-inch dice Mozzarella cheese, shredded Parmesan cheese, freshly shredded	2 qt 3 lb (EP) 3 lb 8 oz	Layer ingredients in the following order in each of two 12 × 10 × 2-inch pans: 1. Marinara Sauce, 2 cups 2. Diced zucchini, 12 oz 3. Tomato halves, 12 oz 4. Mozzarella cheese, 1 lb 5. Parmesan cheese, 2 oz Repeat steps 1, 2, and 3. Bake covered for 30–40 minutes or until mixture reaches 165°F.
Parsley, chopped (fresh) (see Notes) Basil, chopped (fresh)	1 oz 1 oz	Remove from oven and uncover. Top each pan with 8 oz mozzarella cheese and 2 oz Parmesan cheese. Sprinkle ½ oz parsley and ½ oz basil on each pan. Bake uncovered for 10 minutes until cheese is melted and lightly browned.

Approximate nutritive values per portion   **Calories** 128

Amount/portion	%DV	Amount/portion	%DV	Amount/portion	%DV		%DV		%DV
Total Fat 8 g	12%	**Cholest.** 2.5 mg	8%	**Total Carb.** 6.3 g	2%	Vitamin A	13%	Calcium	20%
Sat. Fat 4.5 g	23%	**Sodium** 319 mg	13%	Fiber 1.4 g	5%	Vitamin C	21%	Iron	4%
Protein 8 g				Sugars 1.6 g					

Percent Daily Values (%DV) are based on a 2000-calorie diet.

Notes

- Potentially hazardous food. *Food Safety Standards:* Hold food for service at an internal temperature above 140°F. Do not mix old product with new. Cool leftover product quickly (within 4 hours) to below 41°F. See p. 105 for cooling procedures. Reheat leftover product quickly (within 2 hours) to 165°F. Reheat product only once; discard if not used.

- Dried basil and dried parsley may be substituted for fresh. Use 2 Tbsp parsley and 1 Tbsp basil.

- Serve as a vegetable or with pasta for a nonmeat entree.

- 1 lb mushrooms (small whole or quartered) may be substituted for 1 lb of the zucchini.

STIR-FRIED VEGETABLES

Yield: 50 portions   *Portion:* 3 oz

Ingredient	Amount	Procedure
Cornstarch Water	2 oz 1 cup	Combine cornstarch and water. Set aside for last step.
Assorted vegetables (see Notes for suggestions)	5 lb 8 oz (EP)	Cut vegetables into uniform-size thin slices, strips, or diagonal slices to ensure quick cooking. Pat dry before frying.
Cooking oil Garlic, minced Ginger root, fresh, sliced	1 cup 2 cloves ½ tsp	Combine oil, garlic, and ginger root in frying pan. Heat to 350°F and cook slightly. Remove ginger root and discard.
Water chestnuts, sliced, drained	8 oz	Add water chestnuts and prepared vegetables to heated oil. Stir with long spatula in a folding motion. Cook until vegetables are tender-crisp.
Chicken Stock (p. 790) Soy sauce	3 cups ½ cup	Combine stock and soy sauce. Mix quickly into vegetables. Reduce heat. Pour cornstarch mixture over vegetables. Cook and stir just until sauce thickens and vegetables are glazed.

Approximate nutritive values per portion   **Calories** 63

Amount/portion	%DV	Amount/portion	%DV	Amount/portion	%DV		%DV		%DV
Total Fat 5 g	7%	**Cholest.** 0 mg	0%	**Total Carb.** 5 g	2%	**Vitamin A**	3%	**Calcium**	2%
Sat. Fat 1 g	6%	**Sodium** 238 mg	10%	Fiber 0 g	0%	**Vitamin C**	14%	**Iron**	3%
Protein 2 g				Sugars 0 g					

Percent Daily Values (%DV) are based on a 2000-calorie diet.

Notes
- Select vegetables for contrast in color, shape, texture, and flavor. At least three vegetables should be selected. Cut vegetables into small enough pieces to cook quickly. Frozen vegetables should be thawed before stir-frying.
- Suggested vegetables: asparagus cut diagonally, broccoli or cauliflower florets, green beans, carrot strips or diagonal slices, celery slices, sliced fresh mushrooms, snow peas, onion rings, pepper strips (red, green, or yellow), zucchini or summer squash slices or sticks.
- Suggested combinations (total of 5 lb 8 oz): 1 lb 8 oz sliced carrots, 1 lb 8 oz broccoli florets, 1 lb 8 oz celery sticks, 8 oz mushroom slices, and 8 oz sliced onion; 1 lb 8 oz asparagus cut diagonally, 1 lb 8 oz zucchini slices, 1 lb 8 oz cauliflower florets, 8 oz sliced onions, and 8 oz fresh mushrooms; 1 lb 8 oz sliced celery, 1 lb 8 oz pea pods, 1 lb 8 oz julienne carrots, 8 oz green pepper strips, and 8 oz sliced fresh mushrooms.

RATATOUILLE

Yield: 50 portions   *Portion:* 4 oz
Oven: 300°F   *Heat:* 5 minutes

Ingredient	Amount	Procedure
Vegetable oil	⅓ cup	Heat oil in tilting fry pan.
Onion, cut in wedges	8 oz	Add onion and garlic. Cook until tender-crisp.
Garlic, minced	1 clove	
Eggplant, peeled, 1-inch cubes	2 lb 8 oz	Add eggplant. Sauté 2 minutes.
Zucchini	2 lb	Add squash and peppers. Sauté 5 minutes or until vegetables are still crisp and brightly colored.
Green peppers, fresh, 1½-inch strips	2 lb	
Tomatoes, canned, diced	6 lb	Add to vegetable mixture. Simmer for 5 minutes.
Salt	2½ tsp	Scale into two 12 × 10 × 2-inch pans, 6 lb per pan.
Pepper, black	1½ tsp	
Basil, dried, crumbled	1 tsp	
Oregano, dried, crumbled	1 tsp	
Monterey Jack cheese, shredded	1 lb	Sprinkle 8 oz cheese over each pan. Heat in 300°F oven for 5 minutes to melt the cheese. Do not cover. Serve with a spoon.

Approximate nutritive values per portion   **Calories** 73

Amount/portion	%DV	Amount/portion	%DV	Amount/portion	%DV		%DV		%DV
Total Fat 4 g	7%	**Cholest.** 8 mg	3%	**Total Carb.** 6 g	2%	**Vitamin A**	7%	**Calcium**	8%
Sat. Fat 2 g	11%	**Sodium** 246 mg	10%	Fiber 1 g	3%	**Vitamin C**	43%	**Iron**	3%
Protein 3 g				Sugars 2 g					

Percent Daily Values (%DV) are based on a 2000-calorie diet.

Notes   • Sliced Japanese eggplant may be substituted for all or part of the cubed eggplant.
    • Yellow summer squash may be substituted for some or all of the zucchini.

SUMMER RATATOUILLE

Yield: 50 portions   *Portion:* 4 oz
Oven: 350°F

Ingredient	Amount	Procedure
Eggplant, 1-inch cubes (unpeeled)	2 lb 12 oz (EP)	Put eggplant in colander. Sprinkle with salt and let set for 30 minutes.
Salt	1 oz	Rinse eggplant and drain thoroughly. Use eggplant in following step.
Olive oil	4 oz	Heat oil in large fry pan or steam-jacketed kettle.
Onions, ¼-inch slice	1 lb 6 oz (EP)	Sauté onions, garlic, and eggplant until tender,
Garlic, minced	2½ oz (EP)	10–12 minutes.
Zucchini squash, ½-inch slice	1 lb 12 oz (EP)	Add squash to onion-garlic-eggplant mixture.
Yellow summer squash, ½-inch slice	1 lb (EP)	Sauté squash and peppers until heated through and most of the liquid is absorbed.
Red bell peppers, cut in 1-inch square pieces	8 oz (EP)	
Green bell peppers, cut in 1½-inch strips	8 oz (EP)	
Tomatoes, fresh, quartered	1 lb 8 oz (EP)	Add tomatoes and spices. Stir to combine.
Salt	1 Tbsp	Pan in 12 × 10 × 2-inch pans. Bake uncovered 20 minutes
Pepper, black	½ tsp	
Red pepper, crushed	¼ tsp	
Basil, fresh, coarsely chopped	1 oz	
Oregano leaves, dried	1 tsp	

Approximate nutritive values per portion   **Calories** 44

Amount/portion	%DV	Amount/portion	%DV	Amount/portion	%DV		%DV		%DV
Total Fat 2.4 g	4%	**Cholest.** 0 mg	0%	**Total Carb.** 5 g	2%	**Vitamin A**	4%	**Calcium**	1%
Sat. Fat 0.3 g	2%	**Sodium** 367 mg	15%	Fiber 1.6 g	6%	**Vitamin C**	28%	**Iron**	2%
Protein 1 g				Sugars 2 g					

Percent Daily Values (%DV) are based on a 2000-calorie diet.

Note   ● Potentially hazardous food. *Food Safety Standards:* Hold food for service at an internal temperature above 140°F. Do not mix old product with new. Cool leftover product quickly (within 4 hours) to below 41°F. See p. 105 for cooling procedures. Reheat leftover product quickly (within 2 hours) to 165°F. Reheat product only once; discard if not used.

VEGETABLE TIMBALE

Yield: 40 portions or 1 pan 12 × 20 × 2 inches   *Portion:* 3 oz
Oven: 300°F   *Bake:* 2 hours

Ingredient	Amount	Procedure
Eggs	16 (1 lb 9 oz)	Beat eggs.
Salt	2 Tbsp	Add salt, margarine, and milk.
Margarine, melted	5 oz	
Milk	1½ qt	
Spinach, chopped, frozen	3 lb	Cook spinach (p. 825). Drain well. Add to egg mixture. Mix until well blended.
		Pour into greased 12 × 20 × 2-inch pan. Set into another pan with 3 cups hot water in it. Bake at 300°F for 2 hours. Test with a silver knife as for custard. Cut 5 × 8. Serve with 1 oz Cheese Sauce (p. 749).

Approximate nutritive values per portion   **Calories** 84

Amount/portion	%DV	Amount/portion	%DV	Amount/portion	%DV		%DV		%DV
Total Fat 6 g	9%	**Cholest.** 80 mg	27%	**Total Carb.** 4 g	1%	**Vitamin A**	32%	**Calcium**	10%
Sat. Fat 2 g	9%	**Sodium** 423 mg	18%	Fiber 1 g	3%	**Vitamin C**	7%	**Iron**	4%
Protein 5 g				Sugars 2 g					

Percent Daily Values (%DV) are based on a 2000-calorie diet.

Notes
- Potentially hazardous food. *Food Safety Standards:* Hold food for service at an internal temperature above 140°F. Do not mix old product with new. Cool leftover product quickly (within 4 hours) to below 41°F. See p. 105 for cooling procedures. Reheat leftover product quickly (within 2 hours) to 165°F. Reheat product only once; discard if not used.
- Spinach, broccoli, brussels sprouts, asparagus, or any combination of these vegetables may be used.

Variation
- **Chicken Timbale.** Use 32 eggs (3 lb 8 oz); 1 oz salt; 1 lb margarine, melted; 1 tsp white pepper; 12 oz bread crumbs; and 6 lb chopped cooked chicken. Mix melted margarine, bread crumbs, and milk. Cook for 5 minutes. Add beaten eggs, seasonings, and chicken. Bake as for Vegetable Timbale. Cut 6 × 8. Serve with Béchamel Sauce (p. 750).

GRILLED OR ROASTED MARINATED VEGETABLES

Yield: 50 portions   *Portion:* 3 oz
Oven: 400–500°F

Ingredient	Amount	Procedure
Vegetables (see suggestions listed in Table 19.2)	12 lb (EP)	Prepare vegetables per instructions in Table 19.2.

Marinade:
  Vegetable Marinade (pp. 784, 785)
  Balsamic Vinegar Marinade (p. 786)
  Vinaigrette Marinade (p. 787)
  Herb and Garlic Marinade (p. 787)
	3 qt	Marinate vegetables 10–15 minutes. Drain marinade from vegetables before grilling or roasting. **Save marinade.**
		Baste vegetables once or twice with marinade while grilling or roasting.
		Reserved marinade may be heated to 165°F and drizzled on vegetables when served.
		
		(See grilling and oven roasting instructions that follow.)

GRILLING INSTRUCTIONS

1. Clean grill grids thoroughly. Clean as often as necessary to keep vegetables from sticking.
2. Preheat grill grids until very hot. Place drained vegetables on grill. Turn often. Brush marinade on vegetables after each turn.
3. Grill vegetables until desired doneness. Serve warm or at room temperature.

OVEN ROASTING INSTRUCTIONS

1. Preheat oven to according to Table 19.2. Oven must be hot enough to caramelize the vegetables but not so hot as to dry them out.
2. Place vegetables on a lightly greased sheet pan in a single layer. Do not overcrowd or they will steam rather than roast. For large quantities of vegetables, roast separately and combine prior to service. For smaller quantities, put the slower cooking, hard vegetables to the outside of the roasting pan (vegetables will cook faster on the outside of the pan).
3. Turn vegetables often during roasting. If cooking different kinds of vegetables on the same pan, remove the vegetables as they become tender. Brush marinade on vegetables after each turn.
4. Roast vegetables until desired doneness. Serve warm or at room temperature.

Notes
- Potentially hazardous food. *Food Safety Standards:* Hold food for service at an internal temperature above 140°F. Do not mix old product with new. Cool leftover product quickly (within 4 hours) to below 41°F. See p. 105 for cooling procedures. Reheat leftover product quickly (within 2 hours) to 165°F. Reheat product only once; discard if not used.
- Vegetables may be roasted without first marinating. Follow the ratio: 1 lb vegetable, 1–2 oz olive oil, ½–1 tsp kosher salt, 1 Tbsp fresh finely chopped herbs (oregano, rosemary, sage, thyme). Combine vegetables, salt, and herbs in a bowl. Toss to coat. Follow roasting instructions.

Variations
- **Garlic and Fennel Seed Roasted Vegetables.** Do not use a marinade. Mix and set aside 3 Tbsp olive oil with 2 Tbsp crushed fresh garlic and 2 Tbsp toasted fennel seeds (see p. 782 for toasting spices). Toss vegetables in ½ cup olive oil, 1 oz salt, and 1 tsp black pepper. Roast vegetables according to instructions. When vegetables are *al dente*, remove from oven and toss with oil, garlic, and fennel seed mixture. Roast 10 minutes longer. Remove from oven and toss with 1 oz chopped fresh parsley and ¼ cup balsamic vinegar.
- **Mashed Potatoes and Roasted Vegetables.** Serve 5 oz Mashed Potatoes or Roasted Garlic Mashed Potatoes (p. 856) surrounded by 3–6 oz of roasted vegetables (not potatoes, unless sweet potatoes). Serve garnished with chopped fresh parsley. Drizzle Mashed Potatoes with olive or nut oil if desired. Serve for a nonmeat entree.

- **Sesame Roasted Vegetables.** Do not use a marinade. Mix and set aside 2 Tbsp sesame oil, 2 Tbsp crushed fresh garlic, 2 Tbsp crushed fresh ginger, and ⅓ cup soy sauce. Toss vegetables in ⅓ cup sesame oil, 1 oz salt, and 1 tsp black pepper. Roast vegetables according to instructions. When vegetables are *al dente,* remove from oven and toss with oil, garlic, ginger, and soy sauce mixture. Roast 10 minutes longer. Remove from oven and toss with 2 Tbsp toasted sesame seeds and ¼ cup rice vinegar (see p. 782 for toasting seeds).

- **Sherry Roasted Root Vegetables.** Select root vegetables from Table 19.2. Follow the ratio: 1 lb vegetable, 2 oz olive oil, 3 oz dry sherry, 1 tsp kosher salt, and 1 Tbsp fresh finely chopped thyme. Combine vegetables, salt, and thyme in a bowl. Toss to coat. Follow roasting instructions.

TABLE 19.2 Timetable for roasting vegetables

Vegetable	Preparation Instructions[1,2,3]	Temperature	Time[4,5]
Asparagus	Leave whole.	450°F	15 min
Green or Wax Beans	Leave whole.	450–500°F	15 min
Beets	Do not peel or coat with oil. Wrap in foil.	350°F	45–60 min (baby)
			60–75 min (medium)
			1½–2 hr (large)
Belgian endive	Slice in half lengthwise.	450°F	25 min
Carrots	Slice into ¼–½-inch slices or 1–2-inch sections, or split in half lengthwise.	425°F	20–40 min (depending on size)
Celery root	Cut away thick skin. Cut bulb in half or cube.	425°F	30–40 min
Corn on the cob	To roast in husks, roll back husks and remove silks. Fold husk back against corn ear. May remove husk entirely and coat with oil.	500°F	20–30 min (in husks) 15 min (husks removed)
Eggplant	Peel globe eggplant if desired. Slice ½-inch thick (round or lengthwise). When roasting whole, prick with fork before roasting. For Japanese eggplant, split lengthwise.	400°F	20–25 min (slices) 40–60 min (whole)
Fennel	Cut into wedges.	425°F	15 min
Garlic	Slice off top of entire head. Drizzle with oil. Cover tightly.	425°F	45 min
Kohlrabi	Peel; cut into matchsticks or cubes.	425°F	15 min
Leeks	Split in half lengthwise.	450°F	20 min
Mushrooms	Leave whole, cut into thick slices, or quarter. (Watch carefully so as not to overcook)	450°F	20–30 min
Okra	Leave whole.	450°F	15 min
Onions	Leave whole, cut in half, or slice.	450°F	20–30 min (slices) 20–30 min (whole pearl) 30–40 min (whole mature)
Parsnips	Peel and slice into ¼–½-inch slices or 1–2-inch sections, or split in half lengthwise.	425°F	30 min
Peppers (sweet bell)	Char pepper's skin under a broiler or over an open flame. Turn to roast evenly. Remove charred skin after first placing in a closed paper or plastic bag for 10 minutes to loosen skin. Peel, seed, slice.	Open flame or broiler	15 min
Potatoes (baking)	Peeled or unpeeled. Cut into wedges.[5]	425°F	20 min
Potatoes (new)	Cut in half.	425°F	20–40 min depending on size
Rutabagas	Quarter or slice into ½–1-inch pieces.	450°F	35 min
Squash, (summer/ zucchini)	Slice small squash lengthwise in half. Larger squash may be cut into 1-inch thick slices.	450°F	15 min (small halves and slices)
Squash, (winter)	Peel and dice, or cut into wedges or ½-inch slices.[5]	350–375°F	20–30 min
Sweet Potatoes	Peel if desired. Cut into wedges.[5]	500°F	15–20 min
Tomatillos	Peel off papery skin. Rinse and let dry.	425°F	15 min
Tomatoes	Cut in half.	425°F	30–45 min (as a side dish) 75–90 min (for sauce)
Tomatoes (cherry)	Leave whole.	425°F	20 min
Turnips	Quarter or slice into ½-inch-thick slices or wedges.	425°F	25 min

[1] Unless noted otherwise, all vegetables are coated lightly with oil, butter, or a marinade and arranged in a single layer on a sheet pan.

[2] Time can be reduced by blanching the larger vegetables until slightly tender.

[3] Before roasting, clean vegetables following preparation guidelines for vegetables, pp. 000.

[4] Roasting time will vary depending on the size of the vegetables, how many are in the pan, and whether they are blanched or not. For best results do not crowd vegetables in the pan.

[5] Turn larger vegetables once during baking, about halfway through.

APPENDIX A

Suggested Menu Items and Garnishes

APPETIZERS

See p. 227.

See p. 227.

ENTREES

Meat

Beef

Roast
  Chuck
  Corned beef
  Pot roast
  Rib eye
  Standing rib
  Sauerbraten
  Smoked beef brisket
Steak
  Broiled or grilled
    Club
    Filet mignon
    Sirloin
    T-Bone
  Chicken-fried steak
  Country-fried steak
  Pepper steak
  Spanish steak
  Steak teriyaki
Ground beef
  Bacon-wrapped beef
  Cheeseburger pie
  Chuck wagon steak
  Salisbury steak
  Meat loaf
  Meatballs
    Italian
    Swedish
    Spanish
    With spaghetti

Beef with pasta or rice
  Beef on noodles
  Beef, pork, and noodle
    casserole
  Beef stroganoff on
    noodles
  Chipped beef and
    noodles
  Chop suey on rice
  Creole spaghetti
  Hungarian goulash
  Pasta, beef, and tomato
    casserole
  Spaghetti and meatballs
  Spanish rice
Other beef entrees
  Beef birds
  Beef liver, braised
    Grilled with onions
    With bacon
  Beef pot pie
  Beef stew
    With vegetables
    With biscuits
    Beef wrap
  Chili con carne
  Creamed beef on
    biscuits or baked
    potato
  Creamed chipped beef
    on toast or baked
    potato
  Fajitas

Green chili stew
Kabobs
Lasagna
Pizza
Stir-fried beef
  With broccoli
  With sugar snap peas
Stuffed peppers
Taco salad casserole

Veal

Veal birds
Veal cacciatore
Breaded veal cutlets
Veal New Orleans
Veal Parmesan
Veal piccata
Veal scallopine

Lamb

Roast leg of lamb
Broiled lamb chops
Lamb stew
Curried lamb with rice

Pork

Pork chops
  Breaded
  Baked
  Barbecued
  Chili seasoned
  Deviled

  With dressing
  Stuffed
Pork cutlets, breaded
Pork roast, loin
  Garlic and peppercorn
  Herbed
  Jeweled
  Teriyaki glazed
  With dressing
Pork roast, fresh ham
Spareribs
  Barbecued
  Sweet-sour
  With dressing
  With sauerkraut
Other pork entrees
  Stir-fried pork
  Sweet and sour pork
  Pork and noodle
    casserole
Pork (cured)
  Bacon
  Frankfurters
    Barbecued
    Cheese-stuffed
  Ham
    Baked glazed
    Grilled slices
    Ham balls
    Ham loaf
    Ham patties
      With cranberries
      With pineapple

Creamed ham on
   spoonbread or
   biscuits
Plantation shortcake
Black beans and ham
   on rice
Ham and cheese
   quiche
Scalloped potatoes and
   ham
Sausage
   Gravy on biscuits
   Patties or links
   With acorn squash
   And egg bake
   Rolls
Scrapple

Poultry

Chicken (quarters or pieces)

Barbecued
Cantonese
Cacciatore
Fricassee
Fried
   Deep-fat
   Oven-fried
   Pan-fried
   Herb baked
   Italian baked
Parmesan
Poached
Stewed
   With dumplings
Tahitian

Chicken Breast (grilled or broiled)

Cheese-stuffed
   With tomato basil sauce
Curried
Dijon
Herb marinated
Sesame mustard
Tarragon
With tomato sauce

Chicken (using diced meat)

Brunswick stew
Chicken à la king or
   creamed
   On biscuits
   On chow mein noodles
   On potatoes
   On spoonbread

In patty shell
Chicken crepes
Chicken pot pie
Chow mein
Hot chicken salad
Chicken and noodles
Chicken rice casserole
Chicken and snow peas
   on rice
Chicken tetrazzini
Chicken and vegetable
   stir-fry
Scalloped chicken
Singapore curry
Spaghetti with chicken
   sauce
Sweet-sour chicken
Szechwan chicken
Cornish game hens,
   orange glazed

Turkey

Roast, with dressing
Steaks, grilled
   Lime tarragon
Scalloped turkey
Turkey à la king
Turkey with dumplings
Turkey tetrazzini

Fish and Shellfish

Fin Fish

Fillets
   Baked
   Breaded
   Deep-fat fried
   Grilled
   Lemon baked
   Poached
Fillet of sole amandine
Fajita trout
Herb marinated
   fish steak
Lemon rice-stuffed cod
Salmon
   Baked (whole)
   Loaf
   Poached
   Scalloped
Scallops
Tuna
   À la king
   And noodles
   Broiled
   Scalloped

Shellfish

Deviled crab
Scalloped oysters
Caribbean shrimp
Creole shrimp
Oriental shrimp and
   pasta
Pasta with clam sauce
Pasta with shrimp sauce
Seafood quiche
Shrimp fried rice
Shrimp peel
See also Entree Salads

Meatless Entrees

Vegetable

Black beans and
   couscous
Cuban and rice and
   tortilla
Broccoli and cheese
   casserole
Broccoli and rice au
   gratin
Cheese and broccoli
   strata
Cheese pizza
Falafel
Hummus
Grilled eggplant
Mushroom souffle
Portabella pepper steak
Quiche
   Leek and roasted
      pepper
   Mushroom
   Spinach
   Vegetable
Sicilian rice and
   vegetables
Spinach cheese crepes
Spinach lasagna
   Lasagna florentine
Spinach soufflé
Tofu, broccoli Szechwan
   and vegetables
      jambalaya
   stir-fry
   sweet-and-sour
Vegetable chow mein
Vegetable fajita
Vegetable lo mein
Vegetable paella
Vegetable timbale
Zucchini corn cakes

Pasta, Rice, and Grains

Baked ziti with four
   cheeses
Barley and vegetable
   medley
Curried rice, beans, and
   vegetable pilaf
Couscous
Garden pasta
Ginger rice
Ginger vegetables and
   barley
Grains and beans
Jalapeño rice
Macaroni and cheese
Orzo pilaf
Pasta primavera
Pasta with vegetable sauce
Polenta
Quesadillas
Red beans and rice
Roasted portabella
   mushroom on orzo
   pilaf
Spanish rice and black
   beans
Roasted vegetables
Spicy Barley
Southwest ziti
Tomato linguine

Cheese and Eggs

Cheese balls on
   pineapple slice
Cheese and broccoli
   strata
Cheese soufflé
   With cheese sauce
   With mushroom sauce
Eggs à la king
Frittata
Goldenrod eggs
Hot stuffed eggs
Nachos
Omelet
   Baked
   Chinese
   Mushroom and cheese
   Spanish
Quesadillas
Quiche
Scotch woodcock
Risotto
Swiss broccoli pasta
Tomato cilantro rice
Vegetarian spaghetti

Sandwich Entrees

Cold Sandwiches

Bacon, lettuce, tomato
Cheese salad
Chicken pocket
Chicken salad
Club sandwich
Egg salad
Ham
  With cheese
Ham salad
Pork loin
Sliced turkey
Submarine
Tuna salad
Turkey club hoagy

Hot Sandwiches

Bacon and tomato on bun
  With cheese sauce
Beef

Barbecued
French dip
Roast beef
Bierocks
Chicken cutlet
Chili dog
Chimichangas
Crab salad
Croissant with sautéed
    garden vegetables
Fajitas
Grilled sandwiches
  Cheese
  Corned beef and Swiss
    on rye
Ham and cheese
Hamburgers
  Barbecued
  With cheese
Hot meat and cheese
Hot tuna grill
Meat loaf

Nacho dog
Patty melt
Quesadillas
Roast pork
Tacos
Tuna melt
Turkey, hot
  And Swiss on whole wheat
Western

Salad Entrees

Chef's salad bowl
  Seafood chef salad
Chicken or turkey salad
  Crunchy
  Curried
  Fruited
  Mandarin
  And bacon
  With orange-avocado
Chicken and pasta salad
Cottage cheese salad

Crab salad
Pasta salad
  Italian pasta salad
Pasta and crab salad
Salad plates
  Chicken and pasta salad
    plate
  Deli plate
  Fruit salad plate
  Marinated chicken and
    fresh fruit
  Salmon, poached
  Shrimp tortellini salad
    plate
  Tuna pasta salad plate
Shrimp salad
  Rice
  Tortellini
Stuffed tomato salad
Taco salad
Tomato cottage cheese salad
Tuna salad

ENTREE ACCOMPANIMENTS

Pasta, Rice, and Cereals

Baked cheese grits
Barley casserole
Broccoli and cheese
    casserole
Broccoli rice au gratin
Bulgur
Couscous
Fettuccine
  With pesto sauce
  Grilled vinaigrette
  Herbed
Noodles
  Buttered
  Romanoff
Orzo
  Lemon
  Pilaf
Pasta wheels with
    vegetables
Penne with garlic
Polenta
Quinoa pilaf
Rice
Basmati pilaf
  With black-eyed peas
  Buttered
  Curried
  Fried

  With almonds
  Asian
  Ginger rice stir-fry
  Green
  Mexican
  Pilaf
  Primavera
  Risotto
  Silician with vegetables
  Toasted herb
  Tomato
See also Meatless Entrees

Potatoes

White Potatoes

Au gratin
Baked
  With toppings
  French
  Herbed
  Lyonnaise
  Stuffed
Creamed
Croquettes
Duchess
Fried
French fried
Hashed brown
Lyonnaise
Mashed

New potatoes
  Buttered
  Creamed
  Creamed with peas
  Lemon seasoned
  In mustard
  Paprika seasoned
  Parmesan
  Roasted
O'Brien
Oven-browned
Potato pancakes
  With applesauce
Potato salad, hot
  or cold
Rissole
Romanoff
Rosettes
Scalloped
  With onion
Shoestring
Sour cream

Sweet Potatoes

Baked
Candied or glazed
  With almonds
  With apples
Mashed
Soufflé

Starchy Vegetables

Corn

On the cob
Creamed
O'Brien
Pudding
Scalloped
Succotash

Beans

Baked beans
Barley and black bean
Bean ragout
Black beans and couscous
Black eyed pea salsa
Grains and beans
Lima beans
  Baked
  Seasoned
Ranch style beans
Red beans and rice
Spicy black beans

Squash

Baked acorn
Mashed butternut or
    hubbard
  With apples
Seasoned spaghetti
    squash

VEGETABLES

Green Vegetables

Asparagus

Seasoned
Creamed
With cheese or
     hollandaise sauce
Vinaigrette

Broccoli

Seasoned
  With almonds
  With crumb butter
  With lemon butter
With cheese sauce
With hollandaise sauce

Brussels Sprouts

Seasoned

Cabbage

Seasoned
Au gratin
Hot slaw
Polonaise
Scalloped

Celery

Seasoned
Creamed with almonds
Creole
With carrots amandine

Green Beans

Seasoned
  With almonds
  With dill
  With mushrooms

Casserole
Creole
Herbed
Southern style
Spanish

Peas

Seasoned
  With almonds
  With lemon-mint butter
  With mushrooms
With carrots
With cauliflower
With new potatoes
With pearl onions
With turnips

Spinach

Seasoned
  With egg or bacon
Creamed
Soufflé
Wilted

Zucchini

Seasoned
Casserole
  With tomato

Other Vegetables

Beets

Seasoned
  Julienne
Harvard
Hot spiced
With orange sauce
In sour cream
Pickled

Carrots

Seasoned
  With parsley
Candied or glazed
Mint glazed
Lyonnaise
Marinated
Savory
Sweet-sour
With celery
With peas

Cauliflower

Seasoned
  With almonds
Creamed
French fried
With cheese sauce
With peas

Eggplant

Baked
Creole
French fried
Parmesan
Ratatouille
Sautéed
Tomato bake

Mushrooms

Broiled
French fried
Marinated
Sautéed

Onions

Seasoned
Au gratin

Baked
Casserole
Creamed
French fried

Parsnips

Seasoned
Browned
Glazed
  With carrots

Rutabagas

Seasoned
Mashed
  With potatoes

Summer Squash

Seasoned
With zucchini

Tomatoes

Baked
Broiled
Herb roasted
Stewed
Stuffed
  With mushrooms
  With spinach

Turnips

Seasoned
Mashed
With peas
See p. 877 for suggested
     combinations for
     stir-fried vegetables.

SALADS AND RELISHES

Vegetable Salads

Salad bar
Mixed green
Tossed vegetable
Tossed greens and fruit
Hawaiian tossed
Marinated garden salad
Vegetable collage

Asparagus

Marinated

Beans

Brown bean
Garbanzo bean
  With pasta
Triple bean

Cauliflower bean
Oriental bean

Cabbage

Cole slaw
Creamy cole slaw
Green pepper slaw

Carrots

Carrifruit
Carrot celery
Carrot raisin
Marinated carrots

Cauliflower

Cauliflower-broccoli
Creamy cauliflower

Cucumbers

Sliced cucumbers and
  onions
Sliced cucumbers and
  tomatoes
German cucumbers

Green Beans

Marinated green beans

Potatoes

Potato salad
Sour cream potato salad
Hot potato salad

Spinach

Spinach-cheese
Spinach-mushroom

Tomatoes

Marinated
Sliced
Sliced with cucumbers
Tomato Basil

Fruit Salads

Acini de pepe
Ambrosia fruit

Waldorf
Apple-cabbage
Apple-carrot
Spiced apple
Grapefruit orange
  With apple
  With avocado
Frozen fruit
Tossed greens with fruit

Gelatin Salads

Perfection
Tomato aspic
Applesauce
Apple cinnamon swirl
Arabian peach
Autumn salad
Blueberry
Boysenberry mold
Cranberry apple
Cranberry mold
Cucumber soufflé
Frosted cherry
Frosted lime
Jellied Waldorf
Lemon cream
Pineapple cheese
Ribbon gelatin
Sunshine

Swedish green top
Under-the-sea

Pasta and Rice Salads

Garbanzo and pasta
Dilled rice
Macaroni
Italian pasta
See also Salad Entrees

Relishes

Fruit

Buttered apples
Cantaloupe or
  watermelon chunks
Cranberry relish
Cranberry sauce
  Baked
Grapes, green or red
Pineapple, broiled
  Spears
Salsa
Spiced fruit
  Apples
  Crabapples
  Pears
  Peaches

Vegetables

Broccoli florets
Carrot curls or sticks
Marinated carrots
Cauliflower florets
Celery sticks
Stuffed celery
Cherry tomatoes
Green pepper rings or
  sticks
Marinated mushrooms
Radishes
Tomato slices or wedges
Turnip sticks or slices
Zucchini sticks or slices

Miscellaneous

Cucumber and melon
  salsa
Olives, green, ripe,
  stuffed
Pickles
  Beet
  Corn relish
  Dill
  Sweet
  Watermelon

SOUPS

Stock soups

Beef alphabet
Beef barley
Beef noodle
Beef rice
Creole beef
French onion
Hearty beef vegetable
Mexican beef
Minestrone
Vegetable beef
  Julienne
Vegetable
Brunswick stew
Chicken bouillon
Chicken gumbo
Chicken noodle
Chicken rice

Chicken with spaetzle
Pepper pot
Turkey vegetable
Tomato barley
Tomato bouillon
Tomato rice
Manhattan clam or fish
  chowder

Cream Soups

Broccoli cheese soup
Cheese soup
Chicken velvet
Cream of:
  Asparagus
  Broccoli
  Cauliflower
  Celery

Chicken
Mushroom
Mushroom barley
Potato
Potato baked
Potato and roasted
  pepper
Spinach
Tomato
Vegetable

Chowders

Clam (New England)
Corn
Fish
Potato
Vegetable
Oyster stew

Bean and Lentil Soups

Black bean
Navy bean
Chili con carne
  Chili spaghetti
  Garden chili
  White chili
Lentil soup
Lentil and black bean
Split pea soup

Chilled Soups

Gazpacho
Vichyssoise

DESSERTS

Cakes

Angel food
  Chocolate
  Frozen filled
  Yellow
Chiffon
  Cocoa
  Orange
  Walnut
Cupcakes
White, with variations
Yellow, with variations
Applesauce
Banana
Boston cream pie
Burnt sugar
Carrot
Chocolate
Coconut lime
Dutch apple
Fruit cake
Fudge
German chocolate
Lady Baltimore
Lazy daisy
Marble
Pineapple cashew
Pineapple upside-down
Poppy seed
Pound cake
Praline
Pumpkin
Jelly roll
Chocolate roll
Ice cream roll
Pumpkin cake roll
Gingerbread

Cookies

Drop Cookies

Butterscotch
Butterscotch pecan
Chocolate
Coconut macaroons
Chocolate chip
Gingersnaps
Jumbo chunk chocolate
Molasses
Oatmeal

Peanut butter
Peanut butter chocolate
  chip
Peanut
Snickerdoodles
Sugar
Whole wheat sugar

Bar Cookies

Brownies
Butterscotch squares
Coconut pecan bars
Date bars
Dreamland bars
Oatmeal date bars
Marshmallow krispie
  squares

Pressed, Molded, and Rolled Cookies

Butterscotch refrigerator
  cookies
Butter tea cookies
Chocolate tea cookies
Christmas wreath cookies
Coconut cookies
Crisp ginger cookies
Filled cookies
Frosty date balls
Oatmeal crispies
Pinwheel cookies
Rolled sugar cookies
Sandies
Thimble cookies

Pies

Fruit Pies

Apple
  Crumb
  Sour cream
Apricot
Berry
Cherry
Gooseberry
Peach
Pineapple
Raisin
Rhubarb
  Custard

Soft Pies

Chiffon
  Chocolate
  Lemon
  Strawberry
Cream
  Banana
  Butterscotch
  Chocolate
  Coconut
  Date
  Fruit-glazed
  Nut cream
  Pineapple
Custard
  Coconut
Frozen mocha
  almond
Ice cream
Lemon
Pumpkin
  Praline
  Pecan
    Cream cheese

Frozen Desserts

Sundaes and Parfaits

Caramel sundae
Hot fudge sundae
Peanut butter sundae
Strawberry sundae
Chocolate parfait
Strawberry parfait

Ice Cream

Butter brickle
Chocolate
Chocolate chip
Chocolate almond
Coffee
Lemon custard
Peach
Pecan
Peppermint
Pistachio
Strawberry
Toffee
Vanilla
Frozen yogurt

Sherbet

Cranberry
Lemon
Lime
Orange
Pineapple
Raspberry

Puddings and Other Desserts

Cream puddings
  Banana
  Butterscotch
  Chocolate
  Coconut
  Pineapple
  Tapioca
  Vanilla
Custard, baked
  Caramel
  Rice
  Bread pudding
  Floating island
Baked date pudding
Lemon cake pudding
Christmas pudding
  (steamed)
Cream puffs
Eclairs
Ice cream puff
Orange cream puffs with
  chocolate filling
Baked apples
Apple dumplings
Apple crisp
Fruit crisp
Fruit cobbler
  Apple
  Apricot
  Cherry
  Peach
  Plum
Fruit and cheese
Strawberry shortcake
Bavarian creams
  Apricot
  Pineapple
  Strawberry
Russian cream
Cheese cake
  With fruit glaze

GARNISHES

Yellow-Orange

Cheese and Eggs

Cheese, grated, strips
Egg, hard-cooked or
    sections
Deviled egg halves
Riced egg yolk

Fruit

Apricot halves
Cantaloupe balls
Lemon wedges, slices
Orange section, slices
Peach slices
Peach halves with jelly
Spiced peaches

Vegetables

Carrots, rings, shredded,
    strips
Banana peppers

Sweets

Peanut brittle, crushed
Sugar, yellow or orange

Miscellaneous

Coconut, tinted

Flowers

Carnations
Daisies
Dandelions
Day lilies
Marigolds
Nasturtiums
Pansies
Rose petals
Snapdragons
Squashblossoms

Red/Pink

Fruit

Cherries
Cinnamon apples
Cranberries
Plums
Pomegranate seeds
Red raspberries
Maraschino cherries
Strawberries
Watermelon cubes, balls

Vegetables

Beets, pickled, julienne
Beet relish
Red cabbage
Red peppers, rings, strips,
    shredded
Pimiento, chopped, strips
Red radishes, sliced, roses
Cherry tomatoes
Tomato wedges, slices,
    broiled

Sweets

Red jelly: currant, cherry,
    loganberry, raspberry
Red sugar

Miscellaneous

Paprika
Tinted coconut
Stuffed olives
Cinnamon drops (red
    hots)

Flowers

Carnations, mini
Geraniums
Rose petals
Nasturtiums

Green

Fruit

Avocadoes
Frosted grapes
Green plums
Honeydew melon
Kiwi fruit
Lime slices or wedges
Maraschino cherries
Mint jelly

Vegetables

Broccoli florets
Celery
Endive
Green pepper strips,
    chopped
Green onions
Lettuce cups
Lettuce, shredded
Mint leaves
Nasturtium leaves
Parsley, sprig, chopped
Spinach leaves
Watercress
Zucchini sticks, slices

Miscellaneous

Capers
Coconut, tinted
Olives
Pickles, burr gherkins,
    strips, fans, rings
Sunflower seeds
Pistachios

White

Fruit

Apple rings
Grapefruit sections

Vegetables

Cauliflower florets
Celery cabbage
Celery curls, hearts,
    strips
Cucumber rings, strips,
    wedges, cups
Mashed potato
    rosettes
Onion rings
Onions, pickled
White radishes

Miscellaneous

Almonds
Popcorn
Sliced hard-cooked egg
    white
Parmesan cheese
Shredded coconut
Marshmallows
Powdered sugar
Whipped cream

Flowers

Carnations
Daisies
Geraniums
Lilacs
Pansies
Rose petals
Snapdragons
Violets

Brown/Tan

Breads

Croustades
Croutons

Miscellaneous

Chocolate, shredded or
    shaved
Cinnamon
Dates
French-fried cauliflower
Mushrooms
Nutmeats
Nut-covered cheese balls
Potato chips
Toasted coconut

Flowers

Pansies

Black

Caviar
Prunes
Spiced prunes
Raisins, currants
Ripe olives
Rye croutons
Truffles

Blue/Purple

Bachelor Buttons
Chive flowers
Chrysanthemums
Geraniums
Pansies
Lavender
Lilacs
Violets

APPENDIX B
Glossary of Menu and Cooking Terms

à la   (ah lah) French. In the manner of.

à la carte   (ah lah cart′) French. On the menu, but not part of a meal, usually prepared as ordered and individually priced.

à la king   French. Served in cream sauce containing green pepper, pimiento, and mushrooms.

à la mode   (ah lah mohd′) French. When applied to desserts, means with ice cream. *À la mode, boeuf,* a well-larded piece of beef cooked slowly in water with vegetables, similar to braised beef.

al dente   (al den′ tay) Italian. The point in cooking pasta at which it is still fairly firm to the bite. The term is sometimes used interchangeably with tender crisp when referring to vegetables.

allemande   (ahl mahnd′) French. A smooth yellow sauce consisting of white sauce with the addition of cream, egg yolk, and lemon juice.

allumette   A small matchstick cut, 1/8 × 1/8 × 1–2 inches.

amandine   Served with almonds.

amaranth   Small grain about the size of a poppy seed. High in protein. Doubles when cooked in liquid.

antipasto   (ahn tee pahs′ toe) Italian. Appetizer; a course consisting of relishes, vegetables, fish, or cold cuts.

AP   As purchased weight. The weight of an item before trimming or other preparation (as opposed to edible portion weight, or EP).

appetizer   A small portion of hot or cold food usually served as a first course.

aromatics   Herbs and spices used to enhance the flavor and fragrance of food.

arroz   (ah ros′) The Spanish-American word for rice.

aspic   A jellied meat juice or liquid held together with gelatin.

au gratin   (oh grah′ ton) French. Made with crumbs, scalloped. Often refers to dishes made with cheese sauce.

au jus   (oh zhu′) French. Meat served in its natural juices or gravy.

bake   To cook in the oven by dry heat.

barbecue   To cook on a grill or spit over hot coals, or in an oven, basting intermittently with a highly seasoned sauce.

bar-le-duc   (bahr luh dük′) French. A preserve made of currants and honey. It frequently forms a part of the cheese course.

barley   Grain low in gluten and high in protein. Quadruples when cooked in liquid.

baron   Double sirloin of beef.

baste   To moisten meat while roasting to add flavor and to prevent drying of the surface. Melted fat or meat drippings may be used for basting.

batch cooking   Dividing the estimated amount needed into smaller quantities and cooking as required to meet the demand.

baton/batonnet   A small stick cut, 1/4 × 1/4 × 2–2 1/2 inches.

batter   Flour and liquid mixture, usually combined with other ingredients, thin enough to pour or drop from a spoon.

béarnaise   (bay ar nayz′) French. Sauce of clarified butter, egg yolks, vinegar or white wine, onion, and spices.

beat   To mix ingredients with a rotating motion, using spoon, wire whip, or paddle attachment to mixer.

béchamel   (bay sha mel′) French. A cream sauce made with equal parts of chicken stock and cream or milk.

beurre   (buhr) French. Butter.

beurre blanc   (buhr blahnk) French. A light colored butter sauce made from butter, shallots, and white wine. May be finished with fresh herbs or other seasonings. Often called "white butter."

beurre composé (burr kom-poz-a) Softened butter with flavorings added. Also known as compound butter.

beurre manié (burr man-yay) A well-blended mixture of 50% softened butter and 50% flour (by weight). Used to thicken and give added sheen and flavor to soups and sauces.

beurre noir (burr nwor) Butter browned in a pan until dark, sometimes flavored with vinegar. Often called "black butter."

beurre noisette (burr nwah-zett) Butter heated in a pan until lightly browned. Often called "hazelnut butter" or "brown butter."

beurre rouge (burr rooge) A reddish colored butter sauce made from butter, shallots, and red wine.

bisque (bisk) French. A thick soup usually made from fish or shellfish. Also a frozen dessert. Sometimes defined as ice cream to which finely chopped nuts are added.

blanch To dip briefly in boiling water.

blanquette (blang ket') French. A white stew usually made with veal, lamb, or chicken.

blend To thoroughly mix two or more ingredients.

bleu (bluh) French. Blue.

boeuf (buff) French. Beef. *Boeuf à la jardinie're* (buff a lah zhar de nyoyr), braised beef with vegetables; *boeuf roti* (buff rotee), roast beef.

boil To cook foods in water or a liquid in which the bubbles are breaking on the surface and steam is given off.

bombe (bahm) French. A frozen dessert made of a combination of two or more frozen mixtures packed in a round or melon-shaped mold.

bordelaise (bor d'layz') French. Of Bordeaux. *Sauce bordelaise*, a sauce with Bordeaux wine as its foundation, with various seasonings added.

borscht (borsht) Russian. A soup made with beets and served with thick sour cream.

bouillabaisse (boo yah bes') French. A highly seasoned fish soup made with two or more kinds of fish.

bouillon (boo yon') French. Clear meat stock.

bouquet (boo kay') Volatile oils that give aroma.

bouquet garni (boo kay' garnee') French. Herbs and spices tied in a cloth bag, used for flavoring soups, stews, and sauces, then removed after cooking is completed.

bourguignon (bohr ghee n'yang') French. In the Burgundy style, especially a beef stew made with red wine (for which burgundy is noted), mushrooms, salt port, and onions.

braise (brays) French. To brown in a small amount of fat, cover, add a small amount of liquid, and cook slowly.

bran The high fiber, outer layer of a cereal grain.

bread To coat food with an egg-milk mixture and then bread crumbs before frying.

brew To cook in liquid to extract flavor, as with beverages.

brine A mixture of salt, water, and seasonings used to preserve food.

brioche (bree ohsh') French. A slightly sweetened rich bread used for rolls or babas.

brochette, à la (bro shet') French. Food arranged on a skewer and broiled.

broil To cook over or under direct heat, as in a broiler or over live coals.

broth A flavorful liquid obtained from the simmering of meats and/or vegetables.

brunoise (broo-nwah) Foods cut into cubes, $1/8 \times 1/8 \times 1/8$ inch. Foods are garnished with brunoise-size cut vegetables.

buckwheat Seed of a plant related to rhubarb. Marketed as buckwheat flour and kasha (roasted buckwheat groats).

buffet (boo fay') French. A table displaying a variety of food.

bulgur Wheat that is parched, steamed, and dried before being ground.

butterfly cut Boneless meat, fish, or shrimp cut nearly in half lengthwise and spread open like the wings of a butterfly to increase surface area and shorten cooking time.

cacciatore (ca chi a tor' ee) Italian. Stewed with tomatoes, onion, and garlic.

café au lait (ca fay' oh lay') French. Coffee with hot milk.

café noir (ca fay' nwar) French. Black coffee, after-dinner coffee.

canapé (can ah pay') French. An appetizer of meat, fish, egg, or cheese arranged on a bread base.

candy To preserve or cook with heavy syrup.

caper (kay' per) Small pickled bud from wild caper bush; used in salads and sauces.

caramelize To heat sugar until a brown color and a characteristic flavor develops.

carte au jour (kart o zhur') French. Bill of fare or menu for the day.

caviar (cav ee ar') French. Salted roe of sturgeon or other large fish. May be black or red.

chantilly (shang te' ye) French. Foods containing whipped cream.

charlotte (shar' lot) French. Dessert with gelatin, whipped cream, fruit, or other flavoring, in a mold, garnished with lady fingers.

chiffonade   (shee′ fahn ahd) French. With minced or shredded vegetables, as in salad dressing.

chill   To refrigerate until thoroughly cold.

chop   To cut food into fairly fine pieces with a knife or other chopping device.

choux paste   (shoo paste) French. Cream puff batter.

chowder   A thick soup of fish or vegetables and milk.

chutney   (chut′ ni) A sweet and sour condiment made of fruits and/or vegetables cooked with sugar, spices, and usually vinegar.

cilantro   The pungent leaf of the coriander plant, also known as *Chinese parsley*. Used to season Oriental and Mexican foods.

clarified butter   Melted butter from which the milk and water have been removed leaving pure butterfat. Clarification raises the smoke point of butter.

clarify   Make clear by skimming or adding egg white and straining.

cloche   (klosh) French. Bell, dish cover. *Sous cloche* (soo klosh), under cover.

coat   To cover entire surface with flour, fine crumbs, sauce, batter, or other food as required.

cocktail   An appetizer, either a beverage or a light, highly seasoned food, served before a meal.

coddle   To simmer gently in liquid for a short time.

compote   (kom′ poht) French. Mixed fruit, either raw or stewed in syrup; a stemmed serving dish.

compound butter   Butter combined with herbs or other seasonings and used to sauce vegetables and grilled or broiled meats. Also known as beurre composé.

condiment   An aromatic mixture, such as pickles, chutney and some sauces and relishes, that accompanies food.

consommé   (kon so may′) French. A clear broth that has been clarified, usually made from two or three kinds of meat.

convection   A method of heat transfer in which heat is transmitted through the circulation of air.

converted (parboiled) rice   A specially processed long grain rice that has been partially cooked under steam pressure, redried, then milled and polished.

coulis   (koo-lees) A sauce made from a puree of vegetables or fruit.

court bouillon   (cor boo yon′) French. Water simmered with seasonings, vegetables, and vinegar or wine. Used for poaching vegetables, fish, and shellfish.

couscous   Pellets of semolina usually cooked by steaming.

cream   To mix fat and sugar until soft and creamy.

crème anglaise   (crem ahn-glas) Vanilla custard sauce. Also called stirred custard.

crème chantilly   (crem chan-tee) Whipped heavy cream flavored with sugar and vanilla.

crème fraishe   (crem fresh) Very heavy cream (35% butterfat), cultured to give it a thick consistency and a slightly tangy flavor; similar to sour cream but not as acidic.

creole   (kre′ ohl) French. Foods containing meat or vegetables with tomatoes, peppers, onions, and other seasonings.

crepe   (krayp) French. Thin, delicate pancake, often rolled and stuffed, served as appetizer, entree, or dessert. *Crepe suzette*, a small, very thin and crisp pancake served for tea or as dessert.

crisp   To make foods firm and brittle, as in chilling vegetables or heating cereals or crackers in the oven to remove excessive moisture.

critical control point   A step during the processing of food when a mishandling or temperature mistake can result in the transmission, growth, or survival of pathogenic bacteria.

croissant   (krwa sang′) French. Crescent; applied to rolls and confectionery of crescent shape.

croquette   (crow ket′) Mixture of chopped, cooked meat, poultry, fish, or vegetables bound with thick cream sauce, shaped, breaded, and fried.

croustade   (krus tad′) A toasted case or shell of bread.

croute, en   (awn croot) A food encased in a bread or pastry crust.

croutons   (kroo tons) Bread cubes, toasted, for use in garnishing soups and salads.

crudités   (croo dee tays′) French. Raw vegetables.

cube   To cut into 1/2-inch squares.

curry   (kur′ ee) Highly spiced condiment from India, a stew seasoned with curry.

cut in   To cut a solid fat into flour with knives or mixer until fat particles are of desired size.

cutlet   Thin slice of meat, usually breaded, for frying; also croquette mixture made in a flat shape.

deep fry   To cook in fat deep enough for food to float.

deglaze   To dilute and wash down pan juices and browned pieces by adding liquid.

de la maison   (de lah may zon′) French. Specialty of the house.

demitasse   (deh mee tahss′) French. Small cup of black coffee served after dinner.

dice   To cut into 1/4-inch cubes.

dot   To scatter small bits of butter or margarine over surface of food.

dough   A mixture of flour, liquid, and other ingredients, thick enough to roll or knead.

drawn butter   Melted butter.

dredge   To thoroughly coat a food with flour or other fine substance.

drippings   Fat and liquid residue from frying or roasting meat or poultry.

du jour   (doo zhoor') French. Of the day, such as soup of the day.

dust   To sprinkle lightly with flour.

eau   (oh) French. Water.

eclair   (ay klair') French. Finger-shape cream puff pastry filled with whipped cream or custard.

egg and crumb   To dip a food into diluted, slightly beaten egg and dredge with crumbs. This treatment is used to prevent soaking of the food with fat or to form a surface easily browned.

egg wash   A mixture of beaten eggs (whites, whole eggs, yolks) and liquid (milk or water), used to coat bread dough prior to baking, to add sheen.

emulsion   A mixture of two or more liquids, of which one is a fat or oil and the other is waterbased, so that tiny globules of one are suspended in the other. Emulsions may be temporary, permanent, or semipermanent.

enchilada   (en chee lah' dah) Mexican. Tortillas filled and rolled, served with sauce.

en cocotte   (ahn ko cot') French. An individual casserole.

entree   (ahn' tray) French. The main course of a meal or a single dish served before the main course of an elaborate meal.

EP   Edible portion. The weight of an item after trimming and preparation (as opposed to AP weight, or as purchased weight).

espagnole   (ays pah nyol') French. Brown sauce.

farci   (far' see) French. Stuffed.

fermentation   The breakdown of carbohydrates into carbon dioxide gas and alcohol, usually through the action of yeast on sugar.

filé   (fee-lay) A seasoning and thickening agent made from dried, ground sassafras leaves. Used primarily in gumbos.

filet or fillet   (fee lay') French. A boneless cut of meat, fish, or poultry.

fines herbes   (fen zerb') French. A mixture of herbs, usually parsley, chervil, tarragon, and chives.

flake   To break into small pieces, usually with a fork.

flambé   (flam bay') French. To flame, using alcohol as the burning agent.

flan   In France, a filled pastry; in Spain, a custard.

florentine   A food containing or placed upon spinach.

fold in   To blend ingredient into a batter by cutting vertically through the mixture, and turning over and over by sliding the implement across the bottom of the mixing bowl with each turn.

fork tender   A test for doneness. When foods are fork tender, they should be easily pierced or cut by a fork.

frappé   (fra pay') French. Mixture of fruit juices frozen to a mush.

french fry   To cook in deep fry.

fricassee   (frik a see') To cook by browning in a small amount of fat, then stewing or steaming; most often applied to fowl or veal cut into pieces.

frijoles   (free hol' ays) Mexican. Beans cooked with fat and seasonings.

frittata   (free-tah-ta) An open-faced omelet.

fritter   A deep-fat fried batter containing meat, vegetables, or fruit.

frizzle   To pan fry in a small amount of fat until edges curl.

froid   (frwä) French. Cold.

fry   To cook in hot fat. The food may be cooked in a small amount of fat (also called *sauté* or *pan fry*), or in a deep layer of fat (also called *deep-fat fry*).

garam masala   A spice blend made from roasted and ground spices. Used often in East Indian dishes.

garde-manger   (garhd e mah zha') French. Pantry chef/station. Responsible for cold food preparation.

garni   (garnee') French. Garnish. An edible decoration or accompaniment to a food item.

gelatinization   A phase in the process of thickening a liquid with starch in which starch molecules swell to form a network that traps water molecules.

glacé   (glah say') French. Iced, frozen, or coated with sugar syrup.

glaze   To make a shiny surface. In meat preparation, a jellied broth applied to meat surface; in breads and pastries, a wash of egg or syrup; for doughnuts and cakes, a coating with a sugar preparation.

gluten   An elastic protein formed when hard wheat flour is moistened and agitated. Gluten gives yeast doughs their elasticity.

goulash   (goo' lash) Hungarian. Thick beef or veal stew with vegetables, seasoned with paprika.

grand sauce   One of several basic sauces that are used in the preparation of many other small sauces. The grand sauces are: demi-glace, veloute, béchamel, hollandaise, and tomato. Also called mother sauce.

grantinée (grah teen ay′) French. To brown a food sprinkled with cheese or bread crumbs; or a food covered with a sauce that turns brown under a broiler flame, or intense over heat.

grate To rub food against grater to form small particles.

grease To rub lightly with fat.

griddle A heavy metal surface, which may be either built into a stove or heated by its own gas or electric elements. Cooking is done directly on the griddle.

grill To cook by direct heat. May be on an open grid over a heat source or on a flat cooking surface such as a griddle.

grind To change a food to small particles by putting through grinder or food chopper.

grits Coarsely ground corn, served either boiled, or boiled and then fried.

gumbo A rich, thick Creole soup containing okra or filé.

HACCP (Hazard Analysis Critical Control Points). An established plan and monitoring system used to minimize or prevent a safety risk or hazard as food moves through a foodservice facility. Requires establishing standards and controls for time and temperature, and safe handling practices.

herbs Aromatic plants used for seasoning and garnishing of foods.

hollandaise (hol′ ahn days) French, of Dutch origin. Sauce of eggs, butter, lemon juice, and seasonings; served hot with fish or vegetables.

hors d'oeuvre (oh durv′) French. Small portions of food served as appetizers.

infusion To steep an aromatic or other item in liquid to extract the flavor.

IQF Individually quick frozen.

Italienne (e tal yen′) French. Italian style.

jalapeño A hot pepper used for seasoning Mexican food.

jardinière (zhar de nyayr′) French. Mixed vegetables in a savory sauce or soup.

jicama Tuberous root used in salads.

julienne (zhu lee en′) French. Food cut into small stick-shape pieces, approximately $1/8 \times 1/8 \times 1$–2 inches.

jus (zhoo) French. Juice or gravy.

jus lié (zhew lee-ay) An arrowroot or cornstarch thickened brown sauce often used as a demi-glace.

kasha Roasted buckwheat groats (the culled crushed seed).

kebobs Marinated meat and vegetables cooked on skewers.

kippers Lightly salted and smoked fish.

knead To work dough with a pressing motion accompanied by folding and stretching.

kolach (ko′ lahch) Bohemian. Fruit-filled bun.

kosher (ko′ sher) Food handled in accordance with the Jewish religious customs.

kuchen (koo′ ken) German. Cake, not necessarily sweet.

lait (lay) French. Milk.

lard To insert small strips of fat into or on top of uncooked lean meat or fish to give flavor or prevent dryness.

lebkuchen (lab koo′ ckhen) German. Famous German cake; sweet cake or honey cake.

leek Seasoning vegetable resembling a large spring onion with wide leaves, always cooked.

legumes The seeds of certain plants, including beans and peas, which are eaten for their earthy flavor and high nutritional value.

limpa Swedish rye bread.

liqueur Sweet and syrupy alcoholic beverage made by mixing or redistilling liquor with fruits, flowers, spices, or other flavorings. Also known as a cordial.

liquor An alcoholic beverage made by distilling grains or other foods.

lox Yiddish. Smoked salmon.

lyonnaise (lee′ oh nayz) French. Seasoned with onions and parsley, as lyonnaise potatoes.

macédoine (mah say dwan′) French. Mixture or medley of cut vegetables or fruits cut in uniform pieces.

maitre d'hôtel (mai tre doh tel′) French. Steward. *Maître d'hôtel butter*, a well-seasoned mixture of butter, minced parsley, and lemon juice.

marinade (mah ree nahd′) French. Mixture of oil, acid, and seasonings used to flavor and tenderize meats and vegetables; French dressings often used as marinades.

marinate To steep a food in a marinade long enough to modify its flavor.

marzipan (mahr′ zi pan) Powdered sugar and almond paste colored and formed into fruit and vegetable shapes.

mask To coat a food with a thick sauce before it is served. Cold foods may be masked with a mayonnaise mixture or white sauce, which gels after chilling.

medallion A small, round piece of meat or fish.

melt To liquify by the application of heat.

meringue (mah rang′) Stiffly beaten egg white and sugar mixture used as a topping for pies or other desserts; or formed into small cakes or cases and browned in the oven.

merunière, à la (meh nyair') French. Floured, sautéed in butter and served with butter sauce and lemon and sprinkled with chopped parsley; usually refers to fish.

Milanaise (me lan ayz') French. Food cooked in a style developed in Milan, Italy. Implies the use of pasta and cheese with a suitable sauce, often béchamel.

mince To chop food into very small pieces—not so fine and regular as grinding, yet finer than those produced by chopping.

minestrone (mee ne stroh' nay) Italian. Thick vegetable soup with beans and pasta.

mirepoix (meer' pwa) French. Mixture of chopped vegetables used in flavoring soup stock, usually 25% carrots, 50% onions, and 25% celery.

mise en place (meez oh plahss') French. The preparation, organization, and setup before production. Term means "everything in place."

mix To combine two or more ingredients by stirring.

mocha (moh' ka) Coffee flavor or combination of coffee and chocolate.

mollusks Shellfish with soft body and no internal skeleton and a hard outer shell.

monosodium glutamate (MSG) White crystalline material made from vegetable protein, used to enhance flavor of food.

Mornay (mohr nay') French. Sauce of thick cream, eggs, cheese, and seasonings.

mousse (moose) French. Frozen dessert with fruit or other flavors, whipped cream and sugar; also a cold dish of pureed chicken or fish with egg whites, gelatin, and unsweetened whipped cream.

mulligatawny (mul i ga taw' ni) A highly seasoned thick soup, of Indian origin, flavored with curry powder and other spices.

napoleons Puff pastry kept together in layers with a custard filling, cut into portion-size rectangles, and iced.

Neopolitan (also *harlequin* and *panachée*) Molded dessert of two to four kinds of ice cream or ices arranged in layers.

Nesselrode pudding Frozen dessert with a custard foundation to which chestnut puree, fruit, and cream have been added.

Newburg, à la Creamed dish with egg yolk added, flavored with sherry; most often applied to lobster, but may be used with other foods.

noisette (nooa zet') French. Nut-brown color; may imply nut-shaped. A small round piece of lean meat.

Potatoes noisette, potatoes cut into the shape and size of hazelnuts and browned in fat.

nouvelle cuisine French. "New Cooking." A culinary movement emphasizing freshness and lightness, and innovative combinations of foods.

oeuf (oof) French. Egg.

oven spring The rapid initial rise of yeast dough when placed in a hot oven. Heat accelerates the growth of yeast, which produces more carbon dioxide gas and also causes this gas to expand.

paella (pä ay' yah) Spanish. Dish with rice, seafood, chicken, and vegetables, usually served in a wide shallow pan in which it is cooked.

pan broil To cook, uncovered, on hot metal, such as a fry pan, pouring off the fat as it accumulates. Liquid is never added.

panfry To cook in a skillet in a small amount of fat.

papillote (pah pe yote') French. A cooking method in which food is wrapped in paper and heated to a high enough temperature so that steam is produced and the food cooks in its own steam.

parboil To boil until partially cooked, the cooking being completed by another method.

parch To cook in dry heat until slightly browned.

parchment Heat-resistant paper used in cooking for lining baking pans.

parcooking Partially cooking a food.

pare To cut off the outside covering, usually with a knife.

parfait (par fay') French. A mixture containing whipped cream, egg, and syrup that is frozen without stirring. May be ice cream layered with fruit or syrup in parfait glasses.

parmiginana (par mee zhan' ah) Italian. Parma style, particularly veal, chicken, or eggplant covered with tomato sauce, mozzarella cheese, and Parmesan cheese and browned under the broiler or in the oven.

pasta Italian. Any of a large family of flour paste products, such as macaroni, spaghetti, and noodles.

paste Soft, smooth mixture of a dry ingredient and a liquid.

pastrami (pahs tram' ee) Yiddish. Boneless meat cured with spices and smoked.

pâté (pah tay') French. Paste, dough; highly seasoned meat paste used as an appetizer.

pâté de foie gras (pah tay d'fwah grah') French. Paste of fat goose livers.

patty shell Shell or case of pastry or puff paste used for individual portions of creamed mixtures.

peel To strip off the outside covering.

persillade (payr se yad') French. Served with or containing parsley.

pesto Italian. A thick pureed mixture of an herb, usually basil, and oil used as a sauce for pasta. May also contain pine nuts, grated cheese, garlic, and other seasonings.

petit pois (puh tee pooá) French. A fine grade of very small peas with a delicate flavor.

petits fours (pe teet foor') French. Small fancy cakes frosted and decorated.

phyllo dough Greek. Extremely thin pastry dough that produces a flaky pastry.

picante A highly spiced tomato sauce used as a condiment with Mexican foods.

pilaf or

pilau (pih lahf or pih low) Turkish. Dish of rice cooked with meat, fish, or poultry, and seasoned with spices. A technique for cooking grains, in which the grain is sautéed briefly in butter, then simmered in stock or water with various seasonings.

piquant (pee kahnt') French. Sharp, highly seasoned.

pizza (peet' zah) Italian. Flat yeast bread covered with tomato, cheese, and meat, or other toppings.

plank Hardwood board used for cooking and serving broiled meat or fish. *Planked steak,* a broiled steak served on a plank and garnished with a border of suitable vegetables.

poach To cook gently in a hot liquid, held just below the boiling point, the original shape of the food being retained.

polanise (po lo nays') French. Dishes prepared with bread crumbs, chopped eggs, browned butter, and chopped parsley.

polenta (poh lent' ah) Italian. Thick cornmeal mush; cheese is usually added before serving.

pollo (po' yo) Italian. Italian and Spanish-American term for chicken.

pomme de terre (pon de taré) French. Potato; literally, apple of the earth.

potage (po tazh') French. Soup, usually of a thick type.

pot-au-feu (poh toh fu') French. Meat and vegetables boiled together in broth.

pot roast To cook large cuts of meat by braising.

prawn Large shrimp.

preheat To heat oven or other cooking equipment to desired temperature before putting in the food.

proof To allow yeast dough to rise.

prosciutto (pro shoot' toh) Italian. Ham, usually thinly sliced and served as an appetizer or as a component in veal dishes.

puff paste Rich dough, made flaky by repeated folding and rolling.

pulse The edible seeds of various leguminous crops (peas, beans, lentils).

puree (pu ray') French. Foods rubbed through a sieve; also a nutritious vegetable soup in which milk or cream is seldom used.

quiche (keesh) Custard, cheese, and seasonings baked in a pie shell and served warm.

quinoa Grain high in protein. Grown primarily in South America.

ragout (ra goo') French. A thick, well-seasoned, rich stew.

ramekin (ram' e kin) Small baking dish for individual portions.

rarebit Mixture of white sauce, cheese, and seasonings.

ravioli (rav vee oh' lee) Italian. Bite-size cases of pasta dough filled with finely ground meat, cheese, and spinach; served with a highly seasoned tomato sauce.

reconstitute To restore concentrated foods to their normal state, usually by adding water, as in fruit juice and milk.

reduce To boil down, evaporating liquid from a cooked dish.

refritos Twice-cooked Mexican beans that are boiled once and fried once. Also called *refried beans.*

rehydrate To cook or soak dehydrated foods or restore water lost during drying.

remoulade (ray moo lad') French. Pungent sauce made of hard-cooked eggs, mustard, oil, vinegar, and seasonings. Served with cold dishes.

risotto (ri sot' toh) Italian. Rice that has been sautéed with onion and other aromatics and then combined with stock. Adding stock slowly while stirring produces a creamy texture with the rice grains still *al dente.*

rissolé (ree sall') French. Savory meat mixture encased in rich pastry and fried in deep fat.

roast To cook uncovered in oven by dry heat, usually meat or poultry.

roe Eggs of fish.

rosette (roh zet') French. Thin, rich batter made into fancy shape with special iron and fried in deep fat.

roulade (roo lahd') French. Rolled thin piece of meat, usually stuffed and roasted or braised.

roux (roo) French. A browned mixture of equal parts flour and fat (by weight) used as a thickener for sauces, soups, and stews.

sabayon (sa by on') French. Custard sauce with wine added.

sachet d'epices or

sachet (sah-shay day-pea-say) French. Aromatic ingredients (herbs and spices) tied in a cheesecloth bag and used to flavor stocks and other liquids.

salsa   A highly spiced tomato sauce used as a condiment with Mexican foods.

sauerbraten (sour brah′ ten) German. Beef marinated in spiced vinegar, pot-roasted, and served with gingersnap gravy.

sauté (soh tay′) French. To cook in a small amount of fat.

savory   Spiced or seasoned foods, as opposed to sweet foods. Also a family of herbs.

scald   To heat a liquid to a point just below boiling; pour boiling water over or dip food briefly into boiling water.

scallion   An onion that has not developed a bulb.

scallop   To bake food, cut into pieces and cover with a liquid or sauce and crumbs. The food and sauce may be mixed together or arranged in alternate layers in a baking dish, with or without crumbs. *Escalloped* is a synonymous term. A thin boneless slice of meat. A shellfish (mollusk).

scallopine (skol a pee′ nee) Italian. Small flat pieces of meat, usually veal, sautéed and served in a sauce.

scone (scahn) Scottish quick bread containing currants.

score   To make shallow lengthwise and crosswise slits on the surface of meat.

sear   To brown the surface of meat quickly at high temperatures.

semolina   Coarsely milled hard wheat endosperm used for gnocchi, some pasta, and couscous.

set   Allow to stand until congealed, as in gelatin and puddings.

shallot   Small onion having a stronger but more mellow flavor than the common variety.

shirr   To break eggs into dish, cover with cream and crumbs, and bake.

shortening   Fat suitable for baking or frying.

simmer   To cook in a liquid in which bubbles form slowly and break just below the surface.

skewer   Pin of metal or wood used for fastening meat or poultry while cooking; or long pins used for holding bits of food for broiling or roasting.

skim   To remove surface fat or foam from liquid mixture.

sliver   To cut into long, slender pieces, as in slivered almonds.

smorgasbord (smor gas bohrd′) Swedish. Arrangement of appetizers and other foods on a table in attractive assortment.

sorbet (sor bay′) French. Sherbet made of several kinds of fruits.

soubise (soo′ bees) French. White sauce containing onion and sometimes parsley.

soufflé (soo flay′) French. A light, fluffy baked dish with beaten egg whites; may be sweet or savory.

soy sauce   Chinese sauce made from fermented soy beans.

spaetzle (spet′ zel) Austrian. Fine noodles made by pressing batter through colander into boiling water or broth.

spoon bread   Southern corn bread baked in a casserole and served with a spoon.

springerle (spring′ er le) German. A Christmas cookie. The dough is rolled into a sheet and pressed with a springerle mold before baking.

spumoni (spoo moh′ nee) Italian. Rich ice cream made in different layers, usually containing fruit and nuts.

stabilizer   An ingredient added to an emulsion to prevent it from separating.

steam   To cook in steam with or without pressure. Steam may be applied directly to the food, as in a steamer, or to the vessel, as in a double boiler.

steam-jacketed kettle   A kettle with double-layered walls, between which steam circulates, providing even heat for cooking stocks, soups, and sauces.

steep   To cover with boiling water and let stand to extract flavors and colors.

stew   To simmer in a small amount of liquid.

stir   To mix food materials with a circular motion.

stir fry   To cook quickly in a small amount of oil over high heat, using light tossing and stirring motion to preserve shape of food.

stock   Liquid in which meat, fish, poultry, or vegetables have been cooked.

stroganoff (stro′ gan off) Russian. Sautéed beef in sauce of sour cream, with mushrooms and onions.

strudel (stroo′ dl) German. Pastry of flaky, paper-thin dough filled with fruit.

sweating   Cooking vegetables (usually) in a covered pan with a small amount of fat over low heat, without browning, until the food softens and releases moisture.

table d'hôte (tabl doht′) French. Meal at a fixed price.

tacos (tah′ cos) Mexican. Rolled sandwiches of tortillas filled with meat, onions, lettuce, and hot sauce.

tamale (ta mah′ lee) Mexican. Highly seasoned meat mixture rolled in cornmeal mush, wrapped in corn husks, and steamed.

tart   Small pie or pastry.

tartar sauce   Mayonnaise to which chopped pickles, onions, and other seasonings have been added; usually served with fish.

tender crisp   The point in cooking vegetables at which they are firm and slightly crisp.

terrine   (tay reen') French. Tureen, an earthenware pot resembling a casserole. *Chicken en terrine* is chicken cooked and served in a tureen.

timbale   Thin fried case for holding creamed mixtures; or unsweetened baked custard with meat, poultry, or vegetables.

toast   To apply direct heat until the surface of the food is browned.

tofu   Bean curd.

torte   (tor' te) German. Rich cake made from crumbs, eggs, and nuts; or meringue in the form of a cake.

tortilla   (tohr tee' yah) Mexican. A round thin unleavened flour or cornmeal cake baked on a griddle.

toss   To mix ingredients lightly without crushing.

tournedos   (tur ne' doe) Spanish. A small round filet of beef. French, a small cut from the tenderloin of beef.

trifle   English. Dessert made with sponge cake soaked in fruit juice and wine and layered with jam, custard, almonds, and whipped cream.

truffle   A dark mushroomlike fungus, found chiefly in France. Used mainly for garnishing and flavor.

truss   To tie or skewer poultry or meat so that it will hold its shape while cooking.

turnover   Food encased in pastry and baked.

tutti frutti   Mixed fruit.

velouté   (ve loo tay') French. A rich white sauce, usually made of chicken or veal broth.

vinaigrette   (vin nay greht) French. A temporary emulsion of 3 parts oil and 1 part vinegar and often seasoned with herbs and spices. Wine or lemon juice is often substituted for some of the vinegar.

whip   To beat rapidly and increase volume by the incorporation of air.

Wiener schnitzel   (ve' ner schnit sel) German. Breaded cutlets, frequently served with tomato sauce or lemon.

wonton   Stuffed dumplings cooked in chicken broth.

Yorkshire pudding   English. Accompaniment for roast beef, a popoverlike mixture baked in drippings of the roast.

zest   Colored peel of citrus fruits, such as orange or lemon, which contains aromatic oil.

zwieback   (tsvee' bahk) German. Toasted bread, crisp and slightly sweet.

Index

A

Abbreviations used in recipes, 225
Acidulated water for fish, 460
Acini de Pepe Fruit Salad, **672**
Acorn squash, 165
    Baked, **870**
    with Sausage, **870**
    Stuffed, **870**
Adult care meal pattern, 20
Agaricus mushrooms, 161
A la King Sauce, **749**
Alcohol flavorings, 187
Almond(s), 184
    blanched, 641
    Butter Sauce, **771**
    Filling, **317**
    toasted almonds, 641
        and Bulgur with Cranberries, **620**
Amaranth, 120
Amaretto Cocoa, **249**
Ambrosia Fruit Salad, **673**
Amounts of food to serve 50, 64–74
Angel Food Cake, and variations, **329**
Angel Pie, **395**
Anjou pears, 151
Appetizers and party foods, 227–244.
    See also Beverages; Sandwiches;
    Soups
    Amount to prepare, 229
    Basic Dip, and variations, **232–233**
    entree party trays, 230
    name suggestions for, 231
    suggestions for, 228–229
Apple(s), 146
    Baked, **430**
    Buttered, **693**
    Cinnamon, **693**
    Cinnamon Swirl Salad, **667**
    Compote, **432**
    Cooler, **261**
    Crisp, **429**
    Crumb Pie, **399**
    Dumplings, **431**
    Fried, **693**

Fritters, **297**
Hot Apple Toddy, **261**
Muffins, **270**
Nut Muffins, **275**
Pancakes, **289**
Pie, **399**
Rings, **693**
Salad (Waldorf), and variations, **670**
Sour Cream Apple Nut Pie, **400**
Spiced, **675**
Stuffing, **557**
Applesauce, **432**
    Cake, **336**
    Gelatin Salad, **667**
Apricot(s), 146
    Bavarian Cream, **427**
    Filling, **360**
    Glaze for Ham, **519**
    Muffins, **270**
    Pie, **401**
    Pineapple Punch, **255**
    Roll, **349**
Arabian Peach Salad, **667**
Arrowroot, 127
Artichoke Dip, Hot, **232**
Artichokes, 153–154
Arugula, 154, 167
Asian. *See also* Stir-frying
    Bean Salad, **645**
    Coleslaw, **649**
    Marinade, **785**
    Orange Ginger Beef Wrap, **726**
    Rice
        Fajita Spiced Catfish with, **461**
        Fried Rice, **598**
        Sushi Style, **610**
    Sesame sauce, **754**
    Shrimp and Pasta, **476**
Asian pears, 152
Asparagus, 154
    with Cheese Sauce, **827**
    cooking of, **827**
    Creamed, **827**
    with Hollandaise Sauce, **827**

Marinated, **652**
Seasoned, **827**
seasonings for, **827**
Soup, Cream of, **810**
Vinaigrette, **827**
Autumn Salad, **667**
Avocados, 146

B

Baba Ghanoush, **238**
Bacon
    Lettuce, and Tomato
        Sandwich, **722**
    Oven-Fried, **522**
    Salad Dressing, **701**
    Sauce, **749, 771**
    Wrapped Beef, **493**
Baked Apples, **430**
Baked Beans, and variations, **833**
Baked Lima Beans, **831**
Baked Potatoes. *See* Potato(es)
Baking Powder Biscuits, **268**
    variations of. *See* Biscuits
Baking procedures, for savory foods,
    195–196
Baking temperatures
    convection oven, 97
    metric equivalents, 95
Balsamic vinegar, 175
Banana(s), 147
    Cake, **337**
    Cream Pie, **404**
    Cream Pudding, **419**
    Deep-Fat Fried, **851**
    Fritters, **297**
    Muffins, **271**
    Nut Bread, **286**
    Punch, **253**
    Whole Wheat Muffins, **271**
Banana squash, 165
Banquet service, 30–35
Barbecue Sauce, **755**
Barbequing procedures, 194–195

Barley, 120
  and Black Bean Salad, **648**
  Casserole, and variations, **614**
  Ginger Vegetables and, **617**
  Spicy, with confetti
    vegetables, **618**
  Tomato Risotto and
    variations, **616**
  and Vegetable Medley, 615
  and Vegetables, **619**
Bartlett pears, 152
Basil, 167
  Garlic Basil Fusilli, **846**
  Oil, **574, 577**
    with Sugar Snap Peas, **574**
  and Parmesan Bows, **574**
Basmati Rice and Lentil Pilaf, **604**
Bâtonnet technique, 212
Batter for deep-fat frying, 99
Bavarian Cream
  Apricot, **427**
  Pineapple, **427**
  Strawberry, **427**
Bay laurel, 167
Bay leaf, 167
Bean(s), 154. *See also* Black beans;
    Green beans; Lima beans
  Baked, **833**
  Boston Baked, **833**
  dried beans, lentils, peas, 173
    preparation of, 560, 826
    varieties of, 826
  and Grains, **632**
  with Pork, **833**
  Ragout, **627**
  Ranch Style, **832**
  Red Beans & Rice, **634**
  Refried, **834**
  Soup, Navy Bean, **805**
  and Tomato Sauce, **760**
  Trio Baked, **833**
Béchamel Sauce, **750**
Beef
  Bacon-Wrapped, **493**
  Beef on Noodles, **593**
  Birds, **512**
  Brisket, Savory, **488**
  Brisket, Smoked, **488**
  and Broccoli Stir-Fry, **541**
  Cheeseburger Pie, **511**
  Chop Suey, **504**
  color guide, color exhibit, VI
  cooking methods, 193–194
  Ginger Orange, **491**
    Wrap, **726**
  Kabobs, **496**
  Liver, and variations, **497**
  Meatballs, **498, 499, 500**
  Meat Loaf, **497**
  Pizza, and variations, **506**
  Pork and Noodle
    Casserole, **592**

Pot Pie, **501**
Pot Roast, **488**
  Savory, **488**
  Yankee, **488**
  primal and retail cuts, 129
  Sauerbraten, **489**
  Short Ribs, Barbecued, **517**
  Soup
    Barley, **794**
    Mexican, **795**
    Noodle, **797**
    Rice, **797**
    Vegetable Beef, Hearty, **796**
  Spanish Rice, **510**
  Steak
    broiling, 483
    Chicken-Fried, **492**
    Chuck Wagon, **494**
    Country Fried, **492**
    Grilling, 486
    Pepper, **490, 850**
    Salisbury, **493**
    Smothered with
      Onions, **492**
    Spanish, **492**
    Swiss, **492**
    Teriyaki, **492**
  Stew, and variations, **501**
    Green Chili, **502**
  Stir-fried, with Broccoli, **541**
    with Sugar Snap Peas, **495**
  Stock, **791**
    with Soup Base, **791**
  Stroganoff, **503**
  Sweet-Sour, **518**
  Taco Salad Casserole, **509**
  timetables for
    braising, 487
    broiling, 485
    cooking in liquid, 487
    direct grilling, 486
    roasting, 480
Beet greens. *See* Spinach
Beets, 154
  cooking of, 836
  Harvard, **836**
  Hot Spiced, **836**
  Julienne, **835**
  with Orange Sauce, **836**
  Pickled, **697**
  Roasted, **835**
  Seasoned, **835**
  seasonings for, 835
  in Sour Cream, **835**
Belgian endive, 157
Berries, 147
Beverages, 245–261
  Cocoa, **249**
  Coffee, 174, 245, **247**
  Punch, 251–260
  Tea, 174, 246, **247**
Bierocks, **729**

Biscuits
  Baking Powder, **268**
  Buttermilk, **268**
  Butterscotch, **268**
  Cheese, **268**
  Cinnamon Raisin, **268**
  Drop, **268**
  Orange, **268**
  Raisin, **269**
  Scones, Scotch, **269**
  Whole Wheat, **269**
Biscuit Topping for Cobblers, **434**
Bishop's Bread, **276**
Bittersweet Icing, **353**
Black beans
  and Andouille Sausage, **630**
  cooking of, 826
  and Corn Relish, **696**
  and Couscous, **628**
    Cuban, **629**
  and Ham on Rice, **630**
  over Rice, **630**
  Salad, **648**
  Soup, **630**
  Spanish Rice and, **633**
  Spicy, **834**
  and Tomato Sauce, **760**
  and Tortilla Casserole, **631**
Blackberries, 147
Blackened Chicken Salad, **679**
Black-eyed peas
  cooking of, 826
  and Corn Salsa, **758**
  Seasoned, **852**
Black forest mushroom, 162
Blanching, 198, 641
Blueberry, 147
  Coffee Cake, **277**
  Gelatin Salad, **667–668**
  Muffins, **270**
  Pancakes, **289**
  Pie, **398**
  Syrup, **778**
Blue Cheese Dip, **233**
Blue Cheese Salad Dressing, **699**
Boiling procedures, 199
Bok choy, 154
Bosc pears, 152
Boston Baked Beans, **833**
Boston Brown Bread, **283**
Boston Cream Pie, **335**
Bouillon, **792**
  Chicken, **792**
  Tomato, **792**
Bouquet Garni, 177, 460
Bowknot Rolls, **309**
Boysenberry Mold, **668**
Braids, **309**
Braising procedures, 198–199
Brazil nuts, 184
Bread Dressing, and variations, **557**
Bread Pudding, **423**

Breads, quick, 263–264
  Baking Powder Biscuits
      variations of. *See* Biscuits
  Banana Nut Bread, **286**
  Bishop's Bread, **276**
  Boston Brown Bread, **283**
  Cheese Straws, **298**
  Coffee Cake, **279**
      Blueberry, **277**
      Dutch Apple, **278**
      Walnut, **280**
  Corn Bread, **281**
  Cranberry Nut Bread, **287**
  Crepes, **292**
  Date Nut Bread, **285**
  Doughnuts, **294**
  Dumplings, **295**
  evaluating, 201
  French Breakfast Puffs, **275**
  Fritters, and variations, **297**
  methods of mixing, 263–264
  Muffins, basic
      Cake Method, 264
      Muffin Method, 263
      variations of. *See* Muffins
  Nut Bread, 284
  Pancakes, and variations, **289**. *See also* Pancakes
      Mix for, **290**
  Pumpkin Bread, **288**
  Quality standards, 265
  Scotch Scones, **269**
  Spaetzles, **295**
  Spoon Bread, **282**
  Waffles, **291**
Breads, yeast, 264–267, 299–317
  Basic Roll Dough, **309**
      variations of. *See* Rolls
  Buns. *See* Buns
  Butter Slices, **299**
  Caramel Crowns, **309–310**
  Cinnamon Bread, **299**
  Cinnamon Rolls, **316**
      variations of. *See* Rolls
  Coffee Cake, **314**
  Cornmeal Bread, **301**
  Crullers, **315**
  Danish Pastry, **315**
  Dilly Bread, **303**
  Egg Bread, **301**
  English Muffin Bread, **304**
  evaluating, 201
  Focaccia, **305**
  freezing, 266
  French Bread, **302**
  Fruit Coffee Rings, **315**
  ingredients, 264–265
  Jalapeño Cheese Bread, **301**
  Kolaches, **315**
  Long Johns, **315**
  Molasses Bran Bread, **306**
  Oatmeal Bread, **306**

Portuguese Sweet Bread, **307**
Potato Bread, **307**
preparation of, 265–266
quality standards, 267
Raised Muffins, **313**
Raisin Bread, **300**
Sandwich Ring Bread, **300**
Swedish Braids, **315**
Swedish Rye Bread, and variations, **308**
Sweet Roll Dough, Basic, **314**
    variations of. *See* Rolls
White Bread, and variations, **299–300, 301**
Whole Wheat Bread, and variations, **300, 301**
Broccoli, 154
  Almond Buttered, **837**
  Cauliflower Salad, **649**
  Cheese Casserole, **454**
  with Cheese Sauce, **837**
  and Cheese Soup, **813**
  and Cheese Strata, **453**
  cooking of, **837**
  with Hollandaise Sauce, **837**
  with Lemon Butter, **837**
  Rice au Gratin, **607**
  Seasoned, **837**
  seasonings for, **837**
  Soup, Cream of, **810**
  Swiss pasta, **569**
Broiling procedures, 194
Brown Bean Salad, **646**
Brownies, **377**
  Butterscotch Chocolate Chip, **381**
  Fudge, **378**
  Fudge Nut, **378**
Brown Sauce, **753**
Brown Sugar Glaze for Ham, **519**
Brown Sugar Syrup, **778**
Brunches, 23–25
Brunswick Stew, **548**
Brussels sprouts, 154
  cooking of, **837**
  Seasoned, **837**
  seasonings for, **837**
Buckwheat, 120
Buffet dinner and luncheons, 25–30
  food presentation and service, 28–30
  Menu Planning, 27
  Styles of service, 35–36
  table arrangement for, 27–30
Bulgur, 122
  with Cranberries and Toasted Almonds, **620**
Buns
  Buffet Submarine, **299**
  Butter, **312**
  Double Cinnamon, **317**
  Gooey, **310**
  Hot Cross, **310, 315**
  Hot Dog, **310**

Burnt Butter Icing, **352**
Burnt Sugar Cake, **338**
Burnt Sugar Syrup, **338**
Butter, 119
  Basil, **779**
  Buns, **312**
  Cinnamon Topping, **317**
  Compound, **779**
  Crunch Topping, **317**
  Curry, **780**
  Dill, **779, 780**
  Drawn, **771**
  Garlic, **779**
  Herb, **779, 780**
  Honey, **716**
  Lemon, **779, 780**
  Mustard, **779**
  Onion, **780**
  Parsley, **779**
  Parsley Lemon, **779**
  purchasing and storage, 119
  Red Pepper, **779**
  Tarragon, **780**
  Whipped, **716**
Buttercup squash, 165
Butterflake Rolls, **310**
Butterfly Rolls, **316**
Buttermilk Biscuits, **268**
Buttermilk Pancakes, **289**
  Mix for, **290**
Buttermilk Salad Dressing, **699**
Butternut squash, 165
  Mashed, **872**
  Mashed, with Apples, **872**
Butterscotch
  Biscuits, **268**
  Chocolate Chip Brownies, **381**
  Cookies
      Drop, **364**
      Refrigerator, **385**
  Cream Pie, **405**
  Cream Puffs, **426**
  Pecan Cookies, **366**
  Pudding, **416**
  Rolls, **316**
  Sauce, **773**
  Squares, **364, 381**

C

Cabbage, 154
  Apple Salad, **650**
  au Gratin, **838**
  Carrot Slaw, **650**
  Chinese, 160
  cooking of, **838**
  Creamed, **838**
  Hot Slaw, **839**
  Pineapple-Marshmallow Salad, **650**
  Polonnaise, **838**
  Salad (Coleslaw), **649**
  Scalloped, **838**

Cabbage, *Continued*
  Seasoned, **838**
  seasonings for, **838**
  Stir-fried, **838**
Caffé latte, 174
Caffé mocha, 174
Cajun Seasoning, **782**
Cake(s), 319–324, 328–351
  Angel Food, **329**
    Chocolate, **329**
    Frozen-Filled, **329**
    Orange-Filled, **329**
    Yellow (sponge), **330**
  Applesauce, **336**
  Apricot Roll, **349**
  baking, 322
  Banana, **337**
  Burnt Sugar, **338**
  Carrot, **334**
  Cheese, **422**
  Chiffon
    Cocoa, **331**
    Orange, **331**
    Walnut, **331**
  Chocolate, **339**
    Chip, **333**
    Roll, **348**
    Sheet Cake, **340**
  coating for pans, 328
  Coconut Lime, **333**
  Corn Cakes, Zucchini, **293**
  Cupcakes, **333**, **340**
  cutting configurations, 323
  Dutch Apple, **335**
  Fruitcake, **344**
  Fudge, **340**
  German Sweet Chocolate, **341**
  Gingerbread, and variations, **345**
  Ice Cream Roll, **348**
  Jelly Roll, **349**
  Lady Baltimore, **333**
  Lazy Daisy, **335**
  Marble, **336**
  methods of mixing, 319–320
  Peanut Butter, **342**
  Pineapple Cashew, **343**
  Pineapple Upside-Down, **336**
  Poppy Seed, **333**
  Pound, **346**
  Praline, **336**
  Pumpkin, **347**
  Pumpkin Cake Roll, **351**
  quality standards, 324
  scaling weight of batter for, 320–322
  Silver White, **333**
  Sponge, **330**
  Starburst, **333**
  types of, 319
  White, 332–333
    Dough-Batter, **333**
    Dry Blending, **332**
  Yellow, **335**

Calzone, Broccoli and Ricotta, **733**
  Ham and Swiss, **733**
  Roasted Vegetable, **733**
Campus Salad Dressing, **699**
Canapés, preparation of, 714
Can sizes, 94
Cantaloupe, 150
Cappuccino, 174
Caramel
  Crowns, **309–310**
  Custard, **423**
  Pecan Rolls, **317**
  Sauce, **773**
Carrifruit Salad, **644**
Carrot(s), 156
  Cake, **334**
  Candied, **840**
  and Celery Amandine, **841**
  cooking of, **840**
  Glazed, **840**
  Lyonnaise, **840**
  Marinated, **656**
  Mint-glazed, **840**
  Parsley Buttered, **840**
  and Parsnips, Glazed, **840**
  Raisin Salad, and variations, **644**
  Savory, **840**
  seasonings for, **840**
  Sweet-Sour, **840**
Casaba, 150
Cashews, 184
Catfish, Fajita Spiced, **461**
Cauliflower, 156
  with Almond Butter, **842**
  Bean Salad, **645**
  Broccoli Salad, **649**
    Creamy, **649**
  with Cheese Sauce, **842**
  cooking of, **842**
  Creamed, **842**
  French Fried, **851**
  with Peas, **842**
  Rice au Gratin, **607**
  Seasoned, **842**
  seasonings for, **842**
  Soup, Cream of, **810**
Celeriac, 156
Celery, 156
  and Carrots Amandine, **841**
  cooking of, **841**
  Creole, **841**
  seasonings for, **841**
  Soup, Cream of, **810**
Celery root, 156
Celery Seed Dressing, **702, 709**
Cephalopods, 136. *See also* Fish and
    shellfish
Cereals, cooking of, 611
Chantilly Salad Dressing, **699**
Chard, Swiss, 156
Checkerboard sandwiches,
    714–715

Cheeseburger Pie, **511**
Cheese(s), 111
  Balls, **451**
  Biscuits, **268**
  and Broccoli Casserole, **454**
  and Broccoli Strata, **453**
  Cake, **422**
  cookery, 437
  firm, 115–116
  fresh, 112
  Grits, Baked, **613**
  hard grating, 116
  natural, 111
  Omelet, **443**
  Party Cheese Ball, **237**
  processed, 111, 116
  Salad Sandwich, **717**
  Sandwiches, Grilled, **728**
  Sandwich Sauce, **749**
  Sauce, **749**
  selecting, 112–116
  semi-soft, 113–114
  soft, 112–113
  Soufflé, **452**
  Soup, **452**
  storage, 117
  Straws, **298**
  Welsh Rarebit, **455**
Chef's Salad Bowl, **677**
  Chicken Bacon, **677**
  Seafood, **677**
Cherry, 147
  Crisp, **429**
  Muffins, **270**
  Nut Rolls, **314**
  Pie, **398**
Chervil, 167
Chestnuts, 184
Chestnut Stuffing, **557**
Chicken
  á la King, **545**
  and Bacon Chef's Salad, **677**
  Barbecued, **539**
  Barley Casserole, **614**
  Blackened, **536**
  with Black Olives, **535**
  breading sequence for, 530
  Breast
    Blackened, **536**
    Cheese-Stuffed, **537**
    Curried, **536**
    Dijon, **536**
    Grilled, and variations, **536**
    with Grilled Tomato
      Sauce, **536**
    Herb-Marinated, **536**
    Sesame Mustard, **536**
  and Broccoli Stir-Fry, **541**
  Brunswick Stew, **548**
  Cacciatore, **538**
  Cajun Wings, **240**
  Cantonese, **538**

Chow Mein, **504**
classes of, 134
cooking methods for, 527–532
Creamed, **545**
Crepes, **544**
Curried, **549**
Deep-Fat Fried, **538**
Fajitas, **735, 736**
Fricassee, **535**
Gravy, **752**
Herb Baked, **539**
Hot Barbecued Wings, **240**
Italian Baked, **539**
and Noodles, **551**
    on Whipped Potatoes, **552**
Oven-Fried, **539**
Pan-Fried, **538**
Parmesan, **539**
and Pasta Salad, **659**
and Pasta Salad Plate, **680**
Pocket Sandwich, **723**
Pot Pie, **550**
preparation for salad, 641
Quesadillas, **744**
and Rice Casserole, **553**
Salad, and variations, **678**
    for variations. *See* Salads, entree
Salad, Hot, **546**
Scalloped, **547**
Singapore Curry, **549**
and Snow Peas over Rice, **542**
soup. *See* Soup(s)
Southern Fried, **538**
stewed, 531–532
Sweet and Sour Wings, **240**
Sweet-Sour, **518**
Szechwan, **543**
Tahitian, **535**
Tarragon Chicken Breast, **536**
Teriyaki, **539**
Tetrazzini, **590**
Timbale, **880**
and Vegetable Stir-Fry, **541**
Chicken-Fried Steak, **492**
Chiffonade, 211
Chiffonade Salad Dressing, **703**
Chiffon cakes. *See* Cake(s)
Child care meal pattern, 18–19
Chilean Salad Dressing, **701**
Chile-Cilantro Sauce, **461, 772**
Chile peppers, 162, 163
Chili
    con Carne, and variations, **800**
    Dog, **524**
    Garden, **801**
    Spaghetti, **800**
    White, **802**
Chimichanga, **740**
Chinese cabbage, 160
Chinese Omelet, **445**
Chinese parsley, 168. *See also*
    Cilantro

Chives, 168
Chocolate
    Angel Food Cake, **329**
    Butter Cream Icing, **354**
    Cake, **339**
    Chiffon Pie, and variations, **411**
    Chip Cake, **333**
    Chip Cookies, **365, 368, 373**
    Chip Muffins, **269**
    Cookies, Drop, **364**
        Tea, **383**
    Cream Filling, **359**
    Cream Pie, **404**
    Cream Pudding, **419**
    Crumb Crusts, **393**
    Cupcakes, **340**
    Doughnuts, **294**
    French, **250**
    Glaze, **358**
    Hot Chocolate, **249**
    Icing, **353**
    Jumbo Chunk Cookies, **369**
    Marshmallow Squares, **382**
    Mexican Chocolate, **249**
    Mint Warmer, **261**
    Mousse, **359**
    Peanut Butter Cookies, **368**
    Pudding, and variations, **417**
    Refrigerator Dessert, **411**
    Roll, **348**
    Sauce, **774**
Chop Suey, **504**
Chowder
    Clam, **816, 820**
    Corn, **815**
    Fish, **816, 820**
    Potato, **815**
    Potato Ham, **818**
    Vegetable, **815**
Chow Mein, Chicken, **504**
    Vegetable, **505**
Christmas Pudding, **425**
    Christmas Wreath
        Cookies, **388**
    Flaming, **425**
Chuck Wagon Steak, **494**
Cider Punch, **259**
    Hot Mulled, **259**
    Spiced, **259**
Cider vinegar, 175
Cilantro, 168
    Chile-Cilantro Sauce, **461, 772**
Cinnamon
    Apples, **693**
    Bread, **299**
    Buns, **317**
    Raisin Biscuits, **268**
    Rolls, and variations, **316**
    Twists, **314**
Citronella grass, 169
Citrus Couscous Salad, **662**
Citrus fruits, 147–149

Citrus Pomegranate Salad, **674**
Citrus Spritzer, **261**
Clam(s), 138
    Chowder
        Manhattan, **820**
        New England, **816**
    Pasta Sauce, **567**
Clarifying stock, 789
Cloverleaf Rolls, **310**
Club Sandwich, **722**
Coarse chopping, 211
Coating for baking pans, 328
Coatings for deep-fat fried foods, 99
Cobbler
    Biscuit Topping for, **434**
    frozen fruit guide for, 398
    Fruit, **433**
    Peach, with Hard Sauce, **433**
Cocktails, Nonalcoholic, **261**
Cocktail Sauce, **764**
Cocoa, **249**
Cocoa Icing, **355**
Coconut, 185
    Cookies, **388**
    Cream Pie, **404**
    Cream Pudding, **419**
    Custard Pie, **407**
    Icing, **353**
    Lime Cake, **333**
    Macaroons, **365**
    Muffins, **269**
    Pecan Bars, **379**
    Pecan Icing, **354**
Cod, Lemon Rice-Stuffed, **466**
Coffee, 174, 245
    Hot, **247**
    Iced, **247**
    preparation of, 245
    Steeped, **247**
Coffee Cake, **279**
    Blueberry, **277**
    Dutch Apple, **278**
    Walnut, **280**
    Yeast, **314**
Coffees and brunches, 23–25
Coleslaw, and variations, **649**
Coleslaw, Creamy, and
    variations, **650**
Collards, 156. *See also* Spinach
Colleges and universities, menu
    planning for, 14–15
Combination Salad Dressing, **700**
Comice pears, 152
Commercial foodservices, menu
    planning for, 15–18
Compound Butters, **779**
Condiments, 175
Confetti Rice, **597**
Confetti Vegetables, Spicy
    Barley with, **618**
Convection oven, time and
    temperatures, 97

Conversion
  U.S. to metric, 44–45
  weight to measure, 45
Cooked Salad Dressing, and
    variations, **700**
Cookies, 325–326, 364–388
  Bar, 377–382
  Brownies, **377**
    Butterscotch Chocolate Chip, **381**
    Fudge, **378**
    Fudge Nut, **378**
  Butterscotch
    Drop, **364**
    Pecan, **366**
    Refrigerator, **385**
    Squares, **364, 381**
  Butter Tea, **383**
  Chocolate Chip, **365, 368, 373**
  Chocolate Chunk, Jumbo, **369**
  Chocolate Drop, **364**
  Chocolate Tea, **383**
  Christmas Wreath, **388**
  Coconut, **388**
  Coconut Macaroons, **365**
  Coconut Pecan Bars, **379**
  Crisp Ginger, **386**
  Date Bars, **380**
  Dreamland Bars, **379**
  Drop, 364–376
  Filled, **388**
  Frosty Date Balls, **384**
  Gingersnap, **371**
  Marshmallow Krispie Squares, **382**
  methods of mixing, 325
  Molasses Drop, **370**
  Oatmeal
    Coconut Crispies, **387**
    Crispies, **387**
    Date Bars, **382**
    Drop, **367**
  Peanut, **372**
  Peanut Butter, **368**
  Pinwheel, **388**
  pressed, molded, and rolled, 383–388
  quality standards, 326
  Sandies, **384**
  shaping and baking, 325
  Snickerdoodles, **374**
  storing, 325
  Sugar
    Drop, **375**
    Rolled, **388**
    Whole Wheat, **376**
  Tea, **383**
  Thimble, **383**
Cooking methods, 191–193
  baking savory foods, 195–196
  barbequing, 194–195
  blanching, 198
  boiling, 199
  braising, 198–199
  broiling, 194

deep-fat frying, 196–197
dry heat, 193–197
en papillote, 200
griddle broiling, 194
griddle frying, 197
grilling, 194
large-equipment requirements, 222
moist heat, 197–200
oven frying, 197
panbroiling, 194
pan frying, 197
parboiling, 198
poaching, 199
roasting savory foods, 195–196
sautéing, 197
simmering, 199–200
steaming, 200
stir-frying, 197
Cooking terms, glossary of, 893–901
Cooling Procedures, 105
Corn, 156
  Cakes, Zucchini Corn, **293**
  Chowder, **815**
  cooking of, **843**
  in Cream, **843**
  Creamed Whole Kernel, **843**
  Fritters, **297**
  as grain, 120
  O'Brien, **843**
  Pudding, **844**
  Relish, **696**
  Salsa, **758**
  Scalloped, **843**
  Seasoned, **843**
Corn Bread, **281**
Corn Bread Dressing, **556**
Cornish Game Hens,
    Orange-Glazed, **540**
Cornmeal Bread, **301**
Cornmeal Muffins, **270**
Cornmeal Mush, Fried, **523**
Cottage Cheese Salad, **689**
Cottage Pudding, **335**
Country Fried Steak, **492**
Court Bouillon, **460**
  Black Bean, **628**
Couscous, 122
  Citrus Salad, **662**
  Israeli Salad, **661**
  with Olives and Roasted
      Tomatoes, 622
  Vegetable, **621**
    Red Pepper, **623**
Crab(s), 138
  and Artichoke Dip, **232**
  Deviled, **472**
  and Pasta Salad, **683**
  Salad, **682**
Cracked wheat, 122
Cranberry, 147
  Apple Salad, **668**
  with Bulgur and Toasted Almonds, **620**

Glaze for Ham, **519**
Juice, Spiced, **259**
Mold, **668**
Muffins, **270**
Nut Bread, **287**
Orange Relish, **694**
Punch, **253, 259**
Relish, **694**
  Baked, **695**
Sauce, and variations, **695**
Scones, **274**
Warmer, **258**
Cream, 118
Cream Cheese Icing, **355**
Cream Pie, and variations, **404**.
    See also Pies
Cream products, 119
Cream Puffs, **426**
Cream Soup, Basic Sauce for, **810**
  variations of, **810**
Creamy Icing, **355**
Crenshaw, 150
Creole Baked Fish, **462**
Creole Soup, **797**
Creole Spaghetti, **584**
Crepes, **292**
  Chicken, **544**
  Fruit Cheese, **544**
  Spinach, **544**
Crescents, **310**
Cress, 157
Crimini mushrooms, 161
Critical control points, 225
Croissant with Vegetables, **743**
Crullers, **315**
Crumb Crusts, **393**
  Crumb Topping, **317**
Crustaceans, 136. See also Fish and
    shellfish
Cucumber(s), 157
  German, **651**
  and Onion in Sour Cream, **651**
  Sauce, **767**
  Soufflé Salad, **668**
  Yogurt Salad Dressing, **711**
Cupcakes
  Chocolate, **340**
  White, **333**
Curly endive, 157
Curly parsley, 170
Currant Muffins, **270**
Currants, 147
Curried Eggs, **442**
Curried Rice, **603, 609**
Curry, Singapore, **549**
Curry Butter, **780**
Custard
  Baked, and variations, **423**
  Filling, **361**
  Pie, **407**
  Rice Custard, **423**
  Sauce, **424, 454**

Cutting food, 209
  bâtonnet technique, 212
  chiffonade, 211
  coarse chopping, 211
  julienne technique, 212
  mincing, 213
  oblique slicing, 213
  rondelles, 214
  tournè, 214
Cycle menus, 3–4

D

Daikon radish, 157
Daily Reference Values, 224
Danish Pastry, **315**
Date
  Bars, **380**
  Cream Pie, **404**
  Filling, **360**
  Muffins, **270**
  Nut Bread, **285**
  Pudding, Baked, **420**
Decimal equivalents of a pound, 88
Decreasing and increasing recipes,
    45–48
Deep-fat frying
  coatings for, 99
  procedures, 196–197
  temperatures for, 98
Deli Plate, **690**
  Wrap, **725**
Desserts, 319–436. *See also* Cake(s);
    Cookies; Pies; Pudding(s)
  Apple Crisp, and variations, **429**
  Apple Dumplings, **431**
  Bavarian Cream, Pineapple, and
    variations, **427**
  Chocolate Refrigerator Dessert, **411**
  Cream Puffs, and variations, **426**
  Custard, Baked, and variations, **423**
  Eclairs, **426**
  evaluating, 201
  Floating Island, **424**
  Fruit and Cheese, **436**
  Fruit Cobbler, and variations, **433**
    Biscuit Topping for, **434**
    guide for using frozen fruit in, 398
  Lemon Refrigerator Dessert, **413**
  Meringue Shells, **395**
  Peach Melba, **778**
  Russian Cream, **428**
  Strawberry Shortcake, **435**
Dessert sauces, 773–778
Deviled Crab, **472**
Deviled Eggs, **450**
Deviled Pork Chops, **516**
Dicing, 210–211
Dietary Guidelines for Americans, 5–6
Dill, 168
Dilly Bread, **303**
Dilly Salad Dressing, **699**

Dinner Rolls, **310**
Dipper equivalents, 220
Dip(s)
  Artichoke, Hot, **232**
  Avocado (Guacamole), **233, 235**
  Basic, **232**
  Blue Cheese, **233**
  Chile-Cilantro, **461**
  Creamy Herb, **233**
  Creamy Onion, **233**
  Dill, **233**
  Guacamole, **233, 235**
  Italian, **233**
  Mexican, Layered, **234**
  Nacho, **236**
  Picante, **233**
  Seafood, **233**
  Summer Fruit, **233**
  Yogurt, **233**
Direct reading tables for adjusting
    recipes, 52–59
  home size recipes, 60–63
  in volume measurement, 54–59
  in weight, 52–53
Disabled persons, foodservices for,
    20–22
Distilled vinegar, 175
Doughnuts
  Cake, **294**
  Chocolate, **294**
Drawn Butter Sauce, **771**
Dreamland Bars, **379**
Dressing, Bread (or Stuffing), **557**
  Apple, **557**
  Bread, **557**
  Chestnut, **557**
  Corn Bread, **556**
  Mushroom, **557**
  Nut, **557**
  Oyster, **557**
  Raisin, **557**
  Sausage, **557**
Dressing Salad. *See* Salad
    dressing(s)
Dried Fruit and Nut Granola, **612**
Duck
  classes of, 134
  roasting of, 532
Dumplings, **295**
  Apple, **431**
Dutch Apple Cake, **335**
Dutch Apple Coffee Cake, **278**

E

Eclairs, **426**
Egg and Pepper Dressing, **699**
Eggplant, 157
  Baked, **845**
  and Chick-pea Ragout on Pasta, **576**
  cooking of, **845**
  Creole, **847**

French Fried, **851**
  Parmesan, **845**
  Peperonata, **846**
  Ratatouille, **878, 879**
  Sautéed, **845**
  seasonings for, **845**
  Tomato Bake, **847**
Egg(s), 109–110
  á la King, **442**
  Chinese Omelet, **445**
  cookery, 437
  Creamed, **442**
  and crumb, for deep-fat
    frying, 99
  Curried, **442**
  Deviled, **450**
  Dilled, **450**
  dried, 111
  fresh, 110
  Frittata, **447**
  frozen, 110–111
  Goldenrod, **442**
  Hot Stuffed, **450**
  liquid eggs, 110
  Omelet, Baked, and variations,
    443, 445
  Pickled, **450**
  Potato Bake, **446**
  Potato Omelet, **444**
  preparation for salad, 641
  procedure for cooking,
    439–440
  processed, 110–111
  purchasing and storage,
    110–111
  Quiche, and variations,
    448–449
  Salad Sandwiches, **718**
  Sauce, **749**
  and Sausage Bake, **446**
  Scotch Woodcock, **442**
  Scrambled, and variations, **441**
  Smoked, **450**
Elderly, foodservices for, 20–22
Endive, 157
English Muffin Bread, **304**
Enoki mushroom, 161
en papillote procedures, 200
Epazote, 168
Equipment. *See* Tools and
    equipment
Equivalents
  can size, 94
  ingredient, 85–86
  metric, for weight, measure, and
    temperature, 95
  ounce and decimal, 88
  weights and measures, 75–84, 89
    for commonly used foods,
      90–93
Escarole, 157
Espresso, 174

Evaluating food quality, 200–204
Extracts, 187

F

Factor method of recipe adjustment, 45–46
Fajitas, **727, 735, 736**
  Catfish with Asian Rice, **461**
  Spiced Trout, **461**
Falafel in Pita Bread, 745
Fats, 187–188
  reducing, 48–49
Fennel, 157
  as herb, 169
Fettuccine, Herbed, **565**
  with Herb Butter Sauce, **582**
  Marinated, **664**
  with Pesto Sauce, **582**
  Vinaigrette, **664**
Fig Filling, **360**
Filé, 127
Filled Cookies, **388**
Fillet of Sole, Amandine, **464**
Fillings, **359–363**
  Almond, **317**
  Apricot, **360, 363**
  Chocolate Cream, **359**
  Custard, **361**
  Date, **360**
  Fig, **360**
  Lemon, **362**
  Lime, **362**
  Marmalade Nut, **363**
  Orange, **362**
  Prune, **363**
  Prune Date, **360**
  scaling weights for, 323
Fish and shellfish, 135–136, 457–477.
    See also Salmon; Tuna
  acidulated water for, 460
  Baked Fillets, **460**
  Bouquet Garni for, 460
  Breaded Fillets, **463**
  Broiled Halibut, **465**
  Caribbean Shrimp, **474**
  Catfish, Fajita Spiced, **461**
  Chowder
    Manhattan, **820**
    New England, **816**
  Creole Baked Fish, **462**
  Creole Shrimp, **475**
  defrosting timetable, 102
  Deviled Crab, **472**
  Fillet of Sole Amandine, **464**
  Fin fish
    buying and cooking guide for, 457
    cooking methods for, 457–460
    timetable for steaming, 459
  Herb Marinated Fish Steak, **460**
  Lemon Baked Fish, **462**
  Lemon Rice-Stuffed Cod, **466**

  Marinade for, **784**
  Oriental Shrimp and Pasta, **476**
  purchasing, 136–140
  Scalloped Oysters, **473**
  shellfish. *See also* Clam(s); Crab(s);
    Lobster(s); Oyster(s); Scallops;
    Shrimp
    buying guide, 140
    methods of cooking, 458
    timetable for steaming, 459
  storage, 140–141
Flat leaf parsley, 170
Flavored vinegar, 175
Floating Island Pudding, **424**
Flour(s), 127
Flowers, edible, 166, 172
Focaccia, **305**
  with Herb Cheese Spread, **243**
Food amounts to serve 50, 64–74
Food availability, 7
Food Cooling and Storing
    procedures, 105
Food production information, 41–63
Food Pyramid, 5
  required servings, 6
  serving sizes, 7
Food quality, evaluation of, 200–204
Food safety, 100–101
Food terms, glossary of, 893–901
Food weights and equivalents in
    measure, 75–84, 89. *See also*
    Equivalents; Weights and
    measures
Frankfurters
  Barbecued, **524**
  Cheese-Stuffed, **524**
  Pigs in Blankets, **526**
  with Sauerkraut, **524**
French
  Bread, **302**
  Breakfast Puffs, **275**
  Chocolate, **250**
  Dip Sandwiches, **732**
  Dressing, **702**
  Green Beans, **828**
  Onion Soup, **809**
  Toast, and variations, **296**
French endive, 157
Fresh produce, 141–145. *See also* Fruit;
    Vegetable(s)
Fried Rice
  Asian Fried Rice, **598**
  and variations, **597**
Frisée, 157
Frittata, Roasted Pepper and
    Basil, **447**
Fritters, **297**
  Apple, **297**
  Banana, **297**
  Corn, **297**
  Fruit, **297**
  Green Chili, **297**

Frosted Cherry Salad, **668**
Frosted Lime Salad, **668**
Frostings. *See* Icing(s)
Frosty Date Balls, **384**
Frozen-Filled Angel Food Cake, **329**
Frozen fruit guide for pies and
    cobblers, 398
Frozen Fruit Salad, **676**
Fruit
  canned, 172–173
  and Cheese Dessert, **436**
  Cobbler, and variations, **433**
    Biscuit Topping for, **434**
    guide for using frozen
      fruit in, 398
  Coffee Rings, **315**
  with Creamy Custard Sauce, **424**
  Crisp, **429**
  fresh, 141, 146–153
    pre-preparation guidelines,
      146–153
    yield, availability, storage,
      142–145
  frozen, 172–173
  Gelatin Salad, and variations,
    545, 667
  Glazed Pie, **404**
  Pies
    with Canned Fruit, **396**
    with Frozen Fruit, **397,** 398
  Punch, basic, **251**
  Salad Bowl, **674**
  Salad Dressing, **709**
    Celery Seed, **709**
    Golden, **709**
    Poppy Seed, **709**
  Salad Plate, **692**
  salads, 670–676
  Slices, **433**
Fruitcake, **344**
Fudge Brownies, **378**
Fudge Cake, **340**
Fudge Sauce, **774**
Fusilli, Basil Fusilli, **846**

G

Garbanzo Bean Salad, **647**
  with Pasta, **647**
Garden Pasta, **585**
Garden Salad, Marinated, **657**
Garden Salad Dressing, **700**
Garlic, 158
  Garlic Basil Fusilli, **846**
  Herb Dressing, **711**
  and Red Pepper Penne, **575**
Gazpacho (Spanish Chilled
    Soup), **821**
Gelatin salads, 667–669
German Cucumbers, **651**
German Sweet Chocolate Cake, **341**
Giblet Gravy, **752**

Ginger
  Ale Fruit Punch, **251**
  bread, and variations, **345**
  Cookies, Crisp, **386**
  Muffins, **345**
  Orange Beef, **491**
    Wrap, **426**
  Rice Stir-Fry, **596**
  snaps, **371**
  Vegetables and Barley, **617**
Glaze
  Chocolate, **358**
  Peanut Butter, **358**
  Powdered Sugar, **359**
Glazes for Ham, **519**
Glossary of menu and cooking terms,
    893–901
Golden brown mushroom, 161
Golden oak mushroom, 162
Golden Punch, **251**
Goldenrod Eggs, **442**
Golden Sauce, **750**
Goose
  classes of, 134
  roasting of, 532
Gooseberry Pie, **398**
Goulash, Hungarian, **589**
Graham Cracker Crust, **393**
Grains, 119–120
  and Beans, **632**
  purchasing and storage, 120–122
Granola, **612**
Grapefruit, 148
  Orange Salad, and
    variations, **674**
  with Salad Greens, **642**
Grape Punch, Sparkling, **251**
Grapes, 149
Gravy
  Brown, **752**
  Chicken, **752**
  Cream, **752**
  Giblet, **752**
  Onion, **752**
  Pan, **752**
  Sausage, **525**
  Savory, **751**
  Vegetable, **752**
Green Beans
  Amandine, **828**
  Casserole, **829**
  cooking of, **828**
  Creole, **830**
  with Dill, **830**
  French, **828**
  Hacienda, **830**
  Herbed, **828**
  Marinated, **652**
  with Mushrooms, **828**
  Provincial, **828**
  Seasoned, **828**
  seasonings for, **828**

  Southern Style, **828**
  Spanish, **830**
Green Chili Fritters, **297**
Green Chili Stew, **502**
Green onions, 160
Green Peppercorn Dressing, **700**
Green Pepper Slaw, **649**
Green Rice, **607**
Greens, 158
  for cooking, 155
  for salads, 155
Griddle broiling
  procedures, 194
  timetable for meat, 485
Griddle frying procedures, 197
Grilled Eggplant Peperonata, **846**
Grilled Sandwiches, **728**
Grilled Vegetable Marinade, **785**
Grilling procedures, 194
Grits, Baked Cheese, **613**
Guacamole (Avocado Dip), **233, 235**

H

Half-and-Half Rolls, **310**
Halibut with Black Bean
    Sauce, **465**
Ham
  Balls, Glazed, **520**
  and Cheese Sandwiches, Grilled,
    728
  Creamed, **521**
  Glazed Baked, and variations, **519**
  Loaf, **520**
  Omelet, **443**
  and Pasta Salad, **659**
  Patties, and variations, **520**
  Plantation Shortcake, **521**
  roasting, timetable for, 482
  Salad Sandwich, **719**
Hamburger Buns, **310**
Hamburgers
  Barbecued, **742**
  Grilled, **742**
  Oven-Baked, **742**
Handtools, basic, 215–216. *See also*
    Knives
Hard Sauce, and variations, **776**
Hawaiian Tossed Salad, **642**
Hazardous foods, 107
Hazelnut, 185
Herb Butter, **779, 780**
Herb Butter Seasonings, and
    variations, **780**
Herbed Fettuccine, **565**
Herbs and spices
  dried herbs, 175, 177, 182
    natural spice blends, 177, 182
    regional flavorings, 182
    teaspoons per ounce, 176–177
    usage for different foods,
      178–181

  fresh herbs, 166–172
    uses of, color exhibit, XI
  natural spice blends, 177, 182
  pre-preparation guidelines, 158
  regional flavorings, 182
  Toasted Spice Blend, **782**
  Toasting, **782**
Hollandaise Sauce, **769**
  Mock, **770**
Home-size recipes, increasing,
    47–48
Hominy, 120
Honey
  Butter, **716**
  Cream Dressing, **700**
  French Dressing, **704**
  Rolls, **317**
  Streusel Topping for Muffins, **269**
  Yogurt Dressing, **700**
Honeydew, 150
Hoppin' John (Rice with Black-Eyed
    Peas), **599**
Hors d'oeuvres, per person, 229
Horseradish Cream Dressing, **700**
Horseradish Sauce, **764**
  Caper Sauce, **765**
  Dill Sauce, **765**
Hospitals, menu planning for, 18–20
Hot Barbecued Wings, **240**
Hot Chocolate, **249**
Hot Cross Buns, **310, 315**
Hot Dog Buns, **310**
Hot Fudge Sauce, **774**
Hot Mustard Sauce, **766**
Hubbard squash, 165
Hummus, Red Pepper, **244**
Hungarian Goulash, **589**

I

Ice cream
  Icing, **353**
  Pie, **414**
  Puffs, **426**
  Roll, **348**
Ice Mold for Punch, **251**
Icing(s), 352–359
  Bittersweet, **353**
  Boiled, **352**
  Burnt Butter, **352**
  Candied Fruit, **353**
  Chocolate, **353**
  Chocolate Butter Cream, **354**
  Chocolate Glaze, **358**
  Cocoa, **355**
  Coconut, **353**
  Coconut Pecan, **354**
  Cream Cheese, **355**
  Creamy, **355**
  Ice Cream, **353**
  Lemon Butter, **355**
  Maple Nut, **353**

Icing(s), *Continued*
  Maraschino Cherry, **353**
  Mocha, **357**
  Orange, **356**
  Orange Butter, **355**
  Orange Cream Cheese, **355**
  Peanut Butter, **356**
  Peanut Butter Glaze, **358**
  Peppermint, **353**
  Pineapple, **357**
  Powdered Sugar Glaze, **359**
  scaling weight, 323
Increasing and decreasing
  recipes, 45–48
Ingredients
  proportion of, 87
  substitutions for, 85–86
  used in standardizing
    recipes, 224
Israeli Couscous
  with Olives and Roasted Tomatoes,
    622
  Salad, **661**
Italian
  Pasta Salad, **663**
  Salad Dressing, **703**
  Sausage Pasta, **580**
  Tomato Sauce, **762**
Italian brown mushroom, 161
Italian parsley, 170

J

Jalapeño Cheese Bread, **301**
Jalapeño Rice, **607**
Japanese radish, 157
Jellied Waldorf Salad, **668**
Jelly Muffins, **270**
Jelly Roll, **349**
Jelly Sauce, **753**
Jicama, 158
Juan canary, 151
Julienne technique, 212

K

Kabobs, **496**
Kale, 158
Kale, cooking of. *See* Spinach
Kasha, 120
Kitchen readiness, 189–190
Kiwi, 149
Knives
  care and safety, 206–207
  cutting techniques, 209–214
  gripping, 209
  guiding, 209
  honing, using a steel, 208
  identification of, 205–206
  sharpening, using a stone, 207
Kohlrabi, 158–159

Kolaches, **315**
Kumquats, 148

L

Ladle equivalents, 221
Lady Baltimore Cake, **333**
Lamb
  primal and retail cuts, 130
  timetable for
    braising, 487
    broiling, 484
    cooking in liquid, 487
    roasting, 481
Lard, 187
Lasagna, **573**
  Spinach, **571**
Lavender, 169
Lazy Daisy Cake, **335**
Leeks, 159
Leftovers, minimizing, 10
Lemon
  Baked Fish, **462**
  Butter, **779, 780**
  Butter Icing, **355**
  Butter Sauce, **771**
  Cake Pudding, **421**
  Chiffon Pie, **413**
    Frozen, **413**
  Cream Mold, **668**
  Filling, **362**
  Pie, **406**
  Refrigerator Dessert, **413**
  Sauce, **776**
Lemonade, **252**
Lemongrass, 169
Lemons, 148
Lentil(s)
  dried, 173
  Pilaf, **604**
  Soup, **804**
Lettuce(s), 155
  pre-preparation guidelines, 159–160
  Wilted, **868**
Lima Beans
  Baked, **831**
  Baked with Peas, **831**
  Baked with Sausage, **831**
  Boiled with Ham, **831**
  cooking of, **831**
  Seasoned, **831**
  seasonings for, **831**
Lime Filling, **362**
Limes, 148
Limpa Rye Bread, **308**
Linguine, Tomato, **583**
Liver
  with Bacon, **497**
  Braised, **497**
  Grilled, **497**
  with Spanish Sauce, **497**

Lobster(s), 138
  Salad, **682**
Lo Mein, Vegetable, **581**
Long Johns, Rolls, **315**
Lovage, 169
Lunches for schools, 11–13

M

Macadamia nuts, 185
Macaroni and Cheese, **564**
Macaroni Salad, **660**
Macaroons, Coconut, **365**
Maitre d'Hôtel Sauce, **771**
Malt vinegar, 175
Mandarins, 149
Mangoes, 150
Maple Nut Icing, **353**
Maraschino Cherry Icing, **353**
Marble Cake, **336**
Margarine, 187–188
Marinade
  Asian, **785**
  Balsamic Vinegar, **786**
  Dry, for meat or poultry, **783**
  Fish, **784**
  Grilled Vegetable, **785**
  Herb and Garlic, **787**
  Herb for Poultry or Fish, **786**
  Honey Balsamic, **786**
  Meat, **783**
  Vegetable, **784, 785**
  Vinaigrette, **787**
Marinàra Sauce, **761**
Marjoram, 170
Marmalade Nut Filling, **363**
Marshmallow Krispie Squares, and
  variations, **382**
Mayonnaise, and variations, **699–700**.
  See also Salad dressing(s)
Measuring equipment, 217
Meat, 127–128, 480–526. *See also* Beef;
  Ham; Lamb; Pork; Veal
  Marinade, **783**
  purchasing, 128–129
  storage, 129–133
  timetables for
    braising, 487
    broiling, 483–484
    cooking in liquid, 487
    defrosting, 102
    griddle broiling, 485
    grilling, 486
Meatballs, **498**
  Barbecued, **498**
  Italian, **498**
  with Spaghetti, **588**
  Spanish, **499**
  Swedish, **500**
Meat Loaf, **497**
  Vegetable, **498**

Mediterranean Barley Pilaf, **614**
Melons, 150–151
Menu planning, 3–20
  cycle, 3–4
  for different types of foodservices,
    11–20
    colleges and universities, 14–15
    commercial, 15–18
    disabled and elderly persons, 20–22
    elementary and secondary
      schools, 11–13
    hospitals, 18–20
  factors affecting, 5–9
  key points in, 9
  patterns, 4
  procedures, 9–10
  steps in, 10
  suggested menu items, 885–891
    desserts, 890
    entree accompaniments, 887
    entrees, 885–887
    garnishes, 891
    meatless entrees, 886
    salads and relishes, 888–889
    sandwiches, 887
    soups, 889
    vegetables, 888
  terms, glossary of, 893–901
  types of, 3–4
Meringue
  for Pies, 394
  Shells and Sticks, **395**
Methods of cooking. *See* Cooking
  methods
Metric equivalents, 95
Meunière Sauce, **770**
Mexican Chocolate, **249**
Mexican parsley, 168. *See also* Cilantro
Mexican Rice, **603**
Mexican Salad Dressing, **703**
Milk, 117
Milk cookery, 438
Milk products, 118
Millet, 120
Mincing, 213
Minestrone Soup, **803**
Mint, 170
Mirepoix, 789
Mise en place, 189
Mixer bowl sizes, 221
Mocha Almond Pie, Frozen, **415**
Mocha Icing, **357**
Molasses Bran Bread, **306**
Molasses Drop Cookies, **370**
Mollusks, 136. *See also* Fish and shellfish
Monosodium glutamate (MSG), 182, 184
Mornay Sauce, **750**
MSG, 182, 184
Muffins
  Apple, **270**
  Apple Nut, **275**

Apricot, **270**
Banana, **271**
Banana Whole Wheat, **271**
Basic (Cake Method), **269**
Basic (Muffin Method), **270**
Blueberry, **270**
Cherry, **270**
Chocolate Chip, **269**
Coconut, **269**
Cornmeal, **270**
Cranberry, **270**
Currant, **270**
Date, **270**
Ginger, **345**
Honey Streusel Topping for, **269**
Jelly, **270**
Nut, **270**
Oatmeal, **272**
Oatmeal Fruit, **272**
Poppy Seed Yogurt, **273**
Raised, **313**
Raisin Nut, **270**
Spiced, **270**
Whole Wheat, **270**
Mushroom(s), 160, 161–162
  Barley Soup, **810**
  French Fried, **851**
  Marinated, **652**
  Rice Pilaf, **603**
  Roasted Portabella, **848**
    on orzo pilaf, **848**
  Sauce, **750, 753, 754**
  Soufflé, **452**
  Soup, Cream of, **810**
  Stuffing, **557**
  types of, color exhibit, XXI
Mustard greens, cooking of. *See*
  Spinach
Mustard Sauce, **765**
  Chinese, **765**
  Hot, **766**
  Savory, **753**

N

Nacho Dog, **524**
Nachos, **236**
  quick, **236**
Nacho Sauce, **236**
Nacho Tostadas, **738**
Napa, 160
Napkin folds, 32, 33
Navy Bean Soup, **805**
Nectarines, 151
Noodles. *See also* Pasta
  with Beef and Pork, **592**
  and Chicken, **551, 552**
  and Pork Casserole, **551**
  Romanoff, **566**
  and Tuna, **470**
  and Turkey, **551**

Nutmeg Sauce, **776**
Nutritional values, 224
Nutrition information, recipes, 224
Nut(s), 184–186
  Bread, **284**
  Cream pie, **404**
  Muffins, **270**
  Stuffing, **557**

O

Oatmeal
  Bread, **306**
  Coconut, Crispies, **387**
  Crispies, **387**
  Date Bars, **382**
  Drop Cookies, **367**
  Muffins, **272**
Oats, 120–121
Oblique slicing, 213
Oil and Vinegar Dressing, **703**
Oils, 188
Okra, 160
Okra, cooking of, 825
Olive(s)
  Israeli Couscous with, **622**
  Sauce, **753**
Omelet
  Bacon, **443**
  Baked, **443**
  Cheese, **443**
  Cheese and Bacon, **443**
  Chinese, **445**
  Grilled Cheese, **443**
  Ham, **443**
  Jelly, **443**
  Mushrooms and Cheese, **443**
  Potato, **444**
  Spanish, **443**
Onion(s), 160
  Baked, **849**
  Butter, **780**
  Casserole, **849**
  cooking of, **849**
  French Fried, **851**
  Glazed, **849**
  Gravy, **752**
  Pearl, Creamed, **849**
  seasonings for, **849**
Orange
  Beef, Ginger Orange, **491**
    Wrap, **726**
  Biscuits, **268**
  Butter Icing, **355**
  Chiffon Cake, **331**
  Chiffon Pie, **413**
  Cream Cheese Icing, **355**
  Cream Puffs, **426**
  Filled Angel Food Cake, **329**
  Filling, **362**
  Glaze for Ham, **519**

Orange, *Continued*
  Icing, **356**
  Rolls, **317**
  Sauce, **776**
Oranges, 148–149
Oregano, 170
Oriental. *See also* Asian
  Bean Salad, **645**
  Coleslaw, **649**
  radish, 157
  Shrimp and Pasta, **476**
Orzo Pilaf, **562**
  Lemon, **563**
Ounces and decimal equivalents, 88
Oven frying procedures, 197
Oyster mushroom, 161
Oyster plant, 164
Oyster(s), 138
  marketing sizes for, 139
  Scalloped, **473**
  Stew, **819**
  Stuffing, **557**

P

Panbroiling procedures, 194
Pancakes, **289**
  Apple, **289**
  Blueberry, **289**
  Buttermilk, **289**
  Mix, **290**
  Pecan, **289**
  Potato, **861**
  Silver Dollar, **289**
  Whole Wheat, **290**
Pan Coating, 328
Pan frying procedures, 197
Pans, 218
  baked products, capacities for, 219
  counter pan capacities, 220
Pan-steaming procedures, 200
Papaya, 151
Parker House Rolls, **311**
Parsley, 170
Parsley Butter, **779**
Parsley Butter Sauce, **771**
Parsnips, 162
  cooking of, 825
  Glazed, **840**
    with Carrots, **840**
Party trays, 230
Pasta, 122, 559, 562–593
  Basil and Parmesan Bows with Sugar
    Snap Peas, **574**
  Beef, Pork, and Noodle Casserole, **592**
  Beef on Noodles, **593**
  with Cheese Sauce, **567**
  Chicken and Noodles, **551**
  Chicken Tetrazzini
    and variations, **590**
  with Clam Sauce, **567**

cooking of, 561
cooking times, 561
Creole Spaghetti, **584**
Fettuccine with Herb Butter
    Sauce, **582**
  with Pesto Sauce, **582**
Garden, **585**
Garlic and Red Pepper Penne, **575**
Ham and Swiss Broccoli, **569**
Herbed Fettuccine, **565**
Hungarian Goulash, **589**
Italian Sausage, **580**
Lasagna, **572, 573**
  Spinach, **570, 571**
Lemon and Herb Penne, **575**
Linguine, Tomato, **583**
Macaroni and Cheese, **564**
  with Ham, **564**
Noodles Romanoff, **566**
Oriental Shrimp and Pasta, **476**
Orzo Pilaf, **562**
Pasta, Beef, and Tomato
    Casserole, **591**
Pasta Wheels and Vegetables, **582**
Pork and Noodle Casserole, **551**
Primavera, **568**
purchasing and storage, 122
Rigatoni and Spinach, **577**
Roasted Eggplant & Chick-pea
    Ragout on Penne, **576**
salads. *See* Salads
shapes and descriptions, 123–126
with Shrimp Sauce, **567**
Spaghetti
  with Chicken Sauce, **586**
  with Meatballs, **588**
  with Meat Sauce, **587**
  with Vegetarian Sauce, **585**
Swiss Broccoli, **569**
Turkey and Noodle Casserole, **551**
with Vegetable Sauce, **580**
Vegetarian Spaghetti, **585**
yields, 561
ziti
  with Four Cheeses, **578**
  Southwest, **579**
Pastry. *See* Pies
Patty Melt, **731**
Pattypan squash, 165
Peach(es), 151
  Cobbler with Hard Sauce, **433**
  Crisp, **429**
  Melba, **778**
  Pie, **398**
Peanut Butter
  Cake, **342**
  Cookies, **368, 373**
  Glaze, **358**
  Icing, **356**
  Marshmallow Squares, **382**
  Sauce, **777**

Peanut Cookies, **372**
Peanuts, 185
Pears, 151–152
Peas, 162
  black-eyed. *See* Black-eyed peas
  cooking of, 853
  Creamed with New Potatoes, **853**
  dried, 173
  with Lemon-Mint Butter, **853**
  with Mushrooms, **853**
  with New Turnips, **853**
  with Pearl Onions, **853**
  Seasoned, **853**
  seasonings for, **853**
Pecan(s), 185
  Pancakes, **289**
  Pie, **409, 410**
  Rolls, **317**
  Waffles, **291**
Peperonata, **854**
  Grilled Eggplant, **846**
Pepper, 182, 183
  Steak, **490, 850**
Peppermint Icing, **353**
Pepper Pot Soup, **808**
Peppers, bell, 163
  Green Pepper Slaw, **649**
  Red Pepper Hummus, **244**
  Roasted, **854**
  Stuffed, **510**
Peppers, chile, 162, 163
Pepper Steak, **490**
Percentage method of recipe
    adjustment, 46–47
Perfection Salad, **669**
Persian, 151
Persimmons, 152
pH values, of selected foods, 106
Pickled Beets, **697**
Pies, 327–328, 389–415
  Angel, **395**
  Apple, Fresh, **399**
  Apple Crumb, **399**
  Apricot, **401**
  Banana Cream, **404**
  Berry, **398**
  Blueberry, **398**
  Boston Cream, **335**
  Butterscotch Cream, **405**
  with Canned Fruit, **396**
  Cherry, **398**
  Chocolate Chiffon, **411**
    Frozen, **411**
    Peppermint, **411**
  Chocolate Cream, **404**
  Coconut Cream, **404**
  Coconut Custard, **407**
  Cream, and variations, **404**
  Crumb Crusts, **393**
  Custard, **407**
  Date Cream, **404**

with Frozen Fruit, **397**
  guide for, 398
Fruit, Glazed, **404**
Gooseberry, **398**
Ice Cream, **414**
Lemon, **406**
Lemon Chiffon, **413**
  Frozen, **413**
Meringue for, **394**
Mocha Almond, Frozen, **415**
Nut Cream, **404**
Orange Chiffon, **413**
Pastry, **389**
  Cheddar Cheese, **391**
  Graham Cracker Crust, **393**
  for One-Crust Pies, **390**
  preparation of, 389
  quality standards, 327
  for Two-Crust Pies, **391**
Peach, **398**
Pecan, **409**
Pecan Cream Cheese, **410**
Pineapple Cream, **404**
preparation of, 327–328
Pumpkin, **408**
Pumpkin Praline, **408**
Raisin, **401**
Raspberry Alaska, **414**
Rhubarb, **398**, **402**
Rhubarb Custard, **403**
Sour Cream Apple Nut, **400**
Strawberry, **398**
Strawberry Chiffon, **412**
Pigs in Blankets, **526**
  with Cheese, **526**
Pilaf
  Basmati Rice and Lentil, **604**
  Rice, **603**
    Mediterranean Barley, **614**
Pimiento Sauce, **750**
Piña Colada, Mock, **255**
Pineapple, 152
  Bavarian Cream, **427**
  Cashew Cake, **343**
  Cheese Salad, Molded, **668**
  Cream Pie, **404**
  Cream Pudding, **419**
  Icing, **357**
  Pie, **404**
  Punch, Blushing, **256**
  Upside-Down Cake, **336**
Pine nuts, 186
Pink Champagne-Style Punch, **256**
Pinwheel Cookies, **388**
Piquant Sauce, **753**
Pistachios, 186
Pitas
  and Falafel, **745**
  Pack a Pita, **726**
  and Red Pepper Hummus, **244**
  Vegetable, **727**

Pizza, **506–508**
  Beef, **506**
    and Mushroom, **507**
  Burger, **737**
  Cheese, **507**
  Garden, **507**
  Pepperoni, **507**
  portioning guidelines, 506
  Sauce, **580**
  temperature guidelines, 508
Placement of food and cover, served
  meal, 34
Planning the menu and special
  events, 22–36
Plantains, 152
Plantation Shortcake, **521**
Plums, 152–153
Poaching procedures, 199
Polenta
  Parmesan, **626**
  Soft Polenta, **625**
    Portabella Pepper Steak over, **850**
Popcorn Rolls, **311**
Poppy seed(s), 186
  Cake, **333**
  Dressing, **702**
  Yogurt Muffins, **273**
Pork. See also Bacon; Frankfurters; Ham
  Birds, **512**
  Chops, Baked, **515**
    with Apples, **515**
    Barbecued, **516**
    Breaded, **515**
    Chili Seasoned, **516**
    Deviled, **516**
    with Dressing, **515**
    Honey Glazed, **516**
    Stuffed, **515**
    Supreme, **516**
  Loin
    Garlic and Peppercorn, **514**
    Herbed, **514**
    Jeweled, **514**
    Rosemary, **514**
    Sandwich, **723**
    Teriyaki Glazed, **514**
  and Noodle Casserole, **551**
  primal and retail cuts, 131
  Sausage Gravy on Biscuits, **525**
  Sausage Rolls, **526**
  Scrapple, **523**
  Spareribs
    Barbecued, **517**
    with Dressing, **517**
    with Sauerkraut, **517**
    Sweet-Sour, **517**
  Stir-Fried, **542**
  Sweet-Sour, **518**
  timetable for
    braising, 487
    broiling, 484

  cooking in liquid, 487
  griddle broiling, 485
  roasting, 482
Portabella mushroom(s), 161
  Peperonata, **848**
  Pepper Steak over Soft
    Polenta, **850**
Portioning equipment, 217
Portuguese Sweet Bread, **307**
Potato(es), 163–164
  American Fried, **861**
  au Gratin, **860**
  Baked, **855**
    Broccoli Cheese-Topped, **855**
    Cheese-Topped, **855**
    Soup, **814**
    Stuffed, **855**
    with Toppings, **855**
  Bread, **307**
  Chips, **857**
  Chowder, **815**, **818**
  cooking of, 856
  Cottage Fried, **861**
  Croquettes, **856**
  Deep-Fat Browned, **857**
  Duchess, **856**
  Franconia, **864**
  French Fried, **857**
  Hashed Brown, **861**
  Herbed Bake, **865**
  Lattice, **857**
  Lyonnaise, **861**
  Mashed, **856**
    Casserole, **856**
    with Chicken and Noodles, **552**
    and Roasted Garlic, **856**
    with Rutabagas, **856**
    and Vegetables, **881**
  New, Creamed, **858**
    Lemon-Seasoned, **858**
    in Mustard, **858**
    Paprika Seasoned, **858**
    Parmesan, **858**
    with Peas, **858**
  O'Brien, **861**
  Omelet, **444**
  Oven-Browned, **865**
  Oven-Fried, **861**
  Pancakes, **861**
  Parsley Buttered, **858**
  Rissole, **865**
  Roasted Red-skinned, **859**
  Romanoff, **864**
  Rosemary Roasted, **859**
  Rosettes, **856**
  Salad, **665**
    Hot, **666**
  Scalloped, and variations, **862**
  Shoestring, **857**
    and Roasted Pepper, **817**
  Soup, Cream of, **810**

Potato(es), *Continued*
  Sour Cream, **863**
  Sweet. *See* Sweet potato(es)
Potentially hazardous foods, 106
Pot Pie
  Beef, **501**
  Chicken, **550**
Pot Roast of Beef, and variations, **488**
Poultry, 527–557. *See also* Chicken;
     Duck; Goose; Turkey
  breading sequence for, 530
  categories and classes of, 134
  cooking methods, 527–532
    braising, 531
    broiling or grilling, 527–528
    deep-fat frying, 528
    oven frying, 531
    pan frying, 528
    poaching, 531–532
    roasting, guide for, 532
    stewing or simmering, 531–532
  Cornish Game Hens, Orange-
     Glazed, **540**
  defrosting timetable, 102
  purchasing, 133
  storage, 133–135
  yields of cooked meat, 71
Pound Cake, **346**
Powdered Sugar Glaze, **359**
Praline Cake, **336**
Praline Pumpkin Pie, **408**
Produce, fresh, 141–145. *See also* Fruit;
    Vegetable(s)
Production
  and kitchen readiness, 189–190
  scheduling, 190
Prune Date Filling, **360**
Prune Filling, **363**
Pudding(s)
  Banana Cream, **419**
  Bread, **423**
  Butterscotch, **416**
  Chocolate, and variations, **417**
  Chocolate Cream, **419**
  Christmas, **425**
  Coconut Cream, **419**
  Cottage, **335**
  Date, Baked, **420**
  Floating Island, **424**
  Lemon Cake, **421**
  Pineapple Cream, **419**
  Russian Cream, **428**
  Tapioca Cream, **418**
  Vanilla Cream, **419**
Puff Shells, **426**
Pumpkin
  Bread, **288**
  Cake, **347**
  Cake Roll, **351**
  Pie, **408**
  Praline Pumpkin Pie, **408**

Pumpkin seeds, 186
Punch, 251–260
  Apricot-Pineapple, Sparkling, **255**
  Banana, **253**
  Banana Slush, **253**
  Basic Fruit, **251**
  Blushing Pineapple, **256**
  Cider, **259**
    Mulled, **259**
    Spiced, **259**
  Cranberry, **253**
    Spiced, **259**
    Warmer, **258**
  Ginger Ale Fruit, **251**
  Golden, **251**
  Grape, Sparkling, **251**
  Ice Mold for, **251**
  Lemonade, **252**
  Mock Piña Colada, **255**
  Nonalcoholic Cocktails, **261**
  Pink Champagne-Style, **256**
  preparation of, 246
  Red Hot Tea, **256**
  Ruby Wine, **260**
  Sangria Sipper, **254**
  Simple Syrup for, **252**
  Spiced Rosé Warmer, **260**
  Wassail, **257**
  White Wine Sangria, **254**

Q

Quality evaluation(s), 200–204
Quality-standards
  cakes, 324
  cookies, 326
  pastry, 327
  Standards
    quick breads, 265
    yeast breads, 267
Quesadillas
  Cheese, **734**
  Corn and Roasted Pepper, **734**
  Chicken, **744**
Quiche, **448**
  Leek and Roasted Pepper, **449**
  Mushroom, **448**
  Sausage, **448**
  Seafood, **448**
  Swiss Spinach, **448**
  Vegetable, **449**
Quick breads. *See* Breads, quick
Quinoa, 121
Quinoa Pilaf, **624**

R

Radicchio, 164
Radishes, 164
Raisin
  Biscuits, **269**
  Bread, **300**

Nut Muffins, **270**
Pie, **401**
Sauce, **767**
Stuffing, **557**
Ranch Style Beans, **832**
Raspberry, 147
  Alaska Pie, **414**
  Sauce, **778**
Ratatouille, **878**
  Summer, **879**
Receptions and teas, 23
  table arrangement for, 26
Recipe adjustment, 44–48
  converting from weight to
    measure, 45
  converting to metric, 44–45
  development and
    construction, 43–44
  direct reading tables, 52–59
  enlarging home-size recipes, 47–48
  factor method, 45–46
  for fat, sodium, sugar reduction,
    48–49
  increasing and decreasing yields,
    45–47
  percentage method, 46–47
Recipe information, 224–225
  abbreviations used, 225
  Basic Recipes, 225
  cooking time and
    temperature, 225
  critical control points, 225
  ingredients used
    in standardizing, 224
  nutrition information, 224
  weights and measures, 225
  yield, 224
Red Pepper Hummus on Pita
    Points, **244**
Refried Beans, **834**
Religious food practices, 8
Relishes, 693–698
  Apple Rings, **693**
  Beet Pickles, **697**
  Black Bean and Corn
    Relish, **696**
  Buttered Apples, **693**
  Cinnamon Apples, **693**
  Corn Relish, **696**
  Cranberry Relish, **694**
    Baked, **695**
    Orange, **694**
  Cranberry Sauce,
    and variations, **695**
  Fresh Tomato, **654**
  Fried Apples, **693**
  Minted Tabouli, **698**
  Sauerkraut Relish, **697**
  Summer Cucumber and Melon
    Salsa, **757**
Reuben Sandwich, **739**

Rhubarb Custard Pie, **403**
Rhubarb Pie, **398, 402**
Ribbon Gelatin Salad, **668**
Ribbon Rolls, **311**
Ribbon Sandwiches, 714
Rice, 121–122
   Asian
      Fajita Spiced Catfish with, **461**
      Fried Rice, **598**
      Sushi Style, **610**
   au Gratin, with Broccoli, **607**
      with Cauliflower, **607**
   basic proportions, 560
   Basmati and Lentil Pilaf, **604**
   with Black-Eyed Peas (Hoppin'
      John), **597**
   and Chicken Casserole, **553**
   cooking of, 594
   Curried, **603, 609**
   Custard, **423**
   Fajita Spiced Catfish with Asian Rice
      and Chile-Cilantro Dipping
      Sauce, **461**
   Fried, **597**
      with Almonds, **597**
      Asian, **598**
      with Ham, **597**
      with Pork, **597**
      with Shrimp, **597**
   Ginger Rice, **595**
   Ginger Rice Stir-Fry, **596**
   Green, **607**
   Hopping John, **599**
   Jalapeño, **607**
   and Lentils with Carrots, **608**
   Mexican, **603**
   Pilaf, **603**
      with Mushrooms, **603**
   Primavera, **606**
   and Raisins, **611**
   Red Beans and Rice, **634**
   Risotto, **600, 616**
   Sicilian, with Vegetables, **605**
   Spanish rice, **510**
      and Black Beans, **633**
   Sushi Style Rice, **610**
   Toasted Herb, **603**
   Tomato Cilantro, **601**
   yields, 560
Rice vinegar, 175
Rigatoni and Spinach, **577**
Risotto, **600, 616**
Roast Beef Sandwich, **732**
Roasted Tomatoes with Israeli
   Couscous and Olives, **622**
Roasting procedures, for savory
   foods, 195–196
Roast Pork Sandwich, **732**
Rolls. *See also* Breads, Yeast
   Basic Dough, **309**
   Bowknots, **309**

Braids, **309**
Buns. *See* Buns
Butterflake, **310**
Butterfly, **316**
Butterhorns, **309**
Butterscotch, **316**
Butter Slices, **299**
Caramel Crowns, **309–310**
Caramel Pecan, **317**
Cherry Nut, **314**
Cinnamon, **316**
   Double, **317**
   Jumbo, **317**
   Raisin, **317**
   Twists, **314**
Cloverleaf, **310**
Crescent, **310**
Dinner, **310**
Glazed Marmalade, **317**
Half-and-Half, **310**
Honey, **317**
Hot Cross Buns, **310, 315**
Kolaches, **315**
Long Johns, **315**
Orange, **317**
Pan, **310**
Parkerhouse, **311**
Pecan, **317**
Popcorn, **311**
Poppy Seed, **311**
Raised Muffins, **313**
Ribbon, **311**
Rosettes, **311**
Rye, **308**
Sesame, **311**
Sugared Snails, **317**
Sweet Roll Dough, Basic, **314**
Twin, **311**
Twists, **311**
Whole Wheat, **311**
Rondelles, 214
Roquefort Dressing, **700, 703**
   Creamy Blue, **699**
Rosemary, 171
Rosettes, **311**
Rounding off weight and
   measures, 89
Roux, 747
Rubs, 748, **781–783**
Ruby Wine Punch, **260**
Russian Cream, **428**
Russian Salad Dressing, **700**
Rutabagas, 164
   cooking of, **856**
   Mashed, with Potatoes, **856**
Rye, 122
Rye Bread
   Caraway, **308**
   Limpa, **308**
   Swedish, **308**
Rye Rolls, **308**

S

Safety guidelines, 100–101
Sage, 171
Salad dressing(s), 641, 699–711
   Apple cider, **708**
   Bacon, **701**
   Buttermilk, **699**
   Campus, **699**
   Celery Seed French, **702**
   Celery Seed Fruit, **709**
   Chantilly, **699**
   Chiffonade, **703**
   Chilean, **701**
   Combination, **700**
   Cooked, **700**
   Creamy Blue Cheese, **699**
   Cucumber Yogurt, **711**
   Dilly, **699**
   Egg and Green Pepper, **699**
   French, and variations,
      702, 703
   French, Thick, **702**
   Fruit, **709**
   Garden, **700**
   Garlic Herb, **711**
   Golden Fruit, **709**
   Green Peppercorn, **700**
   Honey Cream, **700**
   Honey French, **704**
   Honey Lime, **704**
   Honey Yogurt, **700**
   Horseradish Cream, **700**
   ingredients, 641
   Italian, **703**
   Mayonnaise, and
      variations, **699**
   Mexican, **703**
   Oil and Vinegar, **703**
   Poppy Seed, **702**
   Poppy Seed Fruit, **709**
   Roquefort, **700**
   Roquefort Cheese French, **703**
   Russian, **700**
   Sesame Seed French, **703**
   Sour Cream, **702**
   Sour Cream Basil, **700**
   Tarragon, **703**
   Thousand Island, **700**
   Tomato French, **703**
   Vinaigrette, **706**
      Basil, **705**
      Creamy, **707**
      Dijon Mustard, **706**
      Hot for Salad Greens, **708**
      with Pimiento, **706**
      Raspberry, **707**
      Sweet Sesame, **707**
   Yogurt Herb, **710**
   Yogurt Orange, **710**
Salad greens, 155

Salads, 639–711. *See also* Salads,
    entree; Salads, fruit; Salads,
    gelatin; Salads, vegetable and
    pasta
    arranged salads, 639
    Barley and Black Bean, **648**
    Couscous
        Citrus, **662**
        Israeli, **622, 661**
    ingredients, 641
        herbs, Color exhibit XI
    salad bars, 640
        arrangement of, 640
        basic components of, 640
Salads, entree, 677–692
    Chef's Salad Bowl,
        and variations of, **677**
    Chicken, **678**
        Avocado-Orange, **678**
        with Bacon, **677**
        Blackened, **679**
        Crunchy, **678**
        Curried, **678**
        Fruited, **678**
        Hot, **546**
        Mandarin, **678**
        Pasta, **659**
        Pasta Salad Plate, **680**
    Cottage Cheese, **689**
    Crab, **682**
    Deli Plate, **690**
    Fruit Salad Plate, **692**
    Ham and Pasta, **659**
    Lobster, **682**
    Marinated Chicken and Fresh
        Fruit, **679**
    Pasta and Crab, **683**
    Salmon, **687**
        poached on greens, **682**
    Seafood Chef, **677**
    Shrimp, **684**
    Shrimp-Rice, **685**
    Shrimp Tortellini Salad Plate, **681**
    Taco, **677**
    Tomato, Stuffed, and variations, **688**
    Tuna, and variations, **686, 687**
    Tuna Pasta Salad Plate, **686**
    Turkey, **678**
        Hot, **546**
    Turkey Croissant Salad Plate, **691**
Salads, Fruit, 670–676
    Acini de Pepe Fruit, **672**
    Ambrosia Fruit, **673**
    Apple Pear, **671**
    Apple (Waldorf), and variations, **670**
    Citrus Pomegranate, **674**
    Fresh Fruit Salad Bowl, **674**
    Frozen Fruit, **676**
    Fruit Salad Plate, **692**
    Grapefruit
        Apple, **674**
        Orange, **674**

Orange-Avocado, **674**
        Orange-Pear, **674**
    Spiced Apple, **675**
    Tender Greens and Fruit, **643**
    Waldorf, **670**
Salads, gelatin, 667–669
    Apple Cinnamon Swirl, **667**
    Applesauce, **667**
    Arabian Peach, **667**
    Autumn, **667**
    Blueberry, **667–668**
    Boysenberry, **668**
    Cranberry, **668**
    Cranberry Apple, **668**
    Cucumber Soufflé, **668**
    Frosted Cherry, **668**
    Frosted Lime, **668**
    Fruit Gelatin, and variations, **667**
    Jellied Waldorf, **668**
    Lemon Cream Mold, **668**
    Perfection, **669**
    Pineapple Cheese, **668**
    Ribbon, **668**
    Sunshine, **668**
    Swedish Green-Top, **668**
    Tomato Aspic, **669**
    Under-the-Sea, **668**
Salads, vegetable and pasta, 642–666
    Asparagus, Marinated, **652**
    Asparagus Vinaigrette, **827**
    Barley and Black Bean, 648
    Basic Green, and variations, **642**
    Black Eyed Pea and Corn Salsa, 758
    Brown Bean, **646**
    Cabbage Apple, **650**
    Cabbage-Carrot Slaw, **650**
    Cabbage-Pineapple-
        Marshmallow, **650**
    Carrifruit, **644**
    Carrot Raisin, and variations, **644**
    Carrots, Marinated, **656**
    Cauliflower Bean, **645**
    Cauliflower Broccoli, **649**
    Citrus Couscous, 662
    Coleslaw, **649**
        Creamy, **650**
        Oriental, **649**
    Cucumber and Onion in Sour
        Cream, **651**
    Fettuccine, Marinated, **664**
    Fettuccine Vinaigrette, **664**
    Garbanzo Bean, **647**
        with Pasta, **647**
    Garden, Marinated, **657**
    German Cucumbers, **651**
    Green Beans, Marinated, **652**
    Green Pepper Slaw, **649**
    Hawaiian Tossed, **642**
    Hot Potato Salad, **666**
    Israeli Couscous, 661
    Italian Pasta, **663**
    Macaroni, **660**

Mushrooms, Marinated, **652**
    Oriental Bean, **645**
    Pasta, Basic, **659**
    Pasta and Chicken, **659**
    Pasta and Ham, **659**
    Potato, **665**
    Salad Greens with Grapefruit, **642**
    Spinach, **642**
    Spinach Cheese, **658**
        Summer Cucumber and Melon,
        757
    Spinach Mushroom, **642**
    Tender Greens and Fruit, **643**
    Tomato, Marinated, **654**
    Tomato and Cucumber, **655**
    Tomato and Mozzarella, **655**
    Tomato Basil, **653**
        and Romaine, **653**
    Tomato Relish, **654**
    Tossed Vegetable, **643**
    Triple Bean, **645**
    Vegetable Collage, **652**
Salisbury Steak, **493**
Salmon
    Baked Whole, **467**
    Creamed, **471**
    Loaf, **469**
    Poached, **468**
        on Field Greens, **682**
    Salad, **687**
    Salad Sandwich, **721**
Salsa, **756**
    Black Eyed Peas and Corn, **758**
    Fruit, **759**
    Summer Cucumber and
        Melon, **757**
Salsify, 164
Salt, 182, 183
    reducing, 48–49
Sandies, **384**
Sandwich(es), 713–746
    Asian Orange Ginger Beef Wrap,
        726
    Bacon, Lettuce, and Tomato, **722**
    Barbecued Beef, **732**
    Bierocks, **729**
    Calzone, Broccoli, **733**
        Ham & Swiss Florentine, **733**
        Roasted Vegetable, **733**
    Canapés, preparation of, 714
    Cheese Salad, **717**
    Chicken Pocket, **723**
    Chicken Salad, **720**
    Chili Dog, **524**
    Chimichanga, **740**
    Chuck Wagon, **494**
    Club, **722**
    Croissant with Garden Vegetables,
        743
    Deli Wrap, **725**
    Egg Salad, **718**
    Fajitas, **727, 735, 736**

freezing of, 715
French Dip, **732**
Grilled, **728**
    Cheese, **728**
    Corned Beef and Swiss on Rye,
       728
    Ham and Cheese, **728**
    Hot Tuna Grill, **728**
    Turkey and Swiss, **728**
Ham and Cheese, **719, 722**
Hamburgers
    Barbecued, **742**
    Grilled, **742**
    Oven-Baked, **742**
Ham Salad, and variations, **719**
Hot Meat and Cheese, **730**
Italian Sausage, **526**
Meat Loaf, **732**
Meat Salad, **719**
Nacho Dog, **524**
Patty Melt, **731**
Pimiento Cheese, **717**
Pita. *See* Pitas
Pizzaburger, **737**
Pork Loin with Salsa, **723**
preparation of ingredients, 713–714
preparation of sandwiches, 714–715
    checkerboard, 714
    Cheese, **734**
    closed, 714
    grilled and toasted, 714
    Grilled Corn and Roasted Pepper
       Quesadillas, **734**
    open-faced, hot, 714
    ribbon, 714
    rolled, 715
Reuben, **739**
Roast Beef, Hot, **732**
Roast Pork, Hot, **732**
Salmon Salad, **721**
Sandwich Spread, **716**
    Sloppy Joe, **737**
    Southwestern Style Steak
       Wrap, **725**
Submarine, and variations, **724**
Tacos, **738**
Tuna Melt, **731**
Tuna Salad, **721**
    Grilled, **721**
Turkey, Hot, **732**
Turkey Club Hoagie, **722**
Turkey French Dip, **732**
Vegetarian Pocket, **723**
Western, **737**
Whipped Margarine or
    Butter for, **716**
Wraps
    Asian Orange Ginger Beef, 726
    Deli, **725**
    Steak, **725**
Sangria Sipper, **254**
    White Wine, **254**

Santa Claus, 151
Sauce(s), dessert, 773–778
    Butterscotch, **773**
    Caramel, **773**
    Chocolate, **774**
    Custard, **424, 775**
    Fluffy Orange, **775**
    Hard, **776**
       Brown Sugar, **777**
       Cherry, **776**
       Strawberry, **776**
    Hot Fudge, **774**
    Lemon, **776**
    Nutmeg, **776**
    Orange, **776**
    Peanut Butter, **777**
    Raspberry, **778**
    Strawberry, **778**
    Syrup, Blueberry, **778**
       Brown Sugar, **778**
    Vanilla, **776**
Sauce(s), entree and vegetable,
    Marinades, Rubs, Seasonings,
    747–748
    à la King, **749**
    Almond Butter, **771**
    Bacon, **749**
       Hot, **771**
    Barbecue, **755**
    Bean and Tomato, **760**
    Béchamel, **750**
    Brown, **753**
    Cheese, **749**
    Cheese Broccoli, **749**
    Cheese Sandwich, **749**
    Chile-Cilantro, **461**
    Clam, **567**
    Cocktail, **764**
    Compound Butter, **779**
    Cranberry, and variations, **694–695**
    Cucumber, **767**
    Drawn Butter, **771**
    Egg, **749**
    Fish Marinade, **784, 786**
    Golden, **750**
    Gravy, Pan, **752**
       variations. *See* Gravy
    Herb Butter, and variations, **779**
    Hollandaise, **769**
    Horseradish, **764**
       Caper, **765**
       Dill, **765**
    Italian Tomato, **762**
    Jelly, **753**
    Lemon Butter, **771**
    Lemon Herb Seasoning, **781**
    Maitre d'Hôtel, **771**
    Marinàra, **761**
    Meat Marinade, **783**
    Meunière, **770**
    Mornay, **750**
    Mushroom, **750, 753, 754**

Mustard, **765**
    Chinese, **765**
    Hot, **766**
    Savory, **753**
Nacho, **236**
Olive, **753**
Parsley, **750**
Parsley Butter, **771**
Pimiento, **750**
Piquant, **753**
Pizza, **580**
Raisin, **767**
Salsa, **756, 757, 759**
Sandwich Tomato, **580**
Savory Cream, **751**
Seasoned Salt, **781**
Sesame, **754**
Shrimp, **750**
Spanish, **763**
Sweet-Sour, **766**
Swiss Cheese and Mushroom, **750**
Tartar, **768**
Tomato, Zucchini, **761**
types of, 747–748
Vegetable, for Pasta, **580**
Vegetable Marinade, **784,
    786, 787**
Velouté, **750**
White, and variations, **749**
    Mix for, **748**
Sauerbraten, **489**
Sauerkraut Relish, **697**
Sausage
    Balls, **239**
    Creamed and Biscuits, **525**
    and Egg Bake, **446**
    Gravy, **525**
    Oven-Fried, **522**
    and Potato Bake, **446**
    Rolls, **526**
    Stuffing, **557**
Sautéing procedures, 197
Savory, 171
Scaling weights
    for cakes, 320–322
    for icings and fillings, 323
Scallions, 160
Scallops, 139
    Gratin, **477**
Scheduling, production, 190
Schools
    breakfast program, 11
    menu planning for, 11–13
Scones
    Cranberry, **274**
    Scotch, **269**
Scotch Woodcock, **442**
Scrambled Eggs, and variations, **441**
    oven method for cooking, 441
    steamer method for cooking, 441
Scrapple, **523**
Seafood Chef Salad, **677**

Seasoned Salt, **781**
Seasonings. *See also* Herbs and spices
Cajun, **782**
Herb Butter, **780**
MSG, 182, 184
pepper, 182, 183
proportions of, 87
salt, 182, 183
Seeds, 184–186
Serving temperatures, 104
Sesame seed(s), 186
Rolls, **311**
Sauce, **754**
Seed Dressing, **703**
Shallots, 164
Shellfish. *See* Fish and shellfish
Shitake mushrooms, 162
Shortcake, Biscuit, **269**
Old-Fashioned Strawberry, **435**
Shortening, 188
Shortribs, Barbecued, **517**
Shrimp, 139
Caribbean, **474**
count and descriptive names, 140
Creole, **475**
Fried Rice, **597**
and Pasta Oriental, **476**
Peel, **241**
Salad, **684**
Sauce, **750**
Tortellini Salad Plate, **681**
Sicilian Rice and Vegetables, **605**
Simmering procedures, 199–200
Singapore Curry, **549**
Sloppy Joe, **737**
Snickerdoodles, **374**
Sole, Filet of, Amandine, **464**
Sorrel, 171
Soufflé
Cheese, **452**
Mushroom, **452**
Spinach, **869**
Soup(s), 789–822
Alphabet, **797**
Asparagus, Cream of, **810**
Baked Potato, **814**
Basic Sauce for Cream Soups, **810**
Beef
Barley, **794**
Noodle, **797**
Rice, **797**
Stock, **791**
Vegetable, Hearty, **796**
Black Bean, **630**
Bouillon, and variations, **792**
Broccoli, Cream of, **810**
Broccoli and Cheese, **813**
Broccoli Swiss, **813**
Cauliflower, Cream of, **810**
Celery, Cream of, **810**
Cheese, **812**

Chicken Noodle, **798**
Chicken Rice, **798**
Chicken Velvet, **811**
Cream of Chicken, **811**
Creole, **797**
evaluationg, 201
French Onion, **809**
Gazpacho (Spanish Chilled Soup), **821**
Lentil and Black Bean, **804**
Minestrone, **803**
Mushroom, Cream of, **810**
Mushroom Barley, **810**
Navy Bean, **805**
Oyster Stew, **819**
Pepper Pot, **808**
Potato, Cream of, **810**
Potato and Roasted Pepper, **817**
Potato Chowder, **815**
Potato Ham Chowder, Hearty, **818**
Spinach, Cream of, **810**
Split Pea, **804, 806**
Stock, preparation of, 789
Beef, **791**
Brown, **791**
Chicken, **790**
Vegetable, **793**
White, **790**
Tomato
Barley, **807**
Bouillon, **792**
Rice, **807**
Turkey Vegetable Soup, **799**
types of, 789
Vegetable
Beef, **795**
Chowder, **815**
Cream of, **810**
Vichyssoise (Chilled Potato Soup), **822**
Sour Cream Dressing, **702**
Basil, **700**
Southwest Ziti, **579**
Spaetzles (Egg Dumplings), **295**
Spaghetti. *See also* Pasta
with Cheese Sauce, **567**
with Chicken Sauce, **586**
with Clam Sauce, **567**
Creole, **584**
with Meatballs, **588**
with Meat Sauce, **587**
with Shrimp Sauce, **567**
with Vegetable Sauce, **585**
Vegetarian, **585**
Spaghetti squash, 165
Baked, **871**
Spanish
Meatballs, **499**
Omelet, **443**
Rice, **510**
Rice and Black Beans, **633**

Sauce, **763**
Steak, **492**
Spareribs
Baked with Dressing, **517**
Barbecued, **517**
with Sauerkraut, **517**
Sweet-Sour, **517**
Special meals and receptions, 22–36
banquet service for, 30–35
coffees and brunches, 23–25
planning, 22–36
receptions and teas, 23
Spiced Rosé Warmer, **260**
Spices. *See* Herbs and spices
Spinach, 164
Cheese Salad, **658**
Creamed, **868**
Crepes, **544**
Lasagna, **570, 571**
and other greens, cooking of, **868**
Salad, **642**
Seasoned, **868**
seasonings for, **868**
Soufflé, **869**
Soup, Cream of, **810**
Stuffed Tomatoes, **874**
Wilted, **868**
Split Pea Soup, **804, 806**
and Black Bean, **804**
Sponge Cake, **330**
Spoon Bread, **282**
Squash
Acorn, Baked, and variations, **870**
Butternut, Mashed, **872**
Butternut-Apple Casserole, **872**
cooking of, **870–873**
Spaghetti, Baked, **871**
with Clam Sauce, **871**
with Vegetable Sauce, **871**
summer, 165
winter, 164–165
Winter, Mashed, **872**
zucchini, 165
Casserole, **873**
Corn Cakes, **293**
French-Fried, **851**
Ratatouille, **878, 879**
Seasoned, **873**
and Summer Squash, **873**
and Tomato Casserole, **873**
Steak. *See* Beef
Steaming procedures, 200
Steam-jacketed kettle sizes, 221
Stew, Beef, and variations, **501**
Green Chili, **502**
Stir-Fried Beef
with Broccoli, **541**
with Sugar Snap Peas, **495**
Stir-Fried Pork, **542**

Stir-Fried Vegetables, **542, 877**
Stir-frying
    procedures, 197
    seasoned oil for, **877**
Stock
    Beef, **791**
    Brown, **791**
    Chicken, **790**
    Vegetable, **793**
    White, **790**
Storage temperatures, 102
Strawberry, 147
    Bavarian Cream, **427**
    Chiffon Pie, **412**
    Pie, **398**
    Sauce, **778**
    Shortcake, **435**
Streusel Topping, **398**
Stroganoff, Beef, **503**
Stuffed Peppers, **510**
Stuffing. *See* Dressing, bread
Submarine Sandwich, **724**
Substitutions, ingredient, 85–86
Succotash, **831**
Sugar Cookies, **375, 388**
Sugared Snails, **317**
Sugars and sweeteners, 187
    reducing, 48–49
Suggested menu items, 885–891
Summer savory, 171
Sunflower seeds, 186
Sunshine Salad, **668**
Sushi Style Rice, **610**
Swedish
    Braids, **315**
    Green Top Salad, **668**
    Meatballs, **500**
    Rye Bread, **308**
Sweet cicely, 167
Sweeteners, 187
    reducing, 48–49
Sweet Potato(es)
    and Apples, **866**
    Baked, **866**
    cooking of, **866**
    Glazed or Candied,
        and variations, **866**
    Mashed, **866**
    Roasted with Soy Sauce, **859**
    seasonings for, **866**
    Soufflé, **867**
Sweet Roll Dough, Basic, and
    variations, **314**
Sweet Sesame Vinaigrette
    Dressing, **707**
Sweet-Sour Sauce, **766**
Swiss Broccoli Pasta, **569**
Swiss chard, 156
Swiss Cheese and Mushroom
    Sauce, **750**
Swiss Steak, and variations, **492**

Syrup(s), 187
    Blueberry, **778**
    Brown Sugar, **778**
    Burnt Sugar, **338**
    Simple, **252**
Szechwan Chicken, **543**

T
Table arrangement
    for buffets, 27–30
    for receptions and teas, 26
Table cover for served meal, 31
Tables and guides, how to use,
    41–43
Table service for banquets, 32–35
Tabouli, Minted, **698**
Tacos, **738**
Taco Salad, **677**
Taco Salad Casserole, **509**
Tahini and Yogurt Spread, **746**
Tangelos, 149
Tangerines, 149
Tapioca Cream Pudding, **418**
Tarragon, 172
    Butter, **780**
    Chicken, **536**
    French Dressing, **703**
    Turkey Steak, **555**
Tartar Sauce, **768**
Tea, 174
    Hot, **247**
    Iced, **248**
    preparation of, 246
    Russian, **248**
    Spiced, **248**
Temperatures
    for bacteria growth, 102
    convection oven, 97
    deep-fat frying, 98
    for food preparation, 96
    for food safety, 102
    for food storage, 102
    metric equivalents, 95
    for roasting poultry, 532
    for serving and holding, 104
    for serving food, 104
    standards, 106
Teriyaki Glazed Pork Loin, **514**
Teriyaki Steak, **492**
Thimble Cookies, **383**
Thousand Island Dressing, **700**
Thyme, 172
Timbales, Chicken, **880**
    Vegetable, **880**
Time and temperature
    standards, 106
Toasted almonds, 641
    Bulgur with Cranberries and, **620**
Toasted Spice Blend, **782**
Toasting Spices, **782**

Tofu, 173
    and Broccoli Szechwan, **636**
    Stir-Fry, **542**
    Sweet and Sour, **635**
    Vegetable Jambalaya, **637**
Tomatillo, 165–166
Tomato(es), 166
    Aspic, **669**
    Baked, **874**
        Italian and Zucchini, **876**
    Barley Soup, **807**
    Basil and Cheese Pinwheels, **242**
    Basil Salad, **653**
    Bouillon, **792**
    Broiled Slices, **874**
    Cabbage Salad, **688**
    Cilantro Rice, **601**
    Cottage Cheese Salad, **688**
    and Cucumbers, **664**
    French Dressing, **703**
    Herb Roasted, **875**
    Juice Cocktail, **257**
        Hot Spiced, **258**
    Linguine, **583**
    Marinated, **654**
    and Mozzarella Salad, **655**
    Mushroom-Stuffed, **874**
    Relish, **654**
    Rice Soup, **807**
    Roasted Tomatoes, Israeli Couscous
        with Olives and, **622**
    Salad, Stuffed and variations, **688**
    Sauce, Italian, **762**
    Sauce, Sandwich, **580**
    seasonings for, **874**
    Spinach-Stuffed, **874**
    Zucchini Sauce, **761**
Tools and equipment. *See also* Knives
    basic handtools, 215–216
    large-equipment requirements, 222
    measuring and portioning
        equipment, 217
    pans, 218–220
Toppings
    for bread and rolls, **317**
    Butter Cinnamon, **317**
    Butter Crunch, **317**
    Crumb, **317**
    Honey Streusel, **269**
Tossed Vegetable Salad, **643**
Tostadas, **738**
Trio Baked Beans, **833**
Triple Bean Salad, **645**
Trout, Fajita-Spiced, **461**
Tuna
    à la King, **545**
    Broiled with White Beans and
        Tomato, **465**
    Creamed, and variations of, **471**
    Loaf, **469**
    Melt, **731**

Tuna, *Continued*
 and Noodles, and variations, **470**
 Pasta Salad Plate, **686**
  and Rice, **470**
 Salad, and variations, **686–687**
 Salad Sandwiches, **721**
  Grilled, **721**
 Tetrazzini, **590**
Turkey
 á la King, **545**
 carving, 533
 classes of, 134
 cooking methods for, 527–532
 Croissant Salad Plate, **691**
 and Dumplings, **554**
 and Noodle Casserole, **551**
 Pot Pie, **550**
 roasting guide for, 532
 Salad, **678**
  Hot, **546**
 sandwiches. *See* Sandwiches
 Scalloped, **547**
 skinning and boning, 534
 Steak, Creole, **555**
  Lime Tarragon, **555**
 Taco, **738**
 Tetrazzini, **590**
 Vegetable Soup, **799**
Turnip greens, cooking of. *See* Spinach
Turnips, 166
Turnips with Peas, **853**

U

Under-the-Sea Salad, **668**

V

Vanilla Cream Pudding, and
  variations, **419**
Vanilla Sauce, **776**
Veal
 Birds, **512**
  with Sausage Stuffing, **512**
 Breaded Cutlets, **513**
 Cacciatore, **513**
 New Orleans, **513**
 Parmesan, **513**
 Piccata, **513**
 primal and retail cuts, 132
 Scallopini, **513**
 timetable for
  braising, 487
  cooking in liquid, 487
  roasting, 481
Vegetable oyster, 164
Vegetable(s), 823–882. *See also*
  individual vegetables
 Barley and Vegetables, **618, 619**
 Beef Soup, **795**
 boiling, 824

canned, 172–173
canned, directions for heating,
  824–826
Chowder, **815**
Chow Mein, **505**
Collage, **652**
cooking of, 824
Couscous, **621**
dried, directions for cooking, 826
evaluating, 201–202
fresh, 141, 153–166
 cooking, 823–824
 pre-preparation guidelines,
  153–166
 yield, availability, storage,
  142–145
frozen, 172–173, 823–824
Ginger Vegetables and Barley, **617**
grilled or roasted, **881**
 Garlic and Fennel Roasted, **881**
 Sesame Roasted, **882**
 Sherry Roasted Root, **882**
Grilled Vegetable Marinade, **785**
Lo Mein, **581**
Marinade, **784**
Paella, **602**
and Pasta Salads, 642–666
Salad, Tossed, **643**
Sauce for Pasta, **580**
Soup, **795**
 Cream of, **810**
steaming, 824
Stir-Fried, **877**
Stir-Fry, **542**
stir-frying, 824
Timbale, **880**
timetable for boiling or steaming,
  825
timetable for roasting, 883
Vegetarian (meatless) entrees, **886**
Vegetarian Spaghetti, **585**
Velouté Sauce, **750**
Vichyssoise (Chilled Potato Soup), **822**
Vinaigrette Dressing, and variations,
  705–708
Vinegars, 175

W

Waffles, **291**
 Pecan, **291**
Waldorf Salad, and variations, **670**
 Jellied, **668**
Walnut Chiffon Cake, **331**
Walnut Coffee Cake, **280**
Walnuts, 186
Wassail, **257**
Water activity, of selected foods, 106
Watermelon, 151
Wax beans, cooking of, **828**
 Seasoned, **828**

Weights and measures
 rounding off, 89
 used in recipes, 225
Welsh Rarebit, **455**
Western Sandwich, **737**
Wheat, 122
Wheat germ, 122
Whipped Margarine or Butter, **716**
White Bean and Tomato Sauce, **760**
White Bread, and variations, **299–300,
  301**
White Cake, **332–333**
White Sauce, and variations of, **749**
 Mix, **748**
White vinegar, 175
White Wine Sangria, **254**
Whole wheat, 122
 Biscuits, **269**
 Bread, **300, 301**
 Muffins, **270**
 Pancakes, **290**
 Rolls, **311**
 Sugar Cookies, **376**
Wieners. *See* Frankfurters
Wilted Lettuce or Spinach, **868**
Wine and bar service, 36
 bar stocking guidelines, 37
Wine purchasing guide, 26
Wine selection guide, 24–25
Wine vinegar, 175
Winter squash, 164–165
Wrap, Asian Orange Ginger Beef, **726**

Y

Yeast bread. *See* Breads, yeast
Yellow Angel Food Cake, **330**
Yellow Cake, **335**
Yellow crookneck squash, 165
Yellow zucchini, 165
Yield of fruits and vegetables, 142
Yield of recipes, 224
Yogurt
 Herb Dressing, **710**
 Orange Dressing, **710**
 Tahini and Yogurt Spread, **746**

Z

Zesting fruit, 147
Ziti
 with Four Cheeses, **578**
 Southwest, **579**
Zucchini, 165
 Casserole, **873**
 Corn Cakes, **293**
 French-Fried, **851**
 Ratatouille, **878, 879**
 Seasoned, **873**
 and Summer Squash, **873**
 and Tomato Casserole, **873**